# TEUTONIC MYTHOLOGY

## JACOB GRIMM

Translated from the Fourth Edition
with Notes and Appendix by
JAMES STEVEN STALLYBRASS

*Volume IV*
*of four volumes*

DOVER PUBLICATIONS, INC.
Mineola, New York

# DOVER PHOENIX EDITIONS

*Bibliographical Note*

This Dover edition, first published in 2004, is an unabridged republication of the 1966 Dover edition of the work originally published by George Bell and Sons, London, of which volumes I, II, and III were published in 1883 and volume IV in 1888.

*Library of Congress Cataloging-in-Publication Data*

Grimm, Jacob, 1785–1863.
    [Deutsche mythologie. English]
    Teutonic mythology / Jacob Grimm ; translated from the fourth edition with notes and appendix by James Steven Stallybrass.
      p. cm.
    Originally published: London : G. Bell and Sons, 1882–1888.
    Includes bibliographical references and index.
    ISBN 0-486-43546-6 (pbk. v. 1) — ISBN 0-486-43547-4 (pbk. v. 2) — ISBN 0-486-43548-2 (pbk. v. 3) — ISBN 0-486-43549-0 (pbk. v. 4)
    1. Mythology, Germanic. 2. Mythology, Norse. 3. Germanic peoples—Religion. 4. Magic, Germanic. 5. Superstition—Germany. 6. Names, Germanic. I. Stallybrass, James Steven, 1826–1888. II. Title.

BL860.G7213 2004
293'.13—dc22

                            2004043828

Manufactured in the United States of America
Dover Publications, Inc., 31 East 2nd Street, Mineola, N.Y. 11501

# PREFACE.

This Volume, answering to Vol. III. of the last German edition, consists of two parts, a SUPPLEMENT and an APPENDIX.

The SUPPLEMENT is the *characteristic*—as it is the only strictly new—part of this Fourth Edition of Grimm's Mythology. After his Second Edition of 1844, which *was* a great advance upon the First, the Author never found time to utilize any of the new matter he collected by working it into the Text; his Third Edition of 1854 was a mere reprint of the Second; so that the stores he kept on accumulating till his death, and the new views often founded on them and on the researches of younger investigators—Kuhn, Müllenhoff, Panzer, Mannhardt, etc.—all lay buried in the *MS. Notes* that covered the wide margin of his private copy, as well as in many loose sheets. On the death of Grimm, his Heirs entrusted the task of bringing out a Fourth Edition to Prof. ELARD HUGO MEYER, of Berlin, leaving him at liberty to incorporate the posthumous material in the Text or not, as he chose. The Professor, fearing that if once he began incorporating he might do too much, and instead of pure Grimm, might make a compound Grimm-and-Meyer concern of it, wisely contented himself with the humbler duty of keeping it in the form of Supplementary Notes, verifying authorities where he could, and supplying References to the parts of the Text which it illustrates.

As the Supplement hardly amounted to a volume, the Professor hit upon the happy thought of reprinting with it an APPENDIX which Grimm had published to his First Edition, but had never republished, probably thinking it had done its work, and perhaps half ashamed of its humble character. Yet it is one of the most valuable parts of the work, and much the most amusing. It falls into three unequal portions : I. Anglo-Saxon GENEALOGIES. II. SUPERSTITIONS. III. SPELLS. Of the short treatise (30 pp.) on the eight royal lines of our Octarchy, their common descent from Wôden, and their points of connexion with Continental tradition, I will say nothing. The bulk of the Appendix (112 pp.) is taken up with the SUPER-STITIONS. After a number of extracts from Medieval authors, extending from A.D. 600 to 1450, we have a vast array of Modern Superstitions (the German part alone has 1142 articles), mostly taken down from the lips of the common people all over Europe, in the simple language of the class, the "rude Doric" which our polite grandfathers used to apologize for printing, but which in these days of Folklore is, I am told, the very thing that goes down. The Author's view of Superstition, that it is a *survival*, the debased wrecks and remnants of a once dominant Religion, of course inclines him to trace these superstitions, as far as possible, to the Old Faith of the Teutonic nations, of which we have still such a splendid specimen in the Icelandic Edda.—The Appendix winds up with 57 old SPELLS in various languages.

THE TRANSLATOR.

# CONTENTS.

## VOL. IV.

# CHAPTER I.

## INTRODUCTION.

p. 1, note] Paul. Diac. still uses *heathen* in the sense of rustici (Pertz, Archiv 7, 334). demo heidanin commane, Diut. 1, 504$^b$. The abbrev. form *heid* occurs even before Luther: *heide* rhy. leide, G. Abent. 2, 67. dieser zeginer oder *heit*, Keller, Fastnachts-sp. p. 823 (like our *christ* for MHG. kristen, OHG. christani); yet the true genitive is retained in Chr. Weise's Erznarre 190: des jungen *heidens* los werden.——Favorite epithets of the heathen are "wild, fierce, grim": wild heathen, wild men of the wild heath, Anegenge 23, 61. conf. Rabenschl. 1080. Neifen 14, 6. MsH. 1, 152$^a$. die *wuotendigen* heiden, Kaiserchr. 951. More freq. die *übelen* heiden, Diemer 158, 18. 162, 2. Morolt 376 seq. die *bösen* h., Diemer 170, 24. 179, 17. der *übele* h., Pantal. 1034. der *vil arge* h. 1847. den h. *gramen*, Servat. 148 (per contra, hypocrita is transl. *dunni cristâni*, Diut. 1, 239$^b$). Also "dogs," as in Judith 134, 39: þone haeðenan *hund*. Olaf Tryggv. saga, cap. 68: *hund*-heidinn. Svenske vis: hednings-*hund*. Mor. 418: den heidenschen *hunt*. In Willeh. 58, 16 the Sarrazin ride on *dogs* and *hogs*.——Gradually milder terms are used: dat *domme* heidine, Maerl. 3, 128. des *gelouben geste* (strangers to faith), Türl. Wh. 15$^a$. heidinen die *sunder êwe* (without law) lebeten, Roth. 475. People do not like to be taken for heathens: sô bin ich niht ein *heiden*, MsH. 1, 42$^a$. als ich waere ein *heiden* 45$^b$. Yet there is pity for them: swie sie wâren heiden, och was *zerbarmen* umbe sie, Nib. Lament 437; and Wolfram, like Walther, speaks of them quite humanely, Willeh. 450, 15: "Die nie toufes künde Enpfiengen, ist das sünde, Daz man die sluoc alsam ein vihe (a sin to slay the unbaptized)? Grôzer sünde ich drumbe gihe: Es ist gar *Gotes hant-getât*, Zwuo und sibenzec sprâche die er hât," they are God's handiwork, 72 languages wherein He speaks.

pp. 2-4.] Heathens in Italy and at Rome as late as Theoderic, Edict. Theod. 108. Salvianus de gubern. Dei, about 450, contrasts the vices of christian Romans and Provincials with the virtues of heathen Saxons, Franks, Gepidæ and Huns, and of heretical Goths and Vandals; towards the end of bk. 7, he says : ' Gothorum gens perfida, sed pudica est, Alamannorum impudica, sed minus perfida. Franci mendaces, sed hospitales, Saxones crudelitate efferi, sed castitate mirandi ;' and further on : ' Vandali castos etiam Romanos esse fecerunt;' conf. Papencordt 271-2. The Bavarian Ratolf is converted in 788 : *coepi* Deum colere, MB. 28ᵇ, 7. In the times of Boniface and Sturmi we read : Populi gentis illius (in Noricum), licet essent christiani, ab antiquis tamen *paganorum* contagiis et perversis dogmatibus infecti, Pertz 2, 366. Alamanns, who appear in Italy 552-3, are still heathens in contrast to the christian Franks, Agathias 2,1. 1,7. Eginhard cap. 7 (Pertz 2, 446) : Saxones *cultui daemonum* dediti; *cultum daem.* dimittere ; abjecto *daem. cultu,* et relictis patriis caerimoniis. The author of Vita Mathildis (Pertz 12, 575) says of the Saxons and of Widukind's family : Stirps qui quondam *daem.* captus *errore,* praedicatorum pro inopia *idola adorans,* christianos constanter persequebatur.

The Nialssaga cap.101—6 relates the introduction of Christianity into Iceland in 995—1000. Yet at Nerike by Örebro, as late as the 17th cent., they sacrificed to Thor on certain rocks for toothache, Dybeck runa 1848 p. 26 ; and to this day old women sacrifice to rivers, and throw the branch on the stone 2, 3, 15. *vit erum heiðin* is said in Olaf the Saint's time in Gautland, Fornm. sög. 4, 187 and 12, 84. In the Norwegian districts of Serna and Idre, bordering on Dalarne, there were heathens in 1644, Samling (Christiania 1839) 6, 470-1. þa kunni enge maðr Paternoster i Straumi, Werlauff. grenzbest. 20. 37. In Sweden we hear of *Oden's followers* in 1578, 1580 and 1601, Geyer Svearikes häfder 2, 329 ; in a folk-song a woman dreads the heathen that haunt the neighbouring wood : 'locka till Thor i *fjäll,*' Arvidsson 3, 504. Thursday was holy in Sweden till 100 or 150 years ago (p. 191). Relapses into heathenism were frequent there, Hervarars. cap. 20 (Fornald. sög. 1, 512). The secret practice of it was called *launblót,* Fornm. sög. 2, 243.

The Slavs in Pomerania heathens till begin. of 12th century. A heathen festival near Pyritz, and that of Gerovit at Havelberg, Barthold's Gesch. v. Pomm. 2, 34. 76. Giesebrecht's Wend.

gesch. 2, 265. 309. Heathen Rans, Barth. 2, 100-1. Pribizlaus of Mecklenburg baptized in 1164, Svantevit's temple destroyed 1168, Lisch's Meckl. jahrb. 11, 10. 97.——The Slavs betw. Elbe and Oder were Christians for 70 years, then relapsed ab. 1013, Helmold 1, 16; adhuc enim (1147) Slavi immolabant daemoniis et non Deo 68. The Prussians still heathen after conversion of Russians 1, 1.——Some Christians in Hungary in latter half of 10th century, Dümmler's Pilgrim von Passau 36 seq. Some heathens in Esthonia at the present day, Verhandl. 2, 36. The Lapps were still heathen in 1750, Castrén's Reise p. 69.

Mixed marriages were not entirely forbidden, as Chlodowig's example shows. Such too was Kriemhilt's union with the heathen Etzel, but she takes care to have her son Ortliep baptized, Nibel. 1328.

p. 5.] Between heathen baptism (the *vatni ausa*, the *dicare* in nomine deorum, Greg. Tur. 2, 29) and christian baptism, stands the *prim-signaz*, Egilss. p. 265, a mere signing with the cross. Thus, Gestr is 'prîmsigndr, eigi skîrðr,' Fornald. sög. 1, 314. The pains of hell were made to hang on being *unbaptized* (p. 918).——Whoever forsook paganica vetustas (Pertz 2, 342), had to renounce the gods : *den goten entfarn* = get baptized, Türl. Wh. 130ᵃ. To abjure one's faith was *abrenuntiare, abjurare, renegare, reneare*, Ducange; Fr. *renier*, O.Fr. *renoier*, MHG. sich *vernoijieren*, Nib. 1207, 1. Lament 494. *vernoierten* sich von den Kristen, Livl. reimchr. 5719. M. Neth. *vernogerde*, Karel. 2, 75. *vernoyert*, Pajin 2, 519. 831. *vernoyert* rh. verghiert, Maerl. 3, 140. OHG. *antrunneo, ant-trunneo aba-trunneo* = apostata, renegatus, Graff 5, 533. *li cuivers renoié*, Ducange; *tornadie, tornadis* = retrayant. Other phrases : *den touf hin legen*, Livl. r. 6129. *lâzen varn krist* 6385. What is meant by : 'eosque (Hessians at Amenaburg) a sacrilega idolorum censura, qua *sub quodam christianitatis nomine* male abusi sunt, evocavit' in the Vita Bonifacii, Pertz 2, 342 ? probably a christian heresy, as p. 344 says of Thuringians : 'sub nomine religionis *falsi fratres* maximam hereticae pravitatis introduxerunt sectam,' conf. Rettberg 2, 308.——The Abrenuntiations declared the ancient gods by name to be *devils* and *unholds*. All heathen merrymaking, espec. music and dancing, was considered *diabolic*, pp. 259. 618-9. 770. Feasts, games and customs connected with the old worship were

now *diaboli pompa, gelp inti zierida.* Grieshaber's Serm. p. 48 :
da man singet und springet in *des tievels dienste ;* conf. Aucassin
in Méon's Fabl. 1, 385.    Fauriel 3, 190.

p. 5.]  The mental protest against christianity shows itself in
the continuance of the rough heroic conception of Paradise (p.
319).  The christian paradise was often rejected, as by Radbod
the Frisian, who withdrew his foot from the sacred font, because
he did not care to give up the fellowship of his forefathers in hell
and sit with a little flock in heaven, Vita Bonif. (Pertz 2, 221).
Melis Stoke, rymkron. 1, 24.    Comp. the contrary behaviour
of Gudbrand (Maurer bekehrung 1, 537) and of Sighvatr at the
baptism of Magnus, St. Olaf's saga c. 119.   Waldemar likes
hunting better than heaven, Thiele 1, 48.   nit ze himelrîche sîn
woldich vür dise reise, Roseng. 110.   mir waere ie liep bî ir ze
sîn dan bî Got in paradîs, MS. 1, 178ᵃ.   möht aber mir ir hulde
(her favour) werden, ich belibe (I would stay) ûf der erden alhie,
Got liez ich dort die werden (worthies), MS. 2, 16ᵇ.   daz himel-
rîche liez ich sîn, und waere bî in iemer wol alsô, Dietr. drachenk.
131ᵇ.   waz sol ein bezzer paradîs, ob er mac vrô belîben von wol
gelopten wîben?   MsH. 1, 82ᵇ.   si waere getreten durch Flôren
in die helle, Fl. 5784.   si me vauroit miex un ris de vous qu'estre
en paradis, Thib. de N. 69.   kestre ne voudroie en paradis, se
ele nestoit mie 75 ; conf. 113.   The hered. sewer of Schlotheim :
' had you one foot in heaven and one on the Wartburg, you'd
rather withdraw the first than the last,' Rommel's Gesch. von
Hessen 2, 17.   fall from heaven to earth, Schwein. 1, 95.   come
back from paradise, Chans. histor. 1, 43.——Eyvindr, like christian
martyrs, endures the utmost pains inflicted by Olaf Tryggvason,
and will not apostatize, Fornm. sög. 2, 167.   The Hist. S. Cuthberti says : quadam die cum Onalaf cum furore intrasset ecclesiam
Cuthberti, astante episcopo Cuthheardo et tota congregatione,
' quid, inquit, in me potest homo iste mortuus Cuthbertus, cujus
in me quotidie minae opponuntur?   juro per deos meos potentes,
*Thor* et *Othan,* quod ab die hac inimicissimus ero omnibus vobis,'
Twysden 73-4.   The heathenism smouldering in many hearts is
perceptible even in Latin deeds of 1270, Seibertz no. 351.

p. 5.]   A peal of bells was hateful to heathens, and therefore
to giants, p. 950, to dwarfs, p. 459, to witches, p. 1085.

p. 5.]   Even in christian times the heathen gods are credited

with sundry powers. The idols *speak*, Pass. 307, 2 seq. Barl.
342, 8 or *hold their peace*, Pass. 306, 24. 34. The Livl. reimchr.
1433 seq. says :

> Die Littouwen vuoren über sê,
> daz ist genant daz Osterhap,
> als *ez Perkune ir abgot gap* (when P. existed),
> daz nimmer sô harte gevrôs (froze).

Hence the quarrel between the old and new religions was often
referred to an *ordeal* or *miracle*: 'probemus miraculis, quis sit
majoris potentiae, vestri multi quos dicitis dii, an meus solus
omnipotens dominus J. Chr.' cries the christian priest in Vita
Ansgarii (Pertz 2, 702); and the rain falls in torrents on the
heathen Swedes despite their praying, while not a drop touches
him. In Greg. Tur. mirac. 1 cap. 81, the *ordeal of water* decides
whether the Arian or Catholic faith be the right one. In the
legend of Silvester, the Jew sorcerer first kills a bull in the name
of his God, and Silvester brings it to life again by calling upon
Christ, W. Grimm's Silv. xv.—xx.

p. 6.] The Romans too had felled *sacred trees*: 'et robora numinis instar Barbarici nostrae *feriant impune bipennes,*' Claudian
de laud. Stilich. 1, 230. In the same way the Irminsul is destroyed, and Columban breaks the god's images and throws them
in the lake (p. 116. 109). Charles has the four captured Sara-
cen idols smashed, and the golden fragments divided among his
heroes, Aspremont 11ᵇ. 45ᵇ—48ᵇ. Idols are broken in Barl. and
Georg. It is remarkable in Beda 2, 13, that the *Coifi* himself
destroys the heathen temple (p. 92 n.). It was a sign of good
feeling at least to build the old images into the church-walls.

p. 6.] Heathens, that knew not the true God's name, are not
always 'wild, doggish, silly,' but sometimes 'die *werden* heiden,'
Titur. 55, 4, die *wîsen* heiden, Servat. 19. his sylfes (God's)
naman, þone yldo bearn aer ne cûðon, *frôd fœdera cyn þeáh hie fela
wiston,* Cædm. 179, 15.

p. 7.] Trust in one's own strength is either opposed to trust in
gods, or combined with it. In the Faereyînga-s. cap. 23, p. 101 :
'ek trûi â mâtt minn ok megin ' and also 'ek treystumsk hamîngju
(genius) minni ok sigr-saeli, ok hefir mer þat vel dugat '; conf.
' trûa magni,' Fornald. sög. 1, 438. The OHG. *sô mir ih !* (Graff
6, 13) must mean 'so help me I myself.' MHG. has milder

formulas: sam mir Got and *mín selbes líp*! Tristan 215, 2. als
in (them) Got und *ir ellen* gebôt, Ernst 1711. als im sîn manlîch
*ellen* jach, Parz. 89, 22. ich gelove God ind mime swerde, Karlmeinet 122, 34. M. Beheim 266, 22 says : si wolten ûf in (them)
selber stân ; and Gotthelf's Erzähl. 1, 146 makes a strong peasant
in Switz. worship ' money and *strength.*' A giant loses his *strength*
by baptism, Rääf 39. Doubts of God are expressed by Wolfram :
ist Got wîse? . . . hât er sîn alt gemüete, Willeh. 66, 18. 20.
hât Got getriwe sinne, Parz. 109, 30. Resisting his will is 'ze
himele klimmen und Got enterben,' En. 3500.——On men who
pretend to be gods, see p. 385 n.

p. 7 n.] God is threatened and scolded, p. 20. With the
mockery of Jupiter in Plaut. Trin. iv. 2, 100 agrees the changing
of his golden garment for a woollen, and robbing Æsculapius of
his golden beard, Cic. de Nat. D. 3, 34. Friðþiofr said : ' enda
virði ek meira hylli Ingibiargar enn reiði Baldrs,' Fornald. sög. 2,
59 ; and pulled B.'s statue by the ring, so that it fell in the fire
86. King Hrôlfr already considers Oðin an evil spirit, *illr andi*,
1, 95.——*Dogs* were named after gods by the Greeks also ; Pollux,
Onom. 5, 5 cites Κόραξ, Ἅρπυια, Χάρων, Λυκίττας. A dog named
*Locke*, Sv. folks. 1, 135. Helbling's *Wunsch* is supported by a
*Wille* in Hadamar v. Laber 289 and Altswert 126, 23. *Sturm* in
Helbl. 4, 459 may have meant Thunder. The lime-bitch is called
*Heila, Hela*, Döbel 1, 86. Nemnich 720. *Alke* is Hakelberend's
dog, Zeitschr. des Osn. ver. 3, 406. A *Ruland* about 1420, and
*Willebreht*, Ls. 1, 297-8, are exactly like men's names. Many
names express the qualities and uses of the animal, such as *Wacker*,
still in use, and leading up to old Norse, Saxon, Skirian and
Suevic names, Grimm's D. Sag. 468; its dimin., *Wäckerlein, Weck-
herlin, Wickerlein*, Fischart's Spiele 246. 491. Is *Wasser*, the
common name of peasants' dogs in the Mark (Schmidt v. Wern.
253), a corrup. of Wacker? *Wackerlos, Vernim*, dogs in Frosch-
meus. Bbb. 5ᵇ, *Hüterlin* in Keisersb. bilg. 140-4-5. Fondling names
are *Harm*, Ls. 2, 411. Holle im Crane p. 30, *Bärlin*, Garg. 258ᵇ,
*Zuckerl*. Jucundiss. 54. To the Pol. *gromi-zwierz*, bait-hound,
Linde 1, 779ᵃ answers our *Hetzebolt*, Nic. v. Jeroschin 30, 12.
*Bello, Greif, Pack-an, Pack-auf* (Medic. maulaffe 647), *Suoche*,
Fichard 3, 245, explain themselves ; also the Boh. greyhound
*Do-lèt*, fly-to ; O. Norse *Hopp* and *Hoi*, Hrolfkr. saga, *Hopf* in

Eulensp., *Estula* (es-tu-là?), Méon 3, 394-5. Ren. 25355. Not so clear is *Strom* in Fritz Reuter's Journ. to Belligen 2, 98; is it 'striped'? or conn. with *Striun* in Helbl. 4, 456 from striunen, to roam? *Smutz* in Laber 358 must be conn. with *schmötzen*, to counterfeit the hare's cry, Schmeller 3, 479. *Trogen*, Sv. äfvent. 1, 51 is our *Fidel*, trusty. *Gramr*, Fornald. sög. 1, 87. *Gîfr*, *Geri*, two dogs in Fiölsvinns-mâl. *Snati*, Markusson 174ᵃ. *Guldtand* Norske event. 2, 92. *Yrsa*, Fornald. sög. 1, 22, *Ursa* in Saxo. *Bettelmann* in Bürger 474ᵃ and *Stallmeister* in Tieck's Zerbino express social rank, conf. *Malvoisin*, Ren. 1664. It were too bold to conn. *Leppisch* in Pauli Sch. u. ernst 77, with Sâmr = Lapp, in Nialss. 71, or *Goth*, *Goz* with the nation so called (Michel's hist. des races maudites 1, 355. D. Sag. 454); more likely that the Silesian sheepdog's name *Sachs* (Weinhold) meant Saxon; conf. Boh. *Bodrok*, an Obodrite. King Arthur's dog *Cabul*, Nenn. 78. *Cipriân*, dog's name in MsH. 3, 305ᵃ.

p. 8.] Christ and the old gods are often *worshipped together*. People got baptized and believed in Christ, en hêto â *Thôr* til allra storræ̌a. Widukind (Pertz 5, 462) tells, an. 965, of an 'altercatio super cultura deorum in convivio, Danis affirmantibus Christum quidem *esse deum*, sed alios ei fore *majores deos*, qui potiora mortalibus signa et prodigia per se ostentabant.' Æthelbert of Kent let heathen idols stand *beside* christian altars, conf. Lappenb. Engl. gesch. 1, 140. The converted Slavs clung to their old superstitions. Dietmar (Pertz 5, 735) says of the sacred lake Glomuzi: 'hunc omnis incola *plus quam ecclesias* veneratur et timet;' and at Stettin a heathen priest was for raising an altar to the god of the christians side by side with the old gods, to secure the favour of both, Giesebr. Wend. gesch. 2, 301.——It is only playfully, and with no serious intention, that the Minnesong links the name of God with heathen deities:

> Ich hân *Got* und die minneclîchen *Minne* (love)
> gebeten flêlîche nu vil manic jâr,
> daz ich schier nâch *unser drîer* sinne
> vinde ein reine wîp. MS. 1. 184ᵃ.
>     *Venus*, vil edeliu künegîn,
> iuch hât *Got*, vrowe, her gesant
> ze freuden uns in ditze lant. Frauend. 233, 26.

The longer duration of heathenism, especially of Wôden-worship, among the *Saxons,* is perceptible in the legend of the Wild Host, in many curses and the name of Wednesday. There also the custom of Need-fire was more firmly rooted. The Lohengrin p. 150 still rebukes the unbelief of the wild Saxons.

p. 11.] Where there was worship of springs, the Church took the caput aquæ into her department, Rudorff 15, 226-7. In that spell where Mary calls to Jesus, 'zeuch ab dein wat (pull off thy coat), und deck es dem armen man über die sat (over the poor man's crop),' Mone anz. 6, 473, a heathen god is really invoked to shield the cornfield from hail. Quite heathenish sounds the nursery rhyme, 'Liebe frau, mach's türl auf (open your door), lass den regen 'nein, lass 'raus den sonnenschein,' Schmeller 2, 196. Spots in the field that are not to be cultivated indicate their sacredness in heathen times, conf. *gudeman's croft* in Scotland, the *Tothills* in England, Hone's Yearb. 873-4. To the disguised exclamations in the note, add ὦ Δάματερ! and the Armoric *tan,* fire! Villemarqué's Barzas breiz 1, 76; conf. Pott 1, lvii.

p. 12.] To these old customs re-acting on the constitution, to the pelting of idols at Hildesheim and Halberstadt on *Lœtare-day* (p. 190. 783), add this of Paderborn : ' In the cathedral-close at P., just where the idol Jodute is said to have stood, something in the shape of an image was fixed on a pole every *Lœtare Sunday* down to the 16th century, and shied at with cudgels by the highest in the land, till it fell to the ground. The ancient noble family of Stapel had the first throw, which they reckoned an especial honour and heirloom. When the image was down, children made game of it, and the nobility held a banquet. When the Stapels died out, the ancient custom was dropped.'—— Continu. of M. Klockner's Paderb. chron. The Stapel family were among the four pillars of the see of Paderborn; the last Stapel died in 1545, Erh. u. Gehrk. Zeitschr. f. vaterl. gesch. 7, 379. Compare also the sawing of the old woman (p. 782), the gelding of the devil, the expulsion of Death (p. 767), the yearly smashing of a wooden image of the devil, and the ' riding the black lad ' in Hone's Yearb. 1108, Dayb. 2, 467.

p. 12.] The Introduction ought to be followed by a general chapter on the contents and character of our Mythology, including parts of Chaps. XIV. and XV., especially the explanation of how gods become men, and men gods.

## CHAPTER II.

## GOD.

p. 13-15.] The word god is peculiar to the Germanic languages. Guitecl. 1, 31 : terre ou lon claime Dieu *got.* On goddess see beginning of Ch. XIII. *diu gotheit* occurs already in Fundgr. 2, 91. In the Venetian Alps, God is often called *der got* with the Art., Schmeller's Cimbr. Wtb. 125. Is the Ital. *iddio* from il dio, which does not account for *iddia* goddess, or is it abbreviated from domen-*ed-dio,* which, like O. Fr. domnedeu, damledeu, damredeu, comes from the Lat. voc. domine deus? Conf. Diez, Altrom. Sprachdenkm. p. 62.

Got is not the same word as guot, though the attempt to identify them is as old as OHG. (yet conf. the Pref. to E. Schulze's Gothic Glossary, xviii.) : ' *got* unde *guot* plurivoca sint. taz (what) mit *kote* wirt, taz wirt mit *kuote,*' Notker's Boeth. 172. Almost as obscure as the radical meaning of god is that of the Slav. bogh, some connecting it with Sanskr. b'agas, sun, Höfer's Zeitschr. 1, 150. In the Old-Persian cuneiform writing 4, 61 occurs bagâha, dei, from the stem baga, Bopp's Comp. Gram. 452 ; Sanskr. bhagavat is adorandus. Hesychius has βαγαῖος, Ζεὺς φρύγιος (conf. Spiegel's Cuneif. inscr. 210. Windischmann 19. 20. Bopp, Comp. Gr. 452. 581. Miklosich 3). Boh. bůže, božatko, Pol. bozę, bozątko, godkin, also genius, child of luck. Boh. bůzek, Pol. božek, idol.

Beside *guda,* gods, John 10, 34-5, we have *guþa,* Gal. 4, 8. The change of þ to d in derivation is supported by afgudei impietas, gudalaus impius, gudisks divinus. Neuter is daz apgot, Mos. 33, 19. abgote sibeniu, Ksrchr. 65. appitgot, Myst. 1, 229. Yet, beside the neut. abcotir, stands appetgöte (rh. kröte), Troj. kr. 27273, and abgote, Maria 149, 42 ; also masc. in Kristes büchelîn of 1278 (cod. giss. no. 876) : ' bette an *den appitgot.*' abgotgobide in Haupt 5, 458 is for abgotgiuobida. In the Gothic *þó galiuga-guda* for εἴδωλα, 1 Cor. 10, 19. 20, where the Greek has no article, we may perceive a side-glance at Gothic mythology ; conf. Löbe gloss. 76[b]. The ON. *goð* is not always idolum merely, but sometimes numen, as *goð öll,* omnia numina, Sæm. 67[b]. siti Hâkon með *heiðin* goð, Hâkonarm. 21. *gauð,* usually latratus, is a contemptuous term for a numen ethnicorum; conf. geyja, to bark, said of Freyja, p. 7 note.

Our *götze* occurs in the Fastn. Sp. 1181. 1332, where the carved 'goezen' of the painter at Würzburg are spoken of. Gods' images are of wood, are split up and burnt, Fornm. sög. 2, 163. v. d. Hagen's Narrenbuch, 314. Platers leben, 37. So Diagoras burns his wooden Hercules (Melander Jocos. 329), and cooks with it; conf. Suppl. to p. 108 n. Agricola no. 186 explains *ölgötz* as 'a stick, a log, painted, drenched with oil,' Low Germ. oligötze ; but it might be an earthen lamp or other vessel with an image of the god, Pröhle xxxvi. In Thuringia ölgötze means a baking.

p. 15.] To the distortions of God's name may be added : *gots* hingender gans! Geo. v. Ehingen, p. 9. *potz* verden angstiger schwininer wunden! Manuel, Fastn. sp. 81. Er. Alberus uses 'bocks angst,' H. Sachs 'botz angst.' Is potz, botz from bocks (p. 995)? Similar adaptations of *Dieu*, Raynouard sub v. deus; *culbieu*, Méon 4, 462. Ital. *sapristi* for sacristi.

p. 15.] The addition of a Possess. Pron. to the name of God recalls the belief in a guardian-spirit of each individal man (p. 875). The expressions not yet obsolete, 'my God! I thank my God, you may thank your God, he praised his God, etc.,' in Gotthelf's Erzähl. 1, 167 are also found much earlier : hevet ghesworen *bi sinen Gode*, Reinaert 526. ganc *dinem Gote* bevolen, Mor. 3740. er lobte *sinen Got*, Greg. 26, 52. durch *meinen Gott*, Ecke (Hagen) 48. saget *iuwem Gote* lop, Eilh. 2714. daz in *min Trehtin* lône, Kolocz. 186. gesegen dich Got *min Trehtin*, Ls. 3, 10. je le feré en *Mondieu* croire, Renart 3553. 28465. Méon 2, 388. son *deable*, Ren. 278. 390. Conf. '*Junonem meam* iratam habeam,' Hartung, genius.

The 'God grant, God knows' often prefixed to an interrogative, Gram. 3, 74, commits the decision of the doubtful to a higher power; conf. 'wëre Got, Gott behüte,' Gram. 3, 243-4. Got sich des wol versinnen kan, Parz. 369, 3; conf. 'sit cura deum.' daz sol Got niht en-wellen, Er. 6411. daz enwelle Got von himele, Nib. 2275, 1. nu ne welle Got, En. 64, 36.——Other wishes : sô sol daz Got gebieten, Nib. 2136, 4. hilf Got, Parz. 121, 2. nu hilf mir, hilferîcher Got 122, 26; conf. 'ita me deus adjuvet, ita me dii ament, amabunt,' Ter. Heaut. iv. 2, 8. 4, 1.

Got hüete dîn, Parz. 124, 17, etc. Got halde iuch 138, 27. Got lôn dir 156, 15. Got troeste iuch des vater mîn 11, 2. Got grüeze iuch, Iw. 5997. The freq. formulas ' God bless thee, greet thee,' addressed espec. to wine. Often in MHG., ' be it God who ': *Got sî* der daz wende ; der in ner' (heal); der uns gelücke gebe, Er. 8350. 6900. Hartm. Erst. b. 1068.—[Many new examples of ' wilkomen Got und mir' are here omitted.] sît mir *in Gote* wilkomen, Pass. 34, 92. *im* und *den göten* (gods) wille-komen, Troj. kr. 23105. God alone: *Got* willekume here von Berne, Dietr. Drachenk. 60ᵃ. Me and my wife: willekomen mir und ouch *der frouwen mîn*, MS. 1, 57ᵇ. bien venuz *mîner frouwen* unde mir, Parz. 76, 12.

The Supreme Being is drawn into other formulas : dankent *ir* und *Gote*, Lanz. 4702. des danke ich *dir* unde *Gote*, Flore 5915. *Got* und *iu* ze minnen (for the love of), Greg. 3819. nû lâz ich alle mîne dinc an *Godes* genâde unde *dîn*, Roth. 2252. To intensify an assertion : ich fergihe (avow) *Got* unde *iu*, Griesh. pred. 2, 71. nein *ich* und *Got*, Ls. 2, 257 ; like the heathenish ' *Oden* och *jag.*' daz er *sich* noch *Got* erkennet, Walth. 30, 7. *Got* und ouch die *liute*, Greg. 271. *Got* und *reht* diu riten dô în ze heile, Trist. (Massm.) 176, 26. 177, 2. We still speak of complaining to God and the world. One could not but love her, ' da half kein *gott* und kein *teufel*,' Höfer, Lorelei 234. So, ' to her and love ' : ich hân gesungen der *vil lieben* und *der Minne*, Neifen 13, 37. *frou Minne* und *ir*, vil sælic wîp 20, 33. ich wil *dir* und *deinem gaul* zusaufen, Garg. 240ᵇ.

p. 17.] God has human attributes : par les *iaus* Dieu, Ren. 505 ; so, Freyr lîtr eigi vinar *augum* til þín, Fornm. s. 2, 74. par les *pies* quide *Diu tenir*, Méon Fabl. 1, 351. wan dô Got hiez werden ander wîp, dô geschuof er iuwern lîp selbe *mit sîner hant*, Flore 2, 259. The Finns speak of God's *beard*. He wears a helmet, when he is wrapt in clouds ? conf. helot-helm, p. 463, Grîmnir pileatus, p. 146, and Mercury's hat ; den *Gotes helm* verbinden, MsH. 3, 354ᵇ ; conf. the proper name *Gotahelm*, Zeuss trad. Wizemb. 76, like Siguhelm, Friduhelm. As Plato makes God a shepherd, Wolfram makes him a judge, Parz. 10, 27. God keeps watch, as ' Mars vigilat,' Petron. 77 ; conf. Mars vigila, Hennil vigila (p. 749). He creates some men him-self : *Got selbe* worht ir süezen lîp, Parz. 130, 23 ; gets honour

by it : ir schöenes lîbes hât Got iemer *êre,* MS. 1, 143[a] ; shapes
beauty by moonlight : Diex qui la fist *en plaine lune,* Dinaux's
Trouvères Artésiens 261 ; feels pleasure : dar wart ein wuof, daz
ez *vor Got* ze himel was *genaeme,* Lohengr. 71. in (to them)
wurde *Got* noch (nor) diu *werlt* iemer *holt,* Dietr. Drach. 119[a].
So in O.Norse : Yggr var þeim *liðr,* Sæm. 251[a] ; conf. ' unus
tibi hic dum *propitius* sit Jupiter, tu istos *minutos deos* flocci
feceris,' and the cuneif. inscr. ' Auramazdá thuvám dushta biya,'
Oromasdes tibi amicus fiat.

p. 17-8 n.] God's diligence : examples like those in Text.

p. 18.] Many new examples of God's ' anger, hatred, etc.' are
here omitted.——Unser gote sint sô guot, daz si dînen tumben
muot niht *râchen* mit einer donre-strâle, Barl. 207, 13. ' *Got haz*
den lesten ! ' sprâchen die dâ vluhen hin (God hate the hindmost,
cried the fugitives), Ottoc. 76[a]. sô in *Got* iemer *hazze,* MsH. 3,
195[b]. daz in Got *gehoene,* dishonour, Lanz. 3862. er bat, daz
Got sînen *slac* über in vil schiere *slüege,* very soon smite, Turl.
krone 92 ; conf. θεοβλαβής, Herod. 1, 127. Got *velle* si beide,
make them fall, Iw. 6752. ich wil daz mich Got *velle* und mir
*schende* den lîp, Flore 1314. Got si *schende,* MsH. 3, 187[a]. fort
mit dir zu *Gottes boden,* Weise comöd. 39. Got *rech' ez* über sîn
kragen, Ottoc. 352[a]. so muoze mig Got *wuorgen,* Karlm. 368.
nû *brennet* mich der *Gotes zan* (tooth) in dem fiur, Tôdes gehugde
679. sô *entwiche* mir Got, Flore 5277. Got ist an mir *verzaget,*
Parz. 10, 30. ist Got an sîner helfe *blint,* oder ist er dran *be-
toubet* (deaved, daft), 10, 20. die göte gar *entsliefen,* Albr. Tit.
2924.

p. 20.] The irrisio deorum, ON. *goð-gá* (Pref. liii. and p. 7n.)
reaches the height of insult in Laxdæla-s. 180. Kristni-s. cap.
9 ; OHG. *kot-scelta* blasphemia, MHG. *gotes schelter.* Conf. the
abusive language of Kamchadales to their highest god Kutka,
Klemm 2, 318. nû *schilte* ich mîniu *abgot,* scold my false gods,
Lament 481. sînen *zorn huob* er hin ze Gote : ' *rîcher* Got un-
guoter ! ' Greg. 2436-42. sô wil ich iemer wesen *gram* den
goten, En. 7985. The saints scold (as well as coax) God,
Keisersb. omeis 12[d]. *wâfen schrîen* über (cried shame upon)
Gotes gewalt, Wigal. 11558. Got, dâ bistu *eine schuldec* an (alone
to blame), Iw. 1384. Charles threatens him : Karles *tença* à
Dieu, si confust son voisin, ' jamais en France n'orra messe à

matin,' Aspr. 35ᵃ. hé, saint Denis de France, tu *somoilles et dorz*, quant fauz tes homes liges tiens en est li gran torz, Guitecl. 2, 156. nemt iuwer gote *an ein seil* und *trenket si*, drench them, Wh. 1, 83ᵃ. *tröwet* (believes) als daun *S. Urban* auch, wenn er niht schafft gut wein, werd' man ihn nach den alten brauch werffen in bach hinein, Garg. pref. 10. In the Ksrchr. 14737 Charles threatens St. Peter: und ne mache dû den blinden hiute niht gesunden, dîn hûs ich dir zestôre, dînen widemen ich dir zevuore. God is defied or cheated: *biss Gott selbst kompt* (to punish us), haben wir vogel und nest weggeraumbt, Garg. 202ᵃ.

p. 20-1.] More epithets of God. He is hardly ever addressed as dear; but we find: an sînen *lieben* abgoten, Pass. 306, 20. ir *lieben* gote 38, 41. der *zarte* Got, Ls. 2, 285-6. Griesh. 22 (5. 9. 17 of Christ). der *süeze* Got von himel, Griesh., etc. in *svasugoð*, Sæm. 33ᵃ. *tugenhafter* Got, Wh. 49, 16. Got der *gewâre*, Fundgr. ii. 90, 41. *hêre* is said of heathen gods, angels, emperors: ein Venus *hêre*, MS. 1, 55ᵃ. *hâlig* dryhten, Beow. 1366.——God sees, tends, blesses, loves, rewards, honours, pities, forgets: Got der müeze dîn *pflegen*, Herb. 6160. Got *gesegene* uns immer mêre 7732. Got *segen* iuch, Got *lône* dir 8092. Got *minne* dich, Eracl. 644. Got müeze mich *êren*, MsH. 1, 59ᵇ. daz mohte Got *erbarmen*, Wigal. 5342. als im Got *ergaz*, forgot, Herb. 15669. sô mîn Got *ergaz*, Troj. kr. 14072. des (him) hât Got *vergezzen*, der tivel hât in besezzen, Warnung 343. Our God-forgotten, God-forsaken.——The poor are *Godes volk*, Diut. 1, 438; sîne aerme, Maerl. 2, 230; daz *Gotes her* (host), Gute frau 1492; hence proper names like *Godesman*, Trad. Corb. 291, *Godasmannus*, Pol. Irmin. 93ᵇ, *Kotesman*, Trad. Juvav. 131.——The Gen. *Gotes* intensifies the adjs. poor, wretched, ignorant, pure: owê mich Gotes *armen*, Nib. 2090. ich vil Gotes *armiu*, Gudr. 1209, 1. ich Gotes *arme* maget, Dietr. Drach. die Gotes *ellenden*, Ernst 3176. der Gotes *tumbe*, Helmbr. 85. der Gotes *reine*, Marienleg. 189, 428.

p. 22.] Earthly titles given to God: der edel *keiser* himelbaere, Tit. 3382. That of the king of birds: Gott der hohe edle *adler* vom himmel, Berthold 331. The M. Lat. *domnus* is not used of God, who is always Dominus, but of popes, kings, etc., Ducange sub v. O. Fr. *dame dieu*, *dame dé*, Roquef. sub v.; Prov. *dami*

*drieu, damri deu, domini dieus,* Raynouard 3, 68; on *dame* conf.
p. 299 n. Wallach. *dumnedeu* for God, *domn* for sir, lord. Slav.
*knez, kniaz,* prince, is applied to God in Wiggert's psalms, conf.
kneze granitsa in Lisch urk. 1, 9. So ἄναξ, ἄνασσα are used of
kings and gods, espec. ἄνακες of the Dioscuri, and the Voc. ἄνα
of gods only.

p. 22.] God is called Father in that beautiful passage : þonne
forstes bend *Fœder* onlaeteð, Beow. 3218. Brahma is called
*avus paternus,* Bopp's gloss. 217ᵃ, and *Pitamaha,* great father,
Holtzm. 3, 141. 153; conf. Donar as father, p. 167. In the
Märchen, God becomes godfather to particular children : in KM.
no. 126 he appears as a beggar, and gives his godson a horse,
in the Wallach. märchen 14 a cow. The fays, as godmothers,
give gifts. The *grandmother* travels all over the earth, Klemm 2,
160; conf. *anel, baba* (p. 641), *zloto-baba,* gold-grandmother;
*mother* (p. 254).

p. 22.] The Saxon *metod,* ON. *miötudr* may be conn. with
Sanskr. *mâtar,* meter and creator, Bopp's Comp. Gr. 1134, and
mâtâ, mother, creatress ; conf. ταμίας Ζεύς.

p. 23.] In Homer too, God is he that *pours* : Zeus creates,
begets mankind, Od. 20, 202. But Zeus χέει ὕδωρ, Il. 16, 385.
χιόνα, Il. 12, 281. Poseidon χέεν ἀχλύν, Il. 20, 321. Athena
ἠέρα χεῦε, Od. 7, 15. ὕπνον 2, 395. κάλλος 23, 156. χάριν 2,
12, etc. Conf. p. 330, and 'Athena ἧκε κόμας,' let her hair
stream, Od. 23, 156. God is he, 'der alle bilde *giuzet,*' Diut. 2,
241 ; der schepfet alle zît niuwe sêl (souls), di' er *giuzet* unde gît
in menschen, Freid. 16, 25. the angel ' *giuzet* dem menschen die
sêle în,' Berth. 209. God is ' der *Smit von Oberlande,* der elliu
bilde wol *würken* kan,' MsH. 2, 247ᵃ. He fits together : das
*füege* Got, Rab. 554. Got *füege* mir'z ze guote, Frauend. 422, 22.
dô bat si Got vil dicke *füegen* ir den rât, Nib. 1187, 1, like our
eingeben, suggest. sigehafte hende (victorious hands) *füege* in
Got der guote, Dietr. 8082. dô *fuogt* in (to them) Got einen
wint, Rab. 619 ; conf. Gevuoge, p. 311 n. The Minne also fits,
and Sælde (fortune) : dir *füeget* sælde daz beste, Tit. 3375 ; our
' fügung Gottes,' providence. God destines, *verhenget,* MS. 1,
74ᵃ (the bridle to the horse) ; OHG. *firhengan* (even *hengan* alone),
concedere, consentire. He carries, guides : Got *truoc* uns zu dir
in das lant (so : the devil brings you), Dietr. and Ges. 656. mich

hât selber *gewîset* her Got von himel, Keller's Erzähl. 648, 11.
We say 'go with God,' safely, σύν θεῷ βαίνεις, Babr. 92, 6.

p. 23.] Though Berthold laughs at the notion of God sitting
in the sky, and his legs reaching down to the earth, as a Jewish
one, there are plenty of similar sensuous representations to be
gleaned out of early poems, both Romance and German : ' Deo
chi maent sus en ciel,' Eulalia ; etc. alwaltintir Got, der mir zi
lebine gibôt, Diemer 122, 24. wanti Got al mag und al guot wil
99, 18. God is eternal : qui fu et iest et iert, Ogier 4102.

p. 24.] To explain the Ases we must compare *ahura-mazdas*
(p. 984 n.) and Sanskr. *asura* spiritual, living. Svâ lâti *áss* þik
heilan î haugi, Fornald. sög. 1, 437. Rîn *âs-kunn*, Sæm. 248ª.
nornir *áskungar* 188ª. A friðla is called *ása blóð*, Fornm. sög. 9,
322, fair as if sprung from Ases ? þâ vex mer *ásmegin*, iafnhâtt
up sem himinn, Sn. 114. *ásmegir*, Sæm. 94ᵇ. *ásmóðr* opp. to
jötunmóðr, Sn. 109. *ása bragr* stands for Thôr, Sæm. 85ᵇ. Sometimes *âs* seems to mean genius, fairy : in Nials-s. p. 190 a *Svinfells-âs* or *Snæfells-âs* changes a man that lives with him into a
woman every ninth night ; the man is called ' *brûðr* Svinfells-âs,
amica genii Svinfelliani. Here also mark the connexion of âs
with a mountain (fell for fiall ?). The Saxon form of the word
is also seen in the names of places, *Osene-dred*, Kemble no. 1010
(5, 51), and *Osna-brugga* (conf. As-brû, rainbow, p. 732). Note
the OHG. *Kêr-ans*, spear-god, *Folch-ans*, Haupt's Zeitschr. 7, 529.
That *Ansivarii* can be interpreted ' a diis oriundi ' is very doubtful. Haupt's Ztschr. 5, 409 has ' des bomes *as*,' prob. for ' ast '
bough, which may indeed be conn. with ' âs ' beam, for it also
means gable, rooftree, firmament, ἕρμα, fulcrum. Varro says
the Lat. *āra* was once *āsa*, *ansa*, sacred god's-seat, v. Forcellini.
Pott 1, 244, Gr. D. Sag. p. 114. The Gr. *αἶσα* (p. 414) seems un-
connected. Bopp 43ᵈ connects îśvara dominus with an Irish *aes-
fhear aesar*, deus, from Pictet p. 20 ; but this contains fear, vir.

p. 26.] ' Hos *consentes* et *complices* Etrusci aiunt et nominant,
quod una *oriantur* et *occidant* una' says Arnobius adv. gentes
lib. 3 ; does he mean constellations ? conf. Gerhard's Etr. gotth.
p. 22-3. Does *áttûnga* brautir, Sæm. 80ᵇ, mean the same as âsa,
cognatorum ?

p. 26.] As consulting *ragin* appear the gods in Sanskr. *râga-
nas* and Etrusc. *rasena*. The Homeric Zeus too is counsellor,

μῆστωρ, μητίετα. ‘consilio deorum immortalium, consuesse deos
immort.’ says Cæsar B. Gall. 1, 12. 14. The pl. regin occurs
further in Sæm. 32ᵇ. 34ª *nyt regin.* 36ª *vîs regin.* Hâkonar-m.
18 *râð* öll ok *regin.* Sæm. 248ᵇ *dôlg-rögnir.* Also *rögn* : höpt,
bönd, rögn, Sn. 176. ‘wer gesaz bî Gote an dem *râte* dâ diu
guote mir wart *widerteilet?’* allotted, Ms. 2, 180ª. Just as impersonal as the Gen. pl. in OS. *regano*-giscapu sounds another in
Haupt's Ztschr. 2, 208, where Mary is styled ‘kuneginne aller
*magene,’* virtutum.

p. 26n.] The appearing of gods is discussed at p. 336. Saxo,
ed. Müller 118, speaks of *sacra deûm agmina.* The gods live
happy : *deorum* vitam apti sumus, Ter. Heaut. iv. 1, 15. *deus*
sum, sic hoc ita est, Hecyra v. 4, 3. The beautiful and blithe
are comp. to them : þyckir oss *Oðinn vera,* Hâk.-m. 15 ; conf.
Asa-blôð above. gê her für *als ein götinne,* Renn. 12277. ên
wîf ghelîc ere *godinnen,* Maerl. 2, 233. alse ochter *God selve*
comen soude, Lanc. 31321. Conf. the beauty of elves and angels,
p. 449. The I. of Cos seemed to produce gods, the people were
so handsome, Athen. 1, 56. Paul and Barnabas taken for Mercury and Jupiter, Acts 14, 12.

p. 27.] On *sihora armen* conf. Massm. in Haupt's Ztschr. 1,
386 and Holtzm. in Germania 2, 448, who gives variants; sihora
may have been equiv. to frauja. Sigora-freá in Cod. Exon. 166,
35. 264, 8 is liter. triumphorum dominus. A warlike way of
addressing God in Nib. Lament 1672 is, himelischer *degen !*

p. 28.] At the end of this Chap. it ought to be observed, that
some deities are limited to particular lands and places, while
others, like Ζεὺς πανελλήνιος, are common to whole races. Also
that the Greeks and Romans (not Teutons) often speak indefinitely
οι ‘some god’: καί τις θεὸς ἡγεμόνευεν, Od. 9, 142. 10, 141.
τίς με θεῶν ὀλοφύρατο 10, 157. ἀθανάτων ὅς τις 15, 35. τις
θεός ἐσσι 16, 183. τίς σφιν τόδ᾽ ἔειπε. θεῶν 16, 356. ἦ μάλα
τις θεὸς ἔνδον 19, 40. καί τις θεὸς αὐτὸν ἐνείκοι 21, 196. 24,
182. 373. Solemnis formula, qua dii tutelares urbium evocaban-
tur e civitatibus oppugnatione cinctis ambiguo nomine *si deus,*
*si dea,* ne videlicet alium pro alio nominando aut sexum confun-
dendo falsa religione populum alligarent, conf. Macrob. Sat. 3, 9.
Nam consuestis in precibus ‘sive tu *deus* es sive *dea’* dicere,
Arnob. 3, 8. Hac formula utebantur Romani in precibus, quando

sive terra movisset, sive aliud quid accidisset, de quo ambige-batur qua causa cujusque dei vi ac numine effectum sit, conf. Gellius 2, 20 ibique Gronovius.

---

## CHAPTER III.

### WORSHIP.

p. 29.] For veneration of a deity the AS. has both *weorðscipe* reverentia, dignitas, and *weorðung*; the Engl. *worship*, strictly a noun, has become also a verb = *weorðian*. The christian teachers represented the old worship as *diobules gelp* inti *zierida* (pompa). In Isidore 21, 21. 55, 5 *aerlós* stands for impius. Beside the honouring of God, we find 'das Meien *êre*,' Ms. 2, 92ᵇ, and 'duvels *êre*, Rose 11200. D. Sag. 71. Gote *dienen*, Nib. 787, 1. er *forchte* (feared) den Heilant, Roth 4415. Heartfelt devotion is expr. by 'mit *inneclîchen* muote,' Barl. 187, 16. *andachtlîche* 187, 36. 14. mit dem *inneren* gebete. die *andâht* fuor zum gibel aus, Wolkenst. p. 24.

p. 29.] Among most nations, the Chinese being an exception, worship finds utterance in prayer and sacrifice, in solemn trans-actions that give rise to festivals and hightides, which ought to be more fully described further on. Prayer and sacrifice do not always go together : betra er *óbedit* enn se *ofblótit* (al. *óblótit*), Saem. 28ᵇ. The Chinese do not pray, and certainly, if God has no body and no speech, we cannot attribute an ear or hearing to him, conseq. no hearing of prayer. Besides, an almighty God must understand thoughts as easily as words. Prayers, the utterance of petition, gratitude and joy, arose in heathenism, and presuppose a divine form that hears. Odysseus prays to Athena: κλῦθί μευ, νῦν δή πέρ μευ ἄκουσον, ἐπεὶ πάρος οὔποτ' ἄκουσας ῥαιομένου, Od. 6, 325. 13, 356. κλῦθι, ἄναξ 5, 445. Il. 16, 514 ; Poseidon and Apollo are addressed with the same formula. Gods are greeted through other gods: Veneri dicito multam meis verbis salutem, Plaut. Pœn. i. 2, 195. But, besides praying aloud, we also read of soft muttering, as in speaking a spell, Lasicz 48. θρησκεύειν is supposed to mean praying half aloud, Creuzer 2, 285. Latin *precari* (conf. procus), Umbr. *persní*

(Aufrecht and Kirchhoff 2, 28. 167) answers to OHG. *fergón*
poscere, precari, N. Cap. 153, Sanskr. *prach*, Zend. *pereç.* 'tases
persnimu,' tacitus precare, pray silently, 'kutef persnimu,' caute
precare, A. and K. 2, 168-9. 170. Sanskr. *jap* = submissa voce
dicere, praesertim preces, Bopp· 135ᵃ; conf. *jalp* loqui, Lith.
kalbu : faveas mihi, *murmure* dixit, Ov. Met. 6, 327 (p. 1224).
'gebete *käuen*,' chewing prayers, occurs in Bronner's Life 1,
475 ; 'stille gebete *thauen*,' distil, in Gessner's Works (Zurich
1770) 2, 133. 'gebet *vrumen*,' put forth, Gudr. 1133, 1. *beten
und himelspreken*, Gefken beil. 116. daz gebet ist ein süezer
bote (messenger) ze himele, Ernst 20. Or, prayer resounds : daz
dîn bete *erklinge*, Walth. 7, 35. precibus deum *pulsare* opimis,
Ermold. Nigell. 2, 273. Prayer gushes out, is poured out : alse
daz gebet *irgie*, Ksrchr. 2172. M.Neth. gebed *utstorten*, Soester
fehde p. 597 ; now, bede *storten*, preces fundere, like tranen st.,
lacrimas fundere. gepet *ausgiessen*, MB. 27, 353.

p. 29.] Other words for praying : Grk. δέομαι I need, I ask,
ἱκετεύω and λίσσομαι beseech. ON. *heita* â einn, vovere sub
conditione contingenti : *hêt* â Thôr, vowed, Oldn. läseb. 7 (conf.
*giving* oneself to a partic. god, Oðinn, p. 1018-9). OHG. *harên*
clamare, *anaharên* invocare, N. Boëth. 146. OS. *grótian* God,
Hel. 144, 24. 145, 5. Does προσκυνέω come from κυνέω I kiss
(as adoro from os oris, whence osculum), and is it conn. with the
hand-kissing with which the Greeks worshipped the sun; τὴν χεῖρα
κύσαντες, Lucian 5, 133 ; or from κύων? conf. πρόσκυνες, fawning flatterers, Athen. 6, 259, see Pott's Zählmeth. 255. Ἀσπά-
ζεσθαι is also used of dogs fawning upon a master.

p. 30.] A suppliant is not only *bëtoman* in OHG., but *beteman*
in MHG. Hartm. büchl. 1, 263. Prayer, our gebet, is a fem.
*bete :* mîne flêhe und mîne bete, die wil ich êrste senden mit
*herzen* und mit *henden*, Trist. 123, 22 (praying with hands,
folded ?). The MHG. *bëten* is always joined with *an*, as prepos.
or prefix : an welchen got er baete, Servat. 1347. ein kreftige
stat, dô man diu apgot anebat, Karl 10ᵃ. Is it used only of false
gods ? conf. Pfeiffer's Barl. p. 446.

p. 30.] The MHG. *flêhen* supplicare takes the Dative : deme
heiligin Geiste vlên, Wernh. v. Niˑder-rh. 37, 17, etc. But
with the Accus. : den tôren flêhen, Freid. 83, 3. alle herren
flêhen, Walther 28, 33. fleha ze himele *frumen*, N. Boëth. 271 ;

conf. 'gebet vrumen' above. Εὔχεσθαι also takes a Dat.: Διί, Od. 20, 97. Ἀθήνῃ 2, 261. Ποσειδάωνι 3, 43. ἐπεύχεσθαι Ἀρτέμιδι 20, 60 ; conf. εὐχῇ (or ἐν εὐχαῖς, ἐν λόγοις) πρεσβεύειν, φροιμιάζομαι, Æsch. Eum. 1. 20. 21.

p. 31.] Can Goth. *aíhtrôn* and OHG. *eiscôn* be from aigan, and mean wish to have ? OHG. *diccan* occurs in MHG. too : *digete gein Gote*, Altd. bl. 2, 149. *an in gediget*, prays, Kdh. Jesu 91, 4. *underdige* supplicatio, Serv. 3445.

p. 31.] Postures in prayer. Standing : diu *stêt an ir gebete in der kapellen hie bî*, Iw. 5886. *an daz gebet stân*, Zappert p. 23. Bowing : diofo *ginigen*, bend low, O. iii. 3, 28. *sîn nîgen er gein himel gap*, made his bow, Parz. 392, 30. Hagen bows to the merwomen, Nib. 1479, 1. As the road is kindly saluted, so contrariwise : ich wil dem wege iemer-mêre sîn vîent swâ dû hin gâst, be foe to every way thou goest, Amur 2347. The Finnic *kumarran*, bending, worship, is done to the road (tielle), moon (kuulle), sun,(päiwällä), Kalew. 8, 103. 123. 145. diu bein biegen = pray, Cod. Vind. 159 no. 35. On kneeling, bending, conf. Zapp. p. 39. ze gebete *gevie*, Ksrchr. 6051. ze Gote er sîn gebete *lac*, Pantal. 1582. er *viel* an sîn gebet, Troj. kr. 27224. *viel in die bede, int gebede*, Maerl. 2, 209. 3, 247. dô hup er ane zu *veniende :* wo ime daz houbit lac, dô satzte her di fuze hin, Myst. 1, 218. legde *hleor on eorðan*, Cædm. 140, 32. Swed. *bönfalla*, to kneel in prayer. During a sacrifice they fell to the ground ῥίπτοντες ἐς ὦδας, Athen. p. 511. The Ests crawl bareheaded to the altar, Estn. verh. 2, 40. Other customs : the Indians *danced* to the Sun, Lucian, ed. Lehm. 5, 130. Roman women, barefoot, with dishevelled hair, prayed Jupiter for rain. The hands of gods are kissed, conf. προσκυνεῖν. In contrast with looking up to the gods, ἄνω βλέψας, Moschus epigr., the eyes are turned *away* from sacred objects. Odysseus, after landing, is to throw back into the sea, with averted look, the κρήδεμνον lent him by Ino, ἀπονόσφι τραπέσθαι, Od. 5, 350. ταρβήσας δ᾽ ἑτέρωσε βάλ᾽ ὄμματα, μὴ θεὸς εἴη, 16, 179.

p. 32.] Uncovering the head : huic capite velato, illi sacrificandum est *nudo*, Arnob. 3, 43. *pilleis* capitibus inclinarent *detractis*, Eckehardus A.D. 890 (Pertz 2, 84). *tuot ûwere kugelen abe*, und bitit Got, Myst. 1, 83, 25. son *chapel oste*, Ren. 9873 ; conf. 's *chäppli lüpfe*, Hebel 213. *helme* und ouch diu *hüetelîn* diu wurden schiere ab genomen, Lanz. 6838. sînen *helm* er *abe bant* (unbound), und sturzt' in ûf des schildes rant ; des *hüetels* wart sîn houbet blôz, wan sîn zuht war vil grôz, Er. 8963. In 1 Cor. 11, 4. 5, a man is to pray and prophesy with covered head, a woman with uncovered, see Vater's note. Penance is done standing naked in water, G. Ab. 1, 7 ; conf. Pref. lxx. The monk at early morn goes to the Danube to draw water, wash and pray, Vuk ii. 7, beg. of Naod Simeun. The Greeks went to the seashore to pray : Τηλέμαχος δ' ἀπάνευθε κιὼν ἐπὶ θῖνα θαλάσσης, Od. 2, 260. βῆ δ' ἀκέων παρὰ θῖνα . . . . ἀπάνευθε κιὼν ἠρᾶθ'·ὁ γεραιὸς Ἀπόλλωνι ἄνακτι, Il. i. 34.

p. 33.] Arsenius prays with *uplifted hands* from sunset to sunrise, Maerl. 3, 197. in *crucis modum* coram altari se sternere, Pertz 8, 258; conf. ordeal of cross. Praying 'mit *zertânen armen, zertrenten* armen, Zellw. urk. no. 1029. 775. Hands are washed before praying : χεῖρας νιψάμενος πολιῆς ἁλός, in the hoary sea, Od. 2, 261. 12, 336. Helgafell, þângat skyldi engi maðr ôþveginn (unwashen) *líta*, Landn. 2, 12.

p. 33.] Χάρις, gratia, is also translated *anst*. Goth. *anstái audahafta*, gratiâ plena ! OHG. fol Gotes *ensti*, O. i. 5, 18. *enstio* fol, Hel. 8, 8 ; conf. 'gebôno fullu' in Tat., and AS. mid gife gefylled. For ginâda Otfried uses a word peculiar to himself, *êragrehti*, Graff 2, 412. The cuneif. inscr. have constantly : 'Auramazdâ miya upastám abara,' Oromasdes mihi opem ferebat ; 'vashnâ Auramazdaha,' gratiâ Oromasdis.

p. 34.] Other ON. expressions for prayer : blótaði Oðinn, ok biðr hann *líta â* sitt mâl, Hervar. saga c. 15. ôreiðom augom *lítið* ockr þinnig, ok gefit sitjondom sigr, Sæm. 194[a]. mâl ok mannvit gefit ockr maerom tveim, ok laeknis-hendur meðan lifom, ibid.——As the purpose of prayer and sacrifice is twofold, so is divine grace either mere favour to the guiltless, or forgiveness of sin, remission of punishment. Observe in Hel. 3, 18 : thiggean Herron is huldi, that sie Hevan-cuning *lédes âléti* (ut Deus malum averteret, remitteret), though Luke 1, 10 has merely *orare*, and O. i. 4, 14 only ginâda beitôta. He is asked to spare, to pity : ἵληθι, Od. 3, 380. 16, 184. φείδεο δ' ἡμέων 16, 185. σὺ δὲ ἵλεως γενοῦ, Lucian 5, 292. 'taivu ainomen Tapio,' be entreated, Kalev. 7, 243 ; conf. τόδε μοι κρήηνον ἐέλδωρ, Il. 1, 41. Od. 17, 242. (Kl. schr. 2, 458.)

The Hindu also looks to the *East* at early morning prayer, hence he calls the South daxa, daxima, the right. In praying to Odin one looks *east*, to Ulf *west*, Sv. forns. 1, 69. *solem respiciens* is said of Boiocalus, Tac. ann. 13, 55. Prayer is directed to the *sun*, N. pr. bl. 1, 300, and there is no sacrificing after sunset, Geo. 2281. On the other hand, ' *Norðr* horfa dyr ' occurs in Sæm. 7ᵇ. Jötunheimr lies to the North, Rask afh. 1, 83. 94. D. Sag. 981-2.

p. 35 n.] Mock-piety : wolt ir den heiligen die *zehen* (toes) *abbeissen?* Bronner 1, 295. alle heiligen *fressen* wollen, Elis. v. Orl. 251. *götze-schlecker*, Stald. 1, 467. In thieves' lingo a Catholic is *tolefresser*, *bilderfresser*, Thiele 317ª. magliavutts, götzenfresser, Carisch 182ᵇ. Whence comes Ital. bachettone? conf. bigot, Sp. beato. die alte *tempeltrete*, Spil v. d. 10 jungfr. in Steph. 175. du rechte *renne umme id olter*, you regular Run-round-the-altar, Mone schausp. 2, 99. *frömmchen*, as early as Er. Alberus Praec. vitae ac mor. 1562, p. 90ª.

p. 35.] On Sacrifice, conf. Creuzer symb. 1, 171. ' opphir = vota,' Gl. Sletst. 6, 672. Gifts = sacrifices, p. 58. si bråhten ir *obfer* und *antheiz*, Diemer 179, 25. In Latin the most general phrase is rem divinam facere = sacrificare ; we also find *commovere*, *obmovere*, Aufr. u. Kirchh. 2, 165. *Victima*, the greater sacrifice, is opposed to *hostia*, the less, Fronto p. 286. To ' *oblationes* für allen gebilden (before the statues and shrines), ut tenor est fundationis, cedens pastori ' (found. at Rüden, Westph. 1421, Seibertz Quellen d. Westf. gesch. 1, 232) answers the Germ. *wisunga* visitatio, oblatio, Graff 1, 1068, from wìsòn, visitare. *wisod* = oblei, visitatio, Schmeller 4, 180. The Swiss now say *wisen* for praying at the tombs of the dead, Stald. 2, 455.

p. 35.] On *blôt*, *blôstr* see Bopp's Comp. Gr. 1146. Goth. *Guþ blôtan*, Deum colere, 1 Tim. 2, 10. In ON., beside gods' sacrifices, there are *álfa blôt*, p. 448, *dîsa blôt*, p. 402 [and we may add the blôt-*risi* on p. 557]. *blôt-haug* and *stôrblôt*, Fornm. sög. 5, 164-5. sleikja *blôt-bolla*, Fagrsk. p. 63. A proper name *Blôtmâr*, acc. Blôtmâ (-mew, the bird), Landn. 3, 11 seems to mean larus sacrificator, = the remarkable epithet *blotevogel*, A.D. 1465, Osnabr. ver. 2, 223 ; or is it simply ' naked bird ' ? conf. spott-vogel, speivogel, wehvogel [gallows-bird, etc.]. ON. *blôtvargr* = prone to curse, for blôta is not only consecrate, but execrate.

p. 37 n.] Mit der *blotzen* haun, H. Sachs iii. 3, 58ᶜ. eine
breite *blötze*, Chr. Weise, Drei erzn. 194. der *weidplotz*, hunting-
knife, *plötzer*, Vilmar in Hess. Ztschr. 4, 86. die *bluote*, old
knife, Woeste.

p. 37.] *Antheiz* a vow, but also a vowed sacrifice, as when
the Germans promised to sacrifice *if they conquered*, Tac. Ann. 13,
57, or as the Romans used to vow a *ver sacrum*, all the births
of that spring, the cattle being sacrificed 20 years after, and the
youth sent abroad, Nieb. 1, 102. ir obfer unde *antheiz*, Diemer
179, 25. *gehéton wîg-weorðunga*, Beow. 350. aerþon hine deáð
*onsægde*, priusquam mors eum sacrificaret, Cod. Exon. 171, 32 ;
conf. MHG. iuwer lîp ist *ungeseit*, ἄφατος, Neidh. 47, 17. What
means OHG. *frêhtan* ? [frêhan ? frech, freak ?]. N. Boeth. 226
says of Iphigenia: dia Chalchas in friskinges wîs *frêhta* (Graff 3,
818) ; conf. ON. *frétt* vaticinium, divinatio (Suppl. to p. 94), and
AS. 'on blôte oððe on *fyrhte*,' Schmid 272, 368, where fear or
fright is out of the question.

p. 38.] AS. *cweman*, also with Dat., comes near fullafahjan :
'onsecgan and godum *cweman*,' diis satisfacere, Cod. Exon. 257,
25. Criste *cweman* leofran lâce 120, 25. Like AS. *bring* is OHG.
*antfangida*, victima, Diut. 1, 240. What is offered and accepted
*lies* : Theocr. epigr. 1, 2 uses κεῖσθαι of consecrated gifts.

p. 39.] To AS. *lâc* add *lâcan* offerre, conf. placare. *lâc*
onsecgan, Cod. Exon. 257, 30. *lâc* xenium, donum, *lâcdaed*
munificentia, Haupt's Ztschr. 9, 496ᵃ.

p. 39.] On ἀπαρχαί conf. Pausan. 1, 31. Callimach. hy. in
Del. 279. Another definite term for sacrifice seems to be the
obscure Goth. *daigs*, massa, Rom. 11, 16 [is it not dough, teig,
a lit. transl. of φύραμα ?] *Wizót* survived in MHG. too : frône
*wizót*, Servat. 3337. Massmann derives *hunsl* from hinþan ;
Kuhn in Berl. Jb. 10, 192—5, 285 from *hu* to pour, which = θύειν
acc. to Bopp 401. *hunsljada* σπένδομαι 2 Tim. 4, 6. *unhunslags*
ἄσπονδος 3, 3. *ufsneiþan* = θύειν, kill, Luke xv. 23-7. 30, and
*ufsniþans* immolatus, 1 Cor. 5, 7 plainly refer to cutting up the
victim. *Hunsaloa* in the Ecbasis may be either hunsal-aha
(-water) or huns-alah (-temple), Lat. ged. p. 289. 290.

O.Slav. *treba* = libatio, res immolata, templum ; *trèbishche* βωμός.
'qui idolothyta, quod *trebo* dicitur, vel obtulerit aut mandu-
caverit,' Amann Cod. mss. Frib. fasc. 2, p. 64. O.Boh. *třeba*,

Russ. *treba*, sacrifice. O.Sl. *trèbiti*, Pol. *trzebić*, Serv. *triebiti*, purify; conf. the place-name *Trebbin*, Jungm. 4, 625ᵇ. Pol. *trzeba, potrzeba*, oportet, it is needful. Serv. *potreba*, Boh. *potřeba*, need; conf. Lith. *Potrimpus* and *Antrimp, Atrimp*, Hanusch 216-7. D. Sag. 328. Sacrifice is in Lett. *śobars*, Bergm. 142; in Hung. *aldomás*, Ipolyi 341.

p. 40.] The right to emend *áibr* into *tibr* is disputed by Weigand 1997; conf. Diefenbach's Goth. wtb. 1, 12. On τέφρα see my Kl. Schr. 2, 223; Umbr. *tefro* n. is some unknown part of the victim, Aufrecht u. K. 2, 294. 373. May we connect the Lett. *śobars*, plague-offering? Some would bring in the LG. *zefer* (= käfer), see Campe under 'ziefer,' and Schmell. 4, 228; conf. OHG. arzibôr, Graff 5, 578, and ceepurhuc, n. prop. in Karajan. Keisersb., brös. 80ᵇ, speaks of *ungesuber;* we also find *unzuter* vermin, conf. *unáz*, uneatable, *i.e.* vermin, Mone 8, 409. The Grail tolerates no *ungezibere* in the forest, Tit. 5198. The wolf is euphemistically called *ungeziefer*, Rockenphil. 2, 28. The *geziefer* in the pastures of Tyrol are sheep and goats, Hammerle p. 4.

With OHG. *wîhan*, to sacrifice, conf. the AS. *wig-weorðung* above, and Lith. *weikiu*, ago, facio, Finn. *waikutan*.

p. 41.] The *diversity* of sacrifices is proved by Pertz 2, 243, *diversos sacrificandi ritus* incoluerunt; and even by Tac. Germ. 9 : deorum maxime Mercurium colunt, cui certis diebus humanis quoque hostiis *litare* fas habent. Herculem ac Martem concessis animalibus *placant.* pars Suevorum et *Isidi* sacrificat.

To a sacrifice the god is invited, is asked to join : καλέει τὸν θεόν, Herod. 1, 132. ἐπικαλέει τ. θ. 4, 60. ἐπικαλέσαντες τ. θ. σφάζουσι 2, 39. The gods are present at it, Athen. 3, 340-1. Why *bones* are offered to the gods, Hes. theog. 557. *primitiae ciborum* deo offerenda, Athen. 2, 213. The rising *smoke* and *steam* are pleasing to gods, Lucian's Prometh. 19. ἐκ δὲ θυμάτων Ἥφαιστος οὐκ ἔλαμπε, Soph. Antig. 1007. Men *strengthen* the gods by sacrifice, Haupt's Ztschr. 6, 125. They sacrifice to Wêda (Wodan), crying : ' Wedki *taeri !* ' dear Weda, consume! accept our offering, Schl.-Holst. landeskunde 4, 246. The god gives a sign that he accepts : þâ kômu þar hrafnar fljugandi ok gullu hâtt, as a sign ' at Oðinn mundi þegit hafa blôtit,' Fornm. sög. 1, 131.

p. 42.] Part of the *spoils of war* given to the God of the Christians, Livl. Reimchr. 2670—73. 3398 to 3401. 6089. 4696. 11785. 11915. '*brünien, pfert* und *rische man*' are to be *burnt* in case of victory 4700. 4711. If *victima* is from vinco, it must have been orig. a sacrifice for victory, ON. *sigur*-giöf, victim. The *ehren-gang* in Müllenh. Schl.-Holst. s., p. 108 was once prob. the same.

p. 42.] In *expiatory offerings* the idea is, that the wrath of God falls on the victim: clearly so in the *scapegoat*, Levit. 16, 20. Griesh. pred. 2, 119; conf. Grimm on the A. Heinr. p. 160. Also in the *plague-offering* at Massilia, Petron. c. 141.

p. 42.] Forecasting the *future* by sacrifice: *ante pugnam* miserabiliter idolis immolavit (Decius), Jorn. c. 18.

p. 42.] Sacrif. *til ârs* also in Fornm. sög. 10, 212: sîðan gerði uaran mikit ok hallaeri, var þâ þat râð tekit at þeir *blôtuðu* Olaf konung *til ârs* ser. With Hâlfdan's sacrifice conf. the ἑκατομφόνια offered by him who had slain 100 foes, Pausan. iv. 19, 2.

p. 44.] Human Sacrifice seems to have been an ancient practice in most nations, as well as the burning of live men with the dead. On the other hand, capital punishments were unknown or rare. Hercules, ad quem Poeni omnibus annis *humana* sacrificaverunt *victima*, Pliny 36, 5. *Men* were sacrif. to Artemis, Paus. 7, 19; to the playing of flutes, Aufr. u. K.'s Umbr. Sprachd. 2, 377. In lieu of it, youths were touched on the forehead with a bloody knife, O. Jahn on Lycoreus 427; conf. the red string on the neck in the 'Amicus and Amelius.' God, as Death, as old blood-shedder (p. 21), asks human victims. Hence they are promised in sickness and danger, for the gods will only accept a life for life, Gesta Trevir. cap. 17, from Cæs. B. Gall. 6, 16. For sacrificing a man on horseback, see Lindenbl. 68. Adam of Bremen (Pertz. 9, 374) says of the Ests: 'dracones adorant cum volucribus, quibus etiam *vivos* litant *homines*, quos a mercatoribus emunt, diligenter omnino probatos *ne maculam in corpore habeant*, pro qua *refutari* dicuntur *a draconibus*.' While a slave-caravan crosses a river, the Abyssinians, like the Old Franks, make the gods a thank and sin offering of the prettiest girl, Klöden's Beitr. 49. In spring a *live child* is sacrificed on the funeral pile, Dybeck's Runa 1844, 5: î þann tîma kom hallaeri mikit â Reiðgotaland. enn svâ gêck frêttin, at aldri mundi âr fyrri koma, enn þeim sveini vaeri *blôtat*, er aeðstr vaeri þar î landi, Hervar. saga p. 452, conf. 454. On the two Gallehus horns is pictured a man holding a child-victim. Saxo, ed. Müller 121, says of Frö at Upsala: '*humani generis hostias mactare aggressus, foeda superis libamenta persolvit*;' he changed the *veterem libationis morem.* To the ' sacrare aciem ' in Tac. Ann. 13, 57 (p. 1046 n.) answers the ON. *val fela,* Hervar. s. 454. Traces of Child-sacrifice especially in witch-stories (p. 1081), such as tearing out and eating the heart. *Bones* collected and offered up, conf. the tale of the good Lubbe p. 526, and the villa of *Opferbein* now Opferbaum near Würzburg, see Lang's reg. 3, 101 (year 1257). 4, 291 (year 1285).

p. 46.] An *animal* sacrifice was expiatory when offered to the invading plague, p. 610. 1142. Only edible beasts sacrificed : ' cur non eis et canes, ursos et vulpes mactatis ? quia rebus ex his deos *par est* honorare coelestes, quibus *ipsi alimur,* et quas *nobis ad victum* sui numinis benignitate dignati sunt,' Arnob. 7, 16. On *dog*-sacrifice see p. 53. The *colour* and *sex* of an animal were important (p. 54), conf. Arnob. 7, 18—20 ; and in a female, whether she was breeding 7, 22 ; whether it had hair or bristles (p. 75), conf. ' dem junker, der sich auf dem fronhof lagert, soll man geben als off der hube gewassen (grown) ist mit federn, mit borsten,' Weisth. 3, 478. In buying it, one must not bargain, Athen. 3, 102. The skin was hung up and shot at, p. 650.

p. 46.] The people by eating became partakers in the sacrifice, conf. 1 Cor. 10, 18 : οὐχὶ οἱ ἐσθίοντες τὰς θυσίας κοινωνοὶ τοῦ θυσιαστηρίου εἰσί ; p. 41.

p. 47.] On sacrificing *Horses* (p. 664) and its origin, see Bopp's Gl. 24ª, *asvamêdha* ; conf. Feifalik on the Königinh. MS. 103. Tyndareus made Helen's wooers swear on the sacrif. *horse,* and then bury it, Paus. iii. 20, 9. Horses sacrif. by Greeks to Helios ib. 5, Ov. Fasti 1, 385 ; by Massagetæ to the Sun, Herod. 1, 216. *White horses* thrown into the Strymon 7, 113. Illi (Moesi) statim ante aciem *immolato equo* concepere votum, ut caesorum extis ducum et litarent et vescerentur, Florus 116, 21. May the Goth. *aihvatundi,* βάτος, refer to sacrifice ? and was the horse burnt with thorn-bushes, or was the fire kindled by *rubbing* with them ?

The *ora* in the passage from Tacitus might mean men's heads, yet conf. p. 659. It has yet to be determined how far the *bodies,*

*horses* and *arms* of the *conquered* were offered to gods. To dedi-
cate the wîcges-erwe, spoils (Diemer 179, 27), seems Biblical.
Shields and swords offered up to Mars, Ksrchr. 3730. The
Serbs presented the weapons of slain enemies, Vuk Kralodw. 88.

    p. 47 n.] *Horseflesh* eaten by witches (p. 1049) ; by giants,
Müllenh. 444. Foals eaten, Ettn. unw. doctor 338—40. The
Wild Hunter throws down legs of horse, Schwartz p. 11. Plica
Polonica attributed to eating horseflesh, Cichocki p. 7.

    p. 49 n.] *Asses* sacrificed by the Slavs, Büsching 101-2. Cos-
mas speaks of an ass being cut into small pieces ; see Vuk's pref.
to Kralodw. 9. Ass-eaters, Rochholz 2, 267. 271. Those of
Oudenaerde are called *kickefreters,* chicken-munchers, Belg. Mus.
5, 440.

    p. 49.] *Oxen* were favourite victims among the Greeks and
Romans : τοὶ δ᾽ ἐπὶ θινὶ θαλάσσης ἱερὰ ῥέζον ταύρους παμμέλανας
Ἐνοσίχθονι κυανοχαίτῃ Od. 3, 5 ; namely, nine bulls before each
of the nine seats 3, 7. Twelve bulls sacrificed to Poseidon 13,
182. To Athena ῥέξω βοῦν ἦνιν εὐρυμέτωπον ἀδμήτην, ἣν οὔπω ὑπὸ
ζυγὸν ἤγαγεν ἀνήρ. τήν τοι ἐγὼ ῥέξω, χρυσὸν κέρασιν περιχεύας
3, 382 ; conf. 426. 437, *auratis cornibus* hostiae immolatae, Pliny
33. 3, 12. Perseus offers on three altars an ox, cow and calf, Ov.
Met. 4, 755. *bovem album* Marti immolare et *centum fulvos,* Pliny
22, 5. *niveos tauros* immolare, Arnob. 2, 68. At the ' holm-
gang' the victor kills the sacrificial bull, Egils-s. 506-8. *rauð*
hann î nŷju *nauta blóði,* Sæm. 114ᵇ. The wise bird demands 'hof,
hörga marga, ok *gullhyrndar kŷr'* 141ᵃ. In Sweden they still
have *God's cows*; does that mean victims, or priestly dues ? A
loaf in the shape of a calf is *julkuse,* Cavallius voc. verl. 28ᵇ. 37ᵇ.
A *sacrificial calf,* Keller's Altd. erz. 547. The names *Farrenberg,
Bublemons* seem derived from bovine sacrifices, Mone's Anz. 6,
236-7. A *cow* and *calf* sacrif. to the plague, p. 610 ; a *black ox* with
*white* feet and star, Sommer 150; conf. the *cow's head,* Wolf's
März. no. 222. A *red* cow, kravicu buinu, Königsh. MS. 100 ;
conf. *rôte kalbela âne mâl,* Griesh. 2, 118 (from Numb. 19, 2).
diu *róten rinder,* Fundgr. 2, 152. Mone in Anz. 6, 237 remarks
justly enough, that agricultural nations lean more to bovine sacrifices, warlike nations to equine. Traces of bull-sacrifice, D. Sag.
128-9. 32.

    p. 50.] To *majalis sacrivus* answers in the Welsh Laws ' *sus coenalis* quae servatur ad coenam regis,' Leo Malb. Gl. 1, 83. Varro thinks, ' ab *suillo* genere pecoris *immolandi* initium primum sumtum videtur,' Re Rust. 2, 4. porci duo menses a mamma non dijunguntur. porci *sacres, puri* ad sacrificium ut immolentur. porci lactentes, *sacres,* delici, nefrendes 2, 4. (Claudius) cum regibus foedus in foro icit, *porca caesa,* ac vetere fecialium praefatione adhibita, Suet. c. 25. duo *victimae porcinae,* Seibertz no. 30 (1074). A *frischling* at five schillings shall stand tied to a pillar, Krotzenb. w., yr 1415 (Weisth. 3, 513). The *gras-frischling* in Urbar. Aug., yr 1316, seems to mean a sheep, MB. 34[b], 365. *frischig, frischling,* a wether, Stald. 1, 399. opferen als einen *friskinc,* Mos. 19, 8. ein *friskinc* (ram) dâ bî gie, Diemer 19, 19. With friscing as recens natus conf. σφαγαὶ νεοθήλου βοτοῦ, Æsch. Eum. 428. King Heiðrekr has a *göltr* reared, with 12 judges to look after it, Hervar. saga c. 14 (Fornald. sög. 1, 463); conf. the *giafgoltr,* Norw. ges. 2, 127.

p. 52.] Ἄρνα μέλαιναν ἐξενέγκατε, Aristoph. Ran. 847. Men sacrif. a ram, and sleep on *its hide,* Paus. iii. 34, 3. Goats sacrif. to Juno: αἰγοφάγος Ἥρη 15, 7. Nunc et in umbrosis Fauno decet immolare lucis, seu poscet *agno,* sive malit *haedo,* Hor. Od. i. 4, 12; conf. bidental, Suppl. to p. 174. A boy of nine kills a *black goat* with white legs and star, over the treasure, and sprinkles himself with the blood, Sommer's Sag. p. 140; a *goat with golden horns* 150-1. 179. ' diu ôsterwîche gêt *über dehein geiz* ' says Helbl. 8, 299; does it mean that only lambs, not goats, are eaten at Easter? A *black sheep* sacrif. to the devil, Firmenich 1, 206[b]; a *sheep* to the dwarf of the Baumann's cave, Gödeke 2, 240. The Prussian *goat-hallowing* is described by Simon Grunau in 1526, Nesselm. x. Lasicz 54; conf. Tettau and Temme 261. A hegoat sacrif. *with strange rites* in Esthonia on St. Thomas's day, Possart 172.

p. 52.] *Dogs* sacrif. in Greece, Paus. iii. 14, 9; in Umbria, Auf. und K. 2, 379. To the nickelman a *black cock* is yearly thrown into the Bode, Haupt 5, 378. Samogits sacrif. *cocks* to Kirnos, Lasicz 47. When Ests sacrif. a *cock,* the blood spirts into the fire, the feathers, head, feet and entrails are thrown into the same, the rest is boiled and eaten, Estn. ver. 2, 39. σκύμνους παμμελάνας σκυλάκων τρισσοὺς ἱερεύσας, Orph. Argon. 962. The bodies or skins of victims hung on trees, p. 75—9. 650. in alta pinu *votivi cornua cervi*, Ov. Met. 12, 266. incipiam captare feras et *reddere* pinu *cornua*, Prop. iii. 2. 19.

p. 55.] That the victim should be *led round* was essential to every kind of lustration, Aufr. u. K.'s Umbr. spr. 2, 263. κήρυκες δ' ἀνὰ ἄστυ θεῶν ἱερὴν ἑκατόμβην ἦγον, Od. 20, 276.

p. 55.] *Small sacrificial vessels,* which participants brought with them, are indic. in Hâk. goda saga c. 16, conf. 'ask ne eski,' ibid. An altar with a *large cauldron* found in a grave-mound near Peccatel, Mecklenb., Lisch 11, 369. On the Cimbrian cauldron in Strabo, see Lisch 25, 218. Out of the cavern near Velmede a brewing-cauldron was lent when asked for, Firmenich 1, 334[b] [so Mother Ludlam's cauldron, now in Frensham Church]; old copper kettles of the giants were preserved, Faye 9.

p. 57.] Former sacrifices are indicated by the banquets at assizes and after riding the bounds. A victim's flesh was boiled, not roasted, though roasting and boiling are spoken of at the feast of Bacchus, Troj. kr. 16201-99. For distribution among the people the victim was cut up small : the ass, p. 49; the gädda into eight pieces, Sv. folks. 1, 90. 94; Osiris into fourteen pieces, Buns. 1, 508. Before Thor's image in the Guðbrands-dalr were laid every day four *loaves of bread* and *slâtr* (killed meat), Forum. sög. 4, 245-6; conf. Olafssaga, ed. Christ. 26. Gruel and fish are offered to Percht on her day (p. 273); meat and drink to Souls (p. 913 n.); the milk of a cow set on the Brownies' stone every Sunday, Hone's Yrbk. 1532.

p. 57.] *Smoke-offerings* were known to the heathen : incense and bones offered to gods, Athen. 2, 73. *thus et merum,* Arnob. 7, 26. Irish *tusga, usga,* AS. *stôr,* thus, *stêran,* thurificare, Haupt's Ztschr. 9, 513[b]. At each altar they set 'eine risten flahses, ein wahs-kerzelîn und *wîrouches* korn,' Diut. 1, 384. Also *candles alone* seem to have been offered : candles lighted to the devil and to river-sprites (p. 1010. 584). Men in distress vow to the saints a taper the size of their body, then of their shin, lastly of their finger, Wall. märch. p. 288; conf. 'Helena (in templo) sacravit calicem ex electro *mammae suae mensura,*' Pliny 33. 4, 23. The shipwrecked vow a candle as big as the mast, Hist. de la Bastille 4, 315; so in Schimpf u. Ernst c. 403; otherwise a *navicula* cerea, or an *argentea anchora,* Pertz 6, 783-4; a 'wechsîn *haus*' against fire, h. Ludwig 84, 19; or the building of a chapel. Silver *ploughs* and *ships* offered (p. 59 n. 264 n.), D. Sag. 59. Pirates offer a tenth part of their booty, p. 231; conf. ἐνταῦθα τῷ ναῷ τριήρους ἀνάκειται χαλκοῦν ἔμβολον, Paus. i. 40, 4. Stones are carried or thrown on to a grave (otherw. branches, Klemm 3, 294) : on Bremund's grave by pilgrims, Karlm. 138. To sacrifice by stone-throwing, Wolf, Ztschr. 2, 61; to lay a stone on the herma, Preller 1, 250; a heap of stones lies round the herma, Babr. 48. O. Müller, Arch. § 66, thinks these ἑρμαῖα were raised partly to clear the road. Darius on his Scythian expedition has a cairn raised on the R. Atiscus, every soldier bringing a stone, Herod. 4, 92. Each pilgrim contributes a stone towards building the church, M. Koch, reise p. 422. J. Barrington, Personal Sketches 1, 17-8, tells of an Irish custom : By an ancient custom of everybody throwing a stone on the spot where any celebrated murder had been committed, on a certain day every year, it is wonderful what mounds were raised in numerous places, wh'ch no person, but such as were familiar with the customs of the poor creatures, would ever be able to account for. *Strips of cloth* are hung on the sacred tree, F. Faber 2, 410. 420; the passer-by throws a *twig* or a *rag* on the stone, Dybeck 1845, p. 6. 4, 31; or *nålar* 4, 35; the common folk also put *pennies* in the stone, 3, 29, and throw *bread, money* and *eggshells* into springs 1844, 22. si het ir *opfergoldes* noch wol tûsent marc, si *teilt* ez sîner seele, ir vil lieben man, Nib. 1221, 2 (p. 913 n.).

p. 57.] Herdsmen offer bloody victims, husbandmen *fruits of the earth,* D. Sag. 20. 21. *ears* left standing for Wôdan (p. 154 seq.); a bundle of *flax,* Wolf's Ndrl. sag. p. 269; for the little woodwife *flax-stems* or a tiny *hut of stalks of flax,* Schönw. 2, 360-9. *sheaves of straw* made for the gods, Garg. 129[b]. The Greeks offered *stalks* and *ears,* Callim. 4, 283; hic placatus erat, seu quis libaverat *uvam,* seu dederat sanctae *spicea serta* comae, Tib. i. 10, 21; tender *oak-leaves* in default of barley, Od. 12, 357. The Indians had grass-offerings, Kuhn rec. d. Rigv. p. 102, as the pixies received a bunch of grass or needles. Firstfruits, θαλύσια, to Artemis, Il. 9, 534. The *flower-offering* too is ancient, being one of the Indian five, viz. reading the Vedas, sprinkling water, burning butter, *strewing flowers* and *sprays,* hospitality, Holtzm. 3, 123. The Sanskr. *śeṣa* = reliquiae, flores qui deo vel idolo oblati sunt, deinde alicui traduntur; conf. the flower-offering of Saras-

vati, Somad. 1, 120-1, and 'Hallows an offering to the clouds,
Of kutaja the fairest *blossoms,*' Meghadûta 4. ' For Greece, see
Theocr. epigr. 1.    The offering to 'Venus' is *bluomen* und
*vingerlîn,* Ksrchr. 3746.   In Germany they danced round the first
violet, p. 762.    The people call a stone in the forest, three miles
from Marburg, 'opfer-stein,' and still lay *flowers* and corn upon it.
A rock is crowned with flowers on Mayday, Pröhle's Unterharz no.
347. 263.   The country folk on the Lippe, like those about the
Meisner, go into the Hollow Stone on Easter-day, Firm. 1, 334 ;
they think of Veleda, as the Hessians do of Holda.   The same
day the villagers of Waake, Landolfshausen and Mackenrode
troop to the Schweckhäuser hills, where an idol formerly stood,
Harrys i. no. 4.

   p. 59 n.]   *Λεῖβον δ' ἀθανάτοισι θεοῖς,* Od. 2, 432.   *οἶνον ἔκχεον,*
*ἠδ' εὔχοντο θεοῖς,* Il. 3, 296.   Before drinking, they poured some
on the ground to the gods 7, 480; whereas the Scythians spilt
*no wine* (Lucian Toxar. 45), and the German heroes drank minne
without spilling any, D. Sag. 236-7.   poculis aureis memoriae de-
functorum commilitonum *vino mero libant,* Apul. Met. 4 p.m. 131.

   p. 61.]   *St. John's* and *St. Gertrude's minne :* later examples
in Gödeke's Weim. Jb. 6, 28-9, and Scheller 2, 593.   postea
dominis *amor S. Johannis* ministretur, MB. 35ᵃ, 138.   potum
*caritatis* propinare, Lacomblet 487 (yr. 1183).   dar truoc man
im *sand Johanns minne,* Ottoc. 838ᵇ.   *Johannes liebe, J. minne*
trinken, Weisth. 1, 562-4.   trag uns her *sant Johans min,* Keller
erz. 32.   si trinkent alsamt *sant Hans min* 34.   In Belgium they
said : ' *Sinct Jans gelei* ende *Sinct Gertrous minne* sy met u ! '
Men pray to St. Gertrude for good lodging, Eschenb. denkm. p.
240.   In Wolkenstein 114, *minne sanct Johans* means the parting
kiss.  A wife says at parting : setz *sant Johans ze bürgen* (surety)
mir, daz wir froelich und schier (soon) zuo einander komen,
Ls. 3, 313 ; conf. drinking the scheidel-kanne, Lüntzel Hildsh.
stiftsfehde 80.   In ON. ' bad þâ drecka *velfarar minni* sitt,' Egilss.
p. 213.   People give each other *John's blessing* at Christmas,
Weisth. 1, 241-3.   The two Johns are confounded, not only by
Liutpr. (Pertz 3, 363), but in the Lay of Heriger : Johannes
baptista *pincerna* (cupbearer), Lat. ged. des MA. p. 336.

   p. 63.]   On the shapes given to pastry, see p. 501 n.   The forms
or names of *öster-flade* (-pancake), *pfadelat* (patellata), *öster-*

*stuopha* (-scone), p. 781, *furiwiz* (Graff 1, 1104), are worth studying. Günther 647 : ' before this sacred fire thy image now is brought' reminds one of Voetius's straw figure set before the hearth.

The *Carrying-about of divine images* was known to the ancients : Syriam deam *per vicos agrosque* circumferre, Lucian de dea Syria 49. Lucius cap. 36. circumgestare deam, Apul. p.m. 194—6. The Northmen of Guðbrands-dalr carry Thor's image out of his house *into the Thing*, set it up, and bow to it, St. Olafs s., ed. Christ. 23-6. The men of Delbruck carried about a *false god Hilgerio* on a long pole, Weisth. 3, 101 n. May Ulrich of Lichtenstein's progress as *Dame Venus* be explained as a custom dating from the time of heathen progresses ? That also was ' at Pentecost,' from April 25 to May 26, 1227; Whitsunday fell on May 30.

Here ought to be mentioned the sacred *festivals*, whose names and dates are discussed in D. Sag. 71-2. ' Festa ea Germanis *nox* (it was sideribus inlustris, i.e. *illunis*, new-moon), et solemnibus *epulis ludicra*,' Tac. Ann. 1, 50 ; conf. Germ. 24, where the sword-dance is called ludicrum. Beside feasting and games, it was a part of the festival to bathe the goddesses, p. 255.

CHAPTER IV.

TEMPLES.

p. 67.] For names compounded with *alah*, see Förstemann. *Halazes*-stat in Ratenzgowe (Hallstadt by Bamberg), MB. 28, 98 (yr. 889) seems a misreading for *Halahes*-stat; and Halazzes-stat 28, 192 (yr. 923) for Halahhes-stat. For the chap. in Baluze 1, 755 has *Halax*-stat, where Pertz 3, 133 has again Halaz-stat, but Bened. more correctly *Alaga*-stat. But even Pertz 3, 302 has Halax-stat. Dare we bring in the AS. ealgian (tueri) and the Lat. arcere, arx ? D. Sag. 319. Pictet in Origines 1, 227 connects alhs with Sanskr. alka. What means ' alle *gassen* und *alhen*' in the Limbg. chron. p.m. 5 ? With the Alcis in Tacitus conf. the Scythian κόρακοι, φίλιοι δαίμονες = Orestes and Pylades, Lucian's Toxar. 7. D. Sag. 118.

AS. *weoh,* templum: *weoh* gesôhte, Cod. Exon. 244, 6. Doners-
*we* in Oldenburg seems to mean D.'s temple ; and Esch-*wege* in
Hesse may be a corrup. of Esch-weh, though acc. to Förstem 2,
111 it was already in the 10th cent. Eskine-wag, -weg ; conf.
Wôdenes-wege, p. 152 and Oðins-ve, p. 159. Even in OHG. we
find *we* for wih : za themo *we* (al. parawe) ploazit, Gl. Ker. 27.
In ON. Vandils-*ve,* Sæm. 166ᵃ. Frös-*vi,* Dipl. Suecan. no. 1777 ;
Götä-*wi* (Göte-vi) 1776. It is said of the gods : valda *veom,*
Sæm. 41ᵇ. Skaði says : frâ mînom *veom* oc *vöngom,* 67ᵃ. Valhallar til, ok *vess* heilags 113ᵃ ; does vess belong to ve, or stand
for vers ? In Sæm. 23ᵇ (F. Magn. p. 255 n.) ' *alda ve* iarðar,'
populorum habitaculum, is opp. to *útve* = ûtgarða, gigantum
habitacula. The Goth. *veihs,* sacer, OHG. *wih,* is wanting in OS.,
AS., and ON. Cote-*wih,* nomen monasterii (Pertz 7, 460), is
afterw. Göttweih ; conf. Ketweig, Beham 335, 31. Chetewic in
Gerbert (Diemer's Pref. xxi.).

p. 68 n.] *Ara* = *āsa,* ansa, is a god's seat, as the Goth. *badi,*
OHG. *petti,* AS. *bed* mean both ara and fanum, D. Sag. p. 115.
*beod*-gereordu (n. pl.), epulae, Cædm. 91, 27. ad apicem gemeinen
*gunbet,* MB. 29ᵃ, 143 (yr. 1059). *gumpette,* Hess. Ztschr. 3, 70 ;
conf. Gombetten in Hesse. Does the OHG. *ebanslihti* (Graff 6,
789) mean ara or area ?　O. Slav. *kumir,* ara, idolum ; conf. Finn.
kumarran, adoro, inclino me. On other Teut. words for altar,
such as ON. *stalli* and the plur. *hörgar,* see D. Sag. 114-5.

p. 69.] OHG. *haruc* seems preserved in Harahes-heim, Cod.
Lauresh. 3, 187, and in Hargenstein, Panzer's Beitr. 1, 1 ; conf.
*Hercynius.* AS. Besinga-*hearh,* Kemble no. 994. ON. hâtim-
broðom *hörgi* roeðr, Sæm. 42ᵃ. *hof* mun ek kiosa, ok *hörga*
marga 141ᵃ. Thors-*argh,* -*aerg,* -*hary,* now Thors-hälla, Hildebr.
iii. D. Sag. 115. The *hof* sometimes coupled with hörgr occurs
even in MHG. in the sense of temple, temple-yard : ze *hofe* geben
(in atrium templi), Mar. 168, 42. ze *hove* giengen (atrium) 169,
30. den *hof* rûmen (temple) 172, 5 ; conf. ON. *hofland,* temple-
land, Munch om Skiringssal 106-7. D. Sag. 116-7. Likewise
*garte, tûn,* pl. *tûnir, wiese, aue* (p. 225) are used for holy places,
Gr. ἄλσος.

p. 69.] OHG. *paro,* AS. *bearo,* are supported by *kiparida* =
nemorosa, which Graff 3, 151 assoc. with kipârida ; by AS.
*bearewas,* saltûs, Haupt's Ztschr. 9, 454ᵇ, and ' *bearo* sette, *weobedd*

worhte,' Cædm. 172, 7. Lactantius's 'antistes nemorum, luci sacerdos' is rendered '*bearwes* bigenga, *wudubearwes* weard' 207, 27. 208, 7. Names of places : *Parawa*, Neugart. Cod. dipl. no. 30 (yr. 760) ; *Barwithsyssel*, Müllenh. Nordalb. stud. 1, 138 ; ON. *Barey*. The OHG. za themo *parawe*, Diut. 1, 150 is glossed on the margin by 'to deme hoen althere, to demo siden althere,' Goslarer bergg. 343.

p. 69 n.] OHG. *luoc*, specus, cubile, delubrum, Graff 2, 129. in *luakirum*, delubris, Diut. 1, 530ᵃ. *lôh*, lucus, Graff 2, 128. In Rudolf's Weltchr. occurs *betelôch*, lucus, pl. beteloecher. Notker's Cap. 143 distinguishes the kinds of woods as *walden, forsten, lôhen*. The Vocab. optim. p. 47ᵃ has : silva wilder walt, nemus schoener walt, lucus dicker walt, saltus hoher walt. Mommsen, Unterital. dial. 141, derives *lucus* from luere, hallow. There are *hursts* named after divine beings : *Freckenhorst, Givekanhorst* (conf. *Freckastein, Givekanstên*. ok þâr stendr enn *Thôrsteinn*, Landn. ii. 12). It comes of forest-worship that the gods are attended by *wild beasts*, Wuotan by wolf and raven, Froho by a boar.

p. 69.] Worshipping in the still and shady *grove* was practised by many nations. 'Thou hast scattered thy ways to the strangers under every *green tree*' complains Jeremiah 3, 13. κλυτὸν ἄλσος ἱρὸν Ἀθηναίης, Od. 6, 321. ἐν ἄλσεϊ δενδρήεντι Φοίβου Ἀπόλλωνος 9, 200. ἄλσεα Περσεφοναίης 10, 509. ἄλσος ὑπὸ σκιερὸν ἐκατηβόλου Ἀπόλλωνος 20, 278. Athenæus 4, 371-2, celebrates the *cool* of the sacred grove. inhorruit *atrum* majestate *nemus*, Claudian in Pr. et Olybr. 125 (on nemus, see p. 648). in tuo *luco* et *fano*, Plaut. Aulul. iv. 2, 8. *lucus sacer*, ubi Hesperidum horti, Pliny 5, 5. itur in *antiquam silvam, stabula alta ferarum*, Æn. 6, 179. nunc et in *umbrosis* Fauno decet immolare *lucis*, Hor. Od. i. 4, 11. nec magis auro fulgentia atque ebore, quam *lucos* et in iis *silentia* ipsa adoramus, Pliny 12, 1. proceritas silvae et secretum loci et admiratio umbrae fidem numinis facit, Seneca ep. 41. As the wood is *open above*, a *hole* is left in the top of a temple, conf. the Greek hypæthral temples: Terminus quo loco colebatur, super eum *foramen patebat in tecto*, quod nefas esse putarent Terminum intra tectum consistere, Festus sub v. ; conf. Ov. Fasti 2, 671. Servius in Æn. 9, 448. The Celts *unroofed* their temples once a year (ἀποστεγάζ.), Strabo 4, p. 198. A grove in Sarmatia was called ἁλιεύμα θεοῦ, piscatura dei, Ptol.

3, 5.   The Abasgi in the Caucasus venerated groves and woods
(ἄλση καὶ ὕλας), and counted trees among their gods, Procop. 2,
471; conf. the prophetic rustle of the cypresses in Armenia (p.
1110). Even in the Latin poems of the MA. we find : Amoris *nemus*
Paradisus, Carm. bur. 162.  circa silvae medium locus est occultus,
ubi viget maxime suus deo cultus 163.    In Eckhart 186, 32 the
Samaritan woman says, 'our fathers worshipped *under the trees
on the mountain.*'   In Troj. kr. 890 : si wolden gerne hûsen ze
*walde* ûf *wilden riuten.*   Walther v. Rh. 64ᵇ : in einen schoenen
grüenen walt, dar diu *heidensche diet* mit ir abgöten geriet (ruled?).
In stories of the Devil, he appears in the *forest gloom*, e.g. Ls. 3,
256, perhaps because men still thought of the old gods as living
there.    Observe too the relation of home-sprites and wood-wives
to trees, p. 509.

Worshipping on *mountains* is old and widely spread; conf. âs,
aus (p. 25), and the Wuotans-*bergs*, Donners-*bergs*.    Three days
and nights the Devil is invoked on a mountain, Müllenh. no. 227.
Mountain worship is Biblical : 'on this mountain (Gerizim),'
John 4, 20 ; see Raumer's Palest. p. 113.

p. 73.]    Like the Donar's oak of Geismar is a large *holy oak*,
said to have stood near Mülhausen in Thuringia; of its wood was
made a *chest*, still shown in the *church* of Eichenried village,
Grasshof's Mülh. p. 10.

p. 74.]    On *thegathon*, see Hpt's Ztschr. 9, 192, and Wilmans'
essay, Münst. 1857.   summum et principem omn. deorum, qui
apud gentes *thegaton* nuncupatur, Wilkens biogr. of St. Gerburgis;
conf. Wigand's arch. 2, 206.   *tagaton* discussed in Ritter's christl.
phil. 3, 308.   It is Socrates's δαιμόνιον, Plato's τὸ ἀγαθόν, the
same in Apul. apolog. p. m. 278.   Can *thegatho* be for theodo, as
Tehota is for Thiuda ?   Förstem. 1, 1148.

p. 75.]    The *holy wood* by Hagenau is named in Chmel reg.
Ruperti 1071, D. Sag. 497.   *fronwald*, Weisth. 1, 423.    On the
word *bannwald* conf. Lanz. 731 : diu tier (beasts) bannen.
Among holy groves was doubtless the *Fridewald*, and perh. the
*Spiess*, both in Hesse, Ztschr. f. Hess. gesch. 2, 163.   *Friðesleáh*,
Kemble no. 187. 285 ; *Óswudu* 1, 69 is a man's name, but must
have been that of a place first.   The divine grove *Glasir* with
golden foliage, Sn. 130, stands outside Valhöll ; Sæm. 140ᵇ says
Hiörvarð's abode was named *Glasis lundr.*

p. 75.] The adoration of the *oak* is proved by Velthem's Sp. hist. 4, 57 (ed. Le Long, fol. 287): Van ere *eyken*, die men *anebede.*

> In desen tiden was ganginge mede
> tusschen Zichgen ende Diest ter stede
> rechte bi-na te-midden werde,
> daer dede menich ere bedeverde
> tot ere *eyken* (dat si u cont),
> *die alse een cruse gewassen stont,*
> met twee rayen gaende ut,
> daer menich quam overluut,
> *die daer-ane hinc scerpe ende staf,*
> en seide, dat *hi genesen wer daer-af.*
> Som liepense onder den bôm, etc.

Here is a Christian pilgrimage of sick people to a cross-shaped tree between Sicken and Diest in Brabant, and the hanging thereon of bandage and staff upon recovery, as at p. 1167. 1179 ; conf. the heathen *oscilla* (p. 78). The date can be ascertained from Le Long's Velthem.

p. 77.] ' *Deos nemora* incolere persuasum habent (Samogitae) . . . . credebat deos *intra arbores et cortices* latere ' says Lasicz, Hpt's Ztschr. 1, 138. The Ostiaks have holy woods, Klemm 3, 121. The Finnic ' Tharapita ' should be *Tharapila.* Castrén 215 thinks -pila is *bild,* but Renvall says *tharapilla*=horned owl, Esth. *torropil,* Verhandl. 2, 92. Juslen 284 has *pöllö* bubo, and 373 *tarhapöllö* bubo. With this, and the ON. bird in Glasis lundr, conf. a curious statement in Pliny 10, 47 : in *Hercynio* Germaniae *saltu* invisitata genera *alitum* accepimus, quarum *plumae ignium modo colluceant* noctibus ; conf. Stephan's Stoflief. 116.

p. 78 n.] *Oscilla* are usu. dolls, puppets, OHG. tocchun, Graff 5, 365. They might even be *crutches* hung up on the holy tree by the healed (Suppl. to 75). But the prop. meaning must be images. On *church walls* also were *hung* offerings, votive gifts, rarities : si hiezen diu *weppe hâhen in die kirchen an die mûre,* Servat. 2890.

p. 79.] A *Celtic grove* descr. in Lucan's Phars. 3, 399 ; a *Norse temple* in Eyrbyggja-s. c. 4.

p. 80.] Giefers (Erh. u. Rosenkr. Ztschr. f. gesch. 8, 261—

285) supposes that the *templum Tanfanae* belonged at once to the
Cherusci, Chatti and Marsi; that Tanfana may come from tanfo,
truncus (?), and be the name of a grove occupying the site of
*Eresburg*, now *Ober-Marsberg ;* that one of its trunci, which had
escaped destruction by the Romans (solo aequare he makes burning of the grove), was the *Irmensul*, which stood on the Osning
between Castrum Eresburg and the *Carls-schanze* on the Bruns-
berg, some 4 or 5 leagues from Marsberg, and a few leagues
from the *Buller-born* by Altenbeke, the spring that rose by
miracle, D. Sag. 118.

p. 80.]   To the *isarno-dori* in the Jura corresp. Trajan's Iron
Gate, Turk. *Demir kapa*, in a pass of Dacia.   Another *Temir kapa*
in Cilicia, Koch Anabas. 32.   Müller lex. Sal. p. 36.   Clausura is
a narrow pass, like Θερμόπυλαι, or πύλαι alone ;   conf. Schott's
Deutschen in Piemont p. 229.

p. 85.]   As *castrum* was used for templum, so is the Boh.
*kostel*, Pol. *kościel* for church.   Conversely, *templum* seems at
times to mean palatium;   conf. ' exustum est *palatium* in Thornburg ' with ' exustum est famosum *templum* in Thornburg,' Pertz
5, 62-3, also ' Thornburg *castellum et palatium* Ottonis ' 5, 755.
The OS. *rakud* is both templum and palatium.   Beside ' casulae '
=fana, we hear of a *cella antefana* (ante fana?), Mone Anz. 6,
228.

p. 85.]   Veniens (Chrocus Alamann. rex) Arvernos, *delubrum*
illud quod Gallica lingua *vassogalate* vocant, diruit atque subvertit;
miro enim opere factum fuit, Greg. Tur. 1, 32.   The statement is
important, as proving a difference of religion between Celts and
Germans : Chrocus would not destroy a building sacred to his
own religion.   Or was it, so early as that, a christian temple?
conf. cap. 39.

p. 85.]   Expressions for a built temple : ' *hof* âtti hann î
tûninu, sêr *þess enn merki*, þat er nu kallat *tröllaskeið*,' Laxd. 66.
*sal*, Graff sub v. ;   *der* sal, Diemer 326, 7.   AS. *reced*, OS. *rakud*,
seems conn. with *racha*, usu.=res, caussa, but ' *zimborón* thia
racha,' O. iv. 19, 38 ;   conf. wih and wiht.   Later words : *pluoz-
hûs, blóz-hûs*, Graff 4, 1053.   *abgot-hûs* fanum 1054.   The Lausitz
Mag. 7, 166 derives *chirihhâ*, AS. *cyrice*, from circus.   O. Sl.
*tzerky*, Dobr. 178 ;   Croat. *czirkva*, Carniol. *zirkva*, Serv. *tzrkva*,
O. Boh. *cjerkew*, Pol. *cerkiew* (conf. Gramm. 3, 156.   Pref. to

Schultze xi. Graff 4, 481). The sanctuary, ON. *griðastaðr*, is not to be trodden, Fornm. sög. 4, 186; beast nor man might there be harmed, *no intercourse* should *men with women* have (engi viðskipti skyldu karlar við konur ega þar, Fornald. sög. 2, 63.

p. 86.] Heathen places of worship, even after the conversion, were still royal manors or sees and other benefices endowed with the estate of the old temple, like *Herbede* on the Ruhr, which belonged to Kaufungen, D. Sag. 589. Mannh. Ztschr. 3, 147. Many *manors* (also *glebe-lands* acc. to the Weisthümer) had to maintain 'eisernes vieh, fasel-vieh,' bulls for breeding (p. 93). In Christian as in heathen times, holy places were revealed by signs and wonders. A *red-hot harrow* is let down from heaven (Sommer), like the *burning plough* in the Scyth. tale (Herod. 4, 5), D. Sag. 58-9. Legends about the building of churches often have the incident, that, on the destined spot in the wood, *lights* were seen at night, so arranged as to show the ground plan of the future edifice. They appear to a subulcus in the story of *Ganders-heim*, Pertz 6, 309-10; to another, Frickio by name, in the story of *Freckenhorst*, where St. Peter as carpenter designs the figure of the holy house, Dorow. i. 1, 32-3; conf. the story at p. 54 and that of *Wessobrunn*, MB. 7, 372. *Falling snow* indicates the spot, Müllenh. 113; conf. Hille-snee, Holda's snow, p. 268 n. 304. Where the *falcon stoops*, a convent is built, Wigand's Corv. güterb. 105. The spot is suggested by *cows* in a Swed. story, Wieselgren 408; by *resting animals* in a beautiful AS. one, Kemble no. 581 (yr 974).

p. 87.] On almost all our German *mountains* are to be seen *footmarks* of gods and heroes, indicating places of ancient worship, e.g. of Brunhild on the Taunus, of Gibich and Dietrich on the Hartz. The Allerhätenberg in Hesse, the 'grandfather-hills' elsewhere, are worth noting.

---

## CHAPTER V.

### PRIESTS.

p. 88.] Religion is in Greek εὐσέβεια and θρησκεία (conf. θρη-σκεύω, p. 107). κατ' εὐσέβειαν = pie, Lucian 5, 277. *Religio* = iterata lectio, conf. intelligere, Lobeck's Rhematicon p. 65. It is rendered in OHG. glosses by *heit*, Hattemer 1, 423; *gote-dehti* devotio, *cote-dehtigi* devout, *anadaht* intentio, attentio, Graff 5, 163. Pietas, peculiarly, by '*heim-minna* unde *mâg-minna*,' Hatt. 1, 423. *Crêdischeit*, Servat. 762, is sham-piety, conf. p. 35 n. ' Dîs fretus ' in Plaut. Cas. 2, 5 = Gote forahtac, O. i. 15, 3.

p. 88.] *Gudja, goði*, seems to be preserved in the AS. proper name *Goda*, Kemble 1, 242. For ἀρχιερεύς, Ulph. has *auhumists gudja*, Matt. 27, 62. Mk. 8, 31; but *auhumists veiha*, Joh. 18, 13. The priest hallows and is hallowed (p. 93), conf. the consecration and baptism of witches. Göndul consecrates: nû *vigi ek þik* undir öll þau atkvaeði ok skildaga, sem Oðinn fyrimaelti, Fornald. sög. 1, 402. The words in Lactant. Phoenix, 'antistes nemorum, luci veneranda sacerdos,' are rendered by the AS. poet: bearwes *bigenga*, wudubearwes *weard* 207, 27. 208, 7. The priest *stands before God*, ἔναντι τοῦ θεοῦ, Luke 1, 8: giangi furi Got, O. i. 4, 11. The monks form ' daz Gotes her,' army, Reinh. F. 1023. The Zendic *âthrava*, priest, Bopp Comp. Gram. 42. Spiegel's Avesta 2, vi. means fire-server, from âtars fire, Dat. âthrê. Pol. *xiądz* priest, prop. prince or sacrificer, Linde 2, 1164ᵇ; conf. Sansk. *xi* govern, kill, *xaja* dominans.

p. 89.] *Ewart* priest: ein *êwart* der abgote, Barl. 200, 22. Pass. 329, 56, etc. *êwarde*, En. 244, 14. prêster und ir *êwe mêster* 243, 20.

p. 89 n.] Zacharias is a *fruod gomo*, Hel. 2, 24. Our *kluger* mann, *kluge* frau, still signify one acquainted with secret powers of nature; so the Swed. 'de *klokar*,' Fries udfl. 108.——The phrase ' *der guote man* ' denotes espec. a sacred calling: that of a priest, Marienleg. 60, 40, a bishop, Pass. 336, 78, a pilgrim, Uolr. 91. Nuns are *guote frowen*, Eracl. 735. klôster und *guote liute*, Nib. 1001, 2, etc. die *goede man*, the hermit in Lanc. 4153-71. 16911-8, etc. So the Scot. '*gudeman's* croft' above; but the name *Gutmans-hausen* was once Wôtenes-hûsen (Suppl. to 154). *Bons-hommes* are heretics, the Manichæans condemned at the Council of Cambery 1165; *buonuomini*, Macchiav. Flor. 1, 97. 158. The shepherds in O. i. 12, 17 are *guotê man*. Engl. good-man is both householder and our biedermann. Grôa is addressed as *góð kona*, Saem. 97ᵃ; in conjuring: Alrûn, du vil *guote* (p. 1202 n.)

p. 89.] Christian also, though of Germ. origin, seems the

OHG. *heit-haft* sacerdos, from heit=ordo; hence, in ordinem sacrum receptus. MHG. *heithafte* liute, sacerdotes, Fundgr. 1, 94; conf. *eithafte* herren, Ksrchr. 11895. AS. *geþungen*, reverend, and espec. religiosus, Homil. p. 344.

p. 90.] Agathias 2, 6 expressly attributes to the heathen Ala-manns of the 6th cent. *diviners* (μάντεις and χρησμολόγοι[1]), who dissuade from battle; and princes in the Mid. Ages still take clergymen into the field with them as counsellors: abbates pii, scioli bene *consiliarii*, Rudl. 2, 253. Ordeals are placed under priestly authority, Sæm. 237-8. In the popular assembly the priests enjoin silence and attention: silentium per *sacerdotes*, qui-bus tum et *coërcendi jus* est, imperatur, Germ. 11. In addition to what is coll. in Haupt's Ztschr. 9, 127 on 'lust and unlust,' consider the *tacitus precari* of the Umbr. spell, and the opening of the Fastnachts-spiele.

p. 91.] The Goth. *þróþjan, úsþróþjan* transl. μύειν initiare, and γυμνάζειν, exercere GDS. 819; may it not refer to some sacred function of heathen priests, and be connected with the Gallic *druid* (p. 1036 n.), or rather with *þrûðr* (p. 423)? Was *heilac* said of priests and priestesses? conf. 'heilac huat,' cydaris, Graff 4, 874; Heilacflât, Cod. Lauresh. 1, 578; Heilacbrunno, p. 587; Heiligbär, p. 667-8. Priests take part in the sacrificial feast, they consecrate the cauldron: sentu at Saxa Sunnmanna gram, hann kann helga hver vellanda, Sæm. 238ᵃ; so Peter was head-cook of heaven, Lat. ged. des MA. p. 336. 344. Priests maintain the *sacred beasts*, horses and boars, Herv.-s. cap. 14; conf. RA. 592. In beating the bounds they seem to have gone before and pointed out the sacred stones, as the churchwardens did afterwards; they rode especially round old churches, in whose vaults an idol was supposed to lie. Priests know the art of quickening the dead, Holtzm. 3, 145. They have also the gifts of healing and divina-tion: ιατρόμαντις, Æsch. Suppl. 263.

p. 91.] In many Aryan nations the priestly garment is *white*. Graecus augur pallio *candido* velatus, Umber et Romanus trabea purpurea amictus, Grotef. inscr. Umbr. 6, 13. Roman priests and magistrates have white robes; see the picture of the flamen

---

[1] The μάντις interprets dreams, entrails, flights of birds, but is no speaker of oracles, χρησμολόγος, Paus. i. 34, 3. [In Plato's Timæus 72 B, μάντις (fr. μαίνομαι) is the inspired speaker of oracles.]

dialis in Hartung 1, 193. Schwenck 27; amictus veste *alba*
sevir et praetor, Petron. 65. The Cimbrian priestesses in Strabo
are λευχείμονες (p. 55-6), and the Gothic priests in Jorn. cap. 10
appear in *candidis* vestibus. The Gallic druids are arrayed in
*white* (p. 1206), the priest of Gerovit in *snow-white*, Sefridi v.
Ottonis p. 128 (Giesebr. Wend. gesch. 1, 90). In the Mid. Ages
too white robes belong to holy women, nuns. die goede man met
*witten* clederen, Lanc. 22662-70.

The Gothic *pileati* (Kl. schr. 3, 227. GDS. 124) remind us of
the 'tria genera *pileorum*, quibus sacerdotes utuntur: *apex, tutu-
lus, galerus*' in Suetonii fragm. p. m. 335. The picture of a
*bearded* man in Stälin 1, 161-2, is perhaps meant for a priest.
The *shaven hair* of Christian and Buddhist monks and nuns is
probably a badge of servitude to God; GDS. 822.

p. 91.] Snorri goði, like the AS. coifi, rides on a mare,
Eyrbygg. s. 34; and the flamen dialis must not mount any kind
of horse, Klausen Æn. 1077. Hartung 1, 194. Possibly even
the heathen priests were not allowed to eat things with blood,
but only herbs. Trevrizent digs up roots, and hangs them on
bushes, Parz. 485, 21; in a similar way do Wilhelm the saint and
Waltharius eke out their lives, Lat. ged. d. MA. p. 112.

p. 92.] Among gestures traceable to priestly rites, I reckon
especially this, that in the vindicatio of a beast the man had to lift
up his right hand or lay it on, while his left grasped the animal's
right ear. The posture at hammer-throwing seems to be another case in point, RA. 65-6. GDS. 124-5.——Kemble 1, 278
thinks *coifi* is the AS. ceofa, diaconus.

p. 93.] Christian priests also are called 'God's man, child,
kneht, scalc, deo, diu, wine, trut,' or 'dear to God,' conf. Mannhardt in Wolf's Ztschr. 3, 143. Gotes *man* (Suppl. to p. 20-1).
Gotes *kint*=priest, Greg. 1355. Reinh. 714; or=pilgrim, as
opp. to welt-kind (worldling), Trist. 2625. der edle Gotes *kneht*,
said of Zacharias and John, Pass. 346, 24. 349, 23. 60; of the
pilgrim, Trist. 2638. Gotes *riter*, Greg. 1362. ein wârer Gotis
*scalc*, Ksrchr. 6071. OHG. Gota-*deo*, Gotes-*deo*, fem. -*diu* (conf.
*ceile De, culde*, servant of God, Ir. sag. 2, 476). der Gotes *trût*,
Pass. 350, 91. Among the Greek priests were ἀγχίθεοι, Lucian
dea Syr. 31; conf. the *conscii* deorum, Tac. Germ. 10. Amphi-
araus is *beloved* of Zeus and Apollo, *i.e.* he is μάντις. On his

death Apollo appoints another of the same family, Od. 15, 245. 253.

p. 93.] If priesthood could be hereditary, the Norse goði must have been free to marry, like the episcopus and diaconus of the early Christians (1 Tim. 3, 2. 12) and the Hindu Brahmin. Not so the Pruss. *waidlot* or *waidler*, Nesselm. p. xv. and p. 141. To appoint to the priesthood is in ON. *signa goðom*, or *gefa*, though the latter seems not always to imply the priestly office : þeir voro gumnar *goðom signaðir*, Sæm. 117[b]. *gefinn* Oðni, Fornm. sög. 2, 168. enn *gaf* hann (Brandr) *guðunum*, ok var hann kallaðr *Guð-branar*, Fornald. sög. 2, 6; his son is Guð-mundr, and his son again Guðbrandr (= OHG. Gota-beraht) 2, 7. Does this account for *divination* being also hereditary (p. 1107)?

p. 93.] The god had part of the spoils of war and hunting (p. 42), priest and temple were paid their *dues*, whence tithes arose: *hof-tollr* is the toll due to a temple, Fornm. s. 1, 268. On priestly dwellings see GDS. 125.

p. 94.] German divination seems to have been in request even at Rome : haruspex ex Germania missus (Domitiano), Suet. Domit. 16. Soothsayers, whom the people consulted in particular cases even after the conversion, were a remnant of heathen priests and priestesses. The Lex Visig. vi. 2, 1 : ' *ariolos, aruspices, vaticinantes* consulere,' and 5 : ' execrabiles *divinorum pronun-tiationes* intendere, salutis aut aegritudinis *responsa* poscere.' Liutpr. 6, 30 : ' ad *ariolos* vel *ariolas* pro responsis accipiendis ambulare,' and 31 : ' in loco ubi *arioli* vel *ariolae* fuerint.' The ON. *spâ-maðr* is called *râð-spakr*, Sæm. 175[a], or *fram-víss* like the prophet Grîpir 172[a]. 175[a]. þú *fram* um *sér* 175[a,b]. farit er þaz ek *forvissac* 175[a]. þú öll um *sér* orlög for 176[b]. Grîpir *lýgr eigi* 177[b]. Gevarus rex, *divinandi* doctissimus, industria *praesagiorum* excultus, Saxo Gram. p. 115. (conf. p. 1034. 1106). The notion of oraculum (what is asked and obtained of the gods), vaticinium, divinatio, is expr. by ON. *frétt : fréttir* sögðu, Sæm. 93[a]. *frétta* beiddi, oracula poposci 94[a]. geck til *fréttar*, Yngl. 21 (Grk. χρᾶσθαι τῷ θεῷ, inquire of the god). Conf. frêhtan, Suppl. to p. 37; OHG. *freht* meritum, *frehtîc* meritus, sacer; AS. fyrht in Leg. Canuti, Thorpe p. 162.

p. 95.] German women seem to have taken part in sacrifices (p. 56n.); women perform sacrifice before the army of the Thracian

Spartacus (B.C. 67), who had Germans under him, Plutarch Crass. c. 11. The Romans excluded women, so do the Cheremisses, p. 1235-6, the Lapps and the Boriâts, Klemm 3, 87. 111-3.

p. 95-6.] A *druias* Gallicana *vaticinans* is mentioned by Vopiscus in Aurel. 44, in Numer. 13-4; by Lampridius in Alex. Sev. 60. Drusus is met by a *species barbarae mulieris* humana amplior, Suet. Claud. c. 1. Dio Cass. 55, 1. Chatta *mulier vaticinans* Suet. Vitel. c. 14. *Veleda* receives gifts: Mumius Lupercus inter dona missus Veledae, Tac. Hist. 4, 61. A modern folktale brings her in as a goddess, Firmenich 1, 334-5. On *Albruna* conf. Hpt's Ztschr. 9, 240. Of *Jettha* it is told in the Palatinate, that she sought out and hewed a stone in the wood: whoever sets foot on the fairy stone, becomes a fixture, he cannot get away, Nadler p. 125. 292. Like Pallas, she is a founder of cities. Brynhild, like Veleda, has her hall on a *mountain*, and sits in her *tower*, Völs. s. cap. 25. Hother visits prophetesses in the waste wood, and then enlightens the folk *in edito montis vertice*, Saxo Gram. p. 122. The *white lady* of princely houses appears on a *tower* of the castle. The witte Dorte lives in the *tower*, Mullenh. p. 344. When misfortune threatens the Pedaseans, their priestess gets a long beard, Herod. 1, 175. 8, 104. Women carve and read runes: Kostbera kunni *skil rûna*, Saem. 252ª, *reist rûna* 252ᵇ. Ornŷ *reist rûnar* â kefli, Fornm. s. 3, 109. 110 (she was born dumb, p. 388). In the Mid. Ages also women are particularly clever at writing and reading. RA. 583.

p. 98.] To the Norse prophetesses add *Gróa völva*, Sn. 110, and *Göndul*, a valkyr, Fornald. s. 1, 398. 402, named appar. from gandr, p. 1054. 420. *Thorgerðr* and *Irpa* are called both *hörgabrúðr*, temple-maid, and *Hölga-brúðr* after their father Hölgi, p. 114. 637. A Slav pythonissa carries her sieve in front of the army, p. 1111-2; others in Saxo Gram. 827; conf. O. Pruss. waidlinne, Nesselm. pref. 15.

---

# CHAPTER VI.

## GODS.

p. 104 n.] The Goth. *manleika*, OHG. *mannalîhho* (conf. ἀνδριάς fr. ἀνήρ man), lasts in MHG. wehsîne *manlich*, Fundgr. 2, 123.

guldîn *manlîch*, Servat. 2581. 'apud *manlîcha*,' where the image stands, Notizenbl. 6, 168.

p. 105.] Though Tacitus mentions no image in human shape, but only signa and formae (*effigies*que et *signa* quaedam *detracta lucis* in proelium ferunt, Germ. 7, conf. *vargr* hângir fyr vestan dyr, ok drûpir *örn* yfir, Sæm. 41ʰ) ;—yet the expression ' *numen* ipsum, si credere velis,' used of the divine Mother in her bath, cap. 40, does seem to point to a statue.

p. 106.] In the oldest time fetishes—stones and logs—are regarded as gods' images, Gerh. Metron. p. 26. Gr. τὸ βρέτας in the Tragic poets is a god's image of wood (conf. εἰκών), though Benfey 1, 511 says ' of clay ;' ξόανον, prop. graven image fr. ξέω I scrape, often means a small image worn on the person, *e.g.* the Cleo in Paus. iii. 14, 4; ἄγαλμα, orig. ornament, then statue ; ζώδιον, liter. little-animal 15, 8. Statues were made of particular kinds of wood : ξόανον ἄγνου, of the vitex agnus-castus 14, 7 (conf. ramos de *nobilissimo agno casto*, Evag. Fel. Fabri 1, 156-7), as rosaries of mistletoe were preferred. cum paupere culta stabat in exigua *ligneus* aede deus, Tib. i. 10, 20. Irish *dealbh, deilbh, deilbhin, deilbhog*, imago, statua, figura. Beside the Boh. *modla*, idolum (fr. model ? or fr. modliti, to pray ?), we find *balwan*, block, log, idol, Pol. *balwan*, Miklos. *bal'van'*, Wall. *balavanu*, big stone (p. 105 n.), which Garnett, Proceed. 1,148, connects with Armoric ' *peulvan*, a long stone erected, a rough unwrought column.' OHG. *avara* (p. 115-6) stands for imago, statua, pyramis (irmansûl), pyra, ignis, Graff 1, 181 ; conf. *Criaches-avara* (p. 297) ; OS. *avaro* filius, proles, AS. *eafora*. The idea of *idolum* is never clearly defined in the Mid. Ages : the anti-pope Burdinus (A.D. 1118-9) is called so, Pertz 8, 254-5. Even Beda's '*idolis* servire' 2, 9 is doubtful, when set by the side of 'daemonicis cultibus servire ' 2, 5.

p. 107.] On Athanaric's worship of idols, conf. Waitz's Ulfila p. 43. 62. Claudian de B. Getico 528 makes even Alaric (A.D. 402) exclaim : Non ita *dî Getici* faxint *manesque parentum* ! Compare the gods' waggon with *sacer currus* in Tac. Germ. 10 and Suppl. to 328-9 below. Chariots of metal have been found in tombs, Lisch Meckl. jb. 9, 373-4. 11, 373.

p. 108.] That the Franks in Clovis's time had images of gods, is proved further by Remigius's epitaph on him: Contempsit credero mille Numina, quae *variis* horrent portenta *figuris*. On the other hand, Gregory of Tours's account (1, 34) of the Alamann king Chrocus in the 3rd century compelling St. Privatus in Gaul to sacrifice to idols, is vaguely worded: Daemoniis immolare compellitur, quod spurcum ille tam exsecrans quam refutans; on Chrocus conf. Stälin 1, 118.

p. 108 n.] Old idols in churches were placed behind the organ (Melissantes orogr. p. 437—9) in Duval's Eichsfeld 341. 'An idols' chamber was in the old choir,' Leipz. avant. 1, 89—91; 'the angels out of the firewood room,' Weinhold's Schles. wtb. 17[b]; fires lighted with idols, conf. Suppl. to p. 13—15. Giants' ribs or hammers hung outside the church-gate, p. 555 n.; urns and inverted pots built into church-walls, Thür. mitth. i. 2, 112—5. Steph. Stoflief. p. 189, 190. A heathen stone with the hoof-mark is let into Gudensberg churchyard wall, p. 938.

p. 113.] The warming (baka), anointing and drying of gods' images is told in Friðþiofs-s. cap. 9 (p. 63). But the divine snake of the Lombards was of gold, and was made into a plate and chalice (p. 684). The statua ad humanos tactus *vocalis*, Saxo p. 42, reminds of Memnon's statue. Some trace of a *Donar's* image may be seen in the brazen dorper, p. 535. On the arm-rings in gods' images conf. the note in Müller's Saxo p. 42. Even H. Sachs 1, 224[b] says of a yellow ringlet: 'du nähmst es Gott von füssen 'rab,' off God's feet; and ii. 4, 6[d]: ihr thet es Got von füssen nemmen. Four-headed figures, adorned with half-moons, in Jaumann's Sumlocenne p. 192—4. On nimbi, rays about the head, conf. p. 323 and Festus: capita deorum appellabantur fasciculi facti ex verbenis. Animals were carved on such figures, as on helmets; and when Alb. of Halberstadt 456[a] transl. Ovid's 'Illa mihi niveo factum de marmore signum Ostendit juvenile, gerens *in vertice* picum,' Met. 14, 318, by 'truoc einen speht *úf siner ahseln*,' he probably had floating in his mind Wôdan with the raven on his shoulder. Even in Fragm. 40[a] we still find: swuor bî allen gotes-bilden.

p. 114 n.] Gods' images are instinct with divine life, and can move. Many examples of *figures turning round* in Bötticher's Hell. Temp. p. 126. One such in Athenaeus 4, 439; one that *turns its face*, Dio Cass. 79, 10: sacra retorserunt oculos, Ov. Met. 10, 696; one that *walks*, Dio Cass. 48, 43. ἱδρώει τὰ ξόανα καὶ κινέεται, Lucian ed. Bip. 9, 92. 120. 378; deorum *sudasse* simulacra, Cic. de divin. 2, 27. simulacrum Apollinis Cumani *quatriduo flevit,* Augustin. Civ. Dei 3, 11; Lanuvii simulacrum Junonis sospitae *lacrimasse,* Livy 40, 19; lapidum *fletus* = statuarum lacrimae, Claudian in Eutrop. 2, 43. simulacrum Jovis *cachinnum* repente edidit, Suet. Calig. 57. *Flames* burst out from head and breast, Herod. 6, 82. An Artemis *drops her shield,* Paus. iv. 13, 1. Not only are they spoken to (interdiu cum Capitolino Jove secreto fabulabatur, modo *insusurrans* ac praebens invicem *aurem,* modo clarius, nec sine jurgiis, Suet. Calig. 22), but they answer. Being asked, ' visne ire Romam, Juno? ' she *nods* and says *yea,* Livy 5, 22.

The same in Teutonic heathenism. Thôr's image *walks* and *talks,* Fornm. s. 1, 302. As Thorgerð's image bends its hand to keep the gold ring on, Mary's does the same, see above, and Ksrchr. 13142-265-323. Vinc. Bellov. 25, 29 foll. by Heinr. de Hervord ad an. 1049. A Virgin sets the Child down, and *kneels* to it, Marienleg. 228; the Child is *taken from her,* Pass. 144, conf. Ges. Ab. 3, 584. A Mary *receives a shot,* and saves the man it was aimed at, Maerl. 2, 202. A Crucifix *embraces* a worshipper, Keisersb. seel. par. 75ᵈ; *bows* to one who has forgiven his mortal foe, Sch. u. Ernst 1522 cap. 628; 'dat cruce *losede den voet,* unde stotte ene,' kicked him, Detm. 1, 7. An image *bites* the perjurer's hand off, Sch. u. Ernst c. 249; *speaks,* Alexius 444. 490. Maerl. 2, 201; and *turns round,* KM. 1 (ed. 2) xlix. The stone visitant in Don Juan nods and walks. Gods' images *fall from heaven* acc. to the Scythian legend; so does the figure of Athena, Paus. i. 26, 7. Or they are *stolen* from abroad, *dii evocati, e.g.* a Juno (Gerh. Etrusker p. 31), and Artemis from Tauris, Schol. to Theocr. ; conf. Meiners 1, 420-3. So, in the Mid. Ages, relics were stolen. Again, idols are *washed, bathed,* Schol. to Theocr.; conf. the Alraun, p. 1203. They were even solemnly burnt; thus in the Bœotian dædals, every 60 years, 14 oaken images of Hera were consigned to the flames, E. Jacobi's Hdwtb. d. Gr. u. Rom. mythol. 394.

p. 115.] The numbers *three* and *four* in conn. with gods' images occur even later still. At Aign on the Inn near Rottalmünster, next the Malching post-house, a St. Leonard's pilgrimage is made to *five brazen idols,* the biggest of which is called the

*Worthy.* The peasants say none but the worthy man can lift it. If a youth after his first confession fails to lift the figure, he goes to confession again, and comes back strengthened. The festival is called The three golden Saturday nights in September. A girl proves her virginity (also by lifting?). The Austrians have a Leonard's chapel too, yet they pilgrim to Aign, and say 'he is the one, the Bavarians have the right one,' conf. Panzer's Beitr. 2, 32—4. A nursery-tale (Ernst Meier no. 6, p. 38) describes a wooden sculpture in the shape of a horse with four heads, three of which belong to Donner, Blitz and Wetter, evidently Donar, Zio and Wuotan.

p. 118.] Similar to the irmen-pillar with Mercury's image in the Ksrchr., is a statue at Trier which represented Mercury flying, Pertz 10, 132. The Lorsch Annals make Charles find gold and silver in the Irmenseule. There are also stories of mice and rats living inside statues, Lucian somn. 24; in Slavic idols, says Saxo; the Thor that is thrown down swarms with large mice, adders and worms, Maurer bek. 1, 536. What Rudolf of Fulda says of the *Irminsul* is repeated by Adam of Bremen (Pertz 9, 286). 'irmesuwel der cristenheit,' Germania 1, 451, conf. 444. The Roman de Challemaine (Cod. 7188, p. 69) describes the war of the Franks with the Saxons:

En leur chemin trouverent un *moustier*
que li Saisne orent fet pieca edifier.
une idole y avait, que les Saisnes proier
venoient come dieu touz et gloirefier.
quar leur creance estoit selonc leur fol cuidier
quele les puist bien sauver jousticier.
*Neptusnus* ot à non en lonneur de la mer.

One is reminded of the lofty Irminsul by the story of an idol *Lug* or *Heillug,* 60 cubits high, in the Wetterau, Ph. Dieffenbach 291 (heiliger lôh?).

p. 121.] On Caesar's '*Sol et Vulcanus et Luna,*' see GDS. 766. The Indiculus comes immediately after the Abrenuntiatio, in which Thuner, Wôden and Saxnôt have been named; its Mercury and Jupiter therefore stand for German gods, as indeed several German words are used in it: nod-fyr, nimidas, frias, dadsisas. The Abrenuntiatio requires you to give up the *trilogy* Thuner,

Wôden, Saxnôt, and all the unholies that are *their fellows ;* so there *were* three heathen gods, and more. On the trilogy conf. Pref. li. liv., and in Verelius, sub v. blotskap, the passage out of the Trojamanna-s. p. 34, where Brutus invokes Thôr, Oðin and *Geffon.*

p. 122.] Saxo's way of looking at the Norse gods is noticed p. 384-5. The thunder-god, who is *Thoro* at p. 41, and *Thor* at p. 103, he once names *Jupiter.* Besides, he has *Pluto* and *Dis =* Othinus as Valföðr 36. 140-7 ; and *Proserpina =* Hel, 43.

p. 123.] Lepsius, Einl. p. 131, says the Egyptian week had not 7, but 10 days. ' Nine days' time ' is a common reckoning among savages, Klemm 2, 149. To nundinae corresponds ἐννῆμαρ, yet Nieb. 1, 308, and O. Müller Etr. 2, 324 think the Romans had a week of 8 days. The seven-day week is Semitic, was unknown to Greeks or Romans, and rests on a belief in the sacredness of the number 7 ; conf. Nesselm. on the origin of the week (Königsb. deutsche gesellsch., May 22, 1845). Titurel 2753 :

Die sieben stern sieben tugende haltent,

Die muozen alle mensche haben, die dâ zît der tage waltent.

The Provençal names of days in Raynouard sub v. *dia.* O. Fr. de-mierkes for mercre-di, de-venres for vendre-di ; conf. Roquef. suppl. v. kalandre.

p. 125.] MHG.——I. *Sunnentac,* MS. 2, 190ᵇ. Amur 1578. 1609-21. Griesh. 114. 141. *suntac,* Pass. 299, 68. 81.——II. *mâutac,* Frauend. 32; 11. *maentags* 82, 1.——III. *aftermaentag,* Hätzl. lxviiiᵃ. *aftermontag,* Uhl. volksl. p. 723. *zistag* and *zinstag,* Wackern. Bas. hss. 54-7 ; also Schweiz. geschichtsfr. 1. 82-3. 161.· 4, 149. *cinstag,* Weisth. 1, 759. *zinstag,* Dietr. drach. 320ᵇ. Justinger 59, Keisersp. *zistig,* Tobler 458. *eritag,* Fundgr. 1, 75. MB. 27, 89ᵃ (1317). 132ᵃ (1345). Lang reg. 4, 711ᵃ (1300). Grätzer urk. of 1319, etc. ; but ibid. *erchtag,* 1310. Schwabe tintenf. 19. 56. *erctag* in Hartlieb, Superst. H., cap. 31-2. *erichtag,* Beheim, 76, 16. H. Sachs 1, 206ᵈ. Hutten 3, 358. *eretag* in Guben, 48, 32.——IV. *mitwoche,* Bas. hss. 57. *mittoche,* Diemer, 357, 5. von *dem mitechen,* Tund. 44, 27. *des mittichen,* MB. 27, 90 (1317). 27, 98 (1321). *der midechen,* Grätzer urk. of 1320, *mitich, mitichen,* 1338. *midechon,* Griesh. 2, 48. ' an dem nehsten *guctemtag* (!), Schreiber 1, 486 (see p. 124 n).——V. Records of the 14th cent. waver betw. *donresdag* and *donredag*. *Dunrstac*, Pass. 57, 87, etc. *dünderstag, dunders-tag* alw. in Conr. of Weinsbg. *dorstage*, Schweiz. geschichtsfr. 3, 260 (1396). *Dunredagh*, Maltzan 2, 6. Hpt Ztschr. 5, 406. *donredagh*, Maltzan 2, 45.——VI. *phincztag*, Beheim 78, 8. MB. 27, 131ª (1343). *vrîtach*, Griesh. 2, 48. *frehtag*, Grätzer urk. of 1310. *des vriegtages*, S. Uolrich, 1488.

p. 125.] OS.——These have to be guessed from the following later forms: I. *sundach*, Ssp. *sondag*, Pom. 1486. Klempin 488.——II. *mandag*, ibid.——III. *dinsdag*, Cöln. urk. of 1261. Höfer no. 5. *dinstag*, 1316, ib. p. 112; *dynsdais*, p. 277. *dince-dagh*, Pom. urk. of 1306, p. 354. *dinscdag*, Magdeb. urk. of 1320, p. 142. *dinstagh*, Quedl. of 1325, p. 179. *dingstdag*, Ravnsbg. urk. of 1332, p. 258. *dynstag*, Siebertz no. 652. 688 (1315-43). *dinxtdag*, Ditm. landr. of 1447 ed. Michels. p. 32. *dynsthedach*, Detmar 2, 287. *dinschedach*, Weisth. 3, 88. 90. *dyngstedag*, urk. of Maltzan 2, 270. *dincsedagh* 2, 34. *dinghe-stedaghes, dingsted., dynsted., dyngesd.* 2, 179. 210. 207. 142. *dinxstedages*, Hpt's Ztschr. 5, 405-406. *dingstedag*, Hammer-bröker recht. Did any Low German district in the Mid. Ages retain Tisdag? Scarcely: all seem to have forms beginning with din, agreeing with Nethl. dinsdag, and corrup. from the older disendach; hence our present dienstag. *Dinstag* appears as early as 1316 at Schleusingen, 1320-2 at Erfurt (Höfer p. 120. 146. 153). *dingesdag*, Klempin 488.——IV. *gudinsdag, gûdens-dag*, Höfer no. 6. 7. (1261-2). *des mitwekens*, Maltzan 2, 88. in *deme mitwekene* 2, 113. *des mydweken*, Hpt Ztschr. 5, 406. *des middewekenes*, Höfer 166 (in 1323 at Halberstadt). *mitd-wekenes* 370 (in 1331). *medewekes* 360 (in 1324). *middeweke*, Klempin.——V. *dunresdach*, Ssp. *donredag*, Klempin. *dunredagh*, urk. of Maltzan, 2, 6. Hpt 5, 406. *donredagh*, Maltzan 2, 45. ——VI. *vridach*, Ssp. *frigdag*, Klempin.——VII. *sunavent*, Ssp. 2, 66 (one MS. *satersdach*). *sonnavend*, Klempin. *saterdag* is Nethl. and Westph., not Saxon. *saterstag*, Seibertz 724ª (1352). *satirsdach*, Marienlieder. Hpt 10, 80-1. *saterstag*, Spinnr. evang., Cöln 1538, title. In Freidank 169, 15, one MS. changes ' suones tac' into *satersdach*. *soterdag*, Firmenich 1, 301ᵇ; *sorreschteg* 1, 495 at Eupen.

M. NETHL.——I. *sondach*, Decker's Lekensp. 1, 38.——II. *maendach*, Decker ib.——III. *dinxdach*, Decker. *disdag desdag*,

Coremans p. 49. *disendaighes,·* Hedu p. 443. De klerk 1, 804. *disendach,* Uhl. 1, 415.——IV. *woonsdach,* Decker.——V. *donredach,* Decker. *donderdach,* Lanc. 13970.——VI. *vridach,* Decker. den *vrindach,* Lanc. 25310. *sfrîndaghes,* Maerl. 3, 284. *sfrindaechs,* De klerk 1, 708 in 1303.——VII. *saterdach,* Decker. In the Leven van Jezus p. 27-8. 74-5. 234 the Jewish notion of Sabbath is lamely rendered by *saterdach.*

p. 126.] FRIS.——III. *tihsdi, tisdey,* Hpt Ztschr. 1, 107.—— VII. A fuller form 'sn-avend' occurs in the Gen. *snavendes,* Anhalt urk. of 1332, Höfer 163.

North-Fris. forms in Outzen, p. 38.——IV. *Weadansdai,* Landeskunde 4, 248. *Winjsday* in Silt, Müllenh. 167.——V. *Türsdei* and *Tüsdei.*——VII. *in* = evening, eve, as in 'gude *e'en* to ye,' Shaksp. good-*en.*

AS.——IV. Mercoris die, hoc est *Wôdnesdag,* Kemble 5, 94 (in 844).

OE.——III. *tweisdaie.* IV. *wensdaie,* Garner, Procdgs. p. 232.

ON. in Gulaþ. p. 9.——III. *Tysdagr.* IV. *Oðensdagr.* V. Þorsdagr. VI. *Freadagr.* VII. *þvatðagr.*

SWED.——I. *sunnundaghr,* östg. (conf. p. 126 n.). VII. *löghurdagh,* östg.

NORW.——IV. *mekedag.* VI. *Freadag,* Dipl. Norv. vol. 3, no. 787 (in 1445).

JUT.——IV. *Voensdag, voinsdau,* Molb. dial. 653. VI. *Freia.* VII. *Luora,* Foersom, p. 12.

ANGL.——IV. *Vonsdaw.*

p. 127 n.] On the Roman altar in Swabia, see Stälin, 1, 111. On the circle of planetary gods, Lersch in Jb. d. Rheinlande iv. 183. v. 298—314. The 8 figures on the altar may signify the gods of *nundinae.* The Germ. week has Odin in the middle, his sons Tyr and Thor next him : Mars, Mercury, Jupiter.

p. 129.] Snorri too, in his Formâli, has interpretations and comparisons with the Bible and classical mythology. Freyr he identifies with Saturn (p. 217).

p. 130.] The Ests, Finns and Lapps name the days thus :—

EST.——I. *pühhapääw,* holy day. II. *esmaspääw,* first day. III. *teisipääw,* second day. IV. *kesknäddel,*[1] mid-week. V.

---

[1] The Slavic nedélia, orig. Sunday, now means week.

*nelyapääw,* fourth day.   VI. *rede* (redi), fast-day ?   VII. *lau-
pääw; poolpääw,* half-day.

FINN.——I. *sunnuntai.*   II. *maanan.*   III. *tiistai.*   IV. *keski-
wiycko.*   V. *tuorstai.*   VI. *peryandai;* is this Perun's day displaced (conf. *Perendan* below)? or, as the Finns have no F, a
corrup. of Fredag ?   [Prob. the latter, conf. Peryedag; and the
Finns are fond of adding an N.].   VII. *lauwandai.*

SWED. LAPP.——I. *ailek.*   II. *manodag.*   III. *tisdag.*   IV. *kaska
wakko.*   V. *tuoresdag.*   VI. *peryedag.*   VII. *lawodag.*

NORW. LAPP.——I. *sodno beive.*   II. *vuosarg.*   III. *mangebarg.*
IV. *guskvokko.*   VI. *fastobeive* fast-day, and *peryedag.*

## CHAPTER VII.

## WODAN.

p. 131.]   The name of the highest god, whom the other gods
serve *as children their father* (Sn. 23), often occurs in OHG., like
*Herrgott* much later, as a man's name: *Wotan,* Schannat 312,
*Woatan* 318, *Wuotan* 342. 386-9.   Langobardic glosses have
*Odan* and *Godan,* Hpt Ztschr. 1, 557 ; conf. *Godán* 5, 1. 2.   In
the Abren. we find *Woden;* perh. *Wedan* too is OS. (Suppl. to
154) ; on *Wodan* conf. Lisch Meckl. Jb. 20, 143.   AS., beside
Wôden, has *Othan* (Sup. to 5) ; *Oðon,* Sal. and Sat. 83 ; *Eowðen*
(p. 161 n.).   Nth Fris. *Wede, Wedke,* Müllenh. 167.   *Wedki* taeri !
Landesk. 4, 246.   For Norse Oðinn, once *Oddiner,* conf. Munch
on Odd's Ol. Tr. 94.   *Audon,* Yngl. c. 7,   Does *Audun* in Norw.
docs. stand for Oðin ?   *Oden* in Östögtl.=hin onde, Almqvist
371ᵃ.   In the Stockh. Adress-calender för 1842, p. 142, are
actually two men named *Odin.*   Rask, Afh. 1, 377-8, takes the
Lett. *Vidvut* for the Vodan of the Vides (Lettons), while Vogt 1,
141 makes *Widewud, Waidewud* a Prussian king.   With *Vut* in
the Grisons, conf. *Vuodan* in the Valais, of whom M. C. Vulliemin relates in his La reine Berte et son temps, Laus. 1843, p. 3 :
' Un jour on avait vu *Wuodan* descendre le Rhône, telle était du
moins la croyance populaire, *l'épée nue* dans une main, un *globe
d'or* dans l'autre, et criant rigou haiouassou (fleuve soulève toi) !
et le fleuve s'élevant avait détruit une partie de la ville.'   On my
inquiring (through Troyon) if the name in the story was really

Wuodan, the answer was distinctly Yes, and the town destroyed was Martigny. Carisch 182ᵇ has *vutt* idol, which some derive from *vultus*, voult, face, or portrait, others from *votum ;* conf. magliavutts (Sup. to 35 n.).

p. 132.] Wuotan from watan, like θεός from θέειν, Sansk. *vâdanas*, Schleicher in Kuhn's Ztschr. 4, 399. He stands closely conn. with *weather*, OHG. *wetar*, aër, aether, and wind (Sup. to 115) ; he is storm, byr, furia, wild hunter, uma, Ymir, Jumala, spirit ; he is also called Ofnir, Vafuðr, Vafþrûðnir. But why in Sæm. 3ᵇ does Oðinn give önd, and Hoenir ôð, when surely Oðinn should give ôð ? The Bav. *wueteln* is known to H. Sachs : das es *aufwudlet* grün in grün (of herbs) v. 377ᵈ. *wudelt* das kraut auf, v. 378ᶜ ; conf. *Wuotilgóz, Wôdelgeát*, p. 367 n., and Wôden's relation to Geát, p. 164-5. We can put him on a par with Zeus, Indra, Loptr : ἀήρ, ὅν ἄν τις ὀνομάσειε καὶ Δία, Meineke's Fragm. com. 4, 31. Æschylus in Eum. 650 says of Zeus : τὰ δ᾽ ἄλλα πάντ᾽ ἄνω τε καὶ κάτω στρέφων τίθησιν, οὐδὲν ἀσθμαίνων μένει. Zeus merely *touches, breathes upon* Io, and she conceives *Epaphos* (the touched), Æsch. Prom. 849—851. ἐξ ἐπαφῆς κἀξ ἐπιπνοίας Δίος, Æsch. Suppl. 18. 45. ἐφάπτωρ 312. θείαις ἐπιπνοίαις παύεται 576. Ducange sub v. *Altanus* has a peculiar gl. Aelfrici : Altanus *Voden*, quae vox saxonice Wodanum seu Mercurium sonat (conf. p. 162 n.). In Wright 17ᵇ 'Altanus *þoden*,' otherw þoden is *turbo ;* altanus auster is a wind. On *Woldan* see Hpt Ztschr. 5, 494.

p. 132.] With Otfried's *gotewuoto* conf. a Schlettst. gl. of the 9th century : 'sub tyranno, under themo *godowôden*.' Der *wüeterîch*, Servat. 28ᵌ3. ein tobender *w.*, Barl. 254, 21 ; conf. gwyth, p. 150 n. In the Eifel the wild host is called *Wodes*-heer, and a savage monster of a man *Wuodes*-woor, Schmitz 1, 233 In the Wetterau band of robbers was one Werner *Wuttwuttwutt*, Schwenker 574. Pfister 1, 157. 162.

p. 133.] It is not *Sviðr*, gen. Svinns, but *Sviðar* ok Sviðrir, gen. *Sviðurs*, in Sæm. 46ᵇ. Sn. 3. 24. 195.——Beside *valfaðir, herfaðir* (p. 817), Oðinn bears the names *Herjann, Herteitr, Gunnarr*, Lex. myth. 641ᵃ ; conf. *Herjans dîs*, Sæm. 213ᵇ. *fleygði* O. ok î folk umskaut 5ᵃ. *valr lâ þar â sandi* vitinn enum eineygja Friggjar faðmbyggvi (ibi caesi in arena jacuere, dedicati unoculo qui Friggae amplexibus delectatur), Sn. 1848, 236.

Non humile obscurumve genus, non funera plebis
Pluto rapit vilesque animas, sed fata potentum
Implicat, et claris complet Phlegethonta figuris,

Saxo Gram. 36.——The *boar's head* in the Alamann order of
battle is expressly acknowledged by Agathias 2, 8 (Stälin 1, 160).
p. 134.] With Paul the Deacon's account conf. the older
setting in the Prol. leg. Rotharis in Hpt Ztschr. 5, 1. There
*Wodan* and *Frea* remind you altogether of *Oðinn* and *Frigg* in
the Grîmnismâl. O. is called *Sigr-höfundr*, Egilss. 640, and his
dwelling *Sigtûnir*, Yngl. 5. Sn. 15.
p. 136.] On name-giving, ON. nafn-festi, see GDS. 153-4.
With *Hliðsciâlf* conf. Valaskiâlf, p. 817 n. Does OHG. Bughen-
*scelp* belong here? Cod. Lauresh. no. 2597. The Gl. Sletst.
15, 7 have *scelb* fornice, also those in Hpt Ztschr. 5, 196. *scelp*
fornix, Graff 6, 479. *biscilbit* in clida, Diut. 1, 342 ; and clida
belongs to hlið, OHG. hlit, operculum. The Lex. myth. 434
explains Hliðskiâlf as *porta* coeli tremens.
p. 136-7 n.] *God's chair* means also the rainbow (p. 733) ;
*God's little chair*, among the Lausitz Wends, the corpse-bird
(p. 1134). The German märchen of the Tailor who climbs the
Lord's *chair*, of iron-booted Ferdinand, of faithful John and
strong Francis, who arrive at a heaven with many *doors* (conf.
Wolf's Deut. mär. u. sagen no. 5, KM. no. 3, 35, Müllenh. mär.
no. xii.), resemble the Greek notion of Zeus's *throne* and the
several *doors* through which he attends to the prayers, vows
and offerings of men, Lucian's Icaromenippus, c. 25-6.
p. 138.] *Wunsch, wish*, seems akin to Sansk. *vângksh, vânch*
opto, desidero, Bopp Gl. 315ᵃ. Pott 1, 235, which Bopp thinks
identical with Welsh *gwanc*, desire. Wish in O.Fr. is *souhait*
(p. 951n.) and *avel*, pl. aviaux, Ren. 25131, 26828. plus bel lui
nestuest *souhaidier*, Ogier 1, 140. *Wunsch* is god of bliss and
love, who wishes, wills and brings good to men. We still speak
of God as the *giver of all good, all gifts*, Kl. Schr. 2, 327-9.
*Wünschen* is to romance, exaggerate, imagine : sam ez *gewünschet*
waere, Rab. 240. ob ieman *wünschen* solde, Nib. 281, 3. 780, 1.
und der nu *w.* solde, Ecke 202 (Hagen). Also to wish into
being, create, Wigal. 327. 887. 5772. so viel nur immer Gott
Vater *w.* kann, Zingerle 2, 64. mit *wunsch*, by divine power,

Tit. 347; and conversely *verwünschen* to annihilate. *wünschen* lernen, to learn conjuring, Müllenh. 395. 402. [Of *wunsch* as the Ideal, a page and a half of examples is here omitted.]

p. 141.] *Wish* personified appears most freq. in Hartmann, which is the more remarkable, as he got no prompting from his French original. The last line on p. 138 :

> der Wunsch het in *gemeistert* sô, Greg. 1097. Er. 2740.

only reminds us partially of *a* French poet, Thib. de N. 95 :

> beneet soit le *maistre*
> qui tele la fist naistre ;

while Chrestien's Erec has nothing similar, either here, or in describing the horse (Hartm. Er. 7375), or the palace and twenty ladies (8213-77) ; and where Hartm. boasts of his Enite :

> man sagt daz nie kint gewan
> ein lîp sô gar dem *Wunsche* glîch, Er. 330,

Chrestien's Erec 407 has merely :

> que tote i avoit mis s'entente
> *nature*, qui faite l'avoit (conf. vv. 415. 425).

Presently, however, in his :

> ich waene *Got* sînen vlîz
> an si hâte geleit
> von schoene und von saelekeit, Er. 338,

where Chrestien had said, v. 429 :

> onques *Dex* ne sot faire miauz
> le nes, la bouche, ne les iauz,

Hartm. draws nearer to his prototype again. His *Wunsches gewalt* often occurs in later writers :

> beschoenen mit *Wunsches gewalte*, Flore 6927.
> ir lîp aller wolgestalt
> gar in des *Wunsches gewalt*, Meleranz. 8768.
> *Wunsches gewalt* hân, Berth. 239. 240.
> hie *Wunsches gewalt*, hie liep âne leit
> in immerwerender sicherheit, Heinr. Suso in Die ewige weisheit.

But the phrase becomes more and more impersonal :

si hât an ir *wunsch gewalt*, Altsw. 98.

an im lît der *wunschgewalt*, Dietr. drach. 41ᵇ.

drîer *wünsche gewalt*, MS. 2, 145ᵇ (KM.³ 3, 146-7).

geben mit alles *wunsches gewalt*, Pass. 298, 1.

aller *wünsche gewalt*, Uhl. volksl. 1, 21.

conf. ἐξουσίας τυχεῖν παρὰ τοῦ Διὸς αἰτήσασθαι ὅτου ἐπιθυμεῖ, Athen. 3, 24. [Another page and a half of examples is here omitted.]

p. 143 n.] Even Wolfram in Wh. 15, 7 has 'des *Wunsches zil*'; and des *Wunsches paradîs* actually occurs in Barl. 52, 8 and in the Rudolf. Vilmar p. 64.

p. 143.] Wish is the meting, moulding, casting, giving, creating (p. 22, 104 n. 139), figuring, imaging, thinking, faculty, hence also imagination, idea, image, figure. There is about Wish something inward, uttered from within : der Wunsch *tihtet*, Troj. 3096, ûz *tiefer sinne grunde erwünschet* mit dem munde 2960. Apart from the passage in the Iliad, χάρις answers to wunsch, not only in Lucian's Pro Imag. c. 26 p. 52 : κόμην ταῖς χάρισιν ἀπείκασε, but, as God imparts wishing, it is said of Hermes : ὅς ῥά τε πάντων ἀνθρώπων ἔργοισι χάριν καὶ κῦδος ὀπάζει, Od. 15, 319. Beside des Wunsches auc and heilwâc, we have also a *wunschsee* and *wunschbrunne*, Pröhle's Unterharz. s., no. 345 ; a *Wünschberg* in Panzer's Beitr. 1, 116, *Wenschenborch* in Hpt Ztschr. 1, 258, *Wunschilburg* in Henricus Pauper 115, *Wünschelburg* a village near Glatz. 'Joannes *Wunschelberg* doctor vixit circa an. 1400,' Flacius cat. test. verit. 782, in Zarncke's Univ. Leipzig 764 an. 1427, 888 an. 1438. A *Wünschmichelbach*, Baader's Sagen no. 345 ; a *Wünschensuhl* near Marksuhl, Thuringia ; a 'super *Wünsche*' and *Wunscheidorf*, Rauch 2, 198. 200.

p. 143-4.] Förstemann has no name *Wunsc, Wunscio*, which would mean wisher, adopter, but Karajan quotes *Wensco* and *Sigiwunh* (for Sigiwunsc, conf. Sigtŷr), and *Sigewnses*-holz about Eichstadt (for Sigiwunsces-holz), MB. 31, 363, year 1080.——The *Oskmeyjar* are called nunnor Herjans, Oðins meyjar, Sn. 212ᴬ. *Oskopnir* might be connected with it and explained as 'stragem, campum *electionis* aperiens' from *opna* aperire, of which the Völs. saga c. 18 makes *uskaptr*. Beside the *Wûscfreá* of Deira, a later one is mentioned by Beda 138, 19. 153, 5.

p. 145.] As Wuotan sends *wind* and *weather*, and stills the stormy sea, it is said of the christian God: daz er uns alle tage dienet mit *weter* ioch mit *wint*, Diemer 89, 18. In Parzival, Feirefiz ascribes it to Juno that she *daz weter fuocte*, fitted 750, 5; dem Juno ie gap *segels luft* 757, 7; *segelweter fuogte* 767, 3.——— If *yggr* be terror, *yggdrasill* means the horse of dread, the storm-courser, perhaps the rushing god himself, as we know that Oðinn bears the surname *Yggr*, and is always figured as the rider in the air, the furious hunter. In that case *Yggdrasils askr* (Pref. li.) is the stormful god's ash. Oðinn is also *Hróptr*, alte clamans, conf. OHG. hruoft, clamor, Graff 4, 1137: Hróptr glaðr, Hpt Ztschr. 3, 154; Hróptatýr, p. 196. And the surname *Farma-týr, Farma-guð* may not be out of place here, as deus vecturarum nauticarum, from farmr, onus nauticum. *Mefingr*, Sæm. 272ᵃ is perh. conn. with mafr, seamew. Other by-names are *Fengr*, Sæm. 184ᵃ. Völs. saga c. 17, p. 157; *Sváfnir*, Sæm. 93ᵃ; *Fiölnir*, Sæm. 10ᵃ. 46ᵇ. 184ᵃ. Völs. saga c. 17, p. 157 and conf. 136. 193. 200. 323. He is 'inn reginkunngi baldur î brynjo,' Sæm. 272ᵇ.

p. 145.] Similar expressions for dying are: AS. *Dryhten sêcean*, Beow. 373. ON. kenna einom âttûnga brautir *til Oðins landa*, Sæm. 80ᵇ. *far till Oden*, Geyer 1, 123; conf. *gefa Oðni*, Landn. 5, 10. The miser collecting treasures is said in Sweden to *tjena Oden*, Geyer 1, 123. Kl. schr. 3, 197.

p. 145 n.] The conception of Oðinn as an evil being is clear in the ON. '*hvaða Oðins látum?*' quid hoc mali est? shortened to 'hvaða látum,' quid hoc rei est? Wormius mon. dan. p. 11; lât is amissio, mors; conf. our 'was des teufels?' Fornm. sög. 3, 179 has 'ôfögnuðr sendr af *Oðni*,' mischief sent from O.; *Oðinn-dæll* 11, 151 periculosus, insociabilis, difficilis, is interpr. 'iìlr viðfângs' 12, 430; *Oðinndæla* 6, 374 periculum, infortunium, interpr. 'vandraeði, vandamâl, naudsyn' 12, 430. Dæll itself is mansuetus, affabilis.

p. 147.] Oðin's outward appearance is alluded to in many other places; hinn *eineygji* Friggjar faðm-byggvir, Sn. 1848 p. 236. He is *Hengikiaptr*, labeo, cui pendet maxilla, Sn. 146 (p. 1075 n.); *Harbarðr*, Flaxbeard, from hör, linum; to Sigurðr appears the *Longbeard*, and helps him to choose Grani, Völs. c. 13. GDS. 688-9. To Saxo's 'Othinus *os pileo obnubens*' answers his surname *Grîmnir* larvatus, from grîma. As 'Grîmnir' he

shews himself to men in the guise of a beggar to try them, *e.g.* to
Geirröðr; as 'Gestr blindi' to Heiðrekr, as 'Gângrâðr' to Vafþrûðnir. Compare the German märchen of the old Beggar-
woman, KM. 150, whose clothes begin to burn, as Grîmni's did.
In the case of Heiðrekr, Gestr guesses riddles for another, as the
miller or shepherd does for the abbot, Schmidt 85—9. Again
Oðinn appears as the one-eyed *bóndi Hrani*, and bestows gifts,
Hrolf Kr. saga c. 39. 46 (Fornald. s. 1, 77. 94). The Fornm.
s. 5, 171-2 says : 'hann var stuttklaeddr, ok hafði sîdan hatt niðr
fyrir andlitit, ok sâ ôgerla âsjonu hans; skeggjaðr var hann;'
conf. the *blind* (one-eyed ?) *Hatt,* Sv. äfventyr 1, 363.    GDS.
578.    Swed. legend gives Oðinn a pointed hat, *uddehatt,* which
agrees with the peculiar shape of certain tombstones, wedge-
shaped, like a man-trap.    But he is called *hauga-dróttinn,*
Vitterh. acad. handl. 14, 73.    Now uddehatt is usu. a dwarf's
hood or cape of darkness; hence also he appears as 'lord of
dwarfs.'    At the same time the hat is a wishing-hat and Mercury's hat.    He appears as an *old man,* or as a *hunter on high
horse* with three hounds which he gives away to a youth; and
a Smâland story expressly names him *Oden,* Sv. folkv. 1, 212.
*Gammal grâman* gives advice, but may not stay beyond cock-
crow, Arvidsson, 3, 3.    Similar is the *one-eyed witch,* Norske
event. 141-2.——In Germany too we can now find many traces
of this divine apparition.    A *Graymantle,* a *Broadhat* often turns
up in nursery tales, see Haltrich p. 10. 39. 44; an *old man*
fetches the children, p. 4.    He appears as *Old One-eye* 45. 55,
as *Stone-goat* 44, *Wild-cat* 63.    God comes in the guise of an *old
beggar,* stands *godfather,* and gives gifts, KM. no. 26 ; or as a
*grey-bearded mannikin,* Frommann's Munda. 4, 328; conf. the
cld beggar-woman, KM. no. 150; as *One-eyed Flap-hat,* Alsatia
1856 p. 131.    A *grey smith* heals, Hpt Ztschr. 1, 103.    In St.
Martin's cloak and hood Simrock sees Wuotan's wishing-cloak,
Martinsl. xvii.

p. 147.]    When Oðinn hurled the spear, then, says the
Völuspâ, was the first war in the world.    He is *geira dróttinn,*
Egilss. 639.    *geiri undaðr oc gefinn Oðni,* Saem. 27[b].    *marka* sik
*Oðni,* p. 1077.    Under Otto III. a man in a dream, after taking
a pious vow, was *transfixed by two lances* of the martyrs Crispin
and Crispinian, Pertz 5, 787.    The giant *Oden* in Sv. äfvent. 455

(some versions omit the name) possesses costly things, as the god does his *spear*. Out of such notions sprang the OHG. names *Kêrans, Folchans*, Hpt Ztschr. 7, 529. Is this spear more like Apollo's destructive dart, or the sceptre of Zeus (p. 680) ? Is the name of the Lombard royal line of *Gunginge* conn. with *Gúngnir?* GDS. 687-8.

p. 148 n.] In Herod. 4, 15 Aristeas is called Apollo's *raven*, *i.e.* priest, as Porphyry tells us the Magians called the priests of the Sun-god ravens. *Three ravens* fly with St. *Benedict*, Paul. Diac. 1, 26. In Goethe's Faust 12, 127 the witch asks Mephistopheles : But where are your two ravens ?——*Doves* sit on Gold-Mariken's *shoulders*, Müllenh. 403. A dove sits on the head and shoulder of a boy at Trier, Greg. Tur. 10, 29 ; one perches three times on the head of St. Severus, Myst. 1, 226-7, another settles on St. Gregory's shoulder 1, 104.

p. 148.] Flugu hrafnar tveir of *Hnikars öxlum, Huginn* til hauga, enn â hrae *Muninn*, Sn. 322. The ravens daily sent out return at dögurðarmâli 42 ; conf. F. Magnusen's Dagens tider p. 42. fara *Viðris grey* valgiörn um ey, Sæm. 154ᵃ. *hrafnar tveir* flugu með þeim alla leið, Nialss. 80. On *Odens foglar, Odens svalar*, see Sup. to 159.

p. 148.] *Oðin-Neptunus* resembles both Poseidon and Zeus, who rise out of the sea as bulls. Oðinn shows himself to Olaf as a boatman, *nökkva maðr*, Fornm. s. 2, 180 ; and, as the *man in the boat*, fetches Sinfiötli's body, Völs. c. 10. Like him are the divine steersman in the Andreas (Pref. xxiv. xxv.), and the thirteenth man who steers the twelve Frisians, who has the axe on his shoulder, throws it at a well-spring, and teaches them justice, Richth. 439. 440. Yet we also come upon Oðinn *Hnikar* as a *karl af biargi*, Sæm. 183-4.

p. 149.] *Byr, Burr* is Oðin's father, p. 348-9. gefr hann (O.) *byri* brögnom, Sæm. 113ᵇ. A fair wind, ON. *óska-byrr*, is in the Swed. rhyming chron. *önsko bör*. Even the German may very likely have had a *wunsch-bür* as well as wunsch-wint, for we find in Pass. 379, 19 : in kam von winde ein ebene *bür*, die in die segele dâ sluoc. 201, 29 : dô quam ein alsô gelîche *bür*. 380, 78 : daz in wart ein guote *bür*. On the other hand : sô er den *wint* ze *wunsche* hât, Er. 7795. *wunsches weter*, Urstende 125, 85. Got schuof im sanften süezen wint, Ernst 5, 238 (Sup. to 145).

The *himmlische kind* makes *guten wind*, Osw. 960-5. 1220; but also the *storm wind* 1137. 2731. To the Greeks it was Zeus espec. that sent a fair wind : Διὸς οὖρος, Od. 15, 297. Ζεὺς οὖρον ἴαλλεν 15, 475. Ζεὺς εὐάνεμος, Paus. iii. 13, 5. Also a Ἑρμῆς ἀέριος is named 'inter deos qui ad pluviam eliciendam a mago advocantur,' Cass. Dio 71, 19; and Hermes or Theuth was the Egyptians' rain-god 71, 8 (Sup. to 175).

p. 150.] With the AS. dialogue betw. Sat. and Sal., conf. Kemble's Salomon p. 323 : *Mercurius gigas.* In Altd. Bl. 2, 190 the other dialogue is entitled 'Adrian and Ritheus,' and contains the words : 'saga me, hwâ wrât bôcstafas aerest? ic þe secge, *Mercurius se gigant.*' In Småland there rides a man resembling Oðinn, with fiery breath, and a rune staff in his mouth, Hpt Ztschr. 4, 509.——Theuth not only invented letters, but dice : πεττείας, κυβείας as well as γράμματα, Plato's Phædr. 274. And Oðinn is not only the finder of runes, but lord of dice-throwing. An ON. dicer's prayer is (Sup. to 1234) : at þû *Fiölnir* falla lâtir, *þat er ek kasta kann !* F. Magn. lex. myth. 646 (Fiölnir = Oðinn, Sup. to 145). And there was a proverb : þû ert ecki einn î leik, ef *Oðinn styðr þik.* On the Devil as dicer, conf. p. 1007. Players invoked Thôrr and Oðinn, Frigg and Freyja together with Enoch and Elias, Christ and Mary, F. Magn. lex. myth. 646.

p. 150 n.] On *Gwydion* and *Don* see Villemarqué's Bardes bretons 388. The milky way was also called 'Arian rod merch *Don,*' Davies's Mythol. 205. Leo in Hpt Ztschr. 3, 224 derives Gwydion from *gwyd*, mens, μένος (p. 162 n.), like Oðinn from ON. *óðr*, mens. The Irish *dia Geden*, Gael. di ciadain, ciadaoin may indeed be expl. as ceud aoine, first fast; but see O'Brien 168ª.

The sentence in the Prol. legis Salicæ : '*Mercurius Trismegistus* primus leges Ægyptiis tradidit,' comes from Isid. orig. 5, 3. *Tervagan, Tervigant* may have to do with *Trebeta*, Gesta Trev. (Pertz 10, 131).

p. 154.] On *Wodenes-berg, -husen, -wege* conf. Förstem. 2, 1566. in *Wodeneswego* Pertz 8, 604; *de Wodeneswege* 8, 676. *Vudenesvege*, Lisch, Örzen 2ᵇ, 161; *Gudeneswege*, 2ᵇ, 136. Again, *Wodonesberg*, Lacomb. 1, no. 97. 117. *Witanes-berc* (Wuotanes?), Cod. dipl. Juvav. 95 (an. 861). *Mons Mercurii*, Fredegar c. 55. Then, *Wódensbeorg*, Kemble 5, 78. 137. *Woddanbeorg* 3, 457.

*Wônhlinc* 3, 415. 5, 112. 291. *Wôncumb* 5, 78. 137. *Wôdnes-dene* 5, 238. *Wôdnesdîc* 3, 403. 413. 452-5-6. 460-4-6. 5, 215. 238. *Wônlond* 5, 235. 6, 355. *Wôddes geat* 5, 78. 137. *Wônstoc* 3, 227 (Kl. Schr. 2, 57). *Wônâc,* quercus Jovis 3, 458. *Wôn-alre* (-alder) 4, 459. But how are *Wonred, Wonreding,* Beow. 5925-38 to be explained ? OS. *Wetanspeckia* for Wêdanes-speckia (-bridge, wooden bridge), Lünzel 12. 53. Nth Fris. *Wedes-hoog, Wens-hoy, Winis-hog,* Müllenh. 167. Other names in Nordalb. stud. 1, 138. *Weadanask,* Jb. f. Schlesw.-holst. landesk. 4, 248. *Wonsfleth* in Holstein, OS. *Wôdenstorp,* now Wunstorf (Kl. schr. 2, 58), can acc. to Förstem. 2, 1578 be traced back to Wungeresdorf. *Wuninsdorp,* Cæs. Heisterb. 9, 18. *Wôtenes-húsen,* Trad. Fuld. Dronke 38, 221. Cod. Fuld. no. 610 p. 274, now Gutmanns-hausen (Dronke 237[a]). A *Wons-husen* in Weimar, and one near Nidda, Landau's Wetterau 218. *Wonsaz,* Bamb. verein 10, 108. A *Wonsees* betw. Baireut and Bamberg; yet conf. ' in der *wonsass*,' MB. 27, 141, and *wonsassen,* Schm. 4, 80. Kl. schr. 2, 58. A Sigeboto de *Wuonten-geseze* (Wuotanes ?) in MB. 11, 167. About the Fichtelgebirge lie also *Wunsiedel* (Wotanes-sedal ?), *Wonsgehai, Wonsgehäu, Wondsgehäu, Wohns-gehaig,* a village on the Neunberg by Mistelgau, Baireut, Panzer's Beitr. 2, 101. ' flumen quod vulgo *Wotinprunno* dicitur,' Sin-nacher, 2, 635. *Watan*-brunnon, Lacomblet 1, no. 103.

p. 154.] Oðinn is a rider; hence called *Atriði,* he who rides up ? (as Thôrr is *Hlôrriði,* p. 167 n.); conf. also Yggdrasils askr and the story of the World-tree, p. 960. The Hervarar-saga (Fornald. s. 1, 486) has a riddle on Oðinn and *Sleipnir.* On a rune-stone in Gothland is supposed to be carved ' Oden and his eight-legged Sleipnir,' Dybeck 1845, 91. The horse is often mentioned with him : ' om Oden och *hans hästar* ' they say in Upland and Gothland; in Småland they speak of ' Odens *stall* och *krubba,*' Rääf; conf. the ' hunter on high horse,' Sup. to 147. A horse with *six* legs in Haltrich 35-6 ; with *eight* 49; an eight-legged talking sun-steed 101.

p. 155 n.] ' Odinus *pascit equos* suos *in follem inclusus*,' Pâll Vidalin 610 ; conf. ' i bälg binda,' Vestg. lag. p.m. 48. veit ec at ec hêck vindga meiði â naetur allar nîo, geiri undaðr ok gefinn Oðni sialfr sialfum mer, Sæm. 27[b] (see note on KM. no. 146). Charles also *splits a stone* before the battle, Wächter's Heidn.

denkm. 42-3; couf. the story of the Swedish general 45, and
that of Hoier, Benecke's Wigal. 452. In Irish legend too the
divine hero Fin Barre has his horse shod by a mortal smith, and
juggles the fourth leg in, Ir. sagen 2, 85 ; conf. Kl. schr. 2, 450.
p. 157.] In the district of Beilngries, Bavaria, the bunch of
ears is left for the *Waudl-gaul*, and beer, milk and bread for the
*Waudl-hunde*, who come the third night and eat it up. If you
leave nothing, the beaver (bilmer-schnitt) will pass through your
fields. In the last cent. they still kept up a harvest-feast called
*Waudls-mähe*, setting out fodder for the black steeds of *Waude*,
while they drank and sang :—

> O heilige sanct Mäha,
> beschere übers jahr meha,
> so viel köppla, so viel schöckla,
> so viel ährla, so viel tausend gute gährla.

If the reapers forgot, they were told : ' Seids net so geizig, und
lasst dem heilgen S. Mäha auch was steha, und macht ihm sein
städala voll ; ' conf. the less complete account in Panzer's Beitr.
2, 216-7. *Three stalks* are left for *Oswald*, three ears tied three
times round with flowers, viz. the cornflower (centaurea, blue),
the *blotze* (red poppy, papaver rhœas), and camomile. The red
poppy is also called Miedei-magn (Mary's mohn), Panzer 2,
214-5-6. Schm. 2, 555. 608; in Swabia, Her-got's kitele or
mäntele. The Russians leave a sheaf standing for Volos (Veles),
' toward Volos's beard (borod).'

p. 159.] *Oðins-ve* occurs (988) in ' episcopatus *Othenes-
wigensis*,' Lappenb. Hamb. urk. no. 5. *On-sjö, Oden-sjö* in
Skåne, Röstanga-socken, lies over a submerged castle named
*Odinsgård* (see the story in Sup. to 946), Dybeck's Runa 1844,
32-3. In *Ons-källa* were washed the old men that threw them-
selves down the cliff, Geyer 1, 115. *Onsänger* in Småland.
*Odens-brunn* in Upland, Wendel-socken, Dyb. Runa 1844, 90.
With *Wóden worhte weos*, conf. Woldan hewing his church-door,
Wolf's Ztschr. 1, 69. Oðinn, unlike Thôrr, hardly ever occurs
in names of men : Rääf 235-7 gives *Odhankarl, Odhinkarl*.

p. 159.] On the plant-name *Woden-tungel*, -star, see K.
Schiller's Ndrd. pflanzenn. 32 ; conf. 'Ερμοῦ βάϊς, Mercurii
surculus, filix, and 'Ερμοῦ βοτάνιον, herba mercurialis, Diosc. 4,

183-8.——Several birds were sacred to Oðinn : 'korpar, kråkar, skatar bör man icke skjuta, emedan de äro Odens foglar, dem han vid Olofsmässan har hos sig i åtta dagar, då han plocker och tager en stor del af dem. Ardea nigra, en temligen stor fogel af häger-slägtet, kallas Odens svala,' Rääf; see Sup. to p. 148.

p. 160.] Wœns-let suggests ûlf-liðr, p. 207. Kl. schr. 2, 58. Who off a thief has cut the thumbs, To him good luck in throwing comes, Garg. 192ᵃ. Do they say anywhere in Scandinavia Odensfinger, Onsfinger? Acc. to F. Magn. lex. myth. 639 the lungs were sacred to Oðinn and Mercury; conf. the Tables of Blood-letting.

p. 162.] Oðinn, Thôrr, Freyr in Snorri's Edda 131 answers to Oðinn, Asabragr, Freyr in Sæm. 85ᵇ; and invocations in Swed. folk-songs give him the first place : 'hjälp mig Othin, thu kan bäst! hjälp mi Ulf och Asmer Gry!' Arvidss. 1, 69. The same in Danish : 'hielp mig Othin, du kan best! hielp mig Ulf og Asmer Grib!' Syv 48. Asmer Gri=Asa-grim; conf. 'hielp nu Oden Asagrim!' Arvidss. 1, 11.

p. 162 n.] On Zeus τρίτος and Τριτογένεια, conf. Welcker's Trilogie 101-2. At banquets the third goblet was drunk to Zeus: τὸ τρίτον τῷ Σωτῆρι, Passow s.v. σωτήρ. Athena τρίτη, Babr. 59, 1.

p. 162.] Oðinn=Hâr, Sæm. 46ᵃ;=Iafnhâr 46ᵇ;=þriði 46ᵃ. But where do we find Tveggi outside of F. Magn. lex. myth. 644? conf. Egilss. 610, where we can scarcely read Thriggi for Tveggi. On the Sansk. Ekatas, Dvitas, Tritas see Kuhn in Höfer 1, 279. 281-9. Zend. Thraetaono, Thrita, Spiegel's Zendav. 7. 66. Thraetaono=Feridun,=the three-quivered, says Leo 3, 192-5 (1st. ed.).

p. 163.] ON. Vili [weak decl., gen. Vilja] would be Goth. Vilja, OHG. Willo. The strong gen. in 'broðr Vilis,' Egilss. 610 is evid. a slip for Vilja, though we do find the strong nom. Vilir in Yngl. saga c. 3. May we conn. Vili with the Finn. veli, Lap. välja, Alban. βελά, frater ? GDS. 271.

p. 163 n.] Munch 1, 217 thinks Mithothin arose from misunderstanding metod; to me it is plainly Fellow-Othin, like our mit-regent, etc. Saxo's Ollerus is the Eddic Ullr, as is clear from his using a bone for a ship, Saxo p. 46. Yet Ullr seems a jumble of Saxo's Ollerus and Snorro's Vilir, Yngl. c. 3 (Kl. schr. 5, 425): *skip Ullar*, Sn. Hafn. 420 = skiöldr; *askr Ullar* 426. Ydalir, his hall, Sæm. 40ᵇ. *Uller sagr*, F. Magn. lex. 766. *Ullar hylli*, Sæm. 45ᵇ; *hringr U.* 248ª; *U. sefi* = Baldr 93ª, Ullr is Thôr's stepson, Sn. 31. 101·5; boga-, veiði-, öndr-, skialdar-âs 105.

p. 165.] I might have spoken here of Oðin's relation to his wife *Frigg*, p. 299, and to *Skaði*, whom the Yngl. saga c. 9 calls his wife.

---

# CHAPTER VIII.

## THUNAR.

### (Conf. KL. SCHR. 2, 402—438.)

p. 166.] *Donar* stands related to *donen* extendere, expansion of the air (Hpt Ztschr. 5, 182), as τόνος to τείνω, yet tonare is in Sansk. stan, resembling στέντωρ, στόνος and our stöhnen, Kl. schr. 2, 412. In AS., beside *Thunor*, of whom there is a legend (p. 812-3), we have also *Dhôr*, Sal. and Sat. 51. So the rubric over John 5, 17 has þunres-dæg, while that over John 5, 30 has þurs-dæg; and the Norman Dudo calls him *Thur*, Wormius mon. 24. The Abren. has *Thuner*, dat. *Thunare*. MHG. still *dunre*, Pass. 227, 81. Dietr. drach. 110ᵇ. des *dunres* suu (Boaner-ges), Pass. 227, 59 (Kl. schr. 2, 427). For the compound Swed. tordön, Dan. torden, the Norw. has *thordaan*, Faye 5, the Jemtl. *torn*, Almqv. 297, Westgötl. *thorn* and *tånn*. In the Dan. märchen *Torden-vejr* means Thor, as *Donner-wetter* in Germ. curses stands for Donar. The Swed. Lapps call the thunder-god *Tiermes*, Klemm 3, 86-7, Ostiaks *Toruim* 3, 117, Chuvashes *Tóra*, *Tór*, Yakuts *Tanara*, Voguls *Tórom*, Rask's Afh. 1, 44. 33.

p. 167.] ON. *reið* is not only vehiculum, but tonitru: lystir *reið* (al. þruma), Gulaþ. Hafn. 498. Norw. *Thorsreia* tonitru, Faye 5. Danish critics regard *Ökuþôrr* as a different being from Asaþôrr, and as belonging to an older time; yet Sn. 25 places them side by side, and looks upon Thor too as Ökuþôrr, conf. 78. He *drives* a chariot; conf. the Schonen superst. about Thor,

Nilsson 4, 40-4.[1] In Östgötl. the âska is called *goa*; when it thunders, they say 'goa gâr,' Kalen 11ª; *goffur* kör, Almqv. 347, but also *gomor* gâr 384, and *kornbonden* gâr 385. In Holland: 'onze lieve Heer *reed* (drove) door de lucht.' Father God is rolling *d'brenta* (milk-vessels) up and down the cellar steps, Wolf's Ztschr. 2, 54. Can the old *kittel-kar* (kettle-car?) of the giant with *two goats* refer to Donar's chariot? Müllenh. 447; conf. Kl. schr. 2, 422. Thôrr carries a *basket* on his back: *meis*, *iarnmeis*, Sæm. 75ª. Sn. 111. OHG. meisa, Graff 2, 874.

p. 167.] God thunders: die blikzen und die donrelege sint mit gewalte in sîner pflege, MS. 2, 166ᵇ. Zeus raises tempest: ὅτε τε Ζεὺς λαίλαπα τείνῃ, Il. 16, 365; 'what doth Zeus?' meant how's the weather? O. Müller's Gr. gesch. 1, 24. Jupiter, alles *weters gewalt* het er, Ksrchr. 1152 (p. 630). In France: ni oistau nes *Damledeu tonant*, Aspremont 22ᵇ. nes *Deu tonant* ni poistau oir, Mort de Gar. 145-9. noissiez *Deu tonant*, Garins 3, 205; conf. 'si gran romore facevano, che i tuoni non si sarieno potuti udire,' Decam. 2, 1. When a thunderstorm comes on, men say: 'schmeckste *paar öchsel?* merkste a *scheindl?*' Weinh. schles. wtb. 82; 'ecce ubi iterum diabolus ascendit!' Cæs. Heist. 4, 21. The Russians shout words of insult after the retreating tempest, Asbjörnsen's Hjemmet 193.

p. 163.] Thunder is God (or the angels) *playing at bowls*: uns Herr *speelt kegeln*, Schütze 4, 164. die engel *kegeln*, Müllenh. 358; conf. the skittle-playing in the Odenberg, p. 953. Or it is anger, and the thunder-bolt his rod, Pol. bozy prąten.

p. 168.] The same *Taranis* is in the Vedas a surname of Indra the thunder-god, he that passes through, from taran = trans; and so Perun may be conn. with πέρα (but see p. 171, and Kl. schr. 2, 420). Welsh *taran* thunder, Gael. *tairneach, tairneanach*, also *torrunn*. *Taranucnus*, Mone's Bad. urgesch. 2, 184. In Burgundy a town *Tarnodurum*, whose later name *Tonnerre* and 'le *Tonnerrois*,' Jos. Garnier 51, prove that the notion of thunder lay in the old name; conf. Kl. schr. 2, 412.

p. 169 n.] Thôrr heitir *Atli* oc âsabragr, Sn. 211ª, conf. Atli 208ª. The Lapps call their Tiermes *aiyeke*, and his deputy

---

[1] The surnames *Hlórriði*, Sæm. 211ª, and *Eindriði* need not conflict with the statement that Thôrr walks or else drives (p. 167 n.). In Sn. 101 he is called fôstri *Vingnis* ok *Hlôru* (p. 187. 257). In Sn. Formâli 12 *Loride* is called Thôr's son, and *Loricus* Thôrs fôstri, who has a wife *Glora*.

*yunkare, stor-yunkare,* Klemm 3, 86, the Ests their Pikker *wana essa,* old father, Verh. 2, 36-7 ; and the American Indians their Supreme Being the *grandfather,* Klemm 2, 153. With the mountains *Etzel, Altvater* we may perh. associate a high mountain *Oetschan,* Helbl. 7, 1087 (now Öftscher), from Sl. otets, voc. otche, father; conf. Kl. schr. 2, 421.

p. 170 n.] The St. Bernard or Great Bernard is called *Montjoux,* A.D. 1132. On the jugum *Penninum,* deus *Penninus,* see Zeuss 34. 99. Dieffenb. Celt. 1, 170. Several inscriptions ' Jovi *Pœnino, Penino* ' in De Wal no. 211—227. A Mount of joy in Meghaduta 61 ; in Moravia the *Radost,* joy. Finn. *ilo-kivi,* stone of joy, Kalev. 3, 471.

p. 171.] Comes ad *Thuneresberhc* (yr. 1123), Erh. 150; apud *Thuneresberg* 133. Sifrit de *Tonresberc* (1173), MB. 33ᵃ, 44. Sifridus de *Donresberch* (1241-58) 33ᵃ, 68. 90. Of a dragon it is said : er hete wol drî kiele verslunden (swallowed) und den *Dunresberc,* Dietr. drach. 262ᵇ (str. 834). vom *Donresberge,* Hpt Ztschr. 1, 438. A *Donnersberg* by Etteln, S. of Paderborn. AS. *Ðunresleá,* Kemble 3, 443. 4, 105. 5, 84. *Ðunresfeld* 3, 394. 5, 131, conf. 6, 342. *Doneresbrunno,* Ztschr. f. Hess. gesch. 1, 244.

p. 171.] With Slav. *grom, hrom* (Kl. schr. 2, 418) put our LG. *grummeln* of distant thunder, Ir. *crom, cruim* thunder, Fr. *grommeler* growl; also Lith. *grauja* it thunders, *growimmas* thunder.

p. 171.] To Lith. *Perkunas* musza, Nesselm. 411ᵇ, and *P.* grauja, grumena 286ᵃ, add the phrases : *Perkuns* twyksterejo (has crashed), *P.* uźdege (has kindled); *Perkúno* szowimmas (stroke), *P.* growimmas (peal), *P.* żaibas (flash) ; *perkunija* thunderstorm. The Livl. reimchr. 1435 says of him : als ez *Perkune* ir abgot gap, daz nimmer sô harte *gevrôs.* Near Battenhof in Courland is a *Perkunstein* with legends about it, Kruse's Urgesch. 187. 49; a *Perkuhnen* near Libau. *Pehrkones* is hedge-mustard. The Lapps have an evil god or devil *perkel, pergalak,* Finn. *perkele,* Kalev. 10, 118. 141. 207. 327 (Sup. to 987).

p. 172.] In Finn. the oak (tammi) is called God's tree, *puu Yumalan,* Kalev. 24, 98. 105-7. 115-7 ; conf. Zeus's oak p. 184, robur Jovis p. 170. Ju-glans, *Διὸς βάλανος* = castanea, Theophr. 3, 8. 10. Diosc. 1, 145. The oak being sacred to Thôrr, he slays

the giants that take refuge under it; under the beech he has no
power over them. It has been remarked, that lightning pene-
trates twenty times as far into the oak as into the beech, Fries
bot. udfl. 1, 110.

p. 172.] A Swed. folksong (Arvidss. 3, 504) makes Thôrr
live in the mountain: locka *till Thor î fjäll*. Beside *Fiörgvin's*
daughter Frigg, another daughter *Iörð* is called Oðin's wife, and
is mother of Thôrr. But if Thôrr be = *Fairguni*, he is by turns
Oðin's father and Oðin's son; and he, as well as Frigg, is a child
of earth (iörð), Kl. schr. 2, 415. GDS. 119.

p. 173.] Of Enoch and Elias, who are likewise named together
in the ON. dicer's prayer (Sup. to 150), we read in Fundgr.
2, 112:

> sie hânt och die wal (option),
> daz sie den *regin behabin* betalle (keep back rain)
> swenne in gevalle (when they please),
> unt in abir *lâzin vliezen* (again let flow);
> ir zungin megin den himel besliezen (shut up)
> unt widir ûftuon (open),
> sô si sich wellint muon.

The Lithuanians call Lady-day *Elyiós* diena, *Ilyios* diena, on
which it begins or ceases to rain. They derive it from ilyia, it
sets in (to rain); is it not rather *Elias's day?* Elias legends of
Wallachia and Bukowina in Schott. 375. Wolf Ztschr. 1, 180.
On his battle with Antichrist conf. Griesh. 2, 149.

p. 174.] Hominem *fulgure ictum* cremari nefas; terra condi
religio tradidit, Pliny 2, 54. Places struck by lightning were
sacred with the Greeks, and were called ἠλύσια, ἐνηλύσια, because the descending deity had visited them. They were not to
be trampled: hoc modo contacta loca nec intueri nec calcari
debere fulgurales pronuntiant libri, Amm. Marcell. 23, 5. One
peculiar rite was thoroughly Etruscan: such a spot was called
*bidental*, because a *two-year old sheep* was sacrif. there, Festus
sub vv. bidental, ambidens. O. Müller's Etr. 2, 171; the railing
round it was *puteal*, and may be compared to the Ossetic skinpole:
bidental locus fulmine tactus et expiatus ove, Fronto 277. Cattle
*struck dead by lightning* are *not to be eaten*, Westendorp 525.

p. 175.] ὑετός, Umbr. *savitu*, Aufr. u. Kirchh. 2, 268. ὗε δ' ἄρα Ζεὺς πάννυχος, Od. 14, 457. Athen. 4, 73. τὸν Δί' ἀληθῶς ὤμην διὰ κοσκίνου οὐρεῖν, Aristoph. Clouds 373 ; conf. imbrem in *cribrum* gerere, Plaut. Ps. i. 1, 100. Διὸς ὄμβρος, Od. 9, 111. 358. οὔτε Πελοποννησίοις ὗσεν ὁ θεός, Paus. ii. 29, 6. An Egypt. magian conjures the *air-god Hermes* (τὸν ἀέριον) for rain, Cass. Dio 71, 8. *Indra,* who has the thunderbolt, is also god of rain; when he disappeared, it rained no more, Holtzm. 3, 140. 1, 15. In Dalecarl. *skaurman åk,* the shower-man rides=it thunders, Almqv. 258; conf. Goth. *skura* vindis=λαῖλαψ, OHG. *scûr* tempestas, grando, AS. *scûr* procella, nimbus, ON. *skûr* nimbus (Kl. schr. 2, 425).

p. 175.] Another rain-procession in 1415, Lindenbl. 301. Petronius's ' uvidi tanquam mures' is like our MHG. in Eracl. 142ᵇ : sô sît ir *naz als eine mûs* (from Enenkel), wet as a drowned rat. A prayer of the *legio tonans,* likewise under M. Antonine, brings on torrents, Cass. Dio 71, 8. A Hungarian prayer for rain, Ungarn in parab. 90; others in Klemm 2, 160 (Kl. schr. 2, 439—458).

p. 176.] *Pikker,* Kalewipoeg 3, 16. 23. 358. 16, 855. *pikker-taati* 20, 730. On *pikker* and *pikne* see Estn. Verh. 2, 36-7. He is the avenging thrice-nine god, that appears in the lightning, and with *red-hot iron rod* (raudwits) chastises even the lesser gods, who flee before him, like the giants before Thor, to human hearths 2, 36—38. *Pikne* seems an abbrev. of *pitkäinen,* tonitru, which occurs in the Finnic form of the Esth. prayer for rain, Suomi 9, 91, and comes from *pitkä* longus ; *pitkäikäinen* longaevus, the Old=Ukko, says Castrén myth. 39, or perhaps the long streak of the lightning. On *Toro, Toor, Torropel* see Estn. Verh. 2, 92.

p. 176.] *Ukko* blesses the corn, Peterson 106. In a waste field on the coast of Bretagne St. Sezny throws his hammer, and in one night the corn grows up into full ripe ears around it, Bret. Volkss. by Aug. Stöber, prob. after Souvestre.

p. 177.] The Thunder-god must be meant in the story of the *red-bearded* giant and the *carriage* with the golden *he-goat,* Wolf Ztschr. 2, 185-6. With the N. American Indians both Pahmi-oniqua and *Jhächinchiä* (red thunder) are men's names, Catlin tr. by Bergh. 136. 190-1.

p. 178.] The three phenomena of lightning are described as simultaneous in Hes. Theog. 691 : κεραυνοὶ ἴκταρ ἅμα βροντῇ τε καὶ ἀστεροπῇ ποτέοντο. Distinct from fulgur is a fourth notion, *fulguratio* (sine ictu).

p. 178.] *Fulgur* is called *bliks*, as late as Justinger. *Blixberg*, now the ruined castle of Plixburg (Plickhs-perckh in old docs.), stands in the Münster valley near Colmar, oppos. a dwarf's mountain, Schöpflin Als. dipl. no. 1336. des snellen *blickes* tuc, Freid. 375. *himelblicke*, Servat. 397. 1651. Roth. 3536. In Styria, *himlatzen* to lighten, *weterblicke* fulgura, Hpt Ztschr. 8, 137. *wetterleich*, Stalder 2, 447. hab dir das *plab feuer!* H. Sachs ii. 4, 19ᵃ. *blue light* in thunderstorms, Schwab's Alb. 229. Lightning strikes or 'touches': mit blitz *gerührt*, Felsenb. 1, 7. It arises when *sparks* are struck with the *fiery axe*, p. 180ⁿ. 813; af þeim *liomom leiptrir* qvômo, Sæm. 151ᵃ. Κοονίδης ἀφίει ψολόεντα κεραυνόν, Od. 24, 539. ἀργῆτι κεραυνῷ 5, 128. 131. *trisulcum* fulgur, Festus, Varro ap. Non. 6, 2. Sen. Thyest. 1089. ignes *trisulci*, Ov. Met. 2, 848. Ibis 471. tela *trisulca*, Claudian iii. Cons. Hon. 14. genera fulminum *tria* esse ait Caecina, *consiliarium, auctoritatis* et *status*, Am. Marc. 23, 5; conf. O. Müll. Etr. 2, 170. The Etruscans had *nine* fulgurating gods 2, 84. In Romanic, lightning is *camég*, form. also calaverna, chalávera; *straglüsch, sagietta, saetta* lightn. that pierces, also *lütscherna* (lucerna?). Lith. *żaibas* lightn., *Perkuno żaibas* streak of lightn., from *żibeti* to shine, Nesselm. 345. Mere fulguratio, summer-lightn., distant, feeble, that does not strike, the Finns call *Kalevan tulet, K. valkiat*, i.e. Calevae ignes, bruta fulmina autumnalia, or *kapeen tulet*, genii ignes. Lightning is named πῦρ Διός, Hebr. *fire of God*.

p. 178 n.] *Blecken, plechazan*, heaven opening, reminds of the Bastarnae, who thought, when it lightened, the sky was falling on them, Livy 40, 58; conf. Duncker p. 84. In Servian songs *munya* is the vila's daughter, *grom* her brother. *Mèsets*, moon, marries Munya, Vuk 1, 154 n. 229—231.

p. 178.] *Tonitrus* is *toniris chlaccha*, Hattem. 3, 598ᵇ. *tonnerklapf*, Justinger 383. 'thunderclap words,' Fr. Simpl. 1, 231. *dôzes klac*, Parz. 379, 11. Troj. 12231. 14693. *donrescal*, Fundgr. 2, 116. *tonnerbotz*, Garg. 270ᵇ. 219ᵇ, from donerbôz. ON. *skrugga* tonitru, conf. skröggr fulminans. Dan. *tordenskrald, tordenbrag*. LG. *grummel-wier, -schuur, -taaren* (-cloud), Lyra 103. 117, see Sup. to 171. We say thunder *rollt, grollt* [if

distant, grommelt]. As lightn. is a bird's glance, thunder is
the *flapping of its wings*, Klemm 2, 155. Zeus's *eagle* holds his
lightnings, and an *eagle* raises the storm-wind, p. 633; conf. the
bird of Dawn.

p. 179.] *Fulmen* is OHG. *donarstrâla*, Graff 6, 752 and
*laucmedili*, Gl. Jun. 191. Graff 2, 707. *blic-schóz* mit (or, an)
dunr-slegen, Pass. 89, 49. 336, 9. des *donres schuz*, Freid. 128,
8. *donrestrâl* der niht enschiuzet, Turl. Wh. 11ª. *dornstrâl*,
Griesh. 151. die *donerblicke*, Fundgr. 1, 73. `donresblicke*, Freid.
123, 26. des *donrisslac*, Fundgr. 2, 125. 'ob der doner z'aller
frist *slüege*, swann ez *blekzend* ist,' if it struck every time it
lightens, W. gast 203. swaz er der heiden ane quam, die
*sluoc* er alse ein *doner* sân, Rother 2734. dô *sluog* er alsô der
*thoner*, for dem sich nieman mac bewarn, Diemer 218, 8. *schûr-
slac*, Helbl. 8, 888. *wolkenschóz*, Lanz. 1483. *weterwegen*, Pass.
336, 10. 2. OHG. *drôa*, *drewa* is both minae, oraculum, and
fulmen, ictus, Graff 5, 246; because lightn. is a bodeful phenomenon? O. Fr. es *foldres* du ciel, Ogier 1, 146. foudre qi *art*,
Guiteclin 2, 137. Le tonnerre a sept différentes formes pour se
manifester aux Polognots. Il tombe en *fer*, alors il brise tout;
en *feu*, il brûle; en *souffre*, il empoisonne; en *genuille*, il étouffe;
en *poudre*, il étourdit; en *pierre*, il balaye ce qu'il environne;
en *bois*, il s'enfonce où il tombe, Mém. Celt. 2, 211.

p. 180.] On *thunderbolts* see the 9th Bamb. Bericht p. 111.
Beside *donnerstein*, we have *wetterstein, krottenstein*. Again:
*Herre Got*, und liezt du vallen her ze tal ein *stein*, der mir
derslüege, Suchenw. 78, 175. A fragment of thunderbolt *healed
over in the hand* imparts to it enormous strength, Hpt Ztschr. 3,
366. A *donnerstral* of 2½ cwt. hangs in Ensheim church, Garg.
216ª. Vestgötl. *Thors-käjl* (-wedge), Swed. *Thor-viggar* (-wedges),
Sjöborg's Nomencl. f. nordiska fornlemningar 100. Indra's bolt
and flash are *svarus*, from svar, sky, sun, Benfey 1, 457; conf.
ἠλύσια, Sup. to 174. Like *elf-shot* is the Sansk. 'vitulum veluti
mater, ita *fulmen Marutes* sequitur,' Bopp Gl. 364ª; conf. mugi-
entis instar vaccae fulmen sonat 262ª. Athena alone knows the
keys to the thunderbolt chamber, Æsch. Eum. 727, like Mary
in the nursery-tale of the forbidden chamber in heaven. Lith.
' Perkuno *kulka*,' P.'s ball. Serv. *strèlitsa*, arrow.

p. 181.] *Miölnir* reminds of Sl. *m'lniya*, molnia ἀστραπή, which

Miklos. 50 derives from mlèti, conterere. The hammṅ simple, world-old implement, indispensable to nearly every and adopted by not a few as a symbol. At boundaries the *hamarsmark* was deeply graven, a cross with hooked limbs; ⌐L afterwards a crossed oak served for a landmark, Kl. schr. 2, 43. 55. In blessing the cup (signa full) the sign of the hammer was made: hann gerði *hamarsmark* yfir, Hâk. góða saga c. 18. Thor með *tungum hamrum* is also in Landstad 14. Thor's image has a great hammer in its hand, Ol. helga s. ed. Christ. 26. Fornm. sög. 4, 245. That the hammer was portrayed and held sacred, is shown by the passage in Saxo, ed. Müll. 630 : Magnus, inter cetera traeophorum suorum insignia, *inusitati ponderis malleos* quos *Joviales* vocabant, apud insularum quandam *prisca virorum religione cultos*, in patriam deportandos curavit. That was betw. 1105 and 1135. In Germany, perh. earlier, there were *hammers* and *clubs* as emblems of Donar on the church wall, or built into the town-gate ; to which was linked a barbarous superstition and a legend of the cudgel, Hpt Ztschr. 5, 72. To the same cycle belong the tales of the *devil's hammer*, which is also called *donnerkuhl, hammerkuhl,* Müllenh. 268. 601 ; conf. p. 999. Pikne carries lightn. as an *iron rod*, see Sup. to 176.

p. 181.] Thôrr a *foe to giants*, p. 531. As Wôdan pursues the subterraneans, so he the giants. They will not come to the feast where *Tordenveir* appears, p. 189. 537. In Schonen, when it lightens, it is Thor *flogging the trolls*, Nilss. 4, 40. der (tievel) wider unsih vihtet mit *viuren* (viurînen, fiery) *strâlen*, Diemer 337, 9.

p. 181.] *Hamer* sla bamer, sla busseman dot ! Müllenh. 603 ; conf. Hermen sla dermen, p. 355. bim *hammer !* Corrodi Professer 16. 58. Vikari 11. tummer und hammer, Prof. 96. 'May heaven's *forked lightn.* bury you 10,000 fathoms underground ! ' du widertuo ez balde, oder dir nimet der *donner in drîn tagen den lîp*, Wolfd. 331, 3. 4 (Hpt Ztschr. 4). A Danish oath is 'ney *Thore gud !* ' Warmii Mon. Dan. 13. dass dich der *Donnerstag* (Thursday = Thor), Ph. v. Sittew. 2, 680. *donnstig !* du *donnstiys* bub ! Gotthelf's Erz. 2, 195-6. The Lithuanians, says Æn. Sylvius, ascribe to *Percunnos* a great *hammer*, by means of which the sun is rescued from captivity, Æn. Sylv. in den Kurländ. send. 2, 6. N. Preuss. prov. bl. 2, 99 ; conf. Tettau u. Temme

28. Lith. ' kad *Perkuns* pakiles deszimt klafterin tave i zeme itrenktu ! " may P. arise and strike thee 10 fathoms into the earth, Schleicher ber. der Wiener acad. 11, 108. 110. The Etruscans ascribed the hammer to *Mantus*, Gerh. 17.

Beside the hammer Thôrr had his *megin-giarðar*, fortitudinis, roboris cingula, and *iarn-greipr*, chirotecas ferreas, Sn. 112-3. er hann spennir þeim (megingiörðum) um sik, þâ *vex honum ás-megn hâlfu*, Sn. 26. þâ spenti hann *megingiörðum* 114. This belt of might reminds us of Laurîn 906. 890. 1928: zebrechent sîn *gürtelin*, dô *hât er von zwelf man kraft*. A girdle imparts *strength* and *wisdom*, Wigal. 332, and shews the right road, 22-3. A girdle that *stills hunger*, Fierabras 209 ; conf. the hunger-belt. A *victoriae zona* in Saxo ed. Müll. 124. Like Thôr's girdle is the *blue band* in Norske folkev. no. 60, p. 365. 374-6. Müllenh. Schl.-holst. mär. 11. Moe's introd. xlvi.

p. 183.] In the Alps the salamander, whose appearance betokens a storm, is called *wetter-giogo*, Schott's Germans in Piedmont 300. 346. A female stag-beetle carries red hot coals into houses (Odenwald).

p. 183 n.] The *barba Jovis* is held to have healing power, Caes. Heisterb. 7, 15. Jovis herba, *hus-loek*, Mone's Quellen 289[a]. *hús-louch*, Mone 8, 403. *donder-loek*, crassula major, Mone's Qu. 283[b]. *dundar-lök*, Dybeck 1845 p. 61. *Jovis caulis*, sempervivum magn., Diosc. 4, 88. AS. *þunor-wyrt*, barba J.; *houseleek* planted on cottage-roofs, Hone's Yrbk. 1552 ; conf. p. 1214. The Swiss call the donnerbesen *hexenbesen*, witch's broom, Stald. 2, 42. Nemnich calls glecoma hederacea *donnerrebe*, gundrebc. The *donnernessel*, urtica dioica, resists thunder. Finn. *Ukon*-tuhnio, fungus, fomes; *U.* nauris, rapa; *U.* lummet, caltha palustris; *Ukkon*-lehti, folium (lappa). Jovis colus, $\Delta\iota\grave{o}\varsigma$ $\mathring{\eta}\lambda\alpha\kappa\acute{\alpha}\tau\eta$, clinopodium, verbena, Diosc. 3, 99. 4, 61. Jovis madius, catanance, herba filicula 4, 132. $\mathring{\iota}\epsilon\rho\grave{\alpha}$ $\tauo\hat{\upsilon}$ $\theta\epsilon o\hat{\upsilon}$ $\phi\eta\gamma\grave{o}\varsigma$ at Dodona Paus. 1, 17. Jovis arbor, Ov. Met. 1, 104. A *thunder-tree* in Tyrol, Wolf Ztschr. While redbreast and beetle attract lightning, the wannenweihe repels it, p. 674. It was a universal practice to *ring the church-bells* to drive the *thunder* away, i.e. the heathen god, for bells are Christian. With the Thracians *shooting* was a safeguard against *thunder and lightning* (p. 20), as elsewhere against an eclipse, p. 707.

p. 184.] Note the Henneberg superstition about the haber-geiss or *himmelsziege*, phalangium opilio, a spider (Maler Müller), in Brückner's Henneb. 11. By *horsgök* was formerly meant a real horse, Runa 3, 14-5. The heaven's-goat is in Finn. *taivaan vuohi;* she hovers between heaven and hell, bleating in the air, Schiefn. Finn. wtb. 612. Another Lith. name for it is *dangaus ožys*, Nesselm. 31, and Lett. *Pehrkon ohsols*, Possart's Kurl. 228. The Hŷmisqviða calls Thôrr *hafra dróttinn;* his goats are *tann-gniostr* and *tann-grisnir*, dente frendens, as Lat. *nefrendes* = arietes (or porci) nondum frendentes, that have no teeth yet. Tanngniostr (tooth-gnasher) is also a man's by-name, Kormaks. 54. 134-6.

p. 186.] *Donerswe*, Ehrentraut's Fries. arch. 1, 435. Hpt Ztschr. 11, 378. de *Donrspah*, Notizenbl. 6, 306. It seems *Thuris-lô* in Trad. Corb. is not Thonares-lô, but giant's wood, p. 521; yet AS. *Thunresleá*, Kemble 3, 443. 4, 105. 5, 84. 243. Scand. *Thörsleff*, Molb. dipl. 1, 173; why not Thors-? In Sweden are *Thorsby, Thorshälla, Thorslunda, Thorstuna, Thorsvi, Thorsåker, Thorsång, Thorsås, Thorsö*. On Thorstuna, -åker, conf. Schlyter Sv. indeln. 32. *Thorseng* in Funen, *Thorshöi* in Schleswig, Müllenh. 584. In Norway *Thôrsey, Thórsnes, Thórshof*, Munch om Sk. 107. *Thorsnes*, Landn. 2, 12, took its name from a pillar with Thôr's image being drifted thither. *Thorsharg* = Thorshälla, Hildebr. tom. 3. *Thorsborg*, Gutal. 94, a limestone-mountain 317. *Thorshafn* in Färöe.

p. 187.] To the few German proper names compounded with *Donar*, add *Donarpreht*, Hpt Ztschr. 7, 529. *Albdonar* is conn. with the plant albdona. In Kemble no. 337, for ' Thoneulf' read *Thonerulf*. The Sax. Chron., yr. 920, has Đurcytel. An O. Irish name *Tordealbhach* (= Thoro similis, says O'Brien) is worth noting. *Thorhalli* in the Heiðarvîgasaga. King *Toril*, whose lightning scorches the sea, burns up forests and devours the city (Hpt Ztschr. 4, 507-8), is apparently Thor himself; perhaps Torkil ? for Thorild is fem.; conf. *Thorkarl*, p. 181 n.

p. 187.] Thôr's by-name of *Vingthôrr*, Sæm. 70[a]; *Eindriði*, Sup. to 167, foot-note. He is hard-hugaðr, Sæm. 74[b], as the iötun is hardraðr, p. 528. Again, fôstri *Vingnis* ok *Hlóru* = fôstri *Hlórriða*, Sup. to 167. *Iarðar* burr, earth's son, Sæm. 70[a]. 68[a]. 157; *Fiörgynjar* burr, *Hlóðynjar* burr, *Yggs* barn 52[a]. Is *Veorr*

the same as *verr, vir* ? conf. AS. weor, but the ON. modification
would be viörr.

p. 188.] Thôrr, imagined as a *son* (in the Edda he is either a
youth or in the prime of manhood), does not accord well with the
' old *great-grandfather.*' In Sæm. 54[b] he is a *sveinn*, but in 85[b]
*Asabragr.* Are we to suppose two Donars, then ? That in the
North he may have been feared even more than Oðin seems to
follow from the fact that so many names of men and women
contain his name, and so few that of Odin.

p. 189.] His sons by Iarnsaxa are *Magni* and *Móði*, Sn. 110
(conf. p. 823), he himself being endowed with *âs-megin* and *âs-
móðr*. Iarnsaxa is elsewhere the name of a giantess. He calls
himself *Magna* faðir, Sæm. 76[a]. His daughter becomes the bride
of Alvîs 48[a,b]; is she Thrûðr, robur, whom he had by Sif ? Sn.
101-9. He is himself called *þrúðugr* âss, Sæm. 72[b]. *þrúðvaldr*
goða 76[a]; and his hammer *þrúðhamarr* 67[b].

p. 191.] Neither the *log-pelting* at Hildesheim (with which
conf. 'sawing the old woman,' p. 781-2) nor the *wheel-rolling*
near Trier (Hocker's Mosel-ld. 1852, p. 415) can be connected
with Jupiter. The latter ceremony, mentioned first in 1550 and
last in 1779, took place thus. On the Thursday in Shrove-week
an *oak* was set up on the Marxberg (Donnersb., Dummersb.),
also a *wheel*. On Invocavit Sunday the tree was cut down, the
wheel set on fire and rolled into the Moselle. A wheel, especially
a flaming one, is the symbol of *thunder*, of *Donar ;* hence the
lords of *Donnersberg*, burg-vassals to Cochheim, bear it on their
coat-of-arms, Hontheim 2, 5, tab. v., likewise those of *Roll* (thunder), while those of Hammerstein have three hammers in theirs.
The signum of German legions, the 14th and 22nd, was the *rota:*
there is a tile with ' Leg. xxii.'' and a six-spoked wheel stamped
on it. Mainz and Osnabrück have such a wheel on their
scutcheon, Mainz as escutcheon of the legions (Fuchs's Mainz 2,
94. 106). Krodo in Bothe's Sassenchr. carries a wheel (p. 206 n.).
Has that heraldic wheel anything to do with the term *rädels-
führer*, ringleader ?

p. 191.] On keeping *Thursday* holy, see especially Nilsson 4,
44-5. tre *Thorsdags*-qvällar, Dyb. Runa 4, 37. 43. Cavallius 1,
404. In Swedish fairy-tales spirits appear on *thorsdags-natt*, and
bewitch. If you do any work on Trinity Sunday, the *lightning*

*will strike it;* hence women are unwilling to do needlework that day, Hpt Ztschr. 3, 360. Similar *desecration of holidays* by weaving, spinning or knitting is often mentioned; Servat. 2880:

> wir sâzen unde wâben,
> dô die lantliute êrten disen tac . . .
> schiere runnen diu weppe von bluote,
> daz ez uns des werkes erwante.

A poor girl spins on our Lady's day, the thread sticks to her tongue and lips, Maerl. 2, 219. Of women spinning on Saturday, see Müllenh. 168; they that spool flax in church-time on Sunday, turn into stone, Reusch no. 30. Spinning was forbidden on Gertrude's day and Berchta's day, p. 270-3; among the Greeks on Bacchus's day, p. 911. Nevertheless the yarn spun on such holy days has peculiar virtues, p. 1099; conf. the *teig-talgen,* dough-kneading on Holy Saturday night, Superst. G, v. 194. Yet again: Si quis die Dominico boves junxerit et cum carro ambulaverit, dexterum bovem perdat, Lex Bajuv. vi. 2, 1.

---

## CHAPTER IX.

## ZIO (TIW, TYR).

p. 194.] In Umbrian the nom. was still *Juv,* dat. *Juve,* voc. *Jupater,* Aufr. u. Kuhn Ztschr. 1, 128: *Juveis luvfreis,* Jupiter liber, Mommsen 139. What of Finn. *taivas,* coelum? or even Θοῦρος, the Assyrian Mars (Suidas)? A divergent form, ' vater Zi ' in Müllenh. nr. 410.——Dyaus is not only coelum, but a Vasu-god, who for stealing the cow Nandini has to go through a human life, Holtzm. 3, 101—6. Parallel with the ideas belonging to the root div, are those developed out of Sansk. *sur,* splendeo: *sura* deus, *sûrja* sol, *svar* coelum.

p. 194.] Spiegel, Zendav. 6, connects θεός with *dhî.* Lith. *dievas* god, *deive* goddess, *dievaitiz* (godkin) thunderer, *dievaite* (goddesskin) rain-goddess; conf. Pott's Etym. forsch. 1st ed. 56-7. Benfey's Orient 1, 510.

p. 195.] Wackernagel in Hpt Ztschr. 6, 19 retains *Tuisco* = duplex, and explains it as *zwitter,* two-sexed, just as Lachm. makes tuisc = bimus, two years old; and Müllenhoff agrees with

them 9, 261. In that case Tuisco would have nothing to do with
Ziu, and Tacitus must have indicated the marvellous hermaphrodite nature. It is a question whether Zio, Tio have not per-
petuated himself in the alarm and battle cries zieter, zeter,
tiodute, tianut! and in *ziu dar nâher*, Parz. 651, 11 ; see Gramm.
3, 303. RA. 877. Leo in Hpt Ztschr. 5, 513. Again, did *zie,
tie* (assembly) originally mean divum, as in 'sub divo, dio'?
The Prov. troubadours have *sotz dieu* = sub divo, under the open
sky, Diez's Leb. d. Troub. 166-7 ; yet it may mean sub Deo.

p. 195.] From *div* splendeo (Lith. *zibeti*) come *div, diva*
coelum, and *divan, divasa, divaňa*, contr. *dina*, dies, Bopp Gl.
168. In Caes. B. Gall. 6, 18 Diespiter is called *Dispater*, abl. *Dite
patre*, O. Müll. Etr. 2, 67 ; conf. Dissunapiter, p. 225. The
Etruscan panels have sometimes *Tinia* for Tina.

p. 198.] The Germani sacrificed to their Mars for victory :
*vestita spoliis* donabere *quercu* (Mavors), Claudian in Ruf. 1, 339.
huic *praedae primordia* vovebantur, huic *truncis suspendebantur
exuviae*, Jorn. 5. hostiles *suspendit in arbore* cristas, Cl. in Ruf.
1, 346. Kuhn finds many points of comparison between Wuotan
and the Roman *Mars*, whom he takes to have been originally a
god of spring. Mârs = Mârutas is a by-name of Indra, Hpt
Ztschr. 5, 491-2. To *Týr Vîga-guð* corresponds ' Mars des *wîge
got* ' in En. 5591. Troj. 8140. 8241. Ms. 2, 198ᵇ : Mars *strîtes
got.* Christian writers suppose an angel of victory marching in
the front of battle : coram eo (Ottone imperatore) angelus penes
quem victoria. Mars is a mere abstraction in Erm. Nig. 2, 2 :
straverat adversos *Mars*que *Deus*que viros, and Pertz 8, 228 : jam
per ordinatas omni parte acies *Mars cruentus* cepisset frendere ;
conf. p. 203.

p. 198.] *Ziesburc*, Augsburg, Hpt Ztschr. 8, 587. *Diuspurch*,
Lacomb. 83 (yr 904), *Tusburg* 205 (1065), *Diusburg*, all = Duis-
burg, Thietm. 5, 3. 9. Dûseburg, Weisth. 4, 775. A *Doesburgh*
in Gelders ; *Tussberg, Tyssenberg*, Wolf Ztschr. 1, 337. *Desberg*
near Vlotho, Redecker 59. *Desenberg, Diesenberg ; Tistede*, Hamb.
liber actor. 331-2. *Tiisvad, Tiiswath*, in Jutl., Molb. dipl. 1, 9.
*Zirelberg* near Schwatz in Tyrol, H. Sachs i. 3, 251ᵃ ; conf. p.
298, *Zisa, Zisenburg*, GDS. 541.

p. 199.] Add *Tived, Tisved, Tivebark*, Dyb. 1845, 50-9. MHG.
*zidelbast*, Gervinus 2, 233 ; conf. Zigelinta, p. 1193.

p. 200.] The very old symbol of the planet Mars ♂ stood apparently for the war-god's shield and spear. Here Týr reminds us of Oðinn and his Gûngnir, p. 147. With *tîre tâcnian* conf. *tîrfæst tâcen*, Cod. Exon. 236, 13; *sigortâcen* 169, 3. *sigorestâcen*, *friðotâcen* circumcision, note on Elene 156. Cædm. 142, 29.

p. 202.] Judges often held their court on *Ertag*, see Kaltenb. 1, 563[a, b]. 580[a]; and judgment may mean war, decision, RA. 818-9. Was a sword set up in the court? On *Famars, Fanmars* see GDS. 529. 619.

p. 204.] The trinity of the Abrenunt. requires a *god*, not a mere hero; for that reason if no other, *Sahsnôt* must be Mars, or at lowest the Freyr of the Upsal trinity. With *Saxneát* compare *Iarnsaxa*, Thor's wife, Sn. 110. In Pomerania they still swear by 'doner *sexen*,' in Bavaria 'meiner *sechsen*,' Schm. 3, 193-4; conf. 'mein *six* !'

p. 205.] On the divine *Cheru* see GDS. 612. Lucian supplies additional proofs of the Scythian worship of the sword; Toxaris 38 : οὐ μὰ γὰρ τὸν Ἄνεμον καὶ τὸν Ἀκινάκην. Scytha 4 : ἀλλὰ πρὸς Ἀκινάκου καὶ Ζαμόλξιδος, τῶν πατρῴων ἡμῖν θεῶν. Jupiter Trag. 42 : Σκύθαι Ἀκινάκῃ θύοντες καὶ Θρᾷκες Ζαμόλξιδι. Conf. Clem. Alex. admon. 42. GDS. 231. Priscus, quoted in Jorn. c. 5, ed. Bonn 201, 17. 224, remarks on the sword : Ἄρεος ξίφος ὅπερ ὃν ἱερὸν καὶ παρὰ τῶν Σκυθικῶν βασιλέων τιμώμενον, οἷα δὴ τῷ ἐφόρῳ τῶν πολέμων ἀνακείμενον, ἐν τοῖς πάλαι ἀφανισθῆναι χρόνοις, εἶτα διὰ βοὸς εὑρεθῆναι. The Mars of the Alans is mentioned by Lucan 8, 223 : duros aeterni Martis Alanos. The worship of lance and sword among the Romans is attested by Justin 43, 3 : Nam et ab origine rerum pro diis immortalibus veteres *hastas* coluere, ob cujus religionis memoriam adhuc deorum simulacris *hastae* adduntur; and Suet. Calig. 24 : *tres gladios* in necem suam praeparatos *Marti ultori* addito elogio consecravit. Caesar's *sword*, preserved in Mars's temple at Cologne, was presented to Vitellius on his election, Mascou 1, 117. Later they knelt before the sword at a court-martial, Ambraser liederb. 370; conf. Osw. 2969 :

> dô viel er nider ûf sîniu knie,
> daz swert er an sîn hant gevie,
> und zôch ez ûz der scheide,

der helt des niht vermeit,
daz ort (point) liez er nider.

To Svantevit, Saxo ed. Müll. 824 gives a *conspicuae granditatis ensis*. The Indian Thugs worship on their knees an axe or bill, which is mysteriously forged, Ramasiana (Calcutta 1836.)

The war-god has also a *helmet*, witness the plant named Ἄρεος κυνῆ, *Týr-hialm*, p. 199.

p. 206.] Hrêð-cyninges, Cod. Exon. 319, 4, said of the wicked Eormanric, and therefore probably from hrêð, hrêðe, crudelis (p. 290); while *Hrêðgotum* 322, 3 answers to ON. Reiðgotum. ' *Red red* brengt raed raed,' where the Walloon has ' *Mars, Mars*,' Coreman's Année de l'anc. Belg. 16 ; conf. Ret-monat, p. 290. We are not warranted in referring Hrôðrs (or hrôðrs) andscoti, Hŷmisq. 11, to Týr.

p. 206 n.] Zeuss 23 believes in *Krodo*, and thinks *Reto* in Letzner is the same. *Crodio*, Cod. Lauresh. 1634; *Crodico* 1342. *Crôda*, Kemble 1, 143 ; *Crêda* 1, 159. 177. *Krode duvel*, p. 248. I am not sure but that Nithart's *Krotolf* (Hpt 117) has after all a mythical sound, and it is followed by a similar compliment Üetelgôz, p. 367 n. *Krathabothl* in Lüntzel's Hildesh. 51. *Kreetpfuhl, Kreetkind*, DS. 1, 415. A ' rivus *Krodenbek*,' Falke's Trad. Corb. 612. *Krottorf* in Halberstadt country, conf. *Krottenstein* for Donnerstein.

p. 207.] Simrock thinks Týr is *one-handed* because a sword has only one edge. Does a trace of the myth linger in ' swâ ich weiz des *wolves zant* (tooth), dâ wil ich hüeten (take care of) *mîner hant*,' Freid. 137, 23 ? or in the proverb ' brant stant as dem *dode* (Tio ?) *sîne rechte hant*,' Wolf Ztschr. 1, 337 ? Conf. the Latin phrases : pugnare *aequo, pari, certo, ancipite, dubio, vario, proprio, suo* Marte. Widukind has *coeco* Marte 1, 6, like *coeco furore* 1, 9. When fighters see the battle going against them, they leave off, and acknowledge ὡς πρὸς τὸν θεὸν σφίσιν ὁ ἀγὼν γένοιτο, Procop. 2, 641. The fickleness of victory is known to the Od. 22, 236 : οὔπω πάγχυ δίδου ἑτεραλκέα νίκην (conf. ' ein Hie-und-dort,' Geo. 5748). Victory and luck are coupled together : *sig* und *saelden* geben, Albr. Tit. 2920-33. an *sig* u. *saelden* verderben 2929.

p. 208.] Companions of Mars : circumque atrae *Formidinis*

ora, *Iraeque Insidiae*que, dei comitatus, aguntur, Aen. 12, 335. *Luctus* comitatur euntem (Tisiphonen), Et *Pavor* et *Terror*, trepidoque *Insania* vultu, Ov. Met. 4, 485. *Bellona, Pavor, Formido*, Claud. in Ruf. 1, 342 ; *Metus* cum fratre *Pavore*, De laud. Stil. ; *Impetus* horribilisque *Metus*, In Pr. et Olybr. 78. δείματα πανικά, Procop. 2, 550. panicus terror, Forcell. sub vv. pan, panicus. A panic *foliage-rustling* fright, Garg. 256ᵇ. So the Wend. volksl. 2, 266ᵃ make *Triakh, Strakh* dwell in a dismal haunted spot ; Sl. *triakh, trias*, tremor, is perh. the Goth. þlahs. The Finn. *kammo* =genius horroris, horror. There is an ON. saying : ' *Ôttar* er fremst î flocki þâ flŷa skal ' ; is that from *ótti*, timor ? conf. the Ôttar in Hyndlulioð. ' Thâ skaut (shot) þeim *skelk* î brîngu '
. . ' skaut *skelk* î brîngu ok *ótta*,' where skelk and ôtta are accusatives of skelkr and ôtti, timor. Goth. *agis* disdraus ina, awe fell upon him, Luke 1, 12 ; conf. AS. *Brôga* and *Egesa*, Andr. xxxii. and diu naht-*egese*, Diemer 266, 23. OHG. gefieng thô allê forhta, fear took hold of, T. 49, 5. There is personification also in the Romance ' negus neu pot ir, si nos torna *espavers*, Albig. 4087. A different yet lively description is, ' so that the *cat ran up their backs*,' Garg. 256ᵇ. 218ᵃ. Beside Hilda-Bellona (p. 422) appears a male *Hildôfr*, Sæm. 75ᵇ, like Berhtolt beside Berhta.

p. 208.] *Tŷr*, who in the Hymisqviða accompanies Thor to the abode of Hymir, calls the latter his father, and Hymi's concubine his mother ; he is therefore of giant extraction ; conf. Uhland's Thor 162-3. Is this Tŷr not the god, as Simrock supposes him to be (Edda, ed. 2, 404) ?

---

## CHAPTER X.
## FRO (FREYR).

p. 210.] The Yngl. 13 calls Freyr *veraldar god*, Saxo calls Frö *deorum satrapa*. Goth. *fráuja* stands not only for κύριος, but for θεός. The Monachus Sangall. says (Pertz 2, 733) : tunc ille verba, quibus eo tempore superiores ab inferioribus honorari demulcerique vel adulari solebant, hoc modo labravit : ' *laete vir domine, laetifice rex*!' which is surely ' *frô* herro !' OS., beside frô, etc., has the form *fruoho*, Hel. 153, 1 ; if it had a god's name Frô, that would account for *Frôs-â*, i.e. Frô's aha, ouwa, ea.

AS. has other compounds, freábeorht (freahbeort) limpidus, Lye
and Hpt Ztschr. 9, 408ᵃ; freátorht limpidus 9, 511ᵃ, conf. Donar-
perht; freáraede expeditus (freahræde, Lye); freádrêman jubilare,
freábodian nuntiare; a fem name Freáware, Beow. 4048. In
Lohengr. 150, zuo dem *frôn* = to the holy place. ON. has also a
*fránn* nitidus, coruscus. From Fris. frâna may we infer a *frâ*
dominus? Bopp (Gl. 229ᵇ) conject. that fráuja may have been
frabuja, and be conn. with Skr. prabhu, dominus excelsus; yet
πραΰς, mild, seems to lie near [Slav. *prav* rectus, aequus, *praviti*
regere, would conn. the meanings of probus, πραϝος, and fráuja].

p. 212.] *Freyr oc Freyja*, Sæm. 59. He resembles Bacchus
Liber, Διόνυσος ὁ Ἐλευθέριος, Paus. i. 29, 2, and Jovis lufreis,
liber. From his marriage with Gerðr (p. 309) sprang Fiölnir,
Yngl. 12, 14. Saxo ed. M. 120 likewise mentions his temple at
Upsal: *Frö* quoque, deorum satrapa, *sedem haud procul Upsala*
cepit. *Fröi* gives food to men, Faye 10. The god travelling
through the country in his car resembles *Alber*, who with larded
feet visits the upland pastures (alpe) in spring, Wolf Ztschr. 2,
62; conf. Carm. Burana 131ᵃ: 'redit *ab exilio* Ver coma rutilante,'
and the converse: 'Aestas *in exilium* jam peregrinatur,' ibid.
(like Summer, p. 759); 'serato Ver *carcere* exit,' ib. 135.

p. 213 n.] On the *phallus* carried about in honour of Dionysos
or Liber by the Egyptians, Greeks and Romans, see Herod. 2, 48.
Hartung 2, 140. φαλλοὶ ἑστᾶσι ἐν τοῖσι προπυλαίοισι δύο κάρτα
μεγάλοι, Lucian De dea Syra 16, where more is told about phalli,
conf. 28-9. An '*idolum priapi* ex auro fabrefactum' in Pertz
5, 481. Phalli hung up in churches at Toulouse and Bordeaux,
Westendp. 116. The O. Boh. for Priapus was *Připekal*, Jungm.
sub v., or *Pripegala*, Mone 2, 270 out of Adelgar in Martene 1,
626. Slovèn. *kurenet, kurent*, Serv. *kurat*.

p. 214.] *Gullinbursti*, conf. *gulli byrstum*, Sn. 104. There is
a plant *gullborst*, which in German too is *eberwurz*, boarwort,
p. 1203. The Herv. saga c. 14 (p. 463. 531) in one passage
assigns the boar to Freyr, in the other (agreeing with Sæm. 114ᵃ)
to Freyja. Perhaps the enormous boar in the OHG. song, Hattem. 3, 578, and the one that met Olaf, Fornm. sög. 5, 165, were
the boar of Freyr. In thrashing they make a *pig of straw*, Schm.
2, 502, to represent the boar that 'walks in the corn' when the
ears ripple in the breeze, conf. AS. gârsecg, ON. lagastafr; 'the

wild sow in the corn,' Meier schw. 149. Rocholtz 2, 187; 'de *willen swîne* lâpet drupe,' Schambach 118ᵇ.

p. 215.] On *eoforcumbul* conf. Andr. and El. 28-9. Tristan has a boar-shield, 4940. 6618. Frib. 1944; 'hevedes of wild-bare (boars) ich-on to presant brought,' Thom. Tristrem 1, 75. Wrâsn, wraesen (Andr. 97) in *Freá-wrásnum* is vinculum, and Freyr '*leysir or höptom* (bonds) hvern,' Sæm. 65ᵃ (conf. p. 1231). A helmet in Hrolf Kr. saga is named *Hildisvîn* and *Hildigöltr*. Does '*Helmnôt Eleuther*' in Walthar. 1008-17 conceal a divine Fro and *Liber*?

p. 215.] On the *boar's head* served up at Christmas, see Hone's Tab.-bk 1, 85 and Everyday-bk 1, 1619-20. guldsvin som lyser, Asbjö. 386; the giant's *jul-galt*, Cavallius 26; *jul-hös*, sinciput verrinum, Caval. Vóc. Verland. 28ᵇ.

p. 216.] *Skîðhlaðnir* is from skîð, skîði, asser, tabula; Rask, Afh. 1, 365, sees in it a light Finl. vessel. Later stories about it in Müllenh. 453. The Yngl. saga gives the ship to Oðinn, but in Sæm. 45ᵇ and Sn. 48. 132 it is Frey's.

p. 217.] Freyr is the son of *Niörðr* and *Skaði*, who calls him '*enn fróði afi*,' Sæm. 81ᵃ. She is a giant's, Þiazi's, daughter, as Gerðr is Gymi's; so that father and son have wedded giantesses. The story is lost of Freyr and *Beli*, whom Freyr, for want of his sword, slays with a *buck's horn* or his fist, Sn. 41; hence he is called *bani Belja*, Sæm. 9ᵃ. Freyr, at his teething, receives *Alfheim*, Sæm. 40ᵇ.

Many places in Scand. preserve the memory of Freyr: *Frösö*, Norw. dipl.; conf. *Frósá*, Sup. to 210. *Fröjrak* (Freyraker), Dipl. norv. 1, 542. *Fröslund*, Dipl. suec. 2160; *Fröswi* 1777; *Frösberg* 2066. *Frösåker* in Vestmanl., Dyb. i. 3, 15. Schlyter Sv. indeln. 34. *Fröslöff* in Zealand, Molb. dipl. 1, 144 (yr 1402). *Fröskog* in Sweden, Runa 1844, 88. *Frösunda, Frösved, Frösön, Frötuna, Frölunda, Fröjeslunda*, all in Sweden. *Frotunum*, Dipl. suec. 228. *Fryeled*, in Jönköpings-län is styled in a doc. of 1313 (Dipl. suec. no. 1902) *Fröle* or *Fröale*; a *Fröel* in the I. of Goth-land appears to be the same name, in which Wieselgr. 409 finds *led*=leið, way; may it not be *eled, eld*, fire? *Niarðarhof* ok *Freyshof*, Munch om Sk. 147. *Vróinló*, now Vronen in West Friesl., Böhmer reg. 28. Müllenh. Nordalb. stud. 138. A man's name *Freysteinn* is formed like Thôrsteinn.

p. 217.] Niörðr is called *meins vani,* innocuus, Sæm. 42ª.
Sæm. 130ª speaks of ' Niarðar dœtur niu ; ' nine muses or waves ?
conf. Heimdall's 9 mothers. Niörðr lives at *Nôatûn* on the
sea, and Weinhold in Hpt Ztschr. 6, 40, derives the name from
Sansk. *nîra* aqua, *nîradhi* oceanus ; add *Nereus* and Mod. Gr.
νερόν. Schaffarik 1, 167 on the contrary connects Niörðr and
Niörunn with Slav. *nur* terra. Or we might think of Finn. *nuori*
juvenis, *nuorus* juventus, *nuortua* juvenesco, Esth. *noor* young,
fresh, *noordus* youth ; Lap. *nuor* young. Or of Celtic *neart*
strength, Wel. *nerth,* Hpt Ztschr. 3, 226 ; Sabine *Nero* = fortis
et strenuus, Lepsius Inscr. Umbr. 205. Coptic *neter* god and
goddess, Buns. Egy. 1, 577. Basque *nartea* north, and Swed. Lap.
*nuort* borealis, not Norw. nor Finn. That he was thought of in
conn. with the North, appears from˜' inn *norðri* Niörðr,' Fornm.
sög. 6, 258. 12, 151, where Fagrsk. 123 has *nerðri.*——Places
named after him : *Niarðey,* Landn. 2, 19. *Niarðvík* 4, 2. 4.
Laxd. 364. *Niarðarlögr,* Ol. Tr. c. 102. Fornm. s. 2, 252 (see
12, 324). Munch's Biörgyn 121 ; al. *Marða-lög, Iarðar-lög.* Is
the Swed. *Närtuna* for Närd-tuna ? and dare we bring in our
*Nörten* by Göttingen ? Thorlacius vii. 91 thinks *niarð-lâs* in Sæm.
109ᵇ means sera adstricta, as *niarð-giörð* is arctum cingulum
[niarð- = tight, fast, or simply intensive]. What means the
proverb ' galli er â *giöf Niarðar* ' ? Niörðûngr ? Gl. Edd. Hafn.
1, 632ᵇ.

p. 218.] Rask also (Saml. afh. 2, 282-3) takes the *Vanir* for
Slavs, and conn. Heimdall with Bielbogh. I would rather suppose a Vanic cult among the Goths and other (subseq. High
German) tribes, and an Asic in Lower Germany and Scandinavia, Kl. schr. 5, 423 seq. 436 seq. ' Over hondert milen henen,
Daer wetic (wot I) enen wilden *Wenen,*' Walew. 5938 ; appar. an
elf, a smith, conf. Jonckbloet 284.

p. 219.] Oðin's connexion with Freyr and Niörðr, pointed
out on p. 348, becomes yet closer through the following circum-
stances. Oðinn, like Freyr, is a god of fertility. Both are said to
own Skîðblaðnir (Sup. to 216), both Gerðr, p. 309. Fiölnir, son
of Freyr and Gerðr, is another name of Oðinn, Sæm. 46ᵇ (p. 348).
Skaði, Niörð's wife and Frey's mother, is afterwards Oðin's
spouse.

# CHAPTER XI.

## PALTAR (BALDER).

p. 220.] Acc. to Saxo, ed. M. 124, *Hotherus* is son to Hoth-brodus rex Sueciae, and brother to Atislus (the Aðils of Yngl. s.); Nanna is daughter to Gevarus (OHG. Këpaheri), and no goddess, indeed she rejects on that ground the suit of the divine Balder. Balder seems almost to live in Saxony or Lower Germany; the Saxon Gelderus is his ally and Hother's enemy, and shares Balder's overthrow. Balder has come to Zealand, apparently from Saxony; he never was in Sweden. Saxo makes Nanna fall to the lot, not of Balder, but of Hother, who takes her with him to Sweden. Balder, mortally wounded by Hother, dies the third day. The tale of king Bolder's fight with king Hother is told in Schleswig too, but it makes Bolder the victor, Müllenh. 373; conf. the tale of Balder and Rune 606.

p. 221.] *Paltar* also in MB. 9, 23 (year 837). ' *Baldor* servus,' Polypt. de S. Remig. 55ª. *Baaldaich*, Neugart no. 289. Lith. baltas = white, good (conf. Baldr inn *góði*, Sn. 64), baltorus a pale man; and the notions white and quick often meet, as in Gr. ἀργός, Passow sub v.

p. 222.] A god *Baldach* is named in the legend of St. Bar-tholomew (Leg. aur. c. 118), also in the Passional 290, 28; but in the Mid. Ages they said Baldach for Bagdad, and Baldewins for Bedouins. *Svipdagr*, Menglöð's lover, is the son of Sólbiört (sun-bright) and Gróa. To the proper names add *Ostertac*, which answers best of all to *Bældæg* = dies ignis. Conf. also the Celtic *Bel, Belenus*, p. 613.

p. 222.] Baldr's beaming beauty is expr. in the saying: fätt er *liott â Baldri*; but what means the Icel. saw: *logið* hefir *Baldr at Baldri*, Fornm. sög. 6, 257? From his white eyebrow—a feature ascr. also to Bödvildr, ' meyna *brá-hvíto*,' Sæm. 139ᵇ, and to Artemis λευκοφρύνη—the anthemis cotula is called *Ballerbro*, Fries, udfl. 1, 86; conf. Dyb. 1845, p. 74. He gives name to *Balderes* lêge, Kemble, 5, 117 (863), and *Balteres* eih, oak.

On *Breiðablik*, conf. p. 795; add ' in manigen *breiten blicken*,' Tr. kr. 42475. Midsummer was sacred to Balder, and the Chris-tians seem to have put St. John in his place. The mistletoe,

with which he was slain, has to be cut at that time, Dyb. Runa
1844, 21-2. Do the fires of John commemorate the burning
of Balder's body? In Tegner's Frithiofss. xiii., Baldersbâl is
lighted at Midsummer.—'Hvat maelti (spake) Oðinn, aðr â bâl
stigi, sialfr *i eyra syni* (in his son's ear)?' Sæm. 38ª; otherw.
'*i eyra Baldri*, aðr hann var â bâl borinn?' Fornald. sög. 1,
487. Conf. Plaut. Trinum. 'j. 2, 170 : 'sciunt id quod *in aurem*
rex *reginae* dixerit, sciunt quod Juno fabulata est cum Jove,' *i.e.*
the greatest secrets.

p. 224.] *Höðr* is called *Baldurs bani, B. andskoti*, Sæm. 95ª, ᵇ;
he is brought and laid on the funeral pile (â bâl) by his slayer
the newborn Vali, ibid. The Edda does not make him out a god
of war, nor does the ON. höðr mean pugna; but the AS. *heaðu*
does (Kemb. Beow. vol. 1, and in heaðolâf, Beow. 914), so does
the Ir. *cath*. In Saxo, Hotherus is a Swed. hero, and not blind,
but skilled in the bow and harp (ed. M. 111 : citharoedus 123);
he is favoured by wood-nymphs, and gifted with wound-proof
raiment and an irresistible sword. Is the Swed. tale of *Blind
Hatt*, Cavall, 363, to be conn. with him? Consider Hadolâva,
Hadeln, Hatheleria, Hadersleben; and Hothers-nes (now Hor-
sens?) in Jutland is supposed to be named after him, Saxo 122.
An AS. Heaðobeard, like Longbeard.

*Hermôðr* is in Sögubrot (Fornald. s. 1, 373) called 'bazt hugaðr,'
and 'like Helgi,' i.e. comparable to Helgi. In Beow. 1795 he
is named immed. after Sigemund; he falls into the power of the
Eotens, and brings trouble on his people; again in 3417 he is
blamed. Does Hermôðr mean militandi fessus? OHG. Heri-
muot, Herimaot (never Herimuodi), is against it. *Hermódes þorn*
in Kemb. Chart. 3, 387; 'terra quae Anglice *Hermodesodes* nuncupatur,' Chartol. mon. S. Trinitatis (Guérard S. Bertin 455).

p. 224.] The spell is given p. 1231-2. On Phol, see Kl.
schr. 2, 12—17. F. Wachter in the Hall. Encycl. 1845, art. Pferd,
pronounces *phol* the plur. of a strong neut. noun phol, a foal.
Thus : 'foals and Wôdan fared in the wood.' But the poem
itself uses for foal the weak (the only correct) form *volo;* and
what poet would think of naming the god's horse or horses
*beside*, and even *before*, the god himself? Again, was ever a
running horse said to *fahren?*

p. 226.] Pfalsau is called *Pfoals-owa*, MB. 4, 519 (circ. 1126);

*Phols-hou* 4, 229; and *Phols-u* 4, 219. 222-3. *Phûls-ouua,* Notizenbl. 6, 141. *Phols-owe,* Bair. quellen, 1, 279. To the 'eas'
enumer. in Hpt. Ztschr. 2, 254, add ' des *Wunsches ouwe,*' Gerh.
2308; 'der *juncfrouwen wert,*' Iw. 6326 (Guest 196[b], lille at
puceles); *Gotis-werder* in Prussia, Lindenbl. 31. 150. With
*Pholes-piunt* conf. other names of places also compounded with
the gen. case: Ebures-piunt, Tutilis-p., Heibistes-bunta (Fin.
Wirceb.).

p. 226.] *Pfahlbronn* by Lorch, Stälin 1, 85. *Pohlborn* on the
Devil's Dike, Wetterau, p. 1022-3. Johannes de *Paleborne,* yr
1300 (Thür. mitth. iv. 2, 48); is this our Paderborn? and may
that town, called in L. German Padelborn, Palborn, Balborn, be
one of Balder's burns? *Balborn* in the Palatinate, Weisth. 1,
778-9. *Balde-burnen, -borne,* Böhmer's Reg. 231-2, yr 1302.
Heinrich von *Pfols-prundt,* surgeon, brother of the Teut. Order
about 1460. *Polborn,* a family name at Berlin, In H. of Fritz-
lar, January or February is *Volborne,* conf. the man's name *Voll-
born, Fülleborn,* also *Faulborn,* GDS. 798. [Plenty of Ful-burns,
-becks, brooks, -meres, -hams, etc. in Engl.] A *Pal-gunse* (and
Kirch-gunse) in the Wetterau, Arnsb. urk. no. 439; de phal-
gunse, p. 267; palgunse, p. 298. *Pholnrade,* Thür. mitth. vi.
3, 2. *Pfulnrode,* 4, 47. 66. *Fulesbutle,* Lappenb. urk. no. 805.
812, yr 1283-4, now Fulhsbüttel. *Balderslee* in Schleswig is
supposed to contain *hlie* refugium, and appar. answers to the
place named *Balderi fuga* in Saxo, ed. M. 119.

p. 227.] That *Phol* (Kl. schr. 2, 12) is a fondling form of
Balder, Paltar, seems after all extr. probable; the differ. of initial
does not matter, as Liudolf becomes Dudo.——Beside the Celtic
Bel, we might conn. Phol with Apollo, as an *a* is often prefixed
in Grk. Or with pol in 'Pol; edepol!' by Pollux. Or with
*phol, ful* = boar, p. 996, seeing that eburespiunt answ. to pholes-
piunt, Sup. to 226. In Gramm. 3, 682 I have expl. *volencel,*
*faunus,* Gl. Bern., Diut. 2, 214[b], by fol, fou, stultus. A hero
*Pholus* in Ov. Met. 12, 306. On the Ethiop king *Phol,* see Hpt
Ztschr. 5, 69.

p. 228 n.] On *Ullr* = OHG. Wol, see Hpt Ztschr. 7, 393; better to conn. it with Goth. Vulþus 8, 201; yet see Sup. to 163 n.

p. 229 n.] The whirlwind is called *Pulhoidchen, Pulhaud,*
Schamb. 161; conf. infra, p. 285 n. 632-6. Beside Boylsperg,

we find *Boylborn*, Mittl. Thür. Ver. v. 4, 60. *Fold*, see p.
992 n. In Reinwald's Henneb. Id. 1, 37 we find the phrase 'to
have (or take) something for your *foll*' means 'to lie on the bed
you have made.' Acc. to the Achen mundart 56, the weavers of
Aix call cloth made of yarn that they have cabbaged *follche*, füll-
chen [filch? Goth. filhan, to hide]. In Kammerforst, the old
ban-forest near Trier, which none might tread with *gesteppten
leimeln* (nailed shoes), dwells a spirit who chastises wood-spoilers
and scoffers: his name is *Pulch*, still a family-name in Trier.
And the hill outside the city, down which the wheel used to be
rolled into the Moselle (Sup. to 191), is *Pulsberg*. Near Wald-
weiler is a *Pohlfels*, and in Prüm circuit a *Pohlbach*.

p. 229.] *Forseta-lund* (-grove) in Norway, Munch's Beskriv.
483.

p. 231.] Villa *Forsazi* in pago Lisgau (Förste near Osterode?)
in a charter of Otto III., yr 990, Harenberg's Gandersheim 625.
Falke 483. Walterus de *Forsaten* (Förste by Alfeld), Falke 890,
yr 1197. In Saxonia, in pago qui vocatur *Firihsazi*, Einhard's
Ann., yr 823 (Pertz, 1, 211) with the variants : firihsati, fiuhsazi,
frihsazi, strihsazi, firichsare, *virsedi;* in Ann. Fuld. (Pertz 1,
358) Firihsazi. The deriv. conjectured at p. 232 n., from *fors*,
cataract, seems the safest, GDS. 757.

p. 232.] Later stories of fishermen and sailors at *Helgoland*,
and the carrying about of an image of St. Giet, are in Müllenh.
no. 117. 181. 535 ; conf. p. 597. Similar names, often confounded
with it (see Fornm. sög. 12, 298), are : *Hálogaland*, now Helgeland,
in the north of Norway, and the Swedish (once Danish) province
of *Halland*, called in Ælfred's Periplus *Halgoland*. Ought we
to write Hâlgoland? conf. Heli, p. 388.

---

CHAPTER XII.

OTHER GODS.

p. 234.] *Heimðallr* is expl. by Leo, vorl. 131, as heim-dolde,
world-tree. If *d* instead of *ð* were correct, it might contain the
AS. deal, dealles (note to Andr. 126). Heimðall *viðkunnari* enn
*vörðr* með goðum, Sæm. 85ª, the sverd-ás in *Himinbiörg*, reminds

of the angel guarding Paradise with a sword, El. 755, &c. His blowing a horn when Surtr approaches recalls "the last trump" (þut-haurn, Ulph.), 1 Cor. 15, 52.——A *Himiles-berc* in Mone's Anz. 6, 228; a *Heofen-feld* in Northumb., Lye sub v.——Heim-ðallr is called *Vindler*, Sn. 105, Vindlere in Resen.——Of Finnish gods, Ahti or Lemminkäinen has the sharpest ears, Kalev. 17, 7 (Anshelm 3, 64 speaks of hearing the grass grow).——H. is son of Oðinn by 9 mothers, Sn. 211ª. Laxd. saga p. 392; does it mean his father had 9 wives? The Romans called their Liber *bi-mater*; conf. the name Quatremère.

p. 234.] *Rigr* is *stígandi, gángandi*, Sæm. 100ª. 105ª. In Yngl. p. 20 he is the first Danish king; his son *Danpr* has a daughter Drött, the mother of *Dyggvi*, and a son *Dagr*. Sæm. 106ᵇ names '*Danr* ok *Danpr*' together; conf. F. Magn. lex. p. 670.

p. 235.] *Bragi* is *beckskrautuðr*, scamnorum decus, Sæm 61ᵇ; brother of Dagr and Sigrûn 164; pl. *bragnar* dat. brögnum, simply viri 152ª.

p. 236.] A *Burnacker* in Förstem. 2, 4; *brunnacker* in H. Meyer's Zürch. ortsn. 523. Weisth. 1, 119; hence prob. the man's name Brünacker in Konr. v. Weinsb. 3, 4.

p. 237.] The *eager* on the Trent, Carlyle's Hero-worship. AS. *eagor*; in Bailey's Dict. *eager* = flood-tide. The Finnish sea-god, with beard of grass, sitting on a water-lily, is *Ahto, Ahti*, gen. *Ahin*, Kalev. 22, 301. 29, 13. 15; conf. my Kl. schr. 3, 122.

p. 238.] Like Oegi's helm is the *Exhelmer stein* on a hill in the Kellergebirge, Hess. Ztschr. 1, 245. On *Grímr œgir*, see p. 1017. In the helmet 'lît ein *hiltegrîn*,' Dietr. drachenk. 11; galeae *minaci*, Claudian in Prob. et Olybr. 92; *terribilem* galeam, Virg. Aen. 8, 620.

p. 238.] *Oegir* is a iötunn, Hŷm. 3; a *bergbúi* 2. The ON. *ôgn*, f., = terror and ocean; *ôgnar liomi* = gold, Sæm. 152ª; *ôgorlig* Oegisdottor 153ª; *ôlsmiðr* = Oegir, Egills. 618. What means *Oegis-heimr*, Sæm. 124-5? *Egisleiba, Agistadium*, Hpt's Ztschr. 8, 588; *Agasûl* on L. Zurich 2, 536, formed like Agadora (Eider, p. 239?) *oegisandr*, sea-sand, Barl. 26, 20.

p. 240.] *Hlês* dættr â vîð blêsu. her er sjor kallaðr *Hlêr*, þvî at hann *hlŷr* allra minnz, Sn. 332; hlŷr = egelidus, tepidus,

OHG. lâo, lâwer, Graff 2, 294; 1r. *lir,* Conan 33-4-9. 93. 192-3.
Diarmid 87. 112-4-6 ; also *lear,* Learthonn, T. 7.

p. 242.] As *Logi,* the 'villi-eldr,' Sn. 60, is son to giant
Forniotr, so is *Loki* a son of giant Farbauti. The eating-match
betw. Loki and Logi is like that of Herakles and Lepreus, Athenæ.
p. 412. Paus. 5, 5. Prometheus is chained to the rock by
Hephæstus, Loki by Logi.——Loki, 'sâ er flestu illu raeðr,' is
hateful to the gods : *er öll regin œgja,* Thorl. sp. 6, 38; sâ inn
*lœvîsi* Loki, Sæm. 67[b]; in folksongs 'Loke *leve,*' Wieselgr. 384-5,
in Danish 'Loke *lejemand,*' conf. thè name Liuuiso, Liuiso, Trad.
fuld. 2, 32-43 ; in Norweg. 'hin *onde,*' Hallager, as Oden is in
l. 828 ; for Lokkens havre we have 'den *ondes* hafre, Dybeck runa
1847, 30-1.——There is a saying : 'leingi geingr *Loki ok Thórr*
(=lightning and thunder), lêttir ei hrîðum,' the storm lasts.——
Rask thinks the name akin to Finn. *lokki,* wolf; some may think
it an abbrev. of *Lucifer !* Uhland takes Loki to be the *locker-up,*
*concluder* of all things, as Heimdall is originator. To Logi conf.
*Hálogi* for Hölgi, Sn. 128. 154. F. Magn. lex. p. 981.

p. 243.] 'Ik bede di *grindel an deser helle,*' Upstandinge 553,
seems almost to mean a personal devil.

p. 243 n.] It is true, another race of rulers beside the Ases is
imagined, one of whom, *Gylfi* king of Sweden, sets out as *gangleri*
(pilgrim) to spy out the Ases (Sn. 1. 2. 2, &c.), but is cheated by
them. But this is an imitation of Eddic lays, which make Oðinn
as gangleri and gangráðr travel to the giants, and talk with them.
Sæm. 31-2; conf. *Aegir's* journey to Asgard, and his dialogue with
*Bragi,* Sn. 79, &c.

p. 245.] In Sæm. 37[a] *Fenrir* pursues Alf-röðull, which must
mean the moon, the 'sun of the elves' ; conf. 'festr mun slitna
enn Frecki renna,' Sæm. 7-8. 'man ôbundinn Fenris-ûlfr fara,'
Hakonarm. 23. '*Loki* lîðr or böndum,' Sæm. 96[a] (conf. *iötunn*
losnar 8[a]; is this Loki or Surtr ? Loki is lægiarnlîki âþeckr,
monstro similis 7[a]).——Loki is *caught* by Þiazi, Sn. 81, and
expressively *chained* 70 (conf. Sæm. 7[a]); so is Fenrir 33-4-5;
conf. the chained giant (Suppl. to 544), chained devil (p. 1011),
chained Kronos (p. 832 n.).——Loki's daughter *Hel* esp. makes
it likely that he too was common to all Teut. nations.

p. 247.] AS. *sâtor-lâðe,* panicum crusgalli, is a grass like the
ἄγρωστις sown by Kronos (Suppl. to 1192). One is reminded of

Saturni dolium by '*Lucifer* sedens in *dolio*,' Upstandinge p. 41,
and 'des *tiuvels vaz*,' Hpt's Ztschr. 7, 327. What means the
ON. *scáturnir*, Sn. 222[b] ?

p. 248-9.] Delius pp. 41. 50 cites *krodenduvel, kroden*-heuker,
*kroden*-kind; is the first out of Botho ? In a Hildesheim MS.
of the 16th cent., Frosch-meus, we read : '*pravi spiritus, id est,
de kroden duvels'* in contrast with the good holdes. In Hh.
VIII[a] : '*misshapen as they paint the *kroden teuffel*.'——Jornandes de regn. succ. p. m. 2 has the pedigree ' Saturnus, Picus,
Faunus, Latinus'; conf. p. 673 and GDS. 120.

---

## CHAPTER XIII.

### GODDESSES.

p. 250 n.] The MHG. *gotinne* is in Sæm. 115[a] *gyðja*, yet in
114[b] ey trûði Ottarr â *ásynjor*, and 61[a] heilir *aesir*, heilar *ásynjor!*
conf. πάντες τε θεοὶ πασαί τε θέαιναι, Il. 8, 5. 19, 101. Od. 8, 341.
This word goddess acquired a lower sense, being used by the
people for fair dames and pretty lasses, Liudpr. antap. 4, 13.
' Ermegart Himel-*gotin*,' Rückert's Ludwig 97. What is the
*götin* in Nithart MSH. 3, 288[a], who goes ' unter dem *fanen* ûz
dem vorst, wol *geammet*,' and is led out on the green under *blue
sky* (baldachin), apparently by peasants at an old harvest-festi-
val ? conf. fee, Suppl. to 410.

p. 251.] OHG. *ero*, earth, answers to Ssk. *irâ*, Ir. *ire*, GDS.
55. *Tellus* might be for terulus, as puella for puerula, but the
gen. is telluris, conf. Ssk. *tala*, fundus. *Humus* is Ssk. xamâ.
*Iaîa*, called πρωτόμαντις in Æsch. Eum. 2, corresponds to Ssk.
*gaus, gô*, cow (p. 665), the cow being mother of the world (p. 559):
ὦ γῆ καὶ θεοί, a frequent Attic invocation. ON. *fold* is unpersonal, yet is greeted in Sæm. 194[a]: *heil sû* hin fiolnýta *fold!*
GDS. 60 (p. 254).——*Iörð*, earth, is called Ionakr's tree-green,
oak-green daughter: dottur Onars viði-groen, Sn. 123; eiki-
groent Onars flioð, Fornm. sög. 1, 29. 12, 27. She is daughter
of night in Sæm. 194[a]: heil *nótt* ok *nipt !* but who is *eorðan
bróðor*, Cod. Exon. 490, 23 ? Iörð is also mother of Meili, Thor's
brother, Sæm. 76[a]; Iörð = *Fiörgyn* 80[b] (p. 172).——Of *Rindr* and

her relation to Oðin: 'seid Yggr til Rindr,' Y. amores Rindae incantamentis sibi conciliavit, Sn. 1848. 1, 236. Is AS. *hruse* (terra) contained in *grusebank*, turf-bench, Schm. von Wern. 114?

p. 251 n.] At Attila's grave too the servants are killed: 'et ut tot et tantis divitiis humana curiositas arceretur, *operi depu-tatos trucidarunt*, emersitque momentanea mors sepelientibus cum sepulto,' Jorn. cap. 49. The Dacian king Decebalus buries his treasure under the *bed* of the Sargetia, Cass. Dio 68, 14. Giese-brecht supposes the Wends had the same custom, Balt. stud. 11, 28-9.

p. 252.] *Nerthus* is the only true reading, says Müllenhoff, Hpt's Ztschr. 9, 256; Erthus is admissible, think Zeuss and Bessel. *Nerthus* answers to Ssk. Nritus, terra, Bopp 202[b]; conf. C. Hofmann in Ztschr. der morgenl. ges. 1847. A thesis by Pyl, Medea, Berol. 1850 p. 96 derives it fr. LG. nerder, nerdrig, conf. νέρτερος. Her island can hardly be Rügen (p. 255-6), but perhaps Femern or Alsen, says Müllenh., Nordalb. stud. 1, 128-9. Her car stood in the grove (templum) under a tree, Giefers. 'Nerthus, id est, *Terra mater*' strongly reminds of Pliny's *mater deum* 18, 4: quo anno *m. d.* advecta Romam est, *majorem ea aestate messem* quam antecedentibus annis decem factam esse tradunt.

p. 253.] Though the people now imagine *fru Gode, Goden, Gauden* as a frau, there appears now and then a *de koen* (king) instead, Hpt's Ztschr. 4, 385. Legends of fru Gauden in Lisch, Meckl. jrb. 8, 203, &c. Niederhöffer 2, 91 (conf. p. 925-6-7). Harvest-home still called *vergodensdél* in Lüneburg, conf. Kuhn and Schwartz p. 394-5. The Vermlanders call Thor's wife *god-mor*, good mother. Rask, Afh. 1, 94 derives ON. *Gói* fr. Finn. *koi* (aurora). GDS. 53. 93.

p. 254] Priscus calls Attila's wife Κρέκα 179, 9, Ῥέκαν 207, 17, which easily becomes Herka. Frau *Harke* a giantess, Kuhn 146. 371. *Fru Harke, Arke, Harfe, Harre*, Hpt's Ztschr. 4, 386, 5, 377. Sommer 11. 167-8. 147 (conf. frau *Motte*, 12. 168. 147). A witch's daughter *Harka*, Wolf's Ztschr. 2, 255. *Haksche*, like *Godsche* for Gode, Hpt's Ztschr. 5, 377. Harke flies through the *air* in the shape of a *dove*, makes the fields *fruitful*, carries a stool to sit on, so as not to touch the ground, Sommer p. 12; this is like Herodias (p. 285) and the wandering woman (p. 632. 1058).

p. 254 n.] Mommsen 133 derives *Ceres*, Oscan Kerres, from creare; Hitzig Philist. 232 connects it with Çrîs = Śrî; I with cera and cresco. For *Demeter* the Slavs have *země matě*, mother earth; a dear mother, like (πυρὸς) φίλης Δήμητρος, Æsop (Corais 212. de Furia 367). Babr. 131; conf. Δημήτερος ἀκτή, Il. 13, 323, and 'das liebe korn, getreidelein,' Gram. 3, 665. GDS. 53. The Earth's lap is like a mother's: foldan sceát (= schoosz), Cod. Exon. 428, 22. eorðan sceáta eardian 496, 23. eorðan sceátas hweorfan 309, 22. grund-bedd 493, 3.

p. 255.] On the goddess's progress see Suppl. to 252. With her bath conf. the purifying bath of *Rhea* (Preller 1, 409), whose name Pott would explain by εὐρεῖα = Ssk. urvî fr. urú = varú, Kuhn's Ztschr. 5, 285. The *lavatio Berecynthiae* is described by Augustine, Civ. Dei 2, 4; conf. Vita Martini cap. 9 (W. Müller p. 48). The image of Artemis was washed in seven rivers flowing out of one spring, Pref. to Theocritus; the alraun and alirumna were bathed.

p. 256 n.] The LG. farmer's maxim, 'Mai-mând kold un nat Füllt schünen un fat, is in Swedish 'Mai kall Fyller bondens lador all,' Runa 1844, 6. A similar saw in Bretagne about St. Anne, Lausitzer mag. 8, 51; how is it worded in French?

p. 257.] On *Tanfana* see my Kl. Schr. 5, 415, etc. GDS. 231-2. 336. 622.

p. 263.] From Rodulf's account was probably taken the 16th cent. notice in Reiffenberg's Phil. Mouskes, tome 1. Brux. 1838 app. p. 721: 'Sub Alexandro, qui fuit sex annis episcopus (Leodiensis) et depositus in Conc. Pisae an. 1135, fuit quaedam *prodigiosa* seu *demoniaca navis*, quae innixa rotis et *magice agitata* malignis spiritibus attractu funium fuit Tungris inducta Loscastrum. Ad quam omnis sexus appropinquans tripudiare et saltare cogebatur *etiam nudo corpore*. Ad eam feminae de mane stratis exilientes accurrebant, dum dicta navis citharae et aliorum instrumentorum sonitu resonaret.'——Weavers, whom Rodulf makes prominent in hauling and guarding the ship, have something to do with navigation: in their trade they ply the schiff (shuttle), and that is why they were called marner, Jäger's Ulm p. 636-7. About carrying ships on shoulders Pliny has another passage 5, 9: 'ibi Aethiopicae conveniunt naves; namque eas *plicatiles humeris transferunt* quoties ad catarractas ventum est.'

Also Justin 32, 3 : ' Istri naves suas *humeris* per juga montium usque ad littus Adriatici maris *transtulerunt*.'

Additional traces of German ship-processions and festivals. In Antwerp and Brabant, near the scene of that old procession, there was about 1400 ' eine gilde in der blauwer scuten,' Hpt's Ztschr. 1, 266-7. At Shrovetide sailors drag a ship about, Kuhn's Nordd. sagen p. 369. At the Schönbart-running in Nürnberg, men in motley used at Shrovetide to carry Hell round, including a ship and the Venus Mount ; see Hist. of Schönb.-run. at N., by the Germ. Soc. of Altdorf 1761. Another ship-procession in Hone's Everyday-book 2, 851. In the · ' Mauritius und Beamunt,' vv. 627—894, a ship on wheels, with knights and music on board, is drawn by concealed horses through the same Rhine and Meuse country to a tournament at Cologne ; it is afterwards divided among the garzuns (pages), v. 1040. Is the idea of the *Ship of fools* travelling fr. land to land akin to this ? especially as Dame Venus ' mit dem *ströwen* ars ' (conf. Hulda's stroharnss, p. 269 n.) rides in it, ed. Strobel p. 107 ; ' frau Fenus mit dem stroem loch,' Fastn.-sp. p. 263. Consider too the cloud-ship of Magonia (p. 639), and the enchanted ship with the great band of music, Müllenh. p. 220. The ' wilde gjaid' comes along in a sledge shaped like a ship, drawn by naughty maidservants, who get whipped, Wolf's Ztschr. 2, 32-3. Nursery-tales tell of a ship that crosses land and water, Meier 31. Schambach 18. Pröhle's Märchen nos. 46-7. Wolf's Beitr. 1, 152, &c. Finn. märch. 2, 1[b]. Berchta is often ferried over, and of Oðinn the Sôlarlioð 77 (Sæm. 130[a]) says : Oðins qvon *rœr â iarðar skipi*.

p. 264 n.] At Shrovetide a plough was drawn through the streets by maskers, Büsching's Wöch. nachr. 1, 124, fr. Tenzel. H. Sachs says, on Ash-Wednesday the maids who had not taken men were yoked in a plough ; so Fastn.-sp. 247, 6-7 ; ' pulling the fools' plough ' 233. 10. Kuhn conn. *pfluoc, plôgr*, Lith. *plugas* with the root plu, flu, so that plough orig. meant boat, Ssk. plava, Gr. πλοῖον.

p. 265 n.] Drinking-bowls in ship shape ; argentea navis, Pertz 10, 577. A nef d'or on the king's table, Garin 2, 16-7 ; later examples in Schweinichen 1, 158. 187. An oracle spoke of a silver ploughshare, Thucyd. 5, 16.

p. 265 n. 2.] Annius Viterb., ed. ascensiana 1512, fol. 171[ab] :

'ergo venit (Isis) in Italiam et docuit frumentariam, molendi-
nariam et panificam, cum ante glande vescerentur .... Viterbi
primi panes ab *Iside* confecti sunt. item Vetuloniae celebravit
Jasius nuptias, et panes obtulit primos *Isis,* ut in V. antiquitatum
Berosus asserit. porro, ut probant superiores quaestiones, Vetu-
lonia est Viterbum.' The Lith. *Krumine* wanders all over the
world to find her daughter, and teaches men agriculture, Hanusch
245. The year will be *fruitful* if there is a rustling in the air
during the twelves, Sommer p. 12 (Suppl. to 254).

p. 267.] Goth. *hulþs* propitius is fr. hilþan, halþ, hulþun, to
bow (s. Löbe). Holle, Holda is a cow's name in Carinthia. In
Dietr. drachenk., str. 517-8, &c. there is a giant called *Hulle,* but
in str. 993: 'sprancten für *frowen Hullen* der edelen juncfrowen
fîn.' In Thuringia frau *Wolle, Rolle,* Sommer 10-1. *Holda* in
Cod. Fuld. no. 523. Frau *Holla* in Rhenish Franconia, Frommann 3, 270. 'Die *Holl* kommt' they say at Giessen, 'die
*Hulla*' also beyond the Main about Würzburg, Kestler's Beschr.
v. Ochsenfurt, Wrzb. 1845, p. 29. Frau *Holle* also in Silesia. In
Up. Sax. she was called frau *Helle,* B. vom abergl. 2, 66-7; frau
*Holt* in Wolf's Ztschr. 1, 273.——The *very earliest* mention of
Holda is in Walafrid Strabo's eulogy of Judith, wife of Louis
the Pious :

Organa dulcisono percussit pectine Judith ;
O si Sappho loquax vel nos inviseret *Holda,* etc.

p. 267 n.] With Kinderm. 24 conf. the variant in KM. 3, 40
seq., Svenska äfv. 1, 123 and Pentam. 4, 7. Much the same said
of the dialas, Schreiber's Taschenb. 4, 310 (Suppl. to 410).

p. 270.] When fog rests on the mountain : 'Dame H. has lit
her fire in the hill.' In Alsace when it snows; 'd' engele han 's
bed gemacht, d' fedre fliege runder;' in Gegenbach 427:
'heaven's feathers fly '; in Nassau : 'Dame H. shakes up her
bed,' Kehrein's Nassau p. 280. Nurses fetch babies out of
*frau Hollen teich.* In Transylvania are fields named *Frau-holda-
graben,* Progr. on Carrying out Death 1861, p. 3. She washes
her veil, Pröhle 198. Like Berthe, she is queen or leader of
elves and holdes (p. 456), conf. Titania and Dame Venus.
'Fraue Bercht, fraue Holt' occur in the Landskranna (?)
Himelstrasz, printed 1484, Gefken's Beil. 112. In the neigh-

bourhood of the Meisner, Dame H. carried off a rock *on her thumb*, Hess. Ztschr. 4, 108; a cave is there called *Kitz-Kammer*, perhaps because cats were sacred to her as to Freya (p. 305). On the Main, between Hassloch and Grünenwörth, may be seen ' fra Hulle ' on the *Fra Hullenstein*, combing her locks. Whoever sees her loses his eyesight or his reason. Dame Holle rides in her coach, makes a whirlwind, pursues the hunter, Pröhle 156. 278. 173, like Pharaildis, Verild (357 n.). Legends of *Hulle* in Herrlein's Spessart-sag. 179—184. A *frau Hollen-spiel* (-game) in Thuringia, Hess. Ztschr. 4, 109. The *Haule-mutter* (mother H.) in the Harz, an old crone, makes herself great or little, Harrys 2, no. 6. Pröhle 278; conf. *Haule*-männerchen (dwarfs) in KM. no. 13. She is a humpbacked little woman, Sommer p. 9; walks with a crutch about Haxthausen, Westph.——Again, queen Holle appears as *housekeeper* and *henchwoman* to Frederick Barbarossa in Kifhäuser, exactly as Dame Venus travels in Wuotan's retinue, Sommer p. 6. In Up. Hesse ' meätt der Holle färn ' means, to have tumbled hair or tangled distaff, prob. also night-walking: the Holle at Wartburg looks like a witch, Woeste's Mitth. p. 289 no. 24; conf. ' *verheuletes* haar,' Corrodi professer 59, and a man with shaggy hair is called *holle-kopf*.—— With her *stroharnss* conf. ströwen-ars, Suppl. to 263. Careless spinners are threatened with the *verwunschene frau*, Panzer's Beitr. 1, 84 : she who does not get her spinning over by Sunday will have Holle in her distaff to tangle it; conf. the Kuga (p. 1188-9).

p. 272.] The *Huldarsaga*, tale of the sorceress Huldr, is told by Sturle ; conf. the extract fr. Sturlunga in Oldn. läseb. p. 40. *Huldre-web* in Norway means a soft vegetable material like flannel; and in Faye 42 Huldra is clothed in green. The *hulder* in Asb. 1, 48. 78. 199 has a cow's tail; here it is not so much one hulder, as *many* huldren that appear *singly*. So in the M.Nethl. Rose 5679 : ' *hulden*, die daer singhen '; are these mermaids ? In Sweden they have a *hylle-fru* and a *Hildi-moder*, Geyer 1, 27; conf. Dybeck 1845, 56.

p. 273.] The name of *Perahta*, the bright, answers to Selēnē, Lucina, Luna, therefore Artemis, Diana. Hence she takes part in the Wild Hunt, accompanied by hounds, like Hecatē ; hence also, in the LG. Valentin und Namelos, Berta has become *Clarina* [conf. St. *Lucy*, frau *Lutz*, p. 274 n.].——The Lith. *Lauma* is very like Berhta and Holda : she is goddess of earth and of weaving. She appears in a house, helps the girls to *weave*, and gets through a piece of linen in no time; but then the girl has to guess her name. If she guesses right, she keeps the linen; if not, the laume takes it away. One girl said to the laume : ' Laume Sore peczin auda dûna pelnydama,' l. S. weaves with her arm, earning bread. Her name was Sore, so the girl kept the linen, N. Preuss. prov. bl. 2, 380. Schleicher in Wien. ber. 11, 104 seq. says, the laume is a malignant alp (nightmare) who steals children, is voracious, yet bathes on the beach, helps, and brings linen : a distinct being (11, 96-7) fr. the laima spoken of on p. 416 n. Nesselm. 353<sup>b</sup>.

p. 273 n.] *Werre* is akin to *Wandel-muot*, Ls. 3, 88. 1, 205-8 : frô *Wandelmuot* sendet ir *scheid-sâmen* (seeds of division) 2, 157. in dirre wîten werlde kreizen hat *irre-sâmen* (seeds of error) uns gesât ein frouwe ist *Wendelmuot* geheizen, MS. 2, 198<sup>b</sup>; conf. the seed sown by death (p. 848) and the devil (p. 1012). frou *Wendelmuot* hie liebe maet mit der vürwitz segens abe (dame Ficklemind here mows down love with curiosity's keen sithe), Turl. Wh. 128<sup>a</sup>.

p. 274.] The *meal* set ready for Bertha resembles the food offered to Hecate on the 30th of the month, Athen. 3, 194 ; certain *fish* are Ἑκάτης βρώτατα 3, 146-7. 323. Filling the belly with chopped straw : conf. the *hrísmagi*, Laxd. saga 226. As the *white lady* prescribes a diet for the country-folk (Morgenbl. 1847, nos. 50—52), they tell of a dame *Borggabe* (loan), who gave or lent money and corn to needy men, if they went to her cave and cried ' Gracious dame B.'; conf. OHG. *chorn*-gëpâ Ceres, *sâmo*-këpa saticena, Gibicho ; *wîn*-gebe, MB. 13, 42. *oti*-geba (890 n.). Nycolaus von dem *crumen*-ghebe, an. 1334, Henneb. urk. ii. 13, 30.

p. 277.] Berta, like Holda, is called *mother* in the Swed. märchen p. 366, *gamla* B., trollkäring. In one Swed. tale a fair lady walks attended by *many dwarfs*; the room she enters is filled with them, Wieselgr. 454.——Like the Thuringian Perchta, the *devil blows out eyes*, Müllenh. p. 202 ; care breathes upon Faust, and blinds him ; conf. the curse, ' Your eyes are mine,' N. Preuss. prov. bl. 1, 395, and ' spältle zustreichen,

*aufstreichen* (stroke them shut, stroke them open),' Meier's
Schwäb. sag. 136.——After the *lapse of a year* the woman gets
her child back, Müllenh. no. 472 ; so does the man in the wild
hunt get rid of his hump (Suppl. to 930) ; conf. Steub's Vorarlberg p. 83, Bader's Sagen no. 424, and the Cheese-mannikin
in Panzer 2, 40. On Berhta's share in the Furious Hunt, see
p. 932.

p. 277.] In S. Germany, beside Bertha, Berche, we find ' frau
*Bert, Bertel,* Panzer's Beitr. 1, 247-8. The *wild* Berta wipes her
—— with the unspun flax. At Holzberndorf in Up. Franconia,
a lad acts *Eisen-berta,* clad in a cow's hide, bell in hand ; to good
children he gives nuts and apples, to bad ones the rod 2, 117.

p. 278.] To the Bavar. name *Stempo* we can add that of the
Strasburger *Stampho,* an. 1277, Böhmer's Reg. Rudolfi no.
322 ; conf. *stempfel,* hangman, MS. 2, 2ᵇ. 3ᵃ. In Schm. 3, 638
*stampulanz* = bugbear, 2, 248 *stempen-har* = flax ; conf. Von d.
Hagen's G. Abent. 3, 13-4.——Beside *Trempe,* there seems to
be a *Temper,* Wolf's Ztschr. 2, 181, perhaps sprung out of
Quatember in the same way as frau *Faste* (p. 782 n.), ibid. 1,
292. tolle *trompe* (trampel ?), Rocken-phil. 2, 16-7. In favour
of S having been added before T is *Schperchta* for Perchta,
Mannh. Ztschr. 4. 388. As Stempe *treads* like the alp, she seems
ident. with the alp-crushing Muraue.

p. 279.] In Salzburg country the Christmas-tree is called
*Bechl-boschen,* Weim. jrb. 2, 133. ' in loco qui dicitur *Berten-
wisun,*' Salzb. urk. of 10th cent., Arch. f. östr. gesch. 22, 299.
304. Outside Remshard near Günzburg, Bav., is a wood ' zu der
*dirne* (girl).' The *dirne-weibl* used to be there in a red frock
with a basket of fine apples, which she gave away and changed
into money. If people did not go with her, she returned weeping into the wood. ' Here comes the *dirne-weibl*' said children,
to frighten each other. Seb. Brant p. m. 195 knows about
*Bächten farn,* B.'s fern.

*Berchtolt* is a common name in Swabia, Bit. 10, 306. 770 ;
conf. Berchtols-gaden (now Berchtes-g.), Prechtles-boden-alpe,
Seidl's Almer 2, 73. The *white mannikin* is also described by
Bader no. 417.

p. 280.] When Malesherbes was talking to Louis XVI. of the
fate in store for him, the king said : ' On m'a souvent raconté

dans mon enfance, que toutes les fois qu'un roi de la maison des
Bourbons devait mourir, on voyait à minuit se promener dans les
galeries du château une *grande femme vêtue de blanc*,' Mém. de
Bésenval; conf. 'de *witte* un *swarte* Dorte,' Müllenh. p. 343-4;
and the *Klag-mutter* p. 1135. The same is told of the Ir. *bansighe*,
pl. *mnasighe*, O'Brien sub. vv. sithbhrog, gruagach.

p. 281.] The image of *reine Pédauque*, Prov. Pedauca (Rayn.
sub v. auca), stands under the church-doors at Dijon, Nesle,
Nevers, St. Pourcin and Toulouse. The last was known to
Rabelais: 'qu'elles étaient largement pattues, comme sont les
oies et jadis à Toulouse la reine Pedauque.' This statue held a
spindle, and spun, and men swore 'par la quenouille de la reine
P.,' Paris p. 4. So queen Goose-foot was a spinner; yet her
goose-foot did not come of spinning, for the spinning-*wheel* was
not invented till the 15th cent., Hpt's Ztschr. 6, 135. Berhta
*cum magno pede*, Massm. Eracl. 385. Heinricus *Gense-fuz*, MB.
8, 172. cagots with *goose-foot* or *duck's-foot ears*, Fr. Michel's
Races maud. 2, 126-9. 136. 144-7. 152. M. C. Vulliemin's La
reine Berte et son temps makes out that Berte la fileuse was
wife to Rudolf of Little Burgundy, daughter to the Alamann
duke Burchard, and mother to Adelheid who married Otto I.;
this Berta died at Payerne about 970. To the white damsel is
given a *little white lamb*, Müllenh. p. 347.

p. 285 n.] The whirlwind is called *sau-arsch*, *mucken-arsch*,
Schmidt's Westerwäld. id. 116; in Up. Bavaria *sau-wede*. When
it whirls up hay or corn, the people in Passau and Straubing cry
to it: '*sau-dreck! du schwarz farkel* (pig)!' *Sew-zuyel*, a term
of abuse, H. Sachs v., 347ᵇ; conf. pp. 632. 996. In an old Langobard treaty the devil is *porcorum possessor*.

p. 291.] *Ostara* is akin to Ssk. vasta daylight, vasas day,
ushas aurora, vastar at early morn; conf. Zend. ushastara eastern,
Benfey 1, 28. Lith. *auszta* it dawns, *auszrinne* aurora; *Ausca*
(r. Ausra), dea occumbentis vel ascendentis solis (Lasicz). Many
places in Germany were sacred to her, esp. hills: Austerkopp,
Osterk. in Waldeck, Firmen. 1, 324ᵇ, conf. Astenberg 325ᵃ;
Osterstube, a cave, Panz. Beitr. 1, 115. 280; Osterbrunne, a
christian name: 'ich O., ein edelknecht von Ror,' an. 1352,
Schmid's Tübingen 180.——Her feast was a time of great re-
joicing, hence the metaphors: '(thou art) mîner freuden *ôster-tac*

(-day),' Iw. 8120. mîues herzens ôstertac, MS. 2, 223ᵃ. 1, 37ᵇ. der gernden ôstertac, Amgb. 3ᵃ; conf. Meien-tag. It is a surname in the Zoller country: dictus *der* Ostertag, Mon. Zoll. no. 252-7. Frideriches saligen son des Ostertages, no. 306.

The antithesis of east and west seems to demand a *Westara* as goddess of evening or sundown, as Mone suggests, Anz. 5, 493; consider westergibel, westermâne, perh. westerhemde, westerbarn, the Slav. Vesnà, even the Lat. Vespera, Vesperugo.

p. 296.] On the goddess Zisa, conf. the history of the origin of Augsburg in Keller's Fastn. sp. p. 1361. About as fabulous as the account of the Augsburg Zisa, sounds the following fr. Ladisl. Suntheim's Chronica, Cod. Stuttg. hist., fol. 250 : 'Die selb zeit sasz ain haidnischer hertzog von Swaben da auf dem slos *Hillomondt*, ob Vertica (Kempten) der stat gelegen, mit namen *Esnerius*, der wonet noch seinen (adhered to his) haidnischen sitten auf Hillomondt; zu dem komen die vertriben waren aus Vertica und in der gegent darumb, und patten in (begged him), das er sie durch (for the sake of) sein götin, *Zysa* genannt, mit veld begabet und aufnam (endow and befriend) . . . . Da sprach hertzog Esnerius : wann ir mir swerdt pei den göttern *Edelpoll* und *Hercules* und pei meiner göttin *Zisa*, so will ich euch veldt geben, &c.'

p. 298.] With *Cisa* may be conn. *Cise*, a place in the Grisons, Bergm. Vorarlb. p. 43, and ' swester *Zeise*,' Bamb. ver. 10, 143-4; *Zaissen-perig*, *Zeisl-perg*, Archiv. i. 5, 74. 48. Akin to *Cisara* seems *Cizuris* (Zitgers), a place in Rhætia, Pertz 6, 748ᵃ; *Zeizurisperga*, *Zeiszaris-p.*, *Heizzeris-p.*, *Zeizaris-pergan*, *Zeizanes-perge*, Notizenbl. 6, 116. 143. 165. 138. 259. How stands it finally with *Desenberg*, which Lambert calls *Tesenb.?* Pertz 7, 178. Conf. other names in Mone's Anz. 6, 235, and Disibodo, Disibodenberg, Disenb., Weisth. 2, 168.

p. 299 n.] *Frouwe* heizt von tugenden ein *wîp* (called a *frau* fr. her virtues), Ulr. v. Lichenst. 3, 17 :

als ein *vrou* ir werden lîp (her precious body)
tiuret (cherishes) sô daz sie ein *wîp*
geheizen mac mit reinen siten,
der (for her) mac ein man vil gerne biten (sue) ; Kolocz. 129.

p. 301 n.] A Swed. folksong, not old, in Arvidss. 3, 250 has :

'*Fröja*, du berömde fru, Till hopa bind oss ungetu !' Fröja often
=Venus in Bellm. 3, 129. 132-5. M. Neth. vraei, pulcher. vrî
=vrô, Pass. 299, 74.

 p. 304.] On the etym. of Freya and Frigg, see my Kl. schr.
3, 118. 127. In a Norweg. tale, stor Frigge goes with the cattle
of the elves, Asb. Huldr. 1, 201 ; conf. 206. *Vreke* is found in
Belgium too, says Coremans 114-5. 158; a *Vrekeberg* 126. *Fre-
kenteve*, Pertz 8, 776. *Fricconhorst*, an. 1090, Erh. p. 131. For
Fruike in Hpt's Ztschr. 5, 373 Kuhn writes *Fuik*, which may
mean whirlwind, ON. *fiuka*.

 p. 306. *Freya* and *Freyr* are both present at Oegi's banquet,
but neither his Gerðr nor her Oðr, Sæm. 59 ; yet she is called
*Oðs mey* 5[b], and Hnoss and Gersemi (p. 886) may be her children
by Oðr. When Sn. 354 calls her *Oðins friðla*, he prob. con-
founds her with Frigg (p. 302); or is Oðinn Mars here, and
Freya Venus ? On the distinctness, yet orig. unity, of the two
goddesses, see my Kl. schr. 5, 421-5 ; was Oðr the Vanic name
of Oðinn ? 426-7.——To her by-name *Syr* the Norw. plants
*Siurguld* (Syr-gull ?), anthemis, and *Sirildrot* prob. owe their
names, F. Magn. lex. myth. p. 361 ; while Saxo's *Syritha* is rather
Sigrîðr, conf. Sygrutha, Saxo 329. GDS. 526.——Freya's hall
is *Sessrýmnir, Sessvarnir*, Sn. 28 ; as the cat was sacred to her,
we may perh. count the *Kitzkammer* on the Meisner (Suppl. to
270) among her or Holda's dwellings ; conf. cat-feeding (p. 1097).

 p. 307 n.] *Mani, men* is akin to Lat. monile, Dor. μάνος,
μάννος, Pers. μανιάκης, μανίακον, Ssk: mani, Pott 1, 89. As *menglöð* expresses a woman's gladness over her jewel, a Swiss woman
calls her girdle ' die *freude*,' Stald. 2, 515-6.

 p. 309.] On *Fulla, Sunna, Sindgund*, see Kl. schr. 2, 17 seq.
GDS. 86. 102. Fulla wore a gold headband, for gold is called
höfuðband Fullu, Sn. 128.——*Sôl* is daughter of Mundilföri (p.
703), wife of *Glenr* (al. Glornir), Sn. 12. 126, or *Dagr*, Fornald.
sög. 2, 7. *Fru Sole, fru Soletopp* occurs in pop. games, Arvidss.
3, 389. 432.——*Skaði*, daughter of Þiazi, wife of Niörðr and
mother of Freyr (gen. Skaða, Sn. 82. Kl. schr. 3, 407), aft. wife
of Oðinn and mother of Sæmîngr, Yngl. c. 9.

 p. 309.] In Sn. 119 *Gerðr* is *Oðin's* wife or mistress, rival
to Frigg. There is a *Thórgerðr* hörgabrúðr. A *Frögertha*, come
of heroic race, Saxo Gram. b. 6. Similar, if not so effective as

Gerð's radiant beauty, is the splendour of other ladies in Asb. Huldr. 1, 47 : saa deilig at det *skinnede* af hende; in Garg. 76[b] : her 'rosen-blüsame' cheeks lit up the ambient air more brightly than the rainbow; in Wirnt die welt :

> ir schoene gap sô liehten schîn
> und alsô wunneclîchen glast,
> daz der selbe pallast
> von ir lîbe (body) erliuhtet wart.

p. 310.] On *Syn* and *Vör*, conf. F. Magn. lex. 358-9. Then the compds. *Hervör, Gunnvör ;* OHG. *Cundwara, Hasalwara,* Graff 1, 907; AS. *Freá-waru,* Beow, 4048. I ought to have mentioned the ON. goddess *Ilmr,* fem., though ilmr, suavis odor, is masc.

p. 310.] *Nanna* in the Edda is ' *Neps* dôttir,' Sn. 31. 66, and Nepr was Oðin's son 211. Saxo makes her a daughter of Gevar (Kepaheri), see Suppl. to 220. Sæm. 116[a] speaks of another Nanna, ' *Nökkva* dôttir.' Is ' *nönnor* Herjans,' the epithet of the valkyrs, Sæm. 4[b], conn. with Nanna ?

p. 311 n.] *Fuoge* and *Unfuoge* are supported by the following : er was aller tugende vol, die in diu *Vuoge* lêrte (virtues that decency taught him), Pass. 165, 2. diu *Füegel, Füeglerin,* Ls. 1, 200-8. wann kompt *Hans Fug,* so sehe und lug (look), Garg. 236[b]. daz in *Unfuoge* niht erslüege (slew him not), Walth. 82, 8. *Unfuoge* den palas vlôch, Parz. 809, 19. nu lât (leave ye) der *Unfuoge* ir strît 171, 16 ; conf. fügen (Suppl. to 23).——Quite unpersonal are ; zuht unde fuoge, Greg. 1070. ungevuoge, Er. 9517. 6527. swelch fürsten sô von lande varn, daz zimt ouch *irn fuogen* sô, daz *si sint irs heiles vrô,* Ernst 1800.

p. 311.] *Gefjon* appears in Lokasenna ; conf. p. 861 n. Does hör-*gefn* mean lini datrix ? Sæm. 192[a] ; or is it akin to Gefn, Gefjon ?

p. 312.] Snöriz ramliga *Rân* or hendi giâlfr dŷr konûngs. Sæm. 153[b]. miök hefir Rân ryskt um mik, Egilss. p. 616. Rân lends Loki her *net,* to catch Andvari with, Sæm. 180. Fornald. sög. 1, 152. In the same way watersprites draw souls to them (p. 846). Later she is called *hafs-fruu :* ' *h.,* som râder öfver alla *hvilka omkomma på sjön* (perish at sea),' Sv. folks. 1, 126. ' Blef *sjö-tagen,* och kom til *hafsfruu* ' 132.

ez ist ein geloub der alten wîp,
swer in dem *wazzer* verliust den lîp (loses his life),
daz der sî *von Got vertriben.* Karajan on Teichner 41.

p. 313.] Slôu *î hel*, Vilk. s. 515. *î hel drepa*, Sæm. 78ᵃ. bita
fyl *til hälia* (bite a foal dead), Östgota-lag 213. höfut þitt leysto
*heljo or*, Sæm. 181ᵃ. *Hel* is a person in Sæm. 188ᵇ : 'er þik *Hel*
hafi!' in Egilss. 643 : 'Niörva nipt (Hel) *â nesi stendr.*'——The
*fara til Heljar* was German too (conf. p. 801-2) : Adam *vuor zuo
der helle*, und sîne afterkumen alle, Ksr-chr. 9225. *ze helle varn*,
Warn. 2447. 3220. 3310. ze helle *varn die hellevart*, Barl. 323,
28. *faren* zuo der hell = die, Seb. Brant's Narr. 57, 9. ze helle
varn, Ring 55ᵈ, 27; nu var du in die hell hinab, das ist *din haus*
30; ir muost nu *reuschen* in die hell 20. ich wolte mich *versloffen*
hân zuo der *helle* (Helle), Troj. kr. 23352. von der hell *wider
komen* (come back fr. hades), Brant's Narr. p. m. 207. in der
hell ist ein frau ân liebe (without love), Fastn. 558,13; spoken
of Hellia ? or of a dead woman ? Helle *speaks*, answers the devil,
Anegenge 39, 23. dô *sprach* diu Helle, Grieshaber 2, 147-8.
Bavarian stories of *Held* in Panzer's Beitr. 1, 60. 275. 297. Observe in Heliand 103, 9 : 'an *thene* suarton hel'; conf. p. 804.

p. 315.] Sic erimus cuncti postquam nos *auferet orcus*, Petron.
c. 34. *rapacis Orci aula* divitem manet herum, Hor. Od. ii. 18, 30.
at vobis male sit, malae *tenebrae orci*, quae omnia bella *devoratis*,
Cat. 3, 13. versperre uns (bar us out) vor der helle *munt*, Karajan 44, 1. der hellisch *rachen* steht offen, H. Sachs i. 3, 343ᶜ.
diu Helle gar ûf tet (opens wide) ir *munt*, Alb. v. Halb. 171ᵇ.
nu kan *daz verfluochte loch* nieman *erfullen* noch (that cursed hole
no man can fill), der wirt ist sô gîtic (greedy), Martina 160, 17 ;
conf. ' daz *verworhte hol* ' 172, 41. Yet MsH. 3, 233ᵇ has : davon
sô ist diu *helle vol*.——O. v. 23, 265 :

then tôd then habet funtan   Hell has found Death,
thiu *hella*, ioh firsluntan.   And swallowed him up.

Did Otfrid model this on 1 Cor. 15, 54-5 : ' Death is swallowed
up in victory. O Death, where is thy sting ? O Hades, where
thy victory ? ' Observe the Gothic version : ' ufsaggquiþs varþ
*dauþus* in sigis. hvar ist gazds þeins, *dauþu*? hvar ist sigis
þeins, *halja* ? ' It is a Christian view, that death is swallowed up ;

but most of the Greek MSS. have θάνατε both times, the Vulgate
both times *mors*, whilst Ulphilas divides them into *daupu* and *halja*,
and Otfrid makes hell find and swallow death.  To the heathens
halja was receiver and receptacle of the dead, she swallowed the
dead, but not death.  One Greek MS. however has θάνατε and ᾅδη
[suggested by Hosea 13, 14 ? 'Ero mors tua, O *Mors !* morsus
tuus ero, *Inferne !* '], Massm. 63[bb] ; and ᾅδης, infernus, in Matt.
11, 23.  Luke 10, 15.  16, 23 is in AS. rendered helle.  So in Irish
the two words in the Epistle are bais (death), uaimh (pit) ; in Gael.
bais and uaigh (grave).  The Serv. smrti and pakle, Lith. smertie
and pékla, smack of the Germ. death and hell; conf. Höfer's
Ztschr. 1, 122.——Westerg. in Bouterwek, Cædm. 2, 160, sub
v, *hel*, identifies it with Ssk. kâla, time, death, death-goddess,
and Kâlî, death-goddess.

p, 315 n.]  *Hellevôt* is a n. prop. in Soester's Daniel p. 173.
The following statement fits *Helvcetsluis*, the Rom. *Helium* :
Huglâci ossa in *Rheni* fluminis insula *ubi in oceanum prorumpit,*
reservata sunt,' Hpt's Ztschr. 5, 10.

---

## CHAPTER XIV.

## CONDITION OF GODS.

p. 318.]  The heathen notion of the *power* of the gods is esp.
seen in their being regarded as *wonder-workers,* who did not sink
into *sorcerers* till Christian times; conf. p. 1031. GDS. 770.  The
giants on the other hand were looked upon, even by the heathen,
as *stupid,* pp. 526-8-9.——The longevity of gods (long-aevi, lanc-
lîbon, Notk. Cap. 144) depends on simple food and a soul free
from care (p. 320-4).  So thinks Terence, Andr. 5, 5 : ego *vitam
deorum* propterea *sempiternam* esse arbitror, quod *voluptates*
eorum *propriae* sunt; and the dwarfs ascribe their long and
healthy lives to their honesty and temperance (p. 458).——
*Amrita* (Somad. 1, 127) is derived by Bopp, Gl. 17[a], from *a* priv.
and *mrita* mortuus, hence immortal and conferring immortality ;
and *ἀ-μβροσία* (279[a]) fr. *ἀ-μροσία, βροτός* being for *μροτός.*
Various accounts of its manufacture in Rhode's Relig. bildung d.
Hindus 1, 230.  It arises from the churning of the ocean, says
Holtzmann 3, 146—150, as ambrosia did from treading the wine-

press, K. F. Hermann's Gottesd. alth. p. 304. Doves carry ambrosia to Zeus, Od. 12, 63 ; conf. Athen. 4, 317. 321-5. Ambrosia
and nectar are handed to goddess Calypso, while Odysseus par-
takes of earthly food beside her, Od. 5, 199. Moirai eat the sweet
heavenly food of honey (p. 415 n.). Even the horses of gods have
in their manger ambrosia and nectar, Plato's Phædr. 247. Yet
the gods eat white ἄλφιτον, meal (Athen. 1, 434), which Hermes
buys for them in Lesbos. Ambrosial too is the odour shed around
the steps of deity (Suppl. to 327 end), of which Plautus says in
Pseud. iii. 2, 52 :

> ibi *odos* demissis pedibus in coelum volat;
> eum *odorem* coenat Juppiter cotidie.

What *nectar* is made of, we learn from Athen. 1, 147-8, conf.
166. ζωρότερον νέκταρ, Lucian's Sat. 7. purpureo bibit ore
nectar, Hor. Od. iii. 3, 12. Transl. in OHG. by *stanch, stenche,*
Graff 6, 696 ; in some glosses by *seim,* and if seim be akin to
αἷμα, our honig-seim still shows the affinity of honey to blood
(pp. 468. 902) ; consider the renovating virtue of honey as well as
blood : der *Saelden* honic-seim, Engelh. 5138.——The *spittle* of
gods is of virtue in making blood and mead (p. 902), in brewing
öl (ale): hann lagði fyri dregg *hráka* sinn, Fornald. sög. 2, 26.
Kvâsir is created out of spittle: so came Lakshmi out of the
milk-sea, Holtzm. 1, 130, as Aphroditē from foam, Sri from milk
and butter 3, 150.

p. 320.] The belief of the Greeks in the Immortality of their
gods was not without exceptions. In Crete stood a tomb with
the inscription : ' *Zeus* has long been *dead* (τεθνεὼς πάλαι), he
thunders no more,' Lucian's Jup. tragoed. 45; conf. p. 453 n.
Frigga's death is told by Saxo, ed. M. 44; dead Baldr appears
no more among the gods, Sæm. 63[b] ; then Freyr falls in fight
with Surtr, Týr with Garmr, Thôrr with miðgarðsormr; Oðinn
is swallowed by the wolf, Loki and Heimðall slay each other.
Duke Julius 302-3. 870 (in Nachtbüchlein, 883), says he has
heard that the Lord God was dead (the Pope ?).——Oðinn and
Saga *drink,* Sæm. 41[a]; Heimðall drinks mead 41[b], and always
' gladly ': drecka glöð 41[a]. dreckr glaðr 41[b] (p. 324). Thôrr *eats*
and *drinks* enormously, Sæm. 73[b]. Sn. 86, and a Norweg. tale of
his being invited to a wedding.

p. 321.]   Of a god it is said: ῥηϊδίως ἐθέλων, Od. 16, 198.
ῥηΐδιον θεοῖσι 211; of Circe: ῥεῖα παρεξελθοῦσα, Od. 10, 573.
Zeus can do the hardest things, οὐδὲν ἀσθμαίνων μένει, Æsch.
Eum. 651.   In Sn. formâli 12, Thôrr attains his full strength at
twelve years, and can lift *ten bear's hides at once*.   Wäinämöinen,
the day after his birth, walks to the smithy, and makes himself a
horse.

p. 322.]   *Got* ist noch liehter (brighter) denne der tac (day),
der antlitzes sich bewac (assumed a visage)
nâch *menschen antlitze*.   Parz. 119, 19.

It is a mark of the Indian gods, that they *cast no shadow, never
wink, glide* without touching the ground, are without *dust* or
*sweat* (their garments dustless), and their *garlands* never *fade*,
Holtzm. 3, 13. 19; conf. Bopp's Nalus p. 31.   Even men, going
into a temple of Zeus, cast no shadow, Meiners's Gesch. d. rel. 1,
427.——Oðinn appears as a '*mikli* maðr, herðimikill,' Fornm.
sög. 2, 180-1.   God has a *beard* : bien font a Dieu *barbe de fuerre*,
Méon 1, 310.   faire barbe de *paille* à Dieu, Dict. comique 1,
86-7.   Finn. *to see God's beard*=to be near him, Kal. 27, 200.
Vishnu is chatur-bhuja, four-handed, Bopp's Gl. 118[a]; Siva
three-eyed, ibid. p. 160-1.   Zeus too was sometimes repres. with
three eyes, Paus. ii. 24, 4; Artemis with three heads, Athen. 2,
152.   The Teut. mythol. has none of these deformities in its
gods; at most we hear of a Conradus *Dri-heuptl*, MB. 29[b], 85
(an. 1254).   *Yama*, the Indian death, is black, and is called *kâla*,
niger, Bopp's Gl. 71[b].   Vishnu in one incarnation is called
*Krishna*, ater, niger, violaceus, Slav. *chernyi* (Bopp 83[a]), so that
Cherni-bôgh would correspond to Krishna.——The beauty of the
gods has already been noticed p. 26 n.; that of the goddesses is
sufficiently attested by giants and dwarfs suing for them : Þrymr
wants Freyja, Þiassi Iðun, and the dwarfs demand the last favour
of Freyja.

p. 323.]   *Numen*, orig. a νεῦμα, nutus, means the nod of deity,
and deity itself, as Festus says (ed. O. Müller 173, 17) : numen
quasi nutus dei ac potestas dicitur.   Athena also ' nods ' with her
eyebrows : ἐπ' ὀφρύσι νεῦσε, Od. 16, 164.   Diu (frau Minne)
*winket* mir nû, daz ich mit ir gê, Walth. 47, 10; and Egilss.
p. 305-6 has a notable passage on letting the eyebrows fall.   Les

sorcils abessier, Aspr. 45ᵇ. sa (si a) les sorcils levez, Paris expt.
p. 104. Thôrr shakes his beard, Sæm. 70ᵃ.

The *anger, hatred, vengeance* of the gods was spoken of on
p. 18-9. They punish misdeeds, boasting, presumption. Their
*envy,* φθόνος, is discussed by Lehrs in Königsb. abh. iv. 1,
135 seq.; conf. θέλγειν (Suppl. to 331). τῶν τινος φθονερῶν
δαιμόνων μηχανὴ γέγονε, Procop. 2, 358. τῆς τύχης ὁ φθόνος
2, 178. ἐπήρεια δαίμονος = tantalizing behaviour of a god,
Lucian pro lapsu in salut. 1. Loki loves mischief when he brings
about the death of Baldr. So the devil laughs to scorn : der
tiuvel des lachet, Diut. 3, 52. smutz der tiuvel, welch ein rât !
Helbl. 5, 89. des mac der tiuvel lachen 15, 448 ; conf. the
laughing of ghosts (p. 945).

p. 324.] *Radii capitis* appear in pictures, Not. dign. orient.
pp. 53. 116. Forcellini sub. v. radiatus. Ztschr. des Hess. ver.
3, 366-7. ἀστραπὴν εἶδεν ἐκλάμψασαν ἀπὸ τοῦ παιδός, saw
lightning flash out of his son (Asklepios), Paus. ii. 26, 4. dô
quam unser vrôve zu ime, und *gotlîche schîne* gingen ûz irme
antlitze (fr. Mary's face), D. myst. 1, 219.

p. 325.] The Homeric gods are *without care,* αὐτοὶ δὲ τ'
ἀκηδέες εἰσίν, Il. 24, 526 ; they are blessed, serene, and rejoice in
their splendour. Zeus sits on Olympus, κύδεϊ γαίων (glad of his
glory), τερπι-κέραυνος (delighting in thunder), and looks down
at the smoking sacrifices of those he has spared. Ares too, and
Briareus are κύδεϊ γαίοντες. A god feels no pain : εἴπερ θεὸς γάρ
ἐστιν, οὐκ αἰσθήσεται, Aristoph. Frogs 634. So Grîpir is ' glaðr
konôngr,' Sæm. 172ʰ.——The gods *laugh*: γέλως δ' ἐπ' αὐτῷ
τοῖς θεοῖς ἐκινήθη, Babr. 56, 5; *risus Jovis* = vernantis coeli
temperies, Marc. Cap. (conf. giant Svâsuðr, p. 758). *subrisit
crudele* pater (Gradivus), Claudian in Eutr. 2, 109. Callaecia
*risit floribus* . . . . per herbam *fluxere* rosae, Claud. laus Serenae
71. 89. *riserunt floribus* amnes, Claud. Fl. Mall. 273 ; conf. laughing or sneezing out roses, rings, etc. Athena too is said to
μειδᾶν, Od. 13, 287.

p. 327.] For gods *becoming visible* Homer has a special word
ἐναργής : χαλεποὶ δὲ θεοὶ φαίνεσθαι ἐναργεῖς, Il. 20, 131. θεοὶ
φαίνονται ἐναργεῖς, Od. 7, 201. 16, 161. ἐναργὴς ἦλθε 3, 420.
ἐναργὴς συγγενόμενος, Lucian's Sat. 10.——Gods can appear and
vanish *as they please,* without any outward means : dwarfs and

men, to become invisible, need the tarn-hat or a miraculous herb.
No one can see them against their will: τίς ἂν θεὸν οὐκ ἐθέλοντα
ὀφθαλμοῖσιν ἴδοιτ' ἢ ἔνθ' ἢ ἔνθα κιόντα; Od. 10. 573.——As a
god can *hear* far off: κλύει δὲ καὶ πρόσωθεν ὢν θεός, Æsch. Eum.
287. 375; as 'Got und sîn muoter *sehent* dur die steine,' MS. 2,
12ᵃ; so gods and spirits enter locked and guarded chambers
unperceived, unhindered, Holtzm. 3, 11. 48.   Dame Venus comes
' dur *ganze mûren*,' p. 455-6; the Minne conducts 'durch der
kemenâten *ganze want*,' through the chamber's solid wall, Frib.
Trist. 796.   St. Thomas walks through a closed door, Pass. 248,
26-7.   Athena's messenger εἰσῆλθε παρὰ κληῖδος ἱμάντα, Od. 4,
802.   παρὰ κληῖδα λιάσθη 4, 838.   Loki slips through the *bora*
Sn. 356; and devils and witches get in at the keyhole.

Examples of *sudden appearance*, p. 400; *disappearance*, p.
951-2.   Oðinn, Höner, Loki in the Färöe poem, when invoked,
immediately appear and help.   Sudden appearing is expressed in
ON. both by the verb *hverfa* : þâ *hvarf* Fiölnir, Völsungas. c. 17;
and by the noun *svipr*, Fornald. sög. 1, 402.   Sæm. 157ᵃ. der engel
von himele *sleif*, Servat. 399.   dô sih der *rouh* ûf bouch, der
engel al damit flcuch, Maria 158, 2.   er *fuor* in die lüfte *hin*, die
wolken in bedacten, Urstende 116, 75; conf. 'rîða lopt ok lög,'
and p. 1070-1.   der *menschlich schîn* niht bleib lang, er *fuor*
*dahin*, Ls. 3, 263.   Homer uses ἀναΐσσειν of Ares and Aphrodite:
ἀναΐξαντε, Od. 8. 361; and the adv. αἶψα as well as καρπαλίμως
and κραιπνά, Il. 7, 272.   When Ovid. Met. 2, 785 says of Minerva : ' haud plura locuta fûgit, et impressā tellurem reppulit
hastā,' her dinting the ground with her spear expr. the ease of
her ascent.   Their speed is that of wind : ἡ δ' ἀνέμου ὡς πνοιὴ
ἐπέσσυτο (of Athena), Od. 6, 20.   sic effata *rapit* coeli per inania
*cursum* diva potens, *unoque* Padum translapsa *volatu*, castra sui
rectoris adit, Claud. in Eutr. 1, 375.   *Eros* is winged, Athen. 5,
29.   Winged angels, pennati pueri (p. 505).   Vishnu rides on
Garuda, Bopp's Gl. 102ᵃ.   Indra and Dharma as vulture and dove,
Somadeva 1, 70.   Holtzm. Ind. sagen 1, 81.   Though Athena
appears as a youth in Od. 13, 222, as a girl 13, 288, her favourite
shape is that of a *bird*: ὄρνις δ' ὡς ἀνοπαῖα διέπτατο 1, 320.
As *vultures*, she and Apollo settle on a beech-tree, and look
merrily on at men, Il. 7, 58.   As a *swallow*, she sits on the rooftree amid the fighters, and thence (ὑψόθεν ἐξ ὀροφῆς) uplifts

the ægis, Od. 22, 297; so Louhi sits a *lark* on the window of the smithy (Suppl. to 338), and the eagle in the dream ἕζετ' ἐπὶ προύχοντι μελάθρῳ, Od. 19, 544; conf. the vulture, who the moment he is named looks in at the door, Meinert's Kuhl. 165. 165. Bellona flies away a *bird*, Claud. in Eutr. 2, 230; Gestr, i.e. Oðin, as a *valr* (falcon), and gets a cut in his tail, Fornald. sög. 1, 487-8. Athena στῆ δὲ κατ' ἀντίθυρον κλισίης, Od. 16, 159; si mache sich schoen, und gê herfür *als ein götinne zuo der tür*, Renner 12227. When the unknown goddess steps inside the door, her stature reaches to the roofbeam, μελάθρου κῦρε κάρη, then in a moment she is recognised, Hymn to Aphrod. 174, to Ceres 189. A woman's spirit appears to a man in a dream: sîðan hvarf hun â brott; Olafr vaknaði, ok þóttist siâ *svip* konunnar, Laxd. 122. sîðan vaknaði Heðinn, ok sâ *svipinn* af Göndul, Fornald. sög. 1, 402. *svipr* einn var þar, Sæm, 157ᵃ.

*Fragrance* and *brightness* emanate from a deity, Schimmelpfeng 100-1. Hymn to Ceres 276—281 (Suppl. to 318); a *sweet smell* fills the house of Zeus, Athen. 3, 503. So with the Hebrews a *cloud*, a mist, or the *glory* of the Lord fills the house of the Lord, 1 Kings 8, 10-1; 2 Chron. 5, 13. comarum (of Venus) *gratus odor*, Claud. de nupt. Heaven breathes an *odor suavitatis*, that nourishes like food, Greg. Tur. 7, 1. The bodies of saints, e.g. Servatius, exhale a delicious odour (p. 823); conf. the *flowers* that spring up under the tread of feet divine (p. 330). The *hands* and *feet* of gods leave their *mark* in the hard stone, so do the *hoofs* of their horses (Suppl. to 664). Gods appear in *human form* and *disguise*, Oðinn often as a one-eyed old man, a beggar, a peasant, to Hrolf as *Hrani* bôndi (Hrani is a hero's name in Hervararsaga, Rani in Saxo).

p. 329.] The Indian gods *ride in chariots*, like the Grk: Indra, Agni, Varuna, etc., Nalus 15-6; 7 steeds draw the car of Sûryas the god of day, Kuhn's Rec. d. Rigveda 99. 100; Râtri, night, Uśa, aurora, are drawn by kine. Plato in Phædr. 246-7 speaks of the gods' *horses, chariots, charioteers*, of Zeus driving a *winged car*. Selēnē is appealed to: ποτ' ὠκεανὸν τρέπε πώλους, Theocr. 2,163. ἀστέρες, εὐκήλοιο κατ' ἄντυγα Νυκτὸς ὀπαδοί 2, 166.—— The German gods occasionally *drive* in star-chariots, or the stars themselves have a chariot, pp. 151. 723 n.; conf. the car-processions p. 336; the sun too drives a chariot: Sôl varp hendi

inni hoegri um himiniódȳr, Sæm. 1ᵇ (who is Vagnarunni in Egilss.
610, Oðinn or Thôrr?). But *riding* is the rule, though Loki says
to Frigg : ec þvî rêð, er þû *ríða* sêrat sîðan Baldr *at sölum*, Sæm.
63ᵇ ; even beasts ride in the Beast-apologue, Renart 10277-280-
460-920.

p. 330.] When Athena sits with Diomed in his war-chariot,
the axle groans with the weight: δεινὴν γὰρ ἄγεν θεὸν ἄνδρα
τ᾽ ἄριστον, Il. 5, 888. When Ceres nods, the cornfields shake:
annuit his, capitisque sui pulcherrima motu concussit gravidis
oneratos messibus agros, Ovid Met. 8, 780.

p. 331.] The gods appear in *mist* or *cloud*: Jehovah to Moses
in a pillar of fire, Deut. 31, 15. diva dimovit *nebulam*, juvenique
apparuit ingens, Claud. in Eutr. 1, 390. (Tritonia) *cava* circum-
data *nube*, Ov. Met. 5, 251. The merminne comes "mit eime
*dunste*, als ein wint," Lanz. 181; in the legend of Fosete the god
vanishes in a *caligo tenebrosa*, Pertz 2, 410. A cloud descends,
and the angel steps out of it, Girard de Viane p. 153.——Gods
and dæmons are said to θέλγειν, hoodwink, delude (conf. p.
463-4 of elves, and Suppl. to 322) : ἀλλά με δαίμων θέλγει, Od.
16, 195; of Hermes: ἀνδρῶν ὄμματα θέλγει, Il. 24, 343 : of
Poseidon: θέλξας ὄσσε φαεινά, Il. 13, 435 ; of Athena : τοὺς δὲ
Παλλὰς Ἀθηναίη θέλξει καὶ μητίετα Ζεύς, Od. 16, 298; θεὰ
θέλγει 1, 57; but also of Circe and the Sirens, Passow sub v.
θέλγω. Hera holds her hand over her protégé, ὑπερχειρία, Paus.
iii. 13, 6.——They take one by the hair : στῆ δ᾽ ὄπιθεν, ξανθῆς
δὲ κόμης ἕλε Πηλείωνα, Il. 1, 197 ; by the ear: Κρόνος προσ-
ελθὼν ὄπισθεν καὶ τοῦ ὠτός μου λαβόμενος, Lucian's Sat. 11.

p. 331.] The Grecian gods *sleep*, Athen. 2, 470; yet Ssk.
deus = *liber a somno*, Bopp's Gl. 26ᵃ. A *sick* god is healed by
incense, Walach. märchen p. 228. They are fond of *play* :
φιλοπαίγμονες γὰρ καὶ οἱ θεοί, Plato Cret. ed. bip. 3, 276. The
*kettledrums* of gods resound from heaven, and *flowers* rain down,
Nalus p. 181. 238 (conf. OHG. heaven is hung full of fiddles);
' it would please God in heaven (to hear that music),' Melander
2, no. 449. Got mohte wol *lachen* (at the tatermenlîn), Renn.
11526. Conf. the effects of music on mankind : when Salome is
ill, there come '*zwêne spilman* ûz Kriechen, die konden generen
(heal) die siechen mit irem senften spil, des konden sie gar vil,'
Morolf 1625 ; ' I have my fiddle by me, to make sick people well

and rainy weather jolly,' Goethe 11, 11; the tinkle of bells a cure for care, Trist. 398, 24. 39. 411, 9; song-birds cheer the tôt-riuwesære, Iwein 610. Aucassin's lay drives death away, Méon 1, 380. With the comforting of bereaved Skaði and Demeter conf. Wigal. 8475: ' sehs videlœre, die wolden im sîne swære (heaviness) mit ir videlen vertrîben,' and Creuzer's Symb. 4, 466. Athen, 5, 334. It was a Lith. custom to get the bride to laugh, Nesselm. sub v. prajûkinu. N. Preuss. prov. bl. 4, 312. A king's daughter, who has a fishbone in her throat, is made to laugh, Méon 3, 1 seq. The gods love to deal out largess, are datores, largitores, esp. Gibika (p. 137); conf. borg-geba (Suppl. to 274), oti-geba (p. 890 n.); they are âr-gefnar, öl-gefnar, crop-givers, ale-givers, Höstlöng ii. 2, 11 (Thorl. sp. 6, 34. 42. 50. 68).

p. 334.] *Gods' language* and *men's*, Athen. 1, 335. Lobeck's Aglaoph. 854. 858—867. Heyne on the first passage quoted, Il. 1, 403: quae antiquiorem sermonem et servatas inde appella-tiones arguere videntur. Like ON., the Indians have many words for cloud, Bopp's Gl. 16ª. 209ª. 136ᵇ. 158ᵇ; but do not attribute a separate language to the gods. Yet Somaveda 1, 59. 64 names the four languages Sanskrit, Prakrit, Vernacular and *Dœmonic.* The Greek examples can be added to: Πλαγκτὰς δ᾽ ἤτοι τάς γε θεοὶ μάκαρες καλέουσιν, Od. 12, 61. θνητοὶ Ἔρωτα, ἀθάνατοι δὲ Πτέρωτα, Plato's Phædr. 252. τὴν δ᾽ Ἀφροδίτην κικλήσκουσι θεοί τε καὶ ἄνερες, Hes. Theog. 197. The different expressions attrib. to *men* and *gods* in the Alvis-mâl, could no doubt be taken as belonging to *different* Teut. dialects, so that *Menn* should mean the Scandinavians, *Goðar* the Goths, and *sól* for instance be actually the Norse word, *sunna* the Old Gothic, GDS. p. 768. Kl. schr. 3, 221.

p. 335.] The Norse gods are almost all *married;* of Greek goddesses the only real *wife* is Hera. Gods fighting with heroes are sometimes *beaten,* and *put to flight,* e.g. Ares in Homer; and he and Aphroditē are *wounded* besides. Now Othin, Thor and Balder are also beaten in the fight with Hother (Saxo ed. M. 118), nay, Balder is *ridiculus fugâ* (119); but *wounding* is never mentioned, and of Balder it is expressly stated (113): *sacram corporis ejus firmitatem* ne ferro quidem cedere.

p. 335.] Apart from Brahma, Vishnu and Siva, the Indians

reckoned *thirteen minor* gods, Bopp's Gl. 160[a]. The former were *younger* gods, who had displaced the more elemental powers, Kuhn's Rec. d. Rigv. p. 101. Holtzm. Ind. sag. 3, 126 ; conf. ' got ein junger tôr ' (p. 7 n.). *Young* Zeus, old Kronos, Athen. 1, 473. cot *crôni*, deus recens, Graff 4, 299. The new year (p. 755). GDS. 765.

p. 336.] Mountain-heights are haunts of the Malay gods also, Ausld. 1857, 604[a]. πέτρα, δαιμόνων ἀναστροφή, Æsch. Eum. 23. *Olympus* descr. in Od. 6, 42—46. To the rock-caverns [at Ithaca] gods and men have separate entrances, those by the south gate, these by the north 13, 110-1-2. The Norse gods live in *Asgard*. Hreiðmarr cries to the Ases : haldit heim heðan, be off home from here ! Sæm. 182[b].——They have separate dwellings, but *near* together ; conf. the Donar's oak near Wuotan's mount (p. 170). þâr (î Baldurs-hage) voru *mörg goð*, Fornald. sög. 2, 63. Indian gods too have separate abodes : urbs *Kuvéri*, mons K. sedes, Bopp's Gl. 19[b]. 85[b]. Διὸς αὐλή, Lucian's Pseud. 19. Significant is the ON. : hefir ser um gerva sali, Sæm. 40-1-2.—— The gods sit on thrones or chairs (p. 136), from which they are entreated to *look down* in pity and protection : Ζεὺς δὲ γεννήτωρ ἴδοι, Æsch. Suppl. 206. ἐπίδοι δ' Ἄρτεμις ἁγνά 1031. *lita* vinar augom. The gods' houses are marked by *gates*, Hpt's Ztschr. 2, 535.

p. 337.] The gods often have a *golden staff*, with which they touch and transform : χρυσείῃ ῥάβδῳ ἐπεμάσσατ' Ἀθήνη, Od. 16, 172. 456. 13, 429 ; Circe strikes with her staff, Od. 10, 238 ; conf. Hermes' rod, the wishing-rod (p. 976) and other wishing-gear. Shiva has a miraculous bow, so has Indra acc. to the Vedas. Apollo's bow carries plague ; conf. Oðin's spear (p. 147). In Germ. märchen the fays, witches, sorcerers carry a trans-figuring staff (p. 1084).

Gods are regarded by men as *fathers*, goddesses as *mothers* (pp. 22. 145. 254). They delight in men, ἀνδράσι τερπόμενοι, Il. 7, 61 ; their kindly presence is expr. by the Homeric ἀμφι-βαίνω : ὅς Χρύσην ἀμφιβέβηκας, Il. 1, 37. ὃς Ἴσμαρον ἀμφι-βεβήκει, Od. 9, 198. They love to come down to men ; conf. Exod. 3, 8 : κατέβην, descendi, hwearf (p. 325) ; they stop their chariots, and descend to earth, Holtzm. 3, 8. Nalus p. 15. *praesentes caelicolae*, Cat. 64, 383. Like the Ind. avatâra is a θεοῦ ἐπιδημία (visitation), Lucian's Conviv. 7. Gods are not omnipresent, they are often *absent*, they *depart*, Athen. 2, 470. Jupiter says: summo delabor Olympo, et deus humanā lustro sub imagine terras, Ov. Met. 1, 212. In the Faröe lay, Oðinn, Hoenir and Loki appear *instantly*. (Appearing to a man can be expr. by *looking under his eyes*, Etm. Orendel pp. 73. 45. 83. 102.) The passage: di liute wânden (weened) *er waere Got von himel*, Griesh. 2, 48, presupposes a belief in God's appearing (p. 26 n.). so ritestu heim als *waer Got do*, Dancrotsh. namenb. 128, and: if God *came down from heaven* and bade him do it, he would not, Thurneisser 2, 48. At Whitsun the street was hung with tapestry: als ochter *God selve comen soude*, Lanc. 31321. God (or his image) loves a place where he is made much of: Got möhte lieber niht *gestên ûf der erden* an deheiner stat, Helbl. 15, 584; 'here *dwells* der liebe Gott,' p. 20 n. His return to heaven is expr. by: 'do *vuor Got ze himele* in deme gesuneclicheme bild,' Diemer 7, 19; conf. 'ego in coelum migro,' Plaut. Amph. v. 2, 13.——Gods send *messengers, angels*, those of Greece Hermes, Iris, etc., who *escort* men (p. 875), and inspect and report the goings-on of the world, says a pretty Servian song by Gavrai. It is worth noting in the prol. to Plaut. Rudens, that Arcturus shines in heaven at night, but walks the earth by day as messenger of Jove. Gods assist at christenings (Godfather Death), weddings, betrothals, Holtzm. 3, 8; and Mary too lifts a child out of the font, Wend. märch. 16. They hallow and bless men by laying on of hands: vîgit ocr saman *Varar hendi*, Sæm. 74ᵇ. Apollon und Tervigant, ir beider got, hât *sîne hant den zwein geleit ûf daz houbet*, daz si helfe unberoubet und gelückes (unrobbed of help and luck) solden sîn, mit götlîcher helfe schîn geschach daz ir, Turl. Wh. 112ᵃ; like a priest or father.——Gods deal with men *in their sleep*: a rib is taken out of sleeping Adam, to make Eve; Athena sheds sweet sleep over Penelope, while she makes her taller and fairer, Od. 18, 188; Luck comes near the sleeper, gods raise up the fallen hero, Il. 7, 272. Their *paltry-looking gifts* turn out precious (Berhta's, Holda's, Rübezahl's): the *leaves* turn into *gold*, the more fittingly as Glasir the grove of the gods bears golden leafage.

p. 338.] Metamorphosis is expr. by *den lîp verkêren*, Barl. 250, 22. sich kêrte z'einem tiere 28. Oðinn viðbrast î *vals* lîki,

when Heiðrekr and Tyrfîng attack him, Fornald. sög. 1, 487.
Loki changes into a *mare*, and has a foal (Sleipnir) by Svaðilfari,
Sn. 47. falsk Loki î *lax* lîki, Sæm. 68ᵇ. Sn. 69. Heimðallr ok
Loki î *sela* lîkjum, Sn. 105. Loki sits in the window as a
*bird* 113; conf. Athena as a swallow on the roof-beam (p. 326).
Louhi as a *lark* (leivonen) in the *window* (ikkuna), Kal. 27,
182-5-8. 205. 215 (conf. Egilss. p. 420), or as a *dove* (kyyhky)
on the *threshold* (kynnys) 27, 225-8. 232. Berhta looks in,
hands things in, through the *window* (p. 274); the snake looks
in at window, Firmen. 2, 156. Louhi, pursuing Sampo, takes the
shape of an *eagle*. denique ut (Jupiter) ad Trojæ tecta volarit
*avis*, Prop. iii. 30, 30. Jupiter *cycnus* et candidorum procreator
*ovorum*, Arnob. 1, 136 (pp. 666. 491). In märchens a *bear, eagle,
dolphin*, carries off the princess.

p. 338.] Gods may become men as a *punishment*. Dyaus
having stolen a cow, all the Vasu gods are doomed to be born
men. Eight of them, as soon as born, return to the world of
gods; the ninth, the real culprit, must go through a whole
human life, Holtzm. Ind. sag. 3, 102-6.

p. 339.] Real names (not merely epithets) of gods often
become abstract ideas in Sanskrit. Indra, at the end of a compound, is princeps, dominus, Bopp 40ᵃ; Šrî is prefixed to
other names reverentiae causa, as Šrîganêša, Šrîmahabhârata
357ᵃ. In ON. one âs can stand for another, as Bragi for Oðinn
in the saw, 'nioti bauga sem *Bragi* auga,' Egilss. 455. So
Freya, Nanna, Týr, Baldr become abstract terms (p. 220-1):
*baldr* brynþîngs, *b.* fetilstînga, Fornm. sög. 6, 257. 12, 151. enn
norðri *niörðr* 6, 267. geir*niörðr*=heros, Sæm. 266ᵇ. Conf.
*Gotes* intensive (p. 19).

---

# CHAPTER XV.

## HEROES.

p. 341.] On demigods, great gods, dæmones, conf. Boeckh's
Manetho, p. 488; semidei, heroes, Arnob. 2, 75. The *hero* has
superhuman strength, ON. hann er eigi *einhamr*, Fornm. sög. 3,
205-7; einhamr, einhama signif. mere human strength. It is
striking how the Usipetes and Tenchtheri glorify human heroes

to Caesar, B. G. 4, 7 : ' we yield to none but the Suevi, for whom
*the immortal gods are no match.'*

p. 343.] To *vir*, OHG. *wer*, are prob. akin the Scyth. οἰόρ,
Fin. *uros*, Kal. 13, 64. 21, 275. 290 ; conf. Serv. *urosh* (p. 369 n.).
GDS. 236. Aug. Civ. Dei 10, 21. K. F. Herm. Gottesd. alt.
p. 69. M. Neth. *hêlt* as well as helet, Stoke 3, 4. Notker's
*hertinga*, AS. *heardingas*, El. 25. 130, recall Boh. *hrdina*, Pol.
*hardzina* (hero), conf. Boh. hrdý, Pol. hardy, Russ. górdyi
(proud), Fr. hardi, G. hart, herti (hard). Arngrîm's eleventh
and twelfth sons are called *Haddingjar*, Fornald. sög. 1, 415-6-7.
GDS. 448. 477. himelischer *degen* in the Kl. 1672. *degenîn*,
heroine, Renn. 12291. With *wîgant* conf. the name Weriant
freq. in Karajan. Jesus der Gotes wîgant, Mos. 68, 10. *Kämpe*
may be used of a giant, Müllenh. 267. 277 ; beside cempa, the
AS. has *oretta*, heros, pugil. Is not ON. *hetja* (bellator) strictly
wrestler, fencer ? conf. OHG. *hezosun*, palaestritae, Graff 4, 1073.
GDS. 578. With OHG. *wrecchio*, AS. *wrecca* [whence, wretch,
wretched], agrees best the description of the *insignes* in Tac.
Germ. 31 : Nulli domus aut ager aut aliqua cura ; prout ad
quemque venere, aluntur prodigi alieni, contemptores sui. Diomed is ἀνὴρ ἄριστος, Il. 5, 839. Heroes are *róg-birtîngar*, bright
in battle, Haralda-mâl 16. Serv. *yunák*, hero, *yunáshtvo*,
heroism ; so MHG. die mîne *jungelinge*, Fundgr. 2, 91, conf.
Nib. 1621, 2, and the heroic line of the *Ynglîngar* (p. 346). Ir.
*trean* hero ; also *faolchu* hero, strictly wild wolf, falcon, and
Welsh *gwalch*, falcon, hero ; conf. Serv. *urosh* (p. 369 n.).

p. 344.] Heroes derive their lineage fr. the gods : Sigurðr
ormr î auga is expressly *Oðins aettar*, Fornald. sög. 1, 258 ; the
Scythian Idarthyrsus counts Zeus his ancestor, Herod. 4, 126 ;
and Zeus does honour to Menelaus as his son-in-law, γαμβρὸς
Διός, Od. 4, 569. They are *friends* of the gods : Zeus loves both
champions, Hector and Ajax, Il. 7, 280 ; there are ' friends of
Ares ' and a ' Frey's vinr.' They can multiply the kindred of
the gods. Jupiter's children are reckoned up in Barl. 251, 37
seq.; Alexander too is a son of Jupiter Ammon or Nectanebus by
Olympias. ' Galli se omnes ab *Dite patre* prognatos praedicant ;
idque ab druidibus proditum dicunt,' Caes. 6, 18. Dietrich
descends fr. a spirit, Otnit fr. Elberich, Högni fr. an elf, and
Merlin fr. the devil.

p. 345.]   As Teutonic tradition made Tuisco a 'terrā editus,' the American Indians have a belief that the human race once lived *inside the earth*, Klemm 2, 159.  Though Norse mythology has no Mannus son of Tuisco, yet it balances Goðheimr with a Mannheimr, GDS. 768, conf. Vestmanland, Södermanland, Rask on Ælfred's Periplus 70-1 ; and Snorri's Formâli 12 places a *Munon* or *Mennon* at the head of the tribes.  He, with Priam's daughter Trôan, begets a son Trôr = Thôr, fr. whom descends Loritha = Hlôrriða, conf. Fornald. sög. 2, 13.  GDS. 195.  The American Indians have a first man and maker *Manitu,* Klemm 2, 155-7.  On the mythic pedigree of Mannus and his three sons, see GDS. 824 seq.

p. 346.]   *Ingo* was orig. called *Ango*, says Mannhdt's Ztschr. 3, 143-4.  He is the hero of the Ingaevones, who included the Saxons and formerly the Cheruscans, consequently the Angles, Angern, Engern (GDS. 831. 629. 630), whose name is perhaps derived from his.

p. 350.]   Did Dlugoss in his Hist. Polon. draw fr. Nennius? Jrb. d. Berl. spr. ges. 8, 20 ; conf. Pertz 10, 314.

p. 350 n.]   *Ascafna-burg*, fr. the rivulet Ascafa = Ascaha, is likewise interpr. in Eckehardus' Uraug. as '*Asken-burg* ab Ascanio conditore,' and is a castellum antiquissimum, Pertz 8, 259. 578.  On *Asc* and *Ascanius* conf. p. 572.

p. 351.]   The old Lay of Patricius 19, ed. Leo. p. 32-3, has *Eirimoin* (Erimon).  *Heremon* in Diefenb. Celt. 2[b], 387-9. 391.

p. 355.]   A communication fr. Jülich country says, *Herme* is used as a not very harsh nickname for a strong but lubberly man. But they also say, ' he works like a *Herme,*' *i.e.* vigorously ; and legend has much to tell of the giant strength of Herme ; conf. Strong *Hermel*, KM. 3, 161.  Herman, Hermanbock, Maaler 218[b]. Firmen. 1, 363[b] : ' to make believe our Lord is called *Herm.*' Lyra Osnabr. 104 : ' du menst wual, use Hergott si 'n aulen *Joost Hierm.*'   It is remarkable that as early as 1558, Lindner's Katziporus O, 3[b] says of a proud patrician, who comes home fuller of wine than wit : ' he carries it high and mighty, who but he ? and thinks our Lord is called *Herman.*'  On the rhyme ' Hermen, sla dermen,' suggestive of the similar ' Hamer, sla bamer, sla busseman doet ' (p. 181-2), conf. Woeste pp. 34. 43. Firmen. 1, 258. 313. 360.

p. 357 n.] Other foreign names for the *Milky Way*. American Indian : the *way of ashes*, Klemm 2, 161. In Wallach. fairy-tales, pp. 285. 381, it comes of *spilt straw* that St. Venus (Vinire) has stolen from St. Peter. In Basque : ceruco esnebidea, simply via lactea, fr. eznea milk. Τὰς εἰς οὐρανὸν ψυχῶν νομιζο-μένας ὁδούς, Lucian's Encom. Demosth. 50. Lettic : *putnu zel-ch*, bird-path, Bergm. 66 (so πόρος οἰωνῶν, aether, Æsch. Prom. 281) ; also *Deeva yahsta*, God's girdle 115, or is that the rainbow ? (p. 733). *Arianrod* is also interpr. corona septen-trionalis, though liter. silver-circle. For the many Hungar. names see Wolf's Ztschr. 2, 162-3.

Other Teutonic names. East Fris. dat *melkpath*, and when unusually bright, *harmswíth*, Ehrentr. Fries. arch. 2, 73. With *galaxia* they seem to have conn. *Galicia* ; hence to Charlemagne, at the beginning of the Turpin, appears *James Street*, leading from France to Galicia. In Switzld : der weg uf *Rom*, Stutz 1, 106. Westph.: *mülenweg* (Suppl. to 924), also *wiärstrate*, weather-street, Woeste p. 41 ; so in Jutland *veirveien*, Molb. Dial. lex. 646, as well as *arken* 18. To ON. *vetrarbraut*, winter-way, corresp. the Swed. *vintergatan ;* conf. Gothl. *kaldgotu*, Almqv. 432, unless this be for Karl's-gate. Do *sunnûnpad, sterrôno stráza, wega wolkóno* in Otfrid i. 5, 5 mean the galaxy ? conf. the *path of clouds*, Somadeva 2, 153-7. 58. 61. Journ. to Himavan 1, 106. *Heer-strasze* (-gasse), viz. that of the ' wütende heer,' in Meier's Schwäb. sag. 137-9 ; *herstrasz*, Mone 8, 495 ; Up. Palat. *hyrstrausz, heerweg*, Bergm. 115-8. 124 ; *helweg* (p. 801-2). Most import. for mythol. are : *frauen Hulden strasze, vron Hilden straet, Pharaïldis sidus* (p. 284-5) ; also ' galaxa, in duutsche die *Brunelstraet*,' Naturk. von broeder Thomas (Clariss's Gheraert, p. 278).

p. 361.] As we have Iuuâringes-weg and Eurings-strasz by the side of *Iringesweg*, so in oldish records Eurasburg castle is called *Iringesburg*, Schm. 1, 96. *Irinc* is in Nib. 1968 a young man, 1971-89 a markgraf and Hâwartes man, and in the Klage 201. 210 ze Lütringe geborn. On the meaning of the word conf. pp. 727. 1148. Kl. schr. 3, 234. F. Magnussen in his Pref. to Rîgsmâl connects (as I had done in my Irmenstrasse 1815, p. 49) the *Ericus* of Ansgar and the *Berich* of Jornandes with *Rîgr*, as also the *Eriksgata ;* conf. the devil's name *gammel Erich*

(p. 989). That Erich was a deified king is plain from a sentence in the Vita Anskarii cited above: 'nam et templum in honore supradicti regis *dudum* defuncti statuerunt, et ipsi tanquam deo vota et sacrificia offerre coeperunt.'

p. 363 n.] Suevi a monte *Suevo*, Chr. Salern., Pertz 5, 512. a *Suevio* monte, Hpt's Ztschr. 4, 493. GDS. 323.

p. 365.] On the *castra Herculis* by Noviomagus, Ammian. Marc. 18, 2. With the giant bones of Hugleich at the Rhine-mouth (Hpt's Ztschr. 5, 10) we may even conn. the Herculis columna which stood there (p. 394). On Herc. Saxanus, Mann-hdt's Germ. mythen p. 230; on the inscriptions, Mythol. ed. 1, p. 203. Herculi in *Petra*, Gruter 49, 2. πεδίον λιθῶδες on the Rhone, Preller 2, 147. Wolfram's Wh. 357, 25. 386, 6. 437, 20.

p. 366.] Like *Castor and Pollux*, there appear in Teut. tales two youths, angels, saints, in a battle, or putting out a fire (Suppl. to Pref. xliii. end): '*duo juvenes candidis circumamicti stolis,* animam a corpore segregantes, vacuum ferentes per aërem,' Jonas Bobb. in Vita Burgundofarae (Mabillon 2, 421); conf. p. 836-7. *duo juvenes in albis,* putting out a fire, in Annal. Saxo p. 558. Chronogr. Saxo in Leibn. 122 fr. Einh. Ann., Pertz 1, 348. Again, the angel wiping the sword in Roth's Sermons p. 78, and the destroying angel. Lithuanian legends have a giant *Alcis,* Kurl. sendungen 1, 46-7. *Jalg* eða *Jalkr,* Sn. 3; jalkr = senex eviratus, says F. Magn.

p. 367 n.] Note, in the Pass. 64, 41 : ein *wuotegôz* unreiner = Wuotilgôz: conf. '*wüetgusz* oder groz wasser,' Weisth. 3, 702. and 'in *wuetgussen,* eisgussen und groszen stürmen, 3, 704. Also p. 164, and *Wuetes, Wüetens,* Schm. 4, 203. GDS. 440. 774-5.

p. 368.] *Sigi* is Oðin's son, Sn. 211[a]. So is *Hildólfr,* ibid., 'Harbarð's lord,' Sæm. 75[b], OHG. Hiltwolf. So is *Sigrlami,* Fornald. sög. 1, 413, and has a son *Svafrlami.* So is *Nefr* or *Nepr,* Sn. 211[a], and has a daughter Nanna 31. 66. So is *Sœ-mîngr,* Sn. 211[a], *Semîngr* in Hervarars., Fornald. s. 1, 416; conf. *Sâmr, Sâms-ey,* Rask's Afh. 1, 108. The name of *Gautr,* Oðin's son or grandson, is conn. with giezen (pp. 23. 105 n. 142. 164. 367); on Gautr, Sn. 195. Oðinn is called *Her-gautr,* Egilss. p. 624, alda *gautr,* Sæm. 95[b]. 93[b]; conf. Caozes-pah, -prunno (-beck, -burn), Hpt's Ztschr. 7, 530.

p. 370.] The accounts of *Sceáf* in AS. chronicles are given by Thorpe, Beow. p. 4. In the same way Beaflor sails alone in a ship, a bundle of straw under his head, Mai 35-9, arrives 51-3, sails away again 152 ; the ship gets home 180, 39. Horn also comes in a ship, and sends it home with greetings. A Polish legend says of Piast : qui *primus appulerit* in navicula, dominus vester erit, Procosius p. 47. As the swan-children can lay aside the swan-ring, so can the *Welfs* the *wolf-girdle* or whelp-skin. Klemm 2, 157 has a remarkable story of beautiful children slipping off their *dog-skin.* 'Skilpunt' in Karajan's Salzb. urk. must be for *Skilpunc.* Oðinn is a *Skilfingr,* Sæm. 47. Did the *f* and *b* in Scilfing, Scilbunc arises out of *v* in *skildva?* The Goth. skildus has its gen. pl. skildivê.

p. 371.] Kl. schr. 3, 197. To the *Gibichen-steine* enumer. in Hpt's Ztschr. 1, 573, and the *Gebiches-borse* in Weisth. 3, 344 (borse, Graff 3, 215), add *Geveken-horst,* Möser 8, 337. Dorow's Freckenh. 222, and AS. *Gificancumb,* Kemble no. 641 (yr. 984). The Nibel., which does not mention the Burgundian Gibeche, has a fürste or künec *Gibeke* at Etzel's court 1283, 4. 1292, 2. The Lex Burg. 3 says : apud regiae memoriae auctores nostros, id est, Gibicam, Godomarem, Gislaharium, Gundaharium. Greg. Tur. 2, 28 : Gundeuchus rex Burgundionum ; huic fuere quatuor filii, Gundobaldus, Godegisilus, Chilpericus, Godomarus.

p. 371.] The diffusion of the *Völsûnga-*saga among the Anglo-Sax. is evidenced by '*Välsing*' and '*Välses* eafera' in Beow. 1747-87. The Völsungs have the snake's eye (Suppl. to 392, mid.). The tale of *Säufritz* is told in Bader no. 435.

p. 371 n.] Mars *segumon, vincius,* Stälin 1, 112. Glück 150 says, *segomo* in nom. De Wal. no. 246 (1847). Can it be the same as ἡγεμών, dux ?

p. 373.] Oðinn himself is called *helblindi,* and Helblindi is the name of a *wolf* (p. 246). Beaflor is said to have give birth to a wolf, Mai 132, 9 ; conf. the story of the 12 babies named Wolf, Müllenh. p. 523, and that of the blind dogs, Pliny 8, 40.

p. 374.] *Pillung,* MB. 9, 10 (yr. 769). Hermann *Billing,* Helmold 1, 10. *Billung* in the Sassen-chron., conf. Förstemann 1, 258. 2, 225. Oda, grandmother of Henry the Fowler, was the daughter of a Frankish noble *Billung* and Aeda, Pertz 6, 306. tome *Billingis-hûge,* Gl. to the Ssp. 3, 29 ; conf. regulus Obotritorum nomine *Billug*, Helm. 1, 13. What means '*pillungs ein wênic verrenket*' in the Hätzlerin 180, 37?

p. 376.] In *Eigls-perge*, MB. 28, 2, 173 (Passau urbar.). Juxta portam quae de *Eigeles* (at Cologne), Lacomblet 318, yr. 1134.

p. 378.] The Heldensage p. 288 has *two* sons of Wieland, [full] brothers: *Wittich* and *Wittich von der aue*; conf. Lat. *Silvanus*, a forest-god of secondary rank: Silvani lucus extra murum est avius crebro salicto oppletus, Plaut. Aul. iv. 6, 8. Ought we to read *Viltinus* for Vilkinus? Hpt's Ztschr. 6, 446. Schott conn. *Wate* with Wuotan, Introd. to Gudr. lvi. To things named after Wieland add the *Wielandstein*, Schwab's Alp. p. 136 seq.; after Galans a *pratum Galandi*, now *Préjelan* in Bourgogne, Garnier's Pagi Burg. p. 83. Dan. *Velants-urt*, also *velamsrot*, *vendelsrot*, Dyb. 1845, 49. 50. On *Wielets*-kinder conf. Schm. sub v. Valföður *vél* framtelja, patris artem (mysterium?) enarrare, Sæm. 1ª. Another point of likeness betw. *Wieland* and *Hephœstos* is, that both are masters of forging dwarfs (p. 471-2). Their handiwork was famous: ἔργον Ἡφαίστοιο, Od. 4, 617. 15, 116. οὓς Ἥφαιστος ἔτευξε 7, 92.

p. 380.] '*Mime* the old' in Bit. 138 seems to have a short *i*, and can hardly belong here. Karajan in Verbrüd. von S. Peter has *Mimilo*, *Mimistein*. To *Mimigerneford* (conf. Ledebur's Bructeri p. 328), perhaps from an adj. mîmi-gern, and *Mîmidun* (Mîmidomensis = Mindensis, Lappbg no. 25; Mimende on Weser, Schrader's Dyn. 104), add a third Westph. locality *Mimegersen*, now Memsen in Hoya country, Lappbg no. 48. Again, *Mimmelage* near Osnabrück. *Mimirberh*, perhaps Mimisberh, Pertz 8, 776. The names Memeln-brun, -born, Memel-born, Memilsdorf, Henneb. urk. 2, nos. 153-6. 169. 1, 166. 125, and Memelen-born (Melborn by Eisenach), Thür. Ztschr. 4, 210 suggest the *Mîmis brunnr* of the Edda. With *Mimingus*, silvarum satyrus, agrees the sword's name in En. 5694; conf. Mumminc, Upstdge 137, (Muma in Thidrekss. 65). There are yet to be considered *Söckmîmir*, Sæm. 46ᵇ; *Hoddmîmir* who dwells î holti 37; *Mimsvinr*, *Mimisvinr*, Egilss. 641. Like *Mîmi's head* is Virgil's head which prophesies, MSH. 4, 246. A head of brass prophesies in Val. et Ourson c. 25; enn *spinnen-hoofd* in the Dutch transl. arose perhaps from taking tête d'airain for t. d'araigne. Heads often speak in churches, F. Magn. Edda-laere 2, 264.

p. 383.] On *Tell* conf. Böhmer's Reg. p. 197 and Sinner in the Solothurner Wtb. 1845, p. 198. Th. Platter 87 (abt 1532) names him Wilhelm *Täll*, and Garg. 180ᵇ Wilh. *Dell*, while Rabelais 1, 23 does not mention him. A picture of Tell in Schwzbg's Memorial 116ᵃ. Some stories make the son shoot the apple off the father's head. *Schützeichel* is at this day a family-name at Bonn, Simrock's Edda p. 396.

Many single heroes remain to be considered, such as *Poppo* the strong, Hpt's Ztschr. 3, 239, conf. 8, 347; *Hugleich* 5, 10. Also lines of heroes: stirps *Immidingorum* (Saxon) et *Erbonum* (Bavar.), Pertz 8, 226.

p. 383.] The god must stand at the head of the line, because he passes for the *father* and *grandfather* of the men. Still there remains an enormous difference between gods and men; hence in Saxo, ed. M. 117, the (earthly) Nanna rejects the suit of Balder: nuptiis deum mortali *sociari non posse,* quod ingens naturae discrimen copulae commercium tollat . . . . supernis terrestria *non jugari.*

p. 385 n.] Saxo calls Othin, Thor, etc. merely *opinative*, not *naturaliter* deos (ed. M. 118), and Balder a *semideus* (conf. p. 340); whereupon P. E. Müller om Saxo p. 54 remarks: Odin lived neither before nor after Christ. Old Conrad in his Troj. Kr. 858—911 is not quite of that opinion: ' si wâren liute als ir nu sît, wan daz (they were men like you, only) ir *krefteclîch gewalt* was michel unde manicvalt von *kriutern* und von *steinen* . . . . ouch lepten gnuoge (lived plenty) bî der zît, die *zouberaere* wâren, und *wunder* in den jâren mit *gougelwise* worhten (with jugglery wrought).' How the old gods were degraded into *conjurors*, is shown p. 1031.——Of the *deification* of men there are plenty of examples: ' daz kint waere *mit den goten ein got*,' Pass. 298, 27. The heathen adore *Sigelôt* as a god, Rol. 198, 21. *Ipomidon* will be a god himself, Tit. 3057. 4147-60. er wolde got hien erde sîn, Diemer 139, 24. als er iz waere got 131, 22. mîn wirde gelîch den goten steic, Turl. Wh. 66ᵃ. Of Caligula: ' wart hi so sot, dat hi *wilde wesen god*, ende hi seide openbare dat hi Jupiters broeder ware,' Maerl. 2, 236, conf. 333. ' Grambaut, roi de Baviere, se nommoit *dieu en terre*,' and called his castle *Paradis*, Belle Helène p.m. 23. The Mongols practise the *worship of ancestors, deific. of rulers*, Klemm 3, 194-5; also veneration of saints and relics.

p. 392.] The Greeks required *beauty of form* in heroes as well as gods, Lucian's Charid. 6. 7. Of Charlem. it is said : *anges resemble du ciel ius devolé*, Aspr. 21ᵃ. Heroes share the *lofty stature* of gods. Of *Huglâcus* the legend says : quem equus a duodecimo anno portare non potuit ; cujus *ossa* in Rheni fluminis insula, ubi in oceanum prorumpit, *reservata* sunt, et de longinquo venientibus pro miraculo *ostenduntur* (Suppl. to 365).——*Many-handedness* is often mentioned. Ancient men with *four hands, four feet*, and *two faces*, Plato symp. 189, *four ears* 190. ἐξ γὰρ χεῖρες ἑκάστῳ ἀπ' ὤμων ἀΐσσοντο, Orph. arg. 519. Men with 8 toes, 6 hands, Megenb. 490, 2. 30 ; conf. gods and giants (p. 527). From the three-handed and three or four-elbowed *Heime* (Germ. 4, 17) perh. the *Heimenstein* takes its name, about which there is a folk-tale, G. Schwab's Alb pp. 161—165. A story about ' *so Heyne, so*,' who helps to raise a treasure, in H. v. Herford, Potth. p. 93 ; conf. Brîsînga-men (p. 306). A three-headed figure on the Gallehus horn discov. 1734 (Henneb., plate 2).——Most akin to the gods seem those heroes who are favoured with a *second birth*. (p. 385). The fact of many heroes' names being repeated in their descendants may have to do with this belief, GDS. 441. But Helgi and Svava are genuine *endrbornir*, Sæm. 148. 169. 159ᵇ. As late as in MS. 1, 97ᵇ we read : ' sturbe ich nâch ir minne, und *wurde ich danne lebende*, sô wurbe ich aber umbe daz wîp (I would woo her again).' Contrariwise MS. 1, 69ᵇ : ' sô bin ich doch ûf anders niht *geborn*.' Solinus says Scipio was another of the *Unborn*, and was therefore called Cæsar, Maerl. 1, 401 ; conf. the Lay of Mimmering tand, Danske Vis. 1, 100.——Karna, son of the Sun, was *born with earrings and a coat of mail*, Holtzm. 2, 123-9. 136. wart ie man *mit wâfen geborn*, Krone 10534 ; conf. ' born with a fiddle.' To phenomena occurring at the birth of a hero, add the storm that attended Alexander's, Pseudocallisth. p.m. 12. Alcmena tests Hercules with snakes, which he kills lying *in his cradle*, as Sigmund does Sinfjötli by kneading the dough that had snakes in it, Völs. saga c. 7. Kullervo, when 3 *nights old*, tears up his swathings, Castrén 2, 45. In the Sv. folks. 1, 139. 140, the child walks and talks as soon as born. Of the grown-up hero's strength the examples are countless. Tied to an oak, he pulls it up, Sv. forns. 1, 44. Danske V. 1, 13 ; Beowulf has in his hand the strength of *thirty*, Beow. 756. They *eat* and *drink enormously*, like Thôrr (Suppl. to 320); so Hammer grâ, Sv. forns. 1, 61-2, conf. the giant bride 1, 71-2. Syv. 49.——Heroes have beaming *godlike eyes, snake's eyes, ormr î auga;* so have kings, Saxo, ed. M. p. 70. Aslög's son (Sigurð's and Brynhild's grandson) is called Sigurðr *ormr-î-auga,* gen. Sigurðar orms-î-auga, Fornald. s. 1, 267. 273. 2, 10-4. Fornm. 1, 115. His stepbrothers say : eigi er oss î augum *ormr* ne *frânir snâkar,* Fornald. 1, 268 (conf. orm frânn, Heimskr. 7, 238. Sæm. Hafn. 2, 13). Sigurðr Oðins aettar, þeim er *ormr î auga,* Fornald. 1, 258. Aslög prophesies of her unborn son : 'enn â þeim sveini mun vera þat mark, at svâ mun þikkja, sem *ormr liggi um auga* sveininum '—a false interpretation, for not the eyebrows coiling round, but the inner look (*î* auga) was meant, Fornald. 1, 257. In Sæm. 187[a] he is called 'inn *frân-eygi* sveinn.' brann Brynhildi *eldr or augom* (fire flashed from B.'s eyes) 215[b]. âmun (minaces) eru *augu ormi þeim enum frâna* (Völundr) 156[a]. *hvöss eru augu î* Hagals þŷju (Helgi in disguise) 158[b]. We still say : something great shines out of his eyes. GDS. 126-7.——Other heroes show other marks : on Hagen's breast is a *golden cross,* Gudr. 143-7. 153; betw. Wolfdietrich's shoulders a *red cross,* Hugd. 139. 189. Valentin and Namelos have also a cross *betw. the shoulders,* like the mark of the lime-leaf on Siegfrïed's back, where alone he is vulnerable (as Achilles was in one heel), Nib. 845, 3. 4. Swan-children have a *gold chain* about the *neck,* the reali di Franza a *niello* on the *right* shoulder, Reali 6, 17. p.m. 344 ; conf. the *wolfs-zagelchen* betw. the shoulder-blades (Suppl. to 1097). Of the Frankish hero Sigurd, the Vilk. saga c. 319 says : 'hans horund var svâ hart sem *sigg villigaltar;* sigg may mean a bristly skin, and seems conn. with the legend of the bristled Merowings.[1] In cap. 146 we are told that Sigurd's skin grew hard as *horn ;* and in Gudr. 101, that wild Hagen's skin *hardened* through drinking the monster's blood. No doubt the original meaning was, merely that he gained strength by it. The great, though not superhuman *age* of 110 years is attained by Hermanaricus, Jorn. c. 24. We read in Plaut. mil. glor. iv. 2, 86 : *meri bellatores* gignuntur, quas hic praegnates fecit, et pueri

[1] Thorpe (ad Cod. Exon. p. 511) sees the Merowings in the North-Elbe Maurungani and AS. Myrgingas. Might not these Myrgingas be those of Mercia ?

*annos octingentos* vivunt. The gods bestow *blessings,* the heroes *evils,* Babr. 63.

p. 392.] Strong Franz also holds converse with his *knowing steed,* Müllenh. p. 422. The hero talks with his *sword* as well as his horse, Sv. forns. 1, 65. Klage 847 seq. Wigal. 6514. Drachenk. 161ª. Vilkinas. pp. 54. 160-1. The dying hero would fain *annihilate his sword,* e.g. the Servian Marko and Roland, Conr. Rol. 237, 3.

p. 394.] Where a god, devil or hero *sits,* there is left a *mark in the stone.* Their hands and feet, nay, their horses' hoofs, leave marks behind (Suppl. to 664). ons heren spronc, Maerl. 2, 116. Stone remains wet with a hero's tears : hiute (to this day) ist der stein naz, dâ Karl uffe sâz, Ksrchr. 14937.

---

# CHAPTER XVI.

## WISE WOMEN.

p. 396.] Helen, as daughter of Zeus and Leda, as half-sister of the Dioscuri, is already half divine; but she is also deified for her *beauty,* as her brothers are for bravery, Lucian 9, 274. Flore says of Blancheflur, whom he supposes dead, 2272 :

> iuch het Got ze einer *gotinne*
> gemacht in himelrîche
> harte wünneclîche.

Women have the further advantage over the harder sex, of being kind and merciful, even giantesses and she-devils (Suppl. to 530).

p. 397.] Soothsaying and magic are pre-eminently gifts of women (p. 95). Hence there are more witches than wizards : ' where we burn *one man,* we burn maybe *ten women,'* Keisersb. omeis 46ᵇ. A woman at Geppingen had foretold the great fire, Joh. Nider (d. 1440) in Formic. 2, 1.

p. 398.] *Woman-worship* is expr. in the following turns of speech [Examples like those in Text are omitted]. ich waen, Got niht sô guotes hât als ein guot wîp, Frauend. 1, 6. êrt altôs vrouwen ende joncfrouwen, Rose 2051. van vrowen comt ons alle ere, Walew. 3813 ; for one reason : wir wurden von frowen geborn, und manger bet gewert, Otn., cod. Dresd. 167. daz wir von den lieben frolîn fîn alsamen [zer werlte] komen sîn, M. Beheim 275, 19. Renn. 12268.

p. 400.] The hero devotes himself to a lady's service, *she will have him* for her knight: *ich wil in z' eime ritter hân*, Parz. 352, 24. 'den ritter dienstes biten,' ask for his service 368, 17. *dins* ritters 353, 29. *mîn* ritter und der *dîn* 358, 2. Schionatulander has to serve Sigune 'unter schiltlîchem dache,' under shield-roof, Tit. 71, 4, he was 'in ir helfe erborn' 72, 4; and this relationship is called her fellowship 73, 1.

> do versuocht ich 'n, ob er kunde sîn
> ein *friunt*, daz wart vil balde schîn.
> *er gap* durch mich (for me) sîn harnas *enwec* . . .
> mange âventiure suoht' er *blôz* (bare, unarmed), Parz. 27, 13.

The knights wore scutcheon or jewel, esp. a sleeve, or mouwe, stouche (parts of a sleeve), 'durch (in honour of) die frauen.' The lady is screen, shield and escort to the knight whose sword is in her hand, Parz. 370-1. 'ich wil *in strîte bî iu sîn*' says Obilôte to Gawan 371, 14. Captives must surrender to the conqueror's lady-love 394, 16. 395, 30. 396, 3; she is thus a warrior like Freya, a shield-maiden (p. 423-4). The *sleeve* he wears as favour on his shield has touched the maiden's *naked arm*, Parz. 375, 16. 390, 20. Er. 2292 seq. En. 12035 seq.; a shirt that has touched the fair one's form is the knightly hauberk's roof, Parz. 101, 10; conf. 'es gibt dir gleich, naizwan, ain kraft, wen du im an den rock rüerest (touchest his coat),' Keisersb.'s Spinnerin f. 3ᵈ. Schionatulander nerves him for the fight, and wins it, by thinking how Sigune showed herself to him *unrobed;* which she had done on purpose to safeguard him in danger, Tit. 1247— 50. 1497. 2502. 4104. 4717.

> Sed in cordibus milites
> *depingunt nostras facies,*
> cum serico in *palliis*
> colore et in *clipeis ;* Carm. Bur. 148ᵇ.

Sîfrit *gedâht an daz küssen* daz ver Krîmhilt im hâte getân, dâ-von der degen küene (champion bold) ein niuwe kraft gewan, Roseng. 1866. Man sol vor êrste an Got gedenken in der nôt, Dar-nâch gedenke an die süezen mündel rôt, Und an ir edeln

minne, diu verjagt den tôt, Kolm. MS. 73, 37. 42, 46. For
'thinking of,' see my Dict. sub. v. *andacht* (devotion).——The
ladies too call out to their champion, or they wish : ' The little
*strength* that I have, I would it were *with you !* ' As you like it,
i. 2.——Woman's beauty can split rocks : von ir schoene müese
ein fels erkrachen, MsH. 3, 173ª. It heals the sick : der *sieche*
muose bî in genesen, Dietr. Drach. 350ᵇ. sol daz ein *siecher* ane
sehn, vor fröide wurde er schier gesunt 310ᵇ. ir smieren und ir
lachen, und solde ein *sieche* das ansehn, dem müeste sorge swachen
70ª. A flight to the ladies saves a man : hie sal die zuht vore
gân, nu he under den vrowin ist komin, 4626 ; conf. 4589. A
lady's tread does not hurt flowers : ich waen swelhe trat diu
künegîn, daz si niht verlôs ir liehten schîn, Turl. Wh. 97ᵇ. 152ª.

p. 400.] Sîn pflâgen (him tended) *wise frouwen,* Gudr. 23, 3 ;
they are called *blessed maids* in Steub's Tirol p. 319.

p. 401.] The OHG. *itis* (Kl. Schr. 2, 4 seq.) is still found in
MHG. In the Wigamur 1564 seq. a maiden is called *îdis* (mis-
printed eydes, for it rhymes wîs, prîs 1654-90. 1972) ; she has a
limetree with a fountain of youth. Again, *Itisburg,* Dronke 4, 22 ;
*Idislind,* Trad. Wizenb. (printed Dislith), Pertz 2, 389. *Dis* in
Förstem. 1, 335 ; is Gifaidis 1, 451 for Giafdîs ? Curtius in
Kuhn's Ztschr. connects itis with ἀθήνη, but where is the *s* ? I
prefer to see in it the shining one, fr. indh = lucēre, *êdha, êdhas*
=lignum (Kl. schr. 5, 435). AS. *ides* = freolicu meowle, Cod.
Exon. 479, 2. Both *meowle* and *mawi* have likewise their place
here ; conf. *Meuenloch,* Panzer's Beitr. 1, no. 85. Kl. schr. 3, 108.

p. 403.] ON. *dîsir* appear as parcae : ' vildu svâ dîsir,' so
willed the fates, Höstl. (Thorl. 6, 6) ; *tâlar dîsir* standa þer â
*tvœr hliðar,* ok vilja þik *sâran siâ,* Sæm. 185ª. Sacrif. off. to
them : *dîsablôt, blêtuð dîsir,* Egilss. 205-7. var at *disa blôti,*
reið hesti um *dîsar salinn,* Yngl. 33. Of the suicide : heingdi
sik î *dîsarsal,* Hervarars. p. 454 ; fôr ser î *dîsar sal* 527. *ioddis,*
Sn. 202. Grendel's mother is an *ides,* Beow. 2518. 2701. On
Vanadîs and her identity with the Thracian moon-goddess Bendis,
see Kl. schr. 5, 424. 430 seq.

p. 403.] Brynhild's *hall,* whither men go to have their *dreams
interpreted,* stands on a *hill,* Völs. c. 25 ; conf. hyfjaberg (p. 1149).
*völu leiði,* divinatricis tumulus, Laxd. 328. An *old fay* has not
been out of her *tower* for fifty years, Perrault p. m. 3.——Of

Veleda and the Goth. Waladamarca in Jorn. c. 48 we are reminded by the wise horse Falada in the fairy-tale (p. 659), and by Velentin : *valantinne, volantinne* alternate in Hpt's Ztschr. 4, 437. The *völur* roam about : ek fôr î skôg *völvu líki*, Fornald. s. 1, 135 ; þû var *völvan* 1, 139. Sæm. 154^b. Other prophetesses in Nialss. p. 194-9 : Sæunn *kerlíng*, hon var *fróð* at mörgu ok *framsýn*, en þá var hon gömul miök ; she wanted the weed removed, else it would cause a fire, which came true. In Fornm. s. 4, 46 : *vîsindakona*, sû er sagði fyrir örlög manna ok lîf; conf. p. 408.

p. 405.] Wackernagel in Hpt's Ztschr. 2, 539 thinks *ali*orunas = *hali*orunas = hellirûna. A cave of the *Alraun* in Panz. Beitr. 1, 78—80. mandragora *alruna*, Mone's Anz. 8, 397.

p. 406.] My resolution of ON. *norn* into Goth. navairns, deathgoddess (Kl. schr. 3, 113) is opposed by Müllenhof in Hpt's Ztschr. 9, 255. The 'Nahanarvali' may have been norn-worshippers, Navarna-hali, Goth. Navarnê-haleis, ON. Norna-halir, GDS. 715. 806. Perhaps we ought to look to the Swed. verb *nyrna*, warn, inform, Sv. folkv. 1, 182-3. In Faröe they say *nodn*, nodnar, for *norn*, nornir, as they do kodn, hodn, badn, for korn, horn, barn, Lyngbye 132 ; so Nodna-gjest 474. That *Nürnberg* contains norn is the less likely, as we find it spelt *Nüern*-berc, MSH. 3, 296^b, *Nüeren*-berc, Walth. 84, 17. *Nornborn* seems a corrup. of Nordenborn, like Norndorf, Nornberg, also in Up. Germany. Conf. the Fris. *Non*, Ehrentr. Fries. arch. 2, 82 ; *Nurnhari*, Karajan 83, 6.

p. 408.] Two Germ. truds, *Muss* and *Kann*, take their names, like the three Norns, from simple verbs, Panz. Beitr. 1, 88. OHG. *wurt*, fortuna, Gl. hrab. 964^a ; conf. *giwurt, ungiwurt*, Graff 1, 993-4, and perhaps Goth. *gavairþi*, n. AS. seo *wyrd geweorð*, Cædm. 168, 3. hie *Wyrd* forsweop, Beow. 949. With ' me þæt Wyrd *gewæf* (wove) ' conf. ' wîgspêda *gewiofu* (webs),' Beow. 1347 (p. 415). In Kormakss. p. 267 comes *Urðr at brunni ;* conf. Urðar lokur, Sæm. 98^a. Urðr öðlînga 214^a is like ' dîs Skiöldunga.'——The Norns *shape* our destiny, *skapa* : ömlig norn *skóp* oss î ârdaga 181^a; in Faröe : tea heava mear nodnar *skapt*, Lyngbye 132. In Graff 6, 662, ' steffara = parca ' is for *sceffura* ; *scepfarun* = parcae, Gl. Schlettst. 6, 457 ; they ' *sceppen* 's menschen leven,' Limb. 3, 1275. Vintler v. 146 (see App. Superst. G) speaks of *gach-schepfen*, Pfeiffer's Germ. 1, 238 ; conf. Finn.

*luonnotar,* virgo creatrix, esp. ferri, fr. luon to make : ' kolme neittä luonnotarta,' *tres* sunt *virgines* naturae creatrices.——Norns are of various lineage, Sæm. 188ª :

> *sundr-bornar* miök hugg ek at nornir sê,
> eigoð þaer aett saman,
> sumar ero *ás*-kungar, sumar *álf*-kungar,
> sumar doetr Dvalins (some, daughters of D., a dwarf).

p. 409.] On *nornir, völvur, spákonur, blákápur* conf. Maurer 284. tha *thriu wüfer,* Ehrentr. Fries. arch. 2, 82. die *drei heil-räthinnen,* Panz. Beitr. 1, 56-7-9. 283. Slav. *tri rojenice* or *sujenice,* Valjavec 76—91. Boh. *sudice,* judges, fem. (p. 436). Nornir *ná-gönglar,* nauð-gönglar, Sæm. 187ᵇ, conf. ed. Hafn. 173 ; note the *töfra-norn* (p. 1033).——The Norns *travel :* konur þaer fôru yfir land, er *völvur* voru kallaðr, ok sögðu mönnum *forlög* sîn, ârferð ok aðra hluti, þâ er menn vildu vîsir verða. þessi sveit kom til Virvils bônda, var *völvunni* þar vel fagnat, Fornm. s. 3, 212. völvan *arma* 3, 214. Norns, parcae, fays come *to the infant's cradle,* and bestow gifts ; so does frau *Saelde* in Erec 9900. A *gammal gumma* prophesies at the birth of the prince, Sv. folks. 1, 195 ; three *mör* (maids) get bathed by the girl, and then give gifts 1, 130 (in our Germ. tale it is 3 haulemännchen).

p. 410.]                     *Saeva Necessitas*
*clavos trabales* et *cuneos* manu
gestans ahenea.   Hor. Od. i. 35, 18.

Si figit *adamantinos*
summis vorticibus *dira Necessitas*
*clavos.*                     Hor. Od. iii. 24, 5.

diu *grimme Nôt,* Er. 837. merkja *â nagli Nauð,* Sæm. 194ᵇ. Rûnar ristnar : *â Nornar nagli* 196ª (*clavo,* not fingernail) ; conf. Simplic. 1, 475 (Keller) : when Needs-be rideth in at door and windows.

p. 411.]   Of Greek mythical beings *Calypso* comes nearest the fays, being goddess and nymph ; and in MHG. the goddess *Venus* is ' diu *feine* diu ist entslâfen,' MS. 2, 198ª, while a fay is often called *goddess.* ' götinne = fee,' Hpt's Ztschr. 2, 183. der götinne land, der g. hende, Frib. Trist. 4458. 4503.——In Petronius we already find a personal (though masc.) *fatus :* malus f. (illum perdidit) c. 42. hoc mihi dicit f. meus, c. 77. On the house of the *tria fata* in the Forum, conf. Gregorovius's City of Rome 1, 371-2-3. In the Engadin they are called *fedas, feas*, also *nymphas* and *dialas* : they help in loading corn, bring food and drink in silver vessels ; *three dialas* come to the spinners, Schreiber's Taschenb. 4, 306-7.

p. 412.] On the *tria fata* see Horkel's Abh. p. 298 seq., conf. the *three maidens* in F. v. Schwaben: *twelve* white maidens in Müllenh. p. 348. Fays, like elfins, are of unsurpassed beauty : schoener danne ein *veine*, Trist. 17481. plus *blanche* que *fée*, Orange 5, 3059. plus *bele* que fée ne lerine 5, 4725. pus bela que *fada*, Ferabr. 2767. de *biauté* resanbloit fée, Marie 1, 100. They hold feasts, like the witches (p. 1045-6). In an old poem (?) p. 104-5, *three fays* prophesy at the birth of Auberon, son of Jul. Cæsar and Morgue, when a *fourth* comes in, p. 106 (p. 32 of the prose). The *fates* are gifting a newborn child, when the last one hurries up, but unfortunately sprains her foot (sbotatose lo pede), and lets fall a curse, Pentam. 2, 8.

p. 413 n.] *Fata Morgana* is ' *Fémurgân* diu rîche ' in Lanc. 7185, *Fâmorgân* in Er. 5155. 5229, *Feimurgân* in Iwein 3422. The ' *Marguel*, ein feine ' in Er. 1932 is the same, for she answers to the Fr. ' Morgain la fée.' She is called ' *Morguein* de elwinne,' Lanz. 13654. 19472. 23264 ; ' *Femurga* die kluoge,' Tit. 4376 ; while Wolfram treats the word as the name of a country (p. 820 n.). On the other hand, Trist. 397, 14 : *gotinne* ûz *Avelûn* der feinen lant (fay's land) ; Er. 1930 : der wert *Avalón*, Fr. l'ile d'Avalon. Does this go back to an old Celtic belief? Michelet 2, 15 mentions *holy maids* who dispensed fair weather or shipwreck to the Celts.

p. 414 n.] *Aîσa* seem akin to ἴσος, ἔϊσος and εἴδεναι: ἴσος equally distributed, κατα ἴσα ex aequo, κατ' αἶσαν convenienter, aeque.

p. 415.] Instead of Κατακλῶθες in Od. 7, 197 Bekker reads :

ἄσσα οἱ αἶσα κατὰ κλῶθές τε βαρεῖαι
γεινομένῳ νήσαντο λίνῳ—'

joining κατά to νήσαντο. Lucian's Dial. mort. 19 : ἡ Μοῖρα καὶ τὸ ἐξ ἀρχῆς οὕτως ἐπικεκλῶσθαι. Conf. ἐπικλώθω used of gods and daemons (Suppl. to 858). Atröpos was supposed to be in

the sun, Clotho in the moon, Lachĕsis on earth, Plut. 4, 1157.
For a beautiful description of the *three Parcae* (parca, she who
spares ?　Pott in Kuhn 5, 250) see Catullus 62, 302—321 with
ever and anon the refrain : Currite, ducentes subtemina, currite,
fusi ! also vv. 381—385.

*Nubila* nascenti seu mihi *parca* fuit.　Ov. Trist. v. 3, 14.
Scilicet hanc legem *nentes* fatalia *parcae*
　stamina bis genito bis *cecinere* tibi.　v. 3, 25.
O duram *Lachesin !* quae tam grave sidus habenti
　fila dedit vitae non breviora meae.　v. 10, 45.
Atque utinam *primis* animam me ponere *cunis*
　jussisset quaevis *de tribus una soror !'*　Propert. iii. 4, 28.
*Tres parcae aurea pensa* torquentes.　Petron. c. 29.
Daz het in *vrôwe Chlôtô* sô erteilet ;
ouch was vil gefuoc *vrô Lachesis* daran.　Turl. Krone 7.

Servian songs tell of a *golden thread* (zlatna shitza), that un-
winds from heaven and twines about a man, Vuk 1, 54 (Wesely
p. 68). 57-8.

　p. 416.]　German legend is full of *spinning* and *weaving
women :* kleit daz ein *wildiu feine span,* Troj. kr. 2895. ein
*feine worhte* den mantel, Altd. bl. 2, 231; and fays *weave* mantles
in Charlem. p. 105-6.　*paile* que fist fere une *fée,* Auberi 37.　in
the cave sits an *old spinster,* Kuhn's Westph. 1, 72. Asbiörn.
1, 194; conf. the old *webster,* Rhesa dainos 198.　*Gelücke span*
im kleider *an,* Frauenl. 115, 15.　There are usually *three together :*
*tres nymphae,* Saxo p. 43 (ed. M. 123).　*drei puppen,* Firm. 2,
34.　die *drei docken,* H. Sachs i. 4, 457[d]. die *drei Marien,*
Kindh. Jesu, Hahn 68.　Uhland's Volksl. 756.　lb. 1582, 332.
*three Marys* protect from fire, Panz. Beitr. 1, 67.　*three spinning
Marys,* Uhl. Vksl. 744.　*three old wives* on a three-legged horse,
Müllenh. p. 342.　the *tras feyes,* Alsatia 1853, p. 172-3.　Many
stories of *three women* in *white* or *black,* esp. in Panzer's Beitr.
1, 2. 11-4-6-8. 25-8. 35-6-8. 46-8; they *stretch a line* to dry
the wash on 1, 1. 9. 11-7. 25. 59. 129 n. 271-8; *sing* at the birth
of a *child* 1, 11 ; become visible at *Sun-wend-tag* (solstice), 1,
38-9. 75. 84.　Near Lohndorf in Up. Franconia a lad saw *three
castle-maidens* walking, two had kreuz-rocken (-distaffs) with nine
spindles spun full, the third a stühles-rocken with nine empty

ones; and the others said to her, 'Had you but covered your
spindles once, tho' not spun them full, you would not be lost.'
Panz. Beitr. 2, 136.  A beautiful Moravian story tells of *three
maidens* who marched, scythe in hand, mowing the people down ;
one, being lame, cannot keep up, and is laughed at by the other
two.  She in her anger lets men into the mystery of healing
herbs.  Kulda (d'Elv) 110.

p. 418.]  Jupiter sends out Victoria, as Oðinn does *valkyrs*,
Aug. Civ. D. 4, 17 (p. 435-6).  Their name has not been found
yet in OHG., though Schannat, vind. 1, 72 (yr. 1119) has *Wal-
karie*, femina serva.  With the *skiald-meyar* conf. schild-knecht,
who keeps his lord's shield and hands it to him, as they to Oðinn.
*Maidens* guarding *shield and helmet* occur in the M. Neth. Lanc.
16913. conf. 16678. 17038.  Their other name, *hialm-meyar* is
made clearer by *hild und hialmi*, Sæm. 228ª, *hialm* geta ok
*óskmey* verða 242ª.  The valkyr is named *folkvitr* 192ª.  So,
*megetlichiu wîp* help Charles to conquer, Ksrchr. 14950 seq.;
diu megede suln dir dîne êre widergewinnen 14954 ; der megede
sigenunft 15029.  Aurelian led in triumph ten captive *Gothic
amazons*, Vopisc. in Aurel. 34.  Lampr. Alex. 6320 calls the
Amazons *urlouges wîp*.  Paul Diaconus mentions a fight betw.
Lamissio and the Amazons for the passage of a river.  Adam of
Bremen 4, 19 speaks of 'amazons and *cynos-cephali;*' conf. P.
Diac. 1, 15.  *hunt-houbito* in Graff.  The Krone 17469 tells of
'der *meide* lant,' land of maids.

p, 418 n.]  Hun var vitr kona ok vinsael ok *skörûngr* mikill,
Fornm. 3, 90 ; hon var *skorûngr* mikill, virago insignis, Nialss.
c. 96 ; and Glaumvör is *skörûngr*, Völs. c. 33 (Kl. schr. 3, 407),
*skarûngr*, Vilk. c. 212 ; but in c. 129 skarûngr=hero.  Conf.
skör, f.=barba, scabellum, .commissura ; skar, m.=fungus, inso-
lentia.  OHG. scara=acies, agmen ; scaraman, scario.

p. 419.]  Where is the *garment* mentioned, in which Oðinn
hid the thorn for Brunhild ?  Sæm. 194ª only says 'stack hana
svefn-þorni;' Völs. c. 20 'stack mik svefn-þorni'; Sæm. 228ᵇ
'lauk hann mik skiöldom ok hvîtom.'  On *spindle-stones*, see
Michelet 1, 461.

p. 420.]  Brynhildr or Sigrdrîfa *fills a goblet* (fyldi eitt ker),
and brings it to Sigurd, Sæm. 194ᵇ.  Völs. c. 20.  A white lady
with *silver goblet* in M. Koch's Reise d. Oestr. p. 262.  A maiden

hands the *horn,* and is cut down, Wieselgren 455. Subterraneans offer similar *drink,* Müllenh. p. 576; and a jätte hands a *horn,* whose drops falling on the horse strip him of hair and hide, Runa 1844, 88.

p. 421.] *Nine,* as the fav. number of the valkyrs, is confirmed by Sæm. 228[a], where one of them speaks of *átta systra.* To our surprise, a hero Granmar turns *valkyrja* in Asgard, and bears nine wolves to Sinfiötli, Sæm. 154[b]. Fornald. 1, 139; conf. AS. wylpen, wulpin = bellona.

p. 423.] The valkyrs *ride through the air* (p. 641), like Venus (p. 892) : a thing aft. imputed to witches (p. 1088, &c.). *Twelve women* in the wood, on *red horses,* Fornm. 3, 135. By the expression *Hlackr för,* Hlöck seems to have the task of conducting those fallen in battle to Oðinn or Freyja, Egilss. p. 226. Is *Göndull* akin to gand? Gl. Edd. tom. 1 : '*göndull* = nodulus'; so that Oðin's by-name Göndler, Sæm. 46[b], would mean 'tricas nectens.' The *Rota* in prose Sn. 39 is *Rotho* in Saxo M. 316. An OHG. name *Hilticomâ,* ad pugnam veniens, Cod. Fuld. no. 153 (yr. 798), describes a valkyr; conf. *Hruodicoma,* no. 172; ON. *Hildr und hialmi,* Sæm. 228[a]; AS. *hilde wôman,* Cod. Exon. 250, 32. 282, 15. *Thrûðr* is likewise a daughter of Thôrr. Heilah-trûd, Trad. Fuld. 2, 46. *trute,* Pass. K. 395, 77. *frau Trutte,* Præt. weltb. 1, 23. the *drut* (p. 464).

p. 423.] May we trace back to the walkürie what is said to Brunhild in Biter. 12617? 'ir wâret in iur alten site komen, des ir pflâget ê, daz ir sô *gerne sehet strît,*' you love so to see strife. Brynhildr is 'mestr *skörûngr*' (p. 418 n.). In Vilk. p. 30 she is called 'hin rîka, hin fagra, hin mikillâta,' and her castle *Ségard.* In the Nibel. she dwells at castle *Isenstein* on the *sea ;* is called des tiufels wîp (or brût), and ungehiurez wîp, 417, 4. 426, 4; wears armour and shield, 407, 4, throws the stone running, and hurls the spear; is passing strong 425, 1. 509, 3. 517, 3, and ties up king Gunther on their wedding-night.

p. 424.] Like the *shield-maidens* are Fenja and Menja, of whom the Grottasöngr str. 13 says : î *folk stigum,* brutum *skiöldu . . . . veittum góðum Gothormi lið.* Clarine dubs her Valentin knight, Staphorst 241. They strike up brotherhood with their protégés ; so does stolts *Signild,* Arvidss. 2, 128—130; conf. the *blessed* (dead ?) *maiden,* who marries a peasant, Steub's

Tirol 319. The valkyrs too have swan-shifts, Sæm. 228ᵃ: lêt *hami* vâra hugfullr konûngr âtta systra *und eik borit* (born under oak); conf. Cod. Exon. 443, 10. 26 : wunian under *âc-treo;* and Grottas. str. 11: vârum leikur, *vetr niu* alnar *fyrir iörð neðan.* The wish-wife's clothes are kept in the *oaktree,* Lisch 5, 84-5.

p. 425.] Brynhildr first unites herself by oath to young *Agnar,* and helps him to conquer old Hialmgunnar, Sæm. 194; conf. 174ᵇ. 228ᵃ (Völs. c. 20), where it says 'eiða seldak' and 'gaf ec ungom sigr.' After that she chose Sigurd : svâ er ek *kaus* mer til manns, Völs. c. 25. Such a union commonly proved unlucky, the condition being often attached that the husband should never *ask* the celestial bride *her name,* else they must part; so with the elfin, with Melusina, with the swan-knight. Also with the goddess Ganga, who had married Santanu, but immediately threw the children she had by him into the river, Holtzm. Ind. sag. 3, 95-9. On the union of a hero with the ghostly vîla, see GDS. 130-1.

p. 429.] Valkyrs are to a certain extent *gods stranded* on the world in Indian fashion. They stay 7 years, then fly away to the battle : *at vitja viga,* visere proelia, Sæm. 133; so in the prose, but in the poem *örlög drýgja* (p. 425). The *wisiu wîp* in the Nibel. are also called *merwîp,* diu *wilden merwîp* 1514-20-28, and Hagen *bows* to them when they have prophesied.

p. 431.] The hut of the *forest-women* in Saxo p. 39 vanishes with them, and Hother suddenly finds himself *under the open sky,* as in witch-tales (p. 1072). Gangleri heyrði dyni mikla hvern veg frâ sèr, oc leit ût â hlið sèr : oc þâ er hann sèz meirr um, þâ *stendr hann ûti â slèttum velli,* sèr þâ önga holt oc önga borg, Sn. 77. Such vanishings are called *sion-hverfingar,* Sn. 2.

p. 433.] *Holz-wîp,* Otn. Cod. Dresd. 277; conf. dryad, hamadryad (p. 653). To *cry* like a wood-wife, Uhl. Volksl. 1, 149 : schrê als ein wildez wîp *owê !* Lanz. 7892. The wild woman's *born, gestühl* (spring, stool), Wetterau. sag. 282 ; *wilde fräulein,* Wolf's Ztschr. 2, 59 ; daz *wilde vrouwelîn,* Ecke 172. In Schlüchtern wood stand the *wild houses, wild table,* often visited by the wild folk, Buchonia iv. 2, 94-5 ; a *willemännches haus* and *tisch* (table) near Brückenau, Panz. Beitr. 1, 186 ; conf. daz wilde getwerc (p. 447). Wood-wives are also called *dirn-weibel* (Suppl. to 279), and carry apples in their basket, like the matronae and Nehalenniae. At flax-picking in Franconia a bunch plaited into a pigtail is left for the *holz-fräule* (as part of a sacrifice was laid aside for nymphs, Suppl. to 433 n.), and a rhyme is spoken over it, Panz. Beitr. 2, 160-1. *witte wiwer* in the forest-cave, Kuhn's Westf. sag. 1, 123. The *rauhe* (shaggy) woman appears in the wood at *midnight*, Wolfdietr. 307-8 (Hpt's Ztschr. 4) ; the mother of Fasolt and Ecke was a *rauhes weib* (p. 483). Zander's Tanh. pp. 7. 17 speaks of *wald-schälklein* Cupido. Does *Widukind*, a very uncommon name, mean wood-child ? conf. Widukindes speckia, Lünzel 22. 25.

p. 433 n.] *Weaving naiads* in Od. 13, 107. Fountain-nymphs, daughters of Zeus, are worshipped by Odysseus and in Ithaca 13, 356. 17, 240 ; a part of the sacrifice is laid by for them 14, 435. βωμὸς νυμφάων 17, 210.

p. 434 n.] The reluctance of *Proteus* is also in Virg. Georg. 4, 388—452 ; the same of *Vertumnus*, Ov. Met. 14, 642 seq. Propert. iv. 2.

p. 435.] Ez ne sint *merminne* niet, En. 240, 4. ein *wîse mer-minne*, Lanz. 193. 5767. 3585. 6195. als êne *merminne* singhen, Rose 7896. A captive merwoman *prophesies ruin* to the country as far inland as she is dragged, Firmen. 1, 23. Müllenh. p. 338. Queen Dagmar hears the *prophecy* of a *hav-fru*, D.V. 2, 83—85 (in which occurs the adage : vedst du det, saa vedst du mer). The *mermaid* of Padstow, exasperated by a shot, curses the harbour, and it is choked up with sand. For Melusine the common people say mère Lusine. Danish songs have *maremind* and *mare-qvinde*. 'waltminne = lamia,' Gl. florian. Fundgr. 1, 396. *walt-minna* = echo (p. 452), lamia,' Graff 2, 774. *widuminna*, Cassel ortsn. p. 22.

p. 436.] The *vîla* builds her castle in the clouds, her daughter Munya (lightning) plays with her brothers the two Thunders, Vuk nov. ed. 1, 151-2. She sits in ash-trees and on rocks, singing songs ; talks with the stag in the forest ; bestows gifts, and is a physician (p. 1148), Vuk 151. 149 n., no. 114. 158. She resembles the *devil* too ; holds night-dance on the hill (Vuk sub v. vrzino kolo), teaches pupils to lead clouds and make storms, detains the last man. The vilas are likest the white ladies (Suppl. to 968). With *kliktati* conf. Lith. 'ulbauya volungě,' the woodpecker whines, and MS. 2, 94[b] : 'ir *klokent* als umbe ein fûlen boum ein speht,' as woodpecker about a plumtree.

# CHAPTER XVII.

## WIGHTS AND ELVES.

p. 439.] Augustine C. D. 8, 14 divides animate beings into three classes : 'tripertita divisio animalium in deos, homines, *daemones*. Dii excelsissimum locum tenent, homines infimum, *daemones medium ;* nam deorum sedes in coelo, hominum in terra, in *aëre* daemonum.' The *vettar* have more power over nature than we, but have no immortal soul, a thing they grieve at (p. 517). Fries. bot. udfl. 1, 109.——The Goth. *aggilus*, OHG. *engil*, is not a convenient general term for these middle beings, for it conveys a definite Christian sense. Iw. 1391 uses *geist* for dae-mon: ein unsihtiger geist. *Genius* means having generative power, Gerh. Etr. gods pp. 15. 52. Another general term is *ungethüm*, Schweinichen 1, 261-2. Spirits are also *ungeheuer* (p. 914) : die *übelen ungehiuren*, Ges. Abent. 3, 61. 70-6 ; elbische *ungehiure* 3, 75. The Swed. *rå* too seems to have a general sense : *sjö-rå, tomt-rå, skog-rå, råand*, Runa 1844, 70 ; conf. *ås* (Suppl. to 24 and 498). Mod. Gr. στιχεῖον, Fauriel's Disc. prél. 82, must be στοιχεῖον element, conf. τὸ στοιχεῖον τοῦ ποταμοῦ 2, 77.

p. 442.] The *Victovali, Victohali* are Goth. Vaíhtê-haleis, ON. Vaetta-halir, fr. vict, wiht, wight, and the same people as the Nahanarvali (Suppl. to 406). GDS. 715. Can *vaihts* be fr. vaian to blow, and mean empty breath ? In Hpt's Ztschr. 8, 178 '*iht* (ie-wiht) übles' is half abstract, like Goth. vaíhteis ubilôs; whilst 'eines boesen *wichtes* art' in Lanz. 3693 (conf. 1633) is altogether concrete ; so are, 'diz ungehiure *wiht*,' Ges. Abent. 2, 129 ; dat vule *wicht*, Rein. 3660 ; dat dein proper suverlec *wechtken* (girl), Verwijs p. 33 ; O. Engl. *wight*=being, wife, Nares's Gl. sub v. ; illar *vaettir*, Fornm. 4, 27 ; ill *vaettr* ok örm, Fornald. 1, 487 ; rög *vaettr*, Sæm. 67-8 ; *ô-vaettr*, malus daemon, our *un*-wesen. *land-vaettir* are Saxo's 'dii *loci praesides*' 161. *dii vettrarne*, Dybeck 1845, p. 98. uppå *vegnar vaettir*, ex improviso, Biörn sub v. veginn (slain). The Norweg. *go-vejter*, good wights, whence the *gu-vitter* of the neighbouring Lapps, answer to our *gute wichte*, *gute holden* (pp. 266. 456. 487); de *guden holden*, Gefken's Beil. 99. 124-9. A 15th cent. description of the Riesengebirge has 'umb des *weckirchen* oder *bergmönlins* willen,' Mone's Anz. 7, 425 ; is this word akin to wicht, as well as ar-weggers (p. 454 n.) which might mean 'arge wichte,' malicious wights?[1] Weckerlein is a dog's name, fr. wacker (brisk, wide-awake). *Wihtelín*, p. 441 n., may mean simply a puppet, like tocke, docke: bleierne (leaden) holder-*zwerglîn*, Garg. 253ª. A wichtel-*stube* in Sommer p. 24, a wichtelen-*loch* in Panz. Beitr. 1, 42. Like wiht, *das ding* stands for nightmare, Prætor. Weltb. 1, 27, as *bones coses* does for boni genii, Alex. 289, 24, and M. Lat. *creatura* for something, wight, Ducange sub v.

ON. *kynd*, f., pl. *kyndir*, is genus, ens, Sæm. 1ª. 6ª. 118ª; *kynsl*, *kynstr*, res insolita; Swed. *kyner*, creaturae, Runa 1844, 74.[2] Akin to this word seems MHG. *kunder*, creature, being, thing, also quaint thing, prodigy: was *chunders?* Wackern. lb. 506, 30; conf. 675, 39. 676, 28. 907, 7. 909, 17. solhez *kunder* ich vernam, MSH. 3, 195ᵇ. tiuvels *kunter*, Rol. 223, 22. der tiuvel und allez sîn kunder, Tit. 2668. du verteiltez k., Ges. Abent. 3, 25. bestia de funde sô sprichet man dem k., Tit. 2737. verswinden sam ein k., daz der boese geist fuort in dem rôre 2408. ein vremdez k., MSH. 3, 171ª. ein seltsæne k., Walth. 29, 5. ein trügelîchez k. 38, 9. diu oeden k., MSH. 3, 213ª. das scheusslich kunter! Oberlin 846ᵇ; but also 'hêrlichiu kunder,' Gudr. 112, 4. einer slahte k., daz was ein merwunder, Wigam. 119. maneger slahte k., Wh. 400, 28. aller slahte *kunterlich*, Servat. 1954. k. daz ûf dem velde vrizzet gras (sheep), Helmbr. 145. der krebez izzet gern diu *kunterlîn* im wazzer, Renn. 19669. OHG. *Chunteres* frumere, Cod. Lauresh. 211. M. Neth. *conder*, Brandaen 33. 1667. dem boesem *unkunder*, Dietr. 9859, formed like ON. ôvaettr; conf. AS. tudor, progenies, *untydras*, monstra, Beow. 221.

p. 443.] OHG. 'faunos=*alp*,' Hpt's Ztschr. 10, 369. MHG., beside alp (dô kom si rehte als ein *alp* ûf mich geslichen, Maurit. 1414), has an exceptional alf: sô tum ein *alf* . . . was nie sô *alf* (both rhym. half), Pass. 277, 69 and 376, 6. der unwîse *alf* 302, 90. ein helfelôser *alf* 387, 19. der tumme *âlf* 482. 12. der tôrehte *alf* 684, 40; conf. the name *Olfalf*, Karajan 110, 40.——Perh. a nom. 'diu elbe' is *not* to be inferred fr. the dat. 'der elbe' in

---

[1] Ar-weggers is a name for *earth*-wights: ar-beren=*erd*-beeren, p. 467, l. 3; and *weg*-lin=*wiht*-lin p. 449, last l.—TRANS.

[2] *Skrymsl*, monstrum, Vilk. s. 35, *skrimsl*, Fornm. 4, 56–7, used like kynsl. Ihre says, skrymsl=latebra, Dan. skrämsel terriculamentum; Neth. schrôm terror, ON. skraumr blatero; Skrymir (p. 541).

MS. 1, 50ᵇ, as Pfeiffer p. 75 says the Heidelb. MS. reads ' von *den elben*.' The dwarf in Orendel is *Alban* ; a name *Elblîn* in Diut. 2, 107 ; a mountain-sprite *Alber* in Schm. 1, 47.——With the above *Olfalf* conf. ' ein rehter *olf*,' Roseng. xiii., which comes near MHG. ulf, pl. ülve, but disagrees in its consonant with alp, elbe. On the other hand, ' du *ölp*, du dölp ' in H. Sachs i. 5, 525ᵇ agrees with the latter ; so does *Olben*-berg, Hess. Ztschr. 1, 245.——The quite reg. M. Neth. *alf* (p. 463, last 2 ll.) has two plurals : (1) *alven* in Br. Gheraert v. 719.   met *alven* ende elvinnen, Hor. Belg. 6, 44 ; and (2) *elven* in Maerl.: den *elven* bevelen, Clarisse's Gher. p. 219.   There is also a neut. *alf* with pl. *elver* ; conf. the names of places *Elver*-sele, *Elvinnen*-berg.   A large ship, *elf*-schuite, Ch. yr. 1253 (Böhmer's Reg. p. 26, no. 190) is perh. fr. the river Elbe.—— AS. *œlfinni* means nymphae, dûn-*œlfinni* oreades, wudu-*œlfinne* dry-ades, wæter-*œlfinne* hamadryades, sac-*œlfinne* naiades, feld-*œlfinne* maides, Hpt's Ztschr. 5, 199.   The Dan. assimil. of *ellen* for elven occurs indep. of composition : ' *ellen* leger med hannom,' mente captus est, Wormius Mon. Dan. p. 19.   *ellevild* = Norw. huldrin, Asbiörns. 1, 46-8. 105.   indtagen af huldren 1, 99.   To *ölpetrütsch*, &c. add *elpendrötsch*, Gräter's Id. und Herm. 1814, p. 102 ; Up. Hess. ' die *ilmedredsche* ' ; Fastn. 350 *älpetrüll* ; conf. *trötsch* Mone's Anz. 6, 229.——The adj. from alp is *elbisch* : in *elbischer* anschowe, Pass. 97, 15.   ein *elbische* ungehiure, Ges. Ab. 3, 75. ein *elbischez* âs 3, 60.   *elbischer* gebaere 3, 68.   ich sihe wol daz dû *elbisch* bist 3, 75.

p. 444 n.]   For the Alps there occur in the Mid. Ages ' *elbon* =alpibus,' Diut. 2, 350ᵇ.   uber *elve*, trans alpes, Rother 470. über *albe* kêren, Servat. 1075.   zer wilden *albe* klûsen, Parz. 190, 22.   gên den wilden *alben*, Barl. 194, 40.

p. 444 n.]   Welsh *gwion* = elf, fairy.   On *banshi*, *benshi* see Hone's Every Day b. 2, 1019, O'Brien sub v. sithbhrog (Suppl. to 280).   *beansighe*, Leo's Malb. gl. 37, *sighe* 35.   Hence the name of an elvish being in the West of Engl., *pixy*, *pexy*, *pixhy*, Scotch *paikie*, Jamieson 2, 182, and pixie, Suppl. 219.   For the *cole-pixy*, at fruit-gathering time, a few apples are left on the tree, called in Somerset the *pixhy-hording* (fairies' hoard), Barnes sub v. *colepexy*.   *Picsy-ridden*, i.e. by night-mare ; *pixy-led*, led astray.

p. 445.]   The distinction betw. *âlfar* and *dvergar* appears also in Sæm. 28ᵃ : for *âlfom* Dvalinn, Dâinn *dvergom*.   By *Alfheimr*

Rask understands the southernmost part of Norway, Afh. 1,
86-8; by *dvergar* the Lapps 1, 87. Loki, who is also called *álfr*,
is sent by Oðinn to *Andvari* or *Andþvari* in *Svartálfaheim*, Sn.
136; so Plutarch 4, 1156 derives daemons from the servants of
Kronos, the Idæan Dactyls, Corybantes and Trophoniads.
Curiously *Olafr* is called digri Geirstaða-*álfr*, because he sits in
the grave-mound at Geirstöð, Fornm. 4, 27. 10, 212.——Both
*albs*, *alps* and the Lat. albus come (says Kuhn in Hpt's Ztschr.
5, 490) fr. Ssk. *ribhus;* conf. thie *wízun* man = angels, O. v.
20, 9. die *weissen männel*, Weise's Com. probe 322. Vishnu on
the contrary appears as a *black dwarf*, Meghaduta 58, and again
as a *brown* shepherd-boy 15. Dwarfs are created out of black
bones, ' or *blâm* leggjom,' Sæm. 2ᵇ. Migrating dwarfs are either
*white* or *black* in Panz. Beitr. 1, 14. Still I think it speaks for
my threefold division, that the elves made by witches' magic are
also *black, white* and *red*, where red may stand for brown, though
hardly for döckr. In charms too, the ' worms' equivalent to elves
are always of those three colours; an Engl. spell names ' fairies
*white, red* and *black*,' Hone's Yearb. 1534. And horses black,
brown and white turn up in the fay-procession, Minstrelsy 199.

p. 446.] The dwarf Andvari dwells in *Svartálfaheim*, Sn. 136;
Sn. 16 makes some dwarfs live in the *ground* (î moldu), others in
*stones* (î steinum).

447.] For *dvergr*, Sæm. 49ᵃ has *durgr*. LS. *twarg*, Westph.
*twiark*, L. Rhen. *querge*, Firmen. 1, 511; Up. Lausitz *querx* 2,
264. ' *gituerg*=nanus vel pomilio,' Gl. Slettst. 29, 43. ein
*wildez getwerc*, Er. 7395; getwergelîn 1096. daz *tzwerk*, Keller's
Erz. 632, 3. *wildiu* getwerc, Goldem. 5, 1. Sigen. 21, 9. Ecke
81, 5. A deed of 1137 is signed last of all by ' *Mirabilis nanus*
de Arizberg, nepos imperatoris Heinrici,' MB. 4, 405; was his
name *Wuntertwerc?* (a Mirabilis near Minden, yrs. 1245-82,
Wigand's Wetzl. beitr. 1, 148. 152. Henr. Mirabilis, D. of
Brunswick, d. 1322.——Earth-mannikins do spin, Sup. 993; but
their favourite line is *smith-work;* they are ' *hagir* dvergar,'
Sæm. 114ᵃ. *Knockers* are little black hill-folk, who help to
knock, and are good at finding ore, Hone's Yearb. 1533. The
thunderbolt was also *elf-shot*, conf. Alp-donar (p. 186-7). As
smiths with *cap* and *hammer*, the dwarfs resemble Vulcan, who
is repres. with *hat* and *hammer*, Arnob. 6, 12 ; conf. Lateranus

(Suppl. to 511). Dwarfs were worked on ladies' dresses, *dvergar á öxlum*, Sæm. 102ᵇ.

p. 447 n.] The *korr*, dwarf, dim. *korrik*, is black and ugly, with deep-set eyes and a voice muffled by age, Schreib. Abh. v. streitkeil. p. 80. Welsh *gwarchell*, a puny dwarf, *gwion*, elf, fairy, *gwyll*, fairy, hag. Lith. *karlà, karlèle.* Serv. *malienitza, manyo,* little-one, *star-mali,* old little-one, *kepetz.*

p. 448.] The worship of elves is further attested by the *álfa-blót* performed in one's own house, Fornm. 4, 187. 12, 84; a *black lamb,* a *black cat* is offered to the huldren, Asb. Huldr. 1, 159. In Dartmoor they lay a bunch of grass or a few needles in the pixies' hole, Athenæum no. 991. The *alp-ranke* is in AS. *ælf-bone,* OHG. *alb-dono,* like a kerchief *spread* out by the elves? (p. 1216); *alf-rank,* amara dulcis, Mone's Anz. 6, 448. Other plants named after them are *elf-bläster, elf-näfver,* Dyb. Runa 1847, 31.

p. 451 n.] The adage in the Swiss dwarf-story, ' *sälben tho, sälben gha* ' (conf. issi teggi, p. 1027), is found elsewhere : Norw. ' sjöl gjort, sjöl ha,' Asb. Huldr. 1, 11 ; Vorarlb. ' selb to, selb ho,' Vonbun p. 10 ; ' salthon, saltglitten,' Wolf's Ztschr. The *goat's feet* suggest the *cloven hoofs* of satyrs, for dwarfs too ' dart through the wood on *pointed hoof,*' Dietr. drach. 140ᵃ.——The ill effect of *curiosity* on men's dealings with dwarfs comes out in the following :—A shepherd near Wonsgehäu saw his dog being fed by two dwarfs in a cave. These gave him a *tablecloth,* which he had only to spread, and he could have whatever food he wished. But when his inquisitive wife had drawn the secret from him, the cloth lost its virtue, and the *zwergles-brunn* by Wonsgehäu ran *blood* for nine days, while the dwarfs were killing each other, Panz. Beitr. 2, 101.

p. 451.] *Angels* are small and beautiful, like elves and dwarfs; are called *geonge.men,* Cædm. 146, 28 ; woman's beauty is comp. to theirs, Walth. 57, 8. Frauend. 2, 22. Hartm. bk. 1, 1469. Percival ' bore angel's beauty *without wings,*' Parzif. 308, 2.[1] And dwarfs are called the *fair folk* (p. 452) ; *sgön-aunken,* Kuhn's Westph. sag. 1, 63. Alberich rides ' als ein *Gotes engel* vor dem her,' Ortnit 358. die kleinen briute (she-dwarfs), vrouwen *also diu bilde* getân (done like pictures), Alex. and Antiloie (Hpt's

---

[1] *Pennati pueri* already attend Venus in Claudian's Epith. Palladii ; angels flit round the tower, Pertz 6, 451ᵃ.

Ztschr. 5, 425-6); conf. 'Divitior forma, quales audire solemus *Naïdes* et *Dryades* mediis incedere silvis,' Ov. Met. 6, 452.——On the other hand, Högni, whose father was an alb, is *pale* and *dun* as bast and ashes, Vilk. c. 150; changelings too are ugly (p. 468). We read of *dernea wihti* (p. 441) ; and the red-capped dwarf is *black*, Runa 3, 25. Dwarfs have *broad brows* and *long hands*, Dybeck 1845, p. 94; *grôze arme, kurziu bein* het er nâch der getwerge site, Wigal. 6590 ; and the *blatevüeze* in Rother seem to belong to dwarfs, by their bringing the giants *costly raiment.*——Dwarfs come up to a man's knee, as men do to a giant's: 'die kniewes hôhen .... die dô sint eins kniewes hôch,' Dietr. drach. 299ᵃ. 175ᵃᵇ. 343ᵇ. Dietr. u. ges. 568. 570. Often the size of a *thumb* only: pollex, Pol. paluch, Boh. palec, ON. þûmlûngr (Swed. pyssling: 'alla min fru mors *pysslingar*,' Sv. folks. 1, 217-8; ON. pysslîngr, fasciculus), Lith. nyksztélis, thumbkin, wren, Kl. schr. 2, 432-3. In Indian stories the soul of the dying leaves the body in the shape of a *man as big as a thumb*, Holtzm. Ind. sag. 1, 65. Ruhig says the O.Pr. *barzduckai* is not fr. pirsztas, finger, but fr. barzda, beard, the sub-terraneans being often repres. with long beards.——MHG. names for a dwarf: der *kleine mann*, Ernst 4067. der *wênige man*, Er. 7422. Eilh. Trist. 2874. der *wênige gast*, Er. 2102. *wêniges mennel*, Frib. Trist. 5294. ein gar *wêniger man* mit einer güldîn krône, Ecke 202. ein *wênic twirgelîn*, Alex. 2955. der *kurze kleine*, der *kleine recke*, Dietr. drach. 43ᵇ. 68ᵃ. der *wunderkleine*, Altsw. 91. Serv. *star-mali*, old little-one. An unusual epithet, applied also to slaves and foreigners, is 'le *puant* nain,' Ren. 4857. The Elf-king sits under a great toadstool, Ir. märch. 2, 4 ; and whoever carries a toadstool about him grows small and light as an elf 2, 75. The little man afloat on a leaf in Brandaen is on a par with the girl sailing over the waves on the leaves of a *waterlily*, Müllenh. p. 340 ; conf. nökkeblomster (p. 489).

p. 453.] Hills and woods give an echo: OHG. *galm*, Diut. 2, 327ᵃ ; MHG. *gal* and *hal*, Deut. myst. 2, 286 ; widergalm, Tit. 391 ; die stimme gap hinwidere mit *gelîchem galme* der walt, Iw. 618. They answer: *conscia* ter sonuit rupes, Claud. in Pr. et Olybr. 125 ; *responsat* Athos, Haemusque *remugit*, Claud. in Eutr. 2, 162 ; daz in dâvon *antworte* der berc unde ouch der tan, Nib. 883, 3 ; ein gellendiu fluo, Lanz. 7127 ; si schrei, daz ir der

walt *entsprach*, Bon. 49, 71 ; daz im der berc *entgegenhal*, Er.
7423.——ON. *dvergmáli* qvaᵭ î hverjum hamri, Fornald. 3, 629 ;
*dvergmalenn*, Alex. saga 35. 67. AS. *wudu-mœr*, both echo and
nympha silvestris. The *woodman* calls fr. the wood, Megenb. 16,
20. Böcler's Superst. of the Esths p. 146 gives their names for
the echo : squint-eye, *wood's reply*, *elf-son's cry* ; Possart p. 163-4
says, the mocking wood-elf *mets halias* makes the echo (Suppl.
to 480). Echo is the silvan voice of Faunus, Picus (conf. woodpecker and Vila), Klausen pp. 844. 1141 ; the Mongols take a
similar view of it, Petersb. bull. 1858, col. 70. In the Ir.
märchen 1, 292 echo is not ' muc alla,' but *macalla* or *alla bair*,
Gael. *mactalla*, son of the rock, Ahlw. Oisian 3, 336.

As the ON. saga makes Huldra *queen of dwarfs*, Swedish
legends have a fair lady to rule the dwarfs ; even a *king* is not
unknown, as the *bergkong* (p. 466). The English have a *queen
of fairies*, see Minstr. 2, 193 and the famous descr. of *queen Mab*
(child, doll ?) in Rom. and Jul. i. 4 ; conf. Merry W. of W. v. 4.
Add *Morguein de elvinne*, Lanc. 19472. 23264-396-515. 32457.——
In German opinion *kings* preponderate. The Sörlaþâttr makes
*Alfrigg* a brother or companion of Dvalinn, while Sn. 16 asso-
ciates *Alþiofr* with him, Fornald. 1, 391 ; conf. ' in dem *Elperichis-
loke*,' Baur no. 633, yr. 1332. ' der getwerge künec Bîlêî ' has a
brother *Brians*, Er. 2086 ; Grigoras and Glecidolân, lords of der
twerge lant 2109. Another is Antiloïs (rhym. gewis), Basel MSS.
p. 29ᵇ. On the name of the dwarf-king *Luarîn*, *Luaran*, see
Hpt's Ztschr. 7, 531 ; *Laurin*, Baur no. 655 ; a *Laurins* in the
Roman des sept sages (Keller's Dyocletian, introd. p. 23—29).
With Gibich conf. *Gebhart*, Müllenh. p. 307 ; king *Piper*, or
*Pippe* kong 287. 291-2. Again, the Scherfenberger dwarf, DS.
no. 29 ; *Worblestrüksken* king of earthmannikins, Firmen. 1,
408—410. Albr. v. Halb. fragm. 25 speaks of a *got der twerge*.

p. 453 n.] The lament ' *Urban* is dead ! ' sounds like the
Vorarlberg cry ' *Urhans* (old Jack) ist todt ' (conf. Urian, ur-
teufel, p. 989, and ' the devil's dead,' p. 1011-2), Vonbun p. 4 ;
ed. 2, pp. 2. 7. Fromm. Mundart. 2, 565. *Kilian* is dead,
Winkler's Edelm. 377. *Salome* is dead, Panz. Beitr. 2, 40.
' Eisch, Pingel, Pippe kong, Pilatje, Vatte, Kind ist dôt,' Müllenh.
nos. 398—401. *Habel* is dead, Preusker 1, 57. nu är *Plagg* död,
Runa 1844 p. 44. nû er *Ulli* dauᵭr, Fornm. 1, 211. Ol. Tryggv.

c. 53.   In a Cornish legend a beautiful she-dwarf is buried by
the little folk in Leland church near St. Ives amid cries of *Our
queen is dead ;* conf. Zeus is dead, buried in Crete, thunders no
more, Lucian's Jup. trag. 45.

   p. 454.]   The dwarf's names *Dáinn, Náinn* (mortuus) raise the
question whether elves are not *souls,* the *spirits of the dead,* as
in Ssk. Indras is pitâ Marutâm, father of the winds = of the dead,
Kuhn in Hpt's Ztschr. 5, 488-9.   Of the dwarf Alvîs it is asked :
hvî ertu *följ um nasar,* vartu î nôtt *með ná ?* Sæm. 48ᵃ. *Dvalinn*
âlfr, *Dáinn* dvergr; *Dvalinn* sopiens, *Durinn* somnifer 28ᵃ. *Andvari,* son of *Oinn* 181ᵃ means perh. cautus (Suppl. to 461).
*Finnr* reminds of Fin in the Norrland story (p. 1025), and of
father Finn in Müllenh. p. 300.   *Bivor* may be conn. with dwarf
*Bibunc* in Dietr. drach.——Germ. names of dwarfs : *Meizelín,*
Dietr. dr. 196ᵃ.   *Aeschenzelt,* Ring 233-9.   *Hans Donnerstag,*
Müllenh. p. 578.   *Rohrinda, Muggastutz,* Vonbun pp. 2. 7 ; conf.
*Stutzamutza, Grossrinda,* Wolf's Ztschr. 2, 60. 183.

   p. 455.]   On the *arweggers* see KM³. 3, 195.   Dwarfs live
in holes of the rock : stynja (ingemiscunt) dvergar fyrir *steins
durum,* Sæm. 8ᵇ.   Dvalinn stôð î *steins dyrum,* Hervar. p. 414.
They like to stand in the doorway, so as to slip in when danger
threatens.   A dwarf's hole is in ON. *gauri,* Vilkin. c. 16 (the
*pixies' house* or *hole* in Devon, Athen. nos. 988. 991).   They were
called *veggbergs vîsir,* Sæm. 9ᵃ.   In Sweden, *berg-rå,* bergrået,
Runa 3, 50, *iord-byggar* 1845, 95, di små *undar jårdi* 60, höj-
biergs-*gubbe,* conf. tomte-gubbe (p. 500), god-gubbe.   In Norway,
*hou-boer,* dweller on a height.   In Germany too, wildiu getwerc
live in the *mountain* beside giants, Hpt's Ztschr. 6, 521 ; ' der
hort Niblunges der was gar getragen ûz eime *holn berge,*' Nib.
90, 1 ; a wildez getwerc is surprised ' vor eime *holen berge,*' Er.
7396 ; ' si kument vor den berc, und sehent *spiln diu getwerc,*'
see the dwarfs play, Dietr. dr. 252ᵇ, conf. 213ᵃ ; twerge dwell in
the *Höberg,* Ring 211.   ' Daemon subterraneus truculentus, *berg-
teufel ;* mitis, *bergmenlein, kobel, guttel ;*' again, ' dæmon me-
tallicus, *bergmenlein,*' for whom a ' fundige zech ' was deposited,
Georg Agricola de re metall. libri XII.   Basil. 1657, p. 704ᵇ.

> Gân ûf manegen rûhen *berc,*
> dâ weder katze noch *getwerc*
> möhte über sîn geklummen.   Troj. kr. 6185.

The term *böhlers-männchen* im böhlers-loch, Bechst. 3, 129, must come fr. bühel, collis; conf. OHG. puhiles perc, Graff 3, 42 and the name Böhler. Wend. *ludkowa gorà*, little folk's hill, Volksl. 2, 268ᵃ. in *montanis* (Prasiorum) *pygmœi* traduntur, Pliny 6, 19. People show the *twarges-löcker, wüllekes-löcker, wulweckers-löcker, wünnerkes-gätter,* Kuhn's Westph. sag. 1, 63.——They also live in *grave-mounds*, Lisch 11, 366, in *cairns* (stenrös), and under men's *houses* and *barns*, Fries's Udfl. 109. These are likewise the resort in summer of the courriquets of Bretagne, who sleep on the hearth all the winter. But they cannot endure men's *building stables* over their habitations, which the muck, sinking through, would defile, Müllenh. p. 575. 297. Kuhn, nos. 329. 363 and p. 323. Asb. 1, 150-1. Dybeck 1845, p. 99.[1]—— The name of Subterranean is widely spread: dat *unner-ersch*, das *ünner-eersche*, in Sylt-öe *önner-erske,* Müllenh. 438. 393. 337. de *unner-ärschen* near Usedom. In digging a well, men came upon their *chimney*, and found quite a houseful, Kuhn in Jrb. der Berl. ges. 5, 247. *erdmännel, erdweibel,* Panz. Beitr. 1, 71. Lith. *kaukas*, earth-man, *kaukaras*, mountain-god; conf. semmes deewini, earth-gods, Bergm. 145. In Föhr and Amrum *önnerbänkissen,* in Dan. Schleswig *unner-væs-töi, unner-bors-töi, unnersboes-töi* (töi = zeug, stuff, trash), Müllenh. 279. 281. 337. Elves inhabit a Rosegarden inside the earth, like Laurîn, where flowerpicking is punished, Minstr. 2, 188. 192.

p. 456.] Venus is called a *feine* (Suppl. to 411), een broosche *eluinne,* Matth. de Castelein's Const van rhetoriken, Ghendt 1555, p. 205; conf. the Venus-Minne hovering in the air, and *travelling viewless as a sprite* (p. 892).

p. 458.] *De guden holden* are contrasted with the kroden duvels (Suppl. to 248-9). Mîn *váro holdo,* verus genius, Notk. Cap. 81. Is *holderchen* the original of *ülleken, ülken,* Balt. stud. 12ᵇ, 184, and *üllerkens,* Temme's Pom. sag. 256?[2] *liuflingr* = huldumaðr, Aefintŷri 105.——The Norw. *huldrefolk,* Asb. 1, 77 and Faröe *huldefolk,* Athen. no. 991, are of both sexes, though

---

[1] Two maidens came to a peasant when ploughing, and begged him to leave off, they were going to bake, and the sand kept falling into their dough. He bargained for a piece of their cake, and aft. found it laid on his plough, Landau's Wüste örter, p. 138. So fairies in Worcestersh. repay compliant labourers with food and drink, Athen.

[2] *Arweggers* is perh. to be explained by arwegget = arbeit, Firmen. 1, 363, and means workers; conf. weckerchen, wulwecker.

the females are more spoken of : a female is called *hulder*, Asb.
1, 70, a male *huldre-kall* (-karl) 1, 151. Dybeck 1845, 56 derives *hyll-fru*, *hyl-moer* fr. hyld, elder-tree.——The good nature
of dwarfs is expr. by other names : Norw. *grande*, neighbour,
and Asb. 1, 150-1 tells a pretty story of the *underground neighbour*. Might not the ' goede kinder ' in Br. Geraert 718 come in
here ? A *quoter* and a pilwîz are named together, Hagen's Ges.
Abent. 3, 70 ; ' der *quotaeri* ' is the name of a MHG. poet. Lith.
*balti žmones*, the honest folk, Nesselm. 319[b].——As dwarfs impart to men of their bread or cake, help in weaving, washing
and baking, and serve in the mill (Panz. Beitr. 1, 155), they in
return make use of men's dwellings, vessels, apparatus. So the
pixies in Devon, Athen. no. 991. In winter they move into men's
*summer-huts* (sheelings), Asb. 1, 77, 88. They can thrash their
corn in an oven, hence their name of *backofen-trescherlein*, Gar.
41[a] ; once the strazeln were seen *thrashing in an oven six together*,
another time *fourteen*, Schönwth 2, 300. 299. They fetch men
of understanding to *divide* a treasure, to settle a dispute, Pref.
xxxiii.-iv. Contes Ind. 2, 8. Somad. 1, 19. Berl. jrb. 2, 265. Erfurt
kindm. 26. Asb. p. 52-3. Cavallius no. 8. Wal. märch. p. 202.
KM. nos. 92. 133. 193-7 ; conf. pt. 3, ed. 3, pp. 167-8. 216. 400
(conf. *dividing the carcase* among beasts, Schönwth 2, 220.
Nicolov. 34. societas leonina, Reinh. 262). They let a kind
servant-girl have a present and a peep at their wedding, Müllenh.
326-7 (see, on dwarf's weddings, Altd. bl. 1, 255-6. Naubert 1,
92-3. Goethe 1, 196). Hafbur goes into the mountain and has
his dream interpr. by the eldest ' elvens datter,' Danske v. 3, 4.
They dread the cunning tricks of men ; thus, if you take a *knife
off their table*, it can no longer vanish, Lisch 9, 371. The man
of the woods, or schrat, like the dwarf in Rudlieb, cannot endure
a guest who blows hot and cold, Boner 91. Stricker 18 (Altd. w.
3, 225).—— If on the one hand dwarfs appear weak, like the one
that *cannot carry* Hildebrand's heavy *shield*, Dietr. u. Ges. 354.
491. 593, or the wihtel who finds an *ear of corn heavy*, Panz.
Beitr. 1, 181 ; on the other hand the huldre breaks a horse-shoe,
Asb. 1, 81, fells a pine and carries it home on her shoulder 1, 91.
And in Fairyland there is *no sickness*, Minstr. 2, 193 ; which
accords with the longevity boasted of by dwarf Rudleib xvii. 18,
conf. Ammian. 27, 4 on the long-lived agrestes in Thrace.

p. 459.] The dwarfs retiring before the advance of man produce, like the Thurses, Jötuns and Hunes, the impression of a
conquered race. In Devon and Cornwall the pixies are regarded
as the old inhabitants. In Germany they are like Wends (the
elves like Celts?), in Scandinavia like Lapps. Dwarfs are
*heathen :* ' ob *getouften* noch *getwergen* der bêder künec wart ich
nie,' of either dipt or dwarf, Biter. 4156. The undergrounders
fear not Wode, if he have *not washed ;* conf. Müllenh. no. 500
(p. 458n.). They can't abide *bell-ringing,* Firmen. 2, 264ᵇ, they
move away. In *moving* they leave a cow as a present, Dybeck
1845, 98. The subterraneans *ferry over,* Müllenh. p. 575 ; wichtels cross the Werra, Sommer p. 24 ; three wichtels get ferried
over, Panz. Beitr. 1, 116 ; conf. the passage of souls (p. 832).
As the peasant of the Aller country saw the meadow swarming
with the dwarfs he had ferried over, as soon as one of them put
his own hat on the man's head ; so in the Altd. bl. 1, 256 : when
the hel-clothes were taken off, ' dô gesach he der *getwerge mê wen
tûsunt.*' When the peasant woman once in washing forgot to put
lard in, and a wichtel scalded his hand, they stayed away. The
ülleken fetch water, and leave the jug standing, Balt. stud. 12ᵇ.
184..

p. 461.] Ostgötl. *skot, troll-skot,* elf-shot, a cattle-disease, also
*elf-bläster,* Dyb. 1845, 51 ; conf. âb-gust, alv-eld, alv-skot, Aasen.
Their mere touch is hurtful too : the half-witted *elben-trötsche*
(p. 443) resemble the ' *cerriti,*' larvati, male sani, aut Cereris ira
aut larvarum incursatione animo vexati,' Nonius 1, 213. Lobeck's
Aglaoph. 241. Creuz. Symbol. 1, 169 (ed. 3). The sick in Ireland are *fairy-struck.*——The name *Andvari,* like the neut. *andvar,*
can be interpr. ventus lenis, aura tenuis, though Biörn translates
it pervigil (Suppl. to 454). With *Vestri, Vindâlfr* is to be conn.
' *Vestralpus* Alamannorum rex,' Amm. Marcell. 16, 12. 18, 2 ; it
is surely westar-alp rather than westar-halp, in spite of AS. west-
healf, ON. vestrâlfa, occidens. Erasm. Atberus' Dict. of 1540
remarks : ' mephitis, stench and foul vapour rising out of swamps
or sulphurous waters, in nemoribus gravior est ex densitate silvarum.' In the Dreyeich they say ' der *alp feist* also.'——The
*looks* of elves bewitch, as well as their breath : eft ik sî *entsén,*
Val. and Nam. 238ᵃ. byn yk nu *untzên ?* Hpt's Ztschr. 5, 390.

p. 462.] Elves can get into any place. The âlfr enters the

house 'at *luktum dyrum* öllum,' Fornald. 1, 313.   They steal up
softly, unperceived : 'se geit *op elben-tehnen*,' she walks on elf-
toes, they say about Magdeburg.

p. 463.]   They can make themselves *invisible :* daz analutte
des *sih pergenten* (self-hiding) truge-tievels, N. Boëth. 42.   ein
*unsihtiger geist*, Iw. 1391.   The invisibility is usually effected by
their head-covering, the *nebel-kappe*, Ettn. Maulaffe 534. 542.
Altswert 18, 30.   in mîner *nebelkappen*, Frauenl. 447, 18 ; or
*hele-käppel*, Winsb. 26, 5.   Winsbekin 17, 5 ; and the secret
notches in it are called *käppel-snite* 17. 18.   '*nacht-raben* und
*nebel-käpel*,' Katzmair p. 23-8 (yr. 1397).   It seems they also wear
a *fire-red tschöple*, Vonbun p. 1 ; and a subterranean has the
name of *Redbeard*, Müllenh. p. 438.   The *huldre-hat* makes invisible, Asb. 1, 70. 158-9, like the *thief's helmet ;* the hat is also
called *hvarfs-hatt*, and the boys who wear it *varfvar*, Hpt's
Ztschr. 4, 510-1 ; conf. ' *hverfr* þessi âlfr svâ sem skuggi,' Vilk.
c. 150.   The courriquets of Bretagne wear *huge round hats*.   Men
cry to the dwarfs, 'zieht abe iuwer *helin-kleit !* ' Altd. bl. 1, 256.
Like our dwarfs, the little *corybantes* in antiques wear *hats*, Paus.
3. 24, 4.   Not only Orcus's *helmet*, but his *coat* was known, for
the Romans called the anemone *Orci tunica*, Dioscor. 2, 207.——
Conversely, dwarfs become *visible* to those who *anoint their eyes*
with dwarf-salve, as in the story of the nurse who put the ointment to one of her eyes, and could see the subterraneans, till
they tore out the eye, Asb. 1, 24-5.   Müllenh. p. 298.   Dyb. 1845,
94.——Poems of the Round Table give dwarfs a *scourge*, wherewith to *lay about them*, Lanz. 428. 436.   Er. 53. 96.   Iw. 4925.
Parz. 401, 16.   Even Albrich bore

> eine *geisel* swaere von *golde* an sîner hant,
> siben *knöpfe* swaere hiengen vor daran,
> dâmit er umb die hende den schilt dem küenen man
> sluoc sô bitterlîchen.   Nibel. 463-4.

In Possart's Estl. p. 176 the giants carry whips with millstones
tied to the tails.

p. 465.]   Old poetry is full of the trickery of dwarfs, who are
*kündic* as foxes, *endelich*, Dietr. drach. 17, ' *endelich* und *kec*,'
' brisk and bold,' 346[b].   *bedrogan* habbind sie *dernea wihti*, Hel.
92, 2.   du *trügehaftez* wiht, Barl. 378, 35.   uns *triege* der alp,

Hagen's Ges. Ab. 3, 60. elfs-*ghedroch*, Beatrijs 736. elfs-*ghe-drochte*, Maerl. (Clarisse's Gheraert p. 219). Walewein 5012. enhôrde ghi noit segghen (heard ye ne'er tell) van alfs-*gedrochte*, Hor. Belg. 6, 44-5. Deception by ghosts is also *getrucnisse*, Herb. 12833. ungihiure *drugi-dinc*, Diemer 118, 25. 121, 3. May we conn. with *abegetroc* the M. Neth. *avondtronke?* Belg. mus. 2, 116. In App., spell xlii., an alb has eyes like a *teig-trog* (lit. dough-trough). *Getwâs*, fantasma, is better expl. by AS. *dwaes*, stultus (Suppl. to 916) than by Sl. dushá, soul (p. 826).——Oppression during sleep is caused by the *alp* or *mar* (p. 1246) : mich *drucket* heint (to-night) der alp, Hpt's Ztschr. 8, 514. kom rehte als ein alp *úf mich* geslichen, Maurit. 1414. The *trud* presses, Dietr. Russ. märch. no. 16, conf. frau Trude (p. 423). Other names for incubus : *stendel*, Stald. 2, 397 ; *rätzel* or *schrätzel*, Prætor. Weltb. 1, 14. 23 (p. 479) ; Fris. *woelrîder*, Ehrentr. 1, 386. 2, 16 ; LG. *waalrüter*, Krüger 71ᵇ. Kuhn's Nordd. sag. nos. 338. 358. p. 419 (conf. Walschrand in the M. Neth. Bran-daen) ; Engl. *hag*-rode, -ridden, W. Barnes ; *picsy*-ridden (Suppl. to 444 ; the pixies also, like the courriquets of Bretagne, tangle the manes of horses, and the knots are called *pixy-seats*, Athen. no. 991) ; Pol. *ćma*, Boh. *tma*, Fin. *painayainen*, squeezer, Ganan-der 65. Schröter 50.——Other names for plica : Upp. Hess. *Hollekopp*, at Giessen *morlocke, mahrklatte, Judenzopf.* A child in Diut. 1, 453 :

> hatte ein siechez houbet (sore head),
> des hatten *sich verloubet*
> di *hârlocke* alle garewe.

And Sibilla (antfahs) has hair *tangled as a horse's mane*, Eu. 2701. Scandinavian stories do not mention Holle's tuft or tail, but they give the huldres a *tail*. This matted hair is treated of by Cas. Cichocki de hist. et nat. plicae polonicae, Berol. 1845, who adds the term gwoździec, liter. nail-pricking, cramping.

p. 465.] Dwarfs *ride* : diu phert diu si riten wâren gelîche grôz den *schâfen*, Hpt's Ztschr. 5, 426 ; conf. Altd. bl. 1, 256. Dwarfs mount a *roe*, Ring p. 211. 231. Fairies ride, Minstr. 2, 199. Pixies ride the cattle at night, Athenæum nos. 991. 989. Poike in a *red cap* rides a *white goose*, Runa 1844, 60, as the pygmæi rode on *partridges*, Athen. 3, 440. The ancients kept *dwarfs* and *dogs*, Athen. 4, 427, as men in the Mid. Ages kept dwarfs and fools. Giants, kings and heroes have dwarfs in their retinue, as Siegfried has Elberich, and in Er. 10. 53. 95. 995. 1030 a knight has a getwerc riding beside him and laying on with his scourge; he is called Maledicur, and is aft. chastised with blows 1066. Elegast goes a thieving with Charlemagne. In Wigalois a maiden comes riding, behind whom stands a dwarf with *his hands on her shoulders*, singing songs 1721—36; another getwerc has charge of the parrot and horse 2574. 3191. 3258-87. 4033. *On the train* of a richly bedizened dame *ride little black spirits*, giggling, clapping hands and dancing, Cæs. Heitsterb. 5, 7 (Suppl. to 946).

p. 467.] While the Devonsh. pixies make away with turnips (Athenæum no. 991), our German dwarfs go in for peas, *erbsen ;* hence the name of thievish Elbegast is twisted into *Erbagast*: 'I adjure thee by thy master Erbagast, the prince of thieves,' Ztschr. f. Thüring. gesch. 1, 188. These thievish dwarfs may be comp. to Hermes, who steals oxen as soon as he is born, Hymn to Merc.——Dwarf Elberich overpowers a queen, and begets the hero *Otnit*. An alb begets *Högni*, Vilk. c. 150. The story of 'den *bergtagna*' is also told by Dyb. 1845, p. 94. Dwarfs are much given to carrying off *human brides* and falling in love with *goddesses*, e.g. Freya. The märchen of *Fitchers-vogel* is also in Pröhle's M. f. d. jugend no. 7, where he is called *fleder-vogel ;* conf. Schambach pp. 303. 369.——Little Snowdrop's coming to the *dwarfs' cottage*, and finding it deserted, but the table spread and the beds made, and then the return of the dwarfs (KM. no. 53) agrees remarkably with Duke Ernest's visit to the empty castle of the *beak-mouthed* people. When these come home, the master sees by the food that guests have been, just as the dwarfs ask 'who's been eating with my fork?' Ernst 2091—3145. And these *crane-men* appear in other dwarf stories : are they out of Pliny and Solinus ? '*Gerania*, ubi pygmæorum gens fuisse proditur, *Cattuzos* (al. Cattucos) barbari vocant, creduntque *a gruibus fugatos*,' Pliny 4, 11, conf. 7, 2. Hpt's Ztschr. 7, 294-5. Even the Iliad 3, 6 speaks of cranes as ἀνδράσι πυγμαίοισι φόνον καὶ κῆρα φέρουσαι. On *dwarfs and cranes* see Hecatæus fragm. hist. Gr. 1, 18. The Finns imagined that birds of passage spent the winter in Dwarfland ; hence *lintukotolainen*, dweller among

birds, means a dwarf, Renvall sub v. lintu : conf. the dwarf's
name lindukodonmies, birdcage man. Duke Ernest's flight to
that country reminds of Babr. 26, 10 : φεύγωμεν εἰς τὰ Πυγμαίων.
As the dwarf in Norse legend *vanishes at sunrise*, so do the pixies
in Devonsh., Athenm. no. 991. In Swedish tales this dread of
daylight is given to *giants*, Runa 3, 24. Sv. folks. 1, 187. 191.
p. 469.] The creature that dwarfs put in the place of a child
is in ON. *skiptûngr*, Vilk. 167. 187 ; in Icel. *umskiptíngr*, kominn
af âlfum, Finn. Joh. hist. eccl. Islandiae 2, 369 ; in Helsing.
*byting* (Ostgöt. möling), skepnad af mördade barn, Almqv. 394ᵇ;
in Småland *illhere*, barn bortbytt af trollen, litet, vanskapligt,
elakt barn 351. In MHG. *wehselbalc*, Germ. 4, 29 ; *wehselkalp*,
Keller 468, 32 ; *wehselkind*, Bergreien p. 64. In Devon and
Cornw. *a fairy changeling*, Athenm. no. 989. *Kielkropf* is in
OHG. *chel-chropf* in the sense of struma, Graff 4, 598. To this
day, in some parts, they say kielkropf for what is elsewhere called
*grobs*, *grübs*, wen, either on the apple or at the throat, and likewise used of babies, Reinwald's Id. 1, 54. 78. 2, 69 ; also *butzigel*,
*Adamsbutz* 1, 18 (p. 506-7), conf. kribs, gribs (p. 450 n.).
Luther's Table-t. 1568, p. 216-7 : 'weil er *im kropf kielt.*'
Schm. 2, 290 : *kielkopf*. The Scotch *sithich* steals children, and
leaves a changeling behind, Armstr. sub v. (Leo's Malb. gl. 1, 37).
In Lithuania the *Laume* changes children, hence *Laumĕs apmai-
nytas* = changeling. Boh. *podwržnec*. Wend. *přemeňk* : flog him
with boughs of drooping-birch, and he'll be fetched away, Volksl.
2, 267-8. Similar flogging with a hunting-whip, Sommer p. 43 ;
conf. Prætor. Weltb. 1, 365. It is a prettier story, that the
dwarfs would fain see a human mother put their babe to her
breast, and will richly reward her for it, Firmen. 1, 274ᵇ. The
joke of the 'müllers sun' (p. 468 n.) recurs in the MHG. poem
of 'des muniches nôt,' Hpt's Ztschr. 5, 434. Other stories of
changelings in Müllenh. p. 312-3-5. DS. 81-2. Ehrentr. Fries.
arch. 2, 7. 8.

The singular method of making the changeling blurt out his
age and real character is vouched for by numberless accounts.
A dwarf sees people brew in a hühner-dopp (hen's egg pot,
see eier-dopp, p. 927), and drain off the beer into a goose-egg
dopp, then he cries : 'ik bün so oelt as de *Behmer woelt*, unn heff
in myn läebn so 'n bro nich seen,' Müllenh. no. 425, 1 and 2

(Behmer *golt* in Lisch's Jrb. 9, 371).　A Swed. version in Dybeck
'45, p. 78. '47, p. 38.　Tiroler sag. in Steub p. 318-9.　Thaler in
Wlf's Ztschr. 1, 290.　Pröhle p. 48.　A Lith. story in Schleicher,
Wiener ber. 11, 105.　'As many years as the fir has needles,'
Vonbun 6.　'I've seen the oak in *Brezal* wood' seems old, for
the Roman de Rou itself says of Breceliande forest : 'vis la forest,
è vis la terre,' Note to Iw. p. 263.　That elves attained a great
age, comes out in other ways ; thus Elberich is upwards of 500,
Ortn. 241.

p. 470.]　Elves avoid the sun (p. 444 n.), they sink into the
ground, they look like *flowers*, they turn into *alder, aspen* or
*willow-boughs*.　Plants that grow in clusters or circles, e.g. the
Swed. *hvit-sippan*, are dedic. to them, Fries bot. udfl. 1, 109 ;
so the fairy queen speaks out of a clump of thorns or of standing
corn, Minstr. 2, 193.　Their season of joy is the *night*, hence in
Vorarlberg they are called the *night-folk*, Steub p. 82 ; esp. Midsummer Night, Minstr. 2, 195, when they get up a merry dance,
the *elf-dans*, Dybk '45, 51, taking care not to touch the herb
Tarald 60.　The elfins dance and sing, Müllenh. p. 341.　Whoever sees them dance, must not address them : 'They are fairies ;
he that *speaks* to them shall *die*. I'll wink and couch ; no man
their works must eye,' Merry W. of W. 5, 5.　When the subterraneans have danced on a hill, they leave circles in the grass,
Reusch's Add. to no. 72 ; so the hoie-männlein, who take their
name fr. *hoien, huien* to holla, dance rings into the grass, Leopr.
32-4. 107. 113-8. 129.　Schönw. 2. 342.　These circles are called
*fairy rings,* and regarded as dwellings of pixies, Athenm. no. 991.
The Sesleria coerulea is called *elf-gräs*, Fries bot. udfl. 1, 109 ;
the pearl-muscle, Dan. *elve-skiäl*, Nemn. 2, 682.　Elves love to
live beside *springs*, like Holda and the fays (p. 412) : der *elvinnen
fonteine,* Lanc. 345. 899. 1346-94 ; der *elvinnen born* 870. 1254.

p. 472.]　Dwarfs grant *wishes :*

> ein mann quam an einen berch (came to a hill),
> dar gref hie (caught he) einen cleinen dwerch ;
> uf dat hie leisse lofen balde (might soon let go)
> den dwerch, hie gaf em *wunsche walde* (power of wishing)
> *drier hande* (3 things).　　　　　　Cod. Guelferb. fab. 109.

They are *wise counsellors,* as Antiloïs to Alexander ; and very skilful. Dwarf *Pacolet* in Cleomades and Valentin makes a wooden horse, that one can ride through the air (like Wieland and Dædalus). Not akin to *Pakulls*, is he ? ' Manec *spaehez werc* Ez worht ein *wildez twerc,* Der listig Pranzopil,' Wigam. 2585. *Dáinsleifr* is the name of a *sword* made by a dwarf, Sn. 164 ; and Elberich forged the *rings,* Ortn. 176. In Wigal. 6077 it is said of a *harnasch :*

| | |
|---|---|
| er wart von einem wîbe | It was by a woman |
| verstoln einem *getwerge* | Stolen from a dwarf |
| alrêrst ûz einem berge, | Out of a mountain erst, |
| dâ ez in *mit listen gar* | Where he it with cunning quite |
| het geworht wol *drîzec jâr.* | Had wrought full 30 year. |

The Westph. schön-annken forge ploughshares and gridirons of trivet shape, Kuhn's Westph. sag. 1, 66 ; conf. the story in Firmen. 1, 274ᵃ. The hero of the Wieland myth (HS. p. 323) acts as Hephæstus or a smith-dwarf (p. 444).

  p. 476.] *Bilwiz :* called *pilwiz,* Mone's Anz. 7, 423 ; *billwiz,* unholden, Schleiertuch p. 244 ; Cuonrad de *pilwisa,* Chr. of 1112. MB. 29ᵃ, 232 ; *bilweisz,* Gefken's Beil. 112 ; ' Etliche glaben (some believe) daz kleine kind zu *pilweissen* verwandelt sind,' have been changed, Mich. Beham in Mone's Anz. 4, 451 ; conf. unchristened babes (Suppl. to 918). In Lower Hesse : ' he sits behind the stove, minding the *biwitzerchen,*' Hess. jrb. '54, p. 252 (al. kiwitzerchen). *berlewitz* (p. 1064). an Walpurgs abende, wan de *pülewesen* ausfahren, Gryphius Dornr. p. 93 ; sprechen, ich wer gar eine *büleweesse* 90 ; sie han dich verbrant, als wenn du ein *püleweesser* werst 52 ; conf. palause (p. 1074 n.). In Gelders they say : *Billewits* wiens goed is dat ? also *Pillewits, Prillewits.* The Lekenspiegel of Jan Deckers (of Antwerp, comp. 1330) says, speaking of 15 signs of the Judgment Day (iv. 9, 19. de Vries 2, 265 ; see Gl. p. 374) :

opten derden dach twaren
selen hem die vische baren
op dat water van der zee,
of si hadden herden wee,
ende *merminnen* ende *beelwiten*
ende so briesschen ende criten,

dat dat anxtelic gescal
toten hemel climmen sal.

With beelwiten conf. the *witten belden*, Gefk. Beil. 157.——Bilwitzes have their 'hâr verfilzet,' matted, Barl. 384, 361 (such hair and a shaggy skin Wolfram imputes to Cundrîe and her brother Malcreâtiure, Parz. 313, 17. 25). They conjure : 'conjurers, waydelers, *pilwitten*, black-artists' are named together in a decree of grandmaster Conr. v. Jungingen, Jacobson's Quellen des cath. kirchenr. urk. p. 285. The *bilmerschnitt*, otherw. *biberschnitt*, performed on Easter or Whitsunday, Panz. Beitr. 1. 240; called *durchschnitt* in Leopr. p. 19, conf. Sommer's sag. p. 171. Clementis recogn. 2, 9 (ed. Gersd. p. 44).

p. 478.] *Roggen-muhme :* called *corn-angel*, steals children, Somm. pp. 26. 170. *Rubigo* frumenti is called *aurugo* in Pertz 8. 368, *wintbrant* in Hpt's Ztschr. 5, 201. Did the Romans call the god of corn *Robigo* or *Robigus* ? the Greeks had an Apollo ἐρυσίβιος, mildew-averting, fr. ἐρυσίβη, robigo. A W.Fland. corn-spell denounces the corn-boar as a *duivels zwyntje*, Hpt's Ztschr. 7, 532. The Slavs have a similar field-sprite, a *corn-wife*, who walks at noon : *pripolnica, prepolnica*, fr. polnyo, midday, or *dźiwica*, as in Polish, Wend. volksl. 2, 268; she carries a sickle (conf. p. 1162). Hanusch p. 360-2.

p. 480.] OHG. *scratin*＝fáunos, Hpt's Ztschr. 5, 330. Gl. Slettst. 6, 222. Graff 6, 577. *scraten*＝larvas, Diut. 2, 351ᵃ. The tale of the *schretel* and the water-bear is also in Hpt 6, 174, and reappears in the Schleswig story of the water-man and bear, Müllenh. p. 257. In Up. Franconia the schretel is replaced by the *holzfräulein*, who, staying the night at the miller's in Berneck, asks : 'Have you still got your great *Katzaus ?*' meaning the *bear*. The man dissembles; the wood-maiden walks into the mill, and is torn in pieces by the bear. Beside schretel we have the form *srete*, Mone's Anz. 7, 423 ; conf. srezze vel srate. der *schrättlig*, Vonbun p. 26-7. d' *schrättli* händ a'g'soga, the s. have sucked it dry, when a baby's nipples are inflamed or indurated, Tobler 259ᵃ. *Schrätels* weigh upon the sleeper like the alp, Gefken's Cat. p. 55. *schrata, schratel*, butterfly, Schm. Cimbr. wtb. 167. Fromm. 4, 63. *Pereinschrat*, Rauch 2, 72 ; *Schratental* and *Schrazental* side by side 2, 22 ; so, with the

*Scratman* already cited, we find a 'servus nomine *Scrazman,*'
Dronke's Trad. Fuld. p. 19; conf. *schratele-mannl,* Anobium
pertinax, deathwatch in Carinthia, Fromm. 4, 53. *schratzen-*
*löcher,* -holes, Panz. Beitr. 1, 111. in *Schrazeswank,* MB. 35ᵃ,
109.——Graff 6, 575 has *walt-screchel*=fauni, silvestres homines;
and Schm. 3, 509 distinguishes fr. *schratt, schrättel* an Up. Palat.
*schrahel, schrächel,* which he refers to schrach, schroch, scraggy,
puny. A *scherzen, schrezen* to bleat, Schm. 3, 405, is also worth
considering. The schrächel is charged with tangling horses'
manes. *Schrawaz* is appar. of different origin: Rudbertus
*schrawaz,* MB. 28ᵇ, 138 (yr 1210); Rubertus *shorawaz* 29ᵇ, 273
(yr 1218). The Swed. *skratt* is both fatuus and cachinnus; Finn.
*kratti* genius thesauri; ON. *skrati*=iötunn, Sn. 209ᵇ. *skratta-*
*vardi,* Laxd. 152. The Dan. lay of Guncelin has: 'og hjelp nu
*moder Skrat!* ' Nyerup's Udvalg 2, 180. Sv. forns. 1, 73. On
*altvil,* which corresp. to the Engl. *scrat,* hermaphrodite, see
Hpt's Ztschr. 6, 400 and Suppl. to 498.——The Esths call the
wood-sprite *mets halias,* forest-elf, who is fond of teasing and
who shapes the echo, Possart's s. 163-4; conf. the Finn. *Hiisi,*
*Kullervo* (p. 552). Ir. *geilt,* wild or wood-man, conf. Wel. gwyllt,
wild. But the Pol. Boh. wood-sprite *boruta* is orig. feminine,
inhabiting the fir, like the Greek dryad, hamadryad. Homer
speaks of *spring* and *mountain-nymphs,* Od. 6, 123-4, and *nymphs,*
daughters of Zeus, who stir up the wild goats 9, 154. *Hama-*
*dryads* are personified trees, Athen. 1, 307. So Catull. 59, 21:
' Asian myrtle with emblossomed sprays, quos *Hamadryades deae*
ludicrum sibi *roscido nutriunt humore.*' Pretty stories of the
tree-nymph in Charon, Fragm. hist. Gr. 1, 35; others in Ov.
Met. 8, 771; the forest-women in line 746 seq. are descr. more
fully by Albr. v. Halberstadt 280-1.

p. 480.] The schrats appear *singly;* more finely conceived,
these wood-sprites become *heroes* and *demigods* (pp. 376. 432).
The *Katzenveit* of the Fichtelgebirge suggests *Katzaus* of the
preced. note. *Rubezagel, Rübezahl,* a man's name as early as
1230, Zeuss's Herk. der Baiern p. 35, conf. Mone's Anz. 6, 231;
a Hermannus *Rubezagil* in Dronke's Trad. Fuld. p. 63; *Rieben-*
*zahl* in a 15th cent. MS., Mone's Arch. '38, 425; *Riebenzagel,*
Praetor. Alectr. 178-9; *Rübezal,* Opitz 2, 280-1; ' 20 acres in
the *Rübenzagil,*' Widder's Pfalz 1, 379; conf. sau-*zagil,* Hasin-*zal,*

Arnsbg urk. 410. 426. Strît-*zagel*, n. pr., Lang reg. 5, 107 (yr
1166).

p. 483.]    Garg. 119[b] names together were-wolves, *pilosi, goat-
men, dusen,* trutten, garausz, bitebawen.    On dusii conf. Hattemer
1, 230-1.    Add the *jüdel,* for whom toys are deposited, conf.
Sommer's Sag. 170. 25; 'he makes a show, as if he were the
*gütle.*' H. Sachs 1, 444[b]; ein *güttel* (götze, idol?), Wolfdietr. in
Hagen's Heldb. p. 236; *bergmendlein, cobele, gütlein,* Mathesius
1562, 296[b].——They are the Lat. *faunus,* whose loud voice the
Romans often heard : saepe *faunorum voces exauditae,* Cic. de
N.D. 2. 2; *fauni vocem* nunquam audivi 3, 7; *faunos* quorum
noctivago strepitu ludoque jocanti . . . . chordarumque sonos,
dulceisque querelas tibia quas fundit, Lucret. 4, 582; visi etiam
audire *vocem ingentem ex summi cacuminis luco,* Livy 1, 31;
silentio proximae noctis ex silva Arsia *ingentem* editam *vocem,
Silvani vocem* eam creditam 2, 7.    On Faunus and Silvanus see
Klausen pp. 844 seq. 1141.    Hroswitha (Pertz 6, 310) calls the
forest nook where Gandersheim nunnery gets built '*silvestrem*
locum *faunis monstris*-que repletum.'    Lye has *wudewâsan*
(-wasan?) =satyri, fauni, sicurii, Wright 60[a] *wudewâsan*=ficarii
(correctly) vel invii, O.E. 'a *woodwose*=satyrus' (*wâsa* elsewh.
coenum, lutum, ooze, ON. veisa), conf. '*wudewiht*=lamia' in a
Lünebg glossary of 15th cent.    In M.Neth. faunus is rendered
*volencel,* Diut. 2, 214, fr. vole, foal; because a horse's foot or
shape is attrib. to him? conf. nahtvole (Suppl. to 1054).    Again,
*fauni* are night-butterflies acc. to Du Méril's art. on KM. p. 40.
The faun is also called *fantasma* : 'to exorcize the *fantasima,*'
Decam. 7, 1. *fantoen,* Maerl. 2, 365.——Other names : *walt-
man,* Iw. 598. 622; also in Bon. 91, where Striker has *walt-
schrat*; *walt-tôre* 440; *walt-geselle, -genôz, -gast,* Krone 9266-76,
*wilder man* 9255; *wilde leute,* Bader no. 9261. 346.    With them
are often assoc. wild women, *wildez wip,* Krone 9340; *wald-
minchen,* Colshorn p. 92; conf. *wildeweibs-bild, -zehnte,* a rocky
height near Birstein, Landau's Kurhessen p. 615.    Pfister p. 271;
*holzweibel-steine* in Silesia, Mosch p. 4.    The wild man's wife is
called *fangga,* Zingerle 2, 111 (conf. 2, 51. Wolf's Ztschr. 2,
58); *fanggen-löcher, -holes* 2, 53; in Vorarlbg *feng, fenggi,
fengga-mäntschi,* Vonbun 1—6.    Wolf's Z. 2, 50; conf. *Finz*
(Suppl. to 484).    The ON. *iviðr* may be malus, perversus,

dolosus, conf. Goth. invinds, OS. inwid, OHG. inwittêr dolosus, îviðgiarn, Sæm. 138ᵃ. In Syryän. *vörsa*＝silvae genius, fr. vör, silva.

p. 484.] Of îviðjur and iarnviðjur little is known, but the *skôgs-râ* akin to them was supposed to live in trees, and any wrong done to him brought on sickness, Fries's Udfl. 1, 109 ; he dies with the tree, conf. walt-minne (p. 434), hamadryas. The skogrât has a long tail, Dyb. Runa 4, 88 ; *skogeroa* and *sjögeroa* boast of their deeds and wealth 4, 29. 40.——The *wood-wives* in Germany wail and cry (pp. 433. 1135): 'you cry like a wood-wife,' Uhl. Volksl. 149. The holz-frau is shaggy and wild, over-grown with moss, H. Sachs 1, 273. The *Finz-weibl* on the Finz (Bav.) is spotted, and wears a broad-brimmed hat, Panz. Beitr. 1, 22 (Fenggi in preced. note). Fasolt's and Ecke's mother is a *rauhes weib*, Ecke 231. The holz-weibl spin till 'lichel' comes out, Mosch. p. 4. They dread the Wild Hunter, as the sub-terraneans flee from Wode, Müllenh. p. 372-3. The wild man rides on a stag, Ring 32ᵇ, 34. The Hunter chases the moos-weibla or loh-jungfer (p. 929), and wild men the blessed maids, Steub's Tirol p. 319 ; in the Etzels hofh. the wonder-worker pursues Frau Sælde (p. 943), as Fasolt in Ecke 161—179 (ed. Hagen 213—238. 333) does the wild maiden.——Men on the contrary are often on good terms with them : at haymaking or harvest they rake a little heap together, and leave it lying, for 'that's the *wood-maiden's* due.' In pouring out of a dish, when drops hang on the edge, don't brush them off, they belong to the *moss-maiden*. When a wood-maiden was caught, her little man came running up, and cried : ' A wood-maiden may tell anything, barring the use you can make of *drip-water*,' Panz. Beitr. 2, 161. A thankful little woodwife exclaims : 'bauern-blut, du bist gut,' Börner p. 231. To the *bush-grandmother* on the Saale corresp. the Esthonian *forest-father, tree-host*, Böcler 146.

p. 485.] Dwarfs and woodwives will not have *cummin-bread*, Firmen. 2, 264ᵇ. A wood-maiden near Wonsgehei said to a woman : ' Never a fruitful tree pull up, Tell no dream till you've tasted a cup (lit., no fasting dream), *Bake no Friday's bread*, And God, etc.' Panz. Beitr. 2, 161.——That wood-mannikins and dwarfs, after being *paid*, esp. in gold or clothes, give up the

service of man, comes out in many stories. The wichtels by
Zürgesheim in Bavarian Swabia used to wash the people's linen
and bake them bread ; when money was left out for them because
they went naked, they said weeping : 'now we're *paid off*, we
must *jog* ' ; conf. N.Preuss. prov. bl. 8, 229. Bader no. 99.
Vonbun p. 9 (new ed. 11—15). Panz. B. 1, 40-2-8. 156.    2, 160.
The same of *hill-mannikins*, Steub's Tirol p. 82 ; *fenggamäntschi*,
Vonbun p. 3 ; *nork*, Steub p. 318 ; *futtermännchen*, Börner p.
·243-6 : *Hob*, Hone's Tablebk. 2, 658 and Yearbk. 1533.    A
*pixy*, who helped a woman to wash, disappears when presented
with a coat and cap.  Pixies, who were helping to thrash, dance
merrily in a barn when a peasant gives them new clothes, and
only when shot at by other peasants do they vanish, singing
' Now the pixies' work is done, We take our clothes and off we
run,' Athenm. no. 991.

p. 487.] The *huorco* sits on a *tree-stump*, Pentam. 1, 1.  Ari-
osto's descr. of the *orco* and his wife in Orl. fur. xvii. 29—65 is
pretty long-winded : he is blind (does not get blinded), has a
flock like Polyphemus, eats men, but not women.  *Ogres* keep
their crowns on in bed, Petit poucet p. m. 162-3.  Aulnoy p. m.
358. 539.  Akin to orco is the Tyrolese wood-sprite *nork*, *nörkele*,
*lork*, Steub's Tirol pp. 318-9. 472 and Rhæt. 131 ; conf. *norg* =
pumilio in B. Fromm. 3, 439, *norggen*, *lorggen*, *nörggin*, *nörklein*,
Wolf's Ztschr. 1, 289. 290. 2, 183-4.  To Laurin people call :
' her *Nörggel* unterm tach ! '  Ring 52[b], 2.  The Finn. *Hiisi* is
both Orcus (hell), giant and wood-man.  The Swed. *skogsnerte*,
*skogsnufva* in Fries's Udfl. 110 is a beautiful maiden in front, but
hollow (ihålig) behind ; and the *skogssnua* is described in the
same way, Runa, '44, 44-5.  Wieselgren 460.

p. 488.]  Ein *merminne*, Tit. 5268.  *mareminne*, Clarisse on
Br. Gher. p. 222.  Nennius says the potamogēton natans is called
*seeholde;* conf. *custos fontium* (Suppl. to 584) and the *hollen* in
Kuhn's Westph. s. 1, 200.  τὸ στοιχεῖον τοῦ ποταμοῦ, Fauriel 2,
77.  Other names : wilder *wazzerman*, Krone 9237 ; daz *merwip*,
who hurls a cutting spear at the hero, Roseng. xxii. ; *sjö-rå*, Dyb.
4, 29. 41.  On the *hafsfruu* see Suppl. to 312.

p. 489.]  *Nikhus*, neut., Diut. 3, 25.  Karajan 80, 4.  *nykus*
even in a Wend. folksong 2, 267[a].  *nichessa* = lymphae, N. Cap.
52.  *nickers*, Br. Gher. 719.  Van d. Bergh p. 180 thinks nikker

is for niger: 'zoo zwart als een nikker'; but the idea of black-
ness may have been borrowed from the later devil. *neckers*,
Gefken's Beil. 151. 168. *nickel*-mann, Hpt's Ztschr. 5, 378;
conf. too the ON. Nöckvi, Sæm. 116ᵃ. The supposed connexion
of the R. *Neckar* with *nicor*, *nechar* is supported by the story on
p. 493-4.——Esth. *vessi hallias*, Finn. *weden haldia*, aquae dominus, Possart p. 163; conf. Ahto (Suppl. to 237). The siren,
whom Conrad calls *wasser-nixe*, is also called cajoler, Boh. *lichoples*
(p. 436 n.), and *ochechule*, Jungm. 2, 903, *wochechule* fr. lichotiti,
ochechulati, to flatter. Spring-nixen (f.) are the Swed. *källråden*,
Sv. folks. 1, 123. A pretty Silesian story of the *wasser-lisse* in
Firmen. 2, 334; does this represent *wazzer-dieze*? The Lusch in
Gryphius's Dornrose is Liese, Elisabeth.

p. 490.] The nymphæa is in Gael. *baditis*, AS. *eá-docce*, Engl.
water-*dock*, Bav. *docke*, *wasser-dockelein* (tocke, doll, girl), conf.
seeblatt (p. 654), Swed. *näck-ros-blad*. On *näckrosor*, Dybeck '45,
64-6; *necken* har sin boning bland *neckroserne*, och uppstigande
på dess blad ännu stundom i mån-skens-natten med sitt stränga-
spel tjuser åhöraren, Fries bot. udfl. 1, 108. The water-maiden
sits on leaves of the waterlily, Müllenh. p. 340; a *nix-bitten*
(-bütten) meadow near Betziesdorf, Hess. Ztschr. 1, 245. The
Syryän. kulĭ = genius aquae, kulĭ-ciurĭ = digitus ejusdem.——
Merwomen prophesy, sometimes deceitfully, like Hadburc in
the Nibel. When a *hav-fru* is saying sooth to queen Dagmar,
the phrase is used: 'vedst du det, saa vedst du mer,' D. V. 2,
83-4-5. In Mecklenbg. the *water-möm* sends her prophetic voice
out of the water, Lisch 5, 78. A spectre foretelling death shows
itself on the Danube whirlpool, Ann. Altahenses, yr 1045 (Giesebrecht p. 75); conf. the soothsaying merwomen (p. 434).

p. 491.] The Scotch kelpie takes the shape of a *horse*, whose
presence is known by his *nicker* (neigh); he draws men in, and
shatters ships. Or he rises as a bull, the *waterbull*; the same is
told of the *water-shelly*, and the Danes have a water-sprite *Dam-
hest*, Athenm. no. 997. The nixe appears as a richly caparisoned
*foal*, and tempts children to mount her, Possart's Estl. p. 163.
This *horse* or *bull*, rising out of the sea and running away with
people, is very like Zeus visiting Europa as a bull, and carrying
her into the water; conf. Lucian, ed. Bip. 2, 125. The water-
möm tries to drag you in, she wraps rushes and sedge about your

feet when bathing, Lisch 5, 78. The *merminne* steals Lanzelet
from his mother, Lanz. 181 ; conf. Sommer p. 173.

p. 493.] The merman is *long-bearded;* so has 'daz merwunder
einen *bart lanc, grüenfar* und *ungeschaffen,*' Wigam. 177; its
body is 'in *mies gewunden,*' Gudr. 113, 3. The mermaid *combs*
her hair, Müllenh. p. 338 ; this combing is also Finnish, Kalev.
22, 307 seq. The nixe has but one *nostril,* Sommer, p. 41. The
water-nix (m.) wears a *red cape,* Hpt's Ztschr. 4, 393, *blue breeches,*
*red stockings,* Hoffm. Schles. lied. p. 8. The *beauty* of the nixen
·(f.) is dwelt upon in the account of the *wasserlüss,* Gryph. 743,
and the *wasserlisse,* Firmen. 2, 334. They have *wet aprons,*
Somm. p. 40-5. Wend. volksl. 2, 267ᵃ. The nixe dances in a
*patched gown,* Somm. p. 44. The sea-maiden shows *a tail* in
dancing, Runa 4, 73. Their coming in to dance is often spoken
of, Panzer 2, nos. 192-6-8. 204-8. Like the sacrifice to the fosse-
grim clothed in grey and wearing a red cap, Runa '44, 76, is the
custom of throwing a *black cock* into the Bode once a year for the
*nickelmann,* Hpt's Ztschr. 5, 378 ; and like his playing by the
waterfall is Ahto's seizing Wäinämöinen's harp when it falls into
the water, Kal. 23, 183.

p. 494.] On river sacrifices conf. p. 596. Nixes (m.) demand
their victim on Midsum. day, Somm. p. 39 : 'de Leine fret alle
jar teine ; ' 'de Rume un de Leine slucket alle jar teine,' Schamb.
spr. p. 87. 'The Lahn must have some one every year' they say
at Giessen. 'La rivière de Drome a tous les ans cheval ou homme,'
Pluquet's Contes pop., p. 116. In the Palatinate they say of the
*Neckar:* when it is flooded, a hand rises out of it, and carries off
its victim. On Midsum. night the *Neckar-geist* requires a living
soul ; for three days the drowned man can nowhere be found, on
the fourth night he floats up from the bottom with a blue ring
round his neck, Nadler p. 126. At Cologne they say : Sanct
Johann wel hann 14 *dude mann,* siben de klemme, siben de
*schwemme* (the seven that climb are workmen on scaffoldings) ;
conf. '*putei* qui *rapere* dicuntur per vim spiritus nocentis,' Tertull.
de Baptismo (Rudorff 15, 215).

p. 496.] The injunction *not to beat down* the price (p. 495n.)
occurs also in a story in Reusch's Preuss. prov. bl. 23, 124. In
buying an animal for sacrifice you must *not haggle,* Athen. 3, 102;
the fish aper must be bought *at any price,* 3, 117-8. '*emi* lienem

vituli, quanti indicatus sit, jubent magi, *nulla pretii cunctatione,*' Pliny 28, 13.——Lashing the water reminds us of a nix who opens the way to his house by *smiting the water with a rod*, Somm. pp. 41. 92 ; *blood* appears on the water, 46. 174 ; an *apple* as a favourable sign, Hoffm. Schles. lied. p. 4. Grendel comes *walking by night*, as the râkshasi is called ' noctu iens,' Bopp's Gloss. 188ª. 198ᵇ.

p. 498.] Râ is neut., def. *râet ;* also *râand, râdrottning,* Sv. folks. 1, 233. 74 (Suppl. to 439). Souls kept under inverted pots by the water man occur again in KM. no. 100 and Müllenh. p. 577. *Neptunius, Neptenius* is also transl. *altvil,* Homeyer's Rechtsb. 14. Watersprites *wail,* or in other ways reveal their presence : the sjö-mor *moans,* Dyb. '45, 98 ; conf. ' gigantes *gemunt sub aquis,*' Job 26, 5 ; ἡνίκ' ἔμελλον τὸν ποταμὸν διαβαίνειν, τὸ δαιμόνιόν τε καὶ τὸ εἰωθὸς σημαῖόν μοι γίγνεσθαι ἐγένετο, Plato's Phædr. 242. A tradition similar to Gregory's anecdote is given by Schönwerth 2, 187.

p. 500.] *Penates* were gods of the household store, penus. *Lares* were in Etruscan *lases,* Gerh. Etr. götter p. 15-6 ; *Lasa* = Fortuna. A legend of the lar familiaris in Pliny 36, 70. Was there a Goth. lôs = domus, and did *Luarin* mean homesprite ? Lares, penates, OHG. *hûsgota* or *herdgota,* Graff 4, 151. Home-sprites are called *hus-knechtken,* Müllenh. p. 318, *haus-puken ;* Russ. *domovoy ; tomtar,* Dyb. 4, 26 ; Finn. *tonttu,* Castrén 167. On Span. *duende, duendecillo* conf. Diez's Wtb. 485 ; couroit comme un *lutin par toute sa demeure,* Lafont. 5, 6. A genius loci is also *Agathodaemon,* Gerh. in Acad. ber. '47, p. 203-4 ; conf. the bona socia, the good holden, the *bona dea, bona fortuna* and *bonus eventus* worshipped by the country folk, Ammian. Marc. 582-3. The *puk* lives in cellars, Mone's Schausp. 2, 80-6 ; niss *puk,* niss *pug,* Müllenh. pp. 318. 325 ; nise*buk,* niske*puks* 321-4. MLG. *pûk* (rh. strûk, bûk), Upstand. 1305. 1445. Lett. *puhkis,* dragon, kobold, Bergm. 152 ; conf. *pixy.*

p. 502 n.] So, ' laughing *like pixies.*' [Other expressions omitted.]

p. 503.] To the earliest examples of *kobold,* p. 500 n., add Lodovicus *caboldus,* yr. 1221, Lisch, Meckl. urk. 3, 71 [later ones, including Cabolt, Kaboldisdhorpe, &c., omitted].——To speak ' in *koboldes* sprâche' means very softly, Hagen's Ges. Abent. 3, 78.

A concealed person in Enenkel (Rauch 1, 316) says: ich rede in *chowolcz* wîse. Lessing 1, 292 : the *kobold* must have whispered it in my ear. Luther has kobold in Isa. 34, 14. *cobel*, der schwarze teufel, die teufels-hure, Mathesius 1562, 154ᵇ. *Gobelinus*, a man's name, Mone's Heldens. 13. 15. *Hob*, a homesprite, Hone's Tablebk 3, 657 (conf. p. 503, n. 1).——May we bring in here the *klabauter*-man, *klüter*-man, Müllenh. p. 320, a ship-sprite, sometimes called *kalfater*, *klabater*-man, Temme's Pom. sag. no. 253, Belg. *kaboter*-man ? Nethl. *coubouton*, Br. Gher. 719. The *taterman*, like the kobold, is painted : " mâlet einen *taterman*," Jungeling, 545.

p. 505.] At Cologne they call homesprites *heizemänncher*, Firmen. 1, 467. Knecht *Heinz* in Fischart's Spiel. 367, and knecht Heinrich. A tom-cat is not only called Hinze, but *Heinz*, *Henz*, and a stiefel-knecht (bootjack, lit. boot-servant) *stiefel-henz* (boot-puss), coming very near the resourceful Puss-in-boots. The *tabby-cat* brings you mice, corn and money overnight; after the third service you can't get rid of her, Müllenh. p. 207. A serviceable *tom-cat* is not to be shaken off, Temme's Pom. sag. p. 318. House-goblins, like the moss-folk, have in them something of the nature of *apes*, which also are trained to perform household tasks, conf. Felsenburg 1, 240. The Lettons too have a miraculous cat *Runzis* or *Runkis*, who carries grain to his master, Bergm. p. 152; conf. the homesprites *Hans*, Pluquet's Contes pop. 12, *Hänschen*, Somm. pp. 33-4, 171, and *Good Johann*, Müllenh. p. 323.——On the Wolterkens conf. Müllenh. p. 318. In Holstein they call knecht Ruprecht *Roppert* 319, with whom and with Wôden Kuhn compares *Robin Hood*, Hpt's Ztschr. 5, 482-3. For the *nisken*, and the *nis*, *nispuk*, *nesskuk* consult Müllenh. 318-9. The home-sprite, like the devil, is occas. called *Stepchen*, Somm. 33. 171; and lastly, *Billy blind*, Minstr. 2, 399.

p. 506.] The spirits *thump* and *racket*, Goethe 15, 131. *Klopferle* (knockerling) rackets before the death of one of the family with which he lives, G. Schwab's Alb. p. 227. ' Was für ein *polter-geist handtiert* (bustles) durch die lichten zimmer ? ' Günth. 969 ; *plagegeist*, Musæus 4, 53 ; *rumpel-geist*, S. Frank's Chron. 212ᵇ ; ' ez *rumpelt* staete *für sich* dar,' Wasserbär 112 ; *bozen* or *mumantz* in the millet-field, Reimdich 145 ; *alpa-butz*,

alp dæmon, Vonbun p. 46-7-8. 'Quoth the mother: Nit gang
hinusz, der *mummel* (or, der *man*) ist dusz ; for the child feareth
the *mummel* (man),' Keisersbg's Bilgr. 166ᶜ. To *vermummen*
and *verbutzen* oneself, H. Sachs i. 5, 534ᶜ. Not only *Rumpelstilt*,
but *Knirfiker, Gebhart, Tepentiren* (Müllenh. p. 306-7-8), *Titteli
Ture* (Sv. folkv. 1, 171) must have their names guessed. Other
names : *Kugerl*, Zingerle 2, 278, *Stutzlawutzla*, Wolf's Ztschr.
2, 183.

p. 507.] The *butzen-hänsel* is said to go in and out through
the open gutter, as other spectres pass through the city moat,
Müllenh. p. 191. *Buzemannes*, a place in Franconia, MB. 25,
110-1; *Putzmans*, ib. 218. 387. Lutbertus qui *budde* dicitur,
Gerhardus dictus *budde*, Sudendf. pp. 69. 70. 89 (yr. 1268),
*butzen-antlitz*, mask, Anshelm 1, 408. Garg. 122ᵇ; *butzen-
kleider*, Ansh. 3, 411 ; does *butzen, putzen* strictly mean to mask
oneself ? The Swiss *böög, bögk, bröög* = mask, bugbear, Stald. 1,
202. 230 ; *böggen-weise*, a Shrovetide play, Schreib. Taschenb.
'40, 230; *bögglman*, Lazarillo Augsb. 1617, p. 5 (?). *Bröög*
seems akin to bruogo, AS. brôga = terror, terriculamentum.

p. 508.] On the Fr. *follet*, conf. Diefenb. Celt. 1, 182. The
*folet* allows the peasant who has caught him three wishes, if he
will not show him to the people, Marie de Fr., Fables, p. 140.
The *farfadet* de Poissy comes out of the fireplace to the women
who are inspecting each other's thighs, and shows his backside,
Réveille-matin, p. m. 342. 'Malabron *le luiton*,' Gaufrey, p. 169.
O.Fr. *rabat* = lutin. M.Neth. *rebas*, Gl. to Lekensp. p. 569. In
Bretagne, *Poulpikan* is a roguish sprite, repres. as husband of
the fay, and found in Druidic monuments. Lett. *kehms, kehmis*,
goblin, spectre; also *lulkis*, Bergm. 145. Is *götze*, Uhl. Volksl.
754 a goblin ?

p. 511.] '*Hödeke* howls ' = it is stormy, Hildesh. stiftsfehde
pp. 48. 91. Falke thinks the whole story of Hödeke is *trumped
up*, Trad. corb. 135. *Hütchen* is a little red mannikin with
sparkling eyes, wears a long green garment, Somm. pp. 26-9.
30. 171. In Voigtland they tell of the goblin *Pump-hut*, who
once haunted the neighbourhood of Pausa, always worked hard
as a *miller's man*, and played many a roguish trick, Bechst. in
Nieritz volks-kal. '46, pp. 78—80. The same *Pump*-hut in
Westphalia, Kuhn's Westf. sag. 2, 279; mentioned even in Insel

Felsenbg, Nordh. 1746, 2, 366—370. About Münster they distinguish between *timp-hüte* and *lang-hüte* : the former are small, wrinkled, hoary, old-fashioned, with three-cornered hats ; the latter tall, haggard, in a slouched hat. Timp-hat bestows positive blessings, long-hat keeps off misfortune. They live mostly in the barn or a deserted loft, and slowly turn a creaking windlass. In fires they have been seen to stride out of the flames and strike into a by-way. Conf. the homesprite *Dal-kopp*, N. Pr. prov. bl. 1, 394. Elsewhere they live in a corner *behind the oven,* under the *roof-beam,* or in *gable-holes,* where a board is put out to attract them, Müllenh. pp. 321-2. 332-5-7. Hpt's Lausitzer sag. 1, 56 seq.——The goblin sits *on the hearth,* flies out at the *chimney,* shares the peasant's room, Somm. p. 27-9. Spirits in the cellar, over the casks, Simplic. 2, 264-5 ; conf. Abundia (pp. 286. 1056). The goblin carries things to his master, but can only bring a certain quantity, and will change masters if more be demanded, Somm. p. 27 (see p. 512). He fetches milk from other men's cows, like the *dragon,* the Swed. *bare* (p. 1090) and the devil ; here he encroaches on the witch and devil province. He helps in milking, licks up the spilt drops, Müllenh. p. 325. Goblins curry down and feed the cattle, and have their favourite beasts, Somm. p. 36-7 ; hence the name *futter-männchen,* Börner's Orlagau p. 241-2. A homesprite *bier-esel* in Kuhn's Nordd. sag. no. 225, conf. pp. 423. 521. They speak in a *tiny voice,* ' in koboldes sprâche,' Müllenh. p. 335. Hagen's Ges. Abent. 3, 78 ; and yet: mit *grôzer stimme* er dô schrei 79. As nothing was seen of king Vollmar but his shadow, so is Good Johann like a *shadow,* Müllenh. p. 323. They are often seen in the shape of a *toad,* pp. 355. 330, also as *tom* or *tabby cat* (Suppl. to 505). The Albanians imagine their homesprite vittore as a little snake, Hahn's Lieder 136. A good description of the *kobold* in Firmen. 2, 237-8. The herb *agermund,* Garg. 88^b, seems conn. with *Agemund,* the house-dæmon in Reinardus.

p. 511.] The homesprite being οἰκουρός, agathodaemon (p. 485-6), there is milk, honey and sugar set on the bench for him, as for the unke, Schweinichen 1, 261. In the Schleswig-Holstein stories they must always have *pap* or *groats,* with a *piece of butter* in. The goblin has the *table spread* for him, Somm. p. 32. *Napf-hans* is like the Lat. *Lateranus,* Arnob. 4, 6 ; Lateranus *deus* est *focorum* et *genius*, adjectusque hoc nomine, quod ex laterculis ab hominibus crudis caminorum istud exaedificetur genus . . . per humani generis coquinas currit, inspiciens et explorans quibusnam lignorum generibus suis ardor in foculis excitetur, *habitudinem fictilis* contribuit *vasculis*, ne flammarum dissiliant vi victa, curat ut ad sensum palati suis cum jocunditatibus veniant rerum incorruptarum sapores, et an rite pulmenta condita sint, praegustatoris fungitur atque experitur officio. Hartung 2, 109 says it is *Vulcanus* caminorum deus; certainly Varro in fragm. p. 265 ed. Bip. makes Vulcan the preserver of pots: Vulcanum necdum *novae lagenae ollarum frangantur* ter precatur (conf. p. 447).

p. 512.] A goblin appears as a *monk*, Somm. pp. 35. 172-3. With *Shellycoat* conf. *Schellen-moriz* 153-4. Homesprites demand but trifling wages, as in the pretty story of a serving dæmon who holds the stirrup for his master, guides him across the ford, fetches lion's milk for the sick wife, and at last, when dismissed, asks but five shillings wages, and gives them back to buy a bell for a poor church, using the remarkable words: magna est mihi consolatio esse cum filiis hominum, Cæsar Heisterb. 5, 36. On the Spanish goblin's *cucurucho tamaño*, observe that the lingua rustica already said tammana for tam magna, Nieb. in Abh. d. Berl. Acad. '22, 257.

p. 513 n.] The *allerürken* is a puppet locked up in a box, which brings luck, Müllenh. p. 209; conf. 'he's got an *oaraunl* inside him,' KM. 183 (infra p. 1203). Wax figures ridiculously dressed up, 'which we call *glücks-männchen*,' 10 eben, p. 357; conf. the *glückes-pfennig*, Prediger märchen 16, 17, also the well-known *ducaten-kacker*, and the doll in Straparola (5, 21). KM³. 3, 287. 291. The *Mönöloke* is a wax doll dressed up in the devil's name, Müllenh. p. 209; conf. the *dragedukke*, a box out of which you may take as much money as you will.——A homesprite can be bought, but the third buyer must keep him, Müllenh. p. 322. One buys a *poor* and a *rich* goblin, Somm. p. 33. Such sprites they made in Esthonia of tow, rags and fir-bark, and got the devil to animate them, Possart's Esthl. p. 162; more exactly described in the Dorp. verhandl. i. 2, 89. So the shamans make a fetish for the Samoyèds out of a sheep-skin, Suomi '46, p. 37-8-9.

p. 516.]   On the *manducus*, see O. Müller's Etr. 2, 101 (conf.
p. 1082).   'Quid si aliquo *ad ludos* me *pro manduco* locem? quia
pol clare *crepito dentibus*,' Plaut. Rud. ii. 6, 52.   This too is the
place for *schemen:* 'als dakten sich die schamn (l. *schemen*) ê, do
si *diu kint schrakten mit*,' to frighten children with, Jüngl. 698.
Are *schemen* masks?   conf. 'schönbart' for *schem-bart*, OHG.
scema = larva, persona, like hage-bart, Schm. 3, 362.   Graff 6,
495.   On *Ruprecht* see Kuhn in Hpt's Ztschr. 5, 473.   von den
sogenandten *Rupperten,* die sich 'bunt und *rauch* untereinander
anziehen,' or 'einen *rauchen* pelz,' 3 erzn. 369.   *Knecht Ruprecht*
(or Krampus, Klaubauf, meister Strohbart) is St. Nicolas's *man*,
Ziska's Oestr. volksm. 49, 110.   *Hollepeter,* Wolf's Ztschr. 2, 194.
'dich müez der *Semper* machen g'sunt,' the devil have the curing
of you!   Ring 14$^d$, 5.   To him corresp. old *Grumbus* with the
rod, Firmen. 2, 45, and *Fiele Gig* (fidele geige?) of the Kuh-
ländchen, described in Schlegel's Mus. 4, 119.   Walloon '*hans-
croufe,* valet de S. Nicolas,' our Hans Buckel (croufe = bosse),
Grandgagn. 1, 271.   As Niclas has a man, Gargantua has a *drôle*
in his retinue, Mém. celt. 5, 393-4.   Our knecht Ruprecht is Russ.
*buka,* Gretsch p. 109, Lett. *bubbulis.*   His Styrian name of *Klaubauf* resembles the *winterklaub,* Wolkenst. p. 67.   A *sooty* face
belongs to the phallophorus also, Athen. 5, 254.   St. Peter, who
may be regarded as Ruprecht's representative, when journeying
with Christ, always behaves as a good-natured simpleton.

As people sacrificed to forest-women (p. 432), so they did to
subterraneans, Müllenh. p. 281.   On feast-days the Ossetes place
a portion of the viands in a separate room for the homesprite to
eat; they are miserable if he does not, and are delighted to find
a part of them gone, Kohl's Süd-russl. 1, 295.   A Roman setting
out on a journey took leave of the familiaris : 'etiam nunc saluto
te, *familiaris,* priusquam eo,' Plaut. Mil. gl. iv. 8, 29.

# CHAPTER XVIII.

## GIANTS.

p. 518.]   In some ways men, elves and giants stand related as
men, angels and devils.   Giants are the oldest of all creatures,
and belong to the stone-age.   Here we have to make out more
fully, that giants and titans are the *old nature-gods.*

p. 520.] Mere descriptive epithets of giants are: der *grôze man*, Ernst 469. 4288; der *michel man*, Lanz. 7705; der *michel*, der *grôze*, Altd. bl. 2, 149. So of their country: *unkundigez lant*, Roth. 625, and *der riesin lande* 761 (=iötun-heim, p. 530); of their nation: *unkundigiu diet* 630. The ON. *iötunn*, AS. *eoten* is supported by the dimin. *Etenca* (?). Is *Etionas* (for Oxionas) in Tac. Germ. 46 the same word? Hpt's Ztschr. 9, 256. Surely *hethenesberg, hedenesbg, hettesnasmont, etanasbg* in Chart. Sithiense 158. 80. 160-2 are not heathen's hill nor hätenbg? Graff 1, 370 has *Entinesburc* (conf. p. 525). *Etenesleba*, Dronke 233ᵃ. ——Leo in Vorles. über d. gesch. d. Deut. volks 1, 112 agrees with me in tracing the word to ON. eta, AS. etan; conf. *mann-aeta* (p. 520n. and Şuppl. to 555), the giant's name *Wolfes mage* (Suppl. to 557), and a giant being addressed as ' dû *ungaeber frâz !*' Dietr. drach. 238ᵇ. Ssk. *kravyâd*, Bopp's Gr. § 572. Finn. turilas, tursas, turras = *edax, gluto*, gigas; and this is confirmed by the two words for giantess, *syöjätär*, lit. femina vorax, fr. sjön = edo, and *juojotar*, lit. femina bibax, fr. juon = bibo, Schiefner's Finn. w. 606-8.——Schafarik 1, 141 connects iötun, jätte with *geta* in Massagĕta, Thussagete (p. 577n.). Thorlacius sp. 6, p. 24 thinks *iotar, iötnar, risar* are all one. Rask on the contrary distinguishes *Jötunheimar* (jätternes land) from *Jótland* (jydernes land), likewise Jötunn (gigas) from Jóti (a Jute), Afh. 1, 77-8. GDS. 736; he takes the iötnar to be *Finns* (more exactly Kvaener), and Jötunheimar perhaps Hâlogaland, Afh. 1, 85-6; but in a note to Sæm. 33 he identifies the iötnar with the *Eistir*. Swed. *jätte* och *jättesa*, Cavallius 25. 467. *Jettha, Jettenberg* may be for Jeccha, Jechenberg, as Jechelburg became Jethelberg. *Jetene-burg, Getenburg* occur in deeds of the 13th cent., Wipperm. nos. 41. 60. *Jettenbach* on the Hundsrück, Höfer's Urk. p. 37. The giant's munching, ' mesan,' p. 519, should be *mêsan*, OHG. muosan.

p. 522.] It seems that *þyrja* þioð in Sæm. 82ᵇ does not mean torridorum gens, but stands for þursa, þyrsa. With Dan. *tosse* conf. *dysse*-troll, Sv. forns. 1, 92-8. Grendel is called a *þyrs*, Beow. 846. As the rune *þurs* in ON. corresp. to *þorn* in AS., we have even in ON. a giant named Böl-*þorn*, Sæm. 28ᵃ. Sn. 7; should it be Bâlþorn, fire-thorn? It is strange that Alvîs, though a dwarf, says: *þursa líki þycci mer â þer vera*, Sæm. 48ᵃ. OHG.

*durisis* = Ditis, Hpt's Ztschr. 5, 329[b]. Gl. Sletst. 6, 169. 'mære
von eime tursen,' KM.[3] 3, 275. In Thuringia the *thurschemann*,
Bechst. März. 63. We still say 'der torsch.' To the Austrian
families of Lichtenfels, Tiernstein, Rauheneck and Rauhenstein
the by-name *türse*, Lat. *turso*, was habitual in the 12—15th cents.,
Heiligenkr. 1, 32. 46. 127. 179. 2, 14. 26. Women were called
*tursin*, see Leber's book. *Türsemûl*, peasant's name, MsH. 3,
293[b]. 'in *thurislôun*,' Falke's Trad. Corb. 100-1. 354. Saracho
p. 7, no. 81, ed. Wigand 281-4. 420; *tursen-ouwe*, etc. Mone's Anz.
6, 231; *Thyrsentritt*, E. of Lechthal, Steub's Rhät. 143; *Tirschen-*
*tritt, Dirschentritt*, Gümbel's Bair. Alpe pp. 217. 247; *Dursgesesz*,
Landau's Wüste örter in Hessen p. 377; *Türschenwald* in Salzach
dale, M. Koch 221; *Türstwinkel*, Weisth. 4, 129. Renvall has
Finn. *tursas, turras, turrisas, turri* = giant, *turilas* = homo edax,
vorax; *meritursas*, Schröter p. 135. Petersen p. 42. GDS. 122-3.

Dionys. Halic. 1, 21 thought the Τυρρηνοί were so called because they reared high towers, τύρσεις. That agrees with the
giants' buildings (p. 534-5).

p. 524.] On Hunen-beds and Hunen, see Janssen's Drentsche
oudheden pp. 167—184, conf. GDS. 475. Does the Westph.
*henne*-kleid, grave-clothes, mean hünen-kleid? or hence-going
clothes, as in some parts of Westphalia a dying man's last com-
munion was called henne-kost?——'Als ein *hiune* gelidet,' having
giant's limbs, Troj. kr. 29562; *hiune* is often used in J. v. Soest's
Marg. von Limburg (Mone's Anz. '34, 218); Ortleip der *hiune*,
Ls. 3, 401; 'der groten *hunen* (gigantum),' B. d. kön. 112.
Strangely the *hühnen* in Firmen. 1, 325 are dwarfs, subterraneans,
who are short-lived, and kidnap children, though like hünen they
live in a hill; conf. the *hünnerskes*, Kuhn's Westf. sag. 1, 63-4.
As the ON. hûnar is never quite synonymous with iötnar and
þursar, so the *heunen* are placed after the giants as a younger
race, Baader's Sag. no. 387. GDS. 475.

p. 525.] Other examples of AS. *ent:* gelŷfdon (believed) on
*deáde entas*, AS. homil. 1, 366; on *enta* hláve (cave), Kemble 4,
49; on *entan* hlew 5, 265.——*Entines*-burc, Graff 1, 370; *Enzins*-
perig, MB. 2, 197; *Anzin*-var, Hess. Ztschr. 1, 246, like Ruozel-
mannes var, Mone's Anz. '36, 300; ad giganteam viam, *entisken*
wec, Wien. sitz. ber. 4, 141; von *enten* swarz unde grâ kan ich
nit vil sagen, KM. [3] 3, 275.

p. 525.] Mercury is called ' se *gygand* ' (p. 149) ; die *ghigante,*
*gigante,* Rose 5135-82. Biörn writes *gigr,* Aasen 152[b] has jygger,
*gyvr* for gygr (conf. ' ze Gîvers,' Suppl. to 961) ; *giögra,* Faye
6. A giant is called *kämpe,* Müllenh. pp. 267. 277. Otos and
Ephialtes, gigantes though not cyclopes, are sons of Poseidon,
and the cyclop Polyphemus is another. Acc. to Diut. 3, 59 and
the Parz. and Tit. (p. 690 n.), monsters were born of women who
had eaten forbidden herbs.

p. 526.] Does *Hrisberg* stand for Wrisberg ? Lüntzel's Hildesh. 23. *riesen-kint,* Laurin 2053. 2509. 2604, and enzen-kint,
like menschen-kind, son of man.——A *Lubbes-stein* in Müllenh.
no. 363, p. 272 ; *Lüpperts-grab,* Vilmar in Hess. Ztschr. 4, 79 ;
*Lüppenhart, Lüppental,* Mone's Anz. 6, 229 ; die *Lupbode,*
Pröhle's Unterharz p. 212, conf. lüppe, poison (p. 1151). ON.
*leifi,* gigas, *óleifi,* humanus ; *rumr,* vir immanis, gigas. Whence
comes *trigene* = gigantes ? Graff 5, 512.

p. 526.] *Gifr* = oreas, Sæm. 143[b] (Suppl. to 525). Other
terms for giantess : *fála,* Sæm. 143[b] (conf. p. 992) ; *hâla* 143[b].
144[a] ; *Griðr* in Sn. 113 is the name of a g$\hat{y}$gr, and her staff is
named *Griðarvölr* 114.——*Tröll* is both monster and giant : ertu
*tröll,* Vatnsd. 292 ; þú þykki mer *tröll,* Isl. sög. 2, 365 ; *hâlf-tröll,*
Nialss. c. 106. 120 ; *trölla-skog,* Landn. 5, 5 ; *trölla-skeið,* curri-
culum gigantum (Suppl. to 85) ; in Färöe, *trölla-botn* is giants'
land. *Trollrygr, Trollagrof,* Werlauff's Grenzb. 16. 22. 35. Michel
Beham had heard ' troll ' in Denmark and Norway, says Mone's
Anz. 4, 450 ; but the word had been at home on German soil long
before that : vor diesem *trolle,* Ortn. 338, 2 ; er schlug den *trollen*
Liederb. (1582) 150 ; ein voller *troll* 215 ; *wintertrolle,* Mone's
Anz. 6, 236 ; ' exsurge sede, tu *trolgast,* cito recede ' says a verse
of the 14th cent., Hpt's Ztschr. 5, 463 ; einen *drulgast* laden,
Weisth. 1, 552 ; de *Drulshaghene,* Erhard p. 144 (yr 1118) ; be-
*trullet,* Tit. 5215 (Kl. schr. 4, 336). But whence comes the Fr.
*dróle,* form. *draule?* It is rather a goblin like the M. Neth.
*drollen,* Belg. mus. 2, 116. Kilian sub v. ; conf. Gargantua's
dróle (Suppl. to 516).

p. 527.] *Mylžinum* kalnay, giants' hills, *mylžynum* kapay,
giants' graves, Kurl. send. 1, 46-7. Boh. *obor* appears as *hobr* in
Wend. volksl. 2, 268[a]. On the giants' name *Volot, Velet, Wele-*
*tabus, Wilz,* conf. p. 1081 n. The γίγαντες of the Greeks lived in

Thrace, Paus. 1, 25; conf. the Arimaspi and Cyclopes, and the
Ind. râkshasas (p. 555). To the Hebrews the Rephaim, Anakim,
Nephilim were giant nations, Bertheau's Israel, p. 142-3-4.

p. 528.] The size of giants is expressed in various ways.
Tityos, son of Earth, covers nine roods, Od. 11, 577; Otos and
Ephialtes in their ninth year were ἐννεαπήχεις in breadth and
ἐννεόργυιοι in length 11, 307 (conf. Ἐνιαυτὸς τετράπηχυς, meaning the 4 seasons, Athen. 2, 263). Dante, Inf. 31, 58—66 poeti-
cally fixes the stature of Nimrod at 90 palms, i.e. 54 feet, which
comes to the same as Ephialtes's 9 fathoms. ' Cyclopen *hôch
sam die tanboume*,' tall as firs, Ksrchr. 357; 'ir reicht in kume
*an die knie* (ye reach scarce to their knees), sie tragent *kláfter-
langen bart*,' beards a fathom long, Dietr. u. ges. 621. Ovid's
picture of Polyphemus combing his hair with a harrow, and
shaving with a sithe, is familiar to us, Met. 13, 764.

Giants have *many heads* : the sagas tell of *three-headed, six-
headed, nine-headed* trolds, Asbjörnsen p. 102-3-4; a *seven-headed*
giant in Firmen. 1, 333ᵃ; another is *negenkopp* (9 head), Müllenh.
p. 450; conf. the *three-headed* wild woman in Fr. Arnim's März.
1, no. 8, and Conradus *Dri-heuptel*, MB. 29ᵃ, 85 (254). Pol.
dziewię-sił, Boh. dewĕ-sil, dewĕt-sil (nine-powered) = giant. The
legend of *Heimo* is in Mone's Unters. p. 288 seq., conf. Steub's
Rhät. p. 143. Ital. writers of the 16th cent. often call giants
*quatromani;* giants with 13 *elbows* in Fischart's Garg.; *Bilfinger*
in Swabia are families with 12 fingers and 12 toes; ' cum *sex
digitis* nati,' Hattemer 1, 305ᵃ; conf. ' sextus homini digitus
agnatus inutilis,' Pliny 11, 52.——Even the *one eye* of the cyclops
is not altogether foreign to our giants: in a Norweg. fairytale
*three* trolds have *one eye between them*, which goes in the middle of
the forehead, and is passed round, Jäleträet 74-5; conf. KM. no.
130 (such lending of eyes is also told of the nightingale and
blindworm, KM. ed. 1, no. 6). Polyphemus says: Unum est in
medio lumen mihi fronte, sed instar ingentis clypei, Ov. Met. 13,
850; these one-eyed beings the Greeks called *kyklōpes*, the
Romans *coclites :* coclites qui altero lumine orbi nascuntur, Pliny
xi. 37, 35; decem *coclites*, ques montibus summis Rhipaeis fodere,
Enn. in Varro 7, 71 (O. Müller p. 148); conf. Goth. haihs,
μονόφθαλμος, coecus, Hpt's Ztschr. 6, 11.——A *tail* is attrib. to
the giantess Hrîmgerðr, Sæm. 144ᵃ. Giants, like dwarfs, are

sometimes descr. as *black :* þráinn *svarti* þurs, Isl. sög. 1, 207, conf. Svart-höfði ; a *black* and an *ash-grey* giant in Dybeck 4, 41. 25. As Hrûngnir's head and shield were of stone, Hymi's haus (skull) is hard as stone, Sæm. 56ᵇ. Thôr's wife, a giantess, is named *Jarnsaxa.* The age of giants is the stone-age.

p. 528.] The adj. *nadd-göfgi,* Sæm. 98ᵇ, seems also to express the unbridled arrogance of the giant : *risenmaezic, der werlte widersaezic,* Bit. 7837. The Gr. Λαπίθαι are braggarts, and akin to the Kentaurs.

p. 529.] The 11th cent. spell ' *tumbo saz in berke* . . . . *tumb* hiez der *berc,*' etc., reminds one of Marcellus' burd. p. 29 (Kl. schr. 2, 129. 147-8) : *stupidus in monte sedebat;* and conf. Affenberg, Giegenberg, Gauchsberg (p. 680-1), Schalksberg. Note that the iötunn too is called *áttrunnr apa,* simiarum cognatus, Sæm. 55ª. The Frozen Ocean is named Dumbs-haf. Biörn says the ON. *stumr*=gigas (dummy?); conf. gŷgr, giugi (p. 525). In Fornm. sög. 1, 304 the heathen gods are called *blindir, daufir, dumbir, dauðir.*

p. 530.] On *Forniotr* see GDS. 737. hin *aldna* (gŷgr), Sæm. 5ᵇ. Giants' names : *Ör-gemlir* (our ur-alte), *þruð-gemlir, Berggemlir* (var. -gelmir). The vala has been taught wisdom by the old giants, she says : ec man iötna *ár ofborna,* þá er forðom mik froedda höfðo, Sæm. 1ª. The good faith of giants is renowned : eotena *treowe,* Beow. 2137 ; so Wäinämöinen is called the *old* (wanha) and *faithful* (waka) and *true* (totinen), Kalev. 3, 107 ; so is God (p. 21).——Polyphemus tended sheep, and the Norse giants are herdsmen too :

> sat þâr â haugi oc slô hörpu
> gŷgjar hirðir, *glaðr Egdir.* Sæm. 6ª.

Gŷmir owns flocks, and has a shepherd 82ᵇ. Thrymr strokes the manes of his horses, just as the Chron. Trudonis (Chapeaville 2, 174) speaks of 'manu comam equi delinire.' Giants know nothing of *bread* or *fire,* Fr. Arnim's Mär. 1, no. 8 ; the Finn. giants do *without fire,* Ueb. d. Finn. epos p. 39 (Kl. schr. 2, 98). Yet they have silver and gold, they even burn gold, Dybeck 4, 33-8. 42 ; their horses wear iron rings in their ears 4, 37. 43. They not only bring *misfortune* on the families of man, but bestow *luck* 4, 36, and *fruitfulness* 4, 45. Esp. is the *giantess,* the giant's wife,

sister, mother, *merciful* and *helpful* to heroes (pp. 555. 1007-8).
Altd. w. 3, 179.  Walach. märch. p. 167.

p. 531.]  A latish saga distingu. betw. Jötunheim, governed
by Geirröðr, and Risaland, by Goðmundr, Fornm. s. 3, 183.  The
giants often have the character of older Nature-gods, so that
*iötnar = gods,* Sæm. 93ᵃ.  The Serv. *divovi,* giants (Vuk's Pref. to
pt. I. of new ed.) either means the *divine* (conf. p. 194) or the
*wild ;* conf. divliy = ferus [Slav. div = wonder].   When in our
kinder-märchen nos. 5. 81-2 the *tailor,* the *carter* or the *gamester*
intrude into heaven (Wolf's Ztschr. 2, 2—7), it may well remind
us of the titans storming Olympus ; conf. p. 575 on angels and
giants.——Giants form ties of love with gods and heroes : thus
Polyphemus is a son of Poseidon, Od. 1, 71 seq.  Hrîmgerðr the
giantess wishes to pass a night with the hero, Sæm. 144ᵃ, like
the witch in fairytales and Marpalie in Wolfdietrich.  Freyr
burns with love for Gerðr, Oðinn spends three days in the mountain with Gunnlöd, Gefion the âsynja has sons (bull-shaped) by a
giant, Sn. 1.  Yet hostility betw. gods and giants is the rule :
that these would get the upper hand, but for Thôr's enmity to
them, the Edda states even more distinctly than the Swedish
proverb :

> mikill mundi æt iötna ef allir lifði,
>
> vætr mundi manna und Miðgarði.        Sæm. 77ᵇ.

Conf. *Thors pjäska* ett qvinno troll baktill ihåligt, som tros fly
för blixten in i ett hus, der åskan då står ned, Almqv. 464ᵃ
(pjäska = a dirty woman).  The giant again is *ás-grûi,* terror
asarum.

p. 532.]  *Managolt,* Pistor. 497.  *Managold,* Neug. 77. 355.
On the myth, conf. Kuhn in Hpt's Ztschr. 6, 134.  With Fenja
and Menja, who grind until the cuckoo calls, conf. the mill-maids
and cock-crow, Gr. epigr. 2, 56.

p. 532.]  Fornald. sög. 1, 469 says : ' austan at *Ymis* dyrum ';
and of Ullr : ' Ullr reið *Ymesver,* enn Oðinn Sleipni '; did the
horse belong to Ymir ?  *Frosti, Jökull,* horses' names, Rask's
Afh. 1, 95.  Esth. *kühna isa,* wana *Pakkana,* Böcler 148.  If
Ymir comes fr. *ymja,* stridere, it is akin to Goth. *iumjô,* turba,
noisy crowd.  The noise, the *roar* of giants is known to MHG.,
see Dietr. u. Ges. 391—4. 458. 470 ; is that why they are likened

to bellowing bulls? Rask in Afh. 1, 88 derives the names of *Herkir* and *Herkja* fr. Finn. *härkä*, ox; but we have also a Germ. giant *Harga*, Wolf's Ztschr. 2, 256, conf. Herka (p. 253) and next note, end.——Giants are beings of Night: those of India grow stronger than heroes at *twilight*, and twice as strong in the *night*, Holtzm. Ind. sag. 2, 152. A Schleswig giantess is 'die *schwarze Greet*,' black Meg, Müllenh. pp. 157. 269. 273-5; on the other hand a queen Margareta, pp. 342. 14. 18.

p. 533.] The Greeks also make giants live on *rocks* and *hills*, Od. 9, 113-4. They are animated stones, or consist partly of stone, or they turn into stone. The giant in Müllenh. p. 442 has a stone heart. Hrîmgerðr, surprised by daylight, stands *î steins liki*, Sæm. 145ᵇ; conf. the Swed. tales in Hpt's Ztschr. 4, 503-4. Bader no. 486. Hati iötunn *sat â bergi*, Sæm. 143ᵃ (Suppl. to 530). The gŷgr lives in caves of the rock (hellir); as Brynhildr fares to Hel, a gŷgr cries to her: 'skaltu î gögnum gânga eigi *grioti studda garða* mîna!' through my stone-built garth; and B. answers: 'bregðu eigi mer, *brúðr or steini*,' bride of stone, Sæm. 227 (see p. 551). 'finna þeir *î helli* nockvorum, hvar *gŷgr sat*, hon nefndiz *Thöck*,' Sn. 68. A giant's cave up in the wild mountain, Trist. 419, 10—20. *Berg-búi*=giant is also in Landn. 4, 12, and Sæm. 52; conf. *berges gnóz*, Er. 8043. *Hobergs-gubbe* (p. 536-7). Finn. *kallio*, rupes,=Goth. hallus, ON. hallr, hence *kaleva*, gigas; another Finn. term for giant is *vuoren väki*, power of the mountain. To *þussin af biargi* corresp. *Tössebergs*-klätten, a place in Värmeland, Rask's Afh. 1, 91-2. Note the term *bergrinder*, mountain-cattle, for Gefjon's children by a giant are oxen, Sn. 1. One giant is called *kuh-tod*, cow-death, Müllenh. no. 328; conf. Herkir, Herkja in preced. note. Giants appear as *wolves*, Sn. 13.

p. 534.] The giantess pelts with stones, the giant wears a stone crown, Braunschw. märch. p. 64. Iron will not bite the giant: 'tröll, er þik *bíta eigi iarn*,' Isl. sög. 2, 364. He can only be floored with *gold*, hence Skiold wraps gold about his club, Saxo 8. Grendel too is proof against iron sword: 'þone synscaðan ænig ofer eorðan *irenna* cyst, *gûðbilla nân grêtan nolde*, Beow. 1596. Arnliotr in Hervarars. has *league-boots*, like the ogre in Petit poucet; they denote the swift pace of the giant, hence Diut. 1, 403: 'hine fuor der herre, îlende alse ein *rise* duot (speeding as a giant doth), der zuo loufe sînen muot ebene hât gesetzet.'

p. 535.] Curious old *structures* are ascr. to *giants* or *heathens*: ' *enta* burg, *risón* burg,' Elene 31, p. xxii. Even Tristan's cave of love is called a *giant's building*, Tristr. 419, 18; conf. ' *etenes* bi old dayn had wrought it,' the house in the ground, where Tristan and Isolde lay, Tristrem 3, 17. *Hünen-wälle* are pointed out betw. Etteln and Alfen (Paderborn). The Orientals attrib. old buildings to a people called *Âd*, Hammer's Rosenöl 1, 36; the Celtic legends to *Finn*. All those large *cairns*, and remarkable peaks like St. Michael's Mount and the Tors, are the work of giants. Pausanias ii. 25, 7 mentions a κυκλώπων ἔργον, ἀργῶν λίθων, the smallest of which a pair of mules could not move. *Tyrrhenians* build towers (Suppl. to 522 end).——In O. Fr. poems the builders are giants or heathen Sarrasins or famous men of old: la *roche au jaiant*, Guitecl. 1, 90. 158; un *jaiant* le ferma qui Fortibiaus ot nom, Renaus 177, 7; *Sarrasins* build, Garin in Mone's HS. 219. 251; el mur *Sarrazinor*, Albigeois 6835; el *palais* montent que firent *Sarrasin*, Garin 1, 88; la tor est forte de luevre as *Sarrasins* 2, 199; *croute* que firent *Sarasins* 1, 57-9; as *grans fenestres* que f. *S.*, Mort de Garin p. 146. *Cain* builds a *tower*, Ogier 6644-66; *roche Cayn*, Garin 1, 93-4; or the giant's building is traced to *Jul. Cæsar*, to *Constantine*, Garin (Paris 2, 53). Chron. fontan. (Pertz 2, 284); conf. the work by *Jul. Cæsar* in Thietmar 6, 39.——A legend of the great *cauldron* which the giants were 20 years digging in silence, is told in Halbertsma's Tongvallen p. 54-5. *Stone-heaps* in the woods the Finn calls *hüden pesät*, giants' nests or beds, Kurl. send. 1, 47; a giant's bed already in Il. 2, 783. The brazen *dorper* is like the huge metal figure that stands on a bridge with a *rod of steel*, barring the passage, Dietr. drach. 57[a]. 61[ab]; old Hildebrand says, ' ich klag ez dem der ûf der brücken *stât* ' 62[a]; they all misdoubt the monster 68[b]. 74-5 : ' der *aller groeste viez* (rhy. liez), daz in der tiufel würge! er was grôz unt dâbî lanc, sîn muot was ungetriuwe; er sî lebende oder tôt, er ist ein rehter boesewiht,' be he alive or dead, he is a bad one 83[ab] (on *viez*, see Gramm. 1, 187).

p. 538.] The Gothland *högbergs-gubbe* must have got his name fr. *Hoberg* in the I. of Gothland, Molb. Tidskr. 4, 189. In

Esthonian legend *blocks of granite* are *Kalev's maidens' apron-stones* (Kallewi neitsi pölle kiwwid, Possart p. 177). What was told of giants, is told of the devil: Once upon a time, say the men of Appenzel and the Black Forest, the devil was flying over the country with a sackful of huts: the sack happened to tear, and out fell a cottage here and a cottage there, and there they be to this blessed hour, Schreiber's Taschenb. '41, p. 158.

p. 540.] *Eaters of flesh* give place to *sowers of corn*, hunters to husbandmen, Klemm 2, 25. Giants consider themselves the *old masters* of the land, live up in the *castle*, and look down upon the *peasant*, Haltrich 198. In the I. of Usedom they say (Kuhn in Jahrb. d. Berl. ges. f. d. spr. 5, 246) : 'en risen-mäken hätt auk mål enen *knecht* met *twei ossen* unnen *håken* (plough) in äre schörte (her apron) packt, wil är *dat lütte wörm* durt hätt (because she pitied),' etc. Similar stories of the *earth-worms* who *crowd out* the giants are told in many parts of Sweden, Dyb. 1842. 2, 3. 4, 40. '44. p. 105. '45. pp. 15. 97. '47. p. 34. Rääf's Osterg. 38; in Södermanland, Hpt's Ztschr. 4, 506; in Schleswig, Müllenh. p. 279; in the Mark, Hpt 4, 392; in Westphalia, Firmen. 1, 322; in S. Germany, Bader nos. 375. 387. Panzer 2, 65; conf. Walach. märch. p. 283.

p. 541.] Stories of the giant *clearing out his shoe* or *shaking the sand out of his holsken* (wooden shoes) are in the Ztschr. d. Osnabr. ver. 3, 230-5. Firmen. 1, 274ᵃ. The giant feels three *grains in his shoe*, Hone's Daybk. 2, 1025. Dutch tales to the same purpose in Halbertsma's Tongvallen p. 55-6.

p. 543.] Near Duclair (on the Seine, towards Normandy) stands ' *la chaire de Gargantua :* l'être mystérieux qui l'occupait *pendant la nuit* devait être un géant, que les peuples ont personifié sous le nom de Gargantua,' Revue archéol. xiv. an., p. 214. On G., conf. Bosquet pp. 177. 182. 193-4; with his seat conf. *devil's pulpits* and their legends.

p. 544.] Giants fling *hammers* at each other, Müllenh. no. 586. Panzer pp. 104. 114. Firmen. 1, 302. Rääf p. 38. Hünen *play at bowls*, Balt. stud. xii. 1, 115, like the *heroes* in the mount (p. 953), like *Thôrr* (p. 545) and the *angels* (p. 953 n.). Another Westph. story of giants *baking bread*, Firmen. 1, 302. 372; they throw *tobacco-pipes* to each other, and knock the ashes out 1, 273. A giant is pelted with *stones* or *cheeses*, KM. no. 20.

Dyb. 4, 46. Cavall. 1, 3. 9 ; conf. the story from Usedom (Kuhn in Jrb. d. Berl. ges. f. d. spr. 5, 246). A *captive giant* is to be let go when he's pulled all the hair off a cow's hide, but he mayn't pluck more than one hair in 100 years, Wieselgren 459.

p. 549.] Similar *building* stories in Müllenh. nos. 410-2. Faye p. 13. A Bavarian tale of the *giant builder,* in which a hammer is hurled, Ober-bair. arch. 5, 316-7. A horse brings the stones, like *Svaðilfari,* Haltrich 29 ; conf. old Bayard at Cologne cathedral.

p. 551.] The giantesses spin like the fays, even giants spin, Firmen. 1, 323. In the Olafssaga *Olaf* fights the *margýgr,* and brings away her hand as trophy, Fornm. sög. 4, 56-7-8. *Red-bearded* Olaf is called Olafr *liósiarpr â hâr* 4, 38. His *pipuga skägg* could also be explained as the Dan. *pip-skiäg,* first beard.

p. 552 n.] Instead of the words in Danske v. 1, 223 the Kämpe v. 155 has : sprang til *flinte-sten lede og sorte.* In Norske ev. 1, 37. 2, 28 (new ed. 162. 272): *flyve i flint,* with anger. Norw. Lapp. gedgom, I turn to stone, am astounded. MHG. *wurde* ich danne *zuo eime steine,* Herb. 8362; conf. ille vir in medio *fiat* amore *lapis,* Propert. ii. 10, 48. Conversely : in haeten sine grôzen liste ûz eime herten steine getragen, Mor. 1562. Many Swed. tales of giants whom the first beam of sunrise turns into stone, Hpt's Ztschr. 4, 503-4. Cavall. 27. Norske ev. 162. The mighty king Watzmann is believed to be a petrified giant, Panz. Beitr. 1, 246. Frau Hütt turns into stone because she has rubbed herself with crumbs, DS. no. 233; people sink into the ground because they've trod on a wheaten roll, Giesebrecht's Balt. stud. 12, 126.——Esp. are a *bride and bridegroom* often turned into stone, DS. no. 229. Müllenh. pp. 108-9. 595. Giesebr. Balt. stud. 12, 114-5. 126. These 'bride-stones' are also known to Norweg. legend, Faye p. 4; nay, we find them in France in the *noce pétrifiée,* Michelet 2, 17, and even in the Wallach. märch. 117. Once a shepherd, his sheepdog and sheep were changed into stone by frau *Wolle,* because he had rejected her petition for bread, Somm. p. 11. The Wallachians have a similar story of an old woman, her son and her sheep, Schott 114-5; so have the Servians, Vuk's Wtb. p. 15[a]. Heinr. v. Herford ad ann. 1009 relates after Will. of Malmesb. (acc. to Vincent 25, 10) how people in a Saxon village disturb the Christmas festival by singing and dancing in a churchyard, and how the priest dooms them to dance a whole year; in time they sink up to their hips in the ground, till at the end of the year they are absolved by his Grace of Cologne. The place is in some MSS. called *Colovize;* surely these are the men of *Colbeke* who danced with what they took for stones, DS. no. 232. A 15th cent. version of the story in Altd. bl. 1, 54-5.

p. 553.] *Strong Jack* is sometimes named der *starke Hannel* (perh. Hermel), Siegthal p. 106. Finn. *Hiisi,* gen. Hiiden, Hiidenpoika = wild man of the woods, giant, Salmel. 1, 242. Lapp. *Hiidda, Hiita* is a malign deity, Suomi '44 p. 30. The Esth. tale of *Kallewepoeg* is given more fully in Poss. Estl. p. 174-5. Lönrot, who has collected from 60 to 70 giant-stories, relates in Kruse's Urgesch. p. 177: In the sea near Abo stands a huge *stone,* which the Finn. giant *Kalevampoika* hurled at the *first church* that was built. He was going to the church himself, when he met a man with a sackful of worn shoes, and asked him how much farther it was. The man said, 'You see, I've worn all these shoes through on my way.' Then K. took up the stone and slung it, but it missed the mark and fell into the sea.

p. 555.] ON. 'iötunn sâ er Brûsi hêti, hann var mikit tröll ok *mann-aeta,*' Fornm. s. 3, 214. OHG. man-ezzo, MHG. man-ezze (p. 520 n.), AS. mon-æta, Lith. *vyrĕde,* viros edens. The Polyphemus legend is widely diffused, e.g. Sinbad on his third voyage punches out the eye of a man-eating giant; conf. the story of Eigill, Nilsson 4, 33. Müller's Sagenbib. 2, 612. As the Oghuzian cyclop takes the arrow for a gnat, so in our Ring p. 241: 'ich waen, mich hab ein fleug gestochen.' Similar tales in Konr. v. Würzbg, MS. 2, 205ª. Altd. w. 3, 178; esp. coarse is the version in the Leipzig MS., Altd. bl. 1, 122—7. For the giant, later stories substitute a *murderer,* Mone's Anz. '37, 399. 400; a *robber,* Wal. märch. p. 167-8-9. Poets of the 13th cent. make 12 schâchære (robbers) enter the dwelling of a *turs,* who *eats up* 11 of them, MSS. 2, 331ᵇ. On the merciful giantess, conf. p. 1008.

p. 556.] A giant gets *bigger* as he rises out of the ground, and *smaller* as he sinks in again, Müllenh. p. 266. Giants often take the *shape of an eagle* (p. 633), e.g. Hræsvelgr, Suttûngr, Thiazi, Sn. 80-1; they are born as *wolves* 13. The story of the flying giantess trespasses on Beast-legend, Hpt's Ztschr. 4, 502-3.

p. 557.] Our Court-poets have preserved here and there a genuine feature of the folklore about giants : Tristan taking the giant's *hand* with him (16195) is like Beowulf bringing away Grendel's. Again, the *old giant-father carrying the heroes up a hill* (Daniel in Bartsch xxviii.) occurs not only in Hero-legend, but in Folktale, Müllenh. p. 266. Then, the giants of the Trûtmunt in Goldemar carry *long poles*, Hpt's Ztschr. 6, 521 ; *Runze* swings a tree over his shoulder, Wolfd. 510 ; one giant is named *Boumgarte* 493, 3. Asperiân is styled the giants' *spileman*, Roth. 2161. In Lancelot 17247 seq. are noticed the giants' *ogen verkeren, tanden criselen, hoft queken*. A giant couple in Ecke 7 (Hagen 5, 8) bear the names *vrô Hilte* and *her Grîme*, conf. Grîmr and Hildr, Vilk. saga c. 16. Note the giants' names in Dietr. drach., *Glockenbôz, Fidelnstôz, Rûmedenwalt, Schelledenwalt, Bitterbúch, Bitterkrût, Hôhermuot, Klingelbolt ;* a *Grandengrûs*, Grandgrûs 118ᵇ. 126ᵇ looks Romance, like Grandgosier (great gullet) in Gargantua. *Wolfes-mage* (-maw) reminds of the manservant *Wolves-darm* (-gut) in Helbl. 1, 372, and of the Ssk. *Urkodara* (wolf's belly), Hitzig 308. Norse names: *Ruth i Skut, Rolf i Topp, Hand i Handöl, Elling, Staff*, Dyb. '45, 97-9 (see p. 557). The connexion between giants and gods has been pointed out, Suppl. to p. 531.

---

# CHAPTER XIX.

## CREATION.

p. 558 n.] Conf. *kînent werden* (p. 746 n.) ; *zekein*, Wernh. v. Niederrh. 11, 18. Schelling takes chaos to be the Roman *Janus* = hianus, after Festus sub v. chaos. The material sense is also found in the expressions ' *ingunnen* werden,' secari, N. Arist. 95 ; ' *sîti ingunnen*,' cloven, Diemer 97, 26 ; M. Neth. *ontginnen*, secare, Fergût 3461. 3565 ; conf. Hpt's Ztschr. 8, 18—20.

p. 559.] For the notion of *creating*, the AS. has the word *frumsceaft*, prima creatio : God is *frumsceafta freá*, Cædm. 195, 9. The Gothic renders κτίσις by *gaskafts*. On our schöpfen, bilden, bilde giezen, see p. 23 : wære ich nie *gebildet*, had I never been shapen, Tit. 3283. Creature in the Bible is in OHG. *hant-tât*, manu factum, N. Ps. 18, 2; MHG. *hant-getât.*——Haug thinks *Ymir* the Pers. Gajômars, Gött. Anz. '53, p. 1960. The *birth from feet* or legs seems to be remembered in an O. Fr. poem : *Fanuel,* whom his mother had conceived out of the smell of flowers, touches his *thigh* with a knife that had just cut an apple; the thigh conceives and bears St. Anne; conf. Brahma's creation (p. 571). Ukko yumala rubs his hands, presses them on his left knee, and makes three maidens, Kalevala 9, 39—44.——Giants come before the Ases (p. 530-2) ; the vala sings, 'ek man *iötna âr ofborna,*' Sæm. 1ᵃ; and Saxo divides mathematici into (1) *gigantes,* (2) *magi*=Ases, (3) *homines.* The Indians say the *cow* is *mother of the world,* and must not be killed, Holtzm. Ind. sagen 1, 65. Of *Bör's three sons,* who create man, it is said in Sæm. 1ᵇ : *bioðum ypto,* orbes extulerunt, they set on high the globes of heaven (p. 701).

p. 560 n.] The Indian myth also accepts a creation out of the *egg,* heaven and earth being eggshells, Somadeva 1, 10; conf. the birth of Helen and the Dioscuri out of eggs.

p. 561.] *Askr* and *Embla* are known as *Es* and *Imlia* among the Yenisei Ostiaks, Castrén's Reise in Sibirien. The division into *önd, óðr* and *lâ ok litr* is also found in Plutarch 4, 1154 : ' spirit, soul and body.'

p. 561.] To giants, men appear as *dwarfs :* they nickname us *earthworms,* and the giant's daughter takes the ploughman for a *worm* or beetle (p. 540). As dwarfs are made out of *maggots* in the Edda, so are men out of *ants* in Ov. Met. 7, 642 ; conf. the way *bees* are brought to life (p. 696). As fire is generated by rubbing wood, so are animals by *rubbing the materials* (Suppl. to 1100). Hiisi *makes an elg* out of various stuffs, Kalev. 7, 32 seq.

p. 567.] The two AS. accounts of the *creation of man* (p. 565, text and note) derive blood from fire, whereas the Emsig Code derives it from water, as the Edda conversely does water from blood. The *eight parts* were known to the Indians also (Suppl. to 571.——The Fris. hêli, ON. heili=brain, resembles Lat. coelum, Gr. κοίλη κοιλία, GDS. 681. Godfrey of Viterbo's comparison of the head to the sky, of the eyes to the lights of heaven is repeated in Walther 54, 27 : ' ir *houbet* ist sô wünnenrîch, als ez mîn *himel* welle sîn, dâ liuhtent *zwêne sternen* abe ; ' and in MS. 2, 189ᵇ the eyes are called stars ; conf. himmel and *gaume,*

Hpt's Ztschr. 5, 541.——A *tear* (thräne) is called in MHG. mers trân, wâges trân, Gramm. 1, 170. The Edda accounts for the taste of sea-water by the grinding of salt out of the quern Grôtti. A tear bites, like salt; δάκρυ, lacruma [and tehero, tearas, zähre] comes from dak, to bite. The Etym. magn. 564, 45 says: *Εὐφο-ρίων δὲ βύνην τὴν θάλασσαν λέγει· οἷον—πολύτροφα δάκρυα βύνης—τοὺς ἅλας βουλόμενος εἰπεῖν. Βύνη = ʼΙνώ*, GDS. 300.

p. 570 n.] An Esth. song in Herder p. m. 112 tells of one who shaped him a wife out of wood, gilded her face, and silvered her shoulders. The Egyptian notion as to the origin of the first man comes very near that of the Bible: Ptah or Neph is picto-rially repres. ' turning the clay for the human creation,' Wilkin-son's Egyptians p. 85.

p. 570.] Another Ind. story of the creation in Suppl. to 560 n. The Pers. doctrine is, that heaven and fire were first created, then mountains, then plants, then beasts. From the horns of the first ox sprang fruits, from his blood grapes, etc., Görres 1, 232-3. The description of *Atlas* in Ovid's Met. 4, 657 agrees with the Teutonic myth of creation far more closely than the notion current among the Greeks. He lets Atlas be converted into a mountain-chain: hair supplies the forest, his shoulders and arms the hills, his head the summit, his bones the stones.

p. 571.] The older Ind. myth makes the great spirit, *mahân âtmâ*, produce the first man out of *water ;* Prometheus too forms men of *earth* and *water*, Lucian's Prom. 13; acc. to Horace, Od. i. 16, 13, he tempers the given ' limus ' with every possible ingredient, conf. Babr. 66. The Greenlanders think the first man was made of earth, and the first woman *of his thumb*, Klemm 2, 313, as Eve was of Adam's *rib ;* so Dakshus was pulled out of Brahma's *toe* (Suppl. to 559). The *eight parts* occur even in the Rigveda, Kuhn in Höfer 1, 288.

p. 573.] For analogies in language between *man* and *tree*, see Pott's Zähl-meth. 234—6. *Askr* and other masc. names of trees indicate man, and femin. names woman. *Askr, Embla* begin with the same vowels as Adam, Eve; conf. Es, Imlia (Suppl. to 561).

The term *liut-stam*, nation, is taken wholly from the vegetable kingdom, Otfr. iii. 12, 7. Plants and rocks are not dead, they speak: δρυὸς καὶ πετρὰς ἀκούειν, Plato's Phædr. 275. Men arise out of trees and stones or mud : O *saxis* nimirum et *robore* nati, Stat. Theb. 4, 339 ; qui, *rupto robore* nati, *compositive luto*, nullos habuere parentes, Juven. 6, 12 (conf. die leimînen, p. 569 n.). Men grow out of *pines* in Nonnus (Reinh. Köhler, Halle '53, p. 24) ; jâ werdent solich leut von *bômen* nit geborn, Wolkenst. 61 ; sîner spiez-genôze sweimet einer von dem *obersten birboume*, Ben. 419 ; ' Where people come from ? think I don't know that ? they're torn off *trees* when young,' Ayrer's Fastn. 160<sup>d</sup>; not sprung from a *hazel-bush*, Schelmufsky, 1, 51 ; his father was drowned on the *nut-tree*, his mother carried the water up in her apron (sieve), Brückner's Henneberg 17 ; a child is exposed on an *ash*, and is found there, Marie de Fr. 1, 150—4. In a Finn. fairytale a foundling is called puuhaara, tree-branch; conf. our Fundevogel on the top of a tree, KM. no. 51.——Acc. to Greek legend there were only gods at first, the earth bristled with forests, till Prometheus made men, Lucian's Prom. 12 ; conf. the Prom. legends in Schütze's Excursus i. to Æsch. Prom.; yet Zeus also makes men spring *out of the ground* for Æacus on his lonely isle, Paus. ii. 29, 2. The *throwing of stones*, which turn into men, is descr. in Ov. Met. 1, 411 ; the stones are styled *ossa parentis* 1, 383. 393, as Æschylus and Sophocles call rocks the bones of the earth. This sowing of stones reminds one of *mana-seps* = λαός, κόσμος (p. 793). The Saxons, named after sahs (saxum), are called in the legend from the Eisenacher Rechtbuch in Ortloff p. 700-1 *Kieselinge, petrioli;* conf. ' *kisila* irquiken zi manne,' quicken flints into men, O. i. 23, 47. Giants spring out of stone, and spring into stone again (pp. 532-3. 552) : ' eine, di slug ich *aus eime steine*,' Fundgr. 2, 518 ; ' nun sihet man wol, dasz er nicht *aus einem steine entsprungen* ist,' Galmy 230 ; ' dasz ich *aus keinem stein gesprungen*,' Schade's Pasq. 76, 87 ; ' many a man fancies he is sprung from a *diamond*, and the peasant from a *flint*,' Ettn. Hebamme 15 ; ' gemacht aus *kisling-plut*,' flint-blood (also, donkey's rib), Fastn. 680, 26. 32. For other legends of the origin of nations, see GDS. 780.

p. 576.] Acc. to Plato's Symp. 190 B, there were at first *three* sexes : ἄρρεν, θῆλυ, ἀνδρόγυννον, descended from sun, earth and moon. It is an important statement in Gen. 6, 4, that the *sons of God* (men) came in unto the *daughters of men* (giantesses). Popular legend very remarkably derives *dwarfs* and *subterraneans* from the *fallen angels*, Ir. elfenm. xiii. ; the 'good people' are not born, but dropt out of heaven, Ir. märch. 2, 73 ; the same with the *huldren* in Norway, Asb. 1, 29. Thiele 2, 175 ; while Finn. Joh. Hist. eccl. Isl. 2, 368 says of the *alfs :* ' quidam enim a Deo immediate et sine parentum interventu, ut spiritus quosdam, creatos esse volunt; quidam vero ab Adamo, sed *antequam Eva condita fuit,* prognatos perhibent.' A N. Frisian story has it, that once, when Christ walked upon earth, he blessed a woman's *five fair* children, and cursed the *five foul* ones she had *hidden ;* from these last are sprung the *undergrounders,* Müllenh. p. 279. The same story in Iceland, F. Magnusen's Lex. 842[b]. Eddalären 3, 329. 330. Faye, pref. xxv.——The giant too is called *válandes barn,* Trist. 401, 7. Even the devil tries to *create* (Suppl. to 1024). The Ind. *Visvakarma,* like Hephæstus, fashions a woman at Brahma's bidding, Somad. 1, 173. On ages of the world, and their several races, conf. Babrius's Prologue, and the statue (p. 792 n.). Ovid. in Met. 1, 89—127 assumes four ages, golden, silver, brass and iron. GDS. 1—5. In the age of Saturn the earth-born men went *naked* and free from care, lived on the fruit of trees, and talked with beasts, Plato's Politicus 272.

p. 581.] Παλαιοὶ λόγοι of deluges (κατακλυσμοῖς) are ment. by Plato de Leg. 3, 677. The form *sin*-vluot is still retained in Mauritius 692, also *sin*-fluot in Anegenge 22, 17. 24, 13, but *sint*-vluot already in 25, 18, *sint*-waege 23, 54, *sint*-gewaege 25, 7. Luther still says *sind*-flut, not sündflut. By the *flood* the race of giants is extirpated, Beow. 3377—84. As it subsides, three ravens are let fly (p. 1140) ; conf. the verses in the Völuspâ on the falling of the waters : '*falla forsar, flygr örn yfir,* sâ er â fialli fiska veiðir,' Sæm. 9[b].——In the American story of the Flood the people likewise take refuge in a ship, and send out animals, the beaver, the rat, Klemm 2, 156. *Deukalions Flood* is described in Athen. 1, 409 and the first book of Ovid's Metamorphoses ; conf. Selig Cassel's Deuk. p. 223. 246. In Lucian's account also, all the wild beasts are taken into Deukalion's ark, and live in peace together, Luc. de Saltat. c. 39.——The Indian narrative of the Flood is ' taken from the Bible,' thinks Félix Nève (De l'orig. de la trad. Ind. du Dél., Paris '49) ; the rapid growth of the fish resembles that of Jörmungandr when thrown into the sea, Sn. 32, and of the snake who wishes to be taken to the sea,

Klemm 2, 162; *Manus* himself signifies man, Kuhn's Rec. d. Rigveda p. 107. On the other Ind. story, that of *Satyávratas*, see Polier's Mythol. des Indous 1, 244—7.——German tales of a great flood are told in Vonbun p. 14—16 (conf. p. 982-3). Our people still have a belief that destroying water will break out of mountains, Panz. Beitr. 1, 276-7. German legend makes the flood stream out of the giant's toe, as it does out of Wäinämöinen's toe in Runo 3. The dwarf-story from the Rhine district in Firmen. 2, 49 seems founded on that of L. Thun, DS. no. 45; the dwarf reminds one of the angel who lifts his hand holding a cloth over the city, Greg. Tur. 10, 24.

---

# CHAPTER XX.

## ELEMENTS.

p. 582.] Before the *new* gods came, there prevailed a primitive worship of Nature (p. 335), to which perhaps Cæsar's ' Luna, Sol, Vulcanus' is to be referred; we know the giants stand for primal forces of nature, for fire, air, water, sun, moon, day and night, conf. Plato's Cratyl. 397. 408. And long after, in the Warnung 2243 seq., there still breaks out a nature-worship, an adoring of the bird's song, of flowers, of grass. All mythologies make *some* gods represent the elements: to the Hindûs *Indra* is god of the air, *Varuna* of water; to the Greeks Zeus was the same thing as aether, aër. The Persians worshipped the elements, not human-shaped gods at all, Herod. 1, 131.——The Indians admitted *five* elements: fire, water, earth, aether (akasa) and wind (vaya). The Chinese thought *metal* an element of its own. Galen sets down *four:* warm, cold, dry, wet (can we make these attributes represent fire, earth, air, water?). How the four elements run into one another, is described in MS. 1, 87[a]; H. Sachs knows ' die vier element,' 1, 255; ' erde und wazzer nider swebet, viur und luft ze berge strebet,' says Freid. 109. 24; conf. Renn. 6115. Animals live in all four: 'swaz gêt, vliuzet, swebet,' MS. 2, 183[a]. Men bewailed their sorrows to the elements, to earth, to fire (p. 642).

## 1. WATER.

p. 584.] People sacrificed to groves and *springs :* blôtaði lundin, Landn. 3, 17; blôtaði *forsin* 5, 5 (p. 592) ; and Sæm. 44ᵃ says : *heilög vötn* hlôa (calent). The Hessians sacrificed 'lignis et *fontibus*,' Pertz 3, 343. The Samländer and Prussians denied the Christians access to groves and *springs* lest they should pollute them, Pertz 9, 375 ; conf. Helmold 1, 1. Prayer, sacrifice and judgment were performed at the spring, RA. 799. 'Porro in medio noctis silentio illas (feminas) *ad fontes aquarum in orientem affluentes* juxta hortum domus egressas Herwardus percepit; quas statim secutus est, ubi eas eminus colloquentes audivit, nescio a quo *custode fontium* responsa et interrogantes et expectantes,' Gesta Herw. Saxonis, yr. 1068 (Wright's Essays 1, 244. 2, 91. 108. Michel's Chron. Anglonorm. 2, 70). An Engl. song has 'I the *wel woke*,' Wright's Ess. 1, 245; this is the ceremony of *waking* (watching by) *the well.* On the Bode in the Harz they still offer a *black hen* (?) to the river-god. Before starting the first waggonload from the harvest field, they throw three ears into a *running stream ;* or if there is none, they throw three ears into the *oven-fire* before the waggon enters the stack- yard; if there was no fire, they light one. This is a Bavarian custom, Panz. Beitr. 2, 213. In Hartlieb's book of all Forbidden Arts we read that lighted tapers are set in front of water drawn from three running streams before sunrise, and *man legt dem wasser êre an,* sam Gott selber (see p. 586). The Romans cherished the like reverence for water: 'flumini Rheno *pro salute*,' De Wal. no. 232; genio loci et Rheno *pro salute*,' no. 233; ' deus Rheni,' no. 234. They *greeted* the bath with *bare head* on enter- ing and quitting it, and placed *votive gifts* by the side of springs, Rudorff's Ztschr. 15, 216; they had even *ministri fontis* 15, 217.

p. 585.] As *prunno* comes from prinnan to burn, the Romans spoke of *torrens aqua,* from torrere to broil : ' subita et ex abdito vasti amnis *eruptio* aras habet,' Seneca's Ep. 41; conf. the context in Rudff's Zts. 15, 214. It is said of St. Furseus (d. 650) : ' fixit *baculum* suum in terram, et mox bullivit fons magnus,' Acta Bened. p. 321. The divine steersman in the Frisian Asegabuch, on touching land, *flings an axe* into the turf, and a spring bursts up, Richthofen 440. A *horse's hoof* scrapes open a well (Suppl.

to 664 n.). Brooks gush out of Achelôus's *ox-head*, Soph. Trach. 14. A well springs out of an *ass's jawbone*, Judg. 15, 19. 'Dô spranc ein brunne sâ ze stete ûz der dürren molten,' Servatius 1382, when the thirsting saint had 'made a cross.' A spring rises where a maiden has fallen down, Panz. Beitr. 1, 198. A giantess produces water by——another method, Sn. (1848) 1, 286. The Finns have three rivers formed out of *tears*, Kalev. 31, 190 ; healing fountains rise from the *sweat* of a sleeping giant, Kalevi-poeg 3, 87-9. *Tiberinus* is prettily described in Claudian's Prob. et Olybr. 209—265 ; 'Rhenus *projecta* torpuit *urna*,' in his Rufin. 1, 133. The nymph holds in her right a *marble bowl*, out of which runs the source of the rivulet, Opitz 2, 262 ; she *pours* the Zacken 263, where the poet uses the phrase ' *spring-kammer* der flüsse' ; so in Hebel pp. 12. 38 the baby Wiese lies in silver cradle in her crystal closet, in hidden *chamber of the rock.* At Stabburags well and grotto (Selburg diocese) the people see a spinning maiden who weaves veils for brides, Kruse's Urgesch. pp. 51. 169. 171. OHG. *klingâ, chlinkâ* = torrens and nympha ; conf. nixe, tocke (p. 492 n.).

p. 586.] At the restoration of the Capitol it is said of the Vestals : aqua *vivis e fontibus amnibusque* hausta perluere, Tac. Hist. 4, 53. Springs that a saint has charmed out of the ground, as Servatius by his prayer, have healing power : 'die mit dehei-nen sêren (any pains) wâren gebunden, genâde die funden ze demselben urspringe,' Servat. 1390. Such *medicinal springs* were sought for with rushes, out of which flew a spark, Ir. märch. 2, 76-7. The notion that at holy seasons *water turns into wine*, prevails in Scandinavia too, Wieselgr. 412. Wells out of which a saint draws yield wine, Müllenh. p. 102-3 ; so in Bader no. 338 wine is drawn out of a spring. The well *loses its healing power* when an ungodly man has bathed his *sick horse* in it, Mullenh. no. 126 ; the same after a noble lady has washed her *little blind dog* in it, N. Pr. prov. bl. 2, 44. On the contrary, fountains be-come holy by *goddesses bathing* in them, e.g. those in which Sîtâ bathed, see beginn. of Meghadûta. Whoever has drunk of the well of Reveillon in Normandy, must *return to that country*, Bos-quet 202.

p. 587.] Holy water is only to be drawn in vessels that cannot stand, but must hang or be carried, and *not touch the ground*, for if set down they tip over and spill every drop (so the pulled plant, the fallen tooth, is not to touch the ground, Suppl. to 658 n.). Such a vessel, *fŭtĭle*, was used in the worship of Ceres and Vesta, Serv. ad Æn. 11, 339. Schol. Cruq. ad Hor. AP. 231. Forcell. sub v.; and by the Scots at the Well of Airth, where witnesses were examined, Hone's Daybk 2, 686, 867. Metal vessels of the Wends, which *cannot stand*, have been found in several places, Balt. stud. 11, 31-3-7. 12, 37. The Lettons, in sacrificing, durst not touch the goblet except with their teeth, Hpt's Ztschr. 1, 145. The hot springs at Thermopylæ were called χύτροι = ollae, Herod. 7, 176; conf. *olla* Vulcani.

*Helicbrunno*, MB. 28ᵃ, 63; *heilicprunno* 11, 109. *heiligbrunno*, 29ᵃ, 96. *Helicbruno*, Chart. Sithiense p. 113. *Helicbrunno*, a brook in the Netherl., Waitz's Sal. ges. 55. On *Heilbronn*, see Rudorff's Ztschr. 15, 226; conf. *nobiles fontes* 15, 218. 'Helgi at *Helgavatni*,' Landn. 2, 2: *Helgavatn*, *Urðarvatn* 3, 2. 3. Other prob. holy springs are *Pholesbrunno* (p. 226), *Gôzesbrunno* (Suppl. to 368). A Swed. song names the *Helge Thors källa* in Småland, fr. which water is drawn on *Holy Thursday night* to cure blindness. Others are enumer. in Müllenh. p. 595. Mary is called 'alles *heiles* ein *lûter bach*' or '*heiles bach*,' Altswert 98, 23. 73. When the angel had troubled the water in the pool of *Bethesda*, whosoever then first stept in was made whole, John 5, 4. Rivers were led over graves and treasures (p. 251-2 n.).

p. 588.] A *youth-restoring fountain* is drunk of in May before sunrise, Tit. 6053. Another *jungbrunnen* in the poem of Abor, Hpt's Ztschr. 5, 6. 7 and one in Wigamur 1611-5 by a limetree. M. Neth. *joocht-borre*, youth-bourn, Horae Belg. 6, 223. The eagle renews his youth at a fountain '*chôck-prunnen*,' Karajan 32, 12. 98, 5; conf. Griesh. Pred. 1, 29.

p. 590.] More about Scandin. *pilgrimages to springs* in Wieselgr. 389. 411. A Span. song tells of picking *flowers* on the *Guadalquivir* on *Midsum. morn*, Hone's Daybk 1, 851. At Warsaw, June 24, the girls throw *wreaths of roses* into the Vistula, and watch with joy or sadness their various ways of floating down the stream. This resembles the Midsum. custom of the Cologne women descr. by Petrarch, which Braun also in No. 23 of the Rhein. Jrb. traces to Christianity. The Schweiz. arch. 4, 87 says Petrarch first came to Germany in 1356, but his letter describing the ceremony is dated 1330; in 1327 he saw Laura at Avignon, and then set out on his tour while yet a *youth*. Whom does he mean by the *spiritus pierii* of the Rhenish city? Alb. Magnus lived and taught at Cologne, but died in 1280; his pupil Thomas of Aquino also taught there for a time. Duns Scotus came to C. in 1308, and died there; Meister Eckhart (d. 1329) was at C., so was his pupil Tauler. The University was not founded till 1388.

p. 590 n.] Stieler p. 1402 mentions the following Easter custom: 'Habent Borussi verbum *schmak-ostern*, quod significat obviam quarto post tres dies Paschales oriente die venientes virgis caedere, sicut juventus nostra facit quarto post ferias Natalitias die, et *kindelen* vocant in memoriam innocentium puerorum. *schmack* Borussis ferulam notat.' It is really more correct to derive the word from *smagač*, to flog (see Weinhold in Aufr. and Kuhn 1, 255) than from śmigust, ablution. Easter rods adorned with many-coloured ribbons are called *schmack-ostern*, Jrb. d. Berl. ges. f. d. spr. 10, 228-9. In Moravia *schmeck-ostern*, Kulda (d'Elv.) 114. Weinhold's Schles. w. 85 distinguishes between *schmag-oster* and *dyngus*.

p. 591.] In Norman stories, springs *run dry* when misfortune is nigh, Bosquet 201. Salt and medicinal springs *dry up* as soon as money is asked for them, Athen. 1, 288. A countryman died of consumption after a cool draught from a spring; and immediately it *ceased to flow*, Hpt's Ztschr. 3, 361. When a new spring *breaks out*, it is a sign of dearth, ibid. By the *rising* or *falling* of water in the Tilsgraben the inhabitants foretell a good or bad harvest, Harrys no. 2; conf. Müllenh. p. 104. When Wartha flats in Werra-dale have gone *unflooded* six years running, the farmer can eat off silver the seventh year, they say (Again: when the beaver builds his castle high, the water that year will run high too, Döbel's Pract. 1, 36ᵇ). In Styria the *hungerbrunnen* are also called *hungerlaken*, Wolf's Ztschr. 2, 43. At different periods the *Nile* had to rise different heights— 22, 16, 14 or 12 yards [?]—to meet the wants of the country, Herod. 2, 13. Strabo p. 788. Pliny 5, 10. Parthey's Plut. on Isis and Os. p. 243.

p. 592.] *Whirl*pool is in OHG. *suarb*, *suirbil*=vortex, Graff 6, 897; *sualm*=vorago in aqua, 6, 873; *huerbo* 4, 1237. Gr. χάρυβδις, Pott in Kuhn 5, 255. Serv. *kolovrat*, vortex (lit. wheel-turn) and *buk*, waterfall's roar (bukati, mugire). '*aitwinde*

(vel storm) = gurges, *eedewinde* = vortex,' Vocab. ms. Vratisl.;
*aitveinda* = gurges, Diefenb. 271[b]. Finn. 'korvalle tulinen kosken
pyhän wirran pyörtehelle,' he went to the *firy waterfall* (Sw. eld-
fors), to the holy flood's *whirl*, Kalev. 1, 177; conf. 6, 92. 7, 785.
794-8. 17, 101. 314. 22, 10. 26, 198.——*Waterfall* is in OHG.
*uazarchlinga* = nympha, Graff 4, 504; *wazardiezo* = nympha 5, 237.
*wazzerdurh?* *uenster?* cataracta, Trier. ps. 41, 11. Windb. ps.
41, 11; *laufen*, Stald. 1, 444. Gr. δῖνος and δίνη. The passage
in Plutarch's Cæsar stands: ποταμῶν δίναις καὶ ῥευμάτων ἐλιγ-
μοῖς καὶ ψόφοις. Homer has ποταμὸς ἀργυρο-δίνης, Il. 21, 130;
he pictured waterfalls as horses flying *headlong* : χαράδραι ῥέουσαι
ἐξ ὀρέων ἐπὶ κάρ 16, 392. 'Tis *a being* below stirs up the whirlpool, Leopr. 106; Loki dwells in Frânangrs-fors, Sæm. 68. Sn.
69. At the *Donau-strudel* a spectre gives warning of death,
Ann. Altahens., yr 1045; conf. the women in the Nibelg.

p. 596.] The Greek *rain-goddesses* are the Hours, who guard
the cloud-gate of Olympus, opening or shutting, and by rain and
sunshine ripen the fruits. The Hora has a *goblet*, which she
rinses at the fountain, Theocr. 1, 150. Men also sacrificed to
Zeus and Hera, when short of rain, Paus. ii. 25, 8. Gē (earth)
is repres. in a picture, imploring Zeus for rain 1, 24. The Lith.
diewaitis is god of thunder, *dewaite szwenta* goddess holy, g. of
rain. The Esths call hoarfrost 'mother of mist,' Böcler 147. In
Germany, as late as the 13th cent., dew was honoured as a bene-
volent being, Parz. 748, 28: 'geêrt sî luft unde *tou*, daz hiute
morgen ûf mich reis.' Dew drips from the manes of airy steeds:
of Hrîmfaxi, Sæm. 32[b]; of the valkyria's horse 145[b] (conf. p.
641).——The ceremony reported by Burchard is also quoted in
Mone's Gesch. des heident. 2, 417 from Martin's Rélig. des
Gaules. The Servian and (acc. to Schott) Wallachian custom of
*wrapping round* reminds me of the Hyperborean votive offerings
wrapt in ears of corn and carried by two virgins, Herod. 4, 33.
Creuzer 2, 117. Were the maidens themselves wrapt up? and
can the five περφερέες who escorted them be conn. with the rain-
maiden's name πορπηροῦνα? conf. GDS. 865. In the new ed. of
Vuk's Dict. the dance and rain-song are called *prporyshe* and the
leader *prpatz*. When a priest touched the fountain with an *oaken
bough*, the rain-cloud rose out of it, Paus. viii. 38, 3; so the
French maire dips his foot in the well of Barenton. In Algeria,

when there is a long drought, they throw a few Marabouts into the river, like the Bavarian *water-bird*, GDS. 54. Kl. schr. 2, 445 seq.

p. 598.] Nero was going to *measure* the Alcyonic lake with *ropes*, Paus. ii. 37, 5. The story in Thiele 3, 73 about sounding the lake is Swed. also, Runa '44, 33. L. Wetter cries: '*mät* min längd!' Wieselgr. 459. On the Esth. worship of water, conf. Kreutzwald's Pref. to Kalewipoeg xii., and his and Neu's Myth. lieder 113; at 114 occurs the hauling up of a *goat's skull*.

p. 601.] To the river is sacrificed (pp. 45. 494) a *reindeer*, Castrén's Reise 342. In wading through clear water you utter a prayer, Hesiod's Erga 735; in crossing a river you take an *auspicium*, Rudorff 25, 218. Water-ordeals in the Rhine, RA. 935; conf. the *Fontinalia*, Rudff 15, 221. Lake and river are often personified: in Irish fairytales (1, 86—89. 2, 144—152) the *lake* is *lent out*, and is carried away in a many-cornered cloth. 'Three *loud laughs* the river gave,' Fleming 373. There is a myth of a wood or mountain sprite, who *scatters rivers* into dust, Praetor. Katzenveit p. 102—6; conf. the *stiebende brugge*, Habsb. urbar. 94, 4, i.e. a devil's bridge. In Denmark, on the approach of spring, they say of a god or genius: 'kaster en *warm steen* i vandet,' F. Magnusen's Lex. 958; do they mean Thor?

Curiously the MB. 13, 18. 42 speaks of an Adalbero *filius Danubii;* 13, 96 Alberus *filius Danubii;* 13, 96 Gozwinus *de Danubio*, Albertus et Engelbertus *de Danubio*. And the *Saale, Neckar, Lahn, Leine* are introd. as persons (p. 494 and Suppl.); conf. Hebel's personific. of the *Wiese*.

With the notion of *ouwe, eá* conf. AS. *holm*=mare profundum, though ON. *hólmr* means insula, and OS. *holm* even collis. The Celts too had *holy* islands, Mone's Heident. 2, 377—380.

Our *meer* (sea), neut., though Goth. *marei* and OS. *mari* are both fem., OHG. *meri*, m. and n., has in it something divine: εἰς ἅλα δῖαν, Od. 11, 2 and elsewhere. Ocean is in Lettic *deewa uppe*, God's river, Bergm. 66. To the sea men sacrificed: 'nostri quidem duces *mare ingredientes* immolare *hostias fluctibus* con-sueverunt,' Cic. de Nat. D. 3, 20. Homer furnishes it with a back, νῶτος, which need not imply a beast's figure, for even OHG. has 'mers *buosen*, mers *barm*,' bosom, Graff 3, 154. It can be angry with men: daz wilde mer ist mir *gram*, En. 7659; das

wasser *gram,* das *böse* mer, Diocl. 7336; de *sture* sê, Partonop. 95,
27. It is wild, it storms and raves: *saevum* mare, Tac. Hist.
4, 52; über den *wilden sê,* MS. 1, 72[b]; daz *wilde* mer, Troj. kr.
6922, etc.; des *wilden wâges* fluot, Gerh. 3966, etc.; daz *tobende*
mer, Troj. kr. 5907, etc.; daz *wüetunde* mer, Servat. 3260, etc.;
la mer *betée,* Ogier 2816, Prov. 'mar *betada,*' Rayn. sub v.; de
*ruskende* see, Uhl. Volksl. 200-1; das *wibende wabende* wasser,
Garg. 111; *sîd* wæter, Cædm. 7, 2. The Fris. *salt,* like ἅλς,
means both salt and sea, Ssk. *lavanâmbhas,* mare salsum, Welsh
*hallfor,* salt sea, Ir. muir *salmhar,* AS. *sealt* wæter, Cædm. 13, 6.
Why the sea is salt, is told in Sn. 147. The sea is *pure,* she
tolerates no *blood,* Anno 227-8, just as the ship will have no *dead
corpse,* Pass. f. 379[b]. She 'ceased from her raging' as soon as
Jonah was thrown in.——Real proper names of the sea are: *Oegir*
(p. 237), conf. AS. wæter-*egesa,* and ' diu *freise* der wilden unde,'
Tit. 2567; *Gŷmir,* conf. *gŷmis leoð* qveða, Yngl. sag. c. 36;
*Brîmir,* akin to *brim;* and *Geofen* (p. 239). Names of particular
seas: *wendilmeri, endilmeri, lebermeri,* Graff 2, 820. To Ælfred,
*wendelsœ* is the Black Sea, only a part of the Mediterranean; daz
tiefe *wentelmere,* Diut. 3, 48; *wendelsê,* Tundal 42[a], 4, and often in
Morolt; *wendelzee,* Bergh's Ndrl. volksr. p. 146. Then: *lebermer,*
Wh. 141, 20. Tit. 5448. 6005. Amûr 1730. Fundgr. 2, 4. Hpt's
Ztschr. 7, 276. 294. Wigalois sub v.; in dem *rôten lebermer,*
Barl. 262, 16; *labermer,* Ernst 3210; *leversê,* Walew. 5955; *lever-
zee,* V. d. Bergh 103. 127. With this term conf. the πλεύμων
θαλάττιος, sea-lung, of Pytheas; F. Magn. traces this lung to the
dismembered Ymir. For *gârsecg,* conf. my first ed., Vorr. xxvii.,
and Hpt's Ztschr. 1, 578. Dahlmann in Forsch. 1, 414 explains
*gars-ecg* as earth's edge; Kemble, Gl. sub v. secg, as homo jaculo
armatus! For *gârsecg* in the Periplus, Rask writes *garsege,* but
explains nothing; conf. Cædm. 8, 1. 195, 24. 199, 27. 205, 3.
Beow. 97. 1024. The ON. *lagastafr* is at once sea and sown
crop, Sæm. 50-1; Gudr. 1126-8 has 'daz *vinstermer,*' sea of
darkness. Lastly, *Dumbs-haf, Dauða-haf,* Fornald. sög. 2, 4.——
The sea advances and retires, has *ebb* and *flood* (on ' ebb ' conf.
Gramm. 3, 384 and Kl. schr. 3, 158); on the alleged Fris. and
Sax. equivalents *malina* and *liduna,* see Gramm. 3, 384 note.
The ON. *kôlga* and *ôlga*=aestus maris: ' er saman qvômo *kôlgo
systir* (fluctus undantes) ok kilir lângir,' Sæm. 153[a]. Ebb and

flood are in Grk. ἄμπωτις and ῥαχία, Paus. 1, 3; in Irish *con-traiht* and *robart*, Zeuss 833. The sea-waves are often treated as living beings: 'dâ *nâmen* ez die unden, *diu eine* ez *der andern gap,* unde truogenz verre sô hinab,' the waves caught it, passed it one to the other, etc., Pass. 313, 73. Three *plunging waves* are three witches, and get *wounded;* the *waterspout* is also a witch, Müllenh. p. 225. On the *nine waves,* conf. Passow sub. v. τρικυμία, πεντα-κυμία: ' ἐν τρικυμίαις φερομένῳ,' Procop. 1, 318. In a storm it is the *ninth wave* that sinks the ship, Wright 1, 290 after Leo Allatius; it also occurs in Ir. sagen u. märch. 1, 86. ON. *skafl* = unda decumana, probably no more than a very high one, from skefla, acervare.

## 2. FIRE.

p. 602.] Fire is a living being. With *quec-fiur* conf. *queckiu lieht,* Ernst 2389. You can kill it: *trucidare* ignem, Lucr, 6, 146. You can wake it: æled *weccan,* Cædm. 175, 26; bælfÿra mæst *weccan,* Beow. 6281. It is wild: conf. ' wildfire ' (pp. 603. 179); Logi *villi-eldr,* Sn. 60; Hans *Wilds-fewer,* MB. 25, 375; ein *wildez viur* sluoc in daz dach, Troj. kr. 11317; daz *wilde fiur* spranc ûz den vlinzen herte 12555; daz *grimme wilde fiuwer,* Rab. 659; daz *starke w. f.* 698; daz *w. f.* ûz den swerten spranc 412; daz *grimme f.* als ein loup ûz den huof-îsen stoup (spirted out of the horse-shoes), Dietr. 9325; daz *f.* vlouc *freislîch* ûz helmen u. ûz ringen 8787. It is a devouring beast: *strudende* (desolating) fŷr, Cædm. 154, 15; brond (glêð) sceal *fretan,* consume, Beow. 6024. 6223; in *pabulum* ignis, in *fuatar* (fodder) des fiures, Diut. 1, 496ᵃ; dem viure geben ze *mazze,* as meat, Fundgr. 2, 131. It is insatiable, like hell or avarice, Freid. 69, 5; the fire saith not ' it is *enough,*' Prov. 30, 16; eld, *œled* (fr. alan, nourish) means ignis *pastus,* the fed and steady flame; conf. ἐκ δὲ θυμάτων Ἥφαιστος οὐκ ἔλαμπε, Soph. Antig. 1007. It licks: Lith. ' ugnis *laizdo* pro stogą,' at the roof; conf. tunga, tungal (p. 700); seven kindlings or seven tongues of flame, Colebr. Essays 1, 190. It snatches, filches: fŷres *feng,* Beow. 3525; se fŷr beoð *þeof,* Ine 43, like Loki and the devil. It plays: *leikr* hâr hiti, Sæm. 9ᵇ; *leiki yfir* logi! 68ᵇ; *leikr yfir* lindar-vâði 192ᵃ; *lâcende* lig, El. 579. 1111; lar (fire) *super turrim saliit,* Abbo de b. par. 1, 548. It flies up like a red cock (p. 670): den *rothen hahn* zum giebel

ausjagen, Schottel 1116[b]; der *rothe hahn* kräht aus dem dach,
Firmen. 1, 292[b]; der *gelbe hahn,* yellow cock 1, 208[a]; conf. *blâcan*
fŷres, ignis pallidi, Cædm. 231, 13; fire glitters with seeds of
*gold,* Holtzm. Ind. sag. 3, 194; faces *aureas* quatiunt *comas,*
Catull. 59, 92. It travels, *nigram viam* habens, Bopp's Gl. 83[a].
Holtzm.. 3, 194. In the Edda it is brother to the wind and sea;
so Ssk. *pâvaka,* fire, is lit. cleanser, fr. pû (Suppl. to 632, beg.),
Bopp's Vocal. 205, conf. Gramm. 126 (new ed. 213-6), and
*pavana,* wind, is from the same root, Bopp (conf. Gramm. 124);
besides, fire is called vayusakhi, wind's companion. It flows: daz
viur *flôz,* Livl. reimchr. 5956; in Holstein, when a fire breaks out,
they call it *hot rain,* Schütze 4, 340; and the ON. *hripuðr,* fire,
Sæm. 40[a] seems to be fr. hripa, perfluere.

There was a time when *fire was unknown,* for the giants have
none (Suppl. to 530) : 'fiure was in tiure' dear, scarce, to them,
Gudr. 104, 1. That time is still remembered in Kalevala 16,
247-8 (Castrén 1, 195) and our nursery tales. Fire belonged to
the gods ; it was stolen by Prometheus, and given to men. Acc.
to a Finn. song it is created: an eagle strikes a fire for Wäinämöinen, Petersb. Extract 3. Other traditions make a *little bird*
(rebló, troglodyte) bring it from heaven, Pluquet p. 44. Bosquet
220. A contrast to the fireless time is the Dan. *arild-tid,* fr.
arild, fireplace (ild, fire), Swed. *äril,* focus, Westg. *arell,* Helsing.
*areld.*

p. 603.] Fire is holy : *ignis sacer* meant lightning, Amm.
Marcell. 23, 5; conf. igne *felici,* Grotef. Umbr. 7, 5. Fire is
called *sacrifice-eater,* Holtzm. Ind. s. 1, 24-6, and four times in
Bopp's Gl. 401[b]; eldr så er *aldri sloknaði* was called *vigðan eld,*
Landn. ed. nov. p. 336. Being often found a hostile power, it
was used in cursing, or was conjured by a spell. Other Fr. forms
of cursing are: *male flambe t'arde!* Ren. 20762; *feu arde son*
*musel!* Berte 116; conf. Holland to Yvain p. 222. The fire-cry
in E. Gothland was : *kumbär eldär lös,* Östg. lag 229. *Fire-spells*
are given in Mone's Anz. 7, 422-7. A fire is adjured in these
words : 'brand, stand als dem dode *sein rechte hand!*' be still as
the dead man's hand, Wolf's Ztschr. 1, 337. If you can charm
a fire, it *jumps behind you* while you do it, and you must run for
your life (Meiningen), Hpt's Ztschr. 3, 363. Remigius *puts a fire*
*to flight,* and *locks it up,* Flodoardus 1, 12. *White angels* quench

a fire (Suppl. to xliii. end, and to 366.——Fire can be stifled with *clothes* that have been *worn some time,* whereas in a Lüttich legend the earth-fire attacks some men who wear *new unwashen* smocks, and is flogged with ropes, rods and sticks, Wolf's Ndrl. s. no. 407. To an outbreak of *helle-viur,* which cannot be stamped out, you must sacrifice a *knight* in gorgeous array, Ksrchr. 1138-41. 1160—72. 1229; he tries while on *horseback* to *speak away* the fire, but falls and breaks his neck, Der Causenmacher, a play, Leipz. 1701, p. 152-6, and pref. A fire put out by means of a *horse,* Thür. Ztschr. 2, 505. To extinguish a fire, a woman in childbed, whose feet must *not touch the ground,* is carried to the fire, and uttering *mystic spells* throws a *new-baked loaf* into the flames (Austria). On quenching fires and driving out cattle, see Tettau and Temme's Pr. sag. 263. There are people who see a fire *burning beforehand :* you must then take out the beam they indicate, or *conjure* the fire *into an oak* with a bung, Müllenh. p. 570. Ossian speaks of pulling out *oaks,* so that *fire springs* out of them. ——Fires *leap out of the ground* like water, Paus. ii. 34, 2 : ein michel vûwer sich *truoc ûf* (ûz ?) *der erden munde* (mouth), Pass. 359, 58 ; als *viurîn urspringe* (fiery springs) dâ waeren ensprungen, Lanz. 2590. *Burning mountains* may be seen on seals of the 14th cent., MsH. 4, 280ᵃ, conf. *Pyrmont, Brennenberg.* Fire struck out of a helmet may be caught on a *schoup* (truss of rye), Er. 9206. *Eggs* put out fire : 'holt *lescid van eia,* wâdi ne brennid'; ovorum autem tantam vim esse dicunt, ut lignum eis perfusum non ardeat, ac ne vestis quidem contacta aduratur, Gl. Argentor. Diut. 2, 194ᵃ. *Milk, camel's milk* quenches fire, Ferabr. 3348.

p. 603.] The Indians had three sorts of fire : *common, celestial, frictile,* Holtzm. Ind. s. 3, 112. In Oegir's hall was ' *lýsi-gull* fyrir *elds-liós,*' Sæm. 59. Out of helmets and swords came fire and light : ob in des *fiures* zerinnet (when short of fire), daz kunnen sie wol suochen in *helm-spange,* Tit. 3222 ; among the Ases the *sword gives light,* Sn. 79 ; it shines in the dark, Landn. 1, 5 ; 'sin *swert* hiez si in *bar* nemen sunder sîn gewant . . . daz er'z mit im naeme, sô 'r in die helle quaeme, in die vinster-nisse, daz er im gewisse dâmite *liuhten* solde,' En. 2858 (she bids Aeneas take his *naked sword,* that when he came into hell's darkness, he should *light* him therewith). Virgil, it is true,

makes Aeneas draw his sword (vi. 260. 291), but not to give
light. Again : 'zuch hervor dîn *swert*, dû trage 'z in dîner hand
*bar*, unde *liuhte* dir dâmite' 3172. Nothing of the kind in Virgil.——*Flint-eld* is struck over cattle, Dybeck's Runa '44, 7. If
sparks fly out of a beam that is being hewn, it betokens fire to
the house into which it is built, Müllenh. p. 570.

p. 607.] *Wildfire* is described in Miede's Hasenmelker p. 43.
Needfire must be rubbed by two brothers, or at least two men of
the same Christian name, (Fischer's) buch vom Abergl., Leipz.
1791, p. 177. Some new facts are coll. by Colshorn 231-2.
350-1. The Mecklenbg custom is described by Lisch 6[b], 127;
that of the Moravian shepherds by Kulda (d'Elv.) 123-4. A
giant rubs fire out of stones, Rother 1041 (acc. to two readings).
The *notten* held on Midsum. Night, and twice mentioned in the
Acct bk of Frankfort city, yr 1374, points to the supposed root
hniudan.

p. 608.] Swed. accounts of *gnid-eld* (rubbed fire) run thus :
' Genom *gnideld* tagen i en ekesticke (piece of oak) från ett snöre
(string) som så länge dragits fram och ater (pulled to and fro) i
en hus-dörr, till-dess det blifvit antändt (kindled), och derefter
3 gånger ansyls förd omkring personen, samt med ett serdeles
formulär signad, berökas och botas sjuka kreatur (cattle besmoked
and cured).' Again : 'För samma ändamal borras häl (hole
bored) uti en ek, hvaruti genom en pinne *eld gnides*, dermed
antändes 9 *slags träd*, öfver hvilken kreaturen böra gå'; conf.
Suppl. to 1089 (?).

p. 609.] Cows or calves are sacrif. elsewhere too, to protect
the herd from plague: ' När *kalfvorne* mycket bordö, skall man
våldsamt fatta an vid hufvudet framsläppa honom ifrån kjötten,
och honom verkeligen hals-hugga öfver fähu-sträskeln,' Rääf. A
*live cow* is buried in the ground against murrain, Wieselgr. 409 ;
or *one of the herd* under the stable-door (p. 1142) ; conf. Wolf's
März. p. 327, where a cow's head is cut off and laid in the loft
(see p. 1188).

p. 610.] In Ssk. *needfire* or *wildfire* is called rub-fire, and is
produced by rubbing a male and a female stick together, Böhtling
1, 522, conf. 1, 404. Acc. to Kuhn's Rec. d. Rigv. p. 98, it is
rubbed out of the *arani* (premna spinosa). Holtzm. Ind. s. 3, 122 ;
is this the aihvatundi ? Weber's Ind. stud. 2, 4 says it comes

out of Pranava, the bow and arrow of self (the lotus-flower). The Arabs call the old-fashioned fire-rubbing sticks *zend* and *zendet*, the first being the upper and male, the second the female or lower one with the hole in it; striking steel and stone together is reckoned a barbarism, Rückert's Hariri 1, 648-9. Finn. *hela-valkya* (fr. hela, the spring festival), ignis non ex silice, sed ex lignis duobus vi confricatis elicitus; also *kitkan-valkya*, rub-fire, Renvall 1, 64.

p. 611.] A *perpetual fire* was kept up by the Israelites, Levit. 6, 12-3; and is still by Parsees and Guebers, as among the ancient Persians. Such a fire burned on the altar of Athena Polias at Athens, Paus. i. 26, 7, and in the temple of Pan in Arcadia, viii. 37, 8. Famous oracles maintained ever-burning fires, as that of Delphi, whose priests in time of war conveyed the sacred flame to Platæa, Plut. Numa cap. 9; conf. Valckenaer on Herod. 6, 108; so the fires of Delos were carried to Lemnos, Welcker's Aeschyl. Trilog. p. 247 seq. We know the undying fire of Hestia, Vesta. Colonies took their *sacred fire* with them from the mother-city; if it happened to go out, there alone could they light it again, Larcher on Herod. 1, no. 360. Wachsm. Hell. alterth. i. 1, 102. ii. 2, 118. Münter's Rel. d. Carth. p. 49. The Samogitians nourished a perpetual fire, Lasicz. 56. On the *eternal lamp* in the worship of Mary, see Lange's Abh. v. d. ewigen lampe (Verm. schr., Leipz. 1832) pp. 191—204.

p. 614.] Toland's Hist. of Druids (quoted in Hone's Yrbk 876 seq.) supposes three *bealtines* in the year, May 1, Midsum. eve, Nov. 1. The first of May and of Nov. were called *beltan*, says Villemarqué's Bardes Bretons p. 386-7. GDS. 108. On *Bel*, see Diefenb. Celt. 1, 185, Stokes 349. Jamieson (Daybk 2, 659). The great and little *Bel*, Meier's Schwäb. sag. 297. On *Beltaine*, *Belton eve*, see Stewart's Pop. superst. 258 seq. Brand's Pop. Antiq. 1, 337. Stokes 349. Michelet 1, 452 seq. Ir. sag. u. märch. 1, 275-6. 2, 479. The May fire is also called *koelkerz*, *coelcerth*, Villem. B.B. 232. 385-6-7, but he does not explain the word; elsewh. *coel* is omen, fides, and *certh* signum.——An Armoric folk-song speaks of *eight fires*, and of the *father-fire* being lighted in May, Villem. Barzas breiz 1, 8; Hone's Daybk 2, 659. 866 puts the chief fire on Midsum. Day. *Sambhuinn* means Nov. 1 (O'Brien: samhainn = Allhallows-tide). The Druidic November-

also called *tlachdgha,* tine tlachdgha, O'Brien sub v.
d fires are thus described in O'Connor's Proleg. 1, 24:
nes splendentes faciebant *druidae* cum *incantationibus*
magnis supra eis, et ducebant *greges* quos cogebant *transire
per eos ignes';* conf. O'Brien sub v. bealtine. *Horses' heads* were
thrown into the May-fire in Ireland, Hone's Daybk 2, 595 (as
into the Midsum. fire in Germany, p. 618).

p. 617.] On *Easter-fires,* conf. Woeste p. 288; dat *osterfür an-
boiten,* J. v. Scheppau's Oster-pred. p. 8; das *ostermaen-luchten*
in Wilster-marsch, Müllenh. p. 168. Even in S. Germany, e.g.
about Abensberg in Lower Bavaria, they used at Easter time to
burn the *ostermann.* After service at church a fellow lighted a
candle, ran out into the fields with it, and set the straw Easter-
man on fire. A Paderborn edict of 1781 abolished the *Easter-
fire,* Wigand's Pad. and Corv. 3, 281. 1, 317. Instead of *bocks-
thorn* (p. 616 n.), Groten's Gesch. v. Northeim 1723, p. 7 says:
' On this hill the *bocks-horn* was held within the memory of man.'
The Easter *squirrel-hunt* in the Harz (p. 616) reminds of the
Lay of Igor (Hanka p. 68), where every householder pays a
*squirrel* by way of tax. Akin to Easter-fires are the *Walburgs*
(Mayday) *fires,* Müllenh. p. 168: in Rügen, on Mayday eve, took
place a *molkentoverschen bernen* with fire-bladders (p. 1072 n.),
conf. Osnabr. verein 3, 229; on the Hundsrück the young men
and boys are allowed to *cut wood* in the forest on St. Walburg's
eve, Weisth. 2, 168.

p. 620.] The *sol-stitium* is in Homer τροπὴ ἠελίοιο, Od. 15,
404; ἀμφὶ θερινὰς τροπὰς, Procop. B. Goth. 2, 13; ἀμφὶ τροπὰς
χειμερινάς 3, 27. The Bavar. records have *sunwenden, sunbenden,*
the Aleman. *sungihten:* ' ze *sungihten,*' Weisth. 1, 293. 304.
316—8; ze *singeht* 1, 325; nach *sungehten* 1, 669; ze *sungiden*
1, 322-3; zu *sungihte* 1, 708; zu *singihten* 1, 745; *singiht-tag* 1,
727; *sungeht-tag* 1, 669; *singehtag,* Namenbüchl. p. 114. The
AS. *sungiht,* solstitium, stands in Menolog. for June 24; Schilter
on Königsh. p. 458 has the whole passage. MHG. drî tage vor
*sunegihten,* Lanz. 7051; conf. bette-*gâht,* N. Cap. 46, kirch-*giht*
(-going, Oberlin).——Vor der *sunnewenden,* Bamb. reht. ed.
Zöpfl 154; ' hiute ist der ahte tac nâch *sunewenden,* dâ sol daz
jârzît enden.' Iw. 2940.

Midsummer was a great time for meetings and merrymakings :

'ze einen *sunewenden* dâ Sîfrit *ritters namen* gewan,' Nib. 32, 4;
'vor disen *sunewenden*' Siegfried and Kriemhilt visit Worms
670, 3. 694, 3; and it is during the wedding festivities at Midsummer that Siegfried is killed, as may be fairly inferred, if it is
not expressed. The wedding in the Heunenland is to take place
'zen naehsten *sunewenden*' 1424, 4; and the heroes arrive at
Etzel's court 'an *sunewenden âbent*' 1754, 1. On Midsum. day
the Zurich people carry their hot pottage over the water to
Strassburg, Glückh. schiff, v. 194 seq.——On *sunwend-fires*, see
Panz. Beitr. 1, 210 seq. Sunwent was corrup. into *summit*,
*simmet-feur*, Leopr. 182; *simentfeuer*, H. Sachs 1, 423[d]; *sommer-
feur*, Albertini's Narrenhatz 100; *S. Johannis-fürle*, Germ. 1,
442. A sage remark on the sonwend-fire in Firmen. 2, 703;
*feuia hupfa z' Johanne*, Schuegraf der wäldler p. 31. Always a
*lad and lass* together, in couples, jump over the fire, Leopr. 183;
some wantonly push others in, and spread their coat over the hot
coals, Gesch. v. Gaustall (Bamb. ver. 8, 112). At Vienna, common women, loose girls, danced at the Midsum. fire, Schlager's
Wiener skizzen 1, 270. 5, 352. *Fiery wheels* are driven in
Tyrol and Hungary, Wolf's Ztschr. 1, 286-7. 270-1, and in Austria, Duller p. 46-7; conf. the joy-fires of Swiss herdsmen in the
*Poster*-nights, Stald 1, 209. 210. Prohibitions of the Midsum.
fire, Kaltenbäck's Pantaid. 98[b]. 104[a].

p. 624.] On Engl. *bonfires*, see Hone's Daybk 1, 827. 846.
851-2. Brand 1, 299 seq. In France embers taken home from
a John's-fire, in England any *live coals* are a protection against
magic, Hone's Yrbk 1553. *Brising*, the Norweg. for Midsum.
fires, may be akin to bris = flamma, brisa = flammare (Aasen), conf.
brasa, our prasseln, to crackle. *Midsum. fires* flamed in Sweden
too, 9 sorts of wood being used, and 9 sorts of flowers picked
for posies, Runa '44, p. 22. Wieselgr. 411. In Spain they
gathered *verbenas* in the dawn of St. John's day, and lighted
fires, over which they leapt, Handbk of Sp. 1, 270[b]. A St. John's
fire in Portugal is descr. in the Jrb. d. Berl. sprachges. 8, 373.
'John's folk' is what the Letts call those who bring John's-
wort (hypericum, and raggana kauli, witch's bones), and sing
songs, Stender's Gram. p. 50, Dict. 85[a]; on St. John's morning
a wreath of flowers, or hawthorn, is hung over the doors, Fr.
Michel's Races maud. 2, 147. In Esthonia they light a John's

fire, and gather a bundle of sweet-smelling herbs; these the girls
put under their pillows, and what they dream comes true, Possart's Esthl. p. 172. On the *Zobten-berg* in Silesia (fr. Sobota,
sabbath) the Slavs kept their *sobotky*, Schafarik 2, 407 of transl.;
it is also called ' mons Slesie, mons czobothus,' conf. Dietmar (in
Pertz 5, 855). Moravia too has its John's fires, Kulda (in d'Elv)
111-2. Plato de Legg. 19, 945 speaks of a festival following the
summer solstice.

p. 625.] To Ovid's picture of the Palilia, add that of Tibullus
ii. 5, 87 :

> at madidus Baccho sua festa Palilia pastor
> concinet : a stabulis tunc procul este, lupi !
> ille levis *stipulae* solemnis potus *acervos*
> accendet, *flammas transilietque sacras.*

p. 628.] In Christmas-fires, mark the practice of saving up
the half-burnt *yule-log*, Gefken's Cat. 56. Other fires are the
*Shrovetide fire*, Stalder 1, 356, and the so-called *hoop-driving*
(burning wheel) in Up. Swabia on the first Sunday in Lent, the
N. Frisian *biiken-brennen* on Febr. 22, see Müllenh. p. 167.

p. 630.] Old examples of illumination : Joh. Chrys. Or. in red.
Flaviani c. 4 : ὅπερ οὖν ἐποιήσατε στεφανώσαντες τὴν ἀγορὰν
καὶ λύχνους ἄψαντες.　Greg. Naz. Or. de red. Athanasii 21 p.
391 : ἑῶ λέγειν . . . πᾶσαν φωτὶ καταστραπτομένην πόλιν.
Choricii Gazaei Orr., ed. Boissonade '46 p. 101 : σκεύεσι δὲ
φωτὸς εἰργασμένοις εὐφημοῦμεν τοὺς εὐεργέτας. splendida fuit
illuminatio ; *mos* is fuit *veterum* diebus laetis ac festis.　Ann.
Worm. 1251 (Böhm. Font. 2, 168) : regem *incensis candelis* et
campanis pulsatis singulis diebus festivis denunciare.　*Trees
of candles* were carried in processions, Lünzel's Stiftsfehde
135-6. 279 ; vil liehtes gap dâ *manec rone*, Türl. Wh. 99 [b]
(conf. Sæm. 22 [b] : med *brennandom liosom oc bornom viði*). The
Ksrchr. 91 has *brinnende ólvaz*. Walth. 28, 14 speaks only of
ringing bells : ir werdent hôh enpfangen, ir sît wol wert daz wir
die *gloggen* gen iu *liuten*.

## 3.　AIR.

p. 632.] Wind is in Ssk. *anila*=ἄνεμος, also *pavana*, cleanser,
fr. pû, like pâvaka, fire (Suppl. to 602).　So in Finn. *tuuli* ventus,

*tuli* ignis; conf. 'des *fiuwers wint*,' Gudr. 499, 2, and *viwer-rôter wint*, Nib. 1999, 2. An OHG. *suëp*=aër, Graff 6, 856, ON. *svif* =motus repentinus, vibratio. As Wôdan is the all-pervading æther, *Zeus* is equiv. to aër: ἀὴρ ὃν ἄν τις ὀνομάσειε καὶ Δία, Frag. Philem. in Meineke 4, 32 (Euripides has *aether* for Zeus). In Latin also, Jupiter stands for aër, Valcken. ad Herod. 2, 13; conf. 'plurimus *Jupiter*=michil *luft*,' air, Gl. Sletst. 6, 467; and Servius ad Aen. 1, 51 says *Juno* was taken to mean air. The Greeks *sacrificed* to Boreas, Xen. Anab. (Koch 92). The Scythians worship ἄνεμος as cause of life, and the sword as that of death, Lucian's Tox. 38. GDS. 222. 459. The Finns call a μαλακία (calm) Wäinämöinen's way, *Väinämöisen tie* or *kulku:* the god has walked, and all is hushed; he is named *Suvantolainen* fr. suvanto, locus ubi aqua quiescit. The Norse *Andvari* is a dwarf, but also ventus lenis, contrarius; conf. *Biflidi*, *óskabyrr* (pp. 149. 637), Wüetelgôz (p. 367 n.), þoden (Suppl. to 132 end). In the Mid. Ages Paul and John 'habent dâ ze himile weteres gewalt,' Ksrchr. 10948; they are the *weather-lords*, and their day (June 26) the hail-holiday, Scheff. Haltaus 111.——*Waltwint*=auster, Mone's Anz. 8, 409, because it originates in the forest. The winds have a home: *Vindheim* vîðan byggja, Sæm. 10ᵃ. *Wint, Wintpôz, Wintesbal?* are prop. names, Graff 1, 624. Wind is the windhund (greyhound), Kuhn in Hpt's Ztschr. 6, 131, as Donner, Sturm are names of dogs. Wind is worshipped: 'des solt *der luft* sîn *gêret* (air be honoured) von spers krache,' Tit. 2, 2; 'er *neic gegen dem winde* der dâ wâte von Gotlinde,' bowed to the wind that blew fr. G., Helmbr. 461; 'stâ bî, lâ mich den *wint* anwaejen (let the wind fan me), der kumt von mines herzen küneginnen,' MS. 1, 6ᵇ. Wind is spoken of as a person, it *goes, stands still*: spiritus ubi *vult* spirat, 'der wint waeje als er *welle*,' blow as he would, Barl. 257, 11; 'vlôch (flew) waer die wint ghebôt,' bade, Maerl. in Kästner 18ᵇ. Winds *ride*, Ahlw. on Oisian 2, 278. They guide people: 'quel vent vos *guie?*' Ren. 2127. 3728; 'quel vent vos *maine?*' 2675; 'quel vent vos *mene* et quel *oré?*' 2654=whence come you? conf. 'what *devil, cuckoo* brings you here?' (p. 1013). They are *wild,* Trist. 2415. Greg. 646. 754. Renn. 22962; angry: erzürnet sind die lüfte,' Dietr. u. ges. 393; 'die lüfte solden *zürnen*' at the height of the towers, Servat. 84. The air groans,

mutters, grunts: '*grunzet* fone ungewitere,' N. Cap. 58; '*grôt
wint* ende *gesoech*,' Lanc. 3899 ; ' die winde begunden *swegelen*,'
began to pipe, Servat. 3233; conf. 'up dem windes *horne*,'
Weisth. 3, 231. On *Fönn, Drîfa, Miöll*, see GDS. 685.

p. 632.] Of the *wind's bride* : mit einer *windes-briute* wurden
sie getwungen, Servat. 2302; in nam ein *windes-brût* 2844;
flugen vaster dan ein *w. b.*, Engelh. 4771 ; daz diu *w. b.* gelît,
Hpt's Ztschr. 7, 381; gelîch der *windesbriute*, Troj. kr. 33571.
Luther says *windsbraut* for ventus typhonicus, Acts 27, 14.   Old
glosses have *nimphus, nimpha*, stormwind, Graff 1, 625 ; is this
a misapplication of nimbus ? or a congener ?   In France they
speak of the *whining of Melusine* (p. 434), who in Bohemia passes
for a goddess of wind, and to whom they throw flour out of the
window for her children (Suppl. to 636) ; conf. the whimpering
of the Vila, and the weeping of the Esth. *tuuleema*, wind's
mother, Böcler 146-7.   Is the Swiss *harein*, Stald. 2, 21, fr.
OHG. harên = clamare, Graff 4, 578, or fr. charôn = queri 5, 465 ?
——Other expressions for wind's bride : *wind-gelle* = venti pellex
(snê-gelle), Hpt's Ztschr. 6, 290.   Rocholz 2, 408 ; Bavar. *wind-
gäsperl*, Swab. *wind-gäspele*, Leopr. 101. 120; Bavar. *windsch-
brach, -brausz*, Panz. Beitr. 2, 209 ; *sau-kegel*, Rocholz 2, 187.
OHG. *wanda* = turbo, Graff 1, 761; ON. *roka*, turbo.   Other
OHG. terms: *ungistuomi* = strepitus (MHG. *ungestüm*, vehementia
aëris, Superst. H. cap. 77); *ungewitiri* = tempestas, procella,
Graff 1, 630; *arapeit* = do. do. 1, 407; *heifti* = tempestas, Windb.
308. 313; *unst* = procella, tempestas, AS. *ûst;* with *treip* = agebat
(nubila ventus), Graff 5, 482, conf. ON. *drîfa*, snowstorm, *drîfa
örva*, a storm of arrows.——Heralds of winter were ' *twer* und
sûrin *bîse*,' MS. 2, 193[b]; contrary wind is in MHG. *twer* or *twere*,
and ON. *And-þvari, Andvari* is said to be that as well as a
dwarf's name ; conf. ' von luftes *geduere*,' Himelr. 292 (Hpt's
Ztschr. 8, 153), ' die winde sluogen in *entwer*,' Hpt 7, 378-9.   A
hurricane, squall, flaw, is called *flâge* in Pass. and Jeroschin ;
windes *vlâgen*, Marienleg. 84, 21. 87, 8; die wint ene *vlaghe*
brachte, Rose 13151.   Maerl. 3, 189; Dut. *vlaag*, Gothl. *flagä*,
*vindflagä*, Almqvist 422[b]; ' *rotten* und sturmwinde,' Luther's
Letters 5, 155.   In Slavic it is *vikhr*, Pol. wicher, Boh. wichr;
Lith. *ummaras, vĕsulas*, whirlwind (conf. our provinc. ' eilung,'
M. Neth. ylinge, Wessel's Bibel p. 7, with ON. *êl, jel*, nimbus).

The Greeks had ἄελλα, θύελλα, λαῖλαψ, Ital. fortuna di mare=
storm.

p. 633.] *Zio* resembles Mars and Indras, the god of winds and
of souls, who with his Maruts or spirits of storm makes war on
the giants of darkness, Hpt's Ztschr. 5, 488-9. 6, 131. Wuotan,
the god of the Wild Hunt, sweeps like the storm through
*open doors* (p. 926-7, etc.). Hodeke howls (Suppl. to 511 beg.).
Both wind's bride and devil are called *sow-tail* (p. 996) or hammer
(p. 999) : conf. *sau-kegel*, Rocholz 2, 187 ; in Bavaria *wind-sau*,
Zingerle's Oswalt 83 (αἰγίς, goatskin, hurricane). Frau *Fiuk* or
*Frick* also acts as goddess of wind, Hpt's Ztschr. 5, 376. 6, 131 ;
conf. the *fahrende mutter*, Wolf's Ndrl. sag. no. 518. At a
village near Passau they call the whirlwind *mueml*, aunty :
' mueml ist drin ! ' (m. is also toad) ; or else *schratl*, Schm. 3,
519. 522. The hurricane has hands : ' nu bin ich sturmwinden
alrêrst *in die hant* gevarn,' fallen, Trist. 8848.

p. 635.] Was there a wind named *Vorwitz* (prurient curiosity)?

do kam ein wint geflogen dar,
der ist *virwitz* genant,
in hânt die meide wol erkant
unde ouch die vrouwen über alle lant.     Renn. 84.
sân kumt *her virwitz* gerant
und *loeset* den meiden *úf* (unlooses) *diu bant*. Renn. 268.[1]

Conf. ' der *fürwitz*, so jungfern theuer machet,' Simplic. 1, 568 ;
' hine *fyrwit brœc*,' Beow. 464. 3966, 5565 ; *vurwitz segens*, Turl.
Wh. 128ᵃ (Suppl. to 273 n.) ; 's sticht's der *wunderwitz*, Hebel
157 ; *fürwitz*, der krämer (huckster), Uhl. Volksl. 636. OHG.
*firiwizi* is also portentum, mirificum, Graff 1, 1099 ; ' man saget
mir von kinde, daz keme uns von dem *winde*,' Erlösung 2440.——
As the North had its storm-giant Hræsvelg, Kl. Grooth's Quickborn calls a tempest ' de grote und de lütge *windkerl* '; conf.
' *Gott* füeget den wind,' Rabenschl. 619 ; ' der Gotes geist daz
(saz?) ûf des luftes *vederen*, Aneg. Hahn 4, 72. Αἴολος, φίλος
ἀθανάτοισι θεοῖσι, Od. 10, 2 ; κεῖνον γὰρ ταμίην ἀνέμων ποίησε
Κρονίων, 10, 21. Virgil's Æolus sits in a hollow mountain, and
Juno begs wind of him, Æn. 1, 52. 64; conf. KM. no. 89 : ' weh',
weh', windchen ! ' blow, blow, Windie.

---

[1] Conf. λυσί-ζωνος, ζώνην λύειν. Tibi (Hymenaee) virgines zonula solvunt sinus.
Catull. 59, 53 ; zonam solvere virgineam 65, 28.

Eagles were fixed on gables or the top of a tent pretty often :

le grant tref Karlemaine font contremont lever,
par desor le pomel font *l'aigle* d'or poser,
par devers Montauban en fist le chief torner.

Renaus 151, 2—4.

A golden eagle on the top of the castle, Auberi 73 ; high on the
tent ' ein guldîn *ar*,' En. 9160. On the inroad of the ' Welschen '
in 978, conf. Giesebrecht's Otto II. p. 48. In Kalevala, tom.
2, 12 (1 ed. 17, 341) :

du min *örn*, min sköna fogel,
vänd (turn) åt annat håll ditt hufvnd (head),
tillslut (shut) dina skarpa ögon !

A golden eagle on the roof in Athenæus 2, 259 ; and observe,
that ἀετός is both eagle and gable. The Basque *egoa*, south
wind, is akin to egoa, egaa, egala, wing, Pott 2, 190. In Goethe,
winds wave their noiseless wings. Thunder-clouds are also
likened to the wide-spreading root of a tree, and called *wind-
wurzel* (-root), a sign of hurricane, Schmidt v. Werneuchen 131.

p. 636.] The wind is *fed* with rags or tow, which is thrown to
it, Leopr. 102. In Austria too they offer meal in a bread-shovel
out of the attic window to the storm, saying (Popovitch sub v.
wind) :

nimm hin, mein lieber wind,
trag heim deinem weib und kind,
und komm nimmer !

Instead of *giving the wind food*, a woman says ' I'd rather stab
the *dog* dead,' and throws a *knife* into the yard (p. 632 n.) ; conf.
M. Koch's Reise in Tirol p. 87-8. Winds were thought of as
*meal-devouring dogs*, Hpt's Ztschr. 5, 373-6. 6, 131 ; conf.
Hodeke's *howling* (Suppl. to 633). In a storm at sea a *dove*
appears, flies three times round the ship, one man puts out his
arm and ' de cauda ejus *tres* tulit *pennas*, quas mari intinguens
tempestatem compescuit,' Venant. Fortun. vita Radegundis, Acta
Bened. sec. 1, p. 332. The Gr. θύελλα snatches away, Od. 20,
63-6, like the Norweg. northwind. To hurtful winds *black
lambs* were sacrificed, to fair winds *white*, Aristoph. Ran. 845.
Virg. Æn. 3, 120. For a favourable wind a *he-goat* is hung on

the mast, Hone's Yrbk 1553.   On Irish wind-worship, see Conan
111—5.

p. 637.] Divine, semi-divine or diabolic beings excite wind
(Suppl. to 145): Got füeget den wint, Rabenschl. 619; in Serv.
songs God is implored for wind, Vuk ii. 561. 1089. i. 369 (no.
511). 370 (no. 513). 322 (no. 455); Christ is appealed to, Sv.
vis. 2, 167.   The saints invoked in a storm are called *wazzer-
heilige*, water-holies, Marienleg. p. 85; the martyrs Paul and
John 'hânt dâ ze himele *weteres gewalt*,' Ksrchr. Diem. 335, 1.
*Scrâwunc* in Hpt's Zeitschr. 6, 290 seems the name of a weather-
giant; Fasolt chases a woman in the mountains, Ecke 167, as
Wuotan does; conf. 'mein sohn *Windheim*,' Wolf's Ztschr. 1,
311.   Is there a special meaning in 'der wint von Aspriâne *dóz*,'
whizzed, Roth. 4226? 'Folks said it wasn't a *natural* wind,
they believed there wasn't a *tufel* left in hell, they was all from
home, trying to *bluster* us out of our wits,' Stolle 170; conf.
'quel vent vos guie' etc. (Suppl. to 632 end).   Oxen with their
horns dig the tempest out of a sand hill, Thiele 2, 257. Müllenh.
p. 128.——With Wôdan *óska-byrr* conf. Suppl. to 149.   ON. *byr*,
Dan. *bör*, fair wind.   Low Germ. seamen's words are *bö*, a sudden and passing squall, *böiges* wetter, *donnerbö, regenbö, hagelbö*.
Slav. *búria* = procella, Miklos. p. 6; Serv. *bura*, Russ. *burán*,
hurricane, conf. βορέας.   Boreas helps the Greeks, Herod. 7, 189.
On *Juno*, see Suppl. to 632 beg.   Can Oðin's name of *Viðrir* be
akin to AS. *hwiða*, *hweoðu* = aura lenis, *hweoðrian* = murmurare?
The Slav. *pogóda* is in Lith. *pagada*, fair wind, fair weather.
Mist in ON. is called *kerlíngar vella*, nebula humi repens.

p. 639.] With the provisions of the Lex Visigoth., conf. the
Indiculus Superstit. (in Pertz 3, 20) de tempestatibus and *cornibus* et *cocleis*, and the passage fr. Seneca in Wolf's Ndrl. sag.
p. 693 about χαλαζο-φύλακες, hail-wardens; ἐν Γέταις χαλαζᾶν
is said of Zeus, Lucian 7, 51.

p. 640.] The passage fr. Bartholom. Anglicus is also in Hpt's
Ztschr. 4, 494-5, where Wackernagel understands Winlandia as
*Finlandia*; and it is true the Finns are said to make *fiölkyngveðr*,
Fornm. sög. 4, 44.   In a Lapland epos a maiden has three sorts
of magic *knots*; she unties the first, wind fills the sails and the
ship gets under way; then the second and the third, followed by
storm and shipwreck; conf. Klemm 3, 100.   Such wind-knots a

woman on the Schlei and a witch of Föhr know how to make,
Müllenh. p. 222-5 ; conf. the sailor's belief about wind in Temme's
Pom. sag. 347-8, and the *Hollen* in Gefken's Catal. p. 55.    In
Gervas. Tilb. p. 972 ed. Leibn. (Liebrecht p. 21), is a story ' de
vento *chirothecae* Archiepiscopi Arelatensis *incluso,* et valli ventis
imperviae *illato.'*

p. 641.]    The ἀσκός of Æolus, Od. 10, 19, is also in Ovid's
Met. 14, 224 : Æolon Hippotaden, cohibentem carcere ventos,
*bovis inclusos tergo ;* and 14, 230 : dempsisse ligamina ventis.
Eight whirlwinds are hidden in a *cap,* Schiefner's Finn. m. p. 611
[a formidable ' capful of wind ']. Conf. *setting* the cap this way
or that in Sommer p. 30-1, and *Hütchen, Hodeke.*

p. 641.]    *Hail* is called in Ind. *marutphala,* fruit of the Maruts,
Hpt's Ztschr. 5, 489 ; an ON. name for it is *stein-óđi,* in saxa
saeviens, Egilss. 600, an OHG. apparently *scrâwunc,* Hpt 6, 290.
On *mildew,* conf. Schmeller 2, 567.    Acc. to Jungm. 1, 56[b], *baby*
(grannies) are clouds heaped up like hills.    Our people ascribe
the rising of mountain mist not to animals alone ; at the Kifhäuser they say : ' Oho, *Kaiser Friedrich is brewing,* there'll be
soft weather,' Prætor. Alectr. pp. 69, 70.

p. 641.]    To the Greeks it was Zeus that shed the *snow,* Il. 12,
280-1 ; ἔνιφεν ὁ Ζεύς, Babr. 45, 1.    ' Die tôren (fools) sprechent
(in winter) *snîa snî ! '*    Walth. 76, 1.

## 4. EARTH.

p. 642.]    Ssk. *dharâ,* Gr. χώρα, Bopp's Comp. Gr. p. 304.    Ir.
*tir,* Lat. *terra,* ' akin to torreo, and signif. the *dry,'* Pott 1, 270.
Another Ssk. word is *ksham,* Bopp's Gl. 92[a].    ON. *hauđr,* neut.,
Saem. 120-6-7.    Goth. *grundus* fr. grindan, as our mël, malm,
molte (meal, dust, mould) are fr. malan ; scholle grund; Ph. v.
Sittew. 601.——Epithets applied to the earth's outside : daz *preita*
wasal, Musp. 63 ; *sîd* folde, Cædm. 154, 5 ; on *rûmre* foldan,
Exon. 468, 25 ; εὐρεῖα χθών, conf. Wh. 60, 28.    Altd. bl. 1, 388.
Eracl. 2153 ; ûf der *scibligen* (round) erde, Diemer 214, 23 ; ûf
der *moltigen* erde, Mar. 157, 39 ; diu *vinster* erde, Tit. 5120 ; in
der *rôten* erde, Karaj. 93, 10 ; um ein wenig *rothe* erde, Simpl. 1,
575 ; eorđe *eal-grêne,* Cædm. 13, 3 ; Guds *gröna* jord, Sv. folks.
1, 126.    Does ' terra *viva* ' in Marcellus no. 24 mean grassy ?
conf. viva flamma (p. 611 n.).——But the Earth is also *liebe* erde,

Schweinichen 1, 104; diu *süeze* erde, Wernher v. Ndrrh. 35, 9;
hin *forna* fold, Sæm. 55[b]; 'sicht wie die *heiliy* erd,' looks (black)
as earth, H. Sachs v. 368[b], conf. ἀπὸ γᾶς ἀγίας, Athen. 3, 494;
Swed. '*Guds* gröna jord,' our '*Gottes* boden,' Chapbk of Hürn.
Siegfr., Pol. maulaffe p. 231, Weisen's Com. probe 39; we say
'Hide in *God's earth* for shame!' Dying is called *ze grunde
gân*; conf. '*daz ich bezîte werde dir gelîch*,' soon be like thee,
Wh. 60, 28; 'sich aus dem *staube* machen,' make oneself out of
the dust, scarce.——The earth will take in liquids: fold scal við
flôdi taka, Sæm. 27[b]; but '*bluot* benimet (robs) der erde den
*magetuom*,' maidenhood, Mos. 10, 28; dannoch was diu erde ein
*maget*, Parz. 464, 13. Earth bears not on her breast the man of
blood: 'jâ solte mich diu erde umbe dis mort niht en-*tragen*,'
Ecke 143; 'mich wundert daz mich diu erde geruochet *tragen*,'
still deigns to bear, Greg. 2511; 'den diu erde niht solde *tragen*,'
Wackern. lb. 588, 3. Stricker's Klage 38; conf. 'daz iuch die
erde niht *verslant*,' swallowed, Warn. 3203; 'terre, *car ouvrez*,
si *recois* moi chaitis!' Garin 2, 263; '*heald* þu nu hrûse!' Beow.
4489. So the witch may not touch the *bare earth* (p. 1074), holy
water must not touch the *ground* (Suppl. to 587); whereas to the
saint she offers herself as a seat: 'diu erde *niht en-dolte* daz er
büge sîn gebeine (tholed not that he bent his limbs), si *bôt* sich
her *engeine*, daz er als ûf einem stuole saz,' Servat. 1592. On
*earthquakes*, see p. 816. Men confided secrets to the *earth*,
Lother u. Maller 36-7: 'si klagten sô senlîche, daz in daz *ertrîche*
möhte g'antwürtet hân,' would fain have answered them, Mai 44,
21; they made their plaint to the *stone*, Lisch's Meckl. jrb. 5, 100.
Müllenh. p. 37, or told their tale to the *dead wall*, Arnim's März.
1, 70.

Much might be said on *gold, silver, iron*. To the Finns iron
(rauta, Lapp. route) is *brother* to *water and fire*, Kalev. 4, 29, and
is born of virgin's *milk*. There is *liquid gold* and *milk* in amrita
(p. 317). Gold is called *Frôða miöl*, Egilss. p. 450, *ôgnarliomi*=
oceani lumen, Sæm. 152ᵃ, and *munnfylli* or *munntal iötna*, Sn.
83; conf. 'morgenstund hat *gold im mund*,' though F. Magn. derives
those words fr. mund=hand. Gold placed under a dumb woman's
*tongue* makes her speak, Fornm. s. 3, 117—9; gold is tempered
in dew, Tit. 3698 (Tigrisgold, 4348). On dragons' and griffins'
gold, see pp. 978. 980.

p. 643.]   For Ssk. *khusa*, Bopp in Gl. 78ᵃ. 86ᵇ writes *kuša*
I find a *reincurni* also in Hpt's Ztschr. 5, 364, *reinegras*=alga,
Sumerl. 54.   Putting *earth* or *turf* on the head secures against
magic, Panz. Beitr. 1, 240-1.   Kuhn's Nord. s. p. 378.

p. 644.]   Emigrants took *earth* as well as fire out with them
(Suppl. to 611) ; conf. the strewing of earth in the Old Saxon
legend.   Þôrhaddr var hofgoði i Þrândheimi, hann fýstist til
Islands, ok tôk âðr ofan hofit, ok hafði með ser hofs-*moldina* ok
sûlurnar, Landn. 4, 6.

p. 644.]   Demeter meets Jasion in the *thrifallow*, the fruitfullest
cornland : μίγη φιλότητι καὶ εὐνῇ νειῷ ἔνι τριπόλῳ, Od. 5, 127,
conf. Hes. Theog. 971 and νειὸς τρίπολος, Il. 18, 541; OHG.
*driska*, GDS. 53. 61-2.

p. 645.]   A *mons sanctus* near Jugenheim is mentioned in a
record of 1264; conf. *svetá gorá*=Mt Athos; an ὄρος ἱερόν of
the Getæ named Κωγαίωνον, Strabo 7, 298; a holy mount Θήκης
in Pontus, Xen. Anab. iv. 7, 11.   The mountains named *grand‹
father* are discussed in Hpt's Ztschr. 1, 26.   Two adjacent mountains in Lausitz are named by the Wends *čorny boh* and *bjeły boh*,
black god, white god, Wend. volksl. 2, 285.   The Ossetes
worship their highest mountains (brakabseli, fair mountains),
Kohl's S. Russia 1, 296.

p. 645.]   The notable passage on *rock-worship* in Landn. 2,
12 is as follows : 'hann (Thorôlfr) hafði svâ mikinn *âtrûnað â
fialli* þvî, er stôð î nesinu, er hann kalladi *Helgafell*, at þângat
skyldi engi maðr óþveginn *lîta ;* ok svâ var þar mikil *friðhelgi*,
at þar skyldi engu granda î fiallinu, hvarki fê ne mönnum, nema
sialft gengi brott.   Þat var *trúa* þeirra Þorôlfs fraenda, at þeir
*dœi allir î fiallit* (al. codex : þa þeir dœi, mundi þeir *î fiallit hverfa*
allir).'   And 2, 16 : 'höfðu mikinn *âtrûnað â hôlana*—trûðu
þeir þvî, at þeir *dœi î hôlana* ' (hôll=tumulus, colliculus); conf.
' *dying (vanishing) into the mountain.*'   The Icelander Kodran of
Vatnsdal had a stone at Gilja, to which he and his fathers sacrificed ; they imagined the *âr-maðr* lived inside it, from whom
fruitful years proceeded, Kristnisaga c. 2.——Stones *prophesy*,
Norske ev. no. 30 ; they are *washed, anointed, honoured*, F. Magn.
Lex. p. 961.   When winds are contrary, sailors *wash a blue stone*,
and obtain a fair wind ; they also take *oaths* upon it, Hone's
Yrbk 1553.   People *kneel naked* before the holy stone, Hone's

Daybk 1, 825. 2, 1035. They creep through hollow stones (p. 1166), they go into hollow rocks to present offerings (p. 58) ; conf. the Gibichen-stones, the pottle-stones with pits and holes, Giesebr. Balt. stud. 12, 114. 128. 'De his quae faciunt *super petras*' is the heading of cap. 7 of Indicul. Superst. On stone-worship among Celts, see Michelet 2, 16-7.——In Swed. tales and spells a stone is always '*jord-fast* sten,' one fixed in the earth, Runa '44, 22 ; â *iarðföstom* steini stôð ec innan dyra, Sæm. 99ᵃ ; till en *jord-fasten* sten, Sv. folks. 1, 217. Sv. äfventyr 1, 282-4-8. 305 ; AS. earðfæst. But we also hear of the '*wahsender* bühel,' growing hill, Lanz. 5132 ; and a Slov. riddle, 'kai *raste* bres korenia (what grows without root) ?' has the answer '*kamen*,' stone. A distinction is also drawn between *walgende* and vaste-ligende steine, Leyser 129, 35 ; usque ad *wagoden* stein, Mon. Zoll. no. 1, *wagonden* stein, no. 12 ; *gnappstein*, Stalder 2, 519 ; Dan. *rokke-stene*, Schreiber's Feen 21. These stones by their *rocking* are said to bring on *thunder* and *rain*, O. Müller 2, 340. Stones are often landmarks : zu dem grawen stein, Weisth. 1, 242, an dem blauen stein 2, 661.

p. 646.] Giants and men turn into stone (p. 551-2) ; stones have sense and feeling. It is true we say 'stone-deaf, stone-dead,' *stille sam die steine*, Karl 92ᵇ. 94ᵃ, and Otfried iv. 7, 4 calls them *unthrâtê*, pigri ; yet in Luke 19, 40 'the stones would cry out ;' the stone *holds fast*, Müllenh. p. 142-3. The *pierres de minuit* move at midnight, conf. the *turning-stones* in the Ir. märch. 2, 37—44 ; the stone *turns* round on Christmas night, Harrys 1 no. 34 (conf. Heusinger p. 20), or when bells ring, Dybeck 4, 43. Men complain to stones as they do to earth (p. 642) and fire (p. 629), as if to elemental gods. The stone you complain to *changes colour*, the white turns red, the red blue, Wächter's Statistik pp. 13. 156. 'Si klagten, daz sich die mûrsteine mohten *klieben* herdan,' Klage 977 (so: 'si ruoften, daz diu erde unter in sich mehte haben ûf getân,' opened under them 1073) ; 'stahel, vlins u. stein sih muosen von dem jâmer *klieben*,' Türl. Wh. 3ᵇ ; 'klage, diu flinse het *gespalten*,' split flints, Tit. 3765 ; 'von ir schoene müeste ein vels *erkrachen*,' MsH. 3, 173ᵃ [similar examples omitted] ; 'hiute ist der stein naz, dâ Karl uffe saz, vil heize weinunde,' to-day the stone is wet, whereon K. sat hotly weeping, Ksrchr. 14937. Stones relent in

the story of Hoyer, Wigal. p. 57—9. 452.   Balt. stud. xi. 2, 191.
A stone will not let a false man sit on it, 'ûf der *Eren* (êren ?
honour's) *steine* sitzen,' Lanz. 5178 seq.

<hr/>

## CHAPTER XXI.

### TREES AND ANIMALS.

p. 647.]   As Freidank 10, 7 says that angels are immortal,
that of men the spirit is immortal, but the body mortal, and of
beasts both body and soul are mortal; so Berthold p. 364 allows
being to stones, being and life to plants, feeling to animals.
Schelling says, life sleeps in the stone, dozes in the plant, dreams
in the beast, wakes in man.   The Ssk. a-ga, na-ga (non iens)
= tree, hill, Bopp's Gl. 2ᵃ. 189ᵃ.   So in the Mid. Ages the line is
drawn between ' ligendez und lebendez,' Diemer 89, 24.   Notker's
Boëth. speaks of boume and chriuter (trees and herbs) diu fone
saffe *lebent*, and of *un*living lapides, metalla.   In Esth., beasts
are ellayat, living ones, and plants kasvias, that which lives.——
Not only do wild birds grieve at man's lament, Walth. 124, 30,
and beasts and fishes help him to mourn, Ges. Abent. 1, 8, but
' elliu geschefede,' all created things, May, summer's bliss, heath,
clover, wood, sun and Venus, MS. 1, 3ᵇ; ' gi bom, gras, lof unde
krût (leaf and herb), helpet mi skrigen over lût (cry aloud)!'
Marienklage 386.   Grass and flower fret at misdeeds, and mourn,
Petersb. extr. fr. Kalev. p. 25, and in folksongs wither up.
Bluomen brehent u. *smierent*, MS. 1, 44ᵇ; dô daz spil ergangen
was, dô *lachten* bluomen u. gras, Hagen's Ges. Abent. 1, 464;
die boum begunden *krachen*, die rôsen sêre *lachen*, ibid.   Flowers
on the heath quarrel : ' dô sach ich *bluomen striten* wider den
grüenen *klê* (clover), weder ir lenger waere,' which of them was
taller, Walth. 114, 28; dû bist kurzer, ich bin langer, alsô *stritens*
ûf dem anger *bluomen* unde *klê* 51, 35; vil maniger hande *bluomen
kîp* (chid), MS. 1, 35ᵇ; *bluomen kriegent* umb ir schîn, Lohengr.
p. 154; *bluomen lachent* durch daz gras, der kurzer, dirre lenger
was, Dietr. drach. 1067; conf. Kl. schr. 2, 157.   They have their
rules, Altd. w. 1, their precedences, their meanings and language,
conf. the Flower-games (Suppl. to 909).——Tree-worship was

highly developed among the Indians and Greeks. The Hindûs with elaborate ceremonies marry trees to one another, esp. the mango and tamarind, shrubs like the rose and jessamine, even tanks and stones, Sleeman's Rambles and Recoll. [Horace: vitem viduas ducit ad arbores]. Woycicki, Germ. ed. p. 144-5. For Greeks, see Bötticher. The Germans *wake* tree as well as corn, Zingerle 691 ; bäumchen, *schlaf nicht,* frau Holle kommt . . . bäumchen, *wach auf,* neujahr ist da, Somm. 162. 182; the forest *sleeps* at New-year, P. Dieffenb. Wetterauer sag. p. 274; conf. Gerhard's hymn: 'Nun *ruhen* alle wälder.' Tree-tops wave, and carry messages, Wolf's Ztschr. 2, 161; 'the birches *know* it still,' Gellert 3, 388. Trees *blossom* at a happy event, and *wither* when a death is near, Sueton. Galba 1 ; and like the Emperors, the Greeks had family-trees. Völsung's tree, barn-stockr, stood in the hall, Völs. cap. 2 ; conf. our 'genealogical *tree.*'

## 1. TREES.

p. 649.] Akin to *nimid* is *vernemet* = fanum ingens, Venant. Fort. 1, 9. Diefenb. Celt. 1, 83-4: *silva* quae vocatur *nemet,* Glück p. 17; δρυ-νέμετος, Strabo 567. GDS. 497. Zeuss's Die Deut. derives nemet fr. neamch = coelum, and sees in it a 'sub divo,' therefore a contrast to wood. A Vocab. optim. p. 47ᵃ renders silva wilder walt, nemus schoener walt, lucus dicker walt, saltus hoher walt.

p. 651.] The Lapps shoot *blindfold* at a suspended bearskin, Klemm 3, 14. Dyb. Runa 4, 92. The Amer. Indians hang up a bison-skin on a high pole to the Lord of life, and then cut it up into small pieces, Klemm 2, 164; likewise a deerskin 2, 179. Skins of sacrifices are hung up by Tungûses, Ostiáks, Boriáts, Cherkesses, 3, 106. 125. 114. 4, 91. The golden fleece of the ram was nailed to an oak, Preller 2, 211.

p. 651.] That is a pretty story of the holy *oak,* whose falling leaves people do not touch. When it is cut down and burnt, a dog appears in the ashes, and makes the people take all the ashes back to where the tree stood, Firmen. 1, 358. The oak as a *tree of plaints* occurs in Megenberg, Hpt's Zschr. 4, 255. Messages are delivered to a holy oak, Livy 3, 25. Its great age inspired respect: 'so long as *oak* and earth do stand,' Weisth. 2, 225: 'while the tree is in the ground and the *acorn* thereon,' 3, 779 ;

j'ai vu le *gland* et la gaule, Barzas br. 1, 28. 32.    On oak and
*beech*, see Dyb. '45, 78-9 ; conf. τὴν παλαιὰν φηγόν, Soph. Trach.
171.    'Af fornum *polli*,' ex antiqua pinu, Sn. ed. '48, 1, 308 ; but·
'af eikirotu' 310.——The *ash* was also holy : fraxinus quem
imperiti *sacrum* vocant, Kemble 5, 103 (yr 854).    It is hostile to
snakes, Panz. Beitr. 1, 251-2.    Pliny 16, 14 ; conf. askr Yggdrasill, and note, p. 796.    There was a spell, that gave a *hazel-rod*
the power to flog people in their absence ; in the Atharva-veda a
branch of açvattha has the power of destroying enemies ; conf.
the hazel-wand as wishing-rod (p. 975).    Hasalwara is a proper
name, Cod. Lauresh. 809.    Lett. lasda, lagsda, Lith. lazda = cory-
lus, baculus ; Lazdona = avellanarum deus, god of filberts.

p. 653.]    It is dangerous to build where an *elder-tree* has stood,
Prætor. Weltb. 1, 16.    Of the *rönn*, rowan, a sacred tree, we
read in Dyb. '44, 9 : *rönnen* sade till mannen : 'hugg mig ej,
dä blöder jag,' hew me not, or I bleed, Wieselgr. 378 ; conf. the
Pruss. tale in Tettau and Temme p. 259, and the Finn. *clopua*,
arbor vitæ, 'non cædenda in pratis.'    The evil *Weckholterin*
(juniper) is mentioned in the Herpin, Hagen's Ges. Ab. 3, xi.
The Serv. for juniper, borovitza, is from bor, fir, Lett. paëgle,
because it grows under the fir; and the Swed. *tall* (fir, pine) is
not to be hewn either : do so, and on turning round you'll see
your house on fire, Dyb. 4, 26. 44.    Neither is the hawthorn,
Nilsson 6, 4.

p. 653.]    Have we any Germ. stories of spirits that live in the
*erle* (alder) ?    Goethe's *Erl-king* seems taken from the Fr. *aulne*,
*aune* = alnus and daemon.    Kalis passes out of Nala into the
Vibhitaka, which is regarded as haunted after that, Bopp's Nalus
p. 153.    Holtzm. Ind. sag. 3, 72.    To the *fig-tree* the Indians
present offerings, which are consumed by crows, sparrows and
cranes ; hence their name of sacrifice-eater.    Like the maiden in
the *pine*, the gods are said to live between *bark* and *tree*, Lasicz
46 ; conf. creeping between wood and bark (p. 1085).    Iw. 1208 :
sam daz *holz under der rinden*, alsam sît ir verborgen; O. Engl.
Iw. 741 : als the bark hilles the tre; O. Fr. Iw. p. 146 : li fuz
qui est coverz de lescorce qui sor lui nest (nait).    A *holy oak*
grows out of the *mouth* of a slain *king*, Harrys 1 no. 55.

p. 654.]    In choosing a twig [for a wishing-rod ?] it is important,
first, that it be a new shoot, the sumer-late (p. 975), and secondly,

that it look to the east : â baðmi viðar þeim er *lúta austr limar*,
Sæm. 195ª. Flowers were invoked: es sten dri rosen in jenem
dal, die *rûfent*, jungfrau, *an*, Uhl. Volksl. 87. O sanctas gentes,
quibus haec nascuntur *in hortis numina!* Juven. Sat. 15, 10.

## 2. ANIMALS.

p. 655.] Beasts are commonly regarded as dumb : stumbez
tier, Iw. 7767, stomme bêste, Lanc. 18849. 32919, daz un-
sprechende vihe, Warnung 2704; conf. muta animalia, Dan.
umälende beest, ON. ômâla; ' der lewe zeict im unsprechenden
gruoz,' Iw. 3870. They are ignorant : tier vil ungewizzen, Er.
5843. Yet they not only show sympathy, like stones and plants
(Suppl. to 646-7), but in urgent cases they, like dumb children,
find their tongues; witness Balaam's ass, and : armentaque vulgo
ausa loqui, Claudian in Eutrop. 2, 43 ; attonito pecudes pastore
locutos 1, 3. Oxen talk, Panz. Beitr. 1, no. 255. Nork 12, 377 ;
ox and ass converse in the Bret. volksm. 87-8, but only for an
hour once a year, between 11 and 12 on Christmas night, N.
Preuss. prov. bl. 5, 468. Bosquet p. 221. Beasts can *see spirits :*
Balaam's ass saw the angel with the sword, Numb. 22, 23—33 ;
the dogs see the goddess, horses and hounds are ghost-seers
(p. 667), Panz. Beitr. 1, 118; nay Athenæus 3, 454 says all *birds*
were *men* once.

p. 656.] Conf. Ferd. Wachter's art. PFERDE in the Halle
Encycl., and the beautiful Serv. wedding-song (Vuk, ed. nov. 15,
no. 23. Wesely p. 55). *Sleipnir* is the son of Loki, a god, and
Svaðilfari; from him is descended Sigurð's Grani, Völs. c. 13,
and Grani has 'mans vid,' Fär. qväd. 156. A sagacious trusty
steed occurs in Walach. märch. no. 17, one that gives advice in
Sv. sag. 1, 164 ; and in German, still more in Hungarian fairy-
tales we have wise, helpful, talking horses, Ungr. tatos s. Ispolyi
(conf. p. 392). *Skinfaxi* is a cow's name in a Norweg. tale, Asb.
Huldr. 1, 202.

p. 658.] Nôtt rides on *Hrîmfaxi*, Dagr on *Skinfaxi*. The
Indians thought curly hair on a horse a lucky sign, Bopp's Gl.
34ª. The horse offered up by kings at the ašvamêdha must be
*white*. To ride a white horse is a privilege of gods, kings and
heroes, Pind. Pyth. 4, 117 : λευκίππων πατέρων. A stallion with
three *white feet* and two glass eyes is in Weisth. 2, 618.

p. 658 n.]   Helbl. 15, 293 : ein hengest der noch nie gras an *fulzande* en-beiz.   A *Fülizan* in Ring 49[b], 38.   49[d], 31.   The Serv. for fülizant is xdrebetiak, foal's (zub underst.).   A horse keeps his foal-teeth till his third year, then cuts his horse-teeth, dentes equini, quos nonnisi trimis caballis natura concedit, Pertz 8, 214 ; jouenes polains, quatre dens ot jetés, Ogier 2412 ; dentes equi, qui primi cadunt, alligati facilem dentionem praestant, Forcell. sub. v. dentio.

Collo igitur molli dentes nectentur equini,
   qui primi fuerint pullo crescente caduci.   Serenus sam. 1040.

The same of a child's teeth : pueri qui primus ceciderit dens, ut terram non attingat, inclusus in armillam et assidue in brachio habitus, Pliny 28, 4.  GDS. 154.

p. 659.]   To Swed. *gnägga* corresp. ON. gneggja, Sæm. 144[a], AS. hnägan, neigh.   The Dan. *vrindske* is our brenschen, wrenschen, frenschen ; conf. *wrene* hengst, Lex Sal. p. xxviii. Ssk. vṛiṅh, barrire, Bopp 32[b].   Norw. Dan. *humra*, a low humming neigh.   In Lanz. 474 : ez begunde sîn ros *weien*, trâsen unde schreien ; in Garg. 240[b] : rihelen u. hinnewihelen, 77[b] : hinnewiheln.   Is *wihelen* akin to Prov. evelhier, Ferabr. 3613, and the horse's name Valentin, Ital. Vegliantino?   In Gudr. 1395 : ' man hôrte ein ros *ergrînen* ' when the battle began.   Bellona spumantium ad bella equorum *hinnitu* aures arrigens, Pertz 2, 169.

p. 660.]   Vedrebbe un *teschio d' asino* in *su un palo*, il quale quando *col muso volto* vedesse verso Firenze, Decam. 7, 1. Remember too the gyrating eagle on a roof (p. 633-4), and the dove over a grave (p. 1134-5 n.).

p. 660.]   As to *horses' heads* on gables, see Müllenh. p. 239. Panz. Beitr. 2, 180. 448-9 ; they protect the rafters from wind and weather.   Lith. żirges, roof-rider, from żirgas, horse, Nesselm. 549 ; also ragai, antlers, 426 ; conf. capreoli, tigna ad firmandum, and AS. Heort, Heorot, name of the house in Beowulf.

p. 664.]   The Boriáts dedicate to the herdsmen's god Sulbundu a horse, on which he rides at night, and which they find all in a *sweat* in the morning, Klemm 3, 115.   The horses ridden by spirits or night-wives have stirrup, cord and wool in their sides, and are covered with *drops of wax*, Kaisersb. Om. 42[d]. 43[a]. Kalmuks also consecrate a horse to the god, and let it run loose,

Ledebour 2, 49. Horses scrape up gold, like that of Rammelsberg, or a fountain, like Pegasus; conf. Panz. Beitr. 1, 38-9. 163. 186. 201. The hoof-prints of a god's horse in stone were believed in by the Romans : Ergo et illud in silice, quod hodie apparet apud Regillum, tanquam vestigium ungulae Castoris equi esse credis, Cic. de Nat. D. 3, 5. A sacred white horse walks on water without wetting his feet, Polier 2, 618.

p. 664.] Foremost of victims stands *ašva*, a horse-sacrifice is *ašvamêdha*, Böhtling, 1, 520-4. The significance of a *horse's head* appears in many other customs : it is played upon (pp. 849. 1050-71), thrown into the Midsum. fire (p. 618), stuck on a pole or tied on a person at Christmas, Hpt's Ztschr. 5, 472-4; in fairytales it works miracles, Müllenh. p. 422, often serves as a bridge 34. 146. 544, is nailed up under the town-gate (Falada's), and wooden ones are set on gables (p. 660). GDS. 151.

p. 665.] Sacred *oxen* of Artemis are mentioned in Plutarch's Lucullus p. m. 606. Hârekr keeps a *blótnaut* in the forest, Fornm. sög. 3, 132. On the bull's head in the scutcheon of Mecklenbg, see Lisch, Meckl. jrb. 10, 15 seq.

p. 666.] *Oxen* dig up a hurricane with their horns. A bull-calf is reared to fight the dragon, DS. 142, Müllenh. p. 238. Thiele 1, 125. Nandini is of all kine the best : he that drinketh of her milk remaineth young 10,000 years, Holtzm. Ind. sag. 3, 99. 100. 'The *black cow* crushes him, has trodden him' means 'he is weighed down by want and care:' so trat ihn auch die *schwarze kuh*, Ambraser lieder 147; stor *blaa stud*, Norske ev. 1, 111; conf. Hungar. 'has not yet trod the black cow's heel,' Wolf's Ztschr. 1, 271-2. Beside the cow's name *Auðhumla*, we have designations of oxen, as freyr, iörmunrekr, reginn, Sn. 221ᵃ (ed. Hafn. 587).

p. 666.] A most ancient and fierce *göltr*, worshipped by the people, Fornm. s. 4, 57-8; conf. eburðrung (p. 727). Wackernagel in Hpt's Ztschr. 6, 280 puts a different interpret. on the verses preserved by Notker; but conf. the boar of the Swed. folktale, that goes about grunting with a knife in his back (Hpt 4, 506-7), and the Dan. legend of Lîmfiorden (Thiele 1, 131) : A sorceress gave birth to a pig, and he grew so big that his *bristles* stood up *above the forest-trees* (Notk., burste eben-hô forste), and he rooted up the earth so deep that the sea flowed in to fill the

dike; conf. swine-dike (p. 1023). A rooting black hog foretells
the fall of the city, Müllenh. p. 105; a Malb. gloss calls the boar
*diramni*, earth-plougher, Leo 1, 75. GDS. p. 57. With Ovid's
descr. of a boar, Met. 8, 284 seq., conf. Alb. v. Halberstadt
p. 269, where the tusks are an *eln lanc* (Notk., zene sîne zuelif-
*elnîge*), which is not in Ovid; 'dente minax' we find in Rudl.
16, 90. Vishnu in one incarnation appears on the sea as a boar.
A *white goat* is reckoned wholesome in a horse's stable, Leopr.
226.

p. 667.] The *dog* is named among sacrificial beasts (pp. 48.
53), Kuhn's Westph. sag. 2, 138 : he belongs to Hecate, Klausen's Æn. 1137. The dog knows Odysseus in his disguise;
bitches can scent a Faunus : 'ab ea cane quae femina sit ex
primipara genita Faunos cerni,' Pliny 8, 40, 62; only a dog
with four eyes (nellisilm), i.e. with spots over his eyes, can see a
devil, Estn. verh. 2, 90. A dog will bark before a haunted rock,
Dyb. 4, 25. Dogs go mad if you give them the bones of the
Easter lamb, Keisersb. Om. 52[a]. Peter's dog appears in the
legend of Simon and Peter, AS. homil. p. 372-4. Pass. H. 175.

p. 669.] A name similar to *Vetrliði* is Sumarliði, Fornm. s. 3,
205; conf. Gramm. 2, 505. Other poetic names for the bear in
Sn. 175. 221, e.g. iorekr, equos fugans. To Samoyeds and Ostiaks
the bear is a god, Castrén 235. 342; the Finn. *ohto* is born in
heaven, and brought to earth in a golden cradle; 'to climb on
the bear's shoulders' means to go to heaven; his foam has virtue,
and should be taken up, Kalev. 13, 236. 254. As Oðinn has two
wolves, the Finn. Pahonev has great bloodhounds in his service,
Salmel. 1, 193. It is believed in Scotland that deer can see
spirits, Arvids. Ossian 1, 238. *Felis aurea* pro deo colitur, Pliny
4, 29, 35; cats are poisonous, acc. to Berth. of Regensb. 303;
Unander connects *îres* with our *viel-frass*, glutton. A story in
Klemm 2, 159 makes out that the house-building beaver was
once man.

p. 670.] A *bird* demands that men shall *sacrifice* to him (p.
672); conf. the Lettish bird-cultus (p. 77), Giesebr. Balt. stud.
12, 128. 139. The 'servitium consuetum in blado et volatilibus,'
Ch. a. 1311. MB. 30[b], 61 need not refer to sacrifice; it may be a
mere tribute in corn and poultry. An angel is sent in the shape
of a bird, see Gudrun and Sv. vis. 1, 232-4-5. As wind is repres.

under the form of an eagle, so the *aar* makes air and shade (p. 1133), and the cock perhaps weather, conf. the weathercock.

p. 671.] To the Dan. metaphor corresp. the Low Germ. ' de raude han kreide ut den dack,' Firmen. 1, 292ᵇ. *Cockcrow* announces day : ἐπεὶ δ᾽ ἀλέκτωρ ἡμέραν ἐσάλπισε, Lucian's Ocypus 114. A set phrase in fairytales is : " lou gal canté, e foughé jhour,' Dict. langued. 224; 'cokkes crewe ande hit was daie,' Sevin sages 2536; thaz huan gikundit dages kunftî, O. iv. 18, 34 ; dô krât der han, ez was tac, Altsw. 67, 3 ; skal ek fyrivestan vindhialms brûar âðr *salgofnir sigrþioð veki,* Sæm. 166. It scares away spirits :

Ferunt vagantes daemonas
laetos tenebris noctium
*gallo canente* exterritos
sparsim timere et cedere. Prudentii Hym. ad galli cantum 10.

A *red* and a *grey* cock crow to the spirit, Minstr. 3, 48, also a *white* and a *grey*, 2, 468. A *black hen* is sacrificed to the hill-mannikins (p. 1010). A *black* cock that was *born lame* takes the spell off an enchanted castle, Müllenh. p. 351. Out of a cock's egg is hatched a dragon, Leopr. 78. Of the longest *tail-feathers* of a cock pull out *the right one*, and you'll open any lock that you touch with it, walk invisible, and see everything, Luciani Somn. 28-9. A cock with *white feathers* is cut up, and carried round the vineyard against the wind, Paus. ii. 34, 3. Sacred cocks in Athen. 3, 445.——The cock on the steeple was already interpr. by the Mystics 1, 199 of the Holy Ghost. In Arabic it is called abul-yaksân, father of watchfulness. Fel. Faber in Evagat. 2, 219 thinks : ' Christiani *crucem cum gallo* ex institutione prima habent in culminibus suarum ecclesiarum '; while the Saracens have ' lunam cornutam vel supinam, quia gallus erecto collo et cauda stans speciem habet supinae lunae.'

p. 672.] To Ostiáks the *eagle* is holy, Klemm 3, 122 ; to Indians Garuda is king of birds, Holtzm. Ind. s. 3, 137 ; aquila, angla = Jovis ministra, Grotef. Inscr. Umbr. 6, 8.——The *hawk* was sacred to Apollo, Schwartz p. 16-7. Od. 15, 526 : κίρκος, usu. ἱέραξ, and the Egyptians esteemed it a holy bird, GDS. 51. On *sparrowhawk* and *kestrel* see Suppl. to 675.——Like *Huginn* and *Muninn*, the AS. *hyge* and *myne* habitually go together, Pref. to Andr. xxxix. *Ravens* follow the hero : ' Haraldi

ver fylgðum sîz or eggi komun,' Läsebog 112ᵃ; two ravens are
guardian spirits, Geser Khân 278. The raven, like the eagle, is
displayed on flags (p. 1112) ; he is to the eagle as the wolf to the
bear (or lion). More about the raven in Schwartz p. 42-3.

p. 672.] The *swallow*, OHG. sualawâ, AS. swealewe, ON.
svala, Dan. svale, Lapp. svalfo. Goth. svalvo? hruzda? Dac.
crusta, Lith. kregźde, Gr. χελιδών, Lat. hirundo for χεριδών,
χριδών, Wallach. rèndurea, Alban. delenduse. Lett. besdeliga.
Slav. lastovice, vlastovice, Serv. lasta, lastavitza, Russ. lástochka.
Finn. pääsky, Est. päästlenne, Hung. fetske. The swallow, ὡς
'Aθηναία, is the first to pluck a borrowed plume out of the κολοιός
(daw), Babr. 72, 16 ; in prose however (Cor. 188) it is the owl
(γλαύξ). Mary's needlewoman, who stole the ball of thread, was
turned into a swallow, on which the white spot shows the ball,
Wieselgr. 478. Iðunn, like Procne, is changed into a ' swallow '
acc. to one reading, though the usual reading is ' hnot,' nut. The
swallow's young are born blind, Dyb. '45, 67 ; ' if one of their
chicks grows blind, they fetch a herb, lay it on, and restore the
sight ; hence the herb's name of chelidonium,' celandine, Dioscor.
2, 211 ; and Megenb. says the same about schellwurz (Suppl. to
1194).

p. 672.] The *swan*, OHG. alpiz, MHG. elbez, AS. ylfet, Sl.
labud, lebedï; Gael. eala, ealadh, Ir. ala, eala, Wel. alarch, eleirch.
' Ulfa þytr mer þôtti illr vera hiâ *söngvi svana*,' Sn. 27; *ylfete
song*, Cod. Exon. 307, 6 ; see p. 436 and Schwartz p. 43-4-6. The
Finns call their youtsen a holy bird, pyhä linu, Kalev. 8, 73.

p. 673.] The *stork* is called *odoboro* in Slettst. Gl. 36, 33 ;
*otfer, ötdifer*, Altswert 71. In Lower Germany : *ådebar* langbên,
*hålebåt* langbên, *knepper* (rattler) langbên; in Groningen *aiber*,
*eiber*; in Gelders *uiver*, *heiluiver*, also *heilebaot*, *albaor*, Simrock
no. 335-6 ; *heilebate*, Hor. Belg. 7, 27ᵃ; ' to call the stork *heilbott*
and *otterwehr*,' Froschmeus. Ji viiᵇ. Can we trace it to a Goth.
addja-baira, egg-bearer, or addjê-baura, egg-born ? Kl. schr. 3,
147. 164. Outzen pp. 1. 2 says, adebar = spring's herald.——The
Esth. for stork is tone kurg, Finn. nälkäkurki, hunger-heron ?
Lith. gandras; Lett. swehts putns, holy bird, and melnsprahkliṣ,
black rump; Pol. bocian and Boh. bočan for the black stork, Pol.
czapla and Boh. čáp for the white ; this last is also Boh. 'bohdal,'
God-given, dieudonné, Morav. 'bogdal, bokdal'; conf. εὐσεβέ-

στατον ζῶον, Æsop. Fur. 76. Babr. 13, 7; candidae aves, Jorn. c. 42. The Slavic has also the congener of our stork in str'k, Miklos. p. 87, Russ. sterkh, Serv. shtrk.——A stork foretells the downfall of a city, Jorn. c. 42. Procop. 1, 330; another saves his father, Babr. 13, 8. Storks are men, says the Spinrocken-evang. Samst. 16. In striking harmony with Wolfram's eulogy, the stork in Babr. 13, 5 says: οὐ σπόρον καταφθείρω.

p. 675.] Ovid too has a statue 'gerens in vertice Picum,' Met. 14, 314; on Picus, see Klausen 844-5. 1141. Both picus and pica seem akin to ποικίλος, variegated; or picus and s-pecht, pecker, go together. The Greek for woodpecker is πελεκᾶς, fr. πελεκᾶν, to hack, πέλεκυς, hatchet; Stald. 1, 263 has tann-bicker, = picus martius; Lith. volungē, wood-hacker, is the greenpecker Lith. genys, Serv. zhunia, are also names of the woodpecker; Lett. dsennis, dsilna, is the bee-eater. The Russ. diátel, Pol. dzięcioł, Boh. datel (woodp.) seems conn. with dziécię, ditià, déti (child), perhaps because he was considered a foster-father, as Picus was to Romulus. The Swiss merzafülli is in the Hennebg dialect shortened into a simple merz: ' der merz hackt dich,' Hpt's Ztschr. 3, 360. Beside kliktati, used of the woodpecker's whine (and of the vila's cry, p. 436), we have totrkati = pulsare in arbore, ut picus facit. Lith. ulbauya volungē, the woodp. whimpers, wails. Ukko created the konkelo (greenp.), Peterson 12. Renvall sub v. The pecker kind are treasure-birds (p. 973). Kuhn thinks the woodp. is conn. with fire. What is the meaning of ' hân ich iu den speht erschozzen ? ' Hpt 6, 501.

p. 675.] The sparrowhawk, Boh. krahug, krahulec, krahuljk = falco nisus, Pol. krogulec, Linde 1134ᵇ; Hung. karoly, karvoly. The OHG. for kestrel, wannoweho, wannunwechel, Graff 1, 643, wannewechel in Ziemann, sounds remarkably like the Lett. vehia vannags, sparrowhawk, lit. holy hawk, for Lith. vanagas is hawk, vanagelis little hawk. Garg. 279ᵇ has the exclamation : ir wannenwäher ! This is the name they still give in Swabia to a small bird of prey : they hang little tubs or baskets (wannen) outside their houses for it to build in, and think the house is then proof against lightning, Mone 7, 429. Frisch 2, 422 has wanne-weihe, accipiter tinunculus, and other forms.[1] Does our weihe,

---

[1] Tinunculus is no doubt from tina, a vessel very similar to wanne; see Victor Hehn's "Migrations of Plants and Animals," Engl. transl. (Swan Sonnenschein) p. 487.—TRANSL.

wîo, wîho (milvus, kite) mean sacred bird ? conf. wîvo : 'milvos laedere capitale est' in England, says Leo v. Rozmital 40. GDS. 50.

The *owl* prophesies (p. 1135). The Greeks held it sacred, as bird of night, bird of victory, bird of Athena. The Amer. Indians worshipped it, Klemm 2, 164; and conf. the Esth. tharapila, horned owl (p. 77). Runes were marked 'â nefi *uglo*,' as well as 'â arnar nefi,' Sæm. 196ª. On strix, στρίγξ, see pp. 1039 n. 1045.

p. 678.] The *cuckoo*, by calling out his name, awakens joy, hence his Finn. name of *ilo-käki*, joy-cuckoo, Kalev. 14, 226, munaiset käkeni 5, 196-7 (like Swed. *tröste-gök*) ; yet also *sorrow-cuckoo*, Castrén 292; six gold cuckoos, kuus on kullaista käkeä, Kalev. 14, 31; the sun like a golden cuckoo climbs the sky 27, 265. Lapp. jäkä, Syrïän. kök. Ssk. kôkila, Pott's Zähl-meth. 229. Mark our exclamation 'heida-guguk!' Schulmeisters-wahl 50-1. 83. OHG. *fols*, cuckoo, Graff 3, 517, has never been explained. On the cuckoo, see Reusch in N.Preuss. prov. bl. 5, 321—343; on the gucker, peeper, Leopr. p. 79. Shaksp., at the end of Love's Lab. Lost, quotes a verse on Spring and the cuckoo, and one on Winter and the owl. The cuckoo is summer's warden : swylce geác *mónaðˀ geomran reorde* singeð *sumers weard, sorge beodeðˀ.* He prophesies to unplighted maidens, conf. Runa '44, p. 10; 'waz der kukuk hiure sanc,' this year sang, Mone's Schausp. 131.

p. 680.] *Zitefogel*, a prop. name, Mone's Anz. 3, 13. The peasant's *time-bird* is the raven, Kalenb. p. m. 284-7. In Wilt-shire the people sing : ' The cuckoo's a fine bird, She sings as she flies, She brings us *good tidings*, And tells us *no lies*. She *sucks* the small birds' *eggs* To make her *voiee clear*, And the more she sings " cuckoo," The summer draws near. The cuckoo *comes in April*, Stays the month of May, Sings a song at *Midsummer*, And then a *goes away*.'——An Ukrainian song of the cuckoo in Bodenstedt 57. Acc. to a Germ. song of the 16th cent., the cuckoo 'hat sich zu tod gefallen von einer hohen weide (willow).' The New Zealanders, like the Poles, esteemed the cuckoo a god (catua), Klemm 4, 371.

p. 681.] On the sceptres of Egyptian gods sits the *kuku-pha's head*, Bunsen 1, 435; conf. the figure at 315. 591 with the

kukupha-sceptre, Pindar's Pyth. 1, 10 ἀνὰ σκάπτῳ Διός, and
the variant in Edda, Hafn. 2, 202 Gûngnis ugla. The plates to
Pertz Scr. 8 show a *bird perched* on the sceptres of the Germ.
kings Henry IV. and V. (conf. the eagle on Arthur's sceptre,
Lanc. 30791). The cuckoo is the bird of wedlock and fecundity,
that is why he has ten wives given him, Firmen. 2, 243ª. For
Notker's 'ruoh,' Ps. 57, 11, both Graff 4, 1150 and Hattemer
write *kouh.*——A *Gauchs-perk* occurs in Tirol. urbar. August. a.
1316. MB. 34ᵇ. 360 ; *Gögeleberg*, Panz. Beitr. 1, 28 ; *Goggles-
berg*, Steub's Rhät. 47 ; the Swiss name Guggenbühler presupposes a *Guggen-bühel* (-hill) ; *Girgenberg* in Up. Rhön and
near Hersfeld, Hess. Ztschr. 1, 245 ; conf. Tumbo saz in berge
= Stupidus in monte sedebat=giant. Henn von *Narrenberg*,
Seb. Brant p. m. 131 ; an *Affenberg* near Nürnberg, Ettn.
Unw. doct. 698 ; a *Monkey's mountain* [Jebel Tsatut, the anc.
Abyla] on the African coast opp. Gibraltar. On affenberg,
schalksberg, see Kl. schr. 2, 147. Gên dem *affen-tal* ûzwaten,
Hadamar 444, 4 ; der *affen zît*, Fragm. 14ª.

p. 682.] The cuckoo is reckoned a *miser*, who when the leaves
come out in spring, dare not eat his fill, for fear they should run
short: 'sô der gouch daz êrste loup gesiht, sô getar sich's gesaten
niht, er vürht ez im zerinne,' Freid. 88, 3 : more fully in the
Welsche gast 114ª : conf. Freid. lxxxvii. In Ssk. he is called
'ab alio nutritus,' Bopp's Gl. 209ᵇ. Gothl. *gauk-pigä*, en fägel
som tros ligga ut gökkens ägg, Almqv. 425ᵇ. He eats the hedge-
sparrow's eggs, and puts his own in her nest, Freid. 143, 21.
144, 1—10 ; this is a fact of natural history, Döbel 1, 60. Schubert's Lehrb. p. m. 315. Eckerm. Gespr. mit Goethe 3, 211—5.
When grown up, he is said to devour his (foster-) parents, ibid.
208, and in winter to become a bird of prey. He begins pretty
early to stand for the devil : '*kukuk hiure unde vert!*' this year
and last, an old hand, Helbl. 4, 800 ; ' des wirt guot rât, *kukuk!*'
8, 1234.——Instead of the hoopoo, the *wryneck* takes the place of
servant to the cuckoo: Finn. käen piika, cuculi ancilla, is transl.
'jynx torquilla' by Renvall, 'curruca' by Juslen. The wryneck
is said by Nemnich (sub v. jynx) to come a fortnight earlier than
the cuckoo; Swed. gök-tyta, Wel. gwas y gog, cuckoo's hand-
maid. The *bittern* and the *hoopoo* were once cowherds, Lisch
Meckl. jrb. 5, 77.——The *kibitz, kywit*, peewit, which plays a

prominent part in the märchen of the Juniper-tree, is called
*giritz* in Stalder 1, 448 : ' in plover's reedy swamp (giritze-ried)
enchanted maidens fly.' Other tales of the lapwing in Nares's
Gl. sub. v. The polytrichum comm. is in Finn. *käen petkel*,
cuculi securis ; *gauch-heil* (pimpernel ?), which is not in Graff,
and is sometimes called hühnerdarm, morsus gallinae, is in M.
Nethl. *guychel-hoyl*, Mone 6, 448.

   p. 683.] The *dove*, a holy bird to the Syrians, was in Ssk.
called kapôta and prîtu, Gr. περιστερά, Lat. columba and
palumba, Slav. gólubĭ, Lith. karvélis, balandis, conf. pp. 828.
1134-5 n. Kl. schr. 5, 445 seq. Women speaking a foreign
tongue were called doves, says Herod. 2, 57. Song-birds seem
to have been called *walt-singer*, Geo. 5849 ; their joy and grief
were alluded to (p. 750-4). The *nightingale* passed for a messenger of Mary, Leopr. 79. ' Some say the *lark* and loathed toad
change eyes,' Rom. and Jul. 3, 5. The *wren*, Lith. nyksztélis
(thumbling and wren), Wel. dryw (druid and wren), is called
' petite poulette au bon Dieu,' Bosquet 220-1.[1] Disturbing the
*redbreast* brings lightning on the house 221 ; she covers the face
of a murdered man with leaves, Hone's Yrbk. 64 ; on the *red-
tail*, see Leopr. 80. The *meislin* (tit) has an angel to himself,
Keisersb. Brosäml. 19ᶜ ; hunting the baum-meise is severely
punished, Weisth. 1, 465. The Finn. *tiainen*, Est. *tihhane*, is
helpful, and understands beer-brewing, Schiefner's Finn. märch.
614. Kantel 1, 110. A legend of the *white sparrow* in Rommel's Hess. gesch. 4, 710 from Winkelm. Chron. p. 585. On the
*kingfisher*, see Gefken's Beil. 113.

   p. 685.] Transformation into a *snake* occurs in many fairy-
tales. The cast slough of a snake is called *senectus serpentis* in
Pliny and Marcellus no. 46 (Kl. schr. 2, 134. 150), agreeing with
ON. *elli-belgr* from *elli*, eld ; e.g. at kasta ellibelgnum = vernare.
There is a beautiful legend about the snake in Klemm 2, 162-3 ;
it lives for ever, 154. Its appearing is mysterious, so is its
vanishing, ' des slangen *sluf*,' Freid. 128, 7. In Ssk. it is called
the creeper, wriggler, breast-walker, uraga, Bopp 52ᵇ ; conf.
Genesis 3, 14. The Ind. serpent-sacrifice lasts for years, it com-

---

[1] Why is the wren called king in the Gr. βασιλίσκος, Lat. regulus, It. reattino, Fr.
roitelet, and Germ. zaunkönig ? because of his golden crest ? And is zaunkönig a
transl. of re-at-tino, the zaun (hedge) being an adaptation by folk-etym. of tinus
(laurustinus) ?—TRANSL.

pels all snakes to come up and throw themselves into the fire,
Holtzm. 3, 172-3. 186-8. In the Parthenon at Athens lived a
serpent sacred to the goddess, and had a honey-cake offered to
it every day, Herod. 8, 41. To the Romans also the anguis was
holy, Klausen p. 1014.——A caduceus with figures of snakes in
Pliny 29, 54 (12); and snake-figures may be seen on the Stuttgart todtenbäume. A serpent on a helmet was called *ezidemón*,
Beneke sub v.; 'ezidemon daz edel kunder,' Tit. 3311. Lohengr.
p. 12, where his friedelinne (lady-love) is also alluded to. The
word is traceable to agatho-daemon, the Egyp. miraculous serpent kneph, Gerhard in Acad. Berl. '47, p. 203. Beside saribant
and serpant we find a *sarapandra-test*, serpent's head, Parz. 50,
5. 68, 8. As Ofnir and Sváfnir are the names of two snakes, and
at the same time by-names of Oðinn, so Hermes is closely allied
to the agathodæmon, Gerh. as above 204; and divine heroes,
descended from Oðinn, also inherit the 'snake in the eye' (p.
391). Serpents lick the *ears* of the sleeping Melampus, and on
waking up he understands the speech of birds as they fly past,
and ever after of all beasts that foretell the future to man.
Prophetic Cassandra too, and her brother Helenus, had their ears
licked clean by snakes.

p. 687.] The Greeks called the *home-snake* οἰκουρὸς ὄφις,
genius loci, Gerh. in Acad. Berl. '47, 203; the Albanian *vittore* is
a homesprite, imagined in the form of a little snake, Hahn's
Lieder 136; the Samogitian *giuoitos*, black snakes, are fed and
worshipped as household gods, Lasicz 51-5-6. That of *milk-
drinking* belongs also to the snake-stories in Vonbun p. 24.
Bader nos. 98. 106 (on the mocken, p. 686 n., see Schmeller 2,
549. Stalder 2, 212. Diut. 2, 84). Snakes had drink given
them, Athen. 4, 364; one that sucked milk out of the breast, in
Lucian's Alex. 7. With the Pomeran. story of a snake creeping
into the pregnant woman, conf. Vopisci Aurelian. c. 4: 'pueri
ejus *pelvem* serpentem plerumque *cinxisse,* neque unquam occidi
potuisse; postremo ipsam matrem, quae hoc viderat, serpentem
*quasi familiarem* occidere noluisse'; and Spartiani Sever. 1:
'dormienti in stabulo serpens *caput cinxit,* et sine noxa, experge-
factis et acclamantibus familiaribus, abiit.'——More tales about
the 'schlangen-*krönli*' in Vonbun 24-5. Woeste 50; about the
*king of snakes* in Müllenh. p. 355. Panzer 1, 183; the Ssk.

*Vásukis*, rex serpentum, Bopp's Gl. 158ª. Holtzm. 3, 143-5.
196-7. 157. 163.     A Swed. story tells how the ormar elect ɾ
king, Dyb. '45, p. 100.     A serpent-king has 12 heads; he that
hews them off, and carries them about with him, is *everywhere*
*victorious*, Reusch no. 74 and app.     When an orm is challenged
to fight, he keeps the engagement, Dyb. '45, p. 95-6.     An adder
comes carrying a stone in his mouth, Gesta Rom. ed. Keller
pp. 68. 152 ; conf. *snake-stone*, unke-stone (p. 1219-20).     Under a
hazel on which mistletoe grows, lies a snake with a precious
stone on his head (p. 1207),     The *vouivre* wears but one eye in
the middle of her forehead, and that is a carbuncle ; when she
stops to *drink at a fountain*, she *lays it aside ;* that's the time to
possess yourself of the jewel, and she is *blind* ever after.     The
vouivre flies through the air like red-hot iron, Mém. des antiq. 6,
217 ; the like in Bosquet p. 204-6-9.     'Des Montags nach S.
Peters tach, so *aller wurmichleiche* ze wazzer gât,' Rec. of 1286 in
Gemeiner's Regensb. chron. 1, 423 ; Fâfnir also *skreið til vatz*,
Sn. 138.     Völs. c. 18.     Snakes love to lie beside a spring, Ausland '57, p. 832ᵇ ; but the ash-tree has a spite against the snake,
Panzer 1, 251. 351.

    p. 688.]     The *serpent's healing power* is heard of pretty early :
' if a serpent had bitten any man, when he beheld the serpent of
brass, he lived,' Numb. 21. 9.     *Slaver* from the mouths of three
colubrae runs into the healing, strengthening dish that has been
cooked, Saxo ed. Müll. pp. 123. 193 (in two different stories) :
two snakes are black, one white.     Eating of the white snake
makes you know the language of beasts, p. 193.     DS.² no. 132.
KM.³ 3, 27 (conf. p. 983 and Suppl. to 689. 690).     On the other
hand, venom drips from the *eitr-orm*, Sæm. 69 ; snakes are made
to suck their poison in again with their ' cleinen munden,' Pass.
310, 20.     A Celtic story of the *anguinum* (ovum) made of *ser-*
*pent's drivel* is given in Pliny 29, 3, 12.     On magic wrought by
means of snakes, conf. Spalding, Abh. d. Berl. acad. ; on the
snake as a bridge, and the term bridge's-tail, brûarspordr, see
pp. 978. 732 n.

    The *toad* also (kröte, Gramm. 3, 364) is a venomous beast
available in magic : she carries a stone in her head (p. 1220) ;
she sits on fungus and on mushroom, hence the one is called
*krötenstul*, *toadstool*, Dut. *paddestoel*, LG. *paddenstol*, and the

other *weiss-krötling*. Austrian names, besides krot, are hepping.
braitling, nöting, brotze, auke, Höfer 2, 47. 175; in Bavaria the
male is braste, broz, bratz, Schm. 1, 274, the female höppin
heppin, also muml (aunty), and women are called heppin in con-
tempt 2, 221. Add wetterkröte, donnerkröte, blitzkröte.

p. 689.] *Δράκων* is fr. *δέρκω*, as *ὄφις* fr. the lost *ὄπτω* : 'sharp-
sighted as a lindwurm,' Soester Daniel p. 141 ; Gal. *dearc* = lacerta.
Dragons are akin to snakes, hence the 'multitudo serpentum cum
magno dracone,' Greg. Tur. 10, 1; conf. snake-charming and the
old dragon in Lucian's Philops. c. 12. Dragons worshipped by
the Esths, Adam. Brem. (Pertz 9, 374); portrayed on bronze
kettles, Lisch in Meckl. jrb. 7, 35—38, 14, 326—330, interpr. by
Giesebercht, Balt. stud. 11, 50-1.——A dragon is called *ormr inn*
*fráni*, Sæm. 173ᵇ. 189ᵇ; MHG. *tievels bote*, Wigal. 5080, *tievels*
*trût* 6443 (in 6453 rather the giantess). The *hvit-orm* lives under
the roots of the oak, Dyb. '45, p. 78; but they like best to *lie on*
*gold*, which is therefore called *linnar logi*, Sæm. 181ᵃ; the dragon
that brings you money behaves like a homesprite (p. 511 ? 1020).
The dragon's *fire-spitting* may have arisen from confounding the
kindred notions of fire and poison, Müllenh. in Hpt's Ztschr. 7,
428. A Welsh dragon story in Peredur, Villem. Contes 2, 193.
Like snakes and toads, these 'worms' also carry *stones*, but in
their belly, and so many that you could build half a tower with
them, Dietr. u. ges. 300. The dragon lives 90 years in the
ground, 90 in the limetree, and 90 more in the desert, Van den
Bergh p. 73; these stages of development were evid. suggested
by the changes of the caterpillar and butterfly.

p. 690.] Dragons are hated : '*leiðari* enn manni hverjom *enn*
*fráni ormr* med fîrom,' Sæm. 85ᵃ with the note : 'vermes, in
Speculo regali, vocantur *leiðendi*, odia, quasi res detestabiles.'
Therefore heroes make war upon them : Apis comes to Argos,
and *slays the dragon's brood*, Æsch. Suppl. 262—7. There are
ways of guarding against them, and of killing them : *bläsvorm* in
Mors is a venom-spitting worm; he can blow through seven
church walls, but not through knitted stockings, Molb. Dial. lex.
43. Again : 'för att en orm med säkerhet skall kunna dödas,
ritas först kring honom en ring med *års-gammal hassel-kjäpp*,
innan han slås,' Rääf. Coats of mail are hardened in dragon's
blood : gehert in traken bluote, Ecke 24; ganz al umbe den rant

schilt gemachet von gold und drachenbluot, Wigam. 2105; swert gehert in drachenbluot, Drachenk. 11. It is said of Alexander: 'gebeizet was sîn brunie in eines *wurmes bluote, hurnen* was siu veste,' Diem. 209. Massm. 1300 seq. Another sword tempered in dragon's blood, DV. 1, 265. Sigurðr, after eating *Fáfni's heart*, understood the *language of birds*; Gudrun had eaten some too, Sæm. 211; conf. 'quin et inesse *serpenti* remedia multa creduntur . . . ut possint *avium sermones* intelligi,' Pliny 29, 4 (Suppl. to 688).

p. 691.] In Serv. also *smuk*, serpentis genus, Boh. *smykati*, serpere, ON. *smiuga*; Syriän. *zmey*, snake, Gabelentz p. 8. *Fishes* too deserve attention: Athen. 3, 30-5-6 speaks of a ἱερὸς ἰχθῦς, they were beasts of *Artemis* and *Hecate* 3, 194; conf. *Berhta's* herrings (p. 273).

p. 692.] For *chafer* there is even an Egyp. *cheper*; OHG. *chwât-chever* (dung-beetle), scarabæus, Graff 4, 378, *sun-chever*, brucus, N. 104, 34; Westerw. mai-*kleber*, Ravensb. eckern-*schäfer*; AS. cynges *cafertûn*, aula regia, Ælfr. Homil. 122. *Keverlinge*-burg and *Sceverlinge*-burg, Hpt's Ztschr. 7, 559; 'predium *chäver-loch*' (lôh?), MB. 8, 405. 500 (yr 1160), 'hodie *kefer-loh*' 8, 516, AS. *ceafor-leáh*, Kemble nos. 570. 1088. Conf. OHG. muggi-stat, Graff 2, 654; brem-garten, brem-stall, Schm. 1, 258; bre-garten = kitchen-garden, says Höfer 1, 113; Pregarten, a place in Styria, Rauch 2, 191.——The other term *wibel* occurs in the adjs. *wibel-val, wibel-var*, pale, Herb. 6880. 12867. A Welsh *gwibeden*, musca, *gwiblo*, to fly, swarm. *Κάνθαρος κόπρου σφαῖραν ποιήσας*, Æsop. Fur. 223. Ælian. Hist. anim. 10, 15. Arist. Hist. anim. 5, 19 (conf. Lucian 8, 428). The Cod. Exon. 426, 11 has: 'is þæs *gores sunu* gonge hrædra, þone we *wifel* wordum nemnað;' in the same way bees are supposed to spring from putrefaction (p. 696), flies from the devil's rotting tongue, Walach. märch. 285; and *chuleih*, scarabæus, horse-beetle, *kielecke* or stagbeetle (Schm. 2, 269) seems to have arisen out of *chuo-leih*, and to rest on a belief about the beetle's origin (from cow-dung?), Gramm. 2, 503; conf. scîn-leih, monstrum.

p. 693.] The lucanus cervus (conf. H. Müller's Griechenth. 446) is in Finn. *tammihärkä*, oak-ox, Serv. *yelén*, cervus volans, Engl. *stag*-beetle, *stag*-fly, Fr. escarbot, Swiss *gueger*, cerambyx, holz-*bock*, feuer-*bock*, Stald. 1, 445; *feuer-käfer* in the Harz, where they wrap him in moss, letting the horns stick out, and strike at him blindfold one after the other (as elsewhere at the cock) ; whoever hits him, takes him home (and has luck, or some honour by it ?).——ON. has also *torð-ýfill*, Droplaug. saga p. 10 : *tio synder* sägas förlätas (ten sins forgiven) den som vänder om en *på rygg liggande tordyfvel*, Runa '44, p. 8 ; conf. an Irish tale of the *daol*, Conan 124, and Schiefner on tarwas pp. 4. 5. The Finn. *turila, turilas* denotes a voracious insect that spoils fruit and grass, either melolontha or gryllus migratorius, says Renvall; but the same word means *giant*, conf. our heimo. Any one that sees the *wern*, mole-cricket, shall get off his horse to kill it, for it nibbles away the roots of the corn ; to him that does so, the farmer owes a loaf of bread. The AS. *eorð-ceaforas* = tauri, i.e. scarabæi terrestres, was doubtless modelled on the passage in Pliny.

p. 693 n.] Hung. *cserebogár*, maybug, lit. oak-chafer, oak-worm ; Pol. chrabąszcz, chrząszcz, Boh. magowy chraust, Russ. siplї, O. Sl. sipl, Dobrowsky Inst. 271. Prov. bertals, bertaus, Mahn p. 59. Finn. lehtimato, leaf-worm, melolontha, Swed. löfmatk. Osnabr. eckel-*tiewe*, Lyra 23, also eik-*schawe*, Münsterl. ecker-*tiefe*, Ravensb. eckern-*schäfer* ; Märk. Pom. *zebrehnke* ; Swiss *bugareje*, Stald. 1, 239. Walloon : *balowe, abalowe, biese a balowe* = hanneton, fr. baloier = voltiger, and bizer, OHG. pisôn ; pisewurm = oestrum. Finn. *urolainen*, a large beetle, *uros* = vir, heros, Serv. *urosh* = picus, heros.——Chafers carry a mirror about them : children in the Wetterau hold a cockchafer in their hands, and sing, ' Mennche, weibche, weis' mer emol (do show me) dein spigelche ! ' the outspread wings ? The *elben* are chafers, chry-salids, butterflies, spirits and holden (conf. pp. 1073-4. 1155-6). The *kobold* sits in the box in the shape of a beetle or humblebee, Sommer 33-4. 171-2. Panzer 2, 173. Rochholz 2, 238-9 ; the Dan. skrukke-*trold* is an insect too, but a wingless one. The Pentam. 3, 5 tells of a *fay* that plays with a sweetly humming chafer (scarafone).

p. 695.] The *coccinella*, Ind. *Indragópa*, Indra's cowherd, Bopp 40[a]. Schiefn. on tarwas p. 5 ; Finn. *lenninkäinen*, which sometimes means the beautiful hero Lemmenkäinen ; Engl. *God'lmighty's cow*, Barnes ; *sünnenkind*, sun's child, Schütze 4, 225 ; Austr. *sonnenkalbel*, sun's calf. *Goldwivil*, cicindela, Diut.

2, 94. Boh. *slunéçko* (little sun), *slunečnice*, coccinella, also *linka*, Pol. *stonka*. Serv. *babe* and *mara*, Mary; the girls set it on their finger, and repeat a rhyme, Vuk p. 9[b]. Lith. *děwo yautis*, God's ox, God's birdie; so the glowworm is with us *liebe Gotts lammje*, Alb. Schott, the dragonfly *unser lieben frauen rössel*, horsie, *Gadespferd*, God's horse, Schütze 2, 6, but also *Devil's horse, needle* and *hairpin* (p. 1029), Stald. 1, 276, and *eye-shooter* 1, 119; Finn. *tuonen koira*, death's dog, Boh. *hadi hlava*, snake's head.——The butterfly, Gael. *eunan-dé*, bird of God, Ir. Gael. *dealan-dé* and Gael. *teine-dé*, both fire of God, Ir. *anaman-dé*, anima Dei; conf. Swed. *käring-själ*, old woman's soul, Ihre 2, 529 (see p. 829). Arm. *balafen, malafen, melven; balafennik doué*, petit papillon de Dieu. A butterfly-song of Hanoverian Wendland sounds like the ladybird-song: '*Bottervågel*, sött di, Våder unn moder röpt di, Mul unn nese blött di', thy mouth and nose are bleeding; otherwise '*Midschonke, midschonke*, sött di,' etc. A children's song at Lüben calls the butterfly *ketelböter*, kettle-mender, Firmen. 3, 480.

p. 697.] *Bees* live among men, and the joys and sorrows of the family are duly reported to the beehives, Bosquet 217, esp. the death of the master, 'if you wouldn't have all your hives waste away within year and day' they say in Münsterland. The same thing in Wilts, Berks and Surrey. Bees foretell the future to man (p. 1136): a humblebee in the box gives notice of spring, Panzer 2, 173. 'Apes furtivae' do not thrive, Pliny 19, 7, 37. Bosq. 217. Their home is carefully prepared: 'istud vas lacte et bona herba linivimus,' Acta Bened. sec. 2, p. 133. They have come down from the golden age, Leo's Malb. gl. 1, 119.——Ssk. names for the bee are *madhu-pa, madhu-kara, madhu-lih*, honey-drinker, -maker, -licker; Abrah. a S. Clara calls them *mett-siederl*, mead-boilers, Schm. 1, 165. (Kl. schr. 2, 369). Gr. ἀνθηδών, flower-eater; but she drinks water too, acc. to a law-phrase in the Weisthümer; conf. 'die bin netzen,' to water the bees, Fischart's Gesch. kl. 87[a]. A pretty name is '*pini-súga* (bee-suck)=thymus,' *i.e.* heath. Finn. *mehiläiskanerva*=clino-podium vulg. A queen-bee settles on the lips of a favoured person, Sv. folks. 1, 78.——Their origin is miraculous: 'diu *pie* ist *maget*, wird âne *hîleichiu* dinc geborn,' the bee is maiden, born without nuptial doings, Predigten hrsg. v. Kelle 40. 'Der

Veldtbau,' Strasbg 1556, bk 15 cap. 1 relates after Varro de R. R. 2, 5 how bees spring out of the decaying body of a dead bull. Miklosich brings both *b'tchela*, *pcheló* = apis, and byk = taurus, under boukati = mugire (the hum of the bee?). The Gl. Salom. make wasps come from the rotten flesh of asses, drones from that of mules, hornets from that of horses, and *bees from that of calves*, conf. Diut. 2, 194 : ἵππος ἐρριμένος σφηκῶν γένεσίς ἐστι, Lessing 9, 146 fr. Aelian 1, 28; and bees proceed from the carcase of the lion slain by Samson, Judg. 14, 8. An account of the generation of hornet and bee in Schröter p. 136. Peterson, p. 55. In the Walach. Märch. 284 the white bee turns black.——As the bee in Germ. *weaves* (wift, wabe), in Lith. she *sews* (pri-súti) : ' bittes daug pri-súwo,' the bees have stitched a good piece on. Bees *build: ἔνθα τιθαιβώσσουσι μέλισσαι*, Od. 13, 106; they build a wax palace, Stier's Volksm. 24. On the church wall at Folsbach was carved a hummel-nest, because the people had carted stones to it as diligently as the humblebee gathers honey, Panz. Beitr. 2, 173. A man in Elsass having stolen the Host and thrown it in a field of standing corn, it hung balanced on three stalks, and bees came and built their waben (combs) round it, and over it was reared a chapel, that of the Three Ears ; conf. Hpt's Ztschr. 7, 533. Predigermärch. 10, 12. Boyes Rodolphi de H. p. 257. In Cæs. Heisterb. 9, 8 the bees themselves build a chapel over the Hostie.

In Virgil's Georg. 4, 68. 75. 106 the sovereign of the bees is called rex, and 4, 4. 88 dux, ductor ; ' einen *fürsten* (prince) hânt bîen,' MS. 1, 84[a]; ' volgheden, alse haren *coninc* doen die bien,' Maerl. 3, 343 ; ' alsam diu bin zuo den karn mit fröiden vallent, ob ir rehter *wisel* (var. *wiset*) drinne sî,' MS. 2, 3[a] ; Flem. '*koning* der bien,' Hpt. 7, 533 ; Hennebg. '*der hädherr*, der weisel,' Brückner. Cherkess *psheh*, prince, Klemm 4, 18. The Samogits allowed bees a god of their own, *Babilos*, and a goddess, *Austheia*, Lasicz 48. On the other hand, the Vita S. Galli (Pertz 2, 7) says: in modum parvissimae *matris apis*, conf. mater aviorum (p. 1242) ; *bienen-mutter*, Haltrich 121. Their honey is not everywhere sweet : τὸ γὰρ μέλι ἐν ἅπασι τοῖς Τραπεζοῦντος χωρίοις πικρὸν γίνεται, Procop. 2, 464 ; μέλι Ποντικὸν πικρὸν ἐστι καὶ ἀηδές, Dio Chrysost. Or. 9 (ed. Reiske 1, 289. 290).

The devil appears as a *fly*, so does Loki (p. 999). *Spiders* are akin to dwarfs (p. 471).   Out of all herbs the bee sucks sweetness, the spider poison.   Yet may the spider be of good omen too ; thus the kind enchantress climbs to the ceiling a spider, and drops down a woman, Arnim's März. 1, 52-7 ; conf. *luck-spinner* (p. 1136).   Cobwebs fluttering on the ceiling betoken luck and a wedding, Lisch 5, 88 ; conf. the fortune-telling spider's head (Suppl. to 380 end).   Lastly consider the myth of Minerva and Arachne.

## CHAPTER XXII.

## SKY AND STARS.

p. 700.]   *Himmel* comes from hima = tego ; the root appears without suffix in O. Swed. himi-rike ; Bopp again would derive it from kam = splendere, Gl. 168ᵇ, but this kam in Gl. 65ᵇ means amare, which is more likely to have had the orig. sense of shelter, cover ; and OHG. himil already included the meaning laquear, lacunar.   AS. ' scôp heofon tô *hrôfe*,' and hrôf is roof ; ' sô himil *thekit* thaz lant,' O. ii. 7, 4 ; ' mit dem himel was ich *bedacht*,' bethatched, Tragemund.   We still say ' the sky is my *decke* (ceiling, coverlid), the earth my bed,' or ' the sky is my *hat*,' as the ON. calls it ' foldar *hattr*,' earth's hat.   The sky is a vault, hence ' under heofones *hwealf*,' Beow. 1146.   It may burst open : ' ich wânde der himel *waere enzwei*,' in-two, when it thundered, Dietr. Drach. 122ᵃ. 143ᵃ (on the comparison of heaven to the roof of the mouth, see Hpt's Ztschr. 6, 541).   A variation of the idea in the ON. ' und himin-skautom,' under the skirts of heaven. Sæm. 173ᵇ.   Norweg. *hibna-leite*, *himna-leite* = horizon, Germ. *kimm, kimming*.——After death we may go to *himmel* (not heven) ; but the sun, moon and stars in L. Saxony stand in *heven* (not himmel) ; *heven-scher*, scudding clouds, Brem. Ndrs. wtb. 4, 645. *Heven* seems more the æther, the ' radur, rodor ' of next paragraph. In Austria they call heaven *blo-landl*, Blue-shire ; and OHG. *uflih* = Olympus, supernum.

OS. *radur*, AS. *rodor* (norð-rodor, Cod. Exon. 178, 33) can hardly be conn. with Ssk. rôdas, coelum et terra, Bopp 295ᵇ. Does the (perh. kindred) word *álf-röðull*, m., Sæm. 37ᵃ, mean the moon? With AS. sceld-byrig connect another expression of Cædmon's, 182, 22 : *dæg-scealdes* hleo, day-shield's (?) roof.

p. 701.] Ssk. *târâ*, f., Zend. *štâr*, Gr. ἀστήρ, Lat. *stella* fr. sterna, is expl. by Bopp, Vocal. 179 as that which *is strewn* over the sky; by Benfey 1, 661 as that which *strews* its beams, from root stri. With *sīdus*, Pott 1, 127 compares Lith. swidus, shining, and σίδηρος. It belongs more likely to sīdo, consīdo, as perhaps even stella and star are conn. with *sta*, stand; conf. stalbaum, and 'er (Got) sitzet ûf den himel-*steln*' rhy. zeln, weln, MSH. 2, 236ᵇ. MS. 2, 166ᵇ.——In Vermland, *tungel* = star, Almqv. 391ᵃ. Helsingl. 403ᵃ; in Angermanland, *tongel* = mâne, Almqv. 307ᵇ. In several languages, flame is called tongue, because it licks; in Irish the stars are *rinn*, which answers to the Gael. roinn = tip. In Fundgr. 1, 145 a constellation is called *lieht-vaz*, lamp.

The OHG. girusti of the stars agrees with AS. *hyrste* gerûn, rodores tungel, Cædm. 132, 7; 'each star sat in his own little chair,' KM. 31, 138; 'when it thunders, you're afraid a *tron* will tumble out of heaven,' Garg. 181ᵇ; the λαμπρὰ τράπεζα τοῦ ἡλίου, sun's bright table, Aesop 350. The sun has a tent: 'undir röðuls *tialdi*,' Hervar. s. p. 438 (conf. Psalm 19, 4). The stars are considered sons and daughters: 'da möhten *jungiu sünnelin wahsen* ûz sîm liehten schîn,' little suns grow out of, Wh. 254, 5 (p. 703 end); 'eina *dóttur* berr âlf-röðull,' moon (?) has a daughter, Sæm. 37ᵃ. In Lett. songs the stars are *saules meitas*, sun's girls, *deeva dêli*, sons of God, Büttner nos. 15. 18 (1842).

p. 703.] The *sun* is 'der *werlde schîn*,' MS. 1, 54ᵃ; 'der *hêrschein*,' Fromm. Mundart. 4, 98. 113 (but see Suppl. to 731): se *œðela gleám*, Cod. Exon. 178, 31; *beorht beácen Godes*, Beow. 1134; *skinandi goð*, Sæm. 45ᵃ. 195ᵃ; *heáðo-sigel*, sol e mari progrediens, Cod. Exon. 486, 17 (conf. p. 223). Three suns are spoken of in Nialss. c. 131 end : til þess er þriar sólir eru af himni.——O. Müller thinks sol and ἥλιος come fr. one fundam. form Savelios, see Schmidt's Ztschr. 2, 124 (Kl. schr. 3, 120); Etr. *usil*, Sab. *ausel*. Bopp's Comp. Gram. 42, 1318-9 derives the Zend. *hvare* and Ssk. *sûra*, *sûrya*, sun, fr. svar, svarga = sky; is Sûryas the same word as ἥλιος (for σϝήλιος) and sol? (Pref. liv., GDS. 301). We might also conn. the Goth. *sáuil* with sáuls = columna (Kl. schr. 3, 120).——The sun is descr. as a

*wheel* in Ksrchr. 80; daz *rat* der sunnen, Myst. 2, 180. *Hvel,*
*hweol* is also the spinning-wheel, and in Finn. the sun is called
*God's spindle,* Kalev. 32, 20 (its usual name is päivä, sol and
dies, but also aurinko); conf. the constell. Freyja's-spindle,
and Tertullian's pectines solis, GDS. 107. Before the sun there
stands a *shield;* if it fall, it will set mountain and sea ablaze:

> Svalr heitir, hann stendr sólo for,
> *sciöldr* scìnanda goði;
> biörg oc brim ec veit at brenna scolo,
> ef hann fellr î frâ.       Sæm. 45ª. 195ᵇ.

Ennius (in Varro 7, 73) calls the sun *caeli clipeus,* and the notion
is Slavic too, Hanusch 256.——On the sun as an *eye,* conf. Kuhn
(in Höfer 1, 150), Passow sub vv. ὄμμα, ὀφθαλμός. Li solaus
qui tout aguete, Rose 1550. The sun's eye hidden in the well
seems to be referred to in such names as *Sunnebrunno* near
Düsseldorf, Lacombl. 1, no. 68 (yr 874); *Sonnenbrunne,* Mone's
Anz. 6, 227; *Sunnebrunnen, Sonneborn* in Saxe Gotha, Dronke's
Trad. Fuld. pp. 42. 61; *Sunneborn,* Landau's Hessengau 181;
*Somborn* near Gelnhausen; *Sunnobrunnon,* Werden's Reg. 236,
and *ougenbrunne* 6, 230; conf. Förstemann 2, 1336.——To AS.
*waldres gim, heofones gim,* Cod. Exon. 174, 30, corresp. the Ssk.
diei dominus, *diei gemma* = sol, Bopp 27ª. Other AS. terms are:
*folca friðcandel,* Cædm. 153, 15, *heofoncandel* 181, 34; *rodores*
*candel,* Beow. 3143, *woruldcandel* 3926; *wyncandel,* Cod. Exon.
174, 31.

    p. 704.] The Letts regard the *sun* and *moon* as sister and
brother, Bergm. 120; in Dalecarlia the moon is called *unkarsol,*
Almqv. 261 (is not that Lappish, the junkare's sun?). Goth.
*mêna,* OHG. *mâno,* AS. *môna,* ON. *mâni,* all masc.; Carinth.
*monet,* Lexer's Kärnt. wtb. Yet also: '*diu maenin* beglîmet,'
V. Gelouben 118 (glîmo, gleimo, Graff 4, 289); *diu maeninne,*
MF. 122, 4; *diu mâninne,* Diemer 341, 22. 343, 11. 342, 27;
'*der sun* (*sunne*) und *diu maeninne,*' Karaj. 47, 8 (Ksrchr. 85-
90). MHG. *diu sunne,* Hpt 8, 544. Diemer 384, 6; in Rollenh.
'der harte mond, die liebe sonn.' The Angevins on the contrary
called 'le soleil *seigneur,* et la lune *dame,*' Bodin's Rech. sur
l'Anjou 1, 86; so in Ksrchr. 3754 ' der *hêrre*' seems to mean the
sun, but in contrad. to p. 3756.——The forester kneels to *sun,*

*moon* and *God*, Baader iii. 21 ; 'the *worship'd sun*,' Rom. and Jul.
i. 1. Men prayed towards the sun, N.Pr. prov. bl. 1, 300 ; they
salute him (pp. 737. 749), esp. when rising : ὁ δὲ εἱστήκει μέχρι
ἕως ἐγένετο καὶ ἥλιος ἀνέσχεν· ἔπειτα ᾤχετο ἀπιών, προσευξάμενος
τῷ ἡλίῳ, Plato's Symp. 220. A *feast of the sun* was held in
Dauphiné, Champoll. Dial. p. 11. On the Tartar worship of the
sun, see K. Schlözer 32-3. Among Tungúses an accused man
has to walk toward the sun, brandishing a knife, and crying :
' If I am guilty, may the sun send sickness to rage in my bowels
like this knife !' Klemm 3, 68. Serv. 'tako mi suntza !' Ranke
p. 59. We still say, when the sun shines warm, ' he means well
by us,' Felsenb. 4, 241.——The Moon is called in Ssk. *niśapati*,
noctis dominus, or *naxtréśa, tárápati*, stellarum dominus; in Pol.
*księżyc*, lord of night, and he is shepherd of the stars (Suppl. to
722). The moon is invoked against anger : 'heiptom scal *mána
kveðia*, Saem. 27ᵇ; and is asked for riches. With the German's
naïve prayer to the moon to 'make his money more,' conf. a
Swed. one in Wieselgr. 431. Dyb. Runa '44, p. 125, and the
' monjochtroger,' Wolf's Ztschr. 2, 60. To avert the moon's
evil influence, the Bretons cry to her, 'tu nous trouves bien,
laisse-nous bien !' When she rises, they kneel down and say a
pater and ave, Cambry 3, 35.

p. 705.] The sun and moon have gods assigned them : Bacchus is sol, Ceres luna, Macrob. Sat. 1, 18. Virg. Geo. 1, 5.
Acc. to F. Magnusen, Freyr is sol, Freyja luna ; and four names
of Freyja, ' Mardöll, Horn, Gefn, Sŷr,' or ' Siofn, Lofn, Vör,
Syn' are the moon's phases, Lex. myth. 357-9. Christ is often
likened to the sun, Mary to the moon.——Our saying, that ' die
sonne scheint, der mond *greint*,' is old : M.Neth. ' seder dat die
maen *grên*,' Potter 2, 104; M.HG. 'diu sunne beschînet, diu
maenin *beglîmet*,' V. Gelouben 118 (Suppl. to 704).

p. 707.] In Pohjola, sun and moon get *stolen*; the sun is
delivered fr. *captivity* by Perkun's hammer, N. Pr. prov. bl. 1,
299. Kl. schr. 2, 84. 98 ; conf. ' donec auferetur luna,' Ps. 72, 7.
In eclipses the demon Râhus threatens the sun and moon, Kuhn
in Höfer 1, 149. Holtzm. Ind. s. 3, 151 ; a dragon tries to
swallow the moon, Caes. heisterb. 3, 35, yr 1225 (Kaufm. p. 55) ;
the Swed. sol-ulf is Dan. *sol-ulv*, Molb. Dial. p. 533.——But the
sun may withdraw his light in grief or in anger :

Sunna *irbalg sih* (was indignant) thrâto    suslîchero dâto (deeds),
ni liaz si sehan worolt-thiot (-people)    thaz ira frônisga lioht,
*hinterquam* in thrâti (disgust)    thera armalîchun dâti.
                                             Otfried iv. 33, 1.
ioh harto thaz *irforahta.*                            O. iv. 33, 14.

The sun hides his face before a great sorrow, e.g. at the death of Christ, or that of Von Meran : ' ez moht diu liehte sunne ir schîn dâ von verlorn hân,' Wigal. 8068. Hrab. Maurus in Wh. Müller pp. 159. 160. A fine descript. of a solar eclipse in Pindar, Frag. 74 Boeckh, 84 Bergk. On superstit. practices at the eclipse of 989, Thietmar of Mersebg says 4, 10 : 'sed cunctis persuadeo Christicolis, ut veraciter credant, hoc non aliqua *malarum incantatione mulierum* vel *esu* fieri, vel huic aliquo modo seculariter *adjuvari posse.*'

The dæmon that dogs the moon is called by the Finns *capeet*; the *capeen* try to eat her up, Hiärn p. 37-9; Juslen has ' *capet*, eclipsis lunae.' Now Renvall sub v. *kavet*, gen. kapeen, pl. kapeet, gives only the meanings 'dæmon, genius,' conf. Peterson p. 31; but sub v. *kuumet* he has ' moonlight, genius myth. *lunae inimicus.*' Compare that ' *deducere* lunam et sidera tentat' (Suppl. to 1089 end), to which is added: ' Et faceret si non *aera repulsa* sonent,' Tibull. i. 8, 21; *aera verberent,* Martial 12, 57; cum *aeris crepitu,* qualis in *defectu lunae* silenti nocte cieri solet, Livy 26, 5; conf. Plutarch 4, 1155.

In lunar eclipses the Ossèts shoot at the moon, believing that a malignant monster flying in the air is the cause; and they go on firing till the eclipse is over, Kohl's S. Russia 1, 305; conf. the legend in Cæs. heisterb. Hom. 3, 35 (Mainzer's Ztschr. 1, 233).

p. 709.] The *change of moon* is called ' des mânen wandelkêre,' Parz. 470, 7, ' d. m. wandeltac' 483, 15, ' d. m. wandel' 491, 5. The period of her shining is expr. by: Sô dem mânen sîn zît In der naht herfür gît,' Er. 1773. By new moon we mean the true conjunction of sun and moon; but the Greeks reckoned the νουμηνία from their first seeing the young moon at sunset, therefore some time after conjunction, K. F. Hermann's Gottesd. alterth. p. 226. Full moon is reckoned in with the ' afbräken maan ' [i.e. bruch, wane], Goldschm. Oldenb. volksmed. 144. OHG. *mânôt-fengida*=neomenia, calendae, Graff 3, 415, conf.

fengari p. 701 n.; *anafang mânôdis*, N. 80, 5; MHG. ein niuwer
mâne hât nâch wunsche sich gestalt, er hât *gevangen* harte wer-
declîche,' begun most worthily, MS. 2, 99ᵃ. Welsh *blaen-newydd*,
first of the new. The Esths hail the new moon with: 'Moon, get
old, let me keep young!' Böcler's Ehsten 143. Full moon:
ein *voller mâne*, MS. 2, 83ᵃ; *höifylde*, Molb. Dial. lexic. 'Nova
luna est *cornuta*, unde plena rotunda est,' N. Boëth. 171; from
the moon's horns it was but a step to the *moon's cow*, Pott 2, 252.
The oath of the Fehm-court (RA. 51) has: 'helen und hoden
(conceal) vor sunne, vor mane, vor alle *westermane*'; what means
this last word? The sun is imagined standing in the east, the
moon in the west: 'östen for sol, og *vesten* for *maane*,' Asb. og
Moe 2, 6 seq.

p. 711.] Taga blod emellan (let blood betw.) *ny* och *nedan*,
Folks. 1, 111. Swed. *nedmörk* is the Gr. νὺξ σκοτομήνιος, Od.
14, 457. Superstitions about ned and ny, ned-axel and ny-tänd-
ning, Rääf 110-6. In Dalecarlia, new moon is called *åväxand*,
Almqv. 262ᵇ; in the Edda, halfmoon is 'inn *skarði mâni*,' Sæm.
134ᵇ, as indeed Perkuns *chops the moon in two*, Rhesa 92. 192.
The Scand. ny is MHG. *daz niu*; thus Diemer 341, 22: 'alsô si
an *daz niu* gât, und iewederen (each) halben ein horn hât'; then
342, 27: 'diu mâninne gât niht ze sedele, an *deme niu* noch an
deme *wedele*'; but again 341, 21: 'diu mâninne *chrump* wirt
unde *chleine*.' A statute of Saalfeld, like that of Mülhausen, says
(Walch 1, 14): 'wer da mit uns hierinne in der stat sitzet *nuwe*
unde *wedil* (= a month), u. kouft u. verkouft.' 'Neu u. *völle* des
monds,' Ettn. Unw. doctor 435; 'so hat Luna zwei angesicht,
das ein gen *New* u. *Abnew* gricht,' Thurneisser's Archidox. 147;
'vollmond, *bruch* oder vollschein,' Franz. Simpl. 2, 301.——
Waxing and waning are '*wahsen* unde *swînen*,' Barl. 241, 24;
M. Neth. '*wassen* ende *wanen*,' Rose 4638, conf. p. 709 n. [and
Engl. wan, wane, want, wanhope]. An Ind. myth of the waxing
and waning moon in Holtzm. 1, 5—8. KM.³ 3, 401. The moon
changes about so, his mother *can't cut out a coat* to fit him, KM.³
3, 347. Plut. in Conviv. sept. sap. Aesop. Fur. 396. Corais
325. Garg. 135ᵇ.

p. 712.] Is *wedel* akin to Ssk. *vidhu* = luna? Bopp 321ᵇ.
Passages quoted in preced. note contrast it with new moon; so
'hölter im *wadel* gehouwen,' Hpt's Ztschr. 3, 90; but 'a hole in

his schedel (skull) hewn in *bad wedel*,' Uhl. p. 658.    Ambras. 152.
On wedel, good and bad wedel, and wedeln to wag, see Liliencron
in Hpt 6, 363-4-8.    Kuhn's Ztschr. 2, 131.    *Wadal*=hysopes,
fasciculus hysopi, Diut. 1, 494ᵃ.

p. 715.]    The reverse of what Cæsar says about the Germans
(de B. Gall. 1, 50) is told by Pausanias i. 28, 4 of the Lacedæ-
monians, who would only fight at *full-moon*.    Silver and gold are
brought out at *newen mon*, Sup. G. 108.    ' Quaedam faciunda in
agris potius crescente luna quam senescente; quaedam contra,
quae metas, ut frumenta et caeduam silvam.    Ego ista etiam,
inquit Agrasius, non solum in ovibus tondendis, sed in meo capillo
a patre acceptum servo, ne decrescente luna tondens calvus fiam,'
Varro RR. 1, 37.    Moonlight makes rotten, and barrel hoops cut
by it will rot sooner, Athen. 3, 7; worms get into wood not
rightly hewn: 'hölzer die man nit zu rechter zeit des mons und
monat gehauen hat,' Petr. Mihi 108ᵇ; 'si howent raif (they cut
hoops, the rascally coopers) an dem niwen mân,' Teufelsnetz
11127; elder to be cut by waxing or waning moon, Gotthelf's
Schuldb. 14; more food taken, or less, acc. to the moon,
Bopp's Gl. 122ᵇ.    Without moonlight, herbs lack scent and
flavour, Holtzm. Ind. s. 1, 6. 8; ' *tes mânen tou* ist anagenne,
unde sâmo saphes unde marges ' [Moon's dew is regeneration,
the seed of sap and marrow ?], N. Cap. 25. Drink out of a jug
that the moon shines into, and you'll be moonstruck [lunatic,
sleep-walker ? ], Stelzhamer 47.

p. 720.]    The *moon's spots* are also descr. as a *stag*, Hitzig's
Philist. 283.    In a Greenland story, while the Moon pursues his
sister the Sun, she dabs her sooty hands over his face; hence the
spots, Klemm 2, 314.    The New Zealand view is, that they are
like a woman who sits plucking Gnatuh 4, 360.    The Ranthum
people think the man in the moon is a giant, standing upright at
ebb-time, and stooping at flood, Müllenh. p. 360; but also in the
same neighbourhood he is a sheep-stealer or cabbage-thief, as in
Holland, no. 483; conf. the Wallachian story in Friedr. Müller
no. 229, and the Westphalian in Woeste 40.    In the Ukermark
he carries a bundle of pea-straw, Hpt's Ztschr. 4, 390; 'und
sprechend die laien, es sitz ain man mit ainer dorn-pürd (thorn-
load) in dem monen,' Megenb. 65, 22.    Ettner's Med. maulaffe
speaks of a bundle of wood to fire the moon with.    ' Burno, nom

d'un voleur, que les gens de la campagne prétendent être dans la lune,' Grandgagnage 1, 86. Acc. to Schott, the Old-Chinese tradition makes a man in the moon continually drive his axe into the giant tree kuei, but the rifts close up again directly; he suffers for the sins he committed while an anchoret. At Wallenhausen in Swabia they used to ride races for the dorn-büschele : three lads would start for the goal, the two foremost got prizes, and the third had a bunch of thorns tied on his back. In Bavaria the reapers leave a few ears standing, and dance round them, singing :

O heiliga sanct *Mäha*,
beschér (grant) ma a annasch gahr (year) meha
so vil körntla, so vil hörntla,
so vil ährla, so vil gute gährla,
so vil köppla, so vil schöckla;
*schopp* dich *städala*, schopp dich städala!
O heiliga sanct *Mäha* !

The stalks tied together represent St. Mäha's *städala* (stack), which they *stuffed* full of ears; only we must observe, that in Bavaria the moon is called *mâ*, not mäha, Panz. Beitr. 2, 217 (Suppl. to 157). The *Kotar* on p. 719 n. was a herdsman beloved by the goddess Triglava, who put him in the moon. Finn. *kuutar* = moon, Kalev. 22, 270. 26, 296 or moon-maiden, from *kuu*, moon, Est. *ku*, Morduin. *ko*; and *kuumet* is the pursuer of the moon, Peterson p. 31-3. In Brother Gheraert ed. Clarisse p. 132 the man in the moon is called *ludergehr*; conf. the Saxon hero Liudegêr in the Nibelungen, and Gödeke's Reinfried 90.

p. 720.] *The sun dances* at Easter (p. 291). The Indians say the sun dances, and they in imitation salute him with dancing. Lucian. de Saltat. cap. 17.

p. 722.] The *stars* are said to glister, twinkle, sparkle : sternen *glast*, MS. 2, 5ᵇ; ein sternen *blic*, flash, Parz. 103, 28. The morning stars break out, like fire : swenne der morgensterne ie früeje *úf brast*, MS. 2, 5ᵇ; an der sterren *brunste*, burning, Diut. 1, 352 ; sterre *enbran* u. schein, took fire and shone 1, 351; conf. N. Cap. 97. The sinking, 'rushing down' of stars is in Grk ἀΐσσειν, Eurip. Iph. Aul. 9.——In Hungary 280 native *names of stars* have been collected, Wolf's Ztschr. 2, 160.

Magyar Myth. 582 ; several names occur in Ossian, Ahlwardt 2, 265. 277. 3, 257. Arfvidss. 1, 149. 206 ; Armenian names in Dulaurier's Chronol. armén. '59, 1, 180-1.——Stars were invoked, as Hesperus in Bion 11 ; they were messengers of gods, as Arcturus in the prol. to Plaut. Rudens ; they do errands for lovers, Vuk no. 137. Stars are *kind* or *hostile:* quaeritis et caelo Phoenicum inventa sereno, quae sit stella homini commoda, quaeque mala, Prop. iii. 21, 3 ; interpreting the stars is spoken of in MS. 1, 189[b] ; Prov. *astrucs* (astrosus) meant lucky, and *mal-astrucs* dis-astrous; 'her star is at the *heat* (brunst). . . . till their stars have *cooled down* (versaust, done blustering),' Ph. v. Sittew. p. 614. Stars take part in a man's birth (p. 860) and death (p. 721). They have angels to wait on them, Tommaseo 1, 233. For the misdeed of Atreus, God changed the courses of all the constellations, Plato's Polit. pp. 269. 271.

The stars are the moon's flock, she leads them to pasture, Spee p. m. 163. 210. 227. A Serv. song, Vuk no. 200, says :

> od sestritze zvezde preodnitza,
> shto preodi preko vedra neba
> kao pastir pred bèlim outzama.

What star is meant by *preodnitza* (percurrens), 'who walks athwart the sky, as a shepherd before his white lambs' ? conf. no. 362 :

> osu se nebo zvezdama,
> i ravno polye outzama ;

*i.e.* heaven sows itself with stars, and the wide plain with lambs. So in Pentam. 3, 5 (p. 310) : quanno esce la luna a pascere de rosata le *galinelle* (Pleiades).

On *shooting stars*, see Humb. Kosmos 1, 393 ; they are called *stern-fürwe* (-furbish), Mone 8, 497 ; Austr. *stearn-raispn*, clearing the throat, *stearn-schnaitzn*, snuffing, Stelzh. 135—144 ; Gael. *dreug, dreag.* A star falls from heaven into the maiden's lap, Müllenh. p. 409 ; conf. 'non cadere in terram stellas et sidera cernis?' Lucr. 2, 209. They are harbingers of war, of dying, Klemm 2, 161 ; says the folksong : 'Over the Rhine three stars did fly, Three daughters of a widow die,' Simrock no. 68. ——A comet is ON. *hala-stiarna*, Ir. *boid-realt*, tail-star, Ssk.

*dhûmakétu,* fumi vexillum. The Indians call the tail elephant's tooth, the Chinese a broom, Kosmos 1, 106. In Procopius 1, 167 the star is ξιφίας, sword-shaped, or πωγωνίας, bearded. It foretells misfortune; hence 'we name it the dreadful *scourge* of God,' zorn-rute, anger-rod, Lucae Chron. 249; 'et nunquam caelo *spectatum impune* cometen,' Claud. B. Get. 243, crine vago 247.

p. 723.] The Greeks called Mercury Στίλβων, Jupiter Φαέθων, Saturn Φαίνων, Venus Φωσ-φόρος = Luci-fer, and Mars Πυρόεις, five planets in all; conf. Cic. de Nat. D. 2, 20; so the third day of the week was Πυρόεις, the fourth Στίλβων.——The evening star was also called *tier-stern,* 'darumb daz die wilden tier dan herfür gent (wild beasts then go forth) auz iren walden und holern,' Oberl. 1639. Similar is the Lith. *żwerinné* fr. žwĕris, fera, Boh. *zwjřetnice,* wild star, evening star; conf. AS. *swâna steorra.* Another Boh. name *temnice,* dim star, is like MHG. tunkelsterne. Welsh *gweno,* evening star, Venus. The Lith. has also *wakaninne,* evening star, *auszrinne,* morning star, beside *żwerinné mażoyi* for Mars, and *żwerinné dideyi* for Saturn.—— The day star, ' der *lichte tage-sterre*' of Albr. v. Halb. (Haupt 11, 366), is Serv. *dunitza,* Boh. *dennice,* Russ. *dennitza;* 'der *bringe-tag*' in Scherfer's Grobian 75 is modelled on luci-fer. Der morgensterne, swenne er *ûf gât,* und in des luftes trüebe lât, Iw. 627; der morgenstern *frolockt* reht, ob er brinne, Hätzl. 3ᵃ; ik forneme des morgensternes *slach,* Upstand. 750; 'some say the devil has taken the daystar *captive,* hence the cold and ill weather,' Gutslaf's Wöhhanda p. 265.——The polar star, ON. *hiara-stiarna;* OHG. *leite-sterre,* loadstar, Graff 6, 723; MHG. *leite-sterne,* Trist. 13660,[1] also *mer-sterne,* stella maris, Griesh. 2, 13; *cathlinn der flut* in Oisian 2, 334; in O. v. 17, 31 ' *Polónan* then stetigon,' nom. *Polóni?* conf. polunoci [pure Slav. for midnight!] = septentriones, Graff 3, 334. The Lapp. *tjuold* = palus and stella polaris, because it stands firm as a stake; Americ. *ichka chagatha,* star that goes not, Klemm 2, 161.

p. 724.] Acc. to Sæm. 76ᵃ it was *Thórr,* not Oðinn, that threw Thiassi's eyes into the sky. Theodosius was changed into a star, Claud. de 3 cons. Hon. 172, de 4 cons. 428. John the Baptist's

---

[1] *Leyt-gestirn* in the Wetterau (Höfer's D. urk. 60. Schmidt's Gesch. d. grossh. Hessen 1, 241) is spelt in the Cod. Lauresh. 3128—30. 249. 250-2 Leit-kestre, Leit-castre, Leiz-castro, and has therefore nothing to do with star.

head was placed in the sky (p. 284-5), so was that of Râhu, Holtzm. Ind. s. 3, 151.

p. 725.] Ssk. *rxâs* pl., the shiners (the 7 sages), *rxas* sing., the shiner=ἄρκτος. Indra's *car* is made of the *seven sages;* the constell. may also be called *vâhanam,* waggon, Kuhn in Höfer 1, 159. 161. Holtzm. Ind. s. 1, 30. The Grt Bear repres. the British *Arthur* (confounded with Arcturus), and the Lyre is his harp, Davies's Mythol. p. 187. All the luminaries ride in cars: 'luna rotigerae vagationis,' Kemble 5, 195 (yr. 931). *Charles wain* is over the chimney, 1 Henry IV. 2, 1 ; der *wagen* ist ob dem hus, Keisersb. Brösaml. 70ᵉ ; der *himelswagen* schon die deichsel rückwärts drehet, Scherfer's Grobian ed. 1708, p. 72. An O. Belg. riddle asks who it is that has to go round on the Roodestraat all night in a coach without horses, and appears in the morning : ' *Bruno* heeft een' *koets* ghemaekt Op vier wielen, zonder peerden ; *Bruno* heeft een' *koets* ghemaekt, Die alleen naer Brussel gaet;' meaning the coach in the sky, Ann. de la Soc. d'émul. de la Flandre occid. '42, 4, 368.    *Geticum plaustrum,* Claud. de B. Get. 247 ; and Alanus ab Insulis (d. 1202) in his Anti-Claudian makes allegorical females construct a *heavenly car,* Cramer's Gesch. d. erzieh. p. 204. Festus sub v. *septentriones,* septem boves juncti. Varro 7, 74 : *boves et temo.* Ov. Met. 10, 447. Ex Ponto iv. 10, 39 : *plaustrum.* Gl. slettst. 1, 2 : Virgilias, *sibinstirne ;* and 6, 392. 479 : Majae, Pliadas, *sibinstirnes.*——Ir. *griogchan,* a constell. ; Gael. *grigirean,* Charles wain, otherw. crann, crannarain (p. 729 n.) ; *griglean, griglean meanmnach, grioglachan,* Pleiades. Ir. *camcheachta,* plough, ploughshare, seven stars of the wain. Finn. *otava* or *otavainen,* ursa major, is distingu. fr. *vähä otava,* ursa minor ; yet otava can hardly belong to ohto (ursus). In Kalev. 28, 393-4 *otavainen* and *seitsentähtinen* (seven stars) are used as if synonymous, and both have shoulders. The Lapp. *sarw* is both alces, elk, and ursa major ; in Ostiak too the constell. is called *los,* elk (Klemm 3, 128), and has a head and tail. In Greenl. it is *tukto,* reindeer, Klemm 2, 314. Fabricius 504ᵇ. In American, *ichka shachpo* is supposed to be an ermine with its hole, its head, feet and tail, Klemm 2, 161. The Arabs call the two end stars of the bear's tail *mizar* and *benetnash,* and the third, which is the pole of the wain, *alioth;* the remaining four make the axles.

p. 727.] Orion's belt, Lat. *jugula, jugulae*: 'nec Jugulae, neque Vesperugo, neque Vergiliae occĭdunt,' Plaut. A. i. 1, 119; also *ensis* and *ensifer*, Forcell. sub v. ensis: '*nitidum*que Orionis *ensem*, Ov. Met. 13, 294. In Westgötl. *Frigge-råkken* and *Jacobs staf;* ON. *fiskikallar*, F. Magn. Dag. tid. 105. 'Orion constell. a rusticis vocatur *baculus S. Petri*, a quibusdam vero *tres Mariae*,' Gl. Augiens. in Mone 8, 397; in Schleswig *Mori-rok* and *Peri-pik*, Müllenh. no. 484. Finn. *Kalevan miekka*, Kalevae ensis, also *Väinämöisen miekka* or *vikate* (sithe), Schiefn. on Castrén p. 329; Lapp. *niall, nialla*, which usually means taberna, repositorium; in Greenl. the belt is named *sicktut*, the bewildered, being seal-hunters who lost their way, and were caught up and set among the stars, Klemm 2, 314; conf. the Lappish legend about the Pleiades, below.

p. 729.] Of the 7 Pleiads only *six* are ever seen, Humb. Kosm. 3, 65; quae septem dici, sex tamen esse solent, Ov. Fast. 4, 171 (see p. 728 n.). AS. Gl. 'pliadas, *sifunsterri*,' Oehler 359. Fr. *l'estoille poussinière*, Rabelais 1, 53; las *couzigneiros*, Dict. Languedoc. 127. The Hung., beside fiastik, has *heteveny*. In Serv. märch. pp. 15 and 87 appears a girl with the golden hen and chickens, conf. Vuk no. 10; the Wallach. story tells of a gold *cluck-hen* and *five chicks*, Schott p. 242.[1] Syryän. *voykodzyun*, lit. night-star. The Lith. and Finn. notion of the constellation being a sieve reminds me of Lucian's Timon 3, where the quaking earth is compared to a shaken sieve.——The Pleiades are called in Norweg. Lapp. *nieid-gierreg*, fr. nieid = virgo, and gierreg = samling af en rets besiddere; but in Swed. Lapp. *suttjènes råuko* (Lindahl 406. 443[b]), i.e. fur in frost: the sky, taking pity on a man whom his master had turned out of the house in the depth of winter, covered him with this constellation (F. Magn. in Dag. tider p. 103 gives *tjokka* = heart, which Lindahl has not under tsåkke). Greenl. *kellukturset*, hounds baiting a bear, Klemm 2, 314. Fabricius 188[a]; conf. Welsh *y twr tewdws*, the close pack, i.e. Pleiades, and eburdrung (p. 727). The Amer. Indians worship this constell., Klemm 2, 112. 153. 173.—— Similar to the Lith. name for the Kids, viz. 'ploughman and

---

[1] The lost lamb is looked for at the morningstar, eveningstar, moon and sun, Lith. in Rhesa p. 290-1-2; conf. p. 707-8, and 'coming to the *sun*, and asking him,' Hym. in Cerer. 64.

oxen,' is the Serv. *voluyara* (fr. vol, ox ?), a star that ploughmen know, for when it rises they look out for their oxen. Cassiopeia is Lith. *jostandis*, no doubt fr. josta, girdle. The Hyades, AS. raedgastran. Lye: 'the five in the head of Taurus'; raedgaesnan, Gl. Epin., redgaesrum, Gl. Oehl. p. 336. The Lyre, Boh. hauslička na nebi, fiddle in the sky.

p. 731.] The constellation of the Bear is made out from the animal's head, back and tail. A star with the shape of a child, Pass. 24, 30 seq.; conf. the sun as a spindle (Suppl. to 703 mid.). Most natural of all was the making of stars out of *beaming eyes* (p. 565-6-8), as in the story of Thiassi and the New Zealand one, Klemm 4, 354-5. 388.

The northern lights (aurora borealis) are called *heerbrand, heerschein,* Frommann 4, 114 (Suppl. to 703 beg.) ; Swed. *norr-sken,* Dan. *nord-lys ;* Gael. *firchlis, na fir chlise,* the merry dancers, Welsh *y goleuny gogleddol.* Finn. the fox's fire ; conf. Gesta Rom. c. 78, and note to Keller's Sept sages ccxx.

p. 734.] On names of the rainbow, see Pott in Aufr. and Kuhn's Zts. 2, 414 seq. The ON. Âs-brû is OS. *Osna-brugga,* Massm. Egsterst. 34. Zeuss p. 11 ; regenbogen-*brücke,* Firmen. 2, 45. Ir. and Gael. *blogha braoin,* Carraigth. 54. The ON. *brúar-spordr,* bridge's tail, is further illustr. by a MHG. *sporten,* caudae vulpium, Griesh. 1, 125. 2, 42. The rainbow is called a messenger in Fornm. sög. 9, 518 : grârr regen-*boði* Hnikars stôð â grimmum Göndlar hinni þegna. Pliny 24, 13 (69) : ' coelestis arcus in fruticem innixus'; more plainly 12, 24 (52) : ' tradunt, in quocunque frutice curvetur arcus coelestis, eandem quae sit aspalathi *suavitatem odoris* existere, sed si in aspalatho, inenarrabilem quandam '; and 17, 5 (3) : ' terrae *odor* . . . in quo loco arcus coel. dejecerit capita sua.' Another superstition is, that a *treasure* lies hidden at the foot of the rainbow, Panzer 1, 29.——— Duller p. 35 cites the name *wetter-maal* (county Guttenstein), which I find nowhere else ; *regenboum*=iris, Gl. Sletst. 39, 320. Finn., beside *taivaan-kaari,* heaven's bow, has *vesi-kaari,* water bow, *Ukon-k., sateen-k.,* rain bow. To the Greenlander the rainbow is the hem of a god's garment, Klemm 2, 327. The Poles have dąga, bow, corresp. to Russ. Serv. dugá, but not in the sense of iris, which they call *tęcza.* The Lettic has also *deeva yohsta,* Bergm. p. 124, and the Lith. *dangaus szlota,* heaven's broom. Schmeller 2, 196 has 'die *himel-blüe*, rainbow,' conf. Iris, who gives her name to both rainbow and flower (Perunika, Suppl. to 1216 n.). Ssk. *Indri telum*, Bopp 43ᵃ. The Tartars make a feast when the rainbow appears, Kurd Schlözer p. 11.

The Pohjan-daughter sits on the air-bow (ilman wempele), the sky-bow (taiwon kaari), *weaving*, Kalev. rune 3 beg. There also sit the sun (Päivätär) and moon (Kuutar), to listen to the song of Wäinämöinen 22, 17, spinning gold the while, till the spindles drop out of their hands 26, 296. Ammian. Marcell. lib. xx., end: ' Et quoniam est signum permutationis aurae . . . igitur apud poëtas legimus saepe, *Irim de coelo mitti*, cum praesentium rerum verti necesse sit status.'

---

# CHAPTER XXIII.
## DAY AND NIGHT.

p. 737.] On the origin of ἦμαρ, ἡμέρα, Bopp thinks differently, see Gr. 505. With Dagr as a mythical person conf. Baldæg, Swefdæg; of his son [or father] Dellîngr it is said in Fornald. sög. 1, 468 : 'uti fyri *Dellings* dyrum,' under the open sky. The Edda makes night precede and produce day, conf. 'nox *ducere diem* videtur,' Tac. Germ. 11.

In spite of Benfey, the Ssk. niś and nakt seem to belong to one root. In GDS. 905 I have traced our nacht to nahan. The Ssk. *rajani* seems akin to Goth. riqis, Ir. reag, AS. racu (p. 813 end). Other words for night: Ir. *oidhche, aidche*, Zeuss 257, Gael. *oiche;* Finn. *yö*, Est. *ö*, Hung. *éj*, Lapp. *iya, ya;* Basq. *gaüa, gauba, arratsa, zaroa*. The Greek language has a separate name, νυκτὸς ἀμολγός, for the last third of the night, when dreams are true (p. 1146 mid.); [but also the first third, when Hesperus shines, Il. 22, 317].

p. 737.] Day and night are holy : ἠὼς δῖα, Od. 9, 151. 306; mit Got und dem *heiligen tag*, Hpt's Ztschr. 7, 536-7; so mir der heilige dach! 107, 46. 109, 19; so mir Got u. dat *heilge licht!* 254, 19; so mir dat heilige licht! 57, 1. 105, 30; summer (so mir) der dach, der uns allen geve licht! 14, 50. 119, 1. 69, 21; God ind der *gode dach* 7, 41. 21, 40. 65, 55; so mir der gode dach, so uch der g. d.! 33, 39. 219, 62; durch den guden dach

69, 21. 196, 3. 312, 63; sô mir der guote tac! Ges. Abent. 3,
227; als mir helf der g. t.! 3, 243; dor dere van den goden dage,
Lanc. 44948; bi Gode ende bi den goeden dage, Walew. 155;
Reinaert, coming out of his hole, 'quedde den *schonen dach*',
Rein. 2332; 'Saint Jourdhuy,' Théatre Franç. 2, 47; qui parati
sunt diei maledicere, MB. 26, 9 (n. 1256), conf. 'wê geschehe dir
(woe betide thee), Tac, daz du mich lâst bî liebe langer blîben
niht!' Walth. 88, 16. Of a piece with the above adjurations is
our 'as sure as the *day* stands in heaven'; OHG. theist giwis io
sô *dag*, O. v. 12, 33; MHG. ich weiz ez wârez als den *tac*, Trist.
6646; 'daz ist wâr sô der tac,' Diemer 78, 8.

p. 738.] Day appears as a personality independent of the sun:
'Awake the *god of day*,' Haml. 1, 1; 'hoer tag, den nieman
bergen kan,' Spiegel after Altsw. 191; quasi senex tabescit dies,
Plaut. Stich. v. 1, 8, conf. the Plautian phrase 'diem com-
burere'; mit *molten* den tag *austragen*, Burc. Waldis 272[b]; eya,
tach, weres du veile, Haupt 1, 27; herre, wâ is (how goes) der
tach? En. 297, 18; ez was hôhe ûf der tach 300, 13; waz *wîzet*
mir der tach (got to say against me), daz er niene wil komen? 335,
14; alt und junge wânden, daz von im der ander tac erschine,
Parz. 228, 5.

Uchaisravas, the heavenly steed of day, emerges from the
ocean, Holtzm. Ind. s. 3, 138—140.

> Hunc utinam nitidi Solis praenuntius ortum
> afferat *admisso* Lucifer *albus equo*.   Ov. Trist. iii. 5, 55.

Ἀνίκα πέρ τε ποτ' ὠρανὸν ἔτρεχον ἵπποι
Ἀῶ τὰν ῥοδόπαχυν ἀπ' Ὠκεανοῖο φέροισαι.   Theocr. 2, 174.

The shining mane of day agrees with the ancient notion that
rays of light were hairs; Claudian in Prob. et Olybr. 3 addresses
the sun:

> Sparge diem *meliore coma, crinemque repexi*
> blandius elato surgant temone jugales,
> efflantes roseum frenis spumantibus ignem!

Compare too the expression Donnerstags-pferd, Thursday's horse.

p. 738.] The sun rises: er sôl *rann up*, Fornm. s. 8, 114.
Sv. folks. 1, 154. 240. Vilk. s. 310; *rinnet ûfe* der sunne, Diem.
5, 28; *errinnet* 362, 26; der sunne von dir ist ûz *gerunnen*, MS.
1, 28[a]. Lith. *utżteka* sáule, up flows the sun, fr. tekéti; light

also flows and melts asunder, conf. ' des tages in *zeran*,' Wigam.
3840. '*Morne, da diu sunne úfgât,* u. sich über alle berge lât,'
Dietr. drach. 345ᵇ; swâ si vor dem berge *úfgât,* MS. 1, 193ᵇ,
conf. M. Neth. baren, ontpluken (Suppl. to 743); ê diu sunne
*úfstige,* climb up, Dietr. dr. 150ᵃ; dei sunne *sticht hervor,* Soester-
fehde (in Emmingh.) 664; die sonne begonste *rîsen,* Rein. 1323;
li solauz *est levez,* et li jors essauciez, Guitecl. 1, 241; '*des
morgens,* do de sunne *wart,*' came to be, Valent. u. Namel. 243ᵇ;
'wan dei sunne *anquam,*' arrived, Soester-f. (in Em.) 673, *bricht
an* 627. 682; '*diu sunne úftrat,*' stept up, Mar. leg. 175, 47. 60;
de sonne *baven de bane quam,* Val. u. Nam. 257ᵇ; diu sunne
*was úf hô,* Frauend. 340, 29; bi *wachender* sunnen, Keyserrecht.
Endemann p. 26.

p. 740.] Er sach die sonne *sinken,* Lanc. 16237; diu sunne
*under sanc,* Pass. 36, 40; die sonne *sanc,* soe *ghinc onder,* also
soe dicke hevet ghedaen, Walew. 6110; sô der sunne *hinder gegât*
(LG. hintergegangen?), MS. 2, 192ᵇ; von der sunnen *úfgange* u.
*zuogange,* Griesh. 2, 23; hinz diu sunne *zuo gie* (went-to) 122;
dô diu sunne *nider gie* (went down), Nib. 556, 1; diu sunne was
ze tal *gesigen* (sunk), Wh. 447, 9; ouch *sîget* diu sunne sêre gegen
der âbentzîte (sinks low toward eventide), Trist. 2512; alse die
sonne *dalen* began, Lanc. 16506; alse hi di sonne *dalen* sach,
Maerl. 3, 197; ê sich diu sun *geneiget* (stooped), MSH. 3, 212ᵃ;
zu dal di sunne was *genigen,* Diut. 1, 351; des âbends dô·sich
*undersluoc* diu sunne mit ir glaste, Pass. 267, 51; diu sunne ie
zû ze tale *schóz* (downward shot), Alb. v. Halb. (Haupt 11, 365);
der sunne ze âbent *verscein,* Rol. 107, 23. Ksrchr. 7407;=die
sunne *iren schîn verluset* (loses her sheen), Keyserr. Endem.
p. 210; metter *sonnen-scede* (discessu), Limborch 8, 206.——On
coucher, colcar, collocare, *solsatire,* see RA. 817: einz *vif* soleil
*cochant,* Aspr. 39ᵇ; '*und sôlar siot,*' till set of sun, Sæm. 179ᵇ;
'*untaz siu sizzit,*' until she sitteth, Fragm. 29, 14; e die sonne
*gesässe,* Weisth. 2, 453; bis die sonne *gesitzt* 2, 490; *in sedil gân*
=obire, Diut. 2, 319ᵃ.

(Sunne) gewîted on *west-rodor,* Cod. Exon. 350, 23; west on-
hylde swegelbeorht hinne *setl-gonges* fûs 174, 32; bis die sonne
wider *der forste gibel* schinet, Weisth. 3, 498. Norw. 'solen begyndte at helde mod *aas-randen,*' Asb. Huldr. 1, 1, and 'solen stod
i *aas-kanten,*' 1, 27, went towards, stood at, *aas's edge;* for this

and for *giâhamarr*, conf. F. Magn. Dagens tider p. 15 and Bopp's
Gl. 25ᵇ : '*Asta,* nomen *montis occidentalis,* ultra quem solem occidere credunt;' it came to mean sunset, and at last any downfall:
'Day sinks behind the *best of mountains, Ast*,' Kuruinge 563.
1718. 2393. Holtzm. Ind. s. 3, 183-4. (Pott in his Zählmeth.
264 derives *asta,* sunset, fr. as = dejicere, ponere); 'diu sunne an
daz *gebirge* gie,' Ecke 110; ἔτι εἶναι ἥλιον ἐπὶ τοῖς ὄρεσι, καὶ
οὔπω δεδυκέναι, Plato's Phædo 116; ichn geloube niemer mê, daz
sunne von *Mycêne* gê, Trist. 8283 (Mycenæ in Argolis, Sickler
p. m. 283-4). In a rocky valley of Switzerland, at a certain hour
once a year, the sun shines through *a hole in the mountain-wall,*
and illumines a church-steeple; conf. the sun shining into Belsen
church, Meier's Schwäb. sag. 297.——'Dô diu sunne *ze gaden*
solde gân,' Morolt 1402 ; de sunne geit *to gade,* Brem. wtb. 1,
474 ; ἥλιος κοιμᾶται, Wieselgr. 414 ; de sunne woll *to bedde,*
Firmen. 1, 329. M. Neth. '*die* sonne vaert henen thaerre *rusten*
waert,' Maerl. 3, 124; umb jede abendzeit, ehe die sonne *zu hause.*
kömpt, Brehme B. 1ᵃ; 'Moidla (girls), geit hoim! Die *sun geit
no;* Kriegt koene koen tanzer, Wos steit ihr den do?'——'Eh
die sonne *zu genaden* get,' Weisth. 1, 744. 2, 492 ; e die sunne
under *zu genaden* gienge 3, 510. Does the Goth. *remi-sol, rimi-
sauil,* mean the sun at rest? Hpt's Ztschr. 6, 540; quant li
solaus *ganchi* (tottered), Mort de Garin 144. Note the phrase in
Walewein 8725 : 'Doe begonste die sonne gaen *Te Gode* van den
avonde saen;' conf. Esth. 'pääw lähhäb loya,' the sun *goes to his
Maker* = sets. The light of sunset is thus expr. in MHG.: 'diu
sunne *z'âbunde schein*,' to evening shone, Karl 3525.

　　p. 742.] ON. *glaðr* = nitens and laetus, and we say 'beaming
with joy'; so the beaming sun is called 'Glens beðja *Guð-bliÞ,*'
God-blithe, Edda Sn. Hafn. 1, 330. *Sunnenfroh* (or Sunnenfrö,
Mohr's Reg. v. Fraubrunnen no. 381, yr 1429) may mean 'glad
*as* the sun,' or '*of* the sun,' as in Boner 66, 42. A maiden in a
Swed. song is named *Sol-fagr,* var. *Solfot,* Arfv. 1, 177. 180 ; at
*glädja* sig = to set, Sv. äfvent. 342. At evening the sun's bow
goes to joy : illalla *ilohon,* Kalev. 27, 277. Acc. to Hagen's
Germ. 2, 689 the sun has a golden bed, lies, sleeps on gold : als
di sonne *in golt geit,* Arnsb. urk. no. 824, yr 1355; *gieng* die
sonn *im gold,* Günther 783 ; de sunne ging to golde, Ges. Abent.
2, 319 ; singt als die sonne fast *zu golde* wolde *gehn,* Scherfer

195.——The sun in rising out of the sea, *crackles*, Ossian 3, 131; and the image of the *zolotà bába* (golden granny) utters tones, Hanusch p. 167; like Memnon's statue, Lucian's Philops. 33.

p. 743.] Oannes (the sun) dips in the sea every evening, Hitzig's Philist. 218.

'Ημος δ' ἠέλιος μετενίσσετο βουλυτόνδε, Od. 9, 58. Il. 16, 779.
'Ηέλιος μὲν ἔπειτα νέον προσέβαλλεν ἀρούρας
ἐξ ἀκαλαρρείταο βαθυρρόου 'Ωκεανοῖο
οὐρανὸν εἰσανιών, Il. 7, 421. Od. 19, 433.
'Ηέλιος δ' ἀνόρουσε, λιπὼν περικαλλέα λίμνην,
οὐρανὸν ἐς πολύχαλκον, Od. 3, 1.

*Occiduo* lota *profundo* sidera *mergi*, N. 221. ‘Sage me, for hwam scîne seo sunne swâ reáde on ærne morgen? Ic þe secge, for þam þe heo cymð up *of þære sæ*,’ Altd. bl. 1, 190; nu gengr sól î egi, Alex. saga p. 163. The sun bathes at night, Hpt's Ztschr. 4, 389. N. Pr. prov. bl. 1, 298; ‘dô begund’ ez werden naht, und *sleich* diu sunne nâch ir aht *umbe daz norden-mere*, als ê,’ crept round the northern sea, Geo. 6001; weil die sonne *niedertunkt*, Schmidt v. Wern. 184.——But the sun also goes into the forest. Swed. ‘solen gâr *i skogen*’: sol gâtt *i skog*, Folks. 1, 155; när sol gick *i skog*, Cavall. 1, 96; ‘siþan sol är *undi viþi*,’ got behind the trees, Oestg. 175 (F. Magn. Lex., sub v. landvidi, gives a differ. explan. of vide, viþi); nå nu ned, du sol, i gran-skog, Kalev. Castr. 2, 57. Finn. kule (kulki) päiwä kuusikolle! Kalev. 19, 386. 412; conf. ‘Not yet *the mountain*, but only those houses are hiding the sunshine,’ Goethe's Eleg. What means ‘bis die sonne uf den *peinapfel* kommt,’ (Weisth. 3, 791)? till he gilds the fir cone?

Unz sich der tac *úfmachte*, Hagen's Ges. Abent. 2, 367; der tac der *sleich* in (crept to them) balde *zuo*, MS. 1, 171ᵇ; der tac der *schleicht* wie ein dieb, Hätzl. 23ᵃ; der tac *nâhen* begunde nâch sînem alten vunde, Türl. W. 125ᵃ; die dach *quam*, die *niet onstont*, Maerl. 2, 236, so that he never stands still. The day says: ‘I *fare* away, and leave thee here,’ Uhl. 169; der tac wil niht *erwinden* (turn back, leave off), Wolfr. 8, 18; der morgen niht *erwinden* wil, den tac nieman *erwenden* (keep off) kan, MS. 1, 90ᵇ. ‘Dô der tac *erschein*,’ shone out, Parz. 428, 13. 129, 15; d. d. t. vol *erschein*, Er. 623; der tac sich *schouwen* liez, Livl. 3299;

dô der morgen sich *úf-liez*, und si sîn entsuoben, Pass. 30, 79 ; sich
der tac *entslôz* (unlocked), Urstende 118, 61 ; der tac sich *úz den
wolken* bôt, Türl. Wh. 67ª ; dô si gesâhen den morgen mit sîme
liehte *úfstrîchen*, die vinstre naht entwîchen von des sunnen
morgenrôt, Pass. 36, 51 ; der tac *lúhte schitere* (thin), Serv. 3237.
Dager var *ljus*, Sv. folks. 1, 129.   La nuis sen va, et li jors *es-
clari*, Garins 2, 203.——'Der tac sich *anzündet*,' kindles, Hätzl.
36ª ; dat hi den dach sach *baren*, Walewein 384 ; die men scone
*baren* sach, Karel 1, 376.   2, 1306. 594 ; dat menne (den dach)
*baren* sach 2, 3579, der tac sich hete *erbart*, Eracl. 4674 : sach
*verbaren* den sconen dach, Lanc. 44532. 45350.   Also ontpluken :
'*ontplôc* haer herte *alse die dach*,' her heart flew open like the
day, Karel 1, 1166.   Walew. 3320. 7762 ; conf. 'sîn herte *ver-
lichte* als die dach,' Walew. 9448 ; *ontspranc* die dach, Karel 2,
593 ; die dach *uten hemele spranc*, Walew. 6777. 4885 ; Fr. 'le
jour jaillit ; ' möcht der tac *herspriessen*, Hofm. Gesellsch. 59 ;
Lett. ' deena *plaukst*,' sprouts, buds.   The day stirs : dag *rînit*,
O. i. 11, 49 ; naht *rînit*, O. iii. 20, 15 ; lioht *rînit*, O. i. 15, 19.   ii.
1, 47.   The day is rich, powerful : ' guotes ist er niht *rîche*(r)
wan als des liehtes der tac,' than the day is of light, Cod. Vind.
428, no. 212 ; *reicher* dan der tac, Uhl. 1, 196.——Other expressions for daybreak : ' die Nacht die *weicht*,' gives way, Lb. 1582.
42 ; Niht forð *gewât*, Cod. Exon. 412, 12 ; diu nacht *gemachlich*
ende nam, Frauend. 485, 11 ; uns ist diu naht *von hinnen*, Wolfr.
Lied. 8, 16 ; unz uns diu naht *gerûmet*, Hahn's Stricker 10, 35 ;
so lange bis die schmiede pinken, u. der tag sich wieder *vor-
zeiget*, Ettner's Vade et occide Cain, p. 9.   It is finely said in
the Nib. 1564, 2 : ' unz daz (until) diu sunne ir liehtez schînen
*bôt* (held out) dem morgen über berge ; ' als der morgenrôt der
vinstern erde lieht *erbôt*, Mar. 169, 28 ; unz der ander morgenrôt
der werlde daz lieht *bôt*, Serv. 1839 ; ouch schein nu schiere der
morgenrôt, den diu sunne *sante* durch vreude *vür* (Dawn, whom
the sun sent before him for joy) daz er vreudenrîche kür vogeln
u. bluomen brâhte, Türl. Wh. 69ª.   Simpler phrases are : dô
begundez liuhten vome tage, Parz. 588, 8 ; gein tage die vogele
sungen, Mai 46, 16.   For descrying the dawn they said : ' nû
*kius* ich den tac,' choose, pick out, espy, Walth. 89, 18 ; *kôs* den
morgen lieht 88, 12 ; den morgenblic *erkôs*, Wolfr. Lied. 3, 1 ;
als man sich des tages *entstê*, Wigal. 5544.

p. 744.]   Day is like a neighing steed :

Velox Aurorae nuntius Aether

qui *fugat hinnitu stellas.*   Claudian's 4 cons. Hon. 561.

He cleaves the clouds : der tac die wolken *spielt* (split), MS. 2, 167ᵃ.  So the *crow* with flapping of her wings divides the night, lets in the light ; with her and the AS. *Dæg-hrefn* we may assoc. the ON. names *Dag-hvelp* (quasi young day) and *Dag-ulf*, För-stem. 1, 328.

p. 744.]   Day is beautiful : *beau* comme le *jour*, plus beau que le *jour* ; ils *croissoient* comme le *jour*, D'Aulnoi's Cab. des f. 243 ; *wahsen* als der *tac*, S. Uolr. 328.   Sô der morgen *enstât*, Herb. 8482 ; dô der tac *werden* began, En. 11280 ; die naht lêt, ende het *waert* dach, Karel 2, 1305 (conf. die nacht lêt, die hem verwies, Florîs 1934) ; der tac ist *vorhanden* (here, forthcom-ing), Simpl. 1, 528 ; dô *gienc úf* der tac (went up), Wh. 71, 20 [Similar examples omitted] ; unze *iz* beginne *úfgân*, Diem. 174, 5 ; es *giengen* nicht 14 tage *in's land*, Schelmufsky, conf. p. 633ᵃ ; der tac *gât* von Kriechen, MSH. 3, 426ᵃ.   Diu naht *gie hin*, der tac *herzuo* (or, der morgen *her*, der morgen *quam*, Pass. 47, 89. 329, 53.   307, 68 [Similar ex. om.].——Day comes rapidly : comes *upon the neck of you*, Döbel 1, 37ᵃ ; *an trat* der ôstertac, Pass. 262, 16 ; als der suntac *an gelief* 243, 1 ; dô der ander morgen *úf ran*, Serv. 3410 ; der tac *geflozzen kam*, Troj. kr. 29651 ; der tac *kommt stolken*, Hätzl. 26ᵇ ; der tac *kam einher walken* 28ᵃ ; êr die mane sinke neder, ende *op* weder *rise* die dach, Karel 2, 1194.   He pushes his way up : dô *dranc úf* der tac, Rosen-g. 627 ; begunde *úf dringen*, etc.   [Similar ex. om.] ; dô siben tage *vor-drungen*, Kolocz 162 ; des *tages wîze ôstern* durch diu wolken *dranc*, Wigal. 10861.   He *is* up : des morgens, dô der tac *úf was*, Fragm. 41ᶜ ; nu *was* wol *úf* der tac, En. 7252 ; *ez* was hôhe *úf den* tac 11146 ; dô was *ez verre* ûf den tac 10334.

p. 745.]   The day may be hindered from breaking : 'What have I done to the day ?   Who has *led him astray* ?' En. 1384 ; H. Sachs iii. 3, 68ᵃ (ed. 1561), 48ᵈ (ed. 1588) says of a 'day-stealer' (idler) : 'wilt den *tag in der multer umbtragen* ?' carry him about in thy trough, OHG. muoltra.   There is a *key* to the day, Sv. vis. 2, 214.   Vlaemsche lied. p. 173 ; the key of day is thrown into the river, Uhl. 171 ; 'Had I the day under lock and key, So close a *prisoner* he should be' 169 (conf. the day's answer). The sun is caught in a noose, he cannot continue his journey, and has to be ransomed, Klemm 2, 156.

A phrase used in Wirzburg comes very near the Romance *poindre* : 'der tag *spitzt sich* schon,' points, perks, pricks itself up, H. Müller's Griechenth. 44 ; Illyr. zora *puca*, the dawn shoots. With *à la pointe* du jour, conf. 'matineret *a punta d' alba*,' Mila y Funtals 159. OHG. strîza=jubar (sub ortu), Graff 6, 760 ; lucis diei *spiculum* in oriente conspiciens, Kemble no. 581, p. 106 ; 'der tac die wolken *spielt*,' split the clouds (Suppl. to 744).

p. 747.] The dawn is accompanied by *noise*, esp. by agitation of the air : ich waen ez tagen welle, sich hebet ein *küeler wint*, Nib. 2059, 2 ; diu *luft* sich gein *dem tage ziuhet* (air is drawn towards day), diu naht im schier entfliuhet, Türl. Wh. 65ᵃ. We must conn. aurora and αὔριον (morrow) with aura, αὔρα (breeze) ; and AS. morgen-*swêg* may be akin to *swëgel* (p. 746). 'Sôl ek sâ driupa *dyn-heimum* î,' solem vidi mergi in oceano? mundo sonoro? Sæm. 125ᵇ. The Hätzlerin 30ᵃ speaks of the *gewimmer* (whine, moan, droning) of daybreak ; 'far an eirich *gu fuai mear* a' grien o stuaidh nan ceann glas,' ubi oritur *sonore* sol a fluctibus capitum glaucorum, Tighmora 7, 422 ; Ssk. *ravi* means sol, *rava* sonus, *ru* sonare.——*Alba* is the lux prima that precedes the blush of dawn, Niebuhr 2, 300 ; it is like Matuta, Leucothea. Burguy's Glossaire 350ᵃ explains '*par son*' before '*l'aube*' as 'par dessus, tout à la pointe'; It. *sull' alba*. Our *anbrechen* contains the idea of noise : daz der tac *úf prach*, Diemer 175, 7 ; de dach *up brak*, Hpt's Ztschr. 5, 399. Detm. 1, 50 [Sim. examp. om.] ; day *breaks in* through the windows, Felsenb. 3, 458 ; ich sihe den morgensterne *úf brehen*, MS. 1, 90ᵇ, conf. Lith. *brĕkszti*, to glimmer, dawn ; *erupit cras*, Walthar. 402 ; l'aube *creva*, Méon 1, 291. The noise of daybreak is sometimes to be expl. by the song of the wakening birds : 'der tac wil uns *erschellen*,' ring out, Ges. Abent. 1, 305 ; der süeze *schal* kunt in den tac, Mai 93, 33 ; biz sie erschracte (startled them) der *vogel-sanc* 93, 32. With the Span. 'el alva se *rie*,' conf. Turn. v. Nantes 42, 4 : 'diu sunne in dem himel *smieret*,' smiles. *Crepusculum* presupposes a crepus, which must belong to crepare, as ψέφος murk is akin to ψόφος noise, see Benfey 1, 617 seq. Bopp's Gl. 91.

p. 748.] Bopp's Gl. 53ᵇ connects *uhtvó* with ushas, from ush to burn, as ahtau with ashtân ; die *ucht* is still used in Germ.

Bohemia. *Uhti-bita*=orgia, Gl. sletst. 6, 436, is explained by Wackernagel as dawn-petition, Haupt 5, 324. Diluculo is rend. in OHG. by: in demo *unterluchelinge*, Windb. ps. 260; fruo *unterluchelingen* 206; *dagendeme*, Ps. Trev. 206; an demo *dalithe* 260; *piliothe*, Diut. 1, 530ᵃ. *Falowendi, faloendi*=crepusculum, Graff 3, 496-7 (falo=fulvus, pallidus); prima luce=in der *urnich-den*, Hor. Belg. 7, 36ᵇ, for which AS. has *wóma* (p. 745), beside *glommung, dægrim*=crepusculum (may we connect 'as de dach griemelde'? Frommnan 4, 265). ON. *byrtîng;* and with *dags-brún* is conn. the Fr. female name *Brun-matin*=Aurora, Dict. 2, 325, misspelt Brumatin, Méon 3, 447. MLG. *dageringe*= diluculum, Detm. 1, 178. 2, 546.

The personific. of Tagarôd is also indicated by the men's names *Daghared*, Trad. Corb. 226, *Dagrim* 394. The word is fem. in Gotfr. Hagen 65: an der *dageroit;* but the masc. preponderates, both here and in morgenrôt (see quotations from Mar., Servat., and Türl. Wh. in Suppl. to 743 end); yet ' *die* rotbrünstige morgenröt,' H. Sachs's Wittenb. nachtigal. 'Der tag graut,' turns grey, dawns; conf. 'es graut mir,' it frightens me: des tages blic was dennoch grâ, Parz. 800, 1. Ἡμέρα ἀμφὶ τὸ λυκαυγὲς αὐτό, dies circa ipsum diluculum est, Lucian's Somn. 33; Arab. *dhenebu-ssirhan*, wolf's tail, the first glimmer of dawn, that sweeps over the sky, then disappears, leaving a deeper gloom behind, Rückert's Hariri 1, 215.

p. 748.] Does the obscure word *morgen* actually mean breakfast? Finn. murkina=jentaculum, breakfast-time. Morning, like day, climbs up and is high, hence the name of Dietrich der *Hochmorgen*, Rauch 1, 413. Greek αὔριον ὄρθρος, to-morrow morning; βαθὺς ὄρθρος, Arist. Vesp. 216. Plato's Crito 43 and Prot. 310. Luke 24, 1.

p. 748.] The sense of downward motion in *abend* is confirmed by 'diu sunne begunde senken u. *aben* (sinking and offing) tegelich,' Heinz v. K.'s Kitt. u. pf. 5. AS. *cwild*= conticinium, ON. *qveld;* conf. Goth. *anaqal*=quies. ON. *húm*= crepusculum, AS. *glom*. The ON. röckur=crepusculum (p. 813) is in Swed. *skymming*, Dan. *skumring*, LG. *schemmer, schummer-licht;* conf. Boh. and Russ. sumrak, and the name Simrock [sú-mrak, sú-merki=half-mirk, subtenebrae, fr. mrak, mórok= mirk]. ON. *skoera*, twilight, Olaf helg. s., ed. Christ. 47, 25.

Diu *tunkle*, evening twilight, Osw. 2013-71; OHG. *tunchali*, Graff 5, 435. Swed. *tysmörk*, Dan. *tusmörke* crepusculum (p. 814 n.). Vesperzît, sô diu *sunne schate gît* (gives shadow), Mar. 158, 7; conf. δύσετό τ' ἠέλιος, σκιόωντό τε πᾶσαι ἀγυιαί, Od. 11, 12. 15, 185. Twilight is also *eulen-flucht*, or simply *eule*, owl, Firmen. 1, 268. Si *bran úf* schône sam der âbentrôt, MS. 1, 34ᵃ. ON. *qvöldroði*, aurora vespertina. ' Abentrôt, der kündet *lûter mære*,' Walth. 30, 15. Modern : ' abendroth gut wetter bot,' or ' ab. bringt morgenbrot,' or ' der morgen grau, der abend roth, ist ein guter wetterbot,' Simrock's Spr. 20. 19. 7099. On the other hand : Εὐάγγελος μὲν, ὥσπερ ἡ παροιμία, ῞Εως γένοιτο μητρὸς εὐφρόνης πάρα, Aesch. Agam. 264.

p. 749.] Ssk. *ušas* aurora, dual ušâsâ, Bopp's Gl. 53ᵇ; Lat. aurora for ausosa; Att. ἕως, Ion. ἠώς, Dor. ἀώς, Æol. αὔως ; conf. Ostarâ (p. 290). The blush of dawn is expr. in Ssk. by *narîr*, the virgins, Gött. anz. '47, p. 1482. In Theocr. 2, 147 the goddess rosy-armed is drawn by steeds (Suppl. to 738) ; ' constiteram *exorientem auroram* forte *salutans*,' Cic. de Nat. D. 1, 28 (conf. Creuzer p. 126). On the Slav. *Iutri-bogh* as god of morning, see Myth. ed. 1, p. 349 n.

p. 750.] The origin of '*Hennil, Hennil, wache !*' in the Mark is still unexplained. Observe, that tales are told of *Strong Hennel* as of Strong Hans, and that *honidlo*, acc. to Wend. volksl. 2, 270ᵃ, actually means a shepherd's staff. Like that shepherd in Dietmar, the Roman fetialis, when about to declare war, entered the sanctuary, and waved the shields and lance of the god's image, crying, ' *Mars, vigila !* ' Hartung 2, 168. Serv. ad. Aen. 8, 3.——Both in France and Germany the watchman, the *vrône wehter* (MSH. 3, 428ᵇ), blew the day in with his horn ; his songs were called *tage-lieder, aubades*. ' La *gaite* corne, qui les chalemiaus tint,' Garin 1, 219; les *gaites* cornent desor le mur anti 2, 117. 158; la *guete* cuida que laube fust crevee, il *tret le jor*, et *huche* et *crie*, Méon 1, 195 ; et la *guete* ert desus la porte, devant le jor *corne* et *fretele* 1, 200. ' Der *wahtaere* diu *tage-liet* (pl.) sô lûte erhaben hât,' Walth. 89. 35 (see Lachm. on W. p. 202); den tac man *kündet* dur diu *horn* (pl.), MS. 2, 190ᵇ; diu naht was ergangen, man *seite* ez wolde tagen, Nib. 980, 1 ; wahter hüet hôh enbor, MS. 1, 90ᵇ ; er erschelt ein *horn* an der stunt, dâmit tet er den liuten kunt des tages kunft gewalticlich,

Ls. 3, 311. He cries: 'ich sich *in her gân* (I see him come on), der mich wol erfröuwen mac, *her gât* der liehte schoene tac,' ibid.; smerghens alse die *wachter* blies, Floris 1935; der uns den tag *herblies*, Liederb. of 1582. 28, *anblies* 238; der wechter blost an, Keisersp. Brösaml. 25ᵈ; 'the watchman blows the rest,' Eliz. of Orl. 502; the warder or 'hausmann' blows the day off, he comes of himself, Drei Erzn. p. 443; 'der wechter ob dem *kasten*,' the guard over the coach-boot. Did watchmen carry a mace called *morgenstern?* see Hollberg's Ellefte Juni 5, 9. Frisch 1, 670 says it was invented in 1347.

p. 750.] Day is *beautiful* and *joyous*: der tac schoen u. grîse sîn lieht beginnet mêren, Troj. kr. 9173; daz lieht *mit vreuden* ûf trat, Pass. 329, 54. On the contrary, 'das abendroth im westen *welkt*,' fades, pales, Schm. v. Wern. 253. The morning star is harbinger of day (p. 752 n.): daz im der tage-sterre vruo kunte den tac, Ksrchr. 7885; ἀστὴρ ἀγγέλλων φάος, Od. 13, 94.

Birds rejoice at his coming: ἡνίκα ὄρνιθες ᾄσωσι πρῶτοι, Charon. Fragm. 34ᵇ; ὁ ὄρνις τὴν ἔω καλῶν, Athen. 4, 36: daz cleine süeze *vogellín* kan dingen (reckon) ûf den morgenschîn, u. sich des tages fröuwen muoz, Troj. kr. 20309; nam diu naht ein ende, die *vogel* des niht wolden durch iemans freuden swende verswîgen, wan sie sungen als sie solden (would for no man's pleasure hush, until, &c.), Tit. 5364; noch süezer denne dem voglîn morgens vrône, Frauenl. Ettm. p. 27; de voghel den dach smorghens groette, als hine sach, Rose 7832 (conf. 'den kleinen vogellîn *tröumet ûf esten*,' dream on the boughs, MS. 2, 166ᵇ). Cock-crow announces day: ἐξέργεσθαι ἤδη ἀλεκτρυόνων ᾀδόντων, Plato's Symp. 223; der han hât zwir (twice) gekraet, ez nâhet gên dem morgen, MS. 2, 152ᵃ; as de hanens den dag inkreggeden (crowed-in), Lyra p. 114.

p. 752.] The swift approach of Night, its falling, sinking, is expr. in many turns of speech: ez taget lanc (slowly), u. *nahtet drât*, Teichn. 70; als die nacht mit *aller gewalt* (all her might) herein brach, Drei klügste leute 146. That night breaks in, whereas day breaks forth, has been remarked by Pott 1, 236; yet Goethe says 'die nacht *bricht an*,' Faust 126; cum nox *inrueret*, Greg. Tur. 10, 24; wie die nacht *herbrach*, Katzip. ciᵇ; biss das der abend *hereindrang* (pressed in), Fischart's Gl. schif 1131; *forth* of each nook and corner *crowds* the night, Goethe; dô *viel*

sîn gaeher âbent *an*, Trist. 314 ; diu naht nu sêre *zuo gâht*, Türl.
Wh. 26ᵃ ; die n. *rückt mit gewalt ein*, Maulaffe 569 ; die n. *rasche
quam*, Hpt's Ztschr. 5, 338 ; es *schiesst* (et schütt, it shoots) in
den abend, Schütze 4, 33.   Night came *upon the neck* of us,
Ungr. Simpl. 65.   Ettn. Apoth. 877 ; ' die n. *stösst an*,' bumps
against, Weisth. 1, 305 ; ' it was avent, de n. *anstoet*,' Reineke 4,
1.   'Niht *becom*,' supervenit, Beow. 230 ; conf. εἰς ὅκεν ἔλθῃ
δείελος ὀψὲ δύων, σκιάσῃ δ' ἐρίβωλον ἄρουραν, Il. 21, 231 ; ἤδη
γὰρ καὶ ἐπήλυθε δείελον ἦμαρ, Od: 17, 606 ; as de avent *in't lant*
kem, Müllenh. p. 201,; *trat* de n. *an*, Weisth. 3, 87 ; die n. *betritt*
ihn (tramples) 3, 457 ; conf. ' wan sie die n. *betrift*,' hits 3, 785,
and ' bis die dämmerung *eintrat*,' Felsenb. 4, 63.   2, 599, *herein
tritt*,' steps in 4, 144 ; ' die naht hinzuo *geschreit*,' strode up to,
Troj. kr. 10119 ; ' *nâhet* in diu naht,' nears them, Nib. 1756, 1 ;
' en hadde die n. niet *ane gegaen*,' not come on, Karel 2, 934 ; do
diu naht (der âbent) *ane gie*, Lanz. 3210.   Flore 3497.   Diemer
27, 4.   Frauend. 342, 30.   Iw. 3904 ; *gieng* der abend *her*, Götz
v. Berl. 82 ; hie mite gienc der âbent hin, u. diu naht heran *lief*
(ran), Pass. 47, 84 ; diu vinstere n. her ouch *swanc*, als si in ir
loufe *lief* 36, 41 ; als diu n. hin *gelief* 81, 86 ; diu n. kumt dâher
*gerant*, Dietr. drach. 336ᵇ.

Again, night sinks, bends, falls : der âbent was *zuo gesigen*,
Diut. 1, 351 ; ist diu naht *herzuo gesigen*, Troj. kr. 11718 ; diu
n. *sîget zuo*, Dietr. drach. 154ᵃ ; uns *sîget* balde *zuo* diu n., Lanz.
709 ; diu n. begunde *sîgen an*, Morolt 1620. 3963 ; diu n. *sîget
an*, Dietr. dr. 327ᵇ; diu n. vast ûf uns *neiget* (bends), Hätzl.
192, 112.——Or day sinks, and night *climbs* : dô der tac hin
*seic*, diu n. herzuo *steic*, Dietr. 9695 ; biz der dach nider begunde
*sîgen*, inde die nacht *up-stigen*, Karlmeinet p. 18 ; li jours va a
*declin*, si *aproche* la nuit, Berte 54 ; li jors *sen va*, et la nuis
*asseri*, Garins 2, 157 ; la nuiz *va aprochant*, si *declina* le jor,
Guitecl. 2, 169 ; nu begund diu sunne *sîgen*, u. der âbentsterne
*stîgen*, Zwei koufm. 180 ; ez begunde *sîgen* der tac, Er. 221 ;
à la *brune*, à la *chute* du jour.   Similar are the phrases : der tac
was iezuo *hin getreten*, Pass. 27, 7 ; der tag *gieng* zu dem abend,
Uhl. 1, 246 ; conf. ' dagr *var â sinnum*,' inclined to evening,
Sæm. 104ᵇ.   In the same way : der tac hiemit ein *ende nam*,
diu vinster naht mit trüebe *kam*, Pass. 19, 3 ; der tac *sleich*
hin, u. *kam* diu naht, Freib. Trist. 4705 ; ja *swant* (vanished)

der tac, u. *wuohs* (grew) diu naht, Heinz v. Konst. Ritt. u. pf.
7; conf. Lat. *adulta* nocte; dô der tac *verswant*, G. frau 2013.
2427; LG. '*he lett dagen u. swinen,*' '*schemmern u. dagen,*'
Strodtm. 200. 238. Brem. wtb. 4, 634; 'dô der tac zerstoeret
wart von der vinsternisse grôz, u. diu n. *herzuo geflôz,*' came
flowing up, Troj. kr. 10489; der tac *gefluze* hin 8519; dô der t.
was *ergân*, Diemer 149, 25; 'als der t. was *gelegen,*' lain down,
Ernst 4679; 'dô der t. *lie sînen schîn,*' let be, left off, Troj. kr.
11095; 'der t. sîn *wunne verlât,*' his bliss forsakes, MS. 2, 192ᵇ;
der t. sîn *lieht verlât* 2, 496ᵇ; der t. *lât* sînen *glast*, Troj. kr.
8480; dô des tages lieht *verswein*, Barl. 368, 3; siððan *œfen-
leoht* under heofenes hâdor *beholen* weorðeð, Beow. 821; der tac
*gieng* mit freuden *hin*, dô diu naht ir trüeben schîn über al
die werlt gespreite, Gerh. 4931; æfenscîma *forð gewât*, Cædm.
147, 30; der tac begerte urloubes (took leave) mit *liuhte*, Tit.
3743.

Night catches, grasps: diu naht *begrîfet*, Tit. 3752. Dietr.
dr. 97ᵃ. Heinr. Trist. 4650; die nacht hevet mi hier *begrepen*,
Maerl. 3, 157; unz si *begreif* diu naht, Wolfd. 302, 1; unz daz
si dâ diu n. *begreif*, Mai 39, 5; die nacht kompt *geslichen*, Ld.
1582, 53. Night covers, spreads her mantle: þâ com æfter
niht on lâst dæge, lagu-streámas *wreáh*, Cædm. 147, 32; 'ja
waene diu n. welle uns nicht *wern* mêr,' will not guard us more,
Nib. 1787, 2; die nacht war *für augen*, Drei kluge leute 147;
evening was *at the door*, Pol. maulaffe 171; der abend all bereit
*vor der hand*, Schweinichen 1, 87; dô man des âbindis *intsuob*,
Athis C*, 153.

Night was deemed *hateful, hostile*, Benfey 2, 224: Grk δείλη,
δείελος evening is akin to δειλός timid, δείδω I fear; conf. νὺξ
ὀλοή, Od. 11, 19, *naht-eise* horror noctis, and Shaksp.'s ' grim-
looked night.' The Lith. '*naktis ne brolis*, night is no man's
friend' occurs already in Scherer's St. Gall. Mss. 34ᵃ: die
nacht niemand ze freunde hat, and in H. Sachs 1, 233ᶜ. On
the other hand: 'la nuit porte avis,' conf. to sleep upon a thing.

p. 752.] 'Night has the *victory won*' is also in Rosen-g.
1119; der tac *vertreip* diu vinster naht, Frauend. 344, 31; per
contra: diu n. den t. *het verswant* 271, 25. A full descr. of
night's victory, with ' her *dusky banner* hung on all high towers,'
in Ls. 3, 307.

p. 753.] The notion of night's *gloominess* preponderates!
ἀλλ᾿ ἤτοι νῦν μὲν πειθώμεθα νυκτὶ μελαίνῃ, Od. 12, 291. OS.
*thiustri* naht, Hel. 133, 4, etc.; de *dustere* nacht, Hpt's Ztschr. 5,
393; in dero *naht-finstri* bechlepfet, N. Cap. 13; diu *vinster*
n., Frauend. 339, 30, etc.; diu *tôt-vinster* n., Lanz. 6538; diu
*swarze* n., Herb. 7964. In thieves' lingo, *schwarz* = night;
diu *trüebe* n., Wh. 2, 10. Swiss ' *kidige* nacht,' pitch-dark,
Stald. 2, 98 (kiden = ring out, pierce); bei *eitler* naht, Abele's
Gerichts-h. 1, 391. Uhl. Volksl. 683 (Ambras. Ldrb. 1582, 377).
AS. ' on *wanre* niht,' pale, Beow. 1398; niht *wan* under wolcnum 1295; conf. OS. wanum undar wolcnum, Hel. 19, 20, morgan
wanum 21, 1; *niht-helma* genipu, Cod. Exon. 160, 12; *sceadu-
helma* gesceapu *scríðan* cwômon, Beow. 1293; ON. *grîma*, larva,
means also conticinium, quando omnia quasi obvelata caligine
videntur.——In *voller* nacht (pleine nuit), Schweinich. 3, 59. 87.
234; ' die *geschlagene* n.,' stricken, hushed, Matth. Pred. v. Luth.
p. 27. Philand. 2, 83; *beloken* n., Rein. 2271 (illunis?); nuit
*close*, Babou 219; schon weicht die *tiefe* n., Goethe 12, 242 =
succincta nox, Sid. Apoll. Epist. 3, 3; ἀλλ᾿ ὅτε δὴ τρίχα νυκτὸς
ἐήν, μετὰ δ᾿ ἄστρα βεβήκει, Od. 12, 312. 14, 483, conf. the seven
parts of night, Fernow's Dante 2, 229.——Night is long, νὺξ
μακρή, Od. 11, 373; often called *intempesta nox*, unseasonable
(for work): dum se *intempesta* nox *praecipitat*, Cato de Mor.;
conf. the ON. adj. *niol*, Sæm. 51ᵃ (AS. neol, neowol = prona?).
But also εὐφρόνη, the kindly (comforting?), Hes. Op. et D. 562;
OHG. *kistillandi* naht, Diut. 1, 251; 'dô was diu *süeze* n. für,'
gone by, Lanz. 1115. On *modranect*, see Hattemer 1, 334. The
midnight hour is fittest for deciding the fates of men (p. 858-9).

---

# CHAPTER XXIV.

## SUMMER AND WINTER.

p. 754.] Winter is called bird-killer, οἰωνοκτόνος, Aesch.
Agam. 563, and ' der vogele nôt,' MSH. 1, 53ᵇ. A M. Neth.
poem (Karel 2, 133) says : ' so dat si ten naesten Meye metten
vogelen gescreye porren moghen,' may march out mid the songs
of birds; 'wie der Meie vögelin *vroene* macht,' gladdens, elevates,
MS. 1, 31ᵇ.

p. 755.]  Sl. *iar* (spring) = yêr (year), says Miklos. 110; Zend.
*yâre* (year), Pott 2, 557.  Bopp, conf. Gramm. p. 568.  Kuhn's
Ztschr. 2, 269 connects yêr with ὥρα, *hora*.  Bekker in Monats-
ber. '60, p. 161 says ἔαρ for Ϝέαρ = vēr.  We may also conn.
ἔαρ with ἦρι (early), as our frühling with früh.  Kuhn thinks
ver is for ves, Ssk. vasantas (spring); conf. vasas, vâsara (day),
vasta (daylight).  Ssk. *vatsara* (year), Bopp's Gl. 306ᵇ.  Finn.
*vuosi* (year), Esth. *aast*, conf. Lat. aestas; in Kalev. 1, 248
*vuosi* year, and *kesä* summer, seem synonymous.  Ssk. *samâ,*
annus, is fem. of sama, similis, Bopp and GDS. 72 seq.  Lenz
(spring) is also *langsi, lanxi, lanzig,* Stald. 2, 156; *somer* ende
*lentîn,* Rose 7326.

p. 755.]  Change of season, change of year is expr. by ' diu̯
zît hât sich *verwandelôt,*' MS. 1, 78ᵇ; conf. 'in der *zîte jâren,*'
years of time, Mai 107, 18.  To the Egyptians the year *sails
round,* whilst in German 'unz *umb kam* daz jâr,' Otnit 899; ein
*umbe-gêndez* jâr, Trist. Frib. 1079; ein mând in (a month to
them) des jâres *trit,* Pass. 162, 58; das *rollende* jahr.——In *gui-
l'an-neuf,* gui is mistletoe (p. 1206); conf. our Germ. cries:
' drei *hiefen* (3 blasts on the bugle) zum neuen jahr!' Schm. 2,
156; 'glückseligs neues jahr, drei *hiefen* z. n. j.!' Frisch 1, 452ᶜ
from Besold.  New-year is expr. by 'sô sich daz jâr *geniuwet*
hât' in springtime, Warnung 2291; or 'wann daz jâr *auz-
chumpt,*' out comes, Gesta Rom. Keller 99; do das jar *auskom,*
Weisth. 3, 650; but also by the simple ' New.'

p. 756.]  The idea of the *whole year* is now and then personified, both in wishes and otherwise: Got gebe uns wunneclîche
jâr, Reinh. acc. to var. 2248 (ms. P.K.); guot jâr *gange* si *an*
(encounter them), Kistener 1188; conf. übel-jâr, mal-anno
(p. 1160 end); do das jar *auskom,* Weisth. 3, 650; ehe ein jahr
in das land *kommt,* Drei Erzn. 266; ehe zwei jahre in's land *gehn,*
Pol. maul. 8; daz vünfte jâr *in gie,* Trist. 151, 27; that jâr
*furdor skrêd* (strode), Hel. 13, 23 (conf. AS. forð gewât dæg-rîmes
worn (numeri dierum multitudo), Cædm. 60, 1, see ' dæg-r.
worn' 80, 20. 156, 51); le bonhomme *l'année,* Mém. de l'acad.
celt. 4, 429.  In the Bacchica pompa Ἐνιαυτός appears as a
*giant* with four elbows (τετράπηχυς, 4 cubits high?), bearing
Amalthea's horn, Athen. 5, 198 (Schw. 2, 263).

p. 757.]  Also in Hel. 14, 10 : ' sô filu *wintro* endi *sumaro*'

means the same as AS. fela missera; but 5, 1. 2, where Zacharias
says he was 'tuêntig wintro' old when he married Elisabeth,
and has lived with her 'antsibunta (70) wintro,' he is 90 years
old, and *wintar* stands for year. The AS. midwinter, ON.
miðvetr, appears in M. Neth. as *medewinter*, Lanc. 13879, *midde-
winter* 23907. A computation of *sumor* and *lencten*, Andr. &
El. p. xxiv. Leo's Rectitud. 212-3. The ON. *dœgr* is Swed. *dygn.*
Gudrun says in Sæm. 232[b]: 'fôr ek af fialli *fimm dœgr talið*,'
fared I from the fell 5 days told; conf. F. Magn. Dagens tider,
p. 28. The sacredness of *Midsummer* and *Midwinter*, of St.
John's day, sunnewende (p. 617) and yule, favours the dual
division : on the night of St. John, vigils are kept in field and
lawn under gold-apple tree, Molbech no. 49. Norske eventyr
no. 52. KM. no. 57.

p. 758.] As to a connexion between Tacitus's three seasons
and *Wodan's three progresses*, see Kuhn in Hpt's Ztschr. 5, 493.
It seems to speak for the three seasons, that often only *three
assizes* are recorded in a year; and still more, that *three great
sacrifices* were offered, in autumn til ârs, in winter til grôðrar, in
summer til sigrs, Yngl. s. cap. 8; *tribus temporibus* anni, Lacomb.
no. 186 (yr 1051). Gipsies divide the year into *two* and *six*
seasons, says Pott 1, 66. The Persian, like the Spaniard, had
two springtimes, for Fasli in the Gülistan speaks of the Shah
*Spring*, Shah Summer, Shah Autumn, Shah Winter, and Shah
*New-year* (newrus) = March, who reintroduces the spring. ON.
*haust*, Swed. *höst*, is an abbrev. of herbist, hærfest [Scot. hair'st],
see Gramm. 2, 368. In Up. Hesse also they call spring *auswarts*,
Vilmar's Hess. Ztschr. 4, 52.

p. 761.] Spring is expr. by the phrases : ez was in der zîte
*aller bluomen ursprinc*, Flore 5529; sô die bluomen enspringent
153; von den bluomen wie sie sprungen 821; conf. flos in *vere
novo*, Pertz 5, 735. More vividly personal are the adjs. in : ' der
*lange* frühling,' E. Meier's Schwäb. märch. p. 303; '*vil lieber*
Sumer, der *liebe* S.,' MS. 1, 167[b]. MSH. 3, 212[a]; diu *liebe*
sumerzît, MS. 2, 108[a]; diu *liebe* sumer-wunne, Dietr. 381;
*saelige* sumerzît, MS. 2, 108[b] (our ' die liebe zeit '); and even
' der *heilige* sumer,' Myst. i. 312, 2. To which is opposed 'der
*leidig* winter,' MSH. 3, 215[b]; 'die *felle* winter,' Rose 53. 62.
Both seasons come and go : '*ira* yvers, si *revenra* estez,' Orange

2, 75; OS. *skrêd* the wintar *ford*, Hel. 6, 13; hiems saeva *transiit*,
Carm. bur. 193; swanne der winter *abe gienc*, unde der sumer
ane vienc, Alex. 5094; Neth. die winter *ginc in hant*, Maerl. 2, 8
(like : binnen dien ginc die nacht in hant, Lanc. 46927); als die
winter *inginc*, Lanc. 36044; *geht* der winter *daher*, Götz v. Berl.
246; der *vorder Winterklaub* herwider hat gehauset sich auf
seinen *alten sitz*, Wolkenst. 67; nu *ist* der leide winter *hie*, Ben.
396; der sumer ist *comen in* diu lant, MS. 2, 83ᵃ; pis *kumt* der
sumer *hêre*, Otnit (V. d. Rön) 29; unz uffen S. Urbans tac, danne
*gat* der sumer *in*, H. Martina bl. 250; si jehent, der sumer der
*sî hie*, MS. 1, 67ᵇ; es *geet* ein frischer freier sommer *da herein*,
Bergreien 71; ver *redit* optatum, Carm. bur. 178.——Or, instead
of Summer, it is *May*, as *mai-gesäss* means summer-pasture,
Stalder 293; als der *Meie in gât*, Warn. 1887; an S. Philippen-
tage, sô der Meie alrêrst *in gât*, Frauend. 63, 13; alse die Mey
*in quam*, entie April *orlof nam*, Lanc. 23434; ' dâ hât uns der
Meie sînen *krâm* (wares) erloubet, ze suochen, swaz wir sîner
varwe geruochen,' to pick what we please, MS. 2, 167ᵃ; des
Meien *blic*, Tit. 32, 2; dô man des liehten Meigen *spil* mit
sîner blüete komen sach, Troj. 6889; Meie, die heide grüeze !
MS. 2, 167ᵇ; der Meie hât die heide *geêret* 2, 52ᵃ : ' der winder
twanc die heide, nu grüenet si *im ze leide*,' to spite him, Ben.
453; flower-leaves, whereon ' der May sein *dolden* (umbels)
henget,' Suchenw. 46, 28; des liehten Meien *schar* (company)
stât *bekleit* in *purpur-var* (-hue), MSH. 3, 195ᵇ; flowers are
' des Meien *künne*,' MS. 2, 22ᵃ, and ' *sumer-geraete*' 1, 194ᵇ;
uf Walpurgen tag xv. gebunt *Mei-gerten* (-switches), Weisth.
3, 497; ' giezent nur den *Meien* under ougen !' sings a girl in
MS. 2, 74ᵇ; does it mean ' put the garland on me '?  Mai, dein
*gezelt* (pavilion) gefellt mir wol, Wolkenst. 116.——May has
power : ich lobe dich, Meie, dîner *kraft*, MS. 2, 57ᵃ; des Meies
*virtuit*, Uhl. 1, 178; gên wir zuo des Meien *hôch-gezîte* (hightide),
der ist mit *aller sîner krefte* komen, Walth. 46, 22 (Lachm. is
wrong in note to Nibel. p. 6). So : in der sumerlîchen *maht*,
Parz. 493, 6; der sumer mit sîner *kraft*, MS. 1, 37ᵃ; des Meien
*kraft* sie brâhte dar, der was der mâlaere (painter), Blicker 79;
der winter twinget mit sîner *kraft*, MS. 1, 37ᵇ; des Aberellen
kraft, Hpt's Ztschr. 6, 353, and so of all the months.  With
power is blended goodness : des Meien *güete* u. *kraft*, Muscatbl.

in Altd. mus. 2, 189 ; ze veld u. ûf der heide lac der Mai mit
sîner *güete*, Hätzl. 131, 6. Suchenw. 46, 15 ; des Meigen *güete*,
Hätzl. 159, 584. Troj. 16213 ; conf. thera zîti guâti (Suppl. to
791) ; der Meie hete dô *gevröut* (gladdened) mit der liehten
künfte sîn (his coming) diu wilden waltvogelîn, Partenopier 45,
18 ; sumer, du hâst manege *güete*, Lachm. Walth. xvii. 7. Summer
brings bliss : si jehent, der sumer der sî hie, diu *wunne* diu sî
komen, MS. 1, 67ᵇ ; 'heia *sumerwunne*, swer uns dîn erbunne!'
grudge us thee 2, 63ᵃ ; sît die *sumerw.* alrêrst begunde nâhen 2,
74ᵇ ; er ist komen wider mit gewalde, den der Meige hât vertriben;
sumerw. ist im entrunnen (fled before him) balde, der ist vor im
niht gebliben, Frauend. 507 ; *sumerw.*, nîg dem süezen Meigen,
MS. 2, 22ᵇ ; der *sumerw. güete*, Flore 165 ; zur *somerw.*, Baur
no. 718.——The Germ. Summer or May stands on a par with
the Scand. god Freyr returning from exile (p. 212-3), as indeed
*Maia, Flora, Aprilis* were goddesses to the Romans. A tree
breaks into blossom when a *god settles* upon it :

> seht ir den boum, der dâ stât,
> der loubes vil u. bluomen hât,
> *ein got hât sich dâ nider gelân* (let himself down),
> ân den (without him) môhte ez niht ergân,
> ez ist bî namen Tervigant.      Geo. 2162.

The poet of the Warnung sings :

> nu minnet (ye adore) bluomen unde gras,
> niht in der (not Him who) sîn meister was ;
> wîp unt vogel-gesanc
> unt die liehten tage lanc,
> der sache jegelîche (all such things)
> nemt ze einem *himelriche.*      Hpt's Ztschr. 1, 495.

And still more distinctly :

> einer *anbetet* (one adores) daz vogel-sanc
> unt die liehten tage lanc,
> darzuo bluomen unde gras,
> daz ie des vihes spîse was (cattle's food) ;
> diu rinder vrezzent den *got* (oxen gobble your god); ibid. 1, 500

Green foliage is the gàrment of May and Summer : quoique le bois
reprenne sa *robe d'été*, Villem. Bardes Bret. 215 ; sumer-*kleit* hât

er ir gesniten (cut out), MS. 2, 47$^b$; der Sumer wil rîchen
manigen boum mit loubes *wât* (leafy dress) 2, 83$^a$; heide u. anger
habent sich bereitet mit der schoensten *wât*, die in der Meie hât
gesant (which May has sent them) 2, 83$^a$; herbest, der des Meien
*wât* vellet von den rîsen (cuts fr. the twigs) 2, 105$^a$; vil rîcher
*wât*, die Meie hât 1, 192$^a$; sich hâte *gevazzet* (collected) der walt,
u. schoeniu *kleit* gein dem sumer an-geleit (put on), Maurit. 1684;
in *Meigeschem* walde, Tit. 143, 1; solutis Ver nivibus *viridem*
monti reparavit *amictum*, Claud. B. Get. 168.

p. 762.] Winter is a ruthless ruffian warrior : 'spiteful W.'s
envy' is complained of, MS. 1, 192$^a$; 'der *arge* Winter *twanc*,'
oppressed, ibid.; der W. *bant* (also *twanc*) die heide 2, 78$^{ab}$; nu
ist der blüenden heide *voget* (tyrant) mit *gewalt* ûf uns gezoget,
hoert wi'er mit winde *broget* (blusters) 1, 193$^a$; des leiden
Winters *überlast*, der sî verwâzen (be cursed) u. sîn *roup !* 2, 20$^b$.
Winter has an *ingesinde*, retinue, Hpt's Ztschr. 4, 311; des
Winters *wâfen* tragen (weapons carry), MsH. 1, 328$^a$. But May
is armed too, and fights him : mein ros schrait (my steed strides)
gên des Maien *schilt*, Wolkenst. 115; diu sunne dringet liehtem
Meien dur den grüenen *schilt*, der von loube schaten birt (brings
leafy shade) den kleinen vogellîn, MsH. 1, 150$^b$. His fight with
W. is descr. in detail in the Song of battle betw. Summer and
W., Uhl. Volksl. p. 23. The AS. already has : þâ wæs W.
*scacen*, fæger folden bearm, Beow. 2266 (yet see p. 779 n.);
brumalis est *ferita* rabies, Archipoeta p. 76; Winder, wie ist nu
dîn kraft worden gar *unsigehaft* (unvictorious), sît der Meie
*sînen schaft* hât ûf dir verstochen, MSH. 3, 195$^b$; fuort mich
durch des Meien *her* (host), der mit ritterlîcher wer den W. hât
*erslagen* (slain), Hätzl. 131, 51; winder ist *nider valt* (felled),
Wiggert 37; hin sont wir den W. *jagen* (chase away), Conr. v.
Ammenh. extr. W. p. 51; wol hin, her W., ir müezt ie *ze rûme in*
*bergen*, Frauenl. 369, 16; der sumerwünne den *strît* lân (drop the
strife with), Flore 150. Haupt on Neidh. 45, 12 takes *Aucholf*
to be for oukolf in the sense of krotolf (p. 206); yet also Goth.
auhjôn = tumultuari might be brought in. The names *Maibôm*,
*Meienrîs* (Closener 68) point back to old customs; the island
*Meigen-ouwe*, now Meinau, perh. to an ancient site of the spring
festival.

p. 762.] A sweet May-song in Wolkenst. no. 63, p. 173 : liet,

dâ si mite *enpfâhen* den Meigen. To welcome the spring is in
ON. ' þâ *fagna* þeir sumri,' Maurer 2, 232 ; alle die vogel froelîche
den Sumer singende *enphânt*, MS. 1, 21ᵃ ; *entphâhen* die wunig-
lîchen zît, Diut. 2, 92 ; *ontfaet* den Mei met bloemen, hi is so
schone ghedaen, Uhl. Volksl. 178 ; sleust uns auf (unlock) die tür,
u. *lest* den Sumer *herein*, Fastn. sp. p. 1103; ir sült den Sumer
*grüezen*, u. al sîn ingesinde, MSH. 3, 202ᵃ ; Meie, bis (be) uns
*willekomen*, MS. 1, 194ᵇ ; wis (be) *willekomen*, wunneclîcher Meie
1, 196ᵃ. *May* and *Summer* are distinguished: sint willekomen *frô
Sumerzit*, sint will. der Meie 1, 59ᵃ ; ich klage dir, *Meie*, ich klage
dir, *Sumerwunne* 1, 3ᵇ.

'In den Meien *riden*' was a real custom, Soester fehde p. 660.
The men of Mistelgau near Baireuth sent envoys to Nürnbg. to
fetch Spring. They were given a humblebee shut up in a box
(Suppl. to 697) ; but curiosity led them to peep in, and the bee
escaped. They shouted after it 'na Mistelgau !' and sure enough
the long rain was followed by fine weather, Panz. Beitr. 2, 173 ;
conf. Herod. 7, 162, where a country has the spring taken out of
its year.

p. 763.] The coming of Summer is known by the opening of
flowers, the arrival of birds : der sumer ist komen schône *über mer*
hât uns ze lande brâht ein *wunniclîchez her*, MSH. 3, 226ᵃ, as in
Ssk. spring is called *kusumâkara*, florum multitudinem habens ;
dô man die sumerwunne bî der *vogel reise* erkande, dô lôste der
Mei die *bluomen* ûz den tiefen banden 3, 229ᵇ ; der sumer ist mit
*süezem sange* schône *erwecket* 3, 241ᵇ ; doch kam ich ûf ein heide,
diu was liehter bluomen vol, dâran möht man schouwen wol, ob
der *Mai* ze velde lac, Ls. 1, 199. Nîthart leads the Duchess, with
pipers and fiddlers, to where he has thrown his hat over the (first)
*viol* ; kneels down and raises the hat, ' ir lât den sumer schînen,'
MSH. 3, 202ᵇ ; 's ersti veigerl brock i' dir z'liab, Firmen. 2, 798,
and Voss goes in search of the *first flowers* as spring-messengers,
Goethe 33, 148 ; the *first buttercup* and *hvitsippa* used to be
eaten, Dybeck '45, 68-9, conf. the *first* 3 *cornblossoms*, Superst.
I, 695. 1018. Tussilago, coltsfoot, is called *sommer-thürlein*
(-doorlet) and Merzblume, because it springs up immed. after the
snow has thawed; also filius ante patrem, filia ante matrem,
Nemnich 1515 ; Nethl. *zomer-zoetjes* (-sweetie) =galanthus nivalis.
Clover too is called *summerflower*, visumarus, Kl. schr. 2, 159.

p. 763.] *Chelidonium*, celandine, so called because it comes with the swallow and withers at his going, Dioscor. 2, 211. A spring song in Lucian's Tragopod. 43—53 (ed. Bip. 10, 4) makes *blossom, swallow*, and *nightingale* heralds of spring; if you see the first ploughman ply, the *first swallow* fly, &c., Sup. I, 1086; usque ad *adventum hirundineum* vel *ciconinum*, Sidon. Apoll. 2, 14; *ciconia redeuntis anni* jugiter *nuntiatrix*, ejiciens tristitiam hiemis, laetitiam verni temporis introducens, magnum pietatis tradit exemplum, Cassiod. Var. 2, 14; *Maien-bule, sommergeck*, Dict. 2, 506 sub v. bühl: conf. 'kunden vogel rehte schouwen, sô lobten sie ze *frouwen* für die *liehten sumerzît*, MS. 1, 84ᵃ.

p. 769.] Schwartz de Apoll. 33 compares *Apollo's* fight with the *dragon* to that betw. *Summer* and *Winter*. The song in Wiggert p. 37 says:

> Winder ist *nider valt* (felled).
> Winder, du bist swer sam ein blî (heavy as lead),
> Sumer, du kanst den Winder *stillen* (bring to reason).

In the Nethl. song of battle betw. *S.* and *W.* (Hor. Belg. 6, 125 —146) Venus comes and reconciles the 'brothers'; yet, at the very end, it says Winter has *had to be killed*—evidently the ending of an older song. Other pop. songs of summer in Firmen. 2, 15. 34. On the Eisenach *sommer-gewinn*, see Wolf's Ztschr. f. myth. 3, 157 and Hone's Daybk 1, 339 (conf. the May fetched by May-boys in Lyncker p. 35-6); the straw Winter is nailed to a wheel, *set on fire*, and *rolled downhill*, Daybk 1, 340. In Franconia the girls who carry Death out are called *death-maidens*, Schm. 1, 464. In Jever they have the custom of '*meiboem* setten,' Strackerjan p. 75.*

p. 781.] By the side of May appears the *May-bride*, Kuhn's Sag. pp. 384. 513, otherw. called *bühli, fastenbühli*, Stald. 1, 240. The *plighted pair* are sought for, Somm. p. 151, conf. 180;

---

* Our people's *love of a forest-life*, which comes out esp. at the summer-holiday, is shown in the following passages: ze *walde* gie, Kindh. Jesu 101, 12; (dancing on the meadow before the wood) reigen *vür den walt* an eine wise lange, MS. 2, 55ᵇ; ze *holze* loufen, reigen 2, 56ᵃ; daz dir ze *walde* stât der fuoz (for a dance), Winsbekin 29, 4. Haupt p. 78. Massm. Eracl. p. 609; wir suln *vor* disem *fürholz ligen* durch der bluomen smac u. der vogel gesanc, Wigam. 2472; ich wil *vor disem walde* ein hôchzît machen, u. herladen u. bitten frouwen u. ritter stolz an *diz grüene fürholz* 2477; vor dem walde in eime tal da sach man swenze blicken, die megde wurfen ouch den bal, MS. 2, 56ᵇ; vil schône ze walde, an dem werde, hebent sich die tenze 2, 57ᵇ.

the Swedes call her *midsummars-brud,* Wieselgr. 410.   Dk. Potter's Der minnen loep 1, 30-1.   Antonius de Arena (a Provence
poet, d. 1644) de villa de Soleriis (Souliers), Lond. 1758 informs
us : ' Cum igitur nunc se offerat hilarissimus mensis *Maïus,* quo
tempore omnes populi voluptati et gaudio, laetitiae et omni solatio
indulgere solent, ut inquit gloss. et ibi doctores in l. unica, C. de
*mayauma,* lib. xi, tunc enim apparent herbae frondesque virentes
et garritus avium, corda hominum laetificantes; *Bononiae,* et in
nostra *Provencia,* ac hîc *Avenione,* in viis *reginas* pro solatio
faciunt, *quas viri coguntur osculari.*   Item in dicto mense *Maïo*
amasii, in signum amoris et solatii causa amicarum, *altissimas*
*arbores* plantare solent, quas *Maïos* appellant' ; conf. Forcell. sub
v. majuma.——At Lons le Saunier and St Amour the prettiest
girl is chosen to be *nymphe du printemps,* is adorned, garlanded
and carried round in triumph, while some collect gifts, and
sing :

> étrennez notre *épousée !*
> voici le mois, le *joli mois de Mai,*
> étrennez notre *épousée*
>    en bonne étrenne !
> voici le mois, le *joli mois de Mai,*
>    *qu'on vous amène !*

In Bresse (now dept. Ain) the May-queen or May-bride, decked
with ribbons and flowers, walks first, led by a young man, while
a May-tree in blossom is carried in front.   The words of the song
are :

> voici venir le *joli  mois,*
> l'alouette plante le Mai,
> voici venir le *joli  mois,*
> l'alouette l'a planté.
> le coq prend sa *volée*
> et la volaille chante.

See Monnier's Culte des esprits dans la Sequanie.   In Lorrain
too he is called *joli Mâ.*

   The Italians danced at the spring holiday, Dönnige's Heinr. VII,
191 ; conf. the May-feast as descr. in Machiav. Stor. Fior. 1, 109.
149.   In ancient Italy, under stress of war or pestilence, they
vowed a *ver sacrum,* i.e. everything begotten and born that spring,

Niebuhr 1, 102. The Servian Whitsun queen is called *kralitza*, Vuk sub v.

p. 782 n.] Vier *frone vasten*, Meinauer's Naturl. p. 8; in der *fronfasten*, in den fronfasten, Keisersb. Om. 42-3. Did they have a matron go about muffled at that season? Er. Alberus in Fab. 39 says of a disorderly dressed female: 'sie gieng gleichwie ein *fassenacht*'; die liebe *frau fastnacht* u. den *jungherrn von fronfasten*, Bienenk. 49^b.

p. 784.] Does an AS. riddle in Cod. Exon. 417-8 refer to the *flying summer*? 'spinneweppe, daz sumers zît im gras ûf grüenen wisen lît,' Albr. v. Halb. 124^b. An Ital. proverb traces the spring gossamer to three Marys (see p. 416 n.): 've' quant' hanno *filato* questa notte *le tre Marie!*' conf. Indiculus 19: 'de petendo (pendulo?) quod boni vocant sanctae Mariae,' and Nemn. sub v. fila divae virginis. *Mädchen-* or *Mättchen-sommer* is supp. to mean Matthias' summer, from its appearing on that saint's day. Yet we read: de *metten* hebbt spunnen, Müllenh. p. 583. Now *Metje* is Matilda, Brem. wtb., and we actually find a 'Gobelinus de Rodenberg dictus *Mechtilde-sumer*,' Seibertz 2, 286 (yr 1338). Matthidia in Clemens' Recogn. becomes Mehthild in Ksrchr. 1245. Flying gossamer is called in India *maruddhvaǵa*, Mârut's flag, Hpt's Ztschr. 5, 490.

p. 786.] In England on May 1 the *hobby-horse* is led about, and also a bear, Haupt 5, 474; conf. the erbes-bär, Somm. p. 155-6. *Pingster-bloemen*, *Pinkster-blomen*, Whitsun-flowers, is the name given to the merry processionists at Jever, Strackerj. p. 76, and in Westphalia, Firmen. 1, 359. The Whitsun sleeper is nicknamed *pfinst-lümmel* (-looby) also in Mone's Schausp. 2, 371; in Silesia *rauch-fihs*, Berl. jrb. 10, 224. In Russia the *lieabed* on Palm Sunday is scourged with rods, Kohl's Russ. 2, 186. On *taudragil* see GDS. 509.

---

## CHAPTER XXV.

### TIME AND WORLD.

p. 791.] *Wîle, stunde*, Graff 4, 1224, *zît, wîle, stunde*, Uolr. 1554, and *stund, weil, zeit*, Wolkenst. 161 stand side by side; so our '*zeit* u. *weile* wird mir lang,' I feel dull. Wîle occurs even

with a numeral : unz (until) *drîe wîle* kômen hin, Servat. 2652.
As *Χρόνος* was a god, and *Καιρός* is called a graybeard, Tommaseo 3, 15. so is diu *wîle* personified, conf. *wîl-sœlde*, pp. 857 n.
863 ; ' der wîle *nîgen*,' bowing to w., MSH. 1, 358ᵃ ; *undanc* der
wîle *sagen*, Kl. 274 ; gêrt sî (honoured be) *diu wîle* unde *dirre
tac*, Parz. 801, 10 ; *saelic* wîle, saelic zît, MSH. 1, 296ᵃ, conf.
AS. *sael* = felicitas and tempus opportunum ; gistuant thera zîti
*guati* = instabat tempus, O. iv. 9, 1, conf. des Sumers güete, p.
760 n.——Above all, there is ascribed to Time a coming, going,
striding, advancing, drawing nigh, entering. Ssk. *amasa* time,
from *am* to go, Bopp, see Gramm. 491-2 ; Lith. *amźis*, Armor.
*amzer*, Kymr. *amser*, Ir. *am*. The Lat. *seculum* is fr. *sec* to go, Ssk.
sać fr. sak = sequi (or secare ? Pott, 2, 588). The OHG. *dîhsmo*,
conn. with Goth. þeihs, means processus, successus, advance,
Graff 5, 111. M. Neth. *tiden* = ire, Lekensp. 622. Gramm. 1,
978 ; diu wîle hete sich *vergangen*, Osw. 3443 ; die tît *ghinc vort*,
Maerl. 2, 364 ; þâ seo tîd *gewât* ofer tiber sceacan, Cædm. 9, 1 ;
thô ward thiu tîd *cuman*, Hel. 3, 14. 23-4. 25, 22 ; ein paar
stunden *kommen in's land*, Weise's Lustsp. 3, 198 ; es *giengen*
nicht drei tage *in's land*, Jucundiss. 36 ; ehe zwei jahre *in's land
gehen*, Pol. maulaffe 4 ; thiu tîd was *ginâhit*, Hel. 121, 21 ; *nâhtun
sih* thio hôhun gizîti, O. iv. 8, 1 ; zît wart *gireisôt*, O. i. 4, 11 ;
' swie *sich* diu zît *huop*,' arose, Tit. 88, 4 ; die tît, die nooit noch
*ghelac*, Rose 353 ; weil jetzt die zeit *beigeneigt*, Eichst. hexenpr.
85 ; thio zîti *sih bibráhtun*, O. iii. 4, 1 ; thô *sih* thiu zît *bibráhta*,
O. iv. 1, 7 ; dô *sik* de tîd *bráchte*, Sachsenchr. 205 ; dô *sik
bráchten* dusent u. twehundert jâr 226 ; forð baero (l. *baeron*)
tîd, Cædm. 8. 31 ; nie *sich* diu zît alsô *getruoc*, Trist. 13, 34 ; *sik*
hadde de tîd *gedragen*, Sachsenchr. 213 ; our ' what future time
might *bring with it*,' Irrg. d. liebe 248 ; ' die zeit *bringt's*.'

p. 792.] *Stunde*, hour, often stands for time : ' jâ gie in diu
*stunde* mit grôzer *kurz-wîle* hin,' their time went by with much
pas-time, Nib. 740, 4 ; nâch des Merzen *stunden*, Gudr. 1217, 3.
But the OS. *werolt-stunda* = mundus, Hel. 76, 5. 159, 11. The
M.Neth. also expressed a moment by ' en *stic*,' Rose 1952, and
by the phrases : ' biz man geruorte die brâ,' while one moved the
eyelid, Servat. 342 ; biz ein brâ die andern ruorte 3459 ; alsô
schiere (as fast as) diu ober brâ die nideren gerüeret, Hpt's
Ztschr. 2, 213.

p. 793.] Voss in Luise p. m. 220 ingeniously derives *werlt*, world, fr. werlen, to whirl. The *World* is often apostrophized by Walther 37, 24. 38, 13. 122, 7. In Ssk. the ages of the world are *yuga*, the two last and corrupt ones being *Dvâpara's* and *Kali's*, Bopp's Damay. p. 266. The men of the golden age are themselves called *golden*, Lucian's Saturn. 8. 20 (ed. Bip. 3, 386) ; conf. our Schlaraffenland, Cockaign, GDS. 1. 2. So in Ssk. the plur. of lôka (mundus) = homines ; and OHG. AS. ferah, feorh have ' mid ' prefixed to them, answering to mitil-gart, middan-geard : OHG. *midfiri*, *mittiverihi*, AS. *midfeorwe*. *Manasêps* seems to corresp. to the Eddic *alda ve iarðar*, Sæm. 23[b], populorum habitaculum, terra ab hominibus inhabitata (F. Magn. p. 255 n.), to which is opposed *ûtve* = *ûtgarðar*, gigantum habitacula. And the Gael. *siol*, seed, often stands for people, men.

p. 794.] Ssk. *lôka*, mundus, fr. lôć, lucere? conf. Lat. locus, Lith. laukas = campus ; ' disa *scônûn* werlt' in Notk. Bth. 147 transl. pulcrum mundum. The Hindûs also held by three worlds: heaven, earth and hell, Holtzm. Ind. s. 3, 121 ; *madhyama lôka* = media terra, quippe quae *inter coelum et infernum*, Bopp's Gl. 256[b]; or simply *Madhyama*, Pott 2, 354. The Greeks too divided the world into οὐρανός, γαῖα, τάρταρος, Hes. Theog. 720 (see Suppl. to 806). ON. heimr terra, himinn coelum, heimir infernus? Heimr is opposed to hel, Sæm. 94[b] ; liggja î milli heims ok heljar, Fornm. s. 3, 128 means to have lost consciousness. O. v. 25, 95. 103 puts all three in one sentence: ' in *erdu* joh in *himile*, in *abgrúnde* ouh hiar nidare.' Distinct fr. *middjungards*, earth, is Goth. *miþgards* = medium in the compound miþgardavaddjus, μεσό-τοιχον, Ephes. 2, 14. 'This *myddel-erde*,' Alisaunder p. 1 ; iz thisu *worolt* lêrta in *mittemo* iro *ringe*, O. iv. 19, 7 ; *ert-rinc*, Diemer 118, 23. 121, 1 ; der *irdiske ring*, Mar. 191, 16. Earth is called diu *gruntveste*, Rother 3651; OHG. *cruntfesti* fundamentum, Graff 3, 718. 'Daz *bû* vergieng,' the world perished, Wolkenst. 180. In the centre of the world lies an *old stone*, under it the measuring chain, Temme's Altmark p. 33 ; conf. navel-stone (p. 806). Other names : der maere *meregarte*, Karajan 22, 15 ; der *irdiske gibel*, Mar. 156, 40 ; daz *irdiske tal* 174, 34.

The *world-snake* has its head knocked off by a throw of Thôr's hammer, Sn. 63. Even Fischart in Gesch. kl. 31[b] says : ' When

Atlas wanted to shift the globe to his other shoulder, to see what
the *great fish* was doing whereon the *world* is said to *stand;'*
conf. Leviathan (p. 998).

p. 795.] The world is called ' der *vrône sal,*' lordly hall, Diemer
297, 6, which usu. means heaven; but ' der *sal* ' 326, 7 seems
to be temple. On the other hand: ' diz jâmertal,' vale of sorrow,
Renn. 896; diz *âmertal*, Griesh. Pred. 2, 101; in ditze *chlageliche
tal*, Mar. 148, 2. 198, 33; dieses *jammer* u. *kummerthal*, Schweinichen 1, 17; ' varen ûz disem *ellende,*' misery, Griesh. 2, 15;
ûz disem *ubelen wôftale*, Diem. 301, 2; in disem *angst-hause*,
Drei erzn. 270; von dirre *snoeden werlt*, Frib. Trist. 33.

p. 795.] There are several heavens: acc. to Diut. 3, 41 *ten*
at first, but after Lucifer's fall only *nine*. The Finns too have
*nine heavens*, taivahan yheksän an, Kal. 10, 190. 28, 308-9; vor
froeide *zuo den himeln* (ad coelos) springen, MS. 2, 47[a].

p. 800.] The World-tree is called *askr Yggdrasill* in Sæm. 3[b],
but *Yggdrasills askr* in 8[a]. 44-5. 89[a]; conf. the Low Sax. legend
of the ash (p. 960). Again: *miotviðr* kyndiz (is kindled), Sæm.
8[a]; *miotvið* maeran *fŷrir mold neðan* 1[a]; which is rendered arbor
centralis, for *miöt*=medium, says Magnusen. But Rask reads
myotviðr, and other expositors miötuðr. Is miötuðr the tree the
same as miotuðr, God (p. 22)? Again: ' it *aldna trê,*' Sæm. 8[a];
perh. also the word *aldurnari*, seculum servans 9[b] signifies the
same world-tree.——The *snake* gnawing at the roots of the ash
must mean mischief to it: well, Germ. superstition likewise places
enmity between *snake* and *ash*, Panz. Beitr. 1, 251-2. 351-2. A
somewhat doubtful legend tells of a world-old *druden-baum* on
the top of the Harberg near Plankstellen in Franconia, that its
leaves fr. time to time shed *golden drops, milk* oozed out of its
roots, and under it lay a treasure guarded by a *dragon;* on the
tree sat a great black *bird*, who clashed his wings together and
raised a storm when any one tried to lift the treasure (?)——
Similar to the passage quoted from Otfried is another in iv. 27,
19:

> tho zeintun (pointed to) *worolt-enti* sînes selbes *henti*,
> thaz *houbit himilisga* munt, thie *fuazi* ouh thesan *erdgrunt*,
> thaz was sîn al in wâra umbikirg in fiara
> obana joh nidana.

But O. has nothing about *birds*. Neither has the legend on the

*Wood of the Cross;* but it mentions the spring and the serpent. It makes Seth look in at the door of Paradise and spy a *spring,* which parted into the four rivers Pison, Gihon, Tigris and Euphrates; at the source of the Euphr. stood a withered tree, with a great serpent coiled about it; its root ran deep down into hell, on its crown lay a newborn babe in swaddling-bands. The *serpent* is he of the forbidden fruit-tree, but he answers to Nîðhöggr, the four *rivers* or *springs* corresp. to the three of the Edda, the *child* on the tree-top to the eagle, and the *roots* of both trees reach down to *hell.* But the wood of the Cross only comes of three pips off this tree, which grow up into three other trees. Now where did this legend spring up? and may some *heathen features* have been adopted into it? The Leg. Aurea c. 64 is very brief.

With the Oriental fable of the mouse gnawing at the root of the bush in the well, ought to be conn. the Indian myth of the *thin stalk of grass* hanging over a *precipice,* and unceasingly gnawed by a mouse, Holtzm. 3, 114. The widely spread fable above has even been painted, Mone 8, 279; conf. Benfey's Pantsch. 1, 80. 2, 528. Liebr. on Barlaam p. 330-1.

p. 801.] *Gehenna* is supposed to mean vale of sorrow; pl. *gehennae,* Arnob. 2, 14. Arab. *iahennem,* Pers. *gehinnom;* the Turks, too, retain it in the Koran as *jehenne,* the abode of *eblis,* diabolus. Ἄδης, ἀΐδης is expl. as the invisible (god), fr. ἀϊδής. Hades is addressed as a person: ὦναξ Ἀΐδη, Soph. Trach. 1085; so is the Hebrew Sheol, שְׁאוֹל, שְׁאֹל Gesen. 731[b] [see Hosea 13, 14, and 1 Cor. 15, 55]. Lucian de luctu 2. 3 descr. Hades as a vast and dark subterranean abyss, encircled by the fearful streams of Cocytus and Pyriphlegethontes, and to be reached by sailing over the Acherusian bog.——Dietrich in Hpt's Ztschr. 7, 305, says *Niflhel* is a place of torment too; yet höll in Fischart's Garg. 202[a], is still a mere dwelling place: das (wie dort geschriben steht) 'ein so weite hölle find man kaum, da *all die toden* hetten raum.' Did he take that fr. the passage in Widukind? Simple dying is called faring to hell; hence the Norse expressions *hel-reið* (e.g. Brynhildar), and *fara til Heljar* (p. 313). It sounds purely local in 'si ist *in der helle begraben,*' buried in hell, Kschr. 2530.

p. 801.] Leonidas at Thermopylae bids his men break their

fast, for they will sup in the realm of the dead: hodie apud
inferos coenabimus. 'Thorgerðr segir hâtt: engan hefi ec nâtt-
verð haft, ok engan mun ek fyrr enn *at Freyju*,' not sup till I
sup with F. (yr 945), Egilss. p. 603 ; ' lifið heilir herra, ek man
*hiâ Oðni gista*,' to-day guest with Oðin, Fornald. s. 2, 366 ; conf.
the passage fr. Saxo in Suppl. to 818 (Kl. schr. 5, 354 seq.).

     p. 802.] De olde *helweg*, Urk. of 1518 in Wigand's Corv.
güterb. 229 ; *hellewege*, *helleknochen* 241. Brückner derives the
Henneberg ' hälweg, hälwehr,' boundary, fr. häl (for hagel).
*Herweg* means also the Milky Way, Woeste 41 ; Hans *Helwagen*,
MB. 25, 314 (yr 1469). 316. 384.

     p. 803.] Hellia lies low. Beside the root of a tree of para-
dise Seth looks into *hell*, and sees his brother *Abel's soul*. It is
curious that Brynhild on her *hel-reið* drives through the *halls
of a giantess*, Sæm. 227. Diu *tiefe* helle, MS. 2, 184[b]. Hpt's
Ztschr. 2, 79. In the same sense death is called deep: an thene
*diapun dôd*, Hel. 136, 1, and conversely ' in der *bitteron* hella,'
Grieshaber 2, 33. 44. 65. 76. 97. 108. 122 ; and ' diu helle diu'st
ein *bitter hol*,' MSH. 3, 468[c], when usu. it is death that is bitter.
——The Greek underworld had an opening, through which Pluto
descends when he has carried off Proserpine, Paus. ii. 36, 7,
while Dionysus leads Semelē out of hades across the Alcyonian
lake ii. 37, 5. The Teut. hell has likewise a gateway (mouth),
which is closed up with a grating: fyr *nâ-grindr* neðan, Sæm.
68[a]. 86[a]; hnigin er *hel-grind*, when the grave-mound opens,
Hervarars. p. 347. OS. *helli-porta*, Hel. 97, 17 ; thiu *helliporta*,
O. iii. 12, 35 ; antheftid fan *hell-doron*, Hel. 71, 9 ; de *doir*
vanner *hellen* mot aupen wesen, Slennerhinke, beginn. There is
a *Höllthor-spitze* in Salzburg, M. Koch's Reise 315. Der *helle
invart* is a hole at which all the dead went in, En. 2906—15 ;
dringet in daz *helletor*, Hpt 2, 69 ; diu riuwe (ruth) stêt für der
*helle tor*, Warnung 316.

     p. 804.] OHG. *helli-stroum* = rudens, torrens inferni, Graff 6,
754 ; *Höll-haken*, hell-hook, was the name of a whirlpool in the
Rhine ; Fischart's Glückh. schif 429.

     p. 805.] Plainly Christian are the following notions : ' *minne*
hât ûf erde hûs, ze himel ist reine für Got ir geleite, minne ist
allenthalben *wan ze helle*,' love is everywhere but in hell, Tit. 51 ;
*helle-viur*, -fire, Kchr. 1138 ; daz *winster viur*, MSH. 1, 298[b];

'ich hân *fiwer* u. *vinster* ze der *zeswen* unt ze der *winster*,' to right and left, Todes gehugede 661 ; der helle *fiwerstôt*, Warn. 72 ; in der helle *brinnen* u. *brâten*, Griesh. 2, 76. 108. 123. Yet the heathen fancy of fires darting out of opened grave-mounds, and of *hauga-eldr* in general (Fornald. s. 1, 437), seems conn. with hellfire. On the other hand we hear of helle-*vrost*, Tod. geh. 902. In pop. speech, hell is any dark hole or corner : the tailor throws pieces of cloth ' in die *hölle*,' the prentice jumps up ' aus der *hölle* ' (fr. behind the chest), and makes for the door, Pol. maulaffe 4 ; kroch nach der *hölle* 6 ; geh *hinter'n ofen* in die *hell*, H. Sachs i. 5, 495ᵇ.——The Christian hell has a pool of pitch and brimstone : *bech* unde *swebel*, Diemer 313, 9 ; von deme *bechen* 303, 22 ; *beh-welle* 298, 29. 303, 27 ; die *swarzen pech-velle* (l. -*welle*), Tod. geh. 686 ; die *bechwelligen bache* 899 ; mit *bechwelliger* hitze 929. In the märchen of Dame Holle the *gold-gate* and *pitch-gate* stand opposed, like heaven and hell. Again : in dem *swebel*, Warn. 260 ; in den *swebel*-sêwen (-lakes) baden, Servat. 3541 ; diu helle *stinchet* wirs danne der fûle hunt, Kara-jan 31, 8 ; infer le *puant*. Thib. de Nav. 150 ; *puafine*, Gaufrey p. xxx. The stench of hell may have been suggested by the noxious fumes that rise out of clefts in the earth.

p. 806.] Greek opinion placed Tartarus not inside the earth, but an immense way off it. A brass anvil (χάλκεος ἄκμων) falls *nine days and nights* fr. heaven, and touches earth on the tenth ; it takes *nine more* to reach Tartarus, Hes. Theog. 722—5 ; but Homer makes Hephæstus fall fr. heaven in *one day*, Il. 1, 592. The Lat. Avernus is Gr. ἄ-ορνος, bird-less, 'quia sunt avibus contraria cunctis,' Lucr. 6, 742. An AS. word for hell is *scræf*, cavern, Cædm. 212, 10. MHG. *âbis*, Roth's Dicht. pp. 10. 23 ; ' daz *abgrunde* ' also occurs in Rother 4434 ; ' in der *helle grunde* verbrunne ê ich,' I'd sooner burn, MS. 1, 56ᵃ ; an *grund* grim-maro helliun, Hel. 164, 5 ; der fürste ûz *helle abgründe*, Walth. 3, 12 ; de *hellegrunt*, MB. 5, 138 ; der *bodengrunt* (bottom) der helle, MS. 2, 147ᵇ. In Russ. however [beside the more usual *âd* fr. ἅδης] it is called *bez-dná*, bottom-less, like ἄ-βυσσος. Conf. der erde *volmünde* (fullamunt), Gute frau 2022 ; der erden *bunder* (ON. pundari), Hpt's Ztschr. 2, 131.

p. 806.] On the Delphian *navel* as earth's centre, see Pott's Zählmeth. 267 ; Zeus ascertains it by sending out eagles or

ravens.   To the Irish too *earth's navel* was a stone, Lappenb. in
Allg. encycl. d. wiss., art. Irland 49[b].   A stone in *helles-grunt*
occurs in Uhl. Volksl. 1, 8 ; the *dille-stein* is the stone ' den kein
hund überbal, kein wind überwehte, kein regen übersprehte,' p.
7 ; über *d'hellplata* springen, Vonbun p. 65.   *Dillestein* means
bottom-stone.

p. 807.]   The underworld has its waters, streams : så hon þar
*vaða þraunga strauma* menn meinsvara, Sæm. 7[b] ; *Vaðgelmi* vaða
181[a] ; in der helle *baden*, Engelh. 6050 ; ze helle *baden*, MSH. 2,
259[a]. 260[b] ; in den swebel-sêwen (brimstone lakes) *baden*, Servat.
3541 ; sêle *besoufet* (drenched) in hellepîne, MS. 2, 150[b].   Hell
is a well, a *helle-puzze* (-pit), obene enge (narrow at top), nidene
wît, Wernh. v. N. 41, 5 ; då diu unerfulte *butze* des *abgrundes* ûz
diezen, Todes geh. 896 ; *helle-sôt*, MSH. 3, 463[b] answers to the
AS. *seáð* in the text ; *Hellekessel*, -kettle, a family name at Bonn.
*Susl* in *cwissusle* is appar. the ON. *sýsla*, negotium, cura, labor,
passing over into supplicium, as verk into verkr, dolor ; conf.
*suslbona*, hell-foe, Cædm. 305, 1.

p. 807.]   Hell is said in AS. to be *wyrmsele* and *wyrmum* be-
wunden, Judith 134, 49. 57 ; þaer bið fýr and *wyrm*, Cædm. 212,
9 ; ûz diseme *wurmgarten*, Diemer 295, 25.   There also dwells
the *hell-hound* (p. 996-7. Suppl. to 815)   There were punishments in hell for heathen heroes too : Sigurðr Fâfnisbani has
to *heat an oven*, and Starkaðr 'hefi *ökla-eld*,' Fornm. s. 3, 200 ;
conf. St. Patrick's Purgatory by Th. Wright xi. and 192.

p. 809.]   Leo in Hpt's Ztschr. 3, 226 has a Gael. *mudspuil*,
mutatio, which I have not found in any dictionary.   He only
gets it out of *muth*, mutare, and *spuil*, spolium ; but the OS.
*mudspelles megin* (like iarðar megin) requires a material sense.
That of wood, tree, is supported by Sæm. 9[b] : ' geisar eimi við
aldurnara,' the fire rages against aldurnari, *i.e.* Yggdrasill ?
(Suppl. to 800 beg.).   Lapp. *muora, muorra* [Mong. *modo*] =
arbor ; but Syriänic and Permic *mu*, Votiak *muziern* = land,
Rask's Afh. 1, 39.   Finnic, beside maa, seems to have *moa, mua*,
Castrén's Syriän. Gr. p. 149.

p. 810.]   *Surtr* is a giant, not a god : S. oc *in sváso goð*,
Sæm. 33[a] ; S. ok *aesir* 188[a] ; Surta sefi 8[a] is supp. to mean fire.
Domesday-bk has a man's name *Sortebrand*.   With *Surtr* conf.
Slav. *tchort, čert, czart* = devil [tchorny, czerny = black], p. 993.

Muspellz synir hafa einir ser fylkîng, er sû *biört* miöc, Sn. 72 ; the field on which they encounter the gods is called *Vigriðr*, Sæm. 33ᵃ. Sn. 75, and also *Oskopnir*, Sæm. 188ᵃ.

p. 810.] The world is destroyed by fire. The Indians spoke of ' the *penal fire* of the Last Day,' Holtzm. Ind. s. 2, 90 : ' *destructive* as the L. D.' 2, 86. 99. An Ionic dance was called κόσμου ἐκπύρωσις, Athen. 5, 283. At Rome one foretold ' *ignem* de coelo lapsurum *finemque mundi* affore,' Capitolini M. Anton. 13. The Celts believed the end of the world would be by *fire* and *water* : ἐπικρατήσειν δέ ποτε καὶ πῦρ καὶ ὕδωρ, Strabo 4, 45. 198 : Gael. *brath*, ultimum orbis incendium; *gu là bhrath*, in aeternum, unquam ; conf. Ossian 3, 433. AS. oð *baeles* cyme, till fire's coming = end of the world, Cod. Exon. 200, 28 : unz an die stunde dô allez sol *verbrinnen*, Karajan 50, 15 ; grôzer schal, als *al diu werlt dâ brunne*, Wigal. 7262 : dîn *jâmertac* wil schiere komen, u. *brennt dich* darumbe iedoch, Walth. 67, 19.

p. 812.] On *Antichrist*, conf. Griesh. Pred. p. 150-1 ; ich wêne nu ist *anticrist* den heiden cumen ze helfe, Gr. Rud. 14, 9 ; deable *antecris*, Méon 3, 250; l'ame emporteirent Pilate et *anticris*, Aspr. 9ᵇ. Müllenhoff in Hpt's Ztschr. 11, 391 does not see so much affinity betw. the Muspilli and the Edda.

p. 814.] Beside *aldar rök, ragna rök*, we have *þioða rök*, Sæm. 28ᵇ, *tíva rök* 36ᵃᵇ, *fíra rök* 49ᵃ, *forn rök* 63ᵃ. AS. *racu* is Ssk. *rajani*, night (Suppl. to 737). To this Twilight of the gods O. Schade in his sixth thesis refers the saying : ' it is not yet the *evening of all the days.*'

p. 815.] The stars fall from heaven (Suppl. to 817), the rainbow breaks down. Atlas holds the vault of *heaven* on his shoulders, it must *fall* when he removes them : quid si nunc *coelum ruat?* Ter. Heaut. iv. 2. The Celts ἔφασαν δεδιέναι μήποτε ὁ οὐρανὸς αὐτοῖς ἐμπέσοι, feared the sky would fall on them, Arrian's Anab. 1, 4. GDS. 459. 460. Germ. superstition tells of a little bird (tomtit) that holds his little claw over his head when he sleeps, to shield it in case the *sky fell* in the night.——The ship *Naglfar* is conn. with Naglfari, the husband of Nôtt, Sn. 11 ; it takes as long to build as the *iron-rock* to wear away, which the woman grazes with her veil once in 100 years ; conf. the *cow's hide* being picked clean by the giant (Suppl. to 544).——It was an AS. belief also that the *hellhound* was fought

with : ' sî he toren of *hellehundes* tôðum,' teeth, Kemble no. 715,
yr 1006 ; *hellehunt*, MS. 2, 147ᵇ (Suppl. to 807. p. 996-7). The
*Last Judgment* is like the *tribunal of Minos* in the underworld,
Lucian's Jup. confut. 18, and the *judgment of souls* of the
Mongols, Bergm. 3, 35 ; conf. Michael's balance (p. 859). AS.
notions about the end of the world are preserved in Cod. Exon.
445.

p. 817.] The Archipoeta's poem on the *fifteen signs* is in Hpt's
Ztschr. 3, 523—5. The signs vary in the different accounts, see
Sommer in Hpt 3, 525—530. Wiedeburg p. 139. Lekensp.
Deckers 2, 264. Diemer p. 283—7. Grieshaber p. 152. Mone's
Schausp. 1, 315 seq. MSH. 3, 96ᵇ. The 12th sign in the Latin
poem above is : fixae coeli penitus *stellae* sunt *casurae* (the same
in Griesh.) ; in the Asega-book the 13th : sa *fallath* alle tha
*stera* fon tha himule ; conf. Sæm. 9ᵇ : *hverfa af himni heiður
stiörnur.* The common folk held by other prognostics besides :
when it strikes thirteen and the hens take to crowing, the Judgment-day will come, Hpt 3, 367.——The earth quaked, ON. iörð
*dúsaði*, Sæm. 241ᵇ. The Greeks ascr. the phenomenon to Poseidon, Herod. 7, 129, or some other god : τὴν πόλιν τοῦ θεοῦ σεί-
σαντος, Paus. i. 29, 7, elsewh. to Typhôeus, Ov. Met. 5, 356 ; its
cause is discussed by Agathias 5, 8. The Lith. god of earthquake is *Drebkullys*, Nesselm. pp. 154. 208, fr. drebeti, quake,
and kulti, strike. A New Zeal. story of earthquake in Klemm 4,
359 ; the earth is carried by a tortoise 2, 164.

p. 818.] The *valkyrs* conduct to heaven, as the Hours opened
the cloud-gate to Olympus. So too the *angels* fetch away dying
*heroes :* la vos atendent li anges en chantant, contre vos ames
vont grant joie menant, Asprem. 22ᵇ ; lame emporterent li ange
en chantant 28ᵃ. A cliff in Blekingen is called *Valhall*, and at
two places in Westgotland are Valhall, Vâhlehall : they are the
hills fr. which *old men weary of life* threw themselves into the
*lake* or *brook* running below, in which they were *washed.* Such
water bears the name of *Odens-källa :* in taking possession of
them, the god first washed or bathed them ; conf. Geijer 1, 115
(Suppl. to 832).——Brave men go to Valhöll : sâ var âtrûnaðr
heiðinna manna, at allir þeir er af *sárum* andadisk, skyldu *fara
til Valhallar*, Fagrsk. p. 27. A servant goes not to V. except in
attendance on his lord, Fornald. s. 3, 8. *Vâpna-þing* goes on in

V., for which a son fits out his father by burying his weapons with him, Nialss. c. 80; '*þû vart valkyrja at Alföður, mundo einherjar* allir *beriaz um sakar þinar,*' were glad to be struck down for thy sake, Sæm. 154ᵇ. When Hâkon died a heathen and was buried, his friends gathered round his grave, and in heathen fashion saw him off to Valhöll: *maelto þeir svâ fyrir grepti hans, sem heiðinna manna var siðr til, oc visoðo honom til Valhallar,* Hâkonars. c. 32. Inde *vota nuncupat* (Ringo), *adjicitque precem* uti Haraldus, eo vectore (equo suo) usus, fati consortes ad Tartara antecederet, atque apud praestitem Orci *Plutonem* sociis hostibusque *placidas expeteret sedes,* Saxo Gr. 147; conf. the *prayer* of Waltharius 1167: hos in coelesti mihi praestet sede videri. Valhöll is also called *hâ höll,* high hall (though only the dat. occurs: *hâva höllo,* Sæm. 24ᵇ. 30ᵇ. Sn. 3); and *Hropts sigtoptir,* Sæm. 10ᵃ.

p. 819.] The souls of kshatriyas slain in battle arrive at Indra's heaven, and are his guests, Bopp's Nalas 264; to warriors fallen in fight the gate of heaven is open, Holtzm. Ind. s. 2, 65; conf. ' en infer vont *li bel cevalier* qui sont morts as tornois et as rices guerres,' Aucassin in Méon 1, 355. Both AS., OHG. and MHG. phrases point to a heavenly castle: *Godes ealdorburg,* Dei palatium, Cod. Exon. 441, 8: *rodera ceaster,* coelorum urbs 441, 10. A minute description of the *himilisge Godes burg* (Hpt's Ztschr. 3, 443-4) says: diu burg ist gestiftet mit aller tiuride *meist ediler geist gimmon,* der himel *meregriezon,* der burge fundamenta, die porte ioh die mure daz sint die *tiuren steina* der *Gotes furst helido.* A similar house, glittering with gold and light, occurs in a vision, Greg. Tur. 7, 1; ir erbe solde sîn der *himelhof,* Ludw. d. fromme 2478.

p. 820.] Heaven is ' der *himelische sal,*' Todes gehug. 942; der *vrône sal,* Diemer 301, 3; der *freuden sal* besitzen (possess), Tit. 5788; conf. *freuden-tal* besitzen, in contrast with *riuwen-tal* 3773-4; it is true a castle is also called *freuden zil,* goal of joy, Wigal. 9238. 11615; hverfa â *mun-vega* (pleasure's path) = to die, Egilss. 622. The Mecklenburg noble, who reckons on a merry drinking-bout with Christ in heaven, is, by another account, fr. Pomerania, N. Pr. prov. bl. 3, 477; conf. ' *im samint in* (along with them) *drinchit* er den wîn,' Diemer 103, 5; s'aurai *mon chief* em *paradis flori,* ou toz jors a *joie, feste e deli,* Aspr. 18ᵃ;

ἐν μακάρων νήσοις πίνειν μετὰ τῶν ἡρώων, ἐν τῷ 'Ηλυσίῳ λειμῶνι κατακείμενος, Lucian's Jup. confut. 17.

p. 820 n.] The reading I proposed in Parz. 56, 18 is now
verified by MS. d; conf. *berc ze Fâmorgân* 496, 8, *ze Fâmurgâne*
585, 14, and ' Fâmorgân hiez daz lant,' Türl. Wh. 24ª, see 37ª.
De *glasenburg* upriden, Uhl. Volksl. p. 16. The *glass mountain*
turns up in many legends and märchen: Müllenh. p. 386-7.
Ehrentraut's Fries. arch. 2, 162. Sommer's März. 99 seq.
Bechstein's Sag. p. 67. Akin to the glass castle is the cloud-
castle : mons *Wolkinburg*, Cæs. Heisterb. 2, 318; conf. Böhm.
Cod. Francof. 247 (yr. 1290). Lacomblet's Arch. 2, 11. 19.
Weisth. 2, 713. The Vila builds a *castle on the cloud* with three
gates, Vuk, nov. ed. p. 151. It says in Kalev. 2, 25: *tuulehenko
teen tupani*, build rooms in the air ; conf. the air-castle on the
rainbow (p. 732-3).

p. 821.] Ssk. *dêšas*, land, Zend. paradaêshas, fairest land,
Benfey 1, 438; τὸν παράδεισον=hortum, Lucian's Somn. 21 ;
the garden of the Vandal king is called παράδεισος, Procop. 1,
382, conf. 434. Ir. *parrathas*, O.Sl. *poroda*. The earthly paradise is the *Rose-garden*, conf. its descript. in a Pommersf. MS.
(Hpt 5, 369). Roseng. 1028. Tit. 6044. Another term is
'saltus *wunniló*,' Lacombl. no. 65 (855); conf. 'lust-wald,' pleasure-
park. Weinhold. in Hpt 6, 461 after all connects *neorxena* with
*norna*.——The Slav. *rai*, paradise, Miklosich 73 would derive fr.
*rad*", glad, as nai fr. nad". Boh. *raghrad* or *rai-grad*, paradise-
garden, later hradiště (castle), a plot encircled by a round wall,
in which the Slavs held feasts and games, and sang songs; so
the *gral-höfe*, *grale*. Herod. 3, 26 calls 'Οασις a μακάρων νήσος,
a green island in the sea of sand. ' A land flowing with *milk*
and *honey*,' Exod. 3, 8. Mar. 160, 17, like Cockaign, Lubber-
land, which even the Greeks knew of, Athen. 2, 526—533 [Hor.
Od. ii. 19, 10 : *vini* fontem, *lactis* rivos, lapsa *mella*]. Conf.
milk, honey and blood as food for gods and drink for poets (pp.
317. 415 n.) ; *mellis* lacus et flumina *lactis* erupisse solo, Claud.
Stil. 1, 85.

p. 823.] 'Ηλύσια are places which lightning (the sun) has
struck, Benfey 1, 457 : ἐν τῷ 'Ηλυσίῳ λειμῶνι, Jup. confut. 17 ;
conf. Plutarch 4, 1154. OHG. *sunna-felt*, elysium, Graff 3, 516 ;
*sunno-feld*, helisios campos, Gl. Sletst. 6, 271. AS. *heofen-feld*,

coelestis campus (p. 234) ; *Hefenfeld,* locus in agro Northumbrensi. On ἀσφοδελός, Rom. *albucus,* see Dioscor. 2, 199, with whom Theophrastus agrees, while Galen descr. the plant very differently, see Sprengel on Diosc. 2, 481.

Like the children in our märchen, who fall through the well on Dame Holla's *meadow,* Psyche having jumped off the *high rock,* 'paulatim per devexa excelsae vallis subditae *florentis cespitis* gremio leniter delabitur,' and then finds herself in a *heavenly grove,* Apuleius lib. 4 in fine. Like the *gardens of the Hesperides* is the '*insula pomorum,* quae *fortunata* vocatur,' v. Merlini p. 393; conf. the *sacred apple-wood,* Barzas breiz 1, 56-7. 90, and '*fortunatorum insulas,* quo cuncti, qui aetatem egerunt caste suam, *conveniant,*' Plaut. Trin. ii. 4, 148 ; ἐν μακάρων νήσοις ἡρώων, Lucian's Demosth. enc. 50. Jup. conf. 17. *Champ flory,* la tanra Diex son jugement, quand il viendra jugier la gent, O.Fr. life of Mary in Lassberg's Zoller p. 74; an der *maten* (prato beatorum), Flore 2326. AS. *grêne wongas,* Cod. Exon. 482, 21; þes *wang grêna* 426, 34; þone *grênau wong* ofgifan 130, 34. H. Sachs iii. 3, 84[d] still speaks of paradise as *the green valley.* Welsh *gwynfa,* paradise, strictly white happy land. The dead shall go to *Helgafell,* Eyrb. c. 4; conf. the earthly paradise closed in by high mountains, Tod. gehug. 970—6. The '*goð-borinn Goðmundr'* in the far off realm of paradise, Sæm. 153[b], is *Granmar* in the Völs. saga, conf. Granmars synir, Sæm. 155[b].

p. 823.] *Viðarr* would in OHG. be *Witheri,* Graff 4, 986 ; but *Viðarr, Witheri* is more correct, conf. Sæm. 42[a] : hrîs, gras, við. There is a saying about him : *Viðarr,* er guð enn î Görðum, hann er lîka î Grindarskörðum.

---

## CHAPTER XXVI.

## SOULS.

p. 826.] Ψυχή anima and νοῦς mens are distinct, Plutarch 4, 1154. Beside the fem. seele, we find a neut. ferah with much the same meaning : OHG. *ferah* = anima, Graff 3, 682 (but smala *firihi* = vulgus 683) ; that *ferah* was af them folke, Hel. 169, 28, i.e. departed fr. among men. Pers. *ferver,* spirits, souls,

Zend. *fravashayó*, Benfey's Monatsn. 63-4. 151.  To the fem.
soul stand opp. the masc. *ahma, âtum, geist*=spiritus (p. 461,
l. 7).  At the same time the *animae* as well as animi are *winds*,
ἄνεμοι, as the Sl. *dukh* and *dushá* are fr. dykh-áti, dú-nuti,
spirare.  Hence: animam exhalare, Ov. Met. 6, 247, animam
ebullire, Petron. 62. 42; den geist aufgeben, give up the ghost,
Albr. v. Halb. 123ᵇ; der *âdem* (breath) zuo den luften fuore,
Ksrchr. 13400.  It was feared that a *soul* passing away in a storm
would be blown to pieces by the *wind*, Plato's Phædr. p. 77.——
The soul fares, slips out: stirb lîb, *sêle var !*  Herb. 14040; diu
*sêl* waer im *entsliffen*, Tundal. 44, 31; diu *sêl* sich ûz den liden
(limbs) zôch, als der *sliufet* ûz dem gwande (garment), Servat.
3464; sô sih diu *sêle enbindet* von mennesklîcher zarge, Mar.
153, 5 (Fundgr. 2, 153); 'nu breche Got ir *sêlen bant !*' is inscr.
on a tombstone, Wackern. W. v. Klingen p. 22; wenn mir die
*sel fleuszt* (flows) von des leibes drauch, Wolkenst. 263; von mir
wolde diu *sêle* sîn *endrunnen* (run away), MS. 2, 52ᵃ; dren (fr.
three) *genk* dei seile ut den *munt* (mouth), Soest. fehde p. 625.
The soul escapes through the gaping wound: κατ' οὐταμένην
ὠτειλήν, Il. 14, 518, conf. 17, 86; ψυχὴ λέλοιπε, Od. 14, 134;
is seola was *gisendid* an *suothan weg*, Hel. 169, 27, and what is
more striking: than im that lîf *scriði* (abiret), thiu seola *bisunki*
(mergeretur, elaberetur), 169, 21; conf. Karajan 32, 15 of the
eagle: im *sunkit* sîn gevidere (plumage, to renew itself?).  Souls,
like elves, sail over the water; and the Indian elves are dead
men, Ssk. *marut*, Kuhn in Hpt's Ztschr. 5, 488-9; conf. Nâinn,
Dâinn (p. 453).  The Lith. *wélĕs* f. are manes, and *welûkas*
spectres, Nesselm. 61-2 (Suppl. to 913 end, 968).

p. 828.]  Souls are of *three kinds*, those of angels, of men, of
beasts, says Dietm. of Mersebg (Pertz 5, 739).  Curiously, however, *each* man is credited with *three souls*, two of which perish
with the body, but the third survives: *bustoque superstes evolat*,
Claud. de 4 cons. Honor. 228—235.  Men's *souls* (ψυχαί) go
to the underworld, their bodies (αὐτούς, like *selb* = mîn lîp)
become the prey of dogs and birds, Il. 1, 4.  Of lovers it is
thought, that *their souls intermarry*; the notion must be old,
for we find it in H. v. Veldeke: wir sîn ein lîp und *ein geist*,
En. 6533, and still more clearly in H. v. Morungen: iuwer sêle
ist *meiner sêle frowe*, MS. 1, 57ᵇ; conf. 'ich wolte nit, daz mîn

*sêle ûz* des *besten menschen munde füere,*' *i.e.* pass out of *his* mouth, Berth. 298.——On the *worship of souls*, see p. 913. It is said of the soul: von im fuor ein *glast* (flash) sam ein brinnender louc, Rol. 228, 21; the soul of Mary *shines* in passing out of her body, Haupt 5, 545; souls in parting are *seven times whiter than snow*, Myst. i. 136, 21; ez müegen wol zwô sêle sîn, den ist *ir wîze* her geleit, und klagent ein ander ir arbeit, Ls. 2, 270. In a Lett. song the dead call themselves *rashani*, beautiful, Büttner no. 89; conf. the meaning of *selig*, blessed. When the soul parts fr. the body, a *sweet scent* is perceived, Wh. 69, 12—15. *Flowers* grow on a virgin's grave, Athen. 5, 495, *lilies* out of dead men, Zappert pp. 29. 31. On lovers' graves *two trees* spring up: det växte tvenne träd uppå deras graf, det ena tager det andra i famn, Arvidss. 2, 11. *Vines* grow out of the mouths of the dead, Tit. 5790; *five roses* bloom out of a dead man's head, Maerl. 2, 308.

> sîn tiost doch valte (felled) den edeln Môr,
> daz er die bluomen mit bluot begôz (bedewed) :
> *die gote* des valles *sêre verdrôz* (vexed the gods),
> daz der minnære sus belac (lover so ill bestead) ;
> und waen daz vür (I ween that from) den selben tac
> nâch der âventiure sage
> daz selbe velt niht wan (nothing but) *rôsen trage*,
> sô grôz wart al der *gote klage.*      Türl. Wh. 36[a].

Drops of blood turn into yellow flowers, as a herb grew out of Ajax's blood, Konst en letterb. '43, p. 76[b]; *mannabod* (sambucus ebulus) near Kalmar sprang fr. the blood of slain heroes, Fries Bot. udfl. 1, 110. The *wegewarte* is also called *wegetritt, Hänsel am weg, feldblume auf der wegscheide*, Meinert's Kuhl. p. 6; *wegeluoge* = heliotropium, Mone 8, 401.

p. 829.] Poles with *pigeons* on them were set up over Lombard graves, Paul. Diac. 5, 34 (Kl. schr. 5, 447); sêle alsam ein *tûbe* gestalt, Pass. 391, 37. Souls fly away in the shape of *doves*, Schönwerth 3, 37. Zappert p. 83. St Louis 60, 25. Baader iv. 32 [' When the Persian fleet was wrecked off Mt Athos, *white pigeons* were seen for the first time in Greece,' Charon of Lamps. in Athen. 9, 394; see Victor Hehn's Wanderings of Plants and Animals p. 258-9]. 'Det kommo *två dufvar* af himmelen ned

(down) ; när de foro upp, så voro de *tre*,' when they flew up
again, they were three, Sv. vis. 1, 312-5. 373.——A sennrin bleib
ich ewiglich, und wann ich stirb, wird ich a *schwalbn*, Almer 1,
58. Souls fly about as *ravens*, Michelet 2, 15 ; they swarm
as little *ducks*, Klemm 2, 165 ; *night-owls* rise from the brain of
a murdered man 4, 220. The story of Madej is given more correctly in Wend. volksl. 2, 319, conf. Walach. märch. no. 15. In
Egypt. hieroglyphs the sparrowhawk with a human head is a
picture of the soul, Bunsen's Dingbilder 126. Every soul, after
parting from the body, *hovers* for a time *betwixt the earth and
the moon*, Plut. 4, 1154.

p. 829.] The soul is *winged*, Plato's Phædr. 246-7-8 ; it loses
and then recovers its wings 248-9, conf. Gerhard's Eros, tab. 1
and 5 ; ψυχὴ δ' ἐκ ῥεθέων πταμένη Ἄϊδόςδε βεβήκει, Il. 16,
856. 22, 361 ; ψυχὴ δ' ἠΰτ' ὄνειρος ἀποπταμένη πεπότηται, Od.
11, 222. Lucian's Encom. Demosth. c. 50 says of the dying
orator : ἀπέπτη, evolavit.

The larva, the butterfly is called ὁ νεκύδαλος. Swed. *käring-
själ*, old woman's soul=butterfly, Ihre 2, 529. Ir. *anamandé*,
anima dei=butterfly ; conf. the Faun as night-butterfly (Suppl.
to 483 mid.). When a moth flutters round the candle, the Lithu.
women say somebody's *dying*, and the *soul* is going hence, N. Pr.
prov. bl. 5, 160.

p. 829.] The soul runs out of the sleeper as a *mouse, cat,
weasel, snake, butterfly.* Yama draws the soul out of a dying man
in the shape of a tiny *mannikin*, the man turns pale and sinks,
and when the mannikin comes back, he thinks he has been asleep,
Holtzm. Ind. sag. 1, 65. The soul slips out of the mouth as a
*little child*, Gefken's Beil. pp. 6. 15 and plates 11. 12. It was
believed in Germany as well, that a dying man's *heart* could
pass into a living man, who would then show twice as much
pluck : so Egge's heart seems to have passed into Fasolt,
Diether's into Dietrich (Ecke 197-8), each time into a *brother's*
body ; conf. the *exchange of hearts* betw. lovers, Wigal. 4439.
8813. MS. 1, 166[b], and the *marriage of souls* (Suppl. to 828).
The exchange of figures, the *skipta litum oc hömum* (Suppl. to
1098 end) is another thing. —— On the similar doctrine of
*transmigration* taught by Pythagoras, see Plato's Phædr. 248-9.
Phædo p. 82. Ov. Met. 15, 156 seq. O'Kearney 133. 160.

Gods, by way of punishment, are born again as *men* (Suppl. to 338), men are changed into *beasts* corresp. to their character, *e.g.* by the wand of Circe, RA. p. xiv. Claud. in Ruf. 2, 482 seq. Thorir hjörtr is pursued by a hunter and his hound; struck by a javelin, he falls to the ground, but *out of his body springs a stag*, which again is hunted down by the dog, and killed after a hard struggle, Maurer's Bekehr. 1, 295-6. Animals too have had many souls, like Lucian's cock.

p. 830.] Good souls for a time *hover on Hades' verdant mead*, Plut. 4, 1154. The soul feeds on the *field or meadow of truth*, ἀληθείας πεδίον, λειμών, Plat. Phædr. 248 (in the train of God, συμπορευθεῖσα θεῷ, it looks upon truth, ibid.). On the *green grass* the soul sits down, Feifalik Musp. p. 5. 'He is going to die' is expr. by 'he is just fluttering away.' Souls of the dead *hang* over a *precipice* by a *slender stalk*, Holtzm. Ind. sag. 3, 174. 'A medicine that sent her soul up to the *tip of her tongue*,' Rommel 4, 771. Vulgo dicitur, quod *triginta animae* super *acumen acus* possunt *sedere*, Chmel's Notizenbl. 6, 386, fr. Nicol. v. Siegen's Chron. yr 1489, ed. Wegele '55, p. 344. How many souls can *sit on a nail*, Wigand's Arch. 4, 321.

p. 832.] Souls are *received, drawn on*, by Wuotan, Frouwa, Rân and Hel, by the watersprites, by angels and elves, by the devil (pp. 1001 beg. 1017). Near the places named *Valhall* there is often an *Odens-källa* (Suppl. to 818 beg.), as if Oden, before admitting souls, should bathe them in the clear stream, as the Greeks thought souls were cleansed in the rivers of Hades, and took the draught of oblivion in Lethe. '*Oden* som kom upp ur *Odens-kammare* eller Asne-kåfve, som ligger in Asne-sjö (fordom *Oden-sjö*), at välja de slagne på Bråvallahed, och föra dem *på ett gullskepp*' (Rääf); conf. the story of *Haki*, Ynglînga-s. c. 27. Old sea-kings were supp. to be buried in a *golden ship*, Müllenh. no. 501.——A funeral pile is built up in a *ship*, Saxo Gr. (ed. Müller) p. 235; conf. the *ship-mounds* thrown up over the dead, Worsaae's Vorzeit p. 81-7. A death-ship in Beow. 34; a swan-ship carrying a corpse, Keller's Romv. 670. Jacob's body crosses the sea in a ship without sail or rudder, Pass. 220, 41 seq. Maerl. 2, 341-2, where note the phrase: si bevalen *Gode* te sine *stierman*.——In Friesland souls are supp. to sail over in *eggshells;* people break their *empty shells*, for witches get into them and

plague the soul on her passage. Halbertsma reminds me verbally
of the nail-parings (pp. 814. 1138-9 n.) and shoelace cuttings, Sn.
73 ; the breaking of eggshells is still enjoined by superstition.
An angel leads a shipful of souls, Dante's Purg. 2, 40 seq. The
boatman Tempulagy ferries souls over the lake, Klemm 2, 165.
——On the Etruscan *Charun* (Gerh. p. 17) and the passage-
money, see Lucian's De luctu 10. Boeckh's Inscr. 2, 103-4.
GDS. 681. *Money* is placed under the *tongues* of the dead, three
grains of corn under the dead *Adam's tongue.* In Germ. skeletons, coins are actually found in the mouth, Mainzer Ztschr. 1,
342-3. Lindenschmitt's Todtenlager pp. 16. 51. Haec Stygias
referant munera ad undas, et *calidos* numerent igne *trientes,*
Liudpr. Antop. 2, 26. Green *apples* were also put in the hands
of the dead, Vuk no. 137.

p. 834.] On Procopius's account of the passage of souls to
Brittia, see Werlauff's Procop. p. 7, who himself on p. 10 seq.
takes ‘Brittia’ to be Jutland, ‘Britannia’ Gt. Britain, and
‘Thule’ Scandinavia.——En passant *le lac de l'angoisse,* elle vit
une bande de morts, vêtus de blanc, dans de petites barques,
Villemarqué's Barz. breiz. 1, 169.

p. 835.] A sharp *bridge* leading across the Purgatorial fire,
and the *souls* flying into it black and coming out white, are
mentioned in Walewein 4958. 5825. 5840 (V. d. Bergh 102-3).
Over de *lank-brugge* fard = he dies, Narragonia 123[b] ; conf. the
*sword-bridge* (p. 1082). Angels conduct over the *rainbow-bridge.*
The Arabian bridge of souls is named *Sirát,* Rück. Hariri 1,
229 ; the Chinese too have a *bridge of souls,* Maltebrun's Précis
3, 527. Old-Irish legends about it in O'Donovan p. 440-1. The
cow driven across the bridge by thé soul in the Tundalus-legend
reminds of the *red cow* being led over a *certain bridge* before the
great battle by the Nortorf elder-tree, Müllenh. no. 509. The
Greenlanders believe the soul has to cross an abyss, where *turns*
a narrow *wheel* as smooth as ice, Klemm 2, 317; this is like the
wheel in Wigalois p. 250 seq.

p. 836.] On the *death-shoe,* see Müller's Sagabibl. 2, 171.
Mannhardt's Ztschr. 4, 421 ; conf. Vîðar's *shoe,* Sn. 31. 73 ; ‘säl
ä den, i denne heimen *fatike gjeve sko,* han tar inkje (he need not)
*barfött* gange in *kvasse tynnermo* (al. paa *kvasse keklebro*),’ Norweg. draumkväe 36. A dead woman ‘walks,’ until her shoe,

which they had forgotten to burn, is found and thrown in the
fire, Lucian's Philops. 27 ; conf. Indicul. sup. ' de ligneis pedibus
vel manibus, pagano ritu.' The Blackfoot Indians, like Lithuanians and Poles, believe the soul has to climb a steep mountain,
Klemm 2, 166-7.

p. 838.] Anima de corpore exivit, et *paradisi januam* introivit,
Vita Mathild. c. 16. 18. Prayers to St. Michael are said over the
corpse : di reinen guzzen ir gebet *Sente Michahéle* zu *dróste* sînre
sêle, Diut. 1, 426 ; Michael is ' *trôst* allir sêlen,' Roth. 4438 : he
brings the soul ' in Abraham's barm,' Hpt's Ztschr. 3, 522, conf.
Pfeiffer's Wigal. p. 340.    Other angels may come instead of
Michael : venerunt *duo juvenes, candidis* circumamicti *stolis*, animam a corpore segregantes, vacuum ferentes per aërem, Jonas
Bobb. in Vita Burgundofarae (Mabillon 2, 421) ; conf. the Gemini
(p. 366).

> Got sante eine *engellische schar* (angelic band),
> die nâmen dô der *sêlen* war (care, charge) ;
> si empfiengen (received) an der selben stunde
> iegelîches (each one's) sêle *von sînem munde* (mouth),
> unde vuorten wirdeclîche (worshipfully)
> si in daz êwige himelrîche.
> Oswalt 3097. 3455.

Out of an old man that is dying the *angels* take the *soul* as a
young child (Suppl. to 876 end) ; ir *engel* vil wol wisten, war
(well knew where) ir sêle solten komen, Klage 922.    Angels
*rejoice* over Christians falling in fight, and devils over heathens,
because they get their souls, Türl. Wh. 22-3 ; *two youths* (angels)
and *two black devils* sit by the bedside of the dead, Griesh. 1, 93 ;
angels *and* devils take the souls of schächer (assassins ?), Mone's
Schausp. 2, 321-2.    The soul first lodges with *St. Gerdrud*, then
sails over the *leber-meer* (liver sea), Gryse Ee 1111[b] ; conf. Gefken's Catal. p. 54.

## CHAPTER XXVII.

## DEATH.

p. 840.] Death as messenger of Deity is called *der heilig tod,*
H. Sachs i. 5, 528ᵈ. 1, 447ᵇ. Death receives, fetches, escorts :
sân in der tôt *entphienc,* Uolr. 1253 ; er hât *den* tôt an der hant
(p. 848); her moste haven *den* tôt, Hpt's Ztschr. 2, 183. We
still say ' du kannst dir *den* tod davon holen,' it may be the death
of you, and ' mit *dem* tode abgehen,' but more commonly without
the article : ' *mit tode* abgegangen ist,' Mohr's Reg. ii. no. 234 (yr
1365). MB. 25, 392. 453 (yr 1480) ; conf. *mit tod verscheiden,*
H. Sachs (Göz 2, 16. 19), *mit tôde vallen,* Nib. 2219, 3. Yet
again ; si *beliben* mit *dem* grimmen tôde 1555, 3. Er brâht ir (of
them) vil manegen dahin, dâ er iemer wesen solde, Gudr. 889,
4 ; conf. ' si-ne kumt niht her-widere ' 928, 2 ; ' der *tôt* der hât
die unzuht, daz er nieman deheine fluht zuo sînen friunden haben
lât,' has the ill manners to allow no flight, Klage 1581.——Death
is a departing ; the dead is in OS. called *gifaran,* Hel. 169, 27,
in ON. *fram-genginn,* Sæm. 83ᵃ ; AS. ' he *gewât,*' died, Homil. 1,
330, ' hæfde *forð-sîðod,*' had gone off, Beow. 3105 ; than im that
lîf *scriði,* Hel. 169, 20. Gr. οἴχεσθαι to be gone, οἰχόμενος =
θανών. Gl. sletst. 8, 35 renders moriebatur by ' towita, vel *hina-
zôh.*' Ssk. *prêta,* gone = dead, Bopp 37ᵇ. Dying is called *ûz
varn,* faring out, Wels. gast 5436 ; (he is *daust, drauzen,* out =
dead, Stelzhamer 166. 175) ; *vervarn,* Walth. 23, 23. MS. 2,
138ᵇ ; ' *forðférde,* obiit,' AS. chronol. ; er ist *an die vart* (journey),
diu uns nâch in allen ist vil unverspart, Walth. 108, 6. In the
Ludwigslied ' *hina-vart,*' hence-faring, is opp. to ' hier-wist,'
here-being ; ich red daz ûf mîn *hin-vart,* MSH. 3, 298ᵇ ; er
swuor ûf sîn *hinvart* 301ᵃ ; bis auf mein *hinefart,* Bergreien 127 ;
die *leste fart farn,* Suchenw. xxxiv. 105 ; zuo der *langen vart,*
Lanz. 1949 ; up mine *langhe vaert,* Reinh. 2213 ; ON. *löng gánga,*
Sæm. 222ᵇ ; on *longne weg,* Cod. Exon. 173, 24 ; zuo der *langen
hervart,* Ksrchr. 6304 ; des tôdes *hervart,* Mar. leg. 54, 14.——To
join the great host (p. 847) ; conf. οἱ πλείονες, plures = mortui,
' quia ii majore numero sunt quam vivi ' ; qui abierunt in com-
munem locum, Pl. Casina, prol. 19 ; *verscheiden,* depart, Renn.
21093 ; our ' drauf gehen ' ; *freude lân,* leave joy, Parz. 119, 15 ;
swenn er *dise freude lât,* Wels. gast 4908 ; *látaz,* Islend. sög. 2,

166. 174; *afgeben* gadulingo gimang, Hel. 17, 17; manno drôm
*ageben* 103, 4; *forlêt* manno drôm 23, 7 (conf. *sôhte* im erlo
gimang endi manno drôm 23, 33); die werlt er *begab*, Diut. 3, 89.
67; daz leben *begibt* den lîp, Maria 23; von *zîte gân*, Staufenb.
661; aer he *on-weg hwurfe* gamol of geardum, Beow. 526; *hwearf*
mon-dreámum from 3433; geendode eorðan dreámas, AS.
chronol.; *lîf-wynna brecan*, Beow. 157.——Dying is also called
staying, being left: *blivet* doot, Maerl. 3, 325; ' *biliban*, mortuus,'
T. 135, 24. O. iii. 23, 55. Graff 2, 47; our ' *geblieben*,' left
(dead on the field). Or it is descr. as perishing, οἱ ὀλωλότες, as
going down to the dust, χθόνα δῦναι, Il. 6, 411; *varen onder
moude* (mould), Maerl. 3, 61; *voer ter moude* 3, 152; *til iarðar
hniga* (bend), Alfskongs-s. cap. 13; conf. *bêt ter moude!* Lanc.
44032; manger la terre, mordre la poussière. The Greeks called
the dead δημητρείους, gone home to Demeter (earth), Plut. 4,
1154; *heim-varn*, W. gast 5440; went, was gathered, unto his
fathers.——*Fara til heljar* = mori (p. 802); *gen Tôtenheim* faren,
Braut 55, 6; fara *î dîsar sal*, Fornald. sög. 1, 527 (conf. heingja
sik î dîsar sal 1, 454); fara *î lios annat*, to other light, Sæm.
262ᵃ; sôkien *lioht ôdar*, Hel. 17, 17; de hac luce transire, Lex
Burg. 14, 3; Esth. *ilma minnema*, go to the other world; conf.
μηκέτι ὄντα ἐν φάει, Soph. Philoct. 415. *An fridu* faran (go to
peace), thar êr mîna fordron dêdun, Hel. 14, 22. For dying is a
going to sleep: den *langen slâf slâfen*, Kolocz 285; daz in (him)
der *lange slâf* gevie (caught), Ring 246; conf. *ûf einem strô
ligen*, MS. 1, 25ᵃ.——The dead go to God: *Dryhten sêcean*,
Beow. 373; si sîn *vor Gotes ougen* (eyes), Trist. 18668; *fore
Meotudes cneowum* (knees), Cod. Exon. 164, 19; ' beholding
God's mouth and beard,' Kalev. p. 34; *Gote hete geboten* über
in, Ges. Abent. 1, 298; wenn der grim *tôt* über in *gebiut*, Ls. 3,
124; 'God came with his mercy,' Schwein. 2, 167. 184. 252.
——Various peculiar expressions: ' er hât im den *namen* benomen,' taken the name (life) fr. him, Nib. 1507, 4: *virwandelen*
(change) disen *lîp*, Ksrchr. 6318; des *lebenes ferwandelen*, Diut.
2, 290; den lîp, daz leben, verwandeln, Cod. Vind. 428, no. 154;
'*tyelach moeten betalen*, have to pay the piper, Maerl. 2, 238; er
ist *verschlissen*, slit up, Vict. Jacobi 88; Esth. 'lay down the
breath.' Life is expr. by ' der *sêle walden*,' Ben. Beitr. 86, and
death by ' he is tor *selen gedegen*,' Michelsen Lub. oberh. 42;

*seeltagen,* Haupt 3, 91 ; our 'todes verbleichen,' turn pale of
death. The word *spalten,* split, is often used in conn. with death:
sîn houbet ime *endriu spielt* (split in 3), *enniuniu* (into 9) sich sîn
zunge vielt, Reinh. 2243 ; sîn houbet gar *zespielt,* Lampr. Alex.
6922 ; daz herze ir in dem lîbe *spielt,* Herzmaere 520 ; hans hoved
*brast* udi *ni stykker,* DV. 1, 157 ; we say the heart *breaks* in
death, *bursts* with grief.

p. 841.] The Ind. *Yama* is god of justice, of death and of the
underworld, Bopp's Nalas pp. 201. 264 ; in this last capacity
he is named *Kâla,* the black, Bopp's Gl. 74ᵇ ; he answers to the
Pers. *Jemshit,* Zend. *Yimô.* Yama sends his *messengers,* who
conduct to his dreary dwelling, Kuruinge 1296. 1360. 1643.
Holtzm. Ind. s. 2, 101 ; conf. the *death-angels,* Rosenöl 1, 56-7,
the *angel of death* and *destroying angel* (p. 1182). How the
Tartars keep off the *angel of death* is told by K. Schlözer p. 32-3.
*Hermes* with his wand drives the souls of the suitors to the
asphodel mead, Od. 24, 1—14. 99—101. As Hermes is sent to
men, so is *Iris* to women.——Death drags men away from their
*houses,* their *buildings* : thus Protesilaos leaves his widow a half-
finished house, δόμος ἡμιτελής, Il. 2, 701. *Apollo* and *Artemis*
come regularly and kill off the old people with *painless darts,*
ἀγανοῖς βελέεσσι, Od. 15, 410-1 ; τὴν βάλεν Ἄρτεμις ἰοχέαιρα
15, 478 ; αἴδε μοι ὡς μαλακὸν θάνατον πόροι Ἄρτεμις ἀγνή 18,
202. 20, 60-1. 80. *Charon* ferries over the water; so the *devil*
is repres. with an *oar* in his hand, Woeste p. 49. ' Vallen in des
Tôdes *wâge,*' balance, Warn. 1650; ' ûf des Tôdes *wâge* sweben,'
be poised 3318.——Death is sent by God : Got der *sende* an
mînen leiden man den *Tôt* ! MS. 1, 81ᵃ ; 'sîn wîp diu schrîet
wâfen ûf den *Tôt,* er sî *entslâfen* daz er'n niht welle bestân,' cries
fie upon D., he must have gone to sleep, that he won't tackle the
man, Teichner 75 ; dô ergreif in der Tôt, dô er im sîn *zuokunjt*
*enbôt* (while he to him his arrival made known), sô daz er in
*geleite,* Greg. 20. He knocks at the door : bereite ze ûftuonne
deme *klopphaere,* Uolr. 1329; so in Berno, 'ut *pulsanti* posset
aperire.' He comes as a young man : der *jüngelinc,* der geheizen
ist Tôt, Ls. 2, 373. The Lapland *Yabmen akka,* uxor vel avia
mortis, sits in a *subterr. cave,* and was worshipped as a divine
being, Lindahl's Lex. 82ᵇ ; ich selbe sol hin in daz *hol,* Frauenl.
114, 8 ; des todes *höle* (p. 853, Gossip Death's cavern).

p. 842.] With *mors* conf. Zend. *merethyu*, Bopp's Comp. Gr.
46 ; *schmerz, smart* is expl. differently by Benfey 2, 39. A Norse
word for dead is *dáinn* (p. 453 end) ; conf. Finn. *Tuoni*=mors,
Pluto ; *Tuonen koira*, death's dog=dragonfly ; *Tuonela*=orcus.
Pruss. *gallas*, mors (the Lith. galas, finis ?). Esth. *surm*=mors,
Finn. *surma*. Hung. *halál*, Finn. *kuolema*, Votiak *kulem*, Lapp.
*yabmen*. Death is the brother of *Sleep*, who is also personified :
the dead sleep. It is said of the dead vala : *sefrattu* fyrri, Sæm.
95ᵇ ; κοιμήσατο χάλκεον ὕπνον, Il. 11, 241. As sleep is called
the *sandman*, death is in Esth. called earthman, sandman, *liwa
annus*, Sand-Jack, *liwa peter*, Sand-peter ; conf. Alf. Maury's Du
personnage de la mort, Revue Arch. 4th year, pp. 305—339.

p. 844.] Death comes *creeping* : mors *obrepit*, Pl. Pseud. ii.
3, 20 ; mors imminet, et tacito clam venit illa pede, Tib. i. 10,
34 ; dâ kam der Tôt als ein *diep*, u. *stal* dem reinen wîbe daz
leben ûz ir lîbe, Wigal. 8032 ; der Tôt kumt *geslichen* als ein diep,
Cato 397 (mutspelli also *thiof* ferit, Hel. 133, 4) ; der Tôt
*erslîchet*, wins by stealth, Warn. 3109 ; der tôt hât mich *erslichen*,
Hugdietr. Fromm. 5 ; er ist mir *na' geslichen* (crept after), der
mich *kan machen bla* (blue), Muskatbl. 18, 36 ; der T. *slîcht*
vaste herein, Steph. Stofl. 174 ; daz euch nicht *ubersleiche* der T.
mit seim gereusch, Wolkenst. 31. M. Nethl.: êrt die Dôt *belope*,
Maerl. 3, 191. Dir ist vil *nâhe* der Tôt, Ksrchr. 5084. 11298 ;
conf. AS. *nea-laecan* (Suppl. to 846 end) ; swie mir der T. *úf
dem rücken* waere, on my back, MS. 2, 46ᵇ.——Death is invoked
by men weary of life: er *rief* (cried) nâch dem tôde, Ksrchr.
1724 ; Tôt, *kum* u. toete mich ! Dioclet. 4732 ; nun *kum* Tôt !
Hartm. 1, büchl. 292 ; *kum* Dot ! Mar. kl., after Arnold 28. 440 ;
conf. ἐλθέτω μόρος, Aesch. Suppl. 804 ; O Yama, come, release
me, Holtzm. Kur. 723 ; *kom* T., brich mir daz herz enzwei,
Hagen's Ges. Abent. 1, 301 ; wê dir T., *kum her*, u. *nim* uns alle
*hin*, Mai 150, 12. 155, 4. 162, 4. 164, 13. 178, 27 ; *recipe* me ad
te, mors, amicum et benevolum, Plaut. Cistell. iii. 9 ; nu *kum*,
grimmeclîcher T., u. rihte Gote von uns beiden, MS. 1,17ᵇ ; kum
ein *kleines tödelein*, u. für mich balde von hinnen, Bergreien
84 ; wo bist so lang, du grimmer T. ? komb ! H. Sachs iii. 1,
227ᶜ ; O mors, cur mihi *sera venis* ? Prop. iii. 4, 34, conf. Soph.
Philoct. 796 ; *riep* om die dôt, dat si *quame*, Lanc. 35711 ; dat se
den dôd beide *schulden* unde baden, dat he niht *ensûmede* (delay),

wen dat he *quême,* unde ön (fr. them) dat *levend* to hand *neme,*
Everh, Gandersh. 487[a]; weiz Got, *her Tôt,* ir *müezet her,* Apollon.
235; *nim* mich T., *brich* T. mîn herze! Altd. bl. 1, 288-9; ôwê
T., wes *mîdest* (shunnest) du? Ls. 1, 99; wê T., zwiu *sparst* du
mich? Mai 43, 10. W. v. Rheinau 190[a]; eia T., *mohtes* du mich
getoeten! Steph. Stofl. 181; wallan Daeð, wela Daeð, þat þu
me n'elt fordemen, Kg Leir 160, 20; he dex, la mort *m'envoie!*
Guitecl. 2, 148; T., nu *öuge* dich! Hag. Ges. Ab. 300.——
Death comes to give warning; he may *come to terms* or *be put
off* the first two times, but not the third. Similar to the tale in
Straparola 4, 5 is that of *Pikollos,* Hanusch p. 218. Death *siht
an,* looks *at* a man, Warn. 28; he *beckons* or *points,* Ruf's Adam,
1421.

Death takes men away, like Hild and Gund (p. 422): diu kint
*füeret* hin des Tôdes *wint,* Warn. 1648; daz in der T. hât *hin
genomen,* Ulr. Trist. 20. Frib. Trist. 32; Secundillen het der T.
*genomen,* Parz. 822, 20; der T. hât mich *begriffen* (gripped),
Hugdietr. Oechsle 10; ê iz der T. *begrîfe,* Diemer 348, 9; dô
*ergreif* den vater ouch der T., Gregor. 19; *begrîft* iuch dâ der
T. 413; Den hât der T. verzimmert, boxed up, Suchenw. 16,
167; des Tôdes zimmer 19, 17; conf. *diap* dôdes *dalu* (Suppl. to
803); tôdes *muor,* Türl. Wh. 16[a]. Death, like the devil, has jaws,
a throat, to devour with: vallen in des Tôdes *giel* (gullet), Karl
72[a]; si liefen dem Tôd in den *rachen* (ran into the jaws, Theiln.
der Serben (?) p. 23 (yr. 1685); conf. 'ir welt *in gewissen tôt,*'
certain death, Wigal. 6061; in den tôt rîten 6153; we say '*den
in den tod gehn.*'

p. 845.] Death rides, as the dead lover fetches his bride away
on horseback, Hpt's Altd. bl. 1, 177. Müllenh. no. 224; and so
far back as Sæm. 168[b]: *mâl er mer at rîða roðnar brautir,* âðr
salgofnir sigrþioð veki (ere the cock crows); conf. des *Tôdes wîp,*
Engelh. 3402 n.; ich gezîme dir (I suit thee) wol ze *wibe,* Er.
5896. Like the Schleswig Hel (Müllenh. no. 335), Wode also and
the wild hunter ride on a *three-legged horse;* Wode catches the
subterraneans, ties them together by their hairs, and lets them
hang on each side of his horse, Müllenh. p. 373. On Bœotian
tombstones the dead man stands beside the horse, with the inscription: ἥρως χαίρε, K. F. Hermann's Gottesd. alterth. § 16,
20. Charos ranges the babes on his saddle, see GDS. 140-1.

p. 846.] Death takes prisoners. Yama leads away the *mannikin* he has pulled out of the dying man, *tied to a rope* which he
carries about, Holtzm. Ind. s. 1, 64-5. Rochholz 1, 89 ; ob mich
der Tôt *enbindet*, Wh. 68, 22. Death throws his *net* over us,
Steph. Stofl. 174 ; in des Tôdes *vallen* (snares) beklemmet,
Mart. 11ᵇ ; kâmen zuo des Tôdes *valle*, Livl. 1808 ; in des Tôdes
*lâge* (ambush), Kl. 1356 ; der Tôt im daz leben *stal*, Ottoc. 86ᵃ ;
die in (fr. them) het der T. *verstolen*, Wigal. 9213 ; in het vil
nâch (well-nigh) der bitter T. mit sîner kraft *gezücket hin* (tugged
away) 5956 ; sîn leben het *gezücket* der T. 5129 ; der T. *zücket*
(rhy. niderbücket), Wolkenst. 31 ; unz si der T. *ersnellet* (till
d. snaps her up), Hpt's Ztschr. 7, 331 ; der T. hât mich
*ergangen*, Ecke 58 ; do nu der T. *her drang*, St. Louis 60, 17 ;
thaz tôd uns sus *gi-angti*, sus nâher uns *gifiangi*, O. iii. 24, 14,
*i.e.* brought us to such straits, so nearly caught us ; der Tod
*rauscht* her behend, *r. durch die hecken* her, B. Waldis 149ᵃ. 163ᵃ.
Death as conqueror stands over the prostrate dying man : des
Tôt *gestêt uber in selben*, Pfaffenleben 33 ; conf. Dietr. 1669 : die
sîne (his men) *stuonden über in*. The dying have *fallen due to*
Death, become *his men ;* hence we say ' ein *mann* (ein *kind*) des
Todes' : sonst war er ein *mann* des Todes, Zehn ehen p. 226 ;
conf. Dôdis *vuoter* (food) werden, Fundgr. 2, 108 ; des Tôdes
*spil* (sport), Wigal. 10743, den Tôt *laben* (with fortifications),
ibid.——The dying man *wrestles* with D., Sanders p. 44 ; mit
dem grimmen Tôde *ranc*, Servat. 1771 ; mit dem T. hât sînen
*geranc*, Warn. 174 (the devil wrestles too : mit wem die tievel
haben *gerungen*, Renn. 10727) ; überwunden (vanquished) sich
dem Tôde *ergeben* (surrender), Wigal. 7662. Death is armed :
A.S. *wîga* wælgîfre, Cod. Exon. 231, 8 ; *wîga* nealaeceð 164, 4 ;
*deáð nealaecte*, stôp *stalgongum* strong and hreðe 170, 17 ; wir
ligend auf des Todes *spiez* (spear), Ring 253. He shoots arrows,
like Charos (Kindt 1849 p. 17) : *wæl-pîlum*, Cod. Exon. 171, 15,
*wæl-straelum* 179, 11 ; ûf in sleif des Tôdes *hagel* (hail), G. schm.
158 ; in hât benomen des Tôdes *schûr*, Wh. 256, 6. He is a
*hunter*, MSH. 3, 177ᵃ. He is likened to a *thorn :* darinne der tôt
als ein *dorn in dem Meien blüete*, Wigal. 7628. He has a legal
claim upon man : galt der dôt haer *scout* (solvit morti debitum),
Maerl. 1, 430 ; we say ' to pay the debt of nature.'

p. 847.] Death has an army : ' der Tôt fuort in die *gemeinen vart,*' the common journey, Ottoc. 86ᵃ ; 'der T. gebiutet sîne *her-vart,*' army's march, Barl. 397, 32. His badge, his *tácen* (Suppl. to 200), is the pallid hue: des Tôdes zeichen in *liehter varwe,* Nib. 928, 3. 2006, 1; des T. z. wirt schîn (is displayed) in *swarz-gelber* varwe, Warn. 128; des T. *gilwe* (yellow), MS. 2, 166ᵇ. Those who are *veig,* fey, may thus be known, Belg. mus. 5, 113. On the contrary, in Wigal. 6151, a *red* cloth tied to a spear *betokens* that a man shall ride to his death that day :

> An ein sper man im dô bant
> einen samet der was *rôt ;*
> daz *bezeichent* daz er in den tôt
> des tages rîten solde.

Proserpine devotes the dying to Orcus by cutting a lock of hair off them :

> Nondum illi flavum Proserpina vertice *crinem*
> *abstulerat,* Stygioque caput *damnaverat Orco.* Æn. 4, 698.

Iris is sent down to Dido :

> Devolat, et supra caput astitit: ' *Hunc* [crinem] ego *Diti*
> *sacrum* jussa fero, teque isto corpore solvo.'
> Sic ait, et dextra *crinem secat,* omnis et una
> dilapsus calor, atque in ventos vita recessit. Æn. 4, 702.

p. 848.] Death *mows,* Lett. nahwe płavj, Bergm. 69 ; des Tôdes *sichel,* Wolkenst. 278. He is a *sitheman,* Shah-nameh, v. Görres 1, 105-6 ; conf. the 3 maidens that mow the people down with their *sithes,* Kulda in D'Elv. 110.

p. 849.] Death is commonly called the *grim,* Diemer 87, 9. 14. Servat. 1771-92. Hahn's Stricker 11 ; der Tôt in mit *grimme* suochte, Diut. 1, 407 ; ' der *grimme* tôt,' the name of a sword, MSH. 3, 236ᵃ ; der *grimmeclîche* tôt, Hagen's Ges. Abent. 1, 300 ; der *arge* tôt, Ernst 1954 ; der *übel* tod, der *bitter,* Ring 6ᵈ,12. 54ᵇ,26. Fr. '*male* mort ;' ez ist niht *wirsers* danne der tôt, Er. 7935 ; der *leide* dôt, Hpt's Ztschr. 2, 197 (like the devil) ; die *felle* Dôt, Maerl. 2, 133 ; der *gewisse* Tôt, Helbl. 1, 109. Wigal. 6061. 6132 ; er was des *gewissen* Tôdes, Diemer 218, 14 ; '*gewis* sam der Tôt,' sure as d., Lanz. 5881 ; jâ *weistu rehte alsam* den T., Flore 3756 ; ich weiz ez *wârez* (true) als den T., Trist.

119. 17751. 19147. Ulr. Trist. 1964; der *gemeine* T., Hahn 78, 20. 91, 48. Greg. 3769. Schwabensp. p. 179; der *gemeinlìche* T., Klage 534; θάνατος ὁμοῖος, Od. 3, 236; qui omnes manet, conf. Etr. *Mantus* fr. manere, Gerh. pp. 17. 56.

p. 850.] *Dominus Blicero* is called *Bleker* in Coremans 109; dass euch der *blickars* reut! Garg. 134ᵇ; der *blasse menschen-frass* (pale man-muncher), Fleming p. 142; our knöchler, knochenmann, Bony. Death was depicted with frightful aspect: an sînem schilde was der Tôt *gemâlt vil grûsenlîche*, Wigal. 2998; conf. des Tôdes *schild-gemaele*, Tit. 2689, the Harii (p. 950), and the death's-head hussars. On the tomb near Cumae the skeletons are put in a dancing posture, Olfers in Abh. der Acad. '30, pp. 15. 19—22.

p. 852.] '*Friend Hain* is not so easy to buy off,' Hans Wurst doktor nolens volens, Frankf. and Leipz. 1779, p. 39; 'and there *Friend Häyn* did the sexton a kindness,' viz. his wife dies in childbed, Kindleben, Wilib. Schluterius, Halle 1779, p. 114. Jean Paul uses the word in Q. Fixlein p. 170, and Lessing 12, 505 (yr. 1778). But I now find in Egenolf's Sprichw. bl. 321ʰ (under 'sawr sehen'): 'he looks sour, he looks like *Henn* the devil.' The other phrases are all borr. fr. Seb. Frank; this one is peculiar to Egenolf's collection. Conf. '*Heintze* Pik, de dood,' V. d. Bergh 155.——Death stretches the limbs: als sie der Tôt *gestracte*, Ernst 3011; θάνατος τανηλεγής, laying out at length, Od. 3, 238. 11, 171 seq.; 'an deme *Strecke-foisze*,' a place, Arnsb. Urk. no. 493, yr. 1319. *Bleckezahn* is also in Fleming p. 424.

p. 854.] Similar to the expression in H. Sachs, but not so figurative, is the phrase: 'der tôt uns *zucke* daz leben,' jerks the life fr. us, Renn. 20389. Hagen's Ges. Ab. 1, 299. On the *life-candle*, see Wackernagel in Haupt 6, 280—4; daz leben ist unstaete, wan ez *erleschet* der Tôt als ein *lieht*, Altd. bl. 2, 122; the devil (here meaning death) is to come for a man when a *wax-taper has burnt down*, Müllenh. p. 180. On the *torch* of Eros (whose other attribute, like Death's, is the bow), and on his relation to Psyche, see Gerhard's Eros pp. 5. 15. 32. KM.³ 3, 70.——Death is a godfather; see also Phil. v. Sittew. 2, 673-4. In the same way the *hoberges-gubbe*, the *man of the mountain* (miner?) is asked to be godfather (p. 189), Müllenh. p. 289 [In

Shaksp. the jury who convict are godfathers]. As a godfather, it matters much whether you stand at the head or foot: *kopp-vadder*, *stert-vadder*, Schütze 4, 194-5. The Slav. story of *Godmother Smrt* in Wolf's Ztschr. 1, 262-3 may be conf. with our märchen of *Gevatter Tod*, KM. no. 44 and note. On the life-or-death-giving look of the bird *charadrius*, see Plut. Sympos. v. 7, 2. Physiol. in Karajan p. 104.

p. 855.] On the märchen of *Death* and *Jack Player*, see Pref. xvi. xli. The Lith. Welnas is called in Lasicz 48 *vielona*, deus animarum. Beside the Finn. *Tuoni*, there is mentioned a death-god *Kalma*, Schott's Kullervo pp. 218. 235.

---

# CHAPTER XXVIII.

## DESTINY AND WELL-BEING.

p. 856 n.] The Gothic for *feige*, fey, is *dauþ-ublis* (ἐπιθανάτιος), conf. ON. *dauð yfli*, morticinium. *Faeges* forðsîð, moribundi decessus, Cod. Exon. 182, 34; wyrd ne meahte in *faegum* leng feor gehealdan 165, 18. Die *vêge* dôt, Karel 2, 733; *veige* eben todt, Klage 536-9. 1304; sît lie man bî den *veigen* vil der pfaffen ûf dem sande (left with the dying many priests), Gudr. 915, 4; si was ze früeje leider *veige*, Flore 2163; dâ vielen (fell) die *veigen*, Ksrchr. 4909. 7078; dâ gelâgen die *veigen*, 5247. 7803; ' die *veghe* es, hie moet ter moude,' who fey is, must to mould, Walew. 3876; ni sî man nihein sô *feigi* (no mortal), O. i. 11, 10; dâ was der *veige* vunden (found, hit), Trist. 403, 8; conf. der veige rise 401, 18; ir sît *veige* gewesen, Wien. merfart 410. 438; unz der man niht *veige* en-ist, sô erneret in vil kleiner list (so long as he is not fey, a little skill will set him up), Iw. 1299.

p. 857.] Destiny rules over the highest of gods: ὑπὲρ δὲ τῆς κεφαλῆς τοῦ Διός εἰσιν Ὧραι καὶ Μοῖραι, Paus. i. 40, 3. It is expr. by the following terms: ON. *sköp* lêt hon vaxa, Sæm. 249b., OS. *giscapu* mahtig *gimanôdun*, Hel. 10, 18; thiu *berhtun giscapu gimanôdun* 11, 17; *regano-giscapu gimanôdun* 103, 3; conf. torhtlico tîdi gimanôdun 3, 11. Dan. den kranke *skjebne*, DV. 1, 123; conf. den kranke lykke 1, 195.——ON. *örlög*, OHG. *urlac*, MHG. *urliuge*, *urlouc*, Gramm. 2, 790; voru nû endut þau *âlög*, Hervarars. p. 488; and the Sax. compds *orlag-huila*, *orleg-*

*hwîl.*——MHG. *wîl-saelde:* diu *wîlsaelde* ie muoz irgân, Ksrchr.
3493. 3535; conf. 3122-5. 3130. Lanz. 1602. Fundgr. 1, 398;
ein ubel *wîlsaelde,* Ksrchr. 1757. Also the uncompounded *wîle:*
sô hab diu *wîle* undanc! Biter. 11933; sîn *wîle* und sîn tac,
Ksrchr. 3557; '*wîle* u. stunde walzent al-umbe,' fate and the
hour roll round, 3660. 3587. We say 'his *hour* has struck.'

p. 858.] The hour of birth and destiny is determined on by
night: *nôtt* var î boe, nornir qvâmo, þar er auðlîngi aldr umskôpo,
Sæm. 149ᵃ; diu mir wart bescheiden (she was destined for me)
von den *nahtweiden,* dô si êrste wart geborn, Krone 4840.

Even in early times destiny is placed in the hands of gods:

Ζεὺς δ' αὐτὸς νέμει ὄλβον Ὀλύμπιος ἀνθρώποισιν
ἐσθλοῖς ἠδὲ κακοῖσιν, ὅπως ἐθέλῃσιν, ἑκάστῳ.     Od. 6, 188.
κακὴ Διὸς αἶσα.     Od. 9. 55.
ἀνέρος ᾧ τε Κρονίων
ὄλβον ἐπικλώσῃ γαμέοντί τε γιγνομένῳ τε.     Od. 4, 207.
οὔ μοι τοιοῦτον ἐπέκλωσαν θεοὶ ὄλβον.     Od. 3. 208.
ὡς γάρ οἱ ἐπέκλωσεν τά γε δαίμων.     Od. 16, 64.

The last three passages have ἐπικλώθω (I spin for), the term
gener. used of the Fates.

p. 859.] The weighing of destinies, performed by Zeus in the
Iliad, is called 'weighing of souls' by Welcker, Cycl. 2, 189, just
what Christian legend ascribes to St. Michael:

Sant Michel richtet ûf sîn wâge (holds up his balance),
    und henket sich der vâlant dran (though the devil hangs on),
doch schaffet er niht, der swarze man,
    wan sîn slecken ist umbsus (his trickery is in vain).
        Conr. v. Dankrotsch. Namenb. 118.     Berthold p. 17.

p. 860.] The *stars* have influence esp. on birth: tam *grave*
*sidus* habenti, Ov. Trist. v. 10, 45; *vonar-stiarna* flaug. þâ var
ec foeddr, burt frâ briosti mer. hâtt at hun flô, hvergi settiz, svâ
hun maetti hvîld hafa, Sæm. 126ᵇ; 'because their star is *at heat,*
or it has *cooled down* (versauset),' Phil. v. Sittew. Soldatenl. p.m.
149. Other omens attending the conception and birth of a child
are mentioned in Pref. xliv. xlv.

p. 862.] In the unavoidableness of fate there is something
*cruel* and *grudging.* The luckiest and best men perish at last:

sît sturbens *jâmerlîche* von zweier edelen frouwen nît (women's jealousy), Nib. 6, 4; wie liebe mit *leide ze jungest lônen kan* (love may reward with woe at last) 17, 3; als ie diu liebe *leide ze aller-jungiste gît* (turn to woe) 2315; æ koma *mein* eptir munuð, Sæm. 129ᵃ; conf. these views of the world's rewards, and Lehrs' Vom neide p. 149.——To the possession of *costly things* is attached *misfortune* and ruin. In the tale of Tyrfîng it is the splendid *sword* that kills; conf. the fatal sword (p. 205). So the horse of Sejanus proved a *fatal steed*, Gellius 3, 9. Lehrs' Vom neide p. 154. To the same category belong the *Nibelung's hoard*, the *alraun* and *gallows-man* (p. 513 n.). And a union with goddesses and fays makes men unhappy (p. 393).

The Norse *fatalism* comes out in: 'ingen man är starkare än *sitt öde*,' no man is stronger than his fate, Sv. folks. 1, 228. In Vestergötland and Schonen they say: det var hanom *ödt*, GDS. 125-6. M. Neth. dat sîn *sal*, dat *moet* sîn, Karel 2, 1561. MHG. poets have: daz geschach u. *muose sîn*, Türl. Wh. 29ᵃ; wan ez *solt et sîn*, Parz. 42, 6; ez *muoz alsô wesen*, Nib. 1482, 1; swaz *geschehen sol*, daz *geschiht*, Urstende 104, 48. Helmbr. 1683. OS. that it *scolda giwerthan* sô, bethiu ni mahtun si is bemîthan (avoid), Hel. 150, 19. 152, 4. Fr. tot avenra ce quen *doit avenir*, Garin 2, 201.——AS. n'æs ic *faege* þâ git (I was not fey yet), Beow. 4289; conf. ' ez sterbent wan (none but) die *veigen* die doch vil lîhte heime dâ muosen sterben, Tit. 1799; nieman sterben *mac* (can die), unz im kumt *sîn lester tac*, Kl. 103; nieman ersterben mac, ê im kumt *sîn endes-tac*, Lanz. 1613.——Ego vero nihil impossibile arbitror, sed utcunque fata decreverunt ita cuncta mortalibus evenire, Apul. p. m. 87; mir geschiht niht, wan mir *geschaffen* ist, ez muoz nû sîn, MSH. 3, 80; ist ez dir *beschaffen*, Helmbr. 1297; muoz ez wesen, u. ist dir *beschaffen*, Laber p. 200; sei es uns mit heil *beschaffen*, Wolkenst. 178; *beschaffens* glück, Ambras. lied. p. 224-5-7.——Mir ist niht *beaht*, Flore 1184; diu ist dir *erahtôt* (intended), Griesh. 2, 18; dem si rehte *erahtôt* ist 2, 19.——Ih ward *giboran* zi thiu, O. iv. 21, 30; wer zuo *drîn helbling* ist geborn, Diut. 1, 325; ze *drîn scherphen* geborn, Renn. 15886; dur sanc (for song) bin ich *geborn*, MS. 1, 53ᵃ; er wart zer fluht *nie geborn*, Wh. 463, 19; ich wart *in dîne helfe erborn*, Tit. 72, 4; Christianchen ist nicht *für mich geboren*, Gellert 3, 168. We say: es ist mir *angeboren*.——Til lykke *lagt*, DV. 3, 5;

Dan. 'er det saa *laget*, saa faaer det saa blive'; ez gêt keinem anders dan im wirt *úfgeleit*, Mich. Beham's Vom unglauben 4 [necessity is *laid upon* me, 1 Cor. 9, 16].——'Swaz dir *enteile* is getân, des enwirt dir niht benomen,' you can't fail to have, En. 82, 6. 87, 21. 117, 1; deme si *beschert* was, ê si wurde geborn, En. 3993 : nieman gelouben sol an daz wort ' ez ist ime *beschert*,' Germania 3, 233ª; dem galgen *beschert*, Renn. 16815; êst iu *beschert*, u. en-mac niht anders sîn, Flore 4588; uns wirdet cnuogiz *kespirre* ioh *peskerit* N. Arist., *beskerit* unde *beskibet* 94; waz ist uns beiden *beschert* u. *bescheiden*, Herb. 14054. We say : es ist mir *beschieden, verhängt, bestimmt, geschickt*.——Lith. *lemtas*, ordained; was einem *geordnet* sei, dem entrinne man nicht, Gotthelf's Erz. 1, 292; es sei so *geordnet*, u. was sein muss, muss sein 1, 284; *zugeschrempt*, Keisersb. Von koufleuten 89ᵇ. Geistl. lewe 50ᶜ; ez ist mir sus *gewant*, Parz. 11, 8.——More antique are the phrases :

οὐ γάρ πως καταδυσόμεθ' ἀχνύμενοί περ
εἰς Ἀίδαο δόμους, πρὶν μόρσιμον ἦμαρ ἐπέλθῃ.   Od. 10, 174.
μοῖραν δ' οὔτινά φημι πεφυγμένον ἔμμεναι ἀνδρῶν.   Il. 6, 488.

AS. gæ þâ *wyrd* swâ hio *scel*, Beow. 905; sô habed im *wurd-giscapu Metod gimarcod*, Hel. 4, 13, conf. 18, 10. 45, 14.

p. 863.] *Weal* and *luck* are all but personified in the phrases : kum, *glück*, u. schlag' *mit haufen drein*, Docen's Misc. 1, 279; ein garten, den glück u. heil *buwet*, Mohr reg. v. Frauenbr. no. 386, yr. 1434; heil, *walde* iz! Diut. 1, 353; des *helfe* mir gelücke! Nib. 1094, 4; mine *helpe* God ende *goet geval!* Walew. 286; *an's* mi God ende *goed geval!* Karel 2, 3609; mîn heil, nu *linge* (prosper)! Altsw. 14, 31. 96, 4; Silvio *volgete* grôz heil, En. 13138; die wîle (meanwhile) sîn heil *vor gienc*, 7251; to snatch the luck that *was going* to another, Unw. dokt. 358; those that luck *pipes to* may dance, Docen's Misc. 1, 282; when God and good luck *greet* him, Simpl. 1, 536; daz in daz heil *verfluochet* (curses him), Hartm. 1, büchl. 782.——Without personification : si liezen die vart *an ein heil*, 3297; waere daz *an* mînem heile, MS. 1, 193ᵇ; vart iuwer strâze (go your way) *mit quotem heile*, Iw. 832; ze heile *komen*, MS. 1, 75ª; heiles *vurt* waten (wade the ford of), Suchenw. xxxiii. 35; *quotes mannes* heil, Hpt's Ztschr. 2, 179; ich *trowe* mîme heile, Nib. 2102, 4; mîme heile ich gar *verteile*, MS. 1, 83ᵃ ; du maht mîn heil *erwenden* (canst thwart), Walth. 60, 18; ich *danke 's* mîme heile, Nib. 1938, 4 ; conf. mîn saelde sî *verwâzen* (cursed be), Mai 174, 4 ; mîn saelde ich *verfluoche*, Flore 1182 ; ich *ziuhe ez ûf* (I lay it all upon) die s. mîn, Lanz. 3162 ; doch *zürn ich* an die s. mîn 4300.——More peculiar are : 'wünschet daz mir ein heil *gevalle*,' befall, Walth. 115, 5 ; conf. M. Neth. *gheval*, luck, Huyd. sub. v., and our Veldeke's ' daz si mêre (increase) min *geval* ' 1, 21ᵃ; des heiles *slüzzel* (key) in verspart freude, Altd. bl. 2, 236; *verlorn* het er daz heil, Alex. 3389. ' Wünschen *heiles vunt*,' a find of luck, Altd. bl. 1, 339. MS. 2, 190ᵃ. MSH. 1, 357ᵇ. Mai 64, 10. Haupt 7, 117 ; *heile* bruoder, *fröiden vunt*, Dietr. drach. 303ᵇ; der *Saelden vunt*, MSH. 1, 359ᵃ ; *glückes vunt* 351ᵇ.——Glück, heil and saelde are named side by side : doch sô was *gelücke* u. Sîfrides *heil*, Nib. 569, 2 ; *heili* joh *sâlida*, O. Ludw. 5 ; man saget von *glucke* u. von *sâlden*, Herb. 6770 ; sô möht ime *gelücke* u. *heil* u. *saelde* u. *êre* ûfrîsen, Walth. 29, 31 ; *gelücke* iuch müeze *saelden* wern (may fortune grant), Parz. 431, 15. *Gelücke* is distinguished fr. *heil*, Herb. 3238. 15465 ; conf. τύχη, μοῖρα, εἱμαρμένη, Lucian 3, 276 ; *dea Fortuna*, Pl. Pseud. ii. 3, 13.

There is a *white* fortune and a *black*, a *bright* and a *dark : thiu berhtun giscapu*, Hel. 11, 16. 23, 17 ; þâ *beorhtan gescœft*, Cædm. 273, 20.

> Eia, glücke ! eia, heil !
> nu hâst du mir daz *swarze teil* (black side)
> allenthalben zuo gekart (toward me turned) ;
> mir sint die *wîzen wege* verspart (barred),
> dâ ich wîlen ane ginc (whereon I whilom went).
>
> Herb. 15465—69.

Frommann p. 321 understands this of the moon's light or dark disc, and seems to derive the ' wheel of fortune ' altogether fr. the lunar orb. Conf. Lett. ' ak mannu *baltu deenu!* ' my white day, Bergm. 76 (see p. 1138).

p. 864.] Of *Saelde's* vigilance I have some more examples [Omitted]: mîn S. *erwachet*, Ls. 2, 509 ; swer si nu solde schouwen, des S. was *niht entslâfen*, Türl. Wh. 46ᵃ. And the same of Luck and Unluck: hadde mi *mîn gheluc ghewaect*, Marg. v. Limbg 1, 1226 ; our *unluck wakes*, Günther 1014 ; my *luck* is fast *asleep* 212 (conf. Dan. 'den *kranke lykke*,' DV. 1, 195; den *kranke skjebne* 1, 123). M. Neth. die *Aventure wacht* (p. 911); *erwachet* sîn *planet,* Chron. in Senkenb. 3, 459; *fortunam* ejus in malis tantum civilibus *vigilasse,* Amm. Marc. 14, 10, conf. ' at vos *Salus servassit,* Plaut. Cist. iv. 2, 76. The *Laima* (Suppl. to 877) also *sleeps* and *wakes up,* Büttner no. 761. Luck is coaxed: sê, *gelücke,* sê, Walth. 90, 18.——Similar phrases : mîn weinender *schade* (hurt) *wachet,* MSH. 1, 102ª; *skade vaker,* Aasen's Ordspr. 210; ' to *wake* a sleeping *sorrow,*' Oedip. Colon. 510. ON. *vekja* Nauð, Sæm. 194ᵇ (var.), like *vekja víg* 105ª. *Vreude* diu ist *erwachet,* diu ie verborgen lac (lay hid), MS. 2, 99ª; conf. *wach auf, fried,* Fastn. 39, 1 ; bî werden man (to noble-minded men) sô *wachent wibes güete,* MS. 1, 190ª; ir güete u. bescheidenheit ist gên mir *entsláfen* 1, 26ᵇ ; ir *genâde* (favour) mir muoz *wachen* 1, 33ª; wil ir diu (*minne*) ze herzen nâhen *wachen,* MSH. 1, 316ᵇ. Nemesis, vengeance, sleeps and wakes. ' A place where a certain *danger waked,*' Serb. u. Kroat. 10.

p. 866.] Fortuna, like Ver Sælde (Hagen's Ges. Ab. 1, 409), waits long *at the door,* and is not admitted, Dio Cass. 64, 1 ; mir ist verspart (barred) der *Saelden tor,* Walth. 20, 31 ; der *S. tor* entsliezen (unlock), Dietr. drach. 179ª; conf. Hpt's Ztschr. 2, 535 and dream-gate (Suppl. to 1146 beg.). In the same way: ' sliuz mir ûf der *vröuden tor,*' unlock me the gates of joy, MSH. 1, 356ª; gein dem süezen Meien stênt offen *fröiden tor,* MS. 2, 108ª; der *fröiden tor* ist zuo getân (shut) 2, 198ᵇ : thro' *portals wide* poured joy into her house, Gotthelf 2, 203 ; thy luck comes in *at every gate,* Fabricius's Haustafel (V. f. Hamb. gesch. 4, 486) ; der *genâden tor,* Hpt 4, 526.——Exulatum *abiit salus,* Plaut. Merc. iii. 4, 6; ' des solt in *Saelde wíchen,*' quit them, Albr. Tit. 2344 ; diu *S.* mir *entwíche,* MS. 2, 20ª; conf. ' da unse heil *von uns trat,*' Pass. 40, 80 ; ' heill er *horfin,*' gone, Völs. c. 11 ; ' la *Fortune passa,* elle part à ces mots,' Lafont. 5, 11 ; conversely : ' *zuo gienc daz unheil,*' on came mischief (Suppl. to 879). Saelde von uns *vonit,* Athis F, 20 ; *S.* wont im bî, u. *vont,* Heinr. Krone 56ᵈ; dar Saelden *ane genge,* Hpt 4, 525 ; daz dich daz gelücke *angê,* Diocl. 4376. 8759 ; alles glück *wehete* (blew) dich *an,* Unw. doct. 617.——Luck approaches one who *sleeps* at the well-side, Babr. 49, 2 ; predestined luck comes *overnight,* Ambras. 247 ; conf. ' falling *asleep* betw. two lucks, Altd. bl. 2, 175;

an Saelden wunsches *arm entsláfen,* Tit. 1248. Ipsa, si vellet, *Salus* his circumfusa, ut *vulgo loquimur,* eos salvare non posset, Liutpr. Legatio 13. Er was *ûf* der *Saelden wege,* Ernst 1843; conf. ' sô verst *ûf gelückes ban,*' MS. 1, 88^b; *hôhe getrat* ze Saelden, Mar. 164, 30; ich kan si wol *erjagen* (hunt her down): si-ne welle sich mir mê *versagen* (refuse me more) dan si sich deheime (any one) *versagte,* der si ze rehte *jagte,* Greg. 1529. ' Ir Saelde diu *sach* sie an,' looked on her, Mar. 187, 20; we say 'smiled upon,' conf. τὴν τύχην προσμειδιῶσαν, Lucian's Asin. 47, Fortuna arridet. ' Ich muoz *ir gruoz* verdienen,' earn Fortune's greeting, Greg. 1527; Got u. das glück *grüszet,* Simpl. 1, 536; daz mich vrô Saelde *erkande* (recognised), MS. 2, 99^a; sô *volgt* dir S. *nách,* MSH. 3, 224^b; mîn frô S., wie sie mîn *vergâz* (forgot me), Walth. 43, 5. ' Einer gelücke *erslîchet,* daz der ander niht wol kan *erloufen,*' one *creeps* up to her, another can't *run* her down, MSH. 3, 297^a; das glück *erschleichen,* Fischart's Gesch. kl. 95^b. Uhl. Volksl. 584. Ambras. 102; ' luck wants to be boldly *galloped up* to,' Polit. stockf. p. 240.——' Gelücke ist uns *verswunden,*' vanished, Altd. bl. 2, 150; ' wie in gelücke flôch,' fled, Ottoc. 713^a; ' vrou Saelde *kêret* mir den *nac,*' turns her neck (back), Frauenl. 447, 22; fortuna *malefida,* Rudl. 1, 11; fortuna *vetus,* 1, 66; vrou S. ist *wilder* dan ein rêch (roe), MSH. 2, 315^a, conf. ' gelücke *lief entwerhes,*' ran athwart, Troj. 12598; S. wird *pflücke,* Kolocz 100; daz *wiltwilde* gelücke *springt,* MS. 2, 147^b. ' In der Saelden *huote* varn,' travel in her keeping 1, 88^a; wîsen ûz vrou S. *huote,* MSH. 1, 339^a; conf. ' cum fortuna ludere,' be her playmate, favourite, Pertz 2, 79.——' Der Saelden *stabe,* dâ sult ir iuch an *stiuren,*' staff whereon ye shall lean, MSH. 3, 462^a; sitzen ûf der S. *kür* 1, 93^a (MS. 1, 36^a); daz iuch vrô Saelde *lâze* widerkêren (send you back), Troj. 9359; wie dich diu S. *fuorte* (led), Hpt 4, 524. ' Diu S. mich *an sich nam,* si *riet* mir,' advised me, Wigam. 4119; ' den *ir S.* daz *geriet,*' for so her luck advised, Wh. 451, 4; ' daz sie diu S. *tuon hiez,*' what S. bade her do, Eracl. 54; ' dar *sîn S.* hât erdaht,' wherever his luck thought good, Parz. 827, 17. ' Diu S. ir mit flîze *pflac,*' carefully tended her, Wigal. 8950; vrou S. ir *stiure gap* sîner ammen (bestowed her gifts on his nurse), diu sîn phlac, dô er in der wiegen (cradle) lac,' Er. 9898; von der Saelden *gebe,* Altd. bl. 2, 218; nû het diu *vrowe Saelikheit* allen-wîs an in geleit (on him set) *ir vil staetigez*

*marc*, Greg. 1063 ; der Saelden *gundes teil*, Krone 4833.——Er
sitzet in S. *vogel-hûse*, Renn. 19512 ; kaeme ich ûf der S. *stuol*,
Partenop. 93 ; der. S. *dach* (roof), MS. 1, 191ᵇ ; daz uns decke
dîner S. *van* (flag), MSH. 1, 339ᵇ ; entsliezen ûf (unlock) der S.
*schrîn*, Dietr. drach. 94ᵇ ; aller S. *grunt* 105ᵃ. 303ᵇ ; der S. *seil*
(rope) 239ᵇ. 257ᵃ ; der S. *vaz* (cask), Hag. Ges. Ab. 1, 461 ; sich
daz (beware lest) dîn muot iht trunken gê von des gelückes *stoufe*
(bowl), Frauenl. 116, 19 ; von gold ein S. *vingerlîn* (ring), Lanz.
4940 ; daz *golt* der S., Tit. 4914. 5028 ; *Saeldenberc*, Mone 1,
346. 7, 319.——Der S. *zwîc* (twig, Suppl. to 977) ; ein *zwî* daran
diu Saelde *blüejet*, Hpt 4, 527 ; sîn S. *blüete*, Wh. 463, 9 ; ez
grüenet mîner Saelden *rîs* (twig), Winsbekin 6, 4 ; wo sein *glücks-*
*grasl graint*, Stelzhamer 36 ; gelücke ist *witen* hie *gesât* (widely
sown), Dietr. drach. 187ᵃ. It is prettily said : das glück *abbla-*
*ten* (disleaf), Fastn. sp. 1143, as if to pluck off the flower of luck ;
' luck *brings roses*,' Ldrb. of 1582, 225 ; grozmechtig *krut-körb*
*voll* glück (huge hamperfuls), Fastn. sp. 884, 24, conf. ' gelück
in einem *kreben* (korb, basket) finden,' Hätzl. 85ᵇ ; der Saelden
*stücke* (pieces, items ?), Parz. 734, 24 ; hât-er darzuo der S. *swert*,
Altd. bl. 2, 229 ; der S. *slac* (blow), Iw. 4141, conf. ' ne nos
Fortuna *sinistro cum pede* prosternat,' Gesta Witigowonis 477 ;
' at first she can't take in her luck, by and by she'll snap at its
*fists*,' Schoch's Stud. D 3ᵇ ; der S. *swanz* (tail) hât dich umbe-
vangen, Hpt 4, 520. ' Der S. *tou* sîn herze hât genetzet,' S.'s
dew has drenched his heart, MSH. 3, 173ᵇ ; ' bliss comes *dewing*
down,' Goethe 14, 74, conf. ' alles heils ein *lûter bach*,' limpid
stream, Altsw. 98, 23 ; ' luck *snows* upon us in large flakes,'
Phil. v. Sittew. 2, 665.——Observe the plur. *saelden*, like ' heillir
horfnar' (p. 864-5 n.): thên *sâlidon* intfallan, O. ii. 4, 89 ; er
mohte *sînen saelden* immer sagen danc, Nib. 300, 2 ; waere 'z *an*
*den s.* mîn, Reinh. 436. In Tyrol (15th cent.) a *frau Selga* rides
at the head of the nightly host, Germania 2, 438, but she may
be the selige, blissful, not our Saelde. Conf. the Indian goddess
of prosperity *Šri*, Holtzm. 3, 150, the ἀγαθὴ Τύχη, the *bona*
*Fortuna*, Gerh. in Acad. ber. '47, p. 203-4.

p. 869.] On *fortune's wheel* see Wackernagel in Hpt 6, 134
seq. Cupid also has a wheel: vorsor in *Amoris rota* miser,
Plaut. Cist. ii. 1, 4. Fortunae *sinistrorsum* sibi *rotam* volvere
sentit, Pertz 8, 235, conf. the image in Carm. burana p. 1 ;

*volubilis rota* transeuntis mundi, Kemble no. 761 (yr 1038) ; *rota fatalis* in Hemmerlin, Reber p. 236 ; videns fortunam, ut solet, *ludicra rota* reciprocare, Eckehardi casus S. Galli (Pertz 2, 88). The mere turning of the wheel denotes the mutability of fate, Fauriel's Poésie Prov. 3, 509. Serb. märch. no. 42, p. 198. Meghadûta ed. Schütz p. 41 str. 107, and the passage fr. Plutarch, ibid. p. 109.

Gelücke ist *sinewel* (spherical), Wh. 246, 28 ; der liute heil ist *ungewegen* u. *sinwel*, Bit. 12440. Fortune rises and falls, like a *wheel* in motion, Meghad. 108 ; daz *rat* der *frô Fortûne*, Turlin's Krone 7 ; Marîe, du *heiles* u. *gelückes rat*, Hpt 4, 523 ; dat *rat* van *avonturen*, Rein. ed. Will. 6183 ; mir gêt der *Saelden schîbe* (wheel), Engelh. 4400 ; dô unser *schîbe* ensamt gie (together went), Warn. 3048 ; wil mir der S. *schîbe* gân, als si dicke (oft) hât getân, Dietr. drach. 12 ; *gelückes rat* umbe trîben, Troj. 13322 ; als sich kêret (turns) des gelückes *rat*, Pass. 32, 62 ; in bezôch der werlde gelückes *rat* 356, 15 ; si vuoren (rode) ûf gelückes *rade*, Flore 845, conf. ' auf *gelukes choken* varen,' Suchenw. 27, 115 ; ich lige iemer *under* glückes *rade*, MS. 2, 194ª ; ic was te hoghe gheseten (sat too high) op dat *rat der aventuren*, Marg. v. Limb. 1, 185 ; Woldemares *schive* in groten lukken hadde lopen (run), Detm. 1, 99 ; gelückes *balle*, Tit. 2368 ; unglücke daz gê si an (befall them), darzuo der *laster* (infamy's) *schîbe* müeze in allen gên in hant ! Dietr. dr. 143 ᵇ.

Saelde *is* sometimes called *blind :* sprich niht ' Saelde sî *blint*,' des si niht ist, Cato 442 ; sia mâletôn (her they painted) *plinda*, Notk. Boëth. 42 ; and *avonture* is blind, Rose 5067, or blindfolded 5858. Notker in Boëth. 43 translates ' deprehendisti *coeci* numinis ambiguos vultus' by ' nû bechennest tû daz analutte des *sich pergenten* (skulking) truge-tieveles.' To Gotfrid's ' *glesîn* glücke ' add the ' fortuna *vitrea* ' of the Archipoeta p. m. 237.

p. 869.] Der *Saelden kint*, Freid. 134, 2 ; Gabriel salutes Mary as such, MSH. 3, 18ª ; frou *Saelde* und *Heil*, ir kint, Krone 15827. 23094, conf. ' sit in the middle of God's lap,' Drei kl. leute 159 ; *mignon*, Lafont. 5, 5 ; *frou S.* ir stiure gap sîner ammen, diu sîn phlac, dô er in der wiegen lac (in his cradle lay), Er. 9898. ' Der *Saelden bote*,' messenger, Pantal. 172 ; *Seldenbut*, Urk. of Hanover ; des sî mîn *Saelde* gein im *bote*, Parz. 416, 4. Like Saelden bote are also : *Triuwen bote*, Engelh. 6332 ;

*Eren bote*, honour's m., Frauend. 487, 13. 479, 28; der *E. holde*, Athis C 82. Er. 9962; der *E. kneht*, Engelh. 4152; der *S. holde*, Lanz. 1996; der *S. hûs-genôz*, housemate, Wh. 3, 125ª; der *S. schol*, Er. 2401; der *Unsaelden kneht*, Hartm. 2, büchl. 626; der fürste *selden herre*, Heldenb. (1590), 110ᵇ, et passim.

p. 873.] Of *frau Fortuna*, a kind of Venus, there is a legend in Altd. bl. 1, 297. With Fortunatus conf. *Faustus*. The *wishing-hat* carved out of a finger-nail, Schiefner on Kalewipoeg pp. 146. 154, resembles Nagl-far (p. 814). On the miraculous making of *cloths*, see Rommel 2, 342 fr. the Ann. Erf. in Menken 3. There is frequent mention of a *girdle* that gives strength (Suppl. to 182), the strength of 12 men, Laurin 1966. 2441, or allays hunger, Ferabr. 2752. 2800; ON. *hûngurband*, our *schmacht-rieme*. Saxo ed. Müller 114 mentions an ' *armilla* possessoris opes *augere* solita,' a ' *tunica ferrum spernens* ' 118, an ' *insecabilis vestis* ' 122; conf. the *growing mantle* in Lanz. 5812, the *seamless coat*, the κρήδεμνον of Ino, Od. 5, the *breost-net broden*, Beow. 3095, the *bread-pocket* in Wigal. 4469. 5843.——Discordia makes herself invisible by a *ring*, Troj. 1303-24, and the like magic lies in the ring with a nightingale in it, Morolt 1305; conf. the ring of Gyges, Plato's Rep. 359. 360. *Seven-league boots*, bottes de sept lieues, Perrault 167. Aulnoy 367. St. Columban has a *wishing-staff* (p. 976).——If Amalthea (Athen. 4, 345. 371) and Fortuna have a *horn-of-plenty*, ' *Fortuna cum cornu* pomis, ficis aut frugibus *pleno*,' Arnob. 6, 25 (conf. ' nam haec allata *cornu-copiae* est, *ubi inest quicquid volo*,' Plaut. Pseud. ii. 3, 5); so has our old Otfrid i. 10, 5 a *horn heiles*, and Wolkenst. p. 61 a *Saelden-horn*, conf. *Gif-horn*. It is an odd thing to speak of sitting down on the *bull's horns*, i.e. pillars, *of wealth*, Pentam. Liebr. 2, 112.

——To make a *wishing-net*, you burn a small boat, and sow flax in the ashes, which shoots up in two days, is picked, baked and braked in two days more, and spun, knitted and stitched in another two days, Kalev. 26, 188; conf. Schröter p. 19. *Wishing-dice* in H. Sachs ii. 4, 114ᶜ. On the *stone of victory*, see p. 1220. *Indra's spear* that *never misses*, that *of itself* comes *back* to the hand, and even when he lends it to others, returns to *his* hand (Holtzm. Ind. s. 2, 137-8. 155), and the javelin that *flies back* of its own accord (Ov. Met. 7, 684), are like Thôr's hammer, like the *sword that gives victory* in Saxo ed. Müll. 115, like the one

that *brandishes itself* in Dybeck ii. 28, and *l'arc qui ne faut*
in the O. Fr. Trist. 1716-45.——The Ssk. *manoratha,* wheel of
thought, may be the same as the wheel in Wigalois, conf. Saelde's
wheel and her glove, Krone 22855. 23093. Similar to *Skiðblaðnir,*
the navis plicatilis (p. 216), is a *tent* in Lanz. 4898 seq., which
folds up, and can with ease be carried by a maiden.    In the land
of the Æthiops ' est locus apparatis epulis semper refertus, et
quia *ut libet vesci volentibus* licet, ἡλίου τράπεζαν appellant, et
quae passim apposita sunt affirmant innasci subinde divinitus,'
Pomp. Mela 3, 9; see Herod. 3, 17-8, where the earth itself
covers the table with meats overnight; conf. the city wherein
the *blessing should abide,* Gellert 1, 194; before the *Gral* all
manner of meats and drinks stood ready, Parz. 238, 10. 239, 1
(the Gral suffers no vermin in Salvaterra, Tit. 5198; the name
*Graalanz* as early as 10th cent., Irmino 49[b]).——A *wishing-tree*
that bears clothes, trinkets, etc., and wine, Meghadhûta ed. Schütz
p. 25-7; like the tree in our fairy-tale, fr. which the child shakes
*dresses* down.   The wishing-cow *Kâma-duh* means ' milkable at
will,' Bopp's Gl. 70[b]. Weber 5, 442; acc. to Hirzel's Sakunt.
153 *Nandini* is the lucky cow that grants all wishes; add the
ass that utters gold, peau d'âne, and the hen that lays golden
eggs.   On the *contest for wishing-gear,* see Pref. p. xxxiii.

p. 874 n.]   On *lucky children* and their *cauls,* see Röszler 2,
xcv. xcvi. and 337.   KM.[3] 3, 57; wir bringen allesamen ein *rot
wammesch* uff erden (pellem secundinam), das mûss darnach der
man (husband) unter die stegen vergraben, Keisersp. Wannen-
kremer 109[d].   In AS. the caul is *heafela, hafela,* Andr. p.
127-8 n.; MHG. *hüetelin, batwât,* Hpt 1, 136-7, *kindbälgel,* Mone
8, 495, *westerhûfe* in the Ritterpreis poem, *westerhuot,* Karaj. 27,
6; conf. the *westerwât* preserved in churches, N. Cap. 83, and
the baptismal shirt of healing power, Dresd. Wolfdietr. 160-1-2;
stera, *vaselborse,* pellicula in qua puer in utero matris involvitur,
Hoffm. Hor. Belg. 7, 19[b].   Lith. *namai kudikio,* child's house,
Nesselm. 414.   ON. Hlöðr is born with *helmet* and sword (p.
389). GDS. 121.

p. 876.]   Every man has an *angel of his own,* but so have
some beasts, Keisersp. Brosäml. 19[c].   Agreeing with Cæsar
Heisterb., the Pass. 337, 46 says : daz einer iegelichen menscheit
*zwêne engel* sint bescheiden : einen *guoten,* einen *leiden* iegelich

mensche bî im hât. Every man has *his candle in the sky*, Hpt 4, 390 (see Suppl. to 722 end). Dô sprach der *engel wol-getân* : 'ich was ie mit dir, unt woldest nie *gevolgen* mir (obey me); von ubele ich dich chêrte (turned), daz beste ich dich lêrte,' Tund. 46, 60; ich bin der *engel*, der *dîn pfliget*, Ges. Abent. 2, 255; wil du *dînem engel* schenken (wîn), Griesh. 2, 50; *angleus* Domini te semper praecedat, comitetur ac subsequatur, Vita Mahthild. c. 20.——In Otfr. v. 4, 40 the angel says to the women : jâ birun wir in wâra iu *eigenê giburâ*=your servants. The angel is called *wîsaere*, director, Helbl. 7, 249. 331, an invisible voice 7, 263. 293. 355; dû hâst gehôrt ein stimme, die *sîn engel* sprach, Pass. 158, 79; (der werlde vluot) manigen hin verdrücket, ob in dar-ûz niht zücket (plucks him out) *sîn engil* mit voller kraft, 337, 41. The angel *rejoices* over his protégé, MSH. 3, 174ᵇ.——The heathen think an old Christian has a young one inside him, and when he is dying the *angels take a baby* out of his mouth, Ottoc. 440-1 [see a mosaic in the cath. of San Michele Maggiore, Pavia]. On English guardian-angels, see Stewart's Pop. superst. 4, 16-7; on Indian, Somadeva 2, 117. Hermes is an escort, πομπαῖος, to men, Aesch. Eum. 91.

p. 877.] Biarki's *bear*-fylgja is in Petersen's Hedenold 1, 210-3 ; a similar *bear* in Fornald. sög. 1, 102-5; Gunnar's fylgja, the *biarndýr*, in Nialss. c. 23. As swans are guardian-angels, *ravens* are a kind of attendant spirits to heathens : Haraldi ver fylgðom (p. 671). On 'gefa nafn ok fylgja lâta,' see GDS. 153-4.——*Hamíngja* means luck, Fornm. sög. 4, 44; *gœfa ok h.* 4, 26; *î hamíngju tauti*, in the riot, full swing, of luck, Biörn sub v. taut; ef *hamíngja fylgir*, 7, 280; *fylgjor* hans höfðo *vitiað* Heðins, Sæm. 147ª. Glûm's dream of his father-in-law's *h.* appearing as a *dîs*, who towered above the hills, is in Vîgagl. sag. c. 9.——Engl. *fetch* : 'I had seen *her fetch*,' Hone's Daybk. 2, 1011-3-6-7; in some parts of Scotl. *fye* for fetch 1019 ; 'to see his *double* 1012; *wiff, waff, wraith, swarth* 1019-20. Ir. *taise*, Conan 105 ; conf. Wilh. Meister, where some one *sees himself* sitting; the *white lady*, the *banshie*.

p. 877.] The Slav. *dóbra srétia*, Vuk 3, 444, *srétia*=luck 788, looks very like Ssk. *Śri*, Bopp 356ᵇ [but s-ret-ati=convenire, ob-ret-ati=invenire, etc.]; srétia is bestowed by *U-súd*, destiny. 'I am *thy luck, thy brother's luck*,' Serb. märch. no. 13. The

Lettic *Laima*, Nesselm. 351, is distinct fr. Laume 353; Lith. also *Laima* = Gk. *Λαιμώ*, Lat. Lamia (p. 500 n. Suppl. to 864 mid.): *Laima lĕme* sauluzês dienatę, Rhesa dain. p. 10. She is comp. in Bopp's Gl. 296ª to *Lakshmi*, abundantiae et felicitatis dea.

p. 879.] Misfortune comes, goes: chumet *ein unheil*, Karajan 5, 2. 19, 15; zuo gienc in beiden *daz unheil*, Diut. 2, 51, conf. daz leit gieng ire zuo 2, 50; hie trat *mîn ungelücke* für, Parz. 688, 29; *unglück* wechst über nacht, u. hat ser ein breiten fusz, Mathesius (1562) 279ª; Swed. quick som en *o-lycka*. Trouble does not come alone; nulla calamitas sola; das *unglück* was mit gewalt da, Herbenst. 330; *t' on-geval* dat es mi bi, Karel 1, 699; *on-spoet* (unspeed) comt gheresen, Rose 8780; *unheil* unsir râmit (creams, thickens), Athis F 21; 'where has *misfortune* had you, that you look so gory?' Reise avant. (1748) p. 107; *unheil* habe, der iz haben wil! En. 12859; si hat des *ungelucks jeger* mit seinen henden umbfangen gar (U.'s hunter has her tight), Keller's Erz. 157, 10; sie reitet *ungelücke* (rides her), Beham in Wien. forsch. p. 47ª; *unfal* reitet mich, Ambras. lied. 92, 9; conf. Death riding on one's back (Suppl. to 844 beg.); was euch *unfal* geit, Murner 2832; *Unfalo* in Theuerdk; *un-gevelle*, Flore 6152; *unheil* mich fuorte an sînen zöumen (reins), Engelh. 5502; riet mir *mîn unheil* (advised me), Er. 4794; undanc begunde er sagen ('gan curse) sîme grôzen *unheile*, Kl. 403 L.; sîn *ungelücke* schalt, Lanz. 1951; *mîn Unsælde*, Nib. 2258, 1; *Unsælde sî* verwâzen! Helmbr. 838; *Unselden-brunne*, Mone's Anz. 6, 228; *Unsælde* ist heiles vîent (foe), Flore 6158; '*misf.* is at the door, in blossom,' Fromm. 4, 142; *ungelückes zwîc* (twig), Cod. pal. 355, 116ª [the oppos. of Saelden-zwîc, wishing-rod, Suppl. to 977 beg.]; *ung. winde*, MS. 1, 84ᵇ; thut ein *ungelück* sich aufdrehen (turn up), H. Sachs iii. 3, 8ª. The *shutting misf. up* in an 'eicher' is like fencing-in the Plague and spectres, Müllenh. p. 196; the devil too gets wedged in a beech-tree, Bechst. Märch. 42; si haben *unglück* in der kisten (trunk), Fastn. sp. 510, 8.

# CHAPTER XXIX.

## PERSONIFICATIONS.

p. 880.] Like the Gr. πρόσωπον is the Goth. *ludja*, Matth. 6, 17, conf. Gal. 4, 19. I have found MHG. *schîn* = εἶδος in two more places : des lewen *schîn*, Bon. 67, 42 ; sînen *schîn* (image), Lanz. 4926. Personification does not give rise immed. to *proper* names, for these tolerate no article (Gramm. 4, 405. 595), but to such names as ' der Wunsch, diu Sælde, der Hunger.'

p. 884.] To personified *elements* I have to add the Slav. *Pogóda* (p. 637), conf. Byr ; *Ignis, Aqua, Aër, Veritas* in Scherz u. Ernst (1522-50) cap. 4, (1555) c. 354. H. Sachs i. 255 ; *Frosti, Logi, Skiálf* (tremor), Yngl. sag. c. 22. We say of *Snow*, ' there's a *new neighbour* moved in overnight' (pp. 532. 761). ' *Hrîm* and *Forst, hâre hildstapan* lucon leoda gesetu,' Andr. 1258 and Pref. p. xxxv. The Esths worship Cold (külm) as a higher being, Peterson p. 46. Finn. *Hyytö, Hyytämöinen* = gelu ; *Aeryämöinen* is the wrathful genius of severe cold. MHG. *Rîfe* (p. 761).——Was ' die *Heide*,' the heath, thought of as a person? she blushes for shame, Walth. 42, 21. Men blessed the *Way*, and bowed to it (p. 31 n.). The name of *Hlîn* the âsynja is echoed back in AS. *hlîn*, Cod. Exon. 437, 17, as the name of a tree. The George in Reinbot's allegory is a child of *der Sunne* and *diu Rôse*, and is called *Rôsen-kint*. On Nŷji and Niði, see above (p. 700). With the two femin. names of months in AS., *Hrede* and *Eástre*, conf. the Roman *Maia, Flora, Aprilis*, who are goddesses in spite of the months Maius and Aprilis being masc.

p. 887.] The *sword*, the biter, is often made a person of. Ssk. *asi-putrî* = culter, lit. Sword's daughter ; conf. ON. *sultr* (p. 888). KM.[3] 3, 223. The ON. *alr*, awl, is brother to the dwarf or the knîfr, Sn. 133. Does ' *helm* ne gemunde *byrnan* sîðe' in Beow. 2581 mean ' the helmet forgot the coat of mail'? On *rhedo*, see GDS. 606. Strange that a warrior's garb is in Beow. 903 *Hræðlan* lâf, but in 4378 [*Hre*]ðles lâfe ; conf. herge-wäte, RA. 568. A *ship* on touching land is addressed as a living creature (p. 1229 ?).——It is a confirmation of *Brîsînga men*, that the OS. *Throt-manni*, monile gutturis, is the name of the town Dortmund, and *Holtes-meni*, monile silvæ, Trad. Corb. no.

321, afterwards called *Holtes-minne* 384, is the present Holz-minden. With *Hnoss* is perh. to be conn. the OHG. female name *Neosta*, Förstemann 1, 960; ON. kvenna *hnoss* = mint. *Mann-gersimar* occurs in Thidr. saga p. 153. What means the M. Neth. 'want haer met *gersemen* doeken'? Rose 11001; is gärs-uma the truer division of the word? Gramm. 2, 151. Light is thrown on the maiden *Spange* by *auð-spaung* ûngri, feminae juvenculae, Kormakss. p. 186; conf. *mouwe* = maiden and sleeve, fetter (Kl. schr. 5, 441), *erenberga*, both shirt and Erem-berga, *schilt-vezzel* (-fetter) = scutiger, squire, Oswalt 3225. In the same way as *Hreda, Hnoss, Gersemi, Menja* (p. 306-7) and the Rom. *Carna*, dea cardinis (Ov. Fasti 6, 101—168), are to be expl. the gods' names *Loki* and *Grentil*. A beautiful woman was often compared to some goddess of female ornament : *hodda Sif, hodda Freyja, hringa Hlín* in Kormakss. 26 means simply a lady adorned with rings. On the same footing as the goddesses of nuts, bees, dough, etc. cited by Lasicz p. 48-9 stand the Puta, Peta, Patellana, Viabilia, Orbona, Ossilago, Mellonia in Arnob. 4, 7. 8, and the goddesses of grains in Augustine's De Civ. D. 4, 8 (Rhein. jrb. 8, 184) and many more in the same author; conf. Robigo, Rubigo (p. 477 end).

p. 887.] Men *greeted* the player's die, *bowed* to it, Jüngl. 389. On *Decius*, see Méon 4, 486-7. *Hazart* geta arriere main, Ren. 18599; *Hasars*, Myst. de Jubinal 2, 388-9. *Dvápara* et *Kali* sunt nomina tertiae et quartae mundi aetatis, et daemones harum aetatum, Nalus p. 213, conf. Holtzm. 3, 23-9 and Pref. xi.; the dice-playing of Yuzishthira and Sakuni was celebr., also that of Nala and Pushkara, Holtzm. 2, 1—11. 3, 23-9. MHG. ' her Pfenninc,' MS. 2, 148ᵃ.

p. 888.] Victory is personified in the AS. phrase : *Sigor* eft âhwearf *œsc-tîr wera*, Cædm. 124, 25. Similarly : ' deme *Orloge* den hals breken,' break the neck of battle, Detmar 2, 555; ' *Hederlein* brother to *zenklein* ' (hader, zank = quarrel), H. Sachs i. 5, 538ᵈ; ' der *Rewel* beiszt,' repentance bites, Luther 9, 472ᵇ; ' der *Zorn* tritt,' anger steps, Pantal. 86. On Φόβος, *Pavor* and the like, see above (p. 207-8).——Goth. snau ana ins *Hatis*, ἔφθασεν ἐπ' αὐτοὺς ἡ ὀργή, 1 Thess. 2, 16; ' an dem hât *Haz* bî *Nîde* ein kint,' in him hate had a child by envy, MS. 1, 75ᵃ; kâmen ûf des *Nîdes* trift, Pantal. 754. Envy, like Φθόνος, is a dæmon; there was a form of prayer to keep him off, Lehr's Vom neide 144 seq.; Finn. *Kati*, genius invidiae; we say ' Envy looks, peeps, out of him.' The OHG. *Inwiz*, masc., may be the same, though the Roman *Invidia* is feminine. ON. *Topi* oc *Opi*, *Tiösull* oc *Ópoli* vaxi þer târ meδ trega, Sæm. 85ª.——Πλοῦτος, the god of wealth, is blind; the Ssk. *Kuvéra* is ugly, with three legs and eight teeth, Bopp 78ª; *Rîcheit*, Er. 1584.——*Hunger*, se þeod-sceaδa hreow rîcsode, Andr. 1116, conf. our ' hunger reigns '; *Hunger* is the best cook, Freid. 124, 17; der *H.* was ir beider koch, Wigam. 1070; *Honghers* cameriere, Rose 4356; der *H.* koch, der *Mangel* küchen-meister, Simpl. 25; we say ' *Schmal-hans* is head-cook here '; bald legt sich *Schm.* in das zimmer, Günther 1050, conf. ' her *Bigenot* von *Darbion*, her *Dünne-habe*, MS. 2, 179ª; dô lag er ûf daz *hunger-tuoch* (-cloth), Fragm. 22ª; am *hunger-tuch* neen (sew), H. Sachs ii. 2, 80ᶜ, etc. (Göz 1, 192. 2, 52); der *Hunger* spilt (gambols), Suchenw. 18, 125; dâ vât *Frost* u. *Durst* den *H.* in daz hâr, u. ziehent (clutch H. by the hair, and drag) gar oft in al dur daz hûs, MS. 2, 189ª; il est *Herbot* (affamé), Trist. 3938; ther *Scado* fliehê in gâhe! O. ii. 24, 37.——Sleep, as well as death, is called *Sandmann* (Supp. to 842): can it possibly mean one who is *sent?* conf. ' dô *sant* er in den *slâf* an,' Anegenge 15, 47; but the other is called *Pechmann* (pitch-man) as well, Schm. sub v., and *Hermann*, Wend. volksl. 2, 269ª. Sleep, a brother of Death, comes in the shape of a bird (p. 331), and sits on a fir-tree (see Klausen p. 30), like the sun sitting on the birch as a bird, and lulling to sleep, Kalev. rune 3. A saint says to Sleep: ' com, *quaet knecht*, com hare dan! Maerl. 3, 197. *Sleep* looks in at the window, Kante-letar 2, no. 175; he walks quietly round the cottages, and all at once he has you, Hebel p. 223; den *Schlaf* nicht austragen, i.e. not spoil one's peace, Höfer 3, 89. Deus *Risus*, Apul. p. m. 105. 111. *Selp-hart*, Wackern. lb. 902. Renn. 270. *Virwitz* (Suppl. to 635 beg.).

p. 890.] Attributes of gods come to be regarded as separate beings, and then personified (Lehrs' Vom neid p. 152), esp. as females. *Copia* was set before the eyes in a ' simulacrum aeneum, *cornu copiae Fortunae* retinens,' Marcellini comitis Chron. p. m. 51. *Care* is a neighbour: γείτονες καρδίας μέριμναι, Aesch. Septem 271; conf. ' ist *zwível* (doubt) herzen nâchgebûr.' *Necessity* (diu

Nôt) parts, *Nauðr* skildi, Kl. schr. 112-3; si vâhten als den
liuten touc (as became men), die ez diu *grimme Nôt* bat, Er. 837;
conf. 'als in mîn wâriu sculde bat,' as my just right bade him do
1246. Der *Rât* (advice), masc., has children by *Scham*, *Treue*,
*Wahrheit*, all fem., Helbl. 7, 50. A host of such personifications
(Fides, Patientia, Humilitas, Superbia, Luxuria, Sobrietas, etc.)
we find already in Prudentius (circ. 400), esp. in his Psychomachia,
with due epic embellishment; conf. Arnob. 4, 1 : Pietas, Con-
cordia, Salus, Honor, Virtus, Felicitas, Victoria, Pax, Aequitas.
The Zendic has two female genii, *Haurvatât* and *Ameretât* (whole-
ness and immortality), often used in the dual number, Bopp's
Comp. Gr. pp. 238—240. The *World* is freq. personified (pp.
792n. 850), and even called 'frau *Spothilt*,' Gramm. 2, 499.

Otfr. iii. 9, 11 says : 'sô wer sô nan biruarta, er *fruma* thana
*fuarta*,' whoso touched, carried off benefit, as we talk of carrying
off the bride; *frum* u. *êre*, Hpt's Ztschr. 7, 343-9. Cervantes in
D. Quix. 1, 11 says finely of Hope, that she shews the *hem of her
garment*: la Esperanza muestra la orilla de su vestido. OHG.
*Otikepa*, MB. 13, 44. 46. 51 *Otegebe*, *Outgebe*; conf. *Borg-gabe*
(Suppl. to 274).

Such phrases as 'he is goodness *itself*' rest on personification
too : vous êtes la *bonté même*. Avec la biauté fu *largesce sa suer*
et *honors sa cousine*, Guitecl. 1, 116.

p. 892.] Personifications have hands and feet given them,
they dwell, come and go. The Athenians have the goddesses
Πειθώ and Ἀναγκαίη (persuasion, compulsion), while in Andros
dwell Πενίη and Ἀμηχανίη (poverty, helplessness), Herod. 8, 111.
Ἀλήθεια (truth) has *fled* alone into the wilderness, Babr. 127.
Aesop 364. Another name for *Nemesis* was Ἀδράστεια, unescap-
ableness. Exulatum abiit *Salus*, Plaut. Merc. iii. 4, 6; terras
*Astraea* reliquit, Ov. Met. 1, 150; fugêre *Pudor Verum*que
*Fides*que 1, 129; paulatim deinde ad superos *Astraea* recessit
*hac comite*, atque duae pariter fugêre *sorores*, Juv. 6, 19; *Virtue*
goes, and leads *Luck* away with her, Procop. vol. 2, 407.

Aller *Freuden füeze* kêren (turn) in den helle-grunt, Warn.
1206; gewunnen si der *Fröiden stap*, Dietr. dr. 200[b]; diu mac
mir wol ze *Froeiden hûse* geschragen (var., mich wol ze Fr. h.
geladen), MS. 1, 9[a]; conf. Fr. *tor* (Suppl. 866 beg.). *Krutchina*,
affliction, jumps out of the oven, Dietr. Russ. märch. no. 9.

*Carrying Frô-muot on the hands* resembles the *levatio imperatoris et novae nuptae*, RA. 433. '*Fromut-loh* cum feris ibi nutritis' must be a bear-garden, Dronke's Trad. Fuld. p. 63. Haupt in Neidh. 135 thinks Frômuot is simply Cheerfulness.——*Gherechticheit*, die sware was, *vlo* tachterst, Rose 5143; conf. Frauenlob's poem on *Gerechtigkeit*, Hpt's Zeitschr. 6, 29. *Minne, Trouwe* es ghevloen, Rose 5141; diu *Triwe* ist erslagen, Tôd. gehugde 268; *Treu* ein wildbret (head of game), Schweinichen 1, 13; ver *Triuwe*, ver *Wârheit*, Helbl. 7, 38; der Triuwen *klûse* (cell), Engelh. 6295; der Tr. *bote* 6332; in Tr. *pflege* (care), Winsb. 8, 8, conf. 'der *Zühte* sal' good breeding's hall 8, 7; St. *Getruwe* (trusty) and *Kümmernis* (sorrow), Mone 7, 581—4; nieman wil die *Wârheit* herbergen, Müllenh. no. 210; *Pax* terras ingreditur *habitu venusto*, Archipoeta ix. 29, 3.

p. 893.] Der *Eren bote* and *E. holde* (Suppl. to 869); *frouwen E. amîs*, Frib. Trist. 61; daz *Ere sîn geverte* sî, Türl. Wh. 125ᵇ; frô E. und *ir kint*, MS. 2, 151ᵇ; an *Eren strâze* gestîgen, Pass. 47, 80; *Ere ûz pfade* gedringen, Ben. 450; in der *Eren tor* komen 551, 26; sîn lop (praise) was in der *E. tor*, Frauend. 81, 14; sitzen ûf der *E. banke*, Gr. Rud. 11, 20; saz ûf der *E. steine*, Lanz. 5178, conf. Er. 1198. Wigal. 1475; der *E. büne* hât überdaht, Engelh. 230; der *E. dach, kranz*, Rauch 1, 319; verzieret nû der *E. sal*, Walth. 24, 3; ûz *frou E. kamer* varn, MS. 2, 151ᵃ; der *E. tisch*, Suchenw. 4, 152; der *E. pflüege*, Amgb. 2ᵃ; in der *E. forste*, Gold. schm. 1874, conf. 'in der *Sorgen forste*,' Engelh. 1941; der *E. krône* treit (wears), Roseng. 908; treit der *E. schilt* 914; der *E. zwî* (bough), Hpt 4, 546; er ist der *E. wirt* (host), MS. 2, 59ᵃ; *mantel*, da frou *Ere* hât ir brüste mit bedecket, Amgb. 18ᵇ; ver *Ere*, Wapenmartîn 6, 55.

*Vrô Minne*, MS. 1, 16ᵃ. The girl's question about Minne is in Winsbekin 34, 8; der *Minnen bode*, Partenop. 80-4-6. 101; der *M. kraft*, Ulr. v. Lichtenst. 35, 15; diu *Minne* stiez ûf in ir *krefte rîs* (thrust at him her wand of power), Parz. 290, 30; der *Minnen stricke* (toils), MS. 1, 61ᵃ; *Minne u. Wîsheit*, Flore 3740; *frau M.* presents herself to two maidens as *teacher* of love, with a rod (einem tosten) in her hand, and gives one of them blows, Hätzl. 165; a woman appears as M.'s *stewardess* 159ᵃ. Can Liehtenstein's progress as *queen Venus* be conn. with a mythical custom (p. 259)?——'*Vrou Mate* (moderation) is ên edel vorstinne,'

Potter 1, 1870; *Máz,* aller tugende vrouwe, Pantal. 120; *Maezic-heit* bint ûf die spen (to teach the baby temperance?), Suchenw. xl. 144; *Zuht, Mâze, Bescheidenheit,* Mai 176, 13; *Zucht* u. *Schame* stânt an der porte, u. huotent, Hpt 2, 229; ze hant begreif sie diu *Scham,* Anegenge 17, 31.   18, 22; diu *Riuwe* was sîn frouwe, Parz. 80, 8; der *Riwe tor* 649, 28; diu *Vuoge, Füegel* (p. 311 n.). A fairy castle under charge of *Tugent,* its 8 chambers with allegoric names painted by *Sælde,* is descr. in Geo. 5716 seq.

p. 895.]   The entire Roman de la Rose is founded on allegories; and in such there often lies a mythic meaning.   *Before sunrise on Easter morn,* appears the maid beside the *fountain* mid the flowers, Hätzl. 160ᵃ; the lady that appears is approached but *once in ten years* 143. 376; under a limetree in the wild wood, the *fair lady washes* her hands 143ᵇ; a *dwarf* in the forest leads to the *three Fates,* H. Sachs v. 333ᵇ, or the *wild lady* leads one about 1, 272ᶜᵈ. ——In the Trobadors a singing bird allures the poet into a wood, where he finds three maidens chanting a threnody, Diez's Leb. d. troub. p. 145.   Frau *Wildecheit* leads the bard by her bridle-rein to a level ground beside a brook, where Dame *Justice, Mercy* etc. sit judging, Conr. Klage der kunst; in his Schwan-ritter, Conrad says *wilde aventiure.*   A poet snatches up his staff, comes upon a fair flowery field, where he meets the *Minne-queen,* Hagen's Grundriss p. 438, or to a lovely child by a forest-fountain 442.   There is a similar description in Helbl. 7, 28: the poet in the morning reaches a wild rocky waste, sees two ladies in white veils, *Joy* and *Chivalry, wailing and wringing their hands;* he helps them to their feet when they faint, but now the Duchess of Kärnten is dead, they will go *among men no more,* they live thenceforward in the wild.   Again, in Ls. 2, 269: on a green field the poet finds *Dame Honour* fallen to the ground in a faint, also *Manhood* and *Minne:* they *lament* Count Wernher of Honberg. Or take the Dream of *seven sorrowing dames* in MSH. 3, 171—3: *Fidelity, Modesty, Courtesy, Chastity, Bounty, Honour* and *Mercy* bewail the Düringer and Henneberger; conf. the 'siben übelen wîbe, *Vrâzheit, Unkiusche, Gîtekeit, Zorn, Nît, Trâcheit, Hoffart,*' Diut. 1, 294—6.   The *ladies lamenting* the death of kings and heroes remind us of the *klage-frauen, klage-mütter* (p. 432), and the *wood-wives* ill-content with the world (p. 484).   At the end of Euripides's Rhesus the *muse* mourns the prince's death;

in Od. 24, 60 the *nine muses* come round the corpse of Achilles, and bewail his end. The lonely tower as the habitation of such beings occurs elsewh. too, as '*turris Alethiae*' in the Archipoeta; conf. '*Mens bona, si qua dea es, tua me in sacraria dono*,' Prop. iv. 24, 19.

p. 896.] Diu *Schande* (disgrace) vert al über daz lant, MSH. 3, 448ᵇ; sô hât diu *S.* von ir vluht, Kolocz. 129; ver *S.*, Renn. 12231; swa vrô Ere wol gevert, daz ist *vrô Schanden* leit, MS. 2, 172; in *S. hol* verklûset 2, 147ᵇ. *Unêre* laden (invite dishonour) in daz hûs, Uebel wîp 815; *Untriuwen* bant, Wigal. 10043; *Unminne*, MS., 1, 102ᵃ; *Ungenâde* (ill-will) hât mich enpfangen ze ingesinde (for inmate) 2, 51ᵇ; *Unbill* (injustice) knocks at the door, Fischart in Vilmar p. 4; diu *Werre* (p. 273 n).—— *Wendelmuot* (Suppl. to 273 n.); conf. '*frowe Armuot* (poverty) muose entwîchen, von ir hûse si flôch,' fled, Er. 1578; ez het diu *grôze A.* zuo im *gehûset* in den glet, diu *A.* mit jâmer lît, Wigal. 5691; sît mich diu *A.* alsô jaget, Pass. 352, 89; das uns schon *reit* (rode us) *frau Armut*, H. Sachs i. 5, 523ᵈ; conf. ' reit mich gross *Ungedult*,' impatience 524ᶜ; *frau Elend*, Hätzl. 157-8 (there is a Fr. chapbook about *bonhomme Misère*). *Missewende* von ir sprach, daz ir teil dâ niht en-waere, MS. 1, 84ᵃ; *Missevende* diu im niht genâhen mac 1, 85ᵃ. Wê, wer wil nu *Sorgen* walten? diu was mîn sinde (housemate) nu vil manegen tac 1, 163ᵇ.

p. 898.] Φήμη θεός, Hes. Op. 761-2; Φάμα carries rumours to Zeus's throne, Theocr. 7, 93. There is a Lat. phrase : scit *Fama*, scit cura deûm, Forcell. sub v. scio. *Famaque nigrantes* succincta pavoribus *alas*, Claud. B. Get. 201; *volat fama Caesaris* velut velox equus, Archipo. ix. 30, 1. Rumour is to the Indian the song of a *by-flown bird*, Klemm 2, 132; a species of Angang therefore (p. 1128). Another phrase is: fama *emanavit*, Cic. Verr. ii. 1, 1; *manat* tota urbe rumor, Livy 2, 49. So in German: daz *maere* wît *erbrach*, Pass. 285, 20. 71, 41; daz *m.* was *erschollen*, Mai 228, 22. Lanz. 9195; von dem uns disiu *m. erschellent* (these rumours ring), Ecke 18; daz *m. erschal* in diu lant überal, ez en-wart *niht* alsô *begraben*, Kolocz. 85; daz *m. ûz schal* (rang out), *ûz quam*, Herb. 14372-4; dese *mare ute schôt*, Maerl. 2, 203. 3, 340; alse die *mare dus* (abroad) *ût sprang*, Hpt 1, 108; daz *maere breitte* sich (spread), Herb. 502. 1320. 17037, or :

wart *breit* 2460. 13708; daz *m.* nû *wîten* began, Türl. Wh. 28ᵃ; die *mare ghinc* harentare, Maerl. 3, 190. Kästn. 2, 1768; daz *maere* wîten *kreis* (circulated), Servat. 1856; die *niemare liep* (ran), Walewein 9513. 11067. Lanc. 35489; *nymare lôpt,* Lanc. 26165; doe *liep* die *niemare* dor al dit lant 25380. 47053; die *mare liep* verre ende sere, Maerl. 3, 193; es komen neue maer *gerant,* Wolkenst. 63; daz m. wîten *umme trat,* sich *umme truoc,* Pass. 221, 93. 169, 32.——In the same way: *word is gone,* Minstr. 3, 92; *sprang þæt word,* Homil. 384; dat *word lep,* Detm. 2, 348. 358. 392, dat *ruchte lep.* 2, 378. 391. We say the rumour goes, is noised. Viel schiere *vlouc* (quickly flew) daz *maere,* Ksrchr. 957. 8415; sîn m. *vlouc* wîten in diu lant, Pass. 204, 24; von ir *vlouc* ein m., Trist. 7292; daz m. *vlouc* dahin, Troj. 13389; schiere *vlouc* ein m. *erschollen,* Türl. Krone 68; dô *fluoc* daz m. über mer, Herb. 13704; harte snel u. balt *flouc* daz m. ze Rôme, Pilat. 398; diu starken m. wîten *vlugen,* Servat. 459; diu m. vor in heim *flugen,* 2393; dô *flugen* diu m. von hûse ze hûse, Wigal. 34, 3. So: der *scal* (sound) *flouc* in diu lant, Rol. 215, 7; des *vlouc* sîn *lop* (praise) über velt, Hpt 6, 497; daz *wort* von uns *fliuget* über lant, Herzmære 169; ON. sû *fregn flŷgr.* More striking is the phrase: diu *maere* man dô *vuorte* (led) in ander künege lant, Nib. 28, 3. Instead of maere: *frou Melde,* Frauend. 47, 29. Ksrchr. 17524; *Melde* kumt, diu selten ie gelac (lay still), MS. 2, 167ᵃ; *M.,* diu nie gelac, MSH. 1, 166ᵃ; *M.,* de noch nie en-lac, Karlm. 159, 43; drî jâr sô lac diu *M.,* Tit. 824; vermârt in *M.,* Lanz. 3346; *M.* brach aus, Schweini. 2, 262. Der wilde *liumet* was vür geflogen, Troj. 24664; nu fluoc dirre *liumt* gelîche über al daz künecrîche, Walth. v. Rh. 136, 43. *Rumor* = maere, Rudl. 1, 128. 2, 80. 121. 173; *Rumour* speaks the Prol. to 2 King Henry IV. Lastly: '*quidi* managa bigunnun *wahsan*' reminds one of the growth of maere.

## CHAPTER XXX.

### POETRY.

p. 900.] On the connexion of the idea of *composing* with those of *weaving, spinning, stringing, binding, tacking,* see my Kl. schr. 3, 128-9.[1] The poet was called a *smith,* songsmith; in

---

[1] *Deilen* unde *snoren,* Sassenchr. p. 3; die leier *schnüren* (to string) in Spee 299.

Rigveda 94, 1 : huncce hymnum Agni venerabili, *currum velut faber,* paramus mente, Bopp's Gl. 260[b].——With *scuof, scóp,* poëta, conf. OHG. *scoph-sanc,* poësis, Graff 6, 253 ; *schopfpŭch* (-book), Karaj. 86, 6 ; in den *schopf-buochen,* Ernst 103 ; conf. Lachm. on Singing p. 12 ; marrêr *scopf* Israhel, egregius psaltes Isr., Diut. 1, 512[a].——With ON. *skáld-skapr* should be mentioned an OHG. *scaldo,* sacer, Graff 6, 484 ; conf. Gramm. 2, 997. Holtzm. Nib. 170. The Neth. *schouden* is M. Neth. *scouden.* ——With the Romance terminology agrees ' poësis =*findinge,*' Diut. 2, 227[b] ; daz *vand* er (indited), Helmbr. 959 ; die *vinden* conste, ende *maken* vêrse, Franc. 1919 ; de *makere,* die de rime *vant* (invented) 1943 ; er *vant* dise rede, Mone '39, p. 53.—— AS. *gidda,* poëta, can be traced in other Aryan tongues : Ssk. *gad,* dicere, loqui, *gai,* canere, *gatha, gîta,* cantus ; Lith. *giedóti,* sing, *giesme,* song, Lett. *dzeedaht, dzeesma ;* Slav. *gudú,* cano fidibus, *gúsli,* psaltery, Dobrowsky p. 102.——On the Celtic *bard,* see Diefenb. Celt. 1, 187 ; *bardi,* vates druidae, Strabo p. 197 ; Bret. *bardal,* nightingale. Ir. *searthon,* chief bard.

p. 901.] On the effects of song we read : þaer wæs *hæleða dreám,* Beow. 987 ; huop ein *liet* an, u. *wart frô,* Hartm. 2, büchl. 554 ; einen *frölich geigen* (fiddle him into mirth), Wigal. p. 312, conf. 332. We often meet with AS. ' giedd *wrecan,*' Cod. Exon. 441, 18 ; sôð gied *wrecan* 306, 2. 314, 17 ; þæt gyd *âwræc* 316 20 ; þe þis gied *wræce* 285, 25 ; conf. vröude *wecken,* Türl. Wh. 116[b].

p. 905.] The poet or prophet is νυμφόληπτος, seized by the nymphs (muses), Lat. lymphatus. He is *goð-málugr,* god-inspired, Sæm. 57[b] ; Gylfi gaf einni *farandi konu* at launum skemtûnar sinnar. . . . en sû kona var ein af *Asa aett ;* hon er nefnd *Gefiun,* Sn. 1. *Gandharva* is a name for the musical spirits who live in Indra's heaven, Bopp 100[b]. God sends three angels into the world as *musicians ;* and *angel-fiddlers* were a favourite subject in pictures. We have the phrase : ' der himmel hängt voll geigen.'

*Kvâsir* =anhelitus creber, Sn. 69 ; see Biörn sub v. qvâsir.

Inditing is also expr. by *füegen* (to mortise), *richten* (righten), Hpt 6, 497 ; *richtere,* Roth. 4853 and concl. ; *berihten,* Freid. 1, 3 ; eines *mezzen,* Dietr. 190 ; *wirken,* Herb. 641 ; daz liet ich *anhefte* (tack on) ûf dîne gnâde volle, Mar. 148, 5 ; der diz maere *anschreip* (jotted down), Bit. 2006. The M. Neth. *ontbinden* =translate, Maerl. 3, 73. 48 ; in dietsce wort *ontb.* 352 ; in dietsch *onbende* 228 ; in dietsche *ontb.,* Rose 29. Walew. 6 ; conf. AS. onband beado-rûne, Beow. 996.

Oðin's *spittle* makes beer ferment (p. 1025 n.) ; '*spittle* that speaks *drops of blood*,' KM. no. 56, note. Lisch in Meckl. jrb. 5, 82 ; a door, when *spat upon*, answers, Müllenh. p. 399, conf. *fugls hráki* (p. 682 beg.). On 'blood and snow,' see Dybeck '45, p. 69 : som *blod* pả *snö.* The entire Mid. Age had a story running in its head, with a playful turn to it, about a child made of snow or ice. The 10th cent. already had its '*modus Liebinc*'; an O. Fr. poem of the same import is in Méon 3, 215, a MHG. in Ls. 3, 513 and Hpt 7, 377 ; in Scherz u. Ernst c. 251 (1550, 183) the child is called *eis-schmarre*, scrap of ice, conf. Burc. Waldis 4, 71 and Weise's Erznarren p. 23. Franciscus makes himself a wife and child of snow, Pfeiffer's Myst. 1, 215. Whoever drank of the *dýri miöðr* (precious mead), the honey mixt with Kvâsir's blood, became a *skáld :* thus the poet prays for a single *trahen* (tear) out of the Camênæ's *fountain*, Trist. 123, 38.

Oðinn gains Oðhroerir fr. Suttûng, who then pursues him ; so Wäinämöinen, after winning Sampo, was chased by Louhi in eagle's shape (p. 873). Oðinn himself says in Hâvamâl 23[b] : 'Oðhroerir er nu uppkominn â alda ves iarðar,' and in 24[a] it is said of him : '*Suttúng* svikinn hann *lêt sumbli frâ*, ok graetta Gunnlöðu. Other names for the drink : *Yggs full*, Egilss. 656 ; *Yggjar miöðr* 657 ; *Viðris full* 665 ; *Viðris þýfi* 608. With *arnar leir* (eagle's dung) conf. *leir-skáld*, muck-poet, Dan. *skarns-poet*, Olafsen's Prize essay p. 5. Like the mead, Player Jack's soul is distrib. among gamesters.

Like *wôð-bora* is *sôð-bora*, also vates. The *d* in Goth. *veitvôds*, testis, seems to exclude it, yet d and þ are sometimes confounded. F. Magnusen transl. *Oðhroeri* ingenii excitator ; Biörn makes *hræri* obturaculum lebetis. On the relation of Oðr to Oðinn, see Suppl. to 306.

Oðinn bestows the gift of poesy on Starkaðr. '*Apes* Platonis infantuli *mel labiis* inferebant,' John of Salisb. de Nug. cur. 1, 13. When St. Ambrose lay in his cradle, a *swarm of bees* settled on his *mouth.* The Muse drops *nectar* into the shepherd Komatas's mouth, and *bees* bring *juice of flowers* to it, Theocr. 7, 60—89. Whom the Muses *look upon* at birth, he hath power of pleasant speech, Hes. Theog. 81—84. The gods *breathe upon* the poet, Ov. Met. 1, 2-3-4.

p. 906.] To Hesiod *tending lambs*, the Muses hand a spray of laurel, and with it the gift of song, Theog. 22—30. In Lucian's Rhet. praec. 4 he being a *shepherd* plucks leaves on Helicon, and there and then becomes a *poet*. The muses come at early morn :

Mirabar, quidnam misissent *mane Camenae*,
    ante meum stantes sole rubente torum ;
natalis nostrae signum misere puellae,
    et manibus faustos ter crepuere sonos. Prop. iv. 9, 1.

Conf. the story of the Kalmuk poet, Klemm 3, 209. 210, and *poor shepherds'* visions of churches to be built (Suppl. to 86). GDS. 821.

p. 908.] The first lay in Kanteletar relates the invention of the five-stringed harp (kantelo) of the Finns. Kalev. 29 describes how Wäinämöinen makes a harp of various materials. Kullervo fashions a horn of cow's bone, a pipe of bull's horn, a flute of calves' foot, Kal. Castr. 2, 58. When *Wäinämöinen* plays, the birds come flying in heaps, Kalev. 29, 217, the eagle forgets the young in her nest 221. When *Wipunen* sings, the *sun* stops to hear him, the *moon* to listen, *Charles's wain* to gather wisdom, *wave* and *billow* and *tide* stand still, Kalev. 10, 449—457; conf. Petersb. extr. p. 11. In the Germ. folksong the *water* stops, to list the tale of love, Uhl. 1, 223-4.

Den ene begyndte en vise at qväde,
    saa faart over alle qvinder,
*striden ström* den stiltes derved,
    som förre vor vant at rinde. D V. 1, 235.

A song makes tables and benches *dance*, Fornald. sög. 3, 222. KM. no. 111. Sv. fornvis, 1, 73. Stolts Karin with her singing makes men *sleep* or *wake*, Sv. vis. 1, 389 or *dance* 394-6. For the power of song over birds and beasts, see DV. 1, 282. Sv. vis. 1, 33. On Orpheus, see Hor. Od. i. 12, 7 seq.; conf. the Span. romance of Conde *Arnaldos*.

p. 909.] Poets assemble on *hills* (as men did for sacrifice or magic), e.g. on the Wartburg : au *pui*, où on corone les biaus dis, Couron. Renart 1676. Does the poet wear garlands and flowers, because he was orig. a god's friend, a priest ? The jeux floraux offer *flowers* as *prizes for song :* violeta, aiglantina, flor dal gauch (solsequium). The rederijkers too name their rooms after *flowers ;* is it a relic of druidic, bardic usage ?

p. 911.] The ON. *Saga* reminds one of the Gr. Φήμη, of whom Hes. Opp. 762 declares: θεὸς νὺ τίς ἐστι καὶ αὐτή. She converses with Oðinn, as *Φάμα* conveys rumours to Zeus (Suppl. to 898 beg.). Musa is rendered *sängerîn*, Barl. 252, 7; 'ladete musas, daz wâren *sengêren* (rhy. eren),' Herb. 17865; but again, '*musê*' 17876.——*Aventiure* answers to *bona fortuna* (bonne aventure), bona dea, *bonus eventus*, Pliny 36, 5. Varro RR. 1, 1; *vrouwe* Aventure, Lanc. 18838; in the Rose the *goddess Aventure*=Fortuna 5634, who has a wheel 3933. 4719. 5629. 5864; *t' hûs der Aventuren* 5786. 5810-39 ; *jonste* de Avonture, Stoke 1, 39; maer d' Aventure was hem *gram*, Maerl. 3, 134; den stouten es *hout d' Aventure* 2, 46, like 'audaces fortuna juvat'; alse di die Av. es *hout* 2, 93; der Aventuren *vrient*, ibid.

---

# CHAPTER XXXI.

## SPECTRES.

p. 913.] In Mone 6, 467 men are divided into living, *hovering, doubtful* and dead. Souls that cannot find rest in Hades and returning wander about the grave, are mentioned in Plato's Phædo p. 81. The dead were worshipped : *sanctos* sibi fingunt *quoslibet* mortuos, Concil. Liptin. Feasts were held in honour of them, as the Pers. *ferver-feast*, Benfey's Monats-n. 151, the Russ. corpse and soul feasts, Lasicz 58. Souls were prayed for, Benf. Mon. 168-9, conf. soul-masses, Nib. 1221, 2.——To near (not to remote) ancestors the Indians offered up *food* and *drink*, Bopp's Gl. p. 143[b] n. 198[a]. 79[b]; conf. Weber on Malavik 103. One of these sacrifices was *udaka-karman*, water-libation for the dead, Böhtl. and Roth's Wtb. 1, 908 ; so χοὴν χεῖσθαι πᾶσι νεκύεσσι, viz. meal, wine and water were poured into a hole, Od. 10, 517—520. 11, 25—29. The souls eagerly *drink up* the *blood* of victims, which restores them to their senses, Od. 11, 50. 89. 96-8. 148. 153. 228. 390. The shades live on these libations, Luc. de luctu 9. The Lith. *wéles* fem. means the figures of the dead, Mielcke 1, 321; to the Samogitian goddess *Vielona* a particular kind of cake was offered: cum mortui pascuntur, Lasicz 48. 50. *Food* and *drink* is laid on the grave for the souls, Pass. 166, 84—93.

On *manes, Mania,* see Gerh. Etr. g. 16; '*in sede Manium*' = in the bosom of the earth, Pliny 33, 1. On *lares,* see Lessing 8, 251 ; *domesticus lar, hamingia,* Saxo Gram. 74.

p. 915.] *Geheuer,* not haunted, is also expr. by *dicht,* tight, Sup. I, 768 : nu bin ich *ungehiure,* Wigal. 5831; I asked mine host, was he sure no *ungeheuer* walked the stable, Simplic. K. 1028 ; it is *unclean* in that house, Nürnberger 11. In Notker '*manes*' is transl. by *unholdon,* in AS. by *hell-waran* (habitantes tartarum).

Spuken (haunt, be haunted) is also called *wafeln,* Kosegarten in Höfer 1, 377; AS. *wafian,* ON. *vafra, vofra, vofa,* MHG. *waberen.* ON. *vofa* = spectrum ; AS. *wœfer-syne,* OHG. *wabarsiuni* = spectaculum, Graff 6, 129. Kl. schr. 5, 437. The dead lie '*heilir î haugi,*' at peace in the cairn, Hervar. p. 442 ; svâ lâti âss þik (God leave thee) *heilan î haugi* 437. They appear in churches at *night* or in the *dawn,* and perform services, wedding, burial, etc.; the sight betokens an approaching death. Dietmar (Pertz 5, 737-8) gives several such stories with the remark : ut dies vivis, sic *nox* est concessa defunctis ; conf. the story in Altd. bl. 1, 160, a Norweg. tale in Asbiörnsen's Huldre-ev. 1, 122 and Schelling's Last words of the vicar of Drottning. As Wolfdietrich lies *on the bier at night,* the ghosts of all whom he has killed come and fight him, Wolfd. 2328—34; conf. Ecke 23 (differ. told in Dresd. Wolfd. 327—330); also the tale of the *ruined church* with the coffin, Altd. bl. 1, 158. KM.[2] no. 4. In the Irrgarten der Liebe the cavalier sees at last the ghosts of all his lovers, p. 610. Such apparitions are said to announce themselves, sich *melden, anmelden,* Schm. 2, 570. Schönleithner 16. Conf. Dict. sub. v. '*sich anzeigen.*'

p. 915.] To ON. *aptra-gánga* add *aptr-göngr,* reditus, Eyrb. 174. 314; *gonger,* Müllenh. p. 183. For 'es geht um' they say in Bavaria '*es weizt* dort,' Panz. Beitr. 1, 98. Schm. 4, 205-6 ; in Hesse '*es wandert,*' in the Wetterau '*es wannert,*' conf. *wanken,* Reineke 934 ; Neth. *waren, rondwaren,* conf. 'in that room *it* won't let you rest,' Bange's Thür. chron. 27[b]. The ON. *draugr* is unconn. with Zend. *drucs,* daemon, Bopp's Comp. Gr. p. 46.

p. 916.] Instead of talamasca, we also find the simple *dala,*

larva, monstrum, Graff 5, 397; *talmasche*, De Klerk 2, 3474.
The Finn. talma (limus), talmasca (mucedo in lingua), has only
an accid. resembl. in sound. AS. *dwimeru*, spectra, lemures,
larvae nocturnae, *gedwimor*, praestigiator, *gedwomeres*, nebulonis,
*gedwomere*, necromantia, Hpt 9, 514-5. The MHG. *getwás* agrees
(better than with Lith. dwase) with AS. *dwaes*, stultus, for *getwás*
means stultus too, Eilh. Trist. 7144. 7200. 7300. An ON.
*skráveifa*, fr. *veifa*, vapor, and *skrá* obliquus? *Vampires* are
dead men come back, who *suck blood*, as the Erinnyes suck the
*blood of corpses*, Aesch. Eum. 174 [or the ghosts in the Odyssey];
conf. the story of the brown man, Ir. märch. 2, 15.

p. 918.] The Insel Felsenb. 3, 232 says of *will o' wisps*:
'from the *God's acre* rise yon flames, the *dead* call me to join
their rest, they long for my company.' ON. *hræ-lios*, corpse-
light, *hrævar-lios*, *hrævar-eld*. *Vafr-logi*, flickering flame, is seen
about graves and treasures in graves (pp. 602. 971); conf.
Sigurd's and Skirni's 'marr, er mic um *myrqvan* beri *vísun*
*vafrloga*,' Sæm. 82ª.——Wandering lights are called 'das *irre-*
*ding*'=ghost, Schelmufsky 1, 151; der *feuer-mann*, Pomer. story
in Balt. stud. xi. 1, 74; *brünniger mann*, Stald. 1, 235; *laufende*
*fackel*, Ettn. Unw. doctor p. 747. AS. *dwás-liht*. M. Neth.
*dwaes-fier*, Verwijs p. 15; *lochter-mane*, Müllenh. p. 246. Wend.
*bludnik*, Wend. volksl. 2, 266ᵇ; Lith. *baltwykszlé*, Lett. *leeks*
*ugguns*, false fire; Lapp. *tjolonjes*, Lindahl 475ᵇ; conf. KM.³ 3,
196.——On *girregar*, conf. Beham (Vienna) 377, 21; 'einen
*girren-garren* enbor-richten, einen teuflischen schragen mit
langem kragen,' Hag. Ges. Ab. 3, 82. The kobold's name
*Iskrzycki* is fr. Sl. *iskra*, spark; and in Hpt 4, 394 the *lüchte-*
*männchen* behave just like kobolds. In the Wetterau *feurig*
*gehn* means, to be a will o' wisp.

*Unbaptized children* are cast into the *fire*, Anegenge 2, 13. 11,
'5. 12, 12; they go to *Nobis-kratten*, Stald. 2, 240; they shall
not be buried in the holy isle (p. 600 n.); vile si dâ vunden
*lûterlîcher kinde* vor der helle an einem ende, dâ die muder wâren
mite tôt, En. 99, 12, whereas '*ôsten* (ab oriente) schulen diu
*westir-barn* in daz himilrîche varn,' Karaj. 28, 12. Unchristened
babes become *pilweisse* (p. 475), as untimely births become *elbe*
(p. 1073); the unbaptized become white *létiches*, Bosquet 214,
or *kaukas*, Nesselm. 187ᵇ.

p. 920.] The Lat. *furia* is fr. furere, OHG. purjan, Dict. 2, 534; it is rendered *helliwinna*, Graff 1, 881; *hell-wüterin*, Schade's Pasq. 100, 9. 103, 25. 117, 79 with evident reference to *Wuotan* and *wüten* to rage. Uns ist der tiuvel nâhen bî, oder *daz wüetende her*, Maurit. 1559; erst hub sich ein scharmutzeln (arose a scrimmage), wie in eim *wilden heer*, Ambras. lied. p. 151. Uhl. 1, 657. Other names for the Wild Host: die *wilde fahrt*, Wolf's Ztschr. 1, 292-3; in Styria, das *wilde gjaid* (hunt) 2, 32-3; in Bavaria, das *gjoad, wilde gjoad*, Panzer 1, 9. 16. 29. 37. 63. 85. 133; in Vorarlberg, das *nacht-volk* or *wüethas*, Vonbun p. 83; der wilde jäger mit dem *wüthis heer*, Gotthelf's Erz. 1, 221; in the Eifel, *Wudes* or *Wodes heer*, Wolf's Ztschr. 1, 316. Firmen. 3, 244ᵇ; *joejagd, jöjagd*, Osnabr. mitth. 3, 238—240.

p. 924.] Als im der *tiuvel jagete nâch*, Livl. reimchr. 7274. The devil is called a *weideman*, hunter, Merwund. 2, 22, and in return the wild-hunter in the Altmark is a *hell-jeger*, Hpt 4, 391. 'Hark, the *wild hunter*, passing right over us! The hounds bark, the whips crack, the huntsmen cry holla ho!' Goethe's Götz v. B. 8, 149, conf. 42, 175. Fischart in Lob der laute p. 100 had already made an adj. of the hunter's name: *Heckelbergisch* geschrei, büffen u. blasen des jägerhorns; conf. supra (p. 924, l. 2) and *Hachelberg* in the Rheinharts-wald, Landau's Jagd p. 190.——Another version of the *Hackelberg* legend is given by Kuhn in Hpt's Ztschr. 5, 379; conf. supra (p. 146-7). Can this be alluded to in a stone sculpture let into the wall of Diesdorf church (Magdeburg country), representing a man whose left leg is appar. being wounded by a sow? Thüring. mitth. vi. 2, 13 and plate 7 no. 5. Somewhat different is the story of the one-eyed wild-sow, whose head laid on the dish gives the master of the hunt a mortal wound, Winkler's Edelm. 371. The whole myth resembles that of Adonis, and the Irish story of *Diarmuid' na mban* p. 193. H. D. Müller (Myth. der Gr. stämme ii. 1, 113) compares it to that of Actæon.——*Dreaming of the boar*, Rudl. 16, 90. Waltharius 623; a boar wounds the Sun in her cave, Rudbeck quoted in Tenzel and Mannling p. 205. *Hackelberg* must hunt for ever: albie der lîb, diu *sêle* dort sol *jagen* mit *Harren* (his hound) êwiclîchen, Laber 568. Of him who hunts *till the Judgment-day*, Firmenich 1, 344. Müllenh. p. 584. In a Westph. folktale picked up orally by Kuhn, giants call to

*Hakelberg* for help, he raises a storm, and removes a mill into the
*Milky-way*, which after that is called the *Mill-way*. In Catalonia
they speak of ' el *viento del cazador*,' Wolf's Ztschr. 4, 191. In
Frommann 3, 271 *Holla* and *Hackelbernd* are associated in the
wild hunt, unless Waldbrühl stole the names out of the Mythology;
in 3, 273 a ' Geckenbehrnden' of Cologne is brought in.  *Tut-*
*osel* is fr. *tuten*, bo-āre, Diut. 2, 203[b]; τυτώ ἡ γλαύξ, a sono tu tu,
Lobeck's Rhemat. 320.

p. 927.] The wild hunter rides through the air on a *schimmel,*
white horse, Somm. p. 7; conf. *schimmel-reiter* p. 160.  *Filling*
*a boot with gold* occurs also in a Hessian märchen, Hess. Ztschr.
4, 117, conf. Garg. 241[a]; *shoes* are filled with gold, Roth. 21[b];
a shoe-full of money, Panzer p. 13.

The wild hunter is called *Goi*, Kuhn's Westf. sag. 1, 8, and the
dürst in Switz. is sometimes *gäuthier*, Stald. 2, 517; do they
stand for *Goden?* Dame Gauden's *carriage* and *dog* resemble
the Nethl. tale of the hound by the hell-car, Wolf p. 527.

p. 930.] A man went and stood under a tree in the wood
through which the *wild hunter* rode. One *of the party* in passing
dealt him a blow in the back with his axe, saying, ' I will *plant*
*my axe* in *this tree;*' and fr. that time the man had a hump.
He waited till a year had passed, then went and stood under the
tree again. The same person stept out of the procession, and
said, ' Now I'll take my axe out of the tree;' and the man was
rid of his hump, Kuhn's Nordd. sag. no. 69; conf. *Berhta's*
*blowing* (p. 276-7), a witch-story in Somm. p. 56.  Schambach
pp. 179. 359.  Vonbun p. 29 the schnärzerli (36 in ed. 2).  Wolf's
D. sag. no. 348-9.  Panzer 1, 17. 63.

In the Fichtel-gebirge the *wild hunter* rides *without a head,*
Fromm. 2, 554; so does the *wölen-jäger, jolen-jäger,* Osnab.
mitth. 3, 238—240; also the *wild h.* in the Wetterau, Firmen. 2,
101; he walks headless in the wood betw. 11 and 12 at noon,
Somm. p. 7; the wild h. halts at one place to feed horses and
hounds, p. 9. In Tirol he chases the *Salg-fräulein,* Wolf's Ztschr.
2, 60. 35; he baits the *loh-jungfer,* Somm. pp. 7. 167; so giant
*Fasolt* hunts the *little wild woman,* Eckenl. 167. 173.

p. 931.] Houses with their *front and back doors* exactly
opposite are *exposed* to the passage of the *Furious Host* (Meiningen), Hpt 3, 366; conf. the open house-door (p. 926-7), the

sitting over the door (p. 945 end). The *hell-jäger's* cry 'Wil ji mit jagen (hunt with us) ?' is also French : '*part en la chasse !*' Bosq. 69. The story fr. W. Preussen is like a Samland one in Reusch no. 70.

Iu Swabia the wild hunt is also called the *mutige heer*, Schwab's Schwäb. Alp p. 312. Leader of the *Muthes-heer* is Linkenbold, who in the Harz is called *Leinbold*, ibid.; there is a *Linkenbolds-löchle* (-hole) there. However, in a Swabian poem of 1486 beginning 'Got mercurius,' the wild hunt is called '*das wilde wûtiss-her.*' A frau *Motte* roams in Thuringia.

At Ottobeuern *lovely music* used to be heard at Christmas time. If any one put his head out of window to listen, and to view the march of *Wuete*, his head swelled to such a size that he could not pull it in again. The full *delicious enjoyment* was had by those who kept snugly behind closed doors. The procession passed along the fron-weg up the Guggenberg, or into the devil's hole at the Buschel, where a treasure lies guarded by the poodle. On this *delicious music* of the night-folk, see Vonbun p. 35.

p. 933.] *Unchristened infants* are the same as the subterra-neans and moss-folk, whom Wode pursues and catches, conf. p. 483 and Müllenh. p. 373. The child's exclamation, 'Oh how warm are a mother's hands !' is like those of the gipsy-woman's child, 'There's nothing so soft as a mother's lap' and 'there's nothing so sweet as a mother's love,' Müllenh. no. 331 ; Lith. *motinôs rankos szwelnos*, mother's hands soft, Mielcke 1, 284. Kraszewski's Litva 1, 389. In Germ. fairy-tales the dead mother comes in the night to nurse her children, KM.[3] 3, 21 ; conf. Melusine, Simr. p. 80. Müllenh. no. 195-6-7 ; hvert *fell blôðugt á briost* grami, Sæm. 167[b]; a similar passage in Laxd. saga p. 328.

The wild host, like the dwarfs, get *ferried over ;* the last that lags behind is girded with a rope of straw, Panz. 1, 164.

p. 935.] De la *danza aérea á* que están condenadas las *Hero-diadas* por la muerte del bautista, Wolf's Ztschr. 4, 191. In Wallachia Ḍina (Zina) = Diana with a large following hunts in the clouds, and you see where she has danced on the grass ; she can strike one lame, deaf or blind, and is esp. powerful at Whit-suntide, Wal. märch. 296.

p. 936.] An *Eckehart* occurs also in Dietr. 9791. On the

*Venusberg,* see Simr. Amelungen-l. 2, 315. We find even in Altswert 82 : dirre berc was *fro Venus,* conf. 80, 9. 83, 7. H. Sachs has *Venusberg* iii. 3, 3ᵇ (yr 1517). 6ᵇ (1518). 18ᵇ (1550). A witch-trial of 1620 says : auf *Venesberg* oder *Paradies* faren, Mone 7, 426. There is a *Venusbg* by Reichmannsdorf in Grä-fenthal distr. (Meiningen), near Saalfeld. A M.Neth. poem by Limb. 3, 1250. 1316 says Venus dwells in the *forest.* The earliest descript. of the *Horselberg* is by Eoban Hessus in Bucol. idyl. 5, at the beginn. of the 16th cent. :

> Aspicis aërio sublatum vertice montem,
> qua levis occidui deflectitur aura Favoni,
> *Horrisonum* Latio vicinus nomine dicit (by a Latin name),
> qui Nessum bibit undosum Verarimque propinquum.
> Isthoc ante duas messes cum saepe venirem,
> ignarus nemorum vidi discurrere *larvas*
> saxa per et montes, tanquam nocturna vagantes
> terriculamenta, et pueros terrere paventes,
> quas *lamias* dicunt quibus est *exemptile lumen,*
> quas *vigiles* aiunt *extra sua limina lyncas*
> esse, *domi talpas,* nec quenquam cernere nec se.

Conf. Victor Perillus's poem on the *Hörselberg,* yr 1592 (Jrb. d. Berl. spr. ges. 2, 352-8) ; it is called *Haselberg* and *Hörselbg* in Bange's Thür. chron. 1599, p. 57-8. Songs about Tanhäuser in Uhl. no. 297, and Mone's Anz. 5, 169—174 ; a lay of *Danhäuser* is mentioned by Fel. Faber 3, 221.

p. 937.] At the death of our Henry 6, *Dietrich von Bern* appears on horseback, rides through the Mosel, and disappears, HS. p. 49. In the Wend. volksl. 2, 267ᵇ the wild hunter is called *Dyter-bernat, Dyter-benada, Dyke-bernak, Dyke-bjadnat.* In one story 2, 185 he is like the Theodericus Veronensis whom the devil carries off. *Diter Bernhard* in Dasent's Theophilus 80 ; *brand-adern* (barren streaks) on the plains are called by the Wends *Dyter-bernatowy puć,* D.'s path. Yet, acc. to Panzer 1, 67 it is a *fruitful season* when the wilde gjai has been ; and where the Rodensteiner has passed, the *corn stands higher,* Wolf p. 20. The wild host goes clean *through the barn,* Panz. 1, 133.

p. 939.] As early as the First Crusade (1096) it was asserted that *Carl* had woke up again : Karolus resuscitatus, Pertz 8,

215; conf. the kaiser in the Guckenberg near Gemünd, Bader
no. 434, and the Karlsberg at Nürnberg, no. 481.

p. 940.] On *Schnellerts*, see Panzer 1, 194 and the *everlasting
hunter of Winendael*, Kunst en letterblad '41, p. 68. Reiffenb.
Renseign. 214. The setting-out of a *carriage with three wheels*
and a *long-nosed driver* is descr. in the story of the monks crossing the Rhine at Spire, Meland. 1, no. 664 (p. 832). *Copiae eques-
tres* are seen near Worms in 1098, Meland. 2, no. 59; battalions
sweeping through the air in 1096, Pertz 8, 214; conf. Dionys.
Halic. 10, 2; higher up in the clouds, two great armies marching,
H. Sachs iii. 1, 227ª.

p. 943.] Something like Herne the Hunter is *Horne the
Hunter*, otherwise called *Harry-ca-nab*, who with the devil hunts
the boar near Bromsgrove, Worcest. (Athenæum). The story of
the *Wunderer* chasing Frau Saelde is in Keller's Erz. p. 6; conf.
Fastn. sp. 547. Schimpf u. ernst (1522) 229. (1550) 268.

p. 946.] Where Oden's lake (On-sjö) now lies, a stately
mansion stood (herre-gård), whose lord one *Sunday went a hunting* with his hounds, having provided himself with wine out of
the church, to load his gun with, and be the surer of hitting.
At the first shot his mansion sank out of sight, Runa '44, 33.
Here the huntsman is evid. *Oden* himself.——Among the train
of *Guro rysserova* ( = Gudron the horse-tailed, Landstad pp. 121.
131-2) is Sigurd Snaresvend riding his Grani (Faye 62). The
members of the troop go and sit over the door : the like is told
of devils, who lie down *in front of lit-hiuser* where drinking,
gaming, murdering goes on, Berthold p. 357; and of the
Devil, who sits during the dance, H. Sachs 1, 342ᵃᵇ; 'setz nur
die seel auft überthür' iii. 1, 261; sein seel setz er uff über thür,
lats mit dem teufel beissen, Simpl. pilgram 3, 85.——Northern
names for the spectral procession are : oskareia, haaskaalreia,
juleskreia, skreia, Asb. og Moe in the Univ. annaler pp. 7.
41-2; julaskrei'i, julaskreid'i, oskerei, oskorrei, aalgarei, jolareiae,
Aasen's Pröver 27-8. 31; conf. Thorsreið (p. 166) and *husprei,
hesprei*, thunder. Lapp. *julheer*, Klemm 3, 90.

p. 949 n.] The very same is told of *Örvarodd* as of Oleg,
Fornald. s. 2, 168-9. 300; conf. a Transylv. tale in Haltrich's
Progr. p. 73.

p. 950.] On Holda's sameness with Fricka, see Kl. schr. 5,

416 seq.   The Gauls too sacrificed to *Artemis*, Arrian de Venat.
c. 23. 32.   *Hecate* triviorum praeses, Athen. 3, 196 ; men took
a sop with them for fear of the *cross-roads* 2, 83, for *Hecate's*
hounds 7, 499 ; Ἑκάτης δεῖπνον means the bread laid down where
three roads met, Luc. Dial. mort. 1 and 22 (note on Lucian 2,
397) ; feros *Hecatae* perdomuisse *canes*, Tibull. i. 2, 54.

p. 950.]   The appalling guise of the *Harii* (GDS. 714) recalls
our death's-head cavaliers. At the outset of the Thirty-years
War there were Bavarian troopers called Invincibles, with black
horses, black clothing, and on their black helmets a white death's-
head; their leader was Kronberger, and fortune favoured them
till Swedish Baner met them in Mecklenburg, March 1631.
Frederick the Great had a regiment of Death's-head Hussars.
In recent times we have had Lützow's Volunteers, the Black
Jägers, the Brunswick Hussars. Does a coat-of-arms with a
death's-head occur in the days of chivalry ? We read in Wigal.
80, 14: an sînem schilde was der *Tôt* gemâlt vil grûsenlîche
(Suppl. to 850). Remember too the terror-striking name of the
legio fulminatrix, κεραυνοβόλος. Secret societies use the symbol
of a death's-head; apothecaries mark their poison-boxes with the
same.

----

# CHAPTER XXXII.

## TRANSLATION.

p. 952.]   *Verwünschen* is also exsecrari, abominari.   OS. *farwâ-
tan*, devovere, OHG. *farwâzan*, *withar-huâzan*, recusare, Graff 1,
1087. As abominari comes fr. omen, so *far-huâtan* fr. *hvât*,
omen (Suppl. to 1105 n.). Beside the Fr. *souhait* (which Génin
Récr. 1, 201 would derive fr. sonhait, as couvent fr. convent,
etc.) we have also *ahait* in Thib. de N., and the simple *hait*=
luck, wish. For its root, instead of OHG. heiz, ON. heit, we
might take the Bret. *het*, Gael. *aiteas*=pleasure. De *sohait*, de
*dehait*, Guitecl. 1, 169.

*Disappearing* (verschwinden) and *appearing again* are ἀφανῆ
γενέσθαι and φανερὸν γενέσθαι, Plato's Rep. 360. Frequent is
the phrase ' to vanish *under one's hand* ' ; conf. the clapping of
hands in cases of enchantment (p. 1026) : thaz thu hiar *irwunti*

mir *untar theru henti*, O. i. 22, 44; *verswant* den luten *under den handen*, Griesh. Sprachd. 26 [Late examples omitted]; *ze hant* verswant der kleine, Ortnit 141, 4; vile schiere her verswant *von sînen ougen zehant*, daz her en-weste, war her bequam, En. 2621; *vor iren ougen* er virswant, Hpt 5, 533; verswant *vor sînen ougen*, Krone 29606 [Simil. ex. om.].——Der engel sâ *vor im* verswant, Wh. 49, 27; dô der tiuvel *hin* verswant, Barl. 3027; dô der winder gar verswant, Frauend. 409, 17; solde ein wîp vor leide sîn verswunden MS. 1, 81ᵃ; der hirz vorswant, Myst. 1, 233; in den *wint* gâhes (suddenly) verswunden, Mar. 159, 7; daz verswant *mit der luft*, Pass. 369, 91; der engel *mit der rede* verswant, Hpt 8, 171; the devil says 'ich *nuoz* verswinden,' MSH. 3, 174ᵃ: '*von hinnan* stêt mîn begirde (desire), Got müeze dich in huote lân!' alsus *swein* diu gezierde, Diut. 2, 251-2; Sant. Servace dô *verswein*, Servat. 3317 [Ex. om.].——*Voer* ute haren ogen, Karel 2, 990; de duvel *voer dane* alse *ên rôc* (smoke) te scouwene ane, Maerl. 2, 237; *Var-in-d'wand*, N. pr. ring 33ᵇ, 30. 36ᶜ, 28. 36. To begone = OHG. *huerban*, ON. *hverfa*: Oðinn *hvarf* þâ, Sæm. 47; oc nu *hverfur* þessi alfur sô *sem skuggi*, (as a shadow), Vilk. c. 150; brottu *horfinn*, ibid.; *flô* þâ *burt*, Fornald. s. 1, 488, conf. *seykvaz*, sink away, Sæm. 10ᵇ. 229ᵇ.—— The translated *sleep*, like Kronos p. 833 n.; Gawan falls asleep on a table in the Grals-halle, and awakes next morning in a moss, Keller's Romvart 660. Vanishing is often preceded by thunder: ein *grôzer slac*, Heinr. u. Kun. 4215. Erf. märch. 84. 160; ' there came a *crash* (rassler), and all was sunk and gone,' Panz. 1, 30; Gangleri hears a *thunder*, and *Valhöll* has vanished, he stands in the fields, Sn. 77.

p. 953.] The shepherd Gyges steps into a *crack of the earth* made during storm and earthquake, finds a giant's corpse inside a brazen horse, and draws a ring off its hand, Plato's Rep. p. 369. *Translation* is imprecated or invoked in the following phrases: in te ruant montes mali, Plaut. Epid. i. 1, 78; κατὰ τῆς γῆς δῦναι ηὐχόμην, Lucian 3, 156. 5, 202; χανεῖν μοι τὴν γῆν ηὐχόμην 9, 68. 8, 18.——Oedipus is swallowed up by the earth, Oed. Col. 1662. 1752; conf. '*slipping in* like the schwick' (p. 450 n.); die *lufte* mich *verslunden*, Hpt 5, 540; λᾶαν ἔθηκε, Il. 2, 319; λίθος ἐξ ἀνθρώπου γεγονέναι, Lucian's Imag. 1; der *werde z'einem steine!* MS. 1, 6ᵃ; hon (Goðrun) var buin til at *springa* af harmi,

Sæm. 211 ; du-ne hetest ditz gesprochen, dû waerst benamen *ze-brochen*, Iw. 153. We talk of bursting with rage (p. 552 n.), i.e., in order to jump out of our skin : er wolte aus der haut fahren, Salinde 13.

　　p. 958.] A *translated hero* is spoken of as early as 1096 : Inde fabulosum illud confictum de *Carolo magno*, quasi de mortuis in id ipsum *resuscitato*, et *alio nescio quo* nihilominus *redivivo* (before Frederick I. therefore), Pertz 8, 215 (Suppl. to 939). *Frederick* is supposed to lie at Trifels in the Palatinate also, where his bed is made for him every night, Schlegel's Mus. 1, 293. Then the folktales make *Otto Redbeard* also live in the Kifhäuser, and give him frau *Holle* for housekeeper and errandwoman, Sommer pp. 1. 6. 104 ; he gives away a *green twig*, which turns into gold, p. 2 ; in the mountain there is *skittle-playing* and 'schmaräkeln,' p. 4. A legend of Fredk Redbeard in Firmen. 2, 201ᵃ. A giant has *slept at the stone-table in the mountain* these 700 years, Dyb. Runa '47, 34-5. Not unlike the Swed. folktale of a blind giant banished to an island are the stories in Runa '44, pp. 30. 43. 59. 60 : in every case the *belt* given is strapped *round a tree* (conf. Panzer 1, 17. 71. 367), but the other incidents differ. Such giants call churches de *hvita klock-märrarna* 4, 37, and the bell *bjelleko*, Dyb. '45, 48. '44, 59 ; the blind grey old man reminds one of Oden. Acc. to Praetor. Alectr. p. 69, Kaiser Frederick seems to have cursed himself into the 'Kiphäuser.'——On the Frederick legend, see Hpt 5, 250—293. Closener p. 30-1 (yr 1285). Böhmer's Reg., yr 1285, no. 830, conf. 824-6. Kopp's Rudolf pp. 736—749. Detmar 1, 130 (yr 1250). Of Fredk the *Second*, the Repgow. chron. (Massm. 711) says straight out : ' bî den tîden sege-men dat *storve* keiser Vrederic ; en dêl volkes segede, he *levede*; de twivel warede lange tît ; ' conf. ibid. 714. Another name for the auricula is *berg-kaiserlein* ; does it mean the wonder-flower that shows the treasure ? —— Fischart's Geschicht-kl. 22ᵇ says : *auff dem keyser Friderich stan* ; Schiller 120ᵇ (?) : und nebenher hatten unsere kerle noch das gefundene fressen *über den alten kaiser* zu *plündern*. Phil. v. Sittew. Soldatenl. 232: fressen, saufen, prassen *auf den alten keyser hinein*. Albertini's Narrenh. p. 264 ; heuraten *auf d. a. k. hinein*. Schmeller 2, 335-6 : immer zu *in d. a. kaiser hinein* sündigen, *auf d. a. k. hinauf* sündigen, zechen, i.e. without thinking of paying.

p. 961.] The sleeping Fredk reminds one of *Kronos sleeping* in a cave, and *birds* bringing him *ambrosia*, Plut. De facie in orbe lunae 4, 1152-3 (see p. 833 n.). *Arthur* too and the knights of the Grail are shut up in a mountain, Lohengr. 179. Lanz. 6909. Garin de L. 1, 238; si jehent (they say) er lebe noch hiute, Iw. 14. Raynouard sub v. Artus. Cæsarius heisterb. 12, 12 speaks of *rex Arcturus in Monte Giber* (It. monte Gibello); conf. Kaufm. p. 51 and the magnet-mountain ' ze *Givers*,' Gudr. 1135-8. 564 (KM.³ 3, 274). Other instances: *könig Dan*, Müllenh. no. 505; the *count of Flanders*, Raynouard 1, 130ª; *Marko* lives yet in the wooded mountains, Talvj 1, xxvi.; so does the horse Bayard. On the search for Svatopluk, *Swatopluka hledati*, see Schafarik p. 804.

p. 968.] The *white lady's bunch of keys* is snake-bound, Panzer 1, 2. A *white maiden* with *keys* in Firmen. 2, 117; *drei witte jumfern*, Hpt 4, 392; *three white ladies* in the enchanted castle, Arnim's März. no. 18 ; conf. the Slav. *vilas* and *villy*, spirits of brides who died before the wedding-day, who hold ring-dances at midnight, and dance men to death, Hanusch pp. 305. 415; dancing *willis*, Mailath's Ungr. märch. 1, 9 ; Lith. *wéles*, figures of the dead.

p. 969.] A certain general plants an *acorn* to make his *coffin* of, Ettn. Chymicus 879. There is some likeness betw. the story of Release and that of the Wood of the Cross, which grows out of three pips laid under Adam's tongue when dead. That the pip must be brought by a little bird, agrees with the rowan sapling fit for a wishing-rod, whose seed must have dropt out of a bird's bill (Suppl. to 977 beg.), and with the viscum per alvum avium redditum (p. 1206); conf. the legend of the Schalksburg, Schwab's Alb. p. 32. You must fell a tree, and make a cradle out of it; the first time a baby cries in that cradle, the spell is loosed, the treasure is lifted, H. Meyer's Züricher ortsn. p. 98; conf. the tale in Panzer 2, 200. 159. Other conditions of release : to draw a waggon up a hill the wrong way, to buy a piece of linen, to hold the white lady's hand in silence, Reusch p. 437; with your mouth to take the key out of the snake's mouth, Firmen. 1, 332; to kiss the worm, or the toad, or the frog, wolf and snake, Müllenh. p. 580. Somm. Sagen p. 21. Meyer's Züricher ortsn. p. 97.

p. 971.] Men do bury *treasures in the ground:* the Kozácks

are said to keep all their money underground ; thieves and robbers bury their booty, dogs and wolves pieces of meat. The Marsians buried the Roman eagle they had captured in a grove, whence the Romans dug it out again, Tac. Ann. 2, 25.——The treasure is called *leger-hort*, Renn. 17687. 2505 ; ON. *taurar* = thesauri, opes reconditae. '*Shogs* not the treasure *up* toward me, That *shining* there behind I see ?' Goethe 12, 193. The treasure *blooms*, Panzer 1, 1 ; 'for buried gold will often *shift about*,' Irrgart. d. liebe 503 ; the cauldrons *sink* three ells a year, Dybeck 4, 45. Once in 100 years the stones off the heath go down to the sea to drink, and then all treasures of the earth lie open, so that one need only reach them out ; but in a few winters they come back, and crush those who don't get out of the way in time, Bret. märch. 88—93. The treasure *suns* itself, Panzer 2, 16. 30. It *cools* (glüht aus), Müllenh. p. 203-4. Treasure-gold turns to *coal*, Lucian's Timon 1, 110. Philops. 7, 284 ; conf. the legends of Holla, Berhta, Fredk Barbarossa and Rübezal. The *coals* of a glowing treasure turn to gold, Reusch no. 25-6-7. *Glimmering fire* and *coals* of a treasure, Dieffenb. Wetterau p. 275.——*Signs* of a treasure : when a hazel bears mistletoe, and a white snake suns himself, and treasure-fire burns, Reusch no. 15. Where treasures lie, a blue fire burns (Hofmannswaldau), or light finds its way out of the earth, Leipz. avent. 2, 40 ; it *swarms* with insects, etc. (pp. 692-4).——The treasure-lifter is stript and plunged up to his neck in water in a tub, and is left till midnight to watch for the coming of the treasure, Cervant. Nov. de la gitanilla p. m. 106. A beshouted treasure *sinks*, Wetterau tale in Firmen. 2, 100 ; conf. AS. *sinc* = thesaurus, opes. Some good stories of treasure-lifting in Asbiörnsen's Huldr. 1, 142-3-4. Ghosts have to give up buried weapons : saemir ei draugum dŷrt vâpn bera, Fornald. s. 1, 436. A connexion subsists betw. treasures and graves : the *hauga eldar*, grave-fires, indicate money, Egilss. 767. The hoard does *not diminish* : sîn wart doch niht minre, swie vil man von dem schatze truoc, Nib. 475, 12.

p. 972.] The *wonder-flower* is said to blossom either on Midsummer night alone, or only *once in* 100 *years*. If any one, having spied it, hesitates to pluck it, it suddenly vanishes amid thunder and lightning ; conf. britannica (p. 1195-6), fern (p. 1211). Preusker 1, 91-2. Before the eyes of the shepherd's man a *wonder-flower grows up* suddenly out of the ground; he pulls it, and sticks it in his hat; as quick as you can turn your hand, a *grey mannikin* stands there, and beckons him to follow; or else, the moment the flower is stuck in the hat, the *white lady* appears, Firmen. 2, 175. The wonder-flower gets caught in the shoe-buckle, Somm. p. 4, as fernseed falls into the shoes (p. 1210), and also ripens or blossoms on Midsum. night, pp. 4. 165. ——It is called *schlüsselblume*, Panzer 1, 883, *wunderblume*, Wetterau. sag. p. 284. Phil. v. Steinau p. 77; Pol. *dziwaczek*, Boh. *diwnjk*, wonderflower. The three *blue* flowers effect the release, Firmen. 2, 201ª. A Schleswig story makes it the *yellow* flower, and the cry is: *Forget not the best*, Müllenh. p. 351. Another formula is: ' wia meh as da verzötarist (squanderest), om sa minder host,' Vonbun p. 5.——As early as the 15th cent. *vergisse min nit* occurs as the name of a flower, Altd. w. 1, 151; a gloss of the time has: *vergiss-mein-nicht* alleluja, Mone 8, 103; *vergis-man-nicht* gamandria, ibid. *Vergiss nit mein* is a blue flower, Uhl. 1, 60. 108. 114-6. 129; blümlein *vergiss nit mein*, Ambras. liedb. pp. 18. 251. Bergr. 37. 70; blümelain *vergiss ni main*, Meinert 34; *vergiss mein nicht*, Menante's Gal. welt p. 70. Swed. *förgät-mig-ej*, Dybeck '48, 28; Boh. *ne-zapoměnka*, Pol. *nie-zapominka*, Russ. *ne-zabúdka*, conf. Weim. jrb. 4, 108; das blümlein wunderschön, Goethe 1, 189.——The *heel cut off* him that hurries away, Firmen. 2, 176. In a story in Wächter's Statist. p. 175-6 the wounded heel never heals. A proverb says: 'Tis what comes after, hurts your heel.

p. 974.] The *spring-wurzel* is in OHG. *sprinc-wurz*, lactarida, lactaria herba, Graff 1, 1051, or simply *springa* 6, 397. Does *piderit, diderit* (usu. diterich, picklock) also mean a spring-wurzel? Firmen. 1, 271. The springw. or wonderflower is sometimes called *bird's nest*, Fr. *nid d'oiseau*, plante apéritive, vulnéraire, qui croît au pied des sapins; it opens boxes (folktale in Mone 8, 539), and makes invisible, DS. no. 85. Again, it is called *zweiblatt, bifoglio*, and is picked off the point of bifurcation in a tree; does it mean a parasite-plant like the misletoe? It must have been regarded as the nest of a sacred bird: thus of the *siskin's nest* it is believed that the bird lays in it a small precious stone to make it invisible, Hpt 3, 361; conf. Vonbun's Vorarlbg 63; Boh. *hnjzdnjk*, ophrys nidus avis, ragwort, Pol.

*gniazdo ptasze* (see Linde 1, 728[b]).——On the *green-pecker,* Fr. *pivert,* see Am. Bosq. p. 217-8, and *baum-heckel,* Musäus 2, 108; picos divitiis, qui aureos montes colunt, ego solus supero, Plaut. Aulul. iv. 8, 1. On the legend of the *shamir,* conf. Hammer's Rosenöl 1, 251. Altd. w. 2, 93. Pineda's Salomon (Diemer p. 44), *samir.* Diem. 109, 19; *thanir,* Gerv. Tilb. Ot. imp. ed. Leibn. p. 1000; *thamur,* Vinc. Bellovac. 20, 170; *tamin,* Maerl. in Kästner 29[a]. In Griesh. Predigt. p. xxv. is the story of the *ostrich* 2, 122.

p. 977.] The Swed. *slag-ruta* is cut off the *flyg-rönn,* bird's rowan (or service) tree, whose seed has fallen fr. the beak of a bird, Dybeck '45, 63; it must be cut on Midsummer eve out of *mistletoe boughs,* Runa '44, 22. '45, 80. Dan. *önske-qvist,* Engl. divining-rod, *finding-stick.* Germ. names: der *Saelden zwîc,* Altsw. 119. 127, conf. ungelückes zwîc (Suppl. to 879 end); *glücks-ruthe,* Lisch in Meckl. jrb. 5, 84; *wünschel-ruote* sunder zwisel (without cleft), MSH. 2, 339[b]; *wunschel-rîs,* Tit. 2509. 5960-82, *w.* über alle küneginne, 1242, *wünschel-berndez rîs* 1728; alles heiles *wünschel-rîs,* Troj. 2217; mîns heils *wünschel-ruote,* Altsw. 118; der *wünschel-ruoten* hort, Dietr. drach. 310[a]. Nu *hât gegangen* mîner künste ruote, MSH. 3, 81[a].——The idea of the wishing-rod was not borrowed fr. Aaron's magic wand; on the contrary, our poet of the 12th cent. borrows of the former to give to the latter: Nim die gerte *in dîne hant,* wurche zeichen manikvalt; *ze allen dingen ist sie guot, swes sô wunsget dîn muot.* Not a word of all this in Exod. 7, 9; the wishing-rod however did not serve the purposes of harmful magic. Conf. the *virgula divina,* Forcell. sub v.; Esth. *pilda,* GDS. 159.——The wishing-rod must have been cut at a fitting time and by clean hands, Kippe die wippe 1688, D 4[b]: it is a hazel-rod, and holy, Vonbun pp. 6. 7. 64; a hazel-bough, Fromm. 3, 210; a white *somer-laden heslin stab,* Weisth. 3, 411. 461. Stories of the wishing-rod in Kuhn p. 330. Müllenh. p. 204; of the old wünschel-stock, ib. no. 283. On the manner of holding it, see Hone's Yearbk 1589. It is called *schlag-ruthe* because it anschlägt, hits [the nail on the head]; hence *slegel,* cudgel? conf. Parz. 180, 10—14, and the hazel-rod that *cudgels* the absent (Suppl. to 651 end).

p. 977.] One must drive a *white he-goat* through the stable, to lift a treasure that lies there, Hpt's Ztschr. 3, 315.

p. 980.] The *devil* is by the treasure, and he is blind too, like Plutus (Suppl. to 993). The Ssk. *Kuvêra*, a hideous being, is god of wealth. *Dit-* is the same as *divit-*, Pott 1, 101. When money is buried, the *devil* is appointed *watchman*, Müllenh. p. 202-3, or a *grey man* on a *three-legged* white horse guards it 102. Finn. *aarni* or *kratti* is genius thesauri, conf. *mammelainen* below. AS. wyrm *hordes hyrde*, Beow. 1767. Fâfnir says : er ek *â arfi lâ* (on the heritage lay) miklom mîns föðor, Sæm. 188ᵇ ; meðan ek *um menjom* lag, ibid. 'Lanuvium *annosi* vetus est *tutela draconis ;*' maidens bring him food :

> Si fuerint castae, redeunt in colla parentum,
> clamantque agricolae 'Fertilis annus erit !' Prop. v. 8, 3.

Dragons *sun* their gold in fine weather, Runa '44, 44, like the white maidens. Some good stories of the roving dragon in Müllenh. p. 206 ; conf. the dragon of Lambton, Hpt 5, 487 ; he is also called the *drakel*, Lyra p. 137, the *wheat-dragon*, Firmen. 2, 309. The n. prop. *Otwurm* in Karajan begins with *ôt*=eâd, conf. ôt-pero. Heimo finds a *dragon* on the Alps of Carniola, kills him and cuts his tongue out ; with him he finds a rich hoard : locum *argento septum* possedit, in quo *aurea mala* habuit, Mone 7, 585 fr. Faber's Evagatorium.——W. Grimm (HS. p. 385-6) thinks the *ring Andvara-naut* was the most essential part of the hoard, that in it lay the gold-engendering power and the destiny, but German legend put in its place the *wishing-rod ;* note however, that such power of breeding gold is nowhere ascribed to Andvara-naut. Sigurd first gave it to Brunhild (Fornald. s. 1, 178), then secretly pulled it off again (187). Siegfried in the German epic, after winning the treasure, leaves it in charge of the dwarfs, does not take it away therefore, but gives it to Chriemhilt as a wedding-gift, and as such the dwarfs have to deliver it up, Nib. 1057—64. Once it is in Günther's land, the Burgundians take it from her, and Hagen sinks it in the Rhine 1077, 3 ; conf. 2305-8. Hagen has merely hidden it at Lochheim, intending afterwards to fish it up again, conf. 1080. So likewise in Sæm. 230: 'Gunnar ok Högni tôko þâ gullit allt, Fâfnis arf.' On the fate bound up with the gold-hoard in the ON. (and doubtless also in OHG.) legend, see Hpt 3, 217. Finn. *mammelainen*, mater serpentis, divitiarum subterranearum custos

(Renvall) reminds one of ON. *môdir Atla* = serpens, Sæm. 243[b]. Golden geese and ducks also sit *underground* on golden eggs, Somm. sag. p. 63-4.

p. 981.] In some stories it is the *old man* in the mountain that, when people come in to him, *crops their heads bald*, Somm. p. 83 ; then again the spectres wish to *shave the beard* of a man as he lies in bed, Simpl. K. 921. 930. In Musäus 4, 61 both get *shorn*.

p. 983.] With *Lurlenberge* conf. ' ûz *Lurlinberge* wart gefurt sîn stolze eventure,' Ritterpr.[b], and *Lurinberc*, Graff 2, 244. Or *Burlenberg* might be the *Birlenberg* of Weisth. 4, 244. On the sunken *or de Toulouse* and *or de Montpellier*, see Berte 20.——Sinking is preceded by a *crash* (Suppl. to 952 end) : heyrði hann *dyna mikla*, Sn. 77 ; there was a *bang*, and all was sunk and gone, Panz. 1, 30 (in Schm. 3, 125 a loud *snore*) ; then comes a *crack*, and the castle once more is as it was before, Kuhn's Westf. sag. 2, 250 ; a fearful *crash*, and the castle tumbles and disappears, Schönwerth 3, 52.——Near Staffelberg in Up. Franconia lies a great pond, and in it a great fish, holding his *tail* in his *mouth* ; the moment he *lets it go*, the mountain will fly to pieces and fill the pond, and the flood *drown the flats of Main and Rhine*, and everything perish, man and beast, Panz. 2, 192. A *little cloud* on the horizon often announces the bursting-in of the flood or violent rain, Müllenh. p. 133. 1 Kings 18, 43-4 (Hpt 8, 284). An *angel* walks into the sinking city, Wolf's Niederl. sag. 326. Of the foundling Gregor, who came floating on the flood, it is said : der sich hât *verrunnen* her, Greg. 1144. After the flood, the baby is left up in a *poplar-tree*, Müllenh. p. 132. In the legend of the Wood of the Cross also, a newborn child lies on the top of a tree. On the name *Dold*, see GDS. 758.

---

## CHAPTER XXXIII.

### DEVIL.

p. 986.] Schwenk's Semiten 161 says the Devil is a Persian invention. On *Ahuromazdâo*, see Windischm. Rede p. 17-8 ; the cuneif. inscriptions have *Auramazda*, Gr. Ὠρομάσθης. *Ahura* is the Ssk. asura, Böhtlg 555 ; and Benfey in Gött. gel. anz. '62,

p. 1757 conn. *mazda* with Ssk. medhás, medhâm = vedhâm. The Ind. asura is evil, the deva good; the Pers. ahura is good, the daêva bad; so heretics repres. Ahriman, the devil, as the first-born son of God, and Ormuzd or Christ as the second. The Yezids worship the devil mainly as one originally good, who has rebelled, and may injure, may at last become a god again, and avenge himself.——Lucifer falls out of heaven (p. 241); the angels fall *three nights and days* fr. heaven to hell, Cædm. 20, 12; sie fielen *drî tage volle*, Karaj. Denkm. 42, 9; Hephæstus falls *a whole day* fr. Olympus to Lemnos, Il. 1, 592. As God creates, the devil tries to do the same; he sets up his *chapel* next the church (p. 1021); he also has 12 *disciples* ascr. to him, Berthold 321; conf. devil's pupils (Suppl. to 1024).

p. 987.] Ulphilas translates even the fem. ἡ διάβολος by diabula, pl. *diabulôs*, slanderers, 1 Tim. 3, 11. Among corruptions of the word are: Dan. *knefvel, snefvel*, Molbech's Tidskr. 6, 317; Arab. *eblis, iblis;* prob. our own 'der *tausend!*' conf. dusii (p. 481) and daus, Dict. 2, 855. Lith. *děvalus, děvulus* = great god, Nesselm. 140ᵃ. Devil, Devilson occur as surnames: Cuonradus *Diabolus* de Rute, MB. 8, 461. 472; *filii Tiufelonis* (Suppl. to 1019 end); Beroldus dictus *Diabolus*, Sudendorf's Beitr. p. 73, yr 1271; Cunze gen. *Duflis heubit*, Arnsb. urk. 787. ——The Finn. *perkele*, devil, Kalev. 10, 118. 141. 207. 327 and Lapp. *perkel, pergalek* (Suppl. to 171 end) are derived fr. *piru*, cacodaemon, says Schiefn. Finn. namen 611.

*Satanas* in Diemer 255, 10; *satanât* in Hpt 8, 155. 355 (the odious *s.*). Karaj. Sprachdenkm. 52, 3; a pl. *satanasâ* in O. v. 20, 4. The word sounds like *scado* (p. 989), *skohsl* (p. 1003), above all like *Sœtere, Saturn* (p. 247).

p. 991.] Der tievel gap den *rât* (advice), wander in bezeren ne hât, Fundgr. 2, 87; als ez der tiufel *riet*, Nib. 756, 9; der tiuvel mir daz *riet*, Frib. Trist. 2207. The devil is called *niht guotes:* we say 'it smells here like no good things'; Lett. *ne labbais*, the not good; Lapp. *pahakes*, the bad one. He is called *der ubel âtem* (breath), Fundgr. 2, 18; unreine *saghe untwas*, Bruns 324-5; conf. Swed. *Oden hin oude*, Ihre's Dial. lex. 123ᵃ; der *arge tumbe*, Martina 160, 23, as we say 'stupid devil'; *arger wiht*, Diut. 1, 470; der *sûre* wirt (sour host), Helbl. 2, 587; ûz des *bitteren* tiefels halse (throat), Griesh. 52; den *leiden* duvelen (odious d.), Hpt 2, 197; der *leidige* tifel, Mos. 52, 18; *leding*, Cavall. Voc. Verland 40ª; *lâjing, lâje*, Wieselgren 385; *liothan*, Dybeck '45, 72; der *greulich* hat dich herein getran (brought), Uhl. Volksl. p. 801. Lith. *bĕsas*, devil, conf. *baisus*, grim. Finn. *paha, pahoillinen*, devil; Esth. *pahalainen, pahomen*, Salmelainen 1, 179. 193. 234.——In Scand. the devil is also called *skam, skammen* (shame), Ihre's Dial. lex. 149ᵇ. Dyb. '45, 3. 55. 77. Is he called the *little* one? 'whence brings you der *lützel* here?' Gryphius's Dornr. 56, 8. The *live, bodily* devil, or simply 'der *leibhaftige*,' the veritable, Gotthelf's Käserei 356; *fleischechter leibhafter* teufel, Garg. 229ᵇ; ich sei des *leibhaftigen* butzen 244ª; der *sihtige* tiuvel, Berth. 37; des *sihtigen* tufels kint, Dietr. drach. 212ᵇ. 285ᵇ; conf. *vif maufé*, Méon 3, 252; ainz est *deables vis*, M. de Gar. 178.——*Antiquus hostis* occurs also in Widukind (Pertz 5, 454); our *Urian* resembles Ur-hans, Old Jack (Suppl. to 453 n.); *u-tüfel*, Gotth. Erz. 1, 162. 177. 253. 275. 286, *ur-teufel* 2, 277; d' *oude* sathan, Maerl. 2, 300; de *uald* knecht, de *uald*, Müllenh. p. 265. The household god of the Tchuvashes, *Erich* (Götze's Russ. volksl. p. 17) recalls '*gammel* Eric.'——ON. *andskoti* = diabolus, hostis; ther *widarwerto* (untoward), O. ii. 4, 93. 104; *warc* = diabolus, Graff 1, 980; *helle-warc*, Diut. 2, 291; conf. ON. *vargr*, lupus, hostis (p. 996). Der *víent*, Pfeiffer's Myst. 1, 131; der *vînt*, Helbl. 1, 1186; der *leide vient*, Leyser 123, 11. 38; *lâð-geteona*, Beow. 1113, is said of sea-monsters, but it means 'hateful foe,' and might designate the devil.——Der helsche *dief*, Maerl. 2, 312; der *nacht-schade*, said of a homesprite, Rochholz 1, 295 (Kl. schr. 3, 407). Ein *unhuld*, Hagen's Heldenb. 1, 235. With the fem. *unholdâ* in OHG. hymns conf. 'daz wîp, diu *unholde*,' Pass. 353, 91; in *Unhulden-tal*, Bair. qu. 1, 220; and the Servian fem. *vila* in many points resembles the devil. *Uberfengil, ubarfangâri*, praevaricator, usurpator, seems also to mean the devil in contrast with angels, Hpt 8, 146.

p. 992.] Der ubele *vâlant*, Diemer 302, 28; der *v.*, Karaj. 89, 14; diu *vâlendîn*, Cod. pal. 361, 74ᶜ; *vâlantinne*, Krone 9375. 9467; diu ubele *v.*, Mai 170, 11; disem *vâlande* gelîch 122, 21; dû *urkiusche* der *vâlande* 172, 16; ein vil boeser *vâlant*, Türl. Wh. 136ᵇ: swaz der *v.* wider in tet (against them did), Welsch. gast 5177; des *vâlandes* spot (mock), Warn. 2426; des *v.* hant

1358. The word occurs in the Erec, not in the Iwein, Hpt's Pref. xv. I find Conr. of Würzbg has not altogether forborne its use: der leide *vâlant*, Silv. 4902 ; wilder *v.*, Frauenl. 382, 15 ; der *v.* müez si stillen 123, 19. It occurs but once in M. Neth. poets: die quade *valande*, Walew. 8945; (distinct fr. it stands *vaeliant* = *vaillant* 9647, and *faliant, valiant*, Lanc. 21461. 24643). ——Du pöser *feilant*, Fastn. sp. 578, 21 ; böser *volant* 926, 11 ; *volandes* man, Hpt 5, 20. 31 ; der schwarze *voland*, Mülmann's Geiszel 273 ; der *volland*, Ayrer 340ª; *volant* in witch-trials of 1515 (Wolf's Ztschr. 2, 77); den sol der böse *voland* holen! Lichtwer 1758, 128. In the Walpurgis-night on the Blocksberg, Mephistopheles calls himself *junker Voland*, squire V., Goethe's Faust, p. m. 159. In Thuringia (at Gotha) I heard ' Das glab der *Fold!* ' devil believe it. *Völundr, Wayland* seems unconn. with vâlant, whose *v.* is really an *f*.

p. 993.] The devil is *lame* in a Moravian story (p. 1011), the same in Wallachia, Fr. Müller nos. 216. 221 ; conf. Thôr's lame goat (p. 995). He is *blind*, Lith. *aklatis ;* his eyes are put out with melted lead (p. 1027). He is *black :* ne nos frangat demon *ater*, Chart. Sithiensc p. 8 ; *tenebrosus* hostis, Münter's Tempelh. 158 ; der *swarze* meister, Hpt 1, 277 ; von dem tiuvel hoert man wol, wie er *swerzer* sî dan kol, u. ist doch unsihtic (yet invisible), Ls. 3, 276 ; die *swarzen* helle-warten, Servat. 3520. In Tirol and the Up. Palatinate he is called *grau-wuzl*, Schm. 4, 208. He wears *grey* or *green* clothes (p. 1063), and, like the dwarfs, a *red cap*, Müllenh. p. 194. The African Negroes paint the devil *white*, Klemm 3, 358. 364.

p. 995.] The devil's *horn* partly resembles the hone in Thor's head (p. 373) ; conf. ' gehurnte *helle ohsen*,' horned ox of hell, Hpt 8, 151. 236. He has a *tail :* ' tied to the devil's *tail*,' Keisersb. xv. Staffely 41-3. 59. Schärtlin p. 226 ; the troll too has a tail, Dyb. Runa '44, 73, the Norw. huldre a *cow's tail*. He has a *hen's* and a *horse's foot*, Lisch's Meckl. jrb. 5, 94, a *horse's* foot and a *man's*, Müllenh. p. 197. Deoful *wam* and *wlite-leás*, Andr. 1170.

p. 997.] The devil has horns and *cloven feet*, Wolf's Ztschr. 2, 63 ; his *goat's feet* peep out, Mone 8, 125, as *goat's feet* and *claws* are ascr. to dwarfs (p. 451 n.) ; daemones in specie *caprarum*, Acta Bened. sec. 1 p. 33 ; devil as *stein-geisz* [wild goat,

Capricorn?], Haltrich p. 44. Pfeiff. Germ. 1, 484; die bös teufels *ziyen* (she-goats), i.e. witches, Keller's Altd. erz. 192, 22. With '*bocks* lid' agrees '*des tiuvels glit*,' limb of the d., Pass. 377, 24 (Suppl. to 1019 end); *box-scheis* habe ir sele! Lindenbl. 123; 'to pluck a *horn* out of the devil,' Garg. 17[b]. Here belong the surnames *Hellbock, Höllbock*, Denkschr. der k. k. acad. 5, 20.

The devil is named *Säu-reussel* (sow's snout), and finds bells, Ph. Dieffenb. Wanderung p. 73; duivels *zwîntje* (pigs), Hpt 7, 532 (Suppl. to 478). The hog for breeding is called *fuhl*, Weisth. 2, 528. There is a hero's name, *Ur-swîn*, Dietl. 5253; conf. ur-ber, ur-kämpe, ur-sau, ur-schwein. The devil is called a *luhs*, lynx, MS. 2, 6[b]. 7[a]; a *hare*, Panz. Beitr. 1, 137; an *ape*, because he apes God (Suppl. to 1024 beg.).

The devil was 'der vil ungehiure *helle-wolf*,' Hpt 5, 520; die *helle-wargen* 7, 376; abstrahis *ore lupi*, Erm. Nigell. 4, 370. GDS. 329. 333.

*Helle-hunt* = Cerberus, Gl. sletst. 4, 32. Renn. 289; der übele *hunt*, Diemer 309, 22, der *helle-hunt*, der *hunt* verwâzen (accursed), 314, 2. 13; vuor der übermuote *hunt* alsô tiefe an den helle-grunt 4, 26; *nit-hunt*, dog of spite, Helbl. 2, 264; devil seen in *dog's* shape, Pass. 203, 59.

p. 999.] Acc. to Gryphius's Sonett. 1, 1 the devil is called *höllen-rabe;* he appears 'in *swarzer vogele* bilde,' Ksrchr. 4314; der höllische *geier*, vulture, Meinert p. 165; das hat sie der *geier* gelernt, Lessing 2, 446; die höllische *agalaster* (magpie), der satan, Pol. maulaffe 195, conf. Parz. 1; *helle-gouch*, Krolewicz 3879, conf. the cuckoo and his clerk (p. 681-2); de bunte *kiwit* hahl se! Hanenreyerey 1618 A v[b]; fört juw (brings you) de *kiwit* nu weer her? B viii[e]. He has *goose-feet, crow's feet*, Thür. mitth. vi. 3, 67. 70.

The *serpent* in Paradise was wrongly supposed to be the devil, Schwenk's Semit. 162. He is called der *lintwurm*, Mar. 148, 28; der alde *helle-trache*, Pass. 13, 23. 101, 47; der *hellewurm* 106, 27; *celidrus*, Erm. Nigell. 2, 191, fr. χέλυδρος, water-snake. Leviathan is transl. in AS. by *sœ-draca;* he is descr. 'cum armilla in maxilla,' Vom geloub. 601, and there is 'ein *rinc* ime in sîne *nasen* gelegit' 541; conf. 'in des tiuveles *drozzen*,' throat, Rol. 244, 29; den hât des tiuvels *kiuwe* (jaw) verslunden, Warn. 540.

*Belzebup*, Karaj. 52, 3; *Belsebúc* in Fragm. of Madelghîs;

*Besebuc,* Walew. 8244; *drukhs* fem. as a fly, Spiegel's Avesta 124. A spirit is shut up in a *glass* as a *fly,* MS. 2, 13-4, or in a *box,* Leipz. avant. 2, 41; there is a *devil* in the *glass,* both in the legend of Zeno in Bruns, and in that of the scholar and robber in H. v. Herford, yr 995 and in Korner.

p. 1000.] The devil as a *hammer* (slege), Kemble's Sal. and Sat. 146. 177. He is called *Hemmerlein,* Ambras. lied. 142. As Donar's hammer gradu. becomes a fiery sword, it is also said: ein *fiurec swert* der tiuvel hât, Hpt 5, 450 (p. 812. Suppl. to 1013 end). The devil *rolling* like a *millstone* resembles the troll *rolling* like a *ball,* Nilsson 4, 40.

p. 1002.] The devil is 'der alde *hellewarte,*' Pass. 23, 18. *helle-wirt* 99, 11, der alde *hellewiht* 293, 94; er rehter *helleschergen gouch,* Mai 156, 40; *hellescherje,* Tit. 5468. 5510; *hellescherge,* Helbl. 2, 603; *hellefiur,* Berth. 56; there is a man's name, *Hellitamph* (-smoke), MB. 14, 424; der *fürst ûz helle* abgründe, Walth. 3, 12, as we say 'the prince of darkness.' With *hellegrâve* (p. 993) connect the prop. names *Helcrapho,* Böhmer's Font. 2, 185, and Herman der *hellengrave, hellegrave,* Mon. zoller. no. 305 (yr 1345). no. 306.

The devil dwells in the *North:* cadens Lucifer . . . traxit ad *inferni* sulfurea stagna, in *gelida aquilonis parte* ponens sibi tribunal; hunc *ferocissimum lupum* Agnus mitissimus stravit, Raban. Maur. De laud. crucis, fig. 10; '(Lucifer) chot, wolti sizzin *nordin,*' Diem. 94, 16; entweder zu den genâdin oder den *ungenâdin,* sive ad austrum sive ad *aquilonem,* Leyser 135, 34. In the N. lies Jötun-heimr (p. 34), and the devil is considered a giant, as Loki and Logi are of giant kin; önskar honom (wishes him) längt *nordan till fjälls* (at the devil), Sv. vis. 2, 163.

They say in Småland, 'drag till *Häckenfjälls!*' Cavall. p. 25ᵃ. On *Hekla, Heklu-fiall,* see Bartholin p. 356—360; fewr im *Heckelberg* (Mt Hecla), Fischart in Wackern. 2, 470.

By desser kerken buwet (builds) de düvil einen *Nobis kroch,* Agricola's Sprikworde (1528) n. 23 bl. 14ᵃ; *nobis-haus,* Mone 8, 277; in *nobis haus,* da schleget das hellisch fewer zum fenster hinaus, Er. Alberus's Barfusser Münche Eulenspiegel u. Alcoran (Wittemb. 1642) bl. E 4; 'so fare they on to *nobishaus,* where flame shoots out at the window, and bake their apples on the sill,' Schimpf u. ernst (1550) c. 233; 'hush, thou art now in *nobis-*

*hauss'* = purgatory, H. Sachs (1552) iii. 3, 44$^{rw}$; ir spart's (the
Reformation) in *Nobiskrug,* Fischart's Dominici leben (1571) x$_2$$^b$.
*Nobis Krucke,* Meland. Jocoseri. (1626) p. 548; 'send down to
*nobiskrug,*' Simpl. 3, 387; 'How Francion rideth in a chair into
the *Nobiskrug* (abyss, dungeon),' Hist. des Francions (Leyd.
1714), Tab. of cont. ix. In Celle they sing the cradle-song:
mûse-kätzen, wô wut du hen? ik wil nâ *nâbers krauge* gân. On
*Nâbers-kroch, Nobels-krug,* see Kuhn in Hpt 4, 388-9. Leo
{Malb. gl. 2, 42) derives 'nobis' fr. Ir. *aibheis,* abyss; *aibhistar*
is said to mean devil.

p. 1004.] AS. *scocca* is found on German soil too: Adalbertus
*scucco,* Annal. Saxo (Pertz 8, 690). Seyfriden dem *steppekchen,*
MB. 16, 197 (yr 1392). The devil's name *Barlabaen* is also in
Walew. 9741; *Barlibaen,* Limb. 4, 959; *Barnebaen, Barlebos,*
*Barlebaen,* V. d. Bergh 11. 12. 275-6; *borlebuer,* said of a boor,
Rose 2804. The word *frimurc* in Türl. Wh. 136$^a$, *fêmurc* in
Cod. pal., reminds of Fêmurgan (p. 820 n.).——Names of devils:
*lasterbalc,* schandolf, *hagendorn* (conf. p. 1063), *hagelstein,* Berthold 56; ein tiuvel genannt *lesterlinc,* Hag. Ges. Abent. 2, 280;
*lästerlein, schentel,* Fastn. sp. 507-8-9. Does ON. *kölski* = satanas,
still very common in Iceland, mean senex procax? Swed. 'hin
*hâle,*' the devil; Vesterb. *snogen,* the bald, Unander 36, conf.
*kahl-kopf* in Gramm. 2, 374; Östgöt. *skammen, skrutt, skräll,*
Kalén 17$^b$ (Suppl. to 991 mid.). In Vorarlberg *jomer* and *höller*
are devils' names, Bergm. p. 94, *jammer* otherwise denoting
epilepsy, convulsion (p. 1064).

Euphemisms for the devil (p. 987 mid.) are: the *God-be-with-*
*us;* Meister *Sieh-dich-für* (look out, mind yourself), Ettn. Unw.
doct. 241; *Et-cetera,* Ital. *ceteratojo.* Gipsies call God *devel,* and
the devil *beink,* Pott p. 67. The Dan. gammel Erik is in Norw.
*gamle Eirik, gamle Sjur,* Aasen 124$^a$. On *Hemmerlin,* see Suppl.
to 1000; *Martinello* (p. 1064). *Pinkepank* in Hpt 6, 485.
*Schimper-schamper, Schimmer-schemmer.*

p. 1006.] The devil appears as the *hunter in green,* Schleicher
213, as *Green-coat* in witch-stories, KM. no. 101. In Östgötl.
*Oden* means devil. His army is called a *swarm:* des tivelis
*geswarme,* Rol. 120, 14; der tiuvel hât ûzgesant sîn *geswarme*
204, 6; *geswerme,* Karl 73$^b$; des tiefels *her* (host), Griesh. 2,
26. Verswinden sam ein kunder, daz der boese geist fuort in

dem *rôre* (reeds), Tit. 2408; der teufel fährt in wildes *geröhricht,* H. Sachs v. 344-5-6.

p. 1009.] De olle *riesen-moder,* Müllenh. p. 444, the *giant's* old *grandmother* 450, Brûsi and his *mother worse* than he, Fornm. sög. 3, 214, all remind us of the devil's mother or grandmother: des übeln teufels *muoter,* Wolfd. and Saben 487; u brachte hier ter stede die *duvel* ende *sin moeder* mede, Karel 2, 4536: frau Fuik is held to be the *devil's grandmother,* Hpt 5, 373; 'yes, the devil should have had him long ago, but is waiting to find the fellow to him, as his *grandmother* wants a *new pair of coach-horses,'* Gotthelf's Swiss tales 4, 51; der tüfel macht wedele drus, u. heizt der *grossmutter* den ofe dermit (to light his granny's fire with), Gotth. Erz. 1, 226; de düvel und ock sîn *môder,* Soester Daniel 8. 11; 'if you are the devil, I am his *mother,'* Praet. Weltb. 2, 64; 'who are you, the devil or his *mother?'* Simpl. 1, 592; conf. 'ist er der tufel oder sîn *wîp?'* Dietr. dr. 159ᵃ; des tiuvels *muoter* u. sîn *wîp,* Hätzl. 219ᵃ; diu ist des tiuvels *wîp,* Nib. 417, 4; des übelen tiuvels *brût* (bride) 426, 4. Mai 172, 10. Conf. *Death's mother* (p. 840-1); 'from Jack Ketch to Jack's *mother* he went,' Pol. colica p. 13.——To the pop. saws about sun and rain, add the N. Frisian: 'when it rains and the sun shines, witches are buried at the world's end.' There are *many* devils: steht in *tausend teufel* namen auf! sauf (drink) in *tausent t.* namen! Dict. 1, 230.

p. 1011.] The devil demands a *sheep* and a *cock,* Cæs. Heisterb. 5, 2; or a *black he-goat,* Müllenh. p. 41, a *black cock* and *he-cat* 201, a *black* and a *white goat* 203. With the curious passage fr. H. Sachs agrees the following: Of a heretic like that, you make a new-year's present to Pluto, *stuck over with box,* Simpl. 3, 5. p. 287. Boar's heads and bear's heads are still garnished so, and even Asiatics put fruit in the bear's mouth. 'The devil shall yet thy *bather* be,' Froschm. J. 2ᵃ (Suppl. to 247).

p. 1012.] A *stinking hair* is pulled out of *Ugarthilocus; seven hairs* off the sleeping devil or giant, like the *siben löcke* (Luther, Judg. 16, 19) off Samson's head, Renn. 6927. Diu helle ist ûf getân, der tiufel der ist *ûzgelân* (let out), Dietr. dr. 211ᵇ. 121ᵃ. 143ᵇ; Lucifer waere *ûz gelân,* Tirol in Hpt 1, 20; 'tis as though the fiend had *burst his fetters,* Eliz. of Orl. p. 270; le diable est *déchaîné,* Voltaire's Fréd. le gr. 23, 118.——With the phrase 'the *devil's dead*,' conf. 'Ulli er dauðr' (p. 453 n.). Other expressions: des tiuvels *luoder* = esca diaboli, MSH. 3, 227[b]; 'the d. may *hold the candle* to one that expects the like of him,' Nürnberger 254; 'of the *d.* and the *charcoal-burner*,' Fastn. sp. 896, 12; 'looked like a *field full of devils*,' Zehn ehen 177; 'we *avenge the devil* on ourselves,' En. 1147; thieves go out in *odd* numbers, so that the d. can't catch one of them, Ph. v. Sittew. 2, 686—690; c'est *l'histoire du diable*, eine *teufelsgeschichte*. There was a *Geschichte' vom henker*, Gotthelf's Uli 148.

p. 1013.] The devil's *seed* occurs also in Dietr. dr. 281[b] and Boner's Epilog 51. His sifting: hînet *riteret* (tonight riddles) dich Satanas alsam *weize*, Diem. 255, 10. Fundgr. 1, 170. His snares: wie vil der tubil *úf* uns *dont* (tendiculas ponit), Hpt 5, 450; παγίς is in Gothic either *hlamma*, 1 Tim. 3, 7. 6, 9 (ON. hlömm = fustis), or *vruggó*, 2 Tim. 2, 26; des tivels *netze*, Mone's Anz. '39, 58; des tiefels *halze*, Griesh. 2, 93; des tiuvels *swert*, Ls. 3, 264 (p. 999 end); daz vindet der tiuvil an sîner *videln*, Renn. 22629.

p. 1014.] As Wuotan and angels carry men through the air, so does God, but much oftener the *devil* (p. 1028): sît dich *Got* hât her getragen, Hätzl. 167, 43; der arge *válant* truoc in dar, Laur. 822; noch waen (nor dream) daz si der *tiuvel* vuorte, Livl. 1425; der *t.* hât in her brâht, Greg. 1162. der t. hât mir zuo gebrâht, Helbl. 1, 641. iuch brâhte her der *tievel* ûz der helle, Hpt 1, 400; die *duvel* brochte hu hier so na, Rose 12887; nu over ins *duvels* geleide, Karel 2, 4447; in trage dan wider der *tüfel*, Diocl. 5566-89; welke *duvel* bracht u dare? Lanc. 1528; brochte jou die *duvel* hier? Walew. 5202; conf. 'waz *wunders* hât dich her getragen? Wigal. 5803; welch *tivel* het dich hiute hin? Hahn's Stricker 14. We say 'where's the *d.* got you?' i.e. where are you? wo *hât* dich der henker? Fr. Simpl. 1, 57. The Greeks too said: τὸν δ' ἄρα τέως μὲν ἀπήγαγεν οἴκαδε δαίμων, Od. 16, 370; τίς δαίμων τόδε πῆμα προσήγαγε; 17, 446; ἀλλά σε δαίμων οἴκαδ' ὑπεξαγάγοι 18, 147.——To the curses add: der *tiuvel* neme! Herb. 6178; daz si der *tievel* alle erslâ! Archipo. p. 233; our 'zum teufel!' conf. 'woher *zum t.?*' Eulensp. c. 78; louf *zu dem t.*, wa du wilt 89. Like our 'red beard, devil's weird' is the phrase: 'dieser *fuchs*, der auch euer *hammer* ist,' Raumer's Hohenst. 2, 114 fr. Hahn's Mon. 1, 122. The devil

*laughs* to see evil done, hence : des mac der tiuvel *lachen*, Helbl.
4, 447 (Suppl. to 323 end) ; ' you make the devil *laugh* with your
lies,' Garg. 192ª.

p. 1015.] The devil ' over-comes us ' like a *nightmare*. In a
tale of the 10th cent., he calling himself *Níthart* joins the histrio
*Vollarc*, invites and entertains him and his fellows, and dismisses
them with presents, which turn out to be cobwebs the next
morning, Hpt 7, 523. *Strengthening a negative* by the word
' devil': den *teufel* nichts deugen, Eliz. of Orl. 447 ; der den
*tüfel* nützschit (nihtes ?) kan, Ls. 2, 311 ; conf. ' hvaða Oðïns
lâtum ? ' (Suppl. to 145 n.) ; our ' the *devil* (nothing) do I know ; '
*teufels* wenig, Ph. v. Sittew. Soldatenl. p. 191, our ' verteufelt
wenig.' Does ' das hat *den teufel gesehen* ' in Lessing 2, 479 mean
' seen nobody' or ' that is terrible ' ? *Welcher teufel* (= who ?),
Berth. ed. Göbel 2, 11. With ' drink you and the devil ! ' conf.
' heft hu de *duvel dronken* ghemakt ? ' Rose 13166. With ' the d.
first and God after ' agrees : in beschirmet (him protects neither)
der *tiuvel* noch *Got*, Iw. 4635.

p. 1016.] The Jewish view of *possession* may be gathered fr.
Matth. 12, 42—45 ; other passages and an Egyp. fragment are
coll. in Mannhdt's Ztschr. 4, 256—9. Possessed by devils is in
Goth. *anahabaidans* (fr. haban) fram ahmam unhrainjaim, Luke 6,
18 ; MHG. ein *beheft* man, demoniac, Uolr. 1348 ; *behaft*, Diemer
324, 25. Servat. 2284 ; ob dû *beheftet* bist, MS. 2, 5ª ; *beheftete*
lute, Myst. 1, 135. 147 ; ein *behefter* mensch, Renn. 15664-85.
5906 ; sint mit dem tievel *haft*, MS. 2, 82ᵇ ; mit dem übelen
geiste *behaft*, Warn. 350 ; der tievel ist in dir *gehaft*, Ecke
123 ; *tiufelhafte* diet (folk), Barl. 401, 25.——We say behaftet or
besessen : mit dem tiuvel wart er *besezzen*, Ksrchr. 13169 ; der
tivel hât in *besezzen*, Warn. 344 ; *obsessus* a daemone, Böhm.
Font. 2, 323 ; *tiuvel-winnic*, Servat. 783 ; *tiuvel-sühtic* 1079 ;
*gevangen* mit dem tiuvel, Fragm. 36ª ; des boten ich zuo's wirtes
maget mit worten hân *gebunden*, MS. 2, 11ª ; die den viant *hebben*
*in*, Maerl. 3, 234. ON. þû *hefir* diofulinn *î þinni hendi*, Vilk. s.
511, i.e. he makes thy hand so strong ; daz iuwer der t. müeze
*pflegen* (tend) ! Herb. 2262 ; der t. müeze in *walden* 9747 ; daz
iuwer der t. *walde* 14923. 18331 ; der t. müeze *walden* iuwer
untriuwe 16981 ; *var* in einen rostûschaer, Helbl. 7, 744 ; *vart*
in ein gerihte, *sliefet* in den rihtaere 7, 750.——A devil says :

sine ut *intrem* in *corpus tuum*, Cæs. Heisterb. 10, 11; an evil
spirit, whom the priest bids depart out of a woman (yr 1463),
asks leave to *pass into* others, whom he names, M. Beh. 276-7;
hem *voer* die duvel *in't líf* (body), Maerl. 2, 293; der tiuvel *var*
im an die *swart*, Helbl. 15, 434; reht als waere *gesezzen* der
tuvel in daz *herze* sîn, Dietr. dr. 117ᵃ; en scholden dre söven
düvel darum *bestan*, Kantzow 2, 351; nu *friz in dich* den tiufel
der dîn suochet, MS. 2, 135ᵇ.——'The d. *looks* out of her *eyes*,'
H. Sachs 1, 450ᵃ; der t. aus dir *kilt*, Kell. Erz. 327, 15, *kal* 328,
23 (and the reverse: *Got* ûz ir jungen munde *sprach*, Parz. 396,
19); der t. ist in dir gehaft, der *fiht ûz dînem líbe*, Eckenl. 123.
Devils in the body are like the *narren* (fools) inside a sick man,
who are cut out as the devils are cast out. The devil is driven
out through the nose with a ring, Joseph. Antiq. 8, 2. 5. Diseases
wait for the patient to *open his mouth* before they can pass out,
Helbl. 7, 101. Mit dem *Bösen curieren*, adjuvante diabolo aegros
sanare, Leipz. avantur. 1, 271. Virtues also pass in and out,
Helbl. 7, 65. 102. 113.

p. 1017.] As the gods diffuse *fragrance*, legends medieval and
modern charge the devil with *defiling* and changing things into
muck and mire: der tiuvel *schîze* in in den kragen! Helbl. 5,
107; Sathanae *posteriora* petes, Probra mul. 220; welcher t. uns
mit den Heiden hete *beschizen*, Morolt 3014; der t. lauft u.
*hofiert* zugleich, Simpl. 178; *cacat* monstra, Reinard. 4, 780; die
seind des teufels letzter *furz*, Rathschlag in Parnasso (1621 4to,
p. 33).——The devil *lies* and *cheats*: der *truge-tievel* (p. 464),
conf. 'driugr var *Loptr* at *liuga*, Sn. '48. 1, 29; ein tiuvel der
hiez Oggewedel, der ie die êrsten *lüge* vant, MS. 2, 250ᵇ; dem t.
*an's bein lügen*, Rother 3137. He is called 'des *nîdis vatir*
Lucifer,' Diemer 94, 20.

p. 1019.] Making a *covenant* with the devil, Keisersb. Omeiss
36-8; he bites a finger of the witch's left hand, and with the
blood she signs herself away; or he smites her on the face,
making the *nose bleed*, Mone's Anz. 8, 124-5. The devil's *mark*
(p. 1077); *hantveste* (bond), dâmide uns der duvil woldi bihaldin,
Wernh. v. N. 61, 33. He will make his servant rich, but requires him to *renounce God and St. Mary*, Ls. 3, 256-7. An old
story told by the monachus Sangall. (bef. 887) in Pertz 2, 742:
Diabolus cuidam *pauperculo* . . . . in humana se obviam tulit

specie, pollicitus non mediocriter illum esse ditandum, si *societatis vinculo in perpetuum sibi delegisset adnecti.* A similar story in Thietmar 4, 44 speaks of *prope jacēre* and *servire.* One has to *abjure God and all the saints;* the d. comes and *gives the oath,* Hexenproc. aus Ursenthal p. 244-6. Roaz hât beidiu sêle und leben *einem tievel geben,* der tuot durch in wunders vil, er *füeget im allez* daz er wil, Wigal. 3656-9. 7321—6; when R. dies, the devils come and fetch him 8136. Giving oneself to the d. for riches, Berth. ed. Göbel 2, 41; wil er *Got verkiesen* unde die sêle verliesen, der *tûbel* hilfet ime derzuo, daz er spâte und fruo tuon mac besunder vil manicfalden wunder, Alex. 2837.——*Kissing* the devil (pp. 1065 last l., 1067 last l., 1071); dich *en-vride der tievel* (unless the d. shield thee), du-ne kanst niht genesen, Nib. 1988, 2. The d. *fetches* his own, as Oðinn or Thôrr takes his share of souls: der hel-scherge die *sînen an sich las* (gathered his own unto him), Loh. 70. The *child unborn* is promised to the d. (p. 1025), Altd. bl. 1, 296-7, as formerly to Oðinn : *gâfu Oðni,* Fornm. sög. 2, 168; conf. *gefinn Oðni* sialfr sialfum mer, Sæm. 27[b]. With *Bearskin* conf. the ON. *biarn-ólpu-maðr,* Kormakss. p. 114; the Hung. *bearskin,* Hungar. in parab. p. 90-1; Völundr sat â *berfialli,* Sæm. 135[a]; lying on the bearskin, Schweinich. 2, 14; wrapping oneself in a *bear's hide,* KM. no. 85; getting sewed up in a *bearskin,* Eliz. of Orl. 295.

One who is on good terms, or in league, with the devil, is called devil's comrade, partner, fellow: *vâlantes man,* Rol. 216, 7; des *tiveles higen* 156, 4; der *tiuvels bote,* Hpt. 6, 501; *t. kneht,* Iw. 6338. 6772; ein *tûbels knabe,* Pass. 172, 59. 175, 16. 296, 27; our 'teufels-kind,' reprobate; filii Tiufelonis habent Tiufelsgrub, MB. 12, 85-7; Morolt des *tiuvels kint,* Mor. 2762; wâren ie des *tivels kint,* Trist. 226, 18. The *polecat,* Lith. *szeszkas,* is called devil's child, because of its smell? iltisbalg (fitchet-skin) is an insulting epithet. *Helle-kint,* Griesh. 2, 81; des *tiuvels genóz,* Trist. 235, 29; slaefestu, des *t. gelit* (lith, limb)? Pass. 377, 25; alle des *tievels lide,* Hpt 8, 169; *membrum diaboli,* Ch. yr 1311 in Hildebrand's Svenskt dipl. no. 1789 p. 15 (p. 997). What does *düvelskuker* mean ? Seibertz 1, 631.

p. 1024.] The devil has in many cases taken the place of the old giants (pp. 1000, 1024); so the Finn. hiisi gradually developed into a devil. One Mecklenbg witch-story in Lisch 5, 83

still retains the giant where others have the devil; conf. KM.[3] 3,
206-7. The *devil* that in many fairy-tales appears at *midnight*
to the lone watcher in a *deserted castle*, reminds one of *Grendel*,
whom Beowulf bearded in *Heorot*.——The devil mimics God,
wants to create like Him : he makes the *goat*, KM. no. 148, and
the *magpie*, Serb. märch. no. 18; conf. Märch. of Bukovina in
Wolf's Ztschr. 1, 179. 180. He builds Bern in three nights,
Pref. to Heldenb. Where a church is built to God, the d. sets
up his *chapel* hard by : in the play of Caterina, Lucifer cries to
the devils, ' habet ûch daz *kapellichen vor den greten*,' ad gradus
ecclesiae, Stephan p. 172. In tales of the *church-building devil*
they make a wolf run through the door ; conf. a song in Uhland's
Volksl. p. 812 and the story of Wolfgang in M. Koch's Reise 413.

> S war just ein neu-gebautes nest,
> der erste bewohner sollt' es taufen ;
> aber wie fängt er's an ? er lässt
> weislich den *pudel* voran erst laufen.
>
> Wallenstein's Camp, p.m. 33.

Mephistopheles hates *bells*, Faust p.m. 433. Tales of *devil's
bridges* in Müllenh. p. 274-5 ; such a one is also called ' die
*stiebende* brücke,' Geschichtsf., heft 7 p. 36.

There is a *devil's stone* near Polchow in Stettin district, on
which the d. takes his noonday nap on Midsum. day ; it becomes
as soft as cheese then, and the evil one has left the print of his
limbs on the flat surface, Balt. stud. xi. 2, 191. xii. 1, 110. A
*devil's chamber* lies between Haaren and Büren (Paderborn).
*Devil's kitchens*, Leoprechting 112-3-7. A field named *teufels-
rütti*, Weisth. 1, 72. The Roman fortifications in Central and
S. Germany are also called *pfal-hecke, pfal-rain, pfal-ranke ;*
Er. Alberus fab. 25 has *pol-graben*, Jaum. Sumloc p. 17; die *boll,
poll-graben*, conf. the iron *pohl*, Steiner's Main-gebiet 277-8 ;
*bulweg*, ibid.; *wul, wulch* in Vilmar's Idiot. 102, conf. art. *Pfahl-
mauer* in Hall. encyclop.——It seems these Roman walls were not
always of stone or brick, but sometimes of *pfäle* (stakes) : Spar-
tian, as quoted by Stälin, speaks of ' *stipitibus* magnis in modum
muralis sepis funditus jactis et connexis' ; and Mone's Bad.
gesch. 2, 5 mentions ' pali,' our *pfäle*. Near the Teufels-mauer
is situated a *Pfahls-buck*, Panz. 1, 156, and in the Wetterau a

*pohl-born* (Ukert p. 281), just like *Pholes-brunno* (p. 226).——On
the other hand the devil's wall is not only called *schwein-graben*,
but also *sau-strasse*, Stälin 1, 81-5. 97. Ukert p. 279 ; and if
the former is said to have been 'thrown up by a *gockel-hahn*
(cock) and a *schwein*,' it puts us in mind of the boar that roots
up earth, and bells out of the earth, Firmen. 2, 148; conf. supra
(pp. 666. 996) and the ploughing cock (p. 977). ' In *beren-loch*,
daz man nempt des *tüfels graben*,' Segesser 1, 645. On a giant's
wall in Mecklenbg lies a *teufels back-ofen* (Ukert p. 314), just
as the people call grave-mounds 'baker's ovens,' ibid. p. 280.
Other places named after the devil'in Mone's Anz. 6, 231.

p. 1024.] 'Devil take the *hindmost !* ' Garg. 190ᵇ, conf.
sacrificing the last man to *Mars* 227ᵃ. So the vila consecrates
12 pupils on vrzino kolo, and the twelfth or *last* falls due to
her, Vuk sub v. vrzino kolo (Suppl. to 986 end). The same with
the 12 scholars at Wunsiedel, Schönw. 3, 56, and the student
of Plesse 3, 26. Again : ' wâ sît ir *ze schuole* gewesen ? hat iu
der *tufel* vorgelesen ? ' lectured to you, Dietr. dr. 157ᵇ.——The
devil's taking the shadow reminds us of the schatten-busze
(shadow-penance) in German law. The Indian gods cast no
shadow, which is as it were the soul of a man, Klemm 2, 309.
*Catching the shadow* is also Wallachian, Schuller's Argisch 17.
Müllenh. p. 554. Winther's folke eventyr p. 18. Icel. story of
Sæmund, Aefintyri p. 34-5. Chamisso's legend is known in
Spain : ' hombre que vendió su sombra,' Mila y Fontals 188.

p. 1028.] The *hushing of the child* in the legend of Kallund-
borg church is the same as that of the giant's child (p. 548).
Similar stories in Schönwerth 3, 61. Müllenh. p. 300-1. A *cock*
that is carried past, *crows* and puts the devil out in his building,
Sommer p. 53. Schönw. 3, 60. Disappearance takes place after
thrice *clapping the hands*, Dybeck 4, 32 (nos. 31 and 33). With
the story of ' *self done, self have*,' conf. p. 450-1 n. ; the tale of
the water-nix and Selver-gedan, Hpt 4, 393 ; the Engadine story
of the diala and the svess, Schreiber's Taschenb. 4, 306. Vonbun
pp. 5, 6 (ed. 2 p. 8); the Lapl. story of giant Stallo, Nilsson 4,
32 ; and the Norse one of Egil, ibid. 4, 33. Müll. Sagenb. 2,
612.

p. 1029.] The *division of crops* between the peasant and the
devil is also in Müllenh. p. 278. ' To raise *corn* and *turnip* ' is

the formula of agriculture : 'ryþia undir *rughi* ok *rôvum*,' rye
and turnips, Östgöt. lagh pp. 217. 220.

p. 1029.] The dragonfly is called *devil's horse* : Finn. *pirum
hevoinen* = daemonis equus, *pirum piika* = daemonis ancilla.   A
priest's wife is the *devil's brood-mare*, App. Spell. xxxiv.   Nethl.
*duivel's-kop* (-head) = typha, our tuttil-kolbe, deutel-kolbe.
Teufels-rohr, conf. Walth. 33, 8.   *Devil's thread* is acc. to Vilmar
the cuscuta epilinum, called rang in the Westerwald.   A farm
named *duvel-bites gutol*, Seibertz 391 (1280).

---

## CHAPTER XXXIV.

### MAGIC.

p. 1031.]   Got *wunderaere*, Gerh. 4047 ; Got, du *w.*, Ad. v.
Nassau 230 ; Got ist ein *w.*, Helmbr. 1639 ; Krist *w.*, Walth. 5,
35 ; Got *wundert*, Engelh. 455. 491.

> Nû möhte iuch nemen wunder,
> waz göte wâren bî der zît ?
> si wâren *liute, als ir nû sît,*
> wan daz ir krefteclîch gewalt
> was michel unde manecvalt
> von kriutern und von steinen.—Troj. kr. 858.

(what were gods in those days ?   Men like you, except that their
power over herbs and stones was much).   All gods are *magicians*,
ibid. 859—911 ; Terramer calls Jesus a *magician*, Wh. 357, 23 :
Thôr's image speaks, walks and fights, but *by the devil's agency*,
Fornm. sög. 1, 302—6 ; a statue of Freyr gets off the chariot and
wrestles 2, 73-5 ; *tiuvele* wonent darinne (inside them), Rol. 27,
8.——The *grâl* makes men magic-proof even to the fifth of kin :
die edel fruht vom grâle, unz an die funften sippe keines zoubers
strâle traf in weder rucke, houbt noch rippe, Tit. 2414.   *Mathematici* are classed among magicians ; thus Cod. ix. tit. 18 treats
' de maleficis et mathematicis' ; mathematicus = himil-scowari,
stargazer, Diut. 1, 505[a] ; math. = tungel-witega, steor-gleaw,
Hpt's Ztschr. 9, 467[b] ; vaticinatores et mathematici, qui se Deo
plenos adsimulant, Jul. Pauli sentent. 5, 21.

p. 1034.] The bad is the *not right* : es geht *nicht mit rechten dingen* zu; 'das ich solcher frawen sei, die mit *bosen stucken* umbgen,' Bodmer's Rheing. 424 (yr 1511). ON. *fordœðu-skapr, fordœðu-verk* (misdoing) = veneficium ; *fordeþ-scipr,* Gutalag 77 ; *fördœþa,* Östg. lag 225. AS. *mân-fordœdlan* = malefici, Beow. 1120. Gl. to Lex 1 § 2. Dig. de obseq. par. (indignus militia ·udicandus est qui patrem et matrem maleficos appellaverit) : hoc est qui matrem dixerit *affactoratricem.*——OHG. *zoupar,* Graff 5, 580-1-2. MHG. *den* selben zouber, Hartm. büchl. 1, 1347, *daz* zouber 1318. *Daz* z. = magic potion : mir ist *zouber* gegeben, Herb. 758, and : Circe kunde trenke geben, sulich *zouber,* sulche spîse 17631. M. Lat. *zobria* f., Mone's Anz. 7, 424 ; mit *zouber* varn, MS. 1, 73ᵇ. Curiously in the Dresd. Wolfdietr. 162 : kein z. dir kan *gewinken* (rhy. trinken) ; *tover* en ontfoerdene mi, Karel 1, 1469 ; si zigen in *zouberlícher* dinge, Trist. 272, 2 ; *zouber-liste,* Eracl. 1062 ; *zouberliste* tragen, MS. 1, 78ᵇ, z. hân 99ᵇ.——Umme-gan (go about, meddle) mit *toverye* und *wyckerie,* Burmeister's Alterth. 25 (yr 1417) ; *tovern* u. *wykken,* ibid. ; *witken,* Bruns Beitr. 337 ; *wickerie, bote, wichelie,* Gefken's Beil. 141, *toverie, wickerie* 124. Welsh *gwiddan,* witch. OHG. *wichôn* saltare, gesticulari, Graff 1, 708 ; conf. Hpt 3, 92. AS. *hweoler* = augur, *fugle hweoler,* fr. hweol, wheel. Lett. *deewaredsis* who sees God and discovers hidden things, conf. devins (p. 471). Buttmann 2, 256 derives χράω, I divine, fr. grabbing, grasping; conf. Grîpir (p. 471).——*Weis-hexen,* Gryph. Dornrose 90, 27 ; *wizanunc,* divinatio, *wizzigo,* vates, Gl. Sletst. 6, 699 ; ein *wizzag gewaere,* MS. 2, 189ᵇ ; *vitka líki* fara, Sæm. 63ᵃ ; Engl. *wizard.* ON. *gan,* 'magia,' Biörn ; but 'inconsultus gestus,' Nialss. p. 683ᵃ. AS. *hwata* = omina, divinationes, Can. Edg. 16 (Suppl. to 1107 beg.). Lat. *veratrix,* soothsayer, sorceress ; *verare,* to say sooth, conf. *veratrum,* hellebore. Lith. *wardyti,* to work magic. ON. *satt eitt* sagðak, I said a sooth, Sæm. 226ᵇ. OHG. *wâr-secco,* divinator; der *warsager* tut mir warsagen, H. Sachs ii. 4, 12ᵇ, unser *w.* 13ᵇ, the one who practises in our village, as among Finns and Lapps, Suomi '46, p. 97-8. Fara til *fiölkunnigra* Finna, Fornm. s. 2, 167 ; *kŷnga,* magica, Laxd. 328; in Cavall. Voc. verl. 38ᵃ *kyng,* sickness. *Leikur,* witches, versiformes, Gróttas. 11. Betw. Lauterbach and Grebenau a divineress was called *e bló kend,* a blue child.

p. 1037.] Spoken magic, spell, is in MHG. *galster*, Lanz. 7011 ; mit *galster-liste*, Fundgr. 2, 100 ; *galstern*, Stald. 1, 417. *Carminator, carminatrix*, MB. 16, 242 (yr 1491). *Vermeinen*, bewitch, Schm. 2, 587 ; *vermaynen* ad oculos, dentes, Mone's Anz. 7, 423 ; *verschiren*, fascinare, Diut. 2, 214b ; *verschieren*, *beswögen*, Müllenh. p. 560 ; *verruochen* u. *vermeinen*, Ges. Abent. 3, 78 ; homines *magicis artibus dementare*, Lamb. p. 214 (yr 1074). Kilian has *ungheren*, work magic, *unghers*, maleficus, *ungher-hoere*, malefica, *unghers eyeren* volva, q. d. manium sive cacodaemonum ova. Van den Bergh p. 58 has Fris. *tjoenders* en *tjoensters*, wizard and witch. *Ougpente*, fascinatione, Gl. Sletst. 25, 149.

ON. *seiðr*, magic : Gunnhildr lêt *seið efla*, Egilss. 403 ; *seið-staðr* or *-stafr*, Laxd. 328 ; conf. Lapp. *seita*, Castrén's Myt. 207-8. *Boiling* of herbs (p. 1089), of stockings (p. 1093).

MHG. die *buoze* versuochen, try remedies, charms, Morolf 916 ; sühte *büezen*, heal sickness, Freid. 163, 16 ; de tene *böten*, cure toothache, Hpt 3, 92 ; *boeten*, Gefken's Beil. 151. 167 ; *boterie* 124. 175-7 ; *zanzeln*, work magic, Mielcke 36a.

*Lupperie*, Gefk. Beil. 109. 112 ; *lâchenîe*, Troj. kr. 27. 234 ; *lâchenaere* 27240, conf. 963 ; *stria* aut *herbaria*, Lex Alam. add. 22.

ON. *bölvísar* konor, witches, Sæm. 197b (p. 988) ; *frœði*, scientia, esp. magia nigra (suppl. to 1044).

Nethl. terms for sorceress, witch : *nacht-loopster* (-rover), *weer-makster*, weather-maker, *luister-vink*, mutterer in secret, *grote kol*, great horse ; op *kol* rijden, work magic, Weiland sub v. kol ; in ma *anwôt* sein, be bewitched, Wolf's Ztschr. 2, 54. Necroman-ticus habebat cucullum ac tunicam de *pilis caprarum*, Greg. Tur. 9, 6 ; conf. indutus pellibus 10, 25.

The AS. *drŷ*, magus, comes not fr. δρῦς, oak (p. 1215 end), but fr. Ir. *draoi*, with a pl. *draoithe*, of which the Romans made *druidœ*, Leo's Malb. gl. 1, 23. Davies in Celt. res. had derived it fr. Wel. *derwydd*. Spells were read out of a book : sîn zouber *las*, Pass. 171, 25 ; ein pfaffe der wol zouber *las*, Parz. 66, 4 ; 'ich hân von allem dem *gelesen* daz ie *geflóz* u. *geflouc*' says the soothsayer, Troj. kr. 19057 ; in den swarzen buochen lesen, Ksrchr. 13234. Finn. *lukia*, to read, but in the Runes always to conjure, Castr. Pref. p. x.——Ze *Dolet* ich niht lernen wil von der nigromanzîe, MS. 2, 63b ; zu *Toletum* die ars necromantica

lernen, Cæs. Heisterb. 5, 4, conf. Jubinal's Mystères 1, 396;
noch sô lernet man die list in einer stat zuo *Tolêt*, diu in His-
paniên stêt, Herb. 562, conf. Fromm. p. 225 and *ze Dolêt* (p. 1048
beg.); ein stat heizet *Persidâ*, dâ êrste zouber wart erdaht, Parz.
657, 28. The *travelling scholars* roam fr. school to school, and
learn black art, H. Sachs ii. 4, 19ᵈ; conf. devil's pupils, disciples
(p. 1024). *Cain* lêrte sîniu chint (taught his children) dei zouber
dei hiute sint, Diut. 3, 59.

p. 1038.] MHG. *liezen* = augurari : stille *liezen*, Er. 8687; ich
kan vliegen u. *verliezen*, MS. 1, 89ᵃ; *sahs-luzzo*, magus, Hattemer
1, 259ᵇ. *Zouberse* too is sortilega, Wolf's Ztschr. 2, 72; kanstu
von zouber meisterschaft, die *wirf an sie* (throw it on her),
Laurin 1675. With Swed. *tjusa* to conjure, conf. Dan. *kyse*,
terrere. *Burt* = sortilegium, *burten*, conjure, divine, Gefken 99;
conf. Lith. *burtas* lot, *burti* prophesy, *burtininkas* lot-caster, and
Lett. *burt* witches, *burtneks* sorcerer. The lot speaks : ' al dar-
nâch daz *lôz geseit ;* seit ez *wol, misse-seit* ez,' as the lot shall say,
yea or nay, MS. 1, 156ᵃ.——*Gougulares list*, O. iv. 16, 33; *caucu-
lare*, magus, Hpt 3, 382; mit *goucgeles liste*, Fundgr. 2, 99,
*goucgelâre list* 99. 100; de *gouchelâre*, MB. 8, 482; ein *goukel*,
Eracl. 1110; *gokell* onder den hoet, Ferg. 2772; under 'm huot
*gaukeln*, Suchenw. 29, 45. May we take it as conn. with *gouch*,
gowk, cuckoo? the Dan. for gowk and conjure are *gjög* and
*göjgle*, but the OHG. *kouh* and *koukalôn*. Frère Barbarin in
Flores practises sleight-of-hand, and is called *encanteor*. ON.
*sion-hverfîngar* = praestigiae, Sn. 79; AS. *gedwimor, gedwymor* =
fantasma, praestigium.

There is an old word, OHG. *hliodar*, AS. *hleoðor* = sonus, vaticinium, ON. *hlioð* merely sonus; OHG. *hleodar-sâzo* hariolus,
necromanticus, *hleodar-sizzeo, hleodar-sezzo* ariolus, *hleodar-sâza*
vaticinium, Graff 6, 302-4; *lioder-sâza*, Hattemer 1, 261; in
cervulo = in *lioder-sâza* , coragius = *liodir-sâzo*, Gl. Sletst. 23, 3. 8;
conf. Superst. A; the diviner then *sits* in a chair? The *sahs-
luzzo*, magus, Graff 6, 91. 2, 322, appar. divines with a knife or
sword.

p. 1039.] Magic is ascribed chiefly to *women*. Priestesses,
prophetesses, were old, grey-haired (p. 96-7): Sibylla ' saz *antfus*
(unkempt) an irme bete-hûs,' En. 2694; *gróz* u. *grâ* was ir daz
hâr, u. harte verworren (tangled) als eines pferdes mane 2698;

daz *mies* lokehte hienc ir ûz den ôren 2708. Neapol. *scirpia*,
brutta strega, fr. scirpus, a kind of rush. A *wunder-altez* wîp
interprets the dream upon her oath, Walth. 95, 8; *vielle sorciere*,
Méon 3, 159; a soothsaying *foster-moder*, Arvidss. 2, 5; *kerlînga
villa*, Sæm. 169; *alter wibe* troume, Türl. Wh. 82ª; 'a devil-
ridden root-delver, spell-speaker, and wizzened old herb-hunter,'
Garg. 189ª. Ir. *cailleach* means a *veiled* woman, *old* woman,
witch.——*Herdsmen* too are sorcerers: 'for, you see, we shepherds, cut off from the world, have our thoughts about many
things while the silly sheep are grazing,' Voss's Idyls 9, 49.

p. 1041.] *Hegitisse* = eumenides, *hägtis* = striga, Gl. Jun. 378,
381; *hazzisa* = eumenides, Gl. Sletst. 6, 273; *haghetissen*, Br.
Gheraert 717, conf. *hezosun* = palaestritae, Graff 4, 1073. *Hage-
disse* = lizard (OHG. egidehsa), Gemmula Antwerp. in Hoffm.
Horae Belg. 7; in the Ring 210-1 it is called *häxe*, 219 both *häxe*
and unhold. Is the Lith. *kékszĕ*, harlot, formed fr. *hexe*, as
keksztas fr. heher, a jay? In the Ring p. 230 a witch is called
*Hächel*, sorceress; conf. '*hägili*, stâ!' stay, little witch, 57. The
Swiss *hagsne* = hexe (Stald. 2, 10) may hark back to OHG. *hah-
sinón* subnervare [hamstring, cut the *hächse*, hough], for a witch
*unnerves* (comedere nervos, p. 1081 last l.); conf. Fris. hexna,
hoxna, hoxne = poples.

p. 1042.] Oðinn is called *galdrs föðr*, Sæm. 94ª. The Vilkina-
saga names a sorceress *Ostacia*, who learnt magic of her stepmother (see p. 1055). Other names of witches in Skâldskap.
234. A sorceress is a *vala* or *völva*: seið-staðr mikill, þóttust
menn þâ vita, at þar mundi verit hafa *völu leiði* nockud (sagae
tumulus), Laxd. p. 328. She is also called *flögð*: *flögð* â Heiðar-
skôg, Fornm. 3, 122; Nethl. *nacht-loopster*, *grote kol* (Suppl. to
1037 mid.); conf. *rœrði* sîn gand, *fôr* at seiða, Vilk. saga c. 328.

p. 1044.] Gera *seið-hiall mikinn;* appar. a platform to hold a
good many: þau fœrdust þar â upp *öll* (all), þau kvâðu þar *frœði*
sîn, en þat voru *galdrar*, Laxd. 142.

p. 1045.] For *masca*, the Lomb. Glosses have *nasca*, Hpt's
Ztschr. 1, 556; conf. talamasca (p. 915). With *striga* connect
στρίγξ owl, who waylays children, and is kept off by hawthorn,
Jv. Fast. 6, 130—168; στρίγλα in Leo Allatius; στίγλος (γόης).
DC. Another word for mask is *schem-bart*, Schm. 3, 362.
Oäger's Ulm p. 526: nu sitze ich als ein *schempart* trûric, Renn

17998; *scema* = larva, Graff 6, 495-6; LG. *scheme* in Voss; Nethl. *scheem, scheme,* shadow; conf. *scheine* in Frauenl. 174.

p. 1046.] On *chervioburgus,* see Malb. gl. 2, 153-4. Müllenhoff (in Waitz p. 287, and Mone's Anz. 8, 452) compares it with the κερνοφόρος of the mysteries. A Tyrolese legend tells of roving night-wives and their *cauldron,* Germania 2, 438. In our nursery-tales *witch* and *old cook* are the same thing, KM. no. 51. Lisch's Meckl. jrb. 5, 82.——On a hill or mountain named kipula, or kipivuori, kipumäki, kipuharja (sorrow's mount, hill, peak), stands Kivutar before a *cauldron* (kattila, pata), brewing plagues. In Kalev. 25, 181, is mentioned a parti-coloured milking-pail (kippa), 182 a copper bushel (vakka), 196 kattila. Acc. to Renvall a witch is *panetar, panutar.* A butterfly is called *kettelböter* (-heater), and whey-stealer, milk-thief (p. 1072).

p. 1047.] A *salt-work* is a sacred gift of God, and protected by the law of nations, Rommel 8, 722. *Salt* is laid on tables and altars: sacras facite mensas salinorum apposito, Arnob. 2, 67; salinum est patella, in qua diis primitiae cum sale offerebantur. Egyptians hated salt and the sea; their priests were forbidden to set salt on the table, Plut. De Iside 32.——The interchange of H and S in *hal* and *sal* is, acc. to Leo (in Hpt 5, 511), syntactic in the Celtic tongues, and Gael. *sh* is pron. *h.* *Hallstadt* is more corr. spelt *Hallstatt,* M. Koch's Reise 407. Ssk. *sara* = salt. Lat. *halec,* herring, is akin to ἅλς, salt, GDS. 300 [So Sl. *seldĭ,* ON. *sîld,* herring, means salt-water fish; but Teut. *häring* = *heer*-fisch, bec. it goes in hosts, shoals, Hehn's Plants and Anim. 411].

p. 1050.] Witches eat *horseflesh,* Wolf's Ztschr. 2, 67. The pipe at the dance of trolls inside the hill is a *horse-bone,* Afzelius 2, 159; conf. a Pruss. story in N. Preuss. prov. bl. 1, 229.

p. 1051.] The Witches' Excursion takes place· on the *first night in May,* Lisch's Meckl. jrb. 5, 83. Wolf's Zts. 2, 68. 'The Esth. witches also assemble that night,' says Possart p. 161; others say the night of June 23-4, *i.e.* Midsum. Eve. 'They ride up Blocksberg on the *first of May,* and in 12 days must *dance the snow away;* then Spring begins,' Kuhn in Hpt's Zts. 5, 483. Here they appear as elflike, godlike maids.

p. 1053.] Witches' Mountains are: the *Brückelsperg,* Wolf's Zts. 1, 6; several *Blocksbergs* in Holstein, Müllenh. p. 564;

*Brockensburg,* Dittm. Sassenrecht 159. GDS. 532; the *unhol-denperg* near Passau occurs already in MB. 28[b], 170. 465. 'At the end of the Hilss, as thou nearest the Duier (Duinger) wood, is a mountain very high and bare, named *uf den bloszen zellen,* whereon it is given out that witches hold their dances on Walpurgis night, even as on Mt Brocken in the Harz,' Zeiler's Topogr. ducat. Brunsv. et Luneb. p. 97. Betw. Vorwalde and Wickensen (Brunswk) stands the witches' mount *Elias.* Near Brünighausen is *Kukesburg,* already named in the Hildesh. dioces. circumscr., conf. Lünzel p. 31-8, which Grupen calls *Kokesburg,* named after the devil's *kitchen.* Witches' hills in Holstein, and their trysts in N. Friesland, are in Müllenh. no. 288-9. A witch-mtn near Jülchendorff, Mecklenbg, Lisch 5, 83; is *Koilberg* another? Gefk. Catal. 111. In Sommer pp. 56. 174 the Brocken is called *Glockersberg.* Similar places are the Franconian *Pfetersberg* near Marktbürgel, and the Alsatian *Büchelberg,* conf. *buhilesberc, pückelsberg,* Graff 3, 135; for other trysts of witches in Elsass, see Alsatia '56, p. 283. Dwarfs as well as witches haunt the *Heuberg* or *Höperg,* Ring 211 : *witches' horses* flew over Höperg 234. In Tirol they meet on the *Schlernkofel,* Zingerle's Hexenproc. 37; seven more places are given in his Sitten 32 and Alpenburg 255. 262.——In Bleking the Swed. trysting-place is called *Jungfru-kullen,* Wieselgr. 398; in fairy-tales *Blå-kulla* or *Heckenfjell,* Cavallius 447-8. The vila holds her dance on the mountain-top (vr), *vrzino kolo;* there also she initiates her pupils, Vuk sub v. vrzino kolo. '*Łesogora* seu Bloksbarch,' Ceynowa 13, exactly translates *Kalenberg,* fr. *lysy* bald, Linde 2, 1318-9. Finn. *kipula* or *kippumäki,* see Peterson p. 72-3 (Suppl. to 1046). In Moravia the witches meet on Mt *Rádošt,* a Slavic mont-joie, Kulda. In Persia another name for Mt Demavend is *Arezûra,* where daevas and wizards assemble, Spiegel's Avesta 2, cxiv.

p. 1054.] In Vilk. cap. 328 ' rœrdi sîn *gand* ' seems to mean ' rode into the air.' There is a dwarf named *Gand-âlfr,* Sæm. 2[b], and a valkyrja *Göndul* (p. 421). The Hächel rides on a *wolf,* Ring 230-7; witches fly on *goats,* 210-1. Matth. v. Kemnat names unholde and *nachthusser* together; does the word contain thusse, durse? In Passion 4, 85 it says : daz ist ein *naht-vole,* den guoter werke tages-lieht lât gesehen wênec iht. The Vatnsdœla p. 106 cap. 26 thus descr. a sorceress and her extraordinary turn-out: þar fer þâ *Liot*, ok hefir *breitiliga* um sik bûit, hun hafði *rekit fótinn fram yfir höfuðit*, ok *fór öfug*, ok retti *höfuðit ût â millum fótanna aptr*; ófagurligt var hennar *augnabragd*, hversu hun gat þvî tröllsliga skotit. Verlauff's note p. 107 says, the (old) Gullþoris saga cap. 17 descr. the similar figure cut by a sorceress, to dull the enemies' weapons.

p. 1061.] *Troll-dances* descr. in Afzelius 2, 158-9. A remarkable story in Lisch's Meckl. jrb. 5, 83 tells of a *giant* giving a feast on a mountain, and *thumblings* dancing on the table before him; the rest is like other witch-stories. H. Sachs v. 343[bc] says witches hold their dances and weddings on a great *beech-tree*. A musician comes upon a witches' dance, and has to play to them, Firmen. 2, 383-4.——AS. *niht-genge*, witch; conf. *nahtegese, naht-eise* (note on Andr. xxxii); *nacht-ridders*, Br. Gher. 715; *nacht-volk*, Voubun p. 34-5. Wolf's Zts. 2, 53; glauben, die lüte des *nachtes farn*, Gef k. Beil. 24; ON. *Nâtt-fari*, a man's name, Landnam. 1, 1; *varende vrauwen* = witches, Belg. mus. 2, 116. Br. Gher. 717; *ausfahrerin*, Judas erzsch. 2, 107; *nahtfrawe* in Mone 8, 408 means midwife; *nacht-frala* is the plant mirabilis jalappa, belle de nuit, Castelli 205. The Thessalian witches also fly by night: φασὶ δὲ αὐτὴν καὶ πέτεσθαι τῆς νυκτός, Lucian's Asin. 1. In Servia the magicians and their pupils travel with the vila. The *unhuld* fetches bottles of wine out of cellars, H. Sachs i. 5, 532[b]. A story in Pertz 2, 741 of a pilosus who fills bottles.

p. 1061.] *Dâse* looks like AS. *dwaes*, fatuus; but in Reinaert 7329 *dasen*, insanire, rhymes with verdwasen, so it can hardly be the same word as dwasen. The Gemm. Antwerp. (in Hoffm. Hor. Belg. 7) has *dase* = peerts-vlieghe, hornet, and in the Mark they still speak of a *dasen-schwarm*, Schmidt v. Wern. 276-7. MHG. ' *daesic* hunt,' Frauenl. 368, 2. Heimdall is called *hornþytvaldi*, Sæm. 92[b].

p. 1064.] Other herb and flower names for the devil and for witches in Wolf's Zts. 2, 64. *Schöne* is even OHG. : Scônea, a woman's name. *Gräsle, Kreutle, Rosenkranz*, Keller's Erz. 195. The elfvor change into flowers or branches by day (Suppl. to 470 beg.). Is not the devil also called *Hagedorn*, like the minstrel in Berthold 56? Is *Linden-tolde* (-top) a witch? Ring 235.——

The devil often makes a handsome figure: daemon *adolescentis venusti* speciem induens, Cæs. Heisterb. 5, 36; hence the names *Frisch, Spring-ins-feld, Fleder-wisch, Schlepp-hans* (yr 1597), Thür. mitth. vi. 3, 68-9. The 'sieben *flederwische* (goosewing dusters)' are witches, Panz. Beitr. 1, 217; aller *flederwische* u. *maikäfer-flügel* gesundheit (health)! Franz. Simpl. 1, 57. 49; hinaus mit den *flederwischen!* Ung. apotheker 762. Other names: *Zucker, Paperle.* Names of devils in the Alsfeld Passion-play are coll. in Hpt. 3, 484—493.

p. 1069.] Witches take an oath *to do the devil's will;* see in Geschichtsfreund 6, 246 the remarkable confession of a witch of Ursernthal (yr 1459). The *devil's bride* sits up in the *tree* with her 'kalt-samigen stink-bräutgam, Garg. 72ᵇ; devil and witch hold dance and *wedding* on *trees* and *boughs,* H. Sachs v. 343ᵇᶜ. In records even of the 12th cent. occur such surnames as 'Osculans diabolum, Basians daemonem, Demonem osculans, Bèse diable,' Guérard's Prolegom. to the Cart. de Chartres p. xciv. What does 'osculans *acnionem*' there mean?——Tres mulieres sortilegae Silvanectis captae, et per majorem et juratos justiciatae (yr 1282); the bishop claims that they belonged to his juris-diction, Guér. Cart. de ND. 3, 341. And even before that: Judices tanquam *maleficam* et *magum* miserunt in *ignem,* Cæs. Heist. 4, 99; this was at Soest, beginn. of 12th cent. In Eng-land: Proceedings against dame Alice Kyteler, prosec. for *sorcery* 1324 by Rich. de Ledrede bp. of Ossory, ed. by Th. Wright, Lond. '43, Camd. Soc. xlii. and 61. A *strega* of 1420, who turned into a *cat,* Reber's Hemmerlin p. 248. About the same time Wolkenstein p. 208 says of old women:

> *zauberei* und *kupel-spiel,*
> das machen si nit teuer (not scarce);
> es wird doch ie eine versêrt
> mit einem heissen *feuer.*

'Vil *fewers* zu! ist der beste rat (plan)' thinks Matth. v. Kemnat p. 117; while on the contrary H. Sachs 1, 532ᵉ saw clearly that

> des teufels eh' und reuterei (weddings and ridings)
> ist nur gespenst und fantasei (mere dreams);
> das bock-faren kumpt aus misglauben (superstition).

An Engl. treatise on Witches and Witchcraft by G. Gifford 1603 has been reprinted for the Percy Soc. '42.——The burning and strewing of the ashes is found as early as Rudl. 6, 49 : Rogo me comburatis, *in aquam cinerem jaciutis*. Fornm. sög. 2, 163 : Klauf hann þå þôr î skîður einar, lagði î eld, ok *brendi at ösku*, sîðan fêkk hann ser lög nökkurn, kastaði þar â öskunni, ok gerði af graut, þann *graut gaf hann blauðum hundum* (al. grey hundum); conf. supra (p. 189).

p. 1075.] The witch holds up her *left* hand in taking the oath to the devil, Geschichtsfr. 6, 246. On the nature of the *mark* printed on her by the devil, see Mone's Anz. 8, 124-5. The Greeks too believed that the Thessalian sorceresses anointed themselves with a *salve*, Lucian's Asin. 12-3. Apuleius p. m. 116-7; vil kunnen *salben den kübel* (tub), das si *obnan ausfarn* (fly out at the top), Vintler (Sup. G, 1. 180). A witch is called *fork-rider*, Garg. 47ᵃ ; she rides *calves* and *cows* to death (p. 1048 mid.) ; she has *wings*, Müllenh. p. 212. The witch's or sorcerer's flight through the air is the god's *rîða lopt ok lög* (air and fire) ; conf. the skipper and his man sailing on water, air and land, Müllenh. p. 222.——In the midst of the witches the Devil sits on a *pillar* (=irmensûl), Mone's Anz. 8, 130 ; he sits with them on the *tree*, holds dance and wedding on *trees* and *boughs* (Suppl. to 1069 beg.). There are banquets of witches, as there are of fays : their viands are tasteless as rotten timber, or they suddenly change to *muck;* so all the food the Huldre brings turns into *cow's dung*, Asb. Huldr. 1, 49. 51. Sometimes the devil plays the *drone-pipe*, Thür. mitth. vi. 3, 70. With the young witch set to *mind the toads*, conf. the *girl* and three *toads* in Lisch's Jrb. 5, 82.——Witches turn the milk, skim the dew, lame the cattle, and brew storms. The mischief is chiefly aimed at the corn-fields and cattle (p. 1106): they draw milk out of a *knife*, Asb. Huldr. 1,176. Wolf's Zts. 2, 72. Müllenh. p. 222; they stretch a *string*, and milk out of it, Mone 8, 131, or cut a *chip* out of the stable-door for the same purpose 5, 452-3; they milk out of an *awl* or the *neck* (handle-hole) *of an axe*, Keisersb. Omeiss 54ᵃ, illustr. by a woodcut; the senni milks out of *four taps in the wall*, Fromm. 2, 565. Witches make *butter* by churning water with a stick, Müllenh. p. 224; they '*filch* people's milk fr. them,' M. Beham in Mone 4, 454 ; they are called *molken-tover*,

Mone's Schausp. 2, 74 (Upstandinge 1116); conf. App., Spell
xxxvii : ' Up thro' the clouds and away, Fetch me *lard* and *milk*
and *whey !*' Witches gather *dew*, to get people's butter away,
Müllenh. p. 565; conf. AS. *deáw-drîas*, Cædm. 3795 (Bout.),
Grein 101; towe daz *gelesen* wirt (gathered dew), Notk. Cap.,
conf. *thau-schlepper, tau-dragil* (p. 786).——They *darn* peace or
no peace into the bridal bed ; they *plait discord in*, by plaiting
the pillow-feathers into *wreaths* and *rings*, Müllenh. p. 223.
Hence the tales about the old wife that's worse than the devil :
' in medio consistit virtus, like the devil between two old wives,'
Garg. 190[b]. An old woman having caused a loving couple to fall
out, the devil was so afraid of her that he reached her the promised pair of shoes at the end of a stick. Witches ' nemen den
mannen *ir gseln*,' M. Beham in Mone 4, 451. Grasping, beating,
stroking, blowing, breathing, eyeing are attrib. to witches (p.
1099), as they are to healing women.——In their magic they use the
*hands of unborn babes*, Fastn. sp. p. 1349. Thieves cut the *thumb*
off an unborn child, and light it : as long as it burns, every one
in the house sleeps ; *spinam humani cadaveris* de tecto pendunt,
and nobody wakes, Cæs. Heist. 6, 10 ; ' du haddest ok ens *deves
dumen* bavene henghen an de tunne ' is said to the cheating inn-
keeper, Mone's Schausp. 2, 87 (a thief taken at Berlin in 1846
had a green herb sewed into her petticoat, her *herb of luck* she
called it) ; *ungemeilit kint* [unbetrothed ?] are employed in sorcery,
Ksrchr. 2102. 2590 ; conf. ' lecta ex *structis ignibus* ossa,' Lachmann's emend. of Prop. iv. 5, 28. It is ' thought that the *alb*
(nightmare) cometh of *untimely births*,' M. Beham in Mone 4,
450. These are divided into *black, white* and *red* (Hpt. 4, 389),
which seems to support my division of elves into black, light and
brown.——The caterpillar *devil's cat* (Stald. 1, 276) reminds one
of *katze-spur*, a hairy caterp. so called in the Palatinate; conf.
Russ. *gúsenitza*, Pol. *wąsienca*, Boh. *hausenka*, Langued. *diablotin;*
ON. *bröndûngr*, variegata, Swed. *kålmask.* The butterfly is
called *pfeif-mutter*, Schm. 1, 30, *fifun-trager*, Alb. Schott 291 ;
conf. pipolter, fifolter. The witch is delivered of *will o' wisps*,
Thür. mitth. vi. 3, 69.——Witches carry magic in their *hair*,
therefore we cut it off: this already in M. Beham's Wien p. 274 ;
conf. the weichselzöpfe (plica Pol.). The witch chains her lover,
the devil, with *yarn* spun in a churchyard, Thür. mitth. vi. 3, 70.

Witches *float* on water, as Goðrûn says of herself: 'hôfo mik, *ne drekðo* hâvar bâror,' Sæm. 267ᵃ; 'hon mâtti *eigi söcqva*,' she might not sink 265. The unsightly German witch is paralleled by the Finn. Pohjan akka *harvahammas* (thin-toothed), Kalev. 2, 187. 205. 5, 135.

p. 1077.] Heathen features are the witches' consumption of *horseflesh* or even *man's flesh,* also their *dislike of bells.* With the witch's *blood-mark,* and with *Death's mark,* conf. ' stakins (στίγματα) Fráujins ana leika baíran,' Gal. 6, 17. It is remarkable that a witch *cannot weep;* she has watery eyes, but sheds *no tears.* In the Tirol. Inquis. (Pfaundler p. 43): sie sprotzt mit den augen, *weint ohne thränen.* Exactly the same is said of Thöck : ' Thöck mun grâta *þurrum târum* (with dry tears) Baldrs bâlfarar.' Here the witch answers to the giantess.

p. 1080.] To lie under a *harrow* defends you fr. the devil: stories in Müllenh. no. 290. Firmen. 1, 206ᵇ. He that puts a *piece of turf* on his head will not be seen by witches, Panz. Beitr. 1, 240-1. Wearing Gundermann's garland makes you see witches, Somm. p. 58. The priest can tell witches by their *round hats,* Ceynowa p. 14.

p. 1082.] Pol. *iędzona* means old witch, eater of men, esp. of children; conf. *iędza,* a fury. Wicked women with *white livers* are also known in France, *white-livered* men in Schambach 123ᵃ. Witches poke straw into the heart's place: þer î briosti liggr *halmvisk,* þar er hiartat skyldi vera, Fornm. s. 2, 208; Walther *Ströwinherz,* Schreiber's Frib. urk. 2, 161. In Petron. c. 63 : strigae puerum involaverant, et *supposuerant stramentitium vavatonem;* and just before : videt *manuciolum* de *stramentis* factum. At a witches' feast, boys were usually killed, boiled or roasted, and eaten up; which reminds us of heathen practices, and those of giants. Such killing, cooking, and eating of children is an antique and vital feature, KM. nos. 15. 51-6, conf. supra (pp. 1045 end. 1058—60). Kettle and cooking are a part of magic.

p. 1083.] A *beast* crawls into the sleeping woman's mouth Wolf's Ndrl. sag. 250, and note p. 688; or a *snake* creeps out of it, Walach. märch. p. 103. A *white mouse* slips into the dead man's mouth, Somm. p. 46 ; ' but alas, in the midst of her song a *red mousie* popt out of her mouth,' Faust p. m. 165 ; a *bee* flies out of one's mouth, Schreib. Taschenb. 4, 308. As the white

mouse runs up the rampart in Fischart's play, so witches indoors
run up the *wall* to the *rafters*, Process v. Ursernthal.——With
the iron bridge of king Gunthram's dream, conf. the *sword-bridge*
in the Rcm. de la charrette pp. 23. 84 (Suppl. to 835). When
the witch is setting out, she lays a *broom* or a *halm of straw* in
the bed by her sleeping husband, Mone 8, 126. With OHG.
*irprottan*, tranced, connect '*inbrodin* lac,' Lachm. Ndrrhein. ged.
p. 9, and 'in *hünnebrüden* gelegen,' Reim dich p. 52. Our
entzückt is in MHG. '*gezucket* anme geiste,' Diut. 1, 466; als in
*zuckete* der geist, Uolr. 1331. We also say 'rapt, caught up,
carried away.'

p. 1083.] With the Servian *starting-spell* agree the Moravian,
Kulda in D'Elvert 92-3. German formulas in Mone 8, 126.
Panzer 1, 251. Müllenh. no. 291. Lisch's M. jrb. 5, 85. With
them compare : *oben hinaus, nirgens an!* Callenb. Wurmld (?) 86;
*hui oben aus, und niergend an*, Agricola's Spr. 217. Kl. red.
(? 1565) 113[a]; *hei op hei an, stött nernich an*, N. Preuss. prov. bl.
1, 229. The cry of pursuit is in Schönw. 1, 139; so Aschen-
püster (Cinderella) cries: 'behind me dark, before me bright;'
Scand. *lyst foran, og mörkt bag*, Norske event. 1, 121; *ljust för
mig, mörkt efter mig*, Sv. äfvent. 1, 410. 427; *hvidt fremun, og
sort bag*, Abs. 421. But '*herop og herned til Mönsaas*,' Asb.
Huldr. 1, 179, is another thing. An Engl. spell for faring to
Elfland is : '*horse and hattock! with my top!*' Scot. bord. 2,
177-8. Völund's speech: 'vel ek, verða ek â fitjom!' is appar.
a flight-formula, for he soars up immed. after, Sæm. 138[a].——
When a sorceress anoints her shoulders, *wings* sprout out, Stier's
Ungr. märch. p. 53. Faust uses a *magic mantle* to fly up; conf.
the remarkable tale of a *dwarf* who spreads out his *cloak*, and
lets a man *stand on it* with him, H. Sachs i. 3, 280[bc].

p. 1085.] The good people (p. 456) cut themselves horses out
of switches, Erin 1, 136. The *magic steed* must be bridled with
bast, or it runs away, Reusch p. 23-4. In Pacolet's wooden horse
one has only to turn the tap to right or left, Val. et Orson c. 26
(Nl. c. 24). A *hose-band* tied round the shank lifts into the air,
Eliz. of Orl. 505.

p. 1086.] The German witches too are hindered in their ex-
cursions by the *sound of bells*. If they are late in coming home,
and the matin-peal rings out from a church, hei[r] career stops as

if paralysed, till the last tone has died away. The witch abuses the *bell*, Panz. Beitr. 1, 20.

p. 1089.] ' Carmine *grandines avertere*,' is as old as Pliny 17, 28. Hail being in grains, it is strewn out by bushelfuls: τῆς χαλάζης ὅσον μέδιμνοι χίλιοι διασκεδασθήτωσαν, Lucian's Icarom. 26. ' You *hail-boiler!*' is a term of abuse, Mone's Schausp. 2, 274. German witches scatter a powder with cries of *alles schauer, alles schauer!* The day before Walburgis night, a merry cobbler mocked his maid : ' Take me with you to Peter's mount!' When evening fell, there came a *storm*, nigh shook his doors and shutters down; well knew the cobbler what it meant. The Esths know how to *produce cold :* if you set two jugs of beer or water before them, one will freeze and not the other; see Wulfstân's journey. The weather must be *well boiled :* if the pot is *emptied too soon*, your labour is lost, Mone 8, 129. 130. The Kalmuks have the same kind of weather-making, Klemm 3, 204. ——Witches *boil apple-blossoms*, to spoil the fruit crop, Mone 8, 129. Dull on the fir-tree pours out hail, Panzer 1, 20. Says an old woman dripping wet, ' I've had this weather *in my back* this fortnight.' When the huntsman heard that, he struck her over the hump with a stick, and said, ' Why couldn't you *let it out* sooner then, old witch as you are?' Simplic. 1, 287. Witches make *stones roll* (ein rübi gan) into the hay and corn fields; also *avalanches*, Proc. v. Ursernthal 245—8. The shower-maidens feed on beshowered (lodged) corn, Panzer 1, 88. Hence Ph. v. Sittew. and the Fr. Simpl. 1, 53. 68 call the witch ' old *weather ;* ' elsewh. she is *hagel-anne, donnerhagels-aas* (-carrion), 7 Ehen p. 78; *shower-breeder, fork-greaser.* Witches are *weather-makers*, Wolf's Ndrl. s. 289. A witch drops out of the *cloud*, Bader nos. 337. 169. The Servian vila *leads clouds* (vode óblake) and *makes weather*, Vuk sub v. vrzino kolo ; she teaches her pupils the art. Our Germ. phrase, ' the *old wives* shake out their petticoats ' = it snows, suggests the Wallachian witch who throws off her petticoats. The Indians of Surinam say their sorcerers have thunderstorms, violent showers and hail at their command, Klemm 2, 168.——The O. Fr. poets name heathen kings ' roi *Gaste-blé*,' Guillaume 4, 179. 256 and ' roi *Tempesté*,' 4, 257. 26; conf. Mätzner 257 and *Tampasté* in Wolfram's Wh. 27, 8 (rhym. with *Faussabré* for Fauche-pré, or blé ?) 46, 20. 344, 7. 371, 3. 442,

39. A Thessalian sorceress fetches the *moon* down from the sky, and shuts her up in a box, Aristoph. Clouds 749. At vos, *deductæ* quibus est fallacia *lunæ*, Propert. i. 1, 19; tunc ego crediderim vobis et *sidera* et *amnes* posse cytacæis *ducere* carminibus i. 1, 23; illic et *sidera* primum præcipiti *deducta* polo, *Phœbe*que serena non aliter diris verborum obsessa venenis palluit, Lucan. Phars. 6, 496; cantus et e curru *lunam deducere* tentat, et faceret si non aera repulsa sonent, Tib. i. 8, 21; hanc ego de cœlo *ducentem sidera* vidi, i. 2, 45; te quoque, Luna, *traho*, Ov. Met. 7, 207; in hac civitate, in qua mulieres et *lunam deducunt*, Petr. c. 129.

In Esthonia the witches *knead* stalks of rye together, and repeat a spell over them; unless the *knots* are soon found out and burnt, the crop is sure to fail, Possart p. 164, conf. 162.

p. 1091.] In transforming, the sorcerer touches with his staff: ῥάβδῳ ἐπιμάσσεσθαι, Od. 13, 429, conf. 16, 172. Venus *touches* the mouth of Ascanius with her *feather*, En. 802; and Dido *catches it* (the magic) from his lips 815. *Mice are made* out of fallen pears, but without tails, Firmen. 1, 276[b]; conf. the red mouse (Suppl. to 1083 beg.). *Young puppies* made, Simpl. 2, 296-7 (ed. Keller), conf. 328. Acc. to Renvall, *bjära* is the Finn. *para*, genius rei pecuariæ lac subministrans; conf. Lencquist De superst. 1, 53. Castrén 167-8. Ganander's Myth. Fenn. 67, even Juslenius sub v. para. In Angermanl. it is called *bjara*, Almqv. p. 299; in Vesterbotten, see Unander sub v. *bara;* the Gothl. vocab. in Almqv. p. 415 describes it as *småtroll med tre ben.* Esths make a *homesprite* out of an *old broom*, Verh. 2, 89; did Goethe take his Apprentice fr. Lucian's Philops. 35-6 (Bipont. 7, 288)? Even a man is *made* out of *wood*, and a *heart put inside* him; he walks about and kills, Fornm. s. 3, 100.

p. 1093.] *Wax-figures* were placed on doors, at cross-roads, and on the graves of parents, Plato De legg. 11, 933; in another passage (of Plato?) Anacharsis speaks of Thessal. sorceresses and their *wax-figures;* the *waxen image* of Nectanebus, Callisth. p. m. 6. At a synod of 1219 Archbp Gerhard of Bremen condemns the Stedingers as heretics, charging them with 'quaerere responsa daemonum, *cereas imagines facere,* a phitonissis requirere consilium, et alia nefandissima tenebrarum exercere opera,' Sudendf's Registr. 2, 158; 'quaerunt responsa daemonum, *cerea simulacra* faciunt, et in suis spurcitiis erroneas consulunt phito-nissas,' Bull of Greg. 9 (1233), ibid. 2, 168. On *wax-figures*, see Osnabr. verh. 3, 71.——M. Lat. *invultuor*, praestigiator qui ad artes magicas *vultus* effingit; *invultare*, fascinare, Fr. envoulter, Ducange sub vv. invultare, vultivoli. They tried to copy the features of the man they were going to bewitch in the wax or clay puppet; they solemnly baptized it, gave it sponsors, and anointed it. When they pricked it with a needle, the man felt a sharp pain; if they pricked the head or heart, he died. They tried to have an Easter candle out of the church, to do the work by. Sticking needles into a wax-figure occurs in Kemble's Chartae, Pref. lix. lx., and the story in Müllenh. p. 233; conf. imago argentea (Suppl. to 1175 end). Ferebatur *imaginem* quan-dam ad instar *digiti*, ex Egipto adlatam, adorare; a qua quotiens responsa quaerebat, necesse erat homicidium aut in summo festo adulterium procurare; conf. Pertz 10, 460 and the thief's thumb (Suppl. to 1075 end).——*Cutting out the footprint* answers to τηρεῖν τὸ ἴχνος καὶ ἀμαυροῦν, vestigium observare et delere (blur), by planting one's right foot on the other's left print, and one's left on his right, and saying: ἐπιβέβηκά σοι, καὶ ὑπεράνω εἰμί, conscendi te, et superior sum! Lucian's Dial. meretr. 4. GDS. 137.

*Things that make invisible* are: the tarn-helm (p. 463), the bird's nest (Suppl. to 974), the right-hand tail-feather of a cock (to 671 mid.), fern-seed (p. 1210), the ring, rather the stone in the ring (p. 911), Troj. 9203. 9919, and the sonnenwedel (helio-trope) laid under a stone, Mone 8, 614.

p. 1097.] Pliny 8, 34: Homines in lupos verti rursumque restitui sibi, falsum esse existimare debemus. Unde tamen ista vulgo infixa sit fama, in tantum ut in maledictis *versipelles* habeat, indicabitur. An OHG. name *Weriwolf* occurs already in the 9th cent., Hpt 12, 252, and in Samland the name *Warwolf*. A *wer-wolf* in H. Sachs ii. 4, 16ᶜ, *meerwolf*, *beerwolf* in Ettn. Unw. doct. 671. *Werwatz* (watz = brood-hog) is a family name at Drei-eichenhain; is it formed like werwolf? *Loups garous*, Bosquet p. 223 seq.——To change yourself into a *fox*, *wolf* or *cat*, you use an ointment, Proc. v. Ursernth.; or shift the buckle of a certain *strap* to the *ninth hole*, Reusch in Preuss. prov. bl. 36, 436 and 23, 127. GDS. 152; conf. the old leather strap,

Firmen. 1, 213. People with a wolf-girdle are *úlf-heðnar :* is
that conn. with our *heiden, heiden-wolf* for unbaptized child, in
Waldeck *heid-ölleken ?* Papollere '60, p. 8.——By putting a slip
of wood (spruoccolo) in one's mouth, one becomes a she-bear,
and man again on taking it out, Pentam. 2, 6. If you dash
grass against the stem of a tree, wolves spring out of it,
Remigii Daemonol. (1598) pp. 152. 162. Sigefridus dictus *wolf-
vel,* MB. 1, 280, but *wolvel* (Wölfel ?) 8, 458. The gods send
Idun a wolfskin : *vargs-belg* seldo, *lêt î faraz,* lyndi breitti, Sæm.
89ᵃ.——Were-wolf stories in Müllenh. nos. 317—320. Firmen.
1, 363. 332. 212-3. Lekensp. 2, 91-2. ON. î varg-skinns ôlpu,
Fornm. s. 10, 201 (ôlpa, ûlpa = toga, vestis). A were-wolf may
be known by a *wolfs-zagelchen* (-tail) betw. the shoulder-blades,
Reusch no. 75 and note ; by a little 'raugen *wolfs-zagel*' growing out of the back betw. the shoulders, Preuss. prov. bl. 26, 435.
117. 172.

    p. 1098.] The witch appears as a *fox,* Schreib. Taschenb. 4,
309 ; as a *three-legged hare,* Somm. Sag. 62 ; as a *kol-svört ketta,*
Fornm. s. 3, 216. 220. Sv. forns. 1, 90 seq. Men protest : 'by
*catten,* die te *dansen* pleghen *tswoendaghs !* ' Belg. mus. 2, 116.
If a girl has fed the cat well, the sun shines on her wedding-day,
N. Preuss. prov. bl. 3, 470. Good stories of witches in Müllenh.
pp. 212—6 ; also that of the cat's *paw* being chopt off, its turning
into a pretty female *hand,* and the miller next morning missing
it on his wife, 227 ; and that of the witch who is ridden as a
horse, who is taken to the farrier's to be shod, and lies in bed
in the morning with horse-shoes on her hands and feet 226. 600.
Mone 8, 182. So in Petron. c. 62 a were-wolf has been wounded
in the neck ; presently a 'miles' is found in bed, having his
neck doctored : intellexi illum *versipellem* esse, nec postea cum
illo panem gustare potui. The ôfreskr in the evening sees a bull
and a bear fighting ; the next day two men lie wounded in bed,
Lundn. 5, 5.——Transformation into a bear or fox, a swan or
raven, is frequent. In Walewein 5598 : tenen vos *verbreken ;*
and 785 : *versciep* hem. ' Er *entwarf sich zu,*' he changed into,
Myst. 1, 214, etc. A bride turns into a *swan,* Müllenh. p. 212 ;
a man becomes a *hawk* or *falcon,* and comes flying to the tower,
Marie 1, 280, conf. 292. Women often change into toads : wesen
ene *padde,* en sitten onder die sille, Walew. 5639 ; gienge ich als

ein *krete* gât, u. solde bî eime zûne gân, Herb. 8364.——I must here remark, that *verða at göltum* in ON. tales does not mean turning into a swine, but running about wild like a boar, Ver-lauff on Vatnsd. p. 106-7. The magicians and enchantresses in our fairytales often change men into wolves, bears, cats, dogs or swine; the witches of a later time have no longer the power. Circe's formula, when turning men into *swine* by a stroke of her rod, was : ἔρχεο νῦν συφεόνδε, Od. 10, 320. The Lapland sorcerers *send* bears, wolves, foxes, ravens, to do mischief to men : such beast is then called *tille*, Lindahl 474ᵃ.

It is a different thing when *two persons exchange figures*. This ON. *skipta litum* or *hömum, skipta litom ok látom, vixla litum* is appar. effected by mere will, without spell or clothing, e.g. betw. Sigurd and Gunnar, Sæm. 177-8. 202-3. Völs. sag. c. 27, betw. Signy and the sorceress, Völs. 7. It happens esp. among born brothers, who are so like as to be taken for one another; but in the Nib. 337, 3. 429, 3. 602, 2 by the tarnhût which makes invisible. In the same way the wrong wife or lover is smuggled into bed at night, as Brangaene for Isot, conf. Berthe au grand pied and the Fabliau of the hair-cutting. A later and coarser version of this is the mere *exchange of clothes*.

p. 1099.] Magic lies in the *nails* : des zoubers ort-habe (seat) ligt an den *nagelen*, Geo. 57ᵇ. Magic is fixed in the *hair* : consider the elf-lock, elf-knot (p. 464); witches have *all the hair shaved* off them, see story in Klemm 2, 168. M. Beheim 273, 26. 274, 7. Magic is taken out of the *hair*, Wolfdietr. 548; conf. *wolf's hair* above.——Magic can *make us proof* against sword and bullet, shot and stroke; e.g. by a thread of silk, RA. 183. One so made proof is called a *frozen* man, Ettn. Unw. doct. 641. 653. 683, *iron* man, ON. *harð-giörr*, poison-proof, Sæm. 170; Kyrtil *bitu eigi iarn*, Landn. 2, 7. 3, 4. The *wound-spell* makes invulnerable ; but it can be neutralized by first hiding a knife in the ground and then wounding with it : this is called *unloosing the spell*, H. Sachs v. 347ᶜ (conf. '*digging* something *in* for a man,' iii. 3, 7ᵈ), and the exorcist *banntuch-macher, hart-macher*, Gutslaf's Wöhh. 207. 337. Othello 3, 4 has a magic *kerchief* wrought by a *sibyl*: 'the worms were hallowed that did breed the silk.' A *St. George's shirt* is made of yarn that was spun on a *Saturday*, Superst. G, v. 182.

p. 1100.] Witches are accused of *grasping, stroking, dazzling*: 'she made a *clutch* at me that will last as long as I live,' Bodmann's Rheingau p. 425, yr 1511 ; or 'ein boser angriff, böser schlag, herz-griff.' They *tread* the cattle ; they 'bringen einen wehthum zu halse,' they learn you what *dazing* (hoodwinking) means, Bodm. Rh. 908, yr 1505. Magic is wrought by *rubbing* : the rubbing of wood brings forth a squirrel, of chips a marten, of leaves a bee, of feathers a flight of grouse, of wool a flock of sheep, Kalev. 13, 160. 220. 280. 17, 328. 467 ; conf. the märchen of the three brothers, who rub feathers, hair and scales, and immed. eagles, bears and fish come to their aid.——Widely spread is the belief in the magic of the eye, Grenzboten '60, no. 26. Βλέμμα, ἀναπνοή and ὀφθαλμός βάσκανος are already in Plutarch's Sympos. v. 7 ; nescio quis teneros *oculus* mihi *fascinat* agnos, Virg. Ecl. 3, 108. Engl. *evil eye*, Ir. the *balar*, Conan p. 32 ; the blink o' an *ill ee*, Hone's Dayb. 2, 688. His diebus ei (Chilperico) filius natus est, quem in villa Victoriacensi nutrire praecepit, dicens 'ne forte, dum *publice videtur*, aliquid *mali incurrat* et moriatur,' Greg. Tur. 6, 41. MHG. *twerhe ougen*. On the evil eye, see N. Pr. prov. bl. 1, 391—3 ; der *blick* slangen toetet, wolve schrecket, strûz-eiger (ostrich-eggs) bruetet, ûzsatz (leprosy) erwecket, u. ander krefte hât gar vil, Renn. 18016 ; men spit in a pretty girl's face for fear of the evil eye, Ir. märch. 2, 64.

p. 1101.] Sâ ze hant ir rôter munt *einen* tûsent stunt (times) sô schoenen (*rôsen*, underst.) *lachet*, MS. 1, 11ᵃ. The name *Rosenlacher* is in Michelsen's Lub. oberh. 271. Baur's Arnsb. 158 ; conf. 'ad Ruozinlachan,' Notizbl. 6, 68. 'To *laugh roses*,' Athen. 5, 498. It is derived fr. heathen beings of light, Mannhdt's Germ. mythen 149. 439 ; *camillen-bluomen ströuwen*, swen sô lieplich *lachen* wil ir munt, MSH. 3, 212ᵇ.

p. 1102.] A *kiss* makes you *forget* everything, Müllenh. p. 400. Pentam. Liebr. 1, 231 ; so does a *bite of the apple*, Norske folke-ev. 2, 47. Helen, like Grimhild, makes a magic potion, mingling spices with the wine, Od. 4, 220—230 ; so does Circe 10, 235. The Färoese still call the draught of oblivion *ouminni*, Qväd. p. 178. 180. The Servians make their *voda zaboravna* of mountain-herbs, Vuk 2, 612-3. Conf. φίλτρον, love-potion ; mein-blandinn miöðr, Völs. saga c. 25 ; scheidel-tranc gebrûwen,

Amgb. 15ª. Incendia inter epulas nominata aquis sub mensis profusis *ab-ominamur*, Pliny 28, 2.

p. 1103.] Silence is a safeguard against magic: Saxo's 'ne *incauto effamine* maleficiis locum instruerent' (p. 659). Incantations are in Serv. *urótzi*, gen. uróka, Boh. aurok, conf. Jungm. sub v. ne-urocny, ne-uroka [reku, I speak]. The Slav. formula against bewitching is 'kamen-mira' [stone of peace?]; conf. *seines zeichens, ihres zeichens*, Schmidt's Westerw. id. 335, and the phrases: salva venia! God forefend (save the mark)! When a man looks startled, the Serv. formula is: 'zatchudio-se prebiyenoi golièni,' he's amazed at his broken leg, Vuk sub v. zatchuditi-se, and Sprichw. p. 87. When something painful or mischievous is said, the answer is: 'u nashega tchabra gvozdene ushi,' our tub has iron ears (handles), Sprichw. p. 334.——On *spitting* as a protection from magic, see Schwenk's Röm. myth. 399. The cyclop, when admiring his own beauty, spits in his lap three times, to avoid baskania: ὡς μὴ βασκανθῶ δέ, τρὶς εἰς ἐμὸν ἔπτυσα κόλπον· ταῦτα γὰρ ἀργαῖά με κοτυτταρὶς ἐξεδί-δαξεν, Theocr. 6, 39. The cock-pigeon spits on its young to keep off sorcery, Athen. 3, 456-8; et eum morbum mihi esse, ut qui me opus sit *insputarier?* Plaut. Capt. iii. 4, 21.——An *ear of corn* protects from magic: *ags* við fiölkýngi, Sæm. 27ᵇ. In the *threshold* of the house-door you bore a hole, put in *hallowed herbs*, and peg them in with a *harrow's tooth*, Mone 6, 460 (p. 1078). Throw a *fire-steel* over anything ghostly, and you are master of it, Dybeck '44, 104—6; conf. the power of the *eld-stål* over the giant, Cavall. 1, 39; *ild-staalet*, Folke-ev. 2, 82; a *flint-eld* is struck over the cow, Dyb. 4, 27 and over enchantresses 4, 29; or a knife is flung '44, 63. 4, 33. A *magic circle* is drawn: gladio circa illos *circulum* fecit, monens sub interminatione mortis, ut infra circulum se cohiberent, Cæs. Heist. 5, 4. On Indian sorcery, conf. Central-blatt '53, 255.

---

# CHAPTER XXXV.

## SUPERSTITION.

p. 1105.] Gr. δεισιδαίμων superstitious, δεισιδαιμονία superstition. Tac. Germ. 45 speaks of the *superstitio* of the Aestyans. Pott 1, 157 derives the word fr. stare super, to *stand by* or *before*

the god or altar. Wend. *vièra* faith, *přivièra, pšivièra* superstition [Russ. suye-vèrie]. With the Swed. *vidske-pelse* agrees
in part the OHG. *unscaf* superstitio, *unscaflîhho* superstitiose,
Graff 6, 453 ; there are also *unpiderpi* 5, 219 and *ubirfenkida*, Gl.
Sletst. 25, 327 both = superstitio; *ubarwintelingun* superstitiose,
Mone's Anz. '35, 89. AS. *ofertaele* superstitiosus, Lye. Later
words : *geloubelîn*, Krolewitz 3753 ; *swacher gloube, ungeloube*,
Er. 8122-39. We have also *köhler-glaube*, collier's faith, and in
the Quickborn *höner-globe*. Superstitiones religionis rubigines,
Garg. 187ᵃ. On superstition, see Nilsson 6, 3. Hes. Opp. 705—
826.

p. 1105 n.] Klemm 3, 201-3 divides magic into explorative
and active. A foretoken, presage, is in Lat. *portentum* from
portendo, *ostentum* from ostendo, *monstrum* from monstro
[moneo ?], Cic. Div. 1, 42 and Forcellini ; *prodigia* coelestia,
prope quotidianas in urbe agrisque ostentantia minas, Livy 2, 42.
OHG. *fora-pouchan*, fore-beacon, *fora-zeichan*, foretoken; *bîzeichen*,
Windb. Ps. 323. 367. Signs appear before the Judgment-day,
bef. a death, a dearth, a war. To curse all *signs*, Hebel 332.

p. 1107.] OHG. *drewa* oraculum, *droa* fulmen, Graff 5, 246.
AS. *hwât* omen, divinatio, also *hwâtung*, OHG. *hvâz* (p. 951),
conf. *hwâtend* iris (p. 1216 n.) ; *fugel-hwâte* divinatio per aves.
AS. hwetton hige, *hael sceáwedon* (on the voyage), Beow. 407 ;
OHG. *heil-scouwunge* augurium, Graff 6, 556 ; *hel-scouwinge*, Partonop. 20, 13 ; *heilge scowede* augurium, Sumerl. 2, 41 ; *hêl-
scowinge*, Bilderdyk's Verscheidenh. 3, 143. Frauenl. p. 142
uses *künden* for prognosticate. Again *kiesen*, choose = look out
for (in ref. to weather, Gramm. 4, 848), conf. Swed. tjusa (p.
1037). *Children* esp. are used in divination and casting lots ;
conf. *pure children*, Superst. H, cap. 55-6-7. 83.

p. 1107.] A remarkable method of acquiring the gift of divination occurs in the Swed. *ârs-gâng*, Hpt's Ztschr. 4, 508 seq.
Both that and the power of healing are passed on from *women* to
*men*, from *men* to *women*, conf. Firmen. 1, 318. Sommer's Sagen
p. 171. As in Superst. I, 996, so in Müllenh. 399 the gift of
spirit-seeing is transferred by treading on the *left* foot and
looking over the *right* shoulder. *Prevision* is the faculty of
presentiment intensified to actual seeing and hearing : a *foreseer*,
*forepeeper* beholds funerals, armies in march, battles, also unim-

portant things, such as a harvest-wagon that will upset in the
yard in ten years' time, the figures and clothing of servants yet
unborn who are lifting him off the ground, the marks on a foal
or calf that shies to one side; he hears the tap of the hammer on
coffin lids, or the tramp of horse. These *vorkiekers* always
perceive with only *one* sense, either sight or hearing: they cannot
hear what they see, nor see what they hear. They are *witch-
seers, god-seers, devil-seers.*——In ON. a ghost-seer is *ôfreskr*,
Landn. 3, 14. 4, 12. 5, 5 (p. 344); or does '*ôfreskir* menn sâ
þat' in these passages mean that even ó-fresk men could see
it? for Biörn Haldorson (sub vv. freskr, ôfreskr) maintains that
*freskr* is the seer, and *ôfreskr* the non-seer; which seems right
enough, provided that freskr means cat-sighted, from fres (felis).
Our nursery-tales tell of these cat-eyed men with an eye for
mice, KM.[3] 3, 198; then there is the giant who gets cat's eyes
put into his head. Another term is *fronsk,* som natten til en
höitids dag, isär Jule-natt, kan forud-sige det til-kommende,
Molb. Dial. lex. 138. *Frem-syn* is to be acquired by smearing
with *riisormsod,* or by looking at a funeral procession through
a *skagle-öiet,* Moe's note.

p. 1109.] On *sieve-running,* see Müllenh. no. 272. Tett. and
Tem. Preuss. sag. p. 284. *Erbe-sib* crispula, a plant's name,
Sumerl. 56, 37. To detect the thief, a *hoop is driven,* Panzer's
Beitr. 1, 210; *three plates* are laid for him, containing bread, salt
and lard, Hpt 7, 538; *dishes shaken,* and *froth observed,* Tett.
and Temm. p. 260. Balt. stud. xii. 1, 37-8; 'when in a *sword*
he sees the *stolen thing,*' Troj. kr. 27412 (the sword holds in it a
spirit, Frauenl. p. 142-3: ich hâte in eime *swerte* von âventiure
einen *geist,* daz er mir solde *künden*). Prophesying from *icicles,*
Panzer 2, 549; by *throwing a Bible open* (an early practice),
Greg. Tur. 4, 16.

p. 1110.] The *lot is cast :* lêton tân wîsian þâ se tân gehwearf
Andr. 1099. The 'temere ac fortuito *spargere*' of Tacitus is
like ON. '*hrista* teina,' to shake the twigs, as in Sæm. 52[a]:
*hristo* teina, ok â hlaut sâ. M.Neth. si *worpen cavelen,* Jesus c.
229, conf. '*jacere* talos in fontem,' Sueton. Tib. 14. Rudorff 15,
218. Goth. hlauts imma *urrann,* ἔλαχε, Luke 1, 9. GDS. 159;
ez was in sô *gevallen,* Livl. chr. 5724, ez was im wol *gevallen*
1694, in was der *spân gevallen* wol 2483, in *viel* dicke wol ir *spân*

7239; dat *lôt viel,* Maerl. 2, 169, die *cavele viel* 2, 60. We say
'to whom the happy *lot* has *fallen.*'
The Scythians too divined by *sticks,* Herod. 4, 67 and Nicander
(Ur. Sk. p. 659); the Alani, Amm. Marcel. 31, 2; the early
Saxons, Beda 5, 11 (mittunt sortes, *hluton mid tânum*); the
Frisians, whose Lex Fris. tit. 14 says : *teni lana munda obvoluti.*
So the Greek suppliants bear in their hands λευκοστεφεῖς
νεοδρέπτους κλάδους, Aesch. Suppl. 333, σὺν τοῖσδ' ἱκετῶν
ἐγχειριδίοις ἐριοστέπτοισι κλάδοισι 22, λευκοστεφεῖς ἱκτηρίας
191, κλάδοισι νεοδρόποις 354 (κλάδ-ος is hlaut-s, hlôz); ἐρίῳ
στέφειν, Plato Rep. 3, p. 398. Hermann's Gottesd. alt. p. 105-8
(raw wool is laid on the stone, Paus. x. 24, 5). The Slavs cast
lots with *black* and *white* sticks, Saxo (Müll. 827), and divined by
the odd or even lines in ashes, ibid.——Drawing lots with *willow-
leaves,* Ettn. Maulaffe 703; with *stalks* of corn, Vuk no. 254.
RA. p. 126; sortiri ex *sitella* (bucket), Plaut. Casina, see Forcell.
sub v. sitella; 'sors Scotorum,' Dronke's Gl. Fuld. 12. There
were *lot-books* to divine ·by: diz *lôss-buoch* ist unrehte *gelesen*
(wrongly read), Wiener mer-vart 556 ; a *lóz-buoch* in Cod. Vind.
2976 (Hoffm. 209). 2953 (H. 366) ; *loss-büchlein,* Ph. v. Sittew.;
*lösseln* and *lössel-buch,* Schm. 2, 504; *lössel-nächte,* Frisch 1,
623 ; *lösslerei, lösslerin.*

p. 1111.] On this *motion of boughs,* from which the Armenians
divined, see N. Cap. 20. Machen *viur úz den spachen* (p. 1121
mid.); conf. Superst. H, c. 80, in dem *fewre* sehen; D, 38r. and
140r., *fúr-*sehen. With 'der *tisch in der hant*' conf. '*mensa
volae,*' Finn. *onnenpöytä,* luck's table, fr. onni = fortuna.

p. 1112.] The Romans also spoke of *drawing water in a sieve:*
cribro aquam, Plaut. Ps. i. 1, 100 ; imbrem in cribro, Pliny 28, 2.
Our 'emptying the pond with a sieve,' Sommer's Sag. pp. 13,
94.

The Gauls prophesied from the σφαδασμός (convulsions) of one
devoted to death, when his *back* was pierced with a sword, Strabo
4, p. 198; the Cimbrians from the blood and entrails of their
sacrificed prisoners 7, p. 294, Lat. *exti-spicium.* The Malays
also divine from the *entrails* of slaughtered beasts, Ausland
'57, p. 603[b].

p. 1113.] An ein *schulder-bein* er sach (looked),
      des quam sîn herze in ungemach (became uneasy).

Er sprach: ' die Littouwen lîden nôt,
mîn bruoder ist geslagen tôt,
ein her (army) in mînem hove lac (has lain)
sît gester bis an disen tac ! '
*Daz* bein hât manigem sît gelogen (lied).

Livl. chr. 3019. Ocellos habens in *spatulis* = humeris, Pertz 8,
385; expositione ossium *spatulae* ala in suis *spatulis*, Fridericus
imp. De arte ven. 1, 26. Inspection of shoulderblades is known
to Kalmuks (Klemm 3, 199), Tunguses and Bedouins (3, 109).

p. 1115.] The Romans also divided *pisces* into *squamosi* and
*non squamosi*, Festus p. 253. W. Goethe's Diss. p. 19. In
Levit. 11, 9 and Deut. 14, 9 fish that have *fins* and *scales* are
pron. eatable; conf. Griesh. 146.

p. 1117.] The rat wishes the cat joy when she *sneezes*, Avada-
nas 2, 149, 150; πταρμὸς ἐκ τῶν δεξιῶν, Herm. Gottesd. alt.
p. 186; Ἔρωτες ἐπέπταρον, Theocr. 7, 96; haec ut dixit, Amor,
sinistra ut antea, *dextra sternuit* approbationem, Catull. 44, 17;
atque, ut primum e regione mulieris, pone tergum eius maritus
acceperat sonum *sternutationis* . . . solito sermone *salutem* ei
fuerat *imprecatus*, et iterato rursum, Apul. Met. lib. 2, p.m. 211.
The ' Got helfe dir ! ' is also in Myst. i. 103, 10 ; swer ze vremden
*niesen* sich rimpfet (crumples up), daz ist ouch *verlorn*, Ettn.
Frauenl. p. 70.

p. 1117.] Ringing in the ears: ἐβόμβει τὰ ὦτα ὑμῖν, Luc.
Dial. mer. 9; aures *tinniunt*, Pertz 9, 265 ; sine oren *songhen*,
Walew. 9911.——*Supercilium salit*, a good omen, Forcell. sub v.
superc. On prophetic *jerks in the limbs* among Orientals, see
Fleischer in Rep. of Leipz. acad. d. w. '49, p. 244.

p. 1119.] The spells in Burns's Halloween are for discovering
one's future *lover*. On Christmas Eve the sleeping fowls begin
crowing, if a girl is to be married soon, Firmen. 2, 377. *Wax*
may be poured instead of lead, Mone's Anz. 7, 423 : ceram in
aquam fundere, Lasicz 56.

p. 1119.] *Angang*, what meets you on setting out, ἔωθεν,
mane, ἐν ἀρχῇ, ἐν θύραις, ἐπὶ τῇ πρώτῃ ἐξόδῳ, is significant.
M. Neth. ên goet ghemoet, Rose 2715; *gude* u. *bose motte*, Gefk.
Beil. 100. Swed. *mot*, möte ; *lyks-mot*, evil meeting. Gr. δυς-
άντητος [*ill-met* by moonlight, proud Titania] = boding ill ; so

δυς-κληδόνιστος [fr. κληδών, omen]. A titulus in the Salic Law
treats ' de *superventis* vel exspoliationibus.'

p. 1124.] On *angang* among the Thugs, see Convers. lex. d.
geg. iv. 2, 55; on the Greek belief in it, Lucian's Pseudol. 17 (ed.
Bip. 8, 72) and Eunuch. 6 (Bip. 5, 208). Theophr. Charact. c.
16 (conf. Kopp De amuletis p. 42). 'Consider too, that the *flight*
and *song* of all the *birds* look favourable; if these be not *joyful*
*signs*, I have clean forgot the art; no bird of *black* feather, no
*raven, starling, crow* nor *ouzel* have I seen. Three *merry* men
have met me, three men named *John*. Not once have I stumbled,
and wellnigh do I believe the *stones move* out of my way or
flatten them before me. The folds of my garment hinder me
not, neither am I weary, every mother's son greeteth me, no *dog*
hath *barked* against me, Wirsung's Cal. J 2^b. To *run across* one's
*path* is always bad, Büttner's Lett. lieder p. 255.

p. 1126.] Meeting an old woman is called *karing-möte*, Afzel.
2, 148. 'Unlucky to meet a *red-haired woman* bef. any one
else in the morning,' O'Kearney 132. 'The first thing that
meets me, were it even a *parson*, a *beggar* or an *old woman*,'
Goethe in Weimar jrb. 5, 458; wizzet, wem der (unsaelige lîp)
*anegenget* an dem *morgen fruo*, deme gît ungelücke zuo, Walth.
118, 16 (conf. 'also wol ir *g'anegenget* was,' Diemer 206, 23).
Doch hân ich ie gehoeret wol, daz man.die *priester schiuhen* sol
(should shun) ze sô-getânen sachen, Heinz v. Kost. Ritter u. pf.
303; on the other hand: swer in zuo einem mâle gesach, der
wânde sîn vürwar (hoped verily to be) deste saeliger ein jâr, Gute
frau 970. Who looks at *early morn* under the fair one's *eyes* is
safe from sorrow all that day, Hätzl. 148^b.——For hunters the
*skogs-râ*, for fishers the *hafs-fru* is unlucky meeting, Afzel. 2, 148.
150. No woman with spindle or distaff may tarry in my lord's
mill (bann-müle), Weisth. 2, 25. To meet one that is *lame of the*
*right foot*, or *gelded*, or *effeminate*, is unlucky, Lucian 5, 208;
conf. Brodæi Misc. in Grævii Thes. 2, 509; (eunuchus) pro-
cedentibus omen, Claudian in Eutrop. 1, 125. *Parsons' journeys*
are a sign of rain, Prætor. Alectr. 163. About meeting a *black*
or a *white monk*, see Spinnr. evang. Friday 10; about a *sword*
being handed by a woman, ibid. Wednesd. 20.

p. 1128.] The Lapps carefully observe what *beasts* they meet,
Klemm 3, 90. There are beasts which are not to be *named* in

the morning : αἰσχίῳ θηρίων τῶν πρωΐας ὥρας ὀνομασθῆναι δυσ-
κληδονίστων, Luc. Amores 39. Meeting with a *hare* bodes no
good, Wolf's Deut. sag. no. 370 ; turn thee home if a *hare run
across thy path*, Keisersb. Vom lewen 63ᵇ. On the *hare* and the
*wolf*, Lappenberg's Eulensp. p. 144.——The encounter of a wolf
estimated variously : ' Sed gravius mentes caesorum *ostenta lu-
porum* horrificant ; duo quippe lupi sub principis ora, dum
campis exercet equos, violenter adorti agmen, et excepti telis,
immane relatu, *prodigium miramque notam duxere futuri*,' Claud.
B. Get. 249.——' Sei weren einen *wulf* op dem wege vangen
(caught), dei quam utem holte gegangen, des freueden sei sik all
int gemein,' all rejoiced, Soester fehde p. 667 ; ' the colonel held
this *brush with the wolves* to be a *good omen* that they should
yet further come upon unlooked for booty,' Simpl. 2, 74. Men
wish the *wandering fox* luck on his journey, Ettn. Unw. doct.
240. Do wart en *catte* lopende vor dem here (army), Detm. 1,
154.

The *weasel* is changed into a *fair lady*, Babr. 32 ; it is called
νυμφίτζα, Lobeck's Path. 360 ; other names in Nemnich sub. v.
mustela. Does *froie* in Reinh. clxxii. answer to It. *donnola*, or
is it conn. w. M. Neth. *vraeie*=pulcra, venusta ? conf. *damoiselle
belette*, Lafont. 3, 17. In the Renart it is called *petit porchaz*, in
the Reinaert *clene bejach*. ON. *hreisiköttr* is ermine. Auspicio
hodie optumo exivi foras, *mustela murem* abstulit præter pedes,
Plaut. Stich. iii. 2, 6. A legend of the mustela in Marie 1, 474.

p. 1129.] Ὄρνις came to mean any auspicium, whether of
birds or not, Aristoph. Birds 719—721. A bird-gazer οἰωνίστης,
Il. 2, 858; ὄρνιθας γνῶναι, Od. 1, 159; διαγνῶναι πτήσεις ὀρνίθων,
Paus. i. 34, 3 ; οἰωνῶν σάφα εἰδώς, Od. 1, 202; ὄρνιθας κρίνων,
Hes. Op. 826. ' Telemus Eurymides, quem nulla *fefellerat* ales,'
Ov. Met. 13, 770 ; nunc ave *deceptus* falsa 5, 147 ; δυς-οιώνιστος,
Luc. Eunuch. 6.——OHG. *fogalrarta* augurium, *fogalrartôn*
augariari, Graff 2, 536; *fogilrartôd* auspicium, Gl. Sletst. 22, 3.
AS. *fugel-hwâte* augurium (Suppl. to 1107). Boh. *kob, koba*,
divination by flight of birds ; *koba, kuba*, falcon. Not every bird
is adapted for divination : ὄρνιθες δέ τε πολλοὶ ὑπ' αὐγὰς ἠελίοιο
φοιτῶσ', οὐδέ τε πάντες ἐναίσιμοι, Od. 2, 181 ; *fugl frôð-hugadr*,
Sæm. 141ᵃ ; *parra, cornix, picus, pica* are augurales, Aufrecht in
D. Zeitschr. 1, 280.——Men watched the flight as well as the

song, Holtzm. Ind. sag. 2, 44; quae voces avium? quanti per
inane volatus? Claud. 4 cons. Hon. 142; die *ferte* dero fogelo,
unde dero *singentôn rarta,* unde die heilesoda dero *in rihte* fure
sih *fliegentôn,* N. Cap. 17; ir vogel in vil wol sanc, Livl. 7240.
The Malays prophesy from the *flight* and *cry* of birds, Ausl. '57, p.
603-4, and war and husbandry are determined by them.――Uf
einem *tach* (roof) stuont ein *krâ,* si schrei vast 'ha ha ha ha, narre
bistu da!' fool that you are, V. d. Hagen's G. Abent. 2, 449; ez
hab ein *swerziu krâ* gelogen (lied), MS. 2, 80ª; chant *sinistre* et
*criard* du corbeau, Villemarq. Bard. bret. 167. On the language
of ravens and crows, and on birds divided into castes like men,
see Monats-ber. d. acad. '59, p. 158-9. Bulletin de Pétersb. '59,
p. 438.――Auspicio, *avi sinistra,* Plaut. Epid. ii. 2, 2; *qua* ego
hunc amorem mihi esse *avi* dicam datum? Plaut. Cas. iii. 4, 26;
*dira avis,* Sueton. Claud. 22. Pulcherrimum augurium, *octo*
*aquilae petere silvas* et intrare visae (signif. 8 legions), Tac. Ann.
2, 17; a Servian song addresses the high-soaring far-seeing
*eagles,* Vuk 1, 43 no. 70 (Wesely p. 64). Fata notant, stellaeque
vocant *avi*umque *volatus,* totius et subito malleus orbis ero,
Richerius 4, 9. Böhmer's Font. 3, 51. Luther says somewhere:
If thou see a little bird, pull off thy hat, and wish him joy,
Schuppius 1121; ichn' weiz waz vogels *kegn in vlog,* Jeroschin
132ᶜ.

     p. 1131.] A flight to your *right* is lucky, to your *left* unlucky,
GDS. 982 seq. *Parra dextera, cornix dextra, picus sinister,* Grotef.
Inscr. Umbr. 6, 5. 7.

> τύνη δ' οἰωνοῖσι τανυπτερύγεσσι κελεύεις
> πείθεσθαι, τῶν οὔτι μετατρέπομ' οὐδ' ἀλεγίζω,
> εἴτ' ἐπὶ δεξί' ἴωσι πρὸς Ἠῶ τ' Ἠέλιόν τε,
> εἴτ' ἐπ' ἀριστερὰ τοίγε ποτὶ ζόφον ἠερόεντα. Il. 12, 237.

The Greeks often mention the *eagle:*

> ἐπέπτατο δεξιὸς (right hand) ὄρνις,
> αἰετὸς (eagle) ἀργὴν χῆνα φέρων ὀνύχεσσι πέλωρον
> ἥμερον ἐξ αὐλῆς. Od. 15, 160.

> αὐτὰρ ὁ τοῖσιν ἀριστερὸς (left hand) ἤλυθεν ὄρνις,
> αἰετὸς ὑψιπέτης, ἔχε δὲ τρήρωνα πέλειαν. Od. 20, 242.

> τῷ δ' αἰετὼ (two eagles) εὐρύοπα Ζεὺς

ὑψόθεν ἐκ κορυφῆς ὄρεος προέηκε πέτεσθαι. Od. 2, 146;
and then: δεξιὼ (right hand) ἤϊξαν διά τ᾽ οἰκία, κ.τ.λ. 154.
Again, the *hawk*:

ἐπέπτατο δεξιὸς ὄρνις,
κίρκος (hawk), Ἀπόλλωνος ταχὺς ἄγγελος, ἐν δὲ πόδεσσι
τίλλε πέλειαν ἔχων, κατὰ δὲ πτερὰ χεῦεν ἔραζε
μεσσηγὺς νηός τε καὶ αὐτοῦ Τηλεμάχοιο. Od. 15, 528.

The flight of the *mouse-hawk* is carefully scanned by the Kalmuks, Klemm 3, 202. We read of δεξιὸς ἐρωδιός (heron) in
Hipponax, Fragm. 50, of δεξιὴ σίττη (woodpecker), Fragm. 62;
*ardeolae* (herons), altero oculo carentes, optimi augurii, Pliny 11
37. 52. *Hrafn* flýgr *austan* af hâ meiði (tree), ok eptir honom
*örn* î sinni; *þeim* gef ek *erni* (to that eagle) efstum brâðir, sâ
mun â blôði bergja mînu, Hervar. cap. 5; *hrafn* qvað at hrafni,
sat â hâm meiði, Sæm. 149[b]. Similarly: *þâ* qvað *þat kráka*
(crow), sat qvisti â (on bough), Sæm. 106[b]; *cornix* avis divina
imbrium imminentium, Hor. Od. iii. 27, 10. Herm. Gottesd. alt.
§ 58; rostro recurvo turpis, et infernis tenebris obscurior alas,
*auspicium* veteri sedit *ferale* sepulcro, Claud. in Eutrop. 2, 230;
nuper *Tarpeio* quae sedit *culmine* cornix, ' est bene ' non potuit
dicere, dixit ' erit,' Suet. Domit. 23.——*Martens vögelken*, Firmenich 1, 139. 140; Sunte *Maartens veugeltje* zat al op een
heuveltje met zijn rood rood rokje, Halbertsma's Tongvallen p.
45; Engl. *martin*, hirundo minor, Nemn. p. 164; Fr. *martinet*,
le petit martinet. There was a society of *Martins-vögel* in Swabia
in 1367, Landau's Ritter-ges. p. 15.* Dös vögerl aum tannabam
(fir) *steht* auf *oanm fuss*, hat a zetterl im schnaberl, von meinm
dearndel (girl) ann gruss, Seidl Almer 1, 24. The *chátaka* drinks
nothing but rain, catching the drops as he flies; he brings luck
when he flies on your *left*, whereas most birds signify good on the
*right*, Max Müll. Meghadûta, p. 59.

p. 1132.] Ἡ σίττη (a pecker) καὶ εἴ τι τοιοῦτον ὄρνεον δεξιὰ
πρὸς ἔρωτας φαίνεται. Ἐγὼ μὲν, ὦ Λεύκιππε, δεξιὴ σίττη!
Didymus apud schol. Aristoph. Av. 704; πετόμεσθά τε γὰρ καὶ
τοῖσιν ἔρωσι σύνεσμεν, Av. 704, conf. Meineke's Choliambi p.
122-3. *Pies* en *nombre impair*, signe de malheur, Bosquet 219.

* *neue hant*, Vindler in Hpt 9, 79; uf die *alten hant* zierlich gemacht, Götz v.
Berlich. ed. Zöpfl p. 14; künigin bin ich der *newen hand*, J. v. Morsheim, beginn.

On the *starling's* flight, Ettn. Maulaffe 704.   *Alban,* espèce
d'oiseau de proie, prob. de vautour, Fauriel's Albig. p. 664.

The heathen Arabs bef. Mahomet: one who has gone out turns
back immed. on seeing a *raven.*   Yet it is a good sign if a *pair*
of ravens, *messaud* and *messauda* (m. and f. for lucky) cross one's
path in *equal flight;* else a croaking raven is called the *bird of
parting,* bec. he foretells a separation.   There is a bird whose cry,
heard from the right, brings blessing to a house: it is called
*sakuni, sakunta,* afterw. *kapnyala,* Kuhn on Vrihaddêvatâ p. 117.
p. 1133.]   The *over-flight* of some birds is significant:

> Zwoa schnee-weissi *täuberli* (dovelings)
> sänt *übawärts g'flogn,*
> und hiaz hat mich mein dearndl (girl)
> schon wiedä bitrogn (fooled me again).   Seidl Almer 34.

*Pigeons* also fan the king while he dines, Athen. 2, 487.
Again :

> Ob im vant er einen *arn* (eagle),
> des schoene was seltsaene ;
> er was im, in waene (I ween),
> gesant von Gote ze gemache (comfort) :
> mit einem vetache (wing)
> *treip er im den luft* dar (fanned the air),
> mit dem andern er im *schate bar.*          Servat. 1330.

Albert. Magn. De *falcon.* c. 4 : ' Ego enim jam vidi qui sine
ligaturis intrabant et exibant, et nobis comedentibus super
mensam veniebant, *in radio solis se extendentes coram nobis,* quasi
blandirentur nobis.'   While Marcian sleeps, an *eagle* flies above
him, giving *shade,* Procop. 1, 326.   A *shading peacock's tail* is
worn by ladies, Vilk. saga c. 213 and Vuk 4, 10 ; a *peacock fan,*
Claud. in Eutr. 1, 109 ; *pfaewîne huote,* Kolocz. 184 [on ' peacock
hats from England,' see Hehn's Plants and Anim., Lond. '85].
With *óminnis hegri* connect ' iwer iegeslîchen hât diu *heher*
(OHG. hehara) an geschrîet ime walde,' the jay has cried a spell
over you all, Wh. 407, 11.

p. 1134.]   A *sihle singing* on your *right* brings luck, Büttn.
Lett. lied. pp. 248. 266.   The sight of the first *wagtail* is significant, Klemm 2, 329, and to Kalmuks that of the *snake* 3, 202-3.

The neighing of horses, sneezing of cats, howling of dogs, each
is an omen : dir het diu *katze* niht *genorn*, Helbl. 1, 1392 (Suppl.
to 1115); on the howling of dogs, see Capitolinus in Maxim. jun.
c. 5. Pausan. iv. 13, 1.

p. 1136.] Leo in Thür. mitth. iv. 2, 98 connects the Goth.
*hráiva-dubó* with *divan* and *daubs, deáf* [Hehn's Plants and
Anim. 258]. '*Bubo* habet nomen a voce sua, et moratur in
cavernis petrosis vel muris antiquis, et differt a noctua solum in
magnitudine, quia est major ea, et bubo dicitur *letalis* vel *mor-
talis,* quia *mortem annuntiat,* unde dicunt quidam naturales, quod
sit animal habens dilectionem naturalem ad hominem, et propterea ponit se supra vestigium hominis, et post mortem festinat
ad amandum cadaver, et dicunt aliqui quod generetur ex medulla
spinae in dorso hominis,' Stephan's Stofl. 118.

> Ter omen
> *funereus bubo letali carmine* fecit.   Ov. Met. 10, 453.
> Tectoque profanus
> incubuit *bubo*, thalamique in culmine sedit.   6, 431.

*Infausto bubone,* Claud. in Eutr. 2, 407; a *bubo* prophesies to
Agrippa, Joseph. 18, 6. 19, 8 (Horkel p. 494); *bubo, cartae funebris
lator,* Marbod's Carm. 1577.   Hipponax in Meineke's Choliambi
p. 112 calls its κρυγὴ (screeching) νεκρῶν ἄγγελός τε καὶ κῆρυξ.
As the Lett. *uhpis,* hoopoo, is a bird of ill-omen, our *hûwe* (bubo)
heralds a speedy death in the Herod story, Pass. 157, 51—72.
159, 76—83; der leidic *hûwaere,* der *naht-hûwer,* Albrecht's
Ovid 177[b]. 345[a]; trûric als ein *unflaetec hûwe,* Renn. 17993.
The screech-owl, *kauz* or *käuzlein,* cries : ' Come along, come
along !' that's twice the *death-bird* has called to me, Kehrein's
Nassau 41 [To Russian children the owl cries *shubu,* (I'll have
your) fur-coat]. The same kind of thing is the *scuwût* on the
tree, Maerl. 2, 323. 348 and the *vöglein kreide-weiss* (chalk-
white), Musæus 5, 28.——The word *klag-mutter* reminds of
Berhta, of the white lady, the fylgja and the banshee, bansighe
(pp. 279. 280).   On the Wendish wailer, *God's little chair,* see
Wend. volksl. 2, 269[b]. Somm. p. 169. A death is foretold by
' la poule qui chante en coq,' Bosq. 219.   Other omens of death
are : When the *dead in churches* are seen or heard at night
by the living, it bodes a new event to these, esp. death : **quando-**

cunque a viventibus haec audiuntur vel videntur, *novum aliquid*
signat, Pertz 5, 738. The same if you hear a *grunting* or *sawing*
at night 5, 738-9; conf. deathwatch, next paragr.

p. 1136.] The wood-worm we call *todten-uhr* is termes pulsa-
torius, the Engl. *deathwatch* scarabæus galeatus pulsator, Hone's
Yrbk 823; ich hör ein würmlin *klopfen*, Garg. 278[b]; the death-
smith who *thumps* in window frames and walls, Gellert 3, 148.
Finn. *yumi* and *seinärautio*, wall-smith; conf. the tapping home-
sprites.

p. 1136.] *Swarms of bees* betoken a fire: molitasque examen
*apes* passimque crematas, perbacchata domos nullis *incendia*
causis, Claud. B. Get. 241. Bees that fasten on you, Aelian's
Var. 12, 40. Pliny 8, 42; bee-swarms and spiders, Bötticher's
Hell. temp. 127; ea hora tantae *aranearum telae* in medio populi
ceciderunt, ut omnes mirarentur; ac per hoc significatum est, quod
sordes hereticae pravitatis depulsae sint, Paul. diac. 6, 4. A
flight of *small birds*, a shoal of *salmon*, are a sign of *guests*,
Justinger 271. 379. The *alder-beetle* flying south is lucky, north
unlucky, Kalewipoeg, note on 2, 218.

p. 1137.] Other omens of death are *bloody weapons*, a *rustiny*
*knife*, KM. no. 60; but also *flowers*, Altd. w. 2, 187. Hpt 3,
364. *Corpse-candles*, mists in churchyards, prefigure a dead
body, Hone's Daybk 2, 1019; an expiring lamp is a sign of
death, Altd. w. 2, 186 (weather also was foretold by *divinatio ex*
*lucernis*, Apuleius ed. Ruhnk. lib. 2, p. 116). *Elmo's fire, Sant-*
*elmo, blawe liechter*, Staden's Reise p. 102; ûf dem maste dar
enboben [enhoben?] ein vackeln-licht so schône quam, Marienleg.
p. 87. A *crackling* flame may denote a blessing:

> Et succensa sacris *crepitet* bene *laurea flammis,*
> omine quo felix et sacer annus erit. Tibull. ii. 5, 82.

So to Kalmuks the *fizzing* of meat when roasting, and the *self-*
*lighting* of an extinguished fire, Klemm 3, 203; retulerunt quidam de ipso (abbate Sangallensi) agonizante, quod audierant
*voces plangentium* et *bullitionem caldariorum* (yr 1220).

The *room-door opens* of itself when there is a death, Lucae
260-9. When a board or shelf tips over, it is called *death-fall*,
Bair. kinderlehre 23. ON. *fall* er farar heill; in *lapsu* faustum
ominatus eventum, Saxo Gr. 73. On the other hand, *stumbling*,

the foot catching, is of ill-omen in Eurip. Heracl. 726 seq.; ter
*pedis offensi* signo est revocata, Ov. Met. 10, 452; sed, ut fieri
assolet, *sinistro pede* profectum me spes compendii frustrata est,
Apuleius p. m. 80. Getting up too early, wrongly, is fatal: si
wâren *ze vruo* des morgens *ûf-gestân*, die muosten dâ daz leben
lân (lose), Livl. 1255; sumelîch *ze vruo* hate des morgens *ûf-
gestân*, der muoste dâ ze pfande lân den lîp 3859.

p. 1137.] The notion that *several ears on one stalk* signify
peace, is apparently derived fr. the Bible, Gen. 41, 22; a stalk
*with* 15 *ears*, Weller's Anm. 1, 221. A double ear is Lett.
*yummis*, dim. *yummite*, Büttner 2818. Good hap or ill is fore-
seen by tying together two *ears of standing corn*, and seeing
which will shoot up higher, Dybeck '45, p. 52. Pilgrimages to
*Our Lady of the Three Ears*, Keisersb. Brösaml. 56[d].

p. 1138.] Things *found* are esp. operative for good or harm,
e.g. *four-cornered*, *four-leaved* clover, Simplic. 1, 334. L. Sax.
sagen no. 190; a *whole grain* in the loaf, Serenus samon. 935.
Things *inherited*, Müllenh. no. 315; *begged*, Wolf's Ndrl. sag.
p. 414; *worn* (pp. 602-3. 1093); rings made of *gibbet irons*, Luc.
Philops. 17. 24; fingers of a *babe unborn* (p. 1073 n.).

p. 1139.] Goth. *dagam vitáiþ* = dies observate, Gal. 4, 10.
Ἡμέρα μέλαινα, μὴ καθαρά, ἀποφράς (fr. φράζω), see Lucian's
Pseudologista (ἡ περὶ τῆς ἀποφράδος), conf. ed. Bip. 8, 434; so
ἀποφράδες πύλαι, Porta Scelerata 8, 58. Dies *fastus, nefastus,
nefandus, nefarius, infandus*, per quem nefas fari praetorem;
dies *inauspicatus, ater*. Henry IV. died on a Tuesday, *die
Martis*, qua etiam cuncta sua praelia, *paganico* nimirum *auspicio*,
perpetrare consuevit, Pertz 8, 240. Napoleon avoided *Fridays*,
Wieselgr. 473. AS. nellað heora þing wanian on *Monandæg* for
anginne þære wucan, AS. hom. 100.

p. 1140 n.] With *Wisantgang* conf. Wisantes-steiga, Wisantes
wanc (Neugart). Should we read *Wolf-bizo* (-bit), or *Wolf-bízo*
(-biter), like bären-beisser, bullen-beisser (-dog)? Cattle *killed
or bitten by wolves*, are wholesome fare, Spinnr. evang., Friday 9.
Gr. λυκόβρωτος, and Plutarch discusses 'why *wolf-eaten mutton* is
sweeter,' Symp. 2, 9. *Wolfleip* Graff 1, 850; *Wolfleibsch*, Kopp's
Gesch. d. Eidgen. 2, 557; *Wulflevinge*, Gosl. berggesetze p. 339;
Ulricus dictus *Wolfleipsch*, der *Wolfleipscho*, Ch. yrs 1260—65.
Neugart nos. 972. 981. 990-5; *lupi praeda*, Marcellus no. 53.

p. 1141.] Juvenes . . . missurum se esse, in quas *dii* de-
dissent *auguriis* sedes, ostendit, Livy 5, 34. The Hirpini were
led by the *wolf*, hirpus, the Picentini by the *pecker*, picus, the
Opici by the *bull*, ops ? Wackern. in Hpt 2, 559. Mommsen's
Röm. gesch. 1, 76. *Bull* and *sow* as guides, Klausen's Aen.
1107; *cows* indicate where a church is to be built, Wieselgr. 408;
*milch-cows* show the site of the future church, a black *bull* that
of the castle, Müllenh. p. 112-3; a *heifer* leads Cadmus to the
spot where he is to settle [two milch-kine bring the ark, 1 Sam.
6, 7].——The Franks are shown their way by the *Rune*, Guitecl.
2, 35; a *white hart* walks before them as God's messenger, Ogier
1, 12; and a Westphal. family-name *Rêasford* (Deeds in Möser)
points to a similar event. A Delaware climbed through the
mouth of an underground lake into daylight, killed a *stag* and
took it home, then the whole tribe moved to the sunny land,
Klemm 2, 159. A *horse* points out the place for a church, Müllenh.
p. 111-2. *Mules* show where the convent of Maulbronn in the
Black Forest is to be founded. A *hare* guides, Paus. iii. 22, 9.
——*Ravens* are indicators, Müllenh. p. 113; the three in the
Icelandic narrative, flying off one after another, strongly remind
us of Noah. The *dove* guides, Hrosvitha Gandesh. 253. 261—6.
A vision reveals that a *bird* sitting on the top of the hill will fly
up, and must be followed: it flies on before, then alights, and
pecks the ground on the spot where stones may be quarried to
build the church with, Pertz 6, 310; *doves* guide Aeneas to the
golden bough, Aen. 6, 191—211. The *lark*, Paus. iv. 34, 5; the
*clucking hen* at Bremen, Brem. sag. no. 1; the *heathcock* rising,
Schüren's Chron. p. 3; fribolum de *ansere* quasi dominam suam
deducente, Pertz 8, 215 yr 1096, conf. Raumer's First Crus. 1, 69.

p. 1144.] In a dike threatened by the sea a child is buried
alive, Müllenh. no. 331. Thiele in Danmarks folkes. 2, 63.
Honsdam in Flanders, V. d. Bergh 261 (Kl. schr. 2, 73). Fair
weather was obtained by walling up a *peck of barley* and a *bowl
of water*, Rocken-philos. 6, 88. A Königsberg story tells how
they took a fallen woman's child, a year and a half old, set it
down in a hollow stone, with a slice of bread-and-butter in each
hand, and then walled it in, leaving only an opening at the top;
in the morning the child was gone, but after that the building
of the wall went on unhindered, N. Preuss. prov. bl. 465. At a

place called the Nine-ways, as many boys and girls were buried alive by the Persians, Herod. 7, 114. Vortigern's tower keeps falling down : ye shall *wet* the foundation-stone with the *blood of a boy* born of woman without man, Merlin 1, 67. 72-5; under it lie two dragons, 1, 91; conf. Thib. de Navarre 2, 160. Like the girl inclosed in Copenhagen wall is the child who is set before a table with apples, and kept shut up in the cave for a year, Müllenh. p. 354.——It is an oft-recurring feature, that what is built in the day is pulled down in the night, as in the Bamberg legend of the cathedral toads, Balt. stud. 10, 32-4. Hanusch 186. Müllenh. pp. 112-3. 128. 177. 542; troll ned-refvo om nätterne hvad som byggdes om dagen, Wieselgr. p. 408; a wall is torn down 15 times, Somm. p. 9; much the same is told of the tower at Enger, Redeker's Sagen p. 41. 'Tradition says, that as fast as the workmen built it up by day, it would *at night* be carried off by invisible hands, and placed on the spot where it now stands' (a Devonshire leg.), Chambers's Pop. rhymes 14[a]. Conversely, a wall broken down by day grows again overnight, Müllenh. p. 349; conf. the tree that is cut down, and sprouts again (p. 960).

p. 1145.] O. Sl. *s"n"*, Serv. *san*, Russ. *son*, Pol. Boh. *sen*, Lith. *sapnas*, dream. Lith. *mègas*, Lett. *meegs*, Pruss. *maiggus*, somnus, Russ. *migáti*, wink. ON. *dûr* levis somnus, nubes somni; höfugr *blundr*, sopor, Sæm. 93[a]; er þer *svefn* höfugt? Laxd. 120. '*Troume sint trüge*' says the proverb in the Hätzlerin 126-7; *traum trug*, Frankl. 21. 46.——OHG. *troum-sceido*, *-sceidari*, -interpreter, lit. divider, Graff 6, 439; conf. ὑποκρίνασθαι, Od. 19, 535. 555; *iafnan* dreymir fyrir veðrum, Völs. saga c. 25, and dreams are still made to refer to rain. AS. *swefen-racu*, -interpretation, *swefen-raccere*, -expounder. Slav. *gadáti*, guess, somnia conjicere; Swed. *gissa* drömmen; 'elvens aldste datter' is to guess the dream, DV. 3, 4; nu hefi ek þyddan draum þinn, Gunnl. s. ormst. c. 2; den troum *betiuten* = deuten, MS. 2, 115[a]. Griesh. 1, 98; *ontbinden*, untie, Rose 6134; *conjectura*, Plaut. Rud. iii. 1, 20. Curc. ii. 1, 31.

p. 1146.] A dream *comes out*, *appears; rann up* en sömn, Sv. vis. 1, 299; wie der troum wolte *úzgên*, Griesh. 2, 133; der traum ist *aus*, Ayrer 177[d]. Fichard's Frankf. arch. 1, 130. There is a *gate* of dreams, Hpt 2, 535; ἐν ὀνειρείῃσι πύλῃσι,

Od. 4, 809 ; ἐν πύλαις ὀνειρείαις, Babr. 30, 8; conf. the myth in
Od. 19, 562—9. A dream-vision, ὄψις, comes repeatedly and
flies away, Herod. 7, 12. 14-5. 17-8-9. A dream appears,
Griesh. 1, 98. Flore 1102; *erscheine* mir'z ze guote, Reinh. 73;
hence ' einen troum er *gesach*,' Ksrchr. 5473, troum *irsehen* 2921.
AS. hine *gemétte*, there met him, he dreamt, Cædm. 223, 20 ;
*geméted* wearᵭ 225, 21 ; *assistit* capiti, Claud. De b. Gildon. 329 n.
——'Der troum *ergienc*,' came about, Ksrchr. 611 ; ' dîn troum
*irgê dir ze heile !* ' turn out well, 1373; we say ' comes true.'
Οὐκ ὄναρ, ἀλλ' ὕπαρ, not dream, but truth, Od. 19, 547. 20, 90 ;
ὕπαρ ἐξ ὀνείρου, Pindar; iwer troum wil sich *enden*, Flore 1117.
A dream is a messenger of God : sagde im an svefne, slâpandium
an naht, *bodo Drohtines*, Heliand 21, 12. Dreams are *heavy* and
*light :* stärke drömme, DV. 3, 3 ; ' ob iu nu *ringer* getroumet,'
milder, better, Ben. 438. A beautiful dream is *weidenlîche*, feasting the eye, Ls. 1, 131; *muowent* uns troume ? Ksrchr. 2948.——
Dreams of *birds* are esp. frequent : mir (Uote) ist getroumet
hînte (last night), wie allez daz *gefügele* in disme lande waere tôt,
Nib. 1449, 3. Vilk. c. 336; mir troumte hînte in dirre naht,
*zwên falken* vlugen mir ûf die hant, Morolt 2876 ; a dream of a
*raven* and an *eagle*, Orendel Ettm. p. 92, and the like in Gunnl.
s. ormst. c. 2. Fornald. sög. 1, 420. Penelope dreams of an
*eagle* killing her pet geese, Od. 19, 536 ; conf. Aesch. Persæ 205.
Darzuo müeze im von *eiern* (of eggs) sîn getroumet, i.e. bad
dreams, MS. 2, 152ᵇ; swer sich zuo lange wolde sûmen, deme
muoste von *eiern* troumen, Türl. Wh. 87ᵃ.——Dreams of *bear*
and *boar* hunting, Tit. 2877-8 ; of a *boar*, Krone 12157, a *dragon*,
Rab. 123-4. Dreaming of *beasts* may be traced to Guardian-
spirits and Transmigration, says F. Magn., Edda-l. 4, 146.
Dreams of a *tree growing up*, Ruodl. 16, 90, of a *shipwreck*, Krone
12225, a *burning house*, Lachm. Ndrrhein. ged. 18-9, a *bridge*,
Kl. schr. 3, 414, a *tooth falling out*, Keisersb. Bros. 48ᵃ; mir'st
getroumet *ab der guoten*, MS. 2, 115ᵃ.

    p. 1147.] ' Der *lôr-boum* habet tia natura, ube sîn ast (if a
branch of it) ûf'en slâfenten man geleget wirt, taz imo *wâr*
troumet,' he dreameth true, N. Cap. 13. The dream ' under a
tree ' in Mar. 155, 21 may be for rhyme's sake alone : ' als einem
man der da gelît, begrifen mit swârem troume, slâfend unter
einem boume,' conf. troum, boum, Wigal. 5808. A dream in a

*pigstye* comes true, Fornm. s. 10, 169. The first dream in a *new house* is important, Günther 640.——Night is descr. as *svefn-gaman, draum-niorun,* Sæm. 51ᵃ. Dreams before the *dawn* are true : Lenore starts up at dawn fr. heavy dreams; ' ir getroumde' at ' *tage-rât,*' after ' han-krât,' En. 5234; 'troumen *gein dem tage,*' towards day, Bit. 9630 ; 'in the *morning hour,* that is called the time of *golden* sleep,' Fastn. sp. 1302 ; mir troumde *nâch mitternacht,* wie mir der dûme swaere (that my thumb festered), und der nagel abe waere, Eracl. 3712; conf. ἐναργὲς ὄνειρον νυκτὸς ἀμολγῷ, Od. 4, 841. Lilia dreams on her *wedding-night,* Gesta reg. Francor. in Mone's Anz. 4, 15 ; der *erste traum* treugt nit, er pflegt wol wahr zu werden, C. Brehmen's Gedichte J 1ᵇ.

p. 1147.] On dreaming of a *treasure on the bridge,* see Kl. schr. 3, 414 seq. One is *waked out of a dream* by cry of dismal crow, Walth. 95, 1, by the crowing cock, the calling servant, Ls. 1, 149. Dô taget ez, und muos ich wachen, Walth. 75, 24: ende ic ontspranc, ende doe wart dach, Rose 14224 ; and with that I woke, Agricola 624, and after that it dawned 625 ; dô krâte der han, ez was tac, Altsw. 67, 3. To *speak out of a dream :* ich en-sprich ez niht *úz eime troume,* Parz. 782, 13 ; ir redet *úz eime troume,* Reinh. p. 202. He *fought* (in a dream), Lachm. Ndrrh. ged. p. 18-9.

---

# CHAPTER XXXVI.

## SICKNESSES.

p. 1150.] Apollo is called ἰατρό-μαντις, Aesch. Eumen. 62 ; Apollo *Grannus* was invoked by the sick, Stälin 1, 67. 112. Wise leeches were *Kasiapa,* Holtzm. 3, 164-5 ; *Iapis* Iasides, Aen. 12, 391 ; *Meges,* Μέγης, Forcell. sub v.; *Dianoecht,* Keller on Irish MSS. p. 93. The Greeks venerated the Scythian *Toxaris* after his death as ξένος ἰατρός, Lucian's Scytha 2 ; Ζαμόλξιδος ἰατροί, Plato's Charmides p. 156. The *grey smith* appears to the sick man in his sleep, and with his pincers pulls the nails and spear out of his hand, foot and side, Hpt's Ztschr. 1, 103. An *angel* reveals the remedy in a dream, Engelh. 5979. 5436; an *angel* visits the sleeper, and gives a willow-bough to stop the murrain, Müllenh. 238. *Saints* heal (p. 1163 end ; Pref. xxxviii.)

GDS. 149.——*Women* are often skilled in leechcraft: *Angitia*
instructs in herbs and healing, Klausen 1039. As Wate became
a leech through a *wildes wîp*, a herbalist traces his art up to
'*madame Trote de Salerne*, qui fait cuevre-chief de ses oreilles,
et li sorciz li penden a chaaines dargent par desus les epaules ';
she sends her men to all countries in search of herbs, 'en la
*forest* d'Ardanne por ocirre les bestes sauvages, et por traire les
oignemenz,' Rutebeuf 1, 256 (Another herbman calls himself
*hunter of Arden-wood* 1, 470). ' Unde communiter *Trotula*
vocata est, quasi *magistra operis ;* cum enim quaedam puella
debens incidi propter hujusmodi ventositatem, quasi ex ruptura
laborasset, cum eam vidisset *Trotula*, admirata fuit, etc.' Medici
antiqui (Venet. 1547) 75[a]; she is named in Chaucer's C.T. 6259.
Acc. to Jöcher she was a physician of Salerno, but the book De
morbis mulierum was written by a doctor who used her name.
——Othinus puts on female disguise, calls himself *Vecha*, and
passes for a she-doctor, Saxo Gram. ed. M. 128; conf. AS. *wicce*,
saga (p. 1033). *Three nymphs* prepare a healing strengthening
food for Balder, Saxo Gr. ed. M. 123 (vigoris epulum 194).
Queen *Erka* is a leech, Vilk. saga c. 277 ; and *Crescentia* is endowed with healing power (p. 1152). The *meer-frau* in the Abor,
like the Scotch mermaid, gathers the healing herb on a mountain,
Hpt. 5, 8. *Fâmurgân* knows herbs, makes plasters and salves,
Er. 5212. 7226. Iw. 3424. There was a leech named *Morgan
tud*, says L. Guest 3, 163; but that is the name of a healing plant
3, 164; conf. Ben. note to Iw. 3424. *Isôt*, diu künegîn von
Irlande, diu erkennet maneger hande *wurze* u. aller *kriute* kraft
u. arzâtlîche meisterchaft, Trist. 175, 32. The *wasser-jungfer*
knows healing herbs, Firmenich 1, 23 ; a *meer-weib* gives help in
childbed, Müllenh. p. 340. En gumma sade, hon kände väl de
*gamles skråck*, men trodde dem ej ; hon viste huru man kunde fâ
hjelp af dem, men att det var syndigt, Fries's Udfl. 1, 108. The
*wilde fräulein* knows the root that will heal a wound, Ecke 173—
5. At Staffelbach the *wood-maidens'* came out of the wood, and
cried to the people : ' esst bimellen und baldrian, so geht euch
die pest nicht an '; therefore at harvest a bunch is left standing
for the wood-mannikin. The *vila* of the woods is a lièkaritza,
and demands a heavy fee, she is angry if you refuse, and poisons
you, Vuk no. 321 ; conf. 2, 50 and the *pere-jungfer* with her

healing fountain, Alsatia '55, p. 216 (a place in Thuringia was called 'in süezer *heilinge*,' Graff 4, 867). The name of the Norse *Eir* reminds one of 'Ιρος, 'Ιρος 'Αιρος [so called because he carried messages], Od. 18, 6. 7. 73, and of 'Ιρις the divine messenger. To *Hyfja*-berg corresponds the Finn. *Kipu*-mäki, *Kipu*-vuori, *Kipu*-haria, mount of pain.——Women heal, they bind up wounds, Roquefort on Marie 2, 198—202 ; *frowen* die die tiefen wunden ir lieben vriunden bunden, Servat. 1779 ; do *sênten* (segenten, blessed) im die wunden die *frouwen* al ze hant, Rosen-g. 1997 ; dede si sine wonden wel besien ere jong-frouwen, diere vroet ane was, Lanc. 22651 ; a *virgin* knows 'der crude cracht,' power of herbs 11999 ; a *woman* gives a magic salve, Ecke 155-6. Herdsmen, shepherds can heal men, for they are expert in treating cattle, Varro RR. 2, 1. When a patient dies, his doctors are killed, Greg. Tur. 5, 35.

p. 1152.] A physician was in Fris. called *lêtze ;* ON. *líkna* ok *laekna*=lenire et mederi, Sæm. 236ª ; Gael. *liagh*, whence Leo in Malb. Gl. 1, viii. derives all the others ; Scot. *lighiche*, physician ; OHG. *láchituom*, medicine. AS. *from*, medicus, Matth. 9, 12 ; conf. OHG. *frumi* thaz wîb, heal the woman, O. iii. 10, 19, thia fruma neman 14, 50, fruma firstelan 14, 39. OHG. *grâvo*, chirurgus, Graff 4, 313 ; Fris. *grêva*, Richth. 786. MHG. *wîse man*, V. d. Hagen's Ges. Abent. 2, 121. On our *arzt, arznei*, see Graff 1, 477 ; *arzenare*, N. Boeth. 217 ; *arsatere*, medicos, Lanc. 42631, *ersatre* von wonden 1988 ; *arzatinne*, Trist. 33, 38 (what is *diet-arzt*, Garg. 72ª ?) ; *arza-díe*, Ksrchr. 7483-93 ; *erzenîe*, Wh. 60, 23.——Leo in Malb. Gl. 2, 38 derives OHG. *luppi* from Gael. *luibh*, herba ; si machent ûz krût ein *gestüppe* (pulverem), daz ist guot ze der *lüppe*, Hätzl. 217ª : Swed. *löfja*, läka ; *löfjor*, medicamenta ; *löfjerska*, vis qvinna, Almqv. 390 ; *lublerin*, venefica, Mone 7, 424. Diu zouuerlicha *hant*, herbipotens manus, N. Boeth. 197 ; diu *chriuter* unde diu *gift-hant* der Circe 198 ; *hant-gift*, Mone 7, 423-4. Tit. 4518 ; so gloubent eteliche an boese *hantgift*, Berth. 58 ; der Saelden h., Silv. 534 ; edel *h.* geben, Troj. 11188 ; sûre *h.* 25043 ; dats goede *hantgifte*, Rein. 6906 ; elsewhere *hantgift* is strena, étrenne ; leidiu *h.*, Troj. 12334. The Lex Salica 19 says : si quis alteri *herbas dederit bibere*, ut moriatur. The sense of 'poison' is evolved out of each of these three words, from *herba* (lubi ?), from *dare* (gift), from *bibere* (potio) ; for potio, liter. a drink, has become the Fr. *poison*; conf. 'à *enherber* (to poison) m'aprist jadis une Juise,' Berte p. 103. Ducange sub v. *inherbare.*——A herbman or quack was called in Bavaria *wald-hansl, wald-mann*, Schm. 4, 63-4; *würzler* umb Bingen, Garg. 172ᵇ, *krautnirer* 188ᵇ, teufels-gerittene *wurzel-telberin*, abgeribene *kraut-graserin* 189ᵃ, *alraun-delberin* 104ᵃ. '*Swiss women* get their 100 *herbs* on *Donnersberg* in the Palatinate, said they were stronger there than in Swiss-land,' Eliz. of Orleans p. 283 ; ich waiz ain *mairin*, diu vil mit dem kraut würkt, Megenb. 386, 32. *Old wives* pick *herbs* on John's day betw. 12 and 1, for then only have they power ; with the stroke of 1 it is gone ; they grow on Pilgerberg alone, Müllenh. p. 222. *Krût tempern*, Hartm. büchl. 1, 1307. Troj. 10635; ein *temperie* als wir *gemischet* nemen, Wh. 420, 2 ; luft *tempern* u. *mischen*, MS. 1, 87ᵃ. Another verb is OHG. *lochôn*, prop. mulcere, fovere : ir eigut siuchi *gilokôt*, O. v. 20, 76 ; conf. ἰάομαι, ἰαίνω, fovere, orig. said of wounds.

    p. 1152.] Our kropf (goitre ?) is called *king's evil*, because it was cured by the king's touch ; 'those who have it, on *drinking* from the Count of Habsburg's *hand*, are made whole,' Reber's Hemmerlin p. 240. Schimpf u. E. 1, 27. It seems a *godfather* could cure his godchild of some diseases : ' *godfather* and *foal's tooth* in urgent cases are too weak ' (p. 658 n.). Among American Indians the knowledge of healing herbs descends from father to son, Klemm 2, 169 ; the family of Diokles can cure disease and disablement, Paus. iv. 30, 2. Health is regained by touching the *hem*, also by *magic song* : Serv. *bayati*, incantare morbum, dolorem. To feel the pulse is in MHG. *die âdern begrî-fen*, MS. 2, 23ᵇ ; conf. *ein âdern grîfen*, Reinh. 2018 ; si *marhte* mit dem vinger sîn *âder-slân* (throbbing), Eracl. 3033 ; der *kraft-âdern slac*, Barl. 188, 22.

    p. 1153.] 'Nomina morborum vernacula' in J. Fr. Löw ab Erlesfeld's Univ. medicina pract., Norimb. 1724. Sickness is *siuche*, Uolr. 1038. 1109. En. 10833 ; MLG. *suke ;* MHG. *siechtuom*, diu *suht*, Fundgr. 2, 46 ; *gesühte*, Warn. 2192 ; siech von *ungesühte*, Walth. 20, 4. Fragm. 46ᵇ ; *ersochte*, Hpt 8, 167 ; *werlt-siech*, En. 12908 ; die *siechen* u. die *weichen*, G. schm. 494, conf. ON. *veikr*, infirmus. *veiki* infirmitas, AS. *wâc*, Engl. *weak*. *Siec* ende *ongedaen*, Lanc. 15338. *Unmahti*, invaletudines, O. iii.

5, 2, *unmahti*, infirmi 9, 5; OHG. *ni mıc ni touc*, non valet;
MHG. *niht en-mac*, aegrotel, Hagen's Ges. Ab. 3, 63; daz ich
nie *ne mac*, Ksrchr. 821; *ungewalt*, invaletudo, En. 10230-551;
Slav. *ne-dúg*, morbus; Boh. *ne-mósh*, Russ. *ne-mótch*, infirmitas.
*Unvarnde*, aeger, Türl. Wh. 60ᵇ.—— The contrary: *wolvarnde*
u. gesunt, Iw. 3430. OHG. *kisúnt*, MHG. *gesúnt*, M. Neth.
*gesónt* (sound, well), hence *ungesunt*, Poor Heinr. 375. *Unganzî*,
infirmitas, O. iii. 4, 34, *ganz*, integer, 2, 22. 32; M. Neth. *gans*,
whole, *gansen*, to heal, Maerl. 1, 313. 2, 359. Jesus p. 136;
*genesen*, and *gansen* side by side, Maerl. 1, 313. The grand word
for sanus is Goth. *háils*, OHG. *heil*, ON. *heill*, OS. *hêl*, AS. *hál*,
Engl. *whole*; sanari is Goth. *háils visan, gaháilnan*, while salvari
is Goth. OHG. *ganisan*, AS. *genesan* with Acc. (p. 1244 n.).——
' Ghenesen ende *becomen*,' Maerl. 3, 97; OHG. *chúmig*, infirmus,
*chúmida*, morbus. M. Neth. *evel*, our *übel* [so, king's *evil*]. AS.
*ádl* ne yldo, Beow. 3469, from *ád*, fire, heat? (Suppl. to 1166
end); *ádl* oððe îren 3692; *ádl* oððe ecg 3523; *ádlig*, aeger.
Dan. *uminden, umänen*, an indefinite disease, Molb. Dial. lex.
p. 630, conf. ON. *ómynd*, monstrum, forma laesa. What means
' lâgi *dawalônti*,' O. iii. 2, 7, moriens? (Graff 5, 346). Dole ich
diz *gebénde*, Ksrchr. 12704; conf. ON. *afbendi*, tenesmus, Dan.
*bindsel*, constipation.——More general are OHG. *suerido*=suero;
*ouc-suero, maga-suero*, Graff 6, 888. OHG. *wêwo*, woe, pain;
manegen *wên* vertreip, Servat. 1077. AS. *ece*, ache, *tóð-ece*.
AS. *coð, coðe*, morbus, pestis; *bân-coða*, m., Cod. Exon. 163, 23.
MHG. ' er *lent*,' he is laid up, Parz. 251, 16; die *geligrigen*,
infirmi, Mohr's Reg. Frauenb. nos. 328. 235; die suht *ligen*,
Hpt 4, 296. Gramm. 4, 620; mi *legar* bifêng, Hel. 135, 12;
*legar-fast* 121, 16; *bette-rise, ligerlinc*, Griesh. 116. 124; *bet-rise*,
Urstende 123, 69. Servat. 3180 (is *pet-ritto* in the Strasb. spell
the same thing?); an *rese-bette* ligen, St. Louis 90, 13; le *gisant*,
jacens, Lafont. 5, 12; conf. ' sô *stüende* ich *úf* von dirre nôt, u.
waere iemer mê gesunt, Walth. 54, 9. Peculiar is OHG. *winnen*,
furere, laborare morbo, *gewinnen* (the fever), conf. ON. *vinna*.
In Cassel they say *aufstützig* for ill: ein pferd *aufstützig* worden,
Cav. im irgarten 53.

p. 1154.] Sickness appears as a *divine dispensation* in νοῦσος
Διός, Od. 9, 411; ir wâre diu suht *gescehen*, Fundgr. 2, 46. Sickness seizes: ἄῤῥωστος is infirmus; our *an-gegriffen*; mich hât

ein siech-tage *begriffen,* Diocl. 6016; in *ergreif* diu misel-suht,
Poor Heinr. 119; *angriffen* von einem boesen wind, von einem
teufels kind, Mone 6, 470; gesuhte *bestêt* uns (tackles us), Hpt
1, 272; dô begunde ein suche *râmen* der vrowen, Pass. K. 425,
20; *wærc ingewôd,* morbus invasit, Cod. Exon. 163, 29; him
færinga âdl *ingewôd* 158, 21. Our *anfall* (attack), morbus;
*anvellig,* infectious, Mone 8, 499. Goth. ' vas *ana-habaida* brinnôn
mikilai,' Luke 4, 38; da wolt' mich hân *ergrummen,* ich *weiz niht
waz,* Hugdietr. Fromm. 146; in *stiez an* einiu kelte, Fragm. 19[b];
in Mecklenbg, if a man is taken ill at harvest time, they say
' the harvest-goat has *gestoszen* (butted at) him '; den hete der
siechtuom sô *begint* (rhy. kint), Uolr. 1523.——The contrary:
den siechtuom *überwinden* (win over), Wigal. 5991; unz der
siechtuom vom im *flôch,* Hpt 5, 278; diu suht *entweich* (ran
away) 8, 188. Iw. 3446; sô muozen dir *intwîchen* dîne suhte,
Ksrchr. 838; daz gesüht begund in *fliehen,* Ecke 176; diu suht
von ime *flôz,* Diemer 325, 7.——The *νοῦσοι* approach men *αὐτό-
ματοι,* and *σιγῇ, ἐπεὶ φωνὴν ἐξείλετο μητίετα Ζεύς,* Hes. Opp.
102. Mulierculae plures . . . . a *daemoniis vexantur* (yr 1075),
Pertz 5, 128. The witch cooks, brews diseases; so does the
Finn. *Kivutar* (Suppl. to 1046); she is called ' kipiä neito,'
Schröter 34, ' kipu tyltö, kipulan näto,' Peterson 75, ' kipunen
eukko,' Kalev. 25, 96. 179; worrying grey *dogs* howl around her,
Pet. 74; she wears gloves and shoes of pain, Kal. 25, 183-4. In
Lith. they say ' ligga ne *sessû,*' the sickness is no sister, does not
spare.

p. 1155.] *Febris* for fervebris, ferbris; Gael. *fiabhar;* MHG.
*biever,* Freid. 74, 9. *Dea Febris,* Aug. Civ. D. 2, 14. 3, 12. 25.
AS. *âdl* þearl, *hât* and heorogrim, Cod. Exon. 160, 30; bân-
cofa *âdle on-æled* 159, 15; *âdl* me innan *æle* 166, 5; conf. Gael.
*teasach,* febris, fr. *teas,* calor, fervor. Dei heizen fieber *lascht* er
dô (he leashes them?), Diem. 325, 5; *sôttar brîmi,* morbi aestus,
Egilss. 637. Hippocrates often has *πῦρ* for *πυρετός : παρθένον
πῦρ ἔλαβε* 3, 6 (*γυναῖκα ῥῖγος ἔλαβε* 1, 5).——The OHG. *rito* is
Norw. *rid,* Aasen 379[b]; are we to conn. it with ON. *hrîð,* procella? Lye too, by the side of *rideroð,* febris, gives *hrið-âdl,
hrîðing,* febris, *hrîðian,* febricitare; conf. ' in bestuont der minne
schûr,'* Parz. 587, 13, and Herbort 12836 calls the minne an
*elbisch viure : Riten* winnanti, febre laborans, Graff 1, 876; *rite*

‚iouh *fieber,* Diut. 3, 45 ; der *rittige,* febricitans, Griesh. 115 ; sô
hat ir êre den *riden,* Hpt 1, 437. M. Neth. *rede* and *redine,*
Mone's Ndrl. lit. 335. Belg. mus. 10, 52 ; bevaen met enen *rede,*
Maerl. 3, 188. 168. 237-8 ; viel in den *r.* 3, 269 ; quam mi an de
*r.* 3, 78 ; hadde enen groten *r.* 2, 79 ; genasen van den *r.,* Hpt.
1, 104 : den vierden *r.* (febr. quartan.), Franc. 2882. Nu muze
der *leide ride* Fukarde vellen ! Karlm. Lachm. 110 ; schütte in
der *rite !* Pass. 45, 32 ; habe den *riden* u. die *suht* umb dînen
hals ! Morolf 715 ; das sie der *jar-rit* schüt ! Garg. 242ᵃ ; die
*corts ridene !* Walew. 6164 ; conf. Gl. to Lekensp. p. 573 ; das
dich gê der *schütler* an ! H. Sachs iii. 3, 8ᵈ ; kam sie an der
*frorer,* Altd. bl. 1, 56 ; ' break the *neck* of the fever,' Ettn. Unw.
d. 792. Fever rides a man, as poverty does, H. Sachs i. 3, 245ᶜ.
——In Boner's fable the *rite* is made a butterfly (= alp, nightmare), no doubt, that he may the better converse with the flea ;
conf. Fastn. 36, 55. Keller's Erz. 330. Like Petrarch, H. Sachs
i. 483 has a dialogue betw. the *zipperlein* (gout) and the *spider*
(Kl. schr. 5, 400 seq.). The spell in Bodm. Rheing. alt. p. 710
speaks of ' 72 *riten* ' ; that in Mone 7, 421 of ' 77 *ritten* ' ; Kulda
132 of ' 99 fevers.'——Other names for fever : M. Neth. *koorts,*
febris, *saghe,* Rein. 391. AS. *gedrif ; drif.* MHG. der *begir ?*
Flore 1005 ; to die of a *schlirige* fever, Garg. 241ᵃ, conf. *schlir,*
ulcer 259ᵃ, *schlir-geschwür* 236ᵇ. At Louvain fever is called *quade*
*méster.* OHG. *it-slac,* febr. recidiva, Graff 6, 773, *it-slaht* 777 ;
*avar-sturz,* relapse ; conf. ' modica *pulsatus* febre,' Greg. Tur. 2,
5. ' *Winter* und *sumer* ' are a disease (cold and hot fits of ague
alternating ?), St. Louis (Rückert) 59, 28. 80, 21. Lat. *quer-*
*quera,* shivering fit. MHG. *quartanie,* febr. quart., MSH. 3,
178ᵇ ; *kartanie,* Wartb. kr. str. 51. Gr. ἠπίαλος, Luc. Philops.
19. In O. Fr. they said ' trembler la fièvre,' Méon 3, 88. Rutebeuf 1, 290. Rénart 10150. Lith. *paszta-kielě,* fever-bird (kielě,
siskin). Lett. *drudsis* vinnu yahi, fever rides him, Bergm. 68.
Der *rôte suche,* Myst. 1, 104. *Flores beatae Mariae,* erysipelas,
Ducange sub v. flores ; Ital. rosalia.

p. 1156.] Gout, OHG. *giht, fargiht,* Graff 4, 142 ; vor zorne
si daz *giht* brach, Mai 69, 2 ; daz mich diu *giht* zubrochin hât,
Ksrchr. 2776. 4293, conf. ' die alten dô der huoste (cough) brach,
V. d. Hag. Ges. Ab. 2, 290 ; swen negt (whom gnaws) daz *giht,*
Renn. 9897 ; swie daz *giht* in stunge, Helb. 1, 70 ; dâ ist si

müende daz *gegihte,* Ulr. Trist. 1512; in die *gichter* fallen, Eliz.
of Orl. 41 ; *vergiht,* Tôdes geh. 548. Servat. 728. 786. 1573. Hpt
6, 493.    Austr. ' kalt *vergicht,*' arthritis vaga ; *icht,* Hpt 1, 104.
Nethl. *jicht ;* die *jôcte,* Maerl. 2, 79 ; *juchtech,* paralyticus 2, 112.
317. 338; do vil em dat *jodute* in de been, Detm. 2, 482 ; is this
gout or terror ? (the *huk,* angina uvularis, is allayed by the spell :
' *Hode-joduth !* I cannot gulp the pot-hook down,' Lisch's Meckl.
jrb. 6, 191 ; the *hetsch,* or the *keller-gschoss* bumps against me,
H. Sachs iv. 3, 76ᶜ ; den *heschen* gewinnen, Suchenw. 18, 238 ;
*hesche* schlucken) ; unz in dô sluoc daz podagra, Ksrchr. 5854.
ON. *ökla-eldr,* Fornm. s. 3, 200 ; AS. *ecilma, œcelma,* podagra,
*deaggede, deag-wyrmede,* podagricus, *deaw-wyrm,* podagra.  *Ko-
synþies,* petits cousins, Belg. mus. 8, 183.   Boh. *dna,* gout ; Pol.
*dma,* prop. blast, breathing upon.

    p. 1157, line 6, a short paragr. was omitted from the text, viz. :
" A burning tumour at the finger-nail (παρωνυχίς) is called the
*worm,* the *runabout worm,* the *unnamed* (bec. one was shy of
uttering the creature's name), the *evil thing ;* Engl. *ringworm*
[mistake for whitlow ?], Scot. *ringwood,* for which R. Chambers
quotes two spells (see Suppl.)."]    The flying gout travels : fon
*farendum* and fon *fretma,* Richth. 246, 14.    Daz *wilde viure,* ignis
sacer, is called *Antonien feuer, Antoni feuer,* Ettn. Unw. d. 136-7,
*Tönges-feuer* (Tony's f.), Fischart, *Antonien rach, plag,* erysipelas,
skin-inflammation ; bec. the Saint and his monks received such
patients into their hospital ? conf. Keisersb. Omeiss 52.    AS.
*bân-coðe,* ossium morbus, ignis sacer.   Gothl. *flaug-ild,* erysip. on
the face, Almqv. 423ª, conf. ON. *flog.*   M. Neth. de *rode guchte,*
Maerl. 2, 290, gutta rosea ; now *roze drup,* our *roth-lauf,* St.
A.'s fire.——Typhus carbuncularis acutissimus is called *landslip,
devil's shot.* ' Of sacred fire are several kinds : one about a
man's waist is called *zoster* (girdle), and kills if it *begirdle* him,'
Pliny 25, 11 (26, 74).    For this gout we find the names *mane-
wurm, hâr-wurm,* Fundgr. 2, 238.   The name of *gichter* (gouts)
is also given to cramps and spasms, Stald. 1, 443.    A tumour
at the finger-nail is in Plattd. *fit* [*whit-low,* white fire ?], der
*ungenannt wurm,* Mone 6, 462 ; AS. *wyrm,* see Gramm. 1, 416
ang-nägle, ongneil ; die *ungenannten,* Stald. 2, 423 ; *bös thier* 1,
207.    Elves suck at children's fingers and toes by night, Dyb.
Runa '48, p. 33.

p. 1157.] Apoplexy is in Grk πληγὴ θεοῦ. Lith. stábas. Got gebe den heiden sînen *slac!* Livl. chr. 5220; het *sloghene Gods plaghe,* Maerl. 2, 348; plag di de *röring!* Müllenh. p. 191; daz *berlin* (fr. bern, to strike?); der *tropf,* Karaj. Kl. denkm. 46, 14. 51, 4; das dich die *drüs* (glanders) rür! H. Sachs v. 364ᶜ; hab dir *drüs* u. das herzeleid! v. 367; hab dir die *drüs* in's herz hinein! v. 344ᵃ: conf. *dros* (p. 1003 mid.).

p. 1158.] Epilepsy: diu *vallunde suht,* Servat. 1572. Uolr. 1092. Ksrchr. 6491; diu *vallende suht* brach, Hpt 8, 185; fanra lerha *fallanda ewele,* Richth. 246; dat *grote evel,* Hpt 1, 104; das *höchste,* Ettn. Maul. 307. On the Rhön Mts, das *arm werk,* Schm. 4, 139. Slovèn. *svetiga Bálanta bolézen,* St. Valentine's evil. Lith. *nûmirrulis,* falling sickness. In the Wetterau, das *thun.* Austr. die *frais,* whence Serv. *vras.* OHG. *winnanti,* epilepticus, Graff 1, 876. Das dich der *tropf* schlag! Fischart. Nethl. *drop, drup, marks-tropf,* Mone 6, 470. Icel. *flog* (Suppl. to 1234).——*Goute* ne *avertinz,* Rutebeuf 1, 257; *avertin de chief* 1, 471; *male goute* les eulz li crieve (put out his eyes)! Trist. 1919. Ren. 1702; *male gote* te crieve loil! Ren. 21198. 25268; la male gote aiez as dens! 14322. Ducange sub v. gutta quotes many kinds; *avertin, esvertin,* Méon 1, 391. OHG. *mánóthuílíno,* moon-sick, lunaticus, Graff 1, 443 (out of its place). Concidere ad lunae incrementa, καταπίπτειν πρὸς τὴν σελήνην, Lucian's Toxar. 24. Nasci=lentigo, Graff 2, 1105. As there are 77 nöschen, so '77 sorts of zahn-rosen,' Hpt 4, 390; '77 shot and 77 plagues,' Superst. spell xxxix.; '77 worms,' Mone 6, 462; *siben suhte* darzuo nemen, Kschr. 6076, wielde 6095. What is the *unnamed disease?* Mone's Schausp. 2, 373.

Our ohn-macht, fainting fit, is called *un-maht,* Er. 8825. Roth. 3015; si kam in *unmaht,* Flore 1055, vor *unm.* si nider-seic (sank) 1223; in *unm.* vallen, Reinh. 593; OHG. mir *unmahtet,* N. Boeth. 131; si vielen in *unkraft,* Kl. 1562; haer begaven *al die lede,* so dat si in *onmacht sêch,* Karel 1, 128; *therte* begaf haer alte male, so dat si *sêch* in *ommacht* 1, 241; viel in *onmaht,* Lanc. 17215; viel in *ommacht,* Maerl. 2, 222; von *âmaht* si niderseic, Flore 1224; si kam in *âm.* 1230; diu *âm.* vaste mit im ranc (wrestled hard), Hpt 5, 277; *âm.,* Engelh. 6303; zwô *âmehte* si enpfienc, Gute frau 1650; *abkraft,* H. Sachs v. 349ᵇ.——Viel in *marmels,* Troj. 10742; *marmels* hingeleit, Oberl. de Conr. herbip.

52. Si lâgen in *unsinne*, Kl. 1978. 1566-71 ; vergaz der *sinne*
1563 ; dô verlôs ich alle mîne *sinne*, MSH. 3, 207ᵇ; *unversunnen*
lac, Kl. 2092. Wh. 46, 27. 61, 19; si viel hin *unversunnen*,
Parz. 105, 8. Se pâmer, pasmer, Ferabr. 2801, se plasmet 3640,
plasmage 2962. We say, my *senses* forsook me ; *animus* hanc
reliquerat, Plaut. Mil. gl. iv. 8, 37. Si lac in einem *twalme*, Er.
6593 ; daz im vor den ougen sînen *vergie* (passed away) *sunne*
unde *tac*, Laurin Ettm. 829 ; er viel vor leide in unmaht, er-n'
weste ob ez waere *tac* oder *nacht*,Reinh. 595. Sendschreiben p. 53;
er was *úz siner gewalt*, Herb. 10500, conf. 10604.——Mir *ge-
swindet*, Gramm. 4, 231 ; daz ir *geswand*, Schreiber 2, 64 ; ir was
*geswunden*, Fragm. 42ᵇ ; im *geswant*, Flore 2178. 2241; *swinden*,
Jüngl. 656. *Beschweimen :* AS. *swima*, deliquium, Engl. *swoon ;
heáfod-swima*, my *head swims*. Wan in daz houbet diuzet von
gesühte, Warn. 2192 ; ime *entsweich*, Reinh. 564 ; *beswalt*,
Partonop. 18, 13. 34, 14; *ontmaect*, Lanc. 12042.——The contrary : er *kam zuo sih*, Flore 1066, *zuo ir selber kam* 1232.
Schreiber 2, 64; *zuo im selben quam*, Gr. Rud. Hᵇ 13 ; *zuo ime
selvin bequam*, Roth. 3035, conf. Lanz. 1747 ; *biz er bequam*,
Wigal. 5796 ; doe hi *bequam*, Maerl. 2, 222. Lanc. 17216 ; was
*vercomen weder*, Karel 1, 158; sîn *herze im widertrat*, Pass. 192,
65; *herze gewinnen*, Servat. 3431; sich *versinnen*, Parz. 109, 18.
Wh. 61, 29 ; sich widere *versan*, Er. 8836 ; er wart *verriht*,
Flore 2230, *kam ze gerechen* 2231; do si *wart ze witzen*, Kschr.
11925. Our 'bei sich sein'; sumne ego *apud me ?* Plaut. M.G.
iv. 8, 36.

p. 1159.] ON. *qveisa*, colica, conf. Goth. *qaisv*, ὠδίς (Suppl. to
1212 end ; *grimme muoter*, Mone 8, 495 ; *bärmuter*, Garg. 182ᵇ,
*bärvatter* 69ᵇ; *wärwund*, Stald. 2, 435. Dysentery, der *rôte suche*,
Myst. 1, 105 ; er gewan den *durchgang*, Diocl. 4645 ; Nethl.
*roode-loop*, dysent. (not our roth-lauf). On *úzsuht*, see Gramm.
2, 794; der *rothe schaden*, Stald. 2, 306. Gotthelf's Sag. 5,
160-1 ; M. Neth. *menisoene, melisoene*, Maerl. 3, 177 ; O. Fr.
*menoison*. Lung disease : daz *swinde ?* Myst. 1, 104. Schm. 3,
539; OHG. *serwên*, tabescere, Graff 6, 271. 281 ; Swiss *serbet*,
Stald. 2, 371 ; *schwienig*, Vonbun in Wolf's Zts. 2, 54 ; *swin-
segen*, Mone 6, 461 ; *schwîn, schwein ; verzehrendes wesen*, consumption, Leipz. avant. 1, 142.

Stitch in the side, pleurisy : ON. *tac*, OS. *stechetho*, Hpt. 5,

200. Our *darm-winde* (twisting of bowels), conf. Lith. klynas, iliaca passio; *miserere*.

Dropsy : Swed. *månads-kalf, mån-kalf*, conf. the story of the 'frater Salernitanus,' Aegid. de medic. p. 167.

p. 1159.] Abortus : ON. *konnuni leystiz höfn*, foetus solvebatur, abortum fecit; Bavar. *hinschlingen* is said of a cow, Schm. 3, 452 ; die frau hat mit dem fünften kinde *umgeworfen*, Claudius in Herder's Remains 1, 423. Goth. *fitan*, our kreissen, to have throes : *zimbern*, parturire, Hag. Ges. Ab. 1, 12. Throes are called ὠδῖνες or βολαί, throws of Artemis, Procop. 2, 576 (Suppl. to 1177 mid.). 'To give birth to' we express by 'come down with, bring into the world,' or simply *bring*, Schweinichen 1, 38 ; Swiss *trohlen, trollen, zerfallen*, fall in pieces (come in two), Stald. 1, 307 ; MHG. *ze kemenâten gân*, Hugd. 107. Mar. 163, 22 ; ON. at *hvíla*, Vilk. sag. c. 31 ; die frau soll zu stuhl [Exod. 1, 16]. Es fieng an zu *krachen*, Garg. 102[b] ; die *balken knackten* schon, da *fiel* das ganze *haus*, C. Brehmen's Ged. (Lpz. 1637) H 3[a]. J 3[b] ; conf. O. Fris. *bênene burch*, bone castle (womb), Richth. 623[b] ; *fallen* und *in zwei stück brechen*, Dict. sub v. frauenbauch ; se is *dalbraken*, broken down, Schütze's Holst. id. 1, 196 ; glückliche *niederbrechung*, safe delivery, Claudius in Herd. Rem. 1, 383 ; si ist *entbunden* von ir nôt, Mai 129, 2. *Schütten, werfen*, used of animals.

p. 1160.] If the newborn infant cries, it has the *heart-disease*, and is passed three times between the rungs of a ladder, Temme's Altmark p. 82 ; *blatt* und *gesper, blatt* u. *herzen-gesper*, Mone 6, 468-9 ; ir tuo daz *herze* vil wê, Hag. Ges. Ab. 2, 178 ; der *klam*, Kolocz. 185, angina ? fr. klemmen, to pinch. ' Der *herz-wurm* hat sich beseicht' of cardialgy and nausea ; stories of the *heart-worm* in Frisch 447[b]. Ettn. Hebamme 890. O'Kearney 180. A Stockholm MS. informs us : ' Wannen ein vrowe entfangen hevet, so pleget gemeinliken bi der vrucht to wassene (grow) ein *worm*, dei hevet vlogele alse ein vledermues (bat) unde einen snavel as ein vogel, unde dei worme wesset op mit (der) vruht ; unde wan dei vrowe geberet hevet, al-to-hant over cleine dagen stiget (climbs) *hei op to deme herten* der vrowen, unde dan to lesten so hellet (holds) hei der vrowen herte, also wan men menit dat dei vrowe genesen si, so stervet dei vrowe rokelose, dat men nicht en-weit wat er schellet (ails her).' If expelled with the fœtus :

' dei *oppe deme assche wesset*, dei vrucht heit gemeinliken *kutten-slotel*.'——Si viennent li *ver* ès cors, qui montent jusquau cuer, et font morir d'une maladie c'on apele *mort-sobitainne*, Ruteb. 1, 257. ' Grew in his heart the *zage-wurm*,' shrink-worm, Burc. Waldis 174ª; die *wurme* ezzent uns daz *herze*, Diemer 290, 10; the miser's *heart-worm*, Festiv. of Conan 180.——*Bulimus*, vermis lacertae in stomacho hominis habitans, Oehler's AS. gl. p. 276; bulimus, *werna*, Diut. 168. *Wurme* wuohsen in ime houbet (in their heads), Kschr. 715. 852; ' the *worm* in man or beast, that we call *faztun* (?),' Mone 8, 406.

Toothache, MHG. *zan-swer*, Freid. 74, 10 (Kl. schr. 2, 115). Headache caused by cross black elves, Hpt 4, 389. Spasms in head and breast with cough are called *tane-weczel*, J. Lindenbl. p. 167 (yr 1404), conf. *bauer-wetzel*, Gr. βήξ. *Tana-weschel* is personified in Fastn. sp. 468. ON. *qvef*, cough, cold in head. In the Wetterau: *krammel* im hals, rasping in throat; *woul*, violent catarrh, conf. OHG. *wuol* (1181-2).

p. 1160.] *Gelesuht* u. *fich*, Diut. 3, 45. Marcellus no. 100; *fik* in the chest, Mone 8, 493; bleeding, running *vig* 8, 409. ON. *gula*, morbus regius, jaundice; morbo regio *croceus* effectus, Greg. Tur. 5, 4.——MHG. *misel-suht*, Servat. 728. 1570; *musilsuht*, Ksrchr. 4293; hiez (bade) die misels. *abe-gân* 726. 4067; *misel-siech*, Urst. 123, 69. ON. *lík-þrâ*, lepra, Fornald. s. 3, 642. Biörgyn p. 107; *líkþrár*, leprosus. M. Neth. *packers*, leprosus, Maerl. 2, 227; *lasers*, *lazers*, Kausler's Altn. denkm. 1, 482-3; OHG. *horngibruoder*, leprosi, Graff 3, 301; MHG. *made villic*, *made-wellic*, *aissel-villic*, Myst. 1, 418; O. Slav. *prokaza*, lepra, Miklos. 34; Gael. *lobharach*, *muireach*, leprosus. The Lex Roth. 180 has 'leprosus aut daemoniacus,' and 233 ' mancipium lepr. aut daem.'——The Sl. *trud* is in Jungm. tetter, ringworm, in Miklos. 94 dysenteria, hydropisis. OHG. *hrub*, scabies, conf. Graff 4, 1155; AS. *hruf*, ON. *hrufa*. *Citir-lús* vel *rúdigê*, Gl. Sletst. 25, 169; *citaroh*, Graff 4, 1155; *tetra-fic*, Hattemer 1, 262ᵇ; *zetern*, flechte, Hpt 4, 390; AS. *teter*, Engl. *tetter*, impetigo; Austr. *zitterich*. Gr. λειχήν impetigo, Sl. *lishái*, Serv. *litai*. A kind of itch is in Austr. *bam-hakl*, woodpecker. ——ON. *skyrbiugr*, Dan. *skjörbug*; schorbock, Garg. 149ª; *schar-bock*, *scorbut*, scorbutus. AS. *þeor* on fêt, in eágum. The *burzel* is a contagious disease, Augsb. chr., yr 1387. Mone 6, 257;

*bürzel, gunbürzel,* Frisch 1, 157. 383. Sl. *kratel,* an ailment that makes one leg shorter, Vuk sub v.; MHG. ir bein (legs) diu habent die *müchen,* Frauenl. p. 192, our *mauke,* malanders, Frisch. A bleeding boil is called *hund schüttler,* Panzer 2, 305; daz yn daz *knallen-ubel* angee! Fries's Pfeiferger. p. 118 (yr 1388).

p. 1160.] Entré sui en *mal an,* Aspr. 15ᵃ.

p. 1163.] Smallpox: Serv. *kraste.* Die blattern (pocks) fahren auf, Lpz. avant. 1, 271. *Urschlechten, urschlichten blattern,* conf. urslaht, Gramm. 2, 790.——The story of a *daemonium meridianum* is told by Cæs. Heisterb. 5, 2. The ' destruction that wasteth at noonday' is trans. in AS. psalms ed. Thorpe p. 253 *on midne dæge mære deoful;* in Wiggert's Fragm. p. 3 von theme *diuuele mittentagelichen;* in Windberg ps. p. 431 vone aneloufe unde *tiuvele deme mittertagelichen;* in Trier ps. von aneloufe unde deme *divele mitdendegelicheme;* conf. the midday mannikin, evening mannikin, Börner 249. *Pshipolnitza,* Wend. volksl. 2, 268; conf. metil and kuga (p. 1188). At noon the gods take their siesta, the ghosts can range freely then, and hurt mankind : a shepherd in Theocritus will not blow his reed while Pan takes his noonday nap. With the spell of ' the *hünsche* and the dragon,' conf. ' *rotlauf* und drach,' Hpt 7, 534. ' God send thee the fever, or the boils, or the *hünsch!'* so prays the peasant against his fellow man, Keisersb. Sins of the lips 38ᵃ.

p. 1163.] There are healing drinks, magic drinks : *drinc of main,* potus corroborans, Erceldun's Tristram 2, 40-2; *drinc of might,* philtrum 2, 48. 51; conf. ôminnis dryckr (p. 1101); *li lovendris,* Trist. ed. Michel 2106 (for 3 years); Engl. love-drink, Fr. boivre damour 2185. A sick man is *fiddled back to health,* supra (p. 331); into his trifling wound she *blew,* Gellert 3, 426. A blind king is cured by washing in the *water of a chaste wife,* Herod. 2, 111. H. Estienne's Apol. pour Herodote. Keisersb. Omeiss 52ᵈ. (Pref. xxxviii).

p. 1165.] Ich kan die leute *messen,* Gryphius's Dornr. 90; *meten,* Gefk. Beil. 167 : ' the third woman declared he had lost the *measure,* and she must *measure* him again,' Drei erzn. p. 361 ; berouchen u. *mezzen,* Hag. Ges. Ab. 3, 70. Is this alluded to in ' ich *mizze* ebener dan Gêtz, diu nie dehein man übermaz'? Helbl. 3, 327 ; *messerinnen,* Ettn. Maul. 657. Carrying a *jewelled chain* about one is a remedy, Bit. 7050—55 (Suppl. to 1218 mid.).

p. 1166.] Whether a man is troubled with the *white folk*, is determined thus: Take 3 *cherry twigs*, and cut them into *small pieces*, saying, ' one not one, two not two, etc.' up to nine, till you have 81 pieces; throw these into a bowl of water, and if they float, the patient is free of the white folk; but if some sink, he is still afflicted with them in the proportion of the sunken sticks to the swimming ones. In Masuria, N. Preuss. prov. bl. 4, 473-4.

p. 1166.] We pour *water* on one who has fainted: daz man mit *brunnen* si vergôz, unde natzte-se under'n ougen, Kl. 1566; si lac in unsinne unz (senseless till) man mit *wazzer* si vergôz 1978. Wet grass is laid on those that swoon, Ls. 2, 283. To strike a *fire*, or to puff it, is good for a burn in the foot, erysipelas and sore eyes, Müllenh. p. 210.

p. 1168.] Poenit. Ecgb. (Thorpe p. 380): (þa *cild*) æt wega gelætum þurh þa eorðan tihð. Creeping through *hollow stones*, Antiqv. ann. 3, 27; conf. Kuhn ou Vrihaddêvatâ in Weber's Ind. stud. 1, 118-9. *Hollow round stones* are fairy cups and dishes, Scott's Minstr. 2, 163. These are often ment. in old records: ad *durechelen stein* (yr 1059) MB. 29ª, 143; *petra pertusa*, Procop. 2, 609; *pierre percée*, Schreib. Taschenb. 4, 262-3 (Kl. schr. 2, 42). ——At Lauenstein a ruptured child is pulled through a *split oak by its godfathers* bef. sunrise; the more carefully the tree is then tied up, the better will the rupture heal; but no one will have that oak, for fear of getting the rupture. The same thing is done with a *young maiden ash*, Barnes p. 326. Sometimes the hair merely is cut off and passed through, Meier's Schwäb. sag. 528. A horse is cured by putting a silver penny inside the split of an aspen or hazel, Mone 6, 476.——In England they often pull a sick child through an *ash*, Athnm '46, Sept. 5, no. 984. They tie the tree up with thick string, or drive *nails* into it. Trees so nailed together are often met with in the woods: one was found full of nails, Hone's Tablebk 2, 466; conf. the Vienna ' stock am eisen,' Ziska's März. p. 105. If you have the toothache, walk silently into a wood on a Thursday morning, take a nail with you, pick your teeth with it, then drive it into *a tree*, Nilss. 4, 45. There is a tree near Mansfeld studded all over with nails, DS.

no. 487. In England a child that has the hooping cough is *drawn three times* through an opening in a hawthorn hedge. Apâlâ, afflicted with a skin-disease, offers a Soma-sacrifice to Indra, who in token of gratitude heals her by drawing her through *three openings in his car*, Weber's Ind. stud. 1, 118. 4, 8.

p. 1172.] When a headache will not go, they *wind* a string three times *round the man's head*, and hang it up in a *tree* as a noose; if a *bird* flies through it, he takes the headache along with him, Temme's Altmk p. 83. If you *lay* a child's chemise, in which it has suffered the schwere noth (fit of epilepsy), on the *cross-ways*, the disease will pass over to him who walks, rides or drives that way, Medic. maulaffe 167. A hatchet-wound is healed by *tying up the tool* that dealt the dint.

> Herre, mit Gotes helfe
> wil ich, daz *reine welfe*
> iuwer kint wol generen (keep alive). Diocl. 4504.

Jaundice can be transferred to the *lizard*, Mone 7, 609. Sick men are wrapt *in the hide* of a newly killed *stag*, Landulph. in Muratori 4, 81. Wilman's Otto 3, 244. A sickly child is *swathed in the skin* of a newly slaughtered sheep (in Shamyl's camp), Allgem. Ztg '56, p. 3323[b]. The *superimposition of warm flesh* occurs in a witch-trial, Schreib. Taschenb. 5, 213.

p. 1172.] The *deer-strap* must be cut off the live animal, Agric. Vom hirsche p.m. 238-9; conf. ' man sol den *erhel-riemen* (lorum nauseae) *snîden* dem der smacke (sapor) wil verderben, Tit. 2621. The tooth of a weasel killed in a particular way is picked up from the ground with the left hand, wrapt in the *hide* of a newly killed *lion* (or maiden *hind*), and laid on the gouty feet, Luc. Philops. 7. On the healing virtue of a *chamois-bullet*, doronicon, see Ettn. Unw. d. 180. A skin-inflammation is called *wolf*:

> Der siechtuom ist des êrsten klein,
> und kumt den herren in diu bein,
> und ist geheizen der *wolf*. Ottok. 91[b].

p. 1173.] Kl. schr. 2, 146. Certain *worms* or *beetles* are recomm. for dog-madness. ' Maz-leide buoz ' in the note = cure for queasiness (meat-loathing). There is a health-giving dish,

into which the *slaver* of *black* and *white snakes* has trickled, Saxo
Gr. ed. M. p. 193-4. Ein iglich tier (every beast) daz wurde
gesunt, der im gaebe (if one gave it) *hundes-bluot*, Renn. 19406 ;
*blood* heals wounds, Lanc. 25397-428. In the Engelhart and
Poor Henry, leprosy is cured by the *blood* of innocent babes ;
' man swendet druosen mit nüechterner *speicheln*,' fasting men's
spittle, Renn. 5884.

p. 1173.] A *yellow bird* by his look removes jaundice ; it is
also cured by drinking out of a waxen goblet with a raven-ducat
lying at the bottom, Unw. doct. 147. Biting is good for a bite :
*beiti* (mordax aliquid) vi𝛿 *bitsóttum*, Sæm. 27ᵇ. The huk is
healed by *pot-hooks*, Lisch's Meckl. jrb. 6, 191, hip-gout (?) by
*gelding*, Greg. Tur. 10, 15.

p. 1175.] To the M. Latin *ligamentum* answers the Gr.
παράρτημα, appendage, Luc. Philops. 8 ; *breviis* ac *ligaturis*,
MB. 16, 241 (yr 1491); *obligatores*, Ducange sub v. Pertz 3,
100. Were *wolf's teeth* hung on people like the foal's tooth
p. 658 n. ?

> Ob ieman wolle tumben spot
> und einen *boesen wolves zan*
> mit ergerunge henken dran. Pass. 3, 70.
> Ir truogt (wore) den *eiter-wolves zan*. Parz. 255, 14.

Daz ich minne, ist mir niht *an-gebunden*, ez ist mir an-geborn,
MSH. 3, 233ᵇ. Parentes vero ejus, intelligentes eum diaboli
immissione turbari, ut *mos rusticorum* habet, a sortilegis et ariolis
*ligamenta* ei et *potiones* deferebant, Greg. Tur. Mirac. S. Mart. 1,
26. Accidentibus ariolis et dicentibus, eam *meridiani daemonii*
incursum pati, *ligamina* herbarum atque incantationum verba
proferebant 4, 36. Illa de sinu *licium* protulit *varii coloris* filis
intortum, cervicemque vinxit meum, Petron. c. 131. Finn. *tyrä*,
prop. testiculus, then ' globulus magicus nocivus, instar testicu-
lorum, *hominibus et pecudibus immitti* solitus.' Fromm. on Herb.
p. 230 quotes : *imago argentea*, per incantationum modos multique
artificii virtute constructa, quae adversus incantationes jam factas
est valde potissima.

p. 1177.] In Arabic a conjurer is called *breather on the knots*,
who ties the nestel, and breathes or spits on it, to complete
the charm, Rückert's Hariri 1, 451. Sura 113 of Koran. *Fluoch*

(a curse), der mîne wambe *besperret* (bars up), Mar. 153, 38. The witch throws the padlock over a loving pair at their wedding, to breed hatred betw. them, Bechst. Thür. sag. 3, 219. People choose the same day for being bled, Trist. 380, 3 [this appar. belongs to 1139 ?]. A lighted wick dipt in one's drink, and so quenched, lessens the drinker's enjoyment of love, Marcell. no. 94. Kl. schr. 2, 142.——Labour is obstructed by *nine witch-knots* in the hair, ' the kaims (combs) of care,' Minstrelsy 2, 400. A *shaggy cap* is good for women in *child-bands* (-birth), Herold in Oechsle's Bauernkr. p. 35. A difficult labour is lightened by *making two babies of wax;* or are they merely to deceive the sorceress? DV. 1, 274-9. A man clasps his hands over his knees, and the labour is stopt; they make believe it is over, he lets go, and it goes on again, Asb. Huldr. 1, 20. *Belts* relieve the labour, Ossian, Ahlw. 3, 436. 450 ; þá *tók* Hrani *belt-it*, ok *lagði um hana*, ok litlu sîðar (soon after) varð hun lêttari, Fornm. s. 4, 32.

The Lettish Laima *spreads the sheet under* those in labour ; the zlotá bába watches over births, Hanusch 337. 356. Ἄρτεμις βολοσίη, Procop. 2, 576; αἱ κύϊσκουσαι ἐπικαλεῖσθε τὴν Ἄρτεμιν, ἀξιοῦσθαι συγγνώμης ὅτι διεκορήθητε, Sch. on Theocr. 2, 66. *Juno Lucina,* fer opem, serva me obsecro, Ter. Adelphi iii. 4, 41.

Swelh wîb *diu driu liet* (3 canticles) *hât,*
sô sie ze keminâten gât (takes to her chamber),
*in ir zeswen bevangen* (clasped in her right),
sie lîdet (will suffer) unlangen
kumber von dem *sêre,*
wand in unser Frôwen êre
g'nist sie (she'll recover) des kindes gnaedeclîchen . . .
Swâ *diu buochel driu sint behalten,*
diu Maget wil der walten (Virgin will manage),
daz da nehein kint
*werde krumb noch blint.* Wernher's Maria 128-9.

p. 1177.] The cure for *poisoning* is descr. in Megenberg 275, 27. To the foot of one bitten by an adder is tied a stone from a virgin's grave, Luc. Philops. 11.

p. 1179.] ' Man sol *genaedige heilige* verre in vremden landen suochen,' MSH. 3, 45ᵇ [Chaucer's ' seeken straungë strondës, to fernë halwës ']. The sick are healed on the *grave of the pious priest,* Pertz 2, 82. The myth of the herb that grows up to the skirt of the statue's garment is also in Walth. v. Rh. 138, 21-58 (p. 1191 mid.). *Relics* bring luck, Al. Kaufmann's Cæsarius p. 28, and the M. Neth. poem of Charles, Hpt. 1, 104. Miracles are also wrought on Pinte's grave, Renart 29481.

p. 1180.] Coins were laid at the feet of a statue which had cured, or was to cure, fever; silver coins were stuck on its loins with wax, Luc. Philops. 20.

> Stabat in his ingens annoso robore quercus,
> una nemus; *vittae* mediam *memoresque tabellae*
> *sertaque* cingebant, *voti* argumenta *potentis.* Ov. Met. 8, 743.

A woman cured of toothache thankfully hangs waxen gums on the grave, Pertz 10, 522; a man whom the saint has delivered from chains hangs up a chain, ibid.; so in Cæs. Heisterb. 7, 29. Liberated prisoners hang their chains on the trees in the goddess's grove, Pausan. ii. 13, 3; those in Ma. on the saint's tomb, St. Louis 96, 2; conf. Scheible 6, 988-9. 997 and RA. 674. ' My mother made a vow that she would hang a votive tablet in the chapel if I recovered my hearing,' Bronner's Life 1, 40. Hooks to which diseased cattle had been tied, also crutches after a cure were left lying in the chapel, Müllenh. p. 105, and at healing springs, Ir. märch. 2, 78. In some places the inscription may still be read: ' hat geholfen,' hath holpen, M. Koch's Reise 203. A waxen house is vowed, that the dwelling house may not be burnt down, St. Louis 84, 19.

p. 1182.] To OHG. *sterpo,* pestis, lues, corresp. the AS. *steorfa.* The *schelm* I explain fr. schwert, GDS. p. 235-6: der *schelme* gesluoc, Hpt 5, 552; der *schalm* slüeg überal, LS. 2, 314; eh dich der *schelm* schlecht, Garg. 102ᵇ; der *sch.* schlägt, Mone's Bad. gesch. 1, 219; *schelmen-grube, -gasse, -acker* 1, 215 seq. Leopr. 75-6; *keib* und *schelm,* Mone's Anz. 6, 467-8, *schelmig* u. *kebig* 8, 407.——OHG. *suhtluomi,* pestilens, corruptus, Graff 2, 212; *staramilo, stramilo* 6, 712. Diut. 1, 279; der *brechen,* plague, Panz. Beitr. 1, 23; dying of the *brechen,* H. Sachs 3, 64ᶜ (cholera?); *pisleht,* pestis, Graff 6, 778 (=sleht, clades, Diut. 1, 183); der *gêhe tôt* in Pass. 316, 90 is apoplexy; der *schwarze tod* Müllenh. no. 329; ' how a pestilence could thus fall fr. the stars, and overrun the world,' Ph. v. Sittew. Zauber-becher p. 238;

die pestelenz *stöszt an*, Platter's Life 66. 71-2.——The Serv.
*kratel* is a fabulous disease that kills in one night, worse than the
plague ; the dead man has *one foot shorter* than the other, hence
the name (krátak, curt, Suppl. to 1160 end). *Ποινή* is a personif.
plague that robs mothers of their children, Paus. i. 44, 7. With
Apollo conf. Oðinn in Sæm. 5ª : *fleygðï* Oðinn, ok î fôlk um
*skaut* (shot). The Lettons think it an omen of pestilence, if the
*auskuts* shears the backs of the sheep in the night, Bergm. 142.

p. 1183.] The angel that smites all in Ezek. 9 is called der
*slahende engel*, Diemer 327-8. 2 Sam. 24, 16-7. Deliverance
from the plague is effected by a snow-white angel, Greg. Tur. 4, 5.
Angels and devils go about during the plague, Sommer p. 55 ;
der sterbe *erbïzet* (bites to death, an angel with drawn sword),
Griesh. 2, 28 ; raging death *rides* through the city on a pale
horse, Judas 1, 327 ; in times of pestilence, Hel (m.) *rides* about
on a three-legged horse, butchering men, Müllenh. p. 244 ; ich
hör auch das *menlin* kum, pestilenz, es fahet an (begins), Keisersb.
Om. 24.[1]

p. 1184.] The black death rises as a *black fog*, Müllenh. no.
329 ; the plague comes in sight as a *blue mist*, Somm. p. 73, as
a *cloud*, a *viper*, Villemarq. Bard. bret. 120. The plague, in the
shape of a *fog*, winds into a wasps' hole, and gets *plugged in*,
Kulpa in D'Elv. 110 ; she comes in at the window, a *black* shape,
passes into a bored hole, and is *pegged in*, Kehrein's Nassau 54.
*Φοῖβος ἀκερσεκόμης λοιμοῦ νεφέλην ἀπερύκει*, Luc. Alex. 36.
N. Marc. Cap. 30. ——The plague proceeds from the *throats* of
pursued wolves, Forcell. sub v. Hirpi. Et nata fertur pestilentia
in Babylonia, ubi de templo Apollinis, ex *arcula aurea*, quam
miles forte inciderat, spiritus pestilens evasit, atque inde Parthos
orbemque implesse, Capitolinus in Vero 8. With the plague that
is conjured into a lime-tree, agrees the *spider* that is bunged in
and let out again, which also runs about the country as a *sterbet*,
Gotthelf's Erzähl. 1, 84.

p. 1189.] The Great Plague is called pestis *flava*, Welsh *y fâd
felen*, San Marte's Arthur-s. 29. 323. With the leg. of Elliant
conf. Volksmärch. aus Bret. p. 185—8. Souvestre 206-7. On

---

[1] *Domus Thiederici*, Thietm. Merseb. 4, 21 ; Ἀδριανοῦ πύργος, τάφος, Procop. B.
Goth. 2, 22 ; *turris Crescentii* or *Dietrichs-haus* in the leg. of Crescentia and the
Two Dietrichs. In Wackern. Lb. 990, Ditterich builds the *Engel-borg;* it is called
*Sorsen-burg* in Myst. 1, 103.

the Lith. *Giltine,* see N. Preuss. prov. bl. 8, 471-2. German plague-stories may be seen in Woeste's Volks-überl. 44, Panz. Beitr. 1, 29 and Wolf's Ztschr. 2, 83. The *pest-frau* is *dressed in white,* Bader no. 431. The plague creeps, crawls in the dark, Schmidt's Westerw. id. 89. The Swed. Plague-boy reminds of the girl who in Denmark indicates deaths to the kindred *with a twig,* Molb. Hist. tidskr. 4, 121 ; three plague-women walk through the town with *scythes.* The plague-maiden appears in *wet garments* and with a *little red dog,* Bunge's Arch. 6, 88.—— When pestilence rises out of Mit-othin's grave, the body is *dug up* and *hedged in with stakes,* Saxo Gr. ed. Müll. 43 (Suppl. to 609). The abating of plagues by *burying in a hill* occurs in Sagebibl. 3, 288. The *cow's-death,* an enormous bull, approaches like the plague, Müllenh. no. 328. In time of plague, the first *head of cattle* that falls is *buried* with a young shoot or a willow planted in its mouth, Superst. I, 838. Müllenh. no. 327 ; or a bull is *buried alive,* Panzer 2, 180, a *calf* or *cow* sacrificed (pp. 608. 1142). At Beutelsbach near Stuttgart, an old woman during a cattle plague advised that the hummel (parish-bull) should be *buried alive :* wreathed in flowers they led him in state to a deep pit ; three times the mighty beast broke his way out, but the third time he choked. Hence the Beutelsbacher are named Hummelbacher.——The plague flies at people's necks as a butterfly, *fillerte,* Woeste's Volks-überl. 44-5. The *Kuga,* like Berhta, can't bear to see the dishes not washed up. A strange bird sings from the tree : ' Eat pimpernel, and you'll all be well ! ' Herrlein's Spessart 217. Rochholz 2, 390-1 ; somewhat differently in Schöppner no. 962. Leoprechting 101. Bader no. 270. Panzer 2, 161. Schönwerth 2, 380. 3, 21.

<hr>

## CHAPTER XXXVII.

## HERBS AND STONES.

p. 1190.] Acc. to Galen (De fac. simpl. 6, 792-3) a Greek, *Pamphilus,* about the time of Claudius, wrote of herbs in alphabetic order, collecting their names and the superstitions about their virtues in sacrifices and incantations. Were the book extant, it would be valuable for mythology and language.

Possibly the names of plants interpolated in MSS. of Dioscorides are out of Pamphilus.

## 1. HERBS.

p. 1191.] Kein dinc hât ûf der erden an kreften alsô rîchen hort (of powers so rich a store) sô *steine, kriuter* unde *wort,* Troj. 10860; *steine, krût* sint an tugenden rîche, *wort* wil ich darobe (above them) an kreften prîsen, MS. 1, 12ᵇ; quae *carmine* sanet et *herbis,* Ov. Met. 10, 397. *Wurzen* kraft u. aller *steine* meister- schaft, MS. 1, 195ᵇ; *würze* des waldes u. *erze* (ores) des *goldes* u. elliu abgründe, diu sint dir Herre künde, MS. 2, 230; der *steine* kraft, der *würze* wâz, Wh. 2, 14. What is the distinction betw. *krût* and *wurz?* Ein *krût,* des *würze* (whose aroma) er wunden helfen jach (asserted), Parz. 516, 24, conf. 516, 27 : er *gruobse,* i.e. the wurz (= wurzel, root). Kraut is *picked,* wurzel *dug out;* flowers too are *picked* (Walth. 39, 16. Hpt 7, 320) or *gathered* (Walth. 39, 1). Also: crût *lesen,* Lanc. 29301.——Ein *edel krût,* Hpt 4, 521; *unedel* bluot (ignoble blood) 7, 321 (p. 1195); durch sîne *edel* ez (daz krût) tragen, Warn. 1944; *tugent-frühtic* kriutel, MS. 1, 88ᵃ; ich brich euch *edle kreuter,* Mone 6, 460; φάρμακον ἐσθλόν, Od. 10, 287. 292; ein *edles kraut* patientia samt dem kreutlein benevolentia, die gaben also süszen ruch, das es mein herz u. sel durchkruch. Healing herbs are ' herbes *demanieres,*' Ren. 19257-69; *surdae,* hoc est *ignobiles* herbae, Pliny 22, 2, not showy, e.g. grass.——Heil-wurz is fetched from an *inaccessible mountain* by the wild merwoman, Hpt 5, 8 (Suppl. to 1192 mid.), as dictamnus is by Venus from *Ida,* Aen. 12, 412. The *Idæan* bed *of flowers* is also in Petron. 127; the Homeric νεοθηλέας ποίης is in Hesiod too, Theog. 576; a woodland bed [of flowers?] is Erek's and Enid's *bette-wât* (-curtain), Er. p. 216. Vuk 1, no. 224; mit rôsen was ich umbestact, Tragemund. Where the maiden *stood* in the garden, *bloom* the fairest flowers, Rhesa dainos 296 ; die boume begunden *krachen,* die rôsen sêre *lachen,* Ges. Abent. 1, 464. Another *planta e capite statuae nascens* is in Athenæus 5, 497. Liebrecht's Gervas. 124. Gesta Rom. K. 138. Moss growing in a *death's head* is supposed to have magic power. There is a superstition about peas sown inside a *skull.*

p. 1192.] Plants are dear to God; He called them forth.

Whether to pick beautiful flowers, or *dur Got stân lân* (for God's love let them stand)? Hpt 4, 500. The marrubium indeed is *gotes-vergeten, gotis-v., gotz-vergessen*, Mone 4, 240-8. 8, 493. 407; *gotis-vergeszene*, Summerl. 57, 51. Θεῶν ἄγρωστις, ῆν Κρόνος κατέσπειρε· Glaucus, having found and eaten it, becomes immortal, Athen. 3, 83-4.——Αἷμα Ἄρεως (blood of Ares), nardus montana, Dioscor. 1, 8, lilium 3, 106; αἷμα Ἑρμοῦ, verbena 4, 60; αἷμα Ἀθηνᾶς chamaepitys 3, 165; αἷμα Ἡρακλέους, crocus 1, 25, centaurium minus 3, 7; αἷμα τιτάνου, rubus 4, 37. So: γόνος Ἡρακλέους, myrtus silv. 4, 144, elleborum alb. 4, 148; γόνος Ἑρμοῦ, anethum 3, 60, buphthalmus 3, 146; γόνος ἥρωος, polygonum 4, 4 (is γόνος here semen, or as the Lat. version has it, genitura?). The flower Αἴας first springs up after the hero's death, Paus. i. 35, 3. Plants often originate from drops of blood (p. 827), as the flower on Sempach field shoots up where Leopold has fallen, Reber's Hemmerlin p. 240. The poison-plant ἀκόνιτον grows out of Cerberus's drivel (Ov. Met. 7, 415. Serv. ad Virg. Geo. 2, 152), as the herb *trachonte* does from dragon's blood, Parz. 483, 6.——Ἀριστολοχία (corrup. into osterluzei) has reference to Ἄρτεμις λοχεία, and is given to women in childbed. Herba *Chironis* alsing, Mone's Quellen 289ᵃ; herba *S. Petri*, ibid. The Pol. *Dziewanna* is both Diana and verbascum thapsus; Boh. *divizna* (wonder-flower) is our himmelbrand (Suppl. to 1196). *Baldrs brâ* stands on a par with *supercilium Veneris*, Diosc. 4, 113 and *jungfrauen aug-braune* (virgin's eyebrow), achillea millefolium, Nemnich; conf. *wild-fräulein-kraut*, achillea moschata, Stald. 2, 451. AS. *Sâtor-lâđe* (p. 247). *Woens-kruid*, angelica? Coremans 53. *Visumarus*, son of summer, of the sun? (Suppl. to 1212 end).——The centaury was first pointed out by the centaur *Chiron;* a herb is named achillea, bec. discovered by Chiron's pupil *Achilles. Venus* culls dictamnus on Ida for her wounded Aeneas, Aen. 12, 412. The μῶλυ plucked out by Hermes is, acc. to Dioscor. 3, 46-7, ruta silvestris and leucoium silvestre. An angel in a dream reveals the sowthistle (p. 1208); the wounded Albert is shown the remedial herb in a dream, Felsenb. 1, 232-4; an angel tells of a remedy in a dream, Engelh. 5437 seq. One herb the *Mother of God* has covered with her cloak, Klose's Breslau p. 102; the empereriz having fallen *asleep* on a rock in the sea, Mary appears and bids her *pull up the herb*

*that grows under her head*, Méon N. rec. 2, 71-3.   Maerl. 2, 226.
Wackern. Lb. 995, 29.   Frau *Babehilt* digs up and grates herbs
for wounds, Ecken-l. 173—6.   The *mermaid* urges the use of
mugwort, the *vila* of odolián (pp. 1208. 1212).   The *vila gathers
herbs* (bere bilye) for Marko, Vuk 2, 218 (ed. '45).

p. 1194.]   In the leg. of Glaucus and Polyidus a *snake* brings
the herb that reanimates the dead, Apollod. Bibl. 3, 3 ; conf.
KM.³ 3, 26.   A *weasel* in the wood culls the red flower that
quickens, Marie 1, 474.   *Birds* pick herbs, and teach their uses
to man, e.g. the spring-wurzel (p. 973).   A *raven* comes flying
with the wound-healing *leaf*, Völs. saga c. 8.   If a *swallow's* chick
grows blind, she fetches a herb, lays it on, and restores the sight;
hence the herb's name of *chelidonium*, celandine, Dioscor. 2, 211.
GDS. 204; and Megenberg tells the same tale of *schell-wurz*
(celandine).[1]   *Harts* shew the hart-wort (hirsch-wurz, -heil),
Megenb. 398, 22—25.   With Norweg. *Tyri-hialm* (Tiwes-helm)
coincides Ἄρεος κυνῆ, Babr. 68, 4.   Does OHG. *wat-wurz*, Graff
1, 768 stand for Watin-wurz ?

p. 1195.]   Mary has the most herbs named after her, see
Fries's Udfl. 1, 87.   Similar to the wine *Liebfrauen-milch* is
Ἀφροδίτης γάλα, Aristoph. in a lost play p. m. 154ᵃ; ἡδύς γε
πίνειν οἶνος Ἀφροδ. γάλα, Athen. 10, 444ᵈ.   *Marien-milch* however is polypodium vulg., said to have grown out of the drops of
milk that Mary scattered over the land, F. Magnus. 361 note;
conf. the Span. *leche* de los viejos, *leche* de Maria = wine.   *Marien
bett-stroh* is Engl. *lady's* bedstraw, *lady in the straw*, Hone's
Yrbk 814.——*Frua-mänteli*, malva rotundifolia, Wolf's Zts. 2, 54.
*Vrowen-hâr, Minnen-hâr*, capillus Veneris, Mone 4, 241 ; conf.
Venus's eyebrow (Suppl. to 1192 mid.).   Nemnich sub vv.
cypripedium, adiantum.   *Marien-thräne*, -tear, resembles Ἥρας
δάκρυον, Diosc. 4, 60.   Labrum, lavacrum, concha Veneris = dipsacus sitibundus, bec. it gathers dewdrops.   *Margarethen-
schöckla*, -shoe, put in a box, becomes a black worm.

[1] A field-flower, euphrasia or myosotis, is called *augen-trost* (eye's comfort),
Nethl. *oghen-troost ;* also *augen-dienst* (Blumentrost, a family name at Mülhausen) ;
conf. ' den ich in mînen ougen gerne burge,' Wolfr. 8, 4 ; ze sumere die ougen
trôsten schoene wise (fair meads enchant the eye); lovely ladies were ὀφθαλμῶν
ἀλγηδόνες, eye-smarts.   Dæges eage, primula veris [?], M. Engl. daies eyghe,
daisy, Alex. 7511.   Clover too is called *ougen brehende*, but Engl. *eye-bright* is
euphrasia.   Ich tuon dir in den ougen wol, Winsbekin 4, 4 ; er ist mir in den
ougen niht ein dorn, MS. 1, 16ᵇ. 2, 98ᵃ; ob ez ir etelîchen taete in den ougen wê,
MS. 1, 68ᵃ. GDS. 209 ; conf. *friedeles ouga*, Mone 8, 405. Hpt. 6, 332.

p. 1195.] Flowers are picked and presented to ladies, Hpt 7, 320. Some herbs engender strife, esp. among women: ononis spinosa, *weiber-krieg*, women's war, Lat. altercum; Serv. *bilye od omraze*, herbs of hate, that makes friends fall out, Vuk 1, 305 (ed. '24). Boh. *bily* is one particular plant, tussilago. Herbs were broken off with the *pommel of a sword*, Lanc. 12013, picked with the *left hand*, bare-footed (see selago). They are gathered acc. to days of the week: on Sunday solsequium, Monday lunaria, Tuesd. verbena, Wednesd. mercurialis, Thursd. barba Jovis, Frid. capillus Veneris, Saturd. crowfoot (? p. 247). Superst. H, cap. 31-2.

p. 1196.] Pliny 26. 5, 14 calls *condurdum* herba solstitialis, flore rubro, quae e collo suspensa strumas comprimit; conf. Plaut. Pseudol. i. 1, 4: quasi *solstitialis herba* paulisper fui, repente exortus sum, repentino occidi.——*Herba Britannica* is called in Diosc. 1, 120 ἅλιμος, οἱ δὲ βρεταννική, in 4, 2 βρεταννικὴ ἡ βεττονική, conf. Diefenb. Celt. 3, 112. Cannegieter de Briten-burgo, Hag. Com. 1734. Abr. Munting de vera herba Brit. Arnst. 1698. C. Sprengel's Diosc. 2, 571. GDS. 679. An OHG. gl. of the 12th cent. has 'herba Brit., *himel-brant*,' Mone 8, 95; perh. '*hilmibranda* = maurella' in Graff 3, 309 stands for himilbranda. *Himmel-brand*, -*kerze* = verbascum thapsus, white mullein, Schm. 2, 196; and *hilde-brand*, verb. nigrum, 2, 178. *Himmelbrand, brenn-kraut*, feld-kerze, unholden-kerze = verb. thapsus, says Höfer 2, 52; *unholden-kraut*, Boh. *divizna*, Jungm. 1, 371[a] (Suppl. to 1192 mid.). Instead of '*hœwen-hýðele*, bri-tannica,' Mone's Quellen 320[a] has the forms *hœwen-hyldele, hœwen-ydele*; may hylde, hilde be akin to helde, heolode (hiding, hidden)?——*Tonnoire*, fleur du tonnerre, coquelicot, poppy, Grandgagnage's Voc. 26; *donner-bart* (-beard) is sedum tele-phium. A fungus ἴτον in Thrace grew *during thunder*, Athen. 1, 238; subdued thunder generates mushrooms, Meghadûta, p. 4.

On *lotus* see Klemm 1, 112-3; lotus caerulea, Bopp's Gl. 39[b]. 46. Sprengel's Diosc. 2, 622; white and blue lotus, Fries's Udfl. 1, 107.

p. 1199.]. Mir wart ein krût *in mîn hant*, Ls. 1, 211; does that mean 'stole in unperceived'? conf. φῦ ἐν χειρί, Passow 2, 1042. Si sluoc daz krût mir *ûz der hant*, Ls. 1, 218. Of the aster atticus, Dioscorides 5, 118 says: ξηρὸν δὲ ἀναιρεθὲν τῇ

ἀριστερᾷ χειρὶ τοῦ ἀλγοῦντος, in the patient's *left hand*. Of the
bark of the wild figtree, Pliny 23. 7, 64 : caprifico quoque medi-
cinae unius miraculum additur, *corticem* ejus *impubescentem puer
impubis* si defracto ramo *detrahat dentibus*, medullam ipsam
*adalligatam ante solis ortum* prohibere strumas. *Three roses* are
picked off in *five picks*, Amgb. 48^b (conf. wishing for 3 roses
on *one* stalk, two roses on *one* branch, Uhl. Volksl. pp. 23. 116.
Reusch no. 12. Meinert's Kuhl. 95 ; offering 3 roses, Uhl. p.
257-8).——A Swed. account of *digging up the rönn* (rowan) in
Dyb. '45, 63. Am abend soltu sie (the vervain) *umkreissen* mit
*silber* u. mit *golde* u. mit *siden* (silk), Mone 6, 474. When the
root is pulled out, the hole is filled up with corn, to propitiate
the earth (Suppl. to 1241). The plant is *plucked suddenly*, and
*covered with the hand* (Suppl. to 1214) : du solt ez (the shoot)
ûz der erden *geziehen vil líhte*, En. 2806 and 2820—5, where
Virgil has no shoot to be pulled up, but a branch to be torn off.
La sainte herbe qu'a son chief trueve . . . *tot en orant l'erbe a
coillie*, Méon N. rec. 2, 73.

p. 1202.] The grasses growing through a sieve remind one of
the words '*þurh aern in-wyxð*' (p. 1244). It is curious too,
that an elder should be considered curative when it grows in a
hollow willow-tree out of seeds that thrushes had swallowed,
Ettn. Unw. d. 161-2. There are herbs, the sight of which allays
hunger : esuriesque sitis *visis* reparabitur herbis, Ecbas. 592.

p. 1204.] The mightiest of magic roots is *mandrake :* abollena
*alrun*, Sumerl. 54, 37. How to pull it out is also descr. in
Oeuvres de Rutebeuf 1, 474 : Ceste *dame herbe* (conf. la mère
des herbes, artemisia, Suppl. to 1212 beg.), *il ne la trest* ne giex
(Jew) ne paiens ne sarrazins ne crestiens, ains *la trest une beste
mue*, et *tantost come ele est traite, si covient morir cele beste*. In
like manner the root Baaras is pulled up by means of a *dog*,
Joseph. 7, 25. Armenian ' *manrakor* or *loshtak*, a man-like root,
is pulled out by a [dog ?] to which it is tied ; in coming out it
*moans in a human voice*,' Artemius of Vagarshapat, transl. by
Busse (Halle '21) p. 106.——Mandragora grows in Paradise,
where the *elefant* goes to look for it, Karajan. Μανδραγόρας.
Πυθαγόρας ἀνθρωπόμορφον, Ῥωμαῖοι μάλα κανίνα, Diosc. 4, 76.
The *alraun* is carved out of a root (p. 513n.). Panz. Beitr. 1, 250.
Un vergier a li peres Floire, u plantés est li *mandegloire*, Flore

244. Mandragora *tvalm*, Mone 8, 95; von senfte der alrûnen
wart mich *slâfen*, Frauenl. 6, 26; ὑπὸ μανδραγόρᾳ καθεύδειν,
Luc. Timon 2 (ed. Bip. 1, 331—3); ἐκ μανδραγόρου καθεύδειν,
Luc. Demosth. enc. 36.——On the *alrûne* in Frauenlob's Minne-
leich 15, 2, Ettmüller says p. 286 : 'they seem to have believed
that *mandrakes* facilitated birth.' This is confirmed by Adam
Lonicerus in his Kreuterbuch (1582) bl. 106ᵃ. '*Alraun* rinden
dienet zu augen-arzneyen. Dieser rinden drey heller gewicht
schwer, für der frawen gemächt (women's chamber) gehalten,
bringet ihnen ihre zeit, treibet auss die todte geburt.' *Alrûnen*
heizit er virbern (he is said to have about him): swenne er wil,
sô ist er ein kindelîn, swenne er wil, sô mac er alt sîn, Cod. Pal.
361, 12ᵇ. 'He must keep an *araunl* by him, that tells him all
he wants to know,' H. Jörgel 20, 3. The *mandragora* is put into
a white dress, and served twice a day with food and drink, Spinnr.
evangel. Tuesday 2; conf. the tale of the gallows mannikin,
Simpl. 3, 811.

p. 1204.] Oðinn sticks the thorn into Brynhild's *garment*
only, and throws her into a sleep (Kl. schr. 2, 276). In Tirol
the schlaf-kunz is called *schlaf-putze*, Zingerle 552. 'Hermannus
dictus *Slepe-rose*,' Hamb. lib. actor. 127, 6 (circ. 1270). The
hawthorn is sentis canina, lignea canis, Athen. 1, 271. Breton
*gars spern*, thorn-bush, in the story of a fair maiden. Nilsson 6,
4.5 maintains that on *barrows* of the bronze age a *hawthorn* was
planted and held sacred; and the same among Celts (Kl. schr. 2,
254. 279).

p. 1207.] *Mistletoe* grows on the hazel, lime, birch, fir, willow,
and esp. oak, Dyb. Runa 2, 16. AS. *âc-mistel*, viscum quer-
neum. *Mistila*, a woman's name, Mone 5, 492. Trad. Fuld. 1,
130. Schannat 445. Many places named after it : *Mistlegau*
near Baireuth; *Mistelouwa*, Mistlau, near Crailsheim, Stälin 1,
599; *Mistelbach*, Frauend. 272, 18. Kaltenb. Pantaid. 184ᵇ;
ad *Misteleberge*, Lacomblet (yr. 1054) no. 189; *Mistelveld*,
Lang's Reg. 2, 397 (yr 1248). 3, 55 (yr 1255). Bamb. calend.
p. 142; *Mispilswalde*, Lindenbl. p. 24; *Misterhult* i Småland,
Dybeck '45, 80. A sword belonging to Semîngr is called
*Mistilteinn* in Hervarars. (Fornald. sög. 1, 416).——*Mistil* =
tuscus (l. viscus), Hpt 5, 326. 364. In some parts of Germany
they call mistletoe *kenster*, *kinster*. Walloon *hamustai*, *hamu-*

*staine*, Grandgagnage 1, 270 and *henistai, hinistrai=* kinster, canister, Grandg. Voc. 23-4. Engl. *misseltoe, misletoe,* Hone's Daybk 1, 1637-8. And *maren-tacke* is misletoe, bristly plant (p. 1247, l. 11).——Nilsson would trace all the Scand. mistletoe cultus to the Druidic, Dybeck '45, 79. 80. Ein *mistlein paternoster*, MB. 18, 547 (yr. 1469); *mischtlin paternoster, mispel* and *aich-mistlin paternoster,* Ruland's Handlungs-b. yrs 1445-6-7. (Pref. viii.) Mistletoe must be cut on a *Midsummer-night's eve,* when sun and moon are in the sign of their power (conjunction?), Dyb. '44, p. 22. For the oak mistletoe to have any power, it must be *shot* off the tree, or *knocked down* with stones, Dyb. '45, p. 80. In Virgil's descr. of the sacred bough, Aen. vi.,

137. *aureus* et foliis et lento vimine *ramus,*
141. *auricomos* quam quis decerpserit arbore *fetus,*
144. *aureus,* et simili frondescit virga *metallo,*
187. et nunc se nobis ille *aureus* arbore *ramus,*

this aureus fetus is merely *compared* to (not ident. with) the croceus fetus of the mistletoe; conf. Athen. 3, 455-7. An oak with a golden bough occurs in a Lett. song, Büttner no. 2723. Armor *huelvar*, aft. *heller*; Wel. *uchelawg, uchelfa, uchelfar, uchelfel, holliach,* Jones p. 391[b]. Lett. *ohsa wehja ⚡lohta,* oak-mistletoe, from ohsols, oak, and ⚡*lohta,* broom, plume; *wehja ⚡lohta* is a plant of which brooms are made. Does wehja mean holy? conf. wehja wannags (Suppl. to 675). Serv. *lepak,* viscum album, also *mela,* of which Vuk p. 394 says: If a mistletoe be found on a hazel, there lies under that hazel a snake with a gem on his head, or another treasure by the side of it.

p. 1208.] Welsh *gwlydd* usu. means mild, tender, *gwiolydd* is violet. *Valerian* is in Finn. *ruttoyuuri,* plague-wort; another Boh. name is *kozljk.* A rare word for valerian is *tennemarch,* Nemnich. Mone 8, 140[a]. Hpt 6, 331. Worthy of note is the Swed. tale about the mooring of *Tivebark* and *Vendelsrot,* Dyb. '45, p. 50. The Serv. name *odolián* resembles a Polish name of a plant, dołęga, for dołęka means upper hand; conf. Vuk's Gloss. sub. v. odumiljen. *Odilienus* is a man's name, Thietmar 4, 37; so is Boh. *Odolén* (Kl. schr. 2, 393). *Nardus* is fragrant, esp. the Indica; nardus Celtica is saliunco. Νάρδος πιστικὴ πολύτιμος, John 12, 3 is in Goth. nardus pistikeins filu-galaubs.

p. 1208.]    Acc. to Martin's Relig. d. Gaules, *Belinuntia* comes
fr. Belenus (Diefenb. Celt. 1, 203.  Zeuss p. 34), and is a herba
Apollinaris ;  Apollo is said to have found it, Forcell. sub v.
Russ. *bêlena*, Pol. *bielun*, Boh. *blen, bljn*, Hung. *belendfu*.  Engl.
*henbane*, gallinae mors.

p. 1208.]    On *eberwurz*, see Reuss's Walafr. Strab. Hortulus
p. 66.  Great power is attrib. to the carlina, Dyb. '45, p. 72.
Another thistle is in Sweden called *jull-borste*, ibid., reminding
us of the boar *Gullin-bursti* and of eberwurz.    As Charles's
arrow falls on the sow-thistle, so does Cupid's on a flower to
which it imparts miraculous power, love-in-idleness, Mids. N.
Dr. 2, 2 ; and other healing herbs are revealed in dreams.    In
another dream a grey smith appears to the same king Karel,
and with his pincers pulls nails out of his hands and feet, Hpt
1, 103.

p. 1209.]    An AS. Herbal says of *Betonica :* þeos wyrt, þe
man *betonicam* nemneð, heo bið cenned on maedum and on
claenum dûnlandum and on gefriðedum slowum.    seo deah
gehwaeðer ge þaes mannes sawle ge his lichoman (benefits soul
and body).    hio hyne scyldeð wið (shields him against) unhyrum
*niht-gengum* and wið *egeslicum gesihðum* and *swefnum*.    seo
wyrt byð swyðe hâligu, and þus þû hi scealt niman on Agustes
mônðe *bútan îserne* (without iron), etc.  MHG. *batónie* (rhy.
Saxônie), Tit. 1947 : *betoene* (rhy. schoene), Hätzl. 163, 86.
Κέστρον Ῥωμαῖοι οὐεττονικὴν καλοῦσι, Diosc. 4, 1.

*Verbena* is akin to veru and Virbius, says Schwenck pp. 489.
491 ; it stands for herbena, says Bergk.    It is sacred, and therefore called ἱεροβοτάνη and *herba pura*, qua coronabantur bella
indicturi, Pliny 22. 2, 3.  25. 9, 59.  Wolfg. Goethe's Dissert.
p. 30-1.  It is called περιστερειόν, bec. pigeons like to sit by it ;
also *ferraria*, Diosc. 4, 60 : ἡ σιδηρῖτις 4, 33-4-5.  OHG. *isarna*,
*isenina*, Graff 3, 864.  1, 491 ; *isincletla* 4, 555.  Sumerl. 24, 9 ;
*isenarre*, Sumerl. 40, 54; *iserenbart* 66, 40.  MHG. *isenhart*,
Mone's Anz. 4, 250 and Quellen 309ᵇ.  *Eisen-kraut*, as we still
call it, is thrown into St. John's fire (p. 618) ; conf. ' Lay aside
the Johnswort and the *vervain*,' Whitelaw p. 112.  Nethl. *izer-
krûd*, Swed. *jern-ört*, Dan. *jern-urt*.  There was a spell for *digging up vervain*, Mone 6, 474.  AS. *æsc-wyrt*, Hpt. 5, 204 ;
*æsc-þrote*, Lye sub v.  GDS. 124.

p. 1209.] *Madelger* ist ain gut crut wurtz. swer si grabn wil, der grab si an Sant Johans tag ze sun-benden (solstice) an dem abent, und beswer si also dri-stund (adjure it 3 times thus): ' Ich beswer dich, *Madelger*, *Ain wurtz so her*, Ich manen dich des gehaiz den dir *Sant Pettrus* gehiez, Do er *sinen stab dri-stund durch dich stiez*, Der dich usgrûb Und dich haim trûg : Wen er mit dir umb-fauht (whom he with thee begirds), ez sy fraw oder man, Der mug ez in lieb oder in minn nimer gelaun. In Gotz namen, Amen.' wihe si mit andern crutern. Kräuter-heilkunde (yr 1400) in the Giessen Papierhs. no. 992, bl. 143.

p. 1211.]. *Fern*, *bracken*. Gr. πτέρις fr. its feathery foliage.* Lat. *filix*, It. *felce*, Sp. *helecho*, Fr. *fougère*. Filix herba, palmes Mercurii (Suppl. to 159) ; filicina, filix minuta, AS. *eofor-fearn*. Celt. *ratis*, Wel. *rhedyn*, Bret. *raden*, Ir. *raith*, *raithneach*, Gael. *raineach* (conf. reinefano), Pott 2, 102. Adelung's Mithr. 2, 68 from Marcell. c. 25 (Kl. schr. 2, 123). Finn. *sana-yalka* (word-foot), Esth. *sona-yalg*, Böcler's Abergl. gebr. d. Esten 144. Lith. *bit-krĕsle* (bee's chair) = tanacetum vulg., Nesselm. 226. 331. Serv. *pouratish*, tansy, tanacetum crispum (fr. po-vratíti, to turn back ? ON. *burkni*, filix, polypodium, Swed. *bräken*, Vesterb. *fräken*, Dan. *bregne*. Again, ON. *einstapi*, Jonsson's Oldn. ordboc, Norw. *einstabbe*, *einstape*, Aasen 79[b]. Nemnich sub v. pteris. Swed. *ormbunke*.——Den wilden *varm* treten, Parz. 444, 7. 458, 17 ; latentis odii *filix* excrevit, Dietmar in Pertz 5, 736 ; *filex* iniquitatis exaruit 5, 742. Fernseed *makes invisible*, Wolf's Ztschr. 2, 30 : we have the receipt of *fernseed*, we walk invisible, 1 Henry IV. 2, 1 ; Swed. *osynlighets gräs*. As fernseed in Conrad is thrown to the shad (schaid-visch, Beheim 281, 28), so bugloss, which is said to blind all animals born blind, is scattered to fishes, Rudl. 12, 13. 1[b], 28. 32—48. After walking naked to the cross-roads and spreading out a pockethandkerchief, one expects *fernseed*, Zehn ehen 235.——On Christmas night, high and low used to walk in the *fernseed ;* there you might wish for anything in the world, the devil had to bring it. The Wend. volksl. 2, 271[a] makes it blossom at Mid-summer *noon :* get hold of the blossom, and all the treasures of

---

* So, from the Slav. *par-iti*, to fly, *pero*, wing, feather, Hehn derives not only the redupl. Slav. and Lith. *pa-part*, *pa-prat*, but the Teut. *farn* and even the Celt. *ratis* which stands (more Celtico) for pratis. Hehn's Plants and Anim. p. 484.—TRANSL.

earth lie open before you. Conf. the Slovèn. riddle : 'kay *tsvete
brez tsveta ?'* what blossoms without blossom ? Answ. *praprot.*
In Tirol, if you step on an *irr-wurz,* you immed. find yourself
plunged in a bog or a carrion-pit. A story of the *irr-kraut* in
Stöber's Neujahrstollen 32-3 ; conf. Lett. songs in Büttner nos.
1593. 1912.

    p. 1212.] *Artemisia,* Fr. armoise, O. Fr. *ermoize,* is called in
Champagne *marrebore* or *marreborc* (marrubium?), which is supp.
to mean la mere des herbes (Rutebeuf 1, 257), as in fact artemisia is called herbarum mater in Macer. Rutebeuf's Dit
de l'erberie 1, 257 makes *ermoize* the first of healing herbs : Les
fames sen ceignent le soir de la S. Jehan, et en font chapiaux
seur lor chiez, et dient que goute ne avertinz ne les puet panre
n'en chiez, n'en braz, n'en pie, n'en main ; mais je me merveil
quant les testes ne lor brisent, et que li cors ne rompent parmi,
tant a l'erbe de vertu en soi.——The Germ. word for it occurs as
a man's name *Peybos* (yr 1330), Bamberger verein 10, 107, and
*Beypoz* (yrs 1346-57) 10, 129. 136-8. 145. Even Schannat no.
348 has the name *Beboz* (see Kl. schr. 2, 399. Dronke's Trad.
Fuld. 420) ; and ' *beyposs* = artemesia ' in Vocab. Theuton.
(Nuremb. 1482) d. 7ª. At last, in Vocab. ex quo Eltuil 1469,
' attamesia = *byfuyss,*' and also ' incus = eyn anfusse,' the *f* in both
being appar. Mid. Rhenish.\* ' *Bismolten,* artemisia, est nomen
herbe, volgariter *byfus* in ander sprach bock,' Voc. incip. Teuton.
' *Bibes* ist ain crut : wer fer welle gaun, der soll es tragen, so wirt
er nit müd sere uf dem weg, der tüfel mag im och nit geschaden ;
und wo es in dem hus lit, es vertribt den zober,' Heilmittelbuch
of 1400 in the Giess. hs. no. 992, bl. 128ᵇ. ' Artemisia, *beyfuss,
sonnenwendel,*' J. Serranus's Dict. Latino-Germ. (Nürnb. 1539)
66ᵇ; ' in dem *bifüs,*' Mone's Anz. '34, 337. Superstitions about
it, Panz. Beitr. 1, 249. ' St John's coals (touchstones) are found
fr. noon to vespers of John's day *under the beyfuss* ; alias non
inveniuntur per annum,' Mone 7, 425.——Artemisia is *zimber,
zimbira* in Hattemer 3, 597ª ; *hergott-hölzel* in Nemnich p. 466.
A.S. *tagantes helde* = artemisia (tragantes, for τραγάκανθα ?),
Mone's Quell. 320ª (conf. p. 1216 n.). OHG. *stapa-wurz, stabe-w.,*
abrotonum, Graff 1, 1052. Sumerl. 60, 2 ; our *stabwurz,* southern-

---

  \* The corruption of *bibôz* into ' our meaningless beifuss ' is a fair example of
Folk-etymology : the herb is good for the pedestrian's *feet.*—TRANSL.

wood. OS. *staf-wurt*, dictamnum, dittany, Diut. 2, 192. Arte-misia is *buggila* in Hattemer 1, 314[ab] and Mone 8, 400; *bugel* 6, 220; *bugge* 8, 405; *buggul*, Voc. opt. p. 51[a]; φασὶ δὲ ἐν ταῖς ὁδοιπορίαις μὴ παρατρίβεσθαι τοὺς βουβῶνας, ἄγνου ῥάβδον ἢ τῆς ἀρτεμισίας κρατουμένης (groin not galled if one carry a switch of agnus castus or artemisia), Diosc. 2, 212. Gallic πονέμ, Dacian ζουόστη (conf. ζωστήρ, girdle), GDS. 208. Diefenb. Celt. 1, 172. Ir. *mugard*, AS. *mucg-wyrt*, GDS. 708. Boh. *černo-byl*, Pol. *czarno-byl*, Slovèn. *zhernób* (black herb); Serv. *bozhye drutze*, God's little tree.

To Gothic names of plants, add *vigadeinô*, τρίβολος (Suppl. to 1215). On equisetum, see Pott's Comm. 2, 27. OHG. *gren-sinc*, nymphæa, potentilla, clavus Veneris, Graff 4, 333; MHG. *grensinc*, Mone's Anz. 4, 244-6. In a Stockholm MS. we find the spell: Unse leve vrowe gink sik to damme, se sochte *grensink* den langen. do se en vant, do *stunt he un bevede*. se sprak: 'summe den soten Jesum Crist, wat crudes du bist?' 'Junk-frowe, ik hete *grensink, ik bin das weldigeste kint*. ik kan den kettel kolen, ik kan alle dink vorsonen, ik kan den unschuldigen man van den galgen laten gan; de mi bespreke un ineges dages up breke, dem were God· holt und alle mannen kunne un golt sulven.' in den namen des Vaders un des Sons, etc. Is grensinc fr. *grans*, prora, bec. it grows in front of your boat?

*Clover*, trifolium, Dan. *klever*, Germ. *klee : nübblättlets klee* (p. 1079 mid.). Esp. significant is the four-leaved (p. 1137 end): *klewer veer*, Müllenh. pp. 410. 557; *clover cinquefoil*, Bret. märch. 89. 93; to send trefoil and wine, Arch. v. Unterfranken iv. 3, 169. Clover is called *himmel-kraut* in Bavaria: schön *blüet's himel-kraut*, Schm. 2, 196, conf. *himel-blüe*, rainbow, *himel-brand*, mullein (Suppl. to 1196); *hergotts-brot* (-bread), head of clover blossom, Schm. 2, 231, conf. *brosam-kraut*, Superst. I, 369; *Gotis-ampher* (-sorrel), alleluja, Sumerl. 54, 35.——Icel. *smári*, trifol. album; Jutl. *smäre*. ON. *qveisu-gras*, trifol. fibrinum, good for colic and hysterica passio (Suppl. to 1159 beg.). Swed. *väpling :* superstit. of the *fyr-väpl., fem-vapl.*, Dybeck '48, p. 22. Gall. *visumarus*, Diefenb. 1, 46 (Suppl. to 1192 mid. Kl. schr. 2, 156. 171). Ir. *shamrock*, in O'Brien seamrog (Kl. schr. 2, 156), GDS. 302. Welsh *meillionen*, Armor. *melchen*, *melchon.* Clover used in Persian sacrifices, Herod. 1, 132.

p. 1213.] Our *gunder-männlein, gundel-rebe*, is a tiny blue
flower, whereas OHG. *gunde-reba*=acer, maple; *gunderebe*, acer,
balsamita, Mone 7, 600. In a charm: '*guntreben gêr* (maple
shoot?), I toss thee up to the clouds,' Mone 6, 468.

p. 1213.] Morsus diaboli, *devilsbit*, see Dybeck '45, 52. AS.
*ragu* (ragwort) is glossed by 'mosicum, mossiclum,' perh.
mosylicum; otherw. ragu is robigo. Lye has also 'Cristes
maeles ragu, Christi crucis mosicum, herba contra ephialten
valens.' Schubert p. 197 : *ragwurz*, orchis.

Serv. *stidak* (shamefaced), caucalis grandiflora : it has a white
blossom, with a little red in the middle. This red, they say, was
greater once, but grew less every day, as modesty died out among
men, Vuk sub v.

*Holder* (wolf's-claw?), when eaten, causes vomiting or purging,
acc. as it was shelled over or under one, Judas 1, 169. Lycopo-
dium complanatum, ON. *jafni*, Dan. *jävne*, Swed. *jemna*, Vesterb.
*jamm*.

p. 1214.] A plant of universal healing power is *heil-aller-welt*,
agrimonia, Mone 8, 103; *aller frowen heil*, MS. 2, 48[a]; *quotes
mannes heil*, Hpt. 2, 179. Lisch's Meckl. jrb. 7, 230 ; conf. the
ointment *mannes heil*, Iw. 3452. Er. 7230.

p. 1214.] *Dorant* seems a corrup. of andor, andorn (hore-
hound): trail your shirt in blue *tharand*, N.Pr. prov. bl. 8, 229.
Gothl. *tarald,* äggling, ett gräs för hvilket trollen tros sky, Almqv.
464[a]. Hold up thy skirt, that thou graze not the white *orand!*
M. Neth. *orant*, Mone 6, 448. Holst. *gäler orant*, Müllenh. no.
425.——'A herb that says, Be *wol-gemut*, (of good cheer)!'
Hoffm. Gesellschaftsl. 136; die braune *wolgemut*, Ambras. lied.
p. 212. Pol. *dobry mysli*, good thoughts. The plant must be
plucked *hastily*, and *hidden* : ἐμμαπέως τὸν ὀρίγανον ἐν χερὶ
κεύθει, Athen. 1, 262 ; ὀρίγανον βλέπειν, look sour, as though
you had bitten marjoram.

*Porst, porse* is strewn under the table, to sharpen a guest's
appetite, Fries's Udfl. pp. 109. 110 ; conf. *borsa*, myrtus, Graff
3, 215.

p. 1214.] OHG. *hart-houwi* (-hay) must, I think, be the
*harten-aue* which the girl 'murkles' to find out if her lover loves
her, Firmen. 2, 234. Fiedler's Dessauer volksr. 98. In Sweden
this hypericum perforatum has to be one of the *nine sorts of*

*flowers* that make the Midsum. nosegay; the picking of it is descr. in Runa '44, p. 22-3 : you lay it under your pillow, and notice what you dream. Again, that plant with St-John's-blood sap (Müllenh. p. 222) is the hart-heu, Schub. p.m. 184. Schütze's Holst. id. 1, 117-8.

OHG. *reinfano,* Graff 3, 521, Swed. *renfane,* tansy, seems to be sacred to elves, Fries's Udfl. 1, 109; it helps in difficult childbirth. Does the name denote a plant that grows on boundaries [rain = strip of grass left betw. hedgeless cornfields] ? conf. *rein-farn,* Kl. schr. 2, 44.

p. 1214.] Was *widertân* orig. widar-dono, formed like ælf-þona ? yet it is *wedertam* in Sumerl. 55, 49. The country-mouse in Rollenhagen, when visited by the town-mouse, lays down a bundle of *widderthan,* that gleams like a red poppy. *Widerthon-moos* (-moss) is polytrichum commune, Schub. p.m. 210, otherwise called golden *frauen-haar* (conf. the holy *wood-moss* of the Samogitians, and the special gods for it, Lasicz 47). Frisch calls *widerthon* a lunaria; the osmunda lunaria is named *ankehr-kraut* (sweep to-), and is supp. to give cows good milk :

> Grüsz dich Gott, *ankehr-kraut !*
> ich brock dich ab, u. trag dich nach haus ;
> wirf bei meinem kuhel (lay flesh on my cow) finger-
> dick auf.                            Höfer 1, 36.

p. 1215.] *Weg-wîse* = solsequium in Albr. v. Halb. 129ᵇ; *wege-weis* = cichorium intybus, Nemnich; conf. AS. *for-tredde,* our wege-tritt. Dâ wênic *wege-rîches* stuont, Parz. 180, 7; other names are *weg-luge* (Stald. 2, 439) from 'luogen,' and ' *Hänslein bei'm weg* ' (or is it ' *häuslein* bei dem weg,' as in Fischart's Onomast. 221 ?). Serv. *bokvitza,* plantago, fr. bok = side; Boh. *čekanka,* fr. čekati = wait [Russ. *popútnik, podorózhnik,* fr. pútĭ, doróga=way].——Dicitur quod *tres rami corrigiolae* (wegetritt) collectae in nomine Trinitatis et cum oratione dominica, suspensi in panno lineo, maculam oculi sine dubio tollunt, Mone 7, 424. Das edle kraut *weg-warte* macht guten augenschein, Ambras. lied. p. 18 ; item es spricht alwärtus, die *wegwart-wurtzeln* soltu niecht essen, so magstu nit wund werden von hauen noch von stechen, Giess. papier-hs. no. 1029 (conf. p. 1244). ' Advocati consueverunt se munire *sambuco* et *plantagine* ut

vincant in causis' is Bohemian, like that about the child's caul
(p. 874n.). The above names remind us of Goth. *vigadeinô*=
tribulus (Suppl. to 1212 mid.), as the Gr. βάτος is perhaps from
βαίνω, and the Lat. sentis akin to Goth. sinþs, via ; yet conf. Kl.
schr. 5, 451 seq. GDS. 211.

p. 1215.] Of the *leek* an ON. riddle says : ' höfði sînu vîsar â
helvegu, en fôtum til sôlar snŷr,' his head points to hell, his feet
to heaven ; to which Heiðrekr answers ' höfuð veit î Hlôðynjar
skaut, en blöð î lopt,' Fornald. s. 1, 469 (conf. the βολβοί in
Aristoph. Clouds 187—193). *Sâra-lauk* sióða, boiling wound-
leeks, means forging swords 1, 468. With the leek men divine,
Dyb. '45, p. 61 ; it drives evil spirits away, Fries's Udfl. 1, 109.
*House-leek*, sempervivum tectorum, Swed. tak-lök, wards off
misfortune 1, 110. ' Radix allii victorialis' is *neun-hömmlere* in
Stald. 2, 236 ; in Nemnich *neun-hemmerlein, sieben-hemmerlein*.
OHG. *surio, surro*, m., cepa, porrum, Graff 6, 273.

p. 1215.] The *rowan* or *rönn* (Dyb. '45, 62-3) is called wild
ash, mountain ash, vogelbeer-baum, sperber-baum, AS. *wice*,
Plattd. *kwieke*, Wolf's Ztschr. 2, 85. Men like a staff made of
*pilber-baum*, sorbus aucuparia, Possart's Estl. 163. Finn. *pihlava*,
sorbus, is planted in holy places : *pihlayat* pyhille maille, Kalev.
24, 71. 94. Renvall sub v.

p. 1216.] *Hab-mich-lieb* and *wol-gemut* (Suppl. to 1214) are
herbs of which wreaths were twined, Hätzl. 15ᵇ; 'ein krenzlîn
von *wolgemuot* ist für sendez trûren guot,' good for love-sick-
ness 162-3.

p. 1216.] A wort, that the mermaid dug on the mount that
might not be touched, makes whoever eats it understand the
*wild beast, fowl and fish*, Hpt. 5, 8. 9. A herb accidentally picked
opens to him that carries it the *thought and speech of others*, Ls.
1, 211-8. Herb chervil *blinds* or gives *double sight*, Garg. 148ᵃ.
Ges. Abent. 2, 267. Whoever carries herb *assidiose* in his hand,
commands spirits, Tit. 6047. When the dew falls in May on
the herb *parbodibisele*, one may harden gold in it, Tit. 3698-9.
Cattle are made to eat *three blooming flowers*, the *blue* among
them, so as not to be led astray into the mountains. Hpt 4, 505.

p. 1216 n.] AS. *ælf-þona* is expl. by *þona* or *þone*, palmes,
pampinus, conf. OHG. *upar-dono*, sudarium ; is *alb-dono* then a
cloth spread by the elves ? If ælf-þone be fem. and = OHG.

alb-dona, *dona* must be pampinus (our dohne, springe or noose),
coil, tendril, and so *alfranke* (p. 448), Hpt 5, 182. AS. *helde*
is sometimes ambrosia. Is *hwátend* (iris Illyrica) equivalent to
soothsaying flower? for *Iris* is at once messenger of the gods,
and rainbow, and a plant which the Slavs call *Perunica*, thunder-
flower. Finn. *wuohen miekka*, caprae ensis, is also iris, sword-
lily.——Other notable herb-names in AS. are: *Oxan-slippa*,
primula veris, E. *oxlip, cowslip*, Dan. *oxe-driv, ko-driv*, Swed.
*oxe-lägg*. *Hundesfreá*, centauria. *Eofor-þrote*, apri guttur, scilla.
*Lust-môce*, ros solis, Nemnich drosera, Stald. 1, 336 egelkraut.
——*Mädere*, venerea, Mone's Quell. 320[b]; Lye has *mäddere*,
rubia, E. *madder ;* Barnes sub v. *madders, mathers*, anthemis,
cotula. *Metere*, febrifuga, Sumerl. 56, 58; and melissa, *metere*
57, 59 (Suppl. to 1244). *Muttere, mutterne*, caltha, Stald. 2,
226; Finn. *matara, mattara ;* 'lus gun mhathair gun athair,'
flower without mother or father: ' a plant resembling flax, which
grows in springs,' Armstr. 368[b].——*Weoðo-bend*, cyclamen con-
volvulus, E. *woodbind, withe-bind*, M. Neth. *wede-winde*, Maerl. 3,
205; conf. *weendungel :* 'ik kenne dat kruud, sede de düvel, do
hadde he *weendungel* freten,' Brem. wtb. 5, 218 (AS. *þung*, pl.
*þungas*, aconitum, helloborus).——*Mageðe, magoðe*, buphthalmus;
conf. '*hay-maiden*, a wild flower of the mint tribe,' Barnes.
*Biacon-weed*, chenopodium, goose-foot, Barnes. *Gloden*, caltha;
also *gladene, glœdene*. *Boðen*, lolium; conf. *beres-boto*, zizania,
*meres-poto*, Graff 3, 81. *Leloðre*, lapathum. *Gearewe*, millefolium, yarrow, OHG. garewâ. *Æthel-ferding, -fyrding*, a
wound-healing plant, from ferd, fyrd = army, war? *Brôðer-wyrt*,
herba quaedam strictum pectus et tussim sanans, Lye. *Hals-wyrt*,
narcissus, from *hálsian* to make whole?

Peculiar OHG. names: *olsenich*, Mone's Quell. 285[b]; *olsnic*,
baldimonia, herba thuris, Sumerl. 55, 11. 57, 26. Ducange sub
v. *ramesdra*. Graff 2, 512. *Striph, stripha*, Graff 6, 751. *Ert-
gallá*, AS. *eorð-gealle*, centaurea major, cornflower. *Hrosse-húf*,
Graff 4, 1180. Add the plant-names in the Wiesbaden glosses,
Hpt 6, 323.

Names still in use: *brändli*, satyrium nigrum, Stald. 1, 216,
small, but scented; it is the Romance *waldser, valser*, Mone's
Anz. '39, 391 (gerbrändli?), conf. *wald-meisterlein*, asperula
odorata, M. Neth. *wal-mêster*, Mone 6, 448. *Herba matris silvae*,

Wallach. *mama padura,* wood-mother, wood-wife, Schott 297.
*Manns-kraft,* geum urbanum, Hess. Ztschr. 4, 81.    *Tag und
nacht* 4, 94.    Sumerl. 58, 29; Ssk. *dies et nox* in one word,
Bopp's Gl. 27[b]; Pol. *dzien i noc,* melampyrum nemorosum, Linde
1, 595[a]. *Partunni-kraut,* stachys alpina, Hess. Zts. 4, 84. *Braut-
treue,* erica, acquires a red tinge, Wächter p. 13; *braut im
haar,* Sommer's Sag. p. 61.——*Berufs-kraut,* anthyllis vulneraria,
Somm. p. 61; *vermein-kraut,* maidenhair, Schm. 2, 587; conf.
*beschrei-kr.* (p. 1195). *Eisen-breche,* sferra-cavallo (p. 974), E.
moonwort, lunaria, Hone's Yrbk 1551. *Maus-öhrlein,* mouse-ear,
herba clavorum, nailwort, makes horses willing to be shod
1550. *Rang* = teufels-zwirn, clematis, Vilmar in Hess. Zts. 4, 94.
*Druten-mehl, hexen-mehl,* semen lycopodii, is sprinkled over sore
babies. *Wind-hexe,* rolling flax, a steppe weed, Russ. perekatí-
pole (roll over field), whose balls drift like thistledown, Kohl's
S. Russia 2, 113-4.

## 2. Stones.

p. 1218.]    Rare stones are called ' steine, die kein gebirge nie
getruoc, noch diu erde bråhte für,' Troj. kr. 2954.    They are
known to Jews : it is a Jew that can tell Alexander what stone
it is, Alex. 7075 ; that master of stone-lore, Evax of Arabia, Lanz.
8531. *Boundary-stones, drei-herrn-steine* are pounded to powder,
and drunk as medicine, Ph. Dieffenb. Wander. 2, 73.    Other
healing stones are ment. in Lohengr. str. 652, defensive helmet-
stones in Aspremont 20. 40-1.    A stone that tells you everything,
Norske folke-ev. 1, 188; a stone taken in the mouth gives a
knowledge of foreign tongues, Otnit Ettm. 3, 32—25. Rhön 126 ;
another, put in the mouth, enables you to travel over water, H.
Sachs i. 3, 291[c].    Simplic. 5, 12 p. 548-9; and there was a stone
that made you fly, Ges. Abent. 3, 212-7.    The *stone of fear* keeps
you from being frightened : ' he hung a *schreck-stein* on him,
Pol. maulaffe 298.

> Quattuor in cunctis sunt insita mythica gemmis,
> durities, virtus, splendorque, colorque perennis
>                                        Gotfr. Viterb. p.m. 367[b].

*Rings, finger-rings* derive all their virtue from the stones set in
them.    A vingerlîn that repels magic, and makes you aware of

it, Lanc. 21451 seq.; one that makes invisible (p. 871). So a
*girdle* with a *precious stone* in it makes whole, Bit. 7050—55.
The *orphanus*, wanting in Megenberg, is ment. by Lessing 8,
175-6. Similar to the orphan is the stone *claugestian* on the
helmet, Roth. 4947 seq. þaer se *beorhta beág* brogden wundrum
*eorcnanstânum* eádigra gehwâm *hlífað ofer heáfde;* heáfelan lixað
þrymmê biþeahte, Cod. Exon. 238; his *eágan* ontŷnde, hâlge
*heáfdes gimmas* 180, 7; is seo, eággebyrd (oculus Phoenicis)
*stâne* gelîcast, gladum gimme 219, 3. Hyaena bestia cujus *pu-
pillae lapideae* sunt, Gl. ker. 146. Diut. 1, 239; and Reinhart's
eyes are supp. to be *carbuncles,* Reinh. 916 seq. One stone is
*oculus felis, oculus mundi, bellocchio,* Nemnich 2, 747-8.——
Precious stones take the place of eyes, Martene's Thes. anecd.
4, 6 (Wachsmuth's Sitten-gesch. 2, 258) : in the sculptured skull
of St Servatius, stones blaze instead of eyes. Swed. *ögna-sten,
ögon sten,* eye-stone, means the pupil; Dan. *öie-steen,* ON. *auga-
steinn;* and Alexander's stone, which outweighs pure gold, but
rises in the scale when covered with a feather and *a little earth,*
is an eye-stone, Lampr. Alex. p. 140—3; see Schlegel's Mus.
4, 131-2-3. Gervinus 1, 549 (ed. 3). *Pupus, κόρη ὀφθαλμοῦ,*
Ducange sub v. It is Oriental too to say 'girl of the eye'; yet
also 'mannikin of the eye,' Gesenius, Pref. xliv. (ed. 2). GDS.
127.

p. 1218 n.] Scythis succinum (amber) *sacrium* (not satrium),
Pliny 37. 2, 40; ubicunque quinta argenti portio inest (auro),
*electrum* vocatur 33. 4. 23. *Prûnt-golt,* electrum, Gl. Sletst. 39,
391. Amber is in Russ. *yantárĭ,* Lith. *gentáras, gintáras,* Lett.
*dzinters, zihters,* conf. OHG. sintar = scoria, GDS. 233; Esth.
*merre-kivvi,* sea-stone, Finn. *meri-kivi.* On the confusion of
amber with pearl, see both Schott in Berl. acad. Abh. '42, p.
361 and H. Müller's Griechenth. 43. Pol. *bursztyn,* Boh.
*agšteyn, akšten.* M. Neth. *lammertynstên,* succinus.

p. 1219.] The pearl: ON. *gimr,* m., gemma, Sæm. 134ᵇ, also
*gim-steinn;* AS. *gim, gim-stân.* With MHG. *mer-griez,* conf.
' daz *griezende mer,*' Fragm. 45ᶜ. The *diamond* was taken to be
crystallized water : 'a little frozen wässerli,' Anshelm 2, 21; fon
diu wirt daz îs dâ zi (thereby turns the ice into) christallan sô
herta, sô man daz fiur dar-uber machôt, unzi diu christalla irgluot,
Merigarto 5, 25; conf. *isînê steina,* ice-stones, O. i. 1, 70 and

'crystal made of ice,' Diez's Leb. d. troub. 159. 165. On the
Ssk. *marakata*, see Bopp's Gl. 255-9. 266; *chandra-kárta*, gemma
fabulosa, quae radiis lunae congelatis nasci creditur 118ª.

p. 1221.] The λυγγούριον is also named by Dioscor. 2, 100.
Of a *stag's* tears or eyes comes a stone. The *dragon's head* contains a diamond, Bosquet 205-6. The *toad-stone*, which occurs
e.g. in Wolf's Deut. sag. p. 496, is likewise in Neth. *padde-
stên*, Boh. *zhabye kamen*, O. Fr. *crapaudine*, Roquef. sub v.; the
.French still say of diamonds, ' il y a *crapaud*.'——There is a
serpent's egg, which ' ad *victorias litium* et *regum aditus* mire
laudatur,' Pliny 29. 3, 12. One *Segerus* has a ' gemma diversi
coloris, *victoriosos* efficiens qui ea utuntur,' Cæs. Heisterb. 4, 10.
*Sige-stein*, Eracl. p. 214. Hahn's Stricker p. 49 ; *seghe-stên*,
Rein. 5420 ; *sige-ring*, Hpt 3, 42 ; hüet dich vor (beware of) alter
wîbe gemein, die künnen *blâsen den sigel-stein*, Hätzl. 93ᵇ, 34 ;
*sigelstein snîden*, Wolkenst. 40, conf. ' ein *bickel* giezen,' Fragm.
38ᶜ. Renn. 13424, *bickel-stein*, Fragm. 21ᶜ. Can sigelstein,
sëgelstein have been the *magnet* ? ON. sëgel-steinn, sailing stone.
——The *swallow-stone*, which grows in the crop of a firstborn
swallow, is known to Diosc. 2, 60; conf. Schm. 3, 399 : schürf
(rip) schwalben auf, so vindestu darinne ein roten (red) stain.

p. 1222.] Georg Agricola (1546) De re metallica libri XII
(Basil. 1657) calls *belemnites* alp-schos, p. 703ᵇ ; *brontia* donnerstein, wetterstein, gros krottenstein, *ceraunia* der glatte donn.,
der glat wett., der glatte gros krott. 704ª ; *ombria* donderst.,
wett., grosz krott. 706ª. The thunder-bolt has healing power,
Ph. Dieffenb. Wander. p. 33; the ON. for it is *skruggu-steinn ;*
and we often find Þórsteinn as a man's name, e.g. Egilss. 476.
Another Finnic name for the bolt is *Ukkoisen nalkki*, U.'s wedge ;
Lith. *Laumes papas*, L.'s pap, Nesselm. 277ᵇ. 353ᵇ, and LG. *mare-
tett*, the (night-)mare's teat, N. Pr. prov. bl. 2, 380. Silex is in
ON. *hiegetill*, quasi rorem generans.

p. 1222.] The *diamond* can only be softened by goat's-blood,
Pliny 37, 4. August. De civ. D. 21, 4 ; conf. N. Cap. 69. Er.
8428. Ms. 1, 180ª. Parz. 105, 18.

The *carbuncle* is taken from the unicorn's forehead, Parz. 482,
29 ; hebt den moed van een *Espetin*, want hi draegt karbonkelen
in sin hoorn, Ndrl. Heemskind p. m. 12. The carbuncle shines in
the darkest night, and puts out other stones, Hartm. büchl. 1500.

Reinh. 920. Morolt 45. Gr. Rud. 8, 10 (*Vätte-lys* are in Dan. superstition small stones, which the spirits had for lamps, Molb. Dial. 663). The carbuncle pales its lustre when the hero dies, Rol. 196, 19; it lies 'ze Loche in dem Rîne,' Ms. 1, 15ª. Sommer on Flore p. xxvii. 1667.

The *magnet*: ON. *leiðar-steinn*, Landn. 1, 2; E. *loadstone* [i.e. leading, as in loadstar]. Prov. *aziman, ariman, ayman*, Fr. *aimant*, Sp. *iman.* MHG. *age-stein*, Diut. 1, 60-1. Trist. 204, 14. 36. M. Neth. *tôch-stên* diese up-tôch, Maerl. 3, 124. It has been used in navigation since the 13th cent., Bible Guiot 633—653; legend of the loadstone, Altd. w. 2, 89.

*Stone-coal* is called Türken-blut-stein, stein-öl Turken-blut, Stald. 1, 329.

## CHAPTER XXXVIII.

### SPELLS AND CHARMS.

p. 1224.] On the power of the *three words*, Kalev. 9, 34. 161; conf. Arnim's März. 1, 47. [Tibetian and Mongolian writers dilate on the force of each syllable in the Buddhist formula 'om mani padmi hom.']. Singing and saying turn to magic: ἐπῳδὴ ἰατρῶν, Plato's Charmides p. 156-8; θελκτήριον, charm, incantation; *verba puerpera* dixit (Lucina), Ov. Met. 10, 511. OHG. *pi-galan* (be-sing) in the Mersebg spell; *galdr gala*, Sæm. 97-8-9; *rîkt gôl* Oddr, *ramt gôl* Oddrûn, bitra *galdra* 240ª. Fr. *charme* is fr. carmen: un *bon charme* vos aprendré, Ren. 7650; *carminare* plagam, to charm a wound (away), Altd. bl. 2, 323; conf. 'er *sprach* zer wunden *wunden-segen*,' Parz. 507, 23. The sorceress is *ansprecherin*, Mone's Anz. 7, 424; conf. *berufen, beschreien*, becall, becry, Ettn. Maulaffe 546-7. ON. *orð-heill*, Sæm. 120ᵇ. Finn. *sanoa*, to say = conjure; *sanat*, conjuration, Castrén.

Blessings are pronounced more esp. at morning and evening: swer bî liebe hât gelegen (had a good night), der sol dar senden sînen *morgen-segen*, MS. 2, 169ª; *gesegenen* unde tiefe beswern, Mar. 188, 30 (conf. '*tiefe* fluochen,' p. 1227); *besworn* sîs du *vil tiure!* Ges. Abent. 3, 53; einem die krankheit *absegnen* (bless

one's illness away), Thurneyser 2, 92.——Cursing is MHG.
*verwâzen*: var hin *verwâzen*, MS. 2, 172[b]; nu var von mir *v.*
Ls. 3, 77; nein pfui sie heut *v.*! Tit. 600, 2; *verfluochet* u.
*verwâzen* wart vil ofte der tac, dâ sîn geburt ane lac (the day
that his birth was on), Arm. Heinr. 160; and the contrary:
gehoehet (extolled) sî der süeze tac, dâ dîn geburt von êrste an
lac, Winsbekin 1. To verwâzen answers the O. Fr. *dahê, duhez,
dehait, dahet, dehez, dehé, daz ait*, often preceded by *mal* or *cent*,
Garin 1, 10. 209. 2, 46. Ren. 404. 1512. 9730. 11022. Méon's
N. réc. 1, 202. 232. 4, 12. Orange 1, 202. 2, 151, etc. Trist.
3072. Aspr. 1[a]. 46[b]. 23[b]. Ferabr. lix[a]. As Walloon *haitî*
= sain, and *mâhaitî* = malsain (Grandgagn. 1, 265), we may
suppose a Celtic origin (Suppl. to 952).——Einen *mit fluoche
bern* (smite), Mart. 163[c], mit dem fluoche *seilen* 226[a] (flüeche
*lîden*, Walth. 73, 5; fluoch *bejagen*, MS. 2, 137; in sih selbon
*luadun* (they loaded) mihilan fluah, O. iv. 24, 30); *bîst* unde
*flôk*, Upstand. 1837 (the Goth. beist?); *digen* einen, precari,
imprecari, Gramm. 4, 655. AS. *wyrigean*, maledicere, Homil. 2,
30. ON. *bölva*, diris devovere, Sæm. 186; *röggva*, a diis mala
imprecari (lit. to fold? akin to röggr, röggvar, pallium plicatum?).
O. Slav. *kliáti*, pres. kl'nu, Serv. *kléti*, pres. kunem [Russ.
kliástĭ, klinátĭ], to curse.

p. 1224.] The AS., beside *hwistlian*, has *hwisprian*, to *whisper*. MHG. slangen (snake's) *wispel*, Diut. 1, 58; *wispler*, who
sweetly *wispelt* to the fishes, Gesta Rom. ed. Keller p. 65. OHG.
*winisôn*, to mutter. Apuleius p. m. 79 speaks of *magicum susur-
ramen*. Piping too has a magical effect: il dit un charme
que il avoit aprins, trois fois *siffla*, Garin 2, 104. A shirt laid
lengthwise on the table is *bemurmured* till it stands upright,
jumps about, and lies down again; you judge by this of the
owner's illness, Ettn. Medic. maulaffe 269, 270. Neth. *luisteren*
is both to listen and to speak low; the witch is a *luister-vink,
luister-zuster.*

p. 1226.] MHG. *rûnen* is to whisper: 'daz ir mit ir *rûnet*,
you whisper to her'; 'daz si mit iu niht *rûnen* kan,' MS. 2, 83[b].

Runes were also cut on the roots of trees: risti *á rôtina* rûnir,
riððraði î blôði, qvað sîðan yfir galdra, gêck *öfug* ok *andsælis*
(against the sun) um trêt, með mörg römm um-mæli; he then
throws the wood into the sea, and lets it drift to one's de-

struction, Grettissaga c. 85 ; scera *á rótum* râs *viðar*, Sæm. 29ª.
Rune-sticks had things *wrapt* and *woven* round them, Sæm.
195ᵇ, like the Fris. tênar ; lagði *á stafi* 94ª ; *hete-rúne* bond, Cod.
Exon. 416, 6 ; *inwit-rúne* 279, 7 ; *helli-rúna,* like M. Neth. *hel-scouwinghe*? Parton. 20, 13 ; *hell-raune,* Mathesius 1562, 154ᵇ ;
liosta *hel-stöfum,* Sæm. 145ᵇ, conf. *faesta feikn-stafa* 41ᵇ. For-
nald. s. 1, 436. AS. *fácn-stœf* ; bregða *blund-stöfum,* Sæm. 193ᵇ,
at *gaman-rúnom* 25-6, *i val-rúnom* 160ᵇ, *mál-rúnar* 214ᵇ, rûnar
*viltar* 252ª, *vilt rísta* 252ᵇ.

    p. 1227.] The might of the Word is extolled by Freidank 67, 1 :

> *Durch wort* ein wilder slange gât (snake goes)
> zem manne, da 'r sich toeren lât (lets be fooled) ;
> *durch wort* ein swert vermîdet (forbears)
> daz ez nieman versnîdet (cuts no one) ;
> *durch wort* ein îsen nieman mac
> verbrennen, gluot ez allen tac.

Er sprach *ein wort mit grim,* daz sich *der berc úf-slóz* (opened),
Altsw. 80 ; jâ möht ich sît einen boum *mit mîner bete* (prayer),
sunder wâpen, nider geneigen, MS. 1, 51ª. A *runar-belti* opens
any lock, drives all disease away, Färöiske qväder pp. 228. 286 ;
two dwarfs *cut* vafrlogi *with runes* 138. 140. Song can burst
fetters, Somadeva 1, 134. ON. *þoku-vísur* call up mist and
darkness, Fornm. s. 3, 97-8. A *letter* was tied round the sword,
Wigal. 4427. 7335, as runes had formerly been carved on it.
Men used to bind certain things by oath, e.g. *swords,* Altd. bl.
1, 43. Ligamenta aut etiam *scripta* in contrarietatem alterius
excogitare, Lex. Visig. vi. 2, 4.

    p. 1228.] Let one or two *good wishes* precede the curses :

> Got müeze im êre mêren (add honour) !
> zuo flieze im aller sælden fluz,
> niht wildes mîde sînen schuz (shun his shot) ;
> sîns hundes louf, sîns hornes duz (tooting)
> erhelle im u. erschelle im wol nâch êren ! Walth. 18, 25.

conf. the curse, Ls. 2, 425. Here is a beautiful blessing :

> Der sumer sî sô guot (be so kind),
> daz er die schoene in sîner wunne (bliss)
> lâze wünneclîche leben (let blissful live) !

Swaz wol den ougen tuot (whate'er delights the eye),
und sich den liuten lieben kunne (can please),
daz müeze ir diu Sælde geben,
swaz grüenez ûf von erden gê,
oder touwes obenan nider rîsen muoz (may trickle down),
loup (foliage), gras, bluomen und klê (clover)!
Der vogel doenen (melody) geb der schoenen
wünneclîchen gruoz (blissful greeting)!   MS. 2, 183ᵃ.
Again: ze heile erschîne im tages sunne, nahtes mâne, und
iegslîch stern!   MS. 2, 174ᵃ; dîn zunge grüene iemer, dîn herze
ersterbe niemer!   Trist. 7797; Got lâze im wol geschehen!
MS. 1, 74ᵇ; Got des geve en jummer hêl, dat kraket (so that
it roars), Wizlau 9, 28.

Curses are far more frequent and varied: mîne vlüeche sint
*niht smal*, Beneke 377.   They operate quickly: ein *swinder* fluoch,
MS. 2, 71ᵇ; mit *snellem* fluoche, Tit. 2588; ein *wilder* fluoch,
Wolkenst. 42.   They hold men like a vice: uns *twinget* noch des
fluoches *zange*, MS. 2, 166ᵃ.   They *alight, settle, cling*: solten alle
vlüeche *kleben*, ez müezte lützel liutes leben, Freid. 130, 12; der
fluoch *bekleip*, Hpt 5, 516; dem muoz der fl. *bekliben* 5, 550; der
fl. *klebet* 8, 187.   They *burn* you up, Nalus p. 177.   They take
*flight*, they turn home as birds to their nest, Berth. 63; die flüche
*flohen* um die wette, Günther 163.——Strong above all is the
*curse of the dying* : þat var trûa þeirra î forneskju, at *orð feigs
manns* mætti mikit, ef han bölvaði ô-vin sînum *með nafni* (cursed
his unfriend by name), hence names were suppressed, Sæm. 186ᵃ.
Sigfrit, wounded to death, *scolds*, Nib. 929, 3. 933, 4 (see *schelten*
below).   A faither's blessin' bigs the toun, A *mither's curse* can
ding it doun.   A *mother's curse* is not to be turned aside,
Holtzm. 3, 144.   Effectual too is the *pilgrim's* curse, Gudr. 933,
and the *priest's*, Holtzm. Nib. 117.   The curse of *aged men* that
fear God works fearful woe, Insel Felsbg 1, 22.   *Carters* have
curses on the tip of their tongue, Philander 2, 345; so have
*officers*, Gellert 4, 145.

*Oaths* and *curses* coll. by Agricola nos. 472—502; *spell-bindings*
in Ls. 1, 410-1. 2, 424—8.   Sæm. 85.   Fornald. s. 3, 203-4; a
song of curses on Otto III. in Pertz 2, 153.   De Vries of Hoofts
Warenar 97—100; Servian curses in Talvj 2, 385.   Vuk nos.
152-4-7. 162. 219. 393.

The savage heartiness of the cursing is set forth in a number of strong phrases : ' his cursing was *cruel* to hear,' Ettn. Unw. d. 743 ; ' he set up a *cursing* and *scolding*, no wonder if the *castle had sunk* into the ground, Schweinichen 2, 70 (daz se dâ *fluochten* niemen, unde daz Hagenen kint bleip *unbescholten*, Gudr. 933, 4) ; er fahet an (begins) ze flûchen u. ze schweren, dass das *erdtreich möcht undergon* (?) ; ' cursing, enough to *send stones flying* into the sky,' Käserei 126 ; ' he swore fit to make the *sky bow down*,' Wickram's Rollw. 9 ; ' cursing, so that it *might have thundered*,' Garg. 149ᵃ ; ' cursing, till the *rafters crack*,' Dict. sub v. balke; ' he curses *all signs* (omens), till the floor cracks,' Hebel 44; to curse *all signs*, Stald. 2, 468 (p. 1105 end) ; ' swearing till the *toads jump*,' Firmenich 2, 262 (conf. the krotten-segen, Garg. 230ᵃ) ; ' he curses *one leg* off the *devil's* haunch, and the *left horn* off his head,' Garg. 232ᵃ ; ' he cursed the *nose* off his face,' Schuldban 27 (?).——Ejaculations that call upon God to curse and crush, are the most solemn: daz ez *Got verwâze !* Er. 7900 ; sô sî ich verwâzen vor *Gotes ougen !* Herb. 1068; daz in *Got von himele* immer gehoene ! Gudr. 1221, 4; ' *God's power* confound thee ! ' Melander 2, no. 198; *Hercules dique* istam perdant, Plaut. Cas. ii. 3, 57 ; qui illum *di* omnem *deaeque* perdant 61 : *Got du sende* an mînen leiden man *den tôt*, daz ich von den *ülven* werde *enbunden*, MS. 1, 81ᵃ (p. 1161) ; swer des schuldig sî, den *velle Got* u. nem îm al sîn êre 81ᵇ ; Serv. *ubió gha Bogh*, Vuk (ed. nov.) no. 254.——M. Neth. curses use the word ' over ' in consigning to the devil : nu *over* in duvels ere, Limb. 4, 62 ; *over* in's duvels name 4, 1088 ; nu *over* in der duvele hant 7, 638 ; nu *over* in's duvels geleide, Karel 2, 4447. MHG. der tievel *var* ime *in den munt* (get in his mouth), Reinh. 1642 ; dass dir der henker *in den rachen führe* (in your throat), Felsenb. 3, 443; dass dich ! (devil take, underst.) ; dass dich das wetter verborne, Meland. 2, no. 362; ir letz' die *slach der schauer* u. *kratz der wilde ber*, Wolkenst. 30.——ON. eigi hann *iötnar, gâlgi görvallan*, Sæm. 255ᵃ ; tröll hafi þik allan, ok svâ gull þit, Kormakss. p. 188; far þu nu þar er *smyl* hafi þik (to one's ship on landing), conf. the formula of benediction in Kg Horne, 143.*

---

* With the curse ' daz die *vor kilchen* laegen ! ' conf. also ' Joh. *vor Ckilkun*,' Oestr. arch. 6, 173; ein jâr *vor kilchen* stân, MS. 2, 121ᵃ ; muoter diu ir kint lât *vor spital* oder *kirchen* ligen, Renn. 18376 ; an *ein velt legen* (in unconsecr. ground), Berth. 230. 330 ; *begrebnisse ûf dem velde*, Gefk. Beil. 10.

Du scholt varen in dat *wilde brôk,* Mone's Schausp. 2, 100-1 ; an
den *wilden wolt* 2, 101 ; conf. *'ze holze* varn,' Kolocz 262 ; Klinsôr
und waerest *über sê,* MS. 2, 6ᵃ; versigelen müez er *ûf daz mer*
von wîbe u. von kinde 1, 6ᵃ. Lett. *eiy vilkam,* go to the wolves ;
*vilkeem apendams,* wolves eat thee, Stender 360 ; so ezzen si die
*wilden krân,* Keller's Erz. 196 ; þitt skyli hiarta *hrafnar* slîta,
Sæm. 232ᵃ; dat uch de *raven* schinnen, Karlm. 140, 23 ; des
müezen si die *wolve* nagen, Altd. w. 2, 56 ; ir herzen müezen
*krânvuoz* nagen, MS. 2, 119ᵇ; den vermîden (shun him) *rôsen,*
u. alle *zîtelôsen* (daisies), u. aller *vogellîne sanc* 2, 63ᵃ; ich schaffe
daz ir aller *fröiden strûzen* ie widerspenic müezen wesen 1, 4ᵃ;
Marke du *versink* 2, 79ᵇ; ut te *paries inclinans* obruat, ut te
*afflicta senio arbor caeduave* obruat, Meland. 2, no. 198.——Death,
disease and sorrow are often imprecated : nu *iz* dir (eat to thyself)
den grimmen *tôt,* Ges. Abent. 2, 667 ; wolde Got, waere dîn *houpt
fûl* (rotting in the ground), Renn. 12192 ; daz dich *aezen* die
*maden* (maggots), Helbl. 1, 1212 ; daz diu *ougen* im *erglasen* 2,
512 (a Gaelic curse : *marbhphaisg,* the shroud over thee !) ; sô
er müeze *erknûren* (?) 8, 227 ; hin ze *allen sühten* 2, 745 (conf.
*alles, aller,* Dict. 1, 213) ; sô dich diu *suht benasche* 1, 1202 ; Got
geb dir die *drüs* u. den *ritten,* Pasq. 1, 157 ; diu *suht* an iuwern
lôsen *kragen* (neck), Reinh. p. 302. *Dahaz* aie parmi le *col,* Méon
N. réc. 1, 202. 232 ; *mau-dahet* ait et el *col* et el *nes,* Orange 5,
2650 ; *cent dehez* ait parmi la *cane,* Trist. 3072 ; tu ut *oculos emun-
gare* ex capite *per nasum* tuos, Plaut. Cas. ii. 6, 39 ; dass du die
*nase in's gesicht* behältst, Reuter olle kam. 3, 25-6. 48. 301 ; da
var diu *suht* in iuwer *ôren,* MSH. 3, 438ᵃ; *wé* dir in die *zende*
(teeth), Ben. 324 ; la male *gote* aiez as *dens,* Ren. 14322 ; daz iu
der munt werde *wan* (without) *der zungen,* Parz. 316, 4 ; daz *si*
(the tongue) *verswellen* müeze, u. ouch diu *kel* (gullet), MS. 2, 5ᵃ ;
dîn *zunge* müeze dir werden *lam,* Morolf 1150 ; in müezen *erlamen
die knübel* (their nibblers, teeth ?), Hpt 6, 492. Mod. ' may you
*turn sour.'* Lith. kad tu *suruktum* (shrivel up). *Wâfen* über
diu *ougen,* etc., woe to the eyes wherewith I saw thee, woe to the
arms wherein I held thee, Ettm. Ortn. 7, 2 ; daz er immir *ubil jâr*
muoze haben, Ksrchr. 6958, conf. malannus (p. 1160 end).——
There is a curse beginning ' *Als* leit sî dir (so woe be to thee),
Karajan, Teichn. 41 ; conf. ' *Als* unglück dich (= auf dich ?) fliege,
Kell. Erz. 244, 31 : mîn sêle sî *ungeheilet,* Rab. 79 ; daz si sîn

*g'unéret* (they be dishonoured), MS. 1, 194ᵃ. ON. vön sê su *vættr vers* ok *barna*, Sæm. 214ᵇ; wan, waere er *swerzer dan ein kol*, MS. 2, 100ᵇ; der *werde z'einem steine* 1, 6ᵃ; on the contrary ' Be born a *man*,' Somadeva 1, 7. 1, 81. Vervluochet sî der *tac*, diu *wîle* (day, hour), Mai 137, 38. 138, 1; conf. vloecte die *wile*, Lanc. 12224-755. 16250; sô *hazz* mich *allez daz sî*, Helbl. 15, 677.

p. 1228.] (*Rutam* serentes) prosequuntur etiam cum *maledictis*, Pallad. Rutil. 4, 9. Women *boiling yarn* must keep *telling lies*, or it will not turn white.——A solemn adjuration is in Swed. *mana neder* (to charm down?), Runa '44, 60; M. Neth. *manen*, *bemanen*, Belg. mus. 2, 116-7. Finn. *manaan*, monere, adjurare; *manaus* exsecratio.

p. 1229.] With *hellirûna* take the prop. name *Walarûna*, Karajan 67, 16, and the *sepulcrorum violatrix* mentioned after 'adultera' and 'malefica' in Lex Burgund. 34, 3. Grôa sings nine *galdra* to her son, and the galdr is called *fiölnytr*, Sæm. 97ᵇ. Conversely the child talks with the mother at her grave, Rhesa dainos 22, and Svegder wakes his dead mother in the hill, DV. 1, 264. *Eulogies sung at the grave-mound* are also ment. in Hall-biörn p. 859. *Raising the dead* comes easy to christian saints, but it was more than Zeus could do: τούτων ἐπῳδὰς οὐκ ἐποίησε, Aesch. Eum. 649. '*Linguae defuncti* dira carmina ligno insculpta supponere' forces him to speak, Saxo Gr. ed. M. 38. The tongue sings aloud after the head is cut off, Ecke 239.

p. 1230.] Wolvesdrüzzel's and other magic is ascr. to Simon:

> Bindet man ime die vuoze unde die hende,
> schiere lôsit er die gebende;
> *diu slôz heizit er ûfgân* (bids the locks open),
> nihein îsen mac vor im bestân.
> in hulzînen siulen (wooden posts)
> machet er die sêle,
> daz die liute waenent daz sie leben.
> alde ronen heizit er bern, etc.     Kaiserchr. 2118.

Much the same is told of Oðinn, Yngl. saga c. 7.

p. 1230.] Es *regnet* u. *schneiet* alles von sacramenten u. *flüchen*, Albrecht's Fluch. ABC. 45. Men spoke contemptuously of *aniles veteranarum fabulae,* Pertz 6, 452[b], and *altes wîbes fluochen,* Ges. Abent. 3, 78.

p. 1231.] Kl. schr. 2, 1 seq. *Hera duoder* = AS. hider and þider, Hpt 9, 503[a]. Wright 289[b]. *Suma clûbôdun umbi cuniowidi;* so three white maidens pick and pull at flowers and wreaths, Müllenh. p. 350. Freyr also sets free fr. bonds (Suppl. to 215). Grôa sings:

> Þann gel ek inn fimta
> ef þer *fiöturr* verðr
> borinn at bôg-limum;
> Leifnis elda læt ek þer
> fyr legg af kveðna,
> ok *stökkr* þâ *lâss af limum*
> en *af fôtum fiötur.*          Sæm. 98[a].

Minne sô *bint* die minneclîche, oder aber mich *en-bint* (love bind her too, or unbind me), Keller's Rom-vart 651; conf. *beadorûnan onbindan,* Beow. 996; 'to burst bolts and fetters,' St Louis 86, 7. 96, 2. Dietm. of Mersebg says: legimus, quod unius *captivi vincula,* quem uxor sua putans mortuum assiduis procuravit exequiis, toties *solverentur,* quoties pro eo acceptabiles Deo Patri *hostiae* ab ea *offerrentur,* ut ipse ei post retulit, cum domum suam liber revisit, Pertz 5, 740.——Side by side with bond-spells stand the *wound-blessings:* den *wunt-segen* man im sprach, St Louis 1531; conf. the houpt-segen, ougen-s., pferit-s. and *wunden-segen* in Hpt. 4, 577. By magic spell a *wound* is quickly healed, Holtzm. Ind. sag. 2, 176. The sword also receives blessing: *swertes segen,* Frauenlob p. 77; *segent* er im daz *swert,* Mai 83, 39; *segen dîn swert,* Altsw. 64.

p. 1234.] Kl. schr. 2, 1 seq.; to the passages there quoted p. 12, add: *ze holz varn,* Hpt 2, 539; *ze holze, ze walde varn,* Hahn's Stricker 9, 13. 10, 33. 11, 78; *vuor zi walde,* Diem. 110, 1; dîn setzen ist noch niht *ze holz* (thy stake is not yet lost), Fragm. 23[b]. With the first line of the Spell, conf. *Petrus u. Paulus gingen to holt un to brok,* Lisch 9, 226. Balder's foal must be the horse that was burnt with him, Sn. 18.——One more spell for a lamed horse runs thus:

> Jeg red mig (I rode) engang igjennem et led,
> saa fik min sorte fole vred (my black foal got hurt);

saa satte jeg kjöd mod kjöd, og blod mod blod,
saa blev min sorte fole god.

*Floget* (ON. *flog*, dolor acer) botas genom denna lösning : '*floget*
och *flömdet* skall fly ur brusk och ben i stock och sten, i namn
Fader,' etc. Då att upropas trenne gänger : ' *trollet satt i berget,*
hästen (horse) feck floget, spott i hand, slå i mun, bot i samma
stund,' Rääf. Esthonian spells in Kreutzwald and Neuss p.
97-8-9. 122-3. On the cure for dislocation in Lapland, see
Castrén's Reise 153. Ernst Meier p. 516. We still say of a
platitude, it wouldn't cure a lame jade. To the spell in Cato, add
the formula ' mota et soluta,' Grotefend's Rud. Umbr. 4, 13. A
similar spell in Atharva-veda, 4, 12 : ' Setting up art thou,
setting up, setting the broken bone; set this one up, Arundhatî !
What in thee is injured, what is broken, thy Maker set it right
again, *joint to joint.* Come *marrow by marrow*, and *joint by joint;*
what is gone of thy flesh, and eke thy bone, shall grow ; *marrow
to marrow* be joined, *skin with skin* arise, blood arise on thy
bone; whate'er was broken, set right, O Herb ! Arise, walk,
haste thee away, fair as a chariot runs on wheel, felloe and nave.
Stand firmly upright ! If it broke by falling in pit, or a stone
being thrown have hit, together, as parts of a chariot, *fit limb to
limb the Elf* (ribhu) ! '
    p. 1235.] Cod. Monac. lat. 536 sec. xii. has the spell altogether
in narrative form : *Nesia nociva perrexit vagando per diversas
plateas, quaerens quem laedere posset; cui occurrit Dominus et
dixit : ' Nesia, quo vadis?* ' ' Vado ad famulum Dei N., ossa
fricare, nervos medullare, carnes exsiccare.' Cui dixit Dominus :
' praecipio tibi in nomine Patris, etc., ut deseras famulum Dei, et
*pergas in desertum locum.*' So in *colic of the head or belly*, the
spell-speaking old woman grasps the painful part, presses it
tightly together, and says 9 times : 'in the name of God, etc.,
*lady mother*, I seize thee, I squeeze thee, *do go to rest in thy
chamber* where the Lord created thee,' N. Pr. prov. bl. 3, 472.
In Masuria they say: 'Depart, *ye white folk* (białe ludzie, p. 1157)
fr. this christened Gottlieb, out of his skin, his body, his blood,
his veins, his joints and all his limbs. Far in the sea is *a great
stone*, thither go, thither sail, there drink and there devour, by
the might of God, etc.,' ibid. 3, 474. And for the *evil eye* :

'Dropped the dew from the sky, from the stone, on the earth. As
that dew vanishes, has vanished, is blown away in air, so may
*thrice nine enchantments vanish, perish in air and be blown away,*'
ibid. 3, 475.

p. 1241.]    *Wahs,* wax, is fr. wahsan, to grow, as cera fr.
crescere; conf. 'Des genuhtsam *nam zuo,* als ein *teic* wol *erhaben,*'
grew as a dough well risen, Ges. Abent. 2, 446.   To ' bere þâ
*turf tó cyrcean*' in the AS. bôt (p. 1237 beg.) corresp. the ' *cespitem terrae super altare* ponere,' Kemble no. 177.   The spells in
it, and the laying of a broad loaf in the first furrow, are illustr.
by Pliny 25. 4, 10 : ' hac (radice panaces) evulsa, scrobem repleri
*vario genere frugum* religio est ad terrae piamentum.'    Bebelii
Facetiae p. 72: supplicationes circum agros frugiferos fieri solitae.
As cakes were baked for Bealtine, so were ' Siblett cakes after
wheat-sowing,' Hone's Yrbk 1596.——Old spells spoken at *flax-
sowing* in Schaumburg, Lynker nos. 319, 320, in Bavaria, Panzer
2, 549—551, in Thuringia, Meland. Jocoser. tom. 2 no. 503.
The Wallachians *dance* to the hemp (pentru cinnib), the dancer
*lifting* her arms as *high* as she can, that the hemp may grow
high, Schott p. 302.    At Newyear's midnight the Esthonian
farmer throws a handful of each sort of grain on to the shelf,
crying ' God grant the grain this year may grow *that high,*'
Possart's Estl. 171.

p. 1242.]    In Stricker's farce of the Thieves, *Sant Martín*
professes to guard the oxen in the stall, Hahn pp. 22 —27; and
a blessing for swine says ' *Johannes* videat illos, *Martinus* expas-
cat,' Hattemer 1, 410ᵃ.   The ' Abraham's garden ' in the herdsman's spell occurs elsewh. too : durch den *Abrahemschen garten,*
Orendel 1240; ez leit uns in *Abrahames garten,* MSH. 3, 223ᵇ.
A Finn. song in Kantel. 1, no. 176 says, *Jesus* guards the flock.
*Suvetar* and *Etelä* (mother nature) watch the cattle, Kalevala
(Castrén 2, 50).

p. 1242.]    Haltrich found a Germ. *bee-spell* in the pasteboard
cover of a book (no. 245 of Schässburg school library) entitled
Disput. de Deo, etc. Claudiopoli 1570 : Maria stund auf eim sehr
hohen berg.   sie sach einen suarm bienen kommen phliegen.   sie
hub auf ihre gebenedeyte hand, sie verbot in da zu hant, ver-
sprach im alle hilen u. die beim versloszen, *sie sazt im dar ein
fas,* das Zent Joseph hat gemacht : ' in das solt ehr phlügen (into

this shall ye fly), u. sich seines lebens da genügen.' In nomine, etc. Amen.

p. 1243.] 'They made *willow-flutes* and *elder-pipes*,' Garg. 193ᵃ; han *spelade barken* af all slags träd (could play the bark off any kind of tree), Arvidss. 2, 311 ; han *sp. b.* af hårdaste träd 2, 314; han *lekte barken* af björke, af boke-trä (birch, beech) 2, 317 ; gerath wol (turn out well), pfeifen-holz, *ich pfeif dir* ja wol darzu, oder du wirst zum bolz, Garg. 213ᵃ; will das holz nit zu'n pfeifen geraten, *ich pfeif im dan wol*, so will ich singen, so gerat's zum bolz, ibid. Other rhymes for loosening bark in Woeste p. 20. Firmenich 1, 294. 352. 426. 442. 2, 102. Panzer 1, 269. Fiedler 97.

p. 1244.] What herb is *febrifuga?* for which Sumerl. 56, 58 gives *metere* (Suppl. to 1216 n., mid.); Gl. Sletst. 39, 405 febrefugia *matirna;* Dioscor. 3, 7 centaurium minus, multiradix, 3, 126 conyza, intybus; '*featherfowl*, the plant feverfew,' Barnes. ——A spell like the AS. one, in which the disease is bidden withdraw, is in Serv. called *ustuk*, fr. ustuknuti, to retire; and the herb employed is likewise *ustuk*. Not only witches, but *rats* and *mice* are sung away, as by the famed rat-catcher of Hameln. In Ireland it is a gift of hereditary poets, Proc. of Ir. Acad. 5, 355—366.

p. 1245.] With the AS. idiom agrees the MLG.: ic en-can den *honger* niet *genesen*, Ver Ave in Belg. mus. 6, 414; conf. M. Neth. *ghenesen*, ghenas = sanare, Lanc. 1996. 8458. Maerl. 3, 190. 2, 111 ; but also = sanari, Maerl. 2, 156, was genesen = sanatus erat 2, 135.

p. 1247.] *Maren*, nightmares, Gefk. Beil. 151. *Bocks-mahrte*, spectre, Kuhn in Hpt 5, 490 ; *kletter-m., drück-m.*, Sommer p. 46. Slovèn. *mora*, both mare and nightm., fr. morim (I throttle)? *kiki-mora*, nightm., Hanusch 333. In the eastern parts of Mittelmark, *murraue* means oppressive as nightmare, but also a being like the Harke or Holle of other places, that has tangled eyebrows, that mats the hair and knits up branches of fir trees, Hpt 4, 386. 5, 488. A *drom* of the *mére* = maar-zopf? Diut. 1, 439. *Mare-zitz*, -teat (Suppl. to 1222). Ir. *tromluidhe*, nightm., fr. trom = heavy.——Of 7 boys or 7 girls born in succession, one becomes a nightmare. Nightmares slip through a buckle-hole in your belt, and press you, Müllenh. p. 242-3-4;

dich hât *geriten* der mar, Ges. Abent. 3, 60. Where the maar
has alighted on the corn, it turns black or full of cockles ; the
hop on which she has sat spoils, Wolf p. 689. On maar-spells,
see Hpt 7, 537-8. Altogether like the Hennebg spell is one
fr. Kuhland :

> Olle wasser wote (wade),
> olle baemer blote (un-blade, disleaf),
> olle baege staige (mountains climb),
> olle kieche-speitze maide (spires avoid) !     Meinert p. 44.

And they are found in other parts too, Leopr. 26. Panzer 1, 269.
Kuhn p. 461.

p. 1248.] With the spell ' Sprach jungfrau Hille : *blut stand
stille !* ' conf. the adjuring of blood in Hpt 4, 391, and the
frequent formula : *stant* pluot *fasto !* Kl. schr. 2, 29 ; *stand
still*, du wildes blut ! Mone 6, 469 ; daz du *verstandest*, u. nit
mê gangest 7, 420 ; dô *verstuont* daz bluot vil gar, Walth. v. Rh.
138, 11 ; *verstellen*, to stanch, Mone 6, 460. 7, 420. In a spell
for stanching blood, the history of iron is related, Kalev. rune 3
(nov. ed. 9). There is a plant named *bluot-stant*, Sumerl. 56, 66 ;
a Thracian herb $\check{\iota}\sigma\chi$-$\alpha\iota\mu o\varsigma$, Welcker's Kl. schr. 3, 29. Fris.
' blôd *sketta*,' protect, Richth. 236, 13.——In the names Blut-
stülpe, Blut-gülpe, *stülpen* is to stanch, M. Neth. *stelpen*, Lanc.
3593. Part. 90, 15 ; *stelpte* mans bloet, Lanc. 42658, wonden
*gestelpt* 44470 ; thaz bluot iru *firstulti* = se sisteret, O. iii. 14, 22 ;
and *gülpe* resembles the Norse Gylfi. MHG. daz bluot *ver-
straeten*, Pantal. 228.

> Sîne *wunden* si besach (she examined),
> ir *segen* si darüber sprach.     Wigam. 5267.

' Holy Tumbo *bless* this *wound* away ' (p. 528-9. Suppl. to 1231
end).——Fingerworm-spells, see Happel in Mannhdt's Ztschr.
3, 2. E. Meier's Sag. no. 464-5. A red, a white, and a black
worm in Mone's Ndrl. lit. 337 ; white, black, grey and green in
a Cod. Dresd. M. 21ª. ' Christus in petra sedebat ' sounds like
' Tumbo saz in berke,' Kl. schr. 2, 29 ; Rother ûf eime steine
saz, Roth. 442. [Pillicock sat on Pillicock's hill, K. Lear].

' *God the Lord* went over the land, there met him 70 sorts of
*gouts* and *goutesses*. Then spake the Lord : Ye 70 gouts and

goutesses, whither would ye? Then spake the 70 g. and g.:
We go over land, and take from men their health and limbs.
Then spake the Lord: Ye shall go to an elder-bush, and break
off all his boughs, and leave unto (naming the patient) his
straight limbs. In the name, etc.'——Conf. ' flaugk blatter u.
nicht zubrist, das gebeut dir herr Jesu Christ,' fly, pustule, and
burst not, so bids thee, etc. (1597), Wolf's Ztschr. 1, 280.

p. 1248.] *Zeter* und *weide* liegen in streite, Hpt 4, 390; conf.
' die *hünsche* und der *drache* ' (p. 1163).

p. 1249.] *Animals* are appealed to : ' I pray thee, *swallow,*'
Schm. 3, 362; adjuro te, *mater aviorum* (p. 1242). One's own
powers are summoned up : Finn. *nouse luontoni,* surge vis mea!
Renvall 1, 294ᵇ. Again, there are particular *words* of great
magic power: *berlicke, berlocke! policke, polucke, podrei!* Fr.
Arnim's Märch. no. 8; Fr. *brelique breloque! berlik berloc,*
Biondelli's Dial. 133 ; conf. Boh. *perljk tudes.*

---

# PREFACE.

p. xxiv.] The difference between the *Norse* and the *German*
system of gods appears the more considerable, when we reflect
that our Eru, Phol, Saxnot, Beowulf, Isis, Zisa and Sindgund
were unknown to the North; that in Germany thus far not a
vestige is discoverable of Heimdall, Loki or Hoenir (Färö. Höner,
not Hœner); and that of Meili, the son of Oðinn and Fiörgyn,
hardly anything is known but the bare name.——Thôrr was
preëminently worshipped in Norway, Freyr in Sweden, Oðinn in
Denmark (p. 160-1). Hâlogi, Thôrgerðr and Irpa seem to be
local deities of Hâloga-land (F. Magnusen p. 981).

p. xxiv.] The result of a new religion coming in is *mixture*
with the old, which never dies out entirely. The old faith then
becomes a *superstition,* as Nilsson 6, 3 very clearly shews.

p. xxvi.] When the rage for the outlandish and satiety with
the home-grown had passed away (tanta mortalibus suarum
rerum satietas, alienarumque aviditas, Pliny 12. 17, 38), there
set-in the equally unwarranted *historical and geographical* explanation of Myths, the study of whose inner sense is yet to seek.

Deified heroes and saints, genealogies beginning with a god for
ancestor, mark the point where myth and history touch.

p. xxix.] *Wolfdietrich* has this other point of likeness to
*Odysseus*, that he wears St George's shirt, as O. does the scarf
of Leucothea. A further resemblance betw. the German mythology and the *Greek* comes to light in Artemis and Hecate, who
remind us of Berhta; see the Copenhagen Edda, pref. xxvii. seq.
The ideas of Meleager and Norna-gestr (p. 853 end), of μεσογαία
and middil-gard (p. 794), of ὀμφαλός and the dille-stein (p. 806),
of Cerberus and the hell-hound (p. 997), of κηρύκειον and the
wishing-rod (976-7), and of sieve-turning (p. 1108) are closely
allied; and ἥλιος, ON. sòl, Goth. sáuil, coincide even verbally
(p. 701 end). With *Roman* usage agree our dislocation-spells
(p. 224-5) and lustration of highways, RA. p. 73. On the other
hand, the Zeus-Jupiter is in other nations split up into Wuotan,
Donar and Zio, or Radegast, Perun and Svetovit, or Brahma and
Vishnu, or Gwydion and Taranis.

p. xxx.] *Celtic* influence on Germ. mythology is pointed out
by Leo in Malb. Gl. 1, 39; from it Nilsson 6, 13-4 derives the
mistil-teinn and Baldrs-brand, believing as he does that many
parts of Scandinavia were once peopled by Celts. Their gods
Taranis, Hesus and Teutates answer to Jupiter, Mars and Mercury, see Stälin 1, 111-2. 109. GDS. p. 120.

p. xxx.] To the old words common to the *Slavic* and Teutonic,
add Goth. gulþ, OHG. kold, Sl. zóloto, zláto; Goth. þaúrnus,
OHG. dornu, Sl. trn, teórn. The Sl. Siva=Ceres corresp. to
ON. Sif, Sitivrat to Saturn, Priya to Frowa (p. 303), and Prove
to Frô.

p. xxxiv.] The harmonies of *Indian* mythol. with ours may
be largely added to. Thus the Liliputian floating on a leaf is
similar to Brahma and Vishnu (p. 451), bald-headed Oðinn and
his day of the week to Buddha (p. 129 n. Iduna 10, 231),
Vishnu's wheel to Krodo's (p. 249), Prithivî to Fria (p. 303),
Yama the death-god and his rope, the cow of creation, etc., to
the corresp. German notions, Garuda's wings to our wind (p.
633), madyamalôka to middilgard. Bopp in Gl. 71[b] says Kâli is
akin (not indeed to Halja, but) to hveila, a while.

p. xxxviii.] Points of contact betw. *Paganism* and *Christian-
ism*. On what is christian in the Edda, see Copenh. Edda,

pref. xxvi. seq., and consider the Last Judgment, the angel's trumpet like Heimdall's horn (p. 234), Surtr like 'death *the last enemy*,' 1 Cor. 15, 26. While the heathen often admitted foreign gods into the ranks of their own, and assimilated them, as the Greeks did sometimes to conciliate other nations; Christianity was exclusive, and hostile to all heathen gods. Yet even the Christian church, involuntarily or designedly, has adopted some heathen gods and practices. That saints of the Catholic church often receive divine homage, is acknowl. by Seb. Frank, Zeitb. 2, 243ª; conf. A. W. Schlegel's Oeuvres 1, 219. Kingston's Lusit. sketches, Lond. '45. The saints *heal* (p. 1163 end): the Servians call Kosman and Damian *vratchi*, soothsayers, physicians, Vuk's Wtb. 82; John the Baptist foretells to Aeda the splendour of the race that shall spring from her daughter Oda, Pertz 6, 307. The saints *make rain* (p. 174-5) ; as *water-saints* they bring succour in a storm (Suppl. to 637): nay, nuns in German legends often take the place of *white ladies*, and munkar in Sweden turn up as *jättar*, Runa '44, 13. The saints pacify God's anger :

> Des mugen si in *stillen*,
> swâ er zornic ûf uns wirt.                Pass. 312, 56.
> Müeze sîn unser *vorspreche* (advocate),
> daz Got mit zorne iht reche (not wreak in wrath),
> swâ wir haben gesündet.                Servat. 1705.

God's anger and that of the saints are estimated about equally in curses : ' habbe he Godes unmiltse and Sancti Martines ! ' Kemble 2, 4 ;

> Des haben in Sant Geôrgen haz
> und Gotes vluoch umbe daz !        Helbling 8, 915.

' Hilf Sanct Anna selb-dritt ! '    A. and the other two, Anshelm 3, 252.

Mary above all other saints received a heartfelt adoration, which, if not in the first centuries, yet very early, was promoted esp. by women, Zappert 16. Epiphan. adv. hæres. p. 1058 (ed. Paris, 1622). Like Hulda, she is called ' gudmoder,' Asbjorns. no. 8, and is a ' spinster,' Zapp. 13. If in the legend of Crescentia Peter, like a second Woden, appears as an old man, con-

ducts the heroine back from the rock in the sea, and endows her
with the gift of healing, or himself heals (KM. no. 81); in other
legends Mary takes the place of Peter, and shows the empress a
medicinal herb. Both Christ and Mary leave the print of their
fingers and toes on the rock, like the giants (p. 546), or devils
(p. 1022); conf. 'ons Heren spronc,' our Lord's leap, Maerl. 2,
116. The O.Norw. Gulaþings-laug p. 6 speaks of 'signa til Krist
þacca (thanks) oc Sancta Mariu *til ârs oc til friðar*,' exactly as was
done to Freyr (p. 212). Mary helps in childbirth, bestows rain,
appears among harvesters, kisses and dries them, Maerl. 2, 248.
285-6. She instead of the Dioscuri makes light shine on the
masts (p. 1137 beg.); she or her mother St Anne carries people
from distant lands through the air (Hist. de la Bastille 4, 315), as
Oðinn did (p. 146, Hading), or the devil (p. 1028). They make
two Virgin Marys visit each other, carrying the inferior one to
the grander. Childless couples cry to St Verena, and she gives
them heirs, Pertz 6, 458—460, like Oðinn and Frigg, Völs. saga
c. 2; conf. the beginnings of many KM.

p. xliii.] The christian God merely sends his messengers upon
earth, as in Gregor 2678: swenn dich unser Herre dîner sælden
ermante, u. dir sînen boten sante, den soldest du enphâhen baz.
But the heathen gods *came down* themselves: fôru at kanna heim
allan, Sn. 135. (KM.[3] 3, 146). Zeus, Hermes and Plutus appear
in Lucian's Timon; conf. Aristoph. Lysistrata 808, Birds 1549;
whenever 3 gods seek a lodging, Hermes is sure to be one, GDS.
123. Zeus coming as an unknown guest, a child is served up
for him to eat, Fragm. hist. Gr. 1, 31. The Dioscuri also travel
unrecognised among men, Preller 2, 72.——What the Lithuanians tell of Perkunos's (or the Saviour's) encounter with the
horse and ox, the Esthonian legend relates of Jesus, Neus 435.
Perkunos and Pikullos travel, and give gifts to men, Tettau and
Temme's Ostpr. u. Litth. sagen p. 28. Also the horse, ox and
dog put up at men's houses, and reward hospitality by giving
their years, Babr. 74.

In such wanderings there keeps recurring the antique incident
of the divine visitor granting *three wishes*. 'Theseus Hippo-
lytum, cum *ter optandi* a *Neptuno* patre habuisset *potestatem*,'
Cic. de Nat. D. 3, 31; het ich *drïer wünsche gewalt*, MS. 2, 145;
conf. KM. no. 87. Of this kind is the Breton fairytale of the

artful moustache, to whom Christ and Peter allow 3 wishes: he asks for a pretty wife, the winning card, and a sack in which to shut the devil up. When Peter denies him entrance into heaven, he flings his cap in, and so takes possession. Echoes of the player who wants to get into heaven, and is refused (p. 818 n.), are found in the Warnung 2710—2806; so brother Lustig and Jack the gamester wish to get into heaven, KM. no. 81-2. Lat. poem of Ma. p. 343, conf. the farce of the miller who sits on his sack behind the gate of heaven, Altd. bl. 1, 381. Gamester Jack's request for the tree from which no one can get down resembles a story in Hone's Daybk 1, 447. Panzer 1, 94; the casting of dice for the soul is also in Cæs. Heisterb. 5, 34. Somm. sag. 175-6. The incident of the thieving cook meets us in Aviani Fab. 30: sed cum consumti dominus cor quaereret apri, impatiens fertur cor rapuisse coquus.

Christ, being on a journey with Peter, pulls one ear out of a sheaf, and burns it at the candle; the grains keep spirting out till they form quite a heap. This happens in a barn, where lazy Peter has been cudgelled by a peasant; and he gets another backful of blows in the inn, because he will not play. Then the Lord made for these peasants boughs on their trees, whose hardness blunted their axes, as the request of a rude set of people for vines is also granted, but the wine is as good as their manners. In a farrier's shop Christ cuts a horse's foot off, shoes it, and puts it on the beast again. Peter will not stop to pick up half a horseshoe, but Christ does, and buys cherries with it, which Peter is glad to pick up one by one to quench his thirst. In the merry gest of the blind man whose wife sits up in the appletree, or the LG. poem in Dasent xxvi., Peter and the Lord act the part of Pluto and Proserpine in Chaucer's Marchantes tale, and of Oberon and Titania in Wieland's Ges. 6, 87. Again, Christ walks with two apostles and three disciples, and comes upon the girl carrying water, Wend. volksl. 2, 314. Peter catches the haddock, as the Ases do Loki, and he Andvari; conf. Wolf's Ndrl. sag. p. 706, and his Pref. to Zingerle 2, xx. Peter comes from heaven to earth on leave, H. Sachs iii. 1, 240, also i. 94[b]. St Peter sits on the roof, throwing pears down, and St Claus throws rotten apples up, Garg. 75[b]. Of a like stamp are the folktales of St Jost and the Bavarian, Renner 24583, of St Nicolas and the

Bavarian, Bebelii Facet. p. m. 1136. The return of saints to heaven is thus descr. in the Warnung 1767 :

> Die heilegen habent sich ûfgezogen (hoisted up),
> von der kuppel (dome) sint si geflogen
> ûf zuo ir Schepfaere.

Here also I must call attention to *Peter* and *Paul* coming to aid the Christians in battle, Lohengr. pp. 116—9. 158—160. Pref. lxxxi. Youths (or knights) clothed in white appear on the walls of Rhodes, to repel the Turks, Detmar 2, 417 (yr 1480). Angels too are called *wîges wîse* in Hêlj. 149, 10; they appear two at a time, and armed, p. 989. This shining pair of champions reminds us of the Alci (p. 366), and of the Dioscuri who on their white steeds help the fighters, Cic. Nat. D. 2, 2; conf. ed. Creuzeri p. 213-4. Justin 20, 3. Florus ed. Jahn 14, 14. Suet. Nero c. 1. Klausen's Aeneas 664-5. 707. Maerl. 3, 148. 174. The Galatians quail before the rider on the white horse, Luc. Dial. mer. 13 ; already in Herod. 8, 38 two armed and superhuman beings pursue and slay the foe.

p. xlvi.] The sky darkens when a villain is begotten or born, Pertz 2, 154; but nature rejoiced when Georis was begot, 261 ; conf. the Alexander-legend in Maerl. 1, 264. With Frôði's blissful age conf. O'Kearney's Gabhra p. 104 : 'They say the times were so prosperous and the produce of the earth so abundant, that when the kine lay down the grass reached above the top of the horns. Hence it is said that cows, whenever they lie, give utterance to three moans in remembrance of the good old times that once had been, and lamenting the hard days in which they live.' So we hear of a Truce of God under Numa, Klaus. Aen. 953, and under Solomon, Diem. p. 113-4. The lines fr. Godfrey of Viterbo are based on Isai. 2, 4 : et conflabant gladios suos in vomeres, et lances suas in falces, conf. Passional p. 17. Jorn. de regn. succ. p. 45. Ksrchr. 630.

p. xlviii.] The Germ. reverence for woman is also expr. in : êre wol die muoter dîn, Pass. 224, 25. In a Serv. song a daughter calls her mother 'bèla tzrkvitze,' white little church, Vuk 1, 17. no. 27.

p. xlix.] The good and evil of the New are hinted by Paus. i. 24, 4 in the words : ὅστις δὲ τὰ σὺν τέχνῃ πεποιημένα ἐπίπροσθεν τίθεται τῶν ἐς ἀρχαιότητα ἡκόντων (become old-fashioned), conf. Lessing 8, 246.

p. li.] Even God, Christ and the Holy Ghost came to be imagined as sitting in the wood, as the old gods had been, Pröhle's März. f. d. jugend p. 17.

p. lii.] The descent of all gods from a God of gods is assumed even by Helmold 1, 83. In India Brahma, Vishnu, Siva are the *three* supreme gods; all the rest are under these; their trinity is designated by the sacred word *óm* = *aum*, Brahma being *a*, Vishnu *u*, Siva *m*, Bopp's Gl. 61ᵃ. GDS. 122. Beside this trinitarian view, we find a dual conception of deity according to sex, as father and mother, or as brother and sister: thus arose Niörðr and Nerthus, Freyr (Frô) and Freyja (Frouwa), Berhtolt and Berhta, Faírguneis and Fiörgyn, Geban and Gefjon, Hruodo and Hreda. With the Germ. sunne, masc. and fem., conf. Lunus and Luna, Liber and Libera, GDS. 122.——*Twelve* gods are reckoned by Athen. 5, 330 (conf. Plato's Phædr. 246-7), and by Apuleius p.m. 59; τῶν δώδεκα ὀνομαζομένων θεῶν ἀγάλματα, Paus. i. 40, 2; si undecim deos praeter sese secum adducat Jupiter, Plaut. Epid. v. 1, 4; duodecim deis, v. 2, 3; twelve adityas, Bopp 30ᵃ; tredecim dii exceptis Brahma, Vishnu et Siva, Bopp's Gl. 160; vâro *ellifo* aesir taldir, Sæm. 117ᵇ; 12 ases, 8 asins, Sn. 79. In like manner, Hrôlf's 12 heroes, Sn. 152. Fornald. s. 1, 100, Kaleva's 12 sons, the devil's 12 disciples (Suppl. to 986 end).

p. lii.] The arguments with which the Fathers and authors like Arnobius combat the folly of heathenism in respect of gods, temples, images and sacrifices, would equally condemn a good deal in the Catholic doctrine. Even a worldly delight in spring, flowers and the song of birds is attacked almost as fiercely as polytheism; thus in the Warnung 2243 :

| | |
|---|---|
| Einer anbetet daz vogel-sanc | One man worships the bird's song |
| unt die liehten tage lanc, | and the days so light and long, |
| darzuo bluomen unde gras, | flowers also and the grass, |
| daz ie des vihes spise was : | aye the food of ox and ass : |
| *diu rinder vrezzent den got.* | bullocks munch your god ! |

conf. 2077 seq. 2382 seq. From the Dualism that pits Evil

against Good as a power, our paganism is free ; for our ancestors, like the Greeks, throw Evil on the shoulders of a few inferior deities, or let it come out in mere attributes of the gods.

# APPENDIX.

---

# ANGLO-SAXON GENEALOGIES.[1]

AUTHORITIES: *Beda*, Hist. eccl. 1, 15. 2, 5. *Nennius* (Nyniaw), Hist. Britonum, comp. in 7th or 9th cent.? the MSS. are of the 10th; ed. Gunn, Lond. 1819, p. 61. *Saxon Chron.*, begun at latest in 9th cent., continued and extended; ed. Ingram, Lond. 1823, pp. 15. 23-4. 33-4. 72. 95. *Asserius* Menevensis (d. 906 or 910), beginn. of his De rebus gestis Ælfredi, Lond. 1722, pp. 3. 4. *Ethelwerdus* (d. 1090), in Savile, pp. 833-4. 842. *Florentius* Wigornensis (d. 1118), ed. Lond. 1592, pp. 218-9. 221. 232. 274. 294, and a collective prosapia p. 566. *Simeon* Dunelmensis (circ. 1129), in Twysden p. 119. *Alfredus* Beverlacensis (d. 1138), ed. Hearne, Oxon. 1716. *Ordericus* Vitalis (b. 1075, d. after 1140), in Duchesne's Scr. Norm. p. 639. *Wilelmus* Malmesburiensis (d. 1143), in Savile p. 17. *Ethelredus* or *Ailredus* Rievallensis (circ. 1150), in Twysden p. 350-1. *Henricus* Huntindonensis (ends 1154), in Savile pp. 310, 313—6. *Galfredus* Monemutensis (circ. 1160), in Scr. Angl., Heidelb. 1587. *Radulfus* de Diceto (ends 1196), in Twysden p. 530. *Joannes* Wallingford (d. 1214), in Gale p. 535. *Albericus* trium fontium (ends 1241), in Leibn. Acc. hist. 1, 186. *Matthæus* Westmonasteriensis (14th cent.), Francof. 1601, pp. 99. 142. Thomas *Otterbourne* (ends 1420), in Hearne's Scr. rer. Angl., Oxon. 1732; most of the names dreadfully corrupt. A confused and corrupt Geneal. from a MS. of Nennius, in Gale's Appendix p. 116. The collections in D. Langhorn's Chron. reg. Angl. 1679, 8 are not to be despised: some of the sources he drew from are now lost.[2]

The Anglo-Saxons, who left Germany for Britain in the 5-6th centuries, carried with them data of the descent of their noblest families. These all go back to *Wôden*, and some of them a great deal higher, naming a whole series of gods or

[¹ Conf. J. Grimm 'On Kemble's Geneal. of Wessex,' Munich '36 (Kl. schr. 5, 240 seq.)—EHM., *i.e.* Prof. E. H. Meyer, Editor of Grimm's D.M. ed. 4.]
[² Conf. the Geneal. tables coll. in Pertz 10, 314.—EHM.]

deified heroes as Wôden's ancestors. After the conversion to
Christianity, they tried to connect this line of kings and gods
with the O.T. tradition of the earliest race of man. Such an
attempt to bring their still cherished heathen forefathers into
harmony with the Noah and Adam of Holy Writ can only have
been made very early, immediately after their adhesion to the new
doctrine, at a time when the mind, convinced of the truth of the
Bible story, was yet loth to part with its native tradition. As
a church was often reared on the site of the heathen temple, as
christian and heathen ceremonies were fused together somehow,
and to fortify the new faith the débris of the old soil was thrown
in; so a simple-minded people might be allowed to retain genealogies interwoven with its past glory, and give them as it were
a new groundwork. Later on, such a combination of irreconcil-
able facts would neither have been attempted nor thought
necessary.

Beyond all doubt these pedigrees were pre-christian, were
known to Angles and Saxons in their old home, and therefore
must have been equally diffused among other German nations
on the Continent: every part of them shows connexion with
national names and old heathen poetry. I am inclined to credit
the Frisians, Westphals, and also Franks with possessing similar
genealogies, though the emigrant Anglo-Saxons alone have
preserved them for us.

Our earliest authority for these pedigrees is Beda [d. 735],
and he only mentions that of Kent, yet in such a way that we
may safely suppose he knew them all. Succeeding centuries
furnish fuller accounts.

These lists of names can have no chronological value as regards
the oldest times; it is only in giving the lines of AS. kings that
they become historical. But that detracts nothing from the importance of the legend.

We know that the Anglo-Saxons formed 7 or 8 distinct
kingdoms, founded on a pre-existing diversity in the immigrant
tribes, and thus answering exactly to the difference of their
genealogies. The Saxon Chronicle says the Jutes occupied
Kent and Wight, the Saxons Essex, Sussex and Wessex, the
Angles Eastangle, Mercia and Northumberland. Of Wessex,
the state that soon overtopped and finally swallowed up the rest,

the genealogy is the most fully preserved. Those of Kent, Mercia, Deira (Brit. Deifyr) and Bernicia (Brit. Bryneich, Northumbria) are also handed down in old documents. Less genuine, or not so well accredited in certain names, appear the lines of Eastangle, Essex and Lindesfarn-ey.

It is convenient to divide these genealogies in two halves, a *Descending* series and an *Ascending*. At Wôden's sons they begin to split, in him they all unite. I will take first the several lines that descend from Wôden, and then deal with the older stock, which is the same for all. Here I bring under one view—

### WÔDEN'S POSTERITY.

| KENT. | EASTANGLIA. | ESSEX. | MERCIA. |
|---|---|---|---|
| Wôden | Wôden | Wôden | Wôden |
| Wecta | Câsere | Saxneát | Wihtlæg |
| Witta | Titmon | Gesecg | Wærmund |
| Wihtgils | Trigel | Andsecg | Offa |
| Hengest (d. 489) | Hrôthmund | Sweppa | Angeltheow |
| Eoric (Oesc) | Hrippa | Sigefugel | Eomær |
| Octa | Quichelm | Bedeca | Icel |
| Eormenrîc | Uffa | Offa | Cnebba |
| Æthelbeorht (567) | Tidel | Æscwine (527) | Cynewald |
| | Rædwald (d. 617) | Sledda | Creoda |
| | Eorpwald (632) | Sæbeorht (604) | Wibba |
| | | | Penda (d. 656) |

| DEIRA. | BERNICIA. | WESSEX. | LINDESFARAN. |
|---|---|---|---|
| Wôden | Wôden | Wôden | Wôden |
| Wægdæg | Bældæg | Bældæg | Winta |
| Sigegâr | Brand | Brand | Cretta |
| Swæfdæg | Beonoc | Fridhogâr | Queldgils |
| Sigegeát | Aloc | Freáwine | Ceadbed |
| Sæbald | Angenwit | Wig | Bubba |
| Sæfugel | Ingwi | Gewis | Bedeca |
| Westerfalcna | Esa | Esla | Biscop |
| Wilgisl | Eoppa | Elesa | Eanferth |
| Uscfreá | Ida (d. 560) | Cerdic (d. 534) | Eatta |
| Yffe | | Cynrîc | Ealdfrith |
| Ælle (d. 588) | | Ceawlin [1] | |

[1] Succeeded by the brothers Ceolrîc, Ceolwulf, Cynegils, Cwichelm, Lappenb. 1, 154-6.—EHM.]

I begin with the general remark, that *seven* sons are here ascribed to Wôden (for Bernicia and Wessex keep together till the third generation). But some chroniclers give him only *three* ; thus William of Malmesbury, speaking of the Mercian line, says p. 17 : possem hoc loco istius (Idae) et aliorum alibi lineam seriatim intexere, nisi quod ipsa vocabula, barbarum quiddam stridentia, minus quam vellem delectationis lecturis infunderent. Illud tamen non immerito notandum, quod, cum Wodenio fuerint *tres filii, Weldegius, Withlegius* et *Beldegius,* de primo reges Cantuaritarum, de secundo reges Merciorum, et de tertio reges Westsaxonum et Northanimbrorum originem traxerunt.'

Let us now examine the eight lines one by one.

KENT, the oldest kingdom, founded by the first invaders.— Beda 1, 15 : ' duces fuisse perhibentur eorum primi duo fratres *Hengistus* et *Horsus,* erant autem filii *Vetgisli,* cujus pater *Vecta,* cujus pater *Voden,* de cujus stirpe multarum provinciarum regium genus originem duxit.' [1] Acc. to that, Hengest and Horsa would be only great-grandsons of Wôden, but one MS. supplies a missing link : ' filii *Victgisli,* cujus pater *Victa,* c. p. *Vecta,* c. p. *Voden,*' who is thus great-great-grandfather to those brothers. Herewith agree both Nennius : ' interea tres ceolae a Germania in exilium expulsae Britanniam advenerunt, in quibus dominabantur *Hors* et *Henegest,* qui et ipsi fratres erant filii *Guictglis,* Guictlis filius *Guicta,* Guicta filius *Guechta,* Guechta filius *Vuoden ;* and the Saxon Chron. p. 15 : ' *Hengest* and *Horsa* that wæron Wihtgilses suna, *Wihtgils* wæs Witting, *Witta* Wecting, *Wecta* Wôdning, fram tham *Wôdne* âwôc eall ûre cynecynn, and Sûdhanhymbra eác.' In Ethelwerd the 3 links betw. Wothen and Hengest are *Withar, Wicta, Wyrhtels ;* in Florence of Worc. 566, ' *Vecta* sive *Wehta, Witta, Wihtgisilus ;* in Henry of Hunt. *Vecta, Wicta, Widgils.*

Hengest had a son *Eoric,* surnamed *Oisc* (Oesc), after whom all succeeding kings of Kent were called *Oiscingas ;* after Oisc came *Octa, Irminric, Ethelbert,* Beda 2, 5. Oisc is called *Aesc* in Sax. Chron. and Ethelwerd. Florence has : ' Hengistus, *Oricus*

---

[1] So in AS. : ' wæron thâ ærest heora lâtteowas and heretogan twegen gebrôthra *Hengist* and *Horsa,* hi wæron *Wihtigilses* suna, thæs fæder wæs *Wihta* hâten, and thæs Wihtan fæder wæs *Wôden* nemned, of thæs strynde monigra mægdha *eyning-cynn fruman lædde.*

cognomine *Aesca, Octa, Irmenricus, Aethelbertus.'*——The names
*Hengest* and *Horsa* are taken from the horse; one might also
suspect in Wictgisl, Wicta, Wecta the presence of wicg, OS.
wigg, ON. vigg (equus), conf. Lat. vehere. The ON. Veg-tamr
(way-tame, much travelled), as Oðinn once called himself, stands
apart, though an old king *Wechtam* occurs in Hunibald. The
Wegdam in Otterbourne p. 32 is accus. of Wegda. Will.
Malmesb. p. 17 calls the head of the Kentish line *Weldegius,*
prob. a corruption of Wecdeg. The Traveller's Song, line 43,
brings up a *Witta,* king of the Swæfas (Swabians); could this
name serve to explain the obscure *wittu* in our Hildebrand-lied?

EASTANGLIA.——In Florence 566 (conf. 233): ' *Woden,
Casera, Titmon, Trigilsus, Rothmundus, Hrippus, Wihelmus, Vffa*
sive Wffa, primus rex Orientalium Anglorum,' and 3 kings after
him, *Titellus, Redwaldus, Eorpwaldus.* In Gale's Appendix:
*Woden* genuit *Casser,* genuit *Titinon,* g. *Trigil,* g. *Rodnum,* g.
*Kippan,* g. *Guithelm,* (g.) *Guechan,* ipse primus regnavit in
Britannia super gentem Eastanglorum, Gueca g. *Guffan,* g. *Tidil,*
g. *Ecni,* g. *Edric,* g. *Aldulfh,* g. *Elric;* elsewh. from a differ.
MS.: *Woden, Casser, Titinon, Trigil, Rodmunt, Rippan, Guillem,
Guecha, Guffa, Tidil, Eeni.* In Langhorn: *Caseras, Tilmon,
Trigisilus, Rothimundus, Hirpus, Quicelmus, Vffa.*[1] Of this Uffa,
Henry of Hunt. 315: 'hoc regnum primus tenuit *Vffa,* a quo
reges Orientalium Anglorum Vffingos appellant, quod postea
*Titulus* (al. Titilus) filius ejus tenuit, pater *Redwaldi* fortissimi
regis Eastangle'; and John Bromton's Chron. (Twysden p. 745):
'regnum Eastangliae incepit ab *Vffa* rege, cui successit rex
*Ticulus;* isti duo non fuerunt multum potentes, quibus successit
potentior aliis rex *Redwaldus;* Redwaldo vero defuncto, filius
suus *Erpwaldus* in regno Eastangliae successit.' Of all these,
Beda mentions only *Reduald* (yr. 616).[2] The Sax. Chron. p. 35
relates the baptism of *Eorpwald* in 632; speaks of his father
*Reodwald* p. 32, yr. 617, or (more correctly) *Rœdwald* p. 88, as
one of the mightiest of AS. monarchs. So Will. Malmesb. p.
34: *Redvaldus,*primus idemque maximus apud Orientales Anglos,
a Vodenio, ut scribunt, decimum genu nactus (l. natus).'

---

[1] Otterbourne has only: ' *Woden* genuit *Casere,* a quo regnum Estanglorum
progrediens derivatur.'
[2] Beda 2, 15 (Stevenson 140, 21) does name four: *Eorpuald, Redvald, Tytilus,
Vuffa.*—EHM.]

The older names seem good Saxon. *Hrippa, Hrippus* answers
to Hripo in Falke's Trad. Corb. 7. 104-7. 312 and OHG. Hriffo
in Meichelb. 430. *Rothmund* for Hrôthmund? a name that occurs
in Beow. 2378. *Titmon* resembles Tiadman in Falke 114.
*Trigil* may be the OHG. Drëgil, Wolfdrëgil, Wolfdrigil? though
in that case we should expect Thrigel.[1] *Tidil* is appar. the Tudil
of Falke 37 [and Tital in Schannat no. 426.—EHM.]. *Uffa* is the
OS. Uffo, and prob. the same as the Offas of Essex and Mercia,
for the Trav. Song. 69 says ' *Offa* weold Ongle,' governed Anglia.
*Eorp* in Eorpwald is the OS. Erp, OHG. Erpf, conf. ON. iarpr =
fuscus. *Cwichelm* is a good AS. name (Sax. Chr. 27. 30), of
which Wihelm, Guillem are corruptions.

The *Casera, Caseras* or *Casser* named as Wôden's son is the
same whom the Trav. Song celebrates as ruler of the Greeks,
l. 39 : ' *Câsere* weold ͵Creacum ' ; and l. 151 : ' mid Creacum ic
wæs and mid Finnum, and mid *Câsere*, se the winburga geweald
âhte, wiolane ( = welena) and wilna, and Wala rîces,' who wielded
winsome burghs, wealth, what heart can wish, and Welsh
dominion. Here Saxon legend has turned the Latin *Caesar* into
*Câsere*, and linked him to native kings, perh. in deference to
that early opinion of Wôden's having come from Greekland (p.
163 n.). Among Saxons and Angles of the 5-6th centuries there
was prob. many a legend afloat about an old king *Kêsor*.

ESSEX.—Acc. to Florence : *Woden, Eaxneta, Gesecg, Antsecg,
Sueppa, Sigefugel, Bedca, Offa, Aeswinus, Sledda, Sebertus ;* for
Eaxneta some MSS. have the truer form *Seaxnete*. Henry of
Hunt. 313 : *Saxnat, Andesc, Gesac, Spoewe, Sigewlf, Biedca,
Offa, Erchenwin, Slede, Sibrict* (al. Siberct). Matth. Westm. p.
99 : *Erkenwinus,* qui fuit filius *Offae,* q. f. *Bredecani,* q. f. *Sigewlf,*
q. f. *Spetuae,* q. f. *Gesac,* q. f. *Andessc,* q. f. *Saxuad,* q. f. *Woden.*
Langhorn : *Saxoneta, Gesacus, Andescus, Sueppa, Sigefugelus,
Bedicanus, Ercenovinus.* Alvredus Beverl. : *Woden, Seaxeca,
Gescecg, Andseng, Snoppa, Sigelugel, Becta, Osse, Eswine, Siedda,
Sabertus.*[2]

Of these, Aescwine (Ercenwine) is named as the first king of
Essex, Sæbert (Sigebert) as the first to adopt Christianity in 604

---

[1] Cursor, minister ? conf. Gothic thragjan, currere, and in OHG. glosses trikil,
drikil (verna), prob. the ON. thræel, thrall.
[2] Otterbourne says little, and that beside the mark : ' *Woden* genuit *Watelgeat,* a
quo regum Essexiae prosapia sumpsit originem ' ; conf. Mercia.

(Sax. Chr. 29). Then the name of Wôden's son is very remarkable : *Seaxneát,* evid. the *Saxnôt* named with Thunar and Wuodan in the Abrenuntiatio; in OHG. it would be Sahs-nôz, Sahskinôz.[1] *Gesecg* and *Andsecg* seem to be related in meaning; *Bedeca* answers to the OHG. *Patuhho; Sweppa* is Saxon.

MERCIA.—The Sax. Chr. p. 33-4 : *Penda* wæs Wybbing, *Wybba* Crŷding, *Crŷda* Cynewalding, *Cynewald* Cnebbing, *Cnebba* Iceling, *Icel* Eomæring, *Eomœr* Angeltheowing, *Angeltheow* Offing, *Offa* Wærmunding, *Wœrmund* Wihtlæging, *Wihtlœg* Wôdening. At p. 72 the line is begun differently, and carried up to another son of Wybba : *Offa* wæs Dhincferthing, *Dhincferth* Eanwulfing, *Eanwulf* Osmôding, *Osmôd* Eawing, *Eawa* Wybbing, *Wybba* Creoding, *Creoda* Cynewalding, and so on up to Wôden. In Florence 566 : *Woden, Withelgeatus, Waga, Wihtleagus, Weremundus, Offa, Angengeatus, Eomerus, Icelius, Cnebba, Cunewaldus, Creoda* sive *Crida* primus rex Merciorum, *Wibba;* p. 232, with slight variations : *Penda,* qui fuit *Wibbae,* q. f. *Cridae,* q. f. *Cunewaldi,* q. f. *Cnebbae,* q. f. *Icelii,* q. f. *Eomeri,* q. f. *Angengeati,* q. f. *Offae,* q. f. *Weromundi,* q. f. *Wightleagi,* q. f. *Wagae,* q. f. *Wothelgeati,* q. f. *Wodeni.* In the App. to Nennius (Gale 116) : *Woden* genuit *Guedolgeat,* genuit *Gueagon,* g. *Guithlig,* g. *Guerdmund,* g. *Ossa,* g. *Origon,* g. *Eamer,* g. *Pubba;* ipse Pubba habuit ix filios, quorum duo mihi notiores sunt quam alii, id est, *Penda* et *Eaua.* In Ralph de Diceto p. 446 : *Offa* fuit filius *Wingferd,* filii *Canwlf,* f. *Osmod,* f. *Epa,* f. *Wibba,* f. *Creada,* f. *Cynewald,* f. *Cnibba,* f. *Ycil,* f. *Com,* f. *Angelreu,* f. *Offa,* f. *Wermund,* f. *Witlat,* f. *Woden.* In Matth. Westm. p. 142 : erat enim *Offa* filius *Thinferthi,* q. f. *Eadulfi,* q. f. *Osulfi,* q. f. *Eoppae,* q. f. *Wibbae,* q. f. *Creoddae,* q. f. *Kinewoldi,* q. f. *Cnebbae,* q. f. *Ithel,* q. f. *Eomeri,* q. f. *Angelthean,* q. f. *Offae,* q. f. *Weremundi,* q. f. *Withleig,* q. f. *Wagon,* q. f. *Frethegeath,* q. f. *Wodeni.* In Otterbourne p. 31 : *Woden* genuit *Feothulgeath,* qui genuit *Vaga,* q. g. *Wichebeg,* q. g. *Vermundum,* q. g. *Offa,* q. g. *Engeltheon,* q. g. *Edomerum,* q. g. *Icel,* q. g. *Cnibbam,* q. g. *Kynewaldum,* q. g. *Cridiam,* q. g. *Bilbam,* q. g. *Pendam* primum regem Merciorum. Langhorn seems to draw from Florence : *Vitelgeta, Vaga, Vitlegius, Veremundus, Offa* al. *Uffa, Angongeta, Eumerus, Icelius, Cnebba, Cunevaldus, Crida.*

---

[1] Conf. the Götting. Anzeig. '28, p. 550.

Langhorn, Florence, Matthew and Gale's App. insert betw. Wôden and Wihtlæg two names that are wanting in Ralph and the Chron., *Wihtelgeát* (Frethegeat) and *Waga* (Gueagon). As Florence puts Angen-geát for Angel-theow, his *Vithel-geát* might elsewh. have been Víthel-theow, but Gale too has *Guedol-geat.*[1] Angen (Gale's ' Origon ' is a misreading of Ongon) is unexceptionable, and Angentheow answers to the OHG. name *Angandio,* perh. to ON. Angantŷr, which may be a corrup. of Anganthŷr ; the pure AS. form is *Ongentheow,* Beow. 3931. 4770. 4945-67,conf. *Incgentheow,* Trav. Song 232. *Offa* (miscopied Ossa), which occurs twice in the Mercian line, is likewise found in Beow. 3895. 3910. *Wihtlœg* seems faultless, Will. Malmesb. p. 17 has *Withlegius,* and even *Guithlig* in Gale confirms the short æ or e. Yet Ralph's *Witlat* agrees better with the ON. *Vigletus* in Saxo Gram. 59 ; and it is a point of importance to our whole inquiry, that the series *Vigletus, Vermundus, Uffo* of the Dan. genealogy (Saxo Gr. 59—65) [2] is so evid. the same as the Mercian. For Gale's ' Pubba ' (AS. þ for p) read *Wubba, Wibba* = OHG. *Wippo.*[3]

DEIRA.—Sax. Chr. p. 24 : *Ælle* wæs Yffing, *Yffe* Uscfreá-ing, *Uscfreá* Wilgisling, *Wilgisl* Westerfalcning, *Westerfalcna* Sæfugling, *Sæfugl* Sæbalding, *Sœbald* Sigegeáting, *Sigegeát* Swæfdæging, *Swœfdœg* Sigegáring, *Sigegâr* Wægdæging, *Wægdœg* Wôdening, *Wôden* Fridhowulfing. Florence p. 221 : *Ælla* fuit filius *Iffi,* cujus pater *Wuscfrea,* c. p. *Wilgelsus,* c. p. *Westorwalena,* c. p. *Seomelus,* c. p. *Suearta,* c. p. *Sœpugelus,* c. p. *Seabaldus,* c. p. *Siggeotus,* c. p. *Suebdegus,* c. p. *Siggarus,* c. p. *Weadegus,* c. p. *Wodenus ;* and p. 566 with a few variations : *Wo-denus, Weagdegus, Siggarus, Suebdegus, Siggeotus, Seabaldus, Se-fugelus, Sueartha, Seomelus, Westerwalcna, Wilgelsus, Wuscfrea, Iffus* dux, *Ælla* primus rex Deirorum. Otterbourne p. 32 : *Wo-den* genuit *Wegdam,* qui genuit *Sigegarum,* q. g. *Swealdegem,* q. g. *Sigegeat,* q. g. *Etabalem,* q. g. *Stafugel,* q. g. *Westerfalducue,* q. g. *Wigilis,* q. g. *Ustfrea,* q. g. *Uffe,* q. g. *Ella* primum regem Sussex.[4]

---

[1] May we connect Wedelgeát, Widhelgeát with the national name *Wedergeátas,* Beow. 2984. 3224. 4753 ?

[2] The Genealogia runica in Langebek i. 32 has *Vithlek, Vermund, Uffi ;* that at i. 27 gives *Vithlef, Vermund, Uffi.*

[3] On the line of Mercia, to which Offa II (757) belongs, see Lappenb. 1, 222 ; conf. the two Offas above (p. 388) —EHM.]

[4] Some other writers also call the Deira genealogy the Sussex ; yet Sussex lies some distance from Yorkshire.

Langhorn : *Vegdegus, Sigarus, Suebdegus, Siggotus, Sebaldus, Sefugelus, Suarta, Somelus, Vestrofalenas, Vilgisilus, Buscreas, Iffius, Alla.* Gale's App. mixes up the Deira line with the Wessex : *Woden, Beldeyg, Brond, Siggar, Sibald, Zegulfh, Soemil, Sguerthing, Guilgils, Ulfrea, Iffi, Ulli.*

As the Kentish borrowed some names from horses, so does this from birds, *Sœ-fugel* and *Wester-falcna,* whom the Chronicle makes father and son, but between whom the other lists insert two more links, Seomel and Swearta (or Swearta and Seomel). There is also a *Sige-fugel* (al. Sigewulf) in the Essex lineage. I doubt whether *Sea-fola* in the Trav. Song 230 can have anything to do with this.——The mythic *Westerfalcna* has perhaps a right to be regarded as ancestor of the Westphals, for the old form of that national name was *Westfalah,* and we know of a hero in the Wessex line who did give name to a branch of the nation. *Sœ-fugel* and *Sœ-bald* have their first syllable in common. *Swœfdœg* resembles the ON. *Svipdagr,* Sæm. 111 [Hrôlfkr. sag. c. 18—23], *Svibdagerus,* Saxo Gr. 9, though the *f* and *p* are at variance ; and it is worth noting that his grandfather too is *Wœg-dœg,* and the head of the Wessex line *Bœl-dœg.* The relation of *Wœg-dœg* to the Kentish *Wecta* I shall discuss by and by in elucidating the Norse genealogy.

BERNICIA or Northumberland has its first two descendants of Wôden in common with Wessex.—Sax. Chr. p. 23 (yr. 547) : ' her *Ida* feng tô rîce, thonon Nordhanhymbra cynecyn ærost onwôc. *Ida* wæs Eopping, *Eoppa,* Esing, *Esa* Inguing, *Ingui* Angenwiting, *Angenwit* Alocing, *Aloc* Beonocing, *Beonoc* Branding, *Brand* Bældæging, *Bœldœg* Wôdening.' Florence 218 : *Ida* fuit filius *Eoppae,* qui fuit *Inqui,* q. f. *Angenwit,* q. f. *Aloc,* q. f. *Benoc,* q. f. *Brandi,* q. f. *Bealdegi,* q. f. *Wodeni ;* but with variations and additions in the prosapia p. 566 : *Bealdeagus, Brandius, Beornus* (for Benocus?), *Beorno, Wegbrandus, Ingebrandus, Alusa, Angengeat, Ingengeat, Aethelbrihtus, Oesa, Eoppa, Ida* primus rex Berniciorum. Otterbourne : *Woden, Belder, Brond, Benoc, Aloc, Agmintus, Inginus, Ensa, Ropa, Ida.* Langhorn : *Beldegus, Brando, Benocus, Beorna, Vegbrandus, Ingebrandus, Alocus, Angongeta, Ingongeta, Aethelbertus, Esa, Eoppa, Ida.* Bertram's ed. of Nennius gives in an appendix : *Woden* genuit *Beldeg,* g. [*Brand,* g.] *Beornec* [g. *Beorno*], g. *Gethbrond* [g.

*Ingebrandus*], g. *Aluson*, g. *Inguet*, g. [*Ingengeat*, g.] *Edibrith*,
g. *Ossa*, g. *Eobba*, g. *Ida.*——Of these names, *Esa* seems to me
akin to ôs, pl. ês (deus divus), and *Ingui* is the ON. *Ingvi*, conf.
*Ingunar* freyr and Beow. 2638 freá *Ingwina*, 2081 eodor *Ingwina*.
WESSEX.—Sax. Chr. p. 24 : *Cerdic* wæs *Cynrices* fæder,
*Cerdic* Elesing, *Elesa* Esling, *Esla* Gewising, *Gewis* Wiging, *Wig*
Freáwining, *Freáwine* Fridhogâring, *Fridhogâr* Branding, *Brand*
Bældæging, *Bœldœg* Wôdening; the same at p. 95, except the
spelling of Fridhugâr and Brond, and the insertion of *Creoda* be-
tween Cerdic and Cynrîc. The same pedigree stands in an AS.
document printed at the beginning of the AS. Beda of 1643, p. 5,
and in Spelman's Vita Alfredi 1678, p. 199, except that the latter
has Winging for Wiging, and both have the words 'Elesa
Esling, Esla Gewising' on the margin, not in the text. Asser :
*Cynric*, qui fuit *Creoda*, q. f. *Cerdic*, q. f. *Elesa*, [q. f. *Esla*], q. f.
*Gewis*, a quo Britones totam illam gentem *Gegwis* nominant,
[q. f. *Wig*, q. f. *Fraewine*, q. f. *Freothegar*], q. f. *Brond*, q. f. *Belde*,
q. f. *Woden ;* the sentences in brackets are apparently taken from
Florence, and wanting in the MS. Ethelwerd p. 842 : *Cynric*,
*Cerdic, Elesa, Esla, Gewis, Wig, Freawine, Frithogar, Brond,
Balder, Wothen.* Florence 219 : *Cerdicius*, qui fuit *Eslae*, q. f.
*Gewisii*, q. f. *Wigae*, q. f. *Freawini*, q. f. *Frethegarii*, q. f. *Brandii*,
q. f. *Bealdigi*, q. f. *Wodeni ;* again at p. 566 : *Bealdeagus, Bran-
dius, Freodegarius, Friawinus, Wigga, Gewisius, Esla, Elisius,
Cerdicius* primus rex Westsaxonum, *Kenricus.* Simeon of Durh.
119 : *Cinric*, q. f. *Creoda*, q. f. *Cerdic*, q. f. *Elesa*, q. f. *Gewis*, a quo
Britones totam illam gentem *Gewis* nominant, q. f. *Brand*, q. f.
*Belde*, q. f. *Woden* [same as in Asser]. Will. Malmesb. p. 41 :
*Woden, Beldegius, Brond, Fridegarius, Frewinus, Wigius, Giwius,
Eslius, Elicius, Cerdicius, Creodingius, Cinricius.* Ethelred
Rieval. p. 350 : *Woden, Bealdœg, Brand, Freodgar, Frewine,
Wig, Gewis, Eda, Elesa, Ceordic, Creoda, Chenric.* Otterbourne :
*Woden, Bealdeath, Brond, Frectegar, Freawinus, Wicca, Gewisse,
Esla, Flesa, Ceredic.* Langhorn : *Beldegus, Brando, Fredegarus,
Frevinus, Vigga, Geviscus, Esla, Elisius, Cerdicus.*

In this series of Westsaxon names, the chief stress is to be
laid on Wôden's son *Bœldœg* (Beldeg, Beldig, *Belde* in Asser
and those who follow him, *Balder* in Ethelwerd), evid. the Norse
*Baldur* son of Odin; *Freá-wine* too resembles the ON. Freys

vinr, still more *Frowinus* in Saxo Gr. pp. 59, 60 ; *Esla*, like the Northumbrian Esa, may come from ôs, ês. *Gewis* must have been a distinguished hero and sovereign, for a whole race to be named after him ; even Beda mentions the fact, where he says of Cynegils, a successor of Cerdic, 3, 7 : eo tempore gens Occiden-talium Saxonum, quae antiquitus *Gevisse* vocabantur, regnante Cynegilso fidem Christi suscepit (yr 635) ; and again of Bp. Byrinus : sed Britanniam perveniens, ac primum *Gevissorum* gen-tem ingrediens, cum omnes ibidem paganissimos inveniret, etc.

LINDESFARAN.—These were a separate race, who had settled in a small island off the Northumbrian coast, and named it after them Lindesfarena-eá (Beda, 3, 17. 4, 12. Sax. Chr. ann. 780. 793), otherw. Hâlig eáland, now Holy Island. I find their genealogy in Flor. 566 : *Woden, Winta, Cretta, Quelpgilfus, Ceadbed, Bubba, Beda, Eanferthus ;* another edition more correctly makes the fourth name *Queldgils,* the fifth *Caed-baed,* and adds *Biscop* after Beda, *Eatta* and *Ealdfrith* after Eanferth. Bubba's successor was prob. called *Bedeca* or *Baduca* (like one of the Essex line), for Eddii vita S. Wilfridi cap. 3 (Gale p. 45) relates of the Kentish king Erconbert (d. 664) : Rex secundum petitionem reginæ, ducem nobilem et admirabilis ingenii quemdam *Biscop Baducing* inveniens ad sedem apostolicam properantem, ut in suo comitatu esset adquaesivit. Biscop's grandson *Eata* became (Beda 4, 13) one of the first bishops of Lindesfarn ; but the grandfather himself, to judge by his name, must have held the same sacred office, perhaps elsewhere.

### WÔDEN'S ANCESTRY.

So far we have dealt with Wôden's descendants. In treating of his *ancestors,* we shall again have to separate the purely *heathen* ones from those that were added after the Bible genea-logy became known.

Some accounts reach back only 4 generations, others 8 or 16, stopping either at Fridhuwulf, Geát or Sceáf. Generally speak-ing, Sceáf is the oldest heathen name in any of the pedigrees.

| | |
|---|---|
| Wôden. | Finn. |
| Fridhuwald. | Godwulf (Folcwald). |
| Freáwine (Freáláf). | Geát. |
| Fridhuwulf. | Tætwa. |

| | |
|---|---|
| Beaw. | Hathra (Itermôd). |
| Sceldwa. | Hwala (Hathra). |
| Heremôd (Sceáf). | Bedwig (Hwala). |
| Itermon (Heremod). | Sceáf (Bedwig). |

The **Chronicle** p. 23 carries the Northumbrian lineage fr. Ida up to Geát: *Wôden* Freodholâfing, *Freodholâf* Fridhowulfing, *Fridhowulf* Finning, *Finn* Godwulfing, *Godwulf* Geáting; at p. 24 (under Deira), Wôden is called *Fridhowulfing;* at p. 95 (under Wessex) the line is given more fully and exactly : *Wôden* Fridhuwalding, *Fridhuwald* Freáwining, *Freáwine* Fridhuwulfing, *Fridhowulf* Finning, *Finn* Godwulfing, *Godwulf* Geáting, *Geát* Tætwaing, *Tœtwa* Beawing, *Beaw* Sceldwaing, *Sceldwa* Heremôding, *Heremôd* Itermoning, *Itermon* Hathraing, *Hathra* Hwalaing, *Hwala* Bedwiging, *Bedwig* Sceáfing. **Nennius** p. 61 carries the Kentish line up to Geta: *Vuoden* filius *Frealof*, Fr. f. *Fredulf*, Fr. f. *Finn*, F. f. *Foleguald*, F. f. *Geta*, qui ut aiunt filius fuit dei, non veri nec omnipotentis dei, sed alicujus ex idolis eorum, quem ab ipso daemone coecati, more gentili, pro deo colebant. **Asser** p. 4 : *Woden*, qui fuit *Frithowalde*, q. f. *Frealaf*, q. f. *Frithuwulf*, q. f. *Fingodwulf*, q. f. *Geata*, quem Getam jamdudum pagani pro deo venerabantur; qui Geata fuit *Cœtva*, q. f. *Beav*, q. f. *Sceldwea*, q. f. *Heremod*, q. f. *Itermod*, q. f. *Hathra*, q. f. *Huala*, q. f. *Bedwig*. **Ethelwerd** p. 842 : *Wothen*, *Frithowulf*, *Frealaf*, *Frithowlf*, *Fin*, *Godwulfe*, *Geat*, *Tetwa*, *Beo*, *Scyld*, *Scef*. **Florence** p. 218 (under Northumbr.) : *Wodenus*, qui fuit *Frithelasi* (for Frithelafi), q. f. *Finni*, q. f. *Godulfi*, q. f. *Geatae;* but on p. 294 (under Wessex) : *Wodenus*, q. f. *Frithewaldi*, q. f. *Frealafi*, q. f. *Fritheulfi*, q. f. *Finni*, q. f. *Godulfi*, q. f. *Gaetae*, quem Getam jamdudum pagani pro deo venerabantur, q. f. *Cedwae*, q. f. *Beawae*, q. f. *Sceldwii*, q. f. *Heremodi*, q. f. *Itermodi*, q. f. *Hathri*, q. f. *Walae*, q. f. *Bedwigi*. So the Wessex line in **Simeon Durh.** p. 119 : *Woden*, q. f. *Frithuwald*, q. f. *Frealaf*, q. f. *Fridrenwulf*, q. f. *Geta*, q. f. *Cetwa*, q. f. *Beaw*, q. f. *Seldwa*, q. f. *Heremod*, q. f. *Itermod*, q. f. *Hatra*, q. f. *Wala*, q. f. *Bedwig*. **Will. Malmesb.** p. 41 : *Wodenius* fuit Fridewaldi, *Fridewaldus* Frelasii (al. Fridelafii), *Frelasius* Fimi, *Fimus* Godwini, *Godwinus* Gesii, *Gesius* Tectii, *Tectius* Beowini, *Beowinus* Sceldii, *Sceldius* Sceaf, *Sceaf* Heremodii, *Heremodius* Stermonii, *Stermonius*

Hadrae, *Hadra* Gualae, *Guala* Bedwegii, *Bedwegius* Stresaei. **Ethelred Rieval.** p. 351 : *Woden,* q. f. *Fredewald,* q. f. *Freolof,* q. f. *Frederewlf,* q. f. *Fingondwlf,* q. f. *Geta,* q. f. *Gearwa,* q. f. *Beu,* q. f. *Celdwa,* q. f. *Heremod,* q. f. *Itermod,* q. f. *Hathra,* q. f. *Wala,* q. f. *Beadwig.* **Henry Huntingd.** p. 310 (under Kent): *Woden,* filii *Frealof,* f. *Fredulf,* f. *Fin,* f. *Flocwald,* f. *Jeta,* quem dixerunt filium dei, scilicet alicujus idoli. **Ralph** (under Wessex) p. 529 : *Woden,* q. f. *Frederewald,* q. f. *Freolf,* q. f. *Fredewlf,* q. f. *Fringoldwlf,* q. f. *Geta,* q. f. *Geatwa,* q. f. *Beu,* q. f. *Sceldwa,* q. f. *Heremod,* q. f. *Itermod,* q. f. *Bathka,* q. f. *Wala,* q. f. *Beadwig.* **John Wallingf.** p. 535 : *Guodden,* q. f. *Frithewald,* q. f. *Frealaf,* q. f. *Frethewlf,* q. f. *Fingoldwlf,* q. f. *Geata,* quem Geattam pagani jamdudum pro deo venerabantur, q. f. *Cetirwa,* q. f. *Beau,* q. f. *Celdewa,* q. f. *Heremod,* q. f. *Idermod,* q. f. *Hathra,* q. f. *Wala,* q. f. *Beadwing.* **Alberic** p. 186 : *Woden* iste fuit filius *Frithewaldi,* qui *Frelasii,* q. *Finnii,* q. *Godpulfi,* q. *Gethii,* q. *Rethlii,* q. *Bedvii,* q. *Sceldii,* q. *Sceaf,* q. *Heremodii,* q. *Gwale,* q. *Bedwegii,* q. *Steresii.* **Matth. Westm.** p. 142 (under Mercia): *Woden* fuit filius *Frethewold,* q. f. *Freolaf,* q. f. *Frithewlf,* q. f. *Godwlf,* q. f. *Getae,* q. f. *Cethwae,* q. f. *Beau,* q. f. *Selduae,* q. f. *Heremod,* q. f. *Itermod,* q. f. *Hathrae,* q. f. *Walae,* q. f. *Bedwi ;* but p. 166 (under Wessex) :• *Wodenus* fuit filius *Frethewold,* q. f. *Freolaf,* q. f. *Frethwlf,* q. f. *Finni,* q. f. *Godulfi,* q. f. *Getae,* q. f. *Teathwii,* q. f. *Beau,* q. f. *Selduae,* q. f. *Seaf,* q. f. *Heremod,* q. f. *Itermod,* q. f. *Hathrae,* q. f. *Walae,* q. f. *Bedvii.* **Otterbourne** (under Kent): *Woden, Frederwald, Freolf, Fredwold, Fyngoldwelth, Geta, Getwa, Beir, Sceldwa, Herecude, Etermode, Athra, Wala, Bedwich.*

The three generations immed. before Wôden exhibit a number of variations, which I will bring under one view :

| Chron. (Wess.): | Fridhuwald | Freáwine | Fridhuwulf |
|---|---|---|---|
| Asser : | Frithowald | Frealaf | Frithuwulf |
| Ethelwerd : | Frithowald | Frealaf | Frithowulf |
| Flor. (Wess.) : | Frithewald | Frealaf | Fritheulf |
| Simeon : | Frithuwald | Frealaf | Fridrenwulf |
| John : | Frethewald | Frealaf | Frethewlf |
| Ethelred : | Frethewald | Freolof | Frederewlf |
| Ralph : | Frederewald | Freolf | Fredewlf |
| Matthew : | Fredewold | Freolaf | Frithewlf |

*Freáwine* rests then on the single auth. of the Chron., and even there some MSS. have Frealafing, Frealaf. In the following, there is one link wanting :

| Chron. (Northumb.) : | . . . . | Freodholaf | Fridhowulf |
|---|---|---|---|
| Nennius : | . . . . | Frealof | Fredulf |
| William : | Fridewald | Frealaf | . . . . |
| Henry : | . . . . | Frealof | Fredulf |
| Alberic : | Frithewaldus | Frelasius | . . . . |

And some have only one name to shew :

| Chron. (Deira) | . . . . | . . . . | Fridhowulf |
|---|---|---|---|
| Flor. (Northumb.) | . . . . | Frithalaf | . . . . |

But as some retain one name and some another, it is plain that the Wessex genealogy of the Chronicle is the complete and correct thing. *Freáwine* and *Freálâf* may be regarded as identical, no matter that Freáwine occurs again in the descending series of the Wessex line, for certain names often repeat themselves. If we accept the Frithalaf of Florence [and Freodholaf in the Chron. under Northumb.], we have then *Fridho*-wald, *Fridho*-lâf, *Fridho*-wulf in immed. succession.[1]

*Finn* and *Godwulf* are thrown into one as *Fingodwulf* in Asser, *Fingondwulf* in Ethelred, *Fingoldwlf* in John, *Fringoldwlf* in Ralph [*Fyngoldwelth* in Otterb.]. Both are wanting in Simeon, Finn in Matthew, Godwulf in Nennius and Henry. Instead of Godwulf, Nennius gives a *Foleguald* (Folcwald), Henry *Flocwald* and William *Godwine*.

*Geát* (Geata, Geta, Jeta, Gesius) is present in all.

*Tœtva*, Tetwa, Tectius appears also as Cætwa, Cetwa, Cethwa, Cedwa, Cetirwa, and Getwa, Geatwa, Gearwa, Rethlius.

*Beav*, Beaw, Beau, Beawa, Beu, Beo, Beowinus, Bedvius, Beir.

*Sceldva*, Sceldwa, Scyld, Sceldwius, Sceldius, Seldwa, Seldua, Celdwa, Celdewa.

*Heremôd* remains unaltered wherever it occurs, except that Otterb. has Herecude ; but it is wanting in Ethelwerd.

*Itermon*, Itermod, Idermod, Etermode, Stermon ; wanting in Ethelw.

---

[1] [Friðleif suggests the ' jomfrue *Fridlefsborg* ' in the Dan. song of Tord af Hafsgaard, where the Swed. has ' jungfru *Froijenborg*.'—EHM.]

*Hathra*, Hadra, Hatra, Athra, Hathrus, Bathka; wanting in Ethelw.

*Hvala*, Huala, Wala, Guala; wanting in Ethelw.

*Bedvig*, Bedwig, Bedwi, Beadwig, Bedwigus, Bedwegius, Bedwing, Bedwid; wanting in Ethelw.

*Sceáf*, Scef, Seaf is not found in Asser or Florence or any writers that follow these two, but only in the Sax. Chr. and four other authorities (Ethelwerd, Alberic, Will. Malmesb. and Matth. Westm.); and even here with the important distinction, that whereas the Chron. puts him at the very end, as father of Bedwig, the other four bring him in near the middle, as father of Sceldwa and son of Heremôd.

Among the names are a few of more than common interest.

*Fin* is spoken of in the Trav. Song 53 as ruler of the Frisians : ' *Fin Folcwalding* weold Fresna cynne,' which confirms the statement of Nennius that his father's name was Folcwald (or Folcwalda). Again, *Fin* appears in Beow. 2129-55-86. 2286, and still as *Folcwaldan sunu* 2172; so that the Kentish genealogy had preserved his name more truly than the others. Observe too, that it is side by side with Fin that Beow. 2159-86. 2248 introduces *Hengest*, a great name with the [Kentishmen ; must not they have been a Frisian rather than a Jutish race ?

Fin's grandfather, Folcwald's father, *Geát*, was worshipped as a god; this is expressly affirmed by many chroniclers, while Wôden's divinity is passed over in silence. We come across Geát in Beow. 3567-82, and if not in the Trav. Song, yet in another AS. lay (Conybeare 241) : '*Geátes* frige wurdon grundleáse.' The Sax. Chr. and Ethelwerd make no mention of his godhood. Nennius and his transcriber Henry Huntgdn designate him the son of a god, ' filius dei,[1] non veri, etc.'; with him they close the Kentish pedigree, and do not name his father. But Asser and those who follow him, notably Florence, Ralph and John, say of *Geta* himself ' quem dudum pagani pro deo venerabantur,' and then add the names of his father (Cetwa) and ancestors. At the same time they refer, absurdly enough, to a passage in Sedulius (Carmen paschale 1, 19. ed. Arevali. Romae 1794, p. 155), which speaks of the ' boatus ridiculus Gĕtae,' or as

---

[1] In myths the *son of a god* seems often ident. with the god himself, conf. Tacitus about Tuisco and Mannus.

Sedulius says in prose ' ridiculi Getae comica foeditate,' evid. a character in a play of the Old Comedy. That the AS. *Geát* or *Gêt* was from the earliest times, long before the migration to Britain, regarded as a god, will be proved presently by a Gothic genealogy, which quite correctly names him *Gaut*, as in OHG. he would be ,*Gôz* or *Kôz*. In the Grimnismâl (Sæm. 47ᵇ, conf. Sn. 24. 195) *Gautr* is the name that Odhinn bears among the gods themselves.

*Tætwa* is prob. to be expl. by an adj. tæt, lost in AS. but extant in ON. teitr, OHG. zeiz, meaning laetus, hilaris, placidus. [1] Both Teitr and Zeiz, Zeizo were in use as men's names, but the great thing is that Odhinn himself is called *Herteitr* in the Edda, Sæm. 46ᵃ. Tætwa might bear the sense of numen placidum, benignum, the ' gehiure.'

The next three names, in the order *Beaw, Sceldwa, Sceáf*, give us a clear insight into the intimate connexion betw. these genealogies and the ancient poetry of the people. *Beaw, Beo, Beu* is no other than the elder *Beowulf* who appears at the very beginn. of the epic of Beowulf, and is called at l. 37 *Scyldes* eafera (offspring), at l. 16 *Scylding* (S.'s son), and who must be distinguished from the younger Beowulf, the subject of the poem. Beo stands in the same relation to Beowulf as the simple form of a name does to the compound in so many cases. [2]——*Scyld* (Beow. 51) resembles the mythic *Skiold* king of Danes (Saxo Gr. 5), and *Skiöldr* the Skânûnga godh (p. 161) ; Skiöldr in the Edda is Oðin's son (Sn. 146. 193), from whom descend the *Skiöldûngar* (Sæm. 114-5), AS. *Scyldingas*. The termin. -*wa*, which makes *Sceldwa* a weak noun, is also seen in Tætwa as compared with Teitr and Zeiz, and arises out of the third decl., to which skiöldr = shield (gen. skialdar, dat. skildi) belongs, implying a Goth. skildus with gen. pl. skildivê.——In Beow. 7 Scyld is expressly called a *Scêfing*, son of *Sceáf*. About this Sceáf the AS. chroniclers have preserved a remarkable tradition with which his very name is interwoven (sceáf, sheaf, OHG. scoup, scoubis), and which is still current in the districts whence the Saxons migrated. As far as I know, Ethelwerd is the first who alludes

---

[1] Laetus is perh. for daetus (Goth. tatis), as lingua, levir, lautia for dingua, devir dautia.

[2] So Wolf means the same as Wolfgang, Regin or Regino as Reginhart, Dieto as Dietrich, Liuba as Liebgart. Hence Beowulf and Beowine mean one thing.

to it, and that precisely in tracing up the Westsaxon lineage, p. 842 : ' ipse *Scef* cum uno dromone advectus est in insula oceani, quae dicitur Scani, armis circundatus, eratque valde recens puer, et ab incolis illius terrae ignotus, attamen ab eis suscipitur, et ut familiarem diligenti animo eum custodierunt, et post in regem eligunt.' Then, with some variations, Will. Malmesb. p. 41 : ' iste (Sceáf), *ut quidam ferunt*, in quamdam insulam Germaniae Scamphtam (al. Scandeam), de qua Jordanes historio‐ graphus Gothorum loquitur, appulsus navi sine remige puerulus, posito ad caput *frumenti manipulo*, dormiens, ideoque *Sceaf* est nuncupatus, et ab hominibus regionis illius pro miraculo exceptus et sedulo nutritus, adulta aetate regnavit in oppido quod tum Slaswich, nunc vero Eitheisi (al. Hurtheby) [1] appellatur ; est autem regio illa Anglia Vetus dicta, unde Angli venerunt in Britanniam, inter Saxones et Giothos constituta.' And, in almost the same words, Alberic and Matth. Westm.; the former says . ' in Scania insula quae est in Dania,' and again ' Sleswyk, quod Hartebi dicitur.' Matthew : ' in quandam insulam Germaniae, Scandalin nomine' ; adding after manipulo : ' quem patria lingua seaf (l. sceaf) dicimus, Gallice vero garbam.'——An unknown boy, in a ship without oars (RA. 701), sleeping with his head on a corn-sheaf, lands in Angeln, is received as a miracle by the inhabitants, is brought up, and made their king : he and his race must therefore have appeared of sacred and divine origin. This legend, no doubt, is touched upon in the obscure opening of the Beowulf, though the incident is there transferred to Scyld the son of Sceáf; his sleeping on a sheaf of corn is not men‐ tioned, any more than it is by Ethelwerd, whose ' armis circun‐ datus' is more in accord with Beow. 72—81. 93-4-5. The difficult word *umbor-wesende* can hardly mean anything but ' recens natus.' [2] The Trav. Song 64 speaks of a *Sceáfa* as lord of the Lombards. Tales of strange *heroes* arriving *asleep in their ships* must have been early diffused in Germany. [3]

---

[1] Read *Haithaby*, ON. *Heidhabœr*, Heidhaboe, a bp's see in S. Jutland [Schles‐ wig]. Ethelwerd p. 833 : Anglia Vetus sita est inter Saxones et Giotos, habens oppidum capitale quod sermone Saxonico *Sleswic* nuncupatur, secundum vero Danos *Haithaby*.

[2] The acc. masc. like a nom. may perh. be justified, else we must emend it to wesende. A new passage in Kemble p. 253: '*umbor* yceð þâ ær adl nimeð' may mean ' *nova proles* addit (restituit) quos morbus aufert.'

[3] The swan-knight, alone and *asleep*, his head reclined on his shield, arrives in

But the divine repute in which Sceáf and Scyld were held is further enhanced by one or the other being likewise a son of *Heremód,* a simple hero in Beow. 1795. 3417, but a distinctly divine being in the Norse mythology. Hermóðr in the Edda is a son of Oðinn, the AS. Heremód of Itermon. *Itermon* (with long *i*) can be expl. by a lost adj. îtor, îtôr, signifying like ON. îtr praeclarus, eximius ; therefore, vir eximius. *Ittermann* is still a family name in Westphalia.

To *Hathra* I shall return further on ; of *Hwala* and *Bedwig* I have nothing particular to say.

It remains to be told in what way the chroniclers tried to bring these native gods and heroes into line with the earliest generations handed down by Holy Writ.

The Sax. Chr. p. 96, after ‘Bedwig Sceáfing,’ inserts in brackets, as not found in all the MSS. : ‘ id est filius *Noe,* se wæs geboren on þære earce Noe,[1] *Lamech, Matusalem, Enoh, Jared, Malalahel, Cainion, Enos, Seth, Adam* primus homo et pater noster, id est *Christus,* Amen.’ Asser, who knows nothing of Sceáf, gives his place to Shem, and brings the two lines to touch as follows : ‘ *Bedwig,* qui fuit *Sem,* q. f. *Noe,* q. f. *Lamech,* q. f. *Mathusalem,* q. f. *Enoch* [q. f. *Jared*], q. f. *Malaleel,* q. f. *Cainan,* q. f. *Enos,* q. f. *Seth,* q. f. *Adam.*’ The same in Florence p. 294, except that *Seth* is put for Sem, and another *Seth* comes after Enos. Simeon, Ethelred and Matthew, like Asser; but Will. Malmesb. p. 41 has a way of his own : ‘Guala Bedwegii, Bedwegius *Stresaei,* hic, ut dicitur, fuit filius *Noae,*’ and the line goes no further. Is Stresaeus [Alberic’s Steresius] a corrup. of Scefius ? A totally different harmony [of heathen with Hebrew], one that does not touch the AS. lines, is propounded by Nennius p. 54.

Now to sum up the gains accruing from these genealogies to our German Antiquity. Names of gods they offer, in addition to *Wóden* : *Geát, Bældæg, Seaxneát, Heremód,* perhaps *Tætwa.* National names are treasured up in *Gewis, Westerfalcna,* and no

---

Brabant *by ship,* delivers the land, and becomes its ruler, Conrad of Würzb.’s poem 116—122. Lohengrin p. 19. Parz. 824, 27. 826, 24. Here the old Frankish, Frisian and Saxon traditions seem to harmonize [Vishnu also *sleeps* on the serpent *in the sea.*—EHM.].

[1] Is there an intended allusion to the boy sailing in the oarless ship ?

doubt in *Saxneát* himself. Part and parcel of our Hero-legend are, so far as we can still descry, *Scyld, Sceáf, Beaw;* many links are doubtless lost, but the solidarity with the Beowulf Lay and the Traveller's Song is in its full significance not to be over-looked. No less important seems the agreement of a string of names in the Mercian line with statements of Saxo Grammaticus. And in some names that stand side by side, we may detect traces of Alliteration, revealing the wrecks of heathen poems of a long past age, e.g. Hengest and Horsa, Scyld and Sceáf, Fin and Folcwald, Freodhowald and Freáwine.

Part of the Saxon pedigrees we have been examining had found their way, not later than the 13th cent., to Scandinavia, viz. the series from *Wôden* back to *Bedwig* and perhaps one generation more, and also forwards to three sons of Wôden and their descendants. That the names were borrowed is plain from the way Snorri (in the Formáli to his Edda p. 15) preserves their Saxon forms, and adds to many of them 'whom *we* call so-and-so.' Bedwig's father is here given as *Cespheth* (al. Sefsmeg, Sesep, Sescef), which may be the Saxon Scef in disguise; then: 'hans son *Bedvig,* hans son *Atra* er ver köllum *Annan,* h. s. *Itrmann,* h. s. *Biaf* er ver köllum *Biar.* h. s. *Jat,* h. s. *Gudólfr,* [h. s. *Finnr,*] h. s. *Fiarleif* (al. Frialafr) er ver köllum *Fridhleif,* hann átti thann son, er nefndr er (is named) *Vódhinn,* thann köllum ver *Odhinn;* kona (wife) hans hêt *Frigidha* er ver köllum *Frigg.*

It goes on to say, that Odhinn had three sons, *Vegdeg, Beldeg, Sigi.* 1) *Vegdeg* (al. Veggdegg, Vegdreg) rules over *East Saxons;* his son was called *Vitrgils,* and had two sons, *Ritta* (al. Picta, evid. Witta, Wicta) the father of *Heingest,* and *Sigarr* the father of *Svebdegg* er ver köllum *Svipdag.* 2) *Beldeg* er v. k. *Baldr,* rules over *Vestfal;* his son is *Brandr,* his son *Friodhigar* er v. k. *Fródha,* his son *Freovit* (al. Freovin), his son *Yvigg,* his son *Gevis* er v. k. *Gave.* 3) *Sigi* (al. Siggi) has a son *Verir* (al. Rerir); from them are descended the Völsûngar that rule *Franken.*

But at the back of all this Saxon genealogy Snorri places another, which interweaves Greek names, and has nothing in common with the AS. accounts. *Munnon* or Mennon, a king in Troia, marries a daughter of Priam, and has a son *Tror,* thann köllum ver *Thór.*[1] He marries a wise woman named *Sibil*

---

[1 Egilsum sub v. *þrôr* = Odin and Thor.—EHM.]

(Sibylla) er ver köllum *Sif*, their son is called *Loride*, his son *Henrede*, his *Vîngethôr*, his *Vîngener*, his *Môda*, his *Magi*, his *Cespheth*, the link that joins this line to the Saxon.[1]

Similar and more lengthened pedigrees, which add Hebrew to Greek and Latin names, are found in the piece called Frâ Fornjoti ok hans ættmönnum, in the so-called Langfedga-tal (Langebek 1, 2), and at the beginning of one MS. of the Sverris saga (Heimskr. th. 4).

In Fornaldar-sögur 2, 13 we find the following list: *Adam, Seth, Enos, Kaynan, Malaleel, Phareth, Enoch, Mathusalem, Lamech, Nôi, Japhet, Japhan, Zechim, Ciprus, Cretus* edha *Telius* (*Cœlius*), *Saturnus, Jupiter, Darius, Erithonius, Troes, Ilus, Lamidon, Priamus, Munnon* edha *Memnon, Trôrr* er ver köllum *Thôr, Lôritha* er v. k. *Hlôridha, Eredei* er v. k. *Eindridha, Vîngithôr, Vînginerr, Môdhi, Mâgi* er v. k. *Magna, Seseph, Bedhuis, Atra, Trînan, Skialdin* er v. k. *Skiold, Beaf* er v. k. *Biar, Godhôlfr, Burri* er v. k. *Finn, Frialâfr* er v. k. *Bors, Vôdhen* er v. k. *Odhinn*, hann var Tyrkja konûngr, hans son *Skiöldr*, h. s. *Fridhleifr*, h. s. *Fridhfrôdhi*, h. s. *Herleifr*, h. s. *Hâvardr*, and so on down to *Haraldr* hinn hârfagri (fair-haired).

In Langfedga-tal: *Noa, Japhet, Japhans, Zechim, Ciprus, Celius, Saturnus, Jupiter, Darius, Erichonius, Troes, Ilus, Lamedon, Priamus*. Priam's daughter *Troana* marries *Memnon*, whose son is *Tror* er v. k. *Thor;* then follow *Hloridhi, Einridi, Vingethor, Vingener, Moda, Magi, Seskef, Bedvig, Athra, Itermann, Heremotr, Scealdna, Beaf, Eat, Godulfi, Finn, Frealaf, Voden*, thann köllum ver *Oden*, fra honum ero komnar flestar konunga ættir (most kings' races) i nordalfuna heimsins.[2]

At the beginn. of Sverris s. [Fornm. sög. 8, 2]: *Adam, Seth, Enos, Kain, Malaleel, Pharet, Enoch, Matusalem, Lamech, Nca, Japhet, Japhen, Zethim, Chypris, Chretis, Chelis, Saturn, Jupiter, Dardan, Erichonius, Ereas, Ilus, Lamidon, Priamus; Thor, Jorekr, Eredeir, Vingithor, Vinginer, Modi, Magni, Sesep, Bedvig, Attras, Trinam, Hermodr, Skioldr, Biar, Godolfr, Finnr, Frialafr, Odin, Sigi, Rerer, Volsungr, Sigmundr, Sigurdr*, Fafnis-bani.

In looking over this Norse genealogy, we see that its resemblance to the AS. ascending series ends with Bedvig, or at most

---

[1] Conf. F. Magnusen's Lex. Myth. 553-4.—EHM.]
[2] This sentence sounds exactly like that in Beda and the Sax. Chr. (under Kent).

with Sesep, Seskef, Cespheth, which may conceal Sceáf, Seaf; the older names have nothing Saxon about them. First come a few that have a well-defined position in the ON. theogony: *Magni, Módi, Vingnir, Vingithôr, Einridi, Hlóridi, Thôr*, all the immediate kindred of Thôr, who never once appears in the AS. pedigrees. The way they are introduced here is rather remarkable. First *Thôr* himself, whom all the authorities on Norse mythology invariably treat as Oðin's son, is here given out for his forefather, and one removed from him by 16 or 17 generations. Then these intermediate links are brought together curiously enough. In the Edda, *Hlórridhi* is a mere surname of Thôr, not a separate person. *Eindridhi* (Eyndridhi) is another Eddic name for Thôr (Thorlac. Observ. 6, 26), and the same holds good of *Vingthôrr*, sonr Sîdhgrana (Sæm. 48, 80). *Vingnir* does occur sometimes as the name of a giant (Thorl. Obs. 6, 25), but *Módhi* and *Magni* are Thôr's two sons, and therefore brothers (Sn. 76). I do not mean to assert that the author of the pedigree wilfully perverted these by-names and brothers into descendants; a confusion in the popular tradition itself may account for it. And the tacking on to Greek gods and heroes was natural enough at a time when we Germans too were tracing our Franks and Saxons to Ascanius and Alexander. From the Greek to the Biblical genealogy was, to be sure, as great a leap as that from the Anglo-Saxon straight to Noah.

More important to our inquiry is that part of the ON. pedigree which mainly agrees with the AS., but differs in details. *Atra* is rendered by the ON. *Annarr*, for which the AS. would strictly be *Odher*, and that stands some distance from the *Hathra* of the AS. record. *Biaf, Biav* (Beaw) is not far from *Biafr, Biar*, and can hardly be the Norse Biörr. *Iát, Eát* is not glossed by any Norse name; would it be *Gautr? Iotr?*

But what deserves the most attention is the different account given of Wôden's Posterity. Here, as in Will. Malmesb. (see just before Kent), only *three sons* are given him, *Vegdeg, Beldeg, Sigi;* the first two agree with those in Will. M., but *Sigi* has nothing to do with his *Wihtlæg*. The account of the countries they ruled would of course be totally different from his. His *Weldeg, Wihtleg* and *Beldeg* were forefathers of the families that afterwards governed Kent, Mercia and Wessex; but the Formâli

of the Edda is appar. indicating their ancient seats before the
migration : to Vegdeg's line is attrib. *East Saxony*, to Beldeg's
*Westphalia*, to Sigi's *Franconia*. Wôden's immediate descendants were Wecta, Witta, Wihtgils ; those of Odhin are likewise
*Vegdeg, Vitrgils, Victa* (the last two merely changing places) ;
but from that point the two lists differ. Without once naming
Horsa, the Norse genealogist gives Victa two sons, *Heingest* whose
line is carried no further, and *Sigarr* whose son is *Svebdeg*, ON.
*Svipdagr*.[1] But this lands us in the line of Deira, which, after
Wôden and Wægdæg, has *Sigegár, Swæfdæg*. And we now
become aware that *Wecta* of Kent is no other than *Wægdæg* of
Deira, that the two lines were at first one, like those of Bernicia
and Wessex, and that we can no longer count seven, but only
*six sons* of Wôden. So much for Vegdeg and his line.——In the
second line, *Beldeg* is expressly identified with *Baldr*; his descendants are named to the fifth generation, and agree with the
Wessex line, except that *Freodogar* is said to be the Norse
*Fródhi*, that *Wig* is called *Yvigg*, and *Gevis Gaue*.——The third
line is altogether new and unknown to the Anglo-Saxons, starting
with a son of Odhin named *Sigi*, from whom come *Rerir* and the
Völsûngar, rulers of the Franks. This agrees with the beginning of the Völsûnga-saga, which calls *Sigi* a son of Odhin :
from him descend *Rerir* (al. Berir, Beirir), *Völsûngr, Sigmundr,
Sigurdhr*. The word *sig* (victory) is a favourite in this line,
Sigmund's sister being also called *Sign*́.[2] Völsûngr has the
form of a patronymic and national name, pointing to a Valsi or
Velsi, which actually meets us in the *Wœlse* of Beow. 1787, where
*Sigemund* too is found 1743-62.

The same continuation down to Sigurdhr is in the Sverris-
saga, but not in the Langfedga-tal. The ' Fornjot and his
kin ' gives quite a different one : *Skiöldr*, already mentioned
as an ancestor of Odhin, reappears as his son, and from him
descends a line of Norse kings to Harald the Fair-haired.[3]

[1] In Grög. and Fiölsv. m. *Svipdagr* is Menglöð's lover. His father is Sôlbiört
(Sæm. 112ᵃ), his mother Grôa.—EHM. ]

[2] In *Sigurdhr = Sigufrid*, Lachmann (Critik der sage v. d. Nibel. p. 22) conjec-
tures a *god's by-name ;* the line of Deira too has compounds with Sig-. Conf. what
I have said of *sihora* (p. 27) and of Wôden as god of victory (p. 134).

[3] The ordinary Danish genealogy begins : *Odin, Skiold, Fridleif, Frode*, Torf.
Series 279. Suhm's Crit. hist. 1, 355. [Sögubrot (Fornm. s. 11, 412-3): Thôrr,
Oðhin, Skiöldr, Leifr = Fridhleifr, Frôdhi. Prologue to Grôttas.: Skiöldr, Frið-
leifr, Frôi. In the AS. genealogies *Sceldwa* is made an *ancestor* of Wôden:

This last account also contains some not inconsiderable variations in Odhin's Ancestry. The outlandish *Eredei* is transl. into
good Norse as *Eindridhi*, and *Mági* as *Magni*; *Trînan* the corrup.
of *Itrman* is here (as in Sverris-s.), *Hermôdr* is passed over, so
is *Eat* (as in Sverris-s.); on the other hand, at Finn and Frialâf
two names are introduced, *Burri* and *Bors*, which occur nowhere
else in these lists.

With such important deviations in form and matter, we can
scarcely say that these Norse genealogies were borrowed straight
from the AS.; more likely they travelled into Scandinavia from
some Saxon or Frisian district, where they were still cherished,
say in the 10-11th century. The forms Beldeg, Vegdeg, Svebdeg
differ, though slightly, from the pure AS. Bældæg, Wægdæg,
Swæfdæg; Atra from Hathra, Skialdun (Skialdin) from Scelwa,
Biaf from Beaw. The interpolation of Thôr's kindred comes, of
course, from the Norse writer.

But even if a loan took place from the Anglo-Saxons, and at
the later date of the 12-13th century, it matters little to the
intrinsic value of these genealogies. The AS. version is of itself
sufficient to vouch for their high antiquity and their solidarity
with the German system of gods.

It is much to be lamented that in Continental Germany, where
they must have existed, such pedigrees were never jotted down.
Witekind of Corvei, or his predecessor Bovo, could have given
us priceless information about them. A table in Sam. Reyher's
Monum. landgravior. Thuringiae (Menken 2, 829. 830), which
brings the fictitious line of a Saxon king Artharicus down to
'*Bodo* vel *Voden*,' and then foists in '*Vecta* vel Vichtus, *Witta*
vel Wittich, *Witgistus* vel Witgislus, *Hengistus*,' is taken from
Petrus Albinus's (d. 1598) Novae Sax. historiae progymnasmata
(Viteberg. 1585). Albinus had copied an AS. chronicler.

For all that, we catch undoubted echoes of ancient genealogies
in our poems of the 13th century. The Nibel. 88, 3 and 92, 1
preserves the names of *Schilbunc* and *Nibelunc*, and Biterolf 7821
calls them brothers. Now *Scylfing*, *Scilfing* (gomela S.) and the
*Scylfingas* occur in Beow. 125. 4406. 4758. 4970. 5850. 5931.
The Edda (Sæm. 47ᵇ) makes *Scilfingr* a by-name of Oðinn, and

' Sceldwa, Friðuwulf, Freálâf, Friðuwald, Wôden '; so he is in some Norse ones
(supra p. 1729), but usually a *son* of Oðin.—EHM.]

the Hyndlu-lioð in its genealogies (Sæm. 114-5) joins *Skiöldún-gar* and *Skilfingar* in alliteration. The above-mentioned ' Fornjot and his kin' (Fornald. s. 2, 9) counts among the mythic sons of Hâlfdân the Old a *Skelfir*, and derives from him and his son *Skiöldr* those two kindred races : ' that heitir *Skilfínga* ætt edha *Skiöldúnga* ætt.'[1] Here *Skelf* seems a corrup. of *Skef*, for both Beowulf and the AS. pedigrees make Scyld or Sceldwa the son of *Sceáf;* and from such corruption arose the different forms in both countries independently.[2] So we must reckon *Schilbunc* [conf. Schiltunc, Hpt. 1, 7], *Scilfing* as closely interwoven with the old genealogy. In Fornm. sög. 5, 239 *Skiöldr* is described as the national god of Schonen, ' Skânûnga godh' (p. 161).

A still more striking instance of agreement is furnished by the Gothic genealogy which Jornandes, after saying that the ances-tors of the Goths were *Anses*, imparts as follows : · Quorum genealogiam paucis percurram, ut quo quis parente genitus est, aut unde origo accepta, ubi finem efficit [percipiatur?] ; absque invidia qui legis vera dicentem ausculta : horum ergo, *ut ipsi suis fabulis ferunt,* primus fuit *Gapt,* qui genuit Halmal (al. humal, ulmal, hulmul), *Halmal* vero genuit Augis, *Augis* g. eum qui dictus est *Amala,* a quo et origo *Amalorum* decurrit. Et Amala g. Isarnam, *Isarna* autem g. Ostrogotham, *Ostrogotha* g. Unilt (al. Huniul), *Unilt* g. Athal, *Athal* g. Achiulf, *Achiulf* g. Ansilam et Ediulf et Vuldulf et Hermenrich ; *Vuldulf* vero g. Valeravans, *Valeravans* autem g. Vinitharium, *Vinitharius* quoque g. Theode-mir et Valemir et Videmir ; *Theodemir* g. Theodericum, *Theode-ricus* g. Amalasuentham, *Amalasuentha* g. Athalaricum et Mathasuentham de Viderico (l. Eutharico) viro suo, qui affini-tate generis sic ad eam conjunctus est : nam supradictus *Hermenricus* filius Achiulfi genuit Hunnimundum, Hunnimundus autem g. Thorismundum, *Thorismundus* vero g. Berimundum, *Berimundus* g. Videricum, *Videricus* g. *Eutharicum,* qui conjunc-tus Amalasuenthae g. Athalaricum et Mathasuentam, mortuoque in puerilibus annis Athalarico, Mathasuenthae *Vitichis* est socia-tus.'——Here again we see historic kings melting into heroes of the mythic time and into gods ; but the first father of them all,

---

[1 In Sn. 215ᵃ *Skilvingr* is the name of a sword. *Skelfir, Skilfingar* î austrvegum, Sn. 193-4.   *Schilpunc,* Ried no. 68 (yr. 888).—EHM.]

[2] The change of Skef into Skelf may have been encouraged by the better allitera-tion of Skilfing with Skiöldûng, Scylding with Scilfing.—TRANS.

no doubt an *Ans*, is he that arrests our attention. *Gapt* seems to me a corrup. of *Gavt*, *Gaut*.[1] This granted, *Gaut* is no other than our AS. *Geát*, on whose brow the chroniclers are so eager to press the crown of godhood. Now the Edda (Sæm. 47ᵇ) makes *Gautr* a mere by-name of Oðinn, who may therefore be reckoned a later re-incarnation of the same divine being. Thus *Gáuts*, *Geát*, *Gautr*, OHG. *Gôz* stands at the head of the *Amalung* family so famed in song and story.

The Langobardic genealogy of the Gunings or Gugings, preserved in the Prologue to the Laws and in Paul Diaconus, I leave on one side, as contributing little towards clearing up the story of the gods. It is one more witness, among so many, to the propensity of German nations to draw up and hand down lists of their forefathers' lineage.

On that point, who would not remember, first and foremost, the oldest word on the origin of the Germani, as preserved, though but in faint outlines, by Tacitus, and expressly grounded on their 'ancient songs, which are all the history they have'? (p. 344). 'Celebrant carminibus antiquis, quod unum apud illos memoriae et annalium genus est, *Tuisconem*, deum terra editum, et filium *Mannum*, originem gentis conditoresque. Manno tres filios assignant, e quorum nominibus proximi oceano *Ingaevones*, medii *Herminones*, ceteri *Istaevones* vocentur. Quidam, ut in licentia vetustatis, plures deo ortos pluresque gentis appellationes, *Marsos*, *Gambrivios*, *Suevos*, *Vandalos* affirmant.'——As the Anglo-Saxons allowed their Wôden, now *three*[2] sons, now *seven*, the same thing happens here to the offspring of Mannus. There is no further connexion between the two genealogies; but it is curious to find that in the first century A.D., various versions of the people's pedigree are already in vogue, and have reached the Roman's ear. He does not tell us the names of the sons, and in guessing them from those of the tribes they founded, we cannot feel sure of their exact form. Pliny 4, 4 supposes five principal tribes: *Vindeli, Ingaevones, Istaevones, Hermiones, Peucini*; the first are

---

[1] The Gothic *u* might easily be miscopied as a *v* (Ⅴ), and thus mistaken for a *p*, just as the AS. ƿ is made *p* in 'Pubba, Godpulf.'

[2] This number three is always turning up in myths. Noah's 3 sons: Shem, Ham, Japheth. Saturn's: Zeus, Poseidon, Pluton. The Scyth. Targitaus's: Leipoxais, Arpoxais, Kolaxais. The Norse Bör's: Oðinn, Vili, Vê. Fornjot's: Hlerr, Logi, Kâri. Amelunc's: Diether, Ermrîch, Dietmar.

Tacitus's *Vandali*. The head of the Herminones was no doubt
*Hermin*, i.e. *Irmin*, whom legends know of as a godlike hero ;
that of the Vandals *Vandal*, and of the Sueves *Svêf*, *Suáp*, which
reminds one of AS. *Swœfdœg* and ON. *Sváfnir* (another by-name
of Oðinn, Sæm. 47[b]) ; the head of the Gambrivii perh. *Gambar* :
OHG. kambar = strenuus, and the Langobard lineage has an
ancestress Gambara. Such a name as *Mars*, if that was the
source of the people's name, I have nowhere come across ; Tacitus
must have found it very acceptable.

The Ingaevones and Istaevones remain to be considered.
*Ingo*, an OHG. name, which also forms the compounds Ingumâr
(Frank. Hincmar), Ingurât, Inguram, Ingulint, Inguwin, must
previously have been *Ingawo, Inguio*, for Inguio-mêrus occurs
several times in Tacitus, and it also agrees with ON. *Ingvi*. A
corresp. *Isto, Istuio* is wanting. As for the ending -*aevo*, we find
Frisaevo, also a national name, in an inscript. in Hagenbuch
173-5, side by side with Frisius 171-2-4. Ingvi or Yngvi in the
Norse mythology is a byname of Freyr, and Ingvi-freyr, Ingunar-
freyr seems to mean the same thing. With this conf. ' eodor
Ingwina, freá Ingwina,' Beow. 2081. 2638, and above all *Ingwi*
in the Bernician line ; can there remain a doubt that this name
belongs to the oldest period of the Germanic race, nay, that there
hangs about it an air of deity ?——*Istuio* is the great difficulty.
I would not willingly throw suspicion on the reading Istaevones,
though the fluctuation between Tuisto and Tuisco would almost
tempt one to do so. If we read *Iscaevones*, and inferred an
Iscvio, Isco, we might connect this with ON. *Askr*, the first-
created man, or with *Oesc* of the Kentish line, if that be not a
little too *un*mythical. Well, I found a passage in an unknown
compiler (Cod. Vat. 5001 fol. 140),[1] which actually has *sc*, not *st* :
' Tres fuerunt fratres, ex quibus gentes xiii. Primus *Ermenius*
genuit Butes, Gualan-gutos, Guandalos, Gepidos, Saxones. *Ingo*
genuit Burgundiones, Turingos, Longobardos, Baioeros. *Escio*
Romanos, Brictones, Francos, Alamannos.' And, strange to say,
Nennius (ed. Gunn p. 53-4) has something very similar : ' Primus
homo venit ad Europam *Alanus* cum tribus filiis suis, quorum

---

[1] Graff 1, 497 has the passage not only from the Cod. Vat., but from the *older*
Cod. S. Gall. 497 : *Erminus, Inguo, Istio ;* conf. Graff 1, 501 and Pertz's Iter Ital.
and Mon. 10, 314. Mone's Ztschr. 2, 256.]

nomina *Hisicion, Armenon, Neugio.* *Hisicion* autem habuit filios quatuor : Francum, Romanum, Alamannum et Brutonem. *Armenon* autem habuit filios quinque : Gothum, Vala-gothum, Cibidum, Burgundum, Longobardum. *Neugio* vero habuit tres: Vandalum, Saxonem, Boganum. Ab *Hisicione* autem ortae sunt quatuor gentes : Franci, Latini, Alamanni et Bryttones. Ab *Armenione* autem Gothi, Wala-gothi, Cibidi, Burgundi et Longobardi. A *Neugione* autem Bogari, Wandali, Saxones, Turingi.' And then, through many names that have nothing German about them, Alanus's line runs up to Adam. Gale's ed. of Nennius p. 102 reads *Hisicion, Armenon, Negno,* and the last has 4 sons, Wandalus, Saxo, Bogarus, Targus. Evidently Neugio, Negno is a corrup. of *Engio, Enguio,* Armenon of *Ermino,* while Hisicio makes for our supp. *Hisco, Isco.* And that Nennius and the Vatican MS. had not drawn from the same source is plain by the difference in details, despite the similarity of the whole.——The great question remains, whether all these accounts were taken first from Tacitus, and then extended and distorted. Unless we are prepared to maintain that, they are, to my mind, of extraordinary value. MSS. of Nennius are supp. to be of the tenth century; of the Vatican MS., in extracting from it many years ago, I left the age unmarked : it can hardly be older than the 12th century. If we think it likely that any link between them and the passage in Tacitus can be established, it must be of a time before Nennius, and therefore pretty early [conf. GDS. 824-5-9].

*Alanus* has unquestionably arisen by sheer mistaking of the first few strokes, out of *Manus,* i.e. the *Mannus* of Tacitus. This *Mannus* stands at the head of the Teutonic race, exactly as *Wóden* does at that of the Anglo-Saxon. It means man in all Teut. tongues: Goth. man, mann, manna, AS. mon, ON. madhr, gen. manns; so does its derivative mannisk, mannisco, mensch. Perhaps 'the thinking being' from the verb man, munum : an apt designation for God as well as God-created man, and certainly of high antiquity. I do not find it as a by-name of Oðinn or Wôden, but one of his ancestors is *Itermon,* of which the first part îter, îtr may be considered an intensive epithet: homo praestans, hominum praestantissimus. Acc. to that, *Mannus* and *Wóden* stand for the same thing. I throw out the guess, that in heathen songs the god might be called by either name.

Lastly, we turn to Mannus's own father, the earthborn *Tuisco*. What if the word be formed like mannisco, and abbrev. from *tiudisco* ? The O.Fr. *Tydios* was shortened to Thyois, Tyois, Tiois, *Thiodonis*-villa [Dieten-hofen] to Thion-ville. In Gothic dialect the god would be *Thiudiska*, in OHG. *Diutisco*, the off-spring of the people (thiuda, diot) itself. And the national name Teuto, Tiuto (OHG. Dieto) might be near of kin to Tiudisco.—But an entirely different derivation, suggested by Lachmann, seems preferable: Tuisco = *Tvisco*, the twin, δίδυμος, OHG. *Zuisco*, meaning perhaps one of the Dios-curi, the ' Castor Polluxque' of Tacitus (p. 66) ? The form Tuisto least of all lends itself to explanation, though there are some derivatives in -*st*, -*ist*; and to connect AS. Tætwa with Teuto or Tuisto would seem hazardous. Anyhow we shall not explain everything ; it is enough to have proved that in Tacitus's German theogony we see an unmistakable connexion with later traditions.

# SUPERSTITIONS.

A. From a *Sermon of St Eligius* (b. 588. d. 659) contained in the Vita Eligii of Audoenus Rotomagensis (Aldwin of Rouen, d. 683 or 689), printed in D'Achery's Spicileg. tom. 5 ed. Paris. 1661. pp. 215-9.

Lib. 2, cap. 16. Ante omnia autem illud denuntio atque contestor, ut nullas Paganorum sacrilegas consuetudines observetis, non *caraïos* (caragios),[1] non *divinos*, non *sortilegos*, non praecantatores, nec pro ulla causa aut infirmitate eos consulere vel interrogare praesumatis, quia qui facit hoc malum statim perdit baptismi sacramentum. Similiter et *auguria* vel sternutationes nolite observare, nec in itinere positi aliquas *aviculas cantantes* attendatis, sed, sive iter seu quodcunque operis arripitis, signate vos in nomine Christi, et symbolum et orationem dominicam cum fide et devotione dicite, et nihil vobis nocere poterit inimicus. Nullus Christianus observet, qua die domum exeat, vel qua die revertatur, quia omnes dies Deus fecit; nullus ad inchoandum opus *diem* vel *lunam* attendat; nullus in Kal. Jan. nefanda aut ridiculosa, *vetulas* aut *cervulos*[2] aut *jotticos* (al. uleriotcos) faciat, neque *mensas* super noctem *componat*, neque *strenas* aut *bibitiones* superfluas exerceat. Nullus Christianus in *puras* (al. pyras) credat, neque in cantu sedeat, quia opera diabolica sunt; nullus in festivitate S. Joannis vel quibuslibet sanctorum solemnitatibus *solstitia* aut *vallationes* (balationes?) vel *saltationes* aut *caraulas* (i.e. choraulas) aut *cantica diabolica* exerceat. Nullus nomina *daemonum*, aut *Neptunum* aut *Orcum* aut *Dianam* aut *Minervam* aut *Geniscum*, aut ceteras ejusmodi ineptias credere aut invocare praesumat. Nullus *diem Jovis*, absque festivitatibus sanctis, nec in Maio nec ullo tempore in otio observet, neque *dies tiniarum* vel *murorum*, aut vel unum omnino diem, nisi tantum dominicum.

[¹ Ducange sub vv. *caragus, cararius.*—EHM.]
[² Ducange sub v. *cervula.* Gl. Sletst. 23, 3 in *cervulo*, in liodersâza; 23, 4 in *vetula*, in dero varentun tragidi; 23, 8 coragios, liodirsâzo —EHM.]

Nullus Christianus ad *fana* vel ad *petras* vel ad *fontes* vel ad *arbores*, aut ad *cellos* vel *per trivia* luminaria faciat, aut vota reddere praesumat. Nullus ad colla vel hominis vel cujuslibet animalis *ligamina* dependere praesumat, etiamsi a clericis fiant, et si dicatur quod res sancta sit et lectiones divinas contineat, quia non est in eis remedia Christi, sed venenum diaboli. Nullus praesumat *lustrationes* facere, nec *herbas* incantare, neque pecora *per cavam arborem* vel *per terram foratam* transire, quia per haec videtur diabolo ea consecrare. Nulla mulier praesumat *succinos* de collum dependere, nec in tela vel in tinctura sive quolibet opere *Minervam* vel *infaustas ceteras personas* nominare ; sed in omni opere Christi gratiam adesse optare, et in virtute nominis ejus toto corde confidere. Nullus, si quando *luna obscuratur*, vociferare praesumat, quia Deo jubente certis temporibus obscuratur ; nec *luna nova* quisquam timeat aliquid operis arripere, quia Deus ad hoc lunam fecit, ut tempora designet et noctium tenebras temperet, non ut alicujus opus impediat, aut dementum faciat hominem, sicut stulti putant, qui a daemonibus invasos a luna pati arbitrantur. Nullus *dominos* solem aut lunam *vocet,* neque per eos juret, quia creatura Dei sunt et necessitatibus hominum jussu Dei inserviunt. Nullus sibi proponat *fatum* vel *fortunam,* aut genesin, quod vulgo nascentia dicitur, ut dicat ' qualem *nascentia* attulit, taliter erit ; ' quia Deus omnes homines vult salvos fieri, et ad agnitionem veritatis venire. Praeterea, quoties aliqua infirmitas supervenerit, non quaerantur praecantatores, non divini, non sortilegi, non *carugi*, nec per fontes aut arbores vel bivios diabolica phylacteria exerceantur. . . .

Ante omnia, ubicumque estis, sive in domo, sive in itinere, sive in convivio, verba turpia et luxuriosa nolite ex ore vestro proferre . . . . Ludos etiam diabolicos et *vallationes* (ballat. ? *i.e.* saltationes) vel *cantica gentilium* fieri vetate, nullus haec christianus exerceat, qui per haec paganus efficitur, nec enim justum est ut ex ore christiano . . . . cantica diabolica procedant. . . . Nulli creaturae praeter Deo et sanctis ejus venerationem exhibeatis, fontes vel arbores *quos sacros vocant* succidite ; *pedum similitudines quos per bivia ponunt,* fieri vetate, et ubi inveneritis igni cremate, per nullam aliam artem salvari vos credatis nisi per invocationem et crucem Christi. Nam illud quale est, quod si arbores illae ubi miseri homines vota reddunt ceciderint, nec ex eis ligna ad focum sibi deferunt? Et videte quanta stultitia est hominum, si arbori insensibili et mortuae honorem impendunt, et Dei omnipot. praecepta contemnunt. . . .

Nullus se inebriet, nullus in convivio suo cogat alium plus bibere quam oportet ; . . . nullus vel in qualibet minima causa diaboli sequatur adinventiones, nullus, sicut dictum est, observet *egrediens aut ingrediens domum,* quid sibi *occurrat,* vel si aliqua vox reclamantis fiat, aut *qualis avis cantus garriat,* vel quid etiam portantem videat; quia qui haec observat, ex parte paganus dignoscitur. . . . Si quos cognoscitis vel occulte aliqua phylacteria exercere, expedit ut nec cibum cum eis sumatis, neque ullum consortium apud eos habeatis. . . .

Omni die dominico ad ecclesiam convenite, et ibi non causas, non rixas, vel otiosas fabulas agatis, et lectiones divinas cum silentio auscultate.

B. *Indiculus superstitionum* et paganiarum (at the end of the Capitulare Karlomanni of 743 apud *Liptinas.*[1] Pertz 3, 20).

    I. de sacrilegio ad sepulchra mortuorum.

    II. de sacrilegio super defunctos, id est *dadsisas.*

    III. de spurcalibus in Februario.

    IV. de casulis, id est fanis.

    V. de sacrilegiis per ecclesias.

    VI. de sacris silvarum quas *nimidas* vocant.

    VII. de his quae faciunt super petras.

    VIII. de sacris *Mercurii* vel *Jovis.*

    IX. de sacrificio quod fit alicui sanctorum.

    X. de phylacteriis et ligaturis.

    XI. de fontibus sacrificiorum.

    XII. de incantationibus.

    XIII. de auguriis, vel avium vel equorum vel bovum stercore, vel sternutatione.

    XIV. de divinis vel sortilegis.

    XV. de igne fricato de ligno, id est *nodfyr.*

    XVI. de cerebro animalium.

---

[1] [Conf. Hagen in Jrb. 2, 62] Liptinae, an old villa regia, afterw. Listines, in the Kemmerich (Cambresis) country, near the small town of Binche.

XVII.  de observatione pagana in foco, vel in inchoatione rei alicujus.

XVIII.  de incertis locis quae colunt pro sacris.

XIX.  de petendo quod boni vocant sanctae Mariae.

XX.  de feriis quae faciunt *Jovi* vel *Mercurio.*

XXI.  de lunae defectione, quod dicunt *Vinceluna.*

XXII.  de tempestatibus et cornibus et cocleis.

XXIII.  de sulcis circa villas.

XXIV.  de pagano cursu quem *yrias* [Massmann's Form. 22: *frias*] nominant, scissis pannis vel calceis.

XXV.  de eo, quod sibi sanctos fingunt quoslibet mortuos.

XXVI.  de simulacro de consparsa farina.

XXVII.  de simulacris de pannis factis.

XXVIII.  de simulacro quod per campos portant.

XXXIX.  de ligneis pedibus vel manibus pagano ritu.

XXX.  de eo, quod credunt, quia feminae lunam commendent, quod possint corda hominum tollere juxta paganos.

Evidently the mere headings of the chapters that formed the *Indiculus* itself, whose loss is much to be lamented. It was composed towards the middle of the 8th cent. among German-speaking Franks, who had adopted Christianity, but still mixed Heathen rites with Christian. Now that the famous Abrenuntiatio has been traced to the same Synod of Liptinae, we get a fair idea of the dialect that forms the basis here. We cannot look for Saxons so far in the Netherlands, beyond the Maas and Sambre, but only for Franks, whose language at that time partook far more of Low than of High German. I do not venture to decide whether these were Salian Franks or later immigrants from Ripuaria.[1]

C.  From the Collect. of Decrees by *Burchard of Worms* (d. 1024),[2] Colon. 1548.

1, 94.  Interrogatio, 42 [3] : interrogandum, si aliquis sit magus, ariolus aut incantator, divinus aut sortilegus, vel si aliquis vota ad *arbores* vel ad *fontes* vel ad *lapides* faciat, aut ibi candelam

[¹ GDS. 537.—EHM.]      [² D. 1025, Kl. schr. 5, 417.—EHM.]

³ This and the foll. Interrogations are drawn 'e decreto Eutychiani papae (d. 283), cap. 9.'

seu quodlibet munus deferat, veluti ibi quoddam *numen* sit, quod bonum aut malum possit inferre. (Repeated 10, 32.)

Int. 43 : perscrutandum, si aliquis subulcus vel bubulcus sive venator vel ceteri hujusmodi *diabolica carmina* dicat super panem, aut super herbas, aut super quaedam nefaria ligamenta, et haec aut in arbore abscondat, aut in bivio aut in trivio projiciat, ut sua animalia liberet a peste et clade, et alterius perdat. (Reptd. 10, 18.)

Int. 44 : perquirendum, si aliqua femina sit, quae per quaedam maleficia et incantationes mentes hominum se immutare posse dicat, id est, ut de odio in amorem, aut de amore in odium convertat, aut bona hominum aut damnet aut surripiat. Et si aliqua est, quae se dicat, cum *daemonum turba in similitudinem mulierum transformata, certis noctibus equitare* super quasdam bestias, et in eorum consortio annumeratam esse. (Reptd. 10, 29.)

Int. 50 : est aliquis, qui in Cal. Jan. aliquid fecerat quod *a paganis inventum* est, et *dies* observavit et *lunam* et *menses;* et horum effectiva potentia aliquid speraverit in melius aut in deterius posse converti.

Int. 51 : est aliquis, quodcunque *opus inchoans,* qui aliquid dixerat, aut quacunque magica arte aliud fecit, nisi ut apostolus docet omnia in nomine Domini facienda.

Int. 52 : quaerendum etiam, si mulieres in *lanificiis* suis vel in *ordiendis telis* aliquid dicant aut observent.

Int. 54 : est aliquis, qui supra *mortuum* nocturnis horis *carmina diabolica* cantaret, et biberet et manducaret ibi, quasi de ejus morte gratularetur; et si alibi mortui in vigiliis nocturnis nisi in ecclesia custodiantur.

10, 1. Ut episcopi eorumque ministri omnibus viribus elaborare studeant, ut perniciosam et a diabolo inventam sortilegam et maleficam artem penitus ex parochiis suis eradicent, et si aliquem virum aut feminam hujuscemodi sceleris sectatorem invenerint, turpiter dehonestatum de parochiis suis ejiciant . . . . Illud etiam non omittendum, quod quaedam sceleratae mulieres, retro post Satanam conversae, *daemonum* illusionibus et phantasmatibus seductae, credunt se et profitentur nocturnis horis cum *Diana* Paganorum dea, vel cum *Herodiade,* et *innumera multitudine mulierum* equitare super quasdam bestias, et multa terrarum spatia intempestae noctis silentio pertransire, ejusque jussionibus velut dominae obedire, et certis noctibus ad ejus servitium evocari. Sed utinam hae solae in perfidia sua perissent, et non multos secum in infidelitatis interitum pertraxissent! Nam innumera multitudo, hac falsa opinione decepta, haec vera esse credit, et credendo a recta fide deviat, et in errore Paganorum revolvitur.[1]

10, 2. Pervenit ad nos, quosdam, quod dici nefas est, *arbores colere* et multa alia contra christianam fidem illicita perpetrare.[2]

10, 5. Qui divinationes expetunt et more Gentilium subsequuntur, aut in domos suas hujuscemodi homines introducunt, *exquirendi* aliquid arte malefica aut *expiandi* causa, sub regula quinquennii jaceant.[3]

10, 6. Si quis, Paganorum consuetudinem sequens, divinos et sortilegos in domum suam introduxerit, quasi ut *malum foras mittat* aut maleficia inveniat, quinque annos poeniteat.[4]

10, 8. Qui auguriis vel divinationibus inserviunt, vel qui credit ut aliqui hominum sint *immissores tempestatum*, vel si qua mulier divinationes vel *incantationes diabolicas* fecerit, septem annos poeniteat.[5]

10, 9. Auguria, vel sortes, quae dicuntur false sanctorum, vel divinationes, qui eas observaverint, vel quarumcunque scripturarum vel votum voverint vel persolverint ad *arborem* vel ad *lapidem* vel ad quamlibet rem, excepto ad ecclesiam, omnes excommunicentur. Si ad poenitentiam venerint, clerici annos tres, laici annum unum et dimidium poeniteant.[6]

10, 10. Summo studio decertare debent episcopi et eorum ministri, ut *arbores daemonibus consecratae*, quas vulgus colit et in tanta veneratione habet, ut *nec ramum vel surculum audeat amputare*, radicitus excidantur atque comburantur. *Lapides* quoque quos in *ruinosis locis* et silvestribus, daemonum ludificationibus decepti, venerantur, ubi et *vota vovent et deferunt*, funditus

---

[1] Extra. above (p. 283). The whole passage was taken from the Council of Ancyra (yr 314). and is also in Regino's De disc. eccl. 2. 364. but without the words ' vel cum Heriodiade '; the Decree of Gratian II. 26. quaest. 5, 12 § 1 has it complete.

[2] E registro Gregorii Magni.

[3] E concil. Ancyr. cap. 23.

[4] Ex concilio Martini papae (in Spain, abt 572), id est, ex Capit. Martini Bracarensis cap. 71 ; whence also Decr. Grat. II. 26. quaest. 5, 3 § 2.

[5] E poenitentiali Romano.

[6] From the same.

effodiantur, atque in tali loco projiciantur, ubi nunquam a cultoribus suis venerari possint.[1]

10, 14. Mulier si qua filium suum ponit *supra tectum* aut *in fornacem* pro sanitate febrium, unum annum poeniteat.[2]

10, 15. Non licet iniquas observationes agere calendarum, et otiis vacare, neque lauro aut viriditate arborum cingere domos. Omnis haec observatio Paganorum est.[3]

10, 16. Si quis calendas Januarias ritu Paganorum colere, vel aliquid plus novi facere propter novum annum, aut *mensas cum lapidibus vel epulis* in domibus suis praeparare, et per vicos et plateas cantatores et choros ducere praesumpserit, anathema sit.[4]

10, 31. Quicunque *nocturna sacrificia daemonum* celebraverint, vel incantationibus daemones quacunque arte ad sua vota invitaverint, tres annos poeniteant.[5]

10, 34. Laici, qui excubias funeris observant, cum timore et tremore et reverentia hoc faciant; nullus ibi praesumat *diabolica carmina* cantare, non joca et saltationes facere, quae Pagani diabolo docente adinvenerunt.[6]

19, 5 supplies the remaining extracts, the references being to *pages* :[7]

Pag. 193[b] : si observasti traditiones Paganorum, quas quasi hereditario jure, diabolo subministrante, usque in hos dies semper patres filiis reliquerunt, id est, ut elementa coleres, id est, lunam aut solem aut stellarum cursum, novam lunam aut defectum lunae, ut *tuis clamoribus* aut auxilio *splendorem ejus restaurare* valeres, aut elementa tibi succurrere aut tu illis posses; aut novam lunam observasti pro domo facienda aut conjugiis sociandis.

Pag. 193[c] : observasti calendas Januarias ritu Paganorum, ut vel aliquid plus faceres propter novum annum, quam antea vel

---

[1] E concil. Namnetensi (Nantes, yr 895). [Mansi p. 172. cap. 20.]
[2] E poenitentiali Bedae. The poenitentale Ecgberti Eboracensis 1, 33 (yr 748) in Mansi 12, 439. 475 has : 'Si mulier filiam suam super *domum* vel *fornacem* collocet, ideo ut febrim ejus curare velit.'
[3] E decreto Martiani papae.
[4] E decreto Zachariae papae, cap. ii.
[5] E poenitentiali Romano.
[6] E concil. Arelatensi (Arles, of which year ?) can. 3.
[7] Whence did Burchard draw this large chapter 19, 5 extending from p. 188[d] to 201[b]? (His 19, 4 is avowedly from Poenitentiale Romanum, his 19, 6 fr. Poen. Theodori.) The German words in it, 'holda, werwolf, belisa' (pp. 194-8. 201) lead me to think that, here more than anywhere, he puts together what he himself knew of German superstitions, with additions from other collections.

post soleres facere, ita dico, ut aut *mensam* tuam *cum lapidibus vel epulis in domo tua praeparare* eo tempore, aut *per vicos et plateas cantores et choros duceres*, aut *supra tectum domus tuae sederes ense tuo circumsignatus*, ut ibi videres et intelligeres, quid tibi in sequenti anno futurum esset; vel *in bivio sedisti supra taurinam cutem*, ut et ibi futura tibi intelligeres, vel si *panes* praedicta nocte *coquere* fecisti tuo nomine, ut si bene elevarentur et spissi et alti fierent, inde prosperitatem tuae vitae eo anno praevideres.

Pag. 193[d] : interfuisti aut consensisti vanitatibus quas mulieres exercent in suis *lanificiis*, in suis *telis ;* quae, cum ordiuntur telas suas, sperent se utrumque posse facere cum incantationibus illarum, ut et *fila staminis* et *subtegminis* in invicem ita commisceantur ut, nisi his iterum aliis diaboli incantationibus e contra subveniant, totum pereat.

venisti ad aliquem locum ad orandum nisi ecclesiam, . . . id est, vel ad *fontes* vel ad *lapides* vel ad *arbores* vel ad *bivia*, et ibi aut *candelam* aut *faculam* pro veneratione loci *incendisti*, aut panem aut aliquam oblationem illuc detulisti aut ibi comedisti, aut aliquam salutem corporis aut animae ibi requisisti.

Pag. 194[a] : credidisti unquam vel particeps fuisti illius perfidiae, ut incantatores, et qui se dicunt *tempestatum immissores* esse, possent per incantationem daemonum aut tempestates commovere aut mentes hominum mutare.

credidisti ut aliqua femina sit quae hoc facere possit, quod quaedam a diabolo deceptae se affirmant necessario et ex praecepto facere debere, id est, cum *daemonum turba* in similitudinem mulierum transformata, quam vulgaris stultitia *Holdam* (al. *unholdam*)[1] vocat, *certis noctibus equitare debere super quasdam bestias*, et in eorum se consortio annumeratam esse.

Pag. 195[b]: fecisti phylacteria diabolica vel characteres diabolicos, quos quidam diabolo suadente facere solent, vel *herbas* vel *succinos* vel *quintam feriam in honorem Jovis* honorasti.

comedisti aliquid de idolothito, i.e. de *oblationibus* quae in quibusdam locis ad *sepulchra mortuorum* fiunt, vel ad *fontes* aut ad *arbores* aut ad *lapides* aut ad *bivia*, aut *comportasti in aggerem lapides*, aut *capitis ligaturas* ad cruces quae in biviis ponuntur.

Pag. 195[c] : misisti filium tuum vel filiam *super tectum* aut *super*

---

[1] ' Friga holdam ' in Cod. Madrid., see Kl. schr. 5, 416-7.—EHM.]

*fornacem* pro aliqua sanitate, vel *incendisti grana* ubi mortuus homo erat, vel *cingulum mortui* pro damno alicujus *in nodos colligasti*, vel *pectines*, quibus mulierculae lanam discerpere solent, supra funus *complosisti*, vel quando efferebatur funus a domo *plaustrum in duo dividisti* et funus *per mediam divisionem plaustri* asportare fecisti.

fecisti illas vanitates aut consensisti, quas stultae mulieres facere solent, dum cadaver mortui hominis adhuc in domo jacet, currunt ad aquam, et *adducunt tacite vas cum aqua*, et quum sublevatur corpus mortui, eandem *aquam fundunt subtus feretrum ;* et hoc observant dum extra domum asportatur funus, (ut) *non altius quam ad genua elevetur*, et hoc faciunt pro quadam sanitate.

fecisti aut consensisti, quod quidam faciunt homini occiso cum sepelitur ; *dant ei in manum unguentum* quoddam, quasi illo unguento post mortem vulnus sanari possit, et sic cum unguento sepeliunt.

Pag. 195$^{d}$: fecisti quod plures faciunt : scopant locum ubi facere solent ignem in domo sua, et *mittunt grana hordei* locae adhuc calido, et si esalierint grana, periculosum erit, si autem ibi permanserint, bonum erit.

fecisti quod quidam faciunt : dum visitant aliquem infirmum, cum appropinquaverint domui ubi infirmus decumbit, si invenerint aliquem lapidem juxta jacentem, *revolvunt lapidem*, et requirunt in loco ubi jacebat lapis, si ibi *sit aliquid subtus quod vivat*, et si invenerint ibi lumbricum aut muscam aut formicam aut aliquid quod se moveat, tunc affirmant aegrotum convalescere ; si autem nihil ibi invenerint quod se moveat, dicunt esse moriturum.

fecisti pueriles arcus parvulos et puerorum suturalia, et projecisti sive in cellarium sive in horreum tuum, ut *satyri* vel *pilosi cum eis ibi jocarentur*, ut tibi aliorum bona comportarent, et inde ditior fieres.

fecisti quod quidam faciunt in calendis Januari, i.e. in octava natalis Domini ; qui ea sancta nocte *filant, nent, consuunt*, et omne opus quodcunque incipere possunt, diabolo instigante propter novum annum incipiunt.

Pag. 198$^{c}$ : credidisti quod quidam credere solent : dum iter aliquod faciunt, si *cornicula ex sinistra eorum in dexteram illis cantaverit*, inde se sperant habere prosperum iter ; et dum anxii fuerint hospitii, si tunc avis illa quae *muriceps* vocatur, eo quod mures capiat et inde pascatur nominata, *viam per quam vadunt ante se transvolaverit,* se illi augurio et omini magis committunt quam Deo.

credidisti quod quidam credere solent : dum necesse habent ante lucem aliorsum exire, non audent, dicentes quod *posterum* sit, et *ante galli cantum egredi non liceat* et periculosum sit, eo quod *immundi spiritus* ante gallicinium plus ad nocendum potestatis habeant quam post, et gallus suo cantu plus valeat eos repellere et sedare, quam illa divina mens quae est in homine sua fide et crucis signaculo.

credidisti quod quidam credere solent, quod sint *agrestes feminae,* quas *silvaticas* vocant, quas dicunt esse corporeas, et quando voluerint ostendant se suis amatoribus, et cum eis dicunt se oblectasse, et item quando voluerint abscondant se et evanescant.

fecisti ut quaedam mulieres in quibusdam temporibus anni facere solent, ut in domo tua *mensam praeparares,* et tuos cibos et potum *cum tribus cultellis* supra mensam poneres, ut si venissent *tres illae sorores* quas antiqua posteritas et antiqua stultitia *Parcas* nominavit, ibi reficerentur ; et tulisti divinae pietati potestatem suam et nomen suum, et diabolo tradidisti, ita dico, ut crederes illas quas tu dicis esse sorores tibi posse aut hic aut in futuro prodesse.

Pag. 199[d] : fecisti quod quaedam mulieres facere solent et firmiter credunt, ita dico, ut si vicinus ejus *lacte* vel *apibus* abundaret, omnem abundantiam lactis et mellis, quam suus vicinus ante se habere visus est, ad se et sua animalia vel ad quos voluerint, a diabolo adjutae, suis fascinationibus et incantationibus se posse convertere credunt.

credidisti quod quaedam credere solent, ut quamcunque domum intraverint, pullos aucarum, pavonum, gallinarum, etiam porcellos et aliorum *animalium foetus* verbo vel visu vel auditu *obfascinare* et perdere posse affirment.

credidisti quod multae mulieres retro Satanam conversae credunt et affirmant verum esse, ut credas in quietae noctis silentio cum te collocaveris in lecto tuo, et marito tuo in sinu tuo jacente, te, dum corporea sis, *januis clausis exire posse,* et terrarum spatia cum aliis simili errore deceptis pertransire valere, et homines baptizatos et Christi sanguine redemtos, sine armis visibilibus, et interficere et de coctis carnibus eorum vos comedere, et *in loco cordis* eorum *stramen* aut *lignum* aut aliquod hujusmodi ponere, et comestis, iterum vivos facere et inducias vivendi dare.

Pag. 200ª : credidisti quod quaedam mulieres credere solent, ut tu cum aliis diaboli membris in quietae noctis silentio clausis januis *in aërem usque ad nubes subleveris*, et ibi *cum aliis pugnes*, et ut vulneres alias et tu vulnera ab eis accipias.

fecisti quod quaedam mulieres facere solent : prosternunt se in faciem, et discopertis natibus, jubent ut supra nudas nates conficiatur *panis*, et eo decocto tradunt maritis suis ad comedendum ; hoc ideo faciunt, ut plus exardescant in amorem illorum.

*posuisti infantem tuum juxta ignem*, et alius caldariam supra ignem cum aqua misit, et ebullita aqua superfusus est infans et mortuus. (Repeated 19, 149.)

fecisti quod quaedam mulieres facere solent, diabolicis adimpletae disciplinis ; quae *observant vestigia* et indagines Christianorum, et *tollunt de eorum vestigio cespitem* et illum observant, et inde sperant sanitatem aut vitam eorum auferre.

Pag. 200ᵇ : fecisti quod quaedam mulieres facere solent : tollunt *testam hominis* et *igni comburunt,* et cinerem dant viris suis ad bibendum pro sanitate.

fecisti quod quaedam mulieres facere solent, illae dico quae habent vagientes infantes, *effodiunt terram* et ex parte *pertusant* eam, et *per illud foramen pertrahunt infantem* et sic dicunt vagientis infantis cessare vagitum.

fecisti quod quaedam mulieres instinctu diaboli facere solent : cum aliquis infans sine baptismo mortuus fuerit, tollunt cadaver parvuli, et ponunt in aliquo secreto loco, et *palo corpusculum ejus transfigunt,* dicentes, si sic non fecissent, quod infantulus surgeret et multos laedere posset.

Pag. 200ᶜ : cum aliqua femina parere debet et non potest, in ipso dolore si morte obierit, in ipso sepulchro matrem cum infante *palo in terram transfigunt.*

Pag. 200ᵈ : cum infans noviter natus est, et statim baptizatus et sic mortuus fuerit, dum sepeliunt eum, in dexteram manum ponunt ei *pateram ceream* cum oblata, et in sinistram manum *calicem* cum vino similiter *cereum* ponunt ei, et sic eum sepeliunt.

Pag. 201ª : fecisti quod quaedam mulieres facere solent : deponunt vestimenta sua, et totum *corpus* nudum *melle inungunt,*

et sic mellito suo corpore *supra triticum* in quodam linteo in
terra deposito sese hac atque illac saepius *revolvunt,* et cuncta
tritici grana, quae humido corpori adhaerent, cautissime colligunt
et in molam mittunt, et retrorsum contra solem molam circuire
faciunt, et sic in farinam redigunt, et de illa farina *panem* con-
ficiunt, et sic maritis suis ad comedendum tradunt, ut comesto
pane marcescant et deficiant.

Pag. 201ᵇ : fecisti quod quaedam mulieres facere solent : dum
*pluviam non habent* et ea indigent, tunc plures puellas congre-
gant, et unam *parvulam puellam* quasi ducem sibi praeponunt,
et eandem *denudant,* et extra villam, ubi herbam iusquiamum
(hyos-cyamum) inveniunt, quae Teutonice *belisa* ¹ vocatur, sic
nudatam deducunt, et eandem herbam eandem virginem sic
nudam *minimo digito dextrae manus eruere* faciunt, et radicitus
erutam cum ligamine aliquo ad *minimum digitum dextri pedis
ligare* faciunt. Et singulae puellae singulas virgas in manibus
habentes supradictam virginem herbam post se trahentem *in
flumen proximum introducunt,* et cum eisdem virgis virginem
*flumine aspergunt,* et sic suis incantationibus pluviam se habere
sperant. Et post eandem virginem sic nudam, *transpositis et
mutatis in modum cancri vestigiis,* a flumine ad villam inter
manus reducunt.

D. From the *Zurich Pap. MSS.* (Wasserkirch-bibl.) B ²²³/₇₃₀.
4to. written 1393, perh. at Zurich, cert. in Switzld. (Communic. by Wackernagel.)

38. r. . . . du solt nút glöben an *zöber* noch an *luppe*
noch an *hesse* noch an *lachenen* noch an *fúr-sehen* ² noch an
*messen* noch an die *naht-fröwen,* noch an der *agelster schrien,*
noch an die brawen vn̄ der wangen *iucken,* noch an die *batenien,*
noch an deheiner hant dinges das vnglöb si.

140. r. . . . Dis stuk seit (tells) von den *lossern* vn̄ von
den valschen propheten.

Die *losserr* vn̄ die valschen gotförmigen *wissagen* das sint die
lút die inen selben zů-eigenent vn̄ zů-legent (arrogate) etlichú

---

[ ¹ 'Herbam *quantamvis* inveniunt, quae Teutonice *bilisa* vocatur,' Cod. Madrid.,
see Kl. schr. 5, 417. Bilisa sounds like Pol. bilica, bielica, but that is artemisia.
Our *bilse,* henbane, is Pol. bielum, Russ. belená.—EHM.]

[ ² Evid. *fiur-sehen* (fire-gazing), not für-sehen (fore-seeing).—EHM.]

ding, dú allein des waren Gottes eigen sint, ân alles vrlŏb, von ir eignen bosheit vn̄ ir grossen valscheit. Das ist, das sú kúnftig ding vor-wissagent, vnd zúhend da-mit vnzallich vil selen mit inen zů der helle. wan sú begnůget nút (for, not content) an ir selbs bosheit, si wellen ŏch ander lút mit inen ziehen in den ewigen tot, die si betrúgent von des túvels rat mit ir bôsen listen. Nv sint dirre valschen *wissen* vil, das ist, der *lossungen* vnd solicher *wissagung.* Etlich geschihet dur den bôsen geist *phytonem appollinem,* der ein vrhab ist der selben bosheit. Etlich geschihet in dem fúr (fire), dú wirt genemmet *pyromancia.* Ein andrú heisset *aeromancia,* dú geschihet in dem luft. Ein andrú *geomancia,* dú geschihet in dem ertrich. Ein andrú *ydro-mancia,* dú geschiht in dem wasser. Ein andrú heisset (Here begins 140. v.) *nigromancia,* das da ze Latine ist ein toter. Wan dur trúgnússe werdent etwenne geachtet die toten erstanden sin von dem tot, vnd dunket die lút wie si warsagen, vnd entwúrten der dingen, der sú gefraget werdin (for the dead are imagined to have risen, and to prophesy and answer things that they are asked). Vnd dis geschihet dur die anrůffung vnd beschwerung der túvelen.

Hier-vmb súlent ellú Mᵉ (therefore should all men) bekennen vnd fúr war wissen, das ein ieklicher mensche, wib oder man, der da haltet oder vebet (practises) solich *wissagung oder losen* von *zŏber,* oder *bescherten.* oder *luppe.* oder *hezze.* oder *lachnen.* oder *fúr-sehen*[1] oder *messen.* oder der *agelster schrien.* oder *vogel-sang.* oder brawen oder wangen *iucken.* oder von den *bathinien* oder deheiner hant das ungelŏb ist. oder der es gern hört vnd vernimet. oder den gehillet, die es vebent vnd haltent. oder es wol glŏbt, Ald der in ir huz zů in tag (l. gat, goes), Ald der sú in sin hus fůret, vmb das er sú rates frag (or who brings them to his own house, to ask their advice), Der sol wissen, das er sinen kristanen glŏben vnd sinen tuf hat vber-gangen vnd gebrochen. Vnd das er si ein heiden. Ein abtrúniger vnd ein vient Gottes. Vnd wisse sich swarlich in-lŏffen (incurred) oder in-valled in den zorn Gottes. Vnd das er ab súle varn in die ewigen verdampnússe. Es si denne das er vor (unless he first) mit kristenlicher penitencie oder rúw werde gebessert vnd gesůnt Got.

[ [1] Evid. *fiur-sehen* (fire-gazing), not fúr-sehen (fore-seeing).—EHM.]

[Here follows within commas transl. of Burchard 10, 1 above : Illud etiam—revolvitur.] " Ouch ist das nút under wegen ze lassenne oder ze úbersehenne, das etlich *meintetigú wiber*, die da nach dem túvel Sathan bekert sint, vnd mit der túvel verspottung vnd mit fantasien oder trúgnússe sint verwiset, Das die glöben vnd veriehent das si selber vnd ein gróssú *mengi wiben ritten* vnd *varen* mit der *heiden gúttinnen* dú da heisset *Dyana*, oder mit *Herodiade*, uf etlichen *walt-tieren* in der *nacht-stilli dur vil ertriches oder landes*. Vnd das si irem gebot gehorsam sien als einer *gewaltigen fröwen*. Vnd das sú dú selb *gúttinne* ze benemten nechten rúffe zú irem dienst. Vnd hie-von haltent sú. Vnd wôlti Got das dis wiber allein in solicher wis verdorben weren gegen Got, vnd nút vil mit inen gezogen vnd verwiset hettin in das verderben des bôsen (141. r.) vnglöben. Wan ein vnzallichú mengi ist mit diser valschen wis betrogen, die da glöbent das es war si, vnd da-mit das si es glöbent ab dem weg gant des rechten glöben, vnd in-wollen werdent der scheilichen irrunge der heidenen," das si glöben vnd wenen wellen, das ichtes iht gôtliches oder gôtlicher kraft vssert-halb einem waren Got si.

Hier-vmb súlent die priester dur die kilchen, die inen enpholhen sint, dem volk Gottes mit grossem flisse steteklich ob-ligen, vnd inen predien vnd sicherlichen bewisen, das si bekennent werden, das disú ding ellú valsch sint vnd nút sint von dem gôttlichen geist, me das si halten das dis trúgnust ingegebe si, entrúwen (verily) von dem bôsen geist dem gemút der glôbigen werden (arise) solichen wibs gemút (sic omnia), vnd dur vnglöben er si im selber hat undertenig gemachet. Alzehant wandlet er denne aber sich in gesteltnús vnd in glichheit menger hant personen. Vnd das gemút das er gevangen haltet, das betrúget er in dem slaf. Vnd offenbart im ietzent frôlichú ding, denne trurigú, ietz bekant personen, den vnbekant, vnd fúrt die *dur die wildinen* vnd *dur die lender*. Vnd so der unglöbig geist dis trúgnúg allein lidet, so haltet er nút das dis in dem gemút gescheh, sunder in dem libe (body) ; wan wer ist der mensche der nút in trômen vnd in offenbarungen oder gesichten der nechten nút vs-geleitet werde von im selben, da er slaffend meniges siht (sees) das er wachend nie gesach (saw) oder villich niemer gesicht (will see) ? Vnd hier-vmb wer ist

also toreht ald so vnvernúnftig, der disú ellú, dú da allein in dem
geist geschehent, úber ein wenet vnd haltet das es geschehe in
dem libe, etc.

(Fol. 143. r.) . . . . Nv mugent dis valsch vnd vppig
erznien (fulsome remedies) geteilet werden nach den menig-
valtigen dúrften, von der wegen sie geúbt werdent (classed acc.
to their uses). Etlich geschehent von der lút siechheit wegen
oder des vihes. Etlich fúr unberhaftikeit. Etlich fúr die erbeit
der fröwen, die nút gebern mugen. Etlich wider den hagel vnd
das ungewitter. Ander wider allerlei pin. Hier-vmb ist den ze
ratenne, die suslichv ding lident (we advise them that suffer such
things), das sú ellú túuellich gespenst lassent, vnd den allein rates
vmb ir notturf fragen (ask Him alone for counsel in their need)
vnd von im es súchen, von des gewalt ellú ding geschaffen sint,
vnd von des willen ellú ding berichtet werdent. Vnd súllent
sprechen demútklich. 'Herre Got, kum vns ze helf.' Wan
(for) dur vns vermugen wir nihtes nit, sunder vns gebristet (we
fail) ob wir getrúwen haben dur vns. Vnd dar-vmb wer da
lidet siechheit, der hab allein in die barmherzikeit Gottes ein
gútes getrúwen, vnd enphahi (receive) den heiligen fron-lichamen
(Lord's body) vnd das heilige blút vnsers lieben Herren Ihesv
Christi mit festem glöben vnd mit gúter andaht. Vnd begere
öch das gesegnet öli von der heiligen kilchen getrúwlich. Vnd
also nachdem vns der apostel sprichet, so behaltet das gebette
des glöben (prayer of faith) den siechen.

Nu gat aller-meist mit diser úppikeit der zöbrie vmb (what
has the chief hand in sorcery is) die (143 v.) bôs kúndikeit der
valschen vnd schedlichen wiben, als öch glich da-vor geseit (said)
ist. Wan dik (for often) vnd vil als vil es an inen ist, so
enteren vnd versmachent solich die sacrament der heiligen
kilchen. Vnd etwenne wúrkent sú mit inen, das erschrokenlich
öch ze sagenne vnd ze hôren ist allen wol glöbenden Mᵉ (men).
Vnd hier-vmb werdent si gesehen bôser vnd wirser den die
túuel. Wan die túuel glöbent Got vnd fúrhtent in mit zittrunge.
Zú dem dise ân vorht vnd ân zitter gânt (go without fear or trem-
bling). Vnd wúrkent mit Gottes fron-licham vngenemú vnd uner-
lichú ding. Des man ein gliches zeichen oder wunder liset in der
geschrift von eim wib, die in der selben wis unsers Herren fron-
licham enphieng, vnd behúb den in irem mund, vnd gieng also

hin, vnd *kuste iren man, vmb das sin minne grösser wurde zů ir* denne vor. Und zehant wart dú hostie gewandlet in fleisch. Vnd do si des gewar ward, do wolt si unsern Herren wider vs han geworfen. Do wúrkt vnser Herre da sin wunder, das si in weder mocht vsgewerfen noc geslinden (wafer in mouth, she went and kissed her husband, to increase his love for her ; the wafer turned into flesh, and she could neither spit it out nor swallow it), etc.

(Fol. 144. r.). . . . Wie das nv da-vor geseit si, das man miden súle solich erzenie die in solicher túuel-licher wis geschehent. Doch wer der weri der das heilsami krut mit den xij stúken des glöben vnd mit dem pater noster schribe (144. v.) an einen brief, vnd den denne leiti (then laid it) vf den siechen, vmb das Got aller ding schepfer also geeret werde, das en-wirt nút verworfen noch versmachet, so man keins der vorgenanten verworfenen vnd falschen dingen mit dar-zů mischelt. Vnd *zit halten* erznie ze gebenne, vnd zu den lessinen ist öch nút ze verwerfenne. vnd och bedút die der zit war-nement ze seienne (sow) vnd böm ze behöwenne (hew). Vnd zů solichen dingen die zů gebúrschen (farming) werken behörent, die sint dar-vmb nút ze straffene. Wan die natúrlichen bescheidenheit mag man halten oder veben in den dingen. Vnd si heint öch ein sicher bescheidenheit Alsdenne So man kein ander vppig haltunge meinet, noch dar-zů lat gan. Ze verstemmenne suslicher vertůmlicher vnd schedlicher bosheit sol in allen wis geflissen sin, vnd hier zů munder sin die kúndikeit der priester, der selen besorger, Das nút die kristenlich geistlicheit mit disen valschen vorgeseiten dingen werde entreinet vnd verwiset. Vnd wider infalle in die sitten der heideschen vnd túuelschen vnglöben, das ein glöb der menschen gemůt werde vnd si, vnd ein miltikeit der werken An ze betten einen waren Got den Vater vnd den Sun vnd den heiligen Geist, der da ist gebenediet in die welt der welten.[1]

E.   From a paper MS. of the Basle Univ. Libr., fol., 15th cent., marked *A. v.* 19. (Communic. by Wackernagel.)

1. r. a.  Incipit registrum super libro. de supersticionibus ab eximio magistro *Nicolao magni de gawe.* sacre theologie pro-

[1 Conf. the eccles. and non-eccles. benedictions in Hpt's Ztschr. 4, 576.—EHM.]

fessore anno a natiuitate saluatoris M°cccc°xv°. edito secundum
ordinem alphabeti.[1]

10. v. b.   Per hoc statim patet falsitas et error quorundum
fatuorum astronimorum dicencium se posse facere *ymagines* sub
certa constellacione, per virtutes suas cogentes *demones* ut
veniant ad istas *ymagines,* ad operandum quaedam mira et ad
dandum responsa.   Sed veniunt non coacti propter duo, ut
Thomas dicit ibidem (ante : sanctus thomas parte prima. q xiiij)
in solucione 2$^i$ articuli et hoc incertis constellacionibus.   Primo
quidem, ut homines in hunc errorem inducant ut credant aliquod
numen esse in celis.   Sicut vnam vetulam noui, que credidit
*Solem* esse *deam,* vocans eam *sanctam dominam.*

11. r. a.   et alloquendo eum solem. benedixit per eum sub
certis verbis, sub osservancia quadam supersticiosa, que dixit
se plus quam quadraginta annos credidisse, et multas infirmitates
curasse.   Insuper hodie inveniuntur homines tam layci quam
clerici, literati quam illiterati, et quod plus dolendum est, valde
magni, qui cum *novilunium primo viderint, flexis genibus ado-*
*rant. vel deposito capucio vel pileo, inclinato capite honorant*
alloquendo et suscipiendo.   ymmo eciam plures ieiunant ipso die
*novilunij,* sive sit dies dominica in qua secundum ordinacionem
ecclesie non est ieiunandum propter resurreccionis leticiam, sive
quacunque alia die. eciamsi esset dies dominice natiuitatis. que
omnia habent speciem ydolatrie. ab idolatris relicte. de quibus
Jeremie vij scribitur. quod fecerunt placentas regine celi s. lune
offerendo eas ei.   Et quidam volentes hoc palliare dicunt quod
non honorant lunam ieiunando, sed omnes sanctos. quorum
festa et ieiunia incidunt in mēse lunacionis vise.   Ecce qualis
est ista excusacio, etc.

11. r.b.   Sic eciam de mandato quo preceptum fuit, quod
*nidum cum ouis* vel pullis et matre desuper incubante non de-
berent simul seruare, sed matrem permittere auolare. Deut°. xxij.
hoc enim quando inuenerunt, trahebant ad fecunditatem et ad
fortunam, si conseruarentur simul.   Et per oppositum ad infortunium et sterilitatem quod gentile erat.   Sic modo vetule dicunt
*inuencionem acus vel obuli reseruati esse prestigium magne fortune.*
Et per oppositum de inuencione magni thesauri.

11. v. b.   Similiter prohibitum fuit eis ne viri vterentur vesti-

[[1] Several MSS. at Munich.   Gawe is Jauer in Schlesien.—EHM.]

bus mulierum. Et econverso. Et de hac prohibitione dicitur
Deut°. xxij. Non induetur mulier veste virili, nec vir vtetur
veste feminea. abhominabilis enim apud Deum est qui facit,
quia mulieres in veneracione *Martis* induerunt vestes et arma
vivorum. et viri in veneracione *Veneris* vestes mulierum. Sic
nunc fit in hominibus christianis tempore carnis privii, quando
seruiunt deo ventris et dee Veneris. tam viri quam mulieres.
Item *incisiones* fecerunt *super mortuos* ad placandum Deum, ut
vehemenciam doloris de *morte thaurorum* exprimerent. quod
adhuc multi faciunt christiani de *morte thaurorum* suorum, quod
utique est de specie plutonis. *Stigmata* vero et figuras adhuc
et christiani faciunt et vocant *breuia.* et in propriis codicibus,
cartis alijsque in rebus videlicet in metallis reseruant. que
ydolatria vera sunt, ymmo christiane religioni contraria sive
aduersa.

12. r. a. Sed quia obseruaciones *sompniorum,* auguriorum,
*constellacionum, sternutacionum, obuiacionum, dierum* et *horarum,*
*stigmatum, caracterum, ymaginum,* et *impressionum* astrorum non
solum vicine sunt ydolatrie, sed eciam vere ydolatrie cum radici-
bus et intime sunt perscrutanda (l. exstirpandae ?) quibus omnibus se fraus *antiqui serpentis* immiscet, quemadmodum prius
dictum est.

12. v. b. Sed forte adhuc diceres. videtur vtique quod
*demones* proprie generent, quia compertum est et apud wulgares
communiter dicitur, quod filij *demonum incuborum* mulieribus,
eorum filijs subtractis, ab ipsis demonibus *supponantur.* et ab
eis tanquam proprii filij nutriantur. propter quod eciam *cambiones*
dicuntur, eciam *cambiti* vel mutuati, et mulieribus parientibus,
propriis filijs subtractis, suppositi, hos dicunt macilentos, semper
eiulantes, lactis eosque bibulos, ut quod nulla vbertate lactis
vnum lactare sufficiunt. 13. r. a. Hij tamen, postquam in
terris commorati sunt, dicuntur euanuisse. . . . Ex quo
patet quod tales pueri non generantur a demonibus, sed sunt
ipsimet *demones.* sicut eciam possent apparere in specie vetularum rapiencium pueros de cunis, que wlgo *fatue* vocantur,
de nocte apparentes et paruulos ut apparet *lauare* et *igne assare,*
que demones sunt in specie vetularum.

F.  From a paper codex of the 14th (15th?) cent., in the
library at St. Florian.  (Communic. by Chmel.)

1. So ain fraw pracht wirt zu dem chind, so *czeucht* sy dem
chind *ainen zwelf-poten,* so stirbt das chind an tauff nicht (conf.
39 and H, 50).

2. item an dem Vaschang-tag, so *werseyt* sy *prein* an *die dillen,*
velt er herab, so stirbt er des iars.

3. item *milich essent* sy des nachts, so waschent sy weis des
iars.

4. item *ayr* (eggs) *essent* sy, so wernt sy nicht hertt an dem
pauch des iars.

5. item so man an dem Oster-tag legt man *würst* (sausages)
vnder das chrawt vnd ain *gens* (goose). welcher die würst siecht,
der siecht des iars chain slangen, vnd wer der gens ist (eats),
der gewint des iar des chalten siechten nit.

6. item den *spekch* (lard) den man weicht mit den praitigen,
do *smirent* dy pawrn (farmers) den *phlüg* mit, so mag man sew
nicht zaubern.

7. item an dem Weihnacht abent, so get ainew zu ainen
*scheiterhauffen* vnd zuht ain scheuit (pulls a log) aus dem hauffen
[in] des teufels nam. pegreifft sy ain langs, so wirt ir ain langer
man (conf. 49).

8. item an dem Vaschang-tag, steigt ains avf *ainen pawn*
(tree) vnd schrait ' *alheit!* ' mit schelt-warten ' *trag die phaim
her haim,* '[1] so wirt des iars nicht natig.

9. ee man zu der metten an dem Weihnachtag get, so greifft
ains *vnder die pankch* vnd nymt ain hant-uolle *molten* (mould)
heraus. vint es *etwas labentigigs* in den molten, so stirbt es des
iars nicht.

10. so man die *palm* haim-trait von kirchen, so legent sy
sew ee *in die chue chrip* (lay it first in the cows' crib), ee das
sy sew under das tach (roof) tragent. so gent die chue des iars
gern haim.

11. item die *pürsten* die man zu den *palm* stekcht, do pürsten
sy das viech (they brush the cattle) mit, so wernt sie nicht lausig.

12. item *palm* legent sy *under das chrawt* hefen, so vallent
nicht fleugen (flies) in das chrawt.

[1 ' ja izz hie haim nicht olheit,' Helbl. 8, 594.—EHM.]

13. item si tragent *vmb das haws,* ee si sew hin-in tragent, so essent die fuchs der huner (fowls) nicht.

14. item an dem Weinacht-tag zu metten-zeit get man *mit liecht* zu ainem *prunn* (well), vnd *lügt in den prunn;* siecht es sten in dem prunn ain man, so nymbt es des iars ainn man.

15. 'ich pewt dir *plater* u. *fel* pey der heiligen sel die parn (born) ist zu Iherusalem vnd tauft im Jordan, das du nicht en-peitest der mess vnd des ampts, pey dem Vater vnd Sun vnd dem heyligen Geist.' vnd sprich z p͞r n͞r, vnd tue das drey mal.

16. item so ainen von *taten vischen* trawmt (dreams of dead fish), sol ains sterben aus dem selben haus.

17. item so ain viech nicht gen mag (if a beast cannot walk), so pintt man im ain *pant* (bindeth a band) an ainem *Suntag* vmb, vnd macht den chnoph oben zu, so wirt im sein puzz.

18. item so ain chue ain erst-chalb trait, so nympt die peyrinn ain *aichen-laub* (farmer's wife takes an oak-leaf), vnd stekcht en mitten ain *nadel* darin, vnd legt es en mitten in den sechter, vnd nympt dan das *vberruckh* mit dem *hor* vnd *spindl* ab dem rokchen, vnd stekcht es auch en mitten in den sechter, so mag man der chue nicht nemen die milich, vnd des ersten milcht sy in den sechter, do das ding inn stekcht die selb chue [am ersten], die weil das dinkch dar-inn stekcht.

19. so man die chuee an die waid (pasture) treibt, so grebt (buries) man ain *e͞kk͞l*[1] *unter den gatern,* vnd treibt das viech dar-vber, so mag man sew nicht zaubern.

20. item *Sand Blasen wasser* gibt man ze trinkchen den iungen huenrn vnd gensen (fowls and geese), ee man sew ab dem nest nymbt, so trait sew der fuchs nicht hin, vnd sind sicher von dem orn.

21. item so aine ain *chalb verchauft* (sells), so sneyt sy dem chalb das wedl ab ab seinem swenczl (cuts the tuft off its tail), vnd des hars ab dem rechten arm, vnd gibts der chue ze essen. so rert sy nicht nach dem chalb.

22. item so aine der andern ir *milich* wil *nemen,* vnd macht das sy pseichent, so nymbt sy drey *chroten* (toads) auf ein *mel-mülter* ain abichen, vnd traitz der chue für, dy *lerft* dy chroten in sich,

[1 The word means steel.—EHM.]

so ist ir nachpawrin irer milich prawbt (bereft), vnd sy hat dy milich.

23. item so ains stirbt, so hant etleich den glauben (some think), di *sel hab nicht rueb* (ruh, rest?), uncz man ir aus leitt.

24. item etleich sprechent, die weil man lewtt (toll), so wert die *sel* peichtich. etleich sprechent, so sich die sel schaid von dem leichnam, so sey sy die erst nacht hincz Sand *Gerdrawten*, dy ander nacht pey Sand *Michel*, die dritt wo si hin verdint hab (has deserved).

25. item ettleich glaubent, die *sel* genn aus den *weiczen*[1] an der Sambstag-nacht, vnd sein heraussen vncz an den Mantag, so müssen sy wider in die *pen*.

26. item ettleich essent nicht *fleichgs* des Phincz-tags in der chottemer,[2] so sterbent sy nicht in dem sterb.

27. item so ainem die *oren seusent* (one's ears ring), so habent sy den glauben, man red vbl von inn.

28. item so ainem die chnie geswellent, so get es zu ainer frawn die *zwendling* getragen hat, vnd heist sey (bids her) im *ain faden spinnen*, den pintz (this he binds) vber die chnie, so wirt him pas.

29. item das die *hüner haubat* werden (chicks be tufted), so sy die henn anseczt, so *hult* sy ain *zuczl an*, vnd macht ainen *chnoph auf dem haupp*, vnd halt in also auf dem haupp, so geschiecht es.

30. item an dem Sunnbent-tag (solstice), so geht aine *ersling auf allen viern mit plassem leib* zu irs nachtpahirn *tar* (backwards on all fours, naked, to her neighbour's gate), vnd mit den fuzzen steigt sy ersling an dem *tar* auf, vnd mit ainer hant halt sy sich, vnd mit der andern *sneit* sy *drey span* (cuts 3 chips) *aus dem tar*, vnd spricht, zu dem ersten span spricht sy ' Ich sneit den ersten span, Noch aller milich wan.' zu dem andern auch also. zu dem dritten spricht sy ' Ich sneit den dritten span, Noch aller meiner nappaurinnen milich wan.'[3] vnd get *ersling auff allen viern* her wider dan haim.

31. item die swangern (pregnant) frawn *messent ain dacht* noch Sand *Sixt* pild (measure a wick by St Sixtus's image), als lank

---

[1] Souls come out of Purgatory (OHG. wizi, AS. wîte) every Saturday.
[2] Thursday in the Whitsun Ember-days (quatember).
[3] ' Wan milich ' in orig.

es ist, vnd guertns (gird it) vber den pauch, so misslingt in nicht an der purd (birth). oder des *man's gurtl* gurtn se vmb.

32. item so man in den *Rauch-nachten* auf *ain tisch siczt*, so habent des iars dy lewt vil aiss.

33. item in der lesten *Rauch-nacht* tragent sy ain ganczen *laib* vnd *ches* (loaf and cheese) *vmb das haus*, vnd peissent (bite) darab. als manig pissen man tan hat. so vil *schober* (stacks, cocks) wernt im auf dem veld.

34. das man das viech des iars nicht schindt (not have to skin as carrion). item in den *Rauch-nachten* so *schint* man nicht *sponholz* (not rend laths, shingles), noch *reibscht* (rummage) an den ofen nicht, noch *lakchen* (shreds, litter) macht in der stuben. so wernt nicht in den velden plas fleckch (bare patches). Aber vmb das raissen dy spen vber den offen, das tüt man darvmb, das der habern nicht prantig wert (oats be not blighted).

35. item in den *Vnder-nachten* trait man nicht *reitter* (sieve) vber den hof, das das viech *nich da-durich luey*, das es nicht werd schiech, noch hin scherff.

36. item *durich ain reitter saicht* ainew (if a girl sift), so tanczt man mit ir vor fur (in preference to) die andern (conf. 60).

37. item an dem Weihnacht-morgen haist man die *ros rennen gen wasser* (horses run against water), vnd wirft der (if he throw) ainn aphl in das wasser die weil es trincht, das der *aphl gegn dem ross rinn*, so wirt das ross resch zu arbait des iars.

38. item so ainem trawmt wie der ofen nider sey geuallen, so stirbt aintweder wirt oder die wirtin (master or mistress).

39. die schwangern frawn, so sew zu Gotz tisch gent, an demselben tag *ziechent* si dem chind ainen *XII poten*, so stirbt das chind nicht (conf. 1).

40. so zway chon-lewt die *erst nacht pey ligent*, welchs *ee entslefft*, das stirbt ee (whichever sleeps first will die first).

41. item man *windt* nicht *wid* (not twist osiers) in den *Under-nachten*, das sich dy lewt in *kranchait* nicht *winten* (writhe).

42. item man *haspht* nicht, so wirt das viech nicht *haspen*.

43. item an dem Weihnacht-abend, noch an dem *rauchen*, so *messent* die lewt 9 *lefl wasser in ain hefen* (measure 9 spoonfuls iuto a pail), vnd lassent es sten vncz an den tag, vnd *messent her-wider auf*. ist sein mynner (less of it), das dy mass nicht gancz ist, so chumpt es des iars in *armüt* (poverty). ist sy gancz, so

*pestet* es (stay as before). ist sein aber mer, so wirt es vberflussikleich *reich*.

44. item man *wirft gruemat* (throw after-hay) vnd *gnietn* [1] *hubern* (oats) in denselben nachten *auf ain dach,* vnd lassentz darauf ligen uncz sy ent nement (till those nights end). so gebent's es dem viech's ze essen, so schullen es die *chran* (crows) des iars nicht essen, vnd wernt darzue fruchtper.

45. item *spanholz* schint man nicht, das man des iars des viech nicht schint (conf. 34).

46. item man lokcht dy saw für das tar (entice the pigs outside the gate) an dem Weinacht-margen, vnd gibt in habern *in ainem raif,* vnd sprechent : '*die meins nachtpawrn ain sümpl. die mein œin grumpl.*' so sind sew des iars frisch, vnd seins natpawr krankch. vnd des iars gentz (they go) gern an das veld.

47. item die paum *chust* man (kiss the trees), so werden se fruchtper des iars.

48. item zu dem Weinacht-tag, so man gen metten gedt, so *slecht* ainer *ain holz ab* (chops a stick down) vnd traid's mit im haim, vnd *an dem Sunbent-abent legt er's an das fewr.* so choment all *znaubln* [knüppel, cudgels ?] zu dem fewr, dew in der ganzen pharr (parish) sind.

49. item in den Unter-nachten lauffent dy iunkfrawn an den *sumerlangen zawn* (hedge) des nachts. pegreifft sy ainen *langen stekchen,* so wirt ir ain langer man (conf. 7).

50. item allew *milich-hefen stürzen* sy (turn all the milkpails upside down) *auf den tisch,* vnd *rauchentz* (smoke them). so stilt (steals) man in dy milich nicht.

51. auch so man gen metten get. so der mensch ain *runczt* vnd *get vber sich,* so stirbt er des iars nicht.

52. item in denselben nachten ist chain mensch auf der welt nicht, so hungert es des iars nicht vast, vnd gwint leicht genüg.

53. item zu derselben zeit, so ains *chrophat* ist (has the goitre), so wirt er sein also an (rid of it ?), so ains chlocht, vnd spricht '*se hin mein chroph* an *deinen chroph,*' vnd greifft an den chroph, and *tüt das venster* die weil *auf,* vnd wirft in hinaus, so verget er im glucklaw.

54. item man *nist* (sneezes) nicht in den nachten. so stirbt das viech nicht.

---

[1] Thrashed, beaten, pounded ?

55. item den *rauch-scherben* (censer?) gebnt sy *drey stund* (3 times *vber sich.* so peissent es (bite them) dy . . . nicht des iars.

56. item abdroin *phenning, twecht* man im (a worn-out penny, if one twigs it), an den Weihnacht-tag, so lassent sich dy phening gern gwinen.

57. item wer *wolf* oder *fuchs* nent, dem stet des iars das gewant (clothes) nicht recht.

58. item hent v. oren (hands on ears) habent sy *vber das fewer,* so chumpt chain *or-hol* in das or nicht, noch dy negel swernt (fester) in nicht.

59. item so man ain *taczs* [1] gen kirchen trait fur (past) ain haws, so lauft aine in dem haus hin vnd seczt (a girl in the house runs and sits down) *auf ainm drifüzz,* so wirt ir der selbe man (conf. 65).

60. das man mit ainer *var tancz* (sooner dance with her). ee das sy zu dem tancz get, so sicz auf ainn *drifues,* oder sy *saicht durich ain reitter.* so tancz man mit ir *var* für die andern (conf. 36).

61. ain schuester, so er schuech zu-sneyt (cuts out shoes), so legt er das *leder auf ain stül,* so let es sich pald verkauffen (soon sold).

62. item an ainem Freytag sneid chaine ab ainen *pachen* (pock, pimple). so wert dy saw nicht phinnig (measly).

63. item so ain chind geporn wirt, vnd hat ainen *raten rinkch vber den hals* (red ring round the neck). es wirt erhangen.

64. item wer VII paternoster spricht, vnd den . . . . iar gancz aus, der lebt das iar aus. spricht er dew p̄r. n̄r. nicht aus, so stirbt er des iars.

65. item so man ain *tacz* gen kirchen trait (59), siecht es ain mensch im haus fur-tragen (carry it past), so spricht es ' *mert* [2] *es das fewr* mit dem *elkl* (19), so stirbt chains aus dem haus nicht.

---

[1] *Taz*, tax, due, offering? Höfer 3, 220.
[[2] Merren, to stir, Schm. 2, 611.—EHM.]

G. From *Hans Vintler's* 'Blume der Tugend' comp. in 1411
(acc. to the Gotha MS.).[1]

Die zaubry die ist Got fast vnwerd,
auch sprechend sy 'mich hautz gelert (has taught it).
ain münch, wie möchtz pösz gesin (be bad) ?
daz sprich ich py den trewen mein,
das man ain sollichen munch oder pfaffen      5
also soltt straffen (should so chastise),
das sich zechen stiessend daran ;
wann sey (for they) sind alle samt jm pan (ban),
die den glauben also fast krenken (sorely wound religion). . .
wann es ist wider dich, du hôchstes Gût,      10
alles das man mit zaubry tût ;
vnd wie fast es wider dich ist (how much it is against),
dannocht findt man (they shall yet find) zû disser frist,
die zaubry dannocht pflegen (who yet practise).
Ettlich wellent *pfeyl auss-segnen* (pretend to bless arrows),   15
do wellent si dem *tewffel bannen,*
das sy jn bringent gût (bring them wealth) zû-samen ;
so wellent ettlich war-sagen (soothsay),
vnd vil wellent den *tewffel fragen* (ask)
wa gût lig (where riches lie) vnd edel gestain.      20
Do habent denn ettlich gemain (are in league)
mit der *pössen Erodiana* (wicked Herodias),
do wellent gelauben (believe) ettlich an *Diana,*[2]
die da ain falsche göttin ist ;
vnd auch ettlich mainent (think) haben den list (skill)   25
als sey die lewtt kundent schiessen (can shoot people)
durch alles gemüre (walls), vnd [3] *giessen* (cast)
*wechssinew pild* (waxen images) mangerlay ;
so wissen dissew das *vogel-geschray* (-cry)
vnd auch darzû die *trem auslegen* (dreams interpret) ;   30
ettlich kunnent *den schwert-segen* (sword-charm),
das sy nicht auf diser erden
van kaimen dorf erstachen werden (can be stabbed) ;

---

[1] The text is often corrupt, and I was not able to use the Augsbg ed. of 1486
(Panzer 1, 164. 2, 58); conf. Adelung's Püterich p. 34—38.
[2] Orig. : an die dyadema.
[3] Orig. has this ' vnd ' at beginn. of line.

ettlich kunnent *an fewr* erkennen
wie sich die sach hie sol enden ; 35
so kunnen ettlich *jn der hand*
schouwen (see) eyttel laster vnd schand.
Vil allte weib kunnend den handel (trade)
zu lieb oder findtschafft (enmity) ;
ettlich gebent *losz-búcher* krafft, 40
vnd ettlich kundent *patonicken graben* (dig betonica),
vnd vil wellent *den eys-vogel* haben,
so nutzen ettlich den *allrawn* (madrake) ;
vnd ettlich glaubent an die *frawn*
die haisset *Precht mit der langen nas.* 45
so send ir vil die yehen, das (many who affirm, that)
die *hand-gifft* [1] sy alz wol getan (is so wondrously made),
das sie sy von ainen man
pesser (better) denn von den andern ;
vnd vil die wellend nit wandern (will not travel) 50
an den *verworffen tagen* (accursed days) ;
so send denn vil, die hie haben
glauben, es pring grossen frum (benefit),
ob jn (if to them) des morgens ain *wolf* kum,
vnd ain *has* (hare) pring ungelücke ; 55
vnd ettlich lütt hand die dücke,
das sy den tewffel petten an (adore),
*stern, sunnen,* vnd auch den *maun.*
Vil wellent *auf oblaut schriben,*
vnd das fiepper da-mit vertryben ; 60
ettlich segnent für daz *zene-we* (toothache),
so hand ettlich den *fierde kle*
das sy daunon gauglen sechen (thereby juggling see) ;
ist auch vil, die da yechen,
sy kunnend *vngewitter* (storms) *machen ;* 65
vnd ettlich zaubrer die wachen
dem *stern Venus* vmb die mynne (love) ;
so send auch ettlich, die schlinden (swallow)
*drey palmen* an dem palmtag,
vnd ettlich segnen den *schlag* 70
mit ainer *hacken* auf ainen *trischublen* (179),

[¹ Hantgift, Troj. 12334 ; Oberl. sub v. (=strena).—EHM.]

vnd ettlich stellen auss den kublen (tubs)
das *schmalz* (grease), die weil man's rûrt (stirs) ;
ettlich der lewt fûrt
das sey send jnvisibilis,                                        75
vnd ettlich habent den *piffys* (beifuss, mugwort).
So sprichet menger tumer lib (silly body),
die *teutte* [trute ?] sey ain altes weib
vnd kunne die lütt sugen (suck people),
vnd ettlich lütt die gelauben                                    80
der *albe* mynne die lutte ; [1]
so sagt manger die *tewtte*,[1]
er hab den *orken* gar eben gesechen (just seen) ;
vnd ettlich die yechen,
das *schrättlin* sy ain klaines kind,                             85
vnd sy alz ring (as small) alz der wind,
vnd sy ain verzwifflotter gaist (lost spirit).
So glaubent ettlich aller-maist,
das *der sigel-stein* hab die kraft
das er macht sygehafft (victorious),                             90
vnd vil wissen der erkennen sitt (?).
So nutzend (avail) auch vil die *erd-schnitt* (slices of earth)
zu mangerlay zaubry (for many kinds of magic) ;
vnd ettlich schribent auf daz *ply* (blei, lead)
vnder der *Crist-messz* fur den wurm ;                           95
so nemen ettlich fur den sturm
den *elsen-paum*, hôr ich sagen ;
vnd ettlich wellent kol graben
wann sy den ersten *schwalm* sechen.
vill kunden jn jr *gwand spechen* (spy in their clothes)        100
ob es glucklich sull gaun (go luckily) ;
so habent vil lütt den waun (fancy)
das *verbene* daz selb krutt (herb)
mach die lewt ain ander trut (fond of),
wann man sy grab (dig it up) ze abend ;                          105
vnd auch vil pösz lütt die gend (bad people go)
des nachtes *durch verschlossen tür* (closed door) ;
vnd ettlich lütt tragen herfür (bring out)
silber vnd gold, alz ich hör yechen (as I hear tell),

---

[1] Should it not be 'mynne die *tewtte*' and 'manger der lewtte' ?—TRANS.

wenn sy *newen mon* sechen;                         110
so tragent ettlich lutt auss
das *wasser* alles *auss dem husz,*
wenn man *totten traitt* (carry the dead)
fur (past) das hus, als man saitt;
so send ettlich alz besint,                             115
wenn man jn *junge honer* (fowls) bringt,
so sprechend sy 'blib (stay) her-haim
als die fud pey meinem pain (bone leg)!'
Und vil die yechen *die weg-wart* (plaintain)
sey gewesen (was once) ein fraw zart,                120
vnd wart jrs půllen (waits her lover) noch mit schmertzen.
ettlich legent *des widhoffen hertze* (lay a hoopoo's heart)
des nachtes auf die schlauffende lütt (on sleeping folk),
das es in haimlich ding betütt (suggest)
vnd vil zaubry vnrain (unclean);                  125
die sechend an dem *schulter-pain* (by a shoulder blade)
das (what) menschen sol beschehen (happen);
vnd ettlich die yechen (affirm)
das sy (that it is) nicht gůt daz man
den *tenggen schůch* leg an (left shoe put on)         130
*uor dem gerechten* des morgens frů;
vnd vil die yechen, man stel der ků
die *milch* aus der wammen.
do send ettlich der ammen (nurses),
die selben nement die *jungen kind*               135
do sy erst geporen synd,
vnd stossend's (push them) *durch ain hole*
do ist denn nichtsz wole,
oder es werd ain horen-plässel darusz [horn-blase, p. 1061].
auch treibt man mit der *fleder-muss* (bat)          140
menig tewschlich spil (juggling tricks);
vnd ist des vngelaubes so vil,
das ich es nit gar sagen kan.
Do habent ettlich lütt den waun (fancy)
das sy mainent, vnser leben (they think our life)      145
das unsz daz die . . . geben,[1]
vnd das sy vns hic regieren (govern us).

[1 The Innsbrk. MS. fills the gap. 'die *gach schepfen.*'—EHM.]

so sprechend ettlich [von?] *diernen* (Maids),
sey ertailen (apportion) dem menschen hie auf erden.
vnd ettlich sendent die *pferde*                                    150
fur elenpug (elbow) vnd auch für rencken (dislocat.);
Vnd auch vil lütt die gedencken
vnd habent sein auch gantzen syn (feel quite sure),
sy mugent nicht haben gwin (make gains)
des tages, und sy fechten [1]                                       155
ain pfeyfflin, als sy yechen.
es spricht manger : ' ich bin gogel,
ich haun gesechen *Sant Martis vogel*
hewt (to-day) an dem morgen frû,
mir stosset (befalls) kain vngelück nit zû.'                        160
do wellent ettlich da-pey,
wenn es *vngewitter* sey (is a storm),
das sey alles von der münch wegen (because of monks)
die da gand affter der wege (going their ways) ;
vnd auch ettlich mainent sicherlich,                                165
wenn der *rapp kopp*,[2] daz tütt ain lich (means a corpse).
Ettlich habent denn ainen newen fund,
sy behatten den pisz jn dem mund (wafer in mouth)
wenn man *Aue Maria lütt* (rings).
do send denn ettlich *prwtt* (brides),                             170
die legent jr hemmet (chemise) an jrs mans ort (place).
so kan auch manger drew wort (3 words)
das er nymmer tewrer wirt ;
so ist ettlicher hirt (herdsman)
der sein *vich segnen* kan (his cattle bless),                     175
das jm kain *hase* (hare) tret dar-von (dar-an?) ;
vnd ettlich nement jrew *kind*,
wenn sy ain wenig *kranck* sind,
vnd legent's ouf ain *dryschuffel ;*
uil kunnen salben den kubel (grease the tub),                      180
das sy obn-an ausz faren (fly out above).
ettlich *spynnen* am Samps-tag *garen* (yarn),
vnd machend dar-usz *Sant Iorgen hemd* (shirt) ;
vnd send ettlich so behend (nimble)
das sy varent hundert meyl                                         185

---

[1] For ' unz sy sechen,' until (unless) they see ?    [2] Si corvus ructet.

dar in ainer kurtzen weil.
Ettlich *prechend* den lutten *ab* (break off people's)
die *pain* (bones, legs), als ich gehört hab,
vnd legent dar-ein *porst* (bristles) vnd *kol.*
mangew maint, sy kund auch wol      190
segen (charms) hyn vnd her wenden ;
ettlich die lütt *plendent* (strike blind)
mit ainer hand von dem galgen ;
vill wend den *taig talgen* [1]
an der *hailigen Samps-tag nacht.*      195
Manger auch *karacteres* macht
ausz *pirmit virgineum* (ber-mutter ?),
ettlich puctieren den linium
jn der kunst (art of) geometria,
so nympt der denn oben *praw* (eyebrow)      200
uon den *gerechten augen*
vnd daz *plût von den krawen* (blood of crows),
vnd macht dar-usz zaubery ;
manger nympt ain *järiges zwy* (year-old twig)
von ainen wilden *hassel-pawm.*      205
So send denn ettlich frawen
die *erschlingen vmb die kirchen* [2] *gen*
vnd hiassent die *totten auf-sten* (bid the dead arise),
vnd niement den *ring* (knocker) *von der kirchen tür*
*jn die hand,* vnd ruffend ' her für ' (cry ' come forth '),      210
vnd sprechend ' ich rür disen rink,
stett auf, ir alten pärttling ! '
do send auch ettlich man,
sie nement *von dem galgen* ain *span* (lath),
vnd legent den vnder die kirch-tür,      215

---

[1] For *talken,* knead the dough.
[2] The MS. has *kuechen,* kitchen ; which seems out of place, yet occurs again in
the *Strolling Scholar,* from which I will extract a corresp. passage (Aw. 2, 55-6):

| | |
|---|---|
| Mit wunderlîchen sachen | gên des lichtes *mânen schîn ;* |
| lêr ich sie (I teach her) denne machen | die lêr ich dâ ze velde sîn, |
| von *wahs* einen *kobolt,* | die lêr ich *koln waschen,* |
| wil sie daz er ir werde holt ; | die lêr ich *brunzen* in die aschen, |
| und *töufen* in dem brunnen, | die lêr ich *brant betrechen,* |
| und *legen an die sunnen,* | die lêr ich *morchen brechen,* |
| und *widersins umb die küchen gân.* | die lêr ich *batônien graben,* |
| . . . . . . . . . . . | die *ungesprochen traben,* |
| So beginn ich sie dan lêren | die ler *nahtes nacket stên,* |
| den ars des nahtes kêren | die *erslingen gên dem fiure gên.* |

so solt kain pfennig gaun hin für ;
vnd ettlich nützend den *strangen* (rope)
da ain dieb (thief) an ist erhangen ;
vnd an der *Ravch-nacht wirffet man* (they throw)
die *schůch* (their shoes), als ich gehort han,        220
*uber daz haubt* (head) *erschlingen* (from behind),
vnd wa sich der spitz kert hyn (where the tips point to),
da sol der mensch beliben (stay).
Vnd vil lutt die tribent (perform)
wunder mit dem *hůff-nagel* (horseshoe nail),        225
vnd ettlich steckend *nadel* (needles)
den lutten jn die magen (stomachs) ;
vnd sämlich laund nicht jagen (let not hunt)
die *hund* auf der rechten fert (track).
ettlich send so wol gelert (well taught),        230
das sy an sich mit gewalt (perforce)
nemen ainer *katzen* gestalt (shape).
so findt man den zaubrinin vnrain (unclean),
die den lütten den *wein*
*trinkend* auss den *kelern* verstolen,        235
die selben haisset man vnuerholen.
So send denn ettliche,
wenn sy sechend *ain liche* (see a corpse),
so *raunent* (whisper) sy *dem totten zů*
vnd sprechend ' *kum morgen frů* (tomorrow morn)        240
vnd sag mir, wie es dir dort gee.'
So faret man vber see
die lewt mit gůttem winde ;
vnd ettlich nement jre kinde
wenn es nit geschlauffen mag (cannot sleep),        245
vnd treitz herfür an die hayttren tag,
vnd legtz für sich (before her) ain *aichin prandt*,
vnd nympt ain *scheitt* (log) jn sein hand
vnd *schlecht* (beats) *den prand mer denn zwir* (twice).
so gett ain andrew (other woman) denn py jr        250
vnd spricht ' waz newestu ? '
' da nae ich hie nu
meins kindes mass-laid vnd *nacht-geschrey* (-crying)
vnd alle main zunge en-zway.'

So send denn ettlich also getan, 255
wenn sy den *or-mutzel* han,
so nemend sy ain küssy (pillow) in die hand
vnd schlachend's an den schlauf (temple) zehand
vnd spricht ' flewch, flewch, *or-mützel !*
dich jagt ain küssi-zypfel.' 260
manig zaubrerin die sein,
die nement ain *hacken* (hatchet) vnd *schlachen wein*
auss ainer dur aichin saul (oaken post) ;
vnd ettlich machen mit dem *knul* (ball)
*vaden* (of thread) mangerlay traufferey (trickling) ; 265
so nempt manger *gersten-pry* (barley-pap)
vur dryaffel, hôr ich sagen.
Mangew wil den *dieb laben* (thief revive)
der an dem galgen erhangen ist ;
auch habent vil lütt den list (art) 270
das sy nützen daz *totten-tûch* (shroud) ;
vnd ettlich stelen aus der prûch
dem man sein geschirr gar ;
so *farent* ettlich mit der *far* (=naht-fare)
*auff kelbern* (calves) vnd auch *pecken* (böcken, goats) 275
durch stain vnd stecke.

H. From Doctor *Hartlieb's* (physician in ordinary to duke
    Albrecht of Bavaria) Book of all forbidden arts, unbelief
    and sorcery ; written in 1455 for Johans, markgraf of Bran-
    denburg. (Cod. Pal. 478. Another MS. at Wolfenbüttel is
    mentioned in Uffenbach's Reisen 1, 310).[1]

Chap. 31-2. Of journeying through the air. In the vile art
of **Nigramancia** is another folly that men commit with their
magic *steeds,* which come into an *old house,* and if a man will, he
sits thereon, and rides in a short time a great many mile. When
he gets off, he *keeps the bridle* only, and when he would mount
again, he *jingles the bridle,* and the horse comes back. The steed
is in truth the very Devil. Such sorcery requires bat's blood,
wherein the man shall sign himself away to the Devil with

[¹ Additions in Mone's Anz. 7, 315.—EHM.]

unknown words, as 'debra ebra.' This kind is common with certain princes: Your Grace shall guard you thereagainst.

To such journeys men and women, the *vnhulden* by name, use also an ointment that they call *vngentum pharelis.* This they make out of *seven herbs,* plucking every herb on a day proper to the same, as on Suntag they pluck and dig solsequium, on Mentag lunaria, on Erctag verbena, on Mittwoche mercurialis, on Phinztag barba Jovis, on Freitag capilli Veneris; thereof make they ointment, mixing some blood of birds and fat of beasts, which I write not all, that none be offended thereat. Then, when they will, they besmear *bench* or *post, rake* or *fire-fork,* and speed away.

Ch. 34. To make *hail* and sudden *shower* is one of these arts, for he that will meddle therewith must not only give himself to the devil, but deny God, holy baptism and all christian grace. This art none practise now save *old wives* that be forsaken of God. Hear and mark, august Prince, a great matter that befell me myself in the year of Christ's birth 1446. There were some women burnt at *Haidelberg* for sorcery, but their true instructress had escaped. The next year came I as envoy from *München* to His S.H. the Palatine duke Ludwig, whom God save, for if any prince shall be upheld by his faithfulness, then is he evermore with God. In the same days came tidings, that the instructress was now taken. I prayed the Prince to let me have speech of her, and he was willing. He had the woman and the chief inquisitor brought to a little town named Götscham, into the house of his high steward, Petter von Talhaym. I obtained of the Prince the favour, if the woman taught me to make *shower and hail,* that he would let her live, but she should forswear his land. I went alone into a chamber to the woman and the inquisitor, and craved to know of her lore. She said she could not learn me this thing but—if I would do all that she learned me. I asked what that was, and so it did not anger God nor go against christian faith, I would do it. She lay with one leg ironed, and spake these words: 'My son, thou must deny God, baptism and all the sacraments wherewith thou art anointed and sealed. After that thou must deny all the saints of God, and first Mary his mother, then must thou give thee up body and soul to the *three devils* that I name to thee, and they will grant thee a time to live, and promise to perform thy will until the time be ended.' I said to the woman: 'What shall I do more?' She said: 'Nothing more; when thou desirest the thing, go to a private chamber, call to the spirits, and offer them that. They will come, and in an hour make *hail* for thee where thou wilt.' I told her, I would do none of these things, for that I had said before, if she could impart to me this art, so that I neither offended God nor harmed religion, I would set her free. She answered that she knew no other way. And she was delivered up again to Hans von Tailhaim, who had her burnt, for he had taken her.

Ch. 50.    There is another 'unbelief' (*un*-gelaube = heresy ?), if one have lost anything, there be those that beswear a *loaf*, and stick therein *three knives* to make three crosses and a *spindle* and an *enspin*[1] thereon, and two persons hold it on the *unnamed finger*, and he beswears by the holy *zwölf-boten* [12 messengers, apostles ? see F, 1. 39.]

Ch. 51.    Others *bless a cheese*, and think he that is guilty of the theft cannot eat of the *cheese*. Although some *soap* be given for *cheese*, yet it is a sin.

Ch. 55-6-7.    When a master of this art (**Ydromancia**) will search out a theft, dig up treasure, or know of any secret thing, he goes on a Sunday *before sunrise* to *three flowing springs*, and draws a little out of each in a clean polished glass, brings it home into a fair chamber, and there *burns tapers before it, doing honour to the water* as unto God himself. Then he taketh a *pure child*, sets the same in a fair seat before the water; and standing behind him, speaketh certain strange words in his ear. After that he readeth strange words, and bids the *pure child* repeat them after him. What the words mean, can no master expound more than that a person thereby puts away God and gives himself to the foul fiend. So the master having the lad before him, bids him say what he sees, asking after the theft or treasure or what else he will. The child's simplicity makes him say he sees this or that, wherein the foul fiend takes part, making the false appear in the place of the true.

Ch. 58.    There be divers ways of *drawing the water*; for some fetch it from running waters, putting the same in a glass; others from standing pools, and boil it in honour of the spirits whom

[1 Schmeller 3, 570.—EHM.]

they suppose to have power over the waters, the lord and prince of them all being *Salathiel*, as the masters declare.

Ch. 60. Some women sprinkle their herbs and plants with *hallowed water*, supposing that the worms shall not come thereat; that is all an 'unbelief.' There be some courtiers, when they get *new spurs*, do plunge them with the *rowels* in a *holy-well*, saying that what they strike therewith shall in no wise swell; that is all an 'unbelief.' Some sorceresses go to a *mill wheel*, and catch the *water that flies off the wheel* in the air; with this water they ply all manner of sorceries for loving and for enmity. And who so may not be good man (husband), they help him therewith that he can be good man; that is all an 'unbelief.'

Ch. 61. There be bad christians that carry on sorcery with divers waters, as that of the blest and hallowed *font*, wherein lies every christian's health and wealth, therewith they juggle and do much that is not meet to be written; yea, an old wife that hath gotten font-water, she thinks to have borne off the prize,

Ch. 63. Another trick with water. Two persons take two things, as *little sticks or straws*, *rings* or small *coins*, and name one after one person and the other after the other, and if the two things *run together on the water in a basin*, then shall those two come together; but if one flee from the other, they come not together, and whose thing fleeth first, his shall the blame be. And the masters of this 'unbelief' also prove thereby, whether of two wedded folk shall soonest die for they think that whichever *sinketh* soonest shall die first.

Ch. 67-8. Now will I write of the fourth art that is forbidden: it is called **Aremancia,** and has to do with *air* and whatsoever flies or lives therein. The art is very strong among the heathen, whose 'unbelief' therein is so great, that they honour the first thing that appeareth to them in a day, and worship it that day for their god. And evil christians do much 'unbelief' therewith, for they say, if a *hare do meet* them, it is a misfortune, and if a *wolf meet* them, it is a great luck. Of 'unbeliefs' there be many in divers beasts. Some say that if *birds fly to one's right hand*, it signifies great gain and luck, and if they *fly to the left* (glinggen) *side*, it signifies unluck and loss. All that is an 'unbelief.' There be those that have great faith in an *eagle* (aren), and think whensoever he *fly pocket-side*, it promiseth great luck or gain.

And so great is the faith of some, that they *shift their pocket to the other side;* if then the *eagle also turn him round*, as may often hap, then have they the fullest faith, and think it cannot fail . . . . Without doubt the Devil is the right inventor and inspirer of the art; he it is that changeth himself into the said *birds* that he may deceive men.

Ch. 69.   There be also princes, poor and rich, that hold their hunting on certain days, and when this or that *wind* doth *blow;* that is all 'unbelief.' . . . Some men do wear *high feathers* in their hats, that they may know *whence cometh the wind*, supposing that in sundry matters they have luck against the wind, and in others with the wind: that is all an 'unbelief' and sorcery.

Ch. 73.   There is one more 'unbelief' in this art, that is, when a man *sneezeth*, whereby the brain doth naturally clear itself, they hold it to be a great sign of luck or unluck, and draw forecasts therefrom, such as, if the *sneezes* be *three*, there are *four thieves around the house.* If they be *two*, the man shall rise, and lie down another way to sleep; but if *thirteen*, then is it exceeding good, and what appeareth to him that night shall in very deed come to pass. Also in the morning, when a man goeth from his bed, the *sneezes* shall mean other things again; the things are many, and it is all a downright 'unbelief.'

Ch. 74.   Again, some natural philosophers do say that this *sneezing* cometh very nigh the *stroke* (apoplexy). For should the crude humours remain obstructed in the brain, and not come out, the stroke would strike the man right soon; therefore do some masters call it the minor applexia, i.e. the lesser stroke. For, when a man sneezeth, he is of many of his limbs in nowise master, but of God's grace it lasteth not long, the better for him.

Ch. 77.   There are also people, and verily great princes, that do utterly believe and suppose, when *great uproars* come, that then great *treasons* are afoot: that is a great delusion.

Ch. 79.   We find some sorceresses that make an *image* or *atzman of wax* and other things. This they make at certain hours, and utter certain known and unknown names, and *hang it up in the air*, and as the wind stirs it, they think the man in whose name it is made shall have no rest. All this is a great 'unbelief' and sorcery. Some do the same with an *aspen-leaf*, writing their sorcery thereon, and think thereby to breed love between people. Of such *atzmannen* I have read much in the Art Magica, where the constellations are brought in, and also some strange words, and very many foreign things besides. All this is downright sorcery and a wicked 'unbelief.' And I have heard say much, how that *women* make such *atzmans*, and *roast* them by *a fire*, thereby to chastise (kestigen) their husbands.

Ch. 80. There be women and men, which dare to make *fires*, and in the *fire* to see things past and to come. The masters and mistresses of this devilish art have particular days, whereon they have wood prepared for them, and when about to practise their art, they go to a *private place*, bringing with them the poor silly folk unto whom they shall prophesy. They command them to *kneel down*, and after worshipping the *angel of the fire*, to offer sacrifice unto him. With the sacrifice they kindle the wood, and the master looks narrowly into the fire, marking well what shall appear to him therein.

Ch. 83. The art of **Pyromancia**[1] is practised in many divers ways and forms. Some masters of the art take a *pure child* and set him *in their lap*, then lift his hand up and let him look into *his nail*, and beswear the child and the nail with a great adjuration, and then speak in the child's ear three unknown words, whereof one is *Oriel*, the others I withhold for fear of offending. After that they ask the child whatsoever they will, thinking he shall see it in the *nail*. All this is a right 'unbelief,' and thou christen-man shalt beware thereof.

Ch. 84. Another deceitful trick in the art is, that the masters take *oil* and *soot* from a *pan*, and anoint also a *pure child*, be it *girl* or *boy*, namely his hand, doing much the same, and *raise the hand against the sun* if the sun be shining, else they have *tapers* which they raise against the hand, and letting the child look therein, ask him of what they will; their belief is, that what the child tells them must be true; they know not, alas, how the devil mixeth himself therein, making far more of wrong to appear than that of right.

Ch. 88. The masters and their like do also practise the art in a common *looking-glass*, letting *children look thereinto*, whom in like manner they strongly beswear and whisper hidden words unto, and think to search out many things therein. That is all

[¹ Fiur-sehen, Altd. bl. 1, 365.—EHM.]

an ' unbelief' and the devil's jugglery and trickery. Beware, O christian, I warn thee right faithfully. The same thing they do in a *beautiful bright polished sword,* the masters thinking that some one may haply ask about wars and such deadly matters; then, if the *sword* be one that hath *killed many men,* the *spirits* shall *come all the sooner and quicker.* If one will ask of pleasure and peace, find out arts or dig up treasure, then shall the *sword* be clean and *maiden* (unvermailigt, unwedded, i.e. unfleshed). I know a great prince: whoso bringeth him an old *worn-out sword* (haher swert), hath done him much honour.

Ch. 90-1. In Pyromancia are many more 'unbeliefs,' esp. one that is thought to be infallible, and is the vilest and worst, for the more firmly men believe in such sorcery, the more is it sin. The thing to be done is, that *boys* shall see in a *crystal* things to come and all things. It is done by false castaway christians, to whom dearer is the devil's delusion than the truth of God. Some have an exceeding *clear and fair-polished crystal* or *parille* [beryl? pearl?], they have it consecrated and keep it very clean, and gather for it frankincense, myrrh and the like; and when they will exercise their art, they wait for a very *fine day,* or have a *clean chamber* and many consecrated candles therein. The masters then go to bathe, taking the *pure child* with them, and clothe themselves in *pure white raiment,* and sit down, and say their magic prayers, and burn their magic offer- ings, and then let the *boy look into the stone,* and whisper in his ear hidden words, which they say are mighty holy, in truth the words are devilish. After that they ask the boy whether he sees aught of an angel. If the boy answer yea, they ask what colour he is of? and if he say *red,* the masters declare that the *angel is angry,* and again they pray, and sacrifice to the devil again, and thereat is he well pleased. Then if the boy say the *angel is black,* the master saith the angel is *exceeding wroth,* we must pray yet again, and *burn* more *lights;* and they pray once more, and sacrifice with incense and other things . . . . And when the devil thinks he hath had service enough, he makes appear the *angel in white.* Then is the master glad, and asks the boy, what hath the *angel in his hand?* and ceaseth not to ask till he says 'I see a writing in the angel's hand.' Then he asketh on, until he see letters: these letters the master collects, and thereof maketh words, until he has that which he desired to know.

Ch. 94. It hath chanced doubtless, that certain priests were so captivated by these *visiones*, that they took the *sacred patenas*, whereon at Mass the elements are changed into God, and have made the children look into them, believing that holy angels alone could appear therein, and no devils. These have mightily mistook, etc.

Ch. 96. Another trick of sorcery that is set down to Pyromancia. . . . The masters take and melt *lead* or *tin*, then *pour it into a water*, and soon take it out again, and beswear the *colour* and *little pits* of the lead or tin, and declare things past or future thereby, which is all an ' unbelief.'

Ch. 102. Know besides, that men do also look at *fingers*, whether the *little finger* reach *beyond the last joint of the ring-finger*. They say that is a sign of great luck, and the farther it reaches, the greater the luck; but if the *little finger* be *even with the said joint*, the man shall be unfortunate. Heed it not, good christian, it is a trifle.

Ch. 103. There is a folk strolleth about much in the world, named *Zygainer* (gipsies) : this people, both man and wife, young and old, do greatly practise the art, and mislead many of the simple, etc.

Ch. 106-7-8. Of a fortune-teller whom Dr Hartlieb knew, and who gave out that the art *had been in her family* for ages, and *at her death the grace would descend to her eldest* (daughter). The woman is well looked upon, and bidden to people's houses. I asked her to impart her cunning unto me. She was willing, bade me wash my hands, and dried them with her own, and bent her face very close to my hands, and told me things that cannot possibly happen to me.

Ch. 115-6. **Spatulamancia** is of the seven forbidden arts one, and is done by a cunning outlandish artifice. When I consider all the arts, I find no other ' unbelief' that hath so little ground, indeed I think it to be a mockery. . . . The masters of this art take a *shoulder* of a dead *ox* or *horse, cow* or *ass ;* they have said when I asked them, that next to a *man's shoulder*, which is best, *any great animal's shoulder is good*. They wash well the shoulder with wine, and thereafter with *holy water ;* they tie it

up in a *clean cloth,* and when they will practise the art, they untie
it, and carry it to a place *outside of roof,* then *gaze into the
shoulder,* and think it *changes* after every question. They have
neither lights nor sacrifice, yet it is a great 'unbelief' to wash
the shoulder with holy water, and to think the shoulder changes
for their questions. Their faith is so great that they ask for no
reasons of the art: they speak out of their own head whatsoever
comes into it, to solve and settle the questions. . . . They
think they can search out all things.

Ch. 120. The masters of this art have also lavg [MHG. louc,
flame? or lauge, lye?] and observe what *colours* the *shoulder* has
at the ends, in the middle and in all the parts; and according to
these the devil suggests to them what to believe and say.

Ch. 121. First I will write of the *goose-bone* (genns-pain).
On St Martin's day or night, when they have eaten the goose,
the eldest and the wise do keep the *breast-bone,* and let it dry till
the morning, and then examine it in every particular, before and
behind and in the middle. Thereby they judge of the *winter,* if
it shall be *cold, warm, wet* or *dry,* and are so firm in their faith,
that they wager their goods and chattels thereon. And thereon
have they an especial 'loss' (lot-drawing) that shall not and
cannot fail, to tell whether the *snow* shall be much or little; all
this knoweth the *goose-bone.* Aforetime the *old peasants in desert
places* dealt in this matter, now is the 'unbelief' grown in kings,
princes, and all the nobility, who believe in such things.

Pag. 76ᵇ. 77ᵃ. Moreover I will write thee a thing that lately
a great victorious captain told me, in whom prince and peasant
put great confidence, one for his deeds, another for his wisdom, a
third for his faith that he had kept alway in every need to his
own prince. This good man on St Nicolas day in this year
1455 said to me, 'Dear master, how shall the winter be this year,
as ye star-gazers opine?' I was quick and quick (hasty?) as I
still am, and spake, 'Lord Saturn goes this month into a fiery
sign, likewise other stars are so disposed, that in 3 years no
harder winter shall have been.' This dauntless man, this
christian captain drew forth of his doublet that heretical 'unbelief,' the *goose-bone,* and showed me that after Candlemas an
exceeding great frost should be, and could not fail. What I had
said he said yet more, and told me that the *Teutonic Knights* in

*Prussia* had waged all their *wars by the goose-bone,* and as the *goose-bone* showed so did they order their two campaigns, one in summer and one in winter. And furthermore he spake these words, 'While the Teutonic Order *obeyed the bone,* so long had they great worship and honour, but since they have left it off, Lord knows how it stands with them.' I said, 'Had the T. O. no other art, help or stay than the *goose-bone,* then should their confidence be small.' With that I parted from my rich host.

Pag. 76ᵃ. This know the physicians well, and say that the disease named bolismus ⸱ (βούλιμος) or apetitus caninus can by no eating or drinking be stilled, but by medicine alone; for all food passeth undigested through the body, whereby the flesh falls away, but the bones remain great as ever; and this makes the child so unshapely, that men call it a *changeling* (wächsel-kind).[1]

---

## I. EXTRACTS FROM MODERN COLLECTIONS.

### a. From the *Chemnitzer Rocken-philosophie.*

1. Whoever goes into a childbed chamber, carrying a basket, must *break a chip off the basket,* and put it in the cradle; otherwise he will take the child's or mother's *rest* (sleep) away.

2. When a mother wants to know if her *child is becried* (bewitched), let her lick its forehead: if becried, it will taste salt; then fumigate with *sweepings from the four corners* of the room——with shavings off the *four corners of the table*——with *nine sorts of wood.*

3. Who *pulls out* an article from the wash *upside down* or *leftwards,* will not be becried.

4. Boil *frauen-flachs, szysche* or *ruf-kraut,* bathe the sick man in the water, and leave the bath under his bed: if he is becried, it will shrink; if not, not.

5. If you are taking much money, put some *chalk* to it, then *bad folk* cannot get any of it back.

6. Wash your money in clean water, and put *salt and bread* to it, then the *dragon* and bad folk cannot get it

7. Women boiling yarn should *tell lies* over it, or it won't turn white.

8. To walk over *sweepings* is unlucky.

9. If you call a young child *little crab,* it will be stunted, for crabs crawl backwards.

10. If you set out on a journey, and a *hare* runs across your path, it bodes no good.

---

[1] At the end of pag. 78ᵇ stands the name of the copyist: 'Clara Hätzlerin.' In the same handwriting is Cod. Pal. 677.

11. In drinking out of a jug, do not *span* the lid with your hand, or the next drinker will have *tension of the heart*.

12. Do not buy your children *rattles*, nor allow any to be given, else they are slow in learning to talk.

13. For tongue-tied children it is good to eat *beggar's bread*.

14. If in leaving home you have forgotten something, *don't go back* for it, but have it fetched by another; else everything is thrown back (goes wrong).

15. If a stranger comes into the room, he shall *sit down*, so as not to take the children's *rest* away with him (see 1).

16. When you cover a table, put some *bread* on at once, or a corner of the cloth will trip some one up.

17. Men shall not stay in the house while the women are *stuffing feathers* into the beds, else the feathers will prick through the bed-tick.

18. Set the *hen* on to hatch while people are coming out of church, and you'll have plenty of chicks crawl out.

19. If you want large-headed chickens, wear a fine large straw-hat while you set the *brood-hen* on.

20. The *straw for a nest* should be taken out of a marriage-bed, from the man's side if you want cocks, from the woman's if hens.

21. After washing in the morning, don't *flirt the water* from your hands, or you'll waste your victuals that day.

22. Never rock an *empty cradle :* it rocks the baby's *rest* away.

23. The first time a baby's *nails* want paring, let the mother *bite them off*, else they learn to pilfer.

24. When about to stand godfather or godmother, *borrow* something to wear, and your godchild will always have credit.

25. If you call children *alt-männichen, alt-weibichen*, they'll be stunted, and have wrinkles on the forehead.

26. If you want children to live long, call the boys *Adam*, and the girls *Eve*.

27. If a child is to live 100 years, the *god-parents* must be fetched from *three parishes*.

28. If you take a child into the *cellar* under a year old, it will grow up timid.

29. If you let it look into the *looking-glass* under a year old, it will grow up vain.

30. Children that *cry at the christening* don't grow old.

31. If the first children take their *parents' names*, they die before the parents.

32. If a *dog* looks into the *oven* when you are baking, the *loaves* will be loose (? erlöset), or the crust leave the crumb.

33. If there is dough in the trough, don't sweep the room till it is carried out, or you'll *sweep a loaf* away.

34. The *vinegar* spoils if you set the cruet on the *table*.

35. If a *woman within six weeks* after confinement walks a field or bed, nothing grows on it for some years, or everything spoils.

36. If a woman dies in the *six weeks*, lay a mangle-roller or a book in

the bed, and *shake up and make the bed* every day till the six weeks are up, or she cannot rest in the ground.

37. Do not blow the baby's *first pap*, and it will not afterwards scald its mouth with hot things.

38. Would you wealthy be, cut the *loaf* quite evenly.

39. Eat not while the *death-bell tolls*, or your teeth will ache.

40. If *red shoes* are put on a child under a year old, it can never see *blood*.

41. If a woman with child stands and eats before the *bread cupboard*, the child will have the *wasting-worm* (mit-esser, fellow-eater); see 817.

42. To *mend* clothes on the body is not good.

43. If you *sew* or *mend* anything on Ascension-day, the lightning will come after him that wears it.

44. Eating cracknels on *Maundy Thursday* keeps fever away.

45. If you *stride over a child*, it will stop growing.[1]

46. Who works *in wood* will not be wealthy.

47. Never shew a light *under the table* where people sit, lest they begin to quarrel.

48. God-parents shall buy the child a *spoon*, lest it learn to dribble.

49. If a woman who is confined put a *black stomacher* on, the child will grow up timid.

50. In the six weeks don't take a child *inside your cloak*, or it will be gloomy, and always meet with sorrow.

51. He that *lends* money at play will lose.

52. He that *borrows* for play will win.

53. Let a mother who is nursing go *silently* out of church three Sundays, and every time blow into her child's mouth, and its teeth will come easily.

54. Between 11 and 12 the *night before Christmas, the water is wine.* Some say, water drawn at 12 on Easter night will *turn into wine*.

55. When lights are brought in on *Christmas-eve*, if any one's shadow has no head, he will die within a year; if half a head, in the second half-year.

56. In the *Twelve nights* eat no lentils, peas or beans; if you do, you get the itch.

57. One who is about to stand sponsor shall not make water after he is drest for church; else the godchild will do the same in bed.

58. If you go out in the morning, and an old woman meets you, it is a bad sign (see 380).

59. Don't answer a *witch's* question, or she may take something from you.

60. *Stone-crop* planted on the roof keeps the thunderbolt aloof.

61 Get out of bed *backwards*, and everything goes contrary that day.

62. If the *Jüdel* won't let the children sleep, give him something to *play* with. When children laugh in their sleep, or open and turn their

---

[1] My brother too *stept with one leg* over me, saying ' Oho Thömilîn, now wiltow grow no more! ' Life of Thomas Plater, p. 19.

eyes, we say 'the *Jüdel plays* with them.' Buy, without beating down the price asked, a new little pot, pour into it out of the child's bath, and set it on the oven: in a few days the *Jüdel* will have *sucked every drop out.* Sometimes *eggshells,* out of which the yolk has been blown into the child's pap and the mother's caudle, are hung on the cradle by a thread, for the *Jüdel* to *play* with, instead of with the child.

63. If a *loaf* is sent away from table uncut, the people are sure to go away hungry.

64. If you spill *salt,* don't scrape it up, or you'll have bad luck.

65. If you tread your *shoes* inwards, you'll be rich; if outwards, poor.

66. If you have the *jaundice,* get the grease-pot stolen from a carrier's cart; look into that, and it will soon pass away.

67. If a *dog* howls the night before Christmas, it will go mad within a year.

68. Great evil is in store for him who harms a *cat,* or kills it.

69. If the *cats* bite each other in a house where a sick man lies, he will die soon.

70. A woman *churning butter* shall stick a three-crossed knife on the churn, and the butter will come.

71. *Splinters* peeling off the boards in the sitting-room are a sign of stranger *guests.*

72. When the *cat* trims herself, it shews *a guest* is coming.

73. If *magpies* chatter in the yard or on the house, *guests* are coming.

74. If a *flea* jumps on your hand, you'll hear some news.

75. If a child does not thrive, it has the *Elterlein:* shove it a few times into the oven, and the *E.* is sure to go.

76. To kill *spiders* is unlucky.

77. Let a newborn child be dressed up fine the *first three Sundays,* and its clothes will sit well on it some day.

78. If women *dance in the sun* at Candlemas, their *flax* will thrive that year.

79. If a stranger looks in at the *room-door* on a Monday, without walking in, it makes the husband beat his wife.

80. If a man buys or gives his betrothed a *book,* their love will be *overturned* (ver-blättert, when the leaf *turns over,* and you lose your place).

81. In making *vinegar,* you must look sour and be savage, else it won't turn out good.

82. If your *ears ring,* you are being slandered.

83. A *hen* crowing like a cock is a sign of misfortune.

84. He that fasts on *Maundy Thursday* will catch no fever that year, and if he does he'll get over it.

85. He that lends the *first money he makes* at market, gives away his luck.

86. When at market selling goods, don't let the *first customer* go, even if you sell under value.

87. A man shall not give his betrothed either *knife* or *scissors,* lest their love be *cut in two.*

88. Bathing the children on a *Friday* robs them of their *rest.*

89. If you are fetching water *in silence,* draw it *down stream.*

90. Draw crosses on your doors before *Wallpurgis-night* (Mayday eve), and the witches will not harm.

91. In going to bed, leave nothing *lying on the table,* else the oldest or youngest in the house can get no sleep.

92. If a woman going to be churched meet a *man,* she'll have a *son* next time; if a *woman,* a *girl;* if nobody, no more children; if two people, twins.

93. If you *sneeze* before breakfast, you'll get some present that day.

94. Don't let *fire* and *light* be *carried out of your house* by a stranger, it is taking the victuals away from the house.

95. A new *maidservant* shall look into the *oven's mouth* the first thing, she'll soon get used to it then (see 501).

96. If you are having *flax sown,* give the sower a fee, or the flax will spoil.

97. If a single woman on Christmas-eve *pour melted lead* into cold water, it will shape itself like the tools of her future husband's trade.

98. If you have a *wooden pipe* or *tap* turned for you out of a birchtree growing in the middle of an *anthill,* and draw wine or beer through it, you'll soon have sold your liquor.

99. He that cuts *bread* unevenly, has told lies that day.

100. *Single women* that want husbands shall, the night before *St Andrew's day,* call upon that saint *naked,* and they'll see their sweetheart in their sleep.

101. When a *maid* wants to know if she shall keep her place, let her on Christmas-eve turn her back to the door, and *fling the shoe* off her foot *over her head :* if the tip of the shoe is towards the door, she'll have to go ; if the heel, she will stay.

102. If a *maid* wishes to know what sort of hair her lover will have, let her *grope backwards* through the open door on Christmas-eve, and she'll grasp the hair in her hand.

103. Whoever finds by chance a hare-laurel (? hasen-lorber) in the wood, and eats it, will have his share of the *hare* wherever he goes.

104. He that looks in the *mirror* at night, sees the devil there.

105. To find out if she'll get a husband during the year, let the damsel knock at the *hen-house* on Christmas-eve or at midnight: if the *cock* cackles, she'll get one; if the *hen,* she won't.

106. If children in the street ride with *spears and banners,* there will be a war; if they carry each other on *crosses* (Banbury chairs) a pestilence.

107. If you are out of money, mind the *new moon* does not peep into your empty purse, or you'll be short of money the whole month.

108. If the *stork* builds on your roof or chimney, you will live long and be rich.

109. To know if her lover will be straight or crooked, a girl must go to a stack of wood on Christmas-eve, and with her *back to it, pull out a log;* as the log is, so will the lover be (see F, 7).

110. To know what he is called, let her *stretch* the first piece of *yarn* she spins that day *outside the house-door,* and the first man that passes will be a namesake of her future husband.

111. Never set a *gridiron* or *trivet* over the fire without putting something on it; she that does so will have an apron (puckers) on her face.

112. Let a woman, when going to bed, *salute the stars in the sky*, and neither hawk nor vulture will take her chickens.

113. In putting *straw* into a bed, don't leave the *knots in the strawbands*, there's no sleeping on them.

144. A woman going to market will get better prices for her wares if on getting up she put her *right shoe* on first.

115. He that wears a *shirt* woven of *yarn*, that a girl *under seven* has spun, will find luck in it (see 931).

116. If it rain on *John's-day*, nuts will spoil and harlots thrive.

117. Onions, turned in their bed on *John's-day*, turn out fine.

118. The maids shall not weed the cabbage-beds on *Bartlemy's day*; Bartlemy is putting [orig. throwing] heads to the cabbages, and would be scared away.

119. If you find a *four-leaved clover* [shamrock], hold it dear; as long as you have it, you'll be happy (see G, 62).

120. A *raven* or *crow*, that sits cawing on a sick house, betokens the patient's death.

121. Shepherds must *not name the wolf* during the *Twelves*, or he will worry their sheep.

122. If a child has a *date-stone* about him, he does not fall, or is not much hurt.

123. When you go into a *new house* or room, what you *dream the first night* comes true.

124. If a woman or maid loses her *garter* in the street, her husband or lover is unfaithful to her.

125. When a woman is going to bed, she shall *move her chair from the place* where she has sat, or the *alp* will weigh upon her.

126. While *a fire burns on the hearth*, lightning will not strike the house.

127. A calf born on St. *Velten's* (Valentine's) day is of no use for breeding.

128. If a *wolf, stag, boar* or *bear* meets you on a journey, it is a good sign.

129. He that finds a *horse-shoe*, or a piece of one, has luck (see 220).

130. The flax or tow that a maid leaves *unspun on the distaff* of a Saturday, does not make good yarn, and will not bleach.

131. Let the father put a sword in the baby's hand directly it is christened, and it will be bold and brave.

132. When a boy is born, let his feet *push against his father's breast*, and he will not come to a bad end.

133. As soon as a girl is born, seat her *on her mother's breast*, and say 'God make thee a good woman'; and she will never slip or come to shame.

134. If a *spider crawl on your coat* in the morning, you'll be happy that day.

135. If a man on a journey meets a *woman* who is *spinning*, it is a bad sign; let him turn back, and take another road.

136. If the clock strikes while *bells are ringing*, it betokens fire.

137. Don't lay a new-born child *on its left side* first, or it will always be awkward.

138. On *Walpurgis-eve* let him that has cornfields fire his gun over them, and the witches cannot hurt the corn.

139. A *blue cornflower* pulled up by the roots on Corpus Christi day stops nose-bleeding, if held in the hand till it gets warm.

140. Root out the reeds in a pond or the thorns in a field on *Abdon-day* (July 30), and they will not grow again.

141. If a woman's neck or throat *itches*, she will soon go to a christening or wedding; if her head *itches*, it means blows.

142. Bright Christmas, dark barns; dark Christmas, light barns.

143. Whoever hurts or even sees an *earth-hünchen* or a *house-adder*, is sure to die that year.

144. Smear the point of your sword with ear-wax, it will melt your enemy's courage.

145. When two nursing mothers drink at the same time, one *drinks* the other's *milk* away. And when two people begin drinking at the same moment, one *drinks* the other's *colour away*.

146. If you eat *bread* that another has bitten, you'll become his enemy.

147. If a woman lets another person wipe *hands* on her *apron*, that person will hate her.

148. *Swallows* building on a house bring poverty, *sparrows* riches.

149. A *hoop coming off a cask* on Christmas-eve shews that some one in the house will die that year.

150. If the *light* on the altar *goes out* of itself, it shews the priest is going to die.

151. A woman gets rid of *earache* by wrapping a man's breeches round her head.

152. When the maids are making *tinder*, they must tear pieces out of men's shirts; tinder made of women's shifts does not catch.

153. Tying *wet strawbands* round the orchard-trees on *Christmas-eve* makes them fruitful.

154. Fruit-trees clipt at *Shrovetide* are proof against worm and caterpillar.

155. To keep a *cat* or *dog* from running away, chase it *three times* round the *hearth*, and rub it against the chimney-shaft.

156. If a *man* sees a *wolf* before the wolf sees him, he need fear no harm; but if the *wolf* saw him first, he is in danger : some say he will be *dumb*, or *hoarse*.

157. *John's blood* (plantain), culled at noon on John's day, is good for many things.

158. If a *magpie* sits chattering on the infirmary, before noon, and *looking our way*, the meaning is good : if after noon, and seen *from behind*, it is bad.

159. The *howling of dogs* bodes misfortune.

160. A *swarm of bees* hanging on to a house signifies fire.

161. The *lark* sings as long before Candlemas as she is silent after.

162. If a *bachelor* and *spinster* stand sponsors to a child, the priest shall plant himself between the two, or they will always be falling out.

163. A man shall not marry his gossip (fellow-sponsor), for, every time they come together as man and wife, *it thunders.*

164. Let him who gets the *first can* of beer out of a cask run away fast, and the rest of that beer will soon go off.

165. Don't let a *baby* tread *barefoot* on a *table :* it will get sore feet.

166. After putting the *candle* out, don't leave it *upside down* in the candlestick; else nobody can wake if thieves should come.

167. A boy born in the *Venus-morningstar* gets a wife much younger than himself; in the *Venus-eveningstar* one much older. And the contrary with girls.

168. On rising from a meal, don't leave any of your *bread* behind; if any one takes it and throws it over the gallows, you won't escape hanging.

169. An *elder* planted before the stable door guards the cattle from sorcery.

170. He that has about him a *string* with which a *rupture* was bound up, can lift the heaviest load without danger.

171. A piece of wood off a *coffin* that has been dug up, if concealed among your cabbages, keeps away the caterpillars.

172. Eat no soup at *Shrovetide*, or you'll have a dripping nose.

173. On *Nicasius-eve* write the saint's name on the door in chalk, and you rid the house of rat and mouse.

174. If the carter plaits a *snake's* or *adder's tongue* into his whip, his horses can pull the biggest loads out of the ditch, and will not over-drink themselves.

175. Make nests for the hens on *Peter's-day*, and many's the egg they will lay.

176. A woman with child, who stands *godmother*, shall not lift the babe out of the *font* herself; else one child dies, the christened one or hers.

177. If the first person you meet in the morning be a *virgin* or a *priest*, 'tis a sign of bad luck; if a *harlot*, of good.

178. If a *weaned* child is put to the breast again, it grows up a blasphemer.

179. If a *woman with child* pass under a *waggon-pole*, she'll go over her time.

180. The *seventh son* is a lucky man, for healing, planting, or doing anything.

181. Malefactors on the rack pin a paper to their back with Psalms 10th and 15th written on it : they can stand the torture then without confessing.

182. If you have *bread* and *salt* about you, you are safe from sorcery.

183. For a fever : Take three bits of *stolen bread*, spit in two nutshells, and write this note : 'Cow, will you go to your stall, Fever (*frörer*, ague), go you to the wall.'

184. If a *mouse* has gnawed at your dress, it means mischief.

185. If the women or maids are *washing sacks*, it will soon rain.

186. To *sneeze* while putting your shoes on, is a sign of bad-luck.

187. To put a clean *shirt* on of a Friday is good for the gripes.

188. Eating *stolen cheese* or *bread* gives you the hiccough.

189. If you dig *devil's bit* the midnight before St John's, the roots are still *unbitten*, and good for driving the devil away.

190. *John's wort* drives witches away and the devil; that's why he out of spite pricks holes in all the leaves with his needle.

191. When a person dies, set the *windows* open, and the *soul* can get out.

192. For a child to grow up good, its godmother or the woman that carries it home from church must immediately *lay it under the table*, and the father take it up and give it to the mother.

193. A year without *skating* is bad for the barley.

194. If they are building a *weir* across the river, it will not rain in that country till they have done.

195. Put a *goose* through your legs three times, give her three mouthfuls of chewed bread with the words 'Go in God's name,' and she'll always come home.

196. He that has fits of *cold fever* shall crawl to a running stream, strew a handful of *salt* down-stream, and say : ' In God his name I sow for seed this grain, When the seed comes up may I see my *cold* friend again.'

197. The first time you hear the *cuckoo* in spring, ask him : ' *Cuckoo*, baker's-man, true answer give, How many years have I to live?' And as many times as he sings, so many years more will you live.

198. If an unmarried maiden eat the *brown* that *sticks inside* the porridge-pot, *it will rain* at her wedding; and if it rains, the new couple get rich (see 498).

199. To sell your cattle well at market, smoke them with the black ball dug out of the middle of an *ant-hill*.

200. Never hand things over a cradle with the child in it; nor leave it open.

201. A *thief's thumb* on your person, or among your wares, makes them go fast.

202. If you throw a bunch of *inherited keys* at a door when some one is listening outside, the *eavesdropper* is deaf for the rest of his life.

203. Eat *milk* on Shrove Tuesday, and you'll not be sunburnt in the summer.

204. If a bride wishes to rule her husband, let her on the wedding-day dress in a *baking trough*, and knock at the church door.

205. To *wean* a child, let the mother set it down on the floor, and knock it over with her foot; it will forget her the sooner.

206. If a dog runs *between* a woman's *legs*, her husband is going to beat her.

207. Put *money in the mouth of the dead*, and they will not come back if they have hidden a treasure.

208. Toothpicks made of wood that *lightning has struck*, send the tooth-ache away.

209. A *knife* shall not lie *on its back*, for fear of its hurting the angels.

210. If two *clocks* in the town happen to strike together, a married couple will die.

211. A boil will safely heal if squeezed with a *three-crossed knife*.

212. Let the bride arrive at the bridegroom's house *in the dark*, then they'll have every corner full.

213. If a *dog* runs through between two friends, they will break off their friendship.

214. He that would dig up a *treasure*, must not speak a word.

215. To draw *storks* to your house, make them a nest on the chimney *with your left hand*.

216. If you have a swollen neck, go *in silence* to the mill, *steal* the tie from one of the sacks, and tie it about your neck.

217. When you see the first *swallow* in spring, halt immediately, and dig the ground *under your left foot* with a knife; you will there find a *coal* that is good for a year against the ague (see G, 98).

218. In digging for treasure, have *bread* about you, and the spectres can't disturb you.

219. *Godfather's money* (gift) makes rich and lucky.

220. When you have been robbed, drive an accidentally-found *horseshoe nail* (see 129) into the place where the fire always is, and you'll have your own again.

221. *Bastard children* are luckier than lawful ones.

222. At a christening get a mite of *bread* consecrated, and the child's parents will never want for bread.

223. He that counts his money at *new moon* is never short of it.

224. Drop a *cross-penny* on a treasure, and it can't move away.

225. Eat *lentils* at Shrovetide, and money will pour (quellen, swell?).

226. He of whom a boy (or girl) makes his (or her) *first purchase* at market, will have good luck in selling that day.

227. Let a merchant throw the *first money he takes* on the ground, and plant his feet upon it; his business will go the better.

228. For the *cuckoo* to sing after St John's is not good, it betokens dearth.

229. When the bride is fetched home, she shall make *no circuit*, but go the *common road;* otherwise she has ill luck.

230. If a man passing under a henroost is bedropped by the *hen*, it bodes misfortune, if by the *cock*, good luck (see 105).

231. A new garment should *not be put on empty*, something should be dropt into the pocket first for luck.

232. In choosing sponsors, ask an *unmarried woman*, else the child will be unlucky in marriage, and also have no children.

223. He that is lucky when *young* will beg his bread when *old;* and vice versâ.

234. He that carries *wormwood* about him cannot be becried (bewitched).

235. If you find a *needle*, and the *point* is towards you, you'll be unlucky; if the *head*, lucky.

236. Put nothing in your mouth of a morning, till you've had a bite of *bread.*

237. If the first *frog* you see in spring leaps in water and not on land, you may expect misfortune all that year.

238. Move into a new dwelling with a *waxing moon* or at *full moon;* and carry *bread* and *salt* into it, then everybody in it will be full and want for nothing.

239. If you hear *horses neigh*, listen attentively, they announce good luck.

240. If a woman in the six weeks *spin* wool, hemp or flax, the child will be hanged some day.

241. Women shall not brush or plait themselves on a *Friday*, it breeds vermin.

242. If you find money before breakfast, and there is *no wood under it*, it is unlucky.

243. He that was born on a *Sunday* is luckier than other men.

244. If after sunrise on Shrove Tuesday you *thrash* in silence, you drive the moles away.

245. Stand with your face to the *waning moon*, and say : ' Like the moon from day to day, Let my sorrows wear away ' (see 492).

246. Don't leave the *oven-fork* in the oven; if you do, the witches can take a dollar a day from the house.

247. Nothing out of the way shall be built, planted or planned in a *Leap-year :* it does not prosper.

248. If in going out your clothes *get caught in the door* or *on the latch*, stay a while where you are, or you'll meet with a mishap.

249. Pare your nails on a *Friday*, and you have luck (see 340).

250. If you lay a *broom* in a witch's way, so that she must step over it, she turns faint, and can plot no mischief.

251. He that has about him an *owl's* heart, or the stone out of a *bat's* back, or a *hoopoo's* head, will have luck in play (see 329).

252. When the *candle* at night burns *roses* (forms a death's head), there's money or some luck coming next day.

253. Of the *first corn* brought in at harvest, take a few of the first sheaves, and lay them cross-wise *in the four corners of the barn ;* then the *dragon* can't get any of it.

254. If it freezes *on the shortest day*, corn falls in price ; if it is mild, it rises.

255. As many grains as the *theuerlings* (dear-lings, a kind of mushroom) have in them, so many groschen will corn be worth from that time.

256. If you search in vain for something that must be there, the *devil* is holding his hand or tail over it.

257. On your way to market, see that no one *meets* you *carrying water ;* else you'd better turn back, you'll have no luck buying or selling.

258. By the grain of the *first sheaf you thrash*, you may guess the rise or fall in the price of corn, thus : fill and empty a *measure* four times, making *four heaps ;* then put the heaps back into the measure, and level off. If grains fall from any heap, or if they seem short, then in the corresponding quarter of the coming year corn will fall or rise.

259. Lay by some *bread* from your wedding, and you'll never want it.

260. He that keeps and carries about him the bit of coat he brought into the world (the *glücks-haube*), will prosper in everything.

261. He that has about him a bitten-off *mole's paw*, will buy cheap and sell dear.

262. Deduct nothing from the cost of making a child's *first dress;* the more you take off, the less luck he'll have.

263. If the seed you are going to sow be laid *on the table*, it will not come up.

264. The *first baking* after Newyear's day, make as many little *cakes* as there are people in the house, give each a name, and prick a *hole* in it with your finger: if any one's hole gets baked up, he will die.

265. When a child is going to church *to be christened*, lift him *out through the window :* he'll be the stronger, and live the longer.

266. If you are telling something, and you or anybody *sneeze*, the tale is true.

267. If two people *rock* one child, it is robbed of its *rest*.

268. Never burn *straw* that any one has slept on, else he cannot *rest*.

269. If you are taken ill at *church*, you do not easily recover.

270. He that touches *tinder* with his fingers, cannot make it catch.

271. If you scrape *cheese* on the tablecloth, people will dislike you.

272. He that eats much *mouldy bread*, lives to be old.

273. If the man *sharpen* his *knife* otherwise than on the whetstone, there will be strife in the house.

274. Who eats no *beans* on Christmas-eve, becomes an ass.

275. Who eats not of *nine herbs* on Maundy Thursday, gets the fever.

276. He that *sews* or patches anything on *his own body*, shall always take something in his mouth, or he becomes forgetful.

277. If a child in its first year *smell* at anything, it learns not to smell afterwards.

278. Your *blessed bread* (liebe brot) shall not be left lying on its back.

279. To eat up clean what's on the table makes *fine weather* the next day.

280. Let him that has the *hiccough*, put a bare knife in a can of beer, and take a long draught in one breath.

281. If a sick or dying man has *hen's feathers* under him, he cannot die.

282. To *appease* the *storm-wind, shake a meal-sack clean*, and say : 'There, wind, take that, To make pap for your brat !'

283. If after washing you *wipe your hands on the tablecloth*, you'll get warts.

284. When the *bells* ring thick, there is generally some one just going to die; if the church-bell rings clear, it means a wedding.

285. When a bride is on her way to church, if it *rains*, she has been *crying ;* if the *sun* shines, *laughing*.

286. If some one happens to come where a woman is *churning*, and *counts the hoops* on the churn first up and then down, the butter will not come.

287. It is not good to look *over your fingers* or the flat of your hand.

288. If you give a baby part of a red baked apple to eat the first time instead of pap, it will have *red cheeks*.

289. A baby does not thrive if you call it *würmchen* (mite) or *jäckel*.

290. If the *cat* looks at you while she trims herself, you'll get a dressing or a wigging.

291. A cook that lets the dinner *burn on to* the pot, is betrothed or promised.

292. A maiden who is fond of *cats*, will have a sweet-tempered husband.

293. If a woman with child walk *over a grave*, her child will die.

294. He that has a lawsuit, and *sees his opponent in court before* the opponent sees him, will win his cause.

295. When you are in court, pocket your *knife bare*, and you'll win your cause.

296. When any one, old or young, can get no sleep, put a *ruhe-wisch* (wisp of rest) under his pillow, i.e. straw that breeding women lay under their backs; only you must get it away from them without saying a word.

297. If you *pity cattle* that are being killed, they can't die.

298. Never lay *bread* so that the cut side looks away from the table.

299. If you hear a ghost, *don't look round,* or you'll have your neck wrung.

300. Sow no *wheat* on *Maurice's day,* or it will be blighted.

301. It is not good to look *over your head.*

302. If you *lop a tree* on John's Beheading day, it is sure to wither.

303. If a maid who is *kneading dough* clutch at a lad's face, he'll never get a *beard.*

304. If your first godchild be a *bastard,* you'll be lucky in marriage.

305. When you drink to any one, *don't hand him the jug open.*

306. Whoever can *blow-in* a *blown-out candle,* is a chaste bachelor or maiden.

307. He that makes a *wheel over his gateway,* has luck in his house.

308. If a woman in the six weeks fetches *spring-water,* the spring dries up.

309. If you *turn a plate over* at a meal, the *witches* can share in it.

310. When a *witch* is being led to the stake, don't let her touch the *bare ground.*

311. He that gets a *blister* on his *tongue,* is slandered that moment; let him spit three times, and wish the slanderer all that's bad.

312. A patient that *weeps* and sheds tears, will not die that time.

313. When the *heimen* or *crickets* sing in a house, things go luckily.

314. He that sleeps long grows *white,* and the longer the whiter.

315. If on their *wedding day* a bride or bridegroom have a hurt on them, they'll carry it to the grave with them, it will never heal.

316. If the *moon* looks in at the chamber window, the maid breaks many pots.

317. If anything gets in your *eye,* spit thrice over your left arm, and it will come out.

318. When *fogs* fall in March, a great flood follows 100 days after.

319. He that walks over *nail parings,* will dislike the person they belonged to.

320. If a woman that *suckles a boy,* once puts another's child, which

is a *girl*, to her breast, the two children when grown up will come to shame together.

321. He that walks with only *one shoe* or stocking on, will have a cold in his head.

322. When the *fire* in the oven *pops*, there will be quarrelling in the house.

323. Just as long as the *meat* on the table keeps on *fizzing* or simmering, will the cook be beaten by her husband.

324. He whose *women* run away, and whose *horses* stay, will be rich.

325. When the candle *goes out of itself*, some one in the house will die.

326. He that smells at the *flowers* or *wreaths* at a *funeral*, will lose his smell.

327. If you cut off a *stalk of rosemary*, and put it in a dead man's grave, the whole plant withers as soon as the branch in the grave rots.

328. When you eat eggs, crush the shells (witches nestle in them), or some one may get the fever.

329. He that has on him a *moleskin* purse with a *hoopoo's head* and penny piece inside, is never without money (see 251).

330. When the *wind* blows on a *New-year's night*, it is a sign of pestilence.

331. If a man eating soup lays his *spoon* on the table, and it falls with its inner side up, he has not had enough; he must go on eating, till the spoon turns its outer side up.

332. If you cut *bread* at table, and happen to cut one more slice than there are people, there's a hungry guest on the road.

333. If you wear something sewed with *thread spun on Christmas eve*, no vermin will stick to you.

334. Never point with your fingers at the *moon* or *stars* in the sky, it hurts the eyes of the angels (see 937).

335. Keep a *cross-bill* in the house, and the lightning will not strike.

336. In *brewing*, lay a bunch of great *stinging-nettles* on the vat, and the thunder will not spoil the beer.[1]

337. If a woman with child has gone beyond her time, and lets a *horse eat out of her apron*, she has an easy labour.

338. When a wedding pair join hands before the altar, the one whose *hand* is *coldest* will die first.

339. He that *steals* anything at Christmas, New-year, and Twelfthday-eve, without being caught, can *steal safely* for a year.

340. To *cut* the finger and toe *nails* on *Friday* is good for the toothache.

341. At Martinmas you can tell if the winter will be cold or not, by the *goose's breastbone* looking white or brown (see H, ch. 121).

342. Let farmers baptize their maids or souse them with water, when they bring the *first grass* in the year, and they will not sleep at grass-cutting.

343. As a rule, when a *tempest* blows, some one has hung himself.

---

[1] The *thunder-nettle* resists thunder, and is therefore put to young beer, to keep it from turning. On *Grün-donnerstag* (Maundy Thursday) young *nettles* are boiled and eaten with meat. Dav. Frank's Mecklenbg 1, 59.

344. Hens hatched out of eggs that were laid on *Maundy Thursday* change their colour every year.

345. When a child is taken out of doors, don't keep the *upper half of the door* closed, or it will stop growing.

346. If *feathers picked up* on a bourn (between two fields) are put in a bed, a child can't sleep in it; if it is a marriage-bed, the man and wife will part.

347. If you *sing* while you brew, the beer turns out well.

348. Salute the returning *stork*, and you won't have the toothache.

349. When you go out in the morning, tread the *threshold* with your *right foot*, and you'll have luck that day.

350. When a *foot-bath* has been used, don't empty it till next day, or you spill your luck away with it.

351. If you happen to find the *felloe* of an *old wheel*, and throw it into the barn in the name of the H. Trinity, mice will not hurt your corn.

352. A silver ring made of *begged penny-pieces*, and worn on the finger, is sovereign against all diseases.

353. Don't keep putting the *bathing towel* on and off the child, or it will have no abiding place when old.

354. Before a wedding, the bridegroom shall *broach* the beer-cask, and put the tap in his pocket, lest bad people should do him a mischief.

355. Hang your clothes in the sun on *Good Friday*, and neither moth nor woodlouse can get in.

356. Suffer thirst on *Good Friday*, and no drink will hurt you for a year (see 913).

357. In walking to your wedding, it is *not good to look round*.

358. On coming home from your wedding, make a *black hen* run in at the door (or window) first, and any mischief to be feared will fall on the hen.

359. In moving to another town or dwelling, if you lose *bread* on the way, you forfeit your food ever after.

360. In walking into a room, it is *not good to turn round* in the doorway.

361. A woman that has a cold in her head, shall smell in her husband's shoes.

362. After pulling a *splinter* out, chew it to pieces, lest it do more harm.

363. If another looks on while you *strike a light*, the tinder won't catch.

364. If a *woman with child* jump over a pipe through which a bell is being cast, it will lighten her labour.

365. A man can *pray* his enemy *dead* by repeating Psalm 109 every night and morning for a year; but if he miss a day he must die himself.

366. If you steal hay the *night before Christmas*, and give the cattle some, they thrive, and you are not caught in any future thefts.

367. Some houses or stables will not endure *white cattle* : they die off, or get crushed.

368. If a *corpse* looks *red* in the face, one of the friends will soon follow.

369. If after a Christmas dinner you shake out the tablecloth over the bare ground under the open sky, *brosam-kraut* (crumb-wort) will grow on the spot.

370. If you drink in the mines you must not say 'glück zu,' but 'glück auf,' lest the building tumble down.

371. In a dangerous place, if you have a *donkey* with you, the devil can do you no harm.

372. Put feathers in a bed when the *moon's on the wane*, they'll very soon creep out again.

373. If you *twist a willow* to tie up wood in a stable where hens, geese or ducks are sitting, the chickens they hatch will have crooked necks.

374. If you have no money the first time you hear the *cuckoo* call, you'll be short of it all that year.

375. A baby left *unchristened* long, gets fine *large eyes*.

376. If a maiden would have *long hair*, let her lay some of her hair in the ground along with hop-shoots.

377. It is not good to beat a beast with the *rod with which a child has been chastised.*

378. Every *swallow* you have slain makes a month of steady rain.

379. A child's first fall does not hurt it.

380. He that walks between *two old women* in the morning, has no luck that day (see 58).

381. When *swallows* build new nests on a house, there will be a death in it that year.

382. When the cats eat their food up clean, *corn* will be dear; if they leave scraps lying, the price will fall, or remain as it is.

383. To get rid of the *rose* (St. Anthony's fire), have *sparks* dropt on it from flint and steel by one of the same christian-name.

384. In cutting *grafts*, let them not fall on the ground, or the fruits will fall before their time.

385. A *spur* made out of a *gibbet-chain* without using fire, will tame a hard-mouthed horse or one that has the staggers.

386. Hang in the dove-cot a *rope* that has strangled a man, and the doves will stay.

387. He that has *all-men's-armour* (wild garlic) on him can't be wounded.

388. It is not good to burn *brooms* up.

389. In a lying-in room lay a *straw* out of the woman's bed at every door, and neither ghost nor *Jüdel* can get in.

390. A *bride* that means to have the mastery, shall *dawdle*, and let the bridegroom get to church before her.

391. Or: after the wedding she shall hide her *girdle* in the *threshold* of the house, so that he shall step over it.

392. She must eat of the *caudle*, or when she comes to suckle, her breasts will have no milk.

393. On no account shall married people eat of the *house-cock.*

394. He that sells beer, shall lay his first earnings *under the tap*, till the cask is emptied.

395. If you burn *wheat-straw*, the wheat in the field will turn sooty that year.

396. Of a *firstborn calf* let no part be roasted, else the cow dries up.

397. Let no *tears* drop on the *dead*, else he cannot *rest*.

398. When one is *attired* by another, she must not thank her, else the finery will not fit her.

399. The fruit-trees must not see a *distaff* in the Twelves, or they'll bear no fruit.

400. A *maid who is leaving* must make one more mess of pottage, and eat it.

401. He that mows grass shall *whet his scythe* every time he leaves off, and not put it away or take it home unwhetted.

402. When girls are going to a dance, they shall put *zehrwurzel-kraut* in their shoes, and say : ' Herb, I put thee in my shoe, All you young fellows come round me, do ! '

403. When the *sun* does not shine, all treasures buried in the earth are open.

404. If your flax does not thrive, steal a little *linseed,* and mix it with yours.

405. Put the *first yarn* a child spins on the *millwheel* of a watermill, and she will become a firstrate spinner.

406. If clothes in the *wash* be left hanging out till sunset, he that puts them on will bewitch everybody.

407. He that comes in during a meal shall *eat with you,* if only a morsel.

408. If a woman with child step over a *rope* by which a mare has been tied, she will go two months over her time.

409. The *first meat* you give a child shall be roast lark.

410. If a pure maiden *step over* a woman *in labour,* and in doing so drop her *girdle* on her, the woman shall have a quick recovery.

411. When the carpenter knocks the *first nail* in a new house, if *fire leap out of it,* the house will be burnt down (see 500. 707).

412. When the flax-sower comes to the flax-field, let him three times sit down *on the bagful* of seed, and rise again : it will be good.

413. If *sparks of fire* spirt out of a candle when lighted, the man they fly at will get money that day.

414. Beware of washing in water warmed with *old waggon-wheels.*

415. If a child is backward in speaking, take two loaves that have stuck together in baking, and *break them loose over his head.*

416. Strike no man or beast with a *peeled rod,* lest they dry up.

417. *Pick no fruit* [bruise no malt ?] in the Twelves, or apples and pears will spoil.

418. Do no *thrashing* in the Twelves, or all the corn *within hearing of the sound* will spoil (see 916).

419. A shirt, sewed with thread *spun in the Twelves,* is good for many things.

420. He that walks into the *winter corn* on Holy Christmas-eve, hears all that will happen in the village that year.

421. Let not the *light go out* on Christmas-eve, or one in the house will die.

422. It is not good when a *stool* lies *upside down,* with its legs in the air.

423. If a man *puts on a woman's cap,* the *horses* will *kick* him.

424. In sweeping a room, don't *sprinkle it with hot water*, or those in the house will quarrel.

425. As the bride goes to church, *throw the keys after her*, and she'll be economical.

426. On her return from church, meet her with *cake* cut in slices; every guest take a slice, and push it against the bride's body.

427. When the bridegroom fetches home the bride, let her on the way *throw some flax away*, and her flax will thrive.

428. If an infant ride on a *black foal* it will cut its teeth quickly.

429. Move to a new house at *new moon*, and your provisions will increase.

430. If you have *schwaben* (black worms), steal a *drag* (hemm-schuh) and put it on the oven, and they'll go away (see 607).

431. Put a stolen *sand-clout* (-wisch) in the hens' food, and they won't hide their eggs.

432. At harvest, make the *last sheaf* up very big, and your next crop will be so good that every sheaf can be as large.

433. When *dogs* fight at a wedding, the happy pair will come to blows.

434. Hit a man with the *aber-rück* of a distaff, and he'll get an *aber-bein*.

435. If the latch catch, and not the match, a guest will come next day.

436. After making thread, don't throw the *thread-water* where people will pass ; one that walks over it will be subject to giddiness.

437. If you *sneeze* when you get up in the morning, lie down again for another three hours, or your wife will be master for a week.

438. When you buy a *new knife*, give the first morsel you cut with it to a dog, and you will not lose the knife.

439. If a dying man cannot die, *push the table out of its place, or turn a shingle* on the roof (see 721).

440. If you sit down on a *water-jug*, your stepmother will dislike you.

441. If you keep *pigeons*, do not talk of them at dinner-time, or they'll escape, and settle somewhere else.

442. He that sets out *before the table is cleared*, will have a toilsome journey.

443. When children are 'becried' and cannot sleep, take some *earth off the common*, and strew it over them.

444. To look through a *bottomless pot* gives one the headache.

445. In the bridechamber let the inschlit-light *burn quite clean out*.

446. On the three Christmas-eves save up all the *crumbs :* they are good to give as physic to one who is *disappointed*.

447. If you are having a coat made, let no one else try it on, or it won't fit you.

448. If two eat *off one plate*, they will become enemies.

449. Light a *match at both ends*, you're putting brands in the witches' hands.

450. When *fire* breaks out in a house, slide the *baking oven* out ; the flame will take after it.

451. Let a woman that goes to be churched have *new shoes* on, or her child will have a bad fall when it has learnt to run alone.

452. A *spoon*-stealer keeps his mouth open in death.

453. If you happen to *spit* on yourself, you will hear some news.

454. When cows growl in the night, the *Jüdel* is playing with them.

455. If women with child go to the *bleaching*, they get white children.

456. A bride at her wedding shall wear an *old blue apron* underneath.

457. Put your *shoes wrong-wise* at the head of your bed, and the *alp* will not press you that night.

458. If she that is confined stick *needles* in the curtains, the babe will have bad teeth.

459. If a *woman with child* tie a *cord* round her waist, her child will be hanged.

460. If she that is confined *handle dough*, the child's hands will chap.

461. If *glasses break* at a wedding, the wedded pair will not be rich.

462. The first time cows are driven to pasture in spring, let them be milked through a *wreath* of *ground-ivy* (gunder-man).

463. He that goes to church on Walburgis-day with a *wreath* of *ground-ivy* on his head, can recognise all the witches.

464. Cows that have calved, the peasants in Thuringia lead over *three-fold iron*.

465. If a woman with child follow a *criminal* going to execution, or merely cross the path he has gone, her child will die the same death.

466. Mix the milk of *two men's cows*, and the cows of one will dry up.

467. Give no thanks for *given milk*, or the cow dries up.

468. As often as the *cock crows* on Christmas-eve, the quarter of corn that year will be as dear.

469. On Ash-Wednesday the *devil* hunts the *little woodwife* in the wood.

470. He that deals in *vinegar* must lend none, even should the borrower leave no more than a pin in pledge.

471. For headache, wash in water that *rebounds off a mill-wheel* (see 766).

472. A *cock built into a wall* brings a long spell of good weather.

473. If the *Jüdel* has burnt a child, smear the oven's mouth with bacon-rind.

474. If a child has the *freisig* (lockjaw?), cover its head with an inherited fish-kettle, and force its mouth open with an inherited key.

475. *Water* cannot abide a *corpse*.

476. Throw *devil's bit* under the table, and the guests will quarrel and fight.

477. To get a good crop, go out in silence on a certain day, fetch mould from *three inherited fields*, and mix it with your seed.

### b. From the *Erzgebirge about Chemnitz*.

(Journal von und für Deutschland 1787. 1, 186-7. 261-2).

478. At the first bidding of the banns the *betrothed* shall not be present.

479. On a *barren* wife throw a *tablecloth* that has served at a first christening dinner.

480. At a wedding or christening dinner let the *butter-dishes* have been begun, or the bachelors there will get *baskets* (the sack) when they woo.

481. When the bride goes from her seat to the altar, let the bridesmaids *close up quickly*, lest the seat grow *cold*, and the bride and bridegroom's love cool also.

482. If there is a *grave open* during a wedding, all depends on whether it is for a man, woman or child; in the first case the bride will be a widow, in the second the bridegroom a widower, in the last their children will die soon.

483. If a *girl* meets a wedding pair, their first child will be a daughter; if a *boy*, a son; if a boy and girl together, there will be twins.

484. Put a *key* beside the baby, and it cannot be changed.

485. Of a wedding pair, whichever gets *out of bed* first will die first.

486. The godmothers help in making the bridal bed, the straws are put in one by one, and care is taken that no stranger come into the bride-chamber. The bed must not be beaten, but softly stroked, else the wife will get beatings.

487. If a *pillow* fall off the bridal bed, the one that lay on it will die first.

488. On the wedding day, man and wife must *wash crosswise*, then they can't be becried (bewitched).

489. Of the *wedding bread* and roll, some shall be saved, that man and wife may not want. Such bread does not get mouldy, and a piece of it put in their pottage is good for pregnant women who have no appetite.

490. At the prayer for the sick, if there is *perfect silence*, the sick man dies; if any one coughs or makes a noise, he gets well.

491. If a sick man, after receiving the sacrament, ask for food, he will die; if for drink, he will recover.

492. For increasing goitre or warts, fix your eyes on the *waxing moon*, and say three times: 'May what I see increase, may what I suffer cease,' (see 245).

493. *Dogs howling* foretell a fire or a death.

494. *New servants* must not go to church the first Sunday, or they'll never get used to the place.

495. Whatever dishes the sponsor *does not eat* of at the christening-feast, the child will get a dislike for.

496. *Crows cawing* round the house mean a corpse, if only of a beast.

497. If the *church clock* strike while the *death-bell tolls*, there will die in the parish a man, a youth, or a child, according as it is the great, the middle, or the small bell.

498. No bride shall move in when the *moon's on the wane* (see 238); but wealth she will win, who comes riding through rain (198).

499. When you move into a new house, *throw* something alive in first, a *cat* or *dog*: for the first to enter a house is the first to die.

500. When carpenters are felling timber for a new building, if *sparks fly out at the first stroke*, the building will burn down (see 411).

501. Before you go into the sitting-room of your new house, peep *into the copper*, to get used to the place. The same rule for new servants

(see 95); beside which, they have to *creep between the legs* of their masters.

502. Journeymen, the first time they travel, must *not look round*, or they'll be homesick, and can't stay anywhere.

503. Let no strangers into the stable at *milking* time.

504. After candles are lighted, don't *empty a washhand basin* in the street, or the family will fall out the next day.

505. When children shed their first *teeth*, let the father *swallow* the daughter's teeth, and the mother the son's; the children will never have toothache then.

### c. From the *Saalfeld country*.

(Journ. v. u. f. D. 1790. pp. 26—29; conf. Sächs. Provinz. bl. 5, 499—512).

506. On Christmas-eve the girls sit up from 11 to 12. To find out if they shall get married the next year, they *strip themselves naked*, stick their heads into the copper, and watch the *water hissing*.

507. If that does not answer, they take a broom and *sweep the room backwards*, and see the future lover sitting in a corner: if they hear the crack of a whip, he is a waggoner, if the sound of a pipe, a shepherd.

508. Some *rush out of doors naked*, and call the lover; others go to a *cross-road*, and call out his name.

509. A *woman who is confined* must never be left alone; the devil has more hold upon her then.

510. She dare not *sleep* unless some one *watches* by the child, for a *changeling* is often put in the cradle. Let the husband's trowsers be thrown over it.

511. The village children dread the *minister*. The unruliest is hushed by the threat: ' Sit still, or *parson* 'll come and put you in the pitch-pot.'

512. If a girl has *not cleared her distaff* the last day of the year, it is defiled by *Bergda*: this *Bergda* is a shaggy monster.

513. A bride preserves her *bridal wreath* and a piece of *wedding bread;* so long as she keeps that hardened lump, she never wants bread. When man and wife are weary of life, *they eat it soaked in pottage.*

514. After the wedding, one of the bridesmaids hurries home first, gets beer or brandy, and offers a glass to the bridegroom, who empties it and tosses it behind his back: if the *glass breaks*, it is good; if not, not.

515. If one is taken ill suddenly without cause, a *sage old woman* goes, *without greeting* any one, *draws water* from a spring, and drops three coals into it; *if they sink*, he is ' becried '; she then draws nigh, and sprinkles him three times with the water, *muttering:* ' Art thou a wife, let it light on thy life! art thou a maid, may it fall on thy head! art thou a servant, thou art served as thou *hast well* deserved ! ' (See 865.)

516. When cattle are first driven out in spring, *axes, saws* and other iron tools are laid *outside the stable-door*, to keep them from being bewitched.

517. On the great festivals, women do not work after church, or they would be *lamed* and *struck by lightning* (the clouds would come after them).

518. In setting cabbages, women say : ' Stalks (? dursche) like my leg, heads like my head, leaves like my apron, such be my cabbages ! '

519. *Flax* is thus adjured : ' Flax, don't flower till you're up to my knee, etc.' On St John's night the girls, *dance round the flax*, they *strip themselves naked*, and wallow in it.

520. When the *dragon* is taking eggs, butter, cheese and lard to his worshippers, call out the Saviour's name several times, and he'll drop them all.

521. If the bride is coming to her husband's homestead, and the *shepherd drives his sheep* in her way, let her give him a fee, and she'll have luck.

522. If a *whirlwind* falls on the aftermath, 'tis the Evil One wishing to convey it to those who serve him. Cry out, and call him foul names.

523. The hare with his front-teeth often cuts a path across whole corn-fields. They call it *pilsen-schneiden*, and think the *devil* cuts the corn and carries it to his good friends.

524. Old women often cut out a *turf a foot long*, on which their enemy has trodden just before, and hang it up in the chimney : the enemy then wastes away (see 556).

525. On the last day of the year, many eat *dumplings* (strötzel) and *herrings*, else *Perchte* would cut their belly open, take out what they have eaten, and sew up the gash with a *ploughshare* for needle, and a *röhm-chain* for thread.

526. The fire is kept in *all night* before *Christmas day*.

527. He that goes *to the beer on Newyear's day*, grows young and ruddy.

528. A dream in *Newyear's night* comes true.

529. If the butter won't come, put a *fire-steel* or *knife* under the churn.

530. When your hands are soiled with setting cabbages, *wash* them in a *large tub*, and the cabbage will have large heads.

531. In *setting cabbages* a girl can find out if she'll ever get the man she loves. She nips a piece off the root of one seedling, splits the remaining part, and puts the root of another through it ; the two plants are then set close to a stone, and squeezed together tight. If they stick, the marriage will come about.

532. If you force a man to sell you something *cheap*, it won't last you long.

533. In sowing flax, *throw the cloth* that held the seed *high up in the air :* the flax will grow the higher.

d. From *Worms and its neighbourhood*.

(Journ. v. u. f. D. 1790. pp. 142-3-4.)

534. A *crackling fire* betokens strife.

535. So does *spilt salt*.

536. So do *yellow spots* on your finger : if they are too large to be *covered with a finger*, the strife will be serious.

537. If the *left ear sings*, evil is spoken of you, if the *right ear*, good.

538. Let no *fire, salt* or *bread* be given out of a house where a woman lies in.

539. He that has on him a *harrow-nail* (-tooth ?) found on the highway, can recognise all witches (see 636).

540. *Red milk* of a bewitched cow shall be *whipt with switches* while boiling : the pain makes the witch reveal herself and heal the cow.

541. He that goes out *unwashed* is easily bewitched.

542. *Ringing consecrated bells* on Walburgis-night hinders the witches that dance with the devil on cross-roads from hurting any one.

543. If a *coffin* rings *hollow* in nailing down, one more in the house will die.

544. He that is in great trouble shall touch the *great toe of a dead man*.

545. The dead shall be laid with their face *to the east*, lest they be scared by the *winseln* (?) that *swarm from the west*.

546. *Combs, knives, cloths*, used about a dead man, shall be laid in the *coffin*, and be buried with him.

547. If a *pregnant woman* lift a child from the font, either that child or her own will die.

548. If a *loaf* be laid on its brown side, witches can walk in.

549. If a *yellow-footed hen* flies over a jaundiced man, he can't be cured.

550. To sow a strife 'twixt man and wife, *press a padlock* home, while parson makes them one.

551. If a *garment* or *linen* come *before* a dead man's *mouth*, one of the family will die.

552. When there's death in a house, *knock at the wine-casks*, or the wine spoils.

553. If *thirteen* eat at a table, one is sure to die.

554. Into a *whirlwind* fling a knife with crosses on it, and you know the witches who made it.

555. If a *mole* burrow in the house (see 601), and the *cricket* chirp, some one will die; also if the *hen* crow, or the *screech-owl* shriek.

556. If one steals in rainy weather, *cut out his footprint* and hang it in the chimney : the thief will waste away with the footprint (see 524).

557. *Combed-out hair*, if thrown on the highway, lays you open to witch-craft (see 676).


*e.* From *Gernsbach in the Spire Country.*

(Journ. v. u. f. D. 1787. 1, 454·5·6.)

558. Bride and bridegroom, on your way to church avoid the *house-eaves*, and do *not look round*.

559. *Stand close together* before the altar, lest witches creep in between you.

560. During the wedding whichever of you has your *hand above the other's*, shall have the mastery.

561. Let a woman with child, when she has a wash, *turn the tubs upside down* as soon as done with, and she'll have an easy confinement.

562. If sponsors on the christening day put *clean shirts and shifts* on, no witch can get at the child.

563. If at night there's a knock at the door of the lying-in room, never open till you've asked *three times* who it is, and been answered three times; no witch can answer *three times*.

564. In swaddling the babe, wrap a little *bread* and *salt* in.

565. In the bed or cradle hide a *sword* or *knife* with its point sticking out: if the unholde tries to get over mother or child, she'll fall upon it.

566. If at the wash a woman *borrows lye* and *thanks you for it*, she's a witch.

567. A woman that *plumps butter* on a *Wednesday*, is a witch.

568. If you go out and are greeted with 'good morning,' never answer '*thank you*,' but only 'good morning'; then, if one of the greeters be a witch, she cannot hurt.

569. If your hens, ducks, pigs etc., die fast, light a *fire in the oven*, and throw one of each kind in: the witch will perish with them (see 645).

570. When a witch walks into your house, give her a piece of *bread* with *three grains of salt* sprinkled on it, and she can't hurt anything.

571. If the cloth is laid *wrong side up*, people can never eat their fill.

572. If you leave it *on the table all night*, the angels won't protect you.

573. Smear a goitre with the wick out of a lamp that has burnt in a *dying man's room*, and it will heal.

574. If you make a promise to a child, and *do not uphold it*, it will have a bad fall.

575. If a woman set her hen to hatch with her *garters dangling*, her *hair streaming* and her *worst frock on*, she'll have chickens with knobs on their heads and feathery feet (see 19).

576. If any one dies in the house, *shift the beehives, shake the vinegar and wine;* or bees, wine and vinegar will go bad (see 664, 698, 898).

577. When you buy poultry, lead them three times round the *table's foot*, cut a chip off each *corner of the table* to put in their food, and they will stay (see 615).

578. The first time a pig is driven to pasture, make it jump over a *piece of your apron*, and it will readily come home (see 615).

579. If a girl on St Andrew's night melt some *lead* in a spoon, and *pour* it through a *key* that has a cross in its wards, *into water* that was drawn between 11 and 12, it will take the shape of her future husband's tools of trade.

580. To measure a child for clothes *in its first year*, spoils its figure.

581. A *mouse's head* bitten off with teeth, or cut off with gold, and hung about a child, helps it to teethe.

582. The same if you *give* a child an *egg* the first time it comes into a house; though some say it makes them talkative.

*f*. From *Pforzheim*.

(Journ. v. u. f. D. 1787. 2, 341—345.)

583. A *seven year old cock* lays a small egg, which must be thrown over the roof, or lightning will strike the house; if hatched, it yields a *basilisk*.

584. If you've a cold, drink a glass of water through a *three-pronged fork*.

585. He that eats a *raw egg* fasting on Christmas morning, can carry heavy weights.

586. Eat *lentils* on Good Friday, and you'll not be out of money for a year.

587. If the *stork* does not finish hatching an egg, one of the highest in the land will die.

588. *White spirits* such as have buried money when alive, must hover between heaven and earth.

589. At an *eclipse of the sun*, cover the wells, or the water becomes poisonous.

590. If you leave a glass of wine standing between eleven and twelve on Newyear's night, and *it runs over*, the vintage will be good that year.

591. In going out, put your *right foot* out of the door first.

592. *Lizards* were once maidens.

593. A child cannot die peacefully on *fowls' feathers*.

594. It is unlucky to *yoke oxen* on Innocents' day.

595. If you *cross a bridge* or see a *shooting star*, say the Lord's prayer.

396. If you lay a knife down *edge upwards*, you cut the face of God or those of the angels.

597 If you carry a rake *teeth upwards*, or *point up* with your finger, it will prick God's eyes out : it also destroys the *rainbow*.

598. Where the *rainbow* touches the earth, there is a *golden dish.*

599. The gravedigger's *spade clatters* when a grave is bespoke.

600. *Crickets, dogs* and *waybirds* foretell a death by their cry.

601. If a *mole* burrows under the room, the *grandmother* dies (see 555).

602. If the *palace-clock* is out of order, one of the reigning family dies.

603. If *clocks* strike while bells ring for prayers, some one dies.

604. He that *dawdles* makes the devil's bed (see 659).

605. Whoever commits a crime that is not found out in his lifetime, *walks* after death with his *head under his arm.*

606. He that buries money must *walk* after death, until it is found.

607. If you don't pray, the *schwaben* (black worms) steal flour out of your bin.

608. *Schwaben* are got rid of by being put in a box and given to a dead man.

609. *Swallow's nests* and *crickets* bring a blessing to the house.

610. *Don't beat down* the joiner's charge for the *coffin*, if the dead are to rest.

611. Cry to the fiery man : '*Steuble, Steuble*, hie thee, Be the sooner by me!' then *Will wi' the wisp* will come, and you must take him on your back. If you pray, he approaches ; if you curse, he flees.

612. If you find a *treasure*, don't cover it with any clothing worn *next* the skin, or you're a dead man ; but with a handkerchief, a crust of bread. The treasure appears once in seven years.

613. *Wednesday* and *Friday* are accursed witch-days. Pigs first driven to pasture on a *Wednesday*, don't come home ; a child begins school on *Wednesday*, and learns nothing. On *Wednesday* nobody gets married, no maid goes to a new place.

614. Every one has his star. *Stars are eyes of men* [ON.].

615. The first time pigs cross the threshold, make them jump over the *wife's garter*, the *man's girdle*, or the *maid's apron*, and they'll come home regularly (see 578).

616. When a fowl is bought, chase it *three times round the table*, give it *wood off three corners of the table* with its food, and it will stay (see 577).

617. If you lose a fowl, tie a farthing in the corner of a tablecloth upstairs, and let the *corner hang out of window :* the fowl will come back.

618. If you creep *under a carriage-pole*, or let any one *step over you*, you'll stop growing (see 45).

619. Creep *between* a cow's *forelegs*, and she'll never lose a horn.

620. *Pigs* bathed in water in which a swine has been scalded, grow famously.

621. He that stares at a tree on which a *female* sits, is struck *blind*.

622. To make a *nut-tree* bear, let a *pregnant* woman pick the first nuts.

623. If you've the *gout*, go into the fields at prayer-bell time on a Friday.

624. *Rain-water* makes children talk soon.

625. If you laugh till your eyes run over, there will be quarrels.

626. If you are in league with the *devil*, and want to cheat him, *don't wash or comb for seven years ;* or else ask him to make a *little tree grow*, which he can't, and so you are rid of him.

627. The *thorn-twister* (a bird) carries thorns to Our Lord's crown.

628. The *swallow* mourns for Our Lord.

629. If you pull down a *redbreast's* nest, your cow will give *red milk*, or *lightning* will strike your house.

630. When a *tooth* is pulled out, nail it into a young tree, and draw the bark over it; if the tree is cut down, the toothache will return. Take a *sliver* out of a *willow*, and pick your bad tooth till it bleeds, put the sliver back in its place, with the bark over it, and your toothache will go.

631. When a *tooth* falls out, put it in a *mousehole*, and say : 'Give me, mouse, a tooth of bone, You may have this wooden one.' [Rääf 130].

632. If a woman dies in *childbed*, give her *scissors* and *needlecase* (yarn, thread, needle and thimble), or she'll come and fetch them.

633. When a child is dead, it visits the person it was *fondest* of.

634. One *born on a Sunday* can see *spirits*, and has to carry them pick-a-back.

635. Nail up *three pigeon's feathers* of the left wing inside the cot, swing the pigeons you let in *three times round the leg*, and don't let their first flight be on a Friday.

636. Have about you a *harrow tooth* found on a Sunday, and you'll see the *witches* at church *with tubs on their heads ;* only get out before the P.N. is rung, or they'll tear you to pieces (see 539. 685. 783).

637. A child in the cradle, who *does not look* at you, is a *witch*.

638. Take a *crossed knife* with you at night, and a witch can't get near

you; if she comes, *throw the knife at her*, and she'll stand there till day-light.

639. If the *eldest child* in the house ties up the *calf*, witches can't get at it.

640. If a *goat* in the stable is *black all over*, the witch can't get in; nor if the cow has *white feet* and a *white stripe* on her back.

641. Any beast with a *black throat* you've no hold upon.

642. If you are afraid of a witch at night, turn your *left shoe* round.

643. If you meet a *doubtful-looking cat*, hold your thumb towards her.

644. A *drud's foot* (pentagram) on the door keeps witches away.

645. If a thing is bewitched, and you *burn* it, the witch is sure to come, wanting to *borrow* something: give it, and she is free; deny it, and she too must burn (see 569. 692).

646. If your cattle are bewitched, go into the stable at midnight, and you'll find a *stalk of straw* lying on their backs: put it in a sack, call your neighbours in, and *thrash the sack;* it will swell up, and the witch will scream (see 692).

647. Witches pick up money at the *cross-ways*, where the devil scatters it.

648. They can make rain, thunder and a *wind*, which sweeps up the *cloth* on the *bleaching ground*, the *hay* in the *meadow*.

649. They *anoint* a *stick* with the words: 'Away we go, not too high and not too low!'

650. When a witch has *gone up* (in ecstasis), turn her body upside down, and she can't come in again.

651. Under *bewitched water*, that will not boil, put *wood of three kinds*.

652. If a child is 'becried,' let its father fetch *three stalks of straw* from different dung-heaps unbecried, and lay them under its pillow.

### g.  From *Würtemberg*.

(Journ. v. u. f. D. 1788. 2, 183-4).

653. Give no *milk* out of the house without mixing a *drop of water* with it.

654. On the day a woman *is delivered*, or a horse *gelded*, lend nothing out of the house, lest horse or woman be bewitched.

655. If in bed you turn your feet *towards the window*, you get the con-sumption.

656. A *shirt spun by a girl* of from 5 to 7 makes you magic-proof.

657. When a spectre leads you astray, *change shoes* at once, *put your hat on another way*, and you'll get into the right road again.

658. If you talk of witches on a *Wednesday* or *Friday* night, they hear it, and avenge themselves.

659. Who *runs not as he might*, runs into the devil's arms (see 604).

660. Children *dying unbaptized* join the Furious Host.

661. If a bride at the altar *kneels* on the bridegroom's *cloak*, she gets the *upper hand*. And if she gets into bed first, and makes him hand her a glass of water, she is sure to be master.

662. Of a wedded pair, the one that first *rises from the altar* will die first.

663. If at the altar they stand so far apart that you can *see between them*, they'll pull two ways.

664. When a sick man is dying, *open the windows*, and *stop up* all in the house that is *hollow*, or turn it over, so that the soul may have free exit. Also *shift* the *vinegar*, the *birdcage*, the *cattle*, the *beehives* (see 576. 698).

665. See that the dead on the bier have no *corner* of the *shroud in their mouth*.

666. *Fold* your *thumb in*, and dogs cannot bite you.

667. Set the *churn* on a 'handzwehl,' and put a comb under it, and you'll have plenty of rich butter.

668. The first time you hear the *cuckoo* call in spring, *shake your money* unbecried, and you'll never run short.

669. The boundary where a suicide is buried, will be *struck by lightning* three years running.

670. The farmer that goes into another's stable for the first time without saying ' Luck in here ! ' is a witch-master.

671. Step into a court of justice *right foot* foremost, and you'll win.

### *h.* From *Swabia.*

#### (Journ. v. u. f. D. 1790. 1, 441.)

672. Let a woman in childbed take her first medicine out of her *husband's spoon*.

673. In the pains of labour, let her put on her *husband's slippers*.

674. Put water under her bed without her knowing it.

675. A child under three, pushed in through a *peep-window*, stops growing.

676. Hair that is cut off shall be burnt, or thrown into *running water*. If a bird carry it away, the person's hair will fall off (see 557).

677. If a child *learning to talk* says 'father' first, the next child will be a boy; if 'mother,' a girl.

678. If a man drink out of a *cracked glass*, his wife will have nothing but girls.

679. When you've *bought a cat*, bring it in with its head *facing the street* and not the house; else it will not stay.

### *i.* From the *Ansbach country.*

#### (Journ. v. u. f. D. 1786. 1, 180-1.)

680. She that *spins* on *Saturday* evening will walk after she is dead.

681. If a dead man's *linen* be not washed soon, he cannot *rest*.

682. He that eats *millet-pap* at Shrovetide is never out of money.

683. Spin at *Shrovetide*, and the flax will fail. The wheels must all be packed away.

684. If the farmer is tying *strawbands* at Shrovetide, and uses bu
to a sheaf in a whole stack of corn, no mouse can hurt.

685. Have about you *three grains* found whole in a baked loaf, and on
Walburgis-day you'll see the *witches* and *night-hags* at church with *milkpails on their heads* (see 636. 783).

686. In the Twelve-nights neither master-nor man may bring *fresh-
blackened shoes* into the stable; else the cattle get bewitched.

687. He that cooks or eats *peas* at that time, gets vermin or leprosy.

688. If a pregnant woman pass through the *clothes-lines* or anything
*tangled*, her child will tangle itself as many times as she has passed
through lines.

689. If a child has convulsions, lay a *horseshoe* under its pillow.

690. A sick child gets better, if its godfather carries it three times *up
and down the room*.

691. If a mare foals at the wrong time, she must have stept *over a
plough-fork*. If you knock that to pieces, she can give birth.

692. When bewitched with vermin, wrap three in a paper, and *hammer*
on it. The witch feels every blow, and comes in to borrow something: if
you refuse, she can't get free, and will sink under the blows (see 645-6).

693. Never burn a *broom*, and you are safe from Antony's fire.

694. When the Christmas-tree is lighted, notice the people's *shadows* on
the wall: those that will die within a year appear *without heads*.

695. Draw the *first three corn-blossoms* you see through your mouth, and
eat them: you'll be free from fever for a year (see 784).

696. He that passes *palm-brushes* (catkins) over his face, will have no
freckles.

697. Nor he that washes his face during the *passing-bell* on Good Friday.

698. When a man dies, his *bird-cages, flower-pots* and *beehives* must be
differently placed; and you must knock three times on his *wine-casks*
(see 552. 576. 664).

699. It furthers the dead man's *rest*, if every one that stands round the
grave throws *three clods* in.

700. The *comb* and *knife* that have combed and shaved a dead man, shall
be put in his coffin; or the hair of those who use them will fall off
(see 546).

701. If you leave any of the *bread* set before you, you must at any rate
*stow it away*, or you'll have the toothache.

702. If you hand *bread* to a pregnant woman on the point of a *knife* or
*fork*, her child's eyes will be pricked out.

703. If you *sew* or even *thread a needle* on Ascension day, your house
will be *struck with lightning* (see 772).

704. *Lightning strikes* where a *redstart* builds; but a *swallow's nest*
brings luck (see 629).

705. If children bring home the *female* of a *stagbeetle*, get it out of the
way directly, or *lightning will strike* the house.

706. On *Good Friday* and Saturday one dare not work the ground, for
fear of disquieting the Saviour in the sepulchre.

707. If the *last* nail the carpenter knocks in a new house give fire, it

will burn down (see 411. 500); and if the *glass he throws from the gable* after saying his saw *break*, the builder will die; if not, he will live long.

708. He that comes into court, wearing a *shirt* of which the yarn was spun by a girl of five, will obtain justice in every suit.

709. They put *turf* or a *little board* under a dead man's chin, that he may not catch the *shroud* between his teeth, and draw his relations after him.

710. A girl can be cured of *St Antony's fire* by a pure young man *striking fire* on it several times.

711. Who steps *not barefoot* on the floor on Easterday, is safe from fever.

712. If the first thing you eat on *Good Friday* be an egg that was laid on *Maundy Thursday*, you'll catch no *bodily harm* that year.

713. *Three crumbs of bread, three grains of salt, three coals*, if worn on the person, are a safeguard against sorcery.

714. If a woman getting up from childbed lace a *crust of bread* on her, and make her child a *zuller* or *schlotzer* of it, the child will not have toothache.

715. If on the wedding day the bridegroom *buckle* the bride's *left shoe*, she'll have the mastery.

716. If he tie her *garters* for her, she'll have easy labours.

717. Whichever of them *goes to sleep first*, will die first.

718. If you eat the *first three sloe-blossoms* you see, you'll not have the heartburn all that year.

719. To get rid of freckles, take the *first goslings* without noise, pass them over your face, and make them run backwards.

720. Turn the *loaf* over in the drawer, and the *drude* can't get out of the room.

721. If a man can't die, take up *three tiles in the roof* (see 439).

722. If a child has the *gefrais*, put a *swallow's nest* under his pillow.

723. He that lies on *inherited beds*, cannot die.

### k. From *Austria above Ens.*

(Journ. v. u. f. D. 1787. 1, 469—472.)

724. If a *pregnant* woman dip her hand in *dirty water*, her children will have coarse hands.

725. If she *dust* anything with her *apron*, they will be boisterous.

726. If she wear a *nosegay*, they'll have fetid breath, and no sense of smell.

727. If she *long for fish*, her child will be born too soon, or will die soon.

728. If she *steal* but a trifle, the child will have a strong bent that way.

729. If she *mount over a waggon-pole*, it will come to the gallows; if she dream of *dead fish*, it will die.

730. If women come in while she is in labour, they shall quickly *take their aprons off*, and tie them round her, or they'll be barren themselves.

731. In fumigating, throw in some *sprigs* from the *broom* that sweeps the room.

732. When the child is born, she shall take *three bites of an onion*, be *lifted* and *set down three times* in the stool, draw her *thumbs* in, and blow *three times* into each *fist*.

733. In the six weeks she must *not spin*, because the B. Virgin did not; else the yarn will be made into a *rope* for the child.

734. If the child, when born, be wrapt in *fur*, it will have *curly hair*.

735. Put three pennies in its *first bath*, it will always have money; a pen, it will learn fast; a rosary, it will grow up pious; an egg, it will have a clear voice. But the three pennies and the egg must be given to the first beggar.

736. The first *cow that calves*, milk her into a brand-new pot, put three pennies in, and give them with the milk and pot to the first beggar.

737. The smaller the *jug* in which water is drawn for a little girl's bath, the smaller will her *breasts* be.

738. Empty the bath under a *green tree*, and the children will keep fresh.

739. Three days after birth, the godfather shall *buy* the child's *crying* from it (drop a coin in the swathings), that it may have *peace*.

740. If the child still *cries*, put *three keys* to bed in its cradle.

741. If the child can't or won't eat, give a little feast to the *fowls of the air* or the *black dog*.

742. If the baby sleep on *through a thunder storm*, the *lightning* will not strike.

743. The *tablecloth* whereon ye have eaten, fumigate with *fallen crumbs*, and wrap the child therein.

744. Every time the mother leaves the room, let her spread some *garment* of the *father's* over the child, and it cannot be changed.

745. If the *churching* be on *Wednesday* or *Friday*, the child will come to the gallows.

746. Before going out to be *churched*, let the mother stride over the broom.

747. If a male be the first to take a light from the *taper* used in churching, the next child will be a boy; if a female, a girl.

748. On her way home, let the mother buy *bread*, and lay it in the cradle, and the child will have *bread* as long as it lives.

749. Before suckling the child, let her *wipe her breasts three times*.

750. The first time the child is carried out, let a garment be put upon it *on the side aforesaid* (inside out).

751. As soon as you see the child's *first tooth, box his ear*, and he'll cut the rest easily.

### l. From *Osterode in the Harz*.

(Journ. v. u. f. D. 1788. 2, 425—431.)

752. The first time you drive out to pasture in spring, put an *axe* and a *fire-steel* wrapt in a *blue apron* just inside the stable threshold and let the cows step over it.

753. In feeding them the evening before, sprinkle three pinches of *salt*

between their horns, and walk *backwards* out of the stable; then *evil eyes* will not affect them.

754. If the girl wash the cow *unwashed*, the milk will not cream.

755. For the cow not to go more than once with the bull, *a blind dog* must be *buried alive* just inside the *stable door*.

756. When you drive the cow past a witch's house, *spit three times*.

757. Cattle born or weaned in a *waning moon* are no good for breeding.

758. If *swallows' nests* on a house are pulled down, the cows give blood.

759. If a witch come to the churning, and can *count the hoops on the churn*, the butter will not come.

760. *Three grains of salt* in a milk pot will keep witches off the milk.

761. To make *hens* lay, feed them at noon on Newyear's day with *all manner of fruit* mixed.

762. Set the hen to hatch just *as the pigs are coming in*; in carrying her, keep pace with the pigs, and the eggs will hatch pretty near together.

763. Whichever *loses the wedding ring first*, will die first.

764. Let a wedding be at *full-moon*, or the marriage is not blest.

765. The first ' warm-bier ' for an accouchée no one may taste, but only *try with the fingers*, or she'll have the gripes.

766. To cure *ansprang* (a kind of rash) on a child, get a piece of wood out of a *millwheel*, set it alight, and smoke the swathings with it ; wash the child with water that *bounds off the millwheel* (see 471) ; what is left of the wood shall be thrown into *running water*.

767. Wean no child when *trees are in blossom*, or it will be gray-headed.

768. While the babe is unbaptized, no stranger shall come in ; he might not be *dicht* (=geheuer), then the mother's milk would go.

769. If a baby has the *kinder-scheuerchen* (shudder ?), let the ' goth ' if it is a boy, or the godmother if it is a girl, *tear its shirt down the breast*.

770. When a baby is weaning, give it three times a *roll* to eat, a *penny* to lose, and a *key*.

771. On *Monday* lend nothing, pay for all you buy, fasten no stocking on the left.

772. *A stroke of lightning will find its way* to whate'er you work at on *Ascension day* (703).

773. On Matthias-day throw a *shoe* over your head : if it then *points out-of-doors*, you will either move or die that year.

774. On Matthias-day set as many *leuchter pennies* as there are people in the house, afloat on a *pailful of water* : he whose penny sinks will die that year.

775. Water drawn *downstream* and *in silence, before sunrise* on *Easter* Sunday, does not spoil, and is good for anything.

776. *Bathing* the same day and hour is good for scurf and other complaints.

777. If a new *maidservant*, the moment she is in the house, see that *the fire is in*, and *stir* it up, she'll stay long in the place.

778. In building a house, the master of it shall deal the *first stroke* of the axe : if *sparks fly out*, the house will be burnt down.

779. If a *bed* be so placed that the sleeper's feet *point out-of-doors*, he'll die.

780. *Bewitched money* grows less every time you count it: strew *salt* and *dill* amongst it, put a crossed twopenny-piece to it, and it will keep right.

781. A *hatching-dollar* makes your money grow, and if spent always comes back.

782. A woman that is confined must not look *out of window*: else every *vehicle* that passes takes a luck away.

783. He that carefully carries about him an egg laid on Maundy Thursday, can see all *witches with tubs on their heads* (see 636. 685).

784. The *first corn-blossom* you see, draw it *three times* through your mouth, saying " God save me from fever and jaundice," and you are safe from them (see 695).

785. *Three knots* tied in a string, and laid in a coffin, send warts away.

786. If a woman have *seven sons one after another*, the seventh can heal all manner of hurts with *a stroke of his hand*.

### m. From *Bielefeld*.

### (Journ. v. u. f. D. 1790. 2, 389-390. 462-3.)

787. If an *old woman* with *running eyes* comes in, and talks to and fondles a child, she bewitches it ; the same if she handles and admires your cattle.

788. If you walk down the street with one foot *shod* and the other *bare*, all the cattle coming that way will fall sick.

789. If an *owl* alights on the house hooting, and then flies over it, some one dies.

790. *Wicke-weiber* tell you who the thief is, and mark him on the body.

791. *Old women* met first in the morning mean misfortune, *young people* luck.

792. At 11-12 on Christmas night *water* becomes *wine* and the *cattle stand up*; but whoever pries into it, is *struck blind* or *deaf*, or is marked for death.

793. *Healing spells* must be taught in secret, without witnesses, and only *by men to women*, or *by women to men*.

794. The *rose* (Antony's fire) is appeased by the spell: ' *hillig ding* wike (holy thing depart), wike un verslike ; brenne nich, un stik nich ! '

### n. Miscellaneous.

795. If a woman tear her *wedding shoes*, she'll be beaten by her husband.

796. If you've eaten *peas* or *beans*, sow none the same week: they will fail.

797. If she that is confined go *without new shoes*, her child will have a dangerous fall when it learns to walk.

798. For belly-ache wash in brook-water while the *death-bell tolls*.

799. When you've bought a *knife*, give the *first morsel* it cuts to the dog, and you'll never lose the knife.

800. Eggs put under the hen on a *Friday* will not thrive ; what chicks creep out, the bird eats up.

801. He that turns his back to the *moon* at play, will lose.

802. If your *right ear* sings, they are speaking truth of you, if your *left*, a lie; bite the top button of your shirt, and the liar gets a blister on his tongue.

803. If a maid eat boiled milk or broth *out of the pan*, it will soon rain, and she'll get a husband as sour as sauerkraut.

804. *Heilwag* is water drawn while the clock strikes 12 on Christmas night: it is good for pains in the navel.

805. *Waybread* worn under the feet keeps one from getting tired.

806. Have a *wolf's heart* about you, and the wolf won't eat you up.

807. He that finds the *white snake's crown*, will light upon treasure.

808. He that looks *through a coffin-board*, can see the witches.

809. To win a maiden's favour, write your own name and hers on *virgin parchment,* wrap it in *virgin wax,* and wear it about you.

810. He that is born on a *Monday*, three hours after sunrise, about the *summer equinox,* can converse with spirits.

811. It is good for the *flechte* (scrofula) to sing. in the morning, before speaking to any one : de *flock-asch* un de *flechte*, de flogen wol över dat wilde meer ; de *flock-asch* kam wedder (back), de *flechte* nimmermer.

812. A *drut's foot* (pentagram) must be painted on the cradle, or the *schlenz* will come and suck the babies dry.

813. At *Easter* the sun dances before setting, *leaps thrice for joy:* the people go out in crowds to see it (Rollenhagen's Ind. reise, Altstet. 1614, p. 153).

814. If you eat *pulse* (peas, beans) in the Twelves, you fall sick; if you eat *meat*, the best head of cattle in the stall will die.

815. A *death's head* buried in the *stable* makes the horses thrive.

816. When *sheep* are bought and driven home, draw three crosses on the open door with a *grey field-stone* (landmark ?), so that they can see.

817. If a woman that is more than half through her pregnancy, stand still before a *cupboard*, the child will be voracious (see 41). To cure it, let her put the child in the cupboard itself, or in a corner, and, cry as it may, make it sit there till she has done *nine sorts of work.*

818. If a child will not learn to walk, make it creep silently, *three Friday mornings*, through a *raspberry bush* grown into the ground at both ends.

819. When the *plough* is home, lift it off the dray, or the *devil* sleeps *under it.*

820. The milk will *turn*, if you carry a pailful over a *waggon-pole*, or a *pig* smell at the pail. In that case, let a *stallion* drink out of the pail, and no harm is done (conf. K 92, Swed.).

821. What's begun on a *Monday* will never be *a week old :* so don't have a wedding or a wash that day.

822. Plans laid *during a meal* will not succeed.

823. If a woman walk up to the *churn,* and *overcry* it in the words,

'Here's a fine vessel of milk,' it will go to froth, and give little butter. Answer her : 'It would get on the better without your gab.'

824. Do not spin in the open country. Witches are called *field-spinners*.

825. If your *left nostril* bleed, what you are after won't succeed.

826. If it rains before noon, it will be all the finer afternoon, when the *old wives* have *cleared their throats*.

827. Till the hunter is near the game, let his *gun* point *down*, or it will miss.

828. If a corpse *sigh* once more when on the straw, if it remain *limp*, if it *suck-in kerchiefs*, ribbons, etc., that come near its mouth, if it *open its eyes* (todten-blick); then one of its kindred will follow soon.

829. If a corpse change colour when the bell tolls, it *longs for the earth*.

830. Never call the dead by name, or you will *cry* them *up*.

831. If *two children kiss* that can't yet talk, one of them will die [Rääf 129. 132].

832. If *two watchmen* at two ends of the street blow together, an *old woman* in that street will die.

833. If a *stone roll towards* a wedding pair walking to church, it betokens evil.

834. If you *read tombstones*, you lose your memory [Nec sepulcra legens vereor, quod aiunt, me memoriam perdere. Cic. de Senect. 31].

835. Two that were *in mourning* the first time they met, must not fall in love.

836. A thief must *throw* some of what he steals *into water*.

837. At a fire, he whose *shoes catch* and begin to burn, is the *incendiary*.

838. If a farmer has several times had a *foal* or *calf* die, he buries it in the garden, planting a *young willow in its mouth*. When the *tree* grows up, it is *never polled* or *lopped*, but grows its own way, and guards the farm from similar cases in future (Stendal in Altmark. allg. anz. der Deut. 1811, no. 306; conf. Müllenh. no. 327).

839.[1] At weddings, beside the great cake, they make a *bachelor's cake*, which the girls pull to pieces; she that has the largest piece, will get a husband first.

840. A *betrothed pair* may not sit at the same table as the *pair just married*, nor even put their feet under it; else no end of mischief befalls one of the pairs.

841. In the wedding ride the driver may not *turn* the horses, nor *rein* them *in*; else the marriage would be childless.

842. At a christening the sponsors must not take hold of the *wester-hemd* (chrism-cloth) by the *corners*.

843. Those who have lost children before, don't take a baby out by the door to be christened, but *pass it out through the window*.

844. A woman in her six weeks shall not go into a *strange house ;* if she does, she must first *buy* something at a strange place, lest she bring misfortune to the house.

---

[1] Nos. 839 to 864 are from Jul. Schmidt's Topogr. der pflege Reichenfels (in Voigtland), Leipz. 1827. pp. 113—126.

845. Nor may she *draw water* from a spring, or it will *dry up* for seven
years.

846. A corpse is set down *thrice on the threshold* by the bearers; when
it is out of the homestead, the gate is fastened, *three heaps of salt* are made
in the death-chamber, it is then swept, and both broom and sweepings
thrown in the fields; some also burn the bed-straw in the fields.

847. The evening before Andrew's day, the unbetrothed girls form a
circle, and let a *gander* in ; the one he turns to first, will get a husband.

848. Between 11 and 12 on John's day, the unbetrothed girls gather
*nine sorts* of flowers, three of which must be willow, storksbill and wild
rue; they are twined into a *wreath*, of which the twiner must have *spun
the thread* in the same hour. Before that fateful hour is past, she *throws*
the wreath *backwards into a tree ;* as often as it is thrown without staying
on, so many years will it be before she is married. All this must be done
in silence.

849. He that has silently carried off an *undertaker's measure*, and *leans*
it against a *house-door* at night, can rob the people inside without their
waking.

850. A root of *cinquefoil* dug up before sunrise on John's day, is good
for many things, and wins favour for him that wears it.

851. Girls wear a *wasp's nest*, thinking thereby to win men's love.

852. If a man has strayed, and turns his *pockets inside out*, or if a woman
has, and ties her *apron on the wrong way*, they find the right road again.

853. If a child has *fräsel* (cramp, spasms), *turn* one *shingle in the roof*, or
lay the *wedding apron under its head*.

854. At Christmas or Newyear, between 11 and 12, they go to a *cross-
way* to *listen*, and learn all that most concerns them in the coming year.
The *listening* may be from inside a *window* that has the 'träger' over
it; or on Walpurgis-night in the *green corn*.

855. If from the *fires* of the three holy eves (before Christmas, Newyear
and High Newyear) *glowing embers* be left the next morning, you'll want
for nothing all that year.

856. It is bad for a family if the head of it dies in a *waning moon*, but
good in a *waxing moon*. It is lucky when a grave *turfs* itself over. A
reappearance of the dead is commonest on the *ninth day* after death.

857. If a tree's *first fruit* be stolen, it will not bear for *seven years*.

858. The *dragon* carries the dung in the yard to his friends.

859. A woman with child must *not creep through a hedge*.

860. If a corpse is in the house, if a cow has calved, *beggars* get nothing.

861. Servants who are leaving take care not to be *overlapt :* they go, or
at least send their things away, before the new one comes in.

862. A new manservant comes at midday, and consumes his dumplings
on the *chimney-seat ;* the mistress is careful to set *no sauerkraut* before
him that day, lest his work be disagreeable to him. One who is leaving
gets a *service-loaf* for every year he has been in the service.

863. If *three thumps* be heard at night, if the *weh-klage* howl, if the
*earth-cock* burrow, there will be a death.

864. For debility in children : their water being taken in a *new pot*, put

into it the egg of a *coalblack hen* bought without bargaining, with *nine holes* pricked in it; tie the pot up with linen, and bury it after sunset in an *ant-hill* found without seeking. Any one finding such a pot, lets it alone, lest he catch the *buried disease.*

865. In the Diepholt country, headache (de *farren*) is cured thus: a *woman of knowledge* brings two *bowls,* one filled with *cold water,* and one with *melted tallow.* When the head has been held in the water some time, the tallow is *poured into the water* through an *inherited hatchel* (flax-comb), and the woman says: ' Ik geete (I pour).' Patient: ' Wat gütst?' Woman: 'De *farren.*' Then she speaks a spell, the whole process is repeated three times, the water is emptied on a *maple-bush* (elder), the cold tallow thrown in the fire, and the ache is gone. (Annals of Brunswk-Lünebg Churlande, 8th yr, st. 4, p. 596.) See 515.

866. In the country parts of Hildesheim, when any one dies, the grave-digger *silently* walks to the *elder-bush* (sambucus nigra), and cuts a *rod* to measure the corpse with ; the man who is to convey it to the grave does the same, and wields this *rod* as a whip. (Spiel u. Spangenbg's Archiv '28, p. 4.)

867. On Matthias night (Feb. 24) the young people meet, the girls plait one *wreath of periwinkle,* one of *straw,* and as a third thing carry a *handful of ashes;* at midnight they go *silently to a running water,* on which the three things are to float. *Silent* and blindfold, one girl after another dances about the water, then clutches at a prognostic, the periwinkles meaning a *bridal wreath,* the straw *misfortune,* the ashes *death.* The lucky ones carry the game further, and throw *barleycorns* on the water, by which they mean certain bachelors, and notice how they swim to one another. In other cases *three leaves* are thrown on the water, marked with the names of father, mother and child, and it is noticed which goes down first. (Ibidem.)

868. In some parts of Hanover, churching is called *brummie,* because in the villages on such an occasion, the mother and father and the invited sponsors, both of the last baptized and of earlier children, set up a *growling* (brummen) like that of a bear. (Brunsw. Anz. 1758, p. 1026; Hanov. Nützl. saml. 1758, p. 991, where it is *brümmie.*)

869. Of *elder* that grows among willows, they make *charms* to hang on children, *nine little sticks* tied with a *red silk thread,* so as to lie on the pit of the stomach. If the thread snaps, you must take the little bundle off with little pincers, and throw it in *running* water. (Ettner's Hebamme p. 859.)

870. *Amulets* of the *wolf's* right eye, pouch of stones, *blind swallows* cut out of his maw. (Ibid. 862.)

871. Puer si veri *genitoris indusium nigrum* seu *maculatum* involvatur, si epilepsia ipsum angat, nunquam redibit. (Ibid. 854.)

872. When a child dwindles, they tie a *thread of red silk* about its neck, then catch a *mouse,* pass the thread with a needle through its skin over the backbone, and let it go. The mouse wastes, the child picks up. (Ibid. 920.)

873. When an old wife blesses and *beets* (bö:et) *tension of the heart,* she

breathes on the painful part crosswise, strokes it, ties salt and rye-meal over it, and says : ' Hert-gespan, ik segge di an, *flüg van den ribben*, asse Jesus van den kribben!' If the patient be seized with spasms, let him *stretch himself on a plum-tree*, saying: ' Ranke-bom, stand! plumke-bom wasse (wax)!'

874. Some men's mere *look* is so *hurtful*, that even without their knowing it, they put men and beasts in peril of their lives.

875. Some men, by *bespeaking* (muttering a spell), can *pull up a horse in full gallop, silence a watch-dog, stanch blood, keep fire from spreading.*

876. You may recover stolen goods by *filling a pouch* with some of the *earth* that the *thief has trodden*, and twice a day *beating* it with a stick *till fire comes out of it.* The thief feels the blows, and shall die without fail if he bring not back the things.

877. To save timber from the woodworm, knock it with a piece of *oak* on *Peter's day*, saying : ' Sunte worm, wut du herut, Sunte Peter is komen!'

878. If the *nightmare* visits you—a big woman with long flying hair— *bore a hole* in the bottom of the door, and fill it up with *sow-bristles.* Then sleep in peace, and if the nightmare comes, promise her a present; she will leave you, and come the next day in human shape for the promised gift.

879. No *bird will touch* any one's *corn or fruit*, who has never worked on a Sunday.

880. He that was born at sermon-time on a Christmas morning, can *see spirits.*

881. Where the *mole burrows* under the wash-house, the mistress will die.

882. If a *herd of swine* meet you on your way, you are an unwelcome guest; if a *flock of sheep*, a welcome.

883. If the crust of the saved up *wedding-loaf* goes *mouldy*, the marriage will not be a happy one.

884. In some parts the bride's father cuts a piece off the *top crust* of a well-baked *loaf*, and hands it to her with a glass of brandy. She takes the crust between her lips, *not touching it with her hand*, wraps it in a cloth, and keeps it in a box; the glass of brandy she throws over her head on the ground.

885. The first time a woman goes to church after a confinement, they throw *on the floor after her the pot* out of which she has eaten caudle during the six weeks.

886. If a suspicious looking cat or hare cross your path, throw a *steel* over its head, and suddenly it stands before you in the shape of an *old woman.*

887. He that kills a *black cow* and *black ox* may look for a death in his house.

888. If on coming home from church the bride be the first *to take hold* of the *house door*, she will maintain the mastery, especially if she says : "This door I seize upon, here all my will be done!" If the bridegroom have heard the spell, he may undo it by adding the words : "I grasp this knocker-ring, be fist and mouth (word and deed?) one thing!"

889. If *magpies* chatter or hover round a house, if the *logs* at the *back* of a fire *jump over* and *crackle*, guests are coming who are strangers.

890. In setting out for the wars, do not *look behind you*, or you may never see home again. ·

891. If you leave yarn on the spool over Sunday, it turns to sausages.

892. Ghosts are banished to *betwixt door and doorpost;* if a door be slammed to, they are too much tormented (995).

893. Look *over the left shoulder* of one who sees spirits and future events, and you can do the same.

894. If two friends walk together, and a *stone fall between them*, or a *dog run across their path*, their friendship will soon be severed.

895. If in going out you *stumble on the threshold*, turn back at once, or worse will happen.

896. The day before Shrove Sunday many people *cook for the dear little angels* the daintiest thing they have in the house, *lay it on the table at night*, set the windows open, and go to bed. (Obersensbach in the Odenwald.)

897. At harvest time he that gets his corn cut *first*, takes a *willow bough*, *decks it with flowers*, and sticks it on the *last* load that comes in. (Gernsheim.)

898. At the moment any one dies, the grain in the barn is *shuffled*, and the wine in the cellar *shaken*, lest the seed sown come not up, and the wine turn sour. (Ibid.) Conf. 576. 664. 698.

899. On St. Blaise's day the parson holds *two lighted tapers* crossed ; old and young step up, each puts his head between the tapers, and is blessed; it preserves from pains in head or neck for a year. (Ibid.)

900. In some parts of Westphalia a woman dying in childbed is not clothed in the usual shroud, but exactly *as she would have been for her churching*, and she is buried so.

901. The ticking of the *wood-worm* working its way through old tables, chairs and bedsteads we call *deadman's watch :* it is supposed that the *dead man goes past*, and you hear his watch tick.

902.[1] *Set your hens to hatch on Peter-and-Paul's*, they'll be good layers.

903. Pull the *molehills* to pieces on Silvester's, they'll throw up no more.

904. If the *cuckoo calls later than John's*, it means no good.

905. Thrash before sunrise on Shrove Tuesday, you'll drive the moles away.

906. If it freeze on the shortest day, the *price of corn will fall;* if it's mild, 'twill *rise*.

907. *Sow no wheat* on Maurice's, or it will be sooty.

908. Who at John's beheading would fell a tree, will have to let it be.

909. A *March fog*, and a hundred days after, a thunderstorm.

910. When the *wind blows of a New Year's night*, it means a death.

911. At Martinmas you see by the *goose's breastbone* if the winter 'll be cold or not.

---

[1] 902—919 from Schmeller's Dialects of Bavaria, p. 529.

912. Chickens hatched *out of duck's eggs* change colour every year.

913. Who *drinks not on Good Friday*, no drink can hurt him for a year (see 356).

914*a*. Stuff a bed with feathers *in a waxing moon*, and they slip out again.

914*b*. On Ash Wednesday the devil *hunts the little wood-wife* through the forest.

915. If on Christmas eve, or Newyear's day, or eve (?) you *hang a washclout on a hedge*, and then groom the horses with it, they'll grow fat.

916. If you *thrash* in the Rauch-nights, *the corn spoils as far as the sound is heard* (see 418).

917. *Set no hens to hatch* on Valentine's, or all the eggs will rot.

918. *Jump over John's fire*, and you'll not have the fever that year.

919. If a *horse be let blood* on Stephen's, it keeps well all the year.

920. A wound dealt with a knife *whetted on Golden Sunday* will hardly ever heal.

921. If shooting at the butts that Sunday, you wrap your right hand in the rope by which *a thief has hung on the gallows*, you'll hit the bull's eye every time.

922. If a man has a *new garment* on, you give it a slap, with some such words as 'The old must be patched, the new must be thrashed;' and the garment will last the longer.

923. Sick sheep should be made to *creep* through a *young split oak*.

924. If a pregnant woman eat or taste *out of the saucepan*, her child will *stammer*.

925. If on a journey she mount the carriage over the *pole* or the *traces*, the child entangles its limbs in the navelstring (see 688. 933).

926. If a baby cries much in the first six weeks, pull it *through a piece of unboiled yarn* three times in silence. If that does no good, let the mother, after being churched, go home in silence, *undress in silence*, and throw all her *clothes on the cradle backwards*.

927. The first time the horned cattle are driven to pasture, draw a *woman's red stocking* over a *woodman's axe*,[1] and lay it on the *threshold of the stable door*, so that every beast shall step over it (see 752).

928. To keep caterpillars off the cabbages, a female shall *walk backwards naked in the full moon three times* in all directions through the cabbage garden.

929. If a single woman be suspected of pregnancy, let the manservant pull a *harvest-waggon in two*, and set the *front part facing the south* and the *hind wheels the north*, so that the girl in doing her work must pass between the two halves. It prevents her from procuring abortion.

930. When a *cricket* is heard, some one in the house will die : it *sings him to the grave*.

931. A *shirt of safety*, proof against lead or steel, must be spun, woven and sewed by a pure chaste maiden on Christmas day; from the neck down, it covers half the man; on the breast part two heads are sewed on,

---

[1] Any *steel* tool laid on the threshold will do; conf. Reichs-Anz. 1794, p. 656.

that on the right with a long beard, that on the left a devil's face wearing a crown (see 115).

932. The *key-test*: a hymn book is tied up, inclosing a key, all but the ring, which, resting on two fingers, can turn either way; questions are then asked.

933. A woman with child may not pass *under any hanging line*, else her child will not escape the rope. They avoid even the *string* on which a birdcage hangs (see 688. 925).

934. In setting *peas*, take a few *in your mouth* before sunset, keep them in silently while planting, and those you set will be safe from sparrows.

935. The sexton does not dig the grave till *the day of the burial*, else you'd have no peace from the dead.

936. Children *dying unbaptized* hover betwixt earth and heaven.

937. Children must not *stretch the forefinger toward heaven*; they *kill* a dear little *angel* every time (see 334. 947).

938.[1] Many would sooner be knocked on the head than pass *between two females*.

939. One man puts his *white shirt* on of a *Monday*; he'd rather go naked than wear clean linen on Sunday.

940. I know some that think, if they did not eat *yellow jam* on Ash Wednesday, *nine sorts of green herbs* on Maundy Thursday, *plaice and garlic* on Whitwednesday, they would turn donkeys before Martinmas (see 275).

941. Bride and bridegroom shall *stand so close together* that *nobody can see through*.

942. They shall observe the *tap* of their *first beer or wine cask*, and step into bed together.

943. The bridegroom shall be married in a *bathing apron*.

944. He that wipes his mouth *on the tablecloth* hath never his fill.

945. 'Tis not good to have thy garment mended on thy body (see 42).

946. The *last loaf shoved into the oven* they mark, and call it mine host: 'So long as mine host be in house, we want not for bread; if he be cut before his time, there cometh a dearth.'

947. 'On thy life, point not with thy finger, thou wilt *stab an angel!*'

948. 'Dear child, lay not the knife so, the *dear angels will tread it into their feet!*' If one see a child lie in the fire, and a *knife on its back* at one time, one shall soooner run to the knife than to the child (see 209. 596-7).

949. *Cup or can to overspan* is no good manners; who drinks thereof shall have the *heart-cramp* (see 11).

950.[2] It shall profit the sick to smoke them with a *rod* that is broke out of an *old hedge* and hath *nine ends* or *twigs*.

951. Or with *hay* that is fetched *unspoken, unchidden*, from the loft of an *inherited barn*.

---

[1] 938—949 from Chr. Weise's "Three Arrant Fools," Lpzg 1704, pp. 253—7.
[2] 950-1 ibid., p. 360.

952. On the *Absolution nights* (before Advent, before Christmas, before Twelfthday, and Saturday in Candlemas) the Gastein girls, as soon as it is dark, go to the sheep-fold, and *clutch blindly among the flock;* if at the first clutch they have caught a *ram,* they are confident they'll be married that year.[1]

953.[2] Some, in the middle of the night before Christmas, take a *vessel full of water,* and ladle it out with a certain small *measure* into *another vessel.* This they do several times over, and if then they find *more water* than the first time, they reckon upon an increase of their goods the following year. If the quantity remain *the same,* they believe their fortune will stand still, and if there be *less* water, that it will diminish (see 258).

954. Some tie the end of a *ball of thread* to an *inherited key,* and unroll the ball till it hangs loose, maybe an ell, maybe six; then they put it *out of window,* and swing it back and forwards along the wall, saying ' *hark, hark !'* From the quarter where they shall go a wooing and to live, they will hear a voice (see 110).

955. Some, the day before Christmas, cut wood off *nine sorts of trees,* make a *fire* of it in their room at midnight, strip themselves *naked,* and throw their *shifts outside the door.* Sitting down by the fire, they say : ' Here I sit naked and cold as the drift, If my sweetheart would come and just throw me my shift !' A figure will then come and throw the shift in, and they can tell by the face who their lover will be.

956. Others take *four onions,* put one in *each corner of the room,* and name them after bachelors; they let them lie from Christmas to Twelfth-day, and the man whose *onion then buds* will present himself as a suitor; if none have budded the wedding won't come off.

957. Some, the day before Christmas, buy the *fag-end of a wheat loaf* for a penny, cut a piece of crust off, tie it under their right arm, wear it like that all day, and in going to bed lay it under their head, saying: ' I've got into bed, And have plenty of bread; Let my lover but come, And he shall have some.' If the bread looks gnawed in the morning, the match will come off that year; if it's whole, there's no hope.

958. At midnight before Christmas-day, the men or maids go to the stack of firewood, *pull one log out,* and look if it be straight or crooked; their sweetheart's figure shall be according (see 109).

959. Some, on Christmas eve, buy *three farthings* worth of *white bread,* divide it in *three parts,* and consume it *along three streets,* one in every street; in the third street they shall see their sweetheart.

960. The night before Christmas, you take two *empty nutshells,* with tiny wax tapers in them, to stand for you and your sweetheart, and *set them afloat* on a dishful of water. If they come together, your suit will prosper; if they go apart it will come to nought. (Ungewiss. Apotheker p. 649.)

961. If a master is left in the lurch by his man, or a girl in the family

[1] Muchar's Gastein p. 146.
[2] 953—9 from Praetorii Saturnalia, Lips. 1663.

way by her lover, you put a certain penny in the *pan of a mill,* and set the mill going. As it turns faster, such anguish comes upon the fugitive, that he cannot stay, but neck and crop he comes home. This they call ' making it hot for a man.' (Beschr. des Fichtelbergs, Lpzg. 1716. 4, p. 154.)

962. To discover what the year shall bring, they plant themselves on a *cross-roads* or *parting of ways* at 12 the night before Christmas, stand stockstill without speaking for an hour, whilst all the future opens on their eyes and ears. This they call ' to go hearken.' (Ibid. p. 155.)

963. On Andrew's day fill thee a glass with water : if the year shall be moist, it *runneth over;* if dry, it *standeth heaped atop.* (Aller Practic Grossm.)

964. On Andrew's eve the maids mark *whence the dogs bark;* from that quarter comes the future husband.

965. They tie a *farthing* to their *great toe,* sit down on the way to church, and look among the Matin-goers for their bridegroom. (Tharsander 1, 84.)

966. To know if an infant be bewitched, put under its cradle a vessel full of running water, and drop an *egg* in ; if it *float,* the child is bewitched. (Val. Kräutermann's Zauber-arzt 216.)

967. Evil persons in Silesia did upon a time have a *knife forged,* and therewith cut but a *little twig* off every tree, and in a short time all the forest perished. (Carlowitz's Sylvicultur p. 46.)

968. The *oak* is a prophetic tree : in *gallnuts* a fly betokens war, a worm dearth, a spider pestilence (conf. 1046).

969. Wood felled in the dog-days *will not burn.*

970. A *piece of oak* passed lightly over the body in silence, before sunrise on John's day, heals all open sores.

971. The *elsbeer*-tree is also called dragon-tree : branches of it hung over house and stable on Walburgis-day keep out the flying dragon.

972. *Oak* and *walnut* will not agree : they cannot stand together without (one ?) perishing. So with *blackthorn* and *whitethorn:* if placed together, the white one always gets the upper hand, the black dies out.

973. Cut no timber in the *bad wädel* (waxing moon): timber [schlagholz = strike-wood) felled at new-moon is apt to strike out again; that felled in a waning moon burns better.

974. When a *sucking babe* dies, they put a bottle of its mother's milk in the coffin with it; then her milk dries up without making her ill.

975. If you have warts, nail a big brown snail to the doorpost with a *wooden hammer;* as it dries up, the wart will fade away.

976. If an *old woman* meet you at early morn, and greet you, you must answer ' As much to you ! '

977. Some people can *stop a waggon of hay* on its way, so that it will not stir from the spot : knock at every wheel-nail, and it will be free again.

978. In a *thief's footprints* put burning tinder : it will burn him and betray him.

979. If a swallow fly into the stable, and pass under the cow, she will

give blood for milk: lead her to a cross-way, *milk* her 3 times *through a branch*, and empty what you have milked backwards over her head three times.

980. A bunch of wild *thyme* or *marjoram* laid beside the milk keeps it from being bewitched.

981. If you walk once round your *garden-fence* on Shrove Sunday, not a plank will be stolen out of it for a year to come.

982. If you have many snails on your land, go before sunrise and take one snail from the east side; then by way of north to the west, and pick up another; then to the north; then by way of east to the south: if you put the four snails in a bag, and hang them inside your chimney, all the snails on your land will creep into the chimney, and die.

983. If, in cutting the vegetables in autumn, a *molehill* be found under the cabbage, the master will die.

984. In Westphalia, when a loaf is cut, they call the upper crust *laughing-knost*, the under the *crying-knost*. When maid or man goes out of service, they get a *jammer-knost* (wailing-crust), which they keep for years after.

985. When children have the *schluckuk* (hiccough?), their heart is growing.

986. The first *stork* a peasant sees in the year, he falls on the ground, rolls round, and is then free from pains in the back for a year.

987. On buying a cow from another village, you give beside the price a *milk-penny*, so that her milk may not be kept back. At the boundary you turn her three times round, and let her *look at her old home*, to banish her regret.

988. Many fasten *fern in blossom* over the house-door: then all goes well *as far as the waggon-whip reaches*.

989. On the first day of Lent, boys and girls run about the fields like mad, with blazing wisps of straw, to drive out the *evil sower*. (Rhöne).

990. The first night of Christmas the people of the Rhön roll on *un-thrashed pea-straw*. The peas that drop out are mixed with the rest, which improves the crop.

991. On Innocents' day, every adult is *flogged* with a *rod*, and must ransom himself with a gift. The trees too are beaten, to promote their fertility.

992. Whoso doth any sewing to bed or clothing on a Sunday, cannot die therein till it *be unripped*.

993. If you rise from the spinning-wheel without twisting off the strap, the *earth-mannikin* comes and spins at it: you don't see him, but you hear the spindle hum.

994. A beggar that would pay his debt in full ought to say as many paternosters as it would take *blades of grass* to *cover the bread* given him. As he cannot, he says ' God yield ye! '

995. Never slam the door: *a spirit sits between*, and it hurts him (892).

996. The first child christened at a *newly consecrated font* receives the gift of seeing spirits and things to come, until some one out of curiosity step on his *left foot* and look over his *right shoulder*; then the gift passes

over to him. But that can be prevented by the sponsors dropping a straw, a pin or a piece of paper into the basin.

997. He that is always praying, and prides himself on it, *prays himself through heaven*, and has to mind geese the other side.

998. If you *drop bread-and-butter*, and it falls on the buttered side, you have committed a sin that day.

999. When girls are weeding, they look for the little herb ' *leif in de meute*' (love meet me), and hide it about them : the first bachelor that then comes towards them is their sweetheart.

1000. Whoever builds a house must use *bought, stolen* and *given* timber to it, or he has no luck: a belief so general in Lippe, that even a large farmer who has wood of his own, will steal a beam, then go and accuse himself, and pay for it.

1001. When the *holy weather* (lightning) strikes, it can only be *quenched with milk*, not with water (conf. 1122).

1002. In weeding flax, the girls pull up the weed Red Henry (mercury ?): whichever way the root grew, from there will come the sweetheart; if it grew straight down, the girl will die soon (conf. Dan. Sup. 126).

1003. Whoever is the first to see the *stork* come in, and to bid it welcome, not a tooth of his will ache that year.

1004. If you go to bed without *clearing the table*, the youngest in the house will get no sleep.

1005. If a maid have not spun her distaff clear by Sunday, those threads will never bleach white.

1006. She that sets the gridiron on the fire, and puts nothing on it, will get an *apron in her face* (be wrinkled).

1007. If you stand a new broom upside down behind the street-door, witches can neither get in nor out.

1008. If a woman nurse her babe sitting on the *boundary-stone* at the cross-way, it will never have toothache.

1009. *Children born after the father's death* have the power of blowing away skin that grows over the eyes for three Fridays running.

1010. Why give ye not the *bones* of the *Easter lamb*, that is blessed, unto dogs ? They will go mad, say ye. Ye may give them, it harmeth not (Keisersb. Ameisz. 52).

1011. Wouldst *lame a horse* ? Take of a tree stricken by hail, and make thereof a nail, or of a new gallows, or of a knife that hath been a priest's cell-woman's (conf. priest's wife, Spell xxxiv), or the stump of a knife wherewith one hath been stuck dead ; and *push it into his hoofprint.* (Cod. Pal. 212, 53ᵇ.)

1012. To know how many ' good holden' are conjured into a man, he shall draw water in silence, and drop burning coals out of the oven into it : *as many coals as sink to the bottom*, so many good holden has he in him.

1013.[1] If a *tempest* lasts three days without stopping, some one is *hanging* himself.

---

[1] Nos. 1013—1104 from the New Bunzlau Monthly for 1791-2.

1014. Who bathes in cold water on Easterday, keeps well the whole year.

1015. If you go out on important business, and an *old woman* meet you, it is unlucky; if a *young girl,* lucky.

1016. When the *night-owl* cries by day, a fire breaks out.

1017. If you look at a *babe in swaddling-bands,* cross it and say 'God guard thee !'

1018. Whoever sees the *corn in blossom first,* and eats *nine of the blossoms,* will keep free from fever (conf. 718).

1019. If a *howling dog* holds his head up, it means a fire; if down, a death.

1020. Whoever on St. John's Eve puts as many John's worts as there are people in the house, *into a rafter of his room,* naming the plants after the people, can tell in what order they will die : he whose plant withers first will die first (conf. Dan. Sup. 126).

1021. It is not good to *point with your finger* at *where a thunderstorm stands.*

1022. Blood let out of a vein should always be thrown into running water.

1023. Let no milk or butter be sold out of the house *after sunset.*

1024. Moles are removed from the face by letting a dead person's hand rest on them till it grow warm.

1025. The rainwater left *on tombstones* will send freckles away.

1026. If you see *blue fire* burn at night, throw a knife into it, and if you go there before sunrise, you will find money.

1027. Hairs that comb out should be burnt : *if a bird carries them to its nest,* it gives you headaches, or *if it be a staar* (starling), staar-blindness (cataract).

1028. When the *schalaster* (magpie?) cries round the house, guests are near.

1029. If you have the *hiccough,* drink out of your jug (mug) *over the handle.*

1030. When it *rains in sunshine,* the sky drops poison.

1031. Let a sold calf be led out of doors *by the tail,* and the cow will not fret; let a bought cow be led into stable *by the tail,* and she'll soon feel at home.

1032. When the *floor splinters,* suitors are coming.

1033. When a hanged man is cut down, give him a box on the ear, or he'll come back.

1034. If the *moon* shine on an *unbaptized* child, it will be moonstruck.

1035. If the *dead man's bier falls,* some one will die in 3 days ; it will be one that did not hear it.

1036. If your *right hand itch,* you'll take money; if your *left,* you'll spend much.

1037. When a sudden shiver comes over you, *death is running over your grave.*

1038. If the *altar-candle goes out* of itself, the minister dies within a year.

1039. If you run in *one* boot or shoe, you lose your balance, unless you *run back the same way*.

1040. A horse goes lame, if you drive a nail into his *fresh footprint* (conf. 1011).

1041. On Christmas-eve *thrash* the garden with a flail, with *only your shirt on*, and the grass will grow well next year.

1042. As long as *icicles hang from the roof in winter*, so long will there be flax on the distaff the next year.

1043. If a *straw* lies in the room, there is *snow* coming.

1044. *Good Friday's rain* must be scratched out of the ground with needles, for it brings a great drought.

1045. If the godfather's letter be *opened over the child's mouth*, it learns to speak sooner.

1046. *Flies in gallnuts* betoken war, *maggots* bad crops, *spiders* pestilence (conf. 968).

1047. *Rods* stuck *into the flax-bed* keep the cattle unbewitched.

1048. *Three knocks* at night when there's nobody there, some one at the house will die in 3 days.

1049. If a woman dies in childbed, wash out her *plätsche* (porringer) directly, or she will come back.

1050. If bride and bridegroom on the wedding day put a *three-headed bohemian* (a coin) under the sole of their right foot, it will be a happy marriage,

1051. *Snow* on the wedding day foretells a happy marriage, *rain* a wretched.

1052. If you stir food or drink with a *knife*, you'll have the cutting gripes ; if with a *fork*, the stitch.

1053. When one is dying hard, lay him on the *change* (where the ends of the boards meet), and he'll die easy.

1054. Give your pigeons drink out of a *human skull*, and other people's pigeons will come to your cot.

1055. When *hens crow*, a fire breaks out.

1056. A house where *cock, dog* and *cat* are *black*, will not catch fire.

1057. One where the *chain-dog is burnt to death*, will soon be on fire again.

1058. If the butter won't come, whip the tub with a willow rod, but *not* one *cut with a knife*.

1059. To win a maiden's love, get a *hair* and a *pin* off her unperceived, *twist the hair round the pin*, and throw them backwards into a river.

1060. If by mistake the pall be *laid over the coffin wrong side out*, another in the house will die.

1061. When you buy a dog, a cat or a hen, *twirl them 3 times round your right leg*, and they'll soon settle down with you.

1062. Under a sick man's bed put a potful of nettles : if they *keep green*, he'll recover; if they *wither*, he will die.

1063. A *worn shirt* shall not be given to be a *shroud*, else he that wore it will waste away till the shirt be rotten.

1064. If a women in childbed *look at a corpse*, her child will have no colour.

1065. A *hanged man's finger* hung in the cask makes the beer sell fast.

1066. If it *rain* on the *bridal wreath,* the wedded pair will be rich and fruitful.

1067. In measuring grain, *sweep the top towards you,* and you sweep blessing into the house; if you *sweep it from you,* you send it into the devil's hand.

1068. If a child's navel sticks out, take a *beggar's staff* from him *silently,* and press the navel with it cross-wise.

1069. To make a broodhen hatch *cocks* or *hens,* take the straw for her nest from the *man's* or the *woman's* side of the bed.

1070. He that has *white specks* on his thumb-nails, he whose *teeth stand close together,* will stay in his own country.

1071. If wife or maid lose a *garter* in the street, her husband or lover is untrue.

1072. To find out who has poisoned your beast, cut the creature's *heart* out, and hang it pierced with 30 pins, in the chimney; the doer will then be tormented till he come and accuse himself.

1073. Wheat, sown in Michael's week, turns to cockle; barley, in the first week of April, to hedge-mustard.

1074. If you have fever-frost (ague), go in silence, without crossing water, to a hollow *willow tree, breathe your breath into it three times, stop the hole up quick,* and hie home without looking round or speaking a word: the ague will keep away.

1075. Young mayflowers picked before sunrise, and rubbed together under your face, keep *summer-freckles* away.

1076. A woman with child shall not sit down on any box that *can snap to under her,* else her child will not come into the world until you have *set her down* on it again and unlocked it three times.

1077. If you see *dewless patches* in the grass before sunrise, you can find money there.

1078. Let linseed for sowing be poured into the bag from a good height, and the flax will grow tall.

1079. If you have fever, *walk over nine field-boundaries in one day,* and you'll be rid of it.

1080. Or: *hunt a black cat* till it lies dead. It is good for epilepsy to drink the *blood* of a *beheaded man,* and then *run as fast and far* as you can hold out.

1081. On Christmas-eve make a *little heap of salt* on the table : if it melt over night, you'll die the next year; if it remain undiminished in the morning, you will live.

1082. Whoever on St Walpurg's eve puts all his *clothes* on *wrongside out,* and *creeps backwards* to a *cross-way,* will get into witches' company.

1083. If the *reel hung awry,* and the *thread dangled downwards,* when a child came into the world, it will hang itself. If a *knife was lying edge upwards,* it will die by the sword.

1084. The smallest box in the house is usually placed before the child-birth bed : if any one sit down on it, and it *snap to of itself,* the woman will never be brought to.bed again.

1085. As many times as the *cock crows* during service the night before Christmas, so many böhmen will the quarter of wheat fetch the coming year.

1086. Whosoever shall spy the *first ploughman ply*, and the *first swallow fly*, on a year of good luck may rely.

1087. If a spinster in spring time, when birds come back, see *two wagtails together*, she'll be married that year.

1088. If a bridal pair on their way to the wedding meet a *cartload of dung*, it betokens an unhappy marriage.

1089. Before sowing barley, let the seed run *through a man's shirt*, and the sparrows will spare it.

1090. If you eat *peeled barley*, apoplexy cannot strike you while there is a grain of it left in your stomach.

1091. If you strike a *light* on the *corner of the table* or *fireplace*, the 'brand' (blight) will fall on your millet.

1092. When the women are going to wash, every one in the house must *get up in a good temper*, and there will be fine weather.

1093. Spinsters on St John's-eve twine a *wreath of nine sorts of flowers*, and try to throw it backwards and in silence *on to a tree*. As often as it falls, so many years will they remain unmarried (conf. 848).

1094. If a chip in the fire in wintertime has a *large catstail*, it is a sign of *snow;* and if the catstail splits down the middle, of *guests*.

1095. It is not good to *walk over sweepings* (see Swed. 1).

1096. Children beaten with rods off a *broom that has been used*, waste away.

1097. If you want your cows to give much milk, buy a *summer* from the *summer-children*, and stick it over the stable-door.

1098. The first time the cows are driven to pasture, you tie *red rags* round their tails, so that they cannot be bewitched.

1099. If you want the witch to have no hold over your cattle, shut a *bear* up in their stable for a night : he scratches out the hidden stuff that holds the magic, and when that is gone, they are no longer open to attack·

1100. Flax bought on St Lawrence day will get 'burnt' (blasted).

1101. If you had something to say, and forget what, step out *over the threshold* and in again ; it will come into your head again.

1102. Let a beemaster *at honey harvest give away* to many, and the bees will be generous to him.

1103. On Christmas-eve put a stone on every tree, and they'll bear the more.

1104. When a girl is born. lay over her breast a *net* made of an *old* (female) *cap*, and the *alp* (night-elf) will not *suck her dry*.

1105. On Allhallows-eve young folks in Northumberland throw a couple of nuts in the fire. If they lie still and burn together, it augurs a happy marriage; if they fly apart, an unhappy (Brockett p. 152).

1106. When the bride is undressing, she hands one of her stockings to a bridesmaid, to *throw* among the assembled wedding-guests. The person on whom the *stocking falls* will be married next (ibid. 218).

1107. Bride and bridegroom, at the end of the wedding, sit down on the bridal bed in all their clothes except shoes and stockings. Each brides-maid in turn takes the bridegroom's stocking, stands at the foot of the bed with her back to it, and throws the *stocking with her left hand over her right shoulder*, aiming at the bridegroom's face. Those who hit will get married soon. The young men do the same with the bride's stocking (ibid.).

1108. On St Mark's-eve some young people watch all night in the church-porch, and see the spirits of *all that are to die that year* go past, dressed as usual. People that have so watched are a terror to the parish : by nods and winks they can hint men's approaching deaths (ibid. 229). In E. Fries-land they say such people ' can *see quad* ' (bad).

1109. On Christmas-eve the *yule-clog* is laid on, and if possible kept burning 2 or 3 days. A piece of it is usually kept *to light the next year's log with*, and to guard the household from harm (ibid. 243). If it will not light, or does not burn out, it bodes mischief.

1110. In spring, when the farmer goes afield, and turns up the first furrows with unbolted plough, he sprinkles this *earth in the four corners of the living-room*, and all the fleas retire (Krünitz 1, 42).

1111.[1] *Dogs* and *black sheep* have also the gift of ' *seeing quad*,' and you may learn it of them. When the howling dog has a vision, look through *between his ears*, and *lift his left leg;* or take him on your shoulder, and *so look between his ears*. If you wish to be rid of the art, you can transfer it to the dog by *treading on his right foot* and *letting him look over your right shoulder*.

1112. Whichever way the howling dog points his muzzle, from the same quarter will the coming corpse be brought.

1113. Sometimes the steeple-bells give out a dull *dead clang :* then some one in the parish will die soon (conf. 284). When the death-bell tolls, whichever side of it the tongue touches last, from that side of the village will the next corpse come.

1114. If a cabbage-plant blossoms *the first year*, or gets white places on its leaves, a misfortune will happen in the owner's house.

1115. A house *beside which a star has fallen* will be the first to have a death.

1116. It betokens war when the *cherry-tree blossoms twice* in a year.

1117. When the *sun shines on the altar* at Candlemas, expect a good flax-year.

1118. A witch can hurt cattle by *skimming the dew off the grass* in their pasture.

1119. *Eggshells* should be *smashed up small;* else the witch may harm the men that ate out of them, and the hens that laid them.

1120. If you find something eatable, throw the first mouthful away, or witches may hurt you.

1121. When 7 *girls* running are born of one marriage, one is a *were-wolf*.

1122. When lightning strikes, the fire can only be *quenched with milk* (conf. 1001).

---

[1] 1111—1123 E. Friesl. superst. (Westfäl. Anz. for 1810, nos. 68—72).

1123. If you *point* your finger *at the moon*, you'll get a wooden finger.

1124. Wisps of *straw*, taken out of a *bed* on which a *dead man has lain*, and stuck up in the cornfield, keep the birds away.

1125. Birds are kept out of the corn, if in harrowing you go to the left, and say a certain spell, but you must have learnt it from *one of the opposite sex*.

1126.[1] If a child look *into a mirror*, and cannot yet speak, it is not good.

1127. Two babes that cannot talk shall *not* be let *kiss one another*.

1128. *Crickets* or *ofen-eimichen* bring ill-fortune.

1129. Ye shall *not spin* nor *wash* while a dead person is yet above ground.

1130. *Three drops of blood* falling from one's nose signifieth something strange.

1131. On the sea one shall not say *thurm* or *kirche*, but *stift, spitze* and the like.

1132. One shall not speak the while *another drinks*.

1133. It is not good that *two drink together*.

1134. *Wood*, when it lies on the fire, and by reason of wetness letteth out air and *fumeth*, it signifieth chiding.

1135. When a mess, though it be off the fire, *still simmers in the pot*, 'tis good warrant there be no witches in the house.

1136. *Pocks* can be sold, and he that *buys* gets not so many as otherwise.

1137. When one hath to do out of doors, and *turneth about in the door*, and goes not straightway, it is not good.

1138. *Itching of the nose* signifies a sudden fit.

1139. If a *nail* being driven into the coffin bends, and will not in, another shall follow soon.

1140. Go not into service on a *Monday*, nor move into a house, nor begin aught, for it shall not live to be a week old.

1141. To stretch over the cradle is not good, thereof comes *tension of the heart*.

1142. When ye move into a house, if ye bring *salt* and *bread* first thereinto, ye shall lack therein nothing needful.

---

[1] 1126—1142 from 'Des uhralten jungen leiermatz lustigem correspondenz-geist,' 1668, pp. 170—176.

# K. SCANDINAVIAN.

## a. SWEDEN.[1]

PERSONAL PRONOUNS:

| | He. | She. | It. | They. |
|---|---|---|---|---|
| N. | han | hon (Dan. hun) | det | de (Obsol. the) |
| G. | hans | hennes | dess | deras (Dan. deres). |
| D.A. | honom | henne | det | dem (Obsol. them). |
| | (Dan. ham) | | | |

POSS. PRON. : M.F. *sin*, N. *sit*, Pl. *sina*, his, her, its, their (own), Lat. *suus*.

INDEF. ART. : M.F. *en*, N. *et*.

INDEF. PRON. : *någon, något* (Dan. *nogen, noget*), some, any. *Ingen, intet*, none.

DEF. ART. : usually a Suffix : M.F. -*en*, -*n*, N. -*et*, -*t*, Pl. -*ne*, -*na*. Thus in No. 9, *sko-n*, the shoe; *fot-en*, the foot; *golfv-et*, the floor; in No. 12, *skor-na*, the shoes.

PASSIVE formed by adding -*s* to the Active: No. 19, *löga-s*, is or are bathed; *lägge-s*, is or are laid.

An initial *j* or *v* (Engl. *y, w*) is often omitted before an *o* or *u* sound: *år* year, *ung* young; *ord* word, *urt* wort.

SWED. often changes *ld*, *nd* to *ll, nn* : *skulle* should, *andre*, *annars*, etc. other. The reverse in DAN.: *falde* fall, *mand* man.

1. Ej må man möta *sopor i dörren*, om man vil bli gift det året (one must not meet sweepings in the doorway, if one would get married that year).

2. Om en flicka och gosse *äta af en och samma beta*, bli de kära i hvar-andra (if a girl and boy eat off one morsel, they get fond of each other).

3. Midsommars-nat skal man lägga 9 *slags blomster under hufvudet*, så drömer man om sin fäste-man eller fäste-mö, och får se den samma (dreams of his or her betrothed, and gets to see them).

4. Ej må ung-karl (young fellow) gifva en flicka *knif* eller *knap-nålar* (pins), ty de sticka sönder kärleken (for they put love asunder).

5. En flicka må *ej se sig i spegelen* sedan ned-mörkt är, eller vid ljus (not look in her glass after dark or by candle), at ej förlora manfolks tycket (not to lose men's good opinion).

6. Bruden skal laga (the bride must contrive), at hon *först får se brud-gummen*, så får hon husbonda-kastet (mastery).

7. Hon skal under vigslen (at the wedding), för samma orsak (reason) *sätta sin fot framför hans* (in front of his).

---

[1] Nos. 1—71 from Erik *Fernow's* Beskrifning öfver Wärmeland (Götheborg 1773, pp. 254—260); 72—109 from *Hülphers's* Beskrifn. öfver Norrland, 4 (Westerås 1780, pp. 308—310); 110—125 from Johan *Odman's* Bahusläns beskrifn. (Stockh. 1746, pp. 75—80).

8. Äfven för samma skäl (reason) skal hon laga, at hon *sätter sig först ned i brud-stolen* (sit down first in the bridal chair).

9. För samma orsak skal hon, liksom af våda (accident), *släppa skon af foten*, eller *näs-duken* (drop her shoe or kerchief), eller något annat *på golfvet* (floor), som brudgummen af höflighet bugar sig (politely stoops) at hjelpa til rätta. Hans öde blir, at kröka rygg under hela ägtenskapet (bend the back all his married life).

10. Bruden skal stå *brudgummen nära*, at ingen framdeles må *tränga sig dem imellan* (no one in future squeeze in between them).

11. De hålla (they hold) i kyrkan *et band* eller *kläde imellan sig*, at de måga bli ensame tilhopa (dwell in unity together).

12. Bägge böra hafva *pengar i skorna* (both should have coins in their shoes), at mynt må aldrig tryta (never run short).

13. Den som (the one who) under vigslen *lutar* (turns) *från den andra*, dör (dies) först; äfven-så den som ser bäst ut (looks best).

14. Bruden skal *taga med så många fingrar på bara kroppen* (touch her bare body with as many fingers), under det hon sitter i brud-stolen, som hon vil hafva många barn (as she wishes to have children).

15. At hon må få lätt barn-säng (easy child-bed), skal hon, vid hemkomsten från kyrkan, til *vänster spänna ifrån buk-hjolen* om hon ridet, men *fimmel-stången* om hon åket (undo leftwards the saddle-girth or the traces).

16. At bruden må bli god mjölk-ko, *möter hännes moder* hänne på gården, då hon kommer ur kyrkan, *med et mjölke-glas*, at ut-dricka.

17. Til mat (for food) på första barn-sängen, skal hon förse sig (provide herself) med en *kaka* och en *ost* (cheese), som hon har hos sig ligande (lying by her) i brud-sängen.

18. När barn äro nyss-födde, lägges (when babes are newly born, there is laid) en *bok under deras hufvud*, at de må bli nimme at läsa (quick at reading).

19. När de första gången lögas (when they are bathed the first time) *lägges penningar i vatnet*, at de må bli rika. En pung (purse), med pengar uti, *sys* ok *kring halsen* (is sewed also round the neck).

20. Något af *fadrens kläder* bredes på *flicko-barn* (is spread over girl-babies), och *modrens kjortel på gosse*, at få tycke hos andra könet (to find favour with the other sex).

21. Modren bör *möta* barnet *i dörren*, när det föres bort (when it is carried off) til christendom; men när det föres hem, sedan (after) det är döpt, skal man *möta* det *i dörren* med en *bröd-kaka*, at det aldrig må fattas bröd (that it may never want bread).

22. Så länge barn ej fådt namn, må *ej elden släckas*, (the fire go out).

23. Ej må man gå *mellan eld och spen-barn* (between fire and sucking babe).

24. Ej må man sent *bära in vatten*, där (bring water in late where) spen-barn är, utan at *kasta eld deruti* (without putting fire therein).

25. Ej må någon som (Let no one that) kommer in i huset, taga et barn i sina händer, utan at förut *taga i elden* (without first touching the fire).

26. När barn få snart tänder, vänta de snart *nya syskon* efter. (If children teethe quickly, they expect new brothers and sisters soon).

27. Om barn *trifvas* gerna *i varmt vatten*, bli de horaktiga.

28. Ej må man *vagga tom vagga* (rock an empty cradle), ty barnet blir grätt och olåtigt.

29. När et *först-födt barn*, som är född med tänder (born with teeth), biter öfver *onda betet* (the evil bite), så blir det läkt (it will be healed). See 37.

30. Barn må ej på en-gång *läsa* och *äta* (at once read and eat), ty det får trögt minne (sluggish memory).

31. Barnet skal först taga i (touch) *hund*, men ej i *katt*.

32. Om barn *leka med eld*, (play with fire) få de svårt at hålla sit vatten.

33. Barn som är afladt före vigslen (begotten before marriage) skal *modren* sjelf *hålla vid dopet* (hold at the font), eljest blir det icke ägta (else not legitimate); men är det född förut (if born before), skal hon *hålla det på armen* när hon står brud (is married).

34. Om den sjuke får *främmande mat* (stranger's food), blir han frisk.

35. För läke-medel (medicine) bör man *ej tacka* (not thank), ty det har ingen verkan (for then it has no effect).

36. Ej må man gå öfver grafvar med öpet sår (open sore), ty det läkes sent eller aldrig (heals late or never).

37. *Onda betet* botas (is cured) af förstfödt barn med tänder (see 29).

38. Ej må man före morgonen omtala (talk of), om man *sedt spöke* (seen a spectre), at ej bli kramad och spotta blod.

39. Sedan *nedmörkt* är (after dark), må man ej gå til vatten, et ej få *onda betet*.

40. För samma orsak (reason), eller ock at ej bli kramad, skal man spotta 3 gånger (spit 3 times), då man *går öfver vatten* sedan *nedmörkt* är.

41. För den sjuka bör man låta bedja (have the sick prayed for) *i* 3 *kyrkor*, dock bör gerna där-ibland vara (but among them should be) en *offer-kyrka* så-som Gunnarskog, Visnum, Rada, om man bor dem så när (lives near enough). Det måste då hastigt slå ut, antingen til helsa eller döden (speedily issue either in healing or death).

42. Stora fiskars *tänder* böra *upbrännas*, at bli lyklig i fiske. (Big fishes' teeth should be burnt, to be lucky in fishing).

43. Man bör ingen tilsäga (tell no one), då man går åstad at fiska; och ej omtala, antingen (nor talk about whether) man får mycket eller litet (see 109).

44. Ej heller bör *någon främmande* (nor must any stranger) få se hur micket fisk man fått.

45. När man ror ut från landet at fiska, må man *ej vända båten ansöls*.

46. Knapnålar (pins) *fundna i kyrkan* och där gjorda til *mete-krokar* (and there made into bait-hooks) nappa bäst, eller äro gäfvast.

47. Går *qvinfolk* (if a female walks) *öfver mete-spö*, nappar ej fisken.

48. *Stulen fiske-redskap* (stolen fishing-tackle) är lyklig, men den bestulne mister lyckan (the person robbed loses the luck).

49. Ej må man *köra lik* (drive a corpse) til kyrka, ty hästen blir skämd (the horse gets shy).

50. Ej må man *lysa under bordet* (shew a light under the table), at ej gästerne skola bli *o-ense* (get dis-united, quarrel).

51. Ej må man *vända om* (turn back), då man går i något ärende (any errand), at det icke må aflöpa illa (turn out ill).

52. För knapnålar må man *ej tacka*, ty de tappas bort (get lost).

53. *Qvinfolks möte är ondt*, om det ej är en *lönhora*.

54. Kommer en främmande in, der *ljus stöpes* (where candles are being dipped), skal han *taga i elden*, eljest losnar talgen af ljusen.

55. Ej må man *spinna* om *Torsdags qväll* (evening), eller i Dymmel-veckan (Carnival); ty det spinner efter om natten (spins on all night).

56. Kommer främmande in, der *korf kokas*, spricker han sönder.

57. Om någon som har *onda ögon* (evil eye) ser då man slagtar, har kreaturet ondt för at dö (the beast dies hard).

58. Slår man (if you beat) kreatur med *vriden vidja* (turned wood), får det tarm-topp (bowel-twisting).

59. Vänder man toflor eller skor *med tån in åt sängen* (slippers or shoes with the toes towards the bed), så kommer *maran* (the mare) om natten.

60. *Påsk-afton* skal man göra *kors* (Easter-eve, make a cross) öfver fähus-dörren (cowhouse-door) för troll-käringar.

61. När man *ligger första gången i et hus*, skal man räkna bjelkarna (count the rafters), så blir sand (comes true) hvad man drömer.

62. Om man *glömer* något (forget something) då man reser bort (sets out), är godt hopp för de hema varande (home-stayers), at den resande kommer tilbaka; men *se sig tilbaka* (to look back) är ej godt märke.

63. När *kattor tvätta* sig (wash), eller *skator skratta* (magpies scratch) vid husen, vänta de främmande (they expect strangers). Har en sölaktig mat-moder eller vårdslös piga icke förr sopat golfvet (not before swept the floor), så bör det då vist ske (be done then).

64. Den som om *Jul-dagen först kommer hem* från kyrkan, slutar (will finish) först sin ande-tid.

65. Om man går 3 *gånger kring kål-sängen* (round the cabbage-bed) sedan man satt kålen, blir han fri för mask (free from slugs).

66. Om *qvinfolk* klifver *öfver skaklor* (climb over the shafts), skenar hästen eller blir skämt.

67. När *väf-stolen* tages ned (loom is taken down), skal man *kasta et eld-kol* där-igenom (burning coal through it); så får man snart up ny väf.

68. Lägges *eld i karet* före mäskningen, surnar ej drikat (if fire is put in the vessel before malting, the drink will not turn sour).

69. Jul-afton *kastar* man *stifvu råghalms strå i taket* (rye-straws into the roof). Så många strå som fastna, så många trafvar råg får man det året.

70. *Tom säk* må ej bäras *oknuten* (empty sacks not to be carried untied). Går en *hafvande* hustru där-efter, så blir hännes foster aldrig mätt (baby never satisfied). Men råkar en *ko* (but if a cow chance) på den olykliga vägen, så tar (gets) hon sig aldrig kalf.

71. Då man lögar sig, sättes *stål i vatnet* (in bathing, steel is put in the water), och *näcken* bindes sålunda: ' *Näck, näck*, stål i strand ! far din var en stål-tjuf, mor din var en nål-tjuf; så långt (so far) skal du vara hår-

ifrån, som detta rop höres (as this cry is heard).' Och då ropa alle med full-hals: ' *Ho hagla* ! '

72. Om kornet väl vil mylla sig (moulds well), är tekn til god års-växt (year's-growth). När gödningen om våren (manure in spring) skåttas af kälan, hvaräst den legat öfver vinteren, *kastas någre korn in, brakningen.* Likeså, när man sår (sows), bör en *näfva-mull läggas i säd-skorgen* (handful of mould be put in the seed-basket); den dagen bör ock *ej tagas eld* ifrån gran-gården.

73. Om Påsk-lördag blåses (on Easter Saturday they blow) med en lång lur genom fähus-gluggen (through the cowhouse window); *så långt ljudet då hörs* (far as the sound is heard), så långt bort-blifva o-djuren (beasts of prey keep away) det året.

74. När man söker efter boskap i skogen (seek cattle in the wood), och *råkar en käkling* (talg-oxe) på högra handen (and a fatling turn up on your right), skal det sökta finna igen.

75. Släppes svinen (if the swine are let out) Lucii dag, *få de ohyra* (uncanny); likeså sägas de bli *åker-gängse*, om de komma ut at Påskafton.

76. Går man vilse (astray) i skogen, skal man *stul-vända sig* (vända ut och in på kläderna), så kommer man til rätta (see Germ. 852).

76 *b.* Om boskapen Mikelsmäss-afton *köres tyst in* (are driven in silently), skal han vara rolig (quiet) i fähuset hela året.

77. När kon blir sprungen af oxen, bör man *med kokslef slå henne på ryggen*, annars bottnar hon (får ej kalfven från sig).

78. När *askan* (ashes) *brinner väl ihop* (together), görs boskapen väl til (blifver dragtig, breed well).

79. At boskapen skal sjelfmant (may of themselves) komma hem ur skogen, måste sparas af *Fet-Tisdags mat* (some of Shrove Tuesday's food saved up), at ge då den (against when they) om våren först släppes ut.

80. Vid första hö-ladningen (hay-loading) säges, at då *drängen* (if the lad, manservant) först får in sin hö-famn (fathom of hay), skal ox-kalfvar födas; men tvärtom, då *pigan* (and the contrary if the maid) har förträdet.

81. Om den, som byter sig til en häst (if he who acquires a horse) eller annat kreatur, låter det *äta af en jordfast sten*, så trifves det väl. Några hår af svansen bindas ok för den orsaken uti spiället.

82. När en byter sig til hemman (homestead), bör *litet fyllning* tagas ifrån gamla stall och fähus, och läggas *i hvar spilta* elles bås i det nya, at kreaturen må trifvas. Äfvenså sättes en *stor gran* i fähus-dörren, at kreaturen må gå der-igenom första gängen.

83. Alt fullgjordt arbete *korsas öfver* (all finished work has the sign of the cross made over it).

84. Om man *Fet-Tisdag* går i ränbaka at åka på skida, ok mäktar stå utan at falla kull (without falling), skal det året blifva *långt lin* (the flax be long).

85. *Garnet* får *ej tvettas i nedan* (not washed downwards), ty då blir det grått.

86. Om alt är under lås (lock and key) *Michelsmäss-afton*, skola tjufvar ej göra skada (thieves do no harm) det året.

87. Om et *korn* eller annat finnes *under bordet* (if some grain or other be

found under the table), då der sopas (swept) Ny-års morgon, skal blifva ymnog års-vext (pretty good harvest).

88. När man på de 3 första säses-dagar (days of sowing) sätter 3 *stickor i en myr-stak* (ant-hill), får man se, hvilket säde bäst lyckas : *kryper myran öfverst* på den 3, blifver den lykligast.

89. Är sjö-redskap stulen, bör den *rökas med vriden eld* (if sea-tackle is stolen, it should be smoked with need-fire).

90. Vil vörten ej rinna genom råsten, bör man sätta en *ull-sax emellan banden och råstkaret.*

91. När brännvins-pannor vora i bruk (use), troddes (it was believed) at bränningen geck bäst i nedanet, om pannan då var förfärdigad; och tvärtom (and v.v.).

92. Då *svin* kommo at *lukta* eller *smaka* (smell or taste) af brännvins-ämnet (vapour), skulle hela bränningen förolyckas, så framt ej en *häst feck blåsa* (would be a failure, unless a horse blew) i pannan eller piporna (see Germ. 820).

93. Påsk-natten *ligga i strumpor* (stockings) var at förekomma (prevent) skabb.

94. När *lomen* ses flyga och strika öfver isen, skal bli många *o-ägta barn* det året. Den som *dåras* af honom, får såra händer (see 119).

95. *Gropar* vårtiden på gården (cracks in the yard in springtime) betyder at någon snart skal dö i huset.

96. Om någon mistänkt kom (suspicious person came) i gården, skulle man, at undgå (escape) spådoms säudningen, äntingen *slå* henne (either beat her) *så at bloden rann*, eller *kasta eldbrand* efter en sådan (such a one).

97. När bruden är klädd, bör hon först få se brudgumen *i sin skrud*, at äktenskapet må blifva kärligt.

98. När bruden kommer från kyrkan, skal hon sjelf *spänna ifrån* eller *sadla af* (unharness or unsaddle) hästen, at hon måtte lindrigt få barn.

99. Äfven bör hon då först gå i kok-stugan (kitchen), och *se i sop-vrån*, at hennes föda må bli tilräkelig.

100. Dansar bruden *med pengar i skona* (money in her shoes), kan ingen trolldom bita på henne.

101. När en qvinna lyktat sin väf (has finished her weaving), och tar en *spjelka*, som *sutit i väfskelet, rider' derpå ut genom dörren*, och möter en man, så skal den hafvande hustrun, hon tänker på (the woman she thinks of), få et goss-barn ; men tvärtom (and v. v.).

102. Dricker hafvande hustrun *ur breda kärl* (out of a broad vessel), blir barnet bred-mynt (wide-mouthed).

103. Går hon genom et *hag-skott*, d. ä., der gårds-balken slutas, skal hon få fall-sjuka.

104. Om barnet får sofva (go to sleep) i *christnings-kläderna*, skal det ej bli okynnigt (not be stupid), utan godt.

105. När *spjäll* om qvällen *skjutes*, hafva de ock fordom haft en särdeles (special) sång : ' Skjuter jag mitt sqjäll sent om en qväll (late of an evening), . . . aldrig (never) skal min eld släckas ut.'

106. Den som *först kommer från kyrka* Jul-dagen, tros (is believed) först få så och berga (sow and reap), samt vara främst i alt arbete (all work).

107. *Tvät-vattn* utslås aldrig *efter sol-gången* (washing-water is never emptied after sunset), utan at *deri stickes eld* (without fire being put therein) i stället för spottning om dagen.

108. Då boskapen först om våren utsläppes (let out in spring), *gå de öfver eld i et rykande fnöske* eller annat ämne (vapour).

109. Man bör gå bort, *utan at saga til*, eller *möta någon*, om fiske i vissa sjöar skal lyckas (if fishing in certain lakes is to prosper; see 43).

110. Ibland (among) the storre amuleter äro *bo-trä* (dwelling-trees), stora *hogar* och *berg*, uti hvilka man tror (believes) *underjordskt folk* bo; så akta de sig högeligen, at icke allenast *intet hugga* (are careful, not only to hew nothing) *af slikt bo-trä*,—til undvikanda (avoidance) af o-lycka, som skedde in Foss-pastorat för 2 år sen, tå en bonde inbillade sig (imagined) at han fådt sin o-lycka, för thet han allenast *högg en gren* (cut a branch) *af slikt bo-trä*, ok giorde knä-fall ok bad om förlåtelse, hvarföre han blef skriftad ok måste plikta;—utan ok hålla the särdeles (but also keep espec.) *Torsdags qväller* så heliga, at the hvarken töra hugga elle spinna, at icke *tomte gubbarne* (lest the homesprites), som *bo i sådanne bo-trä* när vid gården, må fortörnas (be offended) och vika bort med all välsignelse.

111. The låta intet gärna (willingly) någon brud få *god häst*, at rida på, ty om hon intet er mö (for if she be no maid), blir han aldrig god therefter.

112. Tå the äro fäste eller vigde (betrothed or married), lagar bruden, at ingen kommer at gå *emellan brudgummen ok henne*, ty eliest tro the, at the bli snart skilge genom döden eller eliest (soon parted by death or otherwise).

113. När bruden kommer til bröllops gårdsens ägor (wedding house's grounds), komma the emot brudgummen ok henne med brännevin, ock dricka til hela foliet (whole party) från kyrkan : tå hon *slår bägaren med dricken bak om sig* (throws the cup of brandy behind her), *så långt* (far) *hon kan*, i hopp, at hennes ägo-delar skola blifva förmerade (increased).

114. *Måten* (the food) *står på bordet*, natt ok dag, så länge bröllopet påstår (lasts), i then tron, at brude-folken aldrig skal fattas (lack) mat eller dricka.

115. Få the *barn*, så låta the intet gerna sina barn döpas på samma dag the äro födde (born). Hvarföre the dömma (deem), at the barn, som om *Söndag* födas ok döpas, intet skola länge lefva. Men (but) lefva the, tror man, at intet tröll eller spöke (no witch or bogie) kan giora them skada.

116. *Döpelse-vatnet*, ther i (baptism-water, wherein) barnen döpte äro, söka the micket efter, thet the sedan, om the prästen o-vitterligit kunna få, (can get it unknown to the priest), bruka (use) til at bota siukdommar med.

117. Til sina siuka (to their sick) kalla the intet gärna *prästen*, förrän the ligga på thet yttersta (till the last extremity); ty the tro, at the o-felbart (without fail) dö, sedan the tagit Herrans helga nattvard (supper).

118. Hustrorna akta noga (watch strictly) sina barn : tils the bli döpte, ha the altid *stål* ok *sy-nåler* (needles) *i barnets kläder*, at the icke af spöken skola blifva förbytte (not become booty of bogies).

119. Om våren äro the micket rädde för *fogle-rop* (much afraid of birds' cries) at the icke skola *dåras* (fooled) af them, särdeles *göken* (esp. the cuckoo); therföre gå the 1 April ok Maji aldrig ut fastandes (never go out fasting). See 128.

120. Om en flicka, enka (widow), eller karl blir *dårad*, tror then samma sig bli gift (fancy they'll be married) thet året; om gamla ok gifte bli *dårade*, befara the thet året svåra siukdommar eller olycks-fall.

121. Somlige bruka slå sina späda (backward) barn 3 *slag med riset i ändan*, innan mödrarna gå i kyrkan, eller hålla sin kyrko-gång (churching); og tå mena the, barnen skola få *godt minne* (memory).

122. Som (as) the i gamla dagar dyrkat elden (worshipped fire), så ha the ok, här så väl som än i Norriget, brukat *dricka eldborgs skål* [1] hvar Kyndel-mässo (ty 'kindel' på gammal Giötiska betyder lius): hvarföre, när the skulle *dricka eldborgs skål*, täden the 2 *stora lius* ok satte på golfvet (lit 2 great candles and set them on the floor), emillan hvilka lades et hyende (a pillow between), på hvilket alla som i huset voro, then ene efter then andre, skulle sätta sig ok *dricka eldborgs skål* med dricka i en trä-skål (wooden cup). Ok när the utdruckit, skulle skålen *kastas bak öfver hufvudet i golfvet. Hvälfdes* tå skålen öfver-ända (if the cup tipped over), trodde the at then skålen kastat (he who threw it) skulle thet året dö; men *stod han rätt upp*, vore tekn at han skulle lefva.

123. Innan dager har hustrun (housewife) lagt eld i bak-ugnen, ok tå thet bäst brunnit, haft tilreds en smör-klening (buttered slice) på kake-bröd, jämte en skål öl (ale). Therpå har hon kallat alt sitt hus-folk ihop (together), ok stält them i en half-måne mit för ugns-holet (oven's mouth). Ok tå the alla under *knä-böjande* ok *lyck-önskan* (luck-wishing) atit en bit af smör-kleningen ock druckit hvar (each) sin drick *eldborgs-skål*, sen hafva the kastat thet öfvriga af kleningen ok dricken *uti elden*, i tro (belief) at thet året bli bevarade för elds-våda (safe from fire-accidents).

124. Så ha the ok brukat *tända eld* på then halmen *lik ha legat* (burn the straw a corpse had lain on), ok thet strax efter liket blifvit burit til grafva, tå the noga sedt på *röken* (watched the smoke). Om han *slagit ned på gården*, tå the säkert trodt (firmly believed) någon af närmaste släkten (kindred) på gården skulle snart följa efter. Men ther *han gik långt i högden eller längden up ivädret* (air), skulle siukdomen ok döden flytta sig ther bän i öster eller vester, som röken for (E. or W., as the smoke went).

125. På det liket icke skulle spöka (that the dead might not haunt), brukade the at *strö hö-frö* (strew rye-seed) på kyrko-vägen ok grafven, tå the mänte (then they thought) at Satan ingen makt hade (see 150).

## b. DENMARK.[2]

126. Det er skik (custom), at pigerne (girls) paa S. Hans-dag plukke de saa-kaldte *S. Hans urter* (worts, herbs), og sätte dem i bjelkerne (beams) under loftet, for at (so that) de deraf kunne slutte sig til det tilkommende (guess the future). Saaledes pleie de (thus they are wont) at sätte en *urt for sig* og en *for kiäresten* (sweetheart); og hvis disse da *voxe sammen* (if these grow together), betyder det bryllup (marriage). Ogsaa sätte de saadanne (such) urter i bjelken for deres paarörende (relatives), at de deraf maa kunne vide (know), hvo der skal have langt liv, og hvo et stakket

---

[1] Drinking the fire's health ; prevalent esp. in Krokstad and Nafverstad.
[2] From *Thiele's* Danske Folkesagn 3, 95—124.

(and who a short). *Voxer urten op, i-mod loftet* (toward the ceiling), da er det gode tegn ; men *voxer den nedad* (downwards), da betyder det sygdom og död.

127. Naar piger og karle ville have at vide, hvo der skal skifte (leave), og hvo der skal blive (stay) i huset, da *kaste de en skoe over hovedet* mod dören. Falder (falls) da skoen saaledes, at *hälen vender* (the heel points) *mod dören*, da betyder det, at personen skal blive; men *vender taaen mod dören*, da er det tegn til, at han skal skifte.

128. Seer man *första gang* i aaret *gjögen* (cuckoo), medens man endnu (still) er fastende, da hedder det 'gjögen *ganter* os !' (i Fyen : 'g. *daarer* os !'); og er det et mandfolk, skal han i dette aar *ikke hitte* kreaturer (not find cattle) eller andet hvad han monne söge. Er det en pige, maa hun vel vogte (guard) sig for ung-karlene, at hun ikke bliver gantet (fooled) af dem. Er det gamle folk, da have de vel aarsag til at frygte (reason to fear) for sygdomme (see 119).

129. Naar tjeneste-folk (servants) gaae i tjeneste, da maa de vel give agt paa, hvem de möde (notice whom they meet). En *gaaende* betyder ondt, men *ridende* godt.

130. Naar tyende (servants) första-gang see *storken flyende*, da betyder det, at de endnu i samme aar skulde komme at skifte. Men see de den *staaende*, da skulle de blive i deres tjeneste.

131. Naar noget er *bort-stjaalet* (stolen), da kan man lade (let) en smed *slaa öiet ud* paa tyven (knock the thief's eye out).

132. For at optage en tyv, besynderligen mellem tyendet (espec. among servants), har det tilforn väret skik, at lade *soldet löbe* (it was the custom to let the sieve run). Husbonden pleiede (used) da at tage et *sold*, og sätte det i lige-vägt *paa spidsen af en sax* (balance it on the points of scissors), derpaa at opremse navnene (then call out the names) paa alle sine folk, og vel give agt paa soldet, som ufeilbarligen (unfailingly) *kom i bevägelse* (motion), naar tyvens navn nävntes.

133. Naar noget er *bort-stjaalet*, da skal man henvende sig (resort) til de saa-kaldte *kloge folk*, hvilka have den evne, at de kunne tvinge (force) tyven til at bringe det stjaalne igjen.

134. Fra Jule-dag til Nyt-aars-dag maa man ikke sätte nogen ting, *som löber rundt*, i gang (set nothing that runs round a-going), altsaa hvarken *spinde* eller *vinde*.

135. *Jule-nat* vid midnats-tid *reiser qväget sig* på stalden (the cattle rise in their stalls).

136. Naar man Jule-aften sidder til bords, og önsker at vide, om nogen blandt de tilstede värende (wish to know if one of those present) skal döe inden näste Jul, da kan man erfare dette, naar man gaaer *stil-tiende* udenfor og *kiger* ind *igjennem en vindues-rude* (go silently outside, and peep in through a pane). Den som man da seer at sidde ved bordet *uden hoved* (without head), skal döe i det kommende aar.

137. Ved gjeste-bud (feast) er det ikke godt at sidde *tretten* (13) till bords, thi da maa en af dem döe forinden (before) aaret er omme.

138. Om *Fredagen* skal man skjäre (pare) sine nägle, da faaer man lykke. Naar man har klippet sine nägle eller sit haar, da maa det *afklippede* enten

*brändes* eller *graves ned* (either burnt or buried); thi dersom onde menne-sker faaer fat paa saadant (for if bad men get hold of such), da kunne de dermed forgjöre (undo) den person, som har baaret det.

139. Hvo der finder en *afbrudt sye-naal* (broken needle) paa gulvet, förend han har läst sin morgen-bön, faaer enten hug eller onde ord (blows or ill words).

140. Staaer *öinene aabne* paa et liig (if the eyes of a corpse stand open), betyder det, at snart nogen af samme familie skal fölge efter.

141. *Kläder* og linned-stykker, som have tilhört en *afdöd* (belonged to one dead), henfalde og gaae let i-tu (to pieces), altsom legemet *forraadner* (rots) i graven.

142. Man maa ei give et liig *gang-kläder* af en endnu levende (of one yet living) med i graven; thi altsom kläderne forraadne i jorden, saa vil ogsaa den, som har baaret (he who has worn) disse kläder tilforn, tid efter anden forsvinde og hentäres (day by day waste away).

143. Naar talgen (tallow), som sidder omkring et *brändende lys,* böier sig ligesom en hövle-spaan (shaving), da betyder det, at nogen skal döe, og er det sädvanligen (usually) den, til hvem hövle-spaanen peger (points).

144. Naar man om morgenen finder *blaa pletter* (blue spots) på sit legeme, da er det *dödning-kneb,* og har det slägtninges eller kjäre venners (kins-man's or dear friend's) när fore-staaende död at betyde.

145. Naar en *skade* (magpie) sätter på huset, da kommer der fremmede (strangers).

146. Naar man förste-gang om aaret hörer *gjögen* at kukke (cuckoo sing), da skal man spörge : 'Hvor gammel bliver jeg?' eller ogsaa: 'Hvor länge skal det vare, indtil det eller det skeer (till so and so happens)?' Og giver den da svar ved at kukke (answer by cuckooing).

147. Naar man finder en *fire-klöver,* eller en *tvilling-nöd* eller en *skilling,* skal man vel gjemme det (save it up), eftersom sligt bringer lykke.

148. Naar man vil see *djävlen,* eller have med ham at gjöre (to do), skal man gaae *tre gange om kirken,* og tredje gang standse ved kirke-dören, og enten raabe : 'Kom herud!' eller ogsaa flöite igjennem nögle-hullet.

149. Naar man önsker at vide, om en afdöd mand har i levende live havt med fanden at bestille (dealings with the devil), da skal man *kige igjennem seletöiet* paa de *heste* (peep through the harness of the horses), som träkke hans liig-vogn; og hvis det saa har väret (if it was so), da vil man see en *sort hund* at sidde bag (black dog sit at the back) paa vognen.

150. Frygter man for spögerie, skal man *ströe hör-fröe* for dören, da kan intet spögelse komme over dör-tärsklen (threshold). See 125.

151. Naar man slaaer en *heste-skoe* fast paa dör-trinnet (nail a horse-shoe on the doorstep), da kan intet spögerie komme derover.

152. Naar man om morgenen kommer alt-fortidligt (too early) i kirken, da kan det vel hände (happen), at man seer de *döde,* hvorledes *de sidde i stole-staderne.*

153. *Troldene* tör (dare) ikke nävne Korsets navn (the Cross's name), men kalde det blot '*hid og did*' (merely Hither-and-thither).

154. Naar man er paa fiskerie, da maa man vel vogte sig for at *trätte*

*om fangsten* (guard against quarrelling over the lake); ej heller maa man *mis-unde* (grudge) andre, thi da forsvinde fiskene strax fra stedet.

155. Er nogen död, som frygtes for, at han vil gaae igjen (who you fear will come again), da kan man hindre sligt ved at *kaste en skaal-fuld vand* (cupful of water) *efter liget*, naar det ud-bäres.

156. Det er daarligt at skyde (silly to shoot) paa et spögelse, thi *kuglen farer tilbage* (ball flies back) paa den, som ud-skyder. Men lader man bössen med en *sölv-knap* (silver-button), da vil den visselig träffe.

157. Den tredje nat efter begravelsen pleie de döde at gaae igjen.

⁷58. En frugtsommelig (pregnant) kone maa ei gaae over et sted, hvor man *har selvet en kniv*, thi det volder en sväar forlösning. Men naar man i forveien spytter tre gange paa stedet, da har det ei fare (no danger).

159. Naar et barn *veies* strax, som det er födt (weighed as soon as born), da vil det siden ei trives (not thrive afterwards).

160. Naar man löfter et barn *ud af et vindue*, og *tager det ind* igjen *gjennem et andet* (in again through another), da vil det aldrig siden blive större (never grow bigger).

161. Naar en *barsel-qvinde* döer uden at vare bleven forlöst (dies without being delivered), da vil hun fyrretyve uger derefter föde (give birth 40 weeks after) i graven. Derfor gives hende *naal, traad, sax* (needle, thread, scissors) og andet sligt med, at hun selv kan sye börne-töiet (sew the baby-linen).

162. Det er et godt middel imod tand-pine (remedy for toothache), först at tage en *hylde-pind* i munden (elder-twig in mouth), og der-näst stikke den i väggen (wall) med de ord : ' Viig bort, du onde aand (go, evil spirit) ! ' Saa er ogsaa gavnligt mod kold-feber (good for ague), at stikke en *hylde-pind* i jorden, dog uden at mäle (without speaking) et ord der-ved. Da holder feberen sig til hyldepinden, og hänger sig ved den, der u-heldigviis först kommer til stedet.——In a MS. of 1722 : Paganismo ortum debet superstitio, *sambucum* non esse exscindendam; nisi prius rogata permissione, his verbis : ' *Mater sambuci, mater sambuci*, permitte mihi tuam caedere silvam ! ' Videmus quoque rusticos orsuros caesionem arboris *ter exspuere*, quasi hac excretione *vettas* aliosque latentes ad radicem arboris noxios genios abacturos. Passim etiam obvium, quod bacillum vel fracturi vel dissecturi, partem abruptam abscissamve non projiciant in terram, nisi ter in extremitatem fragminis exspuerint, cujus quidem rei aliam non norunt rationem, quam curasse, ne quid sibi a vettis noceatur.

163. Af *bryst-benet* (breast-bone) paa *Mortens-gaasen* kan man see hvorledes (how) vinteren vil blive. Det hvide deri (white therein) er tegn paa snee, men det brune paa meget stärk kulde. Og er det at märke, at den *forreste* deel ved halsen spaaer (part by the neck foretells) om vinteren *för* Juul, men den *bageste* (hindmost) om vinteren *efter* Juul.

164. Oft händer det, at söefolk i rum söe see et *skib* (ship), i alle maader som et andet, at seile forbi (sail past), og i samme stund forsvinde (vanish)' for deres aasyn. Det er *dödning-seileren*, som varsler om (announces), at et skib snarligen (soon) skal gaae under paa det samme sted.

165. Naar man taler om *skadelige dyr* (noxious beasts), da maa man ikke

nävne deres rette navn, men omscrive det (periphrase it), og saaledes kalde rotterne (call rats) ' de lang-rumpede,' musene (mice) ' de smaa graa.'

166. Naar man vil vide sin tilkommende lykke i det nye aar, da skal man tage et *bröd,* en *kniv,* og en *skilling,* og dermed gaae ud at see *maanen, naar nyet tändes* (moon newly lighted). Og naar man da slaaer op (opens) i en Psalme-bog, vil man af dens indhold kunne slutte sig til det vigtigste (guess the weightiest).

167. Naar en pige ved midnat ud-spänder *mellem fire kieppe* den hinde, i hvilken föllet er, naar det kastes (stretch betw. four sticks the afterbirth of a foal), og derpaa *nögen kryber der-igjennem* (creep naked through it), da vil hun kunne föde börn uden smerte (without pain). Men alle de drenge (boys) hun undfanger, blive *vär-ulve,* og alle de piger blive *marer.*[1]

168. *Skjer-Torsdag-aften* (Maundy Thursd.) kaster bonden *öxer* og *jernkiler paa de besaaede agre* (axes and iron bolts on the sown fields), og fäster *staal* paa alle döre, at ikke gamle kjerlinger (lest old witches) skulle skade ham.

169. Naar en kommer til kirke *Skjer-Torsdag,* og haver da, uden selv at vide det, et *höneke-äg* (chicken's egg), det er, det förste äg en höne lägger, paa sig; saa vil han see alle de qvinder, der ere hexe, at gaae lige-som med *sie-bötter* eller *malke-bötter paa hovedet* (see Germ. 783).

## L. FRENCH.[2]

1. Le 24 décembre, vers les six heures du soir, chaque famille met à son feu une énorme bûche appelée *souche de noël.* On défend aux enfans de s'y asseoir, parceque, leur dit on, ils y attraperaient le gale. Notez, qu'il est d'usage dans presque tous les pays, de mettre le bois au foyer dans toute sa longueur, qui est d'environ 4 pieds, et de l'y faire brûler par un bout. See 28.

2. Le jour de la fête de la Trinité quelques personnes vont de grand matin dans la campagne, pour y voir lever *trois soleils à la fois.*

3. Le 24 Juin, jour de Saint Jean, quelques personnes vont aussi sur une montagne élevée, et y attendent le lever du *soleil,* pour le voir *danser.*

4. Les herbes et plantes médicinales, cueillies la veille de la *Saint Jean,* passent pour avoir plus de vertus, surtout contre certains maux.

5. La coupe de cheveux ne doit se faire que lorsque la *lune* est *nouvelle,* sans cela les cheveux ne pourraient plus pousser. On ne doit point jeter la recoupe des cheveux sur la voie publique, les sorciers pourraient y jeter un sort.

6. Les linges, qui ont servi au pansement des maux, ne doivent être ni brûlés ni jetés dans la rue, pour les mêmes motifs.

---

[1] ' Om bruden kryper *genom en sela* (horse-collar), får hon barn utan möda, hvilke dock skola blifva *maror.*' Westerdahl's Beskrifning om Svenska seder, p. 28.

[2] From Mémoires de l'académie celtique: Nos. 1—10 (Commercy en Lorraine) 3, 441—450 and 4, 83-4. Nos. 11—13 (Sologne) 4, 93-4. Nos. 14—20 (Chartres) 4, 242. Nos. 21-2 (Gironde) 4, 268. Nos. 23—28 (Bonneval) 4, 428. Nos. 29—32 (Pyrénées) 5, 386—390. Nos. 33—35 (Bonneval) Mém des antiquaires 1, 239—242.

7. Si quelqu'un meurt, on voile les glaces de sa chambre.

8. Lorsqu'une personne est gravement malade, on a soin d'observer, si quelque *hibou, chouette* ou *chathuant* viennent voltiger autour de l'habitation.

9. *L'hirondelle* est un oiseau d'heureux présage; aussi ne la dérange-t-on jamais. Détruire son nid, c'est détruire ou atténuer les heureuses destinées, qu'on y attache en faveur de la maison.

10. *L'araignée* est un signe de bonheur, et annonce particulièrement de l'argent pour la personne, sur laquelle elle est trouvée. Plus une étable est garnie de toiles d'araignées, plus elle est digne de regards de la Providence.

11. Si une *jeune taure s'égare* la première fois qu'elle est mise aux champs, les Solonaises vont jeter deux liards dans la serrure, se mettent à genoux, et disent tout haut cinq pater et cinq ave, qu'elles addressent au bon saint Hubert ; cette prière faite, elles sont bien sûres que les loups respecteront la taure, fût-elle au milieu d'eux, et qu'ils la rameneront même à la bergerie.

12. Dans la *nuit* du jour *de noël*, jusqu'à midi, les chevaux, les vaches, les bœufs, les taureaux, les ânes *parlent*. Ces animaux se plaignent ou s'applaudissent du traitement de leurs maîtres. Ce don de la parole leur arrive seulement avant minuit sonnant, et finit à midi du jour de noël, ou plutôt si la personne, qui les soigne, est coupable d'un péché mortel.

13. Le même jour de noël il ne faut pas mettre paître les bêtes à corne avant midi, parceque de suite *elles se battraient,* et se blesseraient certainement.

14. La veille de noël, pendant la généalogie qui se chante à la messe de minuit, tous les *trésors cachés* s'ouvrent.

15. Dans la plupart des églises de campagne on fait encore aujourd'hui des offrandes de la *première gerbe de froment* coupée dans un champ. Ces premices de la moisson ne reçoivent d'autres ornements qu'en paille plus ou moins façonnée. Cette gerbe est presque toujours surmontée d'une croix aussi en paille.

16. L'usage des *brandons* est consacré partout les premier et second dimanche de carême. On va brûler dans les champs, ou sur les chemins vicinaux, des flambeaux formés de paille en chantant : ' *Brandons,* brûlez pour les filles à marier ! ' [1]

17. Quand le mari met *l'anneau* au doigt de la mariée, il ne le porte que jusqu'à *la second jointure.* Celle-ci doit donc vîte le pousser à la *troisiéme,* afin d'empêcher le malefice des sorciers, qui n'ont que cet instant du passage de l'anneau, pour l'opérer la nouûre de l'aiguillette.

18. Les mariés entendent la messe à genoux. A l'évangile on a soin de remarquer lequel des deux époux *se lève le premier ;* on en augure que c'est lui qui sera le maître.

19. Au moment qu'on montre le bon dieu de la messe, ceux qui se trouvent placés auprès des mariés, leur *frappent trois petits coups sous les*

---

[1] Conf. Mém. des antiquaires 1, 237 : ' Brandelons, brûlez par ces vignes, par ces blés ; brandelons, brûlez pour ces filles à marier.' Puis on s'écrie : ' Mais les vieilles n'en auront pas.'

*talons*, avec le manche d'un couteau, pour empêcher qu'ils ne deviennent jaloux.

20. En sortant de l'église, on conduit la mariée en face d'une image de la vierge, auprès de laquelle est attachée une quenouille garnie de chanvre, on la lui présente ; elle *file deux ou trois aiguillées*, et l'emporte chez elle ; elle fait filer ou file le reste, et rend ensuite, *avec l'écheveau de fil* qui en est provenu, cette même quenouille, qu'elle a eu soin de garnir d'autre chanvre.

21. Un enfant mâle *qui n'a pas connu son père*, a la vertu de *fondre les loupes*, en les touchant pendant trois matinées de suite, étant à jeun et récitant quelques prières.

22. Le cinquième des enfans mâles venus au monde et de suite, *guérit les maux de rate* par le simple attouchement répété.

23. A-t-on chez soi une *poule*, qui *chante comme le coq*, on se dépêche de la tuer ou de la vendre, dans la crainte qu'elle n'attire quelque malheur sur la maison.

24. Est-on en voyage, si l'on rencontre dans son chemin des *pies par nombre impair*, c'est malheur.

25. Quand on veut savoir, quel mari ou quelle femme on épousera, il est d'usage de se lever, le *premier jour de mars*, au coup de minuit et pendant que l'heure sonne. On marche trois pas en avant de son lit, en prononçant ces paroles : 'Bon jour *Mars*, de Mars en Mars, fais moi voir en mon dormant la femme que j'aurai en mon vivant ! ' On revient à son lit en marchant en arrière ; on se recouche, on s'endort, on rêve, et l'homme ou la femme qui apparaissent alors, sont le futur époux.

26. Ceux qui possèdent de *mouches à miel*, ont grand soin, lorsqu'il meurt quelqu'un dans la maison, d'aller d'abord annoncer à chaque *ruche* l'évènement fâcheux, qui vient d'avoir lieu, et d'y attacher ensuite un petit *morceau d'étoffe noire*. Sans cela, ils périraient bientôt.

27. La veille de Saint Jean un *feu de joie* est allumé dans un carrefour. Au milieu du feu on place une longue perche, qui le domine, et qui est garnie de feuillages et de fleurs. Le clergé se rend en grande pompe au lieu de la cérémonie, allume le feu, entonne quelques chants, et se retire ; ensuite les assistants s'en emparent, *sautent par dessus*, et emportent chez eux quelques *tisons*, qu'ils placent sur le ciel de leur lit, comme un préservatif contre la foudre.

28. La veille de noël, avant la messe de minuit, on place dans la cheminée de l'appartement le plus habité une *bûche*, la plus grosse, que l'on puisse rencontrer, et qui soit dans le cas de résister pendant trois jours dans la foyer ; c'est ce qui lui a fait donner le nom de *tréfué*, tréfoué, trois feux (see 1).

29. Une jeune fille qui désire savoir son futur époux, se lève avant le jour le *premier mai*. Elle prend un seau, qu'elle nettoie avec une branche de romarin, et s'achemine vers quelque fontaine solitaire. Rendue là, elle se met à genoux sur le bord de la fontaine, fait une prière, plante sa branche de romarin dans un buisson voisin, et remplie son seau de l'eau de la fontaine. Elle attend alors le *lever du soleil*. Aussitôt qu'il commence à paraître sur l'horizon, elle s'approche du seau, en *trouble l'eau avec la main*

*gauche*, et dit ces trois mots : ' Ami rabi vohi ! ' Elle doit répéter *neuf fois* la même chose, et avoir fini lorsque le soleil paraît en entier. Alors, si elle n'a été vue par personne, ni en venant à la fontaine, ni pendant les cérémonies qu'elle y a faites, elle voit *au fond du seau* la figure de celui, qu'elle doit épouser.

30. Un jeune homme, pour connaître la couleur de cheveux de celle, qui doit être sa femme, fait, la veille de S. Jean, *trois fois le tour du feu de joie*, prend un *tison enflammé*, le laisse éteindre dans sa main gauche, et le soir, avant de se coucher, le met sous le chevet de son lit, enveloppé d'une chemise qu'il a porté trois jours. Il faut que tout cela se fasse les yeux clos. Le lendemain matin, au lever du soleil, le jeune homme trouve, autour de son tison, des cheveux de la couleur que doivent avoir ceux de sa future épouse.

31. Il est d'usage de se marier *à jeun*. On croit, que ceux qui y manqueraient, sans des motifs bien puissants, n'auraient que des *enfants muets*.

32. Les époux ont grand soin, le jour de leur mariage, de mettre du *sel* dans leur poche gauche avant de se présenter à l'eglise. Ce sel empêche le nœud de l'aiguillette.

33. La *rosée* de la nuit de la *S. Jean* guérit la gale, et le *premier seau* tiré d'un puits à l'instant du minuit, qui commence le jour de S. Jean, guérit de la fièvre. Près de Nogent-le-Rotrou il y a une *fontaine* célèbre pour sa vertu curatrice pendant toute la nuit, veille de S. Jean. Hommes et femmes entrent dans ses eaux et s'y lavent : nulle idée d'indécence ne trouble la cérémonie.

34. Le *feu de S. Jean* ne brûle pas, on peut en prendre à la main les tisons enflammés.

35. Pour se défendre de la puissance des *bergers sorciers*, on met du *sel* dans sa poche, et en passant devant le berger on dit tout bas : ' Berger sorcier, je ne te crains ni te redoute.'

## M. ESTHONIAN.[1]

1. Marriages take place at the time of *new moon*.

2. If the suitor rides to the house where he goes a-wooing, he is careful not to take a *mare*, else there would be only *daughters* born of the marriage.

3. When the bride is betrothed, a *red string* is tied round her body; and when the wedding is completed, she must so inflate herself as to break the string. A sure preventive of difficult confinements.

4. In many places the young couple *run out of church*, hand in hand, at the top of their speed, to secure rapid progress in their business.

5. When the bride is fetched, if she *falls on the way*, it betokens the early death of her first three or four children.

6. If they see the suitor arrive on horseback, they hasten to *undo his saddle-girth*. This also tends to facilitate childbirth in the future wife.

---

[1] Etwas über die Ehsten (Leipz. 1788, pp. 55–88). Nos. 93–99 from Hupel's Topogr. nachr. von Lief- und Ehst-land (Riga 1777. 2, 134—145).

7. The bride must not come out *by a gate* through which a *corpse* has lately been carried out.

8. When the bride is fetched in, she must wear no chains or bells, but be led in *in solemn silence;* else she will have restless noisy children.

9. Directly the wedding is over, the strongest of the relations or guests *lifts the bride and bridegroom aloft,* thereby to heighten their married bliss.[1]

10. As soon as the wedded pair have stept into their house, a *watchman* must stay a good while *by the household fire,* that no stranger may come near it, and contrive secret sorcery to their hurt.

11. The moment the bride enters, she is led through every part of the house, parlours, bedrooms, bathrooms, stables and gardens; and is bound, as she holds her husband's happiness dear, to drop *ribbons* or *money* into each part, even into the *well* and the *fire.*

12. When she sits down, they set a *male child* in her lap, that she may have the power to bear men-children.

13. In some parts they used, during the wedding feast, to stick *two swords into the wall* over where the bride and bridegroom sat; the one whose *sword* kept up the *longest vibration,* would *live longest.*

14. At the meal they are wilfully wasteful of the *beer,* and *spill* it about, so that superfluity may house with the happy pair.

15. Whichever of the pair *first goes to sleep,* dies first.

16. *Rain on the wedding-day* means frequent weeping for the wife.

17. At the marriage-feast they set *two candles before bride and bridegroom;* the one whose light goes out first of itself, is sure to die first.

18. The bridegroom's attendant cuts a *small piece* off a whole loaf, butters it, and puts it *in the bride's mouth.* Her children will then have a small smooth mouth.

19. In bringing the young wife into the husband's house, they *pull down the fence* on both sides of the entrance, that she may drive in swiftly without hindrance. Then her confinements will come off quickly and easily.

20. Women with child are careful, in lighting a fire, not to throw the wood in *against the branches,* else they would have a difficult labour.

21. A difficult labour is lightened by the husband *striding over the wife.*

22. No pregnant woman will sit on a *water-vessel,* lest she have too many *daughters,* or the fruit be lost in the water.

23. If two pregnant women *sneeze* together, they will have *daughters;* if their husbands sneeze, *sons.*

24. In beginning a loaf, a pregnant woman cuts a very *small slice* first, that her children may have pretty little mouths.

25. To *change* the *bastels* (bast-shoes) once a week in the middle of pregnancy, and to throw *salt three times* behind oneself shortly before confinement, will ease the labour.

26. None shall step *over the feet* of a pregnant woman, lest her children get crooked misshapen feet.

[1] RA. 433.

27. A newborn babe is not placed at once in the mother's arms, but first laid at her feet, that *her left foot may touch its mouth ;* then it will not be rebellious.

28. A newborn baby's *bath-water* is emptied on the most out-of-the-way spot, lest, if many trample on it, the child be down-trodden and despised.

29. The midwife with the baby shall, soon after the birth, take the *uppermost seat at table ;* it will then be more highly esteemed.

30. Never pass anything *over the baby's head,* or it won't grow; if such a thing happens, pull the hair on the top of its head upwards.

31. What a baby *first clutches at,* shows what will be its favourite occupation.

32. The first time a babe is laid in the cradle, they put a *knife,* a *cross-key,* and some *red yarn* beside it; these defend it from sorcery.

33. One born on one of the *last days of a week,* will marry late or never.

34. If a married woman has *boys* only, it is a sign of war; if *girls* only, of peace.

35. When a priest visits a sick man, they watch the gait of his horse as he draws near. If the *horse hangs its head,* they despair of the patient's recovery.[1]

36. A *funeral* must on no account cross a cornfield, even when it lies fallow.

37. By a corpse they lay a *brush, money, needles,* and *thread.* Some brush the dead man's head, and lay the *brush* beside him, to bring him peace.

38. Some drive *a nail into the threshold* every time a person dies in the house.

39. The *vehicle* that has carried a corpse is not admitted *within the gate* at once, but left outside for a time; else more of the family would follow.

40. The *straw* on which the sick man died, is all carried out and burnt: by *footprints in the ashes* they can tell if the next loss will be of man or beast.

41. If one dies at *new moon,* he takes all the luck with him; if in *Shrove-tide,* he is buried as plainly as possible.

42. On All Souls day every family makes a *feast* for its *departed* members, and visits the churchyards. In some parts they set food for the deceased on the floor of a particular room. Late in the evening the master of the house went in with a pergel (a lighted brand split down its length), and invited the deceased by name to eat. After a time, when he thought the souls had made a hearty meal, he, while *beating his pergel to pieces on the threshold,* bade them go back to their places, and not trample the rye on their way. If there was a bad crop, it was ascribed to the souls having been entertained too scantily.[2]

43. About the Judgment-day the Esthonian has the notion that all the churches will then *topple over towards the North.* He cannot bear the thought of being buried in that part of the churchyard.

---

[1] Conf. Hupel's Topogr. Nachr. 2, 146.    [2] More fully in Thom. Hiärn 1, 49.

44. Till the baby is baptized, it has a hymnbook laid under its head, and *a fire kept up* beside it, to ban the devil, and keep him from changing the child.

45. During baptism they fix their eyes on the baby, to see if it *holds its head up* or *lets it sink down*. If up, it will have a long life; if down, a short.

46. Sometimes, during the service, the father *runs* rapidly *round the church*, that the child may be gifted with fleetness of foot.

47. If by bribing the sexton they can get the *baptismal water*, they dash it *as high as they can* up the wall. The child will then attain high honours.

48. During baptism you must *not talk*, or the child will talk in its sleep.

49. Don't have a *baptism* directly after a *burial*, or the child will follow the dead.

50. Leave the chrisom baby's *hands free*; it will then be quick and industrious.

51. During baptism a sponsor shall *not look about him*, or the child will see ghosts.

52. Many tie *rings to the swathings* of a chrisom boy, to make him marry early.

53. They do not like a child to be *baptized* on another child's birthday.

54. In the chrisom child's clothes some insert, unobserved, *money, bread,* and *garlic;* then the first two will never fail him, and the last protects from sorcery.

55. *A chrisom child's sleeping* shows it will not live long.

56. When *none but girls* are brought to the font, they will go unmarried long, perhaps always.

57. No sponsor *eats flesh* just before the christening, else the baby will have toothache.

58. Parents who lose their first children call the next ones *Adam* and *Eve*, and they live (see Germ. 26).

59. They will have no christening on a *Friday*; on *Thursday* it has more power.

60. A child christened on a *Friday* grows up a rogue, and comes under the hangman's hands.

61. *Thunder* comes of *God chasing the devil, overtaking him, and dashing him down.* During the storm they make doors and windows fast, lest the hunted devil take refuge in their house, and, as God is sure to catch him up, the house be thunderstruck.

62. Some during a storm fasten *two knives* outside a window, to prevent being struck.

63. Many, the *first time they hear thunder* in the year, take a stone, tap their forehead with it three times, and are free from headache for a year.

64. Anything struck by *lightning* they muse over gravely, especially certain riven rocks; they think the *devil*, having *taken refuge* in or under them, was there surprised and slain.

65. Many take the *rainbow* to be *Thunder's sickle*, with which he *punishes malignant under-gods* who try to injure men.

66. Many believe in the power of man to raise *wind,* and to change its direction. For this purpose they would hang up a *snake,* or set up an *axe,* in the direction whence they wished for a wind, and try to *allure it by whistling.*

67. A sudden noise on *New-year's night* foretells the death of an inmate.

68. They give wild beasts periphrastic names, and avoid their real ones, when they have to speak of them. The fox they call *Hallkuhb* (grey-coat), the bear *Layfalgk* (broad-foot).

69. The first time they drive their cattle out in the year, they bury *eggs under the threshold* over which they must pass, whereby all discomfort is banned away from them. Once, when a cattle plague broke out, it was found that they *buried one head of the herd under the stable door,* as a sacrifice to Death, and to stay the murrain.

70. If the cattle return from pasture, still *chewing grass,* there will be a hay-famine.

71. They send the wolf to the rightabout by sprinkling *salt on his track.*

72. A great *howling of wolves* at early morning foretells plague or famine.

73. Formerly the Ehsts believed, when they heard a great howling of wolves, that they were *crying to God for food,* and he then *threw them dumplings down from the clouds.*

74. If the wolf carries off a sheep or pig, they *let something fall,* of their clothes or of what they have in their pockets, believing that the wolf will then find his load too heavy, and drop his prey.

75. Some wear the tip of a *hen's wing* about them, and think it promotes early rising.

76. They do not like to name the *hare* often, they think it tempts him to come and damage their rye-grass.

77. If a *cock* or *hen* walking in the yard trails a *straw after it,* there will soon be a corpse in the house, its sex depending on that of the fowl.

78. You can enable a *hen* to lay eggs by beating her with an *old broom.*

79. Some, the first time of driving out cattle, put an *egg before the stable-door;* the beast that treads on it is ripe for death, and they try to sell it.

80. They gladly sell the *first calves* of young cows, where the mistress is her own mother's *first child;* such a calf cannot thrive.

81. The *yoke* just *taken off* or about to be *put on* must not be laid on the bare ground, or it will chafe and wound the ox.

82. A *fire* may be checked by *throwing in a live black hen as a sacrifice.*

83. In clearing out the corn and flour bins, leave a *little behind,* or it will bring misfortune.

84. No farmer is willing to give *earth off his cornfields,* he thinks it is parting with a good piece of his prosperity.

85. Let no one *step over your girdle;* it brings on the itch.

86. One is careful not to be beaten with *dry twigs,* it brings on consumption or leanness.

87. In *cutting a new loaf* they *throw some aside;* from a full cup they let *some drops fall on the ground.* It is a sacrifice to the Invisible Spirit.

88. Many a man looks glum if you try to find out the *depth of his well*, it would dry up if you did.

89. One does not like giving all the money in his purse at once; if it can't be helped, let your *spittle* fall in the purse.

90. They are anxious not to have *clothes-props* stolen : their loss runs them short of ash.

91. The first time the cowherds drive home in the year, they are on arriving *sprinkled with water;* it is thought to be wholesome for the cattle.

92. *No shearing of sheep at seed-time,* for then the wool does not grow again properly.

93. *Dung fallen off the cart* is not to be picked up again : it breeds vermin.

94. At flax-picking there is *no talking,* no question answered, no greeting returned; otherwise the flax does not answer well.

95. If the first that dies in a farmer's new abode be a *beast with hairy legs,* a blessing rests on the house; if a *bird with bare legs,* the farmer mopes, dreading losses and poverty.

96. At night when candles are lighted, the *people sigh* and cross themselves.

97. Every time they kill anything, if only a fowl, they put a *piece of it* behind the cattle-shed *as a sacrifice.*

98. On the accursed spot where a house was burnt down, they never build a new one; if, in laying the ground-beam, a single *spark is kindled* by a by-blow, it foretells a new fire, and they look out another place to build on.

99. On the site where a cowhouse is to be built, they first lay rags and herbs; if *black ants* creep on to them, it is a good sign; if *red ants,* the place is pronounced unfit to build on.

100. A *whirlwind* is the work of evil spirits : where you see dust gathering, you should *throw stones* or a *knife* into the heart of the whirl, and pursue it with cries.

101. At a wedding the bride *treads on the* bridegroom's *foot,* that she may never be oppressed by him.

102. *Red streaks* in the sky shew that the *dragon* is setting out; a *dark* hue in the clouds, that he comes home with booty. Shooting stars are little dragons.

### N. LITHUANIAN.[1]

1. When the elf is *red,* he brings people gold; when *blue,* corn or ill-luck.

2. It is not good for a corpse to lie so that it can be *seen in the glass;* some say the dead man gets up and looks at himself. Better hang it elsewhere.

3. On New-year's eve *nine sorts of things*—money, cradle, bread, ring, death's head, old man, old woman, ladder, and key—are baked of dough,

---

[1] Besseldt in Büsching's Wöch. Nachr., b. 3 (Breslau 1817). pp. 223.·339.

and laid under nine plates, and every one has three grabs at them.  What he gets will fall to his lot during the year.

4. The same evening every girl takes *tow* or *flax*, rolls it into a little *ball*, sets it alight, and tosses it up.  She whose ball rises highest, or burns longest, will get married that year.

5. If you spin on Shrove Tuesday, the flax will not thrive; if you go for a *drive* there will be good flax.  All over Lithuania they *drive* on that day; if the gentlefolk don't themselves, they let their servants.

6. Sow *peas* when the wind sets from a soft (rainy) quarter; then they will boil well.

7. Grass *mown* under a *new moon* the cattle reject, or eat reluctantly.

8. The death of the master or mistress must be told the *horses* by *jingling the keys*, also to the other cattle, especially the *bees*.  Otherwise the cattle fall, the trees decay, and the bees die out or move.

9. If a *hare* runs across your path, it means bad luck; a *fox* on the contrary a safe journey and good news.

10. If you take *needle* in hand on Good Friday, the lightning will be after you (see Germ. 43).  All work on that day is fraught with mischief.

11. Girls must be weaned by a *waning moon*, or they'll have too large a bosom; boys at *full moon*, that they may grow big and strong; but no children during the *passage of birds*, else they'll be restless and changeable.

12. When visitors drive away, *don't sweep* your floors directly after; it would bring them ill-luck on their journey.

# SPELLS.

I. *AS. spell for pricking pains.* Harl. MSS. no. 585. fol. 186 (communic. by Price). See p. 1244.

II. *AS. spell for fertilizing land.* Oxf. MSS. no. 5214 (Jun. 103). See p. 1236.

## III. *Exorcismus ad pecudes inveniendas.*[1]

Ne forstolen ne forholen nân uht thäs dhe ic âge, ne mâ the mihte Herod (no more than H. could) urne Drihten. Ic gethohte s̄c̄e Eád Elênan, and ic gethohte Crist on rôde âhangen. svâ ic thence this feoh tô findanne, näs tô othfeorganne and tô vîtanne. näs tô othvyrceanne and tô lufianne. näs tô odhlædanne. *Gârmund,* Godes dhegen, find thät feoh, and fêre thät feoh. and hafa thät feoh and heald thät feoh, and fêre hâm thät feoh. thät he næfre n'äbbe landes thät he hit odhlæde, ne foldan thät odhfêrie ne hûsa thät he hit odhhealde. Gif hit hvâ gedô, ne gedige hit him næfre binnan thrim nihtum. cunne ic his mihta his mägen and his mihta and his mundcräftas. eall he veornige svâ er *vudu veornie,* svâ *bredhel theo* svâ *thistel.* se dhe his feoh odhfergean thence. odhde dhis orf odhehtian dhence. amen.

This man sceal cvedhan dhonne his ceápa, hvilcne man forstelenne. cydh, ær he ænig other vord cvedhe : Bethlem hâttæ seo burh, dhe Crist on geboren väs. seo is gemærsôd ofer ealne middangeard. svâ dheos dæd vyrthe for mannum mære. per crucem x̄p̄i. And *gebide* the thonne *thriva eást,* and cvedh thriva: † x̄p̄i ab oriente reducat. and thriva *vest,* and cvedh : crux x̄p̄i ab occidente reducat. and thriva *sûth,* and cvedh thriva: crux x̄p̄i a meridie reducat. and thriva *north,* and cvedh: crux x̄p̄i abscondita sunt (fuit?) et inventa est. Judeas Crist âhengon. gedidon him dæda thâ vyrstan. hælon thät hi forhelan ne mihton. svâ næfre theos dæd forholen ne vyrthe. per crucem x̄p̄i. Gif feoh sy undernumen. gif hit sy *hors, sing on his feotere* odhdhe *on his bridel.* gif hit sy *other feoh, sing on thät hofrec,* and ontend dhreo candela, and drŷp on thät ofrec veax thriva. ne mäg hit the manna forhelan. Gif hit sy *inorf, sing on feover healfa thäs hûses* and æne on middan: crux x̄p̄i reducat. crux x̄p̄i per furtum periit, inventa est. Abraham tibi semitas vias, montes concludat Job et flumina, Isac tibi tenebras inducat. Jacob te ad iudicium ligatum perducat.

[1] Nos. III. IV. from Wanley's Catal. 114-5 (conf. 110ᵇ. 186ᵃ. 198ᵇ. 275ᵃ). corrected by Kemble's transcripts. Many more AS. spells might be culled out of MSS. cited by Wanley, pp. 44. 83. 223. 231-2-4. 247. 304-5.

### IV. *Benediction.*

Ic me on thisse gyrde belûce, and on Godes helde bebeode, vidh (against) thane sâra sîce, vidh thane sâra slege, vidh thane grymma gryre, vidh thane micela egsa, the bidh æghvam lâdh, and vidh eal thät lâdh, the in tô lande fare. *Sige-gealdor* ic begale (sing), *sige-gyrd* ic me vege. vord-sige and veorc-sige. Se me dege ne me merne gemyrre. ne me maga ne gesvence. ne me næfre mînum feore forht ne gevurdhe. ac gehæle me Aelmihtig and Sunu frôfregâst ealles vuldres vyrdig Drihten. Svâsvâ ic gehŷrde heofna scyppende Abrahame and Isace and svylce men, Moyses and Jacob and Davit and Josep and Euan and Annan and Elizabet, Saharie and ec Marie môdur xps. and eác thæ gebrôdhru Petrus and Paulus and eác thûsend thira engla. clipige ic me tô âre vidh eallum feondum. Hi me fêriòn and fridhion and mîne fêre nerion. eal me gehealdon, men gevealdon. Vorces stîrende sî me vuldres hyht. hand ofer heáfod hâligra rôf sige-rôfra sceote sôdh-fästra engla biddu ealle blîdhu môde thät me beo *hand ofer heáfod*. Matheus *helm*. Marcus *byrne* leoht lîfes rôf. Lucas mîn *svurd* scearp and scîreg. *scild* Johannes vuldre gevlitegôd. vega Seraphin. Fordh ic gefare. frind ic gemête. eall engla blæd. eádiges lâre. bidde ic nu God sigere Godes miltse sidhfät gôdne. smylte and lihte vind veredhum vindas gefran circinde väter simblige häledhe vidh eallum feordum. Freond ic gemête, vidh thät ic on this älmihgian (sic) môte belocun vidh thâ lâdhan. se me lîfes eht on engla blâ blæd gestathelôd, and inna hâlre hand hofna-rîces blæd, thâ hvile the ic on this lîfe vunian môte. ·amen.

### V. *Adjuratio contra grandinem.*

(Munich MS. of 11th cent., Cod. Tegerns. 372.)

Signo te *aer* nomine Domini . . . . adjuro te *diabole* et *angelos* tuos . . . . adjuro vos . . . . ut non feratis *grandinem* neque aliquam molestiam in terminum istum, et non habeatis dicere coram Deo, quia nemo vobis contradixerit. contradicat vobis Deus et Dei filius, qui est initium omnium creaturarum. contradicat vobis sancta Maria . . . . adjuro te *Mermeut*, cum sociis tuis, *qui positus es super tempestatem,* per illius nomen te adjuro, qui in principio fecit coelum et terram. adjuro te *Mermeut* per illius dexteram, qui Adam primum hominem ad imaginem suam plasmavit. adjuro te *Mermeut* per Jesum Christum filium Dei unicum . . . . conjuro te *daemon* et *satanas* . . . . te conjuro, ut non habeas hic potestatem in isto loco vel ini sto vico nocere nec damnum facere, nec tempestatem admittere nec pluviam valentissimam jacere, etc.

A German *weather-spell* in a later Munich MS. (Cgm. 734, f. 208) has: 'ich peut (bid) dir *Fasolt*, dass du das wetter verfirst (removest) mir und meinen nachpauren ân schaden (without hurt).'

### VI. *For a sick Horse* (p. 1235).

(from Cod. Vindob. theol. 259, bottom of right-hand page.)

Petrus Michahel et Stephanus ambulabant per viam. sic dixit Michahel. Stephani equus infusus. signet illum Deus. signet illum Christus et erbam comedat et aquam bibat.

VII. *Contra malum malannum.*

(from a Bonn MS. of 1070–90, in Wackernagel's Wessobr. Gebet 67–70.)

Cum minimo digito circumdare locum debes ubi apparebit, his verbis: ich bimuniun dih *suam* pî Gode jouh pî Christe. Tunc fac crucem per medium † et dic: daz tû niewedar ni gituo noh tolc noh tôt houpit. item adjuro te per Patrem et Filium et Spiritum sanctum ut amplius non crescas sed arescas.

VIII. *For a bloody flux.*

(Cod. Vindob. R. 3282, fol. 32. Twelfth cent.)

Dere hêligo Christ was geboren ce Betlehêm,
dannen quam er widere ce Jerusalêm,
dâ wart er getoufet vone Johanne
in demo Jordâne,
duo verstuont (stood still) der Jordânis fluz
unt der sîn runst.
alsô *verstant dû bluot-rinna*
durch des heiligen Christes minna,
dû verstant an der nôte,
alsô der Jordan tâte
duo der guote sc̄e Johannes
den heiligen Christ toufta.
verstant dû *bluot-rinna*
durch des heiliges Christes minna.

VIIIᵇ. *Blessing on a Journey* (Diut. 2, 70).

Ic dir nâch sihe, ic dir nâch sendi mit mînen funf fingirin *funvi undi funfzic engili.* Got dich gisundi heim gisendi. *offin* sî dir daz *sigi-dor,* sami sî dir daz *slegi-dor*[1] (s. l. for 'selgidor'; query, sælde-dor?). *bislozin* sî dir daz *wagi-dor,* sami sî dir daz *wâfin-dor.*[2] des guotin sandi Uolrichis segin vor dir undi hindir dir undi obi dir undi nebin dir sî gidân, swâ dû wonis (dwellest) undi swâ dû sîs, daz dâ alsi guot fridi sî, alsi dâ wæri, dâ mîn frauwi sandi Marîe des heiligiu Cristes ginas (was recovering).

IX. *The same* (An Engelberg Cod.; Diut. 2, 293).

Herre sc̄e Michahêl hiute wis-tu (be thou) N. sîn *schilt* und sîn *sper.* mîn frouwa sc̄a Maria sî sîn *halsperge* (hauberk). hiute muoze er in deme *heiligin fride* sîn, dâ Got inne wâre, dô er in daz paradîse châme. Herre Got dû muozist in *bescirmin* vor wâge und vor wâfine, vor fiure, vor allen sînen fîandin gesiunlichen und ungesiunlichen. er muoze alse wol *gese-*

---

[1] Gate of the flood; conf. *Egi-dor,* vol. i. 239.
[2] Conf. MS. 2, 198ᵇ: 'der *fröiden tor* ist *zuo getân.*'

*ginôt* sîn sô daz heilige wizzòt wâre, daz mîn herre scē Johannes mîme herrin dem almehtigen Gote in den mund flôzte, do er'n in deme Jordâne toufte. amên.

In nomine Domini. daz heilige lignum domini *gisegine* mich hiute, undenân und obenân, *mîn bûch sî mir beinîn, mîn herze sî mir stâhelîn, mîn houbet sî mir steinîn* (my belly of bone, heart of steel, head of stone). der guote scē Severîn der phlege mîn, der guote scē Petir unde der guote scē Stephan *gesegineigin* mich hiute for allir mînir fîande gewâfine. in nomine Dei patris et Filii et spiritus sancti. alse milte und alse linde (soft) muozistu hiute sîn ûfin mîme lîbe (body) swert und aller slahte gesmîde, sô miner frouwun scē Mariun sweiz (sweat) wâre, dô si den heiligin Crist gebâre. Pater noster.

### X. *From a Munich MS.* (Hoffm. Fundgr. 343).

Ich slief mir hiute suoze
datz mînes Trehtîns fuozen.
daz heilige himel-chint
daz sî hiute mîn *fride-schilt.*
daz heilige himelchint bat mich hiut ûf stan,
in des namen und gnâde wil ich hiut ûf gân,
und wil mih hiute gurten
mit des heiligen Gotes worten,
daz mir allez daz holt sî (be gracious)
daz in dem himel sî,
diu *sunne* und der *mâne*
und der *tage-sterne* scône.
mîns gemuotes bin ih hiute balt,
hiute springe ih, Herre, in dînen gewalt
sant Marîen lîchemede
daz sî hiute mîn *frid-hemede.*
aller mîner vîende gewâfen
diu ligen hiute unde slâfen
und sîn hiut alsô palwahs
als wære miner vrouwen sant Marîen vahs,
dô si den heiligen Christum gebære,
und doch ein reiniu mait wære.
mîn *houpt* sî mir hiute *stœlin,*
deheiner slahte (no kind of ) wâfen snîde dar în.
mîn swert eine wil ih von dem *segen* sceiden (exempt from the
　　　spell),
daz snîde und bîze allez daz ih ez heize,
von mînen handen
und von niemen andern ;
der heilige himel-trût
der sî hiute mîn *halsperge* guot.

XI. *Tobias's blessing on Tobit's journey.*

(Braunswg. nachr. 1755, p. 321. Hoffm. Fundgr. 261).[1]

Der guote hêrre sante Tobîas,
der Gotes wîzage (prophet) was,
sînen lieben sun er sande
sô verre in vremdiu lande.
sîn sun was ime vile liep,
unsanfte er von ime schiet (parted),
umbe in was im vil leide (very sad),
er sande in uber vierzec tage-weide (40 days' journey).
Er sprach : " der Got der vor niemen verborgen (hidden ist,
und des eigen schalc (servant) dû bist,
der an niemanne wenket (is faithless),
die armen vil wol bedenket,
der müeze dich hiute behüeten
durch sîne vaterlîche güete
über velt, durch walt
vor aller nœte manec-valt,
vor hunger und gevrœrde.
Got müeze mîn gebete erhœren,
sô dû slâfest oder wachest
in holze oder under dache.
dîn vîende werden dir gevriunt,
Got sende dich heim vil wol gesunt
mit vil guotem muote
hin heim zuo dînem eigen-guote.
*gesegenet* sî dir der *wec* (way),
uber strâze und uber stec,
dâ vor und dâ hinden
gesegenen dich des Hêrren vünf wunden.
ietweder halben dar en eben
gestê dir der himelische degen.
in Gotes vride dû var,
der heilige engel dich bewar.
der *lip* (body) sî dir *beinîn*,
ez *herze* sî dir *steinîn*,
ez *houbet* sî dir *stœhelîn*,
der *himel* sî dir *schiltîn*,
diu helle sî dir vor versperret,
allez übel sî vor dir verirret (miss its way),
ez *paradîs* sî dir offen,
alliu wâfen sî vor dir verslozzen (shut up),
daz si daz vil gar vermîden (avoid)
daz dich ir dekeinez steche noch en-snîde (none prick or cut).

[1] First 4 lines borrowed ; see Eschenbg's Denkm. p. 279. Tobias segen-spr.
H. Sachs 1, 439ᵈ.

der mâne und ouch diu sunne
diu liuhten dir mit wunne.
des heiligen geistes siben gebe
lâzen dich mit heile leben.
der guote sante Stephan
der alle sîn nôt überwant (overcame his trouble)
der gestê dir bî (stand by thee),
swâ dir dîn nôt kunt sî.
die heiligen zwelf boten (apostles)
die êren (commend) dich vor Gote,
daz dich diu herschaft gerne sehe.
allez liep müeze dir geschehen.
sante Johannes und die vier êvangeliste
die râten dir daz beste,
mîn frouwe sante Marîe
diu hêre unde vrîe.
mit des heiligen Kristes bluote
werdest dû geheiliget (ze guote),
daz dîn sêle (sô dû sterbest)
des himel-rîches niht verstôzen werde
nâch den weltlîchen êren.
Got gesegne dich dannoch mêre.
sante Galle dîner spîse pflege (thy food prepare),
sante Gêrtrût dir guote herberge gebe (lodging give).
sælec sî dir der lîp (body),
holt (kind) sî dir man unde wîp,
guot rât (counsel) dir iemer werde,
daz dû gæhes lôdes (sudden death) niene ersterbest."
Alsô segente der guote
Santobîas sînen sune,
und sande in dô in ein lant,
ze einer stat, diu hiez ze Mêdiân,
diu burc diu hiez ze Râges:
sît wart er vil frô des.

    .     .     .       .     .

Got sande in heim vil wol gesunt
mit vil guotem muote
hin heim ze sînem eigen-guote.
Alsô müezest dû hiute gesegenet
des helfen hiute die heiligen namen drî,
des helfe hiute diu wîhe,
mîn liebe vrouwe Marîe,
des helfen mir alliu diu kint
diu in dem himel-rîche sint,
und der guote Santobîas
und sîn heiliger trût-sun. amen.

## XII. *For stolen goods.*[1]

(MS. of 1347 at Sant Paul in the Lavant valley.)

Darnach dise nachgende gebette, daz soltu dri-stunt sprechen in eim gadem (chamber), daz dich niemen irre (disturb), so *kument darin engel* und sagent dir daz du fragest :

" Der heilig Crist vuor von himele mit engeln manegen, do fuort er an sinen henden en Frones-bilde (Lord's image). under einem boume er geraste (rested), do entslief er so vaste. do komen die leidigen diebe, und verstalen im sin Frones bilde. do er erwachte, trurete er so vaste. do sprach diu genedige min frowe sant Marie, ' des sol guot rat werden, wir sulen uf diser erden von dem heiligen kinde daz dink noch hi-naht (to-night) vinden.'—Sabaoth Herre, ich bitte dich durch din einborn sun Jesum Christum, daz du vergebest mir min sünde, und gib mir ein guot ende. Jesu Crist, des waren Gotes sun du bist. ich bit dich, und man dich, daz du dis dinges verrihtest mich."

Disen selben segen maht du ouch sprechen, so dir oder eim andern diner guten fründen *üt* (aught) *verstolen wirt*, daz gar schedelich si und redelich, nüt umb kleine üppig sache, nuwent da ez noturftig und redelich si ; wande (for) so di segen ie edeler und ie besser sint, ie minre (the less) sü helfent da man sü bruchet unnotdurfteclich (spells lose their virtue if used on trifling occasions).

## XIII. *Exorcism of Gout* (MS. at Göttweich ; of 1373).

Ich virbeden dir, gycht, bi der heylgir wandillungin. vnd bi den heylgin V wunden vnsers herren Jesu Christi. vnd bi deme bluode dat Gote vyt (out of) sinen V wunden ran. vnd bi dem erstin menschin dat Got vf erden ye gemacht, oder ye liz geborren werden. Ich virbeden dir bi den *drin nagelin*, de Gode durch sine hende vnd durch sine vusze wrde geslagen. Ich virbeden dir bi den *vyer hulden* (4 *gracious ones*) *de da stuonden vf zweyn vuoszin* vnd sprachin vys (out of) zweyir muodir libe, ' wer si bede van rechtir lybden, vmme allis dat mogelich is, des wulden si in geweren.' dat was Maria, Godis muodir, vnd was Jesus Christus. vnd was min frauwe sancte Elsebe, vnd was myn herre sancte Johannes der deufir. Ich virbeden dir bi deme bebinden vrdeil (varying verdicts) das Got wil gebin ubir mich vnd ubir alle doden und lebenden. Ich virbedin dir bi deme fronen cruce vnsers herren Jesu Christi, da he de martil ayn leyt (suffered) durch mich vnd alle cristeneyt. Ich virbedin dir bi der gotligir kraft de da ist in hymil vnd in erden, dat du mir Godes knegthe (servant) nyt in-schades an allen minen glederen (limbs), an haubde, an hirne, an augen, an cenden (teeth), an armen, an henden, an vingeren, an rippen, an rucke, an lenden, an huffin (back, loins, hips), an beynen, an vuozin, an cein (toes), an aderen (veins), noch an allen, da ich mich mach keren (may turn) oder wenden. Des helfe mir de Godis kraft, vnd dat heylge graf, da Got selve inne lach (lay), da her bebede (quaked) allit dat da was. Pylatus sprach, ' hais du gesugthe odir gegichte?' neyn, ich in-han sin nyt.—It sy vrauwe oder

---

[1] Nos. XII. XIII. XIV. communic. by Hoffmann.

man, der düse wort ubir yme dreyt, der sal sigchir sin (may be sure) dat in
de geychte nummer gelemen kan (never can lame). Ich geleufe dat keyn
wif noch keyn man, der düse wort ubir sprechen kan. want der sunder
(for the sinner) an deme cruce genade gewan. De mach mich Godis knegt
N. gesunt an selen und an libe, as Maria was, do si irs lieben kyndis genas
(got well). amen.

XIV. *Herdsman's charm* (see p. 1241).

XV. *For the blowing Worm* (Cod. Pal. 367, 173[b]).

Dis ist eyn guter *seyn vor den blasinden worm :* " Der gute herre senthe
Iob der lak in deme miste. her clagete deme heilge Criste, wi syn gebeyne
essen die worme cleyne. Do sprach der heilge Crist. wen nymandt besser
ist. ich gebite (bid) dir, *worm,* du siest wies (white) adir swartz, geel adir
gruene adir roet. in desir stundt siestu in dem pferde toet. in Gotis
namen amen." Nota. man sal das pferdt nennen alz is geharet is (by hue
of hair; see XXXV).—Dis ist eyn *seyn vor den pirczil :* [1] "Horestu, *worm*
yn fleische und in beyne. vornem was das heilge euangelium meyne. du
seist weis, swartz adir geel, grüne adir roet. der gebutet myn herre senthe
Iob in desir stunt siestu in desem pferde toet. in Gotis namen amen."
Nota. man sal deme pferde treten uf den vorder-fuss, und sal ym runen
(whisper) in das rechte oer desen segn (conf. RA. 589).

XVI. *Conjuring a magic Horse* (Cod. Pal. 212, 45[b]).

Wiltu machen ein pferd das dich trag wo du wilt, so nymb ein plut von
einer fledermaus (blood of a bat). wen es dan nacht ist, so *gang zu einem
haus* heimblich *an das ende sin.* und schreib an die haus-tur und die
. . . . in namen omnii. geapha. diado. wen du si geschriben hast,
so gang dan ein weil, und kom dan herwider, so findestu ein *ros* bereit *mit
satl und mit zaum* (bridle) und mit allem gezeuge. Wen du dan uf das ros
wilt sitzen, so *tritt mit dem rechtem fuss in den linken stegreif,* und sprich
die beschwerung : " Ich beschwer dich, ros, bei dem Vater und bei dem
Sone und bei dem heilgen Geist, und bei dem schepfer himelreichs und
erdreichs, der alle ding aus nichts gemacht hat. Ich beschwer dich, ros,
bei dem lebendigen Got und bei dem waren Got, bei dem heiligen Got,
das du an meinem leib noch an meiner sel noch an meinen glidern nit
geschaden mugst, noch mit keinerlei hindernus." So sitz frolich uf das
pferd, und solt dich nit segen, und forcht dich nit. Wan du komst an di
stat do du gern werest, so *nymb den zaumb* vnd *grab in under die erden.*
Wan du das ros wilt haben, so nymb den zaumb und *schutel in vast,* so
komt das ros. So beschwer es aber (again) als vor, und sitz doruff und rit
wo du wilt, und *lug* (look) *das du den zaumb wol behaltest* (keepest).
verleurstu den zaumb, so mustu das pferd wider machen.[2]

---

[1] *Bürzel, gun-birzel.* Frisch 1, 157[c]. 383[a].
[2] Conf. supra, Hartlieb, p. 1768. The importance of bit and bridle in magic
horses is seen in the story of King Beder in the Arabian Nights.

## XVII. *Conjuring the Hedge-stick.*[1]

Geh zu einem zaun-stecken und sprich: *Zaunstecken, ich weck dich!*
min lieb das wolt ich. ich beger (desire) vil mer, dan aller teufel her
(host). Her zu mir, so rür ich dich zaunstecken. alle teufel müssen dich
wecken, und füren (lead thee) in das haus, do mein lieb get in und aus.
dass du müssest faren in die vier wend (4 walls), wo sich mien lieb hin ker
(turn) oder wend! es ist aller eren wol wert. ich send ir einen *bock* (zum
pfert). Ich ruf euch heut alle gleich. bei den *drei negeln* reich. und
bei dem rosen-farben blut, das Gott aus seinen heiligen wunden floss.
ich beut (bid) euch teufel her. ir bringet zu mir mein lieb N. her, *zwischen*
(twixt) *himel und erden, das es nit berür* (touch) *die erden, fürt es ob allen
baumen her*, als man Maria thet, do si fur in ires Kindes reich."——Und
nim die caracteres alle zu dir, und blas dreimal auf die hant, und schlage
dreimal gegen in (them), so mügen sie dir nit geschaden.

## XVIII. *Against Wolves, etc.*

Christ sun gieng unter thür, mein frau Maria trat herfür: 'Heb uf
Christ sun dein hand, und versegen mir das viech und das land, das *kein
wolf beiss*, und *kein wulp stoss*, und kein dieb komm in das gebiet. Du
herz trutz markstein, hilf mir das ich kom gesunt und gevertig heim!'
(Conf. XL[b].)

## XIX. *Das die Wolf das viech nit essen.*

Ich beschwer dich, *Wolf-zan* (-tooth), bei dem vil heiligen namen, und
bei dem vil heiligen Barn, den unser liebe frau trug an irem arm, das
du noch alle dein genossen das viech nit beissen noch stossen. Es muss
dis nacht sein als war und als vast, als das heilig paternoster was, das Got
aus seinem munde sprach.

## XX. *On Going Out.*

Hude (to-day) wil ich uf sten, in den heilgen friden wil ich gen, do
unser liebe fraue in gieng, do sie den heilgen Crist inphieng. Noch hute
wil ich mich gorten (gird) mit den heiligen funf worten, mit den heilgen
sigeringen, mit allen guten dingen. *Allez daz dages alt sy daz sy mir holt!*
unser lieben frauwen zunge sy aller miner fiende münde! amen.

## XXI. *For a Journey.*

Ich dreden hude (I tread to-day) uf den phat, den unser herre Jesus
Cristus drat. der si mir also süss und also gut! nu helfe mir sin heilges
rose-farbes blut, und sin heilge funf wunden, das ich nimmer werde
gefangen oder gebunden! von allen minen fienden mich behude, daz
helfe mir die here hude (heavenly care), vor . . . . fliessen, vor

---

[1] Nos. XVII–XXXVII from Mone's Anzeiger for 1834, p. 277; the same Anz. for
'34, p. 46, has a Wound-spell and a Blood-spell from a Wolfenb. MS.; and those
for '33, p. 234, and '37, p. 464, a spell against sorcery, and a few against
fire.

swerten und vor schiessen, vor aller slacht ungehüre, vor schnoder gesell-
schaft und abentüre ; das alle mine bant von mir enbunden werde zu
hant (at once), also unser here Jesus inbunden wart, do er nam die himel-
fart !

### XXII. *Ain schöner segen, alle Sebtemer zu thun.*

Am Mantag vor der Fronfasten (ember-week). der Mantag is kräftiger
dan die Fronfasten. *vor aufgang der sonne, unbeschrauen.* sprich also :
" Hier ein, in dese hof-stat gehe ich 'nein. solche land beschliesst
(encloses) Got mit seiner aignen hand. er beschliesst sie also fest mit
dem süssen Jesu Crist, disen gibel oben und disen gibel unden. diser
gibel unden, der ist mit engeln uberzogen verbunden. *Feuer vom dach,
dieb vom loch, rauber vor der thür !* unser liebe frau trit heut selbst
darfür, das ave-maria sei vor der thür, das paternoster der rigel (bolt)
darfür. und was der lieb h. Lorenz hat gegert, das hat der heilig Crist
bewert, das niemant stärker ist dan der heilig Crist, der gehe herein
und nemb was hier innen ist. im namen † † † amen." 15 pat., 15 ave, und
credo.

### XXIII. *Against Hail.*

Item, *mach den pfeil* (*i.e.* figure of an arrow) *auf die erden gegen dem
wetter,* oder auf ein deller (plate), und setz in gegen dem wetter ; und nim
ein weich-brun (holy-water pot), und spritz dreu kreuz gegen dem wetter
im namen, u. s. w. und sprich : " Ich peut (bid) dir, *schaur* und *hagl,* in
der kraft der *heilgen drei nagl,* die Jesu Cristo durch sein heilge hend
und fuss wurden geschlagen, er du kumbst zu der erd, das du zu wind
und wasser werd, im namen etc." mach dreu kreuz mit dem weich-
brun gegen das wetter.

### XXIV. *For a Fire.*

Wellent ir feuer leschen (quench), so sprechent wie hernach folgt ; auch
*das ir ain prant* (brand) *von demselbigen feuer in der hand habt,* wo aber
solliches nit beschehn möcht, sol es dannacht mit andacht gesprochen
werden : " 'Unser lieber herr Jesus Christus gieng uber land, und er fand
einen riechenden prant, den hueb er uf mit seiner gotlichen hant, und
gesegent disen riechenden prant, das er nimer weiter kum. in dem namen
etc." und darzue bett 5 p. 5 a. 1 cr.

### XXV. *Against Fire.*

Wer feuer verhüet, dass sein haus und statel nit prinnent werd, der
mach alweg mit der hand ein creuz, und sprech wie hernach folgt : " *Mein
haus das sei mir umbeschwaifen mit engelischen raifen,* mein haus sei mir
bedeckt mit einer englischer deck ! das helf mir Gotes minn, der sei
alzeit haus-vater und wirt darin ! "

### XXVᵇ. *For a Fire.*

Sprich: "*Feuer*, ich gepeut (bid) dir in dem namen Jesu, das du nit weiter kumest. *behalt* (hold in) *dein funk und flammen*, wie Maria ir jungfrauschaft und er (honour) behalten hat vor allen mannen. das sei dem feuer zue puess zelt (counted as quittance) in namen etc."

### XXVI. *Against Fever.*

*Zwig, ich buck dich, Rett nů mid mich* (twig, I bend thee, fever, void me)[1] bi dem heiligen nagel, der unserm lieben herren Cristo Jesu durch siu rechten hand ward geschlagen! und als menig blûts-tropf dar-von ran, als meniger *rett mid mich*, und gang mir ab! im namen u. s. w.

### XXVII. *Against Diseases.*

Ich stand uf den mist (dunghill), und ruf zu werden Crist, das er mir buss (rid me of) die rechten *sporen-fuss*, und das *heupt-gescheub* und den *herz-ritten*, und allen seinen sitten, und *gel-sucht* und *sibenzich gesucht*; und ist ir keiner mer (any more), den buss mir Gott der herre, und gang aus her *ruck-bein*, und gang aus her *ripp*, und gang ab in das wilt zorach! das buss dir der man, der den tot an dem heilgen creuz nam.

### XXVIII. *Against the Worm.*

"Ich beschwör dich, *Wurm* und *Würmin*, bei der waren Gottes minn, und bei der waren Gothait gut, das dein aiter (matter) und dein blut werd lauter und auch rain (pure) als unser lieben frauen gspint, die sie gab Jesu Crist irem lieben kint! im namen Got des vaters etc." Item, *nim den gerechten dumen* (right thumb) *in die gerechte hant.*

### XXIX. *The Same.*

"*Wurm*, bist du dinne, so beut ich dir bei sant . . . . minne, du seiest weiss, schwarz oder rot, dass du hie ligest tot!" Ist's ain vich (animal), so streichend im mit der rechten hand über den rucken ab. ist's dan ain mensch, so *nemend im den finger* (take his f.) *in die hand*, und sprechend 5 vatter unser, 5 ave Maria und ain globen (belief).

### XXX. *Against Ague.*

Grüss dich Gott, vil-heiliger tag! nimm mir mein 77 *kalt-wee* ab; is eben einer drunder, der nit zu erbitten ist, so nem mir's der lieb herr Jesus Crist, der am heilgen fran-kreuz verstorben ist. in dem namen u. s. w.

### XXXI. *To be worn under the right arm 24 hours.*

Es giengen drei selige brüder aus in guter frist (time),[2] begegnet inen herr Jesus Christ. unser lieber herr Jesus Christ sprach: 'Wo welent ir hin!'——'Wir welent hinter den zaun (hedge), wir welent *suchen das*

---

[1] *Rett*=rite (febris). 'Mit der metten dû mich *mit!*' Kolocz 263.
[2] A spell in Keisersp. Ameis 50ᵃ begins: 'Es giengen drei brüder über feld.'

*kraut* (seek the herb) das zue allen wunden guet ist, es sei gleich *gehauen* oder *gestochen*' (a cut or a stab). Unser lieber herr J. Cr. sprach: 'Gant auf Messias berg, nement die wol von denen schafen, und das moes von denen steinen, und das öl von denen bemen.' druck darein und darauf, so heilt die wunde von grund auf, es sei gleich *gehauen* oder *gestochen* oder *brochen*, wie es möcht ergangen sein, so sol es weder *geschwelen* oder *schweren* (swell nor fester), sol auch keines eiters begeren (conf. XXXIX). Wie Lucas auf Severines-berg hat gesprochen, wie die Juden unsern herrn J. Chr. umb unschult haben gestochen. das walt Got der vatter u. s. w.

### XXXII. *A fine charm for Stanching Blood.*

In unsers herren Gottes herz da *stuenden* (stood) drei rosen. die erst ist sein dugent, die ander ist sein vermögen, die dritt ist sein will—*Pluet steh still!* im namen u. s. w.

Another: Longinus der man, der unserm herren Jesu Crist sein gerechte seiten hat auf-getan (opened), daraus rann wasser und bluet—ich beschwöre dich, *bluet*, durch desselbigen bluets ehre, das du *nimer bluetest mere!* im namen u. s. w.

Another: O Got, der immer ewig ist, der aller menschen hilf und trost ist—ich büt dir, *blůt*, das du *stil standist*, als die menschen am jungsten tag (last day) *still stan* müssend, die nicht nach Gottes willen hant getan (have done).

### XXXIII. *For the Nail in a horse's eye.*

Welches ros (whose horse) den *nagel* het in dem ougen, der sol ain stro nemen ain nacht, als dick er mag, und sol im sin atem (breath) in das oug nüchter kuchen (breathe, fasting), und sol mit seinem finger gen dem oug grifen, und sol sprechen: "Ich gebüt dir's, *Nagel*, bi dem vil hailgen Gottes grab, da Got in selber lag unz an (until) den hailgen Oster-tag, das du verschwinist, *Nagel*, und dörrest (dwindle and dry up), als die Juden taten, die verschwinend und verdorrenden. das gebüt der Vatter u. s. w."

### XXXIV. *For the Worm in horses.*

Welches ros (whose horse) die würm in dem gederm (guts) hat, und in dem magen, der sol das ros mit seinem linken fuss stossen, und sol sprechen: "*Wurm*, und al di *würm*, die in dem ros sind, das euch des ros lib, flaisch, gederm und bain also laid sige (as loathsome be) ze niessen und ze bruchen, und euch das als unmar (distasteful) sig, als unserm Herren aines *pfaffen wip, die des tüfels velt-merch* (field-mare) *ist*, als was müssent ir (so surely may ye) in dem ros-flaisch sterben. das gebüt euch u. s. w."

Welches ros den *uss-werfenden* (vomiting) *wurm* hat, der sol sprechen: "Ich gebüt euch, *wurm* und *würmin*, das du des rosses flaisch und bain und al sin lip [lassest], das dir darin sig als wind und als we, und dir darinne sig als laid, als S. Petern was unsers Herren marter, do er vor den richtern und den Juden floch; dar dir darinne werd als we, unz das er das wort gesprech, das S. Peter sprach, do er ze Rom ze dem ersten in das münster trat; das ir uss dem ros fliessend, oder aber heruss fallend, oder in dem ros sterbend, und ewer d'heiner nimmer lebend werde. das gebüt euch der man der die marter und den tod laid (suffered)."

### XXXV. *For a Horse.*

Item ain pfärt, das sich *strichet,* so züch es unter den himel an ainem Sontag frü *vor der sunnen ufgang,* und *ker dem ros den kopf gegen der sunnen,* und leg dine zwen dumen (thumbs) crüz-wis uber ain ander, und halt die hend umb den fuss, doch *das sie den fuss nit an rüren* (not touch), und sprich: "Longinus war ain Jud, das ist war. er stach unsern Herrn in sein siten, das ist war (und nem das pfärd bei der varb), das si dir für das streichen gût!"

### XXXVI. *On losing a Horse-shoe.*

Item ain pfärd, das ain isen verliert, so nim ain brot-messer (bread-knife), und umb-schnit im den huf an den wenden von ainer fersen (heel) zû der ander, und leg im das messer crüz-wis uf die solen, und sprich: "Ich gebüt dir, *huf* und *horn,* das du als lützel zerbrechist, als Got der herr die wort zerbrach, do er himel und erd beschûf." Und die wort sprich dri-stunt nach einander, und 5 pat. n. und 5 ave Maria ze lob; so trit das pfärd den hûf nit hin, bis das du glichwol zû ainem schmit komen magst.

### XXXVII. *Wo man die Milich stelt.*

Nimb weich-wasser (holy water) und spreng's in den stall, nimb gun-reben (ground-ivy), geweicht salz und mer-linsen (duckweed): ich gib dir heut gunreben, merlinsen und salz; *gang uf durch die wolken und bring mir schmalz und milich und molken!*

### XXXVIII.[1] *Against the Holdichen.*

Fahr aus, und fahr ein in N. wie bist du hereingekommen? du sollt gedenken, dass du da wieder heraus kommst. wer dich herein gebracht hat, soll dich wiederum herausbringen, er sei *hei* oder *sei;* und sollst einen beweis (sign) von dir geben, dass man siehet, dass du hinweg bist.

Another: Das walte Got und der teufel! fahr hin da du nutze bist, und thu wie ich empfangen habe!

Another: *Alle in und alle ut!* so spricht die liebe jungfrau sente Ger-drut.

Another: Wolauf *elb* und *elbin, zwerg* und *zwergin,* unterwärts und ober-wärts. du sollst zu dem und dem, du sollst *seine beine necken* (torment), du sollst *sein fleisch schmecken,* du sollst *sein blut trinken, und in die erde sinken!* in aller teufel namen.

Another: Du *elben* und du *elbinne,* mir ist gesagt, du kannst *den könig von der königin bringen,* und *den vogel von dem nest.* du sollst noch ruhen

---

[1] Nos. XXXVIII. XXXIX. from Voigt's Quedlinburg Witch-trials.

noch rasten, du kommst denn unter den busch, das du den menschen keinen schaden thust.

Another: Op unsers Gottes berge ist unsers herrn Gottes born (well), in unsers herrn Gottes born ist unsers herrn Gottes nap (bowl), in unsers herrn Gottes nappe ist unsers herrn Gottes appel, liegt sente Johannis evangelium, das benimmt einem (rids one of) die *bösen dinger*. der liebe Gott wolle helfen, dass es vergehe, und nicht bestehe!

Another: Joseph und gardian die giengen vor Gott den herrn stan; da sie vor Gott den herrn kamen, trauerte (sorrowed) Joseph also sehre. Es sprach Gott mein herre: 'Joseph, warum trauerst du so sehr?'—'Die *unternsen kleine* wollen ausfaulen (the underground tinies want to rot) mein fleisch und meine beine.'—'Ich verbiede es den *untersen kleinen*, das sie nicht ausfaulen mein fleisch und meine beine!'[1]

Another: Die heiligen Drei Könige giengen über das feld, do *mutten ihnen* (met them) *alp* und *elbin*.[2] *Albinne*, das solt du nicht thun, kehre wieder um.' im uamen u. s. w.

Another: *Hebbe-mutter* und *hoch-mutter*, lege still ein deinem blode, als Jesus lag in seiner mutter schote.

### XXXIX. *Against Diseases.*

Unser herr Jesus Christus und dieser wasser-fluss. ich verbüsse dir, *sieben und siebenzig schuss* (77 shot); *sieben und siebenzig seuche*, die seind mehr denn wir verbüssen; weichen von diesem geruch (?) *neunerlei geschuss!* das sei dir zur busse gezählet (counted as quittance). im namen etc.

Es giengen drei Salomen über einen öl-berg, sie giengen über eine grüne aue, da begegnet ihnen Marie unse liebe fraue: 'Wohin ihr drei Salomen?' —'Wei willen hen-gahn ut, und *seuken* mangerlei *god krut* (see XXXI), dat *stikt nicht*, dat *brikt nicht*, dat *killt nicht*, dat *swillt nicht*.' im namen u. s. w.

Unse leve frue ging still over land. se gesegene desen *hilligen brand*, dat he *nich quillt* oder *schwillt* und *inworts fritt!*

Wollet ihr hören des Herrn wunder grot, da Jesus Christus von Marien auf den erdboden schot, in einer hilligen spangen, damit sie den herren Jesum Christ empfangen. sie trug ihn unterm herzen vierzig wochen ohne schmerzen, sie trug ihn gen Betlehem in die stadt, da Jesus drinne geboren ward. Sie schickten ihn über das wilde meer, es wäre noth sie hinter ihn kämen, drei scharfe dornen mit sich nähmen. das eine was de harte nagel, de ward dem heiligen Christ durch hände und füsse geschlagen. Die falschen Juden waren oft behende (quick), sie warfen ihm ein dornen kron auf sein haupt, dass ihm sein rosin-farbnes blaut durch seinen braunen bart floss. Johannes thät einen hellen schrei: 'Hilf Gott, mir bricht mein herz entzwei. die mutter Gottes will| gar verderben, J. Christus wird gar am kreuze sterben.' Wie he do gestorben was, do verwandelt sich laub und gras, und alles was auf dem erdboden was. Ut welken munde (out of

---

[1] A similar formula in the little Book of Romanus (Görres's Volksbücher, p. 205).
[2] The orig. has absurdly 'alfinadi alfinie,' evid. for the L. Sax. *alf indi elfin*.

SPELLS. 1863

whose mouth) dies gebet wird gesprochen, der wird (may he be) *nicht gehauen* oder *gestochen*, dem wird *kein haus verbrant*, kein jungfräulich herz wird auch zu schanden, keiner frauen . . . . gelungen! das helf mich Gott und seine heiligen fünf wunden.

### XL. *Fragm. of a prayer against Fire and Tempest.*

#### (Andr. Gryphius' Horribilicr. p. 768.)

Das walte der es walten kann! Matthes gang ein, Pilatus gang aus, ist eine arme seele draus (i.e., out of hell). 'Arme seele, wo kommst du her (from)?'—'Aus regen und wind, *aus dem feurigen ring.*'

### XL.ᵇ *Beginning of a Spell* (14th cent.).

Unser Herr saz und stunt under der kirch-tür, da kam sein lieb traud muter gangen (herfür): 'Draut son, mein herre, wie siezest du trawren so sere?'——'Ach, herczen-liebew muter mein, solt ich nit trawrig sein?' Da kom ich an *bulwechs perg* gangen, da *schoz mich der bulwechs*, da *schoz mich die bulwechsin*, da *schoz mich als ir hin-gesind* (all their household), etc. Conf. XVIII.

### XLI. *For a Fire.*

A fire can be charmed, if he that speaks the charm *ride three times round the flame;* it will then go out. But the third time, *the fire makes a rush at him,* and if it catch him, he is lost.——'Feuer, stand stille um der worte willen, die S. Lorenz sprach, da er den feurigen rost ansach (looked at the burning gridiron).'

Another: 'Gott grüsse dich, *liebes feuer,* mit deiner flamme ungeheuer! das gebeut (bids) dir der heilige mann Jesus, du solt stille stan, und mit der flamme nit für bass gan (no further go)! im namen etc.'

Another: 'Feuer-glut, du sollst *stille stehn,* und wie das liebe Marien-kind die marter am kreuze hat ausgestanden, der hat um unserer sünde willen all *still gestanden.*'——While uttering these words three times, one shall *take a little earth from under one's right* (or *left*) *foot, and cast it in the fire* (conf. a Danish spell in Nyerup's Morskabsl. 200).

### XLII. *Against Elbe.*

Ich beschwöre dich, *alb,* der du augen hast wie ein kalb, *rücken wie ein teig-trog,* weise (shew) mir deines herren hof!

Ihr *elben,* sitzet feste, *weicht* (budge) *nicht aus eurem neste!* Ihr *elben,* ziehet fort, weicht bald an andern ort!

Im thume steht die rosenblume, sie ist weder braun noch fahl. so müssen die *hüf-dinger* (hip or thigh elben) zersteuben und zerfahren (disperse), und kommen der hirtischen Margareten in's teufels namen an! (Carpzov's Pract. rer. crim., pars 1, quæst. 50, p. 420).

In *burying her elben,* the witch puts a little wax, some threads of flax, and some cheese and bread in the grave with them, and accompanies the action with the words: 'Da, *elben*, da, wringet das *wachs*, spinnet das *flachs*, esset den *käse*, esset das *brot*, und lasst mich ohne noth!' (Elias Casp. Reichardt's Verm. beitr. 3, 369).

### XLIII. *For Fever, etc.*

Fieber hin, fieber her! lass dich blicken nimmer mehr! fahr der weil in ein wilde au! das schaft dir ein alte frau. Turtel-täubchen ohne gallen; *kalte gichtchen*, du sollst fallen!

For *worm in the finger*. Gott vater fährt gen acker, er ackert fein wacker, er ackert *würme* heraus. einer war weiss, der ander schwarz, der dritte roth; hie liegen alle würme todt.

For *ulcered lungs*. Scher dich fort, du schändliches *brust-geschwür*, von des kindes rippe, gleich wie die kuh von der krippe! (see Superst. 873).

For *barm-grund*. To uproot this eruption, wash in a pool where cats and dogs are drowned, saying the words: 'In dit water, worin versupen manch katt und hund, darin still ik di barmgrund. im namen u. s. w.' (Schütze's Holst. Id. 1, 70).

### XLIV. *For the Gout.*

Before daybreak on the first of May, the gouty man must go into the wood, there silently let three drops of his blood sink *into the split of a young pine*, and having closed up the opening with wax from a virgin bee-hive, must cry aloud: 'Give you good morning, *Madam Pine, here I bring you the gout* so fine; what I have borne a year and a day, you shall bear for ever and aye! Earth's dew may drench you, and heaven's rain pour, but gout shall pinch you for evermore!' (Ernst Wagner's A B C eines henneberg. fiebel-schützen, Tüb. 1810, p. 229).

### XLV. *For Women in Labour.*

Unser liebe frau und unser lieber herr Jesus Christ giengen mit einander durch die stadt:[1] ' Ist niemand hier der mein bedarf (has need of me)? Liegt ein krankes weib, sie liegt in kindes banden. Gott helf ihr und ihrem lieben kind von einander! das thu herr Jesu Christ, der schliess auf (may he unlock) schloss, eisen und bein!'——Conf. the following in Mone's Anz. for 1834, p. 278: Ich bitte dich, Maria und Jesu Christ, das mir das schloss verschlossen ist, der Maria ruhet unter ir brust, das mir das schloss wider uf wisch (fly open).

### XLVI. *To forget Women* (conf. ON. *ô-minnis-öl*).

Ich weiss wol wo du bist, ich sende dir den vater herrn Jesu Christ, ich sende dir der treusten boten drei (three messengers), die auf erden und himmel sind, den einen in dein gemüte, den andern in dein geblüte, den dritten in deines herzens block: Gott gebe dass *alle weiber und mägde in deinem herzen verstocken* (moulder)! Ich sende dir den süssen herrn Jesum, den süssen herrn Christum, die stumpfen *nägel drei*, die Gott dem

---

[1] Many such beginnings, e.g.: 'Christ and his mother came out of a wood, went over field and went over land, up hill, down hill, faggot in hand, etc.'

herrn wurden geschlagen, den einen durch seine hände, den einen durch seine füsse, den dritten durch sein herze: Gott gebe dass du müssest *vergessen alle weiber in deinem herzen !* im namen etc.

### XLVII. *To stop Thieves.*[1]

Wie Maria im kinde-bette lag, drei engel ihr da pflagen (tended). der erste hiess S. Michael, der ander S. Gabriel, der dritte hiess S. Rafael. da kamen die falschen Juden, und wollten ihr liebes kindlein stehlen. Da sprach Maria: ' S. Petre, bind!'——Petrus sprach: ' Ich hab gebunden mit Jesu banden, mit Gottes selbst-eignen (very own) handen.' Wer mir ein diebstal thut stehlen, der muss stehn bleiben wie ein stock, über sich sehen wie ein block. wann er mehr kann zählen (count) als sterne am himmel stehn, alle schnee-flocken, alle regentropfen, wann er das alles kann thun, mag er mit dem gestolen gut hin-gehn wo er will. wann er's aber nicht kann, so *soll er stehn bleiben mir zu einem pfand* (pledge), bis ich mit meinen leiblichen augen über ihn sehe, und ihm ur-laub (leave) gebe, wieder zu gehn.

### XLVIII. *To root one to the spot.*

Hier stand so fest, als der baum hält sein äst (boughs), als der nagel in der wand (wall), durch Jesum Marien sohn; dass du weder schreitest noch reitest, und kein gewehr (weapon) ergreifest! In des Höchsten namen solt du stehn.

### XLIX. *The Same.*

Ich thu dich anblicken, drei bluts-tropfen sollen dich erschricken in deinem leibe, der erste mit einer leber, der zweite mit einer zunge, der dritte mit einer mannes kraft. Ihr reitet oder geht zu fuss, gebunden sollt ihr sein so gewiss und so fest, als der baum hält seine äst (boughs), und der ast hält seine nest, und der hirsch (hart) hält seine zungen, und der herr Christus uns hat das himmelreich errungen (won); so gewiss und wahr sollt ihr stån, als der heil. Johannes stand am Jordân, da er den lieben herrn Jesum getaufet; und also gewiss und wahrhaftig solt ihr stehn, bis (till) die liebe göttliche mutter einen andern sohn gebähret, so gewiss solt ihr sein gebunden zu dieser tag-zeit und stunden (hour) !

### L. *To make oneself Beloved.*

Ich trete über die schwelle (threshold), nehme Jesum zu meinem gesellen (companion); Gott ist mein *schuh,* himmel ist mein *hut* (hat), heilig kreuz mein *schwert;* wer mich heute sieht, habe mich *lieb und werth !* So befehl (commit) ich mich in die heilige drei benedicts pfennung (keeping?), die neun-mal-neun (9 × 9) geweihet und gesegnet sein; so befehl ich mich in der heil. Dreifaltigkeit leuchtung; der mich heute sieht und hört, der habe mich *lieb und werth.* im namen etc.

[1] Similar Danish spells in Nyerup's Morskabsl., pp. 197-8.

*LI. To make oneself Invisible.*

Grüss euch Gott! seid ihr wol-gemut (are ye merry)? habt ihr getrunken des herrn Christi blut?——'Gesegne mich Gott, ich bin wol-gemut, ich habe getrunken des herrn Christi blut.' Christus ist mein *mantel, rock, stock* und *fuss,* seine heilige fünf wunden mich verbergen thun (do hide). *Rep.* 'Gesegne mich—Christi blut.' Christus der herr, der die blinden sehend gemacht, und die sehenden blind machen kann, wolle eure augen verdunkeln und verblenden (darken and dazzle), dass ihr mich nicht sehet noch merket u. s. w.

## SWEDISH.

LII. (from Fernow's Wärmeland, p. 250 seq.)

Sanct Johannes evangelist, han bygde bro (built bridges) för Jesum Christ. vår Herre är min *brynja* (armour), och Jesus är min försvar. ser väl för (provides against) min fall idag och hvar dag, *för den heta eld* (hot fire), *för den hvassa orm* (sharp worm). *för den blinda man,* som alla vähla villa kan. Den ena bön (prayer) för min nöd, den ara för min död, den tredje för min fattiga själ (poor soul).

*Afton-bön* (evening prayer). Jag lägger i vårs Herres tröst, korsa (crosses) gör jag för mit bröst. *signe mig Sol, och signe mig Måne* (sun and moon bless me), och all den *frögd som jorden bär* (joy that earth bears). Jorden är *min brynja,* och himmelin är *min skjöld,* och jungfru Maria är *mit svärd.*

*åter :* Nu går jag te sängje (bed), med mig har jag Guds ängle, tolf (12) te hand och tolf te fot, tolf te hvar ledamot (limb).

*ännu en annan :* Vår herre Jesus rider öfver hede (heath), där *möter han den lede* (evil one). ' Hvart (whither) skal du hän ? ' sade vår herre Jesus. —'Jag skal åt kött *at suga blod.*'—'Nej, jag förmenar dig ; du skal *ur ben och i kött* (out of bone and into flesh), *ur kött och i skinn, ur skinn och ändå at helfvetes pina !* ' genom tre namn.

*At döfva verk* (to allay pain) : Vår herre Jesus rider in på kyrko-gård, där *döfde* han både *verk* och *sår.* Jesus *somnade,* verken *domnade ;* Jesus vaknade, verken *saktnade.* genom tre namn.

## DANISH.

LIII. (from Nyerup's Morskabsl. 200. 201).

*At dölge eg og od* (to blunt the edge and point). Läs disse ord strax naar (as soon as) du seer knivene eller svärdene dragne : ' Stat, *eg og od,* med de samme ord som Gud skabte himmel og jord. stat, eg og od, med de samme ord som Gud skabte sig selv med kjöd og blod i jomfru Mariä liv ! i navn Gud faders etc.'

Vor herre Christus red i herre-färd, dövede han alle dragne svärd ; alle de vaaben (weapons) som han saae, dem tog hane *eg og odde* fra, med sine to händer og med sine ti fingre, med sit velsignede blod, med sin värdig hellig aand (spirit) og med sit hellige kors, med sine tolv engle og med sine tolv apostle. Fra *klod* og ud til *od*, det *hvide skal ikke bide* (white shall not bite), det *röde skal ikke blöde*, förend Christus sig igjen lader föde (till C. again be born), dat er skeet og skeer aldrig mere.

Jesus gik ad vejen fram, der *mödte ham Rylla den lede og gram*. 'Hvor vil du gange?' siger Jesus.—'Jeg vil gaae til N. N.'—'Hvad vil du der?' siger Jesus.—'Jeg vil *hans blod lapt*, jeg vil *hans ben bidt*, og *hans händer slidt*, jeg vil hans hilse fortappe.'—'Nej,' siger Johannes evangelist, 'det skal du ikke gjöre; mens Jesu navn mane dig *af blod i flod!* Jesu navn mane dig *af been i steen!* Jesu navn mane dig *af hold i mold!* Jesu navn mane dig *ud til verdens ende!*

Jesus han sig under espen stod, han svedte vand (water), han svedte blod. Flye *ägte rosen* for ordet (before the word), *som den döde under jorden, som duggen* (dew) *for dagen!* Jeg binder dig med min haand, og med Jesu haand, med jomfru Marias haand, med de ni (nine) gode Guds engler, *med hvid uld* (wool) *og grön gräs* og den hellig Aands sande läst. i navn etc.

Lucia den blide skal flye mig ad vide (sweet St Lucy let me know): *hvis dug jeg skal brede* (whose cloth I shall lay), *hvis seng* (bed) *jeg skal rede, hvis barn jeg skal bäre, hvis kjäreste* (darling) *jeg skal väre, hvis arm jeg skal sove i* (sleep in).

### FROM JUTLAND.

A ligger mä paa mi hyver ley (I lay me on my right side), saa souer n paa *vor frou Frey*. Herud (get out), *Ragirist!* herind, Mari med Jesu Christ! Herud, dit slemme skaan (filth)! herind, Mari med det lille baan!

Tvi! det sätter a mellem *deulen* aa mä (this I'll put twixt the d. and me): 'Du gjör di finger for brey (too broad), aa di taa for laang' sagde jomfru Mari.—'Da skal a *bind dem i en silke-traa*' sagde Jesus; 'vig bort, du *deuel*, aa i 7 ond aander!' Saa sätter a vor Haris 12 engler omkring mä, to ve min hoved, to ve hver a min bien (2 at each leg), to ve mi hyver aa to ve mi venster sie (left side); saa vil a si paa den deuel der skal gjör mä nöy. i Giösus naun, amen.

### LIV. *In anointing with salt for the Gripes* (?).

(fr. Skand. Lit. selsk. Skr. 19, 376.)

Christus gik sig til kirke, med bog i hände; kom selver jomfru Marie gangende. 'Hvi fälder du löd (pale), min välsignede sön?'—'Jeg haver faaet stärk *greb*, min velsignede moder.'

### LV. *Against Gripes*.[1]

Jeg giör at dette menneske for *berg-greb*, for *söe-greb*, for *dödmans greb*, for alle de greb, som falder *imellem himmel og jord*. i de tre navn etc.

[1] Nos. LV—LVIII from Hans Hammond's Nordiska Missions-historie (Kjöbenh. 1787), pp. 119. 120.

### LVI.  *Against Rendsel* (gout, rheumatism).

Jesus gik sig efter vejen frem, der *mödte han slangen* (snake).  'Hvor har du agtet dig?' sagde der herre Jesus.  Saa svarede han : 'til den, som svag er (is weak).'  Saa svarede den herre Jesus : 'Jeg skal dig igien vende (turn thee back), hiem igien sende.  jeg skal sende dig *udi bierget blaa* (into the blue mtn), der skal du staae, saa länge som verden (world) staaer, jeg skal binde dig med mine ti fingre og med tolv Guds engle.' udi tre navn etc.

### LVII.  *For a Broken Bone.*

Jesus reed sig til heede (heath), der reed han syndt (asunder) sit fole-been.  Jesus stigede af, og lägte det (doctored it).  Jesus lagde *marv i marv, been i been, kiöd i kiöd.*.  Jesus lagde derpaa et blad, at det skulde blive i samme stad.  i tre navne etc.

### LVIII.  *Against Qvärsil* (a horse-disease).

Jeg giör at dette best for qvärsil udi 3 navn.  der ere 3 ord som döver (allay) qvärsil : et er *jorden*, det andet er *solen*, det tredie er Jesu Christi moder jomfrue Marie.

### LIX.  *For Nettle-sting.*

When badly stung with nettles, you take a few leaves of *dock, dockon* (rumex obtusifolius), spit on them, and rub the place with them, uttering the words : '*In dockon* (elsewh. *dock*), *out nettle !*'  In Chaucer's Troil. and Cr. 4, 461 : '*Nettle in, dock out.*'  A Mid. Lat. saw : 'Exeat urtīca, tibi sit periscelis amica !'—Brockett's Glossary of North-country words, p. 57.  [*Out nettle, in dock !* Barnes, p. 49.]

---

A more copious Collection of such Incantations (of which but a bare beginning is here made) would be needed to throw a full light on their origin and drift.  But older documents seem indispensable;[1] many are taken down from the people's mouth corrupt and unintelligible.  Their substance is often antique and highly poetic ; some are distinguished by a compressed conciseness, e.g. 'Oben aus, und nirgend an !' or 'Wer mich scheusst, den schiess ich wieder,' and ' Shot me thou hast, I shoot thee again.'

The same incidents, the same turns of expression, re-appear in different countries : a sign of long and wide diffusion.  Thus, the elf or devil, bound on a mischievous errand, is *met* and baulked (XXXVIII. LII. LIII. LVI) ; then again, the *meeting* of those in search of remedies forms a prelude (XXXI. XXXIX).  The successive casting-out from marrow to bone, fr. bone to flesh, fr. flesh to skin, in VI and LII, shews the oneness of the

---

[1] Horst (Zauber-bibl. 4, 363) got a number of Spells out of a 15th cent. parchment at Trier, but does not give them in his book, which has a wearisome abundance of worthless things.  Probably the little Book of Romanus (Görres no. 34) contains available matter.

Old German spell with the Swedish. It is ancient too for protection to be expressed by *gates* (VIII<sup>b</sup>), *hauberk*,[1] *shirt, shield, helmet* and *sword* (IV. X. L. LII), or by a body of *bone*, a heart of *stone*, a head of *steel* (IX. X. XI). Often Alliteration still peeps out through the Rhyme, e.g. in the numbers 77 and 55 (XXX. XXXIX. VIII<sup>b</sup>), and in the AS. spells III. IV.

As alliteration and rhyme are mixed, the contents seem also to combine a worship of Heathen and Christian beings. *Mary* stands side by side with *Earth* and *Sun* (LVIII), also with Earth and *Heaven* (II). *Sun* and *Moon* are invoked in X and LII, and in XXXV the head must be turned toward the *Sun :* a primitive worship of Elements. The Jutish formula LIII retains even the *goddess Freya*, if the translation be correct : ' I lay me down on my right side, so shall I sleep with lady Freya.' Who is *Ragirist ?* (ON. ragr = timidus, malus, conf. *Ragi og Riste !* herud *Ragi Rist*, Antiqv. anm. 3, 44). *Rylla* too in LIII seems a nickname (conf. Rulla s. 2, 298).

Many spells rest on mere *sympathy between the simile and the desired effect.* The blood, the fire, are to stand as still as Christ hung on the cross (XLI, sanguis mane in venis, sicut Christus pro te in poenis; sanguis mane fixus, sicut Christus crucifixus); as Jordan stood at the baptism (VIII); as mankind will stand at the Judgment-day (XXXII). The fire is to keep in its sparks, as Mary kept her maidenhood (XXVI); the worm in the flesh to feel such pain as Peter felt when he saw the sufferings of his Lord (XXXIV); the hoof to break as little as ever God broke his word (XXXVI). Yet sometimes the formula of the simile bears a direct relation to the effect, as in VIII<sup>b</sup>, where a peace is prayed for, like that which prevailed at the birth of Christ.

Our poets of the 13th cent. mention several spells, but quote none. ' Das swert bedarf wol *segens wort*,' Parz. 253, 25; ' swertes *segen* êren,' MS. 2, 233<sup>a</sup>; ' wunden *segen* sprechen,' Parz. 507, 23. Only in Diut. 1, 362 are a few words introduced of a Blessing on a Journey : ' guot sî iu weter unde wint !' An *âbent-segen*, a *morgen-segen*, are alluded to in MS. 1, 184<sup>a</sup>. 2, 36<sup>a</sup>; conf. 1, 161<sup>a</sup>. 2, 207<sup>b</sup>. A morning-blessing composed by Walther stands in his works 24, 18.

---

[1] A MS. at Cambr. Univ. LI. 1, 10 has a Latin spell, entitled *Lorica*, with an AS. interlinear version : ' hanc *loricam Loding* cantavit ter in omni die.' There are 89 lines of rhyme, imploring protection for all parts of the body and in all dangers. The first four lines are :

> Suffragare, trinitatis unitas,
> unitatis suffragare trinitas,
> suffragare quaeso mihi posito
> maris magni velut in periculo.

It is not very poetical, nor always intelligible ; but it is of the 9th cent.

# INDEX TO VOL. IV.